New Testament Judaism

STUDIES IN COMPARATIVE LEGAL HISTORY

New Testament Judaism

Collected Works of David Daube

Volume 2

Edited by
Calum Carmichael

The Robbins Collection *Berkeley*

Robbins Collection Publications
School of Law (Boalt Hall)
University of California at Berkeley
Berkeley, California 94720
(510) 642-5094 fax: (510) 642-8325
www.law.berkeley.edu/robbins

ISBN: 1-882239-04-0 *New Testament Judaism*
ISBN: 1-882239-01-6 Collected Works of David Daube

Library of Congress Catalog Card number: 92-61641

Printed in the USA.

Contents

Section 7: Disciples

Section 8: Studies in Luke-Acts

INDICES

Preface

This is the second volume of David Daube's writings that have been published since 1932 and as of 2000 continue to appear in scholarly publications worldwide. Volume One compiling his work on Talmudic Law appeared in 1992. The present volume brings together his work on the Hellenistic and Rabbinic background to New Testament literature.

Born in 1909, Daube was brought up in a strict orthodox Jewish community in Freiburg-im-Breisgau, Germany, then a city of some 45,000 inhabitants with a Jewish population of around 600, of whom about 150 were Orthodox. Introduced to biblical criticism by Johannes Hempel at the University of Göttingen (where he went on to receive a doctorate on a biblical legal topic), he was told by a teacher at his synagogue, "If you must do it [biblical criticism], do it like a surgeon who has to operate on his father." In 1933 Otto Lenel, who had taught Daube Roman law in Freiburg, sent him to England. Daube became a Research Fellow at Gonville and Caius College, Cambridge, where he did a doctorate in Roman law under W. W. Buckland. Buckland's precise, thorough scholarship (and writing style) greatly influenced Daube.

Daube first became interested in the New Testament at Cambridge. C. H. Dodd invited him to his seminar on the New Testament after meeting him at a tea party and learning of his knowledge of the Aramaic language and Rabbinic sources. Along with Dodd, F. S. Marsh had considerable influence on Daube. Both of them were committed Christians but they never tried to influence Daube's own religious beliefs. "If I might be so courageous I would say that they approved 100 per cent of other sensible religions," Daube once reported to me. Marsh was a chaplain during the First World War and if a Jewish soldier died on the battlefield he read the service for him from Singer's *Prayer Book.* Marsh knew many languages, published little, and was extraordinarily generous with his time to others. In his early publications Daube often acknowledges his indebtedness to Marsh. Daube revered Dodd whom he described as a believer who did not follow dogma but genuinely admitted the truth in other religions. For him the Christian message was about love and peace and he acted on it. Buckland, Dodd, and Marsh once attended a Passover *seder* at Daube's home in Cambridge. One of Daube's most original contributions is his research showing the links between the Passover Haggadah as it existed in first century Palestine and the New Testament (Section 4 of this volume).

The topic of originality readily comes up whenever there is discussion of Daube's work in his many areas of scholarship—Biblical law and literature, Greek and Latin literature, Roman law, and Talmudic law. In my judgment, because of unique factors at play, his most insightful contributions are those in the field of New Testament scholarship. W. D. Davies of Duke University, a seminal figure in the field, who began his scholarly career with Dodd and Daube in Cambridge, affirms Daube's "extraordinary openness to the non-Jewish world that this once Orthodox Jewish scholar has always practiced throughout his life. The extent of this openness is a very, very rare phenomenon among Rabbinic scholars; in my own experience, I consider it unique" (letter on file). Davies goes on to say that "through this openness and largesse of mind and spirit David Daube has helped to liberate both Jews and Gentiles from prejudice and from many traditional blinders."

Another force behind Daube's work was an antagonism that he shared with Albert Schweitzer and many previous German scholars to dogmatic claims made about the New Testament down through the centuries. Guided by an acute historical instinct, by a highly sophisticated sense of how to read a text, by an intimate, rare knowledge of that most baffling of works, the Talmud, and, not least, by imaginative flair—the "muscle of the soul" in Nabokov's phrase—Daube's passion to comprehend the New Testament has yielded results that will, I think, effect a sea-change in attitudes to that body of material. Through one pioneering study after another he has uncovered that part of the history of Judaism he designated New Testament Judaism. After Daube's work it would be eccentric in a negative sense for anyone not to regard New Testament literature as, from beginning to end, Jewish literature of the first century, a body of literature, moreover, not strange or extreme for that period. I once asked him why he had put in the title of his book, *Appeasement or Resistance, and Other Essays in New Testament Judaism* (Berkeley, 1987), the last three words. His reply was a very firm one: "It was a deliberate act." He lamented the pettiness of Jewish scholars who excluded the New Testament from their studies and Christian scholars who carried on a tradition of what he called "theological anti-Semitism."

The famed biochemist Szent-Györgyi declared that his aim in doing scientific work was "to see what everyone has seen and think what no one has thought." That has been Daube's aim in all of his scholarly endeavors. Marvelous as this originality is, it does not contribute to an easy presentation of Daube's results because his stance is usually antithetical to a systematic approach to any body of material. (He viewed Gaius, Blackstone, and Pufendorf as great systematizers in the history of law and jurisprudence, but not equal to the greatest in creativity.) I have not included material on New Testament topics from what is perhaps his most readable book, *Civil Disobedience in Antiquity* (Edinburgh, 1972; to appear in Volume Three). It has throughout a distinctive topic under scrutiny, unlike his *New Testament and Rabbinic Judaism* (London, 1956), included in this volume but with the topics often differently arranged. The reader will find that Daube returns time and again to the same subject matter, but more often than not finds something new to say about it. Such repetition is, as it happens, a feature of the tradition he probes so deeply. The notions underlying the designations Mishnah and Tannaite—the terms come from a verb meaning to repeat—refer to a method of study in New Testament and Talmudic times that involves careful repetitions culminating in expansions. In the Table of Contents I provide a summary of each item so that the reader may have some indication why I place it where I do in the volume.

During the course of the preparation of these volumes I visited Daube in a nursing home in Berkeley, California. At 89 years old he experienced both physical and mental decline. Yet despite his deep regret about his current situation the old—in the sense of years past—Daube continued to show through, such as when he expressed regret that he had not gone in for a more radical exploration of things. He was, nonetheless, delighted to learn that in producing the next volume of his Collected Works I received support from the Robbins Collection, School of Law, University of California, Berkeley, from the Oxford Centre of Hebrew and Jewish Studies, and from Cornell Law School; also from such friends as Alan Watson, School of Law, University of Georgia, Athens, whom he wished to acknowledge not only for assisting me with the Latin and Roman law but for his material generosity to him and to this publication project; and Marie-Theres Fögen, Rechtswissenschaftliches Seminar der Universität Zürich, Switzerland, who assisted me with the German. I am also much indebted to Shalon Parker, doctoral student, University of California, Berkeley, for her assistance in preparing this volume.

In translating a good deal of the Aramaic, French, German, Greek, Hebrew, and Latin, I may have done so unnecessarily in some instances, but I had in mind, among others, undergraduate audiences. In transliterating Aramaic, Greek, and Hebrew I have not been entirely consistent, partly because Daube varies in the method he uses and partly because those who are familiar with the languages will have no difficulties.

On February 24, 1999, two weeks after his ninetieth birthday, David Daube died.

Calum M. Carmichael
Cornell University
Ithaca, New York

Acknowledgements

The following articles are reprinted here by permission of the Union of Liberal and Progressive Synagogues: "The New Testament and Rabbinic Judaism" appeared in *The Liberal Jewish Monthly* 28 (1957): 7–11, 28–31; "The Significance of the Afikoman" appeared in *Pointer* 3 (1968): 4–5.

"The Gospels and the Rabbis" appeared in *The Listener* 56 (1956), was reprinted in *Service International de Documentation Judéo-Chrétienne*, English Edition, 26 (1993): 19–23, and is reprinted here by permission of the British Broadcasting Corporation.

The following articles are reprinted here by permission of the Löwenklau Gesellschaft: "The 'Nails' and the Jews" appeared in "Two Jewish Prayers", *Rechthistorisches Journal* 6 (1987): 195–208; "Judas" appeared in *Rechthistorisches Journal* 13 (1995): 307–30.

"Some Reflections on the Historicity of the New Testament" appeared in the *CCICA Annual* (1986): 1–12, and is reprinted here by permission of the Catholic Commission on Intellectual and Cultural Affairs.

The following selections, reprinted here by permission of University of California Press, appeared in *Appeasement or Resistance, and Other Essays on New Testament Judaism* (copyright ©1987 The Regents of The University of California): "The Old Testament in the New" (pp. 1–38), "Appeasing or Resisting the Oppressor" (pp. 75–119), "The Burdened Convert" (pp. 59–73), and "Temple Tax" (pp. 39–58).

The following articles are reproduced here by courtesy of the Director and University Librarian, the John Rylands University Library of Manchester: "Concerning the Reconstruction of the 'Aramaic Gospels'" appeared in the *Bulletin of the John Rylands University Library of Manchester* 29 (1945): 69–105; "Zukunftsmusik: Some Desirable Lines of Exploration in the New Testament Field" appeared in the *Bulletin of the John Rylands University Library of Manchester* 68 (1985): 53–75.

The following selections, reprinted here by permission of the School of Oriental and African Studies at the University of London, appeared in *The New Testament and Rabbinic Judaism* (1956): "Joseph" (pp. 3–4); "Moses" (pp. 10–12); "Samuel" (pp. 13–16); "Saul" (pp. 17–19); "Elijah" (pp. 20–26); "Ruth and Boaz" (pp. 27–51); "Ye have heard—but I say unto you" (pp. 55–62); "Principles and Cases" (pp. 63–66); "Eye for Eye" (pp. 254–65); "Precept and Example" (pp. 67–89); "Violence to the Kingdom" (pp. 285–300); "Terms for Divorce (pp. 362–72); "Basic Commandments" (pp. 247–53); "Haustafeln" (pp. 90–105); "Public Retort and Private Explanation" (pp. 141–50); "Socratic Interrogation" (pp. 151–57); "The Last Beatitude" (pp. 196–201); "Four Types of Question" (pp. 158–69); "The 'I Am' of the Messianic Presence" (pp. 325–29); "Redemption" (pp. 268–84); "Two Tripartite Forms" (pp. 170–95); "Chronology" (pp. 406–17); "A Supernatural Birth" (pp. 5–9); "Two Incidents after the Last Supper" (pp. 330–35); "A Baptismal Catechism" (pp. 106–40); "Missionary Maxims in Paul" (pp. 336–51); "A Missionary Term" (pp. 352–61); "Rabbinic Authority" (pp. 205–23); "The Laying on of Hands" (pp. 224–46); "Disgrace" (pp. 301–24); "Samaritan Women" (pp. 373–82); "Two Aramaisms" (pp. 383–87); "Amen" (pp. 388–93); "I Speak After the Manner of Men" (pp. 394–400); "Two Symbols" (pp. 401–405); "The Abomination of Desolation" (pp. 418–37); "The Interpretation of a Generic Singular" (pp. 438–44); and "The Offices of a Disciple" (pp. 266–67).

The following publications are reprinted here by permission of the London Diocesan Council for Christian-Jewish Understanding: "Hezekiah" and "He That Cometh" appeared together as *He That Cometh* (London, 1966) and "Wine in the Bible" appeared as *Wine in the Bible* (London, 1975).

The following selections are reprinted here by permission of E. J. Brill: "The Form Is the Message" and "Conversion to Judaism and Early Christianity" appeared in *Ancient Jewish Law* (Leiden, 1981), pp. 71–129, 1–47 (respectively); "The Sudden in the Scriptures" appeared as *The Sudden in the Scriptures* (Leiden, 1964); and "A Reform in Acts and its Models" appeared in *Jews, Greeks and Christians—Religious Cultures in Late Antiquity: Essays in Honour of William David Davies*, edited by R. Hamerton-Kelly and R. Scroggs (Leiden, 1976): 151–63.

"Biblical Landmarks in the Struggle for Women's Rights" appeared in *The Juridical Review* 90 (1978): 177–197 and is reprinted here by permission of the publisher W. Green, The Scottish Law Publisher, 21 Alva Street, Edinburgh, EH2 4PS.

The following articles are reprinted here with the permission of the Cambridge University Press: "The Earliest Structure of the Gospels" appeared in *New Testament Studies* 5 (1959): 174–87; "The Responsibilities of Master and Disciples in the Gospels" appeared in *New Testament Studies* 19 (1972): 1–15.

The following articles are reprinted here with the permission of the Akademie Verlag: "A Prayer Pattern in Judaism" appeared in *Studia Evangelica* 73 (1959): 539–45; "'For they know not what they do': Luke 23:34" appeared in *Studia Patristica* 79 (1961): 58–70.

"Pauline Contributions to a Pluralistic Culture: Re-Creation and Beyond" appeared in *Jesus and Man's Hope*, vol. 2, edited by D. G. Miller and D. Y. Hadidian (Pittsburgh, 1971): 223–45].

"Onesimos" is reprinted from *Christians among Jews and Gentiles*, edited by George Nickelsburg and George W. MacRae, copyright ©1986 The President and Fellows of Howard College, by permission of Augsburg Fortress (pp. 40–43).

"The History of Proselytising" appeared in *Chayenu* 8 (1945): 10–11.

"The Authority of the Church and Private Judgment" appeared in *The Guardian* (London, 1941): 393, 406–407, 418.

"Paul a Hellenistic Schoolmaster?" appeared in *Studies in Rationalism, Judaism, and Universalism: in Memory of Leon Roth*, edited by Raphael Loewe (London, 1966): 67–71.

"Inheritance in Two Lukan Pericopes" appeared in *Zeitschrift der Savigny-Stiftung für Rechtgeschichte*, Rom. Abt., 72 (1955): 326–34, and is reprinted here by permission of Verlag Hermann Böhlaus Nachfolger.

"Shame Culture in Luke" appeared in *Paul and Paulinism: Essays in Honour of C.K. Barret*, edited by M. D. Hooker and S. G. Wilson (London, 1982): 355–72.

"On Acts 23: Sadducees and Angels" appeared in the *Journal of Biblical Literature* 109 (1990): 493–97 and is reprinted here by permission of the Society of Biblical Literature.

"Neglected Nuances of Exposition in Luke" appeared in *Aufstieg und Niedergang der Römischen Welt*, edited by H. Temporini and W. Haase (1985), Part II, Principat, vol. 25.3, Religion: 2329–56, and is reprinted here by permission of the publisher Walter de Gruyter GmbH & Co. Kg.

"Τρία μυστήρια κραυγῆς, Ignatius, Ephesians 19:1" appeared in *Journal of Theological Studies*, 16 (1965): 128–29, and is reprinted here by permission of the Oxford University Press.

Abbreviations

ArOr	*Archiv Orientální*
AV	Authorised Version
BGU	Berliner Griechische Urkunden
BJRULM	*Bulletin of the John Rylands University Library of Manchester*
CH	Code of Hammurabi
CLJ	*Cambridge Law Journal*
CLRev	*California Law Review*
CUALR	*Catholic University of America Law Review*
ET	*The Expository Times*
G	Graeca (The Septuagint)
HL	Hittite Laws
HTR	*Harvard Theological Review*
HUCA	*Hebrew Union College Annual*
ILR	*Israel Law Review*
JBL	*Journal of Biblical Literature*
JJSOC	*Journal of Jewish Sociology*
JJS	*Journal of Jewish Studies*
JLA	*Jewish Law Annual*
JQR	*Jewish Quarterly Review*
JR	*Juridical Review*
JRS	*Journal of Roman Studies*
JSS	*Journal of Semitic Studies*
JTS	*Journal of Theological Studies*
LawHR	*Law and History Review*
LE	Laws of Eshnunna
LHR	*Legal History Review*
LQR	*Law Quarterly Review*
LXX	The Septuagint
MAL	Middle Assyrian Laws
MGWJ	*Monatsschrift für Geschichte und Wissenschaft des Judentums*
MT	The Massoretic Text
NLF	*Natural Law Forum (=American Journal of Jurisprudence)*
NT	*Novum Testamentum*
NTS	*New Testament Studies*
PEQ	*Palestine Exploration Quarterly*
pr.	*principium* [the first, unnumbered, part of a text in some Roman legal sources, including Justinian's *Digest*]
Q (Quelle)	The stratum of tradition common to Matthew and Luke
RIDA	*Revue International des Droits de l'Antiquité*
RJ	*Rechtshistorisches Journal*
Sam	Samaritan
SP	*Studia Patristica*
TLR	*Tulane Law Review*
TR	*Tijdschrift voor Rechtsgeschiedenis (=LHR)*
VT	*Vetus Testamentum*
ZAW	*Zeitschrift für die alttestamentliche Wissenschaft*
ZNW	*Zeitschrift für die neutestamentliche Wissenschaft*
ZSS	*Zeitschrift der Savigny-Stiftung für Rechtsgeschichte*

Tractates of the Talmud

A. Zar.	Abodah Zarah
Ab.	Aboth
Arak.	Arakhin
B. B.	Baba Bathra
B. K.	Baba Kamma
B. M.	Baba Metzia
Bekh.	Bekhoroth
Ber.	Berakhoth
Betz.	Betzah (or "Yom Tob")
Bikk.	Bikkurin
Dem.	Demai
Eduy.	Eduyoth
Erub.	Erubin
Ger.	Gerim
Gitt.	Gittin
Hag.	Hagigah
Hall.	Hallah
Hor.	Horayoth
Hull.	Hullin
Kel.	Kelim
Ker.	Kerithoth
Ket.	Ketuboth
Kidd.	Kiddushin
Kil.	Kilaim
Kinn.	Kinnim
Maas.	Maaseroth
M. Sh.	Maaser Sheni
Makk.	Makkoth
Maksh.	Makshirin
Meg.	Megillah
Meil.	Meilah
Men.	Menahoth
Midd.	Middoth
Mikw.	Miqwaoth
M. Kat.	Moed Katan
Naz.	Nazir
Ned.	Nedarim
Neg.	Negaim
Nidd.	Niddah
Ohol.	Oholoth
Orl.	Orlah
Par.	Parah
Peah	Peah
Pes.	Pesahim
R. Sh.	Rosh ha-Shanah
Sanh.	Sanhedrin
Sem.	Semahoth
Shab.	Shabbath
Shebi.	Shebiith
Shebu.	Shebuoth
Shek.	Shekalim
Sot.	Sotah
Sukk.	Sukkah
Tam.	Tamid
Taan.	Taanith
Teb. Y.	Tebul Yom
Tem.	Temurah
Ter.	Terumoth
Toh.	Tohoroth
Uktz.	Uktzin
Yad.	Yadaim
Yeb.	Yebamoth
Yom.	Yoma
Zab.	Zabim
Zeb.	Zebahim

Other sources

Ab. de R. N.	*'Aboth de Rabbi Nathan*
Abr.	*De Abrahamo*
A.N.	*Attic Nights*
Ant.	*Jewish Antiquities*
Apol. Bar.	*Apocalypse of Baruch*
Apol.	*Apologia*
Bel	Bel and the Dragon
Bell.	*Jewish War*
Decal.	*De Decalogo*
Deipn.	*Deipnosophists*
De Inv.	*De Inventione Rhetorica*
De Or.	*De Oratore*
Derek Eretz Rab.	*Derek Eretz Rabba*
Deus	*Quod Deus Immutabilis sit*
Deut. Rab.	*Deuteronomy Rabba*
Dial.	*Dialogue with Trypho*
Ebr.	*De Ebrietate*
Eccl. Hist.	*Historia Ecclesiastica*
Eccl. Rab.	*Ecclesiastes Rabba*
Ep.	*Epistles*
Esth. Rab.	*Esther Rabba*
Exod. Rab.	*Exodus Rabba*
Gen. Rab.	*Genesis Rabba*
Her.	*Quis Rerum Divinarum Heres sit*
Il.	*Iliad*
I.O.	*Institutio Oratoria*
Jer. Targum	*Jerusalem Targum*
Lam. Rab.	*Lamentations Rabba*
Leg. All.	*Legum Allegoriae*
Lev. Rab.	*Leviticus Rabba*
Mek.	*Mekhilta*
Mor.	*Moralia*
Mos.	*De Vita Mosis*
Mut.	*De Mutatione Nominum*
Nic. E.	*Nicomachean Ethics*
Num. Rab.	*Numbers Rabba*
Od.	*Odyssey*
Onk	Onkelos
Op.	*De Opificio Mundi*
Part. Or.	*De Partitione Oratoria*
P. de R.K.	*Pesiqta de Rab Kahana*
P. de R.N.	*Pirqe de Rabbi Nathan*
P.O.	*De Pythiae Oraculis*
P.R.	*Pesiqta Rabbathi*
Prob.	*Quod omnis probus liber*
Pro Clu.	*Pro Cluentio*
Qap	Genesis Apocryphon
QS	Qumran Scroll
Rhet.	*Rhetoric*
Ruth Rab.	*Ruth Rabba*
Sac.	*De Sacrificiis Abelis et Caini*
S.O.	*Seder Olam Rabba*
Sept.	*De Septenario*
Song of Songs Rab.	*Song of Songs Rabba*
Soph. El.	*Sophistici Elenchi*
Leg. Spec.	*De Specialibus Legibus*
Syb. Or.	*Sybilline Oracles*
T. de Be El.	*Tanna de Be Eliyyahu*
Top.	*Topica*
Virt.	*De Virtutibus*

Glossary

A fortiori: All the more.

A minori ad maius: From the lesser to the greater.

Amoraite: A Rabbi of the period from about 200 to 500 C.E.

Antinomy: Apparent contradictions in Scripture.

Babylonian Talmud: The compilation, completed about 520 C.E. in Babylonia, of the discussions and decisions of the *Amoraites* [q.v.] in the form of a commentary on the *Mishnah* [q.v.]

Baraitha: Frequently the *Talmud* [q.v.]—containing the *Amoraic* [*Amoraite* q.v.], 200-500 C.E. exposition of the law—adduces *Tannaitic* [*Tannaite* q.v.], pre-200 C.E. views besides the *Mishnah* [q.v.] and marks them off as such, as *Tannaitic*. A quotation of this description is called a *Baraitha*.

Boruth: Sayings of a vulgar nature.

Collocatio: Division (of a text).

Condictio: A type of action alleging a civil law debt without mentioning any cause of action, available not only as a contractual remedy, but also on a quasi-contractual basis, where unjustified enrichment could be shown.

Consul: The title of the two, annually elected, supreme magistrates of the Roman republic. Consuls continued to be elected during the empire with various administrative and judicial powers, but the position became increasingly an honorary one until it was abolished by Justinian.

Demonstratio: The part of the formula for a legal action in the *praetor's* edict that makes known the subject matter of the action.

Derekh: Proper way or manner, nature.

Derekh Erets: The rules of decent and prudent conduct in daily intercourse, of morally and socially right behavior to one's fellow men.

Digest: The most important part of the *Corpus Iuris Civilis*. Along with the *Code*, the *Institutes*, and the *Novels*, it formed the compilation of Roman Law which was enacted under the Byzantine emperor, Justinian I (c. 482-565 C.E.), together with that emperor's later laws. The *Digest* consists of passages from classical jurists.

Edictum: A proclamation by a magistrate or the emperor. In the republic, the edicts which had the greatest effect on private law were those of the *praetores* who had control of the courts. Each *praetor* [q.v.] could issue a new edict for his year in office, setting out the actions he was prepared to allow, but in practice he took over much of the material from his predecessors. This led to the development of an almost standard body of rules known as the Edict, containing the numerous praetorial extensions to the civil law. This process survived the transition to empire, but the Emperor Hadrian ordered the consolidation of the Edict early in the second century C.E.; thereafter it does not appear to have been a source of new law.

Gaius: Roman jurist, whose works (e. g., the *Institutes*), composed between 130 and 180 C.E., became an authoritative source of Roman law.

Gemara: A term roughly synonymous with *Talmud* [q.v.]; though *Talmud* refers rather to the work, *Gemara* to the contents.

Haggadah: Teaching designed to guide but not strictly binding.

Halakhah: Binding Rabbinic law.

Hallel: Psalms 113–18

Hekhrea' : A word that is to be connected both to what precedes it and what comes after it.

Lectio difficilior: The more difficult reading.

Maiestas: The term was applied to a number of criminal offenses including treason, sedition, and desertion. In the empire it covered any action which endangered the emperor or his family.

Mekhilta: A probably pre-second century C.E. Rabbinic commentary on the book of Exodus.

Middoth: Hermeneutical rules.

Midrash: A commentary on Scripture.

Midrash Rabba: The collective name for ten commentaries on different books of the Bible (the five Books of Moses, Song of Solomon, Ruth, Lamentations, Ecclesiastes and Esther). Among them are Genesis Rabba and Leviticus Rabba, both compiled in Palestine, the former in the fifth century, the latter in the seventh. The material is partly old, partly late; the bulk may well be *Tannaitic*. Not uncommonly, however, the old material has undergone revision.

Mishnah: The Rabbis of about 50 B.C.E. to about C.E. 200 are called *Tannaites*. At the end of this period Judah the Prince produced an authoritative collection of laws, the *Mishnah*; while another collection, the *Tosephta*, was produced by his pupil Hiyya bar Abba.

Mishpatim: The code of laws in Exod 21:2-23:17.

Noachian Commandments: The seven laws (idolatry, incest or unchastity, shedding blood, profanation of the Name of God, justice, robbery, and cutting off flesh or a limb from a living animal) that God supposedly gave to the sons of Noah as the elementary principles of morality.

Parousia: Imminent arrival.

Patria potestas: the power of a father over his descendants of whatever age.

Peregrinus (Peregrine): In classical times this term usually meant a member of a non-Roman community within the empire, who was subject to the law of his own state and had few of the public or private law rights of a Roman citizen. A special *praetor* [q.v.] dealt with peregrines' transactions. After the *constitutio Antoniniana*, the expression came to be applied to foreigners living outside of the empire.

Praetor: In the republic, an important magistrate second only to the *consules* [q.v.] and who, among other duties, had charge of the administration of private law.

Prozbul: According to Deut 15:2, all loans were remitted in the Seventh Year. Lest this should lead to fraud or oppression (Deut 15:9) Hillel enacted the rule of the *Prozbul*, which was a declaration made before a court of law by a creditor, and signed by witnesses, to the effect that the loan in question would not be remitted under the terms of the Seventh Year law.

Qal waḥomer: "The light and the weighty," inference from the less important to the more important.

Ratio: Reason.

Reductio ad absurdum: The propping-up of a decision by showing the alternative to be in striking contrast to the declared specific objective of the enterprise.

Regula: Rule.

Rusticitas: The manners of country people.

Septuagint: The Greek translation of the Hebrew Bible.

Seres: A verse at first sight illogical made logical by re-arranging its parts.

Talmud: From about C.E. 200 until about C.E. 500 is the period of the *Amoraites* [q.v.]. Their discussions and decisions were compiled in the form of two commentaries on the *Mishnah* [q.v.]: one, the Jerusalemite *Talmud* (sometimes called the Palestinian *Talmud*), completed in Palestine about C.E. 420, the other, the Babylonian *Talmud*, completed in Babylonia some hundred years later.

Tannaite: A Rabbi of the period from about 50 B.C.E. to about C.E. 200.

Targums: The Aramaic translations, or rather paraphrases, of the Hebrew Bible.

Tosephta: See *Mishnah*

Vindicatio: In Roman Law the legal action claiming ownership.

1

The New Testament and Rabbinic Judaism

This section contains items that illustrate how Rabbinic interpretations of the Hebrew Bible illuminate the contents of the New Testament.

The New Testament and Rabbinic Judaism*

1. Rabbinic and Hellenistic Elements in the New Testament

The Hellenistic period began with Alexander the Great, about 330 B.C.E. Greek civilisation was carried abroad by Alexander and his successors and it influenced wide areas in the Middle East and around the Mediterranean. In the process, it borrowed many elements from the areas which it captured; above all, many oriental elements. This was inevitable, since Greece had lost her independence and there was, consequently, no fixed and firm Greek nucleus behind the spreading civilisation. The result was a new culture which we call "Hellenistic." In it the Greek and oriental elements were so intermixed as to produce something quite different from the original civilisation of the Greek states and also from each of the individual oriental cultures.

The question how much of the New Testament is Hellenistic and how much of it is rabbinic presupposes a distinction between Hellenistic culture and rabbinic culture. But scholars have long suspected that, by the time of the New Testament, this distinction was no longer very sharp. Indeed, it can be shown (1) that rabbinism itself was by that time very strongly Hellenistic—almost, though not quite, a part of the general Hellenistic civilisation; and (2) that the New Testament is much less Hellenistic and much more rabbinic than is generally assumed.

The Judaising of Hellenistic Doctrines

To illustrate the first point, I would quote a statement of Hillel—a Rabbi who lived shortly before Jesus—that the soul is an unhappy, oppressed guest in the human body. This idea at once reminds us of prevalent non-Jewish Hellenistic doctrines of the relation between body and soul. It might be argued, perhaps, that this concept of the soul as an unhappy guest in the body could be a purely internal Jewish development and that the Rabbis arrived at it by their own efforts, uninfluenced by the surrounding Stoic and gnostic doctrines of body and soul. But a significant feature of Hillel's statement is that it contains Greek words, so that he must have drawn on some Hellenistic author.

Of course, Hillel and the other Rabbis did not simply adopt Hellenistic doctrines without modifying them. Hillel Judaises the material which he uses. Another statement of his, bearing on the same kind of doctrine, is that to go to the baths is a pious act, because the human body is created in the likeness of God and is therefore worthy of care. Now the institution of baths was a Hellenistic one, and care of the body was emphasised in Hellenistic circles. But Hillel's statement is obviously directed against

* Summary of a Lecture given at the Liberal Jewish Synagogue, London 1957.

excessive rejection of the body as impure, in contrast to the soul which comes from Heaven. Thus, while accepting the notion of the soul as an unhappy guest in the body, he insists that the body is in the likeness of God.

That is the way in which the Rabbis work throughout: they adopt Hellenistic ideas, yet they inject essentially Jewish notions into the material and thereby produce something which preserves the essentials of Jewish tradition but accommodates that tradition to prevalent Hellenistic doctrines. Philo also says that the soul is oppressed by the body, but draws the conclusion, not that one should remain celibate, but that one should enter only into a marriage allowed by the Torah. Clearly, Hillel and Philo make the same kind of use of Hellenistic notions. It was a far-reaching accommodation. The die-hards who were opposed to any import of Hellenistic material were left behind and withered away as Judaism developed. The extreme assimilationists who gave up the essentials of Jewish thought were, in a different way, lost to Judaism. Those who remained were people like Hillel and his followers.

A Hellenistic Construction

A more surprising example of Hillel's adoption of Hellenistic thought is in another field. We are used to the distinction between the Written Torah and the Oral Torah, the Torah which is handed down by word of mouth. We are also used to the derivation of the Oral Torah from the Written Torah, and we know how it is done. We take the text and compare the Gemara, and we see how the Rabbis do it. They base their elaborate decisions on the Written Torah by rather complicated methods of analogy, *a fortiori* and the like: "If this is true of so-and-so, how much more must it be true of such-and-such." What is often overlooked is that their entire construction is Hellenistic. Hillel adopted this construction and he himself tells us from where he got it. But again, he Judaises it.

In the Judaism of Hillel's day, the Pharisees observed the Written Torah plus a large number of traditions which had been handed down on the authority of the Rabbis and Elders, while the Sadducees and the Samaritans observed only the Written Torah. Hillel adopted the Hellenistic construction in order to bridge the gulf between the two parties. His thesis was that the traditions could, by certain methods, be based on, or derived from, the Written Torah. In this way he tried to retain all the traditions, while conceding to the Sadducees that, essentially, they must be contained in the Written Law. Many doctrines in this context that are generally looked upon as typically Jewish are, in reality, Hellenistic. For example, the doctrine that "the tradition is a fence around the Written Law" is taken almost literally from Plato, who says that "ancestral customs and traditions form a cover round the written laws, for their protection." Here too, the die-hards like the B'nai Bathyra who would have nothing to do with Hillel's "new-fangled" Hellenistic approach were left by the wayside, and the extreme Hellenists, who wanted to go much further than Hillel and to say that the Written Law had only allegorical meaning, drifted away and were lost to Judaism. Again, those who were left were Hillel and his followers who, while freely, self-confidently and fearlessly adopting a great deal of Hellenistic thought, adapted it to the essentials of Judaism.

Paul's Use of Rabbinic Doctrine

Now I come to the second point—that the New Testament is much more rabbinic than is generally assumed—and will take a few significant examples. In one of Paul's Epistles we find what is generally accepted as a very Hellenistic way of speaking of Jesus: "He is the image of the invisible God, the first-born of all creation; for in him all things were created, in heaven and on earth, all things were created through him and for him. He is before all things, and in him all things hold together. He is the head of the body, the church; he is the beginning, the first-born from the dead." It is usually assumed that this represents the Hellenistic *logos*, the creative and rational principle of the universe. In fact, some Christian scholars have maintained that this passage is too Hellenistic even for Paul and have therefore declared it to be a post-Pauline interpolation. But it is nothing of the sort. It is good rabbinic doctrine—once it is granted that Jesus is the Messiah. Let us take the first epithet, "He is the image of God." That is the doctrine of Jesus as the second Adam who leads mankind back to the state before the Fall. According to rabbinic doctrine, Adam was, before the Fall, the ideal man "in the image of God," and there are beautiful rabbinic descriptions of his glory and his flawlessness. Then Jesus is characterised by pre-cosmic generation and is said to have helped in the creation of the universe. This again has a rabbinic background. In the Book of Proverbs it is said of wisdom: "The Lord created me [wisdom] as the beginning of his work." The Rabbis deduce from this that, in the first verse of the Bible, we ought to translate *Bereshit* as "By Wisdom." Rabbinic literature also personifies wisdom as a craftsman helping God in the Creation. All the qualities ascribed to wisdom are transferred by the Rabbis to the Torah, because the Torah stands for wisdom. The Torah is personified by the Rabbis, the Torah was created before everything else, and the Torah helped God in the creation of the universe. Indeed, the universe was created not only by the Torah but also for the sake of the Torah. Paul believed that Jesus was the Messiah and, because of that belief, he simply transferred the rabbinic formulations to Jesus. Even of this transfer the roots are to be found in rabbinic literature, for in speculation about the coming Messiah the qualities of the Torah are largely attributed to him. We do find here in Paul a certain accommodation to Stoic doctrine, but the accommodation follows very Jewish lines.

Another striking example is the rôle of natural morality in Paul. The doctrine of natural morality means that, without immediate Revelation such as the Torah, man knows by innate reason the fundamental requirements of morality. This doctrine is important because from Paul it has entered the Christian church. Paul says that "the Gentiles, who have not been given the Law, do by nature what is contained in it, because the Commandments are written in their hearts." This idea is assumed to be Stoic, because the Stoics held that the principle of reason, *logos*, is spread throughout the universe and man participates in it so that, without being specifically told, he knows the fundamental principles of morality. No doubt Paul had heard of this Stoic doctrine, but it was good rabbinic doctrine by his time. The Rabbis spoke of Noachian commandments, seven fundamental moral commandments given to the sons of Noah, which were valid for all mankind. The picture of "a law written on the heart of man" occurs in Jeremiah, who certainly was not a Hellenistic author.

Baptism in Rabbinic Judaism

A good many more such examples could be given. Take baptism, for instance, which is interpreted by Paul and other early Christian writers as dying and rising with Jesus. It is maintained that this notion must have come from the mystery religions. Admittedly, in Hellenistic times, a great part was played in the mystery religions by certain ceremonies which were supposed to bring one into direct communication with God; and there is no reason to assume that Paul and the early Christian writers did not know of these. Nevertheless, the ceremony of baptism, and even its interpretation as dying and rising with Jesus had a perfectly good rabbinic setting in New Testament times.

Proselytes to Judaism had to undergo baptism and it was a much more important rite of initiation than circumcision, because most of them were women and they became converts to Judaism by baptism alone. A well-known early Rabbi of the Mishnah, Rabbi Joshua, declared that baptism alone made a person Jewish, even in the case of a male. He did not go as far as Paul; he did not say that circumcision was superfluous; he said that once a man had become Jewish he must undergo circumcision. But baptism sufficed to effect conversion. Moreover, the notion that it means a rising from the dead is quite Jewish. The Rabbis compare it to a rising from the grave, and indeed construe it as a new birth. The proselyte to Judaism is like a "new-born child" and is treated as such. His sins are forgiven. You might suppose that this is just a manner of speaking, but the Rabbis meant a great deal by it. For example, a Gentile who became a Jew in New Testament times was allowed to marry his sister by the same father. It was not incest, because he was no longer the same person as before. Here you have a serious result of the notion that baptism brings about a new birth. It goes as far as, or even further than, any mystery religion. On the other hand, neither the Rabbis nor Paul would ever conceive of a ceremony as making a man part of God.

Granted, then, that rabbinism is much more Hellenistic, and the New Testament much more rabbinic, than is generally assumed, what is left of non-rabbinic, Hellenistic material in the New Testament? Of course, many details are of this kind; and, in some cases, we can watch the transition from the rabbinic *milieu* to the Hellenistic within the New Testament. After all, the work was read in non-Jewish circles and was meant to appeal to them (just as a good deal of rabbinic literature was meant to appeal to them), so certain changes were made. For example, in the case of the Last Supper, the Eucharist, which Christians are to commemorate again and again, some versions in the New Testament say that Jesus said the *berachah,* the blessing over the bread, and the Hebrew is rendered by *eulogeo,* "to bless." But in other versions this term is replaced by *eucharistheo,* the Greek for "to give thanks." This is not rabbinic; it describes a Hellenistic ceremonial thanksgiving. We can see how a change in terminology was introduced in order to render something more intelligible to non-Jews. There are innumerable details like this.

The Gospels of Luke and John

Naturally, the various writers of the New Testament differ in their degree of Hellenism. John, the author of the fourth Gospel, and Luke, the author of the third, are usually considered to be among the most Hellenistic ones. But John's mentality turns out to be more and more Jewish the more we find out about the Judaism of his time. And now, after the discovery of the Dead Sea Scrolls, a good many notions in John which had been considered quite beyond the pale are known to have been held by the Jews. Again, Luke uses good rabbinic material with great fidelity. I will give a few examples from these two to show where and in how far they are Hellenistic.

John certainly represents Jesus as the *logos,* the rational element, the "Word" manifested in history. But when we examine the relevant passages carefully, we find that fundamentally he is not interested in this philosophical idea, that his fundamental interest is in Jesus and the Jewish way of understanding Jesus. For instance, in the first chapter he refers to Jesus as "the Word that was made flesh, and dwelt among us." But immediately he adds that "no man has seen God at any time: his only begotten son, Jesus, has explained him." No sooner has he proclaimed a Hellenistic philosophical doctrine than he insists on the invisibility of God, that what can be seen is only a manifestation of God: in this essential matter he becomes thoroughly rabbinic. We find this attitude throughout the Gospel.

Luke was, of course, quite different, and he shows his Hellenistic training, above all, by making the story smoother. He cuts out phrases which would sound crude to the Hellenistic reader, for example, the opening Amen ("Verily"); but he does it with mixed success. According to Mark, Jesus on the cross cries out aloud just before dying. Luke omits this. It has been maintained that here again there is Hellenistic influence, and that this is a concession to the gnostic, Docetic heresy. These gnostics held that Jesus himself was never on earth and his body never suffered; that only an appearance of Jesus came down but his celestial body remained in heaven. So it has been maintained that Luke's omission of the cry from the cross is a concession to this spiritualising doctrine. But it is most improbable. Much more probably he omitted it because it was too barbarous for a Hellenistic public. Luke is a fair Hellenistic writer and, in his version, the dress of the story and the whole set-up of it is more elegant than in the other Gospels. If you read Luke without remembering too much of the other Gospels, you will notice that he presents the story of Jesus as a sort of travel story. Such travel stories were fashionable at the time. Luke quite successfully follows the fashion, but this is only superficial and, in essence, he too remains faithful to rabbinic tradition.

The most Hellenistic element in the New Testament is its language. It is not written in Hebrew or Aramaic, it is written in Greek. But even here I should add a warning. A foreign language as such need not, after a while, be a sign of cultural influence. When part of Jewry adopted Yiddish, it was, of course, greatly influenced by German-Polish civilisation; but, after a while, that could no longer be inferred. And today it can probably be said that those Jews in Israel who speak Hebrew are much more modern than those who stick to Yiddish. In New Testament times, many Jewish circles, even in Palestine, had long known and spoken Greek. The Talmud tells us that Gamaliel II, who flourished from about 90 to 110 C.E., had a double curriculum for his pupils: Greek was studied as well as Hebrew. This is reliable information. So it seems that even the writing of the New Testament in Greek, though a concession to Hellenism, is not so great a concession as is often assumed.

2. The Dating of Rabbinic Material in the New Testament

We have to consider how to determine the relative ages of ideas and customs which appear both in the New Testament and in our rabbinic sources. The problem is made more difficult than it need be by prejudices. There is a tendency among Christian scholars to consider as much as possible in the New Testament to be original, or rather, to consider those parts original which seem to them agreeable and worthy, which sometimes means such ideas and customs as happen to be fashionable at the time. For example, in the 19th century it was usual to declare any liberal elements in the New Testament to be original, and any similar liberal trends in rabbinic literature to be later than the New Testament. Today, the school of Karl Barth would quite happily leave the liberal elements to the rabbinic sources and would regard a certain theological authoritarianism as essential to the New Testament and as not so early or so prominent in rabbinic literature. We Jewish scholars, it should be admitted, incline the other way. Our writers on the New Testament—even great scholars like Klausner—tend, whenever they find thoughts or customs which strike them as important and valuable, to say these are rabbinic, and anything that they do not approve of they declare to be originally Christian. Those Jewish scholars who think that universalism is the ultimate word in ethics claim that rabbinic religion had become completely universalistic prior to the New Testament and that any universalistic passages in the New Testament are simply rabbinic; whereas those who insist upon the virtues of nationalism maintain that rabbinic religion prior to the New Testament laid much stress on the nationalist element in life and ethics and that Christians were responsible for a "wishy-washy" universalism.

The rabbinic sources—the Mishnah in the form in which we have it and the more important Midrashim—were completed after the New Testament. This does not mean that the material in them is necessarily later than the material in the New Testament. Suppose that we codified English law today. Although this codification would date from 1956, a good deal of the material in it would be very much older; some, indeed, would date from the early Middle Ages. If we compared our new codification with a tract written in 1700 about theft or the proper treatment of insane persons before the law, we might find in the codification of 1956 much older material than in the tract written in 1700. Or suppose that a thousand years hence all that remained of post-Reformation literature was Rousseau and Churchill's Memoirs. The Social Contract is mentioned in Rousseau and in Churchill. So is pipe-smoking. You might argue from that that the idea of the Social Contract or pipe-smoking arose in Switzerland and came to England 200 years later. But the idea of the Social Contract occurs in Hobbes before it occurs in Rousseau, and pipe-smoking also was taken up in England earlier than in Switzerland.

Criteria for Relative Dating

This kind of thing must be borne in mind when one has to do with the relative dating of New Testament and rabbinic material. Take the red wine that is used for the Seder ceremony. The first Rabbi to mention that red wine is to be used lived in the 4th century. Yet it is clear that the custom was firmly established in New Testament times, for the comparison with blood presupposes red wine. The custom can therefore be shown to antedate the earliest rabbinic mention by some 300 years. Again, the equation of the Suffering Servant in Isaiah with Israel first appears in rabbinic sources in the 12th century. But 900 years earlier, the Church Father Origen writes that this interpretation is current in Jewish circles.

Because of these difficulties, I should like to indicate a few criteria which can guide us in relative dating.

(1) Where the rabbinic sources mention a definite author for a statement it may be assumed that this record is correct. If, for example, we are told that Hillel introduced the *Prozbul*, or that he established certain rules for interpretation, or that Joshua ben Hananiah held noteworthy views about the initiation of proselytes, then, unless we have good proof to the contrary, we may assume that the idea does go back to Hillel or to Joshua ben Hananiah. There are, of course, exceptions. An interesting book on the development of Mohammedan doctrine has recently been published by Schacht. It shows how successive doctrines, after they had gained recognition, were ascribed to the Prophet. The same process took place in Christian literature, even within the New Testament, and some later utterances were attributed to Jesus or Paul. It happened also in rabbinic history: ideas of far more recent origin would be ascribed to Moses, or perhaps to a famous early Rabbi. However, in general, if a certain Rabbi is named as the author of an idea or a custom, that record is reliable. We thus obtain a great deal of rabbinic material which can safely be treated as earlier than, or contemporary with, the New Testament.

Pre-Christian Ideas

(2) If we find several lines converging to the same kind of thought, we can infer that the central thought is earlier than the various indications of it. Even if all the literature of about 1900 were lost, a future scholar might still conclude, from the many different applications of psychoanalysis today, that it was not a new thing in 1956 but must have started at least one or two generations earlier. Similarly in rabbinic literature. The idea of rejoicing in suffering occurs very frequently in rabbinic sources. The question is whether it antedates Christianity. I should say that, as we meet with it in so many connections in rabbinic literature and also, for example, in the Syriac version of the Apocalypse of Baruch, there can be no doubt that it goes back to a date prior to Christianity. Again, the concept of the original Adam as bi-sexual is found in various connections, and the Rabbis inform us that it occurred in some versions of the Septuagint, the Greek translation of the Bible. It is also found in Philo. It must, therefore, antedate the New Testament, a result that has a bearing on the interpretation of the New Testament attack on divorce, which seems to be partly based upon it. Or take the opposition to divorce which is connected in the Gospel of Luke with the eternal validity of the Law. Is this just a whim of Luke or is it a pre-Christian rabbinic idea, whatever its basis may be? Again we find several convergent lines. We find opposition to polygamy and divorce connected with the eternal validity of the Law in the Zadokite fragments, and we find the two connected in an anecdote which is told of Rabbi Simeon ben Jochai. All these traces are spread over entirely different fields, so surely the idea must be pre-Christian.

Points Used as Arguments

(3) Where a Rabbi uses one point to prove another, the point he uses as an argument must be earlier, at least, than the moment of argument; usually it is earlier than the Rabbi himself. This, of course, supplies us with a great deal of material which antedates the Rabbis who use it. To give an example: It is sometimes held that the Rabbis in New Testament times still adhered to the literal interpretation of "an eye for an eye, a tooth for a tooth" and so on. It can be shown conclusively by other evidence that they did not, but I am concerned here with a certain criterion. There is a law in Deuteronomy which says that, in the case of a certain offence, a person shall have her hand cut off. Now at an early date the Rabbis explained that this does not mean that she will literally have her hand cut off; it means that she will have to pay damages. The Rabbis' argument is that, because the provision "an eye for an eye, a tooth for a tooth" means merely monetary damages, therefore the provision also means monetary damages. The interpretation of "an eye for an eye, a tooth for a tooth" as monetary damages must have been firmly established before it could be used to prove that point about another law from Deuteronomy; and that gives us a date earlier than the New Testament. To take another example: A certain 4th-century Rabbi uses the first verse of the Hallel Psalm 113, "Praise, O ye servants of the Lord. . ." to prove another point and he proceeds from the interpretation of the verse that when the children of Israel were free from Pharaoh, they became slaves of God. Since the point he makes is an entirely different one, this interpretation must have been quite accepted before his day. This helps to account for the tremendous role which the notion of the change of master plays in the New Testament. It is a rabbinic notion.

(4) A Rabbi may adduce a verse from the Bible in order to establish a new point, to extract from it a new decision, idea or custom. But often Rabbis adduce a verse in order to base on it an established idea or custom, to clothe an established point with Scriptural authority. In that case it is again obvious that the idea or custom is earlier than the argument. There is a legend in the rabbinic sources of how the young Samuel taught in the temple and was cleverer than the teachers and priests. This is associated with verses in the first chapter of the book of Samuel. The question is, did the Rabbi take these verses and make up the legend from them, or was it current in his time and he just thought that it should be proved from the Bible and so he found the appropriate verses? The latter is probably correct. This would again have a bearing on New Testament material, because the story of the young Jesus teaching in the Temple and of his parents, especially Mary, being worried about him might be a transfer of the Samuel legend. We know from other texts that certain features of Samuel were regarded as Messianic and were transferred to Jesus. The role which Mary plays in this story would have a precedent in the Samuel legend, since it is Hannah who finally saves Samuel from the Temple authorities who are hard on him for his presumption.

The Inconvenient is Presumably Old

(5) The next criterion, which I regard as very important, is a paradoxical one. It is that the inconvenient must be presumed to be old. Our natural inclination, when we find

something which we do not like, is to say, "This does not belong to the main source. It is a later interpolation." An example from the New Testament is the story of the Gadarene swine. It tells how devils entered into them and drove them into the sea. In the Middle Ages, this story was well liked. But it does not fit into the West End of modern London and, therefore, even some of the best Christian New Testament scholars try to explain it away as a Galilean interpolation, and as nothing to do with the ministry of Jesus. We Jews do the same sort of thing. However, if you want to be honest in dating material, you must proceed from the presumption that what you do not like is genuine and old. In rabbinic literature there is a passage which says that Elijah, when he returns at the beginning of Messianic times, will be entitled to alter or abrogate the Law. This statement is as much disliked by traditional Jewish authorities as the story of the Gadarene swine is disliked by modern Christian theologians. It is hardly ever mentioned in Jewish tradition and, where it is mentioned, it is explained away. But the statement has, I think, the presumption of good old age in its favour, and it should be taken seriously. It may underlie a good deal of what Paul taught.

(6) A vast number of ideas and customs, whether in the New Testament or in rabbinic sources, are taken for granted by those expressing or practising them and, therefore, are obviously earlier. Prayer is taken for granted, preaching, the sending of letters, the exercise of various crafts are taken for granted. It is not always easy to decide whether a thing is taken for granted, but often we can be quite sure—especially where the author has no great interest in the matter. By paying attention to this criterion, we may isolate much material which antedates Christianity. In the Gospel of Mark, Jesus in the Garden of Gethsemane prays and then comes back to find his disciples dozing. He addresses them and they reply, but they do not know how to reply properly. Then he goes away again to pray and, when he comes back, he finds them fast asleep. The rule is stated in the Mishnah—and some comparable rule has now been found in the Dead Sea Scrolls—that if one of the participants in the Seder falls asleep, the Seder communion is irretrievably dissolved. In 5th-century rabbinic *halakhah,* we find a discussion about the exact moment of dissolution. The definition is that, so long as you reply when addressed, you are not asleep. The Rabbis actually note that, if you reply but do not know exactly what to reply, you are not yet asleep but are only dozing, and the Passover communion is not dissolved. It is dissolved only when you simply do not hear. This is 5th–century *halakhah,* but it is taken for granted in the story of Jesus in the Garden of Gethsemane; otherwise the double coming would have no point. It is clearly not a New Testament innovation, for Mark has no axe to grind; he is not interested in special Passover Eve customs of this kind and he just thinks of the *halakhah* as natural. We can, therefore, say that, although in rabbinic sources we do not find this *halakhah* until some 400 years later, it antedates the New Testament writings.

Ideas Partly Old and Partly New

(7) There are, of course, many more complicated cases than those I have mentioned. Above all, there are those in which an idea in one form may be fairly new, but some part of it goes back to a much earlier time. There we have to decide exactly how

far it is old and how far new. After the Seder meal, it is customary to open the door and to recite some verses from the Psalms asking God to pour out His wrath on the evil–doers of the gentile world. These verses are not in the ancient Seder liturgy but were put into the Ashkenazi rite during the period of persecution in the Middle Ages. Yet, can we really say that this part of the Seder dates only from the Middle Ages? In a sense, yes. But to some extent it is much older. On Passover Eve, at the end of the meal, the Messiah is expected, and he will bring with him not only peace and redemption, but also judgment. This idea is very ancient; and that is why the verses were put in at this particular place. So as an expression of the arrival of the judge, this part of the Service is, in fact, pre–Christian. My last example is perhaps more fragile. In the Ashkenazi rite, the Seder liturgy ends with that fascinating little song *Chad Gadya.* We know that it was composed in the late Middle Ages, almost at the beginning of modern times, so that, in one sense, it is late. But it ends with the destruction of the Angel of Death; and the idea that the Messianic Age will bring his destruction is very old indeed. There is a passage in a letter written by Paul to be read at Passover to an early Christian community, which is curiously reminiscent of this. It explains that, in the end, Jesus on behalf of God will subdue "all rule and authority and power"; and the last enemy to be destroyed will be Death. This is based on good pre–Christian rabbinic material. Did the main theme of *Chad Gadya,* then, already play a part in the Jewish Passover of New Testament times?

The Gospels and the Rabbis*

The New Testament can be best understood against the background of the Palestinian Judaism of the time. Many scholars have done good work in this respect, but there is scope for further research. Let me give a few examples.

Ruth—A Foretaste of Messianic Fulfilment

In the Gospel according to Luke,[1] the angel, who announces to Mary the birth of a son, declares: "The power of the Highest shall over-shadow thee." And Mary replies: "Behold, the handmaid of the Lord." The use of the verb "to overshadow" in this context is strange and has led to a number of theories by modern writers, none of them satisfactory. The explanation is that the Gospel is alluding to the story of Ruth. When Ruth came to Boaz at night, saying "I am Ruth thine handmaid, spread thy wing over thine handmaid,"[2] she was not yet married to him. This fact created a problem for the ancient Jewish Rabbis: no blemish must attach to the character of Ruth, the prototype of the genuine convert and an ancestress of David and the Messiah. The Rabbis somehow reached the conclusion that the request "Spread thy wing over thine handmaid" revealed exceptional chastity; indeed though appearances might be against her, Ruth was the purest of all women.[3] In the Aramaic vernacular translation, "spread thy wing" could easily become "overshadow"; the two expressions are closely associated.[4]

Luke, by his language, by the use of the verb "to overshadow," and also by the way in which Mary describes herself as "the Lord's handmaid," means to indicate a parallel between this situation and the Old Testament one, as interpreted by the Rabbis. Mary, betrothed to Joseph, was with child; yet, despite appearances, this second Ruth was pure, a virgin. It should be stressed that the Evangelist is fully conscious of the uniqueness of the events he relates. But he would deprive himself of a valuable means of bringing out their significance if he did not refer to earlier incidents in the history of Israel as foreshadowing and throwing light on them. The figure of Ruth in particular was looked upon by many Rabbis as endowed with features pointing forward to Messianic happenings.

* Talk given on the B.B.C. Third Programme and printed in *The Listener*, 6 September 1956. A German version with footnotes, translated by Dr. Ernst Bammel, appeared in *ZNW* 48 (1957), 119–26. The footnotes in this volume are translated from it.

[1] Luke 1:35, 38.

[2] Ruth 3:9.

[3] *Ruth Rab.* on 3:9; *Gen. Rab.* on 39:7.

[4] *ṭallit*, "cloak," *ṭelal*, "shadow," *ṭallel*, "to overshadow."

There is at least one more narrative in the New Testament where she is subtly introduced: the narrative of the miraculous feeding of the multitude. There are five versions in the Gospels of Matthew, Mark and Luke,[5] all of which culminate in a statement like "They did eat and were filled and took up twelve baskets full of what was left." This echoes the notice about Ruth, when she had been invited by Boaz to share his and his people's meal in the field: "She did eat and was filled and left thereof."[6] It is, then, the Christian Messianic community which is compared to Ruth: the meal Ruth received from Boaz is regarded in the Gospels as adumbrating the meal the multitude receives from Jesus. This is not so surprising when we consider the role which the pious speculation of the Rabbis assigned to the feeding of Ruth. Ruth was taken by the Rabbis as standing for her descendants, in particular David or even the Messiah, and Boaz, her host, as standing for God. There is indeed one Rabbi for whom it was a miraculous meal, because though Boaz gave her little, it turned out to be more than enough in her hands.[7]

A FATEFUL SLEEP

The scene at Gethsemane before the arrest is nowadays widely classed as legendary, as embodying a theological maxim but with no claim to historicity.[8] Commentators can discover no natural motivation either for Jesus' request to the disciples to stay awake or for the serious consequences he draws when they do finally fall asleep. There is, however, an adequate motivation to be found in the Jewish setting of the story. According to the Evangelists, Jesus and his disciples form a Passover eve company such as was usual in that period: everywhere in Palestine friends, like-minded people, joined to go up to Jerusalem and celebrate Passover eve as a group—five, eight, ten, any number. There were rules governing the formation and the termination of a company; and some circles were stricter than others in these matters. One rule says that if any member of the company fall asleep, the bond is dissolved between all and incapable of being restored, but if they merely doze it is not;[9] and we are told that a man who dozes is characterised by the fact that when spoken to "he answers but does not know how to answer sensibly."[10]

Clearly when Jesus asks the disciples to stay awake, it is in order to delay the ending of the company; the notice that, on his second return from prayer, "their eyes were heavy neither wist they what to answer him" means that as yet, though dozing, they are not fully asleep; and on his third return, when he finds that they are, he knows that he must go on alone. This is not to minimise the theological moral of the scene; but it is firmly rooted in the rabbinic customs of Passover eve. In the sectarian Manual of Discipline, one of the recently discovered Dead Sea Scrolls, falling asleep in the assembly is treated as a grave offence. Luke's narrative, incidentally, is briefer than Matthew's and Mark's

[5] Matt 14:13 ff., 15:32 ff.; Mark 6:31 ff., 8:1 ff.; Luke 9:10 ff.

[6] Ruth 2:14.

[7] *Ruth Rab.* on 2:14; *b. Shab.* 113b.

[8] Matt 26:36 ff.; Mark 14:32 ff.; Luke 22:40 ff.

[9] *m. Pes.* 10:8.

[10] *b. Pes.* 120b.

shorn of all these technical rabbinic points. We need not decide whether Luke himself did not appreciate them or whether he thought that his readers would be unlikely to.

Jesus' Burial Without "Disgrace"

The rabbinic concepts most easily missed are those which are strange to our way of thinking, not yet established in the Old Testament and no longer prominent in modern Judaism. There was in the New Testament era a curious rabbinic notion of "disgrace,"[11] the influence of which is discernible in the reports about the death of Jesus. The opponents of Jesus seem to have dwelt on the "disgraceful," "scandalous" aspects of his end; the Evangelists, though not denying his suffering, are yet understandably concerned to collect all facts that would mitigate the "disgrace." "Disgrace" as conceived by the Rabbis might befall not only a living person but also a corpse. In general, an executed criminal was first buried in a public plot and only a year later transferred to the family grave.[12] Jesus, according to the Gospel of Matthew, was at once buried in the family grave of Joseph of Arimathaea, newly built.[13] Luke and John do not mention that it was a family grave, but at least they also state that it was a grave where no one had been buried before;[14] so it could not be a public plot used on previous occasions. The Gospel of Mark does not go into this point at all.[15]

Again, as a rule an executed criminal was buried unanointed.[16] According to the Gospel of John, however, Joseph of Arimathaea and Nicodemus anointed the body of Jesus; indeed John emphasises that it was done in the approved Jewish fashion.[17] The Gospels of Matthew and Mark do not include this scene. But here, too, the "disgrace" is relieved: for the anointing of the living Jesus by a woman at Bethany is taken to be an anointing of his dead body in advance.[18] The rite of anointing was performed, in however unorthodox a manner. John, who has the proper anointing after death, does not ascribe to the anointing by Mary at Bethany the significance of a burial rite.[19] The Gospel of Luke neither mentions an anointing after death nor contains the idea of a burial rite by anticipation.[20]

The most serious "disgrace" in the rabbinic sense was such mutilation as might look like impeding bodily resurrection. About the period of the New Testament bodily resurrection became a cardinal tenet of the Pharisees. Such was the importance attached to it that they carried out far-reaching reform of time-honoured institutions of the criminal law.[21] The old methods of stoning and burning were replaced by new ones

[11] *niwwul.*
[12] *m. Sanh.* 6:5 f.
[13] Matt 27:60.
[14] Luke 23:53; John 19:41.
[15] Mark 15:46.
[16] *m. Sanh.* 6:5 f.; Josephus, *Ant.* 4.8.6.202, 4.8.24.264, 5.1.14.44.
[17] John 19:39 f.
[18] Mark 14:3 ff.; Matt 26:6 ff.
[19] John 12:1 ff.
[20] Cp. Luke 7:36 ff.
[21] See Büchler, *MGWJ*, 50 (1875), 550 ff., 683 ff., 704 ff.

of so-called stoning and so-called burning which, though not less cruel, avoided any visible damage to the skeleton, and strangulation became the most acceptable mode of execution.

It is with these trends in mind that we must read the circumstantial and insistent account in the Gospel of John of how it came that Jesus' legs were not broken.[22] The Christians shared the belief of the Pharisees in bodily resurrection; more than that, they affirmed that Jesus, after being crucified, actually walked the earth again. A breaking of the bones would have given a handle to their antagonists. John quotes the Old Testament provision laying down that the Passover lamb must remain intact.[23] Critics hold that his story of the omission to break Jesus' legs is not based on tradition but derives from his wish to assimilate Jesus to the lamb. When we consider the rabbinic concept of "disgrace," it is far more likely that the story does go back to an early stage in the controversy about the risen Jesus. John's starting-point was not the quotation on which he built the story, but the story he supported by reference to the Passover lamb, a symbol, by its intactness, of the assurance of resurrection, individual as well as national.

Four Categories of Questions

At times a consideration of the rabbinic material will illumine not only the meaning of a New Testament narrative but the composition of a chapter. In the Gospels of Matthew and Mark,[24] the following four questions are discussed in the same section:

(1) Is it lawful to give tribute to Caesar?

(2) If a man dies without issue and his widow marries his brother, this one also dies and she marries another brother, and so on till she has been married to seven—when they all rise from the dead, whose wife will she be?

(3) Which is the most important commandment?

(4) How can the Messiah be the son of David seeing that David in his Psalms calls him his Lord?

At first sight there seems to be no rational connection between these questions at all. Yet there is a simple reason for their being put together. The Rabbis of the time divided questions into four categories:[25] questions of wisdom, where you ask concerning a point of law; questions of mockery, where you scoff at beliefs of the community, above all that in bodily resurrection; questions of conduct, where you are interested in the principles of a moral life; and questions of exegesis, where you want an explanation of an apparent contradiction in Scripture. The four questions in Matthew and Mark represent the four categories established by the Rabbis. "Is it lawful to pay tribute?" is a question of wisdom, about a point of law. "Whose wife will the widow of seven brothers be when they rise?" is a question of mockery, ridiculing bodily resurrection. "Which is

[22] John 19:31 ff.

[23] Exod 12:46; Num 9:12.

[24] Matt 22:15 ff.; Mark 12:13 ff.

[25] *b. Nidd.* 69b ff.

the first commandment?" is a question of conduct about the basis of a moral life. And "How can the Messiah be David's son and David's Lord at the same time?" is a question of exegesis, concerning an apparent contradiction in Scripture.

We can be even more specific about the model on which this chapter in Matthew and Mark is designed. It will be remembered that the first three questions about tribute to Caesar, the widow, and the greatest commandment are put to Jesus by various people, while the fourth question, about David's son and David's Lord, is put by Jesus himself. The Jewish Passover eve liturgy refers to four types of sons and the instruction in the meaning of the Passover festival appropriate to each of them.[26] One of the sons puts a question of wisdom, one a question of mockery, and one a question of conduct; but in the case of the fourth, the father himself opens the instruction. This cannot be coincidence. The inference is that the New Testament chapter was composed in close analogy to the Passover eve liturgy, in fact by an early Christian who still celebrated the Jewish Passover and replaced or supplemented a traditional section respecting the old exodus by one, similar in structure, dealing with the ministry of Jesus. It may have been Mark, or perhaps even Peter. In the Gospel of Matthew, the original nature of the four questions seems less fully appreciated than in Mark, and in Luke the entire structure is abandoned.

Apostolic Succession

In a number of cases the results to be gained from a study of the Rabbis have a bearing on live problems affecting Christian law or institutions. The historical discussion of Imposition of Hands and Apostolic Succession suffers from the failure to distinguish between two kinds of Imposition of Hands, designated by different terms in the Hebrew-Aramaic sources: a gentle placing of the hands on a person to be blessed, and a heavy leaning.[27] The gentle placing mediated some beneficial influence. The heavy leaning meant the pouring of one's personality into another being. In first-century rabbinic Judaism this rite of leaning was practically confined to two occasions: the sacrificial cult,[28] when you leaned your hand on the animal to be offered, and ordination,[29] when a Rabbi leaned his hands on a disciple, thereby passing on his personality and creating another Rabbi, another true successor of Moses. Jesus performed Imposition of Hands in the sense of a gentle placing, to bless or to heal.[30] But he never performed it in the sense of a heavy leaning, to ordain. Apart from the fact that he was not ordained himself, the idea of Jesus communicating his personality to another man would be impossible. In the early Church, however, the rite of leaning was extended far beyond its rabbinic range, at least in the circles contemplated in the Acts of the Apostles. There

[26] Haggadah, towards the beginning of the first part.

[27] *śim* or *šith*, "to place," *samakh*, "to lean."

[28] E.g., *m. Betz* 2:4.

[29] E.g., *Siphre* on Num 27:23.

[30] E.g., Matt 19:13 ff. Perhaps "to breathe on" in John 20:22 is chosen in order to avoid a leaning on: see J. Hempel, *ZAW*, 68 (1956), 201 (however, Rabbinic authority is not required for the simple blessing of a placing on of hands).

the distributors of charity, though they were not receiving ordination proper, were appointed in this way;[31] and so were Paul and Barnabas when they were sent out by their fellow teachers on a special mission,[32] though they already ranked among the leaders of the Church and there could be no question of promotion from disciple to master. Of this extended use of the rite of leaning, which reflects an enormous religious self-confidence and enthusiasm, and perhaps some liking for the magic involved, no trace is preserved in the Epistles of Paul.

However, the Christian equivalent of rabbinic ordination appears in the Epistles to Timothy. It is clear that the author had made Timothy a bishop by leaning his hands on him, and that Timothy was entitled to use this method for installing others.[33] Just so, in that age any ordained Rabbi had the right to ordain others.[34] One passage in the First Epistle has created difficulty,[35] where it looks as if Timothy had become a bishop by "the laying on of the hands of the presbytery"—the presbytery, not the author of the Epistles. But the usual translation is misleading. The Greek stands for a rabbinic phrase which signifies "the leaning on to appoint a Rabbi."[36] Properly translated, therefore, the passage says, not that Timothy was installed by "the laying on of the hands of the presbytery," but by "the laying on of the hands for the presbytery," "for the office of an ordained Elder, a Rabbi," or in the new, Christian organisation "by the laying on of the hands for the office of a bishop." This is the earliest evidence of the appointment of a bishop by his master leaning his hands on him; and the rabbinic phrase only underlines the closeness of the transaction to the model of Jewish ordination. At the same time the passage should no longer be quoted as attesting the existence in the Church of that period of a body called the presbytery.

PRONOUNCEMENT ON DIVORCE

The pronouncement by Jesus on divorce, as transmitted in the Gospel of Mark,[37] should be read against the background of contemporary Jewish thought. As an argument against divorce, Jesus quotes a verse from the story of the creation, in the First Book of Moses: "Male and female created he them."[38] At first sight it is difficult to perceive why this verse should support the rejection of divorce; indeed it might be held to favour divorce, since God created male and female, independent beings. The clue lies in the doctrine of the ancient Rabbis,[39] who saw in this verse an allusion to the original Adam before Eve was taken out of him. In the eyes of those Rabbis "Male and female created he them" conveyed the teaching that the original Adam was male and female in one. It

[31] Acts 6:1 ff.

[32] Acts 13:1 ff.

[33] 1 Tim 5:22; 2 Tim 1:6.

[34] *y. Sanh.* 19a.

[35] 1 Tim 4:14.

[36] *semikhath zeqenim.*

[37] Mark 10:2 ff.

[38] Gen 1:27, 5:2.

[39] *Gen. Rab.* on 1:26 f.

does not matter whether or not we agree with their interpretation of this verse: Jesus had to proceed from it. Obviously, understood in this way, the verse was a powerful argument against divorce. In the ideal creation, man and woman had constituted one being. Marriage approaches that state; divorce followed by re-marriage is a denial of it; and it is that whether the wife leaves her husband to marry someone else or—and here we arrive at a consequence diverging from traditional Judaism—whether the husband leaves his wife to re-marry. In either case it is a breaking into two of an original whole. It is on this basis alone that we can appreciate the force of the words added by Jesus: "What therefore God hath joined together, let not man put asunder." Once again the reference is to the ideal world, when male and female had been united.

This view of the pronouncement is confirmed when we look at the controversy about divorce as a whole. Jesus is asked about this issue by the Pharisees. His reply is founded, we submit, on a rabbinic interpretation of the verse he adduces. Later, at home, his disciples ask him again for his opinion on the subject, and now he informs them in so many words that divorce followed by re-marriage is adultery. Why should the disciples ask again in private if the public reply to his enemies has been fully intelligible? That reply, quoting "Male and female created he them," must contain some esoteric, mysterious doctrine. It is the rabbinic doctrine of the original Adam, male and female, of which at least the consequences in respect of marriage were not familiar to the uninitiated.

The "Nails" and the Jews*

In 1942 or 3, when I was doing humanitarian war work in England, I met a Protestant chaplain—I am not sure what his name was, Watson, I think—who felt the need for a more seriously engaged Christianity. Two of his hopes were that the Church would help in improving the social order and in replacing enmity by understanding in relations with Jews. Remember that the welfare state was still in the future and that antisemitic doctrines which dominated the continent had some impact even in Britain. Today he would find many flourishing bodies with whom he could link up—especially in the U.S.A. At that time, it was uphill labour. He founded a group "The Nails," so called because the members were always to carry four nails in a pocket, so as not for one moment to forget about Jesus's sacrifice and the demands flowing from it. He planned a publication where their goals were to be set out in detail; and he asked me, then leading a strictly traditional Jewish life, to contribute an article on how far cooperation between us was possible. Before this volume was ready, the group evaporated. He moved away and we lost touch. But I found a carbon of my typescript and shall here reproduce it without the slightest revision. After that, some reflections.

I.

The object of the movement called "The Nails," to judge by a perusal of its Code, is a closer association of the Christian religion with the common life in our industrialized society. The sponsors of the movement realize that even those who are true Christians at heart are more and more apt to regard religion as something to be practised only on certain definite occasions. The notion of religion as the great principle by which all actions, private or public, must be governed is rapidly disappearing. To revive it, and thereby to make Christianity a living factor in the modern world, is the purpose of the new movement.

II.

For that section of Judaism which is strictly observant, and which for the sake of brevity will be termed orthodox in the following remarks, the same problem does not arise. It is absolutely impossible to be an orthodox Jew and not to consider one's every

* From the second part of "Two Jewish Prayers." The article was dedicated to Käthe Zhao. It opened: "The following pages will be devoted to two prayers, one from Genesis [Vol. 3], the other from the Gemara, which have received little attention. Neither has a place in *The Oxford Book of Prayer*—an excellent volume. One is authored by a vile wretch, the other is not for polite company."

action in the light of God's will. The orthodox Jew has to be careful about what he eats and drinks; about when he sleeps and how long; about his prayers several times a day; about his Sabbath and festivals; about his fast-days. He has to say blessings when he gets up in the morning, before and after meals, on taking a glass of water, on smelling an odorous plant, on seeing a beautiful tree or animal, on seeing a deformed person, after relieving nature ("Blessed art thou, O Lord our God, King of the Universe, who hast formed man in wisdom and created in him many orifices and vessels; it is revealed and known before the throne of thy glory that if one of these be opened, or one of these be closed, it would be impossible to exist and stand before thee; blessed art thou, O Lord, who healest all flesh and doest wondrously"[1]), on going to bed and so on. The slightest deviation from truth is a desecration of God's name; he must set aside a certain time every day for the study of his religion; however poor he may be, he must give a minimum percentage of any earnings for charity; he must visit the sick, he must wash and dress the dead (an office never left to paid servants). This list could be extended *ad libitum* [at will]. The orthodox Jew cannot move a finger without thinking of the religious implications.

III.

This does not mean that orthodox Judaism is a system of mere forms, with no emphasis on higher ideals and faith. Can anyone imagine that orthodox Jews have been practising all those tremendously inconvenient rules throughout thousands of years, and are still practising them, for the fun of it? Admittedly, it is quite conceivable that an individual person might abandon his ideals and faith and yet go on, from habit or other motives, observing the traditional forms of orthodoxy. But why should generation after generation shoulder the burden if it were not for a profound trust in God? The true reason why there is comparatively little discussion in orthodox writings of faith and the wider aims is not that these are lacking, but, on the contrary, that they are taken for granted. They are so firmly established that no laborious teaching is needed: without them, the whole edifice, Sabbath and dietary rules and blessings and all, would fall to the ground. In other words, the orthodox Jew attaches so much importance to the forms because, the goal being clear, "an ever-fixed mark," what matters on this earth is the way to the goal: and the Law, in his eyes, is the guidance that God has given him. For him, the higher ideals and faith constitute the unshakable basis of all religion, as evident as the fact of life itself. But as it is not sufficient to recognize or pay lip-service to them, his main object on earth must be to bear witness to his faith and to stand for his ideals. In this, he believes, the forms support him, by making him mindful of God's will in everything he does. No man is free of sin. But the Law, in the orthodox view, at least helps man not to forget about his task. This is the significance of the forms: they are the means, pointed out by God, of making life at least as holy as possible.

[1] I am quoting this blessing in full since in some modern prayer books it is omitted from a misconceived sense of propriety.

IV.

Two passages may here be adduced (countless others would be equally good), both going back to the age before Constantine. The first is from the Talmud.[2] "Rabbi Simlai said, 613 commandments were given to Moses. . . . Then came Micah and reduced them to three: And what doth the Lord require of thee, but to do justly, and to love mercy, and to walk humbly with thy God?" This Rabbi at any rate looks upon the forms as the means by which a man may carry into practice the eternal ideals of justice and mercy, and express his faith in one omnipotent God. The other quotation is from Josephus.[3] He describes as the great, distinctive feature of the law that "it did not make piety one of the virtues, but it made all virtues—such as justice, wisdom, constancy, complete harmony between all citizens—parts of piety; for, with us, all actions, pursuits and statements have reference to piety towards God." The fear of God is the only source from which any good deeds may spring; and all our good deeds, all our observances of the Law, must rest on that.

V.

As is well known, Christianity at a fairly early stage ceased practising the Law. Of the causes that led to this attitude, suffice it to mention four: first, the attacks on dissemblers in the gospels, secondly, the necessity of smoothing the way for pagan converts, thirdly, the doctrine of Jesus as replacing the Law, and fourthly, the setting up of the new faith as an absolute criterion. First, the gospels contain a good many condemnations of hypocrites who, while saying their prescribed prayers, keeping the Sabbath and observing the dietary rules, do not hesitate to cheat or slander a neighbour (nor is it maintained by the present writer that there were not such hypocrites at the time of Jesus or that there are not such now). From these passages, a large number of early readers must have gained the impression, as even modern readers quite often do, that Jesus disapproved of the forms as such, that he objected to saying the prescribed prayers, keeping the Sabbath and observing the dietary rules as such. The result was that the followers of Jesus thought it their duty to discard the forms. Secondly, the followers of Jesus, under the influence of Paul, decided that it was essential not to confine the new religion to the Jews but to throw it open to pagans as well. Of pagans, however, it was too much to expect that they would submit to the Law: the very form by which alone male pagans could join the community under the Law, circumcision, was quite unacceptable to most. If the pagans were to be included, therefore, the only thing to do was to dispense with the Law—and this was done. The third point also is associated with the name of Paul. He worked out the doctrine that Jesus replaced the Law; that the Law had been necessary, as a "schoolmaster," before the arrival of Jesus; but that henceforth the duty of man was to live, not under the Law, but in Jesus. Logically, this doctrine ought perhaps to have made for a Christian life even more dominated by religion (if that were possible) than the orthodox Jewish. For, logically, what it implied was

[2] *b. Makk.* 23b–24a.

[3] *Contra Apionem* 2.16.170.

not that the Christian should be satisfied with less practice but that no amount of practice should satisfy him at all: he should dispense with blessings on certain occasions, for example, not because there was any secular department in life, but because the whole life—not only certain occasions—was to be uniformly permeated by Jesus. As a matter of fact, however, the doctrine had the opposite consequence. As is only natural, few have been able to live up to it (Francis of Assisi comes to one's mind as one of them). Generally speaking, people found it easier to embrace the negative part of the doctrine, the rejection of the Law, than the positive, the substitution for the Law of an equally exacting task. Fourthly and finally, there is a point which the writer has not come across in the literature on the subject but which, he believes, played a considerable part in bringing about the difference here under notice between Judaism and Christianity. It has been argued above that, for the orthodox Jew, faith is the obvious basis for all action, requiring no demonstration; it is only the way in which faith can best be expressed, the Law, that calls for constant and closest examination. The followers of Jesus, however, introduced a dogma that was anything but obvious, the dogma of Jesus as Messiah and Son of God. In fact, the vast majority of Jews refused to recognize this dogma. Small wonder that those who stuck to it made of it the very touchstone of their community. The acceptance of the dogma became the principal demand of the new religion and thus, whereas in orthodox Judaism faith is the unquestioned element and to practise it man's chief duty, in Christianity practice lost a great deal of its importance and faith came to be deemed the chief aim.

VI.

Needless to say, there has remained a high standard of behaviour which the Christian is expected to attain. Yet in the absence of any definite rules giving definite guidance that standard grows vaguer and vaguer. Indeed, the current view is that to some of the most important provinces of modern life, such as politics or science, it need not be applied at all. The movement of "The Nails" is intended to remedy the situation; and to see to it that the Christian religion is not only professed but also practised, practised not only on Sundays but also during the week, practised not only in private life but also in business, politics, science. The founders have expressed the hope that the movement will be supported by orthodox Judaism, with its long experience of scrupulously practised religion. Let it be said at once: since the movement takes as its basis the Christian religion, and as its symbol a cross made of four nails, obviously, Jews cannot join as members. But this is a minor matter compared with what they can do. They can take part in any measures designed to raise the social, moral, cultural and religious standard of the nation and, in particular, the lower classes.

VII.

It has been frequently observed that "the Hebrew term for to give charity is to do justice."[4] In the orthodox Jewish view, that one man should be wealthy and another des-

[4] Proudhon, *Qu'est-ce que la propriété?*, 2nd ed., vol. I, 202.

titute constitutes a wrong which to redress is no more than simple justice: we are not bestowing favours, we are administering simple justice, when we fight poverty. Any action undertaken by the new movement to abolish want will be welcomed by Jewish orthodoxy. As for education, little need be added to the bidding of the Talmud,[5] "Be heedful of the children of the poor, for from them the Torah shall go forth"; or to quote a text with no specific reference to the poor, Josephus says[6] that "of all things we seek our glory in these, the education of children and the observance of the rules and the piety handed down through the latter." Jewish orthodoxy will welcome any action undertaken by the new movement to improve education and render it more generally accessible. There is no need here to go through the various items of the new movement's programme one by one and to shew how they all suit the orthodox Jewish notion of the duty of man. In fact, it would be surprising if there were any actions contemplated in a genuine Christian programme that orthodox Jews could not support. For Jewish ideals and Christian ideals are so much alike, "two young roes that are twins which feed among the lilies," the common heritage of the two religions and developed further on similar lines throughout the Middle Ages and the modern era, that few differences should exist when it comes to real, practical tasks like building better houses for the poor, making the life of a miner worth living, securing peace within the nation and in the world, and so on. This is not saying that every orthodox Jew must necessarily agree with every detail of the Code of "The Nails"; nor would the authors of the Code themselves maintain (if the present writer interprets them correctly) that none of their points could possibly be disputed by any Christian. When the Code, for instance, in chapter 3, advocates "equal educational opportunities for all children," nobody will deny that this is the ultimate object for which to strive. But surely, it may well be argued even by a most sincerely religious person that, in an imperfect world, one cannot achieve one's ideals by a stroke of the pen; and that, indeed, more might be destroyed than gained by over-hasty reforms. In short, if the new movement, which is not content with a purely theoretical Christianity, is itself to avoid becoming theoretical, it must carefully consider, in each matter that it deals with, what are the measures most likely to prove of real benefit to society. However, these are questions of detail which will be solved as the movement takes its course. The success of the new movement as a whole will depend entirely on the spirit of its Christian members and Jewish friends: they must be resolved, in a world that is growing ever more materialistic, to give an example of humble, unselfish work in the interest of their fellow-beings. Maybe the very fact of Christians and Jews joining in such an effort will mark a step towards the great goal, the fulfilment of the Psalmist's word: "Behold, how good and how pleasant it is for brethren to dwell together in unity."

Thus far 1942. I apologize for unfortunate concepts typical of the period; for example, "the lower classes" at the end of section VI. I took this over from the programme and I do not remember finding anything wrong with it at the time. Well before the end

[5] *b. Ned.* 81a.

[6] *Contra Apionem* 1.12.60.

of the war, the designation "the underprivileged" came to the fore; and, beyond terminology, we have grown more aware of the strong dose of self-satisfaction and narrowness which went into that entire way of seeing things. (No doubt the present one has its own flaws.) Again, in section II, I should have included a few more immediately appealing instances of law's beneficent power. Take the old teaching[7] that the Day of Atonement, while procuring forgiveness to the penitent for sins against God, does not erase a wrong against your fellow unless you have done your best to pacify him. Certain definite practices ensued. Here is one of them: in our small orthodox congregation at Freiburg, on the eve of this Day, members who had had a falling-out in the course of the year called on one another to make it up. To be sure, some quarrels would flare up again; but most did not and even the others had a new chance the following year—as, in a fallible world, but for the ritualism they might not have.

However, what I propose to have a closer look at is the prayer set forth in section II.[8] Nothing like it seems to exist in any other religion. Whereas in Judaism, far from representing some fringe element, it is part of the central tradition. My eldest son was still brought up like me to recite it every time he had been to the toilet; more precisely, to recite it after another, shorter blessing. "Blessed art thou, O Lord our God, King of the Universe, who hast sanctified us by thy commandments and commanded us concerning the washing [raising] of the hands"—for this washing also belongs to the ceremony. (It is attested for the Essenes at least already by Josephus.[9] Note, by the way, how this standard phrase in benedictions over performance of a duty, "who hast sanctified us by thy commandments and commanded us so-and-so," will never allow you to lose sight of the fundamental meaning underlying all the minutiae of the system: sanctification.) In fact, at a fairly early date, the two pieces were made the opening of the regular morning service, to be followed by one having regard to a Jew's main task, "Blessed art thou ... who hast commanded us to occupy ourselves with the words of the Torah." That, then, is how each day starts.

Significantly, the blessing under review conceives of divine care as absolutely universal, speaking of *adham*, the most inclusive word for "man," and *kol baśar*, "all flesh." This is a feature of many Jewish prayers to do with basic bodily needs. The primary portion of grace after a meal celebrates God as provider for "the entire world," "all flesh," "all his creatures"—covering even animals; similarly a briefer thanksgiving for food, to "the creator of many living beings and their wants."[10] The roots of this trend reach back deep into the Old Testament.[11]

[7] Based on Lev 16:30 by Eleazer ben Azariah: *Siphra* on Lev *ad loc.*; *m. Yom.* 8:9.

[8] To be found in Hebrew and English in *Authorized Daily Prayer Book,* transl. S. Singer, 9th ed. (1912), 4.

[9] *Bell.* 2.8.9.149.

[10] *Authorized Prayer Book*, 280, 290.

[11] E.g. Ps 104:11 ff. On its use in the Sabbath afternoon service between Tabernacles and Passover, see I. Abrahams, *Annotated Edition of the Authorized Daily Prayer Book* (1914), CLXXI f. An impressive yet neglected illustration is met in Gen 45:5, 50:20: Joseph's sale was providential in preserving Egyptian lives in a famine as well as in what it did for the Hebrews. In a Boalt Hall lecture *Appeasing or Resisting the Oppressor* [102 ff.], I argue that Caiaphas's prophecy of salvation beyond the nation in John 11:52 harks back to these verses.

As for the genesis of the blessing, to begin with, some crude data. The bulk of it, i.e. all except the concluding benediction "blessed art thou, O Lord, who healest all flesh and doest wondrously," is due to Abaye, around A.D. 300.[12] The conclusion is in a sense older. Apparently Rab, of the first half of the third century, had advised that, after easing oneself, one give thanks: "Blessed art thou, O Lord, who healest the sick." His contemporary Samuel objected that this was to turn everybody into a patient and substituted "who healest all flesh." Samuel's disciple Shesheth found even this too reminiscent of sickness and suggested "who doest wondrously."[13] Finally, Papa, disciple of Abaye and Abaye's friend and rival Raba, favoured a combination of Samuel's and Shesheth's texts—by now in the role of a coda to Abaye's lengthier and more specific prayer.[14] His became the authoritative version.

To go on to the background of the prayer—forty-five years ago, I despised the "progressives" who purged it from their worship. By now, while still admiring it no end, I am just a little less furious, for three reasons. First, it has become clearer to me that part of the blame attaches not to those reformers but to the surrounding culture which would treat them and their faith as uncivilized if sponsoring such coarseness. It was of course hopeless to put up a rational defence—say, to point out the hygiene bound up with this blessing. (It is widely held that if the Black Death struck Jewry somewhat less severely than gentiles, ritual washing before a meal, after relief and on numerous other occasions was a factor.[15]) This is not an area governed by sober discourse. Part of the blame only, since they ought to have stood their ground. Still . . . . Second, developments since then in certain societies in certain periods have caused me to think harder about the price paid for overthrowing shame. (Or guilt, but this does not come in here.) It is a tremendous plus, I am convinced, that in many regions of the U.S.A a paper will not lose its bourgeois readers if it counsels teenagers who are worried about the look of their genitals. But a university course on masturbation? Or, less heavy: was it antiquated brainwashing alone that produced a mild discomfort in some when President Johnson displayed the scar from his hernia operation in public? I well remember my late gentle, wise colleague David Louisell in the sixties questioning the slogan "to let it all hang out." Third, feelings were divided even in Abaye's age.

That he himself—rightly—places excretion below other activities is inferable, paradoxically, from the style reverential to an extraordinary degree, which takes doing considering the intensely worshipful tone of even the standard supplications. As if to make up for the subject, or better, so as to lift it into a sphere where nothing of its baser aspect remains. "It is revealed and known before the throne of thy glory": not simply "before

[12] *b. Ber.* 60b.

[13] Cp. e.g. Enoch 36:4.

[14] L. Goldschmidt, *Der Babylonische Talmud*, vol. 1 (1897), 223, in the margin calls attention to another such conciliatory decision of Papa's in *b. Ber.* 59a.

[15] See G. Herlitz, art. "Black Death," in *Universal Jewish Encyclopedia*, vol. 2 (1969), 368. Alas, the boon misfired. Perhaps precisely because suffering less from the epidemic, the Jews were deemed to cause it by poisoning the wells, and incomparably more were slaughtered in revenge than could have been by the plague at its worst. My Freiburg behaved badly.

thee." (First occurrence of "the throne of thy glory" is in a prayer of Jeremiah.[16]) "To endure and stand before thee": existence depends on the functions in question but its sole purpose is heavenward. (First occurrence of "to stand before God" is in the story of Abraham, when he undertook to plead for any righteous citizens that might dwell in Sodom.[17]) He has broken through, that is, to a rare balance: certain refinements, however valuable in social intercourse, are absurd vis-à-vis the power and understanding that encompass everything.

We have indeed direct evidence of the profound and daring spirit which went into his introduction of this blessing. The Talmudic report of it is preceded by a controversy between him and Aha, another sage of that era. The latter taught that, when entering the privy, one ought to ask one's guardian angels to wait outside. Abaye protested that they might take this seriously, suspending their service just while it was least dispensable—the last thing really wanted. In other words, communication with heaven had no use for polite dishonesties. The appropriate petition to the angels was: "Guard me, guard me, help me, help me, support me, support me, throughout my entering and leaving." No point, he added, in hiding from them our earthly make-up: "for such is the way of the sons of man." (Josephus, in his sketch of the Essenes adverted to above,[18] characterizes excretions as "natural.") It is at this juncture that we are told of his prayer after relieving nature which, in contrast to the earlier ones ("Blessed art thou who healest the sick," "healest all flesh," "doest wondrously"), calls a fig a fig. A devout address to the Lord can be open, should be open.

Plainly the dissension about this prayer is only a dramatic illustration of the problem coming up in countless shapes: where to place the lowlier bodily functions in terms of sacred and profane. Thus, R. Huna—third century—greatly admired a pupil of his, R. Hisda, who had himself become an authority. Yet Rabbah, Huna's son, flagrantly did not cultivate contact with Hisda, so Huna questioned him. Rabbah explained that he had visited Hisda in the past—to be treated, however, not to matters concerning heaven, but to mundane ones such as how to avoid hurting oneself when going to stool. Huna demolished this evaluation: "He is engaged in preserving the lives of God's creatures and you call it mundane matters."[19] Here it may be appropriate to remember the four-

[16] Jer 14:21.

[17] Gen 18:22.

[18] Text with footnote 9.

[19] *b. Shab.* 82a. In *y. Ber.* 11b, he once again reproves his son, and here also for being too narrow—though in a quite different area. Huna, his son Rabbah and his pupil Zeira, by then an accomplished scholar, dined together. Zeira got up to wait on the others (a first-century parallel is recorded in *b. Kidd.* 32b and quoted in connection with Matt 20:26 by H. L. Strack and P. Billerbeck, *Kommentar zum Neuen Testament aus Talmud und Midrasch*, vol. 1 [(1926, repr. 1969)], 838). He brought wine and oil for the end-of-Sabbath ceremony. Now according to the School of Shammai, you had to carry the wine in the right hand, the oil in the left, according to the School of Hillel, the other way round. Zeira carried both in one hand. Which caused Rabbah to ask: "What is your other hand carrying?" His father was enraged by this fault-finding with one doing a selfless act—indeed, remarkably selfless seeing that Zeira was of priestly descent. He ordered Zeira to return to his place and his son to do the serving. On Huna's allergy to self-importance and hypocrisy, see H. Loewe, in C. G. Montefiore and H. Loewe, *A Rabbinic Anthology* (1938, repr. 1974) with a prolegomenon by R. Loewe, LXXIX.

teenth-century anchoress Julian of Norwich. "Food is shut in our bodies" she writes, "as in a very beautiful purse. When necessity calls, the purse opens and then shuts again in the most fitting way. And it is God who does this because I was shown that the goodness of God permeates us even in our humblest needs."[20]

At least three more old-established prayers are disapproved by Abaye on basically the same grounds. One:[21] the customary acceptance by a mourner of his loss, in the course of which he confesses "I have sinned and thou hast not collected from me a thousandth part of my debt." Too theatrical for a genuine offer to undergo an endless series of such blows; if God acted on it, as he might, it would not be welcome. The text substituted by Abaye is not recorded. Perhaps he simply cuts out the florid "and thou hast not collected . . . ." It might be rewarding to compare, and contrast, Old Testament precursors.[22]

The other two disputes—as to how to pray when visiting a bath-house and when visiting a doctor for blood-letting—are preserved in the immediate vicinity of that about going to the toilet.[23] By tradition, a visitor of the baths begs God to keep him from sinning and, should he sin, to count his death an atonement. Abaye here too finds the self-condemnation exaggerated, the man does not truly wish to be taken at his word—to be slain, by way of atonement, for a lapse. Here too no substitute prayer by him is quoted. There is a strong indication that Aha adheres to the conservative line. He, we learn, counsels that, on exiting from a bath-house, one give thanks for being "saved from the fire"—sounds distinctly extremist. The conflict regarding blood-letting, once more between Aha and Abaye, brings out further facets of the problem. Aha's prayer emphasizes that God alone heals and men have no part in it—not even the physician to whom, following convention, one is turning. For Abaye, this is yet another cover-up, almost an attempt to fool the All-knowing. The doctor does promote the cure, under authority from God. The School of Ishmael (second century), Abaye points out, actually discovered a snippet in the Law itself sanctioning this office.[24] I suppose the prayer he prefers would conform to the old one, except for omitting the, to him, spurious alibi. Some five hundred years before, Ben-Sira staked out the general position:[25] "Cultivate the physician,

[20] See B. Doyle, *Meditations with Julian of Norwich* (1983), 28. I am indebted for this reference to my colleague Lawrence A. Sullivan.—A thought: "The purse opening and shutting" in Julian's meditation is very close to "one of the orifices opening and shutting" in Abaye's thanksgiving; and we have three options. 1) In all probability, there is no historical tie. 2) It is possible that the two formulations go back ultimately, to a common source, Galen or the like. 3) Norwich had an important Jewish community prior to the expulsion in 1290. Just conceivably, the Jewish prayer, or fragments of it, reached Julian over half a century later. I could offer parallels from Europe 1925–1985.

[21] *b. Ber.* 19a. It looks as if Joseph, his predecessor as head of the School of Pum Beditha, had contributed to this criticism. Cp. W. Bacher, *Die Agada der Babylonischen Amoräer* (1878), 109 f.

[22] Such as Ps 103:10: "He has not dealt with us after our sins . . . ."

[23] *b. Ber.* 60a. In the case of the bath-house, once again, Abaye seems to be influenced by Joseph. The major modern translators fail to appreciate the clash of opposing principles informing all this material, hence are driven to mispunctuate and even mutilate the prevalent reading: see L. Goldschmidt, *loc. cit.* and M. Simon, *Berakoth*, in Hebrew–English Edition of the Babylonian Talmud, ed. I. Epstein, vol. 1 (1960), 60a towards the end, esp. footnote da. A detailed discussion would add little to my thesis.

[24] Exod 21:19.

[25] Sir 38:1 ff. See G. H. Box and W. O. E. Oesterley, *The Book of Sirach*, in *The Apocrypha and Pseudepigrapha of the Old Testament*, ed. R. H. Charles (1913), vol. 1, 448 f.

for him God hath ordained. God hath created medicines out of the earth and let not a discerning man reject them." Like Abaye, he felt constrained to supply Scriptural proof—so even then there was a "Jewish Science" sect; indeed, as early as in Chronicles it savagely denounces King Asah for taking the other route.[26] However, in Ben-Sira's period such proof might still consist in a respected example and need not yet come from the Law proper.[27] Hence he could invoke the episode[28] when God instructed Moses how to sweeten the bitter waters with the help of a wood: a model cooperation of a beneficent plant, an enlightened human and—ultimate source—"I am the Lord that healeth thee." It may be worth mentioning Aha's benediction when taking leave of the phlebotomist: "Blessed is he who healeth gratis." Impossible to miss the barb: the Lord, sole agent of the recovery, unlike the good-for-nothing bleeder, charges no fee. Ben-Sira looked on an opulent reward as a feather in a doctor's cap. To be sure, it takes the form not of vulgar pay but of a honorarium: "From God he getteth his wisdom and from the king gifts."[29]

It will come as no surprise that, with the Rabbis forming two camps, one purist, the other realist,[30] Abaye is altogether a member of the latter. Here is a striking statement of his.[31] Ishmael, a realist (which, needless to say, does not detract from piety: he died a martyr under Hadrian), had contended that the exhortation "this book of Torah shall not depart out of your mouth day and night"[32] was to be taken with a grain of salt, adjusted to the condition of mortals. For Simeon ben Johai, purist, it meant that you must renounce all worldly occupation and care for livelihood, trusting that God would respond by his saving might. Abaye comments: "Many acted in accordance with Ishmael and succeeded and many in accordance with Simeon and did not succeed." (It may be recalled that he relies on a down-to-earth exegesis of the School of Ishmael in

[26] 2 Chr 16:12.

[27] See my *The New Testament and Rabbinic Judaism* (1956, repr. 1973), 67 ff. [249 ff.], "Zukunftsmusik," in *BJRULM*, 68 (1985), 56 f. [355 f.], and "Example and Precept: From Sirach to R. Ishmael," in *Talmudic Law: Collected Works of David Daube,* Vol. 1, ed. C. M. Carmichael (Berkeley: 1992), 205–11.

[28] Exod 15:23 ff.

[29] A doctor might act for free, of course, even in Talmudic times. That such services were invariably despised by no means follows, as is often held, from the quip or proverb put into the mouth of an injured person on a very particular situation in *b. B. K.* 85a. For a proper exploration of the subject, other noble vocations would have to be compared: teaching, preaching, judging, and so forth. Scripture is rich in material, much of it highly complicated. Think, for example, of Elisha's propagandist motives when refusing the presents of the Syrian general he had rid of his leprosy (2 Kings 5). The same prophet's acceptance of hospitality from a wealthy couple (2 Kgs 4:8 ff.) is remembered by the Rabbis when dealing with etiquette (*b. Ber.* 10b.). Of New Testament passages, it suffices to name Matt 10:10; Luke 10:7; 1 Cor 9:14; 1 Tim 5:18, plus Didache 13:1. On a special aspect of a prophet's honorarium, see my remarks ["Money and Justiciability"] in *ZSS,* 96 (1979), Rom. Abt., 5 f.

[30] Just a useful simplification. See my contribution ["Neglected Nuances of Exposition in Luke–Acts"] to *Aufstieg und Niedergang,* 2329 ff. [see 857 ff.]. As may be seen from the title of this portion of my essay, *Encomium Prudentiae,* I am breaking a lance for the realists—in defiance of my instinctive sympathies.

[31] *b. Ber.* 35b.

[32] Josh 1:8.

the more circumscribed debate as to the physician's role.) Again, when we compare his mottos with those of his lifelong friend and rival Raba,[33] he is the harmonizer, striving "to be beloved above and well liked below," Raba the stringent, proclaiming that if you follow out the Law from selfish motives, "it were better for you not to have been created."[34] Admittedly, there are utterances by the latter in the realist direction: maybe he relaxed once he had his own academy.[35] Abaye's affinity with Wisdom is significant—the motto just cited obviously echoes the ideal of "finding favour in the eyes of God and man"[36]—and so is Raba's with mysticism, à la Simeon ben Johai. It should be borne in mind, too, that the former descends from an exceptionally old and distinguished lineage.[37]

I wonder, in fact, whether an anecdote from the adolescence of this pair may not adumbrate this very divergence.[38] A youngster, though he has not yet reached full puberty, counts toward the quorum for ceremonial grace provided he understands the nature of the addressee. When Abaye and Raba were, say, 12 1/2, they were studying under the same master, the former's uncle, Rabba bar Nahmani. He tested them, asking first to whom grace was directed; both replied "To the All-merciful." Next he asked where the All-merciful resided, and at this they parted company. Raba pointed to the ceiling. Abaye stepped into the open and pointed to the sky. Whereupon their examiner called out: "You are both of you Rabbis already," i.e. far above the requisite standard for communal grace. The Talmud then appends the proverb: "Any pumpkin's quality is predictable from its stalk."

Up to not long ago, I shared the prevalent interpretation of the tale as a glorification of Raba. That he outshone Abaye in dialectical agility is beyond doubt;[39] and this incident is universally believed to be transmitted as demonstrating his overall, innate superiority: even in boyhood, a more or less majestic environment made no difference to his recognition of the One-on-high, while Abaye did welcome a prop. I still take off my hat—or should I say, put on my skullcap—to him. But by now I also sense a trace of the overrational, a lack of vitality, an estrangement from the concrete universe. Abaye is more natural, has a place for the senses, does not totally give over to logic. Interestingly, the story itself contains no evaluation of their respective stands. I have already quoted their teacher's eulogy, indiscriminately extended to both. If he had a preference, he was considerate enough to keep it to himself. The actions of the two are arranged in the sequence I have reproduced: first Raba's pointing to the ceiling, then

[33] *b. Ber.* 17a. I adverted to the two above, text with footnote 14.

[34] A moving prayer ascribed to him further up in *b. Ber.* 17a and found in *Authorized Prayer Book*, 263, fits the perfectionist picture.

[35] Another possibility is that we have been too quick in crediting him with these realist opinions. For instance, the one in *b. Pes.* 50b (quoted by me in *Aufstieg und Niedergang*, 2331 [859]) which makes use of Pss 57:11, 108:5 and goes back to Rab may not have been accepted by him at all.

[36] Prov 3:4.

[37] See *Aufstieg und Niedergang*, 2331 f. [860]. Caiaphas, whose realism I am calling attention to in the lecture cited above, footnote 11, belongs to an eminent high-priestly family.

[38] *b. Ber.* 48a.

[39] See W. Bacher, *op. cit.*, 109, 115.

Abaye's to the sky. Which implies no assessment, at least none ascertainable by us.[40] W. Bacher turns them around and adds two loaded details, whereby Raba emerges triumphant: "Abaye steps outside and points to the sky whereas Raba remains seated [not in the original] and, undeflected [not in the original], points to the ceiling."[41] It is conceivable, then, that the legend is trying to do justice to Abaye no less than to Raba. After all, the former's victory over the latter in being made President of the academy of Pum Beditha shows that his qualities were appreciated. (This is not to exclude his aristocratic provenance as a factor.) Indeed, the terse, riddling account of his election[42] could be hinting at his restraint and tolerance as decisive considerations: his pronouncements, we are told, were less open to refutation than those of Raba and other candidates.

In conclusion, two philological points and one perhaps falling under ethnology. In conformity with English usage, I have put the second person in the "who"-stretch of benedictions: e.g. "Blessed art thou who hast sanctified us." The Hebrew consistently puts the third, "Blessed art thou who hath sanctified us." As has been seen for some time,[43] this is no small matter. In the Hebrew, the bold, direct approach to the Lord, "Blessed art thou," is followed by an awed retreat, "who hath sanctified us."

Abaye is conscious that it would be fatal if one of the artfully constructed ducts "be opened or closed"—meaning "be opened or closed through malfunctioning in a troublesome, dangerous way." The use of a verb to single out an extraordinary instance of what it commonly denotes is a widespread phenomenon; the extraordinary element may be of a negative hue—as here—or positive. To explain it, one would have to compare many related data and, in fact, probe into the mainsprings of speech. It must suffice, therefore, to offer the simplest parallels from English. A schoolmaster who announces that any pupil "talking during class" will be punished means "talking out of order"; he does not mean one who answers when he calls on him, maybe not even one who asks an intelligent question. For a positive variant, we may think of a committee member who in the course of a long meeting gets a previously hostile majority to vote for his side. A follower of his, on returning home, reports to his wife: "I tell you, that guy talks," meaning "talks without giving up, breaking down all resistance."

The ethnical item is not, I bet, recorded anywhere, and, but for this little plaque, would soon be forgotten for good. In the first third of this century, among the rank and file of practising South-German Jews, toilet-paper (often consisting of old newspapers) was known as *asher yotsar Papier. Papier* is German for "paper." *Asher yotsar*, "who hast formed," are the two words with which, following the general introductory formula "Blessed art thou" up to "King of the Universe," the prayer after relieving nature commences: "who hast formed man in wisdom and created in him" and so on. "Who-hast-

[40] I should love setting out my findings about the upward or downward or neutral order chosen by authors—including myself and acquaintances of mine.

[41] *Op. cit.*, 109: "*Geht Abaji hinaus und zeigt zum Himmel, während Raba sitzen bleibt und unbeirrt zur Zimmerdecke hinaufweist.*"

[42] *b. Hor.* 14a.

[43] At least I think so, but I cannot remember my source.

formed-paper," then.[44] I have no idea how far back the designation goes nor how far it extended beyond South-Germany.[45] As for its social setting, I doubt that my mother's brothers, doctors of some eminence at a time when that profession was pretty clannish, employed it—though they never objected. There was not the slightest disrespect or irony or scruple attaching to this usage. Evidently, one sought to avoid a crude reference to defecation: the same motive that led to "toilet paper." No one from age four or thereabouts was not familiar with the thanksgiving recited so often, day in, day out, by everybody. Its distinctive opening provided a ready-made civilised, indeed, religious, term.

[44] I write *yotsar*: that is how it was pronounced—and with the accent on the first syllable. Official Israeli pronunciation agrees with the academic one: *yatsar*, and accent on the second syllable.

[45] Reuven Yaron, to whom I showed the typescript, informs me that it was part of the Yiddish vocabulary in Austria-Hungary at least.

Some Reflections on the Historicity of the New Testament*

It is a great pleasure and honour to speak under the auspices of my admired friend John Noonan. Experience shows that Scripture may be absorbed into the soul with no concern about historicity. My guess is that Bernadette Soubirous of Lourdes or, to cite someone of no fame, my Psalms-reading paternal grandmother, was not exercised by that problem. Yet they lived and died by holy writ. We may find it sublime or ridiculous, commendable or regrettable, or anything in between, but we cannot contest it. However, I am neither competent nor worthy to explore this mystery.

So I go on to my subject, concentrating on the New Testament, or rather, since I must be brief, on the gospels and, within them, on circumstances and events, to the exclusion of the teaching. Actually, I shall narrow down my scope still more: feeling uncomfortable with systems, I shall say little of a comprehensive nature and, instead, focus on the tools of the trade.

The one basic question I shall glance at is: how does an evangelist mean us to understand his testimony? Unfortunately for the scholar, fortunately for the world, the answer is: in countless different ways. Always, obviously, we are to accept at least a nucleus as true in the plain sense. Always: that is to say, not only when he tells us something of extreme importance—as that Jesus preached and healed, had disciples around him, was crucified under Pilate, returned and rose—but also in relatively minor matters, from the meeting with the Baptist to the self-destruction of the Gaderene swine. On the other hand, a great deal is negotiable, so to speak. C. H. Dodd, who guided my first steps in this region and, in a sense, guides me still, remarks that inspiration does not carry inerrancy. That none of our authors would dispute this seems to me evident from their untiring labour to improve on precursors, by addition, excision, reshaping. It would not do to assume that each of them ascribes fallibility to all others but not to himself. Of course, exactly how much is offered as less, or more, than strict datum and exactly what direction we may speculate varies from incident to incident, slightly or enormously.

Here are a few examples. Of Mark, we possess definite information that here and there his sequence follows, not the course of Jesus' activity, but that adopted by Peter for special purposes. Luke, mindful of the, by now numerous, converts of gentile provenance, habitually cuts out Hebrew and Aramaic words; hence no Hosanna at the entry in Jerusalem. Manifestly, in these cases, an absolutely precise account is not even the aim. By contrast, when one writer deviates from another in the distribution between the

* A talk delivered at Dominican School of Philosophy and Theology, Graduate Theological Union, November 2, Berkeley, 1985.

Jews and Pilate of the responsibility for Jesus' death, he does intend to provide a more accurate picture.

Not seldom a report is revised because of some puzzling feature: the reviser does his best, no doubt aware of possible ill-success. Take Peter's denial. (By the way, he at least did follow the arrested Jesus from a distance: with the result that he receives more censure than those who fled. It is the kind of price that is often paid by him who excels. At Delhi in 1961, I asked Nehru whether he was not harder on the West than on Soviet Russia. He said Yes—because he expected more from the former.) He waits around among a crowd outside the High Priest's palace into which Jesus has been taken for interrogation. In Mark, twice, as he is charged with being one of Jesus' gang, he answers: I have no idea what you are talking about. The third time he answers: No, I do not know the man. To Luke, who generally displays subtle psychological insight—perhaps having to do with his profession as a physician—this development sounds implausible and he substitutes the reverse one. Twice, Peter simply disclaims the connection: I do not know him, I do not belong to them. It is only in exasperation, when he keeps being pursued, that he speaks as if he had never gotten within miles of those people: I do not understand what you say. Compelling at first sight, but as it happens I am pretty convinced that Mark is nearer the original tradition. The Jews, used to persecution, had worked out two major guidelines as to how to behave when to admit being Jewish would cost you your life. (Guidelines which recur again and again among hunted groups. They flourished during the National-Socialist regime.) One: caving in in private is less bad than in public. You sit in your study and a thug comes in with a revolver: Are you Jewish? Your "no" at least does not undermine the morale of your co-religionists. Two: saving yourself by evasive speech is preferable to outright renunciation. You are surrounded by a ferocious mob: Are you Jewish? The answer You have the strangest ideas again saps the spirit of your side less seriously than would a straight No. Peter's ordeal starts by a maid of the High Priest's recognizing him and saying to him, You were with Jesus. He replies: I do not get you. It takes place in private and he resorts to evasion. Then he tries to slip away but she comes after him with others she has alerted and repeats the accusation, which he counters as before. By now the scene is public, but he still clings to a verbal cover-up. Finally, the bystanders join the maid in pressing him, things really become threatening, and he swears, I do not know this man. Public and direct, the ultimate defection. Probably, Luke no longer grasps this progression—though it is just conceivable, that, as on occasions already adverted to, he re-writes in deference to his public of whom many would not grasp it. It would lead too far afield to analyze Matthew's and John's treatment of the interlude.

One more illustration of the diversity we have to reckon with when tuning in to an evangelist's claim. In Matthew, Mark, and Luke, Jesus expels the traders from the Temple towards the close of his ministry, in John towards the opening: it is recorded in chapter 21 of Matthew, 11 of Mark, 19 of Luke, but 2 of John. I shall explain later why, by secular lights, the three Synoptics appear to be right. John certainly knows their dating (whether from a complete written work or otherwise does not here matter) but he changes it. Does he, then, regard it as erroneous and wish us to give it up? Not quite.

What he has in mind is the addition of a further level. The community at any rate which preserved all four gospels despite the contradiction must have taken this line. In the down-to-earth sense, the action is carried out near the end. On the plane of prophetic doom, it marks the outset, governing all that ensues. That such is John's intent is corroborated by alterations in substance which accompany that in the timing. In Matthew and Mark, Jesus drives out the delinquents and overthrows their tables. Luke, gentle himself and with a cultured readership, deletes the meddling with the furniture. Which renders John's emphatic choice of the opposite course all the more conspicuous. Jesus personally makes a whip from cords; he attacks not only the guilty humans but also the animals waiting to be sold and sacrificed; and besides overthrowing the tables of the moneylenders, he spills their coins. This is not to be taken *au pied de la lettre.* This is the universal judgment from on high which the New Testament story enshrines (it is not all that it enshrines), placed in front as an omen, ominously. If someone had told John that his grandfather, who was present at the scene, spoke of it as just prior to the catastrophe, John might have replied: "Yes, that is when it happened." I shall not go into his dating of the crucifixion a day earlier than the Synoptics, namely, at the very hour the paschal lambs are sacrificed in the Temple—except to note that we ought to take it in the same way, as set within a visionary frame. Indeed, to some extent, this event, too, he would have us look on as occurring long before, even preceding the discomfiture of the traders: it is pre-realized right at the beginning, in chapter 1, when, at the initial appearance of Jesus, the Baptist exclaims "Behold the lamb of God."

So we are faced with facts, half-facts, conjectures, some with tremendous import, some with less, and there is even import overlaying fact. What lies before us purports to be neither perfect reconstruction nor romance nor allegory *tout court.* Up to a point, certain heathen works, Near-Eastern, Greek, Roman, are comparable—despite a longstanding convention to belittle their religious content. C. K. Barrett, for example, demonstrates how much can be learnt from them. Still, it is up to a point only. The challenge of the Bible is unique and intolerant of easy solutions.

Now I propose to present three routes which I feel got me somewhere: common sense, an opting for the troublesome and a modicum of attention to the background. Common sense I need not define to you, who so clearly evince it by holding your meeting in this area. It may be applied to the divergence between the Synoptics and John in their placing of Jesus' intervention at the Temple. If we accept John's chronology as the correct one in a this-worldly sense, Jesus started out with open violence; there was not the slightest reaction on the part of the administration, Jewish or Roman; he was allowed to go on for several years, during which nothing like that first outbreak was repeated; and then he was put to death. Far less plausible than what we hear from the Synoptics: the near-seditious action was undertaken in his final weeks and did contribute to the determination of the authorities to destroy him. This impression gains in weight from the fact that it is considerably easier to account for a transposition of the episode by John from toward the close to toward the opening—he is endowing it with programmatic status—than for one by the Synoptics the other way round. Needless to add, even common sense can mislead and especially in this field it is to be used with care. Perhaps I may quote a teacher by the name of Kuflik at our tiny orthodox congregation at Freiburg in the late 1920s to whom I confided that I had become interested in Old Testament source-criticism through attending a seminar of Johannes Hempel at Göttingen. What he said was "If you must do it, do it like a surgeon who has to operate on his father."

Opting for the troublesome comprises at least two situations. The first: when we come upon an item we are allergic to, as when Jesus spits into the eyes of a blind man, we ought to think twice before declaring it spurious or interpreting it away. Recently, when investigating the Matthean pericope concerning Temple tax, I marvelled at the multitude of theories designed to get rid of Jesus' prediction to Peter that he would find an appropriate coin in the mouth of a fish. Some of them were highly ingenious; e.g. Jesus was really impressing on Peter that if only he applied himself diligently to his trade, he would earn enough to pay with. Good work-ethics in the place of an awkward, rare quality. Let me remind you that my business is with historicity, dry, one-dimensional; I am fully aware that the result of an unhistorical approach may be valuable in its own right. To continue along my track, however: according as we favour Pharisees, Sadducees, Samaritans, gentiles, the rich or the poor, men or women, adults or children, it is not a bad rule to give the benefit of the doubt to texts that hurt us. I try and often I slip.

As for the second situation under this heading—of two versions, other things being equal, we should choose that which must have been more painful to put down at the time. In Mark, Jesus on the cross laments, My God, why hast thou forsaken me?, and dies after a last cry. In Luke, he prays Father, forgive them, comforts one of two criminals crucified with him and dies commending his spirit to God. Mark's is the more pristine narration. His gloom was hard to endure—as, for sure, it still is, so even from this point of view we must accord it precedence. The conclusion is supported by the fact that some of the best manuscripts of Luke still lack the plea Father, forgive them, and that the oldest Church Fathers indeed ascribe it to James as he is being martyred.

From time to time it is maintained that the entire story of Jesus is a myth. The counter-arguments which have been propounded are overwhelming. For example, how could we account for the references in Paul's epistles, all the stronger evidence for being in the main allusive, taking things for granted, rather than explicit? What is relevant here is that a figure invented would have been more convenient, not "to the Jews a stumbling-block and to the Greeks foolishness." Moses offers a parallel. Granted he is enveloped in plenty of saga. But a major, reliable *Grundstock* [core source] is guaranteed by his failure to reach the land. A leader freely thought up would have succeeded.

In fact, the parallel extends further. So unbearable was his disappointment to some chroniclers that they unmade it. The last scene when he is shown the land from a mountain top, all of it from one end to the other, is not, at its core, just sentimental but a legal conveyance. That is how, in antiquity, you are invested with land: its owner takes you to a nearby height and acquaints you with its circumference—*finium demonstratio*, a pointing out of the boundaries, the Romans called it. We are given to understand, that is, that though he did not literally cross the Jordan, yet he did so juridically, he did take possession by means of this ceremony. The literature on the efforts of the early Christians to mitigate their tragedy is immense. Here is a detail on which I have done research. To be buried like a criminal, unanointed, was a serious disgrace—the Talmudic term is *niwwul*—in New Testament times. The non-believers surely made much of it, and the gospels contain no fewer than three different refutations. One, the woman anointing Jesus at Bethany is held to have been performing an anticipatory burial rite. Two, Joseph of Arimathaea and Nicodemus secretly anoint the body at night. Three, several women would have anointed him at once had it not been for the Sabbath laws—a most effective point against their excessively Sabbatarian antagonists—and by the time they arrive on Sunday, he has risen: a triumphant elimination of *niwwul*. This is not to pronounce on the factualness or otherwise of these three reports. All I am here concerned with is the tendency to lighten the dark. That it affects the descriptions of what was done to Jesus during and after the execution is indisputable if only from the gradual replacement in primitive references to his corpse of *ptoma*, cadaver, by *soma*, body.

Lastly, as for consideration of the authentic milieu. It helps, for instance, to reconstruct the setting of Jesus' baptism. According to Matthew, "he at once came up out of the water and, behold, the heavens were rent." Very odd: why ever should he not have come up at once? Mark writes that "at once, having come up out of the water, he saw the heavens rent." What happened at once, then, was not his coming up but his illumination thereupon. This makes excellent sense. A gentile's conversion takes effect at the moment of emergence from the water; in the words of the Mishnah, "he immerses and comes up, behold, he is like an Israelite." The Baptist deems even Jews in need of conversion and extends the rite to them: that is indeed why he got his epithet. In the case of Jesus, naturally, the culmination is very much out of the ordinary, yet it is embedded in the genuine structure. Matthew mispunctuates (as on another, similar occasion). Instead of "at once, having come up, he saw," he reads "at once having come up, he saw." Thus, as he unravels the participial phrasing, instead of putting "he came up and, at once, behold" etc., he arrives at "he at once came up and, behold" etc. Luke omits the coming up altogether; the heavens open on Jesus' praying. That his version ranks behind Mark only within the limited purview of this lecture is evident.

In Matthew and Mark, three questions are addressed to Jesus one after the other: is it lawful to pay tribute to Caesar?; if a man dies without issue and a brother of his dutifully marries the widow, he also dies childless and another brother marries her and so forth, whose wife will she be on resurrection?; and which is the foremost commandment? Then a question is put by Jesus: how can Scripture speak of the Messiah now as David's son and now as his Lord? Commentators are at a loss to discover a unifying idea and leave us with the feeling that we have to do with an *omnium gatherum* [disparate collection]. In reality, this is about the oldest composite chapter surviving. As Matthew has greatly altered some of the primary features, I shall for the moment base myself on Mark only.

In the Jewish Passover eve recital, four types of disciples or sons are introduced, three of them characterized by their questions about this festival. First, the wise one who is interested in legal specifics and is given a reply it takes wisdom to decode. Paralleled by Is it lawful to pay Caesar?, with a reply equally demanding. Second, the wicked one who by his manner of asking excludes himself from the community God delivered. Paralleled by the gibe at bodily resurrection. Third, the simply pious one who just wants to be told the basic meaning of it all. Paralleled by What is the greatest commandment? The fourth type does not know how to ask. With him, it is up to the master or father who conducts the Seder to pose a problem, such as about an apparent conflict in the Torah's presentation of the redemption. Paralleled by Jesus' riddle, regarding the different designations of the Messiah. Note that whereas the first three questions receive answers both in the Seder recital and in the gospel, the fourth, meant to stimulate, remains unanswered in both. We are in touch here with a Seder celebration of the *Ur* [original]-Christians well before they had perfected their own literary genres for surveying the ministry. They still adhered to the familiar scheme, content with enriching the references to the past exodus with material from the new. Thus, where the traditional exposition mentioned a disciple probing into the law, they added an enquiry of this kind that had been brought before Jesus; the evil questioner cutting himself off from the faithful provided an opportunity for recalling the Sadducean sneerers; and so on. Clearly, in each of the four cases, there was more than one scene in the life of Jesus that could have served as a recent counterpart. The choice accords with my thesis: it reflects those issues on which the young sect, say in A.D. 40, would need guidance most. What did it owe to Rome whose representative had just contributed to the horrid death of its head?; what about bodily resurrection, linchpin of its hope?; what, beyond all minutiae, was expected of one wishing to be a worthy member?; and what about the nature of its Messiah?

Quite likely, it is Peter who created this group when presiding over a Passover eve meal. Earlier on I mentioned evidence, going back to around A.D. 100, according to which Mark is apt to record memorabilia—sayings, above all—not in the order in which they occurred in the course of Jesus' activity but in that in which Peter, his mentor, arranged them to meet the demands of a given occasion. It would be difficult to imagine a better example than the section under review. These four questions were not originally raised in one go or in their present sequence; the one as to the foremost canon, for instance, may have preceded by many months that as to bodily resurrection. They were collected by Peter as the Christian Seder's complement of the traditional quartet; and Mark loyally hands them on in this form. Paying heed to the native sources, then, may result in major re-evaluations. In this case, indeed, it enables us to pinpoint what might be the very earliest channel through which were passed on clusters of reminiscences of Jesus' companions: the Passover eve symposium in the years following the crucifixion. I would add that the provably archaic setting of the chapter cannot but enhance confidence also in its contents—except, of course, for the arrangement.

Not surprisingly, once the four questions entered the stream of transmission on their own, detached from the established Passover model, their role as a rounding off of the latter in the light of the new dispensation was soon forgotten. Matthew is quite unaware of it. For example, the enquiry as to the foremost imperative, which in Mark comes from an honest, unsophisticated seeker, in Matthew has the purpose of entrapping Jesus; of the warm approval bestowed on the questioner in Mark no trace is left in Matthew. As for Luke, he totally separates this question from the other three and uses it for an introduction to the parable of the Good Samaritan. Actually, in the Bibles you have brought along, the Marcan report itself—or, more precisely, the way it is set out—is affected by the disregard of its antecedents. This pericope with the third question now ends "and no one any further dared ask him." A strange consequence of Jesus' praise for the interlocutor, "thou art not far from the kingdom." More than that: Eusebius, ca. 260–340, does not yet incorporate the clause in what goes before. The solution is that the evangelist intends it not as the finale of the third pericope, but as the start of the fourth. Here is the Seder text behind it: "And he who does not know how to ask, you [master or father] open [the discourse] for him." In close correspondence, Mark formulates: "And no one any further dared ask him, and, opening [the discourse], Jesus spoke." N.B. The New English Bible has restored the correct division.

By critical consensus, Jesus' prayer at Gethsemane is a pious legend. This does not diminish its glory, but my topic, pedestrian, pedantic, is historicity. How, it is argued, could anyone have come to know anything about it? He offered it at some distance from his disciples who, besides, were dozing or asleep. That he told them on rejoining them, I have made the following supplication and so on, is incredible on many grounds, one of them his immediate arrest. A strong case for a negative verdict—and none the less a look into notions and customs then prevailing will prompt reservations.

To begin with, a few words about the situation. The little band are in the dark of the night just outside the city, awaiting the climax of their venture, and Jesus repeatedly calls on the others to stay awake. No doubt to a certain extent this is figurative: they are to remain conscious of their task. But the concrete details pervading the account—tarry and wake, their eyes are heavy, sleep and rest—show that, above all, he is anxious for them not to let their physical fatigue get the better of them. At Qumran, it was a grave offense to fall asleep in the assembly. No need to search into the genesis of this rule; it is readily intelligible that where collective action is of true importance, the sleeper constitutes a serious flaw. There is, however, an institution directly pertinent to our narrative. Jesus and his disciples are a *habhura*, a community formed for the joint celebration of Passover eve. Such a community assumes the place of a house, a family; so much so that the provision in Exodus, "In one house shall the lamb be eaten," in the Aramaic version appears as "In one *habhura* it shall be eaten." (In passing—the existence of "families" of this or a similar nature may have facilitated Jesus' dictum that his followers are his true mother and brothers.) The point is that a *habhura* terminates when its members—or even one or two of them, in the rigorist view—fall asleep: no more communal eating of the sacrifice, no more communal hymn, no more communal prayer. This last item is perhaps in Jesus' mind as he urges the company to "stay awake and pray": communal prayer is of particular force. At any rate, that he is concerned about the Seder circle dissolving in this way comes out in a little notice of Mark's. Wherever sleeping at a meeting produces such a major effect, it will be desirable to establish a criterion. Seeing you here before me, for example, I would not be sure how to class you:

some of you are probably quite gone, others in that not unhappy state with the lecture faintly heard as a cradle song. One Rabbinic opinion surviving is that a person is merely dozing so long as "when you call on him, he answers even though he does not know how to respond rationally." The notice, then, that, on Jesus' second return to his disciples, "they did not know what they might answer him," specifies the degree of their severance. What all this points up is Jesus' intense yearning to prolong, if only by hours or less than hours, the present, precious union. Soon there will supervene a fearful test which will prove each of them in isolation and him most severely of all.

In this extremity, surely the fitting mode of prayer is that customary on the point of death; and his entourage cannot but have been aware—he does express his sorrow "unto death" to them. An old Jewish form runs: "I acknowledge, O Lord, that my cure and my death are in your hands. May it be your will to send me a perfect healing. Yet if I die, may my death be an atonement." Jesus prays: "Father, all things are possible unto you. Take away this cup from me. Nevertheless not what I will but what you will." The coupling of temporal request for good fortune and transcending acceptance of a higher decision goes back deep into Old Testament invocation in time of ultimate peril, on the eve of a battle, for instance. A tremendous scene from King David's reign is in point. He has to flee from his capital which is taken over by his rebellious son Absalom. Priests and Levites, siding with him, transport out of Jerusalem into his camp the holy ark, the most powerful source and symbol of might. But he declines: "Carry back the ark of God into the city. If I shall find favour in the eyes of the Lord, he will bring me there again and let me see both it and his habitation. But if he thus say, I have no delight in you, behold, here am I, let him do to me as is good in his eyes." Certainly, Jesus' entreaty would have its own note, with the imprint of his person and adapted to the particular crisis. How far these minute nuances are represented in the text depends on the nearness to him and sensitivity of whoever first set it down. There is good reason, however, to think of it as essentially historical.

Neither Matthew nor Luke preserves the pregnant reminder of the tired companions' disability to give a proper answer—an out-of-date technicality by then. In discussing Peter's denial, I remarked on Luke's psychological acumen. Here we come across another example: it was sadness, he explains, which caused the disciples to sleep instead of praying.

The Old Testament in the New: A Jewish Perspective*

I. Outline

The New Testament frequently cites the Old, from centuries before. Now whenever people base on an ancient text, for a comprehension of the drift it matters little what that text means or, to put it more humbly, what we suppose it to mean; the key lies in what it means to them, which may be quite different. To some extent, this is true even where the text is contemporaneous. Say, you form an opinion or take action inspired by an item in today's *San Francisco Chronicle*. If it is you I am out to understand, I must concentrate not on what the article says but on what it says to you. Even in such a case, the discrepancy now and then will be enormous. However, the likelihood of its being so is less.

Here is an example unrelated to the Bible. To make sense of the itineraries chosen in the age of Columbus by the seekers of Atlantis, the lost island figuring in the Arabian geographers, we must proceed not from where the latter place it but from where the Renaissance voyagers believed they did. Next, for a complaint about the Old Testament by Hamlet, who wishes God had promulgated no law against suicide. Shakespeare has in mind "Thou shalt not murder," assumed in his time to extend to self-killing.[1] Few scholars nowadays go along with this range of the commandment but, as far as an appreciation of the monologue in question is concerned, this is beside the point. Noah's three sons offer further illustrations. Dutch Reformed churchmen in South Africa, in defence of racial oppression, adduce his curse dubbing Ham-Canaan a servant of servants to Shem and Japheth.[2] Fairly logical, given their view that from the one wicked brother are descended the present blacks and from the decent pair of Shem and Japheth the present whites, that the pronouncement is designed to punish all the former and reward all the latter, and so forth. The craziness of their view does not make it any less the explanation of their reliance on this passage. In the first half of the second century A.D., Simon ben Gamaliel II, permitting the writing of the Torah in Greek, appeals to another portion of Noah's oracle: "Japheth shall dwell in the tents of Shem."[3] The force of the

* An expanded version of the George Hitchings Terriberry Memorial Lecture delivered at Newcomb College, Tulane University, on Oct. 26, 1982. I dedicate it in gratitude to my friend David Patterson and his family. Nineteen eighty-two was the year when his admirers around the world celebrated his sixtieth birthday. A German translation by Wolfgang Schuller has appeared as volume 10 (1984) of the series *Xenia* which he edits.

[1] Shakespeare, Hamlet, 1.2.132; Exod 20:13; Deut 5:17.

[2] Gen 9:25.

[3] *y. Meg.* 71c; Gen 9:26.

quotation emerges when we remember that, for the Rabbis, Japheth stood for Hellas and Shem for Jewry. To follow Simon, it is this that we need to know, while how far the identifications coincide with the original meaning is of secondary interest.[4]

My proposition, then—far from novel but too readily neglected—is that, when dealing with the Old Testament in the New, we ought to read it as it was read by the Jews of that era. The references without exception come from their midst, are founded on their interpretation. If this often clashes with the pristine sense (or what we take to be such) it cannot be helped. We must still stick to it. Unless we do, we may miss parts—from relatively minor to very major—of the New Testament message conveyed by means of the reference.

In passing, the chief reason for the widespread disregard of this strategy is that it requires being steeped in the Rabbinic modes of exegesis, and few Christian theologians are. The most excellent collections of Talmudic material bearing on the New Testament cannot fully make up for this shortcoming. Luckily, owing to a variety of factors—one of them, the discovery of the Dead Sea Scrolls—the situation is improving; and at least the number of those explicitly minimizing the importance of what went on among the Jews of the period seems in decline. But I have no illusions. As we know from the fable of the fox and the grapes, to pooh-pooh what we cannot tackle is a natural—and, up to a point, healthy—defence mechanism. I have confessed elsewhere that when, some time ago, a colleague from Sofia sent me his manual on Roman law, in Bulgarian, I laid it aside, comforting myself with the thought that it was unlikely to contain much that was radically new.

II. GOD OF OUR FATHERS

Perhaps I had best begin with a quotation most scholars do treat as distorting the genuine tenor, Rabbi-wise: a clause from the Book of Exodus which Jesus thinks confirms resurrection.[5] More carefully, is represented as thinking; but I shall submit grounds for crediting the report. The reason the incongruity in this instance is widely admitted is that the ratiocination, the "logic"—fancy to us—turning the clause into a proof of resurrection, is offered in full.

Resurrection, a fundamental tenet of the Pharisees, is nowhere mentioned in the Pentateuch—to their grave embarrassment vis-à-vis Samaritans and Sadducees for whom Mosaic directives alone were binding and who rejected this dogma of later provenance. Its upholders, in consequence, were driven to all sorts of twistings of holy writ to convict their opponents of error even by their own standard. For example, Deuteronomy speaks of "the land which the Lord swore to your Fathers to give to them and to their seed." But, the Pharisees argued, the Fathers died before their seed

[4] Jan Vetter, when I told him of this essay, drew my attention to a 1977 Supreme Court decision in *St. Paul Fire and Marine Insurance Co.* v. *Barry*, written by Powell J. and approving of a remark by Mr. Justice Cardozo in 1935, that "words or phrases in a statute come freighted with the meaning imparted to them by the mischief to be remedied and by contemporaneous discussion. In such conditions history is a teacher that is not to be ignored." I am grateful to Walter Pakter for helping me locate these opinions.

[5] Matt 22:31 f.; Mark 12:26 f.; Luke 20:37 f.; Exod 3:6.

reached Canaan; how, then, could God give the land to them as well as to the latter? Answer: because they will return. Mosaic evidence.[6] It was taken seriously enough for the Samaritans to excise "to them" from their version. Nor must they be labelled as fraudulent.[7] They believed they were throwing out an intrusion no less honestly than the Pharisaic masters believed they were uncovering its true contents. The same Gamaliel II in whose name this proof is transmitted, as well as his contemporary Joshua ben Hananiah—around A.D. 100—made use of a grammar-defying method to produce further testimony. Towards the close of Deuteronomy, God tells Moses: "You will be resting with your Fathers, and there will be rising this people and be whoring after the gods of the strangers." The two asserted that "and there will be rising" attached to both the preceding part and the following part, so we obtain (1) "you will be resting with your Fathers and there will be rising"—resurrection, (2) "and there will be rising this people and be whoring"—Israel's lapse.[8]

Jesus confronts the Sadducees with God's self-revelation to Moses: "I am the God of Abraham, the God of Isaac and the God of Jacob." The incident takes place long after the days of the Patriarchs. But plainly, Jesus argues, God must be a God of the living. It follows that they are not departed for ever: they will come back. Mosaic evidence of the same character as Gamaliel's.[9] To do justice to the New Testament sense of the line, no use looking at it from the standpoint of the composer of Exodus; we have to put on Rabbinic spectacles.

This is all that is essential to my thesis. The subject matter is of such weight, however, as to deserve an excursus.

That Jesus invented the syllogism is *a priori* implausible, surely. Fortunately, it can be shown that he did not. It definitely underlies, for example, the doctrine of 4 Maccabees, on which a little more presently; and almost certainly the proofs from Deuteronomy—also with the Fathers in a prototypical role—are offshoots, weaker than the model "I am the God of" etc. which centers on the very opening of the Almighty's decisive intervention in Exodus. It is demonstrable, too, that one had to be no academic to be acquainted with it: that is why I have no qualms as to historicity. It was in fact by his time deeply embedded in the central daily prayer, the Eighteen Benedictions.

As pointed out by Herbert Loewe (in whose home I had my first meal at Cambridge in the thirties), when the Sadducees are declared in this debate "to know neither the Scriptures nor the power of God," the latter term denotes the Second Benediction,

[6] *b. Sanh.* 90b; Deut 11:9, 21.

[7] As they are by Eliezer ben Jose, around A.D. 150, in *b. Sanh.* 90b. For further details, see my comments ["Texts and Interpretation in Roman and Jewish Law"] in *JJSOC* 3 (1961), 23. [See *Talmudic Law*, 201 f.]

[8] *b. Sanh.* 90b; Deut 31:16. The method is discussed by me in ["Alexandrian Methods of Interpretation and the Rabbis"] *Festschrift Hans Lewald*, 1953, 34 ff. [See *Talmudic Law*, 357 ff.] Classical specimens reached the Elizabethans and, if B. Everett, writing in the *London Review of Books*, 18 December 1986, 7, is right, "wisheth" in the dedication of Shakespeare's *Sonnets* faces in two directions.

[9] Virtually conceded on all hands. Still, not a few authorities, believing Jesus to be the originator of this proof, are at pains to elevate it. Thus, K. H. Rengstorf, *Das Evangelium nach Lukas*, 9th ed. (1962), 229, greatly refines its message, while E. Klostermann, *Das Markusevangelium*, 4th ed. (1950), deems it *geistreicher*, "more ingenious," than the ordinary run.

aimed against them and carrying the appellation "Powers."[10] The First Benediction, with the appellation "Fathers," addresses "the God of Abraham, the God of Isaac and the God of Jacob"—from the Book of Exodus. The Second extols him as "powerful" and "Lord of powers" in reviving the dead and also, significantly, as the giver of rain.[11] Clearly, the sequence is determined by that notion that the formulation in Exodus guarantees resurrection. Whether this Benediction was coined in its entirety during the fierce struggles between the sects in the second century B.C. or whether, as has been suggested, the bulk of it dates from before and only the contested principle was inserted in that period, we may leave open, Here, by the time of Jesus, was the Pharisaic case, accessible to everybody. The Sadducees, he is saying, ignore a vital teaching of the Torah, as explicated in the Second Benediction. Luke has cut out this somewhat parochial reprimand, preserved in Matthew and Mark.[12]

Various considerations supporting this approach may be added. For a start, let me dispose of a possible objection: Jesus employs the singular, "power of God," the Talmud the plural, "Powers." Not a serious stumbling block. The plural embraces the several powers appearing in the Benediction—resurrection, rain, provision of good, healing, salvation, even killing—while Jesus concentrates on the first. There is plenty of evidence that singular and plural are not kept rigidly separate in this province, and no doubt the earlier the date, the more fluidity. In the third century still, the question why, traditionally, one speaks of the "powers of rains" in discussing the Second Benediction, is answered: "Because they come down by the power [of God]."[13]

Now for a more positive input. It was usual then to cite important divisions of sacred works by means of conventional, pregnant designations. As it happens, Jesus on the same occasion avails himself of this mode not only for the Second Benediction, "Powers," but also for the verse from Exodus: "Have you not read in the Book of Moses, at the Bush." "The Bush" figures in Rabbinic material as the appellation of the pericope recounting God's first appearance to Moses.[14] In this case, Matthew—against Mark

[10] See C. G. Montefiore and H. Loewe, *A Rabbinic Anthology* (1938); repr. with prolegomenon by R. Loewe (1974), 369. The idea is taken up by R. Loewe, *JTS,* n.s. 32 (1981), 358. But he assumes that the evangelists are no longer aware of Jesus' meaning—which, at least as far as Mark is concerned, seems unwarranted.

[11] Cf. Isa 26:19. I shall return to the mention of rain at the end of II.

[12] Here is a translation (which, sorry to say, does not convey the beauty, strength and depth of the Hebrew): Blessed are you, O Lord our God and God of our Fathers, God of Abraham, God of Isaac and God of Jacob, great, powerful and awesome God, God the Highest, who bestows beneficent kindnesses and possesses all and remembers the kindnesses of the Fathers and brings a redeemer to their children's children for his name's sake in love; King, Helper and Saviour and Shield; Blessed are you, O Lord, the Shield of Abraham." —Second Benediction: "You are powerful for ever, O Lord, who revives the dead, you are mighty to save; who causes the wind to blow and the rain to descend; who sustains the living in kindness, who revives the dead with much mercy, who supports the falling and heals the sick and looses the bound and keeps his faith to those sleeping in the dust; who is like you, O Lord of powers, and who resembles you? King who kills and revives and causes salvation to spring forth; and faithful you are to revive the dead; Blessed are you, O Lord, who revives the dead."

[13] Johanan bar Nappaha in *b. Taan.* 2a.

[14] See H. L. Strack and P. Billerbeck, *Kommentar zum Neuen Testament aus Talmud und Midrasch,* 4 vols. (1924–1929, repr. 1969), 2:28.

and Luke—has dropped the technical detail, along with "the Book of Moses," to replace it by his favourite "that which is said."[15]

To go by Mark, throughout the debate, both Sadducees and Jesus speak of "a rising" (noun) or "to rise" (verb); once only, in interpreting "I am the God of" etc., he substitutes the dead "being waked." Some scholars who have noticed the switch justly attribute it to the idea, well attested in the Talmud, of death as not final annihilation but temporary sleep. The Fathers are alive, just sleeping, waiting to be resummoned.[16] According to 4 Maccabees, the martyrs are convinced that "unto God, they die not, as our Fathers Abraham, Isaac and Jacob died not, but that they live unto God."[17] In the Qumran hymns, at Judgment time, "all the sons of his truth will awake" and "those that rest in the dust" will hoist the banners.[18] What is significant for us is that the so-called Babylonian rescension of the Second Benediction (so-called—it seems to be a product of Palestine just as much as the Palestinian version)[19] explicitly glorifies God as "keeping his faith to them that sleep in the dust." Indeed, it borrows the image from the Book of Daniel where we also meet the verb "to awake": "And many of them that sleep in the dust of the earth shall awake."[20]

The famous pronouncement in 1 Corinthians 15 stands foursquare in this tradition: "Some of them [that saw Christ after his burial] are fallen asleep," "Christ has been awakened from the dead, the first-fruits of them that slept," "we shall not all sleep."[21] Nor is the key word "power" missing: "Sown in weakness, awakened in [or by] power."[22] Of the many other contributions—direct or indirect—to this concern, some concur, some deviate, slightly or markedly. It is a quest touching on the most diverse facets of the infant Church.

English translations, not excepting the most meticulous ones, as a rule put "to rise" or "to raise" even where the Greek has "to be awakened" or "to awake" (transitive). One cause—repeat: one of a dozen—is surely the far greater convenience of the former pair; my parenthesis (transitive) illustrates a drawback of the latter. In German, there is no awkwardness about *auferweckt werden* or *auferwecken*, hence the two are fairly frequent. Actually, German has some difficulty with "to raise": *auferstehen lassen* is clumsy. So in German renderings, it is this term which is apt to be pushed out—by *auferwecken*.[23] Admittedly, the mix-up is provided with justifications—to wit, that, in Greek literature, "to be awakened" not seldom has the sense of "to rise" and "to awaken" (transitive) that of "to raise." However, this happens only in special conditions and a metaphorical

[15] To disentangle the various New Testament writers' systems of citation cannot be my task here. I am content to observe that "that which is said" or "it has been said" is never met in Mark and that whenever Matthew puts it without specifying the source, he is citing the Pentateuch.

[16] See Klostermann, *Markusevangelium*, 126, 180.

[17] 4 Mac 7:19, similarly 16:25. This is not to affirm absolute identity with the attitude of Jesus.

[18] I Qumran Hodayoth 6:29 f., 34.

[19] See Strack and Billerbeck, *Kommentar*, 4, pt. 1:211.

[20] Dan 12:2.

[21] 1 Cor 15:6, 20, 51.

[22] 1 Cor 15:43; cf. 6:14; 2 Cor 13:4.

[23] E.g. Acts 2:24.

flavour nearly always persists. As for the New Testament, though here and there synonymity of the two verbs is reached, in the vast majority of cases it is not, small as the difference may at times be. It is wrong to postulate that the adoption of the noun *anastasis,* "resurrection," "rising," as the chief heading in this domain spells the end of nuances. Roughly, "to be awakened" and "to awake" do remain narrower, evoke a definite mode of coming back. A friend of mine has enrolled in a class on "cooking" in order to learn "to bake." Furthermore, quite apart from any substantive distinction, the verb opted for almost invariably points to a certain historical filiation—which, indeed, can still influence the mood, the aura, of a passage. Helen often uses "to block out" or "to repress" instead of my pedestrian "to forget." She has long given up the axiom that any lapse of memory is due to unwillingness to remember. So the former verbs continue (1) meaningfully, in a few situations where she does assume such a mechanism, (2) as a habit of speech, where it may or may not be at work or even, on occasion, where it most probably is not. No matter what the circumstances, her idiom links her historically to a movement to which I, belonging to an earlier generation and growing up in good, old Freiburg, was not exposed in my formative years. Moral: even where "rising" and "awaking" are equivalent, the choice of one or the other will very likely be a clue to antecedents of the statement.

Once in process, the painting out of shades goes on and on. "Some of them are fallen asleep" etc., adverted to above, in the New English Bible and Anchor Bible runs "some have died," "the first-fruits of them that have died," "we shall not all die." Standardization. I shall not heap excursus on excursus to document my claim but be content with remarking that the trend is demonstrable from very early on. A fragment from the Gospel according to the Hebrews, preserved in Latin by Jerome, has James vow at the end of the Last Supper that he will not eat till he sees Jesus "rise from the sleeping": *resurgere a dormientibus.*[24] The Greek translation of Jerome gives us "from the dead," *ek nekron,* and in Latin writers using Jerome we also come across *a mortuis.* Curiously, whereas Jerome twice speaks of "to rise," *resurgere,* the Greek version puts *anistamai* only the first time and then goes over "to be awakened," *egeiro.* The impact of *a dormientibus,* it appears, was strong enough to evoke this image in the translator even though he gave up "to sleep" in favour of the less specific "dead."

I submit that if, for an experimental period of twenty years, scholars Englished, Germaned, Frenched, etc. the texts in strict compliance with the Greek, it would lead to worthwhile results. Nabakov, I am confident, would have backed me. Far be it from me to recommend this pedantry for Bible lovers not engaged in research. Take Jesus' forecast in John that he will "awaken" the destroyed temple in three days, thinking of his body.[25] Any popular edition must substitute something like "rebuild." Yet scholars even here ought not to slur over the evangelist's selection. I am aware that *egeiro* can denote "to erect a building" without any allusion to sleep. In fact, it may have been commoner in this sense than one might suppose from extant evidence: the correspon-

[24] The Gospel according to the Hebrews 8, from Jerome, *De Viris Illustribus* 2. On a different aspect of the passage, see my *Wine in the Bible* (1974), 14 [455].

[25] John 2:19 ff.

ding Latin *excito,* met in Cicero and Caesar, is, I guess, an imitation. (The Vulgate avails itself of it in this pericope.) Nevertheless, it is decidedly not the most obvious verb in the field. John, in preferring it, conveys a particular notion of resurrection. As for "to die" in lieu of "to fall asleep," perhaps a modern audience likes the blunter word. I would have thought that "first-fruits" was more antiquated. Gretchen's brother, in Goethe's *Faust,*[26] let us note, conceives of death as a sleep to end (at least for the just ones) by being allowed into the presence of God: "*Ich gehe durch den Todesschlaf zu Gott ein als Soldat und brav,*" "I go in to God, through the sleep of death, as a soldier and a good fellow."

It is just conceivable that even Jesus' portrayal of the risen ones as of the nature of angels falls within the orbit of the Eighteen Benedictions. A number of Jewish parallels have been collected; those in Enoch particularly impressive[27] since this corpus was influential at the very inception of Christianity. Here I have in mind the Third Benediction, "Sanctification," which at least when recited in public includes the Thrice-Holy of Isaiah's seraphim.[28] The earthly community, that is, after "Fathers" and "Powers," worships in the manner of the celestial one—maybe in anticipation of the ultimate transfiguration. The first Three Benedictions, it is worth recalling, were seen as belonging together, devoted to praise, the subsequent clusters being petitions and thanks.[29] The implication: the first three do not ask God to exert his might and mercy but acknowledge him as possessed of them.[30]

A few thoughts about Acts. Twice we find Peter and his companions proclaim that "the God of Abraham, Isaac and Jacob" or "the God of our Fathers" has awakened Jesus[31]—doubtless harking back to the stand Jesus took when assailed by the Sadducees. That episode, it will be remembered, is incorporated in all Synoptic Gospels, including that of Luke, author of Acts. Jesus, the choice of language is conveying, placed his trust in the assurance enshrined in this particular self-revelation of God; and the God who had thus revealed himself did prove him right and restore him to eternal life.

In a subsequent section, focusing on Paul, we hear of the Sadducees averring "that there is no resurrection neither angel nor spirit."[32] It is universally agreed that this rep-

[26] Goethe, *Faust,* Part One, Scene: Street in front of Gretchen's house.

[27] See Strack and Billerbeck, *Kommentar,* 1:891.

[28] Isa 6:3. Translation: "We will sanctify your name in the world as they sanctify it in the heavens above, as it is written by the hand of your prophet, And they called one to the other and said, Holy, holy, holy is the Lord of Hosts, the whole earth is full of his glory; those over against them would say Blessed; Blessed is the glory of the Lord from his place; and in your Holy Words it is written, saying, The Lord shall reign for ever, your God, O Zion, from generation to generation, Praise the Lord; from generation to generation we will proclaim your greatness and to the eternity of eternities your Holiness we will sanctify, and your exaltation shall not depart from our mouth for ever and ever, for a great and holy God and King you are; Blessed are you, O Lord, the Holy God."

[29] See Strack and Billerbeck, *Kommentar,* 4, pt. 1:214 ff. The petitions are for Understanding, Repentance, Forgiveness and so on, the thanks for benefactions throughout the ages and in the present.

[30] Oh that we had been spared the Freudians. Today, when your wife compliments you, "You are sweeter than any of the five hubbies I have had before," you suspect that she wants something special.

[31] Acts 3:13 ff., 5:30.

[32] Acts 23:8.

resents them as dismissing angelology. One half of the literature accepts the allegation though it is corroborated in not a single other source and though angels are accredited by the Pentateuch. The other half assumes a blunder, though how that could occur on a topic of such popular interest is hard to imagine. In actual fact, the statement has to do not with angelology as a whole but with the Jesuanic concept of the risen ones as akin to angels. "Resurrection and angel" equals "rising and donning an angel's existence." It is this peculiar species of angel the Sadducees deny—which, indeed, shows them fully at ease with angelology as such. The dissension between Pharisees and Sadducees depicted in this chapter is stirred up by Paul in order to get the former on his side: he protests that those who raged against his sermon on the previous day did so because it expressed faith in resurrection. Perfectly true, no deception: already in the preceding portion about Peter and John, just inspected, we learn that the Sadducees resented "their preaching through Jesus the resurrection of the dead."[33] At any rate, no need whatever for the narrator to drag in angelology in general, while a reminder of the superior understanding of resurrection, by disclosing which Jesus repulsed the Sadducees, is highly appropriate.

There is yet a bit more to it. Remarkable stress is laid in this account on Pharisaic approval of his concept: "the Pharisees confess both,"[34] i.e., not only resurrection but also radical transmutation. Tying in with the concession by some of their scribes that "if a spirit or angel has spoken to him . . . ."[35] Once more, by no means a reference to angels at large. It takes up exclusively the two visions of the risen Jesus detailed by Paul the day before, the first of them in light so overwhelming that no earthly being could dwell in it unblinded.[36] That this momentous aspect of his experience, a direct manifestation of the wholly different make-up of the new body—"we shall be changed" in 1 Corinthians[37]—should have an impact on his listeners is scarcely surprising. But there is absolutely no indication of the scribes going on to wider, unconnected questions. It looks to me as if a rare, specific contact between Acts and the Third Gospel might now gain in import. As in Matthew and Mark, so in Luke, Jesus' view of resurrection obtains Pharisaic assent, but in Luke alone it comes from "certain of the scribes"—the same phrasing as in Acts.[38] We may well be moving in the realm of prefiguring and re-enacting.

It may be asked why, whereas Jesus likened the risen ones to angels, in Acts it is "angel or spirit" or "spirit or angel." "Spirit" would be a legitimate accommodation to an educated public of the period.[39] It alone figures in 1 Corinthians 15. Also towards the end of Luke, where Jesus, risen from the grave but not yet carried up into heaven,

[33] Acts 4:2.

[34] Acts 23:8.

[35] Acts 23:9.

[36] Acts 22:6 ff.

[37] 1 Cor 15:51.

[38] This is wholly compatible with the view of J. M. Creed. *The Gospel According to St. Luke* (1930), 250, that the verse has been suggested by Mark 12:28. What is of interest here is precisely the subtle deviation from the latter in position and formulation.

[39] The chapter on Lord of the Spirit in W. D. Davies, *Paul and Rabbinic Judaism* (1948, rept. 1958), 177 ff., is invaluable for this and related problems.

still has flesh and bones—in contradistinction to "a spirit."[40] ("A ghost"—even in the New English Bible—is sadly misleading and, indeed, vulgarizing.[41] It would be—significantly—an acceptable rendering of *eidolon* in a scene from *The Life of Apollonius.*[42]) In Romans 8, there is much to and fro[43] between God's or Christ's life-giving "Spirit" and the Christian raised by it to become "spirit." Which enables me to end with the bee in my bonnet. Hebrew *ruaḥ,* "breath," "wind," "spirit," has life-giving force in a clause of the Second Benediction briefly introduced towards the beginning of this discussion. During the months between the Feast of Tabernacles and that of Passover, there is inserted into this Benediction the acknowledgment of God as "causing the wind to blow and the rain to fall."

III. Male and Female

According to Matthew and Mark, the Pharisees question Jesus concerning divorce, in the hope of cornering him:[44] they know that he is opposed but, should he say so, he will be spurning the law of Deuteronomy where it is permitted. Jesus triumphs by showing the Scripture itself, in two texts, classes the law as a *pis aller* [second best], tailored to a depraved people. My main business is with the first, which to begin with certainly stood alone: "Male and female created he them."[45]

Why ever should this have borne him out? So God made two species: does this impose an indissoluble bond? From the plain wording, the contrary inference would be almost more plausible. In Isaiah, God speaks of himself as "making peace and creating evil."[46] One would not deduce that an irenic person ought never to give up vice.

The solution lies in the then cherished, esoteric teaching, preserved in Midrash and Philo,[47] that the verse envisages the *Ur*-Adam androgynous, male and female in one. A variant of the Septuagint mentioned by the Rabbis in fact rendered it: "Male and female genitals of his created he him." Obviously, taken thus, it is a tremendous weapon against divorce, as also, let us note, against polygamy. The first human, formed in the image of God, constituted a lasting union of the two sexes. The *Zadokite Fragments,* in combating polygamy and divorce, give pride of place to this very line, calling it "a fundamental principle of the creation."[48] Just so, Jesus demands that this ideal "from the beginning of the creation" guide the community now starting out afresh. In my opinion,

[40] Luke 24:37, 39.

[41] So is Rengstorf's treatment of the scene, *Evangelium nach Lukas,* 285, as analogous to the Walking on the Water in Matt 24:22 ff.; Mark 6:45 ff.—where we hear not of *pneuma* at all but of *phantasma.* Creed, *Gospel According to Luke,* 298 f., does not bring in that incident.

[42] Philostratus, *The Life of Apollonius of Tyana* 8.12 towards the beginning.

[43] Sensitively annotated by C. H. Dodd, *The Epistle of Paul to the Romans* (1932), 116 ff.

[44] Matt 19:3 ff.; Mark 10:2 ff. See my *The New Testament and Rabbinic Judaism* (1956, repr. 1973), 71 ff. [252 ff.], and my oration ["Concessions to Sinfulness in Jewish Law"] in *JJS,* 10 (1959), 1 ff. [*Talmudic Law,* 1 ff.]. A similar attempt will be inspected below, under VII.

[45] Gen 1:27, 5:2.

[46] Isa 45:7.

[47] *Gen. Rab.* on 1:26 f.; *Mek.* on Exod 12:40; Philo, *Op.* 24.76; *Leg. All.* 2.4.13; *Her.* 33.164.

[48] *Zadokite Fragments* 7.1 ff.

at one time, the conclusion followed immediately on this first text: "What therefore God has joined together, let not man put asunder"—the creature may not dare disdain the pattern set up by the creator.

How the exegetes came to peg the androgynous shape of the pristine Adam onto this specific verse I have explained elsewhere.[49] Their doctrine, of course, is reminiscent of Aristophanes' in Plato's *Symposium*.[50] My hunch is that its core hails from the Orient. The Greeks took it over, like many other myths, and elaborated it in their way—achieving a brilliant complexity. Jewish probers into the divine scheme must have found the idea alluring as soon as they reflected deeply on that Adam from whose side God removed Eve; which does not exclude the possibility of their speculations being refertilized by Greek ones in the Hellenistic epoch.

The second text, culminating in "and the twain shall be one flesh," looks far more to the point;[51] indeed, it is its presence which has, so to speak, carried the first, saved it from being a puzzle. It, too, however, as I have tried to show, in the mind of whoever originally affixed it—Jesus himself or an early expositor—exhorts a mankind not yet perverted to aspire to that initial wholeness. This, irrespective of what we may deem the authentic drift in Genesis, gives it its special force in Mark—though probably no longer in Matthew, but I shall not pursue this change.

Why was it added? Because the first text was an argument from example—how God fashioned the world. But the Pharisaic leaders more and more insisted that, in putting forward binding regulations, you must argue from precept. "The two shall be one flesh" had the requisite style. The *Zadokite Fragments* contain three quotations. The first two, examples: "Male and female created he them" and "The animals went in two by two." The third—definitely a supplement—a precept: "The king shall not multiply wives to himself."[52]

IV. EYE FOR EYE

The Sermon on the Mount opposes to the maxim "eye for eye" and so on non-resistance and turning the other cheek.[53] Commentators, oblivious of the amazing change in meaning an Old Testament rule might undergo in the course of a thousand years or so, think of an attack on physical talion.[54] However, this practice had long disappeared; not one instance is traceable in the pertinent sources. Nor need we rely on external evidence alone: the Sermon itself militates against the facile handling. For one thing, it is

[49] See the works cited in footnote 44.

[50] Plato, *Symposium* 189C ff.

[51] Gen 2:24.

[52] Gen 1:27, 5:2, 7:9; Deut 17:17.

[53] Matt 5:38 (cf. Luke 6:29); Exod 21:24. On what follows, see my *The New Testament and Rabbinic Judaism*, 254 ff. [177 ff.], *Civil Disobedience in Antiquity* (1972), 109 f., and *Ancient Jewish Law* (1981), 86 ff. [198 ff.].

[54] See e.g. W. F. Albright and C. S. Mann, *Matthew* (Anchor Bible) (1971), 68. Belonging to a breed of New Testament students who have no desire to run down Judaism, they are distinctly uncomfortable and add a plea that came up around the turn of the century: retaliation acted as a check on blood feud. But, at best, it had done so in the distant past.

not into law reform; its aim is to direct its listeners away from literal ordinance towards ethical and spiritual understanding. For another, suppose the intention were to abolish a regime under which a thug guilty of mutilation has his eye gouged out, his leg cut off or the like: to summarize the new way of doing things by meekness when slapped would be utterly incongruous. The subsequent counsels—if someone sues you for your shirt or bids you accompany him for one mile, let him have your coat as well or go with him two miles, give and lend whenever asked—would be even remoter. No doubt they may be later elaborations. If so, at least the interpolator knows of no connection with talion.

A solid explanation must recognize that, by the time of the Sermon, he who hurt a person was liable to monetary damages, more precisely, five kinds, not, of course, all of them operative in each case: for permanent impairment, for temporary incapacity, for healing expense, for pain and for shaming. Pain and shaming were relative newcomers in this array, not really—i.e. by our lights—the subject of any Scriptural provision. Indeed, very likely, they came in not long before the New Testament era. Here is how the sages brought pain under the talion formula. The formula ends: "burning wound for burning wound, crushing wound for crushing wound, bruising wound for bruising wound."[55] They held that this enumeration of several ways of wounding must add something of consequence to the basic precept of redress—amends for pain, which varies according to the mode in which an injury is inflicted.[56] As for shaming—an even more refined item than pain—the final Rabbinic system derives compensation for it in a, to us, phantastic fashion from an injunction in Deuteronomy, decreeing that a woman who, in order to save her husband fighting with another man, takes hold of the latter's genitals, have her hand cut off.[57] There is good reason to assume, however, that originally (and in the popular view perhaps for a long time) it, like pain, was deemed to be covered by the talion edict. Anyhow, as in many ancient laws, so in the Jewish one, it was a slap and suchlike actions that typified a shaming assault. I cannot here go into why the slap comes to be so widely adopted as a standard example, except to note that one factor is precisely the absence of bodily harm outlasting the moment. If you cut off your enemy's ear or nose, however enormous the indignity resulting, it is to some extent overshadowed by the crude, corporeal atrocity. The offensive thing about a slap is just the indignity—hence when a law gets around to enforcing compensation on this ground, it is a most suitable illustration.[58] The Mishnah, under the head of shaming, lays down: "If a man slapped his fellow, he gives him 200 *zuz;* if with the back of his hand, 400 *zuz.*"[59]

The Sermon takes off from this development of the maxim. Within the new community, if an evildoer humiliates you, far from insisting on the exact amends due to you, you should be ready to suffer yet again. As soon, then, as we take account of how the

[55] The *lex Aquilia* contemplates *urere, frangere, rumpere* ["to burn, to break, (also) to break"].

[56] This line of reasoning is presupposed in *Mek.* on Exod 21:35, where the duty of reparation is extended to the mere causing of pain, without a wound.

[57] *Midrash Tann'aim* on Deut 25:11; *m. B. K.* 8:1.

[58] This, *au fond,* is but another facet of the phenomenon I describe in *Studi in onore di Siro Solazzi* ["On the Use of the Term *Damnum*"] (1948), 139 ff.

[59] *m. B. K.* 8:6.

Old Testament quotation would strike a Jewish audience of the first century A.D., instead of clinging to a stage that had lost all relevance, there is nothing absurd in meekness when slapped as its contrast. "Eye for eye" etc. had been the breeder of an ever more extensive claim in the case of a hurt, with, in the end, redress even for a cuff; it was to this that "turn the other cheek" opposed an alternative route to go. What is more, the following admonition—if sued for your shirt, give up your coat as well—fits, is a natural expansion. I am not at all sure it is the work of a second hand. Should it be, it still remains comforting that the by far earliest annotator of "whoever shall smite you" etc. manifestly takes it as I do.

(Readers under the spell of our modern legal system may find it difficult to understand how damages for battery could be disapproved of as an excessive standing on one's rights. As just explained, however, this application of "an eye for an eye" etc. was a novelty in Jewish law at that time. Whatever its merits, it was bound to interfere with old-accustomed social ease. As a somewhat comparable action looming on the horizon today we might think of, say, that of a ten-year-old child against a parent who has boxed his or her ears; or, to stray a little afield, that of a child aged twenty against a parent who chose an inferior school for him or her or against one whose race or economic condition was from the outset likely to restrict the choice.)

There is a riddle, happily not affecting my main presentation. The Sermon throughout implies that, if only you explore the Sinaitic commandments in depth, advancing from letter to spirit, they will turn out already to contain the new ideals *in nuce* [in a nutshell]. For example, "you shall not murder," if only we take it in fully, already condemns anger. But how could it possibly be maintained that "eye for eye" and so on inculcates meekness? (This problem, *nota bene,* would be even harder if the quotation were still related to actual talion.) One conceivable answer is that, as the Exodus provision runs "you shall give eye for eye" etc., adepts in Rabbinic exposition, when it came to a slap in the face, were able to treat the victim as the addressee: you, the one who has been slapped, shall give cheek for cheek. They might invoke in support such snatches from the prophets as "I gave my back to the smiters and my cheeks to them that plucked off my hair; I hid not my face from affronts and spitting," or "He gives his cheek to him that smites him, he is sated with indignity."[60] Too bold a construction? Not bolder than some of those on behalf of resurrection or, if it be objected that less freedom was allowed in interpreting legal texts (*halakhah*) than historical or doctrinal ones (*haggadhah*), not bolder than the recycling of the statute, just mentioned, concerning an interfering wife. Alas, I see no way of getting beyond speculation.

V. GLUTTON AND WINEBIBBER

So far I have attempted to persuade you that ignorance of what Jewish exegetes made of their material may blunt our insight into the New Testament quotations from it. I now go on to cases where it has resulted in downright failure to recognize the presence of a quotation.

[60] Isa 50:6; Lam 3:30.

All three Synoptics record strictures on Jesus for his unworthy meal company and on his disciples for not fasting like those of the Baptist and other Pharisees.[61] In a section confined to Matthew and Luke—Q, for short—Jesus chides the people for having equally scorned John who did not eat and drink and him who did; of John they said he had a malign spirit (presumably, of melancholy[62]) and of him that he was "a man who is a glutton and a winebibber, a friend of publicans and sinners."[63] It is this strange combination of apparently separate charges which is here of interest.

Let us observe, to begin with, that in its primary thrust at least, the criticism can hardly have been directed against his deviating from John: the latter is never represented as hostile to publicans and sinners. Next, as for the first charge, in two respects it goes substantially beyond that lack of penance among Jesus' followers adverted to above. For one thing, it is levelled not against them but against himself. For another, to be a glutton and winebibber is far worse, on an entirely different level, than not to fast or, for that matter, than to eat and drink, the phrasing employed in this pericope. Gluttony and winebibbing are vices.

Now while the Book of Proverbs and Sirach impress on us their ruinous nature, Deuteronomy actually gives them a niche in the criminal process: the capital indictment of a depraved son by his parents culminates in "he is a feaster and a drunkard."[64] That Jesus' enemies are not just resorting to a ready-to-hand term of abuse but are citing this law becomes plain if we consider its then accepted exposition—to the effect that the clause designates, not a mere reveller, but a reveller surrounding himself with godless associates. For Philo, the worst about such a person is that "he is not only out to do wrong but to join with others in doing wrong."[65] By around A.D. 300, Abbahu goes as far as to declare that not unless he consorts exclusively with dissolute fellows does the legislator's severity apply.[66] It is in view of this line of interpretation that "a glutton and a winebibber" is supplemented by "a friend of publicans and sinners."

The features noted above now fall into place. The focus is not on the contrast with John. The target of the attack is Jesus and not his disciples. He is not rebuked for neglect of self-mortification nor, indeed, for excessive indulgence in the literal sense: it is

[61] Matt 9:10 ff.; Mark 2:15 ff.; Luke 5:29 ff., 7:36 ff., 15:1 ff. On the varying addressees of the strictures, see my article ["Responsibilities of Masters and Disciples in the Gospels"] in *NTS*, 19 (1972), 1 ff. [749 ff.].

[62] *y. Gitt.* 48c.

[63] Matt 11:19; Luke 7:34.

[64] Deut 21:20; Prov 23:20 f.; Sir 9:9, 18:33. The Gospels put *phagos kai oinopotes.* The LXX in Deut 21:20 puts *symbolokopon oinophlygei,* and in Prov 23:20 *ekteinesthai symbolais* for "to be a feaster," *esthai oinopotes* for "to be a drunkard." In Prov 23:21 the Hebrew "feaster" becomes a *pornokopos,* "a fornicator," while "the drunkard" is retained as *methysos.* Greek Sir 9:9 warns against *symbolokopein en oinoi,* "feasting at wine" with another man's wife, 18:33 against being a *symbolokopon ek daneismou,* "a feaster upon borrowing." Philo, *Ebr.* 4.14.359, faithfully quotes the LXX for Deut 21:20 (following it up with the noun *oinophlygia* in *Mut* 37.206.609). Mostly, he uses the root *methys* for "drunkenness." But there is variety, e.g. *polyoinia* in *Ebr.* 6.22.360. "Feasting," too, is represented by diverse expressions; in this paragraph we find *aplestia gastros,* "insatiability of the belly."

[65] Philo, *Ebr.* 7.25.361.

[66] *b. Sanh.* 70b.

difficult to imagine that anyone could ever have thought of this. He is characterized as the stubborn and rebellious son of the code whose crime consists in a general, calculated, incorrigible defiance of those in authority, the feasting and drinking being only its most visible mark. It has been argued that Talmudic jurisprudence defines this son much as psychiatrists since Philippe Pinel define the sociopath, morally deranged though not insane in a way that exempts from culpability.[67] If this is correct—and I think it is—it furnishes strong support to my proposition. The saying as a whole turns out very pointed: John was rejected as giving in to a devil of melancholy, Jesus, the son out of control, as giving in to a devil of disorder.

What conclusions, if any, are to be drawn from this as to the provenance of the invective, is beyond the scope of my topic. I will, however, draw attention to a peculiar notice which may be relevant to further enquiry. The general insult that he is possessed, that he is with Beelzebub or the like, occurs in all four Gospels. But only Mark briefly introduces his family coming to seize him, on the ground that he is beside himself.[68] This does sound like parents taking the first steps against a rabid son: according to Deuteronomy, before proceeding to a public trial, they must seek to put things right by chastening him—and Philo expressly lists physical restraint as appropriate at this stage.[69]

VI. FOR THEIR GENERATION

Luke tells us of a tycoon's agent who, about to be dismissed, forgives all debtors a portion of what they owe;[70] and the laudatory treatment he receives for this is justified by the argument that "the children of this age are wiser than the children of the light for their generation." The dictum has given enormous difficulty. It disappears as soon as we realize that "for their generation" echoes Noah's description as "just and perfect in his generation"[71]—taking it the way it was taken by first-century A.D. Jews.

There went on then a struggle between purists and realists, one of their disagreements relating to behaviour externally meritorious but tied up with questionable concerns: the purists deemed it worthless, the realists—within limits—a second-best.[72]

[67] See M. Rotenberg and B. L. Diamond, *Journal of the History of Behavioral Sciences*, 7 (1971), 29 ff.

[68] Mark 3:21. Klostermann, *Markusevangelium*, 36 f., rightly regards *existemi* here as a medical term for sick excitement—"ecstasy." He adds that, as is well known, it can also denote genuine religious enthusiasm. Maybe this range rendered it particularly attractive to the author of the notice: some kind of double meaning. On a probably second-century Hebrew translation of *exo einai* or *exo gignesthai* in the positive sense, see my note ["Ecstasy in a Statement by Rabbi Joshua ben Hananiah"] in *Niv Hamidrashia* (1972), 60 ff. [*Talmudic Law*, 455 ff.].

[69] Philo, *De spec. leg.* 2.41.232. On some connection between the Deuteronomic law and the story of Eli's misbegotten sons in 1 Sam 1:12 ff., see my *Sons and Strangers* (1984), 13 ff.

[70] Luke 16:1 ff. In what follows, I draw heavily on my essay "Neglected Nuances of Exposition in Luke–Acts," in *Aufstieg und Niedergang der römischen Welt*, ed. H. Temporini and W. Haase (1985), pt. II, Principat, vol. 25:3, Religion, 2329 ff. [857 ff.].

[71] Gen 6:9.

[72] Philo, in his discussion of historical relativity to which I shall return presently, does speak of "a second prize in the contest."

Three Lucan parables contain traces of this problem.[73] The Helper at Midnight satisfies his insistent petitioner not from friendship—this is stated in so many words—but because he cannot bear the undignified scene. The Unjust Steward comes to the debtors' help not from compassion but in order to be saved by them from a degrading life. The Unjust Judge takes up the clamorous widow's case though—as is made crystal clear—still caring about neither God nor man, afraid of public humiliation. Basically, in all three cases, the proper conduct is inspired not by moral virtue but by fear of disgrace. Elsewhere I have connected the prominence of this particular motive with the Third Gospel's shame-cultural affiliation.[74] We are in touch here, I suggest, with Wisdom circles of the time between Jesus and the evangelist. For the purpose in hand it is enough to remark that the verdict is realist. What the Helper, the Steward and the Judge end up doing, while definitely flawed, is none the less an outcome deserving commendation.

However, in addition to the conundrum of the right action with an ulterior aim, the two schools debated that of the person who, living in a degenerate period of history, is unable, despite endeavours in the right direction, to come up to the desirable standard. The realists considered their attitude, making allowance for his environment, to be sanctioned by the line about Noah, splendid "in his generation"—which signified, they maintained, "by comparison with his generation": though not the equal of many later saints, he is given generous credit by Scripture for his relative excellence. It is in precisely this application—found in both Philo and the Midrash[75]—that the phrase serves to explain the praise extended to the agent; and, quite likely, the minuscule change[76] of the original "in his generation" into "for [*sic*] their generation" is designed to ensure the proper understanding—"for" denoting "measured against," "if account is taken of." Those still belonging to the present aeon, of whom he is one, considering their surroundings, rank higher when making such an inadequate effort than the members of the new community.

The substitution of "wise" for "just and perfect" reflects the central values of the circles to whom we owe this expansion of the parable. It is noteworthy that, with all their additional speculation, they do remain alive to the authentic message: the urgent need, in the endtime crisis that has arrived, of seizing the only chance of escape. Noah in both Testaments is the archetype of such salvation,[77] so an appeal to his precedent would be highly effective.

There is, of course, a reason the problem of historical relativity, in contradistinction to that of dubiously motivated service, is brought up only in connection with the Unjust Steward. This parable alone deals with the transition of one age into another, the hero setting an example of successful coping. The theme of the other two parables is the

[73] Luke 11:5 ff., 16:1 ff., 18:1 ff.

[74] See my "Shame Culture in Luke," in *Paul and Paulinism, Essays in Honour of C. K. Barrett*, ed. M. D. Hooker and S. G. Wilson (1982), 360 f. [817 ff.].

[75] Philo, *Abr.* 7.36 ff.; *Gen. Rab.* on 6:9.

[76] Of which I made nothing in my essay "Neglected Nuances."

[77] E.g. Q, Matt 24:37 f.; Luke 17:26 f.

force of prayer, the responses of the earthly Helper and earthly Judge providing an inkling of how heaven will respond. No occasion here, as in the parable about transition, for pondering the different standards of different epochs.

Here is the New English Bible's version of the saying, as good an illustration as any of the helplessness resulting when no heed is paid to what the Rabbis made of the ancient texts. "For the worldly are more astute than the other-worldly in dealing with their own kind." In the first place, this is not what we find in the Greek. In the second place, read as part of the New English Bible's overall presentation of the parable,[78] it makes the principal, who has just given notice to the bailiff for squandering his property, express admiration for a final downright villainy. Incredible and, in addition, completely divorced from primitive Christian concerns.

VII. He That Is Without Sin

When Jesus confounds the would-be executioners of an adulteress, "He that is sinless among you, let him be the first to cast a stone at her,"[79] he is citing the Book of Numbers. In it, a wife her husband suspects of infidelity is subjected to an ordeal which, should she be guilty, will make her rot away in the most gruesome manner. The statute closes: "And the priest shall execute upon her all this law, and the man shall be clear of sin and the woman shall bear her sin."[80] The Rabbis were troubled by the crass inequality between the sexes in this area. They resorted to the following rendering of the final passage, just defensible in Hebrew on over-rigid grammatical grounds: "And if the man is clear of sin, then the woman shall bear her sin."[81] So she is liable to punishment only if her accuser leads a blameless life. In due course, the more sensitive sages concluded that even where the individual husband's morals were unexceptionable, it was unjust to come down hard on an erring woman while the male world as a whole, man as a species, was given to hedonism; and in the sixties A.D., the most eminent of them, Johanan ben Zaccai, abolished the ordeal altogether.[82] Throughout this evolution, the progressives invoked the prophet Hosea for their cause: "I will not wreak vengeance on your daughters when they commit whoredom or on your daughters-in-law when they commit adultery, for you yourselves make off with whores and sacrifice with harlots."[83]

Jesus, then, quotes the verse from Numbers in its current interpretation—at the time the subject of much debate, there being a good deal of resistance—and he extends the principle to the treatment of an adulteress caught in the act, with not a shred of doubt as to her crime. It should be observed that Johanan, too, advocated leniency even in fully proven cases. A simile of his thoroughly approves of a king who, having

[78] Which, like all presentations since Jerome, is mistaken; see my "Neglected Nuances."

[79] John 8:7. For details, see my lecture ["Biblical Landmarks in the Struggle for Women's Rights] in *JR*, n.s. 23 (1978), 177 ff. [See 239 ff.].

[80] Num 5:30 f..

[81] *Siphre* on Num 5:31. As in their treatment of Deut 31:16, about resurrection—see above, under II—so here the desired meaning is attained by wangling, *collocatio*, division.

[82] *m. Sot.* 9:9.

[83] Hos 4:14.

divorced his adulterous wife, is reminded by her friends of her lowly origins where she could not learn right from wrong, and who thereupon remarries her.[84] The excuse, incidentally, is realistic, in line with the pleading of historical conditions we came across under VI: it pleads what we nowadays call social ones.

To Jesus, on this occasion, a Scriptural basis is indispensable. His opponents, as quite a few variants expressly inform us, are out to trap him. They reckon, of course, that he will not condone a stoning; but how can he set himself against an ordinance of the Torah? A mere appeal to fairness—which his words have commonly been thought to constitute—would not have been enough to defeat the schemers. He does stir their conscience but only because he is armed with a text in which their luminaries find fairness demanded for a similar situation. Essentially, he beats them on their own ground, much as that other time—discussed above, under III—when he is asked about divorce, again with a view to trapping him. The questioners know his attitude and hope he will get into difficulty seeing that the Torah permits this measure. Here also he prevails, adducing chapter and verse—in the then accepted sense—for the teaching that indissoluble union befits the ideal kingdom.

It may be worth pointing out that the method resorted to against Jesus—a question meant to embarrass you whichever way you answer it—is extremely old both in popular application and rhetorical art.[85] Jesus himself uses it in the controversy about his authority, when he counter-asks whether the Baptist's activity was from heaven or men. His foes, of course, deem it from men, but if they say so, they will incur the wrath of the populace. Unlike Jesus, they find no way out: "we cannot tell."[86]

VIII. They Ate and Were Satisfied and Took Up What Was Left Over

According to the Synoptics, the multitude fed by Jesus—if we discount minor variations—"ate and were satisfied and took up what was left over . . . ." John expands this but still reflects the original summation.[87] Commentators rightly note the influence of Elisha's feeding of a hundred men who "ate and left over."[88] However, this ending contains only two members—eating and leaving over—in contrast to three in the Gospels—eating, being satisfied and leaving over. There is a second Old Testament text in the background: when Boaz first meets Ruth in the field, at mealtime he hands her corn and "she ate and was satisfied and left over."[89]

[84] *Deut. Rab.* on 10:1.

[85] Aristotle, *Rhet.* 2.23.16.1399a; *Soph. El.* 2.12.173a; *Ad Herennium* 2.24.38.

[86] Matt 21:23 ff.; Mark 11:27 ff.; Luke 20:1 ff.

[87] Matt 14:20, 15:37; Mark 6:42 f., 8:8; Luke 9:17; John 6:11 ff. See my *New Testament and Rabbinic Judaism*, 36 ff. [144 ff.].

[88] 2 Kgs 4:42.

[89] R Ruth 2:14. The LXX here puts its habitual rendering of *śabha'*, "to be satisfied": *pimplemi.* Occasionally, however, we do find *chortazo*, e.g. Ps 17:15 (in LXX 16:15). The latter, incidentally, no doubt represents *śabha'* also in Tob 12:9—where a revised version prefers *pimplemi.* (This version is published by O. F. Fritzsche, *Kurzgefasstes exegetisches Handbuch zu den Apokryphen des Alten Testamentes, Zweite Lieferung* [1853], pp. 71 ff.) Matthew, Mark and Luke all offer *chortazo* while John uses *pimplemi.* In Matt 14:20, 15:37; Mark 6:43, the root *pleres* is met in connection with the baskets "heaped" with the remains.

This source has gone unremarked because, to appreciate its relevance, we have to be aware of what was seen in it by the Rabbis. A typical interpretation which seems to be quite early runs: "She ate, in this world; and was satisfied, for the days of the Messiah; and left over, for the Age to Come."[90] In some expositions, Boaz stands for God and Ruth for her descendant David or the Messiah himself. Again, the word for "corn," *qali*, is equated with *qalil*, which means "slight." So Boaz gives her a slight portion only but miraculously it suffices for her "to eat, be satisfied and leave over."[91] For the Jews of the first century, then, the two feedings by Elisha and Boaz belonged closely together, were largely interchangeable, supplemented one another: they both exhibited the same deeply significant kind of wonder wrought by God through and for his elect at various stages of salvation. We must not indeed forget that, to minds untouched by higher criticism, a testimony from the Book of Ruth, far older than one centering on Elisha, would appear particularly venerable and reassuring.

It is a rich tapestry the evangelists have woven: to the extent that the passage from Ruth plays a role in their narrative, Boaz, the widow's redeemer, becomes Jesus and Ruth he redeems becomes the Messianic community.

IX. THE HANDMAID OF THE LORD

Lastly, the annunciation: "And the angel said ... The Power of the Highest shall overshadow you . . . and Mary said, Behold the handmaid of the Lord."[92] This exchange assumes yet further depth when we perceive its evocation of Ruth, the Messiah's ancestress. She pays a nocturnal visit to Boaz, to whom she is not yet married, offering to become his wife: "I am Ruth your handmaid, spread therefore your skirt over your handmaid, for you are a redeemer."[93] In Hebrew and Aramaic, the mysterious verb is closely related to "to overshadow." They then spend a symbolical wedding night together, without consummation. What it all means in the ancient saga, I have set out elsewhere.[94] For the present discussion, two links with the Lucan chapter are of importance. One, Ruth, in the offer just quoted, is displaying unbounded faith in Boaz: far from taking advantage of her, he will bring about redemption, guide her to her ultimate, exalted fortune. As Naomi put it when she advised the visit: "He will tell you what you shall do."[95] The other, while Goethe, romantically and arrogantly thinking of those primitives as children, admired their doings as idyllic, the Jewish sages, more squeamish yet equally unhistorical in their way, were disturbed by an at-first-sight grave breach of modesty on Ruth's part.[96] By dint of their interpretative art, they proved to their satis-

John 6:13 employs *gemizo*. This much less frequent verb occurs twice in 2:7, which reinforces my suggestion (*New Testament and Rabbinic Judaism*, 45 [151 f.]) as to a profoundly thought-out approximation by John of the bread in the episode under notice and the wine at Cana.

[90] *b. Shab.* 113b.

[91] *Ruth Rab.* on 2:14.

[92] Luke 1:35 ff. See my *New Testament and Rabbinic Judaism*, 27 ff. [137 ff.].

[93] Ruth 3:9.

[94] See my *Ancient Jewish Law*, 33 ff. [489 ff.]

[95] Ruth 3:4.

[96] Not denying that each has a point; neither claiming that children are necessarily idyls.

faction not only that she committed no such infraction but, indeed, that she was the purest of all women; and, significantly, the phrasing used by her plays a major part in their deliberations. "I am Ruth your handmaid, spread therefore your skirt over [overshadow] your handmaid" is contrasted, as expressive of the most sublime chastity, with the shameless invitation the wife of Potiphar extends to Joseph: "Lie with me."[97] By choosing Ruth's words for the climax of his recital, the New Testament author depicts her as prefiguring Mary.

Let me in conclusion touch on an aspect not directly falling under my topic and yet neither quite without relevance. It has to do with style which here, however, more clearly than in many other instances, has been moulded by profound beliefs and feelings. I am referring to the Gospel's masterly, beautiful delicacy of presentation. We may assume that the miraculous birth from the first moment provoked nasty and mocking comments on the part of unbelievers; and that the introduction of Ruth, recognized as above reproach though with appearances equally against her, was in large part calculated to rebut them. Yet there is not a single mention of those low aspersions. It is not as if their existence were denied: that would defeat the purpose. They are relegated into the background, implied instead of spelled out, guardedly alluded to by the in themselves lofty terms "to overshadow" and "handmaid." Thus the readers—or, to be precise, those of them familiar with the heroes and heroines of tradition—would grasp the contention without being confronted by crude ugliness. Matthew, it should be noted, is not so reticent; he relates that Joseph, before being enlightened by a vision, intended to divorce Mary.[98] In Luke, the angelic mood of the annunciation scene is never broken; nothing openly mars the picture; the focus is throughout on the positive, the Spirit's descent and the Virgin's perfect submission in trust. So successful is this achieved that, in the roughly eighteen centuries of the legend's circulation in a gentile world, the polemical point has stayed totally submerged.

This mode of shaping the material has a long history. Two pieces from Genesis and Second Samuel come to mind. Jacob serves seven years for Rachel. But then, after the wedding feast, at night, her father substitutes her elder and less comely sister Leah and it is to her that the bridegroom finds himself joined in the morning.[99] Not a word is said about her participation in the fraud. Obviously, the most docile daughter could not execute that assignment without a considerable contribution of her own. Once more, the troublesome facts are not negated: it would be difficult to do so. They are pushed out of sight. Certainly, we do come across some acute Rabbinic observations[100] and, of course, modern, psychology-oriented reworkers of the story have a ball. None the less, on the whole, the Biblical author manages to deflect our interest, she remains apart, untouched, we just do not think of her—or, for that matter, Rachel's—active involvement. The feat becomes all the more remarkable when we compare the accounts of Sarah's induction into the harems of the kings of Egypt and Gerar.[101] Here it is fully

[97] *Gen. Rab.* on 39:7.
[98] Matt 1:18 ff.
[99] Gen 29:21 ff.
[100] *Gen. Rab.* on 29:22.
[101] Gen 12:11 ff., 20:2 ff.

brought out that she cooperates with Abraham in concealing her married status.

Again, David commits adultery with Bathsheba while her husband Uriah is at the front.[102] Pregnancy results, so the king summons him home to bring news of the campaign and, having received his report, suggests he visit his wife before returning to the army. The child would then have appeared to be Uriah's. The latter, however, refuses to indulge in pleasure at a time his comrades are in the field. Whereupon David sends him back, with a sealed letter to the general requesting that Uriah be so placed in battle as to be sure to fall. The text contains no hint at Bathsheba's complicity in the duping scheme. Indeed, somehow, with supreme skill, our mind is kept off that datum. It is by no means denied—it simply does not occur to us. The odious reality is that the king could not possibly have encouraged her husband to spend a night with her without first initiating her and being assured of her utmost support.

No doubt there are all sorts of differences between these episodes. To name only one, Mary is innocent, Leah and Bathsheba are guilty. But this does not affect what I am talking about: the veiling of anything base. In the case of Leah and Bathsheba, our attention is directed away from their doings, in that of Mary, even from a suspicion: essentially, the same concern—to protect the holy. It is hardly accidental that the three most striking Scriptural examples have regard to sexual relations and, furthermore, show women as recipients of the reverential treatment. It is in the realm of sex that solicitude about the look of things, shame, originates in hoary antiquity;[103] and at a certain stage of civilisation, definitely reached in the Near East by the second millennium B.C., it is women—those you care for at least—who may be endowed with a sanctity so special as to require dissociation from impurity not only in life but also in speech and writing. As for the Third Gospel in particular, I have already—under VI—cited my thesis[104] that it is far more imbued with refined shame culture than the other Synoptics. The way Mary is defended is typical of this component.

I agree with the avant-garde among the young generation that a cover-up remains a cover-up however nobly motivated. Also that, on closer scrutiny, the motive leading to women being placed on a pedestal turn out to include distinctly ignoble elements. Unless we heed these insights, often neglected, we are apt to caricature the past and bungle more than we have a right to in the present. Still, a number of extremists seem to go too far. For one thing, they fail to allow for the individual circumstances of each epoch, its needs, its means, its inevitable limitations. Our own—not excepting our radicals, who, paradoxically, remind me a little of the Rabbinic purists[105]—had better hope for this kind of understanding from future critics. For another thing, too much faith is put in simplistic new formulas: to let it all hang out and complete, unselfish equality of male and female. There is no vision that does not conflict with another, there is nothing entirely good or entirely evil, we must weigh and choose at every step. To me, those

[102] 2 Samuel 11. See my article ["Nathan's Parable"] in *NT*, 24 (1982), 275 ff.

[103] See my papers ["The Culture of Deuteronomy"] in *Orita*, 3 (1969), 33, 40, and "Shame Culture in Luke" [817 ff.].

[104] In "Shame Culture in Luke" [817 ff.].

[105] See above, under VI.

ancient, basically truthful records of interaction between the human—frequently, all-too-human—and the divine are a continuous source of inspiration.

Two ironies. First, a pattern similar to that outlined dominates a far from sacred genre: the detective novel which, from beginning to end, is strewn with heavily disguised occurrences. True, the object is not to prevent an image being stained but to test the reader's intelligence: can he spot the clues? In the end, they will all be brought into the open. As one would expect, the fundamental discrepancy in purpose influences not a few details of the technique;[106] but I shall not enlarge.

Second, what demon moves me, who so treasures the devout considerateness of these tales, to undo it by ruthless analysis?

[106] On rereading this paragraph, I notice that I have slipped from style, with regard to Biblical writers, to technique when coming to the *Krimi*.

Concerning the Reconstruction of the "Aramaic Gospels"*

I. Torrey's Translation of the Gospels

It is sometimes maintained that the four gospels as they have come down to us are straightforward translations of Aramaic originals, with the exception, indeed, of a few small portions. Recently this view has found a brilliant and highly competent advocate in C. C. Torrey. It is not the present writer's object to investigate this vast problem, though it may be permissible to express respectful disagreement. Certainly, it is highly unlikely that Jesus used Greek when talking to his disciples or preaching; or even that he knew a great deal of Greek. (This point has perhaps received too little attention from those who have speculated upon the trial of Jesus before Pilate. That scene will appear none the less pathetic if we assume the presence of an interpreter.) There must, therefore, have existed a nucleus of sayings and stories in Aramaic. But it has been convincingly argued that Greek versions of these, or many of these, were current from an early date and were used by the evangelists or even their sources. Probably some narratives and sayings to be found in the gospels were in Greek from the outset. The truth seems to be that the problem does not admit of a uniform solution to be stated in a few words. The proportion of Aramaic, Greek and other elements (for there are others, among which Hebrew is prominent) varies from one pericope to the next and, quite often, one verse to the next. As for the Aramaic gold, while that may here and there be almost on the surface, as a rule we have to dig through several layers (some of them deep and hard enough to render the work laborious) to reach it; and not infrequently we shall toil all in vain, much as did those inhabitants of the shores of the Rhine who, fascinated as "the midnight moon did lave her forehead in the silver wave," searched their river for the legendary treasure of the *Nibelungen*.

Here a much narrower subject will be discussed. Torrey has given us a new English translation of the gospels,[1] a translation based on the theory mentioned at the beginning of this paper; and he has explained his deviations from previous renderings not only in numerous notes appended to this translation but also in a separate, more recent work.[2] In the latter he classifies his deviations, in order to show what kinds of mistakes we have to expect in a Greek work coming direct from the Aramaic. It may be said to be the purpose of the following remarks to point out some of the mistakes we have to expect in a work like Torrey's. More precisely, Torrey, for whom the gospels are immediate versions

* The author wishes to thank Professor F. S. Marsh for criticism and advice.

[1] C. C. Torrey, *The Four Gospels*.

[2] C. C. Torrey, *Our Translated Gospels*.

of Aramaic originals, is inclined to blame the translator into Greek for any difficulties in the text before us; inclined to solve any problems by alleging that the Aramaic was in order, only the translator into Greek misunderstood it. This procedure has its great dangers, whether Torrey's main thesis is tenable or not. No doubt some passages in the gospels may owe their present form to mistranslation of an Aramaic original. But it is easy to exaggerate and, except for certain particularly favourable cases, impossible to achieve reconstructions that can be regarded as authoritative. A phrase that looks odd at first sight may yet turn out to be in its proper place, on close examination of, say, the Rabbinic background: if we assume mistranslation in such a case, we shall only have made the text suit our modern notions instead of arriving at its true meaning. And who knows enough about the Aramaic of first century Palestine, the little personal peculiarities in the Aramaic of, say, the hypothetical Aramaic Matthew and those in the Aramaic of the man who made him into Greek to be able to reconstruct with authority? The writer happens to have seen a large number of reconstructions of texts from the Digest supposed to have suffered under the hands of Tribonian, Justinian's minister of justice, when he compiled that code from the works of the famous jurists of the first two and a half centuries. But it is greatly to be feared that few of them would cause the original authors anything but annoyance. Yet the task is considerably less complicated than in the case of the gospels, since both Tribonian and the classical jurists whose works he handled wrote in Latin. (The great Roman lawyer Otto Lenel, in the course of discussing similar questions, pointed out that of the German synonyms *da* and *weil*, the former was to be found hundreds of times in his own writings, the latter hardly at all: an interesting and by no means unique example of personal preference for one of two equally good words.) The pitfalls here referred to are only a few out of a great many in the way of him who would rely chiefly on the possibility of mistranslation in dealing with difficulties in the gospels. This is not saying that no account should be taken of that possibility. Far from it. It remains an undoubted merit of Torrey's to have revived interest in a method too often neglected. What it is sought to demonstrate is, first, that only good can come of a certain reluctance to assume mistranslations,[3] and secondly, that reconstructions are apt to go wrong. Unfortunately, even where one does not agree with an explanation by Torrey, it is often impossible to disprove it. In Aramaic, sometimes, the same words may express either a declaration or a question. Torrey says that in Luke 16:8 f., the Aramaic signified "Did the lord of the estate praise his faithless manager?," and that it was the translator into Greek who is responsible for the troublesome "And the lord commended the unjust steward."[4] The present writer prefers the traditional version, just because it is so inconvenient, but this means only that he does not approve of Torrey's suggestion, not that he has refuted it. Nevertheless there are cases where Torrey's treatment can at least be shown to be very problematic, and it is to a discussion of some of these that the following pages will be devoted.

[3] The present writer himself has sinned against this principle in ["ὄχλος in Mark ii.4 (Luke v. 19)"] *ET*, 50 (1938), 138 f., though he has made it clear that his treatment of Mark 2:4 and Luke 5:19 is not meant to provide more than a conceivable solution of a difficulty which may not exist. [See 643 ff.]

[4] *The Four Gospels*, 157 and 311; *Our Translated Gospels*, 56, 59f.

This inquiry, then, is not concerned with the wider question whether or not the four gospels are straightforward translations of Aramaic originals. Two points, however, may be noted. For one thing, should it be possible to prove mistaken significant explanations of Torrey, one's view of his main thesis will inevitably be affected, in however slight a degree. For another thing, even where something like a mistranslation appears established, we must remember that it may have occurred at a stage of the tradition far prior to the evangelist-translator; frequently, it may have occurred before any translation was made, so that we ought to think of misinterpretation of an Aramaic passage by one who handed it on in Aramaic rather than of mistranslation of an Aramaic passage by one who handed it on in Greek. According to Matt 14:2, Mark 6:14, "the powers work in him [John the Baptist]." Torrey contends that the Aramaic used a form which, if written without vowels, could mean this or "the deeds are worked by him" (passive); that, in this context, only the latter meaning can have been intended; and that the translator into Greek mistranslated.[5] But if the first two steps of this argument are conceded, there is nothing to prevent us from assuming that it was at the Aramaic stage itself that the form was misunderstood and replaced by one signifying only "the powers work in him" (active). It follows that even where something like a mistranslation appears established, special evidence is required if we are to be certain that it was the evangelist-translator himself who committed the mistake. A fair proportion of the mistranslations alleged by Torrey, even if believed in, are not of the type that can be ascribed only to the last or, indeed, to any translator into Greek. However, as the wider issue is not raised in this paper, this consideration will not be pursued. The object of these reflections, as already stated, is quite unambitious: to demonstrate that much care should be exercised in inferring mistranslations and attempting reconstructions.

II. Matthew 5:37

Let us begin with Matt 5:37. Torrey's allegation of a mistranslation is unfounded. An analysis of the Rabbinic background shows that the passage, if not superior to its parallel, Jas 5:12, is certainly not the result of clumsiness on the part of a translator.

Matt 5:37, as it stands, says: "But let your communication be, Yea, yea; Nay, nay. . . . " Torrey substitutes: "But let your word 'yes' be yea, and your 'nay' be nay. . . . " He remarks: "The Greek follows the Aramaic exactly, word by word, but the result is mistranslation; the second occurrence of the 'yea' or 'nay' is in each case the predicate. Jas 5:12 has it right."[6] But the matter is a little more complicated than that. True, we might readily conceive of an Aramaic original the meaning of which was as Torrey supposes, though it could also be interpreted (or rather, on this hypothesis, misinterpreted) in the way chosen by the Greek translator. True, Jas 5:12 has a version speaking for Torrey: "But let your yea be yea; and your nay, nay." Yet when we inspect the Rabbinic parallels, the result is strongly in favour of the Matthean text before us.

According to Matt 5:33 ff., you have to avoid oaths; you may swear neither by heaven nor by the earth nor by Jerusalem nor by your head; and you may go no further—if

[5] *The Four Gospels*, 31, 81, 293 and 299; *Our Translated Gospels*, 98 f.

[6] *The Four Gospels*, 11 and 291.

we accept the traditional text—than an emphatic "Yea, yea" or "Nay, nay." Jas 5:12 ends on a somewhat different note. You have to avoid oaths; you may swear neither by heaven nor by the earth nor by any other oath; the most ordinary assurance coming from you should be good enough. This "let your yea be yea, and your nay be nay" Torrey takes as having been behind Matt 5:37 as well. Now it is clear from the Rabbinic discussion of oaths that people were afraid to use the name of God; moreover, the better ones at least saw that swearing by God mostly showed a lack of true reverence. The name of God, therefore, was often replaced by attributes of God or the like. But as even these were feared and respected, less and less solemn expressions might take the place of oaths. For this and other reasons, it became necessary to lay down which phrases constituted an oath and which did not. In *m. Shebu.* 4:13, for instance, it is provided that, for certain purposes, "By heaven and by earth" is not an oath, but "By the Merciful and Gracious" is. In the Babylonian Gemara attached to this Mishnah (*b. Shebu.* 36a), R. Eleazar takes the view that a mere "Yea" or "Nay" may constitute an oath; whereas in Raba's opinion, a "Yea, yea" or "Nay, nay" is required.[7] It is worth noting that several examples of "Yea, yea" and "Nay, nay" being used for emphasis are quoted from Rabbinic sources by Strack-Billerbeck:[8] they were living expressions. Surely all this supplies a sufficient background to Matt 5:37 even as it stands. You may not resort, this is the meaning of the passage, to any of the dodges usual in oaths: all you may do is to say "Yea, yea" or "Nay, nay." And the conclusion that this verse is intended to give us the maximum formula permissible is confirmed by the second half: "For whatever is more than these cometh of evil."

As for the version in Jas 5:12, it is important to observe that the Rabbinic illustrations adduced by Strack-Billerbeck[9] are none of them concerned, like Matthew and the sections from *Shebuoth* cited, with the proper mode of making binding declarations. In other words, none of them are concerned with the problem whether man, so small before God, has the right to take an oath, and what he can do if he has not. In the first case, R. Jose b. Judah comments on Lev 19:36 ("Just balances, just weights, a just *ephah*, and a just *hin*, shall ye have"): "Your Nay shall be just and your Yea shall be just." The second case is the same as the first, except for the additional remark by Abaye: "You should not say one thing with your mouth and think another thing in your heart." In the third case, R. Huna in the name of R. Samuel b. Isaac comments on Ruth 3:18 ("Then said she, Sit still, my daughter . . . for the man will not be in rest, until he have finished the thing this day"): "The Yea of the just is a Yea, and their Nay is a Nay." In all three passages, that is, the theme is not the proper mode of making a binding declaration, but truthfulness and reliability. The two themes are closely related but not quite the same.

[7] These Rabbis, it seems, rather lost sight of the nature of an oath: for us, at any rate, an oath involves the invocation of a superior power. But in this as in every matter, the ultimate test, in the eyes of the Rabbis, was Scripture. As they found there, or thought they found there, mere confirmations and denials with the force of oaths, they regarded it as sufficiently proved that a simple "Yea" or the like might be an oath. Compare also Philo, *Leg. All.* 3.72.203 ff., and *Sac.* 27.91 ff.

[8] See H. L. Strack and P. Billerbeck, *Kommentar zum Neuen Testament aus Talmud and Midrasch*, vol. 1, 336 ff.

[9] *Op. cit.*, 336.

In Jas 5:12 alone they appear to be combined: you may not swear by heaven, the earth or any other oath (this sounds like a reference to the proper mode of giving an assurance)—you may not go back on your mere confirmation or denial (this is an exhortation to be truthful and reliable). Instead of "For whatever is more than these cometh of evil," we find the less specific "Lest ye fall into condemnation."

Dibelius indeed seems to think that Jas 5:12 is confined to the theme of honesty.[10] But this view can hardly be accepted. He relies on Pythagoras, but Pythagoras affords no real parallel. That sage, if we are to believe his biographers, "forbade his disciples to swear by the gods, saying that every man ought so to exercise himself as to be worthy of belief without an oath" (Diogenes Laertius [*Lives of Eminent Philosophers*] 8.22); and advised administrators to surpass the common citizens in nothing but justice, adding that "it was proper that the senators should not make use of any of the gods for the purpose of an oath, but that their language should be such as to render them worthy of belief without oaths" (Jamblichus, *Vit Pyth.* 47). This is a logical line of thought, belonging exclusively to the theme of truthfulness and reliability, but it is different from Jas 5:12. (It does recur, significantly, in Josephus' account of the Essenes, *Bell.* 2.8.6.135: "And while any word counts with them as stronger than an oath, they avoid swearing, deeming it worse than perjury; for he stands condemned from the very outset, they say, who cannot be trusted without an invocation of God."[11]) Jas 5:12 does not contain only a plain warning not to swear and to stand by one's mere word. More precisely, it says not only "swear not," but "swear not, neither by heaven, neither by the earth, neither by any other oath." This distinctly indicates that somewhere in the tradition underlying James stood the problem that is still prominent in Matthew, the problem of dodges (how far are they admissible? which of them constitute oaths? is there a way to do without them?); somewhere in that tradition stood the notion of the oath as abhorrent not because a man's mere assurance ought to be enough, but because God is to be feared and respected; somewhere, in brief, stood the discussion of the proper mode of making binding declarations. Only Jas 5:12, in contradistinction to Matt 5:37, superimposes on this the theme of truthfulness and reliability: it concludes with an admonition to be honest. As a result, it is less compact than either Matt 5:37 (the proper mode of making a binding declaration) or Pythagoras (honesty).

In view of this evidence, it is arguable that Jas 5:12 represents a later stage than Matt 5:37. Matt 5:37, we might hold, is slightly more precise. It tells us not to swear, not even with the help of dodges, but to use the formula "Yea, yea" or "Nay, nay": But let your communication be, "Yea, yea; Nay, nay." Jas 5:12 seems to draw an inference from this teaching. It tells us not to swear, not even with the help of dodges, but to make up by being truthful and reliable: "But let your yea by yea, and your nay, nay." Maybe the technical point of Matthew's "Yea, yea" and "Nay, nay" was no longer understood at a very early date. But this does not necessarily follow: the introduction into the saying of a general, moral maxim is nothing very surprising. However, there is no need here to

[10] M. Dibelius, *Der Brief des Jakobus*, 7th ed., 228 ff.

[11] Compare Philo, *Prob.* 12.84: the Essenes, we are here told, attach the greatest importance to "continued and uninterrupted purity throughout the whole of life, avoidance of oaths, avoidance of falsehood," etc.

decide between the claims of the two versions. The present writer inclines to prefer Matt 5:37: for if the interpretation here attempted is tenable, it forms the conclusion of a homogeneous utterance concerning the proper mode of making a binding declaration, while Jas 5:12 gives the argument a twist so as to lead up to the command to be honest. Dibelius prefers Jas 5:12: for he regards it as a homogeneous utterance concerning honesty, and also as ethically superior to the more legalistic Matt 5:37.[12] (Some help might be got for the question from 2 Cor 1:17 ff., if that passage did not itself give rise to considerable difficulties.) In any case, the position is that we have one version in Matt 5:37, strongly supported by Rabbinic analogy; and another version in Jas 5:12, less strongly supported by Rabbinic analogy, though, according to Dibelius, to be paralleled from Pythagoras. Admittedly, there is here an awkward problem. But to assume a mistranslation in Matt 5:37 and violently assimilate this text to Jas 5:12 is evading the problem, not solving it. It is, at bottom, doing the same thing with modern means that was done in a more primitive way by those ancient editors and scribes who simply corrected Matt 5:37 after Jas 5:12 or Jas 5:12 after Matt 5:37. A glance at the apparatus will show that quite a few, in the course of the centuries, made the two versions agree with one another. Let us not succumb to the temptation.

III. Mark 10:6

Mark 10:6 uses a curious phrase, which Torrey ascribes to mistranslation. There exists so close an analogy, however, in Rabbinic literature that this view must be rejected. The difference between Mark 10:6 and its parallel, Matt 19:4, cannot be dissolved by assuming clumsiness on the part of a translator.

Mark 10:6, in its present form, reads: "But from the beginning of the creation, male and female made he them." Torrey substitutes: "At the beginning, the Creator made them male and female." He remarks: "The text of the verse began: *milqadmin di b'ra*, which might be rendered exactly as in Mark, the subject of the verb (God) being understood. But Matthew, who had the same text (with the words possibly transposed), rendered correctly. See Matthew 19:4, and the note there.[13] *Milqadmin* is the regular Jewish Aramaic for 'at the beginning.'"[14] Torrey further argues that the traditional text of Mark cannot be right, seeing that God made man not at the beginning of creation, but at the end.[15]

[12] The latter reason would seem peculiarly weak, though it is also given as decisive by E. Klostermann, *Das Matthäusevangelium*. 2nd ed., 46 f. For one thing, the transformation of a saying with a legalistic point (Matthew) into one with a general, ethical point (James) is much more likely in this case than the reverse process; yet it is the reverse process that Dibelius assumes. For another thing, is it right to label a version as finer merely because it makes a stronger appeal to the twentieth-century reader? Certainly, James' admonition to be honest suits any modern system of ethics. But is it really finer than the advice to make binding declarations in the form of "Yea, yea" or "Nay, nay" only, if that advice springs (as it does in Matthew) from a genuine acknowledgment of the greatness of God, of God who alone is master of "heaven, the earth, Jerusalem and thy head"?

[13] This note, to be found in *The Four Gospels*, 294, says: "'He who made' renders *di b'ra*, which is the standing phrase for 'the Creator.' See note on Mark 10:6."

[14] See *The Four Gospels*, 91 and 302.

[15] See *Our Translated Gospels*, 3, 12, and 14.

It must be admitted, first, that the Aramaic postulated by Torrey might well mean what he thinks it originally did; secondly, that it might well be translated, or rather, on his hypothesis, mistranslated in a way leading to the text as it stands; thirdly, that if we accept his correction, the troublesome difference between Mark 10:6 and Matt 19:4 disappears; and fourthly, that man was the last, not the first, of God's works—at least to go by the plain sense of the Biblical story rather than certain Midrashic speculations. Torrey could even have added two further points. First, the view that the present Mark 10:6 must be due to mistranslation is not new. Wellhausen and Klostermann held it,[16] though their Aramaic or Hebrew and, consequently, their original saying is vastly different from Torrey's; and on the basis of their reconstruction, the gulf between Mark 10:6 and Matt 19:4 becomes even wider than it now is. (According to them, the Aramaic or Hebrew behind Mark 10:6 meant: "At the beginning of the book of the creation, Moses wrote that male and female made he them.") Secondly, the desire to make these two texts say exactly the same is not new. It has been suggested that Matt 19:4 is corrupt and, at some stage, was absolutely identical with Mark 10:6.[17]

There are, then, a number of arguments in favour of Torrey's opinion; yet those against it are stronger. The first point to make one doubtful is the existence of another passage where Mark uses the term "from the beginning of the creation" while Matthew does not. Mark 13:19 says: "For in those days shall be affliction, such as was not from the beginning of the creation." Matt 24:21 says: "For then shall be great tribulation, such as was not since the beginning of the world."[18] It is true that this time there is no difference in meaning between the evangelists, and also that whereas man, according to the plain Biblical story, was not made "in the beginning of the creation" (which Mark 10:6 in its traditional form might be taxed with overlooking), it is perfectly natural to speak of troubles more fearful than any "since the beginning of the creation" (so that Mark 13:19 is safe on this account). Still, the fact remains that here is another instance where Mark alone employs just this phrase, and where a mistranslation of the kind assumed by Torrey in the case of 10:6 is out of the question.

A far more serious consideration is that *mitt'ḥillath b'riyyatho shel 'olam*, "from the beginning of his creation of the world," is a frequent expression in Rabbinic discourses on the creation. Sometimes, indeed, the phrase is used in its most literal sense. This happens particularly where God's perfect knowledge of everything to come is emphasised. In *Gen. Rab.* 2 we are told: "R. Abbahu taught, From the beginning of his creation of the world the Holy one saw the deeds of the righteous and the deeds of the wicked; according to Psalm 1:6, For the Lord knoweth the way of the righteous, but the way of the ungodly shall perish; or according to Genesis 1:2 f., And the earth was without form and void—these are the deeds of the wicked, And God said, Let there be light—these are the deeds of the righteous.... R. Hiyya the Elder taught, From the beginning of his creation of the world the Holy one saw the temple built, destroyed and rebuilt; according to Genesis 1:1 ff., In the beginning God created—this is the temple

[16] See E. Klostermann, *Das Markusevangelium*, 2nd ed., 110 f.

[17] See M.-J. Lagrange, *Évangile selon Saint Matthieu*, 2nd ed., 367.

[18] Compare also Matt 25:34: "Inherit the kingdom prepared for you from the foundation of the world."

built (with Isaiah 51:16, That I may plant the heavens ... and say unto Zion, Thou art my people); And the earth was without form and void—this is the temple destroyed (with Jeremiah 4:23 ff., I beheld the earth, and lo, it was without form and void ... I beheld, and lo, the fruitful place was a wilderness); And God said, Let there be light—this is the temple re-built (with Isaiah 60:1 f., Arise, shine, for thy light is come ... For behold, the darkness shall cover the earth ... But the Lord shall arise upon thee)." Here, with God seeing the end as he sets to work, we are not very far from Fitzgerald's "Yea, the First Morning of Creation wrote What the Last Dawn of Reckoning shall read."

There seem, however, to have been Rabbis against whom the same charge could be preferred as against Mark 10:6, namely, a use of the expression under notice not in accordance with the strict Biblical account of the creation. *Gen. Rab.* 5a may be adduced: "R. Eleazar taught, From the beginning of his creation of the world the Holy one decreed (the Floods) and said (Genesis 1:9), Let the waters under the heaven be gathered together. How? It is written twice (Amos 5:8 and 9:6), He that calleth for the waters of the sea and poureth them out upon the face of the earth: one reference is to the generation of the Flood and the other to the generation of Enosh." (That there were two floods, one of them earlier than the familiar Flood, namely, in the time of Enosh, is an old Midrashic view.) In this passage, God is represented as having gathered the waters "from the beginning of his creation of the world," despite the fact that the Bible makes this one of the works of the third day. The same Midrash is recorded in *Deut. Rab.* 10 (where it is ascribed to R. Jose b. Zimra) and *Eccl. Rab.* in 3:14, and in these two versions the formulation is even clearer: "Thus spoke the Holy one from the beginning of his creation of the world, Let the waters be gathered" in the former, "From the beginning of his creation of the world it is said, Let the waters be gathered" in the latter. (The interpretation of the Midrash here adopted is Bacher's.[19] A somewhat less plausible way of taking it is to hold that the Rabbis meant to establish a contrast between the gathering of the waters in Gen 1:9 and the pouring out in Amos 5:8 and 9:6, the two Floods constituting a reversal of the original order. For the purpose of this discussion, it does not matter at all which interpretation is preferred: on either of them, the words "Let the waters be gathered" were regarded by R. Eleazar as uttered "from the beginning of his creation of the world.") Obviously, if it could be said that God gathered the waters "from the beginning of his creation of the world," there is no reason why this phrase should have been inapplicable to the creation of man.

But there is one more highly suggestive point: we find what God did "from the beginning of his creation of the world" treated by the Rabbis as an indication of what man ought to do. The relevance of this to the matter in hand is obvious. We have here part of the wider background of an argument like Mark 10:6 in its present form. In *Lev. Rab.* 25 is recorded a discourse of R. Judah b. Simon on Lev 19:23 ("And when ye shall come into the land, ye shall plant all manner of trees for food"[20]): "R. Judah b. Simon

[19] See W. Bacher, *Die Agada der Palästinensischen Amoräer*, vol.2, 51.

[20] This is a Rabbinic interpretation of the verse. The English Bible has: "And when ye shall come into the land, and shall have planted all manner of trees, then. . . ."

opened his discourse by quoting Deuteronomy 13:5, Ye shall walk after the Lord your God. But is it possible for flesh and blood to walk after the Holy one, him of whom it is written in Psalm 77:20, Thy way is in the sea, and thy path in the great waters, and thy footsteps are not known? ... But the explanation is as follows. From the beginning of his creation of the world the Holy one was first occupied with plantation only, as is proved by Genesis 2:8, And the Lord planted a garden eastward in Eden: so you also, when you have entered the land, shall first occupy yourselves with plantation only. This is the meaning of Leviticus 19:23, And when ye shall come into the land, ye shall plant trees." When we consider how carefully the comments on the story of the creation were sifted by the compilers and publishers of tradition, it becomes very probable that there once existed many more arguments of this type than would appear from the material handed down to us.[21] Incidentally, the plantation of Gen 2:8 is here said to have taken place "from the beginning of his creation of the world," though, if we rely on the plain sense of the Biblical story, it cannot have occurred before the third day, on which grass, herb and trees were created (Gen 1:11 f.). It is quite possible, however, that R. Judah did not rely on the plain Biblical story but adhered to a theory according to which the garden of Eden was among the first works of creation (see *b. Pes.* 54a): a theory perhaps supported by an interpretation of *miqqedhem*, "eastward," as "of old," "And the Lord God planted a garden of old in Eden."[22]

An examination of Rabbinic literature, then, shows that it would be rash to attribute Mark 10:6 to a mistranslation and violently assimilate it to Matt 19:4. Precisely what the relationship is between the two texts need not here be discussed. Nor is it necessary to decide whether Mark 10:6 uses the phrase "from the beginning of the creation" loosely, as the equivalent Hebrew is used in *Gen. Rab.* 5 cited above, or whether we have to interpret more literally. We might, for example, think of some Midrashic speculation ante-dating the creation of man. Several such are preserved, and there must have been more in the Talmudic era. We are told that an ideal creation in God's mind preceded the actual one; that God created everything on the first day, only the various works became manifest or extended in a certain succession; and so on. Another way of taking the term in Mark 10:6 literally would be to see in it a reference to the original state of man, when male and female were not yet two separate beings, as opposed to the final state now prevailing. It may be significant that it is precisely the clause "Male and female made he them," the clause quoted in Mark 10:6, on which the Midrash (which has every mark of great antiquity) rests its teaching of the androgynous man, of the first man who was two, male and female, in one. Mark 10:6, should this have to be regarded as relevant, would

[21] A line of thought not dissimilar to that in the section on divorce here under discussion is to be found in The Testament of Zebulon 9:4 (see D. Daube, ["The New Testament Terms for Divorce"] *Theology*, 4, 67) [See 286]. The patriarch warns his children against political division, against division "into two heads, since all that the Lord has made has received one head, and two shoulders, two hands," etc. But the term "from the beginning of the creation" does not occur.

[22] The Jerusalemite Targum paraphrases the word *qodham b'riyyath 'olam*, "before the creation of the world"; whilst *Gen. Rab.* 15 affirms that the word means not that Eden was created *qodhem libh'riyyatho shel 'olam*, "before his creation of the world," but merely that it was created *qodhem l'adam hari'shan*, "before Adam."

imply: "But the very first time that man was created, male and female, in one, made he them." If the verse was intended to be understood in this way, evidently, the argument against divorce was very powerful indeed. However this may be, to alter Mark 10:6 by assuming a mistranslation is, unfortunately, too simple a solution. One remark may be added in conclusion, though it has been made by others before. The fact that Mark 10:6 says, "Male and female made he them," with "God" as the subject merely implied,[23] should not be urged in justification of emendations (and Torrey does not do it). These words are a literal quotation of Gen 1:27 and 5:2, passages with which any Jewish audience, educated or uneducated, was thoroughly familiar: and the insertion of "God" would have made the reference less rather than more intelligible.

IV. Mark 10:12

The next case to be presented is Mark 10:12. Here, indeed, as has long been recognized, we find a saying that can hardly go back to a Jewish environment—though it will be shown that it just conceivably may. But it would be wrong to say, with Torrey, that the flaw was due to a slip of him who translated the Aramaic into Greek. For there still exist some Greek and Latin versions of the passage from which the flaw is absent. Accordingly, if we assume that the saying once was of a more typically Jewish character, the versions adverted to have preserved it intact: and it was changed not in the course of translation, but during its life in Greek. The problem of the relationship between this saying and its parallels, Matt 5:32, 19:9 and Luke 16:8, cannot be disposed of by declaring the former a mistranslation.

Mark 10:12, to go by the commonest reading, says: "And if a woman shall put away her husband, and be married to another, she committeth adultery" or "he committeth adultery." Torrey substitutes: "And if she who has been divorced by her husband marries another, he committeth adultery." The reason he gives is: "The Jewish woman, at this time, *could not divorce* her husband; see Josephus, *Ant. Jud.* 15.7.10, at the beginning. The reading here in Mark was not *pat'ra l'gabrah*, 'putting away her husband,' but *p'tīrā l'gabrah*, 'put away by her husband,' and the following verb was masculine. Observe that this is exactly what is said in Luke 16:18."[24] Once again, however, there is another side to the matter. Certainly, a Jewish wife under Jewish law could not divorce her husband, and Mark 10:12, therefore, sounds odd. Certainly, by emending the passage as Torrey does, we get the same sense as in Luke 16:18, or for that matter, in Matt 5:32b and 19:9b. Only it seems that, in the case under notice, if we adopt the method outlined, we are suppressing an interesting piece of textual—and general—history.

A Jewish woman under Jewish law could not divorce her husband; but she could and, apparently, sometimes did run away from him (*halakh, yasa', parash,* in Hebrew, *n'phaq, p'rash* in Aramaic).[25] The possibility is contemplated by Paul in 1 Cor 7:10 f.

[23] The English Bible says, "God made them male and female" (so also Luther: "*hat sie Gott geschaffen einen Mann und ein Weib*"), and there is ancient authority for this. (See the apparatus.) There can be no doubt, however, that the *lectio difficilior*, without "God," is the better reading.

[24] *The Four Gospels*, 91 and 302; see also *Our Translated Gospels*, 93 ff.

[25] See D. Daube, ["The New Testament Terms for Divorce"] *Theology*, 47, 65 ff. [281 ff.].

Indeed, the rule that a wife ought not to separate from her husband and that, if she does, she ought not to marry another precedes the rule that a husband must not divorce his wife: "Let not the wife depart from her husband. But and if she depart, let her remain unmarried . . . and let not the husband put away his wife." The point is that there is extant a variant reading of Mark 10:12 putting precisely this case. In D, the verse begins: "And if a woman shall depart from her huband," not: "And if a woman shall put away her husband."[26] And, strikingly enough, the same text underlies some versions of the *Itala*. Actually, most of the *codices* known to the present writer have a text compatible with Jewish law; namely, MSS. Cantab. (D), Corb., Mun. and Veron., where the phrase used is *exire a viro* [depart from a husband], MS. Verc., with *discedere a viro* [leaves a husband], and MSS. Bob., Colb. and Holm., with *relinquere virum* [abandon a husband]. According to Nestle's apparatus,[27] the versions of the *Itala* supporting D are only few ("*pc it*"). Strictly speaking, this is true, since the versions with *relinquere virum* do not really render ἐξέρχεσθαι ἀπὸ τοῦ ἀνδρός. They probably go back to a different Greek, lost to us. But the fact here relevant is that *relinquere virum* was possible for a Jewish wife. There is an essential difference between this and *dimittere virum* [dismiss a husband]. Actually, the existence of two Latin forms compatible with Jewish law, pointing to two Greek forms, should render fairly difficult any attempt that might be made to declare all Latin versions of the saying here in question as descended from D, which in turn might be declared as for some reason or other irrelevant. In other words, the existence of different Latin versions compatible with Jewish law seems considerably to strengthen the hand of D.

Clearly, we thus have a basis for a solution far more probable than Torrey's. D and the relevant versions of thc *Itala* have preserved the original form of the saying, with the wife not divorcing, but running away from, her husband. The other, commoner reading, with the wife divorcing her husband, was substituted at an early date. Nor is it difficult to see either how this happened or why the new reading almost completely ousted the original form. For one thing, Mark 10:11, the verse immediately preceding that here discussed, is directed against the husband divorcing his wife. So, indeed, are all remaining synoptic passages dealing with the subject, Matt 5:32; 19:9 and Luke 16:18. Is it too rash to suggest that Mark 10:12 may have been assimilated to these passages, may have been made to refer, like them, to divorcing one's partner instead of to running away from him? (This would not be the only point where we can notice a tendency to assimilate to one another the various utterances concerning divorce.) For another thing, in the Graeco-Roman world, divorce of the husband by his wife was permissible and frequent. Consequently, as soon as Mark 10:12 fell into Hellenistic hands, the version speaking of the woman divorcing her husband would appear perfectly natural. It may be added that the question whether the saying originally concluded with "she committeth adultery" or with "he committeth adultery" is of little moment in this connection.

So far, it has been assumed that the prevalent reading of Mark 10:12, with the wife

[26] καὶ εὰν αὐτὴ ἐξέλθῃ ἀπὸ τοῦ ἀνδρὸς καὶ ἄλλον γαμήσῃ, not καὶ ἐὰν αὐτὴ ἀπολύσασα τὸν ἄνδρα αὐτῆς γαμήσῃ ἄλλον.

[27] E. Nestle, *Novum Testamentum Graece*, 3rd ed., 113.

divorcing her husband, could not have originated in a Jewish milieu. One might conceivably argue, however, in favour of its superiority—though it looks rather unlikely. The very story from Josephus quoted by Torrey, one might, urge, shows that while Jewish law did not allow a woman to divorce her husband, there were circles in which this occurred. It should be observed that Josephus uses the same verb of Salome's action that is found in Mark. (It is true that he has the middle, ἀπολύεσθαι.) "She sent him ... a document, dissolving (ἀπολυομένη) the marriage, contrary to the laws of the Jews," he says of Salome's dismissal of her husband. Moreover, it might be said, there is the case of Herodias. Formally, she did not go quite as far as Salome. She did not, that is, write her husband a bill of divorce but just left him: Josephus records that she was τοῦ ἀνδρὸς διαστᾶσα (*Ant.* 18.5.4.136). Yet she married again while her husband was still alive; and it is strange that such criticism as has come down to us seems directed only against her marrying her husband's brother, not against her re-marrying as such. It is, of course, possible that the crime of incest was considered so monstrous that little mention was made of other weak points about her second marriage; or again, her first husband may have divorced her when she left him. But it remains a remarkable affair.[28]

However, like several of Salome's and Herodias' actions, the ones referred to must have been of a very exceptional character—a slender basis for upholding the commoner reading in Mark 10:12.[29] Besides, if we take the commoner reading, with the wife divorcing her husband, as the better, we shall have to assume that D and the versions of the *Itala* agreeing with it got their text from a source in which the saying had for some reason or other been Judaised. (The possibility of an unwitting alteration with the effect of making the saying Jewish can safely be ruled out.) It is hard to believe in such a secondary harmonisation of the passage with the Jewish ideas on divorce; and the existence of two different Latin forms consistent with Jewish law, on which something was said above, constitutes an additional obstacle in the way of such an explanation. In any case, without settling the claims of the common reading on the one hand and D and some ver-

[28] It is not necessary here to go into details. The difficulties, especially those of a chronological nature, are well known. F. C. Burkitt, *The Gospel History and Its Transmission*, 100 f., takes the saying in Mark as directly referring to the action of Herodias.

[29] I did not consider the accounts of (a) Salome's divorce and (b) Herodias' offence in the article ["The New Testament Terms of Divorce"] in *Theology* 47, cited above. The conclusions that I reached there are not substantially affected, save that to the terms occurring in Josephus which I gave in the last paragraph ought to have been added the following: (a) From *Ant.* 15.7.10.259 f. (1) πέμπειν γραμμάτιον ἀπολυομένη τὸν γάμον, "to send a document, dissolving the marriage," of Salome's illegal action. The same, Josephus remarks, would be legal if done by the husband. (2) προαπαγορεύειν τὴν συμβίωσιν, "to renounce the marriage," of Salome's illegal action. (3) ἀποστῆναι τοῦ ἀνδρός (aorist 2 of ἀφιστάναι), "to separate from the husband," of Salome's illegal action. More precisely, this term, according to Josephus, was employed by Salome in explaining her step to Herod. It may well be that Josephus chose it in this connection because he thought it unlikely that Salome herself would have described her action as what it was: ἀποστῆναι τοῦ ἀνδρός, being intransitive, could be applied to a wife running away from her husband. (4) διαχωρίζεσθαι (passive) καθ' αὐτήν, "to separate by her own decision," of a wife who runs away from her husband. (5) ἐφιέαι, "to dismiss," of a husband divorcing his wife. (b) From *Ant.* 18.5.4.136 and 18.5.1.110. (1) διαστῆναι τοῦ ἀνδρός (aorist 2 of διιστάναι), "to separate from the husband," of a wife running away from her husband. (2) ἐκβάλλειν, "to dismiss," of a husband divorcing his wife.

sions of the *Itala* on the other, we find that Mark 10:12 alone of all synoptic passages concerning divorce contemplates the possibility of a wife leaving her husband. According to the commonest reading, the case put is that of divorce of the husband by his wife. This was not recognised in Jewish law; but it was in Gentile law, and of Salome at least we know that she divorced her husband in spite of what Jewish law said. According to D and a number of versions of the *Itala*, the case put is that of a wife running away from her husband. Of this situation, frequent mention is made in Rabbinic literature; and it is considered by Paul. The passage thus creates a most intricate problem. To assume a mistranslation and violently assimilate it to Luke 16:18, Matt 5:32 and 19:9 is no answer: it is evading the real question.

V. Matthew 26:64, Luke 6:27, John 8:26

In three passages, Matt 26:64, Luke 6:27 and John 8:26, Torrey holds the particle "but" to be a mistranslation of an Aramaic word which, he says, could mean this or "moreover." The view is not tenable. There is no reason to boggle at the passages in their present form; and the only Aramaic text quoted by Torrey does not show that the Aramaic word which he thinks underlies these "buts" could mean "moreover."

In Matt 26:64 we are told that, to the high priest's question whether he was the Christ, Jesus replied: "Thou hast said; but I say unto you, Hereafter shall ye see the Son of man sitting at the right hand of power." Torrey substitutes: "You say it; moreover I tell you, You shall soon see...." He explains: "πλήν, the usual rendering of *b'ram*, is here a mistranslation, for the word meant 'moreover,' as not infrequently elsewhere (thus in Onkelos Genesis 20:12 it renders Hebrew *gam*)."[30] Similarly, Luke 6:27, as it stands, runs thus: "But I say unto you which hear, Love your enemies." Torrey prefers: "Moreover, I say to you who hear..." His comment is: "The word *b'ram* here meant 'moreover also,' not 'but'; see note on Matthew 26:64."[31] There is a third case of mistranslation of *b'ram*, in Torrey's view, John 8:26. In its present form, this verse reads: "I have many things to say and to judge of you; but he that sent me is true; and I speak to the world those things which I have heard of him." Torrey replaces this by: "I have many things concerning you to say and to judge; also he who sent me is a sure reliance . . . ." In justification, he remarks: "See notes on Matthew 26:64 and Luke 6:27."[32] No doubt, in all three cases, Torrey's alteration produces a smoother text. Nevertheless his thesis can be accepted for none of them. The contrasting particles (πλήν in Matthew, ἀλλά in Luke and John) are perfectly intelligible; in Matthew, "moreover" can be shown to be most unlikely. Besides, it is doubtful whether *b'ram* would be capable of the meaning required by Torrey at all.

One argument against Torrey's alteration of these passages may be derived from the very fact, just mentioned, that it produces a smoother text. Reading the Bible, the Old Testament or the New, one again and again comes up against a use of conjunctions not entirely in harmony with our academic logic or rhetoric. Admittedly, a Hebrew or

[30] *The Four Gospels*, 61 and 296.

[31] *Ibid.*, 128 and 308.

[32] *Ibid.*, 202 and 323.

Aramaic "but" has not always the same weight as an English one. Yet the proper procedure surely is to try and acquire some sympathy with that peculiar style, find out what sort of contrast may be at the back of the ancient author's mind. To pick out three passages and change "but" into "moreover" cannot be right. Why not add, say, Matt 11:22, 24 and Luke 10:14? In these pericopes, curses are pronounced against the heartless Chorazin and Capernaum. The places are compared with Tyre and Sodom. The latter, if they had been allowed to witness the works performed by Jesus, would have repented and survived. At this point, Matthew continues, "But [πλήν] I say unto you, It shall be more tolerable for Tyre at the day of judgment, than for you": and Luke has, "But it shall be more tolerable . . . ." Would the logic of this not be improved by substituting "therefore" for "but"? Maybe it would. But the verses under notice never formed part of a scientific treatise; and their authors saw nothing wrong in putting a conjunction that expressed a remoter idea, an idea not on the surface of the text but easily "felt" by an audience accustomed to this manner. In a scientific treatise, we should register a gap in the argument. The present writer is not the first to discover this somewhat arbitrary use of conjunctions in the Bible: it looks to him as if the Rabbis had noticed it. This, it is suggested, may well have been one of the factors contributing to the elaboration of the hermeneutic rules of *Ribbui* and *Mi'ut*.[33] The Rabbis, it seems, felt uncomfortable about certain conjunctions such as *'aph*, *gam*, and *'akh*, and concluded that these must have a very special significance. (The rules will be referred to again below, in discussing the Aramaic text, Onk Gen 20:12, appealed to by Torrey.) Needless to add, in elevated style, the establishing of contrasts is particularly to be expected. All the three passages attacked by Torrey contain important utterances of Jesus; none of them, for instance, a mere narrative account of a journey.

If now the three passages are examined singly, there is first Matt 26:64. It is superfluous here to decide whether the reply given by Jesus to the high priest meant "Yes," "No," "Yes and No," "It is not for me to answer this question" or any of the other nuances that have been proposed. It may be observed, however, that Strack-Billerbeck who, following Dalman, interpret it as a clear "Yes"[34] proceed from two questionable assumptions. They claim that the words σὺ εἶπας equal *'amarta* in Hebrew. But though this is conceivable, they may well equal *'atta 'amarta*, namely, if we regard σὺ as essential, as stressed; and the difference is very considerable. They further claim that in one Rabbinic text (they admit there is only one, and it has *'amarta*, not *'atta 'amarta*), in *Tosephta Kelim*, *'amarta* signifies "You are right, it is so." But even here the word may be taken as far less emphatic. Simon the Saint, severely reprimanded by Eliezer b. Hyrcanus, says: "Rabbi, *'amarta*." This seems to mean: "Rabbi, as thou hast said so, I shall submit." In any case, what Torrey does is to co-ordinate the two clauses concerned, "Thou hast said—I say unto you," in an exact, scientific manner, which the text as it stands does not. In fact, he assimilates the text to the Markan version, in sense though not in wording. According to Mark 14:62, Jesus declared that he was the Christ

[33] For a brief description of *Ribbui* and *Mi'ut*, see H. Strack, *Introduction to the Talmud and Midrash*, transl. from the 5th German ed., 96.

[34] *Op. cit.*, vol. 1, 990.

in so many words: "I am; and ye shall see the Son of man sitting . . . ." Torrey's reconstruction of Matt 26:64 comes to the same: "You say it; moreover, I tell you, You soon shall see . . . ." Such assimilation, tempting though it be, is always risky. In this case, everything speaks against it. It is hard to believe that a significant divergence between Matthew and Mark, occurring in one of the most vital scenes of the New Testament, should be due to nothing but a slip on the part of him who translated Matthew into Greek. It is most improbable that if the author of the present Matthew had had before him an Aramaic word capable of being rendered as "moreover," he would not have gladly availed himself of the opportunity; in other words, most improbable that if he had been enabled by his source to emphasise the reference to the Messianship in Jesus' reply, he would not have done so.[35] Be that as it may, clearly, we have to choose between two alternatives. Either the author of the present Matthew wanted a solemn, unambiguous affirmation of the Messianship; in this case, he would have put "moreover" had there been the slightest authorisation. Or he did not want this; in this case, we can hardly say anything about the (hypothetical) Aramaic original, since he might have put πλήν even if the Aramaic had a slightly different conjunction.

Going on to Luke 6:27, we find this verse opening a series of injunctions like "Love your enemies," "Bless them that curse you." Several interpretations of the particle "but" at the beginning of the verse have been attempted. The one apparently most popular at the present time says that while the section immediately preceding the verse under notice is devoted to condemnations of the rich, who are absent, from 6:27 onwards it is again the disciples present at the sermon that are addressed. After "Woe unto you that are full, Woe unto you when all men shall speak well of you," 6:27 means: "But to you who are here listening I say, Love your enemies."[36] This explanation is quite good enough. (If only we had equally good ones of many "buts" not rejected by Torrey!) It is worth noting that the rules "Love your enemies" and so on are introduced by a contrasting particle (δέ) also in Matthew, in 5:21 ff.; though, indeed, the contrast here is between the old and new ways of life: "Ye have heard that it hath been said, Thou shalt love thy neighbour . . . But I say unto you, Love your enemies."

There remains John 8:26. The present writer is inclined to take ἀλλά here to mean more or less the same as it means in verse 28. (These variations on a theme are by no means rare in John.) If this is correct, we may paraphrase as follows: "I have many things to say and judge of you. But it is not ordinary things, not things that I invent myself and you may accept or reject as you please: he that sends me is true and his things I speak." Bauer would make a different contrast.[37] On his view, we get something like: "I have many things to condemn at the present. But I have to continue since God is true and I must not make my mission dependent on success or failure; his things I have to speak." This is certainly a strong possibility. Obviously, there is no reason to despair and violently eliminate "but" from the text.

[35] Luther translates Luke 22:70 by, "*Er sprach zu ihnen: Ihr sagt es, denn ich bin's*," and John 18:37 by, "*Du sagst es, ich bin ein König*." The A.V. is more reticent.

[36] See J. M. Creed, *The Gospel according to St. Luke*, 92 f., and E. Klostermann, *Das Lukasevangelium*, 2nd ed., 80 f.

[37] See W. Bauer, *Das Johannesevangelium*, 2nd ed., 118 f.

So much for the passages concerned themselves. How strong is Torrey's Aramaic position? He says that *b'ram*, of which πλήν or ἀλλά is a good rendering, not infrequently meant "moreover"; this possibility the evangelist-translators seem to have overlooked. The present writer cannot deny that *b'ram* might be used as denoting "moreover," though he is unable to call any instances to mind and the dictionaries, in so far as they support Torrey's view, are misleading.[38] Of the one illustration offered by Torrey, at any rate, it must be said that it proves nothing, and this despite the fact that he might have appealed to the authority of Dalman's dictionary.[39] Gen 20:12 is a very special case. The situation is this. Abraham has described Sarah as his sister to Abimelech, Abimelech has taken her into his harem, God has threatened Abimelech and commanded him to return her, and now Abimelech blames Abraham for having wronged him. Abraham replies that he acted from fear of being murdered if he told the truth. This comes in verse 11. But he adds another defence, the claim that he did tell the truth: Sarah is his sister, they have the same father, though not the same mother. (Of course, Abimelech, told by the newcomer that the woman with him was his sister, had concluded that she was no more than that.) The precise logical connection of this second defence with the first is difficult to establish. The Hebrew confines itself to noting the sheer fact that here is a further excuse: "And also [*w'gham*], really, she is my sister." The LXX takes a similar line, rendering *w'gham* as καὶ γαρ. But Onkelos may have wished to give prominence to a more particular aspect. He may have wished to stress that, though Abraham was prompted by fear, his actual words contained no untruth. If so, *ubh'ram*, "and yet," was a natural choice: "And yet, in reality, she is my sister."[40] By putting "and yet" he may have intended to make Abraham emphasise that no charge of dishonesty can be preferred against him; "and also" is weaker. That Onkelos was given to introducing his interpretations into the text in the most subtle manner is well known. In any case, the exact relation between the two defences is obscure, deliberately left obscure by the Bible: we have to remember that the second defence is an instance of a method which, in the ancient world, counted as clever and at the same time not quite fair.[41] If in these circumstances the Hebrew co-ordinates the clauses concerned by means of "and also" and Onkelos by means of *ubh'ram*, this does not show that the latter particle could ever be used in the same sense as the former.

As a matter of fact, in the present writer's opinion, there most probably is a deeper reason why Onkelos chose *ubh'ram*. It should be noted that he has another *b'ram* in the same verse: "And yet [*ubh'ram*] indeed she is my sister, the daughter of my father, only [*b'ram* for the second time, *'akh* in the Hebrew text] not the daughter of my moth-

[38] I am preparing a note on the meanings of *b'ram*, in which I hope to show that the particle expresses a contrast even in the few passages where the dictionaries say it does not. Here it will be sufficient to deal with Gen 20:12, the text relied on by Torrey, and the parallel case of Gen 30:34 (see below, 82).

[39] G. Dalman, *Aramäisch—Neuhebräisches Handwörterbuch*, cites this text for *b'ram* in the sense of *auch*, "also."

[40] It is worth remarking that the A.V. goes with Onkelos. Luther, on the other hand, gives a literal rendering of the Hebrew: "*Auch ist sie wahrhaftig meine Schwester*." The ambiguity has its root in the incident itself, and there is little point in requiring exactitude of translators in such a case.

[41] See D. Daube, ["How Esau Sold his Birthright"] *CLJ*, 8 (1942), 1–6.

er." Onkelos disliked using the same word twice in one verse. Where the Hebrew text does it, he preferred to put different, synonymous words (if at all possible) rather than be a faithful reflection of the original.[42] Yet here we find him opening a verse with what is a most offensive *ubh'ram* if repetitions are to be outlawed, whereas the Hebrew has first *w'gham*, "and also," and then *'akh*, "yet." Surely, we have to look for a serious motive. Now Gen 20:12 was a very inconvenient text for the Rabbis. The Rabbis could not admit that Abraham and Sarah had the same father. They could not admit that Abraham, the pious, should have contracted an incestuous marriage like the ordinary "children of Noah." They maintained that Sarah was Abraham's niece, identifying her with Iscah in Gen 11:29. But Gen 20:12 was a stumbling-block. For here Abraham seemed himself to call Sarah his sister. The Rabbis explained that he was not giving the word "sister" its full force: one's grandchildren are, in a way, like one's children, they argued, and therefore, Abraham's niece, his father's grandchild, was, in a way, like his father's child. It was in this weaker sense that Abraham styled her his sister. This was a highly important matter, which Onkelos would be almost compelled to bring out in his translation. Was there a way of doing it?

There was. Reference has already been made to the hermeneutic rules of *Ribbui* and *Mi'ut*. From a very early date (tradition ascribes the invention of the method to Nahum of Gimzo, and of his pupil Akiba we know that he employed it a great deal), the exegetes assumed that certain particles might have a very special significance beyond the one immediately discernible. Thus the particle *gam*, "also," was supposed to extend the statement in which it occurred to something not explicitly mentioned. Exod 19:9 reads: "And the Lord said unto Moses, Lo, I come to thee ... that the people may hear when I speak with thee, and also [*w'gham*] in thee believe for ever." The particle *w'gham*, the Rabbis contend, is chosen in order that the prophets coming after Moses be included: in these also the people have to believe. Obviously, the Hebrew opening of Gen 20:12, "And also [*w'gham*] she is my sister," was rather awkward for Onkelos; it strengthened the statement whereas he was out to tone it down. The Hebrew particle that would have met all difficulties was *'akh*, "yet," "only," πλήν. This particle, for the Rabbis, indicated a limitation not expressed. An early Halakhic application of this rule is to be found in the *Mek.* on Exod 31:13: "Yet [*'akh*] my sabbaths ye shall keep." This verse is interpreted by R. Jose Ha-gelili thus: "The word *'akh* implies a restriction. There are Sabbaths on which thou must rest and there are Sabbaths on which thou mayst not rest [namely, thou mayst not rest if a human life is to be saved]." An illustration from the province of Haggadah is furnished by a comment on Gen 7:23: "And Noah only [*'akh*] remained alive and they that were with him in the ark." The Rabbis deduce that Noah did not remain unhurt; from the *'akh* it follows that "even he spat blood because of the cold." Clearly, it was *'akh*, πλήν, that the interpreters needed at the beginning of Gen 20:12. "And yet, *'akh* she is my sister": this would provide clear Scriptural proof that she was not his sister in the full sense of the word, this would put right that impossible utterance of Abraham. Here, it is submitted, seems to lie the real reason for Onkelos' use of *ubh'ram*, though it resulted in the same word occurring twice

[42] See A. Berliner, *Targum Onkelos*, part 2, 211 ff.

in this verse. This *ubh'ram* by which he regularly translated the Hebrew *'akh*, by which, indeed, he translated *'akh* further on in the very same verse, this *ubh'ram* was designed to suggest—not that the Hebrew text had *'akh* (for an alteration of the Hebrew text itself would have been sacrilege) but that the Hebrew text was to be taken as if it had an *'akh*, as if it had this particle drawing attention to a limitation not expressed. Abraham declared Sarah to be his niece only, not his sister.

Three points may be mentioned in conclusion as supporting this explanation. First, it has been seen for a long time that Onkelos was familiar with, and liked to employ, the methods of exegesis prevalent in Akiba's school.[43] His use of *Ribbui* and *Mi'ut* cannot, therefore, cause any surprise. Secondly, it is important to recall that he manages to make a prohibition of incest of Gen 2:24: "Therefore shall a man leave his father and his mother, and shall cleave unto his wife." According to an early Rabbinic view (the names of Eliezer b. Hyrcanus and Akiba appear in this connection),[44] this verse means that a man shall leave, that is to say, not take, his close relatives when he chooses a wife. Onkelos translates nearly literally, but only nearly: "Therefore shall a man leave the bedroom [*beth mishkabhe*] of his father and his mother . . . . " When we consider that the same expression is used by him in Gen 49:4, the intention becomes quite clear. The latter passage contains Jacob's complaint about Reuben's incestuous commerce with Bilhah, about his "going up to his father's bed."[45] Thirdly, Onkelos, it is submitted, makes exactly the same use of *b'ram* in Gen 30:34 as in the text just analysed. The Bible records how Jacob asked Laban that, in future, if any spotted goats were born amongst the herd entrusted to him, they should be his; and how Laban accepted the proposal with the words, "Behold, would it might be according to thy word." Onkelos renders "behold" by *b'ram*. Why? it is well known that the agreement outlined turned out unexpectedly lucrative for Jacob, who did what the French politely describe as *corriger la fortune* [to better one's luck]. As is natural, the Rabbis claim that he did it in self-defence and that it was Laban who first broke the contract. In fact, according to the Rabbis, the verse quoted, Gen 30:34, proves that Laban lied in the very act of agreeing, or rather, apparently agreeing: the words "behold, would" are interpreted by them as meaning "yes–no." (The Hebrew *hen*, "behold," is equated with the Aramaic *hen*, "yes," and the particle *lu*, "would," is read as *lo*, "no."[46]). "R. Hiyya the Elder said," we are told in *Gen. Rab.* 73, "Everything that Laban arranged with Jacob he retracted ten times even at the outset, for it is written, Yes–no." Onkelos does not hesitate to follow this tradition, vindicating Jacob's honour at the expense of Laban's. That is why he translates, "Only [*b'ram*] would it might be according to thy word": Laban, even while he appeared to consent, was already revoking. Once again, *b'ram* is chosen as introducing a limitation not expressed. Onkelos indicates that the word with which Laban opened his statement is to be construed as a case of *Mi'ut*: Laban meant less than he

[43] See A. Berliner, *op. cit.*, 107 f., 202, 245. There is no need here to inquire whether Berliner is right in using this fact as an argument in favour of an early date of Onkelos.

[44] See H. L. Strack-P. Billerbeck, *op. cit.*, vol. 1, 802 f. Onkelos is not mentioned, however.

[45] See A. Berliner, *op. cit.*, 117.

[46] See J. Levy, *Neuhebräisches und Chaldäisches Wörterbuch, s.v. lo.*

said. To conclude from this passage, as Dalman's dictionary does, that *b'ram* might denote "certainly" or "yes" (*gewiss, fürwahr, ja*) is wrong. The Targum's deviation from the Hebrew "behold" is quite deliberate; by putting *b'ram*, Onkelos makes Laban negate, not emphasise, his acceptance of Jacob's proposal.

The upshot seems to be that, in adducing Gen 20:12 for *b'ram* in the sense of "moreover," Torrey has not taken account of the exceptional nature of this case. In this text, at any rate, and in Gen 30:34 also, not only does *b'ram* not signify "moreover" but, in all probability, it is put as a most weighty *'akh*, "and yet," πλήν.

VI. Matthew 5:48

The last case from Torrey to be investigated is Matt 5:48. His assumption of mistranslation is unacceptable. The Aramaic conjectured by him could have neither the meaning that he supposes it originally had nor the meaning that he supposes the translator mistakenly gave it. The passage can be understood without recourse to emendation of any kind.

Matt 5:48 reads: "Be ye therefore perfect, even as your Father which is in heaven is perfect." Torrey substitutes: "Be therefore all-including [in your good will], even as your heavenly Father includes all." He comments thus: "Be therefore *perfect*," etc., would be mere nonsense, even if it were not wholly unprepared for in this context. Nothing here leads up to the idea of perfection—to say nothing of equaling the perfection of God himself! In this paragraph, vss. 43–47, the disciples are taught that they must show kindness *to all men*; just as their heavenly Father makes no exception. The explanation of the false rendering lies, very obviously in the fact that the form of *g'mar* (certainly used here) was active, not passive, in significance. *H'wo gam'rin* (or, *g'mirin*) meant 'be all-including', making no exception in your kindliness. (On *g'mir* in the active sense, see e.g. Babylonian Shabbath 63a: 'When I was eighteen years of age, I had completed, *g'mir'na*, the whole Talmud'; Babylonian Hagigah 3a: *h'wo g'mire hilkatha*, 'they learned all the Halakoth')."[47] This reconstruction, however, does not commend itself. It is impossible because the Aramaic given by Torrey does not signify what he says, and it is unnecessary because the Matthean text as it stands is in line with Rabbinic thinking.

The first objection to be raised against Torrey's view is that his Aramaic will account neither for the original saying postulated by him nor for the mistranslation. In other words, *h'wo gam'rin* or *g'mirin* could never have meant "be all-including," nor could it ever have been taken as "be perfect." Regarding the former point, *g'mar* signifies "to complete" but not "to include." The difference is small but, in this case, of decisive importance. You can "complete" an action, a work and the like; but if you extend your good will to all men, you do not "complete" them, you "include" them. The latter meaning *g'mar* simply has not got. In the two illustrations adduced by Torrey (if, for a moment, his rendering of them be adopted, though something will be said on it presently), "to complete" and "to include" are rather near one another: "to complete" the whole

[47] *The Four Gospels*, 12 and 291; also *Our Translated Gospels*, 92 ff., 96.

Talmud or all the Halakoth is much the same thing (though not quite the same) as "to include" them. The verbs are far from synonymous, however, when they take persons as direct objects. "To complete" a person might be used with reference, say, to God's finishing Adam by giving him a soul. Here *g'mar* would no doubt be suitable. (It could also be employed as signifying "to destroy" a person or, in the Aphel, "to teach" a person.) "To include" a person means something entirely different. Here *g'mar* would not be suitable, which rules out the original saying as conjectured by Torrey. It is seldom wise to affirm the absence of a certain usage from a large body of literature. But the present writer feels safe in maintaining that there is not a single instance in Talmud or Midrash where *g'mar* denotes "to include a person." It may be added that even if the word did mean "to include," one would still want some evidence that *h'wo gam'rin* could have the abstract, general sense ascribed to it by Torrey. Even if the word did mean "to include," that is, to claim that for "be including everybody in your good will" a preacher in Aramaic might put a mere "be including" would still be assuming a kind of diction of which there is not trace anywhere in the Sermon on the Mount.

It is to be observed, incidentally, that in neither of the two texts cited by Torrey does *g'mir* signify even "to complete": it is used in the technical sense of "to learn," "to study." How, in Babylonia, this meaning grew out of the meaning "to complete" cannot be said with certainty, though Bacher has made a probable suggestion.[48] At any rate, it is "to learn," "to study," that *g'mir* signifies both in *b. Shab.* 63a and *b. Hag.* 3a. In the former passage, R. Kahana declares: "When I was 18 years old, I had learnt, studied, the whole Talmud, yet I did not know that a verse [outside the Pentateuch] could not depart from its plain meaning." The latter passage is concerned with the question whether a dumb person is able "to learn, study" the Law. A story is told of a cure of two dumb people by R. Judah the Prince, whose lectures they had regularly attended for a long time; and it was found that "they were learning, studying, the Halakoth, Sifra, Sifre and the whole Talmud." However, this is a minor matter. What is fatal to Torrey's thesis is that *g'mar* does not mean "to include."

The next step, according to Torrey, was the mistranslation of *h'wo gam'rin* or *g'mirin* as "be perfect." But the phrase could mean this no more than "be all-including." Here it seems that Torrey has rashly attributed to *g'mar* the scope of the English "perfect." In English, though we speak of "a perfect scoundrel" just as well as "a perfect saint," yet the injunction "be perfect" is quite unambiguous: it means "be perfect saints." (Even so, one asks oneself whether this possibility of using "be perfect" for "be perfect saints" may not be due precisely to the influence of Biblical texts like Matt 5:48.) But in Rabbinic language, *g'mar* and all other words belonging to the same root are so neutral that the kind of perfection contemplated must always be expressed. A man may be described as *ṣaddiq gamur*, "a perfect saint," or *rasha' gamur*, "a perfect scoundrel." But he can never be described as, or asked to become, *gamur*: it would simply make no sense. There are parallels in English. A man may be called "a complete [absolute] saint" or "a complete [absolute] scoundrel," but hardly "complete [absolute]"

[48] See W. Bacher, *Die Bibel- und Traditionsexgetische Terminologie der Amoräer*, 28 f.

without any further explanation; and the injunction "be complete [absolute]" would be unintelligible. Once again the writer considers it safe to make a sweeping statement; and to say that there is not a single instance in Talmud or Midrash where *g'mar* or any other form of the verb, standing alone, denotes "to be perfect."

So far, the criticism advanced has been of a negative kind. The second objection against the reconstruction proposed by Torrey is of a more positive nature: it is submitted that Matt 5:48 in its present form is neither nonsense nor unprepared for in the context—provided the Rabbinic background is taken into consideration. The idea that man ought to imitate God occurs in many religions. It is certainly very old in Judaism. It is at least adumbrated in passages like "Ye shall be holy: for I the Lord your God am holy" (Lev 19:2) or "Thou shalt be perfect with the Lord thy God" (Deut 18:13). By the time of the Rabbis, it is almost a commonplace. A collection of relevant texts is given by Strack-Billerbeck.[49] Here it will be sufficient to draw attention to some of those in which we find the idea applied in exactly the way it is applied in Matt 5:43 ff.; that is to say, in which to be like God means to be merciful or, even more specifically, to be merciful to all, good and bad, friends and enemies. First, *Exod. Rab.* 26 is worth mentioning. Commenting on Exod 17:5 ("And the Lord said unto Moses, Go on before the people"), R. Meir said: "What does *'abhor* ('go on') mean? God said to Moses, Be like me: as I repay good for evil, so thou shalt repay good for evil. For it has been said (Micah 7:18), Who is a God like unto thee, that pardoneth iniquity, and passeth by (*w' 'obher*, the same verb as in Exodus 17:5) transgression?" Next a discussion in Sifre Deuteronomy of Deut 11:22 ("To walk in all his—the Lord's—ways") may be quoted. "It has been said (Joel 3:5), Whoever shall be called by the name of the Lord[50] shall be delivered. But how is it possible for a man to be called by the name of God? The words mean, As God is called merciful and gracious (Exodus 34:6), so thou shalt be merciful and gracious and make gifts to all without reward; as God is called righteous (Psalm 145:17), so thou shalt be righteous; as God is called loving (*ibid.*), so thou shalt be loving. This is why it has been said, Whosoever shall be called by the name of the Lord shall be delivered." It should be noted that mercy and graciousness are here defined as the readiness to "make gifts to all without reward"; this is distinctly reminiscent of Matthew. Lastly, there is the story of R. Joshua b. Levi and the Jew who became a Christian and made life difficult for the Rabbi by quoting Scripture for his new faith (*b. Ber.* 7a). One night when R. Joshua went to bed, he tied a cock to his bedstead and decided to curse his enemy in the early hours of the morning: that, it seems, would have been a most effective procedure. But he overslept himself, and when he awoke he concluded: "From this one should learn that it is never seemly to curse, even as it is written (Psalm 145:9),[51] And his—the Lord's—tender mercies are over all his works, and

[49] *Op. cit.*, vol. 1, 370, 372 f. and 386; vol. 2, 159.

[50] The Midrash points *yiqqare'* instead of *yiqra'*; hence the meaning "shall be called by" instead of "shall call on" as in the English Bible.

[51] In *b. Sanh.* 105b and *b. A. Zar.* 4b, where the same anecdote is told, the reference to Ps 145:9 is missing. There is no need here to decide whether it was contained in the original form of the story or not. For the purpose of this discussion it is enough to know that the argument of Matt 5:48 was familiar to the Rabbis.

again (Prov 17:26), To punish is not good for the righteous."[52] God's kindness to all his works (the word *ma'ase* used by the Psalmist includes everything created by God) in this anecdote is made the basis for the teaching that one must not hate even a heretic.

But what seems particularly objectionable to Torrey is the use of the adjective "perfect." Yet it is clear that, for unsophisticated minds, there existed no inconsistency whatever between the duty to be like God and the duty to acknowledge his majesty, between perfection as an aim and the inevitable failure of all attempts to reach it.[53] In fact, the Rabbis did not hesitate on occasion to call certain people "perfect" regardless of the doctrine that nobody ever lived without sin. Basing himself on Gen 17:1, "Walk before me and be thou perfect," a verse the Rabbis early connected with circumcision, Judah the Prince observed (*m. Ned.* 3:11): "Great is circumcision for despite all the commandments that Abraham performed he was not called 'perfect' until he was circumcised." It is quite possible that this remark was directed against the very notion expressed by Matt 5:48, the notion of perfection through the fulfillment of moral ideals only, to the exclusion of ritual.

The question might be asked why Matt 5:48 should insist on "perfection" while the parallel verse, Luke 6:36, says, "Be ye therefore merciful, as your Father also is merciful"; a way of putting it not criticised by Torrey. One possible solution might be to take Matt 5:48 not, as the author has done up to this point, as referring only to 5:43 ff., but as covering the whole section from 5:21 onwards.[54] In other words, Matt 5:48 may speak of perfection because it contemplates not only the one virtue of loving one's enemies but also the acceptance of all the other principles set forth in 5:21 ff., such as freedom from impure desire, abstention from oaths: the verse may be a general summing up, while Luke 6:36 clearly has regard to the love of enemies and similar virtues only. However, it is quite unnecessary to connect Matt 5:48 with the entire section 5:21 ff. The examples cited above from Rabbinic literature distinctly indicate a tendency to regard mercy as God's chief quality; and to prescribe the exercise of mercy as the conduct bringing man nearest to God, to perfection. It is interesting to find a warning in the Palestinian Talmud against this reduction of God's qualities, and man's struggle to be like God, to the exercise of mercy.[55] "Those who paraphrase Leviticus 22:28 thus," R. Jose b. Abin says, "My people, children of Israel, as I am merciful in heaven, so you shall be merciful on earth: A cow or ewe, ye shall not kill it and her young both in one day—they do not right, since they make consist the qualities of God[56] in mercy only." The paraphrase censured by the Rabbi is still extant, namely, in the Jerusalemite Targum, only that the

[52] This is a Midrashic interpretation of Prov 17:26; the English Bible translates, "To punish the just is not good."

[53] See E. Klostermann, *Das Matthäusevangelium*, 2nd ed., 50 ff. An exhortation to perfection is to be found also in Jas 1:4, though it is not said that it must be the perfection of God. If the passage is an echo of Matt 5:48, it is a very remote one. Dibelius observes (*op. cit.*, 73) that in putting τέλειοι καὶ ὁλόκληροι, "James worries about the relativity of all human perfection just as little as other authors of wisdom sayings in similar connections; compare Sir 44:17; Wisdom of Solomon 9:6; Matt 5:48."

[54] See E. Klostermann, *loc. cit.*

[55] See H. L. Strack and P. Billerbeck, *op. cit.*, vol. 2, 159, and vol. 3, 399.

[56] One of the two versions in which this dictum is preserved has "the commandments of God."

Targum says "As our Father is merciful" instead of "As I am merciful." (Ought we to treat the paraphrase preserved in the Targum as a proper version of the saying to be found in Matt 5:48 and Luke 6:36? Ought we to accord it some recognition, beside the passages from the gospels, in considering the oral tradition behind these? The present writer has never found this possibility contemplated. In any case, R. Jose b. Abin, in attacking the paraphrase, most probably meant to attack also, if not mainly, the Christian attitude.) Manifestly, the ground was well prepared for Matthew's use of "perfect." This is not claiming that his version is more original than Luke's.[57] The question of priority need not here be raised at all.

In view, then, of the Rabbinic passages adduced, to which others could be added, Matt 5:48 appears to be in order. God loves both the just and unjust: man must do the same, and thus be perfect like God. This is a line of thought with which the Jewish readers of Matthew at any rate were well acquainted. It has already been noticed that, for the evangelists, there can have existed no inconsistency between the call to be like God and true humility. One further point, however, may be mentioned in conclusion. According to Torrey, the argument of Matt 5:43 ff. runs as follows: (1) Ye have heard, Thou shalt love thy neighbour. (2) I say, Love your enemies. (3) That ye may be the children of your Father, who sendeth rain on the just and the unjust. (4) For if ye love them which love you, do not even the publicans the same? (5) Be therefore all-including like God. Admittedly, point 5 constitutes a perfectly logical conclusion (though, as has been shown, a conclusion no more logical from a Rabbinic point of view than the traditional one). But it is a good deal duller, a good deal less dynamic, than the ending as it stands: Be therefore perfect like God. It is duller and less dynamic even than Luke's ending of the corresponding section, 6:36 (not questioned by Torrey): Be therefore merciful like God. This fact alone would make one hesitate to approve of the emendation.

VII. "Improving" the Ethics of the Gospels

The method of conjecturing an Aramaic original with a different sense from the Greek is particularly dangerous where religious issues are involved. The present writer is not competent to examine the respective merits of various schools of theology. But a word of warning from the purely philological point of view may not be out of place. It is a sound principle in dealing with an ancient work (to be sure, it must be applied with caution), if one has to choose between two readings, to prefer that which must have been less agreeable to the public interested in the work. On the basis of this principle, future historians having before them a Greek supported by old textual evidence but theologically inconvenient and an Aramaic attained by conjecture but theologically pleasing will do well to rely on the former and disregard the latter. Obviously, a modernisation of the ethics of the gospels by postulating a suitable Aramaic is a game as easy as unsafe. (It is also, of course, superfluous.) A very slight misinterpretation by the Greek translator will account for the death of the Gadarene swine. (Lest the following be misunderstood, however, the writer should perhaps adopt the method that he found used in an

[57] J. M. Creed, *op. cit.*, 95 f., prefers Luke, arguing that Matthew has a liking for τέλειος.

edition of Molière. There a footnote is attached to the conversation between Argan and the two Diafoirus's, saying: *C'est comique.*) The Aramaic word used to describe what happened in Matt 8:32, Mark 5:13 and Luke 8:33 was *ṭuph*. This verb could indeed be employed as signifying "to be drowned." In *m. Ab.* 2:7 we are told how Hillel, on seeing a skull floating in the water, exclaimed: "Because thou drownedst (*di'aṭepht*), they drowned thee (*'aṭiphukh*), and at last they that drowned thee (*m' ṭayphayikh*) shall be drowned (*y' ṭuphun*)." The Greek translator, therefore, proceeded from *ṭuph* in this application: hence the present text. But the proper meaning of *ṭuph* is "to swim"; and the translator ought to have taken it in this sense and said, not that "they were choked in the sea," but that "they swam in the sea."

2

Messianic Types

This section explores how the writers of the New Testament transfer to Jesus features, as understood by them, of great figures of the Old Testament.

Joseph

The events recorded in the New Testament, and the manner in which they are recorded, naturally reflect the Messianic speculations current among the Jews of the period. Thus certain features and actions of Jesus recall those of Isaac, Moses, David, Elijah, the Suffering Servant and so on, persons whose lives were popularly looked upon as prefigurations of that of the Saviour, or who were expected actually to play a part in the last days. It is indeed clear that all references to such Messianic types have not yet been noticed. A few examples of this kind may here be given, some admittedly doubtful, others as plain as anything can be in this field.

That the disciple who betrayed Jesus bears the same name as that brother of Joseph at whose suggestion he was sold is probably a mere coincidence. Still, it is interesting that, whereas according to the Biblical account, Judah's intention in recommending a sale was to prevent murder, the Rabbis hold that he ought to have adopted Reuben's attitude and taken Joseph home to his father. In other words, for the Rabbis, by bringing about the sale of Joseph, Judah committed a grievous sin.

Chapter 37 of Genesis ends with the sale of Joseph. Chapter 39 begins by saying that he was brought down to Egypt and goes on to recount what befell him there. Between these two chapters, there is 38, the story of Judah and Tamar, introduced by the words: "And it came to pass at that time that Judah went down from his brethren." The Rabbis are exercised by the position of this story and try to establish a connection with the preceding events. They conclude that Judah's "going down from his brethren" means his being lowered in dignity, or even his being deposed and expelled.[1] One is reminded of John's notice—not to be found in the Synoptics—that Judas, once Satan has entered into him, left the company.[2] However, even this is hardly more than coincidence. The detail in John can be fully explained without assuming any outside influence.

The figure of Joseph, then, does not seem to have been drawn upon by the New Testament writers.

[Editor's note: as the next essay demonstrates Daube changed his view about the figure of Joseph.]

[1] *Gen. Rab.* on 38:1; *Exod. Rab.* on 32:7.

[2] John 13:30.

Appeasing or Resisting the Oppressor*

I.

Probably you expect some advice on how to handle University Chancellors or Law School Deans. But I shall talk on a more sombre subject which has overshadowed a large part of my life: the choice between appeasement and resistance if you belong to a group under the rule of another one fiercely hostile and with absolute power. My main discussion will focus on events of one and a half to two millennia ago; some guidelines from Jewish experience at various stages of Roman supremacy are still worth pondering.

To ease you into the atmosphere of this field, let me begin with a personal reminiscence. I live with a woman[1] with whom I have never won an argument. Once only I came close and even then was routed. Here is what happened. Soon after World War II, in 1948 or '49—years before I knew her—I was lunching in a Strasbourg restaurant with friends. It was a lively place. Yet all the conversation came to a sudden halt as the door opened and three elderly men walked in, one of them obviously central. This reverential hush lasted till well after they had sat down at a table. Then, gradually, people started talking again. I asked my companions for the meaning, and the following story emerged. During the occupation of the city, in retaliation for an act of sabotage, the Commandant of the occupying troops sent out a detachment to conduct a *razzia;* that is to say, the soldiers sealed off four or five blocks downtown, picked up there any males who looked like between fifteen and fifty and took them to the courtyard of headquarters—where they were to be shot. As it chanced, the two sons of the dignitary—ex-Mayor or the like—who had just entered were walking together in the area and got arrested. Somebody immediately informed him. He gained access to the Commandant, the window of whose office in fact gave out to the yard with the twelve or so victims already lined up for the firing. He set forth his plight. The Commandant, nonchalantly waving towards the window, said: "All right, you can have one of them." But he could not bring himself to act on this direction and both were executed. It was that drama, my hosts explained, which accounted for the reaction of the lunchers.

* To Ernst Bammel—since 1955—and his wife Caroline. At the beginning of last academic year, my colleagues Michael E. Smith and Philippe Nonet suggested that I deliver a special lecture at Boalt Hall and, joined by Sanford Kadish, made the arrangements. It came off on 19 February 1986. I wish to express my gratitude to them for a, to me, wonderful occasion.

[1] Between delivery and publication of this address we got married.

When, in the early seventies, I reported this to Helen, she—then at the height of her psychoanalytic venture—did not acclaim the protagonist. He deserved pity, she held, but not homage. He was made a cruel offer, to be sure. But he declined it, not from love of his sons or for the sake of their welfare, but selfishly, because he was afraid of the guilt he would feel later towards the one abandoned to die. The truly heroic thing would have been to act as instructed and then cope, or maybe fail to cope, with the pangs of self-reproach. Certainly his response was very understandable and, yes, meriting compassion, but not admiration. Well, she put this to me of an evening, when I am generally not so good at sustained reasoning with her. As usual, I recovered in the morning, on my way from North Beach to Boalt Hall, and I sensed something off in her thesis. Those people in the café were not all taken in by what would be, basically, an evasion of responsibility. Soon it became clear to me that what they honoured was a refusal of collaboration. By accepting, the petitioner would have involved himself in the entire operation of which, indeed, this sideshow would be a particularly ugly part, bringing out to the full the arbitrary playing with human life.

Before stepping down from my bus, I had worked out to my satisfaction solid proof that it must be his rejection of the tyrant's lure, at enormous cost, which moved the Strasbourgers. Contrast the following case, alike in all respects but this one. A father strolls along the shore with his two children, aged six and four. An unexpected wave sweeps both into the sea. He may just be able to rescue one. If he remains passive because he cannot make up his mind between them, the situation does approximate Helen's assessment; and we shall pity him but not pay him homage. What is the difference? It is that here the calamity is due to a force of nature when, normally, we do our best and deal with the consequences as they unfold. The Strasbourg father was faced by a devilish man-made scheme; and, rather than participate, he sacrificed his progeny. Had the stroller who lost his babes to the ocean appeared at the restaurant, there might well have been some manifestation of sympathy but not conceivably that profound awe. Back with Helen at the end of the day, I expounded it all. She listened—which she does not always do—but what did she say? "Yes, that is correct. But a mother would have taken one home with her."

She is right, of course. Those soundly, nobly motivated objections to ever doing business with Satan are, *au fond*, of a political nature, the ultimate aim being to ensure decent government. In a conflict between such principles and concrete, close, personal bonds, the latter, for women—those not turned into men at any rate—take precedence. Even that abominable thing, collaboration, is outer, means nothing compared with the inner, the immediate, natural tie. Though, for once, having to strike the flag of the mind, she hoisted in its place the more stirring one of the heart. The public at the restaurant was predominantly male. I shall briefly come back to the feminine approach at the close, when adverting to a Marxist one which now and then looks deceptively similar.

A rider about this episode, however, should be added. I have long come to realize that its star ought not to be idolized. How did he get to be warned of what was going on without a moment's delay? A graver question: how did he get to be admitted to the enemy chief, and in the midst of a precarious exploit? Plainly, he had dubious connections. Again, what was the purpose of his visit? To save his sons. Ergo: he would happily have gone off with them, leaving the other innocents to perish; at best, he might feel sorry for them. His anti-collaborationist impulse was triggered by having a ghastly dilemma forced upon him. Still, let us not be too hard: we most of us are not saints ourselves. For that matter, who knows? Besides all the malevolence in the Commandant's proposal there may have been a flicker of mercy.

II.

Moving back now in history, the problem before the Rabbis I shall concentrate on was: what ought a collective—a town, a congregation—to do if the reigning power, enraged maybe by signs of insubordination, or for the fun of it, orders it, say, to hand over that same day three members for public hanging; in the event of defiance, the entire community or half of it or sixty persons will be wiped out. I have published a little tract on this topic.[2] At the time, I bracketed out the relevant New Testament material, reserving it for subsequent consideration.[3] Today is my opportunity.

The initial Pharisaic stand—I shall deal with the Sadducees further on—was unbendingly negative: no one to be surrendered ever, even though extinction will ensue. Clearly, no such scruples are entertained by the Judeans in Judges who, fearing what their mighty Philistine neighbours might do to settle accounts with the indomitable Samson, propose to deliver him up in fetters. It is only his giant strength lent him by the Lord that saves him.[4] A proper ruling was first formulated with regard to heathen thugs asking a company of travellers to let them have one for killing (for having sport with him, would be a likely sixteenth-century euphemism); otherwise they would kill the entire lot. An astonishing variant of this collision in the Old Testament will be presented in due course.[5]) A demand by the Roman masters, the Pharisees contend, is no better. The dogma may indeed have hastened the outbreak of the war against them in A.D. 66. Florus, the procurator, ordered the Jewish leaders of Jerusalem to give up a number of men who had abused him in public; he was told that it was impossible to identify them; whereupon he had his soldiers sack the "upper market," three thousand

[2] *Collaboration with Tyranny in Rabbinic Law* (1965) [*Talmudic Law*, 63–135]. The chief texts are *m. Ter.* 8:12; *t. Ter.* 7:20; *y. Ter.* 46b; *Gen. Rab.* 94 on 46:26 f. E. J. Schochet supplements them by medieval ones in his searching treatise *A Responsum of Surrender* (1973), an edition and analysis of a sixteenth-century Rabbinic advice on a tragic case in Poland. A summary was already furnished in his *Bach = Rabbi Joel Sirkes* (1971), 132.

[3] *Collaboration with Tyranny in Rabbinic Law*, 18 [*Talmudic Law*, 76]. John Noonan complained at once. E. Bammel has inspected the New Testament side, first in a review of *Theologische Literaturzeitung*, 93 (1968): 833 ff., then in a major paper, "*Ex illa itaque die consilium fecerunt...*," in *The Trial of Jesus, Cambridge Studies in Honour of C. F. D. Moule*, ed. E. Bammel (1970), 11 ff. While alive to the strength of his argumentation, I differ in my general approach. A rough overview may be found in my *Civil Disobedience in Antiquity* (1972), 97 ff. Huge gaps remain. If, twenty years hence, Michael, Philippe and Sandy desire an encore, I shall try to assess Josephus's contribution to this terrain. For a minuscule specimen see below, under V, footnote 98.

[4] Judg 15:9 ff.

[5] See below, under V, item 5.

six hundred persons were slaughtered and chances for a settlement rapidly vanished.[6]

Scriptural support was found in Deuteronomy, which makes it a capital crime to sell a fellow-Jew, *scil.* to abroad. More precisely, it condemns sale of "any of your brothers, the children of Israel," the redundant "your brothers" no doubt alluding to the saga of Joseph, sold to the Ishmaelites by his brothers literally.[7] For the Rabbis, in this context, to deliver up a person in return for safety is a selling just as much as if it were done for money. The ruling prevailed both before A.D. 70, while a measure of self-government remained under Roman suzerainty, and for several decennia after.

It became untenable, however, in the Hadrianic persecution following the defeat of Bar-Kochba in 135, when circumcision, Sabbath services, religious instruction were interdicted on pain of death. That these activities continued underground goes without saying, and the Romans went all out to stop them. To go on rigidly disregarding an ultimatum of theirs of the kind in question would in no time have put an end—really an end, no metaphor—to Palestinian Jewry, decimated already. Accordingly, at a secret synod of the Sages, the majority established a distinction. If the authorities request an unnamed victim or number of victims—let us have one or five of you to be executed, or else you will all go—the old maxim applies: the answer is No. However, if they specify—give us Avrom or Avrom, Baruch and Gedaliah—they are to be obeyed. The former demand is utterly barbarous, treating humans like cattle, fungibles. A secondary objection is that the selection is imposed on the community and, whatever procedure it might resort to, trust would be undermined—not to speak of the inevitable burden of guilt. (Volunteers cannot solve the problem, but I shall not go into detail.) Obliteration is better than descent to this level. The latter demand evinces a glimmer of justice, being for someone they have a quarrel with: even if they want a pious scholar because he has taught Torah, at least he is not simply an object replaceable by any other of the same description. Neither will there be the evil selection by the group. Here, then, though the price is horrendous, it may be paid to ensure survival of the whole. (I suppose, under this formula, the head of a congregation of three hundred in 1943, notified to have ready by the next morning twenty of them for transport to extermination, otherwise everybody will be despatched, had to refuse; ordered to have ready twenty designated persons who had contributed to pacifist journals, he had to yield. What about the dread predicament in Bosic's *The Judge*?) The Biblical text invoked in favour of this concession was the narrative of Sheba, a rebel against King David. David's general prepared to storm the city in which he was holding out but offered peace if he were delivered up to him. The residents did toss his head over the wall and the general withdrew: surrender of a named person for the sake of the universality.[8] Evidently, the use of this precedent implied a degree of recognition of Roman rule.

A minority declined to budge. Deuteronomy's was the only right way. Jewry would not go under: God could work a miracle at any time and his people should move him to

[6] Josephus, *Bell.* 2.14.8.301 ff.

[7] Deut 24:7. See C. Carmichael, *The Laws of Deuteronomy* (1974), 212 ff., *Law and Narrative in the Bible* (1985), 261 f., 305.

[8] 2 Samuel 20.

do so by a sincere return. As for Sheba, he defected from the legitimate, heaven-appointed sovereign, nothing to do with the foreign usurpers. It is worth observing that the two factions of the synod were agreed that an individual, threatened with death unless he kills someone, unnamed or named, must choose death—actually, irrespective of whether the other is Jewish or not.[9] The limitation to "any of the children of Israel" does not here apply.

By the third century, the danger had abated and the trend was towards greater firmness. This comes out clearly in a case giving rise to a legend. A Jew sought by the Romans[10] for what must have been something like terrorism was given shelter by a leading Rabbi at Lydda. It should be noticed right away—in view of what will follow—that, palpably, the Rabbi was risking his life. The Romans found out that the criminal was hiding in that city and proclaimed that, unless he was handed over, it would be sacked. At this the Rabbi persuaded his guest to willingly accept his fate. So much for the case: here legend takes over. Up to this incident, the prophet Elijah had paid regular visits to the Rabbi, so they might exchange news about goings-on in paradise and on earth. Now the visits stopped. The Rabbi, disconsolate, prayed and fasted and finally Elijah returned. Asked why he had stayed away, he replied that he did not wish to consort with betrayers—the term is familiar from the deed of Judas, *masar, paradidomi.* The Rabbi defended himself by citing the resolution of the synod. But Elijah declared that those truly devout would not follow that teaching. Strong criticism, and it is not surprising—at this junction we return to reality—that before long another influential scholar advocated a mighty limitation to the synod's concession: even a specific person claimed by the alien power may be transferred only if he is actually deserving of death. (By this criterion, the pacifist journalists were not to be turned over.) The Biblical Sheba, after all, was guilty of armed high treason. Unless the condition is satisfied, the community must allow itself to be slaughtered. The requirement foreshadows modern extradition clauses, but I shall not expand.[11]

Virtually no room is left in the Rabbinic deliberations for the possibility that, now and then, it might be from genuine moderation or even sympathy that a collective is called on to give up a member in order to avoid worse. Whereas, for instance, in Second Samuel's original recital of the Sheba affair, this aspect predominates. Joab is here portrayed as fully concurring with the wise woman who interceded for the city. Though it had abetted the revolt it remained a sacred constituent of the nation, and he would be dismayed if, because he could not otherwise get hold of the leader, he had to go to extremes. The reason for the difference is that the warring factions of Second Samuel were still linked by strong, old bonds.[12] Not so those here under review. The Rabbis had lit-

[9] *y. Sanh.* 21b; *b. Sanh.* 74a.

[10] Or, less probably, by Zenobia, Queen of Palmyra.

[11] Below, under V, item 4, we shall find the Danaides begging for sanctuary at Argos, and the king taking pains to discover whether they are in the right. See my brother Benjamin's *Zu den Rechtsproblemen in Aischylos's Agamemnon* (1938), 78 ff.

[12] According to C. Carmichael, "On Deuteronomic Legislation—Sparing the Mother Bird," *LawHR*, 2 (1984): 288 ff., Deut 22:5 f. alludes to this campaign. If he is right, as I think he is, the lawgiver evidently sees there a worthy compromise: the mother, the city as a whole, is to be let off, and with this proviso, it is

tle cause for thinking that a Roman commander, involved in a serious conflict with the Jews, would ever feel protectively about a community of theirs.

Of course, the high standards of the Sages were not always practised. In the Middle Ages, in particular, in many places sad breakdowns in spirit occurred. A frightened congregation would regard the slightest misbehaviour of a member in the outer world as menacing its existence—not without reason. Motivation mattered little: in fact, one acting from religious zeal was likely to do it again, hence a special threat, a troublemaker. He might be offered up almost before the authorities turned nasty. (There is a foretaste as early as during the serfdom in Egypt.[13]) Still, we have plenty of evidence of a collective, however pressured, faithfully approaching a respected Rabbi for guidance; e.g. when, in 1620, a Kalish Jew was charged with stealing the host,[14] or even from the period of World War II.

III.

Who stands where? The patricians incline to accommodation, their less attached colleagues to going through with it. The majority opinion of the assembly during the Hadrianic terror—viz. that to escape annihilation, a community should sacrifice a member specifically targeted by the government—was propounded by Judah ben Ilai, son of a famous father, an admirer of Roman civilisation, in the end awarded an honour by the Romans. The minority's spokesman, Simeon ben Johai, was a mystic, despised Rome and for many years lived with a price on his head. Nor should we overlook a personal hurt: it was an insider's denunciation which led to his being outlawed. And another: quite possibly, his own father's sympathies and even activities were in flagrant contrast with his.[15] In the next century, Joshua ben Levi, reproved by Elijah, was president of the academy of Lydda, wealthy, on good terms with the proconsul. Similarly, the slightly younger Johanan, who also upheld that majority ruling, was president of the academy of Tiberias and traced his descent back to the pre-exilic epoch. By contrast, we know nothing about the ancestry of Resh Laqish who, by barring any extradition incompatible with justice, virtually preached return to defiance regardless of the consequences. High as he rose, he was never allowed to forget about his adolescence in abject poverty, when he sold himself as gladiator and acquired plebeian habits for good. (Elijah sided with the idealists: the saints in heaven always do that.) It would be simplistic to rush to judgment as to the relative merits, practical or moral, of the two camps; I hope my gut response is not too noticeable. Fortunately, for the purpose in hand, it is enough to locate them.

This brings me to the Sadducees, the aristocrats par excellence—and, indeed, they did anticipate the compromisers among the Pharisees by at least one hundred years. At some stage, Jesus's activity alarmed the more cautious ones of his compatriots: it

quite in order to dispose of undeserving nestlings such as the renegade. None of this is incompatible with my conjectures in *Ancient Jewish Law* (1981), 99 f. [208], but such refinements can wait.

[13] Exod 5:21.

[14] See Schochet, *Responsum of Surrender.*

[15] *b. Shab.* 33b f.; *b. Pes.* 112a. His son stood by him.

seemed about to drive the Romans into "intervening and taking away the place and the nation," into clamping down, that is, by paganizing the Temple and suppressing what self-government endured.[16] The attribution of this misgiving to "the chief priests and the Pharisees" sounds very plausible: the former would enlist as many of the latter as they could. (This kind of conscription is common throughout history. An efficient elite knows when it needs the backing of numbers. I have watched striking instances in my life, among states, among parties within a state, among strata within a denomination, a city, a university and so forth.[17]) Admittedly, there was no formal ultimatum threatening physical extirpation. But if what was feared came to pass, thousands of Jews would die and the loss of the Temple would be almost worse. Remember Philo's defence, less than ten years later, of the Judaeans preparing for collective suicide should Caligula put up a statue of himself in the sanctuary.[18] Viewed thus, therefore, it was the life of a specific zealot versus the future of the entire body, and the high priest Caiaphas argued that "one man should die for the people and the whole nation perish not."[19] He was a Sadducee, scion of an eminent dynasty, appointed not by the Jews but by Valerius Gratus, predecessor of Pontius Pilate. He took the line then to which the majority of Pharisaic leaders found themselves reduced under Hadrian. One of the two sources relating the end of Ullah actually has Joshua ben Levi remind him that "it is better to kill that man [= you] so they may not punish the congregation on his [= your] account."[20] Whether this detail is authentic or not,[21] it does underscore the identity of the synod's position with that of Caiaphas.

Fundamentally, the entanglement was nothing new. Long before, in the second third of the second century B.C., Alcimus, a Hellenizer, elevated to the high-priesthood by the Syrian king, had abetted the latter's fight against the Hasmonaean rebels. The king's general ordered the Temple personnel, whom he knew to loathe Alcimus and be hand in glove with the rebels despite their outward subservience, to hand over Judas Maccabaeus. They swore they were ignorant of his whereabouts; whereupon he, infuriated, told them that unless they handed him over, their Temple would be replaced by one to Dionysos after victory. Well, he was defeated.[22]

That Caiaphas was opposing the original, inflexible Pharisaic No is reflected in his angry language: "You know nothing." Furthermore, he called the abandonment of the

[16] John 11:48.

[17] The corresponding phenomenon in reverse is the support a struggling subjugated group receives from wayward members of the governing one—saints, traitors, mavericks. The patrician Appius Claudius enabled a son of one of his freedmen to publish the secret archives of the pontiffs; Livy, *From the Founding of the City* 9.46.7 ff.

[18] *Embassy to Gaius* 32.229 ff. See my *Civil Disobedience in Antiquity*, 92 ff., and "Three Footnotes on *Civil Disobedience in Antiquity*," *Humanities in Society*, 2 (1979): 79 f.

[19] John 11:50, 18:14.

[20] *Gen. Rab.* 94 on 46:26 f.

[21] In all likelihood, alas, it is something in between: the maxim as such comes down from the beginning of the Christian era via inner-Jewish transmission—not the New Testament, that is—but is put into Joshua ben Levi's mouth after the event. Had he quoted it, it is difficult to see why it would have been dropped by the Jerusalemite Talmud.

[22] 1 Mac 7:6 ff.; 2 Mac 14:3 ff.; Josephus, *Ant.* 12.10.1.389 ff.

person who imperiled all "expedient," "beneficial," *symphero.* The term—of enormous importance in Paul—characterizes conduct deviating from hallowed principle, yet the decidedly superior one because of special circumstances. As things stood, he protested, it was misguided to make a fetish even of a warning with roots so deep in the past as Deuteronomy's against sale of an Israelite. This indeed explains the notable feature, that with not one syllable does he criticize the substance of Jesus's words or deeds: he argues entirely from *raison d'état,* from the overriding, public-necessity-geared reservation to the hard line. Quite likely, the Sadducees already in that period referred to Sheba in corroboration.[23] When Caiaphas exclaimed, "You do not consider, *logizomai,* that it is expedient" etc., he may well have used the verb in the sense "to draw the proper conclusions from the ancient reports." At any rate, this account of his outlook belongs to the invaluable, historical items preserved by John alone.

(Re a twist in the end of Sheba. The appeasers invoked his treatment in support of their readiness to hand over a wanted person to the enemy if the alternative was extirpation of the group. Yet he was not strictly handed over, or better, was handed over only in an over-literal sense: Joab's request was satisfied by the citizens themselves cutting off his quarry's head and throwing it out to him—which had the advantage that none of the besiegers entered the place. The use made of the case is not, however, hard to understand. In most such confrontations, the tyrant would mind as little as Joab whether the individual he was after was surrendered or despatched on the spot; and quite reasonably, the Sages judged the latter a selling, a handing over, no less than the former. The narrow interrelation of the two modes of knuckling under is amply evidenced—not least in New Testament times. What chiefly worried Herod Antipas about the Baptist's near-seditious activity may well have been the Roman reaction to be expected; so he ordered his execution.[24] At some stage, to go by Luke,[25] he had the same intention with regard to Jesus, but eventually found it politic to leave the final deed to the occupying power, handing him over *stricto sensu.* As for John,[26] in the first Caiaphas session, chief priests and Pharisees determined to kill Jesus—presumably somehow or other, themselves or through a convenient agency. As things developed, they saw to his arrest but got the Romans to crucify him: again an actual handing over. The Sages were realistic in having the precedent from Samuel to cover all these situations.)

The evangelist adds a Christological interpretation: owing to divine dispensation, the high priest's utterance constituted a prophecy that Jesus would indeed die for the best, "die for the nation, and not for the nation only but in order that he might gather together into one the children of God that were scattered."[27] Here the archetypal victim of the transaction outlawed by Deuteronomy is directly introduced: Jesus becomes a

[23] I had not gotten this far in my analysis when surmising—*Collaboration with Tyranny,* 60 [*Talmudic Law,* 104]—that it was probably Judah ben Ilai who first held him up as illustrating a reservation to the taboo on sale.

[24] Josephus, *Ant.* 18.5.2.117 ff. No doubt personal rancour, of the sort brought out in the Synoptics (Matt 14:3 ff.; Mark 6:17 ff.; Luke 3:19 f.), was also involved.

[25] Luke 13:31, 23:11 ff.

[26] John 11:53, 10:12 ff.

[27] John 11:51 f.

second, ultimate Joseph. The latter, reunited with his brothers, comforts them: "God sent me ahead of you to preserve life," *scil.* among the heathens, in a famine, "and to save your lives," *scil.* the chosen band.[28] Again, "God brought it to pass to save much people alive," referring to the Egyptians, and "Now I will nourish you and your little ones," referring to his kin.[29] The near-technical term, it should be observed, recurs in Jesus's farewell: "It is expedient, beneficial, for you that I go away."[30]

IV.

Obviously, from the moment of his arrest, Jesus must have reminded people of Joseph[31]—not only the learned few acquainted with the latter's place in the discussion of relations with the outside world but also the unlearned many. As Joseph was disposed of by his real brothers, so Jesus was by one as good as a brother. What is more, his mercenary seller bore the same name as that brother of Joseph who instigated the deed, recommending it as more lucrative than an outright killing would be.[32] Some ancient exegetes do draw the inference that Judah thereby forfeited his privileged rank;[33] presumably this viewpoint was once more widespread than would appear from the sources, on the whole preferring to exonerate him. (To be fair, a later test proved him resolved to bear heavy vicarious affliction: he begged to be enslaved instead of Benjamin when Joseph—not as yet having disclosed who he was—proposed to keep the latter for the theft of the cup found in his sack while permitting the others to return to Canaan.[34]) One might indeed wonder whether the name of the New Testament traitor is not an imaginative transfer from the Old. I think there is good reason—not here to be set out[35]—for refraining from this conclusion. Anyhow, if we did have to do with a nickname (by now it definitely has become one), that would only strengthen my case for an immediate, general recognition of the parallel.

Let me add one more coincidence. Simeon ben Johai's violent propaganda came to the knowledge of the authorities through a favourite disciple, son of proselytes—whose name was Judah. And, for good measure, a dysincidence: you will have noted that it was the Maccabean Judas whom the foreign invader sought to get betrayed—yes, *paradidomi.*

[28] Gen 45:5 ff.

[29] Gen 50:20 f.

[30] John 16:7.

[31] Gen 37:18 ff.; Matt 10:4, 26:14 ff., 21 ff., 45 ff., 27:3 ff.; Mark 14:10 f., 18 ff., 41 ff.; Luke 22:3 ff., 21 ff., 47 ff.; John 13:2 ff., 21 ff., 18:2 ff. In my *New Testament and Rabbinic Judaism* (1956, repr. 1973), 3 f. [91], the role of Joseph is grossly underrated. I so strove to be cautious that the result was as wrong in one direction as overkill would have made it in the other.

[32] Gen 37:26 f.

[33] *Gen. Rab.* 85 on 38:1; *Exod. Rab.* 42 on 32:7.

[34] Gen 44:17 ff. This is a rough statement: no need here to enter into the exact function of the offer in the mind of the cycle's author.

[35] W. R. Farmer's comments on naming in that era are pertinent. In *Maccabees, Zealots and Josephus* (1956), viii, he writes: "Then I noticed how frequently the leaders of seditious activity against Rome bore the same names as the early Maccabees—Mattathias, Judas, John, Eleazar, Jonathan, Simon."

Once the catastrophe was mastered, another analogy would be readily seen: in both cases a despicable wrong opened the road to triumph—to exodus, Sinai and the land in the one, redemption in the other. It is in fact this feature of Joseph's biography, its pointing far beyond itself, which radically distinguishes it from otherwise comparable Near Eastern commemorations of marvellous losings and findings. It is taken up in the Psalter: "He [God] sent ahead of them a man, as a slave was sold Joseph.... And there came Israel to Egypt.... And he sent Moses... and he brought them out... and he gave them the lands of the nations."[36] An *Ur*-Christian brought up in this milieu could hardly miss the link to the present renewal.

John, however, goes much further with his elaborate filling in of Messianic features. (Nothing like it in the other evangelists, except for an isolated pericope towards the beginning of Luke.[37]) When he dwells on the overarching plan which the evildoers help to accomplish and which, in fact, makes their most abject wickedness result in the greatest blessing—to cite just Jesus's reply to the governor: "You could have no power against me except it were given you from above"[38]—the specific texts about Joseph are among his stimuli. "It was not you that sent me hither but God." "You thought evil against me, but God meant it unto good."[39] It has been contended that Paul, in Romans and Galatians, and John, in his Gospel and the First Epistle, independently accord centrality to "the Saviour sent in order that he perform his function": they must be drawing, therefore, on a primitive credal formula.[40] A drawing on the Joseph paradigm is an alternative and, at least as far as John is concerned, preferable explanation, the tone is so alike. Joseph: "God sent me ahead of you for [the furtherance of] life."[41] Fourth Gospel: "God sent his son in order that the world should be saved," immediately following upon "God gave his son in order that every believer should have eternal life"[42]—near enough though with "to give" in the place of "to send." First Epistle: "God sent his son in order that we should live," "God sent his son as propitiation," "God sent his son as saviour."[43] I shall not speculate about a credal formula itself inspired by the miracle in Egypt: too remote a chance.

(It is true that Joseph's statement contains no "in order that," but the emergence of this construction in the New Testament is easily accounted for by its generally increasing popularity.[44] As a matter of fact, two of the pertinent verses in the First Epistle themselves do without it[45] even though, overall, John is affected by the general trend to an

[36] Ps 105:17 ff.

[37] Luke 2:41 ff.; see Appendix below. The way I hear John is greatly indebted to C. K. Barrett's seminal study "The Old Testament in the Fourth Gospel," *JTS*, 48 (1947): 155 ff.

[38] John 19:11. Samson's story, adverted to above, II, footnote 4, is also in point.

[39] Gen 45:8, 50:20.

[40] John 3:17; Rom 8:3; Gal 4:4; 1 John 4:9 f., 14. See M. Hengel, *Der Sohn Gottes* (1975), 24.

[41] Gen 45:5.

[42] John 3:16 f.

[43] 1 John 4:9 f., 14.

[44] See F. Blass and A. Debrunner, *Grammatik des neutestamentlichen Griechisch*, 14th ed. by F. Rehkopf (1976), 314 ff.

[45] 1 John 4:10, "God sent his son as propitiation," 4:14, "as saviour."

extraordinary degree.[46] One difficulty with the other thesis is[47] that Paul, though earlier than John, defines the mission in far more doctrinal fashion, as purposing a higher fulfilment of the law or a ransoming of those under the law. John speaks of to save, to live, propitiation, saviour. With the exception of propitiation—mentioned to remind us how the life celebrated in the previous sentence was made possible—this is all quite basic, and close to the Old Testament. A second objection: "to send" appears as *pempo* in Romans, *exapostello* in Galatians. They are near-synonymous but, if a credal profession were underlying, one would expect no switch. The three passages from John claimed to base on the creed all employ *apostello*—employed as in Genesis; and in the psalm just cited, too, it is *apostello* or *exapostello.* Lastly, in Romans, "in order that" is not really attached to "to send" but to "to condemn": "God, having sent his son, condemned sin in the flesh in order that the higher law be fulfilled after the spirit.")

That so sensitive a typologist should be captivated by those passages in the old narrative is to be expected. Here, within a minimal space—about three verses—are clustered these tremendous slogans of salvation history: "God sends" a saviour from his home to a distant populace, for "to keep alive a multitude of people" among the latter and "maintain a remnant" among his own, destined for "a great deliverance." ("Multitude," "much," *rabh* in Hebrew, *polys* in Greek, often approaches an idealistic "all";[48] it may do so here, and if not, many a devout student will have assumed this sense. Amos hopes God will be gracious to "the remnant of Joseph."[49] "Remnant" and "deliverance"—or other formations from these two roots—are coupled in a fair number of significant texts: "From Jerusalem shall go out a remnant and a deliverance from mount Zion."[50]) The whole of it set in the framework of fatherhood to the alien monarch and dominion over his realm[51]—and, above all, forgiveness.[52] What one might want to explore is how this vision, as sophisticated as generous, comes to occupy its place in Genesis, but this is outside my topic. As for sophistication, to get a full picture, one would have to pay attention to quite a few easily neglected details, such as the notion of "to be angry" over your own misdeed.[53] Nor shall I probe John's deviations from the model. One, at first sight surprising, is his far lesser emphasis on forgiveness. Joseph grants it before his brothers have time to request it, in the same breath as he reveals his identity; and when after his father's death they fear reprisals, acknowledge their culpability and ask his pardon, he weeps, impresses on them that he is a mere human, not God, and promises to care for them—all of them, not excluding Judah. The Johannine Judas is a devil, is lost.[54]

[46] E.g. John 1:27, 4:34. See W. Bauer, *Das Johannesevangelium,* 2d ed. (1925), 32, 69.

[47] As pointed out by Hengel himself; and I agree with him that it is by no means fatal.

[48] See J. Jeremias, art. "*polloi,*" in *Theologisches Wörterbuch zum Neuen Testament,* ed. G. Friedrich (1957), 6:536 ff.

[49] Amos 5:15.

[50] 2 Kgs 19:31; Isa 37:32.

[51] Gen 41:40 ff., 45:8.

[52] Gen 45:5 ff., 50:15 ff.

[53] Gen 45:5. Where does it occur the first time elsewhere?

[54] John 6:70, 17:12.

There are further contacts with the Joseph tradition, though not all equally certain. John tells us that Judas, once Satan has entered into him, "went out" into the night, i.e. ceased to belong.[55] Some Rabbis go as far in their denunciation of Judah's crime as to see in the opening of the next chapter, "And Judah went down from his brothers,"[56] an indication of his expulsion.[57] My remark as to the self-censorship of our sources naturally applies with special force to such drastic interpretations: they would have wider currency two thousand years ago. Again, the city where Jesus meets the Samaritan woman is "near the ground that Jacob gave to Joseph."[58] Conceivably an alert, near the outset, to Jesus taking up Joseph's repudiation of narrowly fixed boundaries.[59] It can be shown, I think, that the young Jesus's rejoinder in Luke that rather than cleave to his parents he must heed the concerns of his heavenly father connects up with Joseph's forgetting—being made to forget by God—his earthly father's house to fulfil his mission abroad.[60] Some repetitive phrasing in the lesson appended to the meeting may be significant: "My meat is to do the will of him that sent me to finish his work," "The works that my father has given me to finish bear witness that the father has sent me"—to which we should add a line from near the end: "I have finished the work that you gave me to do."[61]

Fresh light surely falls on Jesus's warning in John as he takes action against desecration of the Temple: "Make not my father's house a house of trade."[62] Note both "my father's house," used by Joseph, and "house of trade," recalling the foreigners to whom he was sold and who are described as "traders."[63] The lower elements, we are given to understand, are back—or still—at their plots, about to do to the new Joseph what was done to the old. In this pericope, he acts prophetically, programmatically, at the start of his mission.[64] His farewell discourse resumes the typology. "In my father's house are many mansions"[65] brings out the ampleness marking the house of Joseph's supreme father. (Side by side with numerous further references. One of them is to a yet earlier foretaste in the patriarchal cycle, the young Rebekah's welcome of a stranger who has just entered the town with his camels; she does not yet know that he is Abraham's servant. He asks "Is there room in your father's house for us to lodge in?," to which she replies "We have both straw and provender enough and room to lodge in."[66]) This sequel

[55] John 13:30.

[56] Gen 38:1.

[57] *Gen. Rab.* 85 on 38:1; *Exod. Rab.* 42 on 32:7, cited above, footnote 33. This possible ingredient in John's depiction I did ponder in *New Testament and Rabbinic Judaism* [91]; cf. footnote 31.

[58] John 4:5.

[59] This is not to rule out the impact of a general association of Samaritans and Josephites.

[60] Gen 41:51; Luke 2:49; see above, footnote 37.

[61] John 4:34, 5:36, 17:4.

[62] John 2:16.

[63] Gen 37:28.

[64] See my "Some Reflections on the Historicity of the New Testament," *Catholic Commission on Intellectual and Cultural Affairs Annual* (1986), 3 f. [36].

[65] John 14:2.

[66] Gen 24:23 ff., cited at John 14:2 by D. Eb. Nestle, *Novum Testamentum Graece*, 22d ed. by D. Eb. Nestle and D. K. Aland (1956), 276.

speaks of Jesus leaving in order to prepare a place for those around him so that, after reunion, he may fulfil all their desires: the Joseph pattern. Actually, they ought to rejoice at this departure destined to lead to the highest blessings for him and them: just as God turned evil into good in the prefiguration. These gifts are bestowed by the Father, in answer to Jesus's wishes: so behind Joseph stood Pharaoh, occupying the throne.[67]

Even such advanced theological propositions as that their future life in glory is assured by his own, or that they should believe and see the Father in him, if for no other reason in view of his works, belong here. We must bear in mind that, in a sense, Joseph too died and rose. Quite apart from the general affinity between enslavement–liberation and death–rebirth, to Jacob at least it would totally feel that way. He was presented with proof that he whom "he loved more than all his children"[68] had been torn to pieces by a wild beast; and he gave himself up to utter despair. "He refused to be comforted ... I will go down into the grave unto my son mourning."[69] Josephus indeed depicts him as mourning "like an only son's father."[70] When, years later, his other sons told him that "Joseph lives and is ruler through the land of Egypt,"[71] he would not listen and—if we interpret in "fundamentalist" fashion—well-nigh died himself really from such lack of faith: "His heart grew cold for he believed them not." They kept filling him in with details, however, and showed him the carriages Joseph had sent him for his journey—he saw Joseph's works, we might say—so he revived: "His spirit lived." The briefest mention may be made of a verbal point from pursuance of which in earnest we might never return: while Jacob would not be comforted till, after a long time, his spirit lived on taking in the glad tidings, John in this chapter has Jesus promise a Comforter, the spirit of truth, the holy spirit, and that will help in difficult periods.[72]

Luckily, it is demonstrable that, for some at any rate of the first-century exegetes, Jacob's initial disbelief constituted a serious lapse; demonstrable from Josephus's strenuous, direct contradiction of Scripture on this matter.[73] Already the Book of Jubilees seems to have felt it necessary to exculpate the patriarch, ascribing his response to a blackout;[74] and the Jerusalemite Targum and Pirqe de R. Eliezer 38 suppress the datum. Josephus's picture is extreme. Of the wonderful reports, he writes, Jacob "deemed none unbelievable, taking into consideration[75] God's power to perform great works[76] and benevolence towards him even if it was in abeyance for an interval." What deserves particular attention is that Jacob's attitude strikingly accords with that prescribed for the disciples in John. Such is the resemblance, in fact, that one might sus-

[67] Gen 41:40 ff., 45:8 ff., 16 ff.

[68] Gen 37:3.

[69] Gen 37:35.

[70] *Ant.* 2.3.4.38. If the dead is not an only son, or if he can be replaced, a parent will be comforted: 2 Sam 12:24; Job 42:11.

[71] Gen 45:26 ff.

[72] John 14:16 f., 26.

[73] *Ant.* 2.7.1.186 f. See H. St. J. Thackeray, *Josephus* (Loeb Classical Library, 1930), 4:237 note a.

[74] Jub 43:24. An interest in excuses of this type comes out also in 41:25, stressing Judah's ignorance of Tamar's identity when he had intercourse with her.

[75] *Logizomai*, as in Caiaphas's reproach "You do not consider"; see above, with footnote 23.

[76] *Megalourgia.*

pect an old Christian interpolation. It is unlikely, in my view. Note, however, that even on that basis the passage would afford strong evidence in favour of the part the Fourth Gospel, I maintain, assigns to the Joseph drama—the interpolator representing a genuine tradition.

To conclude this section with what at the moment is just an impression: the epic from Genesis, as understood by later generations, may have contributed to facets of atonement in the New Testament. Jubilees, of the second century B.C., makes it dominant in this department of religion: the deed of the brothers took place on the tenth of the seventh month, and that is why the Day of Atonement was ordained for this date. What is more, the offence against the father is the most terrible element of the crime. The news that his son had perished made him weep on the tenth of the seventh month, the yearly atonement commemorates "their grieving the affection of their father regarding Joseph his son."[77] The Dead Sea sect read Jubilees and so, surely, did other fringe movements. Indeed, *non constat* [it is not apparent] that similar constructions were not once more widespread than it looks from our expurgated Rabbinic material.

V.

Here are five headings which do fall under my subject and I feel bad sidetracking them.

(1) Nature of the rulings and sanctions. To quote myself: "We are moving in an uncomfortably ill-defined region where law, morality, politics and practical wisdom combine into a strange mixture." In Hebrew, the forms mostly employed for these directions are ambiguous, translatable by "must," "should" or "may," and if negative by "must not," "should not" or "need not." I quote myself again: "Usually, in legal writings, the context enables us to pick the right nuance. In the province here under consideration, however, owing to its peculiar, indeterminate description, such help is greatly attenuated and a good deal remains nebulous."[78] Take an advice that in such and such circumstances, "they surrender a person." Does this signify "must surrender," "should surrender," "may surrender"? Interpretation will vary—and, up to a point, is meant to vary by the authors—according to period, general conditions, individual philosophy. A mess, more durable than order. In the so-called Haustafeln of the Epistles, incidentally, one of these forms is detectable behind the faulty Greek.[79] I would say that, on the whole, the obligations laid down there belong to the relatively stable category. A directive for slaves in 1 Peter, for example, doubtless means "should": "The slaves should subject themselves to their masters."[80] "May" would be inappropriate.

There are a few strict sanctions in the ancient sources for unjustified surrender and none for unjustified non-surrender. Extra-legal punishment is a different matter. Judas found himself an outcast. He sought expiation in suicide in one version, suffered vio-

[77] Jub 34:12 ff. Translation by R. H. Charles, ed. *The Apocrypha and Pseudepigrapha of the Old Testament* (1913), 2:65.

[78] *Collaboration with Tyranny*, 93, 95 [*Talmudic Law*, 127–28].

[79] See my *Ancient Jewish Law* (1981), 83 f. [196 f.]

[80] 1 Pet 2:18.

lent death at the hand of heaven in another.[81] Simeon ben Johai, having returned to civilized life after years in hiding, recognized the disciple through whom the Romans had obtained their information. He looked at him and he turned into a heap of bones.[82]

(2) The attitude of the victim. Calling for a study in depth. Isaac and Isaiah's Servant of the Lord are resigned and trusting. The former, it is true, starts out naively unaware,[83] but he must have known soon enough. Joseph resembles them in meekness. Frightened and begging for mercy as his ordeal is about to begin,[84] he ends up accepting it thankfully. Sheba surely fought to the end. Ullah acquiesced in his extradition, under gigantic pressure: besides the ultimatum as such, there were the representations of a host who up to then had protected him at heavy risk to himself. It is to Joshua ben Levi's credit that, called a betrayer by Elijah, he did not plead Ullah's consent in excuse. Among Greek playwrights, Euripides is a veritable specialist in the shades of willingness to lay down one's life for others.[85] His Macaria prefers to be slaughtered straightaway to being chosen for slaughter by lot: the latter may be more just but is less gracious.[86] (In the twelve years or so of involvement in medical ethics, I became very aware of the complexity of "voluntarism," say, in donating a kidney to your brother or subjecting yourself to a dangerous experiment.[87]) An extremely intricate case which would have to figure is Jonah:[88] as the boat on which he was fleeing from God was about to sink in a tempest, he got the company to rescue themselves by throwing him overboard—the same man who, little later, resents the reprieve of Nineveh. I shall still have to say a word about another aspect of this near-disaster at sea.

Jesus offers himself up wholeheartedly. Yet, at Gethsemane, he does pray for the cup to pass from him—except in the Fourth Gospel, where his readiness is absolute.[89] It displays the same tendency elsewhere. Thus, Jesus cooperates with Judas to a striking extent.[90] Partly this may be due to the latter being a devil—as I mentioned before—less than human, a mere instrument for a purpose. But it also serves to underline the single-mindedness of the former. As for Gethsemane, John virtually criticizes the other tradition when he puts a rhetorical question into Jesus's mouth: "The cup which my Father has given me, shall I not drink it?"[91] It is uttered, by the way, to stop Peter's armed attack on the band come for his arrest. The incident, therefore, takes the place

[81] Matt 27:3 ff.; Acts 1:18 ff.

[82] *b. Shab.* 34b.

[83] Gen 22:7 f.

[84] Gen 42:21.

[85] See J. Schmitt, "Freiwilliger Opfertod bei Euripides," in *Religionsgeschichtliche Versuche und Vorarbeiten*, ed. L. Deubner, L. Malten and O. Weinreich (1921), vol. 17, pt. 2.

[86] Euripides, *The Children of Hercules*, 543 ff.

[87] See e.g. my "Transplantation: Acceptability of Procedures and the Required Legal Sanctions," in *Ciba Foundation Symposium on Ethics in Medical Progress*, ed. G. E. W. Wolstenholme and M. O'Connor (1966), 197 f.; and "Legal Problems in Medical Advance," The Hebrew University of Jerusalem Lionel Cohen Lecture 16 (1971), 8 ff., rept. *ILR*, 6 (1971): 4 ff.

[88] See my "Jonah: A Reminiscence," *JJS*, 35 (1984): 36 ff.

[89] Matt 26:39; Mark 14:36; Luke 22:42.

[90] E.g. John 18:2; see Bauer, *Johannesevangelium*, 203.

[91] John 18:11, cf. 12:27.

(of course, this is only a fraction of what it does) of one recorded in Matthew and Mark—and omitted by Luke—where Peter will not tolerate Jesus's fateful predictions, no doubt hoping for, if need be, a victorious battle and is rebuffed: "Away from me, Satan, you intend not the things of God but those of men."[92] This connection is verified by the fact that it is only John who identifies the violent disciple as Peter; in all three Synoptics he is anonymous.

In the appendix of the Fourth Gospel, Jesus foresees the crucifixion of Peter, by then grown old and feeble in body. What deserves notice here is the phrasing of his emotions as that ordeal occurs; he will be carried "whither he would not want [to go]."[93] Human nature does assert itself—even in a genuine martyr.

A last point. In Matthew and Mark, as Jesus is taken, the disciples escape. Luke omits this detail. In John, they have no need to flee: Jesus requests the officers, since it is he whom they consider a threat, not to touch the rest.[94] This version is widely assumed to aim at exonerating his companions.[95] It is certainly one aim. But another, more conformable to the text—"of them whom you gave me I have lost none"—is to have Jesus do for his proximate circle the same as for the world at large.[96] He will sacrifice himself for the former no less than for the latter. Once more, a faint echo of the Joseph epic may be perceptible.

(3) Bystanders. (Would be a good title for a reflective essay, taking in all varieties; for instance, that extreme character, the bystander to whatever befalls himself.) Two summary pronouncements in the New Testament are clearly relevant though going far beyond the specific situation of this lecture: "He that is not against us is for us" (originally, Caesar's mode of assessment—secure and noble) and "He that is not with me is against me" (originally, the mode Caesar attributed to his opponents—insisting on visible adherence to the party line).[97] In our day, Hochhuth, his supporters and his critics are among those who have wrestled with the problem of passivity in dilemmas not unlike that here examined.

(4) The line-up. Owing to the vagueness of the dicta, it is not too clear even what constitutes a collective for their purposes and what an outside foe. Caiaphas manoeuvred in defence of the nation, precariously holding up under its Roman overlord. According to John, we saw, Jesus surrendered himself also for the more intimate body formed by his disciples. Joshua ben Levi feared for the congregation of Lydda. Whether Ullah actual-

[92] Matt 16:23; Mark 8:33; cf. Luke 9:22 ff.

[93] John 21:18.

[94] Matt 26:56; Mark 14:50; John 18:8 f.

[95] See Bauer, *Johannesevangelium,* 204.

[96] See C. K. Barrett, *The Gospel According to St. John* (1955), 431, 435.

[97] Matt 12:30; Mark 9:40; Luke 9:50, 11:23; Cicero, *Pro Ligario* 11.35. In connection with Luke 9:50, H. L. Strack and P. Billerbeck, *Kommentar zum Neuen Testament aus Talmud und Midrasch,* 4 vols. (1924–1929, repr. 1969), 2:165, adduce Jose ben Bun, fourth century, who sees in Ps 1:1, "Blessed is the man that walks not in the counsels of the ungodly," the merciful assurance that shunning these counsels equals following those of the just. No doubt there are points of affinity but, on the whole, the setting and focus of the quote make it rather distant from the Caesar-generated proverb. On the Talmudic background, see C. G. Montefiore and H. Loewe, *A Rabbinic Anthology* (1938), rept. with prolegomenon by R. Loewe (1974), 595 f.

ly belonged to it, however, and indeed whether this datum mattered, we cannot say.[98] Right at the beginning, you may remember, I catalogued a quite different, cruder case, a party of travellers given the choice by heathen brigands between handing over one and being murdered all. One common characteristic which does stand out is the vastly superior strength of the harasser. Without exception, the various solutions to the ghastly problem I have inspected were tried out by the Jews in the fixed role of underdogs.

Obviously, even of two more or less equal groups, one may threaten the other with dire consequences unless it delivers up somebody at discretion. My speaking of "more or less equal" is an admission that the situation is not rigidly separable from my principal interest. Still, the Book of Judges offers a good enough illustration.[99] An abominable deed was committed against a Levite visitor in a Benjaminite city. The other tribes gave Benjamin an opportunity to extradite the perpetrators. It was scorned and after prolonged, ruinous fighting Benjamin was defeated. It would indeed have ceased to exist had the victors not taken special measures towards its recovery—a fraternal posture which, as observed above,[100] the Jews did not expect ever of their masters. There is an entire genre of Greek plays about sanctuary to a fugitive from abroad in the face of his country's remonstrations. In the oldest one preserved, the *Suppliant Maidens* by Aeschylus, Argos grants the Danaides asylum though their Egyptian pursuers, claiming them as their brides, have given notice that this will mean war.[101]

Again, nowadays, over a large part of the globe, if a man kills or robs, the public organs are charged with his punishment and his family is supposed to abide by the verdict. In many an ancient society, it was a matter between the two families.[102] Change set in as, more and more frequently, the injured family would gain the cooperation of others. Even at this stage, not seldom the two sides might be fairly balanced, and it took time—and inducements of all sorts—for the abandonment of the malefactor to become automatic. As is well known, there are pockets of the previous system left in states with the most up-to-date judicial institutions.

For a really thorough evaluation of the Rabbinic canons, all these adjoining fields would have to be taken into account.

(5) Theocracy. Somewhat akin to the Jewish wayfarers set upon by savages is the community in the Book of Jonah, and a truer stand on humanity it is difficult to imagine. The crew of the vessel were gentiles, yet far from religious harmony: in the storm, "every man cried to his god." Certainly nothing tied them to the person of Jonah who, immediately on being admitted, withdrew to sleep in a corner and only appeared when the captain woke him so he might implore his god too. The lots proved him to be the

[98] For Josephus, *Ant.* 7.11.8.291, a consideration making it easier for the inhabitants of Sheba's last stronghold to throw him to the wolves was that he was unknown: the Biblical text contains nothing to this effect. See my "A Reform in Acts and its Models," in *Aufstieg und Niedergang der römischen Welt,* pt. 2, Principat, vol. 25, ed. W. Haase (1985), 2350 [835].

[99] Judges 19 ff.

[100] Under II, towards the end.

[101] See B. Daube, *Rechtsprobleme im Agamemnon.* 74 ff.

[102] Plenty of literature. I have tackled some questions in *Studies in Biblical Law* (1947, rept. 1969), 213 ff., and *The Defence of Superior Orders in Roman Law* (1956), 19 f., rept. *LQR,* 72 (1956): 501 f.

stirrer-up of heaven's wrath. Now he introduced himself and exhorted them to hurl him into the waves, thus ensuring their safety. But so strong was their dedication to the bond between any aboard ship that, notwithstanding the danger, they laboured long and hard before they could bring themselves to take this step. (I commute from San Francisco to Berkeley by the first bus about half past five in the morning. There is definitely a degree of comradery between the regulars—and of hostility to the occasional intruder—but I assure you that we do not come up to the standard of those pagan seadogs.) In terms of this discussion, here was a summons, on pain of universal extinction, to extradite a specific individual guilty, as he himself acknowledged, of the crassest dereliction of duty—and these "Noachides" felt like resisting.

Perhaps the most arresting feature of the imbroglio is that the oppressor making the hateful demand was God. By rights, it should not need to be pointed out at all seeing that a large proportion of human sacrifices from inside a collective everywhere are designed to gratify a deity otherwise at odds with it, and often, indeed, the deity wants not a designated individual like Jonah but simply one or more victims no matter who they are—what the Rabbis would not submit to even in an epoch of terror. Thus, at one time, if Rome was in peril, anything born that spring, animal or human, was forfeit to Jupiter.[103] The Theban general Pelopidas, bidden in a dream on the eve of battle to slaughter a virgin—any virgin so long as she had auburn hair—refused.[104] When Korah and other grandees rose against Moses and Aaron, the bulk of the people were ordered to distance themselves from them if they did not wish to share their fate.[105] Those condemned were manifestly guilty, not just an undefined crowd—though their innocent households, let us not overlook, were wiped out with them.[106] In this case it was God himself who executed the sentence; as they had challenged the leadership, it was essential for the answer to come from one standing above both parties. Achan, who appropriated sacred booty from Jericho, was put to death—together with his innocent household—by the community.[107] The latter, to begin with, had been unaware of his offence. But the army got into desperate straits. God informed Joshua that an impious theft was the cause, indicated a method by which to identify the culprit and declared that, unless he was burnt, the people would be rendered no more help. Arguably, in a theocracy, any capital punishment includes an element—from strong to faint—of duress from on high: the villain is offered up lest, if he is not, the community be doomed. Naturally, this is most conspicuous where a crime affects the deity directly, idolatry, for example. But it is traceable elsewhere too: "If a man hates his neighbour and smites him that he dies, your eye shall not pity him but you shall put away the blood of the innocent from Israel, that it may go well with you."[108]

[103] Festus, *De Significatu Verborum,* Pauli Excerpta 379. Far be it from me to pronounce on the question of historicity.

[104] Plutarch, *Parallel Lives,* Pelopidas 21.1.

[105] Num 16:26.

[106] Mitigated in Num 26:11.

[107] Joshua 7.

[108] Deut 19:11 ff.

A thorough comparison of extradition to terrestrial potentates and extradition to supernatural ones would greatly further our understanding of both. Roughly, the latter started by being modelled on the former, but then developed its own momentum and, while constantly receiving fresh impulses from below, in turn exercised strong influence. Just as, say, the picture of God as judge took off from the this-worldly institution, then sprouted more and more traits of its own, and time came when the judge above would be held out for imitation to the original. Similarly, at first, "the exodus was construed as an application, on a higher plane, of social usages familiar from the daily world; once the story in this form had gained currency, however, it in its turn had an enormous impact on social affairs."[109] Some proto-Pharisaic principle of defending to the last a fellow-member of your caravan from human raiders, whatever their motivation, must have been held in profound respect when the sailors of the first chapter of Jonah attempted to enforce it against the Almighty tracking down a deserter.

The extent of overlap may be gauged from narratives where it is scarcely possible to say whether a community confronts an earthly claimant or a higher one. Minos waged war against Attica, supported by the gods who sent pestilence and barrenness. It was the gods, too, who told the Athenians to accept his terms: tribute every few years of a number of youngsters to be devoured by the Minotaur.[110] Were they delivered up to the gods or to the foreign adversary? In David's reign there was a famine and the Lord informed him of the cause, a wrong done the Gibeonites by Saul.[111] Asked what amends they desired, they replied that they wanted seven of Saul's sons whom they would hang up to the Lord—which was done. Extradition to the Gibeonites or to the Lord?[112] I shall not proceed with this.

(Here is a warning should anyone do so. I have confined myself to the area of human sacrifice closest to the central conundrum of this lecture, i.e. where a collective, not to succumb, has to cede one or more of its members to the gods. From this, we must mark off the case where a person in power, not to succumb, has to cede a human possession—a father his son or daughter, a husband his wife, a monarch one or more of his subjects. Jephtha promised the Lord whoever of his household would welcome him first on his victorious return—happened to be his only child.[113] Artemis, offended by Agamemnon, produced a calm so the Greek fleet under his command could not sail against Troy; whereupon he donated to her his daughter Iphigeneia. Though the two situations—a community abandoning a member, a person in power abandoning a subordinate—share obvious similarities, there are also huge political and moral differences and their histories are far from smoothly parallel. By and large, we have before us the distinction between communal responsibility and ruler punishment I advocated for

[109] See my *The Exodus Pattern in the Bible* (1963), 16.

[110] Plutarch, *Parallel Lives,* Theseus 15.1.

[111] 2 Samuel 21.

[112] As well as, in part, to David himself, so to speak, who would welcome their demise. The sacrificer's interest, crudely apparent in this case, will on scrutiny turn out not to be totally absent in quite a few others.

[113] Judg 11:30 ff. Rabbinic exegesis, bent on mitigating his ruthlessness, makes him vow not "whoever would first meet him" but "whatever"—thinking of a goat or a dog: Josephus, *Ant.* 5.7.10.263 f.; *Gen. Rab.* 60 on 24:13. See my "Texts and Interpretation in Roman and Jewish Law," *JJSOC*, 3 (1961): 25 [*Talmudic Law,* 175].

ancient jurisprudence long ago.[114] I noted then that intermediate and mixed varieties abound. Insofar as Jesus was betrayed in order to placate the Romans, his was the very type of extradition controversial between Pharisees and Sadducees. When the First Epistle of John has him sent by his father for a propitiation,[115] he becomes more like Isaac whom Abraham, his father, the person in power, is willing to slay on mount Moriah. Needless to say, as the father in 1 John is God himself, this is not all.)

A final aside about the Book of Jonah. That God seemingly deals with the oarsmen like the grimmest tyrant is in keeping with the entire paradoxical constitution of the work. Its prophet tries to quit his service not because his master is cruel but because he is all-merciful: which makes it a fool's errand to preach that disaster will follow sin. He is forced back and does prove right again. Yet, as the curtain comes down, the wicked Ninevites have repented—for the moment at least—and he himself has learnt—for the moment at least—a lot about God's reasons. Just so, the mariners, having held out for brotherhood under severe testing, reach land and adore the Lord of creation—to the accompaniment, indeed, of a chant by Jonah in the whale's belly.[116] Everything is stood on its head, yet comes out profoundly alright.[117]

VI.

In the late fifties and early sixties I talked on this complex to various audiences, and perhaps my most interesting lecture now would concern their various responses. My poor youngest son was around ten when I asked him what he would do as the mayor if bidden to supply two male citizens—any two—for a spectacular execution, otherwise all males of the town would be shot; and, of course, he was not allowed to offer himself. He replied that he must assume to have been elected for the town's welfare, so he would accede—and then commit suicide. No wonder he has taken himself off to Western Australia, safe from his father. My experience in general was that the less familiar my listeners were with the realities of tyranny, the more unhesitating they were in saying No. Occasionally, when meeting with a lively, informal undergraduate group, I took a vote: who would appease and who would resist? And felt real admiration for the handful with the courage of coming out for compliance.

American academics inclined to be overreliant on unilinear logic. At a law seminar, a number of colleagues took it for granted that the Strasbourg dilemma would remain the same if the Commandant, instead of conducting a *razzia,* had told the parents to bring one boy to be shot or else he would seize both: ergo a mother of the sort Helen had in mind would grab one and take him to headquarters. Utterly mistaken. No

[114] See my *Studies in Biblical Law,* 160 ff.

[115] 1 John 4:10.

[116] Jonah 1:16, "The men offered a sacrifice unto the Lord and made vows," 2:9, "I will sacrifice unto you, I will pay what I vowed"; see "Jonah: A Reminiscence," 41.

[117] Familiarity renders one insensitive to a further, momentous contradiction, not relevant to the subject in hand. We hear of a boat battling a gale, a passenger thrown into the sea and swallowed by a fish, a city utterly depraved—but, throughout, not one person is killed. The same is true of another masterpiece in praise of the misfit: in the whole of *Don Quixote,* including part 1 and part 2, a persiflage, after all, of the knightly exploits then popular, there is not a single killing.

doubt she would thereby be avoiding a double loss. But this does not erase the huge difference of the scenario as a whole, involving—among other things—a brutal act. My hunch is that a mother would be almost less capable of it than a father.

A frequent Marxist approach in East Germany and Russia was to deny any special problem: you simply, as in every situation, take the course most helpful for continuing the war against the class enemy. The Strasbourg father should have saved a son: one more fighter on the right side. Looks superficially like Helen's impulse but is, at bottom, miles apart. In most cases—for example, that just posited: bring us one child in order to keep the other—even the outer results would be different. (I shall be content with hinting at a distinct, highly important aspect: the inadequacy, even within a thoroughly materialistic philosophy, of a mechanical head-count for assessing gain and loss. One could imagine that the shooting of the two brothers, by creating widespread abhorrence, did the occupying power more harm than it would have suffered at the hands of a survivor.) I did, however, hear other views even behind the iron curtain: Marxism is not one rigidly unitary system. Also, now and then, I got one answer from officials in the open debate and another from humbler folks afterwards, in conversation.

As I am putting the finishing touches to this paper, my friend Walter Weyrauch sends me a pioneering study of betrayal.[118] While dealing in depth with Gestapo informants[119]—the inducements, likely and unlikely candidates, their fate—he sketches a comprehensive theory of undercover operations, with glimpses at confidential information in answer to job or credit inquiries and, indeed, at any scholar's pursuit of truth qua gathering of hitherto secret data for "intelligence" purposes. Which puts me in mind of the sixties, when John (now Lord) Butterworth, Vice-Chancellor of Warwick University, got into trouble with the students: they found out that he had scribbled on a youngster's application file which he passed on to the admission committee, "Was co-editor of a radical school-magazine." I was told of this by Alan (now Lord) Bullock at Oxford who, a far more experienced hand at university government, added "He doesn't seem to know what the telephone is for."[120]

Occasionally the question is raised why Jewish suffering attracts more than average attention. I visited Cambodia before the Vietnamese war and fell in love with that civilisation—and I mean the whole civilisation, not just the famous sculptures. It is gone for ever, destroyed by invaders who had as little awareness as an ox that tramples over the black tulip. A holocaust; but, honestly, are there many who care? One factor, however minor, may be precisely what is exemplified by the material before us: a continuous, conscious turning over of the agonies throughout the millennia among those

[118] "Gestapo Informants: Facts and Theory of Undercover Operations," *Columbia Journal of Transnational Law*, 24 (1986): 553 ff.

[119] Incidentally, the account—see above, under III, footnote 15—of how the Romans got to know about Simeon ben Johai's attacks shows that they had informants telling them not only of enemies but also of friends and neutrals: Judah ben Ilai is mentioned as on their side. It very much looks as if the Rabbi's disciple had in fact been such a general informant, though just conceivably he was a careless talker—maybe among his gentile relations—and someone else made the damaging report.

[120] Anticipating Nixon's "Destroy all tapes." The comment has more point in England than in the States, on two grounds. First, even yet, over there, the note has not lost out to the call, so it takes a clever guy to discover where the latter has advantages; and second, even yet, over there, bugging is not commonplace.

afflicted and within each of them, a never-ending re-experience, modified yet enhanced by changes in culture, often refined, at times debased, always rich far beyond the temporary, and—springing from it at once and fostering it—an attempt to draw lessons and provide signposts, tentative though they must be, for succeeding generations plunged into the same gruelling impasse. You cannot be in touch with this mood without feeling that not one sparrow is forgotten before God.[121]

[121] Matt 10:29; Luke 12:6. According to *y. Shebi.* 38d, cited by Strack and Billerbeck, *Kommentar,* 1:582, Simeon ben Johai, when after thirteen years in a cave he had an inkling that conditions had improved, reached his decision to return by observing a man catching birds with a net. Each time a heavenly voice proclaimed salvation, the little creature escaped; and he concluded that since no bird could perish against the Lord's will, surely no human could. How touching that, in this quandary, he made use of the established logic of the *a fortiori.* —On rereading, I cannot leave it at that. *b. Shab.* 33b is simpler and, I guess, later: no birds, and a heavenly voice just counsels the fugitive to go forth from his cave. His contact with the above is manifestly no less intimate in the Jerusalemite version, so why the complication, the indirectness? Because God here behaves like a great teacher with a gifted pupil, supplying a signal but leaving room for interpretation and choice of action. All over the world, wisdom instruction—especially if of an esoteric flavour—cultivates this method. As for Simeon's prowess in the art of inference, I have argued that he learnt from Labeo's *ratio* and *regula* ("Jewish Law in the Hellenistic World," *JLA,* suppl. 2 [1980], 58 ff.) [*Talmudic Law,* 227–29]. With the particular deduction in this case, cf., for example, his gloss on Isa 65:22, "As the days of a tree are the days of my people": the tree is the Torah and since the Torah, created in honour of Israel, will endure throughout this and the next worlds, all the more will the pious ones for whose sake the world was created (*Siphre* Deut 47 on 11:21, see W. Bacher, *Die Agada der Tannaiten* [1890, rept. 1966], 2:146). —Clearly, this final footnote is destined to link up with the beginning. When I rhapsodized to Helen about that reticent, oblique kind of guidance, she remarked that men taught thus but not women; the latter came right out. This seems accurate. I suppose it is explicable by women, so far at least, having their vital teaching experience with infants, where you must be to the point: "Don't touch the hot iron." Men take over at a stage when the abler ones among their charges ought to be steered towards independence.

Appendix: Jesus among the Sages

As is well known, the Lukan tale of the young Jesus among the teachers in the Temple[122] calls to mind numerous cases of future greatness manifested in boyhood. J. M. Creed[123] singles out Cyrus who quite early showed his royal qualities at play,[124] Alexander who was not much older when making an impression on ambassadors he received in his father's absence,[125] Apollonius who at age fourteen surpassed his tutors in wisdom and application[126] and Josephus who in his autobiography relates[127] that he was consulted at that age on points of law by high priests and other notables. Without disputing the relevance of these pieces, I think there is another which has directly contributed to the shaping of the story, namely, the dreams of Joseph, aged seventeen years, in Genesis.[128]

For my purpose it is enough to quote the second one which he reports to his father as well as his brothers. In it, sun, moon and eleven stars prostrate themselves before him. His father rebukes him for his arrogance, at the same time storing the incident in his memory. In Luke, as Jesus's parents leave Jerusalem with their caravan, he, without informing them, stays behind to debate in the Temple. After a day's journey they notice his absence, return and are struck with amazement on finally locating him in the midst of an admiring audience. His mother reproaches him for his unfilial behaviour but he majestically overrides her complaint. The parents do not understand, yet his mother keeps everything in her heart.

That there are weighty differences is obvious. To name a few—Joseph is less far along his road than Jesus. Thus, whereas the former's break with the norm consists in a vision and his promulgation of it, the latter's consists in actions; and whereas the former does not refute the censure meted out to him, the latter does. Again, the dominant role of Joseph's father contrasts with that of Jesus's mother. This is just one illustration of a general datum: the father's attachment is to the fore throughout Joseph's life, the mother's throughout Jesus's. (I am speaking of earthly parents.) Still, the similarities are too striking to be due to chance. Apart from the main theme, i.e. an omen from heaven of glory to come, in both pericopes the hero commits an apparent wrong, upsets traditional authority within the family, assumes a status not yet recognizably his. In both one parent pleads with him and in both in the name of the other parent too: Jacob exclaims "Shall I and your mother and your brothers bow down ourselves?", Mary "Why have you thus dealt with us? Your father and I have sought you." In both, the leading parent, while on one level offended and while far from thorough comprehension, does sense another dimension and will go on pondering the matter. The phraseology is much the

122 Luke 2:41 ff.; see above, under IV, with footnotes 37 and 60.
123 *The Gospel According to St. Luke* (1930), 44.
124 Herodotus, *Histories,* 1.114 ff.
125 Plutarch, *Parallel Lives,* Alexander 5.1.
126 Philostratus, *Life of Apollonius* 1.7.
127 *Vita* 2.9.
128 Gen 37:5 ff.

same: the LXX writes "*ho de pater autou dieterese to rema,*" the evangelist "*kai he meter autou dieterei panta ta remata en kardia autes.*"[129]

With regard to phraseology, there is a further detail of interest. Jesus asserts that he must be "in what are my father's," *en tois tou patros mou.* Creed, representing the prevalent opinion, rightly gives it the sense "in my father's home"—on the basis of Septuagintal usage. Joseph, we learn in Genesis,[130] calls his firstborn Manasseh, *Menashshe* in Hebrew, "for God has made me forget, *nashshani,* all my toil and all my father's house"; the Septuagint renders the concluding words "all that are my father's," *panton ton tou patros mou.* My point is that we have before us not a mere linguistic coincidence, but a harking back of the New Testament narrative to the Old Testament one. The latter brings out a moment when Joseph becomes so filled by his marvellous present as to no longer have a stake in the past. Something of this kind happens to the young Jesus at the Temple. Only Joseph by "my father's home" designates his old world now, under God's direction, left behind, Jesus his new world now totally claiming him—"my true father's home," we might expand. In passing—Mary's address "child," *teknon,* has a remarkable counterpart in Reuven's lament on finding Joseph gone from the pit:[131] "The child is not," with *yeledh* referring to a seventeen-year-old-lad. The Septuagint does justice to the Hebrew though, to be sure, by means of *paidarion,* not *teknon.*

Thirty years ago I wondered[132] whether New Testament writers connected Jesus's treacherous disciple with that brother of Joseph who devised his sale, both bearing the name Judah or Judas; and I said probably not, and indeed that Joseph appeared nowhere to be treated as prefiguring Jesus. By now I am certain that I was wrong on both counts. John's Caiaphas, for instance, in his prophecy about Jesus's death, can be shown to allude to Joseph's saving mission to the Egyptians threatened by famine.[133] I am setting out the documentation in the preceding lecture; and am content here to point out that the episode under review evidently contains hints allied to those in the Fourth Gospel.

No doubt the bulk of the occurrence is pre-Lukan. The easy tone of the discourse with the Sages, highlighted by its elimination from the Infancy Gospel of Thomas, mid-second century,[134] speaks for an early date. Moreover, had he been formulating on his own, he would hardly have depicted the parents as forgetful of the previous predictions by the shepherds, Simeon and Anna.[135] Lastly, I have suggested[136] that the final reference to Jesus's subjection[137] is appended to the nucleus which had a tripartite structure famil-

[129] Naturally, subsequent re-interpretation, too, presents similarities. According to Josephus, Jacob, far from protesting, expresses delight (*Ant.* 2.3.3.15). J.-P. Migne explains (ed. *Scriptura Sacra,* vol. 22 [1862], col. 463) that Mary's "Why have you thus dealt with us?" *interrogatio est, non reprehensionis, accusationis aut querimoniae, sed admirationis* ["The question is not one of blame, accusation or complaint, but of admiration."].

[130] Gen 41:51.

[131] Gen 37:50.

[132] See my *New Testament and Rabbinic Judaism,* 3 f. [See 91 and "Judas," 790 f.].

[133] John 11:52; Gen 45:5 ff., 50:20; Ps 105:17.

[134] Gospel of Thomas 19:2.

[135] Luke 2:15 ff., see Creed, *Gospel According to St. Luke,* 44, 46.

[136] See my *Civil Disobedience in Antiquity,* 47 ff.

[137] Luke 2:51.

iar from many encounters: revolutionary action—protest—silencing of the remonstrants. By Luke's time, with a fair number of homes already fully Christian, Messianic zeal must be tempered with respect for worthy progenitors. Nevertheless, though he is not its author, his choice of the story does prove him to be in sympathy with it. Perhaps, to the considerations met in the literature, we may now add its universalist tendency, its linking Jesus's first public statement—uttered in the holiest of places—with Joseph's work for gentiles, in fact, gentiles who would soon oppress his people. J. Massyngberde Ford[138] has recently argued a sharp division between the infancy legends, reflecting traditional, nationalistic expectations, and the main Third Gospel. Simeon and Anna, she proposes,[139] "may have been anticipating a political leader." Thereafter, however, "Luke will... show that Jesus... is a preacher with... the powerful message... of loving one's enemy in word and deed." The foregoing remarks seem to fit in with her thesis.

[Additional note: In any re-edition of *Appeasement or Resistance* I would briefly comment on yet a further reaction to the demand for one otherwise all will perish. It is found in Ahiqar, Pritchard, *Ancient Near Eastern Texts*, p. 429, ca. sixth century B.C. The bear went to the lambs: "Give me one of you and I will be content." The lambs answered: "Take whichever thou wilt. We are thy lambs." Horrible, yet often realistic.]

[138] See *My Enemy Is My Guest* (1984). Yes, her initial stands for Josephine.
[139] See *My Enemy Is My Guest*, 35.

Moses

There are numerous unmistakable references to Moses—for example, the command to Joseph, after the death of Herod, to "go into the land of Israel, for they are dead which sought the young child's life," which echoes the command to Moses in Midian to "return into Egypt, for all the men are dead which sought thy life."[1] No purpose would be served by enumerating the well-known parallels. It may suffice to draw attention to three points.*

A Prophet without Honour in his Country

The complaint that "a prophet is not without honour save in his country"[2] occurs in several ancient works. No wonder, seeing that it refers to a genuine experience of deplorable frequency. If the New Testament pericopes in which it is to be found are influenced by a Rabbinic anecdote about Moses, they are influenced only as far as the mode of exposition is concerned. The substance is entirely independent.

According to Hama bar Hanina, Moses was removed from his father's house at the age of twelve in order that later, when God sent him to the oppressed Hebrews, they would believe him.[3] Had he grown up at home and then proclaimed to them the name of the God at whose bidding he acted, they would have said that he had simply been informed by Amram, who was in possession of a tradition which Joseph had handed on to Levi and Levi to Kohath—Amram's father.[4] As, however, he had early been removed from his father's house, "the people believed."[5]

The differences between this story and that concerning Jesus's rejection in his native city are numerous and considerable. To name only one: in the case of Moses, the danger of a prophet being rejected in his country was foreseen and averted.

Nevertheless, in Matthew and Mark at least, there are two features, apart from the general idea of the incident, curiously reminiscent of the Rabbinic tale. First, the lengthy enumeration of Jesus's relations—"Is not this the carpenter's son? Is not his mother called Mary? And his brethren James and Joses?"—may correspond to the detailed account of how Moses might have got to know about the name of God—"his father has handed it on to him, for Joseph handed it on to Levi, Levi to Kohath and

[1] Matt 2:20; Exod 4:19.

* [The first one, A Supernatural Birth, is in Section 4, 421 ff.]

[2] Matt 13:57; Mark 6:4; Luke 4:24; John 4:44.

[3] *Exod. Rab.* on 4:18 (following a quotation of 4:27).

[4] For this tradition, cp. *Exod. Rab.* on 3:16 towards the end.

[5] Exod 4:31.

Kohath to Amram." Secondly, the New Testament episode ends by a reference to the people's unbelief, just as the Rabbinic one ends by a reference to their belief.

Hama bar Hanina lived about the middle of the 3rd cent. A.D. If he invented the anecdote about Moses, it is, of course, of little importance to an understanding of Matthew and Mark. But he may well be transmitting, and refashioning, a story that was already current in New Testament times. Perhaps his interest in it was due to what appears to have happened to his father: to go by a somewhat doubtful reading,[6] R. Judah the Prince (about A.D. 200) had refrained from ordaining Hanina because "they cried out against him at Sepphoris as an inhabitant of Sepphoris"; that is to say, he was despised by his fellow-citizens.

INTERCESSION

The third point concerns Moses's mediation between God and Israel. The Bible tells us that when the Israelites had worshipped the Golden Calf, Moses insisted on sharing their fate. According to the Rabbis, he offered to die, or even did die, in order that they might live.

Admittedly, by the time of the New Testament, the idea of a just man giving his life as *kopher*, λύτρον, "ransom" or "expiation," for the community or the sinners was common in Judaism. It is prominent in the Fourth Book of Maccabbees, and Paul would have preferred to be "accursed from Christ for his kinsmen according to the flesh."[7] Nonetheless it is probable that for early Christian writers the example of Moses was of particular significance.

Let us remember that he was considered "the first redeemer" just as the Messiah would be "the last." The antithesis is not extant in utterances prior to the 3rd cent. A.D.,[8] but that may be accidental. Again, the Bible, where it describes his death, calls him "the servant of the Lord."[9] True, it does the same with Joshua.[10] But the passage about Moses interested the Jewish theologians more. It is widely held that those Talmudic texts which identify Moses with the suffering Servant of the Lord in Isaiah are inspired by Christian teaching.[11] They may be, but it is difficult to see why they must be. Further, while the Rabbis contend that each patriarch and prophet "gave his life for Israel" in the sense that he offered it,[12] it is apparently only Moses whose offer was accepted. He could have entered the promised land on condition of cancelling his previous wish that the Israelites should be forgiven the worship of the Golden Calf. But he exclaimed: "Let Moses and a hundred like him die rather than a nail of one of the peo-

[6] *y. Taan.* 68a. Bacher, *Die Agada der Palästinensischen Amoräer,* vol. 1 (1892), 1, n. 2, prefers the version of *Eccl. Rab.* on 7:7.

[7] Strack-Billerbeck, *Kommentar zum Neuen Testament aus Talmud und Midrasch* (thereafter quoted as Strack-B.), vol. 2 (1924), 274 ff., vol. 3 (1926), 260 ff.

[8] E.g. *Num. Rab.* on 6:22.

[9] Deut 34:5. Dante speaks of *Mosé ubbidiente*. My brother Benjamin Daube wondered whether he chose the epithet because its sound suggests *ebed* or *obed* (*'ebhedh,'obhedh*), "servant."

[10] Josh 24:29.

[11] J. Z. Lauterbach, *Jewish Encyclopedia,* 9 (1905), 51, s.v. Moses.

[12] *Mek.* on Exod 12:1.

ple be harmed."[13] Joshua ben Levi, the author of this anecdote, belongs to the first half of the 3rd cent. A.D. The main idea, however, may be far older.

Finally, there is a Midrash dealing with the breaking of the Tables.[14] Moses realized that, under the strict law, the worship of the Golden Calf would mean the end of the nation, since it is laid down that he who sacrifices to idols "shall be utterly destroyed," "shall be *ḥerem*."[15] Therefore, the Midrash continues, "he joined, united (*ḥibber*) his life, self (*'eth naphsho*) with them" and committed the sin of breaking the Tables; whereupon he asked God[16] either to pardon all or to reject him as well—there was now no difference. A legend like this may well have contributed to the notions of all sinners being gathered and saved in Jesus, and of Jesus, sinless, being made sin or curse for others.

It might perhaps be argued that it is the legend which is indebted to Christianity. This, however, is unlikely. The legend is comparatively simple, whereas the Christian notions are very intricate. Moreover, the latter refer so specifically to Jesus that one cannot very well imagine their being watered down and transferred to Moses.

[13] *Deut. Rab.* on 29:4.
[14] *Exod. Rab.* on 34:1.
[15] Exod 22:19 (20).
[16] Exod 32:32.

Samuel

Samuel is no Messianic figure. But in Talmudic literature he is called "the *Rabban*, the foremost master, teacher, of all prophets,"[1] and his prominence among the prophets is recognized in Acts and the Epistle to the Hebrews.[2] Moreover, as God allowed Hannah to conceive him in answer to her prayers, he represents for the Rabbis the righteous child granted to parents who come together "in holiness" (*biqedhusha*).[3]

That the narrative of Samuel's birth influenced the Lukan stories of the birth of the Baptist and the birth of Jesus is well known. The Magnificat, for example, closely follows the song of Hannah. The presentation of the infant Jesus at the Temple probably contains a reminiscence of the presentation of the boy Samuel at the sanctuary of Shiloh.[4] Jesus's parents make a yearly pilgrimage to Jerusalem comparable to that of Samuel's parents to Shiloh. Luke concludes his account of the childhood of Jesus by saying that he "increased in wisdom and age and in favour with God and man"; just so "the child Samuel grew and was in favour both with the Lord and also with men."[5]

In view of these acknowledged parallels, it may be justifiable to call attention to a story about the young Samuel teaching at the sanctuary although it is transmitted by a Rabbi who flourished as late as the middle of the 3rd cent. A.D. We shall come back to this problem of date. The story is[6] that Samuel, when brought to Shiloh by his parents, observed that the priests misinterpreted one of the sacrificial regulations. He remarked on it and was summoned before Eli, where he established his point by a convincing exegesis of a precept from Leviticus.[7] Eli paid tribute to his fine argument. But he also reminded him that anyone teaching a *halakha*, a legal regulation, in the presence of his superior—in this case Eli himself—deserved to be put to death. It was only Hannah's intercession which saved her son. His prophetic qualities, however, were henceforth undoubted.

It is no doubt conceivable that Eleazar ben Pedath, of the 3rd cent., invented this legend in order to give an ampler meaning to three verses in 1 Samuel.[8] "And they slew a bullock"—*scil.* the priests slaughtered it incorrectly; "and they brought the child to Eli"—*scil.* because he had questioned the procedure; "and she said, I am the woman

[1] *y. Hag.* 77a, where Judah the Prince uses the appellation.

[2] Acts 3:24; Heb 11:32

[3] *Tanhuma* on Num 5:13.

[4] Creed, *The Gospel according to St. Luke* (1930), 39.

[5] Luke 2:52; 1 Sam 2:26.

[6] *b. Ber.* 31b.

[7] Lev 1:5.

[8] 1 Sam 1:25–27

that stood by thee here praying unto the Lord"—*scil.* she said so to Eli after he had pronounced the learned boy guilty of a capital offence; "for this child I prayed"—*scil.* though Eli assured her that even if Samuel had to die for laying down a *halakha* in the presence of his superior, God would give her other sons instead, she insisted that it was Samuel, "this child," she wanted to have. If we assume that the legend dated from the 3rd. cent., it has of course no bearing on Luke's story.

We cannot, however, rule out the possibility of its being much earlier. Eleazar ben Pedath may well have done no more than connect it with, "prove it" by reference to, certain verses in 1 Samuel. On this hypothesis, Luke—or his precursors—may have regarded the Rabbinic gifts of the boy prophet Samuel as foreshadowing those of the boy prophet Jesus. We are not concerned with the historicity of the incident reported by Luke. All that is here suggested is that the Jewish model, if it existed in his time may have contributed to his selection of this scene and to his manner of depicting it.

According to the Gospel of Thomas,[9] which also contains the episode of Jesus teaching in the Temple, Jesus reduces the doctors to silence and himself expounds the Law. Creed holds[10] that "in Luke the boy is a genuine learner." There is a great deal of truth in this. But, for one thing, we do not know whether the Gospel of Thomas is entirely dependent on Luke, so that any deviations must be secondary; it may preserve parts of a version of the incident no less old than Luke, though, admittedly, this is far from likely. For another thing, even in Luke, we ought perhaps not to press too much the reference to Jesus "hearing" the doctors and "asking them questions." In the very next sentence we are told how all were astonished "at his understanding and answers." In the Talmudic anecdote concerning Samuel, the boy also begins by asking the priests why they do so and so, and only then goes on to point out their error.

Needless to say, there remain enormous differences between the story about Samuel and that about Jesus. Let us, however, in conclusion, note three remarkable points of correspondence.

First, as his mother rebukes him, Jesus replies: "Wist ye not that I must be in my Father's service" or "in my Father's House?" Samuel's parents left him at the sanctuary from his earliest childhood.

Secondly, the mother of Jesus plays a more prominent part in the episode than his father, and her anxious love for him is touchingly depicted. The same is true of Samuel's mother in the Talmudic parallel.

Thirdly, Jesus "was subject unto his parents" and he "increased in wisdom and age and favour with God and man." Now this sequence of ideas—subjecting oneself and finding favour—is interesting. (We omit the clause which, in Luke, separates them, namely, that Mary kept these things in her heart.) It is to be met with in early Christian catechetical material. Paul in Romans 13 enjoins subordination to the state and other social duties. In the following chapter he deals with vegetarianism and urges that, though no food is unclean, one should have some consideration for the prejudices of a fellow-Christian: "for he that in these things serveth Christ is acceptable to God and

[9] Gospel of Thomas 19.

[10] *Op. cit.*, 45.

approved of men."[11] Similarly, 1 Peter[12] demands subjection to the authorities because "so is the will of God, that with well doing ye may put to silence the ignorance of foolish men." In Luke, to be sure, Jesus gives in not to the state or the prejudices of a fellow-being, but to his parents. This is not, however, a vital difference. He is represented as setting an example of Christian morality, and 1 Peter contains an injunction almost directly applicable to this case:[13] "Ye younger, submit yourselves unto the elder; yea, all be subject one to another and be clothed with humility; for God giveth favour to the humble."

Yet here, too, the evangelist may have had in mind the figure of Samuel. For one thing, let us note that the association of self-abasement with acceptability to God and men goes back to Jewish teaching. According to the *Letter of Aristeas*[14] "it is a principle that God accepts the humble and the human race loves those willing to be in subjection to them." Several hundreds of years later (first third of the 4th cent. A.D.) a favourite saying of Abaye was that a Jew should be yielding to both his co-religionists and gentiles, in order to be agreeeable to God and man.[15] For another thing, apart from the fact that the Rabbis generally ascribe particular humility to Samuel,[16] the Old Testament itself records that whereas Eli's sons were wicked and "hearkened not unto the voice of their father,"[17] Samuel "ministered unto the Lord before Eli the priest";[18] and we have already seen that when Luke wrote of Jesus that "he increased in wisdom and age and in favour with God and man," he was drawing on the Old Testament notice that "the child Samuel grew and was in favour both with the Lord and also with men."

To sum up, considering the late appearance of the Rabbinic legend of Samuel, it would be rash to assert that the Lukan pericope must have been inspired by it. A dogmatic denial of any influence, however, would be equally wrong. The question must remain an open one.

[11] Rom 14:18
[12] 1 Peter 2:13 ff.
[13] 1 Peter 5:5; cp. also Col 3:20.
[14] *Letter of Aristeas* 257.
[15] *b. Ber.* 17a.
[16] E.g. *Tanhuma* on Num 21:7.
[17] 1 Sam 2:25.
[18] 1 Sam 2:11, 18.

Saul

A. General

The case for Saul is worth consideration. Patai, in a recent article,[1] points out analogies between Old and New Testament symbols of royalty. He notes: (1) Samuel recognizes Saul one day after God announced his coming. The Baptist recognizes Jesus one day after announcing his coming.[2] (2) As Samuel sees Saul, God says: "Behold the man I spake to thee of, this same shall reign over my people." As the Baptist sees Jesus, he says: "Behold the Lamb of God which taketh away the sin of the world. This is he of whom I said, After me cometh a man which is preferred before me" etc.[3] (3) Saul's public proclamation follows his choice by means of the oracle. Jesus's public proclamation follows his choice by means of the descent of the dove.[4] (4) When Saul is anointed, the Spirit enters into him, so that he turns into another man.[5] In other ancient installation rites, the person elected dies and is reborn as a god. That this idea was current also among the Hebrews is suggested by passages like this from Psalms:[6] "Yet have I set my king upon the holy hill of Zion. I will declare: the Lord hath said unto me, Thou art my son, this day have I born thee."[7] Possibly Patai might have added two verses referring to Saul himself, namely, those which say[8] that, when he had been fetched from his hiding-place to be acclaimed, "he was higher than any of the people" and there was "none like him among all the people." When Jesus is baptized, the Spirt of God descends upon him, and he is proclaimed to be the son of God.[9] (5) Jair, one of the Judges, "had thirty sons that rode on thirty ass colts, and they had thirty cities";[10] another, Abdon, "had forty sons and thirty nephews, that rode on three score and ten ass colts";[11] Solomon, when crowned, was made to ride on "king David's mule" or "the king's mule";[12] and Zechariah's prophecy about the king, "lowly and riding upon an ass," is well known.[13] Jesus also rides on an ass.

[1] *HUCA* 20 (1947), 154 f., 170, 176.
[2] 1 Sam 9:15 f.; John 1:19 ff.
[3] 1 Sam 9:17; John 1:29 f.
[4] 1 Sam 10:20 ff.; Matt 3:16 f.; Mark 1:10 f.; Luke 3:22; John 1:32 ff.
[5] 1 Sam 10:6, 9. Cf. 16:13, of David.
[6] Ps 2:6 f.
[7] Or 2 Sam 7:14; 1 Chr 17:13; Ps 89:27 f.
[8] 1 Sam 10:23 f.
[9] Matt 3:16 f.; Mark 1:10 f.; Luke 3:21 f.; John 1:32 ff.
[10] Jdg 10:4.
[11] Jdg 12:14.
[12] 1 Kgs 2:38, 44.
[13] Zech 9:9.

B. JOHN

Not all these parallels are equally striking. Perhaps we should distinguish between the Synoptics and the Fourth Gospel. This has all analogies occurring in the Synoptics—the proclamation after a sign from heaven, the descent of the Spirit and the riding on an ass—plus two besides, the recognition one day after the announcement and the presentation opening with "Behold." The value of the first of these two may be diminished by the fact that, in John 1, it is several times that one event succeeds another on the following day.[14] On the other hand, it is just conceivable that the awkward duplication of verses 29–34, "The next day, John seeth Jesus coming and saith, Behold the Lamb of God," by 35–37, "Again the next day after John, looking upon Jesus, saith Behold the Lamb of God," has something to do with the two days of Saul with Samuel.[15] At any rate, whereas those installation rites which the Fourth Gospel has in common with the Synoptics—proclamation after a sign, descent of the Spirit and riding on an ass—appear to come from a general stock of notions concerning installation rather than from the particular narrative of Saul, those peculiar to the Fourth Gospel—recognition one day after the announcement and presentation by "Behold" and so on—are more specifically reminiscent of the latter.

After all, Saul was the first king of Israel and is mentioned as such—not merely as of the tribe of Benjamin—even in Paul's brief historical survey.[16] Moreover, there is a school of Rabbis which explains away any discreditable actions he committed and makes of him an ideal king. Paul was not influenced by it—for him, God "removed" Saul[17]—but John may have been. Once we think of Saul as an ideal king, the whole relationship between the Baptist and Jesus in the Fourth Gospel becomes comparable to that between Samuel and Saul.

C. JESUS'S FLIGHT FROM KINGSHIP

One detail not listed by Patai deserves attention. John tells us that Jesus, when the people "would come and take him by force that they might make him king, departed again into the mountain himself alone."[18] Saul, about to be acclaimed as king, hid and had to be fetched.[19]

In Saul's case, the hiding had been a formal act belonging to the established pattern of coronation.[20] This original significance, however, was no longer understood in New Testament times—though, curiously, the idea of the Messiah hiding until his appearance is common. Of Saul's hiding, the Rabbis invariably say—even those who do not generally idealize him—that it was due to his humility. The incident is one of the

[14] John 1:29, 33, 43. Maybe 2:1 also ought to be understood as one day after 1:43, "the third day" signifying the third day after 1:29.

[15] 1 Sam 9:19 ff.

[16] Acts 13:21.

[17] Acts 13:22.

[18] John 6:15.

[19] 1 Sam 10:21 ff.

[20] Patai, *op. cit.*, 178 f.

great proofs that "he who flies from rulership, rulership will pursue him."[21] Josephus has four paragraphs about it, taking the same line.[22] Whether the Jewish interpretation was influenced by Greek philosophy—Plato held that the man best fitted to govern would not covet the office—may be left undecided.

If the Fourth Gospel alludes to Saul, it must be in the Rabbinic sense. It may not be superfluous to add that this would not affect the question of historicity; there is no reason why John should not depict a true occurrence in language connecting it with an earlier one which, in his view, throws light upon it.

The Sinaiticus is interesting. It reads "the people would take him by force and proclaim him king," *καὶ ἀναδεικνύναι*, instead of "the people would take him by force in order that they might make him king," *ἵνα ποιήσωσιν*, thus more closely approaching the formal language of coronation. It also reads (this time with some support from versions) "Jesus flees," φεύγει, instead of "Jesus departed," ἀνεχώρησεν, thus more directly expressing the idea of flying from rulership.

The upshot seems to be that, while Saul does not figure as a Messianic type in the Synoptics, there is some evidence, however inconclusive, that he does in John.

[21] *Tanhuma* on Lev 1:1. This attitude was far from universally shared. An old Midrash represents Alexander as asking the Elders of the South how a man might become liked by his fellows. They reply: "Let him hate kingship and dominion." But he retorts: "Let him love kingship and dominion and do good to the creatures" (*b. Tam.* 32a.)

[22] *Ant.* 6.4.5.62 ff.

Elijah

Of Elijah we do know that speculations concerning him were present in the minds of those who witnessed or wrote about the events described in the New Testament. They may account for two incidents not so far associated with him: the way in which Jesus is acclaimed on entering Jerusalem, and the rending of the veil of the temple.

A. "Blessed is He that Cometh in the Name of the Lord"

As Jesus is about to enter Jerusalem, the multitude, according to Mark, greets him by a quotation from Psalm 118: "Hosanna; Blessed is he that cometh in the name of the Lord." They also shout: "Blessed is the kingdom of our father David" and so on, but this is clearly Mark's, or his source's, interpretation of the greeting. Matthew understands it in the same way, putting "Hosanna to the son of David; Blessed is he that cometh," etc. Luke refers not to David but to the king in general; and he omits "Hosanna." The multitude cries: "Blessed is the king that cometh in the name of the Lord." John, finally, introduces "the king of Israel": "Blessed is the king of Israel that cometh in the name of the Lord."[1] The question is whether the evangelists are justified in ascribing a Messianic meaning to the greeting, and if so, whether they have given it the right kind of Messianic meaning.

It has long been seen that, in the view of some Rabbis, the verse "Blessed is he" and so on, together with a few that precede it and a few that follow it in the Psalm, was composed when David became king,[2] and will be recited again when the Messiah appears.[3] Unfortunately, though this exegesis definitely existed by the first half of the 3rd cent., we cannot say whether it goes back to the 1st. One point, however, is suggestive. The Rabbis put several lines, not only "Blessed is he" etc., into the mouth of the public welcoming David or the Messiah. For example, when the Messiah appears, the people inside Jerusalem will say, "O Lord, save, I beseech thee" ("O Lord, Hosanna"), those outside, "O Lord, send prosperity," those inside, "Blessed is he that cometh in the name of the Lord," those outside, "We bless you of the house of the Lord," and so they will complete the Psalm.[4] The crowd welcoming Jesus also combines "Save, I beseech thee" and "Blessed is he," two verses at least. Luke, it is true, omits "Hosanna." But its genuineness cannot be doubted. Very likely he considered that it would be unintelligible to Greek readers.

[1] Ps 118:26; Mark 11:9 f.; Matt 21:9; Luke 19:38; John 12:13.

[2] *Targum* Ps 118:22 ff.; *b. Pes.* 119a; see Strack-B., vol. 1 (1922), 876, 849 f.

[3] *Midrash Psalms* on 118:24; Strack-B., vol. 1, 850.

[4] Ps 118:25 ff., *Midrash Psalms* on 118:24.

Let us look at another piece of evidence, from the service at the circumcision of a Jewish boy. All over the world, it begins by the boy being brought into a room where the participants in the service are already assembled, and the latter exclaiming: "Blessed is he that cometh," *barukh habba'*. The child is then placed on a chair called "the throne of Elijah." From this moment, variations occur. In some rites, he is circumcised on this chair, in others he is taken to another, ordinary chair for the circumcision.

The usual explanation of "the throne of Elijah" is that, for the Rabbis, Elijah is the "messenger of the covenant" mentioned in Malachi[5] and as such invisibly supervises every circumcision, every initiation into the covenant of Abraham; therefore a seat must be provided for him. It is, however, possible that, at its inception, the custom symbolized the hope that the child himself would prove to be Elijah: so he must be enthroned, just in case. Rab (of the first half of the 3rd cent. A.D.) interpreted the Psalmist's warning "touch not mine anointed" as directed against unkindness to school-children.[6] The "cup of Elijah" which Jews put on the table on Passover eve may be compared, though, admittedly, it seems to be very much later than "the throne." Some Passover eve, Elijah will arrive. Hence it is necessary every year to have a cup ready for his use.

The differences in rites as to the place of the child during the actual circumcision may reflect a change in interpretation. That rite according to which the boy remains on "the throne of Elijah" may be the older, dating from the period when he was thought of as, conceivably, Elijah. The other rite, according to which he is circumcised on an ordinary chair, may have grown up when this identification of a child with Elijah fell into disfavour—anti-Christian motives would account for this—and when the original idea was replaced by that of Elijah watching the ceremony as an invisible angel.

If, in the New Testament age, some Messianic symbolism was applied to any male child—whether or not it took just this form of "the throne of Elijah"—it becomes far easier to fit the narratives of the adoration of the Magi or the shepherds into a Jewish milieu. The same is true of the miracle which Luke says happened at the circumcision of the Baptist, whom the gospel, in its present form at least, does clearly assimilate to Elijah.

Be this as it may, certain it is that, at the opening of a service at circumcision, Elijah is greeted by "Blessed is he that cometh." The words may be addressed to the angel Elijah accompanying the boy or to the boy *qua* Elijah: in either case are they addressed to Elijah. Once again, however, the question of date is complicated. We cannot trace the greeting beyond medieval collections of Jewish observances.[7] This does not, of course, rule out its existence long before. The authors of those collections tell us that they made them because otherwise ancient traditions would be forgotten. As Malachi announces of the messenger of the covenant that "Behold, he shall come, saith the Lord of hosts," it must have been natural for the Rabbis to connect with him—i.e. with Elijah, the same person in their eyes—the verse "Blessed is he that cometh in the name of the Lord." In

[5] Mal 3:1.

[6] *b. Shab.* 119 b; see Ps 105:15.

[7] Ibn Yarhi, the Tanya, Abudarham. Possibly *P. de R. El.* may be added. In this work (29 at the end), Mal 3:1, "Behold, he shall come," is associated with "the throne of Elijah": an indication, perhaps, that at any rate by this time the greeting "Blessed is he that cometh" was usual in the service at circumcision.

other words, quite apart from the service at circumcision, this was as appropriate a greeting for Elijah as for the Messiah himself or other figures that were "to come." Elijah, it will be recalled, is introduced as "the coming one" in several synoptic pericopes.[8]

On balance, the evidence favours the assumption that the greeting of Jesus by the multitude was of a Messianic character. There is agreement on this point between all evangelists. It is underlined by the prediction Jesus utters according to Matthew and Luke,[9] "Ye shall not see me till ye shall say, Blessed is he that cometh in the name of the Lord"—"Hosanna" is here not included. And several lines of Rabbinic testimony converge to support this interpretation. Exactly which Messianic figure, however, the crowd had in mind is far more dubious. It may have been the son of David, the king or the king of Israel: we need not go into the relation beween these. But it may also have been Elijah.

B. The Veil of the Temple

Mark tells us that, on Jesus's death, "the veil of the temple was rent in twain from the top to the bottom."[10] Codex Bezae and the Itala are even more explicit: "it was rent in two parts," not just "in twain."

Matthew and Luke both put the miracle together with others said to have occurred, the former with an earthquake and opening of graves, the latter with an eclipse of the sun.[11] This, however, throws little light on the specific meaning of the event. As Luke pairs it off with the eclipse, the result is that, in his account, the rending of the veil precedes Jesus's death. But in looking for the original significance, we must start from Matthew and Mark, where it follows it. In modern literature, a good many interpretations are to be found, none of them satisfactory. The latest writer holds that the notice expresses an early *theologoumenon* of the Church, concerning the removal through Jesus's death of obstacles in the way to God.[12]

Most probably, we ought to proceed from the action of Elisha when Elijah ascended into heaven: "And Elisha saw it and he cried, My father, my father, the chariot of Israel and the horsemen thereof. And he took hold of his clothes and rent them in two pieces."[13] In Rabbinic times, there were prescribed occasions on which a man had to rend his garment. In this connection, the incident quoted acquired particular importance. The Rabbis noted the emphatic "he rent his clothes in two pieces" instead of a plain "he rent his clothes"; and, in their usual manner, based on it the teaching that, in certain cases, the two parts into which you have rent your garment may never be sewn together again. The cases are the death of your father, your mother, your teacher of

[8] Matt 11:14, 17:10 ff.; Mark 9:11 ff., maybe also Matt 27:49; Mark 15:36. As a rule, modern editors and commentators quote only Mal 3:23 as Old Testament basis. But 3:1, which alone uses the verb "to come," is absolutely necessary as well. The Elijah who "shall first come and restore all things" derives from the messenger who "shall prepare the way before me, behold he shall come."

[9] Matt 23:39; Luke 13:35.

[10] Mark 15:38.

[11] Matt 27:51 ff.; Luke 23:44 f.

[12] Lindeskog, *Coniectanea Neotestamentica* II (1948), 132 ff.

[13] 2 Kgs 2:12.

Torah, the Patriarch (*Nasi*) or the Father of the Court (*Abh-beth-din*), the receipt of terrible news, the utterance of a blasphemy by someone in your presence, the burning of a Scroll of Law and, finally, the destruction of Judaean cities, the temple or Jerusalem.[14]

When we consider the stress laid in the New Testament on the complete splitting of the curtain into two—or, according to some readings, two parts—from top to bottom, it is safe to find here an allusion to the rite practised as a sign of deepest sorrow. We need not decide whether the death of Jesus is likened to that of a teacher of Torah or to the destruction of the temple. Either or both comparisons may play some part, as also the idea that those responsible for the crucifixion are the real blasphemers, and not Jesus at whose words the High Priest had rent his clothes.[15] It may be noted that Luke, who places the rending of the veil before Jesus's death, thus completely obscuring its original import, omits this gesture by the High Priest.[16] Presumably, he did not think his readers would understand the rite.

The question whether the miracle did in fact happen is not here relevant. We are concerned only with the manner of its representation, which connects it with a mourning rite—and, indeed, with the prototype, in Rabbinic eyes, of this rite, the action of Elisha on Elijah's ascension. It is difficult not to believe that this episode was in the mind of the author of the notice about the veil of the temple.

Support is furnished by the passages concerning the assumption of Jesus at the close of the gospels of Mark and Luke and at the beginning of Acts.[17] True, the authors may no longer be conscious of a connection with the end of Elijah. But at some stage of the tradition such a connection no doubt existed. We need only compare the Lukan "he was parted from them and carried up to heaven" with the description in the Old Testament, "they parted them both asunder and Elijah went up into heaven." The incident of the veil may be regarded as, in a way, adumbrating these references to the assumption.

Among the various explanations in early Christian literature, there is one—to be found in a work of Jewish-Christian provenance[18]—which at least sees in the miracle a sign of mourning, though not for Jesus's death but for the approaching end of the temple. Another point worth a mention is that the word *pargodh*, which in the Targum stands for the curtain separating the holy of holies from the outer chamber, may also denote a tunic. If the story originated in Aramaic-speaking circles, the extension of the custom of rending one's garment to the veil of the temple—the tunic of the temple—must have been particularly easy.

So far we are on safe ground. May we go further? It is tempting to suggest that, in Matthew and Mark, the notice concerning the veil together with some verses preceding and following it forms a much more closely knit pericope than has hitherto been real-

[14] *b. M. Kat.* 25b f.; *m. Sanh.* 7:5 (on blasphemy in particular).

[15] Matt 26:64 f.; Mark 14:62 f.

[16] Luke 22:67 ff.

[17] Mark 16:19; Luke 24:51; Acts 1:2.

[18] Clem. Rec. 1:41: "*lamentans excidium loco imminens* ["lamenting the imminent destruction destined for the place"]."

ized.[19] As Jesus cries out, "*Eli, Eli, lama sabachthani,*" some bystanders think he is summoning Elijah[20] and mockingly remark, "Let us see whether Elijah will come to save him." After this, the rending in two of the veil of the temple, reminiscent as it is of what Elisha did when his master was translated, may well be intended as an answer to the mockery: here is Elijah himself, or one that is greater.

Even the centurion's confession[21] may correspond to Elisha's cry, "My father, my father, the chariot of Israel and the horsemen thereof." In the Targum, "my father" is changed into "my Rabbi," no doubt in deference to the view, recurring in Matthew, that, as a title, "my father" is not ordinarily suitable for human beings.[22] The rest is paraphrased by "who was better for Israel by his prayer than chariots and horsemen."[23]

That the distinction was transferable to other prophets and teachers may be seen from the way king Joash addresses Elisha himself on his last sick bed,[24] "O my father, my father, the chariot of Israel and the horsemen thereof"; and, for Rabbinic times, from the Aramaic version of Chronicles,[25] which speaks of "Moses, the teacher of Israel, whose merit was better for them than horsemen and chariots," and from the story of the last moments of Eliezer ben Hyrcanus (beginning of the 2nd cent. A.D.), on whose death his old antagonist Joshua ben Hananiah quoted the words of Elisha.[26] The centurion's confession is rather different in substance, but its position at least may owe something to the old precedent.

[19] Matt 27:46–54; Mark 15:34–9.

[20] The misunderstanding was possible because in New Testament times *'eli* was not the only form for "my God": the ancient form *'eliya* had not yet died out and was apparently used by Jesus. See Guillaume, "Matthew XXVII, 46 in the Light of the Dead Sea Scroll of Isaiah," *PEQ* (1951), 78 ff.

[21] Matt 27:54; Mark 15:39; Luke 23:47.

[22] Matt 23:9; see Strack-B., vol. 1 (1922), 919.

[23] Cp. Xenophanes, as reported by Athenaeus (*Deipn.* 10.414a f.): "My wisdom is better [for the city] than the strength of men and horses."

[24] 2 Kgs 13:14.

[25] 1 Chr 2:55.

[26] *y. Shab.* 5b ("my Rabbi"); *b. Sanh.* 68a ("my father").

Ruth and Boaz

We now go on to Ruth and Boaz. Their influence has not so far been recognized at all. Yet it would be surprising if a couple so prominent among the ancestry of the Messiah, and possessing so many features capable of a Messianic interpretation, had been absolutely neglected by the authors of the New Testament. As a matter of fact, allusions can be shown to occur in two pericopes at least: the Lukan narrative of the annunciation, and the narrative of the feeding of the multitude preserved in all four gospels.

A. The Annunciation

In the narrative of the annunciation, Mary is made to resemble Ruth.

1. *"To overshadow"*

To substantiate this proposition, it is necessary to find out about the antecedents of the puzzling term ἐπισκιάζω, "to overshadow." It is used on three occasions: once, in Acts,[1] where the sick hope for a cure if "the shadow of Peter overshadows them," another time, by all three Synoptics, in the narrative of the transfiguration, of a cloud which "overshadows" some disciples and out of which a voice proclaims Jesus "my beloved son,"[2] and finally by Luke, in the narrative of the annunciation, of the power of the Highest that is to "overshadow" Mary so that she will bear a son, Jesus.[3]

It is an exact equivalent of Hebrew *ṣalal* or Aramaic *ṭallel*, which, while literally denoting "to overshadow," is very often applied to the descent on a person or object of the divine presence, the Shekhinah. The Hebrew noun *ṣel* or the Aramaic *ṭelal* signifies "shadow" both in the literal sense and in the figurative of "shelter." In addition, the verb can mean "to cover," and the noun "a cover," "a roof," "a tabernacle" or "a booth." Other Aramaic nouns of the same root, *meṭalela'* and *meṭalalta'*, are indeed exclusively used as designating "a cover" or "a booth."

In the Old Testament, *ṣalal* occurs only in two obscure passages; the LXX omits it in the one,[4] and renders it by καθίστημι, "to become quiet," in the other.[5] However, the LXX seems to assume the verb in two further texts, translating it by σκιάζω, "to

[1] Acts 5:15.
[2] Matt 17:5; Mark 9:7; Luke 9:34.
[3] Luke 1:35.
[4] Ezek 31:3 (Hiphil).
[5] Neh 13:19.

shade";[6] and Theodotion manifestly assumes it in yet another, of some theological significance, and translates it by ἐπισκιάζω, "to overshadow"—we shall have to come back to this one.[7] Symmachus employs the verb ἐπισκιάζω in a passage where the Hebrew has the noun *ṣel*, "shade."[8] As for this noun *ṣel*, the LXX normally translates it by σκιά where the notion of "shadow" predominates, and by σκέπη where that of "shelter" predominates.

So much for the Hebrew *ṣalal*. The Aramaic *ṭallel* is very common in the Aramaic versions of the Old Testament, the Targumim, and we shall give a number of typical illustrations presently. In the original text it is to be met with twice. Shallun built a gate and "covered it," "made a roof over it," LXX στεγάζω;[9] and under the tree of which Nebuchadnezzar dreamt, the beasts "sought shadow" (the verb here is in the *Aphel*, *'aṭlel*), LXX σκιάζω, Theodotion κατασκηνόω.[10]

As we propose to show, the use of ἐπισκιάζω in the New Testament can be appreciated only if we proceed from the Semitic equivalent, *ṣalal* or *ṭallel*. Why has this never been done? Two other explanations have stood in the way.

Some scholars hold that the idea in the narrative of the annunciation is the same as in a discourse by Philo,[11] where he gives an allegorical comment on the verse from Genesis:[12] "After that, the sons of God came in unto the daughters of men, and they bare children to them." This means, Philo says, the fellows of darkness, i.e. lies, mating with man's inferior passions and begetting vices; which can only happen "after that," i.e. after the pure rays of reason have ceased to shine and the light of understanding is "overshadowed." However, any connection with Luke is out of the question. No conceivable bridge leads from this application of the verb, in the sense of "to obscure," "to darken," "to keep from light," to the message "the power of the Highest shall overshadow thee."

A second group of scholars argues in this way. In the LXX, ἐπισκιάζω three times represents *sakhakh*, "to cover,"[13] and once *shakhan*, "to dwell."[14] The latter text, referring to the cloud which "abode" on the tabernacle, is clearly relevant to both the transfiguration and the annunciation. Hence (they argue) ἐπισκιάζω in these narratives equals *shakhan*.

[6] 2 Sam 20:6, Hebrew *wehiṣṣil*, of *naṣal*, "and he will escape," a variant of LXX καὶ σκιάσει, "and he will shade"; Jonah 4:6, Hebrew *lehaṣṣil lo*, again of *naṣal*, " to deliver him," LXX τοῦ σκιάξειν αὐτῷ, "to shade him."

[7] Num 11:25, *wayya'ṣel*, really "and he put aside," of *'aṣal*, but looking little different from a Hiphil of *ṣalal*.

[8] Hos 4:13.

[9] Neh 3:15.

[10] Dan 4:9.

[11] *Deus* 1.3.

[12] Gen 6:4.

[13] Ps 91:4 (Hiphil), 140:8; Prov 18:11 (Hiphil). The case of Prov 18:11 is very doubtful. If ἐπισκιάζω is intended as a rendering of *maśkith*, the LXX makes a mistake: this Hebrew noun really derives, not from *sakhakh*, but from *śakha*, and it signifies "imagination." It may, however, be δόξα by which the LXX means to render *maśkith*. If so, ἐπισκιάζω is intended as a rendering of *ḥoma*, "wall," laxly taken in the sense of "protective cover."

[14] Exod 40:35.

But this is a palpable *non sequitur.* The fact that the LXX in one case renders "to dwell" by "to overshadow" does not entitle us generally to identify "to overshadow" with "to dwell." The verb "to dwell," *shakhan,* occurs more than a hundred times and is nowhere else translated by "to overshadow." Of the three texts where "to overshadow" stands for "to cover," *sakhakh,* two are just as relevant as that where it stands for "to dwell," namely: "The Lord shall cover thee with his feathers," and "O Lord, thou hast covered my head in the day of battle."[15] So, obviously, is the passage where Theodotion puts ἐπισκιάζω for what he takes to be *ṣalal*: "The Lord overshadowed them [the elders of the people] with his [Moses's] spirit."[16]

We shall try to indicate the special reasons why the LXX in the instances referred to deems "to overshadow" a suitable rendering of "to dwell" or "to cover." For the moment, it may suffice to remark that the range of *ṣalal* or *ṭallel* is more than wide enough to account for these applications. At any rate, in searching for the Hebrew and Aramaic background of ἐπισκιάζω in the New Testament, the proper course surely is to start from the centre, i.e. from the verbs for "to overshadow," and not from peripheral uses, i.e. from a verb primarily denoting something quite different. As far as Luke is concerned, it is all the more dangerous to rob ἐπισκιάζω of its etymological meaning as in Acts, in the notice about the healings performed by Peter, it is undeniably employed in the most literal sense.

2. *The Transfiguration*

We need not enlarge on this passage from Acts, except to repeat that when we are told of "Peter's shadow overshadowing the sick," it is impossible to assume any other meaning than that of *ṣalal* or *ṭallel.*[17]

In the narrative of the transfiguration, Peter proposes to build three booths, one for Jesus, one for Moses and one for Elijah. Probably he is thinking of the role of the booth on the Feast of Booths, namely, as symbolizing God's immediate guidance and protection. In any case, it is in reply to his proposal that a cloud "overshadows" them.

To illustrate the connotations of the term in this context, it may be observed that the Aramaic for "Feast of Booths" is "Feast of *meṭalayya'* " "*Feast of Covers*"—of the root *ṭallel*, "to overshadow."[18] The Aramaic version of the Biblical section in which this Feast is instituted shows how closely associated are the ideas of the festal booth and the divine presence in a cloud. The injunction "Ye shall dwell in booths seven days" is translated by "Ye shall dwell in *meṭalayya'* seven days,"[19] but in the next verse, for "that your generations may know that I made the children of Israel to dwell in booths when I brought them out of Egypt," the Targum puts "to dwell in the *meṭalletha'* of clouds,"[20] or even "to dwell in the *meṭalletha'* of clouds of glory."[21]

[15] Ps 91:4, 140:8.

[16] Num 11:25.

[17] A suggestion regarding this mode of healing will be made below, 599 under The Laying on of Hands.

[18] *Targum* Lev 23:34 Onk and Jer., Gen 35:14 Jer., Num 29:12, 17, 20 f. Jer., Zech 14:16 ff.

[19] Lev 23:42 Onk; *meṭalalta'* Jer.

[20] Onk.

[21] Jer.

Similarly, where the Bible says "And they took their jouney from Succoth," R. Akiba regards "Succoth" not as a place-name but as standing for "booths" in the sense of "clouds of glory."[22] Several times the Hebrew *sukka*, "booth," is rendered by *ṭelal*, "shadow" or "booth"; as in the verse from Job,[23] "Can any understand the spreadings of the clouds or the noise of his tabernacle," or that from Psalms,[24] "In time of trouble he shall hide me in his pavilion." Isaiah's prophecy,[25] "And the Lord will create upon Zion a cloud of smoke, and there shall be a booth, *sukka*, for a shadow, *ṣel*, in daytime," in the Targum appears as "And the Lord will create upon Zion a cloud of glory which will overshadow it, *'aṭṭel*, and over Jerusalem there will be a booth, *meṭalletha'*, of clouds to overshadow it, *'aṭlel*." It is noteworthy that, under Rabbinic law, in a booth which was to serve on the Feast of Booths, the shaded part had to be larger than the unshaded.[26]

However, quite a few texts are of interest though there is no mention of a booth. During their wanderings in the desert, the Lord's cloud, we learn, "standeth over the people"; according to the Targum, it "overshadows them," *'aṭṭel*.[27] "The cloud of the Lord was upon the tabernacle by day"; according to the Targum, "the cloud of the glory of the Lord overshadowed it," *'aṭlel*.[28] "The cherubim were covering the mercy seat with their wings"; according to the Targum, "they were overshadowing it," *ṭallel*.[29] "The Lord is thy shade," Hebrew *ṣel*, in the Targum becomes "The Lord overshadows thee," *ṭallel*.[30] "Hide me under the shadow of thy wings," *ṣel*, becomes "under the shadow of thy Shekhinah," *ṭelal*.[31] "He shall abide under the shadow of the Almighty," *ṣel*, becomes "in the shadow of clouds of glory," *ṭelal*.[32] "He shall cover thee, *sakhakh,* with his feathers, *'ebhra,* and under his wings, *kanaph,* shalt thou trust," becomes "He shall overshadow thee, *ṭallel*, with the shadow, *ṭelal*, of his Shekhinah and under the shadow, *ṭelal,* of his glory shalt thou trust."[33] "Ye, the wings of a dove" becomes "Ye, the congregation of Israel, which resembles a dove, overshadowed by clouds of glory," *'iṭṭallel*.[34]

Two more uses are remarkable. First, the Aramaic equivalent of the Hebrew phrase "to come under the wings of the Shekhinah," which signifies "to be converted to Judaism," is "to come under the *ṭelal*—cover, shadow—of the Shekhinah."[35] Secondly, we come across in the Targum the expression "to be overshadowed, *'iṭṭallel*, by the spir-

[22] *Mek.* on Exod 13:20.

[23] Job 36:29.

[24] Ps 27:5.

[25] Isa 4:5 f.

[26] *m. Sukk.* 1:1, Lev 23:42 in Jer.

[27] Num 14:14 Onk; it "is a shadow over them," *maṭlul*, Jer., unless the reading *maṭlel* is correct, in which case the meaning is the same as in Onk.

[28] Exod 40:38 Jer.

[29] Exod 25:20, 37:9 Jer.; *'aṭlel* Onk.

[30] Ps 121:5.

[31] Ps 17:8.

[32] Ps 91:1.

[33] Ps 91:4.

[34] Ps 68:14.

[35] Ruth 2:12; Deut 23:16 Jer.

it of prophecy."[36] We have already adverted to a parallel in Theodotion, who uses ἐπισκιάζω of God's "overshadowing" the elders with the spirit of Moses.[37]

Against the background of these quotations, the employment of "to overshadow" in the narrative of the transfiguration appears perfectly natural. Moreover, we can now understand why, in the LXX, ἐπισκιάζω occasionally does service for a Hebrew word the literal meaning of which is by no means the same. Where the Shekhinah was concerned, the verb "to overshadow" was evidently highly popular. That was so not only because it evoked the idea of "the cloud of the Lord," but also because it was respectful and less crudely physical than other terms.

In one text,[38] ἐπισκιάζω, replaces *shakhan*, "to dwell." So, in the Targum, we have seen, *ṭallel* may replace *'amadh*, "to stand,"[39] or be inserted where the Hebrew is without any verb, simply speaking of "the cloud on the tabernacle."[40] In three texts, ἐπισκιάζω is put instead of *sakhakh*, "to cover." Two of them are concerned with the coming down of the Shekhinah to help: "The Lord shall cover thee with his feathers," and "O Lord, thou hast covered my head in the day of battle." In both, the Targum also uses *ṭallel*, "to overshadow,"[41] as it does in another passage where the Hebrew has *sakhakh*: "The cherubum were covering the mercy seat with their wings."[42] It should be remembered that *sukka*, "booth," is connected with *sakhakh*. The third case of ἐπισκιάζω for *sakhakh* is of a different sort: "The rich man's wealth is his strong city, and his opinion of it greatly overshadows."[43] Here ἐπισκιάζω means "to cover," "to form a protective roof." We have already adduced an original Old Testament text where *ṭallel* has this sense.[44] In the Targum, this application of the verb is frequent;[45] and we may again recall the noun *ṭelal*, or others of the same root, in the sense of "booth," *sukka*. Comparable Hebrew phrases are "the shadow, *ṣel*, of my roof," LXX σκέπη,[46] and—quite near the rich man's wealth the opinion of which "overshadows"—"in the cover, *ṣel*, of wisdom, and in the cover, *ṣel*, of money," LXX σκιά.[47]

3. *The Annunciation*

Let us proceed to the annunciation. A fair number of the passages already cited are here pertinent too: all those referring to a descent of the Shekhinah in a general sense, and more particularly, that containing the notion of "being overshadowed by the spirit

[36] 1 Chr 2:55, connecting *śukhathim* with *sakhakh*, "to cover."

[37] Num 11:25.

[38] Exod 40:35.

[39] Num 14:14.

[40] Exod 40:38. 1 Chr 2:55 also belongs here: the Targum derives *śukhathim* from *sakhakh* and puts *'iṭṭallel*, "to be overshadowed by the spirit of prophecy."

[41] Pss 91:4, 140:8.

[42] Exod 25:20, 37:9.

[43] Prov 18:11. Our argument needs little modification if ἐπισκιάζω is intended as representing, not *maśkith*, but *ḥoma*.

[44] Neh 3:15, LXX στεγάζω.

[45] E.g. Exod 36:19 Jer.; 1 Kgs 6:9.

[46] Gen 19:8.

[47] Eccl 7:12.

of prophecy." Gabriel says to Mary: "The Holy Spirit shall come upon thee and the power of the Highest shall overshadow thee." The Spirit and the Shekhinah are here descending at the same time.

There is, however, one text which seems to be specifically responsible for the terminology in question, Ruth's request to Boaz:[48] "I am Ruth thine handmaid; spread therefore thy wing over thine handmaid, for thou art a redeemer."

In Rabbinic literature, Ruth is celebrated both as representative of the true proselyte and as an ancestress of David and the Messiah. Her life is often interpreted as prefiguring Messianic events, and where this is done, Boaz sometimes stands for God himself, or at least speaks and acts as God himself would. Thus his words, "Hearest thou not, my daughter, go not to glean in another field, neither go from hence but abide here by my maidens,"[49] are declared to mean: "Hearest thou not, thou shalt have no other gods before me,[50] this is my God and I will praise him,[51] abide here by my righteous ones."[52]

Further examples will be adduced in discussing the narrative of the feeding of the multitude. At this point, we may be content with observing that an allusion in the narrative of the annunciation to the scene between Ruth and Boaz ought to cause no surprise.

If we turn to the Rabbinic exegesis of Ruth's request, it must be borne in mind that, at this moment, she is not yet married to Boaz. For a man like Goethe, this was only in keeping with the natural, rustic character of the Book of Ruth, in his judgment the sweetest idyll composed in antiquity. But the Rabbis could not see it in this light. They took it for granted that the situation, however awkward it might look at first sight, was reconcilable with the most refined notions of morality. This aspect is indeed accentuated in the case of Mary, who was a virgin. There was an even wider discrepancy between appearances and the truth, and we should only expect one or the other of those who narrated the story to have been conscious of the Old Testament parallel.

Now the Rabbis solve the problem by proving that Ruth's conduct, far from being immodest, is ideal; and, significantly, it is the phrase, "Spread thy wings over thine handmaid," LXX περιβαλεῖς τὸ πτερύγιόν σου ἐπὶ τὴν δούλην σου, on which they dwell in this connection. It is considered to reveal exceptional chastity. Samuel ben Nahman, of the 3rd cent. A.D., contrasts it with Potiphar's wife's shameless "Lie with me."[53] An anonymous Midrash goes as far as to conclude from it that Ruth was the purest of all women. When we add to this the opportunity presented to Rabbinic typologists by the end of the sentence, "for thou art a redeemer," it is obvious that here was a most suitable expression for the New Testament narrative.

Perhaps we should here also draw attention to the Rabbinic legend,[54] transmitted by Resh Lakish, 3rd cent., and resting on the circumstantial report "So Boaz took Ruth,

[48] Ruth 3:9.

[49] Ruth 2:8.

[50] Exod 20:3.

[51] Exod 15:2.

[52] That "maidens" equals "righteous ones" is deduced from Job 40:29; see *Ruth Rabba* on 2:8.

[53] *Gen. Rab.* on 39:7. In *Ruth Rabba* on 3:9, the idea is attributed to R. Berechiah. Clearly, Berechiah had it from Helbo, who was Samuel b. Nahman's pupil.

[54] *Ruth Rabba* on 4:13.

and she was his wife" instead of either "So Boaz took Ruth" or "So she was his wife," that when Ruth married, she—like Sarah and Rebekkah—had no womb, and that God specially prepared her so that she could have a child. No doubt this legend is only a remnant of a vast amount of speculation about the phrase in question and others in its immediate neighbourhood, such as "the seed which the Lord shall give thee [Boaz] of this young woman"[55] or "the Lord gave her [Ruth] conception." The latter expression is certainly peculiar. Yet the Midrash Rabba, in its present form, contains not a single observation on it. Considering the profusion of Rabbinic comments on phrases far less unusual, this can only mean that such observations as existed were deemed unsuitable by the time the Midrash Rabba was redacted. They had become unsuitable owing to the use Christianity had made of these ideas.

But how, it may be asked, did "to spread one's wing over a person" become "to overshadow"? One factor may have been that the cloak worn by pious or scholarly men, and distinguished by "wings," borders, specially made in accordance with the law concerning the showfringes,[56] was called *ṭallith,* from the root *ṭelal*, "shadow." Now the expression "to spread the *ṭallith* over a woman" is used in Rabbinic literature[57] as a refined alternative for "to cohabit with a woman." We may safely assume that it was coined under the influence of two Old Testament passages: one from Ezekiel,[58] where God reminds Jerusalem how "Thy time was the time of love, and I spread my wing over thee," and the other Ruth's request "Spread thy wing." It follows that some Rabbis must have paraphrased this request by "Spread thy *ṭallith*"—which comes very near "Overshadow."

Another point, however, seems even more important. In the verse where Boaz addresses Ruth as having come "under the wings of God,"[59] the Aramaic version translates "under the *ṭelal*—cover, shadow—of the Shekhinah of his glory." Even the Hebrew comments of the Rabbis paraphrase "under the shadow—*ṣel*—of God"; and R. Abin, of the early 4th cent., compares a line from Psalms, "The children of men put their trust under the shadow—*ṣel*—of thy wings."[60]

No doubt there were Aramaic versions translating "Spread thy wing" by "Spread the shadow of thy wing" or simply "Overshadow." Several of the texts quoted earlier on may be compared, for instance: Hebrew, "He shall cover thee with his feathers, and under his wings shalt thou trust," Targum, "He shall overshadow thee with the shadow of his Shekhinah, and under the shadow of his glory shalt thou trust."[61] But even if there were no such versions, the rendering "Spread the shadow of thy wing" or "Overshadow" was the appropriate one as soon as the scene was transferred to a higher sphere, of the kind to be found in Luke. Quite possibly, the mention of "the power" of God, the δύναμις, is

[55] This may at one time have been brought together with Seth, "another seed instead of Abel," as the Messiah's ancestor; see *Gen. Rab.* on 4:25, and below, 677, A Generic Singular.

[56] Num 15:37 ff.

[57] *b. Kidd.* 18b; cf. *Mek.* on Exod 21:8.

[58] Ezek 16:8.

[59] Ruth 2:12.

[60] Ps 36:7; see *Ruth Rabba* on 2:12.

[61] Ps 91:4.

also connected with this elevation to a higher sphere. The Rabbis, where they wish to avoid bluntness, resort to euphemisms like "to lay one's power (*reshuth*) over a woman."[62]

To be sure, the Targum as we have it before us contains a different rendering. But the way it deals with the text speaks in favour of rather than against our thesis. It avoids not only the elevated "Spread the shadow of thy wing," but also the literal "Spread thy wing." What it puts is "Mayst thou take me to wife." For this astonishing introduction of homely—though certainly not shameless—speech there must be a reason. It is in conflict both with the original Hebrew and with all those Rabbinic references to the particular dignity of Ruth's mode of expression.[63]

The explanation is that the version before us is designed to counter some dangerous interpretation of the text, an old one, older than the Targum—the overshadowing by God. It does not matter whether it is directed against a Jewish school or—more likely—against the Lukan narrative itself. In either case it supports the view that the language of the latter is influenced by this passage from Ruth. For if it is directed against a Jewish school, that is the one which has left traces in Luke; and if it is directed against the narrative itself, it is evidence that the public had no difficulty in detecting the allusion to Ruth.

If the original author of the narrative was familiar with Hebrew, he may, indeed, when using "to overshadow," have found an additional attraction in a possible pun: one created in the shadow, *beṣel*, of God might be declared to be created in the image, *beṣelem*, of God.[64] It is not, however, very likely that this pun plays a part, since there is nothing else in the annunciation that would suggest the idea of Jesus as the Second Adam; and the passage from the Book of Ruth is quite sufficient to explain the choice of verb.

It only remains to add that Mary's words, "Behold the handmaid of the Lord,"[65] are still from the same source. "I am Ruth thine handmaid; spread therefore thy wing over thine handmaid," says Ruth to Boaz. This designation of Mary, which has inspired so many wonderful prayers and poems of the Middle Ages, has its ultimate origin in the Book of Ruth.

B. The Feeding of the Multitude

In the narrative of the feeding of the multitude,[66] it is the Messianic, Christian community itself which experiences a miracle foreshadowed in the life of Ruth, while the role of Boaz is now taken over by Jesus. The motif, however, is treated very differently by the Synoptics and John; and it may be best to begin by a general comparison of their versions of the narrative. It will emerge that John has profoundly altered both the form and the substance of the feeding of the multitude as it appears in the Synoptics.

[62] Jer. *Targum* Deut 21:14.

[63] True, the full translation of the Targum is "May thy name be called over thine handmaid and mayst thou take me to wife." But even the first half of this exclamation, based as it is on Isa 4:1, cannot be considered exceptionally refined.

[64] Cp. Gen 1:27.

[65] Luke 1:38.

[66] Matt 14:13 ff., 15:32 ff.; Mark 6:31 ff., 8:1 ff.; Luke 9:10 ff.; John 6:1 ff.

1. *Form*

First, for the question of form. Like them, he starts by putting a transition, "Jesus went over the sea" etc.;[67] the situation, "he saw a great company" etc.,[68] a dialogue introducing the need, the resources and a command of Jesus, "Whence shall we buy bread?" etc., and "Make the men sit down";[69] and the execution of the command, "So the men sat down."[70] But from this point onwards, he goes his own way.

In all the Synoptics, there follow (1) blessing and distribution, and (2) the miracle, namely—leaving out of account variations not here relevant—"They did all eat and were filled and took up of the fragments that remained twelve baskets full."[71] There would be little justification, from the formal point of view, for a threefold division, (1) blessing and distribution, (2) reception of the food, (3) the miracle of the remains. To make such a division would be succumbing to the spell of John, where, as we shall see, it does apply.

In the Synoptics, formally, "They did eat and were filled and took up" constitutes one unit, the miracle. That is to say, we have before us a simple miracle story, telling us how a multitude was feasted—and opulently feasted—with little. It is a necessary feature of a pre-rationing feast that one need not care about every morsel—*"ut reliquiarum sit potius aliquid quam te hinc patiar non satiatum discedere"* ["That there may be something left from the banquet, rather than let you go unsatisfied"] in Cicero's words[72]—and in Rabbinic discussion it is taken for granted that a banqueting-hall is strewn with fragments, small and big.[73] We must also remember that, in those times, pieces of bread served for spoons and forks: in the course of a good meal, many must have been discarded. The same argument, of course, holds good if we think of the fragments not as bits thrown away or dropped, but as a proper part of the meal with which the diners could not cope. Where a meal takes place in the open air, the distinction between food dropped and food not finished up would in any case be fluid.

No doubt even in the Synoptics, this feature of the remains is strongly emphasized, and expressed at greater length than the eating and being filled. We shall come back to this. For the moment, it ought to be realized that a clause does not become a separate item in a narrative pattern by mere emphasis or length. If we had to recount what happened to the poor widow saved by Elisha,[74] it would be: "She sold the oil and paid her debt and she and her children lived of the rest." Surely, that is one unit, though the last member is longer than the rest. It would remain one unit even if we said: "She sold the oil and paid her debt and she and her children lived of the rest until the day when they were gathered unto their people." There is a line in the the Song of Moses: "I will pursue, I will

[67] John 6:1–4. No proper transition in Matt 15:32 ff.; Mark 8:1 ff.

[68] John 6:5.

[69] John 6:5–10.

[70] John 6:10. No special mention of this in Matt 14:19, 15:35; Mark 8:6.

[71] Matt 14:19–21, 15:36–8; Mark 6:41–4, 8:6–9; Luke 9:16 f.

[72] *Top.* 5:25. Cp. also Athenaeus, *Deipn.* 1:13a: "In Homer the feasters do not carry home what is left over but, being sated, leave it behind where the feast took place."

[73] *b. Ber.* 52b.

[74] 2 Kgs 4:7.

overtake, I will divide the spoil."[75] The treatment of this by Handel in *Israel in Egypt* is illuminating. The singer has repeatedly to sing only "I will pursue, I will overtake, I will divide," omitting "the spoil." Then he has to end by an emphatic "I will divide the spoil." Yet the whole clause of three members forms one musical unit throughout.

The Synoptic "They did eat and were filled and took up of the fragments twelve baskets" is no different from either of these cases. However, whether this is admitted or not, one thing seems indisputable: there is in the Synoptics a straightforward, unbroken sequence from eating and being filled to leaving a good deal lying about.

In John, item (1) also is blessing and distribution.[76] But the distribution itself constitutes a preliminary miracle, and thus a preliminary conclusion of the story. Each was given "as much as they would." The supernatural wealth of the host is revealed already at this stage. This is in none of the Synoptics. John's story could perfectly well end here, say, with a remark: "And the people believed in him."

The supreme miracle, however, is yet to come; and it consists, not in a miraculous feast, not in eating and being filled, but exclusively in bread remaining—or probably, if we may anticipate one of our conclusions, in all the bread remaining. The eating and being filled are indeed mentioned, but only incidentally, in subordinate clauses: "when they were filled," and "the fragments which remained unto them that had eaten."[77] It is the least notable details of a story which we are used to seeing dismissed in this fashion: "when they were filled," "unto them that had eaten." In contradistinction to the Synoptics, the gathering of the remains alone is reported in a main clause: "They filled twelve baskets with the fragments which remained."

Moreover, it is brought about by a fresh command of Jesus, to be met with in none of the Synoptics: "He said, Gather up" etc. This command, it may be noted, again contains the key-word "to remain": "Gather up the fragments that remain." The word is not absolutely indispensable here. Further, it is this miracle of the remains which is recognized by the people as the sign of the prophet "that should come into the world."[78] There is no equivalent in the Synoptics.

If we give due weight to the formal position, we shall arrive at this contrast. In the Synoptics, we find (1) blessing and distribution, (2) the miracle, a feasting of many with little, one feature of the feast, the leaving over of ample fragments, being accorded some prominence. In John, we find (1) blessing and preliminary miracle, the plentiful distribution, "as much as they would," (2) a fresh situation, "when they were filled," (3) a fresh command of Jesus, "Gather up," (4) the execution of the command resulting in the culminating miracle, the remains: "Therefore they gathered up, and filled twelve baskets," and (5) recognition of the miracle and inference: "The men, having seen the miracle, said, This is that prophet that should come."

That John is secondary is shown, apart from other considerations some of which will be mentioned later on, by the very form. For one thing, his pattern is highly elaborate compared with the Synoptic. For another, it would have been impossible to refer to

[75] Exod 15:9.
[76] John 6:11.
[77] John 6:12 f.
[78] John 6:14.

the eating and being filled in subordinate clauses, in passing only, had the matter never figured in the main clauses, so that it was gradually taken for granted.

When the story was first told, they must have put it: "And they did all eat, and were filled." They could not then have put it: "And when they were filled," as if it were the most natural thing in the world.[79] The statement that "the Israelites went out of Egypt"[80] must have preceded the hymns depicting the wonders that were done "when Israel went out of Egypt."[81] It is John who deviates from the original form.

Why? What is the purpose of this change? There are two factors.

In the first place, as already remarked, the Synoptics, though keeping the eating, being filled and leaving over in one sequence, do stress the leaving over. Probably they did it because that was the visible, undeniable part of the miracle. There is a vulgar Jewish joke about a Jew who, pressed by a missionary, undertakes to accept half of each Christian tenet; for example, he will believe that Jesus fed a multitude on five loaves, but not that they got enough. Though the joke is modern, the attitude it expresses is as old as miracles. It would be met by "pushing" the objective fact of the copious remains.

John goes a step further. He has only two objective facts as miracles, the plentiful distribution and the remains; and he reduces the subjective elements, the eating and being filled, to the rank of accompanying circumstances. In other words, he is pursuing to its extreme conclusion the course indicated by the Synoptics.

However, this is not the whole explanation. There is something else behind it.

In the second place, then, John has turned a simple miracle story into a parable. For the Synoptics, though there was little food, the multitude ate, were satisfied and left the place full of morsels or victuals unfinished. For John, though there was little food, each was given as much as he liked—a proof of inexhaustible wealth; and when the meal was over, plenty remained, in fact, as we shall suggest, he probably implies that there was as much bread as before if not more—a proof that here was imperishable bread. The exact meaning of this we need not here work out. No doubt the bread he has in mind is not only the true doctrine and life in general, but also, and maybe chiefly, the Eucharist.

In such a parable, the eating and being filled, the very miracle of the simple feasting story, can only be the occasion for the miracle of the remains. Moreover, on this basis, we can explain not only his negative alteration, the cutting down of the eating and being filled, but also his positive ones, the insertion of (a) a special command of Jesus to gather up the remains, and (b) the declaration of the people that this is the expected prophet. The demonstration of the imperishable bread deserves a full-dress introduction and statement of effect on the public.

2. *Substance*

So far we have argued mainly from form. But the two principal results are borne out by the contents and a comparison with other pericopes.

[79] *The Virgin and the Gipsy* by D. H. Lawrence opens: "When the vicar's wife went off with a young and penniless man…" But this is a rather sophisticated device, one purpose of which may well be to *épater* [to shock] *le bourgeois.*

[80] E.g. Exod 12:41.

[81] Ps 114:1.

The one conclusion we reached was that John represents as miraculous only the visible facts of the plentiful distribution and the remains. This is supported by the following details.

The men who recognize Jesus as the prophet do so "having seen" the miracle. That this is no accidental wording is clear from its subsequent repetition in a rebuke Jesus administers to the same people: "Ye saw the miracles."[82] The plural "miracles" here includes Cana. The phrase "to see the miracle," it should be observed, is frequent in John,[83] and a remark like "this beginning of miracles did Jesus in Cana, and manifested forth, ἐφανέρωσεν, his glory"[84] also belongs here.

John's constant use of σημεῖον, "sign," for "miracle," now appears more purposeful. In the Synoptics, the term is employed only in depicting the attitude of the unbelieving who wanted visible evidence. To this, the passage about Herod who "hoped to have seen some sign done by Jesus"[85] is not, as Bauer thinks,[86] an exception; we are here told about Herod's state of mind, the word "sign" is put from his, not from Luke's point of view.

John, on the other hand, by using the word as the legitimate description of Jesus's deeds, impresses on his readers that visible proof was offered to any who had eyes to see. It follows that, when he concentrates on the objective facts in the narrative of the feeding of the mutitude, he is not merely working out a line adumbrated in the Synoptic version before him—even the Synoptics, we saw, stressed the leaving over as the undeniable part of the miracle. He is also giving expression to a general, anti-Synoptic idea of his own, a different evaluation of "signs."

The other conclusion which we have to test is that John makes the miracle consist in the plentiful distribution, a proof of inexhaustible wealth, and above all, in the remains, a proof that here was imperishable bread.

Before enumerating some confirmatory points, however, one reservation may be stated. John nowhere says in so many words that he assigns a new meaning to the remains; and that they are not, as in the Synoptics, just a quantity of food left lying as it dropped or which could not be finished, but all the original bread again or even more. He nowhere says this expressly, he only gives strong hints. This is consistent with his manner on other occasions. But it is the reason why we do not put forward this matter as more than highly probable. What does appear certain is that, whether all the bread or only some of it is restored, John intends to convey the idea of incorruptibilty.

Now for a list of points in support.

The earliest comment on the question is certainly the passage in the apocryphal Acts of John:[87] "Our loaves were preserved entire," ὁλόκληροι ἐφυλάσσοντο. This is exactly the interpretation we are advocating.

[82] John 6:26.
[83] See, in addition to the verses quoted, John 2:23, 4:48, 6:2, 6:30.
[84] John 2:11.
[85] Luke 23:8.
[86] *Das Johannesevangelium*, 2nd ed. (1925), 42.
[87] *Acts of John* 93.

John alone gives us to understand that only bread remained, but no fish: "They filled twelve baskets with the fragments of the loaves." In the Synoptics, the fragments are indeterminate, anything that fell down or was too much to be eaten up; they are just the traces of a huge feast. In one version, we are actually informed that they included fish.[88] In John, the miracle concerns only the bread broken by Jesus, the heavenly food or Eucharist.

John alone mentions the exact number of the loaves a second time in describing the culminating miracle: "They filled twelve baskets with the fragments of five barley loaves." If twelve baskets can be filled with the remains of five loaves, then it is right to infer that the loaves are unconsumed if not more numerous than before the meal.

John alone uses συνάγω for "to gather up the fragments"; it occurs both in the command and execution. This verb, however, may also mean "to join together." The Synoptics all use αἴρω, "to take up." When we consider that it is αἴρω which corresponds to the Hebrew word common in such connections, *naṭal*,[89] John's choice of συνάγω does suggest an ulterior motive. The verb is used in several important sections, for example: "And he that reapeth gathereth fruit unto life eternal."[90] An additional reason of a rather different nature he may have had for putting συνάγω we shall mention when discussing the Rabbinic background of his version.

John alone states the purpose of the gathering up of the fragments "that nothing be lost." The notion is Rabbinic. A man had prepared a banquet for distinguished guests; when they did not turn up, he invited the poor, "that it might not be lost."[91] No doubt one of the objects the Rabbis pursued when insisting on the duty to collect fragments of a meal from the floor was "that they be not lost." The Shammaites urged that the taking up must precede the cleaning of one's hands, since otherwise, as a result of water pouring down, "one would lose" the victuals on the floor.[92] The prohibition of destroying a fruit-bearing tree in Deuteronomy was interpreted very widely. Some held that if a person lived on finer, rarer bread, refusing the ordinary, plentiful sort, he was transgressing that law.[93] However, John, in his usual, subtle fashion, makes the phrase far more significant. "That nothing be lost," with him, means "that all the bread be there again." It is noteworthy that the order is, not "Gather the fragments that they be not lost," but "Gather the fragments that nothing be lost."

In John alone it is the disciples, not the people at large, who gather up. The difference, long recognized, can now be explained. In the Synoptics, the action is merely a characteristic part of the successful feast, on a level with eating and being filled. In John, it is the very sign shown to the people. It must be done by the disciples.

John assigns a conspicuous role to the word "to remain." In the Synoptics, it is not emphasized. We hear of "the taking of the fragments that remained"; and one version—

[88] Mark 6:43.

[89] *b. Ber.* 52b.

[90] John 4:36.

[91] *y. San.* 23c; see Strack-B., vol. 2 (1924), 479.

[92] *b. Ber.* 52b. Superstition may also have played a part: see *b. Hul.* 105b and, for pagan circles, Athenaeus, *Deipn.* 4.149c.

[93] Deut 20:19; *y. Shab.* 140b.

the same which expressly includes fish among the fragments—simply speaks of "the fragments," without adding "that remained."[94] John has it in the order to the disciples, which, as we saw, is not known to the Synoptics: "Gather the fragments that remain, that nothing be lost." The word is here not only superfluous but also somewhat unnatural—unless a deeper sense is connected with it. He also has it in the verse saying that the fragments were gathered. But instead of the Synoptic "fragments that remained," he puts: "fragments which remained unto them that had eaten." In the Synoptics, "that remained" adds little to the sense; the Johannine "which remained unto them that had eaten" is too heavy, too full, to be overlooked. The verb περισσεύω means "to remain" in the sense of "to remain over after use of the rest." On this occasion, John suggests, the people received incorruptible bread, with the paradoxical result that the remains equalled or maybe exceeded the whole. Nothing was found lost, that is, after the disciples had gathered "what remained over unto them that had eaten," i.e "what remained over unto them despite, or even because of, their eating."[95]

The subsequent censure of the crowd by Jesus[96] also is now fully intelligible. Jesus reproaches the people for coming, not because of the signs, i.e. Cana and the remains, but because of the eating and being filled. Had John been a form critic, he might have put it thus: "Ye seek me not because of the main clauses, but because of the subordinate clauses." In John's version of the narrative of the feeding, the handing out of the food "as much as they would" and the gathering of the fragments are described in main clauses, while the actual meal appears only in "unto them that had eaten" and "when they were filled." At any rate, no sharper distinction than we find in this rebuke could be drawn between the eating and being filled, as inessential, and the remains, as the real sign. It sounds almost like an open attack on the Synoptics.

The following verse[97] greatly gains in significance: "Labour not for the meat which perisheth, but for that which endureth," ἐργάζεσθε μὴ τὴν βρῶσιν τὴν ἀπολλυμένην ἀλλὰ τὴν βρῶσιν τὴν μένουσαν. This manifestly alludes to the gathering up of fragments by the disciples ἵνα μήτι ἀπόληται, "that nothing perish." By that action they had demonstrated the incorruptibilty of the Eucharist, and of the divine food in general.

The different verbs for "to eat" and "to be filled" which John uses in the narrative and Jesus's rebuke also suit the thesis we are submitting. In fact, they are another illustration of his extreme care and subtlety in verbal questions.

In the narrative,[98] he tells us about the miracle as he wishes it to be understood. So the Synoptic χορτάξω is replaced by πίμπλημι. The former, "to make absolutely full," would stress the wrong, worldly aspect.[99] Similarly, φαγεῖν is replaced by βιβρώσκω. Both mean "to eat." But the latter, though not essentially more refined, is associated

[94] Mark 6:43.

[95] According to Julius Paulus (quoted by Gellius, A.N. 1.22.9), περισσόν might signify either *quod supervacaneum esset ac non necessarium* or *quod abundans nimis et afluens et exuberans* ["Of what was superfluous and unnecessary" or "of what was too abundant, overflowing and excessive"].

[96] John 6:26.

[97] John 6:27.

[98] John 6:12.

[99] Cp. Athenaeus, *Deipn.* 3.99e, where the refined word to use instead of χορτάζω is said to be κορέννυμι.

with βρῶσις, "the true meat," in the same chapter[100] as well as similar contexts. On the other hand, both χορτάζω and φαγεῖν are kept in Jesus's censure, only a little further on:[101] "Ye seek me because ye did eat, ἐφάγετε, of the loaves, and were filled, ἐχορτάσθητε." Here where the attitude of the vulgar is depicted, the primitive Synoptic terminology is resumed. This, incidentally, is another conclusive piece of evidence that John knew the Synoptic version, and that his own is a development from it.

Of particular interest is the fact that John has treated the marriage at Cana in exactly the same manner as the feeding of the multitude.[102]

It is safe to assume that, though this incident is not represented in the Synoptics, some version of it was current prior to John: his artificial pattern clearly presupposes a simpler one, we might say one of a Synoptic character. Now what must have been the climax of the original story, the turning of water into wine and perhaps the resulting carousal of the party, hardly appear at all. We hear nothing of a carousal, and of the turning of water into wine only in a subordinate clause, in the verse telling how the butler tasted the water "that was made wine";[103] as if it went without saying, as if such a thing happened every day. The point of John's miracle is no longer the providing a large company with wine though there had seemed to be only water, but the providing of superior wine. This alone occupies a main clause: "When the ruler of the feast had tasted the water that was made wine, he saith, Thou hast kept the good wine until now."[104]

Surely the original story culminated in a sentence like: "And the water was made wine and they bare it to the guests and they found it very good." John concentrates exclusively on the quality, just as in the feeding of the multitude. That is the sign.

It may be added that the sign of the true wine, like that of the imperishable bread, is preceded by a second command and a note that this was performed. The first command was that the pots should be filled.[105] This corresponds to the order that the multitude should sit down. It is at this point that the original version must have put the ending: "And the water was made wine" etc. John, however, inserts a fresh command, "Draw out now and bear unto the ruler of the feast,"[106] corresponding to "Gather up" etc. There follows the remark "And they bare," which corresponds to "Therefore they gathered up."

Further, as in the Johannine feeding of the multitude, the sign shown at Cana is followed by recognition and inference. "This beginning of miracles did Jesus and manifested forth his glory, and his disciples believed on him" is an appendix very similar to "The men, having seen the miracle that Jesus did, said, This is that prophet."

But even the preliminary miracle is to be met with again. In the feeding of the multitude, inexhaustible wealth is suggested by each obtaining "as much as they would."

[100] John 6:27.
[101] John 6:26.
[102] John 2:1 ff.
[103] John 2:9.
[104] John 2:9.
[105] John 2:7.
[106] John 2:8.

At Cana, the servants filled those tremendous pots with water "up to the brim."[107]

There is yet another argument for our view: in several respects, the way John has turned the feeding of the multitude from a simple miracle story into a parable is paralleled, or maybe foreshadowed, by an episode preserved in Matthew and Mark, where Jesus reminds the disciples of the feeding.[108]

The miracle is here too treated as a parable, and though there are important disagreements with John, four similarities at least are worth observing. In the first place, no mention whatever is made of eating and being filled. The miracle consists in the remains alone—no matter precisely what significance may be attached to them in these passages. In the second place, it is definitely only bread which remains. The fish is entirely suppressed. In the third place, it is the disciples who are supposed to have taken up the fragments, not the people at large. And in the fourth place, the remains are thought of as a σημεῖον, a visible sign. This we may infer both from the position of the episode, which directly follows a demand by the Pharisees of concrete evidence, of a σημεῖον,[109] and from the fact that the disciples themselves are represented as of little faith. That, in John, visible proof is designed not only for those of little faith but for any who can see, we had occasion to point out before; here we have before us an example of a disagreement.

3. *Old Testament and Rabbinic Roots*

It is time to advert to a few neglected points concerning the Jewish roots of the story.

The Synoptic pattern, as is well known, is highly reminiscent of the feeding of a multitude by Elisha;[110] and so is a good deal of the substance. But the actual miracle is worded in a different way. The men fed by Elisha "did eat and left thereof"; the clause has two members. The Synoptics write: "They did all eat and were filled and took up the fragments that remained." This clause has three members; the reference to being filled is not to be found in the Old Testament narrative. It is surprising that the Old Testament model for the Synoptic version has never been discovered. It is a verse from Ruth:[111] "And Boaz reached her parched corn, and she did eat and was filled and left thereof."

Three things ought to be remembered. In the first place, for the Rabbis, Ruth was one of the outstanding converts. A special law authorizing the reception into Judaism of Moabite women had been enacted for her sake—at least, so the Rabbis taught.[112] What is more, in the very section which ends in her being given to eat by Boaz, he invokes on her the blessing of God, "under whose wings thou art come to trust."[113] This blessing is the Biblical basis for all the Rabbinic expressions representing conversion as coming under the wings of the Shekhinah or the like.

In the second place, Ruth was an ancestress of David and thus of the Messiah.

[107] John 2:7.
[108] Matt 16:5 ff.; Mark 8:14 ff.
[109] Matt 16.1 ff.; Mark 8:11 ff.
[110] 2 Kgs 4:42 ff.
[111] Ruth 2:14.
[112] *y. Yeb.* 9c.
[113] Ruth 2:12.

In the third place, the particular passage in question was interpreted by the Rabbis in a way that must have rendered it a most apt Old Testament testimonial.

For example, "She did eat—in this world, and was filled—for the days of the Messiah, and left thereof—for the Age to Come."[114] Or the three blessed periods are three glorious reigns of descendants:[115] "She did eat—in the days of David, and was filled—in the days of Solomon, and left thereof—in the days of Hezekiah;" or again, "She did eat—in the days of David and Solomon, and was filled—in the days of Hezekiah, and left thereof—in the days of Rabbi Judah." Rabbi Judah the Prince belonged to the house of David. No doubt the third king in such schemes would often be the Messiah.

Occasionally, Ruth is taken as directly standing for one or the other of her descendants, and Boaz for God.[116] Thus where she stands for David, we find this exegesis: "And Boaz said unto her, At mealtime come thou hither—this refers to God calling David to the kingdom; and eat of the bread—this refers to the bread of the kingdom; and dip thy morsel in the vinegar—this refers to the sufferings, *yissurin*, of David; and she sat beside the reapers—this refers to David's temporary loss of the kingdom through Absalom's revolt; and he reached her parched corn—this refers to the kingdom being given him again; and she did eat and was filled and left thereof—this means David eating in this world, his eating for the days of the Messiah and his eating for the Age to Come." Needless to say, all these equations are supported by proof-texts, in the usual Rabbinic fashion.

Ruth may even represent her last descendant, the Messiah, Boaz again standing for God: "And Boaz said unto her, At mealtime come thou hither—this means, Approach to the kingdom—and eat of the bread—this means the bread of the kingdom—and dip thy morsel in the vinegar—this means the sufferings, *yissurin*, as it is said,[117] But he was wounded for our transgressions—and she sat beside the reapers—this means, his kingdom will be turned aside from him for a while, as it is said,[118] For I will gather all nations against Jerusalem to battle and the city shall be taken—and he reached her parched corn—this means, the kingdom will return to him, as it is said,[119] And he shall smite the earth with the rod of his mouth." Presumably in the eyes of the author who makes Ruth stand for the Messiah, "she did eat" etc., would just indicate the rich Messianic feast.

However much or little weight we may attach to any one of these Rabbinic utterances, there is no doubt that the text figures prominently in Messianic speculation. As for the date, one of the interpretations quoted is definitely Tannaitic, of the period prior to A.D. 200.[120] Moreover, R. Johanan or Jonathan of the 3rd cent.,[121] when lecturing on

[114] *b. Shab.* 113b.
[115] *b. Shab.* 113b.
[116] *Ruth Rabba* on 2:14; *Yalqut* ad loc.
[117] Isa 53:5.
[118] Zech 14:2.
[119] Isa 11:4.
[120] *b. Shab.* 113b: "She did eat for this world, and was filled for the days of the Messiah, and left thereof for the Age to Come."
[121] Johanan figures in *Ruth Rabba*, Jonathan in *Yalqut*.

the verse under notice, was able to enumerate ten different allegorical interpretations of the kind adduced. Since we must allow a considerable time for the growth of such a number, we are brought fairly near the New Testament era.

One more interpretation taking a different line deserves attention.[122] The feeding of Ruth was declared miraculous because, it was held, she received little and yet it turned out more than enough. The Hebrew for "parched corn," *qali*, was explained as *qalil*, "slight"; and the passage "he reached her parched corn" was understood in the sense "he reached her little only." The conclusion was drawn that, since she "did eat and was filled and left thereof," a special blessing must either have attached to his hand or have been at work within her, and it was decided that the latter was the case. The date of this statement is about A.D. 300, but in all probability there were earlier, similar ones.

In the narrative of the feeding of the multitude, then, a meal prepared for Ruth by her redeemer, Boaz, is conceived as an adumbration of one prepared for the Messianic community by Jesus. Once this relation is recognized, several features of the Johannine version take on an increased significance.

John alone specifies the nature of the bread as barley bread; in fact he does so twice.[123] This may well be due, not only to the influence of the story of Elisha, who fed a hundred men with twenty loaves of barley,[124] but also to that of the Book of Ruth, where barley is mentioned quite frequently—from the moment that Ruth and her mother-in-law "came to Bethlehem in the beginning of barley harvest."[125]

After all, the barley in Ruth occasionally becomes a Messianic symbol in Rabbinic interpretation. When Ruth left Boaz after her nocturnal visit, he gave her six measures of barley.[126] The Midrash considers it the marriage price. But as it looks a somewhat poor one, it is taken as alluding to six descendants, namely: David, Hezekiah, Josiah, Hananiah, Mishael, Azariah, Daniel and the Messiah. (Note that these are eight, not six. But there is no need to worry. The three friends of Daniel count as one: they are given only one proof-text together.)

The re-interpretation by John of the remains as equalling or excelling the original amount may also be based on an artificial exegesis of a phrase common to both the story of Elisha and that of Ruth. In both, as in the Synoptics, there is an abundant meal, and some food is left over. Incidentally, in these Old Testament narratives, the remains are clearly not pieces dropped or thrown on the ground, but that part of the meal which cannot be finished. John's idea that, though a feast has taken place, the entire bread is again in existence may derive from an over-literal reading of the texts: the men fed by Elisha "did eat and left,"[127] and Ruth "did eat and was filled and left."

The meaning is, of course, "and left thereof"; and the current English version in one case at least[128] adds "thereof" in italics. But John may have felt justified in inter-

[122] *Ruth Rabba* on 2:14.
[123] John 6:9, 13.
[124] 2 Kgs 4:42.
[125] Ruth 1:22.
[126] Ruth 3:15.
[127] 2 Kgs 4:44; Ruth 2:14.
[128] 2 Kgs 4:44.

preting more strictly, "and they did eat, *scil.*, the food, and left, *scil.* the food," or "and she did eat, *scil.* the food and was filled, *scil.* with the food, and left, *scil.* the food"—all the food, not only some. From the strict grammatical point of view, it was possible to supply as object the entire bread; and it was possible whether he proceeded from the Hebrew, *wayyo'khelu wayyothiru, watto'khal wattiśba' wattothar,* or from the Greek καὶ ἔφαγον καὶ κατέλιπον, καὶ ἔφαγε καὶ ἐνεπλήσθη καὶ κατέλιπε.

We have already referred to John's substitution of συνάγω, "to gather the fragments," for the Synoptic αἴρω, "to take them up." But to the reason we have given, another may now be added. In Ruth, the clause "and she did eat and was filled and left" is followed by a verse beginning "and she rose to glean."[129] The Hebrew verb "to glean" is often represented by συνάγω in the LXX; and though the LXX in this passage has συλλέγω, it has συνάγω elsewhere in the Book of Ruth.[130] John may have read "and she did eat and was filled and left and rose to gather"—"to gather" in the sense of "to gather the fragments of the meal." And he introduced this term into the feeding of the multitude.

There is unexpected support for this assumption. In the Hebrew Bible, though "she left" is marked by a *Silluq*, as the last word of the verse, it is pointed, not with a *Qames*, but with a *Pataḥ*. This strongly suggests that, for one school of Rabbis, the verse did not end here but included the words "and she rose to glean." The next verse began by: "And Boaz commanded his young men." Presumably John started from this tradition, according to which "and she did eat and was filled and left and rose to glean" belonged together.

A borrowing from Ruth may account for the strange use of ἐργάζομαι in: "Labour, ἐργάζεσθε, for that meat which endureth. Then they said unto him, What shall we do that we might work the works of God, ἵνα ἐργαζώμεθα τὰ ἔργα τοῦ θεοῦ. Jesus answered, This is the work, τὸ ἔργον, of God, that ye believe on him whom he hath sent."[131]

In the same section where the feeding of Ruth is described, we are told of the blessing Boaz pronounces on her.[132] "The Lord recompense thy work, and a full reward be given thee of the Lord God of Israel, under whose wings thou art come to trust." The verse, we saw, furnished the Rabbis with the technical term for "conversion." The point here to be made is that the Rabbis emphasize[133] that Ruth's "work" consisted in seeking refuge under the wings of God. The LXX has ἐργασία for this "work." John's application of the word sounds like an echo.

This is not to deny that he may be thinking also of the consecration of the Levites,[134] "that they may execute the service of the Lord," ὥστε ἐργάζεσθαι τὰ ἔργα κυρίου. Many of John's references to the Old Testament are "multivalent," deliberately suggestive of several passages.[135]

[129] Ruth 2:15.

[130] Ruth 2:2, 7.

[131] John 6:27 ff.

[132] Ruth 2:12.

[133] *Ruth Rabba* on 2.12.

[134] Num 8:11. Perhaps even of Josh 22:27, though the LXX as we know it has here λατρεύειν λατρείαν κυρίου.

[135] For the background of this feature, see C. K. Barrett, "The Old Testment in the Fourth Gospel," *JTS* 48 (1947), 155 ff.

However, these are matters of detail. What is of greater interest is that with Ruth as the starting-point, the evolution of the pattern of the narrative becomes quite clear. It is, in fact, a strikingly consistent evolution.

In Ruth, we find the plain "and she did eat and was filled and left thereof." Even here, there is a slight emphasis on the leaving over, for the line is obviously ascending: eating—being filled—leaving over. The narrative itself confirms the importance of the latter: a few verses further on[136] we hear that she took the remains home for her mother-in-law.

Just so, in the chapter about a miraculous feast provided by Elisha, we may paraphrase:[137] "and they not only ate but even left thereof." God does not stint his guests. In the narrative of Elisha and the widow's oil cruet too the sufficiency of the divine gift for more than the immediate need is accentuated:[138] "Sell the oil and pay thy debt and live thou and thy children of the rest."

In the Rabbinic comments, the position is unchanged. In form, the three members remain equal, though, in thought, there is always a rise from the first to the third: for example, this world—the days of the Messiah—the Age to Come.

The Synoptics, while still preserving an unbroken sequence, have lengthened the third member and rendered it more colourful, more concrete and detailed: "and they did eat and were filled and took up of the fragments that remained twelve baskets full." We are well on the way to a fundamental change in form. The limit is reached within which a unit can be kept intact when one of its parts acquires excessive weight.

John takes the final step. He breaks off the third member and makes of it a separate unit, provided with its own introduction, i.e. fresh situation and command, and its own conclusion, i.e. recognition of the miracle.

In conclusion, the question may be raised whether there was a stage when the feeding of the multitude was not associated with that of Ruth. Possibly there was, and it is represented by that version—in Mark—which, on the one hand, expressly includes fish among the fragments and, on the other, does not introduce the notion "to remain," περισσεύω.[139] This notion may have been taken over from Ruth after the narrative as a whole was already established.

True, the LXX in Ruth uses καταλείπω. But, first, the LXX frequently translates the Hebrew verb by some form of περισσεύω or a derivative. Secondly, there are cases where one MS. employs the former root and another the latter.[140] Thirdly, how close the two are may also be seen from phrases like τὸ περισσὸν τὸ καταλειφθέν.[141]

[136] Ruth 2:18.
[137] 2 Kgs 4:44.
[138] 2 Kgs 4:7.
[139] Mark 6:42 f.
[140] Judg 21:16, τοῖς ἐπιλοίποις and τοῖς περισσοῖς.
[141] 2 Kgs 25:11; cp. Judg 21:7.

Hezekiah*

First, then, for Hezekiah. All history-writing transfers features of one event or one great personage to another, and, indeed, much history-acting is in imitation of previous occurrences. Whoever nowadays writes about Napoleon is likely to lend him some traits of Caesar, and Napoleon himself—not to mention de Gaulle—would on occasion look to that example. This general phenomenon, that history, whether reflected upon or in the making, harks back to history, is enormously accentuated in New Testament times because, in the then prevalent view, Old Testament events and personages were largely a prefigurement of things to come. It is a commonplace that Jesus in the New Testament is depicted as a new Moses, the real Manna, the true water-giving rock, the perfected Torah; as a new Elijah, returning a dead child alive to the child's mother; as the Suffering Servant foreseen by Isaiah; as a new Adam or, partly at least, counter-Adam, representing all mankind but releasing it from, instead of involving it in, sin. Certainly he is a new King David. Other New Testament characters also are given features of Old Testament ones: Mary now and then appears as another Ruth, a chaste handmaid.[1] The very concept "New Testament" implies a reshaping of the forerunner, the "Old Testament."

What I want to point out in this first part of my lecture is that among Old Testament heroes that have contributed to the image of Jesus in the New Testament is King Hezekiah, so far rather neglected by students of early Christianity. For the Rabbis of the New Testament era Hezekiah was a Messianic figure, whether a Messiah of the past or of the future, or indeed both a past saviour and one to come again. The evidence for this is early and safe. Johanan ben Zaccai, who lived in the period of the destruction of the Temple, at the moment of his departure saw beyond the present and exclaimed to his disciples: "Prepare a throne for Hezekiah, King of Judah, that cometh."[2] (The full statement

* Lecture given October 1966 in the crypt of St. Paul's Cathedral, London. This is the first part of the lecture "He That Cometh" (see 429 ff. for the second part). The lecture began with, "I wish to make two points to-night, which is two points more than I usually make in a lecture. First I should like to draw attention to the influence that the Old Testament figure of Hezekiah has had on New Testament thought, and then I should like to say something about the background of the institution of the Eucharist."

[1] See Daube, *The New Testament and Rabbinic Judaism* (1956), 27 ff. [137 ff.]

[2] *b. Ber* 28b. The Munich manuscript omits "that cometh," plainly in order to shed the Messianic meaning of the utterance: so, correctly, Bammel, *NT* 5 (1962), 224 f. Hezekiah's role is reduced to that of a member of the cortege doing the last honour to the dead scholar. Why this role should necessitate a throne is a question that might well be asked. The re-interpretation underlying this suppression of "that cometh" goes back to a date quite soon after the original utterance: see Strack and Billerbeck, *Kommentar zum Neuen Testament aus Talmud und Midrasch*, vol. 1 (1922), 30, on *y. Sot* 24c. The "throne of Elijah," incidentally, a

is: "Remove the vessels because of the uncleanness[3] and prepare a throne for Hezekiah, King of Judah, that cometh." There is here surely an allusion to the cleansing of the Temple which was Hezekiah's first act as ruler. I shall comment on it in a moment.)

In an ancient Christian document (from about the middle of the second century A.D.), Justin Martyr's *Dialogue with Trypho,* reporting a discussion between the author and a Jew, the Jews are represented as associating with King Hezekiah a highly relevant chapter of Isaiah: it is Hezekiah who is the Immanuel born of a young woman.[4] This is confirmed by Rabbinic sources,[5] where he is regarded as envisaged also by the prophecy "For unto us a child is born."[6] For Trypho he is, too, "the king of glory" of Psalm 24[7] as well as the addressee in the psalm quoted more frequently in the New Testament than any other Old Testament passage: "The Lord said unto my lord, Sit on my right hand."[8] Perhaps I should add a cryptic pronouncement transmitted in the Talmud, to the effect that there will be no Messiah for Israel since they already enjoyed him—a literal rendering would be "ate him"—in the days of Hezekiah.[9] It has recently been maintained that the author of this dictum was not, as is ordinarily held, the Hillel of around A.D. 300, but the elder and more renowned Hillel who flourished around 15 B.C.[10]

Now let me submit a number of significant parallels. Hezekiah is a descendant of David, in blood and in spirit,[11] and the Bible puts him above all kings of Judah before or after: "There was none like unto him."[12] This eulogy is commonly ascribed to a reviser of the original narrative and very likely the critics are right;[13] for my present purpose

---

seat of honour which custom requires at a Jewish circumcision and which, according to *Pirqe de R. El.* 29 at the end, is intended for Elijah as an invisible witness of the ceremony, originally also had a direct Messianic function: any male child entering into the covenant was greeted as, potentially, the deliverer, the throne was his. The Soncino translation of *b. Berakoth*, by Epstein, *Zeraim* I (1948), 174, gives strong support to the a-Messianic tendency. The purpose of Hezekiah's descent is said to be to accompany Johanan ben Zaccai into the next world. Again the throne makes no sense.

[3] *Scil.* the uncleanness caused by a corpse.

[4] Isa 7:14; Justin 43.8, 67.1, 68.8, 71.3, 77.1 f.

[5] *Exod. Rab.* 18 on 12:29, *Num. Rab.* 14 on 7:48. The Rabbis see evidence for this identification in 2 Chr 32:8, where Hezekiah encourages his subjects to resistance against the King of Assyria: "With him is an arm of flesh [*zeroa' basar* in Hebrew, *brachiones sarkinoi* in Greek], but with us is the Lord our God [*we'immanu yahwe 'elohenu, meth' hemon de kyrios ho theos*]." Hezekiah is said (*b. Sanh.* 94b) to have been a vegetarian, by contradistinction to the wicked Pekah son of Remaliah (2 Kgs 15:25 ff.) who devoured enormous quantities of fowl and meat. Though Hezekiah's diet is greens, it is conceivable that the legend derives from Isa 7:15: "Butter and honey shall he eat."

[6] Isa 9:5; *b. Sanh.* 94a etc.; see Strack and Billerbeck, *op. cit.*, vol. 2 (1924), 332.

[7] Ps 24:7; Justin 85.1.

[8] Ps 110; Justin 33.1, 83.1 ff.

[9] *b. Sanh.* 98b, 99a; *'akheluhu.*

[10] See Bammel, *l.c.*, 225 f.

[11] 2 Kgs 18:3; 2 Chr 29:2.

[12] 2 Kgs 18:5; not in 2 Chronicles, but see below, note 56, on 2 Chr 32:31.

[13] E.g. Snaith, *The First and Second Books of Kings* (*Interpreter's Bible*, vol. 3) (1954), 290. The main reason for assuming a revision is that the passage makes Hezekiah superior to the pious reformer Josiah, his great-grandson.

this is immaterial, what counts is that readers in New Testament times had the eulogy before them. They also had before them another suggestive piece of praise: "He rebelled against the King of Assyria and served him not."[14]

The reign of Hezekiah is inaugurated by a cleansing of the Temple—"in the first year, in the first month."[15] Such a cleansing is treated as of the highest importance in both the Synoptics and John, and the latter (unhistorically, I think) places it at the very beginning of Jesus's public activity.[16] The verbal affinity between the Old Testament episode and the New Testament one is not negligible. The decisive word to describe the elimination of the unworthy is *ekballo* both in the Septuagint[17] and in all four gospels. In the New Testament episode it means "to drive out" the traders and money-lenders. In the story of Hezekiah it refers to the "removal" of Greek *akatharsia*, "uncleanness."[18] This is a wide and vague notion, and ancient exegetes must have speculated (as modern ones still do) precisely what might here be envisaged. The term is capable of denoting moral turpitude no less than levitical impurity or idolatrous connection; it might include objectionable professions or ways of carrying on a profession.

After the cleansing of the Temple by Hezekiah there follows a great Passover.[19] Hezekiah sends out messengers, not only to Judah, but also to the other kingdom, Israel, with an invitation to celebrate the feast at his capital. Israel has just been defeated by the Assyrians and seen many of its inhabitants carried off into captivity. Hezekiah admonishes the conquered people to return to God. Most of them laugh at his messengers; the verb *katagelao* found in the Septuagint[20] is used in the New Testament of the crowd's scornful laughter at Jesus as he announces that the daughter of Jairus is merely asleep, not dead. (It occurs in all three Synoptics.[21]) Some however of the rival kingdom humble themselves and come up to Jerusalem. So there is a large, inspired congregation assembled at Jerusalem for this Passover, yet it remains a group of elect ones who have followed the call, surrounded by hostility and disbelief.

Now we come to an elaborate incident which takes place on the occasion of this feast, and which constitutes a crux in Jewish tradition as well as for Christian commentators—in both cases precisely because it seems an astonishing anticipation of distinctive New Testament ideas. The Israelites, the visitors from the northern kingdom, are not clean, have not purified themselves as the law requires of a participant in the feast.[22] This brings about a bold brushing aside by Hezekiah of a Scriptural ruling. We are told that, as these Israelites ate the passover "not as is written," *para ten graphen*

[14] 2 Kgs 18:7, not in 2 Chronicles.

[15] 2 Chr 29:3, 17. The whole episode is absent from the section on Hezekiah in 2 Kings 18 ff.

[16] Matt 21:12 ff.; Mark 11:15 ff.; Luke 19:45 ff.; John 2:14 ff.

[17] Hebrew *hosi'*.

[18] The Hebrew has *nidda* in verse 5, *tum'a* in 16. The former, often associated with menstruation, is a stronger expression than the latter: the usual distinction in English translations of the Bible between "filthiness" and "uncleanness" is about right.

[19] 2 Chronicles 30—not represented in 2 Kings 18 ff.

[20] 2 Chr 30:10; Hebrew *hishiq*.

[21] Matt 9:24; Mark 5:39; Luke 8:53—nowhere else in the New Testament.

[22] Num 9:6 ff. I wish I knew what is behind the notice concerning purification in John 11:55.

in the Septuagint, "contrary to Scripture,"[23] Hezekiah prayed for them: "Let the Lord pardon every heart that prepareth itself to seek God ... though it be not according to the purification of the Sancturary."[24] (In fact, the prayer opens "Let the good Lord pardon." The phrase "the good Lord," *yahwe hattobh* in Hebrew, *kyrios ho agathos* in Greek, is unique, but this is not, as some scholars have held,[25] ground for emendation: the whole story is unique. In any case, this is what Rabbis and New Testament writers had before them.) We meet here both the conviction, so strongly emphasized by Jesus,[26] that it is good will which counts rather than ritual punctiliousness, and an assurance of divine reprieve of the faithful reminiscent of "Thy sins are forgiven thee."[27] Admittedly, the Septuagint has *exilaskomai* for "to pardon, forgive," the New Testament *aphiemi*;[28] but considering the general rarity in the New Testament of any representatives of the former root, this difference is not too relevant.[29]

There is more to come, however. The next sentence says: "And the Lord hearkened unto Hezekiah and healed the people." This is remarkable. No disease has been mentioned, yet the assurance of divine reprieve given by Hezekiah is followed by a divine healing. The sequel is very close to that in the New Testament story where a similar assurance by Jesus to a paralytic is followed by the latter's recovery. No doubt it is possible to understand the Old Testament text in ways that render it less striking and puzzling: instead of "the Lord healed the people" we may translate "the Lord left the people healthy,"[30] or "the Lord spiritually healed, forgave, the people."[31] But whether or not such rationalisations are justifiable, few ancient readers would be inclined to resort to them; and the Septuagint at any rate has *iasato*, "healed."

In some Christian commentaries the extraordinary attitude of Hezekiah to law and motivation is recognized[32]—though only in some, others tend to play it down. The man-

[23] 2 Chr 30:18; Hebrew *belo' khakkathubh*.

[24] I am following the Septuagint. The Hebrew may mean the same, but more probably means that Hezekiah's prayer preceded the breaking of the law: "They ate the passover not as is written, for Hezekiah had prayed for them. . . . " The uncertainty arises from the fact that *ki hithpallel* may be rendered "but indeed, Hezekiah prayed" or "for Hezekiah had prayed."

[25] E.g. Barnes, *The Books of Chronicles* (*Cambridge Bible*) (1899), 262.

[26] Matt 15:1 ff.; Mark 7:1 ff. In the New Testament pericopes, however, the ruling in question—about the washing of hands—is not Scriptural but merely Rabbinic. Hezekiah's precedent is more radical.

[27] Matt 9:2; Mark 2:5; Luke 5:20, 7:48. It is an assurance no matter exactly how we intepret the imperative *exilastho*, "let the Lord pardon"; the use of the third person instead of the direct address, "pardon," lends the expression much force. (The apparatus shews that there was an occasional attempt to substitute the personal address, *exilasai*.) The Hebrew *yekhapper* is translatable as "the Lord may pardon" or "the Lord will pardon."

[28] The Hebrew in 2 Chr 30:18 is *kipper*. Once, in Isa 22:14, the Septuagint does render this verb by *aphiemi*: "This iniquity shall not be purged from you till ye die."

[29] *Exilaskomai* occurs nowhere else in the New Testament; *hilaskomai* only in Luke 18:13; Heb 2:17; *hilasmos* in 1 John 2:2; 4:10; *hilasterion* in Rom 3:25; Heb 9:5.

[30] In this sense, Barnes, *l.c.*, Rudolph, *Chronikbücher* (*Handbuch zum Alten Testament*) (1955), 302, Cazelles, *Les Livres des Chroniques* (*La Sainte Bible*), 2nd ed. (1961), 217.

[31] Slotki, *Chronicles* (Soncino Books of the Bible) (1952), 307. A middle position between these two is taken by Curtis and Madsen, *The Books of Chronicles* (International Critical Commentary) (1910), 475.

[32] See e.g. Cazelles, *l.c.* He inclines to attribute a very advanced sense also to verse 22: the Levites are praised not only for their technical skill in singing but also for their profound understanding of, dedication to, God.

ifold efforts of the Rabbis to explain it away merely underline its true quality.[33] The ultimate object, of course, is common to all: to prove that Hezekiah intended the most meticulous observance of the law. So why a prayer for pardon? That must contemplate, the Rabbis argue, an error which he committed in his interpretation of the law and which he discovered too late. According to one opinion, in order to enable those who were unclean to become clean, he celebrated the Passover not in Nisan, the normal date for it, but in the following month, Iyyar; he was thinking of the Biblical provision to the effect that a person unclean at the time of the feast should postpone it for a month.[34] He was, however, mistaken: as he knew beforehand that a great many persons were unclean, he should have intercalated a month in the calendar, so that the Passover would still take place in Nisan. According to another opinion, this is exactly what he did, but what he should have done was to hold the feast in Iyyar. Yet another opinion is that his error could not have been so gross as this. What he did was, he intercalated a month, which was the right thing to do in principle, but he erred in intercalating a second Nisan, whereas it is only permissible to intercalate a second Adar, the month preceding Nisan. Later authorities make the error even subtler: he intercalated, which was the right thing, he intercalated a second Adar, which was the right thing, but he erred in intercalating it after Nisan had already been declared, sanctified as Nisan.[35] There are further equally ingenious—and artificial—attempts to mitigate the story; but there it is.[36]

Disease and recovery are associated with Hezekiah in more than one way. He himself fell mortally ill and no less a figure than Isaiah foretold him his death. But he prayed and wept and the prophet was sent to him again to tell him that God would cure him—"On the third day thou shalt go up to the house of the Lord." (There is repeated reference to this third day.[37]) At the prophet's bidding a poultice of figs was applied and the King recovered.[38] In the eyes of the Rabbis this was a near-resurrection from the dead, comparable to the raising by Elijah of the son of the woman of Shunem.[39] For them, severe disease and death were always close. (Healing—as also, for example, deliverance from captivity—may be found among God's saving actions in the Second Benediction of the *Shemone-Esre*, the theme of which is the raising of the dead.[40]) In this case, the sick man, with his doom announced by God's messenger, was certainly as good as dead. It is noteworthy that "the gates of hell," *pylai haidou*, which according to Matthew will not prevail against the Church, occur for the first time in the

[33] *b. Sanh.* 12a f.

[34] Num 9:9 ff.

[35] Cp. *b. Ber.* 10b, and see e.g. Schachter, *Sanhedrin I* (Soncino translation) (1935), 54.

[36] Rudolph, *l.c.*, 303, considers that the story was set down by the author of Chronicles in the first decades of the fourth century B.C. with a view to a problem acute in his period: he was advocating a welcoming treatment of pilgrims from the north even if they lacked the necessary knowledge or time to satisfy the usual prerequisites.

[37] 2 Kgs 20:5, 8.

[38] 2 Kgs 20:1 ff., summarized in 2 Chronicles in a single verse, 32:24.

[39] 1 Kgs 4:18 ff.; *b. Ber.* 10b.

[40] Singer, *Authorized Daily Prayer Book* (1891), 44 f. In *Pirqe de R. El.* 31 Isaac, killed and revived, is considered the author of this Benediction; see Strack and Billerbeck, *op. cit.*, vol. 3 (1926), 746, on Heb 11:19.

psalm composed—so the Bible has it—by King Hezekiah on his recovery from this illness.[41]

Rabbinic legend goes even further. Hezekiah introduced curable disease, disease the purpose of which is not to kill but to make people think and repent, disease sent as a warning. Prior to him, once you were ill, you died; at his entreaty the order of things was relaxed. This is of course fanciful, but it bears testimony to the enormous theological significance attributed by the Rabbis to the incidents in the life of this monarch. From then onwards, illness might be a summons to return, you might hope for God to lift it and allow you a new and better life.[42] Another interesting point from this area is that, according to old Rabbinic tradition, Hezekiah hid away a "Book of Remedies"—apparently in order that the sick should repent and trust in God rather than have recourse to medicine.[43]

The great Passover leads to such zest and joy that Hezekiah and the congregation decide to prolong the marvellous event and add a second week: a measure second in daring only to the breach of the law I have already discussed. There is a trace here of the spirit which causes Jesus's circle to dispense with fasting.[44] At the end of this Passover the priests pronounce a blessing over the people, "and their voice was heard, and the prayer came up to his holy dwelling, even unto heaven."[45]

In Rabbinic speculation Hezekiah attaches the utmost importance to the saving of souls in the sense of the making of proselytes: it is a goal that has been pursued from the earliest times down to his.[46] There are many minor items which might be listed. Throughout, being the son of the wicked Ahaz, he symbolizes renewal, regeneration. He was a teacher of his people and, as such, called them "his sons."[47] In his reign a sword planted at the entrance of the schoolhouse threatened those who would not devote themselves to the study of the Torah. Women and children were instructed in the Torah as well as men. Indeed that generation was so immersed in sacred occupation and aspiration that only the minimum was done to gain one's daily subsistence.[48] The Bible itself tells how an angel of God smote the enemies who had been about to overwhelm the King[49]; how he received gifts from many and was honoured by all nations[50]; and how he was given an exceptionally noble burial.[51]

[41] Matt 16:18; Isa 38:10; Hebrew *sha'are she'ol*.

[42] *Gen Rab* 65 on 27:1, "And it came to pass that when Isaac was old and his eyes were dim." Abraham, we are informed, introduced the venerable if withered looks of old age, Isaac (his eyes being dim) the sufferings of old age, Jacob the one brief illness ending in death, Hezekiah the illness susceptible of recovery. In *b. B. M.* 87b; *b. Sanh.* 107b, his role is assigned to Elijah.

[43] *m. Pes.* 4:9; *b. Ber.* 10b; *b. Pes.* 56a.

[44] Matt 9:14 f.; Mark 2:18 f.; Luke 5:33 f.

[45] 2 Chr 30:27.

[46] *y. Ber.* 8b; *Eccl Rabba* on 5:6. Simeon ben Eleazar (second half of the second century A.D.) blames him for his hospitality to heathens, *b. Sanh.* 104a.

[47] *Siphre Deut* on 6:7, referring to 2 Chr 29:11.

[48] *b. Sanh.* 94b.

[49] 2 Kgs 19:35; 2 Chr 32:31.

[50] 2 Chr 32:23, less general in 2 Kgs 20:12.

[51] 2 Chr 32:33; more restraint in 2 Kgs 20:21.

A last major point I would mention before going on to the second part of my lecture is that, according to the account in the Books of Chronicles, Hezekiah was on one occasion left by God.[52] The verb is *'azabh* in Hebrew, *egkataleipo* in Greek, *shebhaq* in Aramaic, just as in the verse from Psalm 22 put in the mouth of Jesus in Matthew and Mark: "My God, my God, why hast thou forsaken me?"[53] He was forsaken by God on that occasion in order to test him, to find out what was in his heart when without divine assistance. And though for a sad moment he was guilty of pride, he humbled himself and did pass the test.[54] (The orthodox view is perhaps still that he did not pass.[55] But this involves the impossible translation of Hebrew *wekhen*, Greek *kai houtos*, by "howbeit," "nevertheless," instead of by "and so." There are other objections, among them precisely that the figure of Hezekiah is elevated to a new height in the Books of Chronicles.[56] It may well be the widespread misinterpretation of this passage which has prevented scholars from drawing a parallel between the forsakenness of Hezekiah and that of Jesus.[57]) I have already noted that the Rabbis identify Hezekiah with Isaiah's Immanuel. As such, he "knew to refuse the evil and choose the good"[58]—which, in their opinion, means that he recognized God and his will without instruction or aid, by his own inner illumination.[59] No doubt the test of loneliness from which he emerged triumphant is seen by them as supporting their exegesis.

May I repeat: I would urge that Hezekiah as a Messianic figure influencing the writing up of subsequent Messianic figures deserves far more attention than he has received.

[52] 2 Chr 32:31, not in 2 Kings. The occasion was the visit of the Babylonian ambassadors, 2 Chr 32:25 f.; 2 Kgs 20:12 ff.

[53] Matt 27:46; Mark 15:34.

[54] So, correctly, Rudolph, *l.c.*, 315; not very differently Cazelles, *l.c.*, 226, Curtis & Madsen, *l.c.*, 492 f.

[55] E.g. Barnes, *l.c.*, 274.

[56] The same trend in the probably interpolated notice 2 Kgs 18:5: see above, note 12.

[57] The misinterpretation coupled with an unawareness of Hezekiah's image in religious circles in New Testament times. Seesemann, art. "*peira*", in *Theologisches Wörterbuch zum Neuen Testament*, vol. 6, ed. by Friedrich (1959), 36, declared the parallel to be purely formal.

[58] Isa 7:15.

[59] *Num Rab* 14 on 7:48.

3

Legislative and Narrative Forms

This section focuses on ethical and legal instruction in the New Testament, and highlights how teachers in antiquity seek to communicate their ideas.

“Ye Have Heard—But I Say Unto You”

In inspecting a few Rabbinic legal and narrative forms in the New Testament, we may perhaps first take a form of law which, in the course of its transfer to the different setting, underwent a considerable change. Yet for a true understanding of the New Testament section containing it, it is essential to take account of its original use and significance.

In Matthew, in the sermon on the mount, we find a series of injunctions intended to illustrate the position of Jesus as upholder, not destroyer, of the Law.[1] They all more or less follow this pattern: “Ye have heard that it was said by them of old time, Thou shalt not kill. But I say unto you, That whosoever is angry with his brother shall be in danger of the judgment.”

This form falls into two parts. The first gives a Scriptural rule narrowly interpreted, the second a wider demand made by Jesus. The first, in Hebrew, would open: “*shema‘tem ma shenne’emar*. The translation “Ye have heard” is not technical enough. In Rabbinic discussion, *shome‘a ’ani*, “I hear,” “I understand,” or rather, “I might understand,” introduces an interpretation of Scripture which, though conceivable, yet must be rejected. For example, an old Midrashic exposition of the fifth commandment begins thus:[2] “Honour thy father and thy mother. I might understand, *shome‘a ’ani*, Honour them with words only.” The Midrash goes on to refute this proposition and to show that the commandment refers not only to respectful speech but also to the duty of maintaining your parents. Quite often, as in this instance, the interpretation introduced by “I hear,” “I might understand,” is primitive, narrow, literal, compared with that accepted in its stead.

In fact, how closely the root “to hear,” “to understand,” is associated with literal interpretation may be seen from the two early technical terms for “literal meaning”: *shamu‘a* and *mishma‘*, “that which is heard.” Furthermore, *hashshome‘a*, “he who hears,” is used in the sense of “he who sticks to the superficial, literal meaning of Scripture” in the hermeneutic rule[3] according “to which a general summary (like the notice concerning man’s creation in the first chapter of Genesis) may be followed by detailed facts (the story of man’s creation in the second chapter) which are merely a repetition giving more particulars; he who hears—i.e. he who takes Scripture literally—will form the erroneous belief that the second account refers to different facts, but in reality it is merely a repetition with more particulars.”

[1] Matt 5:21 ff.

[2] *Mek.* on Exod 20:12.

[3] The 13th of Eliezer ben Ha-gelili’s 32.

There is good reason, then, for translating the first part of the Matthean form by: "Ye have literally understood," or "Ye might understand literally." "Ye have literally understood what was said by them of old time, Thou shalt not kill."

It may be observed that, on this basis, an old puzzle can at once be solved. Twice in the sermon on the mount the words, "Ye have heard" lead up to a quotation not really to be found in the Old Testament: "Ye have heard, Thou shalt not kill, and [only] he who shall kill shall be in danger of the judgment," and "Ye have heard, Thou shalt love thy neighbour and hate thine enemy."[4] The clauses "and only he who kills shall be in danger of the judgment," and "thou shalt hate thine enemy," do not occur in the Pentateuch at all. However, as soon as we proceed from the translation "Ye have literally understood," the additions cease to be troublesome. "To understand" does not necessarily introduce a strict quotation; the quotation may be provided with a comment. The Rabbis remark on the fifth commandment: "I hear, I might understand, Honour with words only." Just so, Matthew writes: "Ye have literally understood, Thou shalt not kill and only he who kills shall be in danger of the judgment." There is here neither error nor falsification. In modern writing, we should mark off the comment by a phrase like *scilicet* [understand]. That was not necessary where the force of "to hear" was properly appreciated.

As for the second part, "But I say unto you," what is its nearest Rabbinic equivalent? The question may be put in a different way: what is the form employed by the Rabbis when they repudiate those interpretations introduced by "I might understand"? Those interpretations are always refuted by some recognized argument. Mostly this is another text from Scripture. Thus the primitive interpretation of the fifth commandment is disproved by a passage from Proverbs:[5] "Honour thy father and thy mother. I might understand, Honour them with words only. But there is a teaching in what another verse says [Proverbs], Honour the Lord with thy substance. So honouring means honouring with food, drink and clean garments." There need not, however, be recourse to another text. The argument against the objectionable, narrow interpretation may consist in a logical deduction—an inference *a minori ad maius* or the like—and, significantly, the usual Hebrew verb for establishing such a deduction is *'amar,* "to say."

Here is an illustration, a comment by R. Judah the Prince on the notice: "And the Lord came down upon mount Sinai."[6] He explains: "I might hear this as it is heard, I might understand this according to its literal meaning, *shome'a 'ani kishemu'o*. But thou must say, *'amarta*: If the sun, one of the many servants of God, may remain in its place and nevertheless be effective beyond it, how much more He by whose word the world came into being."

Evidently, there is a Rabbinic form expressing a contrast between the "hearing," the "literal understanding," of a rule and what we must "say" it actually signifies. Here lies the source of Matthew's pattern.

[4] Matt 5:21, referring to Exod 20:13; Deut 5:17, and Matt 5:43, referring to Lev 19:18.

[5] Prov 3:9.

[6] *Mek.* on Exod 19:20.

At this point, however, the real problem for form criticism only begins. There are striking differences between the Rabbinic form and the Matthean. If our method is correct, they must reflect the differences in setting; or in other words, any deviations in Matthew from the Rabbinic model must be explicable by his changed premises and objects. This is indeed the case. Matthew has adapted an academic form to his peculiar legislative purposes.

In the Rabbinic form, it is the cautious, scholarly, devout interpreter of holy writ who speaks and is spoken to. "I might understand literally"—"I," namely, the scholar investigating the text. "But thou must say"—"thou," namely, again, a scholar investigating, a fellow-scholar addressed in an imaginary debate. To put it differently, the expounder begins by considering a possibility ("I might understand God's descent on mount Sinai literally") and goes on to refute it as if it had been submitted to him by a colleague in the course of discussion ("But thou must say, there are grounds for not taking it in this way").

The setting in life is academic, dialectic exegesis, and this comes out in a further suggestive feature. The refutation, opening by "But thou must say," does not simply contradict the original proposition; it reasons, it shows why another must be substituted. Judah the Prince, when rejecting the literal interpretation of "And the Lord came down on mount Sinai," does not simply declare: "I might understand this literally. But thou must say, the Lord did not come down and his activity reached mount Sinai though he remained in his place." He gives an argument: "But thou must say, if the sun, a servant of the Lord, can remain in its place and yet produce effects elsewhere, how much more the Lord himself."

In the Matthean form, little remains of this atmosphere of self-contained, orderly exposition. Instead of "I might understand literally," we find "Ye have understood literally" or "Ye might understand literally." The interpretation to be discarded is not a possibility turned over in his mind by an exact scholar. It is put into the mouth of a public as yet blind or even antagonistic. Then, the reply also is far from academic in tone. "But I say unto you" replaces the Rabbinic "But thou must say." Note not only the first person, "I say," but also the "unto you," not present in the Rabbinic form. The tone is not academic but final, prophetic, maybe somewhat defiant. Nor is there any reasoning. The correct attitude is simply stated: "But I say unto you, That whosoever is angry with his brother shall be in danger of the judgment," with no argument *a minori ad maius* or the like.

The point is that, in Matthew, we have before us, not a scholarly working out by some Rabbis of a progressive interpretation as against a conceivable narrow one, but a laying down by Jesus, supreme authority, of the proper demand as against a view, be it held by friends or enemies, which would still take the exact words of the Scriptural precept as a standard of conduct. Jesus, supreme authority, lays down the proper demand: this accounts for "But I say unto you, That whosoever is angry" etc. The demand is opposed to a view held among those addressed which would still take the exact words of a precept as basis: this accounts for "Ye have understood literally what is said" etc. The setting in life of the Rabbinic form is dialectic exposition of the Law; that of the

Matthean is proclamation of the true Law. All differences are intelligible once we are clear as to these settings.

But, it might be asked, is it not more likely, despite all this, or because of it, that Matthew's pattern does not come direct from the other? Is not the gulf between mere exposition and authoritative legislation too great to allow us to assume an intimate connection? And may it not be that Matthew created his pattern independently, though indeed using Rabbinic terms?

The answer is that the gulf is very much smaller than we have so far made it to appear. On the one hand, the Rabbinic form is considerably less detached, less academic, than one might think at first sight. The first part, "I might understand literally," in many if not most cases puts an interpretation which is not only theoretically conceivable, but which is actually maintained somewhere, be it by an older school or a contemporary, rival school or—occasionally—a heretical sect. We have repeatedly quoted Judah the Prince's comment on "And the Lord came down on Sinai," which opens: "I might understand this literally." The paragraph immediately preceding this in the Midrash shows that R. Akiba did adhere to a rather literal explanation. Judah the Prince was combating Akiba's view. The phrase "I might understand literally," therefore, is not quite so speculative and peaceful as it sounds. It is not, in other words, quite so far removed from "Ye have understood literally."

This is confirmed by the second part of the Rabbinic form, "But thou must say" and so on. Here an imaginary fellow-scholar is addressed and instructed. The interpretation to be excluded, that is, is represented as favoured by an opponent—a scholarly, friendly opponent, it is true, but still a "thou" in need of guidance.

Moreover, this second part, "but thou must say" and so on, though it advances a recognized logical justification for replacing the literal meaning by a freer, yet in effect does substitute a new, freer meaning. Nor were the religious leaders of the time unaware that exegesis might be tantamount to legislation. That was precisely the reason why Samaritans and Sadducees refused to accept the results produced in this way as binding. We may also recall the parable, preserved in the Talmud itself,[7] of Moses unable to follow a discussion in R. Akiba's academy—so remote is the Law as expounded by Akiba and his disciples from the Law Moses thought he was giving. Clearly, "But thou must say" contains a strong element of discretionary power. The seed is there which, given certain conditions, might develop into the absolute "But I say unto you."

On the other hand, the Matthean form is far milder, less revolutionary, than one might incline to believe. As we mentioned at the beginning, these declarations, "Ye have heard—But I say unto you," are intended to prove Jesus the Law's upholder, not destroyer. The relationship between the two members of the form is not one of pure contrast; the demand that you must not be angry with your brother is not thought of as utterly irreconcilable with the prohibition of killing. On the contrary, wider and deeper though it may be, it is thought of as, in a sense, resulting from and certainly including the old rule, it is the revelation of a fuller meaning for a new age. The second member

[7] *b. Men.* 29b.

unfolds rather than sweeps away the first. That authoritative "But I say unto you" has in it a good deal of the reasoning "But thou must say."

Indeed, it is only when this factor is properly realized that a familiar, serious difficulty disappears. The injunctions under notice, we are expressly informed, are designed as illustrations of "Think not that I am come to destroy" and so on. Yet, on a superficial reading, they appear to illustrate the very opposite: "Ye have heard the Law saying this—But I say something different." It is only by bearing in mind the descent of this pattern from the Rabbinic one outlined that we can solve the problem and understand Matthew's meaning. There is no conflict. Tertullian is right in describing the new Law as *plenius, perfectius, eruditius, instructius* [fuller, more perfect, more learned, more fit] than the old; but he does not describe it as opposed to the old.[8] Matthew's is a Rabbinic gospel.

Three points may be added in support of our thesis. First, Paul, in Romans, also emphasizes that his doctrine means not destroying but upholding the Law.[9] And he also at once proceeds to demonstrate this by a typically Rabbinic use of some texts from Scripture. He does not, indeed, employ the antithesis "I might understand literally—But thou must say," but still he argues in a good, technical, Rabbinic manner. The affinity with Matthew is striking.

Secondly, in the announcement "I am not come to destroy the Law but to fulfil it," the Hebrew behind "to fulfil" is *qiyyem*, "to uphold."[10] It would lead too far afield here to substantiate this proposition, but let us take it as established. One nuance of *qiyyem* which seems to play a part in this passage is "to uphold Scripture" in the technical sense of "to show that the text is in agreement with your teaching." This is a frequent application of the verb, based on the idea that the test of any teaching you propound is whether, proceeding from it, you can give full effect to, "uphold," every word of the Law. For instance, R. Pappias asserted that God, when remarking "The man is become as one of us," likened man to the angels.[11] Akiba vehemently rejected this interpretation: "That is enough, Pappias." Pappias retorted: "But how then doest thou uphold, *qiyyem*, this verse?" Whereupon Akiba explained that it meant "The man has gone one of the two ways, the evil one, of his own choice." The Hebrew *mimmennu* may signify "of us" or "of himself," and Akiba prefers the latter sense: "The man is become as one [*scil.* of the two ways] of himself [*scil.* of his own choice]." This is a typical example of one disputant—in this case Pappias—defying another—Akiba—to prove that, with his view, he can "uphold" Scripture. Sometimes a Rabbi will not wait for the challenge but call on himself in this way. That is to say, having advanced a doctrine, he will immediately himself put the question, "But how do I uphold this or that text?" and conclude by smoothing away the difficulty.[12] Often the "upholding" is done by showing that, though at first blush one might "hear," "understand," a text in a certain manner, in reality its

[8] *Apologia* 45.3.

[9] Romans 3 and 4; see above all 3:31 ff.

[10] See Guillaume, "The Midrash in the Gospels," *ET*, 37 (1926), 394 ff.

[11] Gen 3:22; see *Mek.* on Exod 14:29.

[12] E.g. *Mek.* on Exod 12:5, 6, 11, 34, 20:25.

import is different.[13] Surely, structures like these constitute the background of the Matthean pattern taken together with the heading "I am not come to destroy the Law but to uphold it." This heading takes up a challenge—no matter from what side we assume that it came—and what follows is legislation, yet defence and argument as well.

Thirdly, when we consider the arrangement of this section of Matthew as a whole, we find a general principle put at the head, "I am not come to destroy, Your righteousness shall exceed that of the Pharisees," and the rest consists of illustrations, all of one pattern, "Ye have heard" and so forth. This sequence of principle and cases is very common in Rabbinic literature. We shall presently say a few words about it.

Before doing so, however, we must still add a note concerning the date of the antithesis "I might hear, understand—but thou must say." There can be no doubt that it goes back to the New Testament period. True, we have no direct evidence before R. Ishmael, in the first half of the 2nd cent. But it is so well established by this time that it must be considerably older. This is not to deny that Matthew may have been familiar with an earlier and slightly different variant.

One point is worth mentioning. Ishmael and his school never say "I might hear what is said by them of old time" or "I might hear what is said," but merely "I might hear." When Schechter tentatively suggested a connection between Matthew's "Ye have heard" and the Rabbinic "I might hear,"[14] it was the additional words in Matthew which caused Bacher to dismiss the idea.[15] But the probability is that, originally, the Rabbis also used a fuller version. The alternation in Matthew of "what is said by them of old time" and "what is said" is suggestive: when he wrote, there already was a shorter as well as a longer form. By Ishmael's time, the Rabbis had made a further abbreviation, saying simply "I might hear"—no wonder, considering how very frequently they availed themselves of the phrase in their expositions.

[13] E.g. where Akiba "upholds" Ps 106:20; see *Mek.* on Exod 14:29.

[14] *JQR,* 10 (1898), 11, n. 3.

[15] *Älteste Terminologie der Jüdischen Schriftauslegung* (1899), 190, n. 3

Principles and Cases

Let us now turn to the arrangement of the section as a whole: the proclamation of a general principle, "I am not come to destroy, Your righteousness shall exceed that of the scribes and Pharisees," followed by a series of illustrations, "Ye have heard, thou shalt not kill, but I say unto you, that whosoever is angry with his brother shall be in danger of the judgment; Ye have heard, thou shalt not commit adultery, but I say unto you" and so on. It has been maintained that this form must be Greek. But there is no justification for this view.

In its simpler applications, the form is to be found even in the Old Testament. Nor is this surprising. The form presupposes a certain degree of systematization, but not an exceptionally high one. Once this stage is reached, lawgivers all over the world will find the arrangement convenient. The fifth of Alfred's Laws begins with a general proposition that every church has a right of sanctuary, and then follow details as to the meaning and limits of this.[1] No. 5 of the Laws of Canute runs in Robertson's rendering:[2] "Concerning heathen practices, We earnestly forbid all heathen practices," and then follow details of such practices. Similarly, in Ecclesiastes,[3] there comes first the general principle: "To every thing there is a season and a time to every purpose." After this come the illustrations: "A time to be born, and a time to die; a time to plant" and so on.

Or take a slightly less primitive example from Leviticus.[4] A general introduction, stating that you must not do as the Egyptians and Canaanites do, is followed by the detailed prohibitions of adultery, incest and the like. Admittedly, the introduction is later than the details. But this does not alter the fact that the author who, at some date, prefixed it intended the structure: general principle—particular cases. Actually, had he repeated the idea governing his introduction in the code itself—and it may be assumed that though he did not repeat it expressly, it was in his mind all the time—we should get something not unlike the Matthean scheme: "Do not as the Egyptians and Canaanites do. They commit adultery—you should not. They marry their sisters—you should not," etc.

In Rabbinic literature, we come across far more intricate applications of this form; moreover, it is clear that it is employed quite consciously. One chapter of the Mishnah begins:[5] "If a man wounds another, he is liable on five counts, for injury, for pain, for healing, for loss of time, and for the indignity inflicted." The text goes on to deal with each of

[1] Attenborough, *The Laws of the Earliest English Kings* (1922), 66 f.

[2] *Laws of the Kings of England from Edmund* (1925), 177.

[3] Eccl 3:1 ff.

[4] Lev 18:1 ff.

[5] *m. B. K.* 8:1.

these five points in detail. Another passage[6] opens with the general principle that "If aught that conveys uncleanness by overshadowing is divided and brought into a house, R. Dosa ben Harkinas declares it clean while the Sages declare it unclean." This principle is illustrated by a number of examples: "If a man touches two pieces of carrion, each a half-olive's bulk," and so on. In all cases, according to the principle prefixed, R. Dosa declares the person in question clean, the Sages declare him unclean. Again, the Mishnah enunciates the rule[7] that if a court (a Beth-din) gives a decision inconsistent with a minor, secondary precept only—say, with a mere detail concerning the observance of the Sabbath—it may be presumed to have acted from an innocent error. The implication is that a decision subverting a main institution of the Law—say, one denying any need to observe the Sabbath—must have sprung from wilful defiance. The rule is illustrated by a few decisions which, though they would be wrong, would not be regarded as deliberately wrong. And these examples are all framed in the same way: "The Sabbath as such is regulated in the Law, but it is allowed to carry a burden on the Sabbath. Idolatry as such is regulated in the Law, but it is allowed to bow down before an idol" and so on.

The following case may be of special interest. One section of the Mishnah[8] begins thus: "In these things the School of Hillel changed their opinion and taught according to the opinion of the School of Shammai." To be sure, this is just a heading, not a principle. But this hardly makes any difference in the present connection. At any rate, the general heading is followed by some particular instances, which are just as lengthy as the particular illustrations in Matthew. In all cases the original opinion of the School of Hillel is given, then the argument by which the Shammaites convinced their opponents, and the conclusion is always in the same words: "The School of Hillel changed their opinion and taught according to the opinion of the School of Shammai." That is, we get a veritable refrain. This structure reminds one very much of the sermon on the mount, with its general principle and elaborate yet systematically arranged illustrations.

Perhaps a brief consideration of Tannaitic terminology shows better than any amount of examples how conscious the Rabbis were of the distinction between principle and detail or illustration. It may suffice to adduce four terms.

The word *'abh*, literally "father," "ancestor," is used, in technical language, to denote a comprehensive notion; *toladha*, literally "descendant," signifies a narrower notion falling under it. For instance, "the pit" counts as one of the *'abhoth neziqin*, of the principles of causation of damage—the historical reason being that the opening of a pit into which a beast might fall is mentioned in a legal section of the Pentateuch.[9] Now if you leave broken glass lying about, thus causing damage, this would be a *toladha* of "the pit," a particular instance falling under the principle.[10]

Again, the noun *guph*, literally "body," is employed as meaning a fundamental principle of the Torah. The commandment to keep the Sabbath, for example, is consid-

[6] *m. Eduy.* 3:1.
[7] *m. Hor.* 1:3b.
[8] *m. Eduy.* 1:12.
[9] Exod 21:33 f.
[10] *m. B. K.* 1:1, 3:1.

ered a *guph*, as opposed to any detailed precept concerning the Sabbath, such as the prohibition of carrying a burden.[11] We have seen that a court giving an incorrect decision regarding a detail is presumed to have done so by mistake, whereas the abolition of a *guph*, according to the Mishnah, inevitably betrays a spirit of godlessness.

Of particular relevance is the term *kelal*, literally "the universal," signifying a basic commandment of the Torah and opposed to *peraṭ*, "the individual," which means a detailed rule. It is worth noting that, according to R. Ishmael, who taught in the first half of the 2nd cent., "the basic commandments were made known to Moses at Sinai, but the details in the tabernacle." (For Philo,[12] the Ten Commandments, given by God's own mouth, were the principles of all law, κεφάλαια νόμων, summarizing the special provisions, ἐν μέρει διατάγματα, which latter were given through Moses.) This view was combated by Akiba, for whom all rules, general or detailed, went back to Sinai.[13] The importance of Ishmael's utterance, for our purposes, lies in the fact that, in his eyes at any rate, the form here discussed—first general principle, then particular rules—was good enough to have been the form chosen by God when he gave Moses the Law. God, in Ishmael's opinion, proclaimed the fundamental principles first, at mount Sinai, and only later the detailed provisions.

A similar distinction between *kelal* and *peraṭ*, incidentally, was applied by the Rabbis to the narrative portions of the Bible. The two accounts of man's creation in Genesis, for example, were explained by means of a hermeneutic rule, already mentioned:[14] Scripture sometimes "starts by giving a general summary of an event—*kelal*, the first, brief account of man's creation—and then goes on to relate facts—the second, longer account—which are merely a detailed description—*peraṭ*—of the same thing."

Finally, the interrogative adverb *keṣadh*, "how?" ought to be mentioned. It is frequently to be met with as introducing the illustrations of a general principle. In three of the examples we have adduced, this adverb is inserted between the principle and its illustrations.[15] For instance, there is the principle that if a court gives a decision contrary to a specific provision only, it need not be regarded as having wilfully defied the Law. At this point the question *keṣadh* comes: "How?," "What exactly does this mean?" Whereupon the illustrations follow to which we have already referred—the decision that you may carry a burden on the Sabbath, that you may bow down before an idol, or the like. To give an idea of the way in which this adverb is employed, we may perhaps say that in Matthew, if it were translated into the language of Mishnic discussion, we might well put *keṣadh* between the heading and the rest: "Your righteousness shall exceed that of the scribes. How?, *keṣadh*? Ye have heard," and so on.

The upshot seems to be that it is quite unnecessary to look for a Greek background to the Matthean arrangement. The evidence strongly suggests that it goes back to a thoroughly Jewish milieu.

[11] *m. Hor.* 1:3.
[12] *Decal.* 18 f., *De spec. leg.* 1.1.1.
[13] *b. Hag.* 6a.
[14] Above, in discussing "Ye have heard—but I say unto you."
[15] *m. B. K.* 8:1; *m. Eduy.* 3:1; *m. Hor.* 1:3b.

Eye for Eye

Matthew tells us[1] that Jesus opposed to the old maxim "An eye for an eye" the rule "Resist not evil: but whosoever shall smite thee on the right cheek, turn to him the other also."

The passage raises many problems. First, Luke indeed has the rule "And to him that smiteth thee on the one cheek, offer also the other."[2] But he has not the old maxim "An eye for an eye" to which it is opposed in Matthew. Which, if either, of the two versions is original? Or is it too old-fashioned to suggest that both are, going back to different sermons? (A minor item relevant in this connection is that while Matthew speaks of "the right cheek" and the other, Luke speaks of "the one cheek" and the other.) Secondly, is the rule "Resist not evil" a natural product of the Jewish teaching of the time—or at any rate, of one school of Rabbinic theology—or is there anything new? Thirdly, how far does the passage allude back to the description of the suffering servant of the Lord in the Old Testament and forward to the treatment meted out to Jesus during the trial?

These and several more points cannot here be discussed; and we shall concentrate on two questions only. First, was the teaching of Jesus—or whoever the author of the passage may have been—directed against talion in the literal sense; or in other words, was talion in the literal sense still practised or taught in the circle he addressed? Secondly, what is the significance, for the history of the Jewish law concerning insult, of the connection to be found in this passage between the maxim "An eye for an eye" and the case of smiting a man's cheek? Our answer to the first question will be in the negative; and to the second, that the passage most probably reflects a pre-Talmudic state of the law.

A. Talion

First, then, we submit that the teaching under notice was not directed against talion in the literal sense. For one thing, there are various general considerations making it likely that, by the time of Jesus, retaliation in the case of damage to a person had been superseded by money penalties. Not a single instance of the practice of retaliation is mentioned in the sources. Both Mishnah and Mekhilta reject any literal interpretation of "Eye for eye" and lay down that the wrongdoer has to pay damages.[3] It might perhaps be objected that these works, though containing old material, were not completed until

[1] Matt 5:38 f.

[2] Luke 6:29.

[3] For references, see Strack-Billerbeck, 1 (1922), 341 ff.

the end of the 2nd cent. A.D. (Mishnah) or even later (Mekhilta). But this argument loses much of its weight when we remember that the system of damages of Mishnah and Mekhilta is of so elaborate and subtle a nature—we shall soon have to quote a few illustrations—that we must allow a long time for its growth. In other words, talion must have been ousted by a pecuniary settlement long before the detailed provisions concerning the latter which we find in Mishnah and Mekhilta were established. Consequently, even if we assume that these provisions do not belong to the older material—an unlikely assumption in this general form, though one instance of divergence from the law of the time of the New Testament will be given below—we still arrive at the conclusion that talion can no longer have formed part of the law in the age of Jesus. Had he attacked this principle, he would have been guilty of a strange anachronism.

There are, it is true, two points occasionally adduced for the opposite view.[4] A group of Sadducees, the Boethusaeans, seem to have been in favour of actual retaliation, and their attitude was shared by at least one Talmudic authority, R. Eliezer. It is, however, doubtful whether this doctrine represents a genuine survival of ancient legal ideas; it may well have been a revival due to the Sadducean theory that the Bible ought to be interpreted quite literally and not, as among the Pharisees, in a way that rendered it possible to introduce outside notions. What is more important: it is difficult to see why Jesus should have addressed the words here discussed precisely to the holders of that theory. There is no sign of his singling out Sadducean doctrines anywhere in the sermon on the mount.

The other point sometimes advanced is a paragraph from Josephus,[5] where he says that a man who mutilates another should be mutilated in the same manner, unless the person wronged is satisfied with damages. Now this regulation is not referred to at all in other Jewish sources. It agrees neither with that of the Pharisees nor with that of the Sadducees nor with that of any dissentient authority. It very much looks as if Josephus, when he had to interpret the Biblical maxim "Eye for eye," had gone to Roman law for guidance. The XII Tables do give a regulation somewhat like his.[6] Admittedly it was out of date by the time he wrote. But he was not a lawyer; he had to make the Biblical injunction palatable to his Roman readers; and a provision of the XII Tables known to Festus and Gellius, and obviously a favourite topic of debate, may have been known to him. *Si membrum rupit, ni cum eo pacit, talio esto* [If he destroys a limb, unless he makes an agreement with him, let there be retaliation], says Festus,[7] *Si membrum rupit, ni cum e pacto, talio esto* [If he destroys a limb, unless it were in terms of an agreement, let there be retaliation], says Gellius.[8] In any case Josephus is so much out of touch with the main line, or lines, of Jewish law on this matter that his testimony must be ruled out.

So far we have appealed to external evidence only, and we grant that it might not be regarded as fully conclusive. Actually the principal reason why the question has

[4] See Strack-Billerbeck, 1. c.
[5] *Ant.* 4.8.35.280.
[6] VIII 2.
[7] *De Verborum Significatione*, 363.
[8] *Attic Nights* 20.1.14.

remained controversial up to our day seems to be that nothing but external evidence has ever been considered. (A subsidiary reason is the desire on the part of Christian scholars to make the preaching of Jesus as original as possible and the desire on the part of Jewish ones to explain away any originality.) There is, however, a clue in the text itself.

Its author opposed to the maxim "An eye for an eye" the rule "Resist not evil," and he illustrated the rule by the case where a man has his ears boxed; in this case, he said, the other cheek should be offered. Supposing for a moment the maxim "Eye for eye" had then meant actual talion for mutilation and Jesus had intended to attack this principle, would the case of a slap in the face not have been an excessively weak illustration of his new position? Would it not have been absolutely necessary to give a far more serious example? Would he not have said something to this effect: But whosoever tears out one of thine eyes, forgive him and do not require that one of his be torn out? Certainly, nowadays we can use the exhortation "Turn the other cheek" even for the most serious cases. But we must not take our proverbial use back into the New Testament. The author of this passage cited the offence of smiting a man's cheek, not as a proverbial case covering all kinds of injury, even the gravest, but as the best example available of the situation to which the warning not to demand "An eye for an eye" was to apply. Which shows that he was not combating talion in the case of mutilation.

In fact it shows that he was not thinking of the law concerning damage to a person at all. A slap in the face is a case, not of mutilation, but of insult—a very different thing. From the choice of this example it is evident that he meant to pronounce immoral not the law concerning mutilation but that concerning insult. A man should be meek under an insult, this was his teaching, and not insist on such redress as the maxim "An eye for an eye" would give him—which was such a sum of money for this kind of insult and such a sum for another kind.[9] It follows that, in the eyes of the author of this passage, the maxim "An eye for an eye" governed the law concerning insult, was the basis for the fines to be paid by him who had committed an insult to the person insulted. In the eyes of the author, that is, that maxim, far from enjoining literal talion for mutilation, simply stood for the idea of accurate reparation, the exaction of amends precisely corresponding to the wrong done. In the case of insult there had never been any talion—how could there be?—but always money penalties. Where the maxim "An eye for an eye" is connected with this offence, its horrifying character must have gone; it can have reference only to fines.

All this is argument from purely internal evidence. And the result is that this utterance is the earliest positive testimony preserved to us of that stage of Jewish law where the principle "Eye for eye" had only the refined meaning of restitution by means of money.

Once this is recognized, three points, otherwise incompatible with the verses analysed, become intelligible and indeed provide strong confirmation of the interpretation submitted. In the first place, in the Mishnah also—and in Roman law—the case of smiting a man's cheek serves to illustrate just that situation where there is only insult but no damage to a person. We shall come back to this point later on, but would lay much emphasis on it in the present connection.

[9] A list of fines is quoted from the Mishnah by Strack-Billerbeck., *loc. cit.*

In the second place, neither of the two further examples given in Matthew ("If any man will sue thee and take thy coat, let him have thy cloke also; and whosoever shall compel thee to go a mile, go with him twain") is a case of mutilation. We need not here inquire whether they come from the same hand as the first one, the case of smiting a man's cheek. It is sufficient to remark that whoever put them in their present place did not think of combating retaliation, but regarded the cry "An eye for an eye" as characterizing him who stands on his rights and honour instead of humiliating himself before his fellow-man. He proceeded from the refined Rabbinic meaning of the maxim, from "An eye for an eye" as signifying the claim to accurate, nicely calculated compensation.

In the third place, it is noteworthy that when Jesus quoted the old Biblical maxim, he omitted the first clause "Life for life" and mentioned "Eye for eye, tooth for tooth." This is highly significant. In the case of homicide, the Rabbis did not abolish retaliation, at least not in theory: a murderer was liable to capital punishment, and even he who killed a man unwittingly could save himself only by escaping into a city of refuge.[10] Accordingly, the clause "Life for life" was not divested by the Rabbis of its literal meaning in the way the other clauses "Eye for eye, tooth for tooth" and so on were. The natural result was that the two parts of the maxim drifted apart, in law and in the minds of the people: the clause "Life for life" belonged to criminal law, was connected with the death penalty, the other clauses "Eye for eye" and so on belonged to private law, were connected with monetary compensation. Had this development not yet been completed by the time of the New Testament, had "Eye for eye" still implied actual talion, the omission of "Life for life" would be incomprehensible. It is readily accounted for, however, on the basis of the thesis here proposed. When the passage under notice was written, "An eye for an eye" was no longer interpreted as demanding literal talion but was referred to damages. The separation of "Eye for eye" and so on from "Life for life" was complete, and it did not occur to the author, who was thinking of insult, a matter of private law, to bring in the criminal law clause, "Life for life."

Perhaps we may add that if this part of the sermon on the mount is properly understood, its religious implications come out the more clearly. It is not concerned—not even secondarily—with a certain historical system of punishment. It is concerned with something far more fundamental, namely, the urge to resent a wrong done to you as an affront to your pride, to forget that the wrongdoer is your brother before God and to compel him to soothe your unworthy feelings; and it advocates, instead, a humility which cannot be wounded, a giving of yourself to your brother which will achieve more than can be achieved by narrow justice. Insult, because immediately aimed at the victim's dignity as a human being, and thereby at the image of God was considered by the Rabbis as a terrible sin. For them, one striking his fellow or even one putting his fellow to shame by a hurtful remark, was the typical *rasha'*, "godless man."[11] (The rendering "Resist not the wicked man" or, for that matter, "Do not prosecute the wicked man"[12]

[10] A survey of the law is given by Strack-Billerbeck, *op. cit.*, 254 ff.

[11] *b. Sanh.* 58b; *b. B. M.* 59b.

[12] ἀνθίστημι means "to go to law" or something like it, for instance, in Deut 19:18; Isa 59:12; Jer 14:7 (the Hebrew in these cases has *'ana*) and Isa 50:8 (*'amadh*).

would be no less in agreement with the Rabbinic attitude than "Resist not evil.") It is precisely this most direct attack on your personality which the saying here discussed expects you to bear without resentment. It breathes the spirit of the Rabbinic teaching (Gamaliel II, towards the end of the 1st cent. A.D., Judah ben Elai, middle of the 2nd) that if you are struck you must forgive the offender even though he does not ask your forgiveness,[13] or of a prayer which the Jew says three times a day (if he says his prayers!), in the morning, in the afternoon and in the evening: "My God, unto those that curse me may my soul be dumb, yea, may my soul be as dust unto all."[14]

B. Insult

At this juncture, however, a problem arises which seems completely to have escaped notice. In Rabbinic law as we know it from Mishnah and Mekhilta, the case of smiting a man's cheek does not fall under the provision "An eye for an eye" at all, but under the provision, to be found in Deuteronomy,[15] "Then thou shalt cut off her hand." In other words, in Rabbinic law as we know it, the insulting party's duty to pay a fine to the party insulted is based on that injunction from Deuteronomy. Yet Jesus assumed that it was based on "An eye for an eye": when he demanded that a man should reply to a slap in the face by offering the other cheek, he was illustrating an attitude that leaves behind the old principle "An eye for an eye."

This is a real conflict, which calls for an explanation. We thus come to the second question: Is there any significance for the history of the Jewish law concerning insult in the connection occurring in Matthew between the maxim "An eye for an eye" and the case of smiting a man's cheek, and, if so, what is it?

In order to answer this question, a closer inspection of the Rabbinic law on the matter and its evolution will be necessary. As pointed out already, smiting a man's cheek appears in Rabbinic argument as a typical case of insult, of insult unqualified, without actual damage to a person. The same is true of Roman law, where the praetor's edict gave as example of actionable insult the case of *Aulo Agerio pugno mala percussa est* [Aulus Agerius' cheek was struck by a fist].[16] Indeed already the first Roman codification, the XII Tables, laid down a penalty of twenty-five *asses* for *iniuria*, understanding by this such modes of insult as a box on the ears.[17] There is no reason to assume any influence of Roman on Jewish law (though it is impossible to disprove it). A slap in the face must have been so natural an example of insult in ancient times that the lawyers of various countries would think of it independently of one another. We find it mentioned as part of the humiliating treatment of the suffering servant of the Lord in the Old Testament, we find its insulting character considered in Germanic systems.[18] It should be remembered that mere insulting words were not enough to justify proceedings; that

[13] *t. B. K.* 9:29 f.

[14] Singer's *Prayer Book*, 54, 119, 142, 166.

[15] Deut 25:11 f.

[16] Lenel, *Das Edictum Perpetuum*, 3rd ed. (1927), 398.

[17] VIII 4.

[18] See His, *Das Strafrecht des deutschen Mittelalters*, 2 (1935), 97.

dangerous words such as hostile spells belonged to a different class of delicts altogether, at least for a long period; and that in the case of blows resulting in serious injury such as the loss of a limb, the element of actual damage to a person was very much more important than that of insult—which, be it noted, might be entirely absent, for instance, if there was an honest fight or a mishap. It is easy to see how the kind of insult expressed by a slap in the face became the prototype of insult in the legal sense.

The very term employed by the XII Tables, *iniuria*, reflects this development. The XII Tables declared punishable first *membrum ruptum* [damaged limb (exact meaning unclear)], secondly *os fractum* [broken bone], and thirdly *iniuria* [wrong]. Whereas the two former involved actual damage to a person (no need here to go into the exact difference—a hopeless task), *iniuria* signified harmless blows such as a slap in the face. Why was this word, the native meaning of which is "an unlawful act" or "illegality," used to denote a slap in the face? Were *membrum ruptum* and *os fractum* not also instances of *iniuria* in this wider, untechnical sense? They were, and no doubt the Romans knew it. But it was only in cases like a slap in the face that unlawfulness alone, so to speak, constituted the offence; that the rather abstract notion of "violation of another person's rights" was in the foreground, not concealed behind any more concrete facts like a broken limb or a torn-out eye; that the plaintiff could show the judge no glaring damage but appealed for redress on the sole ground that "a wrong," *iniuria*, had been done to him. Consequently it was cases like a slap in the face, cases of wrong pure and simple, that received the technical appellation of *iniuria*, "unlawfulness proper." It was they which made early lawyers aware of the existence of a thing like violation of another person's rights as such, independent of real damage. As we concluded above, the kind of attack expressed by a slap in the face became the prototype of that spiritual delict, insult.

Whether under Roman influence or no—and probably there was none—the Rabbis used the case of smiting a man's cheek as illustration of the delict of insult. When it came to making this delict actionable, however, they were in some difficulty. In Roman law the XII Tables mentioned the delict, and any reforms desirable were easily effected by the praetor. The Bible, however, had no obvious provision concerning insult. Yet—and this is a point of vital importance for a correct assessment of the evolution—in the view of the Rabbis, if there was to be a regulation, it must have its basis in the Bible. In one way or another, that is, any action that was to lie in the case of insult must be derived from Scripture. We have no details left of the various attempts—for there must have been more than one—that they made to solve the problem. We do know, however, the ingenious method by which it was finally mastered.

The final system as set forth in Mishnah and Mekhilta may be summarized thus.[19] If a man attacked another, there were five kinds of damages that had to be considered; according to the particular circumstances, sometimes it was only one of them, sometimes several or even all, to which the wrongdoer was liable. First, there was compensation for actual damage to a person; secondly, for the pain caused; thirdly, for loss of

[19] See, in the main, *m. B. K.* 8 and Mekhilta on the passages from Exodus to be quoted in the course of the following discussion.

time, incapacity to work; fourthly, for the cost of healing, doctor's fees; and fifthly, for insult. The Biblical basis for the first four the Rabbis found in the *Mishpatim*, the "Judgments," the legal chapters in Exodus. Compensation for actual damage to a person was rested by them on "Eye for eye, tooth for tooth, hand for hand, foot for foot."[20] We have already observed that, for the Rabbis, this provision referred to a pecuniary settlement. Here it must be added that they confined it to the case where real damage has been inflicted on a person, where, for example, an eye or foot has been lost. The second kind of compensation, for pain, the Rabbis deemed to be indicated by the words "Burning for burning, wound for wound, stripe for stripe."[21] By this enumeration of several hardly distinguishable and apparently negligible modes of wounding, the Rabbis argued, the Bible intended to impose on the offender the obligation to make amends for pain even if no physical damage may have resulted, for instance, if he touched another man with a hot spit. For the third kind of compensation, compensation for loss of time, the Rabbis adduced the verse: "Only he shall pay for the loss of time" (literally, "for his ceasing," or perhaps "for his sitting down").[22] The same verse served as basis for the fourth kind, compensation for the cost of healing: "And he shall cause him to be thoroughly healed."

So far, so good. The linking of the first four kinds of compensation with the "Judgments" in the fashion just described may appear artificial to a modern reader, but it is at least intelligible and not vastly different from Roman "interpretations" of statutes and edicts, especially the logic of the Pontiffs, or even from certain feats of English jurisprudence. Of all these four kinds of compensation—or, more cautiously, of all except compensation for pain—even a modern historian has to admit that the beginnings at any rate were really there in the Bible. But what about the fifth kind, compensation for indignity inflicted? Where did the Rabbis get Scriptural authority for this? They got it from Deuteronomy: "Then thou shalt cut off her hand." This provision, if we read it without Rabbinic spectacles, ordains that a woman who commits a certain obscene and vicious crime shall have her hands cut off. According to the Rabbis it ordains that he who insults a man—for example, by smiting his cheek—shall pay damages.[23]

It must be chiefly two factors that account for this surprising Rabbinic use of the law in question. In the first place, the crime originally contemplated must have been exceedingly rare long before the Rabbinic era. But even if it did occur, it could be adequately dealt with under the general rules concerning attack on a person which we have outlined above and some other rules. We are safe, therefore, in assuming that the provision in its original sense had long been a dead letter. It follows that the Rabbis were free to use it for other purposes, or rather, since it was their doctrine that the Bible contained no superfluous provision, that they were compelled to use it for other purposes. They did so by declaring it the basis for compensation in the case of insult. In the sec-

[20] Exod 21:24.

[21] Exod 21:25.

[22] Exod 21:19.

[23] The Siphre, it is true, also mentions the somewhat less astounding interpretation that these verses refer to the duty to prevent a person from serious crime by incapacitating him.

ond place, there was indeed a verbal link—or maybe it was just a little more than that—between the passage from Deuteronomy and the delict of insult. The woman of whom this provision speaks seizes a man by his *mebhushim*, "shameful parts." The Rabbinic technical term for insult suffered was *bosheth*, "shame," coming from the same root. Surely, this also led the Rabbis to see here the Biblical regulation of the delict of insult.

Be this as it may, the fifth kind of damages, damages for insult, was derived by the Rabbis from this Deuteronomic law. It should be noted, however, that even when they had overcome their main difficulty in the matter of insult, and recognized the provision discussed as sufficient Scriptural authority for an action, they had yet to prove one more item, namely, that the words "Then thou shalt cut off her hand" meant no more than monetary compensation. To prove this they made use of one of their traditional rules of hermeneutics, the inference *a minori ad maius*. They argued that, since the maxim "Eye for eye," though referring to the serious case of actual damage to a person, prescribed money compensation only, *a fortiori* the injunction "Thou shalt cut off her hand," which referred to mere insult, had to be considered as prescribing money compensation. We have here, incidentally, another piece of evidence showing that the interpretation of "Eye for eye" as speaking of a pecuniary settlement goes back to a very early date. Clearly, it must have been firmly established by the time that it was employed for reading a pecuniary settlement into other laws such as that from Deuteronomy.

Such, then, is the system of Mishnah and Mekhilta, and it will be agreed that we did not say too much in the first part of this discussion when we maintained that we ought to allow a considerable time for its growth. We can now proceed to answer the question posed above. Jesus looked upon "An eye for an eye" as the principle governing compensation in the case of insult. In Rabbinic law as we know it the principle governing compensation in the case of insult was "Then thou shalt cut off her hand." How is this divergence to be explained? To put it differently, it is plain that Jesus was ignorant of the technical Rabbinic analysis of the delict of insult as it appears in Mishnah and Mekhilta. What can be the reason?

There are two possibilities. One is that he had not penetrated into those details and took it for granted, as presumably anyone not belonging to the learned circles would, that any kind of damages had its basis in the old maxim "Eye for eye." In other words, he was not enough of a scholar to be aware of the distinction between compensation for actual damage to a person and compensation for indignity inflicted, and of the subtle derivation of the latter from the unlikely provision in Deuteronomy. If we take this line, Matthew represents a popular, unlearned view as distinct from academic teaching. From the standpoint of Jewish legal history, incidentally, the result remains much the same if we assume that the author himself was familiar with the Rabbinic technicalities but discarded them out of consideration for his unlearned audience.

We are, however, inclined to prefer the second possibility. This is that in the period when Jesus preached, or when the verses in question were composed, that highly technical treatment of the delict of insult did not yet exist. The Rabbis themselves, that is, in this period still regarded the maxim "Eye for eye" as sufficiently comprehensive to include cases like smiting a man's cheek as well as cases like breaking a man's arm.

It was not till later, say, the end of the 1st or beginning of the 2nd century, that they sought a separate basis in the Bible on which to rest compensation for insult, finally resorting to the law from Deuteronomy. Whether or not the several texts used with reference to damages for pain, loss of time and cost of healing were already fixed in the age of Jesus may be left undecided, though quite probably they were. They all, like "Eye for eye," are from the "Judgments," the legal chapters in Exodus, the principal source of ancient Hebrew private law and the source most relied on by the early Rabbis. "Thou shalt cut off her hand" is the only provision in the system of damages reviewed that lies outside the "Judgments," being taken from Deuteronomy. At any rate, the fact that this provision is introduced from outside furnishes strong support for the second alternative, for the view that when the author of the utterance we find in Matthew started from "An eye for an eye" as demanding compensation in the case of insult, he was in agreement with the then prevailing Rabbinic law. This maxim was still interpreted at the time as prescribing compensation not only for actual damage to a person but also for insult. We may add that in Roman law also, in the XII Tables, *iniuria*, insult, was still placed together with *membrum ruptum* and *os fractum*, and that its separation from those grave cases was a result of gradual development.[24]

If this is true, then not only have we a satisfactory explanation of the problem created by the Matthean passage, but we also have some indication, vague though it be, as to its date of composition. It must have been a comparatively early date, before the delict of insult was severed from "An eye for an eye" and assigned to "Thou shalt cut off her hand." Above all, however, we have here a plain instance—there cannot be many—where the New Testament has preserved to us a pre-Talmudic stage of Jewish private law, a stage far removed from the law of the Bible (monetary compensation instead of talion, and legal consideration of insult as well as of actual wounds) but less advanced than that of Mishnah and Mekhilta (no separate Scriptural texts as yet for compensation for actual damage and compensation for insult, but both resting on "Eye for eye"). That stage might perhaps have been inferred even without this evidence from general considerations respecting the evolution of Rabbinic doctrines and with the help of comparative methods. To have chapter and verse for it, however, is a different matter, especially as we are here moving in a period of Jewish private law on which the light of the sources shines only dimly.

[24] That to some extent they ultimately met again—namely, when the edict on *iniuriae* was extended to serious wounds—is irrelevant to the present discussion. It may be noted, however, that even in its widest application this edict never included the unintentional causing of *membrum ruptum* or *os fractum*; i.e. at least half the field covered by the *membrum ruptum* and *os fractum* of the XII Tables remained outside the scope of the edict.

The Form is the Message

The form of a statement usually reveals a good deal, apart from its content.[1] Of course, it is never possible to appreciate either in strict isolation from the other. However, exclusive interest in material is so common as to justify a call to restore the balance. The fact is that the slightest nuance in style is likely to signify something. A report that "Carter is coming to San Francisco" is not the same as "the President is coming to San Francisco." In the field of legislation, we shall presently see, "If a man steals a sheep, he shall be hanged" is not the same as "Whoever steals a sheep, he shall be hanged," though at first blush one might think so.

Before going on *in medias res*, a reservation: a structure once established is apt to be carried on mechanically, in which case it may tell us more about the past than the present. Take the way mail is addressed. In Germany, where I grew up, I was taught to put first the addressee's name, Hermann Müller, then the place, Ulm, then the street, Kaiserstrasse, and lastly the house number, 12. This order becomes intelligible when we consider that, at one time, mostly, name and place were all that was needed: Hermann Müller, Ulm. Later it became necessary to add the street, yet later the house number. Today the arrangement makes little sense and they are about to adopt the British-American one with its clear progress from particular to general: name, house number, street, place. It is questionable, however, whether even here logic was a factor at the outset. Formerly, a person's dwelling was often more or less part of the name—John Smith the Mill, Peter Low the Oakwood—and it may well have been in this role that house number and street obtained their position before the place on an English address. Arguably, a rational modern address constructed *de novo* would begin with the place, there would follow street and house number, and the name would come at the end.

In law and related areas, where tradition is strong, a good many modalities outlive their meaning.[2] The "whereas" introduction of a statute has a history taking us back to the Greek philosophers' debate as to whether a legislator should set forth his reasons.[3] Yet it became so time-worn that often we are told scarcely more than: "Whereas it is expedient to lay down the following provisions."[4] Or think of the piling up of synonyms—"this object shall not be damaged, injured, hurt, harmed, broken, split,

[1] See Excursus 1, below, 221 ff.

[2] See D. Mellinkoff, *The Language of the Law* (1963), 290 ff.

[3] Plato, *Laws* 4.718 ff.

[4] *Probate of First Offender Act* (1887), J. M. Lely, *The Statutes of Practical Utility*, 3 (1894), 164; *India Church Act*, 1927, *The Statutes printed by authority*, 3rd rev. ed., 19 (1950), 355.

scratched." In a period of hairsplittingly rigid interpretation, it might be a safeguard,[5] but it continued—or should I say, continues?—long after that. (It does remain useful to the lawyer whose client believes such lingo needed and pays for it.)

Still, a vestige at least of the original import normally lingers on. Let us look at the pair "If a man steals a sheep, he shall be hanged" and "Whoever, or he who, steals a sheep shall be hanged." I have discussed it before[6] but present it again because it is such a straightforward—if somewhat boring—illustration, or test, of my theme. A court will certainly come to the same decision no matter which alternative it has before it. The substance, then, is identical—at any rate, for most practical purposes. Yet even here it pays to take notice of the patterns. They turn out to derive from quite distinct evolutionary stages and, furthermore, to carry a little of their primary equipment with them to this day.

The conditional clause goes back to a much older mode of lawmaking than the relative. It tells the occurrence to be regulated, "a man steals a sheep," and all it does to raise it from a story to a model is to put "if" in front. Actually, in Nordic compilations, we find a phrasing even nearer the bare narrative, with no "if" but merely a "now": "Now a slave runs away,"[7] "Now a man becomes a slayer,"[8] "Now a slayer swims out to a boat."[9] And there is the transitional "now if": "Now if men fall in battle."[10] By contrast, the relative clause, "whoever steals" or "he who steals," instead of reciting an occurrence, introduces a person defined by his action: the story is replaced by a category. The step will be best comprehended by thinking of the question to which each of the two forms makes answer. The conditional presupposes the question: "What shall be done if so-and-so happens?"—surely about the earliest enquiry directed to a lawgiver. Answer: "If so-and-so happens, if a man steals a sheep, he shall be hanged." The relative presupposes a question that has advanced far beyond the emergency "if so-and-so happens," being at home with abstraction, thinking in terms of classes: "What shall be done to such-and-such as a class, to whoever steals a sheep?" Answer: "Whoever steals a sheep shall be hanged."

No wonder Hammurabi, the Twelve Tables, the genuine Mishpatim in Exodus,[11] are dominated by "if," while in Neo-Babylonian laws, laws around the time of Augustus,

[5] See my discussion ["The Influence of Interpretation on Writing"] in *BuffLR*, 20 (1970), 41 ff.

[6] I have discussed "If" and "He who" in *Das Blutrecht* etc. and in *Forms of Roman Legislation* (1956) (repr. 1979), 6 ff.; "Thou shalt" in a Lecture at the Oxford Society of Historical Theology, Abstract of Proceedings (1945), 38 ff.; Rules stated as Facts in the same Lecture, 43 ff., in Appended Note to E. G. Selwyn, *The First Epistle of St. Peter* (1946) 2nd ed. (1947), 467 ff., and in *Forms of Roman Legislation*, 68 ff.; "You have heard" in *The New Testament and Rabbinic Judaism*, 55 ff. [167 ff.]; the Fifth Commandment in Lectures (unpubl.) at Institute of Jewish Studies, (Manchester, 1955), and at Department of Hebrew, University College, London, 1957, and in Gifford Lectures 1963 etc., no. 1, "The Fifth Commandment" and no. 2, Deuteronomy; Diagnosis in Lecture at the Oxford Society etc., 39 ff.; Technique and Technician in Lecture at NEH Seminar of Karen Lebaqcz, Berkeley, on Bioethics and Professional Responsibility, 1980 (unpubl.); and Curses in *Das Blutrecht* etc. and in Lecture at Oxford Society, etc., 39.

[7] *Norwegisches Recht*, Gulathing, translated into German by R. Meissner (1935), 57.

[8] *Landrecht des Königs Magnus Hakonarson*, edited and translated into German by R. Meissner (1941), 102 f.

[9] *Norwegisches Recht*, 107.

[10] *Landrecht*, 179.

[11] Exodus 21 ff.

laws in Leviticus,[12] "whoever" is no less frequent. We have to do with a universal phenomenon: it takes a long period of occurrence-orientation to be able to reach category-orientation, and some legal cultures do not get there at all, remain what we might call folk-law. I should add that since I first dealt with this matter, Reuven Yaron has drawn attention to the relative in proclamations like "Whoever is fearful, let him return,"[13] "What man that will begin to fight Ammon, he shall be head."[14] This usage may well have played a major part in the development.[15]

The generalizing, systematizing thrust of the breakthrough from "if" to "whoever" or "he who" comes out beautifully in King Alfred's code. In the midst of a chapter with one "if" after another, there is this provision: "If anyone seeks the King's life, he shall lose his life and all his possessions." Then follows the one exception: "So we ordain for all estates, too, commoners as well as nobles—he who seeks his master's life shall lose his life and all his possessions."[16] The "he who" part is clearly marked as an innovation. Emphatically, dramatically, generously (generously to the ins, that is) it extends punishability from one plotting against the King—very narrow—to one plotting against his superior—all-inclusive. It is here that "he who" makes its appearance.

Once a civilisation has adopted the relative, the legislator can choose between it and the conditional; and closer examination reveals that the intrinsic, primary difference never completely ceases to matter. For example, where a law is subdivided into main case and more special case, often the former begins with "whoever" and the latter with "if," while the converse is extremely rare. There are scores of Roman statutes, senatusconsults and edicts like this one: "Through whosever wickedness a tomb is interfered with [basic offence] against him I shall give an action for 100,000 sesterces. If anyone makes his habitation in a tomb [aggravated offence], against him I shall give an action for 200,000."[17] Just so, a U.S. statute runs: "Whoever wilfully sets fire to any building shall be imprisoned not more than five years. If the building be a dwelling, he shall be imprisoned not more than twenty years."[18] It is most unlikely that the drafters have reflected on the respective values of "if" and "whoever." They instinctively go on observing them, they just feel that this sounds right and the opposite would sound wrong—which makes the evidence all the more impressive.

I now proceed to three patterns which, I suppose, count as characteristic respectively of Old Testament, New Testament and Tannaitic precepts: "you shall" or "you shall not," "you have heard but I say," "one does" or "one does not." "You shall" or "you shall not" is far from widespread. More specifically, it is met neither in the New Testament nor in the Talmud, except, of course, in quotations. The most perfect application is offered by the Ten Commandments: "Thou shall not make an image, bow down

12 Leviticus 20.

13 Judg 7:3.

14 Judg 10:18.

15 See R. Yaron, *The Laws of Eshnunna* (1969), 67 f.

16 *Die Gesetze der Angelsachsen,* edited and translated into German by F. Liebermann (1903), vol. 1, 50 f.

17 O. Lenel, *Das Edictum Perpetuum,* 3rd ed. (1927), 228.

18 Title 18 of United States Code, *Crimes and Criminal Procedure,* Part I, Crimes, Chapter 5, Arson, Section 81.

to them, serve them, take the name of the Lord in vain, do any work on the Sabbath, murder, commit adultery, steal, bear false witness, covet." We may include a slight variation: "There shall not be unto thee other gods."[19] It will be noticed that, throughout, the singular, "thou," is used, as is the negative "shalt not." Hardly accidental: I take it that the singular version of the form preceded the plural one, and, alas, prohibition preceded positive rule.

What is the initial background? Let us begin by observing that the directives purport to emanate from highest, absolute authority. Actually, the translation "thou shalt not" is not quite adequate. In Hebrew, this is indistinguishable from the future, "thou wilt not." (The expert will have no difficulty in substituting the correct terminology of Semitic grammar.[20]) The Septuagint, the New Testament quotations and the Vulgate do put the future, *ou phoneuseis, non occides*. We ought to acknowledge an element going beyond what should not be done, on to what will not be done, in other words, a prophetic-predicting-compelling admixture, a spell. Hence a transgressor would be breaking down a sacred barrier, would be placing himself outside the God-determined order of things. When a father sternly admonishes his children "You will never dishonour the family name," the implications are not dissimilar. (Poor Kelsen. Ought and is are not, then, forever apart. Christian Morgenstern's Korf knew it: "*Weil, so schliesst er messerscharf, nicht sein kann was nicht sein darf.*" ["Because, so he concludes sharply, what may not be, can not be."])

We come across here a feature to which I shall return when analysing Tannaitic diction:[21] laws apparently without sanction may yet contain one. The injunctions under review never provide for human enforcement and only now and then add a reminder of heaven's vigilance—for example, "the Lord will not hold him guiltless that takes his name in vain." But even in the absence of any such clause, my point is that, originally, "thou shalt not" as such carries a threat. So long as it has its full force, comprising "thou wilt not," the consequences of a violation are tremendous—a fall into the abyss.

Next, for the addressee. It is the individual; the male individual, to be precise, as may be gathered from "thou shalt not covet thy neighbour's wife." He is spoken to, put under restraint, in the most immediate and gripping fashion, far more immediate than would be "nobody shall do so and so" or "this or that shall not be done," far more gripping than the paternal caveats of Wisdom which, typically, are without that domineering "thou wilt not" touch. It is up to him to comply with these interdicts: they are supported, as just mentioned, by no this-worldly measures in the event of disobedience.

As to substance, it will suffice to notice the concentration on taboos indispensable to the cohesion of a peculiar, religious community. No casuistry: "Thou shalt not murder"—and not a word as to exactly what the crime consists in or what killings are still permissible or excusable. At the same time, the range covered by the brief list is extraordinarily wide: from false worship to theft, from a gross disruption of peace like adultery to the mere inclination of coveting.

[19] Exod 20:2 ff.; Deut 5:6 ff.

[20] Cp. below., 204 f.

[21] See below, 197 f.

It is with regard to "Thou shalt not covet" that insensitivity to pattern has fostered a major fallacy. We often hear[22] that an early legislator would not be concerned about an inner lapse. Accordingly, it is concluded, either the Ten Commandments, or at least their final exhortations, are late or the verb traditionally rendered as "to covet" in reality signifies a concrete act, say, "to meddle with" or "to start to meddle with."

This reasoning is mistaken. Certainly, there are subtle attitudes primitive tribunals are unable to go into. Negligence is one of them. It would be impracticable in 1200 B.C. Palestine to expect a verdict to turn on its presence or absence in the person arraigned. As for coveting, it never anywhere becomes punishable by the secular arm. A statute "If a man covets another's ox, he shall be fined half his value" would be as utopian today as then. But this does not mean that negligence and coveting are not from time immemorial recognized for what they are and frowned on. No Hebrew, Greek or any other law imposes a penalty on wrath or greed; yet Cain is reproved for the former[23] and Plato asserts that war is caused by the latter.[24] And, while "If a man covets, he shall be fined" would not make sense at any time, in a God-fearing epoch, however remote, "Thou shalt not covet" does. This warning "thou shalt not," which we found to be a communication to the individual of the divine will, with no dependence on any intermediary aid, is highly suitable for inculcating the sinfulness not only of deeds but also of states of mind. The recipient hears: that is what matters. Again, over these prohibitions, we have seen, the Almighty alone stands guard. He, even in the stone age, unlike earthly officers, has no difficulty in unveiling the hidden and determining and carrying out the fitting response.

There is ample corroboration. Just as the deity can deal with internal evil irrespective of external data, so it can with internal good. The King of Gerar, having taken Sarah into his harem under the impression that she is Abraham's sister only, not his wife, successfully reminds God: "In the simplicity of my heart have I done this."[25] Parallels abound.

So we may now ask: what setting would produce just this style—a ban from on high, direct to the conscience,[26] devoid of casuistic addenda and capable of reaching into areas beyond terrestrial power? The answer emerges from those ancient Oriental documents which focus on the kind of wrong "thou shalt not" is primarily meant for. Two quotations. In the Egyptian Book of the Dead, the soul brought before the underworld arbiters affirms: "I have not killed, I have not instigated any killing, I have not defiled myself, I have not stolen, I have not been covetous, I have not told lies." In Babylonia, in serious illness, the gods are asked: "Has he despised father or mother? Has he given petty things and refused important ones? Has he approached the wife of his fellow? Has he shed the blood of his fellow? Has he been sincere with his mouth and false with his heart?"[27]

[22] See my *Roman Law* (1969), 163 f.; also the literature quoted by B. Jackson, *HUCA*, 42 (1971), 197 ff. He does not share the erroneous approach. Nor (as W. D. Davies, who looked through my typescript, reminds me) did C. H. Dodd; see his *Paul to the Romans* (1932), 108 ff.

[23] Gen 4:6.

[24] *Phaedo* 66C ff.; *Republic* 2.373D.

[25] Gen 20:5. See *Ancient Jewish Law*, 51 f., 57 f.

[26] See Excursus 2, below, 225 ff.

[27] See A. Jirku, *Altorientalischer Kommentar Zum Alten Testament* (1923), 87 f.

Here, in final protestation, confession and search into one's past, the scope is precisely that of "thou shalt not," grave lapses inner as well as outer. In death and mortal sickness everyone, high or low, is utterly alone, exposed, forced to account, without helpers and subterfuges, for what he was really up to—all façade being gone. (The medieval *Dies Irae*, figuring in Goethe's *Faust*, contains the lines: *Quidquid latet apparebit*, "All secrets will be revealed," and *Quem patronum rogaturus*, "You will have no protector.") It is, I suggest, this ultimate, desperate situation which, at the outset, the form we are considering envisages. Its essential function is to announce the one route of escape from eternal damnation; or in the imagery of the Book of the Dead, to keep you from being swallowed up by the crocodile instead of stepping into unending bliss. If you stay within the boundaries drawn, and only then, you can face the last jury—one not to be deceived and weighing up your schemes as well as your execution. (My friend Louis Brown of U.S.C. should be pleased: "thou shalt not" may be dubbed the earliest specimen of preventive law, designed to avert the calamitous results of sin.) Hence, at the initial stage, the preoccupation with fundamentals, the omission of ifs and buts, the inclusion of internal depravity. Hence another, very different thing. I am struck again by the tenacity with which the original aura of a phrase clings long after the circumstances of its birth are largely forgotten. To this day, the term "plebiscite" or "plebiscitarian" has a revolutionary ring, a remnant of the struggle of plebeians against patricians.[28] Similarly, "thou shalt not" is still strangely powerful: a quality coming down from that ancient setting, the naked soul's choice between ruin and salvation.

To go on to "one does" or "one does not." "One does": "When the month of Ab comes in, one reduces joy";[29] "He who buys fruits from an Uninstructed separates first tithe and second tithe";[30] "If a buyer of fruits finds among them coins in a bundle, he proclaims them."[31] "One does not": "One does not sell pagans bears or lions or anything dangerous";[32] "He who undertakes to be an Associate does not sell an Uninstructed wet or dry produce and does not receive him if he wears his ordinary garment [presumed to be unclean]";[33] "One does not divide a courtyard unless each co-owner will be left with four cubits."[34] "One does" and "one does not" side by side: "On Purim, women sing dirges for the dead but do not wail";[35] "One does not let children fast on the Day of Atonement but one trains them a year or two before they come of age";[36] "The proselyte brings the first-fruits but does not recite the traditional declaration";[37] "If a man throws a stone in his yard and kills somebody entitled to be there, he goes into exile, if somebody not entitled, he does not go into exile."[38] This pattern springs up in the in-

[28] See my article [" 'Suffrage' and 'Precedent,' 'Mercy' and 'Grace' "] in *TR*, 47 (1979), 240.

[29] *m. Taan.* 4:6.

[30] *b. Sot.* 48a.

[31] *m. B. M.* 2:4.

[32] *m. A. Zar.* 1:7.

[33] *m. Dem.* 2:3.

[34] *m. B. B.* 1:6.

[35] *m. M. Kat.* 3:9.

[36] *m. Yom.* 8:4.

[37] *m. Bikk.* 1:4; Deut 26:3 ff.

[38] *m. Makk.* 2:2.

tertestamental era and, by New Testament times, it predominates.

What we have before us is a rule expressed as a fact (once again, a fusion of is and ought.) Instead of "In the month of Ab, one should reduce joy," we are told, "In the month of Ab, one reduces joy." This twist occurs in many languages, English among them. An old-order parent may reprove a weeping young son: "A boy does not cry." Well, he clearly does, so this is not intended as a portrayal of the situation. It stands for: "A boy ought not to cry."

Roughly, the usage no doubt evolves in these stages. The starting-point is a present occurrence: "They work this morning and do not drink." Next comes a habitual occurrence: "Some people work, others drink." Then a habitual occurrence approved of: "Decent people work and do not drink," "Doctors care for their patients." And finally, the added implication that you should fall in with it. In a speech by the boss to his men or in a class on medical ethics, an observation like, "Decent people work," "Doctors care," readily gains a normative sense. It is this last step which is relevant to my inquiry. Precisely what is its typical milieu, its specific point?

In English, the part of the verb prominent in this structure is the indicative present. The Oxford Dictionary's definition of "indicative" is "stating a thing as a fact."[39] The nearest Hebrew equivalent is the participle, employed in all the above illustrations. The very first paragraph of the Mishnah opens:[40] "From when are they reciting the Shema in the evening?" A more idiomatic rendering will be: "From when does one recite?" And its import is: "From when may one recite?" That the participle has directive force is confirmed by its alternation with modes of the verb more commonly and openly constraining. Here is a provision about school on late Friday afternoon, when it is important not to miss the beginning of the Sabbath: "A master is watching how the children read but he himself should not read."[41] "Is watching" means "may watch"; and the second half, "should not read," does bring in the imperfect. Similar switches are met in the Manual of Discipline of the Dead Sea Essenes: "The priests shall be [imperfect] blessing and all that enter are saying [participle, evidently as good as the imperfect], Amen. And the priests shall continue [perfect with consecutive *waw*] and all that enter shall open [imperfect] and say [perfect with consecutive *waw*], Amen."[42] The same goes for the codes of the primitive Christian community the phrasing of which, we shall soon see, can be inferred from Paul's and Peter's Epistles.

The style plainly covers the religious and the secular, the month of Ab and coins found in a purchase. Since, essentially, the data underlying those precepts are customs—positive, "one does," or negative, "one does not"—the variety of normative shades is considerable. We may have to deduce a strict duty, a must or a must not: "If a man kills somebody entitled to be there, he goes into exile," "must go"; "One does not sell pagans anything dangerous," "must not sell." Or a less strict duty, a should or a should not: "In the month of Ab, one reduces joy," "should reduce"; "On Purim, women

[39] H. W. Fowler and F. G. Fowler, *The Concise Oxford Dictionary*, new ed., rev. H. W. Fowler (1929), 580.

[40] *m. Ber.* 1:1.

[41] *m. Shab.* 1:3.

[42] Manual of Discipline 1.18, 20, 2.11, 18.

do not wail," "should not wail." Or a concession, a may or a need not: "On Purim, women sing dirges," "may sing"; "If a man kills somebody not entitled to be there, he does not go into exile," "need not go." There are further possibilities, such as a denial of effect, a cannot: "The proselyte does not recite the traditional declaration," "cannot validly recite" seeing it speaks of the land "promised to our fathers." Frequently, it is an in-between nuance that prevails; and now and then, indeed, the meaning will remain obscure—for instance, we do not know whether it is may or must.[43]

As already mentioned, this type of guidance acquires currency at some stage between the two Testaments. In fact, it occurs not a single time in the Old nor in any of the ancient Near-Eastern codes, hence must be the Tannaitic lawmaker's response to a fundamental *novum* facing him. This is not hard to identify. It is that immediate revelation has ended, the framework of right living is complete. Legislation by means of "you shall" or "you shall not," transmitting the direct will of God, is, therefore, no longer appropriate. The task now is to interpret the old statutes promulgated from on high and to stabilize their execution. The participle of the correct practice as I would call it, "one does" or "one does not" in translation, sets out what, on elaboration and systematization of the Scriptural material, emerges as the commendable course. (In a way, the development corresponds to one in the domain of worship—from spontaneous Psalm to derivative Benediction.) It is the learned student of the holy text who speaks in "The proselyte brings the first-fruits but does not recite the declaration," the guardian and organizer of ritual in every sphere who speaks in "On Purim, women sing dirges but do not wail." The sober tone, the limitless range, the fluidity in nuances, all chime with such *au fond* secondary activity. The connection with *halakha*, "the walking," the principal Tannaitic term for a recognized ruling, and with *derekh*, "way," a central term for normative custom,[44] is obvious.

Even a decree by the High Priest John Hyrcanus—second half of the second century B.C.—if we may rely on the version offered by the Gemara, is couched in this fashion: "He who buys fruits from an Uninstructed separates first tithe and second tithe." For, however authoritative, it is subsidiary to Biblical law. Its aim is somewhat to make up for the widespread laxity of common folks in paying their dues and, indeed, it forms part of a perennial search of the leaders for solutions at once satisfying the scrupulous and not imposing too heavy a burden. It is a question, not of a divine command, but of working out, under such a command, the proper route to take. I might add that my argument would be scarcely affected should the phrasing before us be unauthentic: it would still be what the Rabbis thought plausible in an edict of this kind.

We can probe deeper. It would have been open to the Tannaites, while avoiding "you shall," "you shall not," to resort to a straight "do," "do not" (the Hebrew imperative being relatively mild—I shall come back to this[45]) or to a circumlocution like "it is

[43] For similar difficulties where the imperfect is employed, see my *Collaboration with Tyranny in Rabbinic Law* (1965), 95 ff. [*Talmudic Law*, 128–31.]

[44] Cp. my remarks ["Negligence in the Early Talmudic Law of Contract (*Pesh'ah*)"] in *Festschrift Fritz Schulz*, 1 (1951), 140 ff. [*Talmudic Law*, 324 ff.]

[45] See below, 201 ff.

needful to do so-and-so," "meritorious," "forbidden," "permissible." These all are quite suitable for derivative provisions and they do indeed occupy a far from negligible place in Tannaitic sources. What is there about "one does," "one does not," that makes it a successful competitor?

Its characteristic, we saw, is the setting forth of a precept as a fact or, to put it negatively, the absence of any reference to obligation such as marks the other styles I have adduced, "you shall," "you shall not," "do," "do not," "it is meritorious," "it is forbidden." Needless to say, a system of duties is presupposed even in concessions like "you may," "it is permissible," granting relief. None of all this in "one does" or "one does not." A simple datum—yet it constrains or exempts no less than those overt prescriptions. To understand the Tannaitic predilection for it, we have to solve this mystery, the acquisition of directive import by an observation.

This occurs because the pattern is meant for an élite—better, for a body believing itself to be an élite: with what justification does not matter. An élite requires only to be informed of the proper behaviour to act accordingly. The implication is: "In a community as superior as this one, such-and-such is done," "not done," "all right if desired," "not *de rigueur*." No need for "must," "must not" and so on. Indeed, anything smacking of compulsion would be out of place. "Dinner jacket is worn," an invitation to All Souls College will say. Wherever the form is genuinely applied (by "genuinely" I mean not by way of completely dried-up routine) this is the spirit behind it. "A boy, or a brave boy, does not cry" appeals to the youngster's pride in being among that choice part of the human species, boys or brave boys. What endows the factual description of a custom with regulatory effect is the addressee's desire to belong to the nobility singled out by this bearing.

There is plenty of confirmative evidence. The etymology of the designation *perushim*, "Pharisees," is uncertain; but doubtless it was widely taken to denote "those keeping apart." What is of direct relevance is that quite a few rules which ended up binding on the whole people demonstrably began as conventions of a select body. It was the company of Associates that engaged to comply with the minutiae of tithes and cleanness, and this original circumscription still comes through in the Mishnah: "He who undertakes to be an Associate does not sell an Uninstructed produce and does not receive him if he wears his ordinary garment." Again, the Qumran Manual stipulates that, when new members are being received, "The priests recount the just exploits of God and the levites recount the iniquities of the children of Israel and all that enter confess after them."[46] This never became the general law, but the form recurs in the Tannaitic norms concerning the reception of a convert: "And two scholars stand by his side and inform him of lighter and heavier commandments."[47]

Significantly, Amoraic authors evince far less partiality for the participle of the correct practice. By their time, Pharisaism has long ceased to be an affair of an élite. It is orthodox doctrine: the pattern continues but, except for special contexts, in a subdued mode.

[46] Manual of Discipline 1.18 ff.

[47] *b. Yeb.* 47b.

On the other hand, in the earliest Christian communities, it does have its full function. It is met in Paul and the First Epistle of Peter. Paul: "One abhors the evil, one prefers one another in honour."[48] Peter: "The servants subject themselves to their masters."[49] If you look up the Greek, you will find it quite ungrammatical. What has happened is that primitive Christian canons which were in Hebrew and used the participle—our present—have been overliterally done into Greek. Even the auxiliary is omitted, good Hebrew but impossible Greek, so that we get: "Abhorring [in the plural] the evil, preferring [plural] one another," "The servants subjecting themselves"—not "They are abhorring, preferring," "The servants are subjecting themselves," just *apostugountes* [abhorring], *proegoumenoi* [preferring]. New Testament scholars, perplexed, when translating, usually substitute an imperative: "Abhor, prefer," "Be subject." This is understandable but, besides covering up the genesis of the texts, it falsifies their particular note. Imperative and "one does" or "one does not" represent very different types of authority. The maxims before us emphasize the specialness of the new fellowship.

It used to be thought that the sections detailing Christian conduct in which these oddly phrased admonitions are found were the work of Paul and that the First Epistle of Peter borrowed from him: it has indeed been a major argument against Peter's authorship of this Epistle. In reality, each independently draws on Hebrew codes of the sect. Otherwise, 1 Peter would surely echo Paul also outside these ordinances, but it does not. Moreover, though its Greek is generally better than Paul's, several times it uses the un-Greek participle for a norm appearing in decent Greek in Paul. The latter instructs slaves in the imperative: "Servants, obey the masters," *hypakouete*.[50] Peter would not have substituted the Hebrew form: it must derive from the source common to both. Whether they themselves are responsible for the Greek or whether, when they wrote, there already were Greek versions in circulation I leave open.

That this haughty style is taken over by a movement one of whose major complaints about the dominant circles is their arrogance[51] is not without irony—tragic irony:[52] the truth is that a band trying to provide a model to the ordinary world around it cannot but consider itself better, in some respects at any rate. Of course, meekness being a chief virtue, "one does" or "one does not" can be adopted only in unawareness of its character. As I pointed out in discussing the choice between "if" and "whoever,"[53] form, unlike substance, tends to be fastened on by instinct rather than deliberation—hence it often lets us in on unavowed attitudes. In the case of the structure under notice, this happens again and again. No one keener on we-are-all-the-same than the scouts. Yet paragraph 2 of the Scouts Law opens, "A Scout is loyal to the King," paragraph 4, "A Scout is a friend to all." They would have spotted no incongruity in a further one: "A Scout is humble."

[48] Rom 12:9 f.

[49] 1 Pet 2:18.

[50] Eph 6:5; Col 3:22—assuming that at least Colossians is authentic.

[51] Rom 2:19, 10:3.

[52] John Noonan, to whom I submitted the typescript, comments: "not too tragic, just natural." He is right, and my appraisal is a hangover from my falsely perfectionist upbringing.

[53] See above, 189.

In passing, contemporary ads are by way of turning from depiction—realistic or fictitious—to prescription. "Top executives use Lilac Waft deodorant." (Captain—first world war—Cyril Falls, for many years military correspondent of *The Times* and attached to All Souls, once remarked to me: "I'll be damned if I get rid of my smell." A gentleman of the old school.) "Successful women buy Gucci shoes." Not quite yet on a level with the conventions of the Associates, but pushing that way. Negatives are rare in this domain, chiefly because you must not openly run down competitors—"A lady does not wear a Woolworth hat"—also, you do not wish to offend that part of the public who, as yet, are unconverted. Still, "The expert jogger does not wear sandals," or "Thoughtful parents do not try to take the place of the Ultimate Lurch therapist with their children" is possible.

Once we grasp the tenor of the participle, we shall not be surprised never to find it with a basic, universal law. A precept "One does not kill" is unthinkable in Rabbinic speech. This interdict is not a special restraint worked out for observance by the faithful. It is different when we come to the problem under what conditions it is or is not in order to kill a man about to commit a sin: "These one saves at the cost of their lives—he that pursues after his fellow to slay him or after a male to force him into intercourse; but he that pursues after a beast or profanes the Sabbath, one does not save them at the cost of their lives."[54] Here the concern is with details of this particular system. Similarly, we would not say in English, "One does not kill," "A boy does not kill," though we might say, "One does not shoot a defenceless enemy," "A boy imbued with Zen does not volunteer for combatant service." Naturally, all depends on the individual culture. In the Rabbinic one, "One does not blaspheme God," "one does not commit adultery," "One does not steal," "One does not have homosexual relations," are almost as inconceivable as "One does not kill." Today, at least "One does not blaspheme God" would readily pass, intended for an elevated milieu. Similar formulations for the other three lapses would make sense in California, and even "One does not kill" may not be far off.

A striking Roman illustration of the pattern is furnished by the set of taboos which, according to Gellius,[55] must be heeded by a priest of Jupiter. Many of them are in the present indicative: "He has no knot in his headdress," "He does not pass under slips trained upwards from vines," "If he loses his wife, he abdicates his office." I am aware that the verbal fidelity of Gellius's quotes cannot be proved. But for my purpose it suffices that an antiquarian of the middle of the second century A.D., and most likely also his source Fabius Pictor, of the middle of the second century B.C.,[56] looked on this form as appropriate for the statutes of a high-ranking fraternity.

Of "you shall" or "you shall not," I said above that, though at first sight it seems sanctionless, this appearance is deceptive. Its meaning shades off into "you will" or "you will not," hence anyone disobeying removes himself from God-ordained destiny, is lost.[57] If we fully take in the élitist setting of the form here analysed, it, too, turns out

[54] *m. Sanh.* 8:7.

[55] Gellius, *Attic Nights* 10.15.9, 13, 22.

[56] Not the more famous third century B.C. annalist.

[57] See above, 190.

far less tame than it looks. It states no penalty for transgression; indeed, it totally refrains from coercive language, it merely describes the distinctive customs of a group. Yet by doing so, it also defines who is and who is not a member. When you reprimand your lad, "A boy does not cry," then, if he does, he proves not to be a true boy. The Tannaitic pattern, as I have tried to show, implies: "In a community as superior as this one, such-and-such is done or not done." It follows, logically, that if you flout the rule, you are not inside. "In the month of Ab, one reduces—literally, they are reducing—joy." If you have fun instead, you are not designated by "one," you do not belong to "them," you fall outside that special crowd. "An Associate does not sell an Uninstructed produce"; if you do sell, you are not a proper Associate. "A priest of Jupiter has no knot in his headdress," "A Scout is a friend to all"; a gallant sporting a rococo coiffure is not a genuine priest of Jupiter, a mean guy is not a real scout. An old division of norms is into *lex perfecta*, announcing a punishment to be inflicted on a transgressor, and *lex imperfecta*, with no such threat. The participle of the correct practice is something of a *lex perfectissima*. Beneath its peaceful semblance lurks an automatic retribution of ultimate severity, exactly the kind suited to an élite, than which nothing worse can befall a person: exclusion from the club.

The mostly widely remembered New Testament form of promulgation is, I guess, "you have heard but I say," in the sermon on the mount,[58] attached to five or six topics: murder, adultery, oath, insulting blows, love of fellow-humans and, maybe, divorce though the phrasing is here abridged.[59] "You have heard that it was said… thou shalt not kill and whosoever shall kill shall be in danger of the judgment. But I say unto you, that whosoever is angry with his brother shall be in danger of the judgment."

Superficially, this sounds as if the old dispensation were being completely overthrown. At once, however, we come up against the introductory assurance, "I am not come to destroy but to uphold."[60] One might perhaps try to brush it aside. It is plainly later than what it prefaces: you do not protest your innocence unless accused. The teachings must have been coined first, they were branded as impious by the establishment who felt menaced, and to this "I am not come" and so on makes reply. How much of the development took place in Jesus's lifetime and how much afterwards I need not here work out. What matters is the relative posteriority of the opening summary: at first sight, it might appear arguable that, for the purpose of defence, it tones down an original, extremist object of the pronouncements. But that this is not so, that, on the contrary, it offers an absolutely correct assessment, emerges when we inspect the form in question more closely.

No doubt, it has a majestic ring and I shall come back to it. But to a Jewish audience of the time, the contrast between hearing and saying, more precisely, between what the Torah is heard to declare and what it should be said to declare, is quite familiar and

[58] Matt 5:21 ff. See the magisterial work by W. D. Davies, *The Setting of the Sermon on the Mount* (1964), 101 ff., 235 ff., 300 f.

[59] Matt 5:31.

[60] On "uphold," Hebrew *qiyyem*, as the most plausible rendering, see my *The New Testament and Rabbinic Judaism* (1956) (repr. 1973), 60 f. [171 f.]

betokens not an annulment of the heard by the said but a refinement: an initial crude understanding—what is heard—is being rectified—so as to become what must be said. On the notice in Exodus that "the Lord came down on mount Sinai," Rabbi Judah the Prince comments:[61] "I might hear this as it is heard, but you must say, If the sun, one of the many servants of God, may remain in its place and nevertheless be effective beyond it, how much more He by whose word the world came into being." To our critical intelligence it is obvious that the Biblical author does have in mind an actual descent of God and few of us will be worried: why should he be less primitive than Hammurabi or Homer? In a sense, then, the Rabbi is repudiating the Pentateuch's theology in favour of one more advanced. Yet this is not how he sees it. For him, whatever the *prima facie* tenor of a text, if we only search deep enough, taking account of all we know in every field, its true meaning will prove to accord with the most ideal standards. In other words, these are never adopted at the expense of Scripture; rather, they are always pointed to by it. The term "to uphold" is conspicuous in this kind of interpretation. Rabbi Akiba and one Pappos debate Job's remark about God: "He is apart and who can turn him?"[62] Against Pappos, who finds God here represented as judging with no regard to right or wrong, Akiba "upholds" the verse by contending that it stresses the irrevocability of a divine sentence without in the least denying its supreme fitness.

The series "you have heard but I say" has close affinity with the Rabbinic approach. Alas, a modern public may find this hard to accept as far as two of the six topics are concerned. I start with the four easy ones. The Decalogue condemns murder—if we ponder law and prophets thoroughly (such is the thought behind its treatment in the sermon) this must include ill-will; adultery—this must include ill-lust; false oath—this must include any dragging down of the sacred; and the commandment to love your neighbour, in view of all else the Bible puts before us, must include love of your enemy. With insulting blows and divorce, things are more complicated. Scriptural law, as understood in Jesus's time,[63] imposes a fine on assault; the sermon on the mount enjoins the utmost meekness on the victim. Scriptural law recognizes divorce, the sermon rejects it. In these cases, is there not an open break with the former religion? Well, not from the then prevailing point of view. The Rabbis manage to reconcile the boldest innovations with sacred writ—by assuming, for instance, that a certain regulation found there constitutes a concession for the mass but ought not to be taken advantage of by the truly devout; and they always discover somewhere in the Bible a text which, they believe, bears them out. Some of them disapprove of private ownership, claiming that insistence on it is depicted in the Book of Genesis as typical of Sodom.[64] Many are opposed to polygamy, and they cite in their support the God-created union between

[61] *Mek.* on Exod 19:20.

[62] *Mek.* on Exod 14:29, referring to Job 23:13. See W. Bacher, *Die Exegetische Terminologie der Jüdischen Traditionsliteratur*, Part I, Tannaiten (1899), 170 f.; *Die Agada der Tannaiten*, vol. 1, 2nd ed. (1903), 318 f.

[63] See my *The New Testament and Rabbinic Judaism*, 254 ff. [177 ff.]

[64] *m. Ab.* 5:10, doubtless based on Gen 14:21 ff. See my lecture ["Concessions to Sinfulness in Jewish Law"] in *JJS*, 10 (1959), 5. [*Talmudic Law*, 5.]

Adam and Eve.[65] Among sects like the Essenes, deviation construed as following out the essential intent of the revealed word is, of course, even more pronounced. Evidently, up to a point, the relation between hearing and saying throughout the proclamations here discussed corresponds to that found in the Tannaitic sources.

Still, it is up to a point only: there are enormous differences. For one thing, the deeper demands taking off from, and contrasted with, the literal ones are all distinctly uncompromising. Further, the very listing of five to six such antitheses one after another—unparalleled in the Talmud—introduces a somewhat revolutionary tone. Again, the form itself alludes to a new aeon. I have not so far mentioned that twice—in connection with murder and oath—a brief clause is added: the proclamation begins not simply "you have heard that it was said" but "you have heard that it was said to them of old time." Surely, the implication is that the immature grasp, to be expected from those groping novices, is not tolerable in the Christian world.

But even the central portion of the form diverges significantly from the Rabbinic model. The latter's setting is scholarly reflection or interchange. The above-quoted passage about God on mount Sinai begins, "I might hear this as it is heard," the sage talking to himself; and it goes on, "but you must say," more precisely, "but thou must say" (the Hebrew employs the singular), directed to an imaginary fellow-sage or disciple. Moreover, this "but thou must say" is followed, not directly by the right solution, but by a consideration leading up to it; not, that is, by a categorical "God's descent was not corporeal" but by "Since the sun, a mere servant of God, may act in the distance without moving, clearly God may." By contrast, the teachings in the sermon start off with a rebuking "you have heard," addressed to the multitude. Then comes—still addressed to them—a sovereign "but I say unto you," and it enunciates the true understanding, not a ground for regarding it as such: "Whoever is angry with his brother shall be in danger of the judgment." I discount some vestigial argumentation in the ban on swearing—"neither by heaven, for it is God's throne" etc.—and also, of course, appended reasoning—like "for if you salute your brethren only, what do you more than others?"

By now you may be fed up with my to and fro, but I shall not apologize: the form expresses the New Testament's complex attitude to the Torah. The latter is of no avail or even injurious if narrowly construed, turned into a tight, arid regime. It is still valid, and only valid, if deference is paid to its ultimate, generous goals, if "your righteousness exceeds that of the scribes and Pharisees." No wonder once this alive, open course is radically pursued, things will no longer be the same as before, to the dismay of conservative circles. The answer given them, "I am not come to destroy but to uphold," is, however, quite genuine: the visionaries are convinced—just like, say, Hillel, Johanan ben Zaccai, the Dead Sea faction—that theirs is the proper insight into the meaning of Scripture.

Here I have to recall yet one more point—a negative finding already adverted to: the New Testament never (save in quotations) employs "you shall" or "you shall not."

[65] *Ab. de R. N.* 2:5a, referring to Gen 2:21 ff. and Job 31:3. See my *The New Testament and Rabbinic Judaism,* 77 [256 f.], and ["Concessions to Sinfulness in Jewish Law"] *JJS,* 10 (1959), 6. [*Talmudic Law,* 6.]

Absent friends can be as conspicuous as present ones[66] and, in this case, neglect of this experience has definitely caused confusion. That the mode of ordinance impressing God's will directly on the individual is entirely missing has weighty implications. Before going further, let me rule out the possibility that the form did once figure in Jesus's preaching and got lost through a vagary of transmission. We may safely assume that, had it occurred anywhere in early Christian tradition, it would have been treasured as a symbol of his supremacy; indeed, it would soon have crept into sayings not originally containing it. The fact is that Jesus is not, in form, presenting another Sinaitic revelation. Admittedly, it is conceivable that a centuries-old reverential instinct would prevent the use of the pattern even after his recognition as the Messiah, a second Moses, Godlike. But even on this basis, there remains something in "you shall," "you shall not," too mighty, too awesome, to be transferred.

Once we are aware of this absence, it is in fact particularly striking in the sermon. After "you have heard thou shalt not kill, but I say unto you," the natural continuation would be "thou shalt not be angry with thy brother." Instead, there is almost—from the formal angle—an anticlimax: "that whosoever is angry with his brother shall be in danger of the judgment," reminiscent—as to form—of a statement like Eleazar of Modiim's (he was Bar Kokhba's uncle):[67] "He who... puts his fellow to shame in public has no share in the world to come." This structure, too, would be worth exploring; here it suffices to observe that, compared with "you shall" or "you shall not," it is sober, grading, classifying. In the same way, "thou shalt not commit adultery" is followed not by "thou shalt not look on a woman to lust" but by "whosoever looks to lust has already committed adultery in his heart": in form, mere exegesis determining the scope of the statute, the act furthest from the central one still falling under it (in a sense at least[68]). Again, to "thou shalt not forswear thyself" it would be simple to oppose "thou shalt not swear at all." What we actually find is "but I say unto you not to swear at all": a very subdued, dependent infinitive—as in the counsel against exacting satisfaction, "but I say unto you not to resist evil." A little further on in the part about oath, "neither mayest thou swear by thy head," *me* with the subjunctive, comes closer to "thou shalt not," which makes the avoidance of the final step all the more impressive. Lastly, "thou shalt love thy neighbour" is widened, not into "thou shalt love thine enemy" but into "love your enemies." This is an imperative with a strong Wisdom component—like "Love the truth" in the *Testament of the Twelve Patriarchs.*[69] "Turn the other cheek," too, belongs here. I shall say something about this form in a moment.

Translations, form-blind, give us "you shall" or "you shall not" quite freely. German, French and other versions adopt an analogous course. In some cases it may not be easy to hit on a pleasing alternative but in others it is. A reverse aberration is found

[66] Cp. my remark on Gideon in *Typologie im Werk des Flavius Josephus* (Bayerische Akademie der Wissenschaften, Philos.-Histor. Klasse, Sitzungsberichte, Heft 6) (1977), 24, English transl. ["Typology in Josephus"] *JJS*, 31 (1980), 33.

[67] *m. Ab.* 3:12.

[68] See my lecture ["Greek and Roman Reflections on Impossible Laws"] in *NLF*, 12 (1967), 49 f.

[69] Testament of Reuben 3:9.

in The New English Bible, in the creation of which my admired friend C.H. Dodd played the leading role. It eliminates "you shall" and "you shall not," substituting: "Do not commit murder," "do not commit adultery," "do not break your oath." The Ten Commandments defanged.

For completeness's sake: the farewell talk of Jesus in John, though inculcating "a new commandment," *entole kaine*, shows no trace of "you shall" or "you shall not." "A new commandment I give unto you, that you love one another."[70] A sage's distilled conclusion, the all-important task he bequeathes which embraces all other tasks, stated solemnly yet quietly, without any break in the didactic mood. The New English Bible cannot bear having the sublime teaching in a subordinate clause. It puts, "I give you a new commandment: love one another." It sounds alright, at a price: the injection of a separate imperative dissipates the original atmosphere.

Do not get me wrong. Had I been on the Dodd-Committee, I would have pointed out the distortions but not, necessarily, have voted against them. A modern version for general use has to strike a balance between accuracy and appeal. This may be the place for a reminiscence. When Dodd was asked to direct the huge project, he discussed with me how to decide. For a considerable time before, he had talked to me about a Life of Jesus as his crowning work. I was very keen on his accomplishing this and, mindful of his fairly recent bout of tuberculosis, was not wholeheartedly in favour of another commitment that would engage him for several years. (My brother died of T.B.) But he felt strongly that the Bible should be freshly translated for each generation and that participation in this enterprise was a more urgent calling than anything else. He did see the translation through and he did write The Founder of Christianity.[71]

To sum up. In the Old Testament form, God's voice compels the individual conscience;[72] obedience means hope, disregard utter ruin. The Tannaitic participle constitutes a painstaking working out of the way of life an élite will pursue on the basis of the hallowed documents. And the antitheses of the sermon on the mount stand in between, representing a fresh impulse on the one hand, a faithful acceptance of the traditional framework on the other.

At this juncture, we might look at the Fifth Commandment—at least I first heard of it as no. 5—"Honour your father and your mother" etc., or, to imitate the Hebrew singular, "Honour thy father and thy mother." Here we meet an imperative, which I labelled above as gentler than "you shall" or "you shall not."[73] In fact, with one dubious exception, it is the only ordinance in the Pentateuch couched in this mood. Commentators slur over the difference from the Sabbath-Commandment, with an infinitive: "To remember the Sabbath day."[74] But though the infinitive is closer to the imperative than to "you shall," "you shall not," it is not the same.

[70] John 13:34.

[71] We now have a discerning biography of Dodd by F. W. Dillistone (1977).

[72] See Excursus 2, below, 225 ff.

[73] See above, 190, 194, 201.

[74] Thus, G. Beer, *Exodus* (1959), 100: *Inf. abs.* = *Imptv.*

The Rabbis see a bidding to marry and beget children in the words God addresses to Adam and Eve, Noah and his sons and Jacob: "Be fruitful and multiply."[75] In reality, they are just a blessing, with not the remotest intention of imposing a duty, legal, moral or religious—as when Jethro releases Moses with "go in peace,"[76] or when we say "farewell," "be well," "enjoy yourselves," "have a good day." Exactly the same words are used when fish and fowl have been created;[77] and the Bible itself speaks of a blessing in both cases, men and animals.[78] The Rabbinic reinterpretation dates from the era of Augustus. Even then it is not whole-hearted, but its consequences in the next two millennia have been tremendous.[79]

What about a number of injunctions accompanied by a warning like "guard this," "guard yourself"? "Guard that which I command you, guard yourself lest you make a covenant with the inhabitants of the land."[80] These imperatives do not, like "Honour your father," convey the substance of the legislation: in the example just cited, the actual law is clearly the ban on a treacherous covenant, "lest you make." They are stereotype, cautionary introductions or closings of a statute with a view to stressing its importance—not to mention the fact that their ultimate provenance overlaps with that of the substantial "Honour."

There are, of course, a great many imperatives in orders for the individual, momentary occasion. God calls on Abraham, "Go from your land,"[81] or on Moses, "Speak to the children of Israel";[82] Judah decides to have Tamar put to death, "Bring her forth and she shall be burnt."[83] These instructions can be quite comprehensive. Abraham, for instance, is exhorted, "Walk before me and be perfect."[84] But it is still not lawmaking for the people at large and valid for future times as well as the present: the reference is exclusively to his personal conduct. Here and there, at first sight, an imperative may look like a law proper, but the impression is deceptive. An invocation like "hear"—"Hear, o Israel, the Lord is one God"[85]—is always in the Pentateuch confined to the particular audience, quite apart from the fact that it is cautionary emphasis resembling "guard," "guard yourself," rather than substance. Or take the passage: "And now, write you this song and teach it to the children of Israel that it may be a witness for me."[86] The opening "and now" shows that what is being demanded is not continuous transmission throughout the generations—as, say, in the law "and these words which I command you this day shall be in your heart and you shall teach them to your children and

[75] Gen 1:28, 9:1, 7, 35:11; *Gen. Rab.* ad 1; *m. Yeb.* 6:6.

[76] Exod 4:18.

[77] Gen 1:22.

[78] Gen 1:22, 28, 9:1.

[79] See my *The New Testament and Rabbinic Judaism*, 78 [257]; *The Duty of Procreation* (1977), 2 ff., 34 ff.

[80] Exod 34:11 f.; cp. Deut 4:9, 12, 28, 24:8.

[81] Gen 12:1.

[82] Exod 25:2.

[83] Gen 38:24.

[84] Gen 17:1.

[85] Deut 6:4.

[86] Deut 31:19.

you shall write them on the doorposts of your houses."[87] The imperative asks for one definite action only: God inspires Moses to a last hymn he is to set down and pass on. A subsequent verse records that the order was executed: "And Moses wrote this song on that day and taught it the children of Israel."[88]

The only exception occurs earlier on in the same chapter: "At the end of every seven years," says Moses to the priests and elders, "you shall [thou shalt, literally] read this Torah before all Israel; gather [gather thou] the people together that they may hear and learn."[89] Obviously, true legislation, and none the less the imperative "gather." I suspect it is due partly to the influence of "gather" in similar contexts where, however, it expresses a special order,[90] and partly to the legislator putting himself in the situation at the end of each septennial when the time for the reading has arrived and the imperative would fit. It may be worth noting that the portion from "gather" onward has been held interpolated because, logically, it ought to come before "you shall read": first, the summons to assemble, then the recital.[91] However, this strikes me as over-critical.

We are left, then, with a unique—or, if you prefer, near-unique—statutory imperative in the Fifth Commandment. Maybe I shall now be told that *kabbedh*, "honour," could be construed as an infinitive. This would give us "To honour your father and your mother," analogous to "To remember the Sabbath day." To this, I have a fivefold repartee. First, it would be unfair, simply because I have laboriously demonstrated the strangeness of a usage, to explain it away. Up to now, everybody has been happy with an imperative here. Secondly, as already hinted, the original settings of the normative imperative and infinitive have anyhow much in common. Thirdly, this infinitive itself, if we discount routine warnings, "to remember," "to guard," figures only about half a dozen times in the Pentateuch. It is so rare that some scholars account for "To remember the Sabbath day" by calling in the even rarer imperative: "to remember" equals "remember."[92] Fourthly, the law speaks not of "father and mother" but of "your father and your mother"; not, indeed, impossible after "to honour" but going better with the direct address, "honour." (The Sabbath Commandment starts off impersonally: "To remember the Sabbath day to keep it holy.") Lastly, *kabbedh* recurs in Proverbs, "Honour the Lord with your substance,"[93] paired off with unmistakable imperatives, "Trust (*beṭaḥ*) in the Lord," "Fear (*yera'*) the Lord."[94]

It is time to ask: First, why is the imperative missing from the codes? Second, what brings it into the Fifth Commandment?

As for question 1, the grammatical unsuitability of this mood for prohibitions may come to mind: you cannot in Hebrew say "Murder not"—a limitation paralleled in many languages. This no doubt excludes it from a huge area. But there remains a mass of pos-

[87] Deut 6:6 ff.

[88] Deut 31:22.

[89] Deut 31:10 ff.

[90] Deut 4:10, 31:28.

[91] C. Steuernagel, *Deuteronomium und Josua* (1910), 111 f.

[92] See G. Beer, *loc. cit.*

[93] Prov 3:9.

[94] Prov 3:5, 7.

itive provisions, never imperatival. Mostly, they use the future—technically, the imperfect—and as a law apparently cannot open with a simple imperfect, we find two varieties. Either the law opens with an imperfect preceded by the infinitive: "To tithe you shall tithe your produce,"[95] "To furnish you shall furnish your slave when you release him."[96] The usual rendering is by means of "surely": "You shall surely tithe," "you shall surely furnish." What interests here is that no quirk of grammar would have prevented an imperative: "Tithe your produce," "Furnish your slave." Or the law places the imperfect at the end: "My Sabbaths you shall guard and my sanctuaries you shall fear."[97] Here, too, an imperative would have been quite feasible. At the close of Ecclesiastes, precisely these two verbs appear: "God fear and his commandments guard."[98] Another frequent phrasing is for a provision to begin with what a layman might look on as a substitute future, technically, the perfect with the consecutive "and" (*waw*): "And you shall offer a lamb,"[99] "And you shall count from the morrow of the Sabbath,"[100] "And you shall love the Lord."[101] Once again, no grammatical obstacle to an imperative. "Eat of my bread and drink of the wine I have mingled," we are admonished in Proverbs, "forsake the foolish and live and go in the way of understanding."[102]

Perhaps you expect me to say something about the jussive-imperfect with *'al* which, much like *me phoneuses* in Greek or *ne occideris* [do not murder] in Latin, serves in the place of a negative imperative, and which does turn up—however sparingly—in the codes. This would lead too far afield, however, and in any case I must leave something for my next visit.

So I proceed to my solution: where it is a question of a rule as opposed to an order on a specific occasion, the Hebrew imperative is far weaker than "you shall." It counsels, recommends, rather than imposes, compels. It is common in Wisdom: "Refrain your foot from the path of the sinners,"[103] "If you have become surety, deliver yourself as a roe from the hunter,"[104] "My son, hear the instruction of your father and forsake not [jussive with *'al*] the teaching of your mother."[105] This is effective education of the young by the old, but it is not the spirit of Pentateuchic legislation, inescapable, the will of God.

And now question no. 2. If, none the less, this mood does surface in "Honour your father and your mother," it is because the Fifth Commandment descends from Wisdom. To avoid misunderstandings, let me say at once that it need not therefore be later or less devoutly religious than the proper statutes. True, the latter are commonly held to antedate the Wisdom collections—Ecclesiastes, Proverbs and so on—but there was

[95] Deut 14:22.
[96] Deut 15:14.
[97] Lev 19:30.
[98] Eccl 12:13.
[99] Lev 23:12.
[100] Lev 23:15.
[101] Deut 6:5.
[102] Prov 9:5 f.
[103] Prov 1:15.
[104] Prov 6:5.
[105] Prov 1:18.

Wisdom among the Hebrews long before these. No one living where they did could have escaped it. Again, the notion of Wisdom—Hebrew Wisdom, in particular—as this-worldly, with little more than lip-service to the divine, has long been seen to be mistaken.[106]

At any rate, the result of form analysis chimes with the contents of the injunction. Respect of the child for the parent is a foremost concern of Oriental Wisdom. The Egyptian Vizier Ptah-Hotep opines, "How good is it when a son accepts what his father says";[107] and I have just adverted to Proverbs, "My son, hear the instruction of your father" and so on. What enormously enhances the role of the theme in Wisdom circles is the fact that the father-son relation is the model for the master-disciple one. Think how often the sage addresses his listener "my son."

There is a further link to Wisdom. The Fifth Commandment—as noticed in the Epistle to the Ephesians[108]—holds out a reward: in Exodus, "that your days may be long," in Deuteronomy, "that your days may be long and that it may be well with you." That piety is beneficial is a characteristic Wisdom idea. In fact, Wisdom is keen on precisely these benefits, long life and well-being. "He that is wise attains old age," we are assured in a Babylonian anthology of bilingual adages.[109] The above-quoted line from Proverbs, "Honour the Lord with your substance," continues "so shall your barns be filled." The Psalmist sings: "What man is he that desires life, loves days to see good? Keep your tongue from evil, depart from evil and do good, seek peace and pursue it."[110] The Wisdom background of this section at least of the psalm is evident not only from the imperatival maxims but also from their introduction in the preceding verse: "Come, children, hearken unto me, I will teach you the fear of the Lord."

Twentieth-century critics postulate the same short *Urform* for each paragraph of the Decalogue: "it is manifest," *es liegt auf der Hand*, that the reference to reward is an accretion.[111] If all they meant were that in the evolution of Hebrew—or any—society, the duty of filial deference is enunciated before a detailed return for it, I would have no complaint. In fact, I would go further: on this basis, the opening word "honour" is secondary compared with "your father and your mother." However, what they have in mind, of course, is not the sequence in which the various concepts grew up in communal thought but the history of the specific text before us. In the original Decalogue, they claim, it actually ran "Honour your father and your mother," period; later, it was provided with an appendix, mentioning a *douceur.* This I cannot accept. The promise hails from the same milieu as the imperative. They are both integral elements of this Wisdom tenet, complementing one another.

[106] See W. Zimmerli, in H. Ringgren and W. Zimmerli, *Sprüche/Prediger* (1962), 132 ff., and my article ["The Culture of Deuteronomy"] in *Orita,* 3 (1969), 51.

[107] See *Ancient Near Eastern Texts,* ed. J.B. Pritchard (1950), 414.

[108] Eph 6:2; cp. Deut 22:6.

[109] See W. O. E. Oesterley, *The Book of Proverbs,* XXXVIII.

[110] Ps 34:13.

[111] See W. Keszler, *VT,* 7 (1957), 2; G. Beer, *loc. cit.*; M. Noth, *Das Zweite Buch Moses, Exodus* (1959), 133.

Significantly, in a sense, the promise is unique just like the imperative. E. Würthwein, writing on *misthos*, "reward," in *Theologisches Wörterbuch,*[112] observes that pre-Deuteronomic legislation predicts retribution for wrongdoing—"if you do not comply, you will suffer"—but no favours for righteousness—"if you comply, it will be to your advantage." With certain modifications not here to be set out, this thesis is correct—except for the one case of "that your days may be long." Würthwein argues that, really, this clause also announces punishment alone: it has the force of "if you disobey, you will die young." Desperate reasoning. By taking this line, we can make a threat of any promise—or vice versa. Your uncle who will pay you a trip to Rome if you pass the exam is really notifying you that he will withhold the cheque if you fail. A law with the death penalty on idolatry is really assuring the orthodox worshipper that he will not be stoned. I am not saying that there are no occasions when such an interpretation may be illuminating, but this is not one of them. We had better admit the irregular positive nature of the long days. Just like the imperative, it is anything but irregular in Wisdom.

While demand and reward thus prove to belong together as primary components of the Fifth Commandment, the latter is something of an erratic block in the code. This should not cause too much surprise: the truth is that, as far as ultimate roots are concerned, we have to do here with a pretty motley compilation. One could not conceive of the Fifth Commandment as originating in the same setting as the Sabbath Commandment, or of either of them in the same as the warnings against murder, adultery and theft. The Rabbis sensed it. In the Noachian world law which they assumed to have been decreed by God after the flood, the Fourth and Fifth Commandments are not represented though murder, adultery and theft are crimes.[113] This is not to underrate the meaningfulness, the marvel, of the Decalogue as a unit, produced at the latest at the moment of promulgation but certainly prepared by earlier developments. Above, in discussing "you shall" and "you shall not," I indicated some factors likely to have been decisive in gluing diverse material together. I believe that rather than construct a fantastic, homogenized *Urform*, we ought to try to find out more about what led to the achievement of this lasting constitution.

A word on the relation between the Fifth Commandment and Deuteronomy. As Deuteronomy, too, is Wisdom-oriented, it, too, makes much both of the desirable attitude between the generations and of the prizes virtue will bring. But it is palpably later than the Fifth Commandment. The Decalogue appears already in Exodus. Deuteronomy itself depicts its version as a rerun shortly before Moses's death. And in the Fifth Commandment, after "Honour your father and your mother," it inserts "as the Lord your God commanded you." The same insertion is found in the Sabbath Commandment. So with regard to these two, there is additional, specific reference to a prior existence. Is the Fifth Commandment perhaps the product of a trend leading up to Deuteronomy? I doubt it. If it were, surely, Deuteronomy would not be without the imperative.[114] In all

[112] See E. Würthwein, in *Theologisches Wörterbuch zum Neuen Testament,* ed. G. Kittel, 4 (1942), 715. M. Noth, *loc. cit.* concurs: "*Zusage bzw. Warnung,*" "promise, or rather, warning."

[113] *b. Sanh.* 56a ff.

[114] On Deut 31:12, see above, 204.

probability, the Fifth Commandment and Deuteronomy represent Wisdom streams. There must have been quite a few from early on; and despite the attractiveness of least resistance, it will not do to treat them as identical. As far as the phrasing of norms is concerned, Deuteronomy, as I have shown elsewhere,[115] while not availing itself of the imperative, does contain its own, telling form, midway between advice and ordinary, statutory decree, but I shall not here enlarge on it.

May I, instead, draw your attention to a little point though it is not directly relevant. As remarked above, the inducement of Exodus is "that your days may be long," to which Deuteronomy adds "and that it may be well with you." The expansion may be intended to bring the reward into line with that for not taking a mother bird together with her young ones or her eggs.[116] There is no other law on a specific matter where the combination long days and well-being occurs.[117] In this philosophy, the protection of the mother bird is allied to the Fifth Commandment: we owe piety to parents even in nature. Remember that Deuteronomy prohibits the army, when building siegeworks against a city, from felling a fruitbearing tree for this purpose.[118] That reverence for progenitors transcends national boundaries comes out in the statute about a woman taken captive in war whom her captor wishes to marry: she is first to spend a month mourning her—heathen—parents.[119] In one or two of these laws, incidentally, it is motherhood to which homage is paid: Deuteronomy generally advances the status of women.[120]

Here is a pattern produced by the confluence of law and medicine, two spheres which throughout the millennia have interacted in manifold ways. Think of the American Jewish family who want the daughter to marry either a doctor or a lawyer. The form I am going to inspect had puzzled me for years until one night, when I indulged my medical-historical curiosity and browsed in Egyptian medical sources, the connection occurred to me.

Some laws of the Pentateuch are composed of three parts: facts, designation, consequences. Thus, the legislation designed to discriminate between murder and unintentional killing contains this paragraph:[121] "And if he smote him with an instrument of iron, he is a murderer, the murderer shall surely be put to death." Part 1 describes the situation, he struck with an iron; 2 subsumes it under a category, he is a murderer; 3 declares what is to happen, he shall be put to death. More precisely, 1 puts the concrete, particular instance, reduced in 2 to its essence, from which follows 3, the verdict applicable to 1. From a narrowly practical point of view, part 2 is superfluous; a court would come to the same decision if it did not exist. The aim is to justify the ruling, to represent it as called for by the logic of the system.

[115] See ["The Culture of Deuteronomy"] *Orita*, 3, 1969, 41 ff.

[116] Deut 22:6.

[117] Deut 4:40, 5:30 concerns good conduct in general. Cp. also Pss 23:6, 34:12 f., 91:16; Prov 3:2, 16; Eccl 8:13.

[118] Deut 20:19 f.

[119] Deut 21:10 ff.

[120] See my illustrations in ["Biblical Landmarks in the Struggle for Women's Rights"] *JR*, 90 (n.s. 23) (1978), 177 ff. [231 ff.]

[121] Num 35:16.

This sequence is met in four chapters only. Besides Numbers 35 about homicide, the following three are pertinent. Leviticus 11, concerning diet: "The camel (1), because he does not part the hoof (2), he is unclean (3). And every creeping thing (1), it is a detestable thing (2), it shall not be eaten (3)."[122] Leviticus 13, concerning leprosy: "And the priest shall see the skin and the hair is turned white (1), it is the plague of leprosy (2), and the priest shall pronounce him unclean (3). And if a man's hair has simply fallen off (1), he is just bald (2), he is clean (3)."[123] Leviticus 20, concerning sexual commerce: "And a man that lies with a male as with womankind (1), abomination have the two committed (2), they shall surely be put to death, their blood is upon them (3)."[124]

The statutes are all priestly in character—which is not surprising: the priests were the group most capable of so subtle yet compact a structure. The provenance is obvious for Leviticus 11 and 13, diet and leprosy. But Leviticus 20 also by its contents and language reveals its nature: it suffices to call attention to the prohibition of intercourse with a menstruating woman,[125] and to expressions like "to uncover the nakedness,"[126] "to uncover the fountain of her blood."[127] As for the list in Numbers 35, marking off ill-will from inadvertence, it, too, presumably came into existence at some sanctuary when a compromise had to be worked out between its claim and those of the victim's kin or the community.

That echoes of the form are detectable in Ezekiel, "Ezekiel the priest,"[128] supports this finding. "When I say to the wicked, You shall surely die, and you do not warn him (1), he is wicked (2), he shall die for his iniquity, but his blood I will require at your hand (3)."[129] Similarly: "And if a man be just and do law and justice (1), he is just (2), he shall surely live (3)."[130] The continuation is looser but still influenced by the same model: "And he begets a son, a robber, who has eaten upon the mountains and defiled his neighbour's wife (1), shall he live?, he shall not live, all these abominations has he done (2), he shall surely die, his blood is upon him (3)."[131] In a couple of Aramaic papyri, it is true, the style is transferred to the area of contract: "If she says so, *scil.* I take away the gift (1), bound she remains (2), she will not be listened to (3),"[132] and again, "And if he does not do so (1), divorce it is (2), he shall do to her the law of divorce (3)."[133] Both documents are from the same scribe—a P fan.

What prompted this form? Certain bodies, priests and lawyers above all, from early had the task of making distinctions—the clean and the unclean, objects fit and unfit for sacrifice, holy and ordinary seasons, the innocent and the guilty, the valid and the void.

[122] Lev 11:4, 41.
[123] Lev 13:3, 40.
[124] Lev 20:13.
[125] Lev 20:18.
[126] Lev 20:11.
[127] Lev 20:18.
[128] Ezek 1:3.
[129] Ezek 3:18.
[130] Ezek 18:5 ff.
[131] Ezek 18:10 ff.
[132] *Aramaic Papyri of the Fifth Century B.C.*, ed. A. Cowley (1923), 18.3, 55.
[133] *The Brooklyn Museum Aramaic Papyri*, ed. E. G. Kraeling (1953), 7.38 f., 206 f.

Gradually, they built up inclusive, coherent orders so that everything might be dealt with in accordance with its classification. In a world where this was the dominant interest, it would be vital, before deciding on a course, to bring the facts under the right heading. Expressed in a form, this meant: facts, heading, decision.

Besides this general background, however, we can discern at least two specific factors. This first has to do with fiction, re-interpretation of narrow norms, irrebuttable evidence and the like. When the provisions laid down for a class are to be extended to facts close to it but outside, it will satisfy an urge for justice, or tidiness, to pronounce them to be within, so that the extension appears well-founded. It is a process constantly going on in legal evolution;[134] to some extent, the current trend of bringing more and more unions under the marriage umbrella furnishes an illustration. In this context, the pattern discussed would be highly appropriate. All five occurrences in the Code of Hammurabi belong here: "If a man has bought silver or gold from a man's son or slave without witness and bonds, that man is a thief, he shall be put to death."[135] So does a Hittite paragraph: "If a member of a guild steals, and the guild do not return the stolen article, they are guilty, all thieves, he [the owner] shall seize them."[136] Three injunctions in the Laws of Eshnunna seem to owe their tripartite structure to this method of widening a class: "If a man brought bride money for a man's daughter but another forcibly deflowered her, it is a case of life, he shall die."[137]

The same urge will be at work if the provisions laid down for a class are to operate whenever certain facts are present though now and then, by way of exception, they do not fall under it: to pronounce them to be within warrants that inflexible operation. The Pentateuch's rule about homicide adduced above is an example: "If he smote him with an iron, he is a murderer, he shall be put to death." In nine out of ten cases, the wielder of a deadly weapon is bent on mischief. It is not feasible, at the time, to examine the individual incident as to whether it may constitute the rare abnormality. Hence, if a workable separation of witting and unwitting is to be achieved at all, it can be only a rough-and-ready one. To kill with an iron instrument statistically falls on the wrong side. The law determines—one is tempted to say, explains—that it is murder, and to be punished accordingly. A Hittite parallel: "If a man seizes a woman in the mountain, the man is wicked, he shall die; but if he seizes her in the house, the woman also is wicked, the woman also shall die."[138] This regulation is particularly valuable for form analysis since the corresponding Biblical one demonstrates dramatically in how different a fashion the same idea can be conveyed. In Deuteronomy 22, the, irrebuttably assumed, connivance of the girl in one case and struggle in the other are depicted in didactic detail in appendices to the respective verdicts: "If a damsel is betrothed and a man finds her in the city and lies with her, you shall stone them that they die, the damsel because she cried not and the man because he has humbled his neighbour's wife. But if a man finds

[134] See my article ["Greek and Roman Reflections on Impossible Laws"] in *NLF*, 12 (1967), 25 ff.

[135] CH 7; cp. 9, 10, 11 and 13. For further aspects, see B. Jackson, *Essays in Jewish and Comparative Legal History* (1975), 66 ff.

[136] HL 49; cp. 35.

[137] LE 26; cp. 24, 58.

[138] HL 197.

a betrothed damsel in the field and lies with her, the man only shall die, but unto the damsel you shall do nothing, there is in the damsel no deadly sin, for he found her in the field and she cried and there was none to save her."[139] Quite unlike the rigorous tripartite pronouncements.

The second factor that must have played a role I alluded to at the start of this section: it takes us to another branch of civilisation. In the ancient Orient, both Egypt and Babylonia, the main stream of the tripartite directive flows, not in legal codifications, but in medical ones. It is in the latter that the scheme (1) facts, or as we should now say, symptoms, (2) designation, or rather now, diagnosis, (3) consequences, or rather, treatment, is common.[140] "If a woman has an issue, say: It is the *achat* disease, apply jaspis with honey."[141] Forty-eight such instructions are met in the Edwin Smith Surgical Papyrus alone. A cuneiform specimen runs: "If his joints are all painful, it is a swollen joint lasting two years, make him rest on leavened meal, with leaven you atone."[142]

In medicine, part 2 is of direct, practical relevance—or at least, has been held to be that—from remotest antiquity to very recent times: treatment must be preceded by diagnosis. There are rational grounds for this and less defensible ones, a mixture which often turns the procedure into a cult. The rational side is stressed by a translator of Hippocrates: "A modern doctor, when called to a case of illness, is always careful to diagnose it, that is, to put it in its proper place in the catalogue of diseases.... Diseases may be similar in symptoms and yet call for different medicines."[143] But over-reliance on the catalogue is common, to the neglect of the peculiar features of a case—not to mention true empathy with the patient. For ancient doctors, the importance of part 2 is even greater, for two reasons. First, understandably,[144] it not seldom brings out the hopelessness of the condition, so that part 3, treatment, becomes non-treatment: "this ailment I shall not tend." Second, even if the sickness appears manageable, at a primitive stage, to conquer it it is thought necessary to discover its name or that of the demon causing it. Maybe more of this belief (even if not without rational ingredients) survives to this day than the profession would care to avow. "A quacksalver," John Webster writes,[145] "is a mountebank of a larger bill than a tailor; if he can but come by names enow of diseases to stuff it with, 'tis all the skill he studies for." At any rate, medicine provides the perfect setting for the sequence of the three parts we are investigating.

The Old Testament statutes about leprosy and food are plainly dealing with questions to some degree of a medical nature; and even the particular chapter about intercourse which contains the form has a faintly medical flavour—remember the tabooing of the menses. This is not to assert that all, or any, of these provisions originated strictly in medical science and from thence invaded religion and law. More probably, they

139 Deut 22:23 ff.

140 See O. Temkin, *Kyklos, Jahrbuch für Geschichte und Philosophie der Medizin,* 3 (1930), 102 ff.

141 From Papyrus Ebers; see O. Temkin, 109.

142 From *Assyrian Incantation against Rheumatism*; see O. Temkin, 127.

143 W. H. Jones, *Hippocrates* (Loeb Classical Library), 2 (1943), IX.

144 On how little could be done by medicine till very recently, see L. Thomas, *Bulletin of the American Academy of Arts and Sciences,* 34, no. 1 (Oct. 1980), 21 ff.

145 *Characters,* No. 24, A Quacksalver.

are due to a priestly class dominating both medicine and diverse other fields—sexual behaviour and the granting of asylum among them. Support for this view is furnished by the portion of the Hittite Laws from which I have already quoted the paragraph concerning rape. The pattern occurs here two more times, used exactly as in Leviticus 20: bestiality—an abomination—capital punishment.[146] There are unmistakable signs of priestly contribution to this section: a ghost seems to figure in one paragraph,[147] exclusion from priestly rank is ordained in another,[148] a differentiation is made between a cow, sheep, dog or pig[149] and a horse or mule.[150] At the same time, no medical notions are in evidence. Priestly interest, without explicit pointers to medicine, is discernible, too, in a part of an Assyrian compilation where, possibly, the diagnosis pattern is employed.[151] These parallels indeed suggest that we have to do with a style widespread among Oriental priesthood in an age prior to the Biblical texts.

What does appear certain is that the medical model was a major agent in its genesis and expansion. After all, the connection between disease, sin and crime and between cure, atonement and punishment prevalent in Hebrew thought and throughout the East—not to forget Greece[152]—is frequently commented on; and it is less astonishing that there exists this form shared by medical prescriptions and other priestly norms than that such a link has not been looked for long before now. The wide range of life covered by the pattern reflects the wide range of priestly sway. Who knows?, it may not be the only one of its kind.

As for its extent in space and time—it is not found in Greek, Roman or Germanic legislation. Yet it does emerge now and then in systems specially keen on the sort of logic it represents. The Austrian Penal Code favours it. "Whoever with intent to kill acts against a man in such a way that this or another man's death results—becomes guilty of the crime of murder—he shall be punished with life imprisonment." "Whoever throws into a well, a cistern, a river or a brook the water of which serves a settlement for drinking or brewing dead cattle or anything else by which the water may become dirty or unhealthy—commits an offence—and shall be punished with arrest from three days to one month."[153] Strangely, it seems to do something for a criminal or a patient to be told that he is being hanged or kept incarcerated for first degree murder or that he is dying from Alibert's Mycosis Fungoides.[154]

May I append an observation respecting another medical arrangement imitated

[146] HL 187, 188.

[147] HL 190.

[148] HL 200 A.

[149] HL 187 f.

[150] HL 200 A.

[151] MAL A51; see R. Yaron, *Biblica*, vol. 51 (1970), 556.

[152] See *Ancient Jewish Law*, 65.

[153] *Strafgesetz über Verbrechen, Vergehen und Übertretungen etc.* (1852), *wiederverlautbart als Österreichisches Strafgesetz* (1945), 134, 136, 398.

[154] Long after writing this, I come across in the *San Francisco Chronicle* (August 9, 1980, People, 11) a tale of an ailment starting in 1970 but receiving its "differential diagnosis" only in 1978: Sclerodoma plus Sjogren's Syndrome. Treatment—or non-treatment—remains much the same as before, but the patient-narrator is lyrical about the christening: "My years of agonizing anxiety, despair and emotional trauma are over."

outside medicine though not in law. Once again, the clue lies in its being of distinctly greater actual utility in connection with medicine.

Technical manuals of classical antiquity often fall into two parts: the technique and the technician.[155] Horace on poetry or Quintilian on rhetoric expounds separately the craft of writing or speaking and the requisite qualities of writer or speaker. It has of course been seen that this division occurs also in medical literature. In my opinion, that is where it arose. In medicine—which I take in a wide sense, including doctors, midwives and the like—the way of life, health, conduct and appearance of the practitioner have an immediate impact on the practice, far more so than in other fields. Mostly, that is, the healer's person is as important as what he does or prescribes. (Admittedly, it is changing now, with the automation of this calling.) So when the work on *The Physician* attributed to Hippocrates treats of the doctor in chapter one and of tumours in the following ones,[156] or when Soranus of Ephesus discusses first the midwife and then midwifery,[157] the student will benefit in the most practical fashion. I am not denying that the scheme makes sense elsewhere too: in fact, this is the reason for its popularity. But its birthplace is medicine to which it is most directly helpful.

Now and then, it may be possible to link a pattern with a particular school of thought. The Talmudic *le'olam* seems to be in point: I would call it the Stoic Ever. "Ever should a man be accustomed to say, Everything that the All-Merciful does he does for the best,"[158] "Never should a man remain in a place of danger and say, They will perform a miracle for me,"[159] "Ever keep in obscurity and last out."[160]

Already the Scriptures represent certain behaviour as constantly incumbent on a person. You may have to observe it "day and night." This is how the good shepherd watches over his flock[161] and God over his people,[162] and how Nehemiah had the rebuilding of the walls of Jerusalem guarded.[163] Above all, unceasing occupation with the law is enjoined;[164] indeed, you must speak of it "when you sit, walk, lie down and rise up."[165] (A terrible prediction of idolatry "day and night" occurs in Jeremiah.[166]) Other expressions used are "at all times" and "continually." The Psalmist will bless the Lord thus,[167] he extols the man who never deviates from righteousness[168] and he calls on us to persist in seeking God.[169] Wisdom knows that a true friend is unshaken by

[155] See E. Norden, *Hermes,* vol. 40 (1905), 481 ff.

[156] See W. H. Jones, *op. cit.,* 303 ff.

[157] See F. E. Kind, Pauly-Wissowa's *Real-Encyclopädie,* vol. 3A:1 (1927), 1119 ff.

[158] *b. Ber.* 60b, R. Huna quoting Rab quoting R. Meir.

[159] *b. Taan.* 20b, R. Adda bar Ahaba quoting R. Jannai.

[160] *b. Sanh.* 14a, 92a, R. Eleazar ben Pedath.

[161] Gen 31:39 f.

[162] Isa 27:3; Ps 121:3 f.; cp. Jer 33:25.

[163] Neh 4:3.

[164] Josh 1:8; Ps 1:2.

[165] Deut 6:7.

[166] Jer 16:13.

[167] Pss 34:2, 40:17; cp. 145:2 "every day."

[168] Ps 106:3.

[169] Ps 105:4; 1 Chr 16:11.

adversity;[170] it exhorts a husband to stay steadfastly attached to his wife;[171] and it advises you, since all must die, to enjoy yourself and keep on wearing festive robes.[172] Often the meaning is not exactly "every minute" but rather "habitually, whenever the appropriate moment arrives." The judges Moses appointed to relieve him were to take any dispute as it came up,[173] the sacrificial code prescribes the offering of one lamb in the morning and one in the evening in perpetuity.[174]

In the first half of the second century A.D. a special form crops up for the enunciation of duties always to be borne in mind: "ever" or "never" (*le'olam* or *le'olam lo'*) should a man do or be so-and-so, or—less common—in direct address, "ever" or "never" do or be so-and-so. It is met neither in the Old Testament[175] nor, say, in Sirach or the Dead Sea texts; nor is it discernible behind the Greek Apocrypha or the New Testament.[176] It is adumbrated in an argument of Joshua ben Hananiah and fully developed by the time of Akiba.

Among its roots must be those cases where with an obligation applicable to a limited area is contrasted one applicable without reservation. Frequently this happens in controversy, one Rabbi advocating a narrower scope, another the ever or never. Where there is a priest, heave-offering is to be given from the best, where there is no priest, simply from that which keeps—but R. Judah holds that "ever one gives from the best."[177] According to R. Eliezer, though rain is wanted only from the end of Tabernacles, it should be mentioned in the Eighteen Benedictions from the first day: to mention it, he urges, is not to ask for it. To which R. Joshua replies that, on the basis of this reasoning, "ever [in summer as well as winter] one would have to mention it."[178] On the Ninth of Ab one works or abstains from work according to local custom, though the disciples of the Sages abstain everywhere. However, Rabban Simeon ben Gamaliel (father of Judah the Prince) favours universal abstention: "ever should a man make himself a disciple of the Sages."[179] This example[180] shows well how these antitheses might help on the growth of the form: the statement just quoted could easily be detached from its original, specific context so as to figure as an independent maxim.

[170] Prov 17:17.

[171] Prov 5:19.

[172] Eccl 9:8.

[173] Exod 18:22.

[174] Exod 29:38.

[175] Some Biblical provisions do contain the word: Exod 21:6; Lev 25:46; Deut 23:6. But it never opens a law and, moreover, its meaning is somewhat different: it refers to the immutability of the state of affairs ordained, "for ever" rather than "ever." At first sight, 1 Chr 16:15 looks like adumbrating the Rabbinic maxims: "Remember *le'olam* his covenant." Even here, however, the emphasis is on the lastingness of the bond. The verse continues: "the words he commanded to a thousand generations." A comparison with Ps 105:8 confirms this interpretation: here it is God who remembers *le'olam*, surely, "for ever."

[176] If one were to make a Hebrew translation of Tob 4:19; Luke 18:1; Col 4:6; 1 Thes 4:17, 5:15 ff., one would use "at all times" and "continually."

[177] *m. Ter.* 2:4.

[178] *m. Taan.* 1:1.

[179] *m. Pes.* 4:5.

[180] Others: *m. Shab.* 16:2; *m. Yom.* 4:5; *m. Sukk.* 5:8; *m. Ket.* 5:7; *m. Men.* 11:2; *m. Neg.* 1:4; *m. Par.* 4:4; *m. Mikw.* 8:3.

Very likely, a decisive role in the evolution was played by Stoic influence. That school was thinking a good deal in terms of ever and never, activities and attitudes to be stuck to or shunned with determined consistency; and its diction reflects this bias. The Stoic ideal, Cicero explains, is "to be in accord with virtue ever."[181] "Ever in promise," he says, "attention is to be paid to the meaning, not to the words."[182] "There should ever be pondered all human things that may befall a man."[183] What Marcus Aurelius finds admirable is "Nothing else to consult even for a moment than reason, ever the same course,"[184] and he tells himself, "Continuously reflect who they are by whom you want to be approved."[185]

Certainly, one need not be a Stoic to tender emphatically general advice. Cicero himself was not one, strictly. Ever and never may be resorted to by any self-confident instructor. Publilius Syrus counsels: "By what means you may ensure your safety, ever reflect."[186] (It is indeed remarkable how rare this phrasing is in his fragments.) Christopher Robin warns his mother: "You must never go down to the end of the town, Unless you go down with me." It remains probable that the Stoic mood was a major factor in this matter.

Considering the popularity of the Stoic system throughout the Empire, we can hardly be surprised it should have had an impact on the shaping of Talmudic principles. The range of the form, too, speaks strongly in favour of this thesis: it is distinctly tied to ethics, refined religion, wise living, philosophy. And some additional support is furnished by the fact that the addressee of these precepts is regularly designated by the rather universal noun *'adham*, "human," "man." It appears even where the rule can be meant only for a Jew: "Ever should a man run to a fulfilment of a commandment, and even on a Sabbath" (when, normally, one walks at a leisurely pace).[187] To be sure, this noun is freely employed also in injunctions not couched in this style: "Nothing is proper for a man on a festival but either eating and drinking or sitting and studying."[188]

The form proved an enormous success, flourishing throughout the Middle Ages and almost to the present day. Tobit reminds his son: "Pour out your bread and wine on the tomb of the just." A twelfth-century Jewish translator adds *le'olam.*[189] For him, such a teaching would not be complete without this particle.

An example of source criticism going astray without the corrective of form criticism is furnished by twelve curses which, according to Deuteronomy, were solemnly laid on twelve crimes as the Israelites entered the promised land.[190] The catalogue has been deemed an *omnium gatherum* [disparate collection] due to the post-Deuteronomic, final

181 Cicero, *De Officiis* 3.3.13.

182 Cicero, *De Officiis* 1.13.40.

183 Cicero, *Tusculan Disputations* 3.14.30.

184 Marcus Aurelius, *Thoughts* 1.8.

185 Marcus Aurelius, *Thoughts* 7.62.

186 Publilius Syrus, *Sentences* 520.

187 *b. Ber.* 66, R. Tanhuma quoting R. Joshua ben Levi.

188 *b. Pes.* 68b; *b. Betz.* 15b, R. Eliezer.

189 Tob 4:17. See D. C. Simpson, "The Book of Tobit," in R. H. Charles, *The Apocrypha and Pseudepigrapha of the Old Testament,* 1 (1913), 213.

190 Deut 27:15 ff.

redactor R: the offences are culled, it is said, "not from the Deuteronomic work but from the whole of the Pentateuch."[191] At first sight, no doubt they do look quite disparate: setting up an image, despising father or mother, removing a landmark, misdirecting the blind, perverting the judgment of the stranger, intercourse with the father's wife, with a beast, with the sister, with the mother-in-law, homicide and sentencing an innocent person to death for a bribe. For the moment, I leave out of account the last imprecation, upon "him who does not uphold all this law." By general source-critical considerations, one would readily be led to the conclusion just quoted.

As soon, however, as we reflect on the form, "Cursed is he who does so-and-so," things appear in a different light. The invocation of divine vengeance is appropriate where, grave as the misdeed is, human justice cannot cope with it; chiefly, that is, because it takes place in secret, or because it is committed by the mighty against the helpless, or because it is of an insidious nature that eludes precise definition. If, with this datum in mind, we go through the list again, it turns out anything but a random, heterogeneous compilation. The first transgression is not just setting up an image but setting it up "in secret." The attribute is in the code itself. In the case of the second, contemptuous treatment of a parent, apart from the fact that the victim will often be loath to publicize it, it may be most difficult to pinpoint a concrete wrongdoing.[192] The third, interference with a boundary sign, is invariably perpetrated by stealth. The fourth, exploitation of the blind, not only implies a decided superiority on the blackguard's part but also can assume so many devious, treacherous shapes—a misleading hint, a handkerchief displayed à la Iago—that even a modern court might have to give up. (It would, of course, be a gross mistake to confine "blind" in this text to its literal meaning.) The fifth, oppression of the alien, is similar: strong versus weak, and countless subtle ways of trampling on him. The sixth is not just slaying but slaying "in secret": again, specified in the code. Then four cases of illicit intercourse—always occurring in private. The same is true of the last crime, of a bribe for a miscarriage of justice; and besides, the judge's powerful position makes earthly retribution unlikely.

The appeal to heaven in these three circumstances—the evil is hidden, done by one who can defy censure or of a kind too vague to be justiciable—is amply documented throughout Scripture, and it plays an enormous part in the laws: "If a person sins in that he hears a curse pronounced [by the victim of an unsolved crime on doer or abettor], and he is a witness whether he has seen it or known of it but does not tell, he shall bear his iniquity,"[193] "If you afflict a widow or orphan and they cry to me, I shall surely hear their cry"[194] and so forth. No wonder the curse is a prominent instrument of intertribal or international coexistence. In the final covenant between Jacob and Laban, the reason—the absence of effective human guarantees—is spelled out: "No man is with us," Laban says, "see, God is witness between me and you."[195] Paradoxically, the

[191] See E. F. Kautzsch and A. Bertholet, *Die Heilige Schrift des Alten Testaments,* 4th ed., 1 (1922), 309.

[192] On the shame-cultural aspect of this curse, see my lecture ["The Culture of Deuteronomy"] in *Orita,* 3 (1969), 38 f.

[193] Lev 5:1, cp. Judg 17:2.

[194] Exod 22:22.

[195] Gen 31:50.

lack of sanction in international affairs constitutes a graver problem today, in the era of UNO, than in those periods of antiquity when God or the gods were held to watch over them.

The spirit of the collection has much in common with that of the Ten Commandments. I incline to a pretty early date. The order of the four sexual sins is noteworthy: father's wife, bestiality, sister, mother-in-law. One would expect the three instances of incest together and bestiality at the end.[196] A possible inference is that the original version of the dooms goes back to before sister and mother-in-law were prohibited, these being subsequently appended to father's wife and beast. It is also arguable, however, that the code is not quite that old and that the strange array results from its drawing on prior legislation: it is that source which grew up in stages, with new taboos tacked on to an existing set instead of being worked in, and the code under discussion does not bother to rationalize the sequence.

A glance at other systems supports my approach. Ancient Greek lists of imprecations cover much the same field as the one in Deuteronomy. Even in Plato, neglect of filial obligations,[197] removal of a landmark[198] and faithlessness to a stranger[199] are still given over to divine chastisement. In commenting on the last-mentioned wrong, Plato, like Laban, explains the need for intervention from on high: "He is without companions or kinsfolk." An inscription of Chios[200] goes further, frankly assigning to the curse last place when all worldly remedies have failed. It starts by imposing a fine on misappropriation of public land. It goes on to lay down that if the officials who ought to exact it fail to do so, they themselves are liable. And what if the higher officials who should make them pay are equally remiss? Now we come to the ultimate resort: they are cursed.

Comparison may also supply a clue as to the standing of the twelfth curse which I have so far neglected—threatening "him who does not uphold all this law." On the stele of Teos known as the *Dirae Teiae*,[201] there are a number of warnings with the structure "Whoever does so-and-so, that man shall perish, he and his house"; and the last two are aimed at a magistrate not properly proclaiming the catalogue and at a person not respecting the stele itself. Imprecations of this and similar kinds are also met in Greece proper. The entire constitution of Solon was protected by a curse—at least Dio says so,[202] enough for my purpose. The twelfth curse, then, may contemplate an attack, in some form or another, on the authority of the norms as such—a crime that certainly belongs to the type to combat which the deity's help is badly wanted.

Perhaps it is worth observing that, if the community in its battle against malefactors turns to the Almighty only as a *pis aller* [second best], it closely mirrors individual

[196] See my *Studies in Biblical Law* (1947) (repr. 1969), 77 ff.

[197] Plato, *Laws* 4.717B, 9.880E f.

[198] Plato, *Laws* 8.842E f.

[199] Plato, *Laws* 5.729E f.

[200] 5653 a 20 in H. Collitz and F. Bechtel, *Sammlung griechischer Dialektinschriften*, 3, pt. 1 (1905), 703.

[201] 5632 in H. Collitz and F. Bechtel, *op. cit.*, 690 ff.

[202] Dio Chrysostomus, *Discourses* 80.6.

behaviour. Indeed, whether we fight against or for something, we prefer to rely on *les gros bataillons* [the masses]. "God's opportunity," in the words of Scott, "is man's extremity." Unquestionably, there lurks here some lack of faith. But, by and large, unless we abdicate responsibility for what little seems to be in our hands, we cannot act very differently. Synagogue preachers like to dwell on Biblical heroes who, in critical situations, both prayed and took all reasonable steps to succeed—say, Jacob when, on his journey home from Laban, he was going to encounter Esau.[203]

By the way, even now, in general people swear (I mean, those who do, none of you, of course) when debarred from effective action. This, to be sure, goes for atheists as well as believers. Yet I wonder—without playing down other factors—whether the primeval role of the curse does not still occupy a little corner in the collective unconscious.

It is contrary to Jewish tradition to end on an ill-omened note,[204] so I must not take my leave of you with curses. Instead, let me remind you that these reflections on legal rules are many of them applicable, *mutatis mutandis*, to rules in other fields, among them the jolly ones of cooking and love-making. A San Franciscan recipe for fondue runs: "Allow bread crumbs to dry slightly... toss the cheeses... stir until smooth."[205] This is descended in direct line from old-time Wisdom—by which, I should note, I mean not only the Hebrew variety but also the classical one, basically alike: for making Greek wine, Cato in his treatise *On Agriculture* writes, "carefully gather ripe grapes, add... a measure of pure salt...,"[206] as to truffles, Apicius says, "boil with leeks."[207] The sage is addressing his disciple. Here are some contemporary amatory directions: "Always have a medical examination before you come to any conclusion,"[208] "Pay a lot of attention to the conditions, time, place, lights on or off,"[209] "Hug her but also tell her that you love her. Kiss him but also tell him that you love him."[210] (The last example might tempt one to investigate upcoming structures, more or less laboured, resulting from the need for evenhandedness between the two sexes.[211]) Equally deriving from antiquity. A newly deciphered hieroglyphic message by a father to his son reads: "Do not take liberties with a woman whose husband is listening to your words."[212] The typical German cookbook prescription of my young days was impersonal, distant and authoritative: "*Man nehme zwei Eier*," "one takes two eggs." I shall not go into its complicated history. Nowadays, the Wisdom infinitive is to the fore: "*Den Braten fünf*

[203] Gen 32:1 ff.

[204] See J. H. Hertz, *The Pentateuch and Haftorahs* (1938), 970, on the repetition of Mal 3:23 after 3:25 in the Lesson from the Prophets.

[205] See The Junior League of San Francisco, *San Francisco à la Carte* (1979), 41.

[206] Cato, *On Agriculture* 24.

[207] Apicius, *On Culinary Art* 7.16.5.320.

[208] See H. Fensterheim and J. Baer, *Don't say Yes when you want to say No* (*The Assertiveness Training Book*) (1975) (New Dell edition 1978, repr. 1981), 154.

[209] *Ibid.*, 155.

[210] *Ibid.*, 138.

[211] For a special, early case in 1 Cor 7:12 ff., see my lecture ["Pauline Contributions to a Pluralistic Culture: Re-Creation and Beyond"] in *Jesus and Man's Hope*, edd. D. G. Miller and D. Y. Hadidian (1971), vol. 2, 240 [551 f.].

[212] See L. M. Boyd's Grab Bag in *San Francisco Chronicle*, November 1, 1980, 29.

Minuten stehen lassen," "to let the roast stand for five minutes." Even the direct address is gaining ground, but as it is based on the polite *Sie*, "you," instead of on *du*, "thou," the tone is not really intimate and paternal.[213] (Another significant change in my lifetime is uniformization: every recipe in a collection is arranged the same way.) From the province of Cupid, there is Nietzsche's "*Du gehst zu Frauen? Vergiss die Peitsche nicht!*,"[214] "You are visiting women? Do not forget the whip," or Goethe's much more philogynous rebuttal of the complaint that a woman will flit from one suitor to another: "*Tadle sie nicht, sie sucht einen beständigen Mann*,"[215] "Do not blame her, she is looking for a constant man."

N.B. The very title of the volume containing the advice about medical check-ups, lights on or off etc., shows the Wisdom imperative: "Don't say Yes when you want to say No." Such titles are common now in this country. "Do it yourself" is proverbial. Twelve minutes at Cody's bookshop gave me, from Business, "Don't bank on it,"[216] "Go for it,"[217] "Make yourself clear";[218] from Health, "Be slim and healthy,"[219] "Eat your way to Health,"[220] "Eat right to stay healthy,"[221] "Improve your Sight without Glasses,"[222] "Live your Health,"[223] "Run to Health."[224] Particularly interesting is "Heal yourself with Vegetables, Fruits and Grains,"[225] a translation: the French original carries the old-fashioned designation "Treatment of Diseases by Vegetables, Fruits and Grains." A seachange on the voyage to the States—though Europe will doubtless catch up before long. Finally, from Psychology, "Don't push the River,"[226] "Get your Message across,"[227] "If you meet the Buddha on the Road, kill him,"[228] "Own your own Life,"[229] "Spare the Couch,"[230] "Stand up!" Speak out! Talk back!,"[231] "Stop running scared."[232] We have to do with a new-established style of title. It is not found, say, in Freud, Jung or even their immediate disciples over here; nor, when I went from Cody's to the store in the Students' Union where they sell books recommended for courses, did I notice a single speci-

[213] See *Brigitte Kochbuch* (1970), 18.
[214] *Also sprach Zarathustra*, Part 1, *Vom alten und jungen Weiblein* i.f.
[215] Goethe's *Gespräche*, ed. F. v. Biedermann, rev. W. Herwig (1965), vol. 1, 343.
[216] By M. J. Meyer (1979).
[217] By M. Douglas (1979).
[218] By J. O. Morris (1980).
[219] By L. Clark (1972).
[220] By I. B. Holbrook (1972).
[221] By D. Burkitt (1979).
[222] By Editorial Committee of *Science of Life Books*, 10th ed. (1975).
[223] By R. and J. Halpern (1980).
[224] By P. D. Wood (1980).
[225] Translation by H. Stern-Montagny (1976), of J. Valnet, *Traitment des Maladies par les Légumes, les Fruits et les Céréales.*
[226] By B. Stevens (1970).
[227] By J. R. Diekman (1979).
[228] By S. B. Kopp (1972).
[229] By R. G. Abell with C. W. Abell (1976).
[230] By D. L. Tasto and E. W. Skje (1979).
[231] By R. E. Alberti and M. Emmons (1975).
[232] By G. Fensterheim and J. Baer (1977).

men—so the chief priests have not yet taken to it. It is a concomitant of a peculiar outgrowth of the—*au fond* marvellous—American zest for experimentation: the reign of gurus who, each with his novel tao to salvation, guide us through the twenty-four hours of the day.

Not by chance it comes hard on the heels of a proliferation of "How to" tracts. "How to" also has its pedigree, going back to the ancient manuals of crafts. Cato heads a paragraph "how (*quomodo*) one should construct a mill,"[233] another one "how one should preserve lentils."[234] The large-scale use of the phrase for entitling whole books implies an immense popularization of technology. Our magi instruct us in the fixing of anything whatever. But whereas at the "How to" stage, we are still allowed to choose our needs, the imperativists-imperialists—"Do," "Do not"—determine these as well as the answers.

This bent explains why the Wisdom imperative in titles frequently shades off into the imperative that expresses a detailed order. "Don't push the River" is still in the nature of a general, profound rule. "Stand up! Speak out! Talk back!" is only partially that; it at least half conjures up the specific occasion on which these directions have to be barked out. Nor is the affinity with advertising slogans accidental. A report on Fat Profits in Diet Aids quotes "Slim down fast without going hungry," "Take weight off and keep it off" and so forth.[235] You are being offered the infallible remedy: there is no excuse for not buying it. Education gives way to dictate, strategy to tactics, and the groves of academe are being turned into workshop or drillground.

I started researching into patterns of love advice in the early fifties, during my period at Aberdeen. The University Library there kept all Erotica locked away in a sort of poison section and even professors had to specially ask for any item they wanted. I have done a few brave things in my life but, believe me, none of them compares to facing the North of Scotland lady at the desk and requesting a copy of the Kamasutra. For that, I feel, I deserve the Victoria Cross.

[233] Cato, *On Agriculture* 19.1.

[234] Cato, *On Agriculture* 116.

[235] In *San Francisco Chronicle*, November 3, 1980, 28.

EXCURSUS 1

"The form of a statement may reveal a good deal, apart from its content." If it is oral, this goes even for intonation, a gesture, a twinkle.

I remember, in my Cambridge days, showing a "gremial" generously helpful to refugees the draft of a lecture which contained a remark I did not mean seriously. I forget what it was, say, "a Roman politician did not lie to his constituency." He boggled at it and when I replied that the class would get me from my manner, also from their by then pretty fair acquaintance with my philosophy and, at a pinch, if they did not, I would sense it and add a quick supplement, he declared that the text by itself ought to convey the intended sense, with no assistance whatever from inflection, personal ties, interaction and the like. Indeed, by and by I learned that even the text itself had preferably be understated. His was a Wykehamist attitude: the classical restraint of an English gentleman extolled, for example, in André Maurois's *Les Silences du Colonel Bramble*. As a teacher, he never procured his flock a "high" and he never let them down—he was dependable and slightly boring. My use of extrinsic aids springs from a far greater, vulgar involvement; and while I frequently manage to carry my public along, now and then, for some reason or other, I fail dismally.

Perhaps the champions of austerity will be less disapproving if reminded of support for me in antiquity. Demosthenes considered declamation the foremost branch of oratory,[236] Aristotle complained about the lack of treatises on the subject,[237] his disciple Theophrastus, taking it up, compared speaker and actor[238] and Cicero coined the phrase "eloquence of the body."[239] It is not, by the way, as if the purists were not acting. Only their object is not to drive home their specific points—that is the need of those who have not yet arrived—but to convey an overall impression of security, impartiality, distance, standing above it. "Dumb, we shout," says an old proverb;[240] "immobile, we run" it might continue." (A parallel can now be found over here: many a guru, a picture of impassivity and disinterestedness, is making it fast.) I grant that their toning down of presentation educated their listeners to spot irony more readily than do continental or American ones. The latter just do not expect it when confronted by a dead-pan face. Economy breeds subtlety.

Of course, there are gradations within the two camps. Reticence in Britain is required more strictly in the academic field than in some others, the political, for instance. "While the speech for the Gregorian Calendar by Lord Macclesfield, a consummate astronomer, was received with yawns, that of Lord Chesterfield who, as he himself tells us, was utterly ignorant of the science, but a captivating orator, chained the attention and won the votes of the House."[241] In the Germany of my youth, though in

[236] Philodemus, *On Rhetoric* 1.196.3; Cicero, *Brutus* 38.142; *De Or.* 17.56, and others.

[237] Aristotle, *Rhet.* 3.1.3.

[238] Cicero, *De Or.* 3.59.221.

[239] Cicero, *De Or.* 17.55.

[240] *Dum tacent clamant.*

[241] See W. Mathews, *The Great Conversers* (1878), 206.

general rules were less rigid, much contempt was felt for unassimilated Jews on the ground of "talking with the hands," *mit den Händen reden*. Personal characteristics, too, come into play. My friendly instructor was uncommonly correct, I—from day one bent on outshining my elder brother—am avid for applause.

English protest against the overrating of frills—not the same as outright rejection—started early. Bacon comments on Demosthenes's view:[242] "A strange thing that that part of an Orator which is but superficial, and rather the virtue of a Player, should be placed so high." Even on the stage, he notes, originally, the quality of acting was of little moment: the earliest authors of tragedies performed themselves and did not call in professional actors. What, then, brought about the imbalance? The stupidity of the mass who goes for glitter: "There is in human Nature generally more of the fool than of the wise." This elitism would become the hallmark of the British public school. Actually, staying with the bare text wards off not only the rabble within the borders but foreigners as well. Already the ancient masters perceived the relevance of the problem to retention or bridging of both class and national divisions. "Anything pertaining to delivery," says Cicero,[243] "conveys a certain meaning naturally. For this reason, the ignorant, the crowd and indeed the barbarians are most moved by it. For words move only one who is conjoined in a society of a common language . . . Delivery, carrying the mind's emotion to the outside, moves all since the minds of all are stirred by the same emotions and it is by the same signs that they recognize them in others and manifest them themselves." Clearly, renunciation of non-verbal, "natural" relish ties in with insularity.

Maybe it can come about only in a highly masculine culture. In a previous publication,[244] I quoted Oscar Wilde to the effect that, in conversation with women, you should listen less to what they say than how they say it. This, *au fond*, is to concede that, less unilinear than men, they will not be confined to one narrow channel of communication. To be sure, what prompted the quip was pure machismo: at the time, feminine fluidity counted as sweet, childlike, a bit treacherous, well below male earnestness. In the same book,[245] I complained that most writers on Roman law were leaving the study of form to the professors of literature and poetry—possibly a result of the same male inflexibility.

Where I go wrong is in transferring what belongs in a live show to the printed page. Often when I write I feel as if talking. As a result, trusting to an imaginary contact, I may express myself in a fashion apt to mislead even a sophisticated reader. Quintilian observes that an audience will detect sarcasm by heeding one or more of three clues: modulation, character of the orator, the statement as such.[246] Whereas my Camford mentors would keep to *rei natura* [the nature of the thing] even in speech, I am apt to rely on *pronuntiatio* [emphasis in diction] and *persona* [personality] even in writing. Exactly where the line ought to be drawn is not easy to determine. Here are a few instances.

[242] Bacon, *Essays*, "Of Boldness" init., cited by Cope, *The Rhetoric of Aristotle*, ed. Sandys (1877), vol. 3, 4.

[243] Cicero, *De Or.* 3.59.223.

[244] *Forms of Roman Legislation* [1956] [repr. 1979], 6.

[245] *Op. cit.*, 1.

[246] Quintilian, *I.O.* 8.6.54.

A recent number of the *California Law Review* celebrated the start of the Jurisprudence and Society Program at Boalt Hall. For people overseas I should explain that university law journals in the States are directed by students who may thoroughly revise a contribution; so I collaborated only on being assured by Dean Kadish that he would keep an eye on things and that no changes would be made without my consent. My article introduced Sophocles as originator of the detective story.[247] I concluded by saying that I would not now discuss the two millennia between him and the modern whodunnit but—last sentence in my draft: "Hopefully, I reserve this study for the silver jubilee of J.S.P." Attached to "hopefully" was a footnote: "Student editors, please note that this is the approved manner of using the adverb." I am sure that, had I been conversing with them, or even had they been pupils of mine and therefore known me well enough, they would have realized that I was inviting them to laugh together with me at the pedantic, repetitious criticism of the extended application that has long gained currency. However, as it was, they thought that I was truly concerned about this grammatical issue and, worse, I doubted their grasp of it. They were seconded by the Dean, otherwise very protective of my idiosyncracies. Evidently, I had failed to link up properly and I rephrased the ending.

In a forthcoming tract on New Testament ethics I write: "There is indeed a blend of shame and guilt mechanism in each civilisation and each individual (except for California where we do without either)—not to mention the fact that a deep enough probing would reveal an intrinsic overlap of the two emotions." John Noonan, whom I asked for his comments, is put off by the inconsistency with another passage where I point out that, in Luke,[248] the invitees to the Great Supper keep up appearances, "tendering apologies that would go down well in the Berkeley hills—I just married, I have arranged to inspect some real estate I bought" etc. I do not think I shall make any change. I cannot believe there will be many who do not see that the aside in brackets is to be taken with a grain of salt.

In the following case, he does catch me out treating the written word as if spoken. I draw attention to a split among the Rabbis between purists, with absolute standards, and realists, taking account of period and milieu. According to the latter, far less is to be required of Noah, living in a godless age, than of Moses or David. I add: "Conduct barely so-so under Carter may be splendid under Nixon." John Noonan urges that the contrast between the two administrations is no longer so sharp as it once seemed. I fully agree with him.[249] In fact, I find Carter's exploitation of his rebirth for the purpose of advancement particularly distasteful. (Though a realist will be aware that, in a Southerner, it is not quite so calculated as it would be in others.) In a lecture, my voice would do all that is needed. Without it, it is only the rise from censorious "barely so-so" to enthusiastic "splendid" that signals tongue-in-cheek—and that is probably too little.

[247] ["Greek Forerunners of Simenon"] *CLRev*, 68 (1980), 301 ff. An expanded German translation will come out as a *Konstanzer Universitätsrede* shortly [*Die Geburt der Detektivgeschichte aus dem Geiste der Rhetorik* (1983)].

[248] Luke 14:16 ff., as contrasted with Matt 22:1 ff.

[249] Written prior to Billygate.

Lastly, describing in a paper on Josephus[250] the court-Jew professor in Europe, I maintain that, while not fully accepted by the gentile colleagues, he is also distrusted by his correligionists: they are conscious that "we are hand in glove with the establishment, careful not to let the inferior contacts intrude overmuch." Helen warns me that few American readers will apprehend the ironical thrust of "the inferior contacts." What I mean is not that Moses Cohen the peddler is in fact less worthy or interesting than Moses Cohen the mathematician or historian but that, in parts of the world, such is the verdict of the arrogant, hidebound ruling set; hence whoever craves there a position of eminence must compromise with prejudice, must not flaunt too much his intimacy with those looked down on. In England, I assume, I shall be understood, in the States, with a higher degree of literal-mindedness, maybe I shall not. Why did I not make myself clearer by recourse to inverted commas: "careful not to let the 'inferior' contacts intrude overmuch"? In general, if you have to announce "here comes irony," I feel it is not worth having. It is possible, however, that my disinclination to this crutch goes back to an attack on underlining I heard in the 1920s from a teacher at my Gymnasium, Ernst Ochs, who could compete with my Cantabrigian mystagogue: "*Das Unterstreichen ist das pöbelhafte Kind des parlamentarischen Zeitalters*," "Underlining is the plebeian child of the parliamentary age."

Rather to my surprise, I discover that the original German version of this piece is quite straightforward, with *Brüder*, "brothers," instead of "inferior contacts"; all the more striking as it was an address to the Bavarian Academy,[251] and as I explained above, it is easier to be ironical in oral communication. Apparently, in my native country, the subject was too loaded for both my audience and me to allow of any *exornatio*, elegant roundabout.

Who knows?—my overdoing it may betray various instincts bearing on power and weakness: to play, to tease, to test, to attract at once and make things difficult, to wield a secret weapon, to entrap, to outwit, to be chased (by friend or foe), to remain in the twilight, to escape full responsibility. In close relationships, Helen insists, irony—*dissimulatio* in Latin—is often a distancing rather than a positive force. She has Plato on her side[252] (also Rilke[253]): his Alcibiades is lyrical about the great moment when he broke through to the true Socrates, who for once dispensed with his habitual deviousness. What made him eager for that miracle in the first place?

[250] ["Typology in Josephus"] *JJS*, 31 (1980), 34.

[251] *Typologie im Werk des Flavius Josephus*, Bayerische Akademie der Wissenschaften, Phil.-Hist. Klasse, Sitzungsberichte (1977), 6, 26.

[252] *Symposium* 216 E.

[253] See the quotations in R. Bly, *Selected Poems of Rainer Maria Rilke* (1979), 188.

Excursus 2

In the Ten Commandments, "God's voice compels the individual conscience." My friend William David Davies, whom I asked to vet parts of the typescript, suggested I substitute "accountability" for "conscience," seeing that the latter word—Latin *conscientia*, from Greek *syneidos* or *syneidesis*—is missing from the Old Testament. He has contributed the authoritative article on it to *The Interpreter's Dictionary of the Bible.*[254]

I was aware, when writing, of what modern theologians make of its absence, but I do not go along with them. I explained my standpoint to William David, and he encouraged me to set it down. Here, then, is what I feel.

Let me start with *tu quoque*: they talk freely about Mosaic "morality," "religion," etc., with no better textual backing. I wonder what the Hebrew for "accountability" may be.

Next, what is meant by saying that a term does occur? In many cases, such as "husband" for *ba'al* or *'ish*, "covenant" for *berith*, "to create" for *qana*, the remoteness of the translation from the original is obvious at a glance. Some measure of discrepancy, however, is always there: not a single Hebrew-English pair is truly alike. The only solution—even if by no means perfect—would be to publish in ancient Hebrew.

In a less quibbling spirit—though absence of a term often betokens absence of the thing, this is far from inevitable. The sources contain no equivalent of "nuclear power": it was not invented. On the other hand, parents taught children long before there were the verbs "to instruct"—let alone the nouns "teaching," "instruction"[255]—and people behaved responsibly or recklessly about spears and fires long before "due care" and "negligence" made their debut. Psalmists and prophets structured their utterances by means of *parallelismus membrorum* [parallelism of members], but the device was christened only by an Oxford professor of the eighteenth century.

There is a further factor of enormous importance: not seldom the late birth or adoption of a word is due to the previous self-understoodness of what it expresses.[256] At this moment, in English, while we do have "vegetarian," we are without a settled label for the less gentle feeder—not because he does not exist but, on the contrary, because he is taken for granted. Common occurrence, that is, may join non-occurrence in being left unnamed. No doubt, we could easily fill the gap; and should current nutrition fads prevail, "meat-and-fish-eater" or "non-vegetarian" will become part of established usage, or perhaps "carnivore" will be extended from the animal world to the human. But the priority of "vegetarian" will remain. Molière's *bourgeois*, before losing his naivety as he trains for the status of *gentilhomme*, has no inkling that he is an author of "prose"—*prorsa oratio*, "straight speech."

[254] Vol. 4 (1962), 671 ff.

[255] On the posteriority of the action noun, see my *Roman Law* (1969), 11 ff.

[256] See my articles ["*Intestatus*"] in *Revue Historique de Droit Français et Etranger*, ser. 4, 15 (1936), 341 ff., ["The Preponderance of Intestacy in Rome"] *TLR*, 39 (1965), 254 ff., and ["Das Selbstverständliche in Rechtsgeschichte"] *ZSS*, 90 (1973), Rom. Abt., 1 (Engl. version ["The Self-Understood in Legal History"] in *JR*, 85, n.s. 18 [(1973)], 126).

The point is that words are coined to designate the striking, not the ordinary; and the striking is often the less frequent, in fact, it may be striking precisely because it is exceptional. I got interested in the phenomenon years ago, when dealing with *intestatus*, "intestate," in the XII Tables of fifth-century B.C. Rome. Scholars were then agreed that, as Latin had only a negative term for a person leaving no will, this figure must have been rare. That seemed to me fantastic: testacy the norm as early as that, and among the have-nots as well as the haves! The correct conclusion is just the opposite. Primeval Latin had no appellation for a person who allowed his estate to go to the law-appointed heirs: everybody did that. It was for the novel, remarkable step of willmaking that a verb was introduced, *testari*. Hence, when the XII Tables wished to say something about the old and still by far most usual way, they had to resort to a negative, *intestatus*. Similarly, *experiri*, "to try out," *auspicari*, "to take to auspices," draw attention to actions which, to begin with at least, are special. There are no verbs for the unexciting conditions without a try out, without auspices. So the doer of the special can be described by a positive past participle, *expertus*, *auspicatus*, but the abstainer, who represents the rule, only by negativing this: *inexpertus*, *inauspicatus*. A passage from King David's dirge about Saul and Jonathan is instructive.[257] "Tell it not in Gath, lest the daughters of the uncircumcised triumph." For the authors of the King James version, "to circumcise" denotes an outlandish measure. Accordingly, in referring to the standard, not endowed with a tag of its own, they make do with the negative "uncircumcised." By contrast, the Hebrews, by the time of this poem, are taken aback by lack of their rite. In the original, therefore, we find a positive adjective, *'arelim*, "those with foreskin." To be sure, squeamishness, too, may have inclined the King James team towards the less direct.

The Greeks never spoke of a *polytheos*, "polytheist." Yet the predicate is listed in Greek dictionaries. Philo, Jewish outsider, made it up. In modern vocabulary, *athéisme* and *polythéisme*, French precursors of "atheism" and "polytheism," preceded *monothéisme*. Sixteenth-century *athée* (Rabelais) was never followed by *monothée*, and *monothéiste* had to wait for *monothéisme*, seventeenth century. *Déisme* is as late as 1660 (Pascal). Both in French and in English, "bigamy" and "polygamy" considerably antedate "monogamy."

No woman in the Pentateuch is said to "love" a parent, suitor, husband or child except Rebeccah who puts one son above the other.[258] A fully developed noun "love" is not met in this corpus at all. In *Fiddler on the Roof*,[259] Tevye asks his wife of many years whether she "loves" him. She finds the question awkward: at their stage, it is inane to bring up, play with, what throughout has been preserved in safekeeping, sacred, central. By putting it, the hero shows himself slightly infected, *angekränkelt*, by the present tendency to cover over insecurity and brittleness with romantic declamation. "Tell him that you love him."[260] After all, the show must appeal to a contemporary audience. (I hope somebody has examined, or will examine, the numerous intriguing deviations

[257] 2 Sam 1:20.

[258] Gen 25:28. Cp. Gen 29:18, 30, 32, 37, 37:3 f., 44:20; Deut 10:15, 21:15 f.

[259] J. Stein, (1964), 80 ff.

[260] See H. Fensterheim and J. Baer cited above, 298.

from Sholem Aleichem.[261]) Though my parents were often at loggerheads, I do not think my father ever needed this kind of reassurance. His son sympathizes with Tevye.

When I lived in England, again and again the German *Schadenfreude*, with no close English parallel, was quoted to me as proving a peculiar German defect. On such occasions, if I was in a bad mood, I retorted that it is superfluous to note that which, literally, "goes without saying": so it was the English who lost. And I was only half-joking. (Among South-German Jewry at least, *neqama*—pronounced *neqome*—the Biblical "vengeance," came very near *Schadenfreude* with, however, slight differences in application.)

We must not, of course, simplify. The everyday nature of a thing is far from the only feature delaying a title, unusualness far from the only feature promoting it. Again, what is thoroughly familiar in one context may be astounding in another; and perhaps, in the course of millennia, most things have astounded sufficiently to be marked out: "friend" and "foe," "sickness" and "health," "to eat" and "to fast," "honest" and "fraudulent." Most things—but by no means all. To "vegetarian," already mentioned, I could add many more examples. There are, as yet, no opposite numbers to "murderer," "arsonist," "cannibal." "Straight" has only recently become available, at San Francisco, as a—faintly pejorative—antonym of "gay."

Basically, language gives an inverted reflection of reality. It is a laughing mirror in which the small appears large and the large small. The Pythagoreans were on to something when they held[262] that we do not notice the music of the spheres because it is with us right from birth; we are like a coppersmith who becomes indifferent to the din around him; and we hear only the petty interruptions. It is moving that, notwithstanding the comparison with a factory, they assumed those galactic sounds to be of marvellous beauty.

Conscience in the Old Testament. What, for instance, about David's charitableness after all who stood in his way are routed? "Is there yet any left of the house of Saul, that I may show him kindness for Jonathan's sake?"[263] But, one might object, it is not openly stated that this motive plays a part; we have to infer it. What, then, about two episodes from the Joseph cycle? One for conscience after a misdeed: his brothers, unaware that he is the high Egyptian official who keeps one of them back as hostage, remember what they did to him long ago.[264] "And they said to one another, We are verily guilty concerning our brother, in that we saw the anguish of his soul; therefore is this distress come upon us." The other for conscience when tempted: Joseph, purchased by an Egyptian grandee who promotes him to majordomo, is urged by his master's wife to be her paramour.[265] "But he refused: Behold, my master keeps no watch over me[266] as to what goes on in his house and all that he has he has put into my hand; he is not greater in this house than I; neither has he kept back anything from me but you, because you

[261] Hodel's engagement which, in the musical, triggers the question, is found in his *The Old Country* (1946), 382 ff.

[262] Aristotle, *On the Heavens* 193.

[263] 2 Sam 9:1.

[264] Gen 42:21.

[265] Gen 39:8 f.

[266] On the phrasing in the original, see below, 228.

are his wife. How then can I do this great evil and sin against God?" Or an illustration of a good conscience:[267] the King of Gerar who takes Sarah into his harem, having been given to understand by her as well as Abraham that she is the latter's sister only, is threatened by God with death for appropriating another man's wife, but bravely pleads: "Will you slay even a righteous nation? Did he not himself say to me, She is my sister, and did she, even she herself, not say, He is my brother? In the simplicity of my heart and the innocency of my hands I have done this." It is hard to believe that a culture possessing the word "conscience" would have to reformulate these narratives.

At this juncture, I should like to raise a problem not discussed in the literature I have looked up: how come that Greek, in picking a term, so concentrates on the rational, on knowledge? As has long been seen, the verb *synoida*, "to know together with," originally refers to the sharing of knowledge with somebody else—which has nothing to do with conscience. Hebrew has the same notion, *yadha' 'eth*. Joseph's remark which, above (in order to avoid confusion) I rendered "my master keeps no watch over me as to what goes on in his house," literally signifies: "my master does not know together with me" and so on. Already two verses before, we are told that his master "left all he had in Joseph's hand and he knew nothing together with him save the bread which he ate," i.e. save what his trusted servant actually provided him with. You can, however, also share knowledge with yourself: say, you attained it on your own or you are alone in having it. This still is not conscience. But from the fifth century B.C. on, *synoida* and its nouns become fashionable where you share knowledge with yourself in the sense of judging yourself according as you do or do not commit a wrong. Whence this tie-up of self-evaluation with awareness?

Before attempting an answer, I would point out that it very soon loses in strength. Certainly, today, it is quite gone. What we mean by "conscience" is no inner knowing but almost an instinct, a moral sense related to guilt. The same is true of German *Gewissen*. If only on this ground, it would be futile to avoid the word in connection with the Old Testament. Today, to recapture something of its pristine application, one would have to turn to "consciousness." But I cannot here go into the similarities and dissimilarities between our "consciousness" movement and ancient doctrines. Historically, the speed with which the rational element gives way to feeling in the Greek suggests that the emphasis on the former must be due to a distinct fifth-century cause.

That period is indeed eminently philosophical. But, more specifically, the key to virtue is widely supposed to lie in information, successful schooling, learning properly taken in.[268] It is quite likely this theory which chiefly leads to the identification of self-judgment with "the sharing of knowledge with oneself." Just conceivably, at its inception, the term is favoured by the opponents of Socrates's teaching[269] that no one transgresses wittingly: he errs, they suggest, a person's choice of right or wrong is the very point of his insight. After all, the earliest extant evidence for *syneidesis* is Democritus, whom Plato resents so much that he never once mentions him (as Nixon

[267] Gen 20:4 f. See *Ancient Jewish Law,* 51 f., 57 f.

[268] See R. Maschke, *Die Willenslehre im Greichischen Recht* (1926), 116 ff.

[269] See *Ancient Jewish Law,* 64 ff.

never mentioned McGovern when they were running against one another). According to Xenophon-Hermogenes,[270] Socrates after his trial uses the verb *synoida*: whereas he can be high-spirited, he says, those participating in the false witness against him must "share knowledge with themselves" of their wicked conduct. No doubt conscience may be involved, but partly at least the phrase here seems to stress secrecy: privately, those fellows are perfectly acquainted with the truth despite their lies in public. It would still be open to Socrates to argue that even in thus lying they proved their ignorance.

To come back to the Old Testament, there are adumbrations of the Greek semantic evolution though, not surprisingly, adumbrations only. I conclude by giving an example. The Second Book of Samuel records that, as King David looks like being ousted by his son Absalom, a relative of Saul's by name of Shimei insults and curses him. After Absalom's defeat, he asks to be pardoned: "Your servant knows that I have sinned."[271] Not simply "I have sinned" but "I know that I have done so." In fact, the subjective aspect is stressed even further. The Hebrew reads not just *ḥaṭa'thi*, "I have sinned," but *'ani ḥaṭa'thi*, "I, even I" or "I myself have sinned."

A freak formulation? Impossible. For though David accedes to the plea, the story continues in the First Book of Kings, when Solomon, mindful of a deathbed wish of his father, finds a pretext under which to have Shimei executed; and what he says to him is, "You know all the evil that your heart knows that you did to my father David."[272] Awareness is here accented to a remarkable degree. More than that: "to know the evil that one's heart knows" is highly reminiscent of "to share knowledge with oneself of an evil." It would not be wildly off to render: "Your conscience tells you how you offended." Commentators have overlooked the motif common to the two portions of the narrative in Samuel and Kings. Some postulate tautology in the latter and cut out "that your heart knows." Others interpret the clause as meaning "of which you are secretly conscious."[273] But while conscience may dwell on the private (as in the Xenophon text just presented), it need not do so. In this case, it definitely does not. Nothing could be more open than Shimei's confession as he pleads for mercy: "Let not my Lord remember that which your servant did perversely that day... Your servant knows that I have sinned." We ought to admit the beginning of something Greek-like here. What accounts for it I have no idea. All I can say is that the entire business of Shimei is full of deep reflection and subtlety.[274]

[270] Xenophon, *Apology* 24.

[271] 2 Sam 19:21.

[272] 1 Kgs 2:44.

[273] See J. Gray, *I and II Kings* (1963), 108.

[274] On one phase of it, see my article ["Shimei and Örn: The Construction of a Restraint"] in *TLR*, 46 (1972), 653 ff.

Biblical Landmarks in the Struggle for Women's Rights*

I count it a high privilege to deliver the first Light of Truth lecture at Osgoode Hall Law School. It was, I understand, the first law school in the British Commonwealth to admit a woman student. Quite apart from this, I trust that my subject is in harmony with the spirit of the series. The relation between the sexes, the most vital facet of social life, is in process of radical revision. As I see it, the principal causes are peculiar to modern civilisation and no well-tested answers are available. Yet it makes sense to take note of the vast experience of former generations and especially that recorded in sacred writ. At the very least it will stimulate our imagination and give us greater freedom in solving our dilemmas. Let me, then, indicate some Biblical milestones on this long trek.

With so much material available, a choice is difficult. I shall present two illustrations from the Old Testament and two from the New.

I.

My first one is a provision in Deuteronomy imposing the death penalty on an adulterous couple.[1] Why should this rank in the present survey? In many cultures, the law of adultery goes through the following evolution. At the outset, the erring wife is, of course, in the hands of her master—usually husband or father. The narrative of Judah and Tamar brings out the extent of a head of house's power over his womenfolk: he condemns, he acquits.[2] But the community does not intervene even against the intruder. It is up to the wronged master to do his best or worst. The result will be unfair both where he has no power and where he has too much; not to mention the risk to the general peace if, as must often happen, it comes to a feud between his family and the offender's.

Next, the community helps calling the latter to account, in the end taking over altogether—that is to say, his punishment is now the business of the state. This does away (one hopes) with the injustice produced by unequal power and with the danger of feuds. However, the wife even in this period is supposed to be dealt with by her husband, or whoever holds *potestas.* He may wring her neck, cut off her nose or let bygones be bygones. She is his puppy, if exaggeration be permitted. Think of a thief who gets your dog to follow him by means of a slice of pepperoni. The authorities will come down on the thief, not on the dog: it is for you to decide whether to give him a thrashing or pat him on the back.

* To Hazel Barnes, admired scholar, humanist and friend.

[1] Deut 22:22. See D. Daube, ["Concerning Methods of Bible-Criticism: Late Law in Early Narratives"] *ArOr,* 17 (1949), 93. I shall not go into the relation of this statute to Lev 20:10.

[2] Genesis 38.

The Trojan War reflects this phase.[3] Helen, consort of King Menelaus of Sparta, elopes with Paris. All the Greek monarchs fight the offender and his people who abet him, till victory is won. But about Helen they do not bother. As Menelaus finds her in the ruins of Troy, his original resolve to run her through with his sword breaks down before her beauty. After 10 years of bloodshed and the sack of a magnificent city, all for her sake, he takes her back with him to be his queen again. Touching, funny, very fortunate for the lady—but also, in a sense, very degrading. From the Bible, the lives of Abraham and David may be adduced. Abraham, for reasons not here to be set out, encourages Sarah to get into a situation where she will be taken into a king's harem.[4] The king cannot, of course, be brought to trial, but that an adulterer violates communally protected standards is clear from the severe rebuke administered by God. By contrast, Sarah is not treated as in the least blameable. Her husband is content: that is good enough. Similarly, David has intercourse with Bathsheba, married to one of his warriors, Uriah; and, as pregnancy results, engineers the latter's death.[5] He need fear no retribution at the hands of the community. Yet its concern is given expression in the announcement to him by a prophet, that he will not escape the avenging arm of the Lord. As for Bathsheba, not a word is said against her. The man in whose hands her fate would have lain has been got rid of. There is no communal interest in her paying for her deed: fortunate and degrading.

Deuteronomy moves on to a further stage: it places the woman under the public criminal process. Quite consciously, too, as may be seen from the formulation: "If a man be found lying with a woman married to a husband, they shall die indeed both of them." Many translations omit the particle "indeed" and put simply: "they shall both of them die."[6] But evidently the legislator is calling attention to the breakthrough: the woman, too, is answerable to the state. Actually, the point is repeated, for the sanction goes on: "the man lying with the woman and the woman." The whole clause, then, runs: "they shall die indeed both of them, the man lying with the woman and the woman." The price for personhood is high: an adulteress will be executed. At least, however, there are the safeguards of a proper tribunal, with its rules of evidence and so forth, as opposed to a husband's discretionary verdict. An analogy of sorts from classical Roman law is the female slave, not falling under the harsh criminal repression of irregular sex; once freed, she does fall under it.[7] Too little attention has been paid to this and similar aspects of manumission.

Pious modern commentators, feeling the need to apologise for the paragraph under discussion, depict it as stressing the stern treatment to be meted out to the adulterer:

[3] A simplification. My statement applies to a certain version of it. There are others, and mostly the deviations from the one I have in mind reflect nuances in the legal presuppositions. A study focusing on this aspect of the differences might be rewarding. The phase here outlined, incidentally, may well be represented by Eshnunna: see R. Yaron, *The Laws of Eshnunna,* 189 ff.

[4] Gen 12:11 ff., 20:2 ff.; cf. 26:7 ff. See D. Daube, *Sin, Ignorance and Forgiveness in the Bible* [1960], 7 ff.

[5] 2 Samuel 11 ff.

[6] E.g. J. H. Hertz, ed., *The Pentateuch and Haftorahs,* 845, using the 1917 version of the Jewish Publication Society of America. The particle is *gham.*

[7] See T. Mommsen, *Römisches Strafrecht,* 691.

the woman must not be the only one to suffer; "there is to be no double standard of conjugal morality in Israel."[8] But this is to appraise the regulation as if it were enacted in the Victorian era, by which time a yet further stage had been reached: the adulteress is torn to pieces while her partner may be admired. In reality, it stresses precisely the adulteress's liability to capital punishment—paradoxically, a momentous advance in her position. We have before us an instructive example of the gulf that may exist between the *prima facie* thrust of a law and that which emerges when it is placed in its historical context. Another lesson to be learnt—a sad one—is that when society bestows a right, it is apt to exact a *quid pro quo.*

Of Deuteronomic laws closely related, three may be quoted. First, the one about a bride accused by her groom of not being a virgin.[9] Previously, this charge no doubt fell within domestic jurisdiction: once again the episode of Judah and Tamar may be recalled. Now it comes before the elders, and the possibility of her getting off is clearly spelled out. Significantly, her mother as well as her father takes part in her defence.[10]

Secondly, the section about a betrothed girl who may or may not have been raped.[11] Deuteronomy gives her a public hearing which, while it will lead to her death if she is found guilty, excludes any reprisals if she proves innocent.

Finally, Deuteronomy brings under the public process also the rebellious son[12]—a landmark in the struggle for children's rights. He, too, suffers death, but he, too, is at least no longer given over to the arbitrary decision of the holder of *potestas.* How far a father could go is shown by the story of Isaac's near-sacrifice.[13] It is worth noting, considering the enhanced status of women in the ordinances just discussed, that in that about the rebellious son father and mother are equals: he disobeys "the voice of his father and the voice of his mother," and "his father and his mother" are to arraign him before the elders. Lest we be carried away, let us reflect that nothing is said about the daughter. Her position is altogether different.

II.

I go on to an entirely different case, the likening of God to a woman. Ordinarily, he acts as a father or some other male figure in authority: king, judge, warrior. In fact, the whole of Scripture—Old Testament, New Testament and Apocrypha—contains only three passages where he is cast in the part of a female, a mother. Two of them are in the Book of Isaiah, one in the portion commonly attributed to the Second Isaiah (Deutero-Isaiah) and one towards the end, in the last of a number of chapters thought to come from various followers of the Second Isaiah (Trito-Isaiah). Maybe they date from not so long after the Deuteronomic legislation just examined. The former runs:[14] "Can a

[8] J. H. Hertz, *loc.cit.*
[9] Deut 22:13 ff.
[10] Deut 22:15.
[11] Deut 22:22 ff.
[12] Deut 21:18 ff.
[13] Genesis 22.
[14] Isa 49:15.

woman forget her suckling, that she should not have compassion on the son of her womb? Yea, these may forget, yet I will not forget you." The latter:[15] "As a man whom his mother comforts, so will I comfort you."

It should at once be pointed out that, contrary to simplistic notions about a patriarchy, the Old Testament female can be extremely powerful and—more relevant to this discussion—the male can behave in ways far from consonant with machismo. The verb "to weep"[16] in the vast majority of cases has a man as its subject. A father may be expected to look after and carry around his child,[17] and God does this for his chosen.[18] Some jobs, like that of shepherd or guardian of a vineyard, involve a great deal of tender care—in fact, though chiefly undertaken by men, they are open also to women;[19] and in many a simile they are assigned to God.[20] Nevertheless, to represent God as a mother is a daring departure from the norm: behind it must lie a deep concern with this aspect of things.

It is a thousand pities we know next to nothing about external and personal factors which produced such passionate engagement. No doubt we have to reckon with a measure of indebtedness to heathen religions. They not only had both gods and goddesses but also were quite liberal in letting them switch their rôles. A neo-Babylonian prayer to Ishtar[21] at first calls her a lioness but further on, as her ferocious potential is stressed, a lion. The Hittite king says to the deity Telepinus: "Of the oppressed and the lowly you are father and mother";[22] and a Hittite official, asking relief from suffering, exclaims: "You, my god, are father and mother to me."[23] But what was it that rendered precisely Deutero-Isaiah and his school open to this influence—if influence there was?

Fortunately, just enough vestiges are left to confirm my view of the two texts cited as enshrining conscious, seriously thought-out innovation. The evidence is particularly strong in regard to the second of them, introducing the comforting mother. The prophet's empathy with women comes out clearly a few verses before. Among the wonders the people will experience when final salvation occurs, he announces: "Before the pangs of labour came to her, she was delivered of a male. Who has heard such a thing, who has seen such things? Is a land brought forth in one day or is a nation born all at once? For as soon as her labour began, Zion bore her children."[24]

This idea is without parallel anywhere else in the Bible: the Messianic lifting of the primeval curse laid on Eve. No need here to settle such details as whether he is referring primarily to an actual increase in population or to the creation of the triumphant

[15] Isa 66:13.

[16] *Bakhah*. See any concordance.

[17] E.g. Num 11:12; Deut 1:31; 2 Sam 12:3.

[18] In Isa 46:3 ff., the remnant of Israel is being carried by God, not only in youth but also in age. For this imaginative seer, God's parental support is not tied to immaturity. What psychoanalysis would say to this I dare not conjecture.

[19] Gen 29:9; Cant 1:6.

[20] E.g. Isa 5:1 ff., 40:11, 63:11.

[21] See J. B. Pritchard, *Ancient Near Eastern Texts relating to the Old Testament*, 383 ff.

[22] See J. B. Pritchard, *op. cit.* 397.

[23] See J. B. Pritchard, *op. cit.* 401.

[24] Isa 66:7 ff.

end-time community; nor even the, for us, more basic question as to the range of his vision—how likely is he to believe, generally, that labour pains will be unknown in the new Jerusalem? The main thrust of his message is unmistakable.

As for Deutero-Isaiah's picture of mother and suckling, the same chapter offers a striking example of the phenomenon I have just called attention to, the sharing of men in female functions: the redeemed Zion will be nursed by the kings of the Gentiles and given suck by their princesses.[25] Trito-Isaiah indeed goes still further and, with extreme boldness, speaks of Zion as sucking the breast of kings.[26]

Resistance to this revolutionary trend was enormous:[27] hence only one more comparison of God to a mother—an animal mother—in subsequent products of Jewish-Christian antiquity. 2 Esdras has him protect his chosen as a hen protects her chicks.[28] Interestingly, in the Rabbinic Midrash the role is assigned to Moses,[29] and in Matthew and Luke to Jesus.[30] There is reason to suspect that Q spoke of God.[31] If so, we may have before us a deliberate removal of the divine image from unworthy association.

Even the cessation of labour pains in the Messianic aeon is rarely taken up. To be sure, the Rabbis claim that, now and then, in special circumstances, a woman gave birth without suffering: Sarah, for instance,[32] or Jochebed when she had Moses.[33] Similarly, in second-century elaborations of the New Testament, Mary is spared any distress.[34] (In Greek myth, Leto experienced no pain at the birth of Artemis.[35]) But universal relief is seldom met. We do find it in a Pharisaic Apocalypse of the end of the first century A.D.,[36] and in an occasional Rabbinic teaching.

It is all the more suggestive that among the few sages attaching weight to Trito-Isaiah's promise is Abbahu of Caesarea, of around A.D. 300, an indefatigable champion of women's causes.[37] Theological ideas are apt to lead to consequences in daily life. If you are satisfied with women being second-class citizens, you had better not push the motherhood of God or the repeal of Eve's condemnation. Abbahu knew what he was doing in invoking a neglected text. Here it may suffice to note that he adhered to that school (ultimately not prevailing) which put women on the same level as men in regard

[25] Isa 49:23.

[26] Isa 60:16. A slight mitigation is introduced by "breast" being in the singular.

[27] Still is. Certainly, for J. H. Hertz, some 40 years ago, to comment on Isa 66:13, "God is our Mother" (*op. cit.* 950), must have taken courage.

[28] 4 Ezra 1:30.

[29] *Lev. Rab.* 25 on Lev 19:23.

[30] Matt 23:37; Luke 13:34.

[31] See J. M. Creed, *The Gospel according to St. Luke,* 187.

[32] S. Buber, ed., *Midrash Tanhuma,* vol. 1, 107, *Wayyera* 37 on Gen 21:7.

[33] Josephus, *Ant.* 2.9.1.218; *b. Sot.* 12a. In the latter discussion, there is also a wider statement, to the effect that all pious women are exempt from the decree.

[34] E.g. *Ascension of Isaiah* 11:14.

[35] Callimachus, *Hymn 3* (*To Artemis*), 24 ff.

[36] *Apoc Bar* 73:7.

[37] *Lev. Rab.* 14 at the end, on Lev 12:2. In J. J. Slotki's translation, *Midrash Rabbah, Leviticus,* 187, the passage in question is printed as if it were anonymous. There is little to be said for this. Quite likely, Abbahu was influenced by Simeon ben Lakish: cf. *b. Ber.* 32b.

to the duty of procreation,[38] that he found it quite in keeping with the nature of divine providence to furnish women with cosmetics[39] and that he taught his daughters Greek.[40] In fact, he was suspected—a unique charge against a revered religious leader—of falsifying a tradition in order to procure authority for this education. Admittedly, in a sense, he was treating them like dolls, much as when young Victorian ladies were instructed in Italian by way of adornment. But we must not judge him as if he lived today: he was far ahead of the bulk of his contemporaries.[41]

Alas, that most advance is halting is borne out even by Trito-Isaiah's remarkable preaching. It does accept the customary preference for male offspring: "Before the pangs of labour came to her, she was delivered of a male."[42] The prejudice is too ingrained, going back to the age of the patriarchs. Rachel, dying in childbirth, by way of solace is informed that she has another son:[43] at a time when Jacob already has 11 sons and one daughter only.

III.

The apostle Paul does not enjoy the reputation of a feminist. Neither should he. Yet in the same letter to the Corinthians in which he calls man the head of woman and debars women from speaking at church meetings,[44] he takes an enormous step forward.[45]

To appreciate it, we must bear in mind that, according to Jewish doctrine, a convert becomes a fresh person.[46] This is meant quite seriously. In principle, if a father and his daughter convert, they can marry; similarly, a mother and her son, or brother and sister. Their old ties have vanished through rebirth. Some time before the New Testament period, however, the Rabbis found that people not grasping the basic idea behind these rules were apt to form a distorted picture of Judaism as indifferent to incest. It was laid down, therefore, that converts ought to refrain from such unions as were frowned on by the heathen host-culture.[47] A father, for example, must no longer marry his daughter; this marriage was disapproved of by the surrounding Gentiles and one could not expect understanding for the notion that, as a result of conversion, their original relationship had ceased to exist. On the other hand, in quite a few regions, say, marriage between brother and sister (especially if they had only the father in common) was still permissible, since not looked on as incest by the outside world.

[38] See D. Daube, *Talmudic Law,* 143 ff..

[39] *Song of Songs Rab.* on 4:15.

[40] *y. Peah* 15c; *y. Shab.* 7d; *y. Sot.* 24c; *b. Sot.* 21b.

[41] In *b. Sot.* 21b, at first sight, he seems to side with a teaching of Eliezer ben Hyrcanos downgrading women. But in reality he is trying to give it a friendlier meaning.

[42] Isa 66:7. The end of 66:8 should perhaps be rendered: "Zion bore her sons"—not "children."

[43] Gen 35:17.

[44] 1 Cor 11:13, 14:34.

[45] 1 Cor 7:12 ff. See D. Daube ["Pauline Contributions to a Pluralistic Culture: Re-Creation and Beyond"] in D. Miller and D. Hadidian, ed., *Jesus and Man's Hope,* 2 [1971], 232 ff. [545 ff.]

[46] E.g. *b. Yeb.* 48b.

[47] E.g. *b. Yeb.* 22a.

Paul adopted this scheme, hence his condemnation of a member of the Corinthian community marrying his stepmother.[48] The pair and their friends had been proud of this liberty[49] bestowed on them, they thought, by their having turned into new beings. But Paul reminded them that theirs was a union avoided by the Gentiles, so to contract it was an egotistic misuse of re-creation.

In passing, it is commonly held that when, in the first two centuries or so, Jews and Christians were accused by pagans of being allowed by their religions to indulge in incest, this was sheer calumny.[50] Plainly, however, an onlooker not crediting a convert with a changed identity might often be honestly shocked. We have before us one of many instances where the defamation of a minority is particularly effective because it contains a grain of truth. In the case of Christianity, the influx of slaves would be an additional factor. Among them, incest had relatively little meaning: a Roman master might breed slaves as we breed setters.[51] Scholarship tends to block out these data, for reasons which would be worthy of a separate *wissenschaftgeschichtliche* [history of scientific enquiry] study.

What about a couple who enter the Jewish faith? The doctrine under discussion implies that their marriage is ended: they are simply no longer the two who were a couple.[52] In practice the outcome is not so harsh, for generally they would go on living together; and, as one mode of concluding a Jewish marriage is by intercourse (the other two being by money and by document),[53] they thereby become husband and wife again. Still, it is a second marriage, a fact with considerable legal consequences into which I shall not go here.

A problem exercising Paul in this epistle was conversion of one only of two spouses.[54] Their marriage was extinct. Technically, therefore, the convert, a fresh person, was rid of any obligation, entitled to re-marry and so on; and (Paul explained) that was indeed all right if the other chose to leave the scene. But if he or she desired to stay on, higher considerations restricted this freedom. (Notice the affinity between the line of thought here and in the case of the incestuous couple.) The pursuit of peace, that is, and the chance of ultimately winning over the non-believer, were so important that there must be no rejection. The convert must keep living with the old partner, their cohabitation making them into spouses once more.

The teaching involved two momentous deviations from the Jewish law prevailing at the time. One was that he recognised marriage to a heathen. For this, there were per-

[48] 1 Cor 5:1.

[49] 1 Cor 5:2.

[50] E.g. M. Conrat, *Die Christenverfolgungen im römischen Reiche*, 31: "*Kaum braucht erwähnt zu werden, dass diese Beschuldigungen grundlos waren*" ("It is scarcely necessary to mention that these charges were groundless").

[51] In the course of time, pre-manumission ties come to be recognized after manumission: e.g. *Digest* 23.2.14.2, Paul XXXV *ad edictum*. This fragment purports to date from around A.D. 200, but some subsequent intervention is not unlikely.

[52] E.g. *y. Yeb.* 12a.

[53] *m. Kidd.* 1:1. The term "to sanctify, consecrate, by intercourse" is met, e.g. in *m. Nidd.* 5:4.

[54] 1 Cor 7:12 ff.; see above, note 45.

haps recent precedents, though incurring official displeasure.[55] What interests here is the second novelty. In Judaism, it is invariably the woman who is consecrated to spouse, sanctified, by the man.[56] Paul in the special situation he was regulating admitted sanctification of the man by the woman. In other words, he judged it irrelevant whether it was husband or wife who converted: even if it was the latter, by intercourse she would sanctify the man to be rejoined with her. He was quite emphatic on there being no difference: "The unbelieving husband is sanctified by the wife, and the unbelieving wife is sanctified by the husband."

To be sure, his motive was not the promotion of equality for women; it was consideration for the children from these reconstituted unions who, but for his revolutionary solution, would not only not be members of the community but indeed born out of wedlock, spurious. More precisely, his argument proceeded thus: the ideal of peace and the hope that the non-believer might come to believe rendered it imperative to continue living with him or her if he or she was willing; and this living together was proved legitimate by the fact that, otherwise, the children would be (in his terminology) "unclean." A fairly sophisticated presentation, making use of a *reductio ad absurdum*: he established his opinion (union valid) by stressing the intolerability of the opposite (union invalid) or rather of its consequences (children spurious). This mode of reasoning was practised a good deal by Rabbis as well as Roman jurists.[57] The particular concern to facilitate the inclusion of offspring in the community was no doubt widely shared in Judaism, though not then acted on with Paul's enthusiasm and courage. Some 80 years later only, the desperate state of Jewry after the collapse of the Bar Kochba revolt led to a far-reaching reform.[58]

Nevertheless, while the apostle did not set out to remedy discrimination, he did end up by doing so in one small corner. To put it differently, for the sake of certain cherished goals, he was prepared to grant women a right normally the prerogative of men. Progress of this nature should not be belittled. It not only testifies to an openness of mind in its author but also, once launched, is apt to develop a momentum of its own. Parallels abound. One may think, for example, of the freeing of slaves to serve in the army in time of war or the offer of scholarships to poor youngsters particularly talented in areas deemed vital by the government. A university allowing its students to formulate their own examination questions would be blazing a trail even if it were done in order to give the professors more time for research.[59]

I shall not, however, pursue the subsequent fate of Paul's message. It must suffice to note that, before long, its original import got completely forgotten. This was chiefly

[55] Testament of Levi 14:6 ff.

[56] The Hebrew verb is *qiddesh*: e.g. *m. Nidd.* 5:4, above, note 53.

[57] On the latter, see D. Daube, *Roman Law* [1969], 176 ff.

[58] See D. Daube, in a forthcoming book on ancient Jewish law [*Ancient Jewish Law* (1981)], chapter entitled "Conversion." [481 ff.]

[59] The Russian exhibition currently on show at the de Young museum includes excellent samples of the realist movement in whose early history 1863 is memorable. In that year, 14 students of the St. Petersburg Academy seceded, after being refused the right to choose their own examination subject. What they had been told to paint was "The Banquet of the Gods in Valhalla."

due to the Church's abandonment of the Jewish—and Pauline—view of a convert as literally a being distinct from the pre-conversion one. The resultant complications Paul had to tackle were no longer understood, and the section in question was re-interpreted. Actually, it furnished the basis for a rather important medieval institution called the "Pauline privilege." Most expositions of it start or end by observing that it is not mentioned in the earliest Christian works.[60] Small wonder: it did not exist.

In Judaism, conversion still counts as a true rebirth. Suppose (as is not unlikely) the fragmentation of the modern family were to produce a relaxation of incest taboos, so that, for example, secular Western systems treated the father's sister as permissible, a nephew and aunt who converted could marry under Jewish law: there would be no danger in such circumstances of people concluding that Judaism encouraged licentiousness, and the Biblical ban does not apply to this pair whose kinship is gone.[61]

IV.

Back to adultery. The scribes and Pharisees, we are told,[62] attempted to trip up Jesus by bringing before him an adulteress caught in the act, reminding him of the death penalty prescribed for this crime[63] and asking him his opinion. The latter is familiar: "He that is without sin among you, let him be the first to cast a stone at her." They slunk away. Whereupon he assured her that he would condemn her no more than the others had done; and he dismissed her, bidding her sin no more. I propose to show that his reply was directed specifically against the unfair treatment of women by men and their laws. It is in fact representative of a strong trend in the Judaism of that period.

The episode did not always belong to the canonical gospels; its present place in John was apparently first assigned to it in the fifth century.[64] This does not reflect on its age. There must have been many narratives about Jesus not taken up by the four recognised evangelists. Actually, the fact that adultery is punishable by stoning points to a date in the first century: early in the second strangling was substituted. In this connection, it may be worth noting that the manner of stoning envisaged—pelting the criminal to death—had begun to be replaced about 100 B.C. by one which seems to leave the skeleton intact, pushing him down from a height; it was only when that did not kill him that stones were thrown. By New Testament times, the unrevised mode survived chiefly where a court was under Sadducean direction or where there was an element of lynching.[65]

It is agreed that Jesus is applying a principle which, variously formulated, occurs many times in the New Testament: "Judge not that you be not judged"; "With what

[60] E.g. *The Oxford Dictionary of the Christian Church* (2nd ed.), 1054, art. "Pauline Privilege."

[61] See e.g. Maimonides, *Mishneh Torah* 5 (Qedushah). 1 (Issure Biah). 14.11 ff. Sweden is already very much on the move.

[62] John 8:2 ff..

[63] Lev 20:10; Deut 22:22; on the latter law, see above, section I.

[64] See C. K. Barrett, *The Gospel according to St. John*, 490 ff.

[65] See D. Daube, *The New Testament and Rabbinic Judaism* [1956], 304 ff. [619 ff.], and ["Origen and the Punishment of Adultery in Jewish Law"] in *Texte und Untersuchungen zur Geschichte der altchristlichen Literatur*, 64 (= *SP*, 2), 109 ff. [See *Talmudic Law*, 167–71]

measure you mete, it shall be measured to you again."[66] Numerous parallels are met not only in Rabbinic literature—"Whenever you are merciful, God will be merciful to you; when you are not merciful, God will not be merciful to you"[67]—but also in pagan. Cicero stresses the incongruity of a charge preferred by a man guilty himself, and adultery is among his illustrations: "You denounce somebody as seducer or adulterer: you should carefully see that there is no vestige of licentiousness in your life."[68] Proverbs all over the world enshrine the idea: "The pot calls the kettle black."[69] One of them even brings in stoning; though not of a judicial kind: "People who live in glass houses should not throw stones."[70]

Not surprisingly, this aspect of the verdict, or non-verdict, "Let him who is free of guilt cast the first stone," was recognised from the start.[71] Nowadays it is certainly quotable with regard to any infringement of the principle: as when a lawyer is to be disbarred on the ground of too brazen advertising; or one aggressive government blames the other for re-arming or sacrificing freedom to military efficiency.[72]

What is not adequately appreciated is the peculiar thrust of the utterance on that first occasion. It means not simply, "Judge not that you be not judged," but rather, "You, regarding yourselves as the more excellent half of mankind, charged with keeping the inferior half in line, by your corruption have forfeited any such title." A modern analogy would be, not just the disbarment of an attorney by colleagues not much better or the criticism levelled by one state against another, but the harsh reaction of whites when a black gets drunk, on the theory that blacks are particularly liable to alcoholic excess; or, indeed, a law faculty's opposition to a female candidate because she is a gossip.

To elucidate the bearing on law enforcement of "Judge not that you be not judged" in its general sense, a less sophisticated situation would do. One would expect a male culprit or a wicked couple; or, for that matter, a poor fellow to be sold for his debts, such as is depicted in the parable of the unmerciful servant.[73] Instead, we find an adulteress, alone—with nobody even asking what has become of her partner in crime—dragged in by an all-male crowd: "the scribes and Pharisees," the text says, but we would know anyhow, since only men could be witnesses and executioners.[74]

[66] Matt 7:1 ff. See W. Bauer, *Das Johannesevangelium* (2nd ed.), 113 ff.; W. F. Howard, "The Gospel according to St. John," in *The Interpreter's Bible*, vol. 8, 593; C. K. Barrett, *loc. cit.*

[67] *y. B. K.* 6c. See H. L. Strack and P. Billerbeck, *Kommentar zum Neuen Testament aus Talmud und Midrasch*, vol. 1, 424 ff.

[68] Cicero, *Against Verres*, 2.3.2.4. Paul, too, instances adultery in Rom 2:22 where, beyond hypocrisy in judging, even hypocrisy in preaching is censured. Judging is reproved in 2:1.

[69] See *Oxford Dictionary of English Proverbs* (3rd ed.), 421.

[70] "*Wer im Glashaus sitzt soll nicht mit Steinen werfen*"; see *Deutsches Sprichwörter-Lexikon*, K. F. Wander, ed., 1695.

[71] Very likely, it was in the mind of whoever is responsible for the present position of the pericope; further on in the same chapter (John 8:15) Jesus says: "I judge no one." See C. K. Barrett, *op. cit.* 279 ff., 491.

[72] Russ Braley, discussing the UN in the *San Francisco Sunday Examiner and Chronicle* (September 14, 1975) writes: "Ambassador Daniel Patrick Moynihan earlier had refused to condemn India for its crackdown on civil liberties—remarking to a news conference, 'If there is a country in the forum without sin, will it please raise its hand?'"

[73] Matt 18:23 ff.

[74] E.g. *Siphre* on Deut 19:17; *m. Shebu.* 4:1.

At the trial of Susannah also the paramour is missing; necessarily, for the accusation is false. However, her calumniators at least fabricate an excuse: he managed to escape and she would not disclose his name.[75] In the present case, there is complete unconcern about the man. One is reminded of the way in which anti-prostitution ordinances are administered to this day.[76]

The formulation "without sin" is significant. It is not to be understood pedantically, "free of the precise sin in question, i.e. adultery"; Jesus is not suggesting that all those he addresses are adulterers *stricto sensu.* Neither, however, is its scope unlimited, "free of any sin, e.g. even of a shady business deal or a violation of the Sabbath": he is not here emphasising general human fallibility. It means free of a serious infraction—by deed or intent—of sexual morality.[77] What he does imply is that they are every one of them given over to lust: the male world is depraved from top to bottom; and, as they get away with it, they ought not to come down harshly on those less comfortably placed.

To grasp the background of the story, we must attend to how the Rabbis dealt with an ancient ordeal where a husband suspects his wife of adultery. It has long been seen that the steps they took are relevant,[78] but not quite how relevant particularly with regard to the question of discrimination.

The Old Testament prescribes a frightening test.[79] She is taken before the priest, humiliated, given a concoction of water and dust to drink and made to say "Amen" to a terrible imprecation should she be guilty: as a result of it, if she is, she will rot away in the most gruesome fashion. There is no corresponding machinery against a man suspected of having slept with a married woman. It is a flagrant case of double-standard.

The procedure still continued in the first century A.D., while the Temple stood.[80] In fact, it furnishes an interesting example of how a group accustomed to being trampled on may develop a real fervour in collaboration with its oppressors. Around A.D. 50 a heathen queen, Helen of Adiabene, converted to Judaism; she made a gift to the Temple of a golden plaque on which the awesome, one-sided law was inscribed.[81]

We must not, indeed, overlook the reality that a wife whose fidelity is in doubt may be importing illicit fruit. In this, her case is very different from her male counterpart. If the Bible does not subject him to a similar trial, neither does it a person, male or female,

[75] Susannah 39 ff.

[76] "*Ihr, die auf unsrer Scham und eurer Lust besteht*" ["You who dwell on our disgrace and your lust"]: B. Brecht and K. Weill, *Die Dreigroschenoper*, towards end of Act II, *Ballade über die Frage*: "*Wovon lebt der Mensch?*," part 2, Jenny.

[77] Compare the Ciceronian "no vestige of licentiousness." The adjective *anamartetos* is very suitable for bringing out this nuance: see W. Bauer, *loc. cit.*

[78] See D. W. Amram, in *Jewish Encyclopedia*, vol. 1, 217, art. 1, "Adultery," quoted by J. D. M. Derrett, *Law in the New Testament*, 187. I. Abrahams, *Studies in Pharisaism and the Gospels*, f.s., 73 ff., is also alive to the fact; he is quoted by C. K. Barrett, *op. cit.* 164. It is a puzzle why these Rabbinic texts are missing from the discussion of the pericope in H. L. Strack and P. Billerbeck, *op. cit.*, vol. 2, 521; they do appear elsewhere in the work (vol. 1, 642, 717; vol. 3, 106).

[79] Num 5:11 ff. Cf. CH 131 ff.

[80] Philo devotes a largish section to it: *De spec. leg.* 3.10.52 ff.

[81] *m. Yom.* 3:10. I. Abrahams, *op. cit.* 74, holds that her action dates from after the abolition of the practice and was designed to revive it: unlikely in the extreme, but it would make no difference to my thesis.

suspected of murder or theft. It can be said, generally, that throughout the history of adultery the husband's fear of having another's child foisted on him plays an enormous part (not much cosmic love here); and viewed from this angle, an unclear situation is in some ways worse than a proven fling. The latter at least leaves no room, in ancient times, for worry about the legitimacy of offspring. Still, while such considerations go a long way towards explaining the bias of the ordeal, its injustice is not thereby removed.

The Rabbis did grow sensitive to it. The inequality between the sexes in the matter of adultery had long been queried in the Hellenistic world. The elder Cato wrote:[82] "If you should take your wife in adultery, you may with impunity put her to death without trial; but if you should commit adultery or indecency, she must not presume to lay a finger on you, nor does the law allow it." He approved of this discrepancy, but he would not have needed to be so strident had there been no opponents.[83] The Augustan legislation of 18 B.C., though still heavily weighted in favour of men, did narrow the gap;[84] and what should here be borne in mind is that it was the kind of legislation of interest not only for jurists but for the educated class at large. Horace, Ovid and Martial allude to it,[85] and it led to indictments of male as well as female V.I.P.s. The monster process of Decius Mundus is retailed by Josephus.[86] Needless to say, there are huge differences in antecedents and spirit between the pagan approach to this tangle and the Jewish one. Nevertheless a modicum of stimulation from the former cannot be ruled out.

Anyhow, the sages by an artifice of interpretation worthy of the Supreme Court make the Old Testament law stipulate that only if the husband himself is blameless will the execration affect a guilty wife.[87] More precisely, they resort to a forced division.[88] Taken in the natural way, the text runs: "If the spirit of jealousy comes upon a man, then shall he set the woman before the Lord and the priest shall execute upon her all this law; and the man shall be clear from iniquity and that woman shall bear her iniquity." The Rabbis treat everything up to the first "iniquity" as protasis, as conditions, of the apodosis condemning the woman: "If the spirit of jealousy comes upon a man and if he sets the woman before the Lord and if the priest executes upon her all this law and [this is the point] if the man is clear from iniquity, then shall that woman bear her iniquity." So for an adulteress to be undone, the man's innocence is necessary no less than the ritual; and clearly, as in Jesus's warning, what is demanded is not merely that he has committed no adultery proper nor, on the other hand, that he has done no wrong whatever, but that he is above reproach in his sexual life.

[82] Gellius, *Attic Nights* 10.23.5.

[83] Livy 24.1 ff. reports on his unsuccessful defence of a law restricting female expenditure. See D. Daube, *Civil Disobedience in Antiquity,* 27 ff.

[84] See T. Mommsen, *op. cit.* 688 ff.

[85] Horace, *Odes* 4.5.21 ff.; Ovid, *Fasti* 2.139 ff.; Martial, *Epigrams* 6.7, 21.

[86] Josephus, *Ant.* 18.3.4.65 ff. See R. S. Rogers, *Criminal Trials and Criminal Legislation under Tiberius,* 32 ff.

[87] *Siphre* on Num 5:31; *y. Sot.* 24a; *b. Sot.* 74b.

[88] On some aspects of Rabbinic *collocatio* (as division is termed by Quintilian, *I.O.* 7.97), see D. Daube ["Alexandrian Methods of Interpretation and the Rabbis"] in *Festschrift Hans Lewald,* 34 ff. [See *Talmudic Law,* 357 ff.] From a rigidly grammatical point of view, the re-interpretation of Num 5:30 ff. undertaken by the Rabbis is just defensible.

In support of their exegesis they invoke the prophet Hosea:[89] "I will not wreak vengeance on your daughters when they commit whoredom or on your daughters-in-law when they commit adultery for you yourselves make off with whores and sacrifice with harlots." The verse is aptly picked. Though it is not, unless we read it through Rabbinic spectacles, concerned with the ordeal in question, it does denounce an outrageous imbalance between what is done by men and what is expected of women.[90] The former are unfaithful to their lord, and in a mode involving the libertinism of heathen fertility cults, yet they insist on chastity in the latter: God disapproves and resolves no longer to take note if women misbehave. The Rabbis did little violence to the spirit of the passage when they found here that mitigation of the curse: it brings perdition only to the impure wife of a pure husband.[91]

The trouble with the doctrine was twofold. For one thing, once hedonism was the rule in the male world, to subject any woman to the grim examination was a mockery, irrespective of the individual husband's mode of life. For another, it was left entirely to heaven to put matters right. Nothing was changed on earth: women were to take it on trust that divine vigilance would prevent a scoundrelly husband from destroying his wife in this way. Religious answers to grievances are often of this kind, hence hampering as well as helpful; and which of the two possible effects prevails depends greatly on the circumstances of the moment. Take the message that somehow, in the end—if need be, in the next world—God will reward the poor and punish their exploiters. It is marvellous, in that it inculcates the right values; but inasmuch as it preaches—or can be taken to preach—passive reliance on an ultimate sorting-out from above, it is apt to benefit a rotten *status quo*.[92] (True, where change is simply impossible, such reliance does provide solace.)

Johanan ben Zaccai, the leading scholar of his generation, did away with the institution,[93] apparently basing himself on the same quotation from Hosea. That must have been in the sixties for, later, his interdict would not have been needed: the destruction in A.D. 70 of the Temple, to which the ceremony was attached, would have spelled the end in any case. One may indeed wonder whether, had the Temple gone on, his measure would have succeeded so easily. Beyond question it created a stir—and not only among the learned. The press, so to speak, was full of it, the progressives in favour, the reactionaries against.[94]

[89] Hos 4:14.

[90] See D. M. Derrett, *loc. cit.*

[91] In the course of time, incidentally, keen as they were on Scriptural proof for everything, they read into Hosea even a reference to the detail adverted to above, that it is not only adultery proper which renders a husband "iniquitous" but any sexual misbehaviour. Hosea, it was pointed out, speaks of associating with worthless unmarried women: *b. Sot.* 47b.

[92] "Vengeance is mine (saith the Lord)," Deut 32:35, is often quoted as an exhortation to leave it to God, though this is not its original meaning. On a significant stage in the treatment of a crime committed in error, see D. Daube, *Sin, Ignorance and Forgiveness in the Bible,* 7 ff.

[93] *m. Sot.* 9:9.

[94] Many scholars, e.g. C. K. Barrett, *loc. cit.*, follow I. Abrahams, *loc. cit.*, who attributes the teaching that a guilty wife will be struck down only if the husband is blameless to Akiba, of the early second century. The evidence, however, is imaginary. In *Siphre* on Num 5:31, an opinion of Akiba's happens to come just before;

There is evidence that, quite apart from other scruples about such a coup, indignation at the double standard was not equally shared by all. This comes out in not a few comments on the developments outlined. In an early third-century compilation, for example,[95] the ordeal is said to have been abandoned, not because the men no longer deserved their privileged status, but because adultery had grown into an open practice—so the test for cases of doubt lost its meaning. It was given up, that is, on the same ground as the ceremonious atonement for an untraced murder:[96] when murders perpetrated in public became the order of the day, it was futile to hang on to a special rite for an unsolved one. No criticism of discrimination in this work, the redactor of which, Hiyya, we happen to know, was something of a misogynist, approving of the line in Ecclesiastes: "I found more bitter than death the woman whose heart is snares and nets."[97]

The *pericope de adultera* in John has its setting in this evolution and the struggles entailed by it. Jesus firmly sides with the view that women are placed at a disadvantage in ways no longer tolerable: if men are keen on exacting retribution from an adulteress, let them first be God-fearing themselves. The foregoing reflections, however, enable us to be more specific concerning his subtlety and effectiveness. His questioners, it will be remembered, are out to trap him. They know that he will disapprove of an execution. But how can he do so without spurning the strict Pentateuchic ruling to which, indeed,

---

but the teaching is quite distinct from it and anonymous. (Abrahams cites also *b. Sot.* 47b: here there is not even the preceding piece. Neither, it may be added, is it met in *y. Sot.* 24a.) K. G. Kuhn in his translation (*Sifre zu Numeri,* 68) is right about it. He is wrong when he goes on to say that *m. Sot.* 9:9 fathers the doctrine on ben Zaccai. This paragraph explains the termination of the ordeal: very different from its representation as working equitably. Neglect of this difference has caused much confusion, such as a major slip in A. Cohen's treatment of *b. Sot.* 47b: *The Babylonian Talmud,* I. Epstein, ed., Nashim VI, Sotah, 251 ff. (L. Goldschmidt is sound: *Der Babylonische Talmud,* vol. 5, 412, 346). By Akiba's time, the test had long been discarded. For this reason alone, the notion that it would function only on behalf of a guiltless husband is unlikely to have originated with him: far more plausibly, it was a step on the road to suppression. Still, there is no absolute certainty as to the order in which things happened. The Rabbis kept refining the institution even after it had become a memory. (In *Talmudic Law,* 146–47, I adduce a second-century modification of a humiliating detail; and see above n. 91, on an even later display of concern to have all minutiae shipshape.) So the sequel (1) abrogation, (2) restriction of efficacy in the interest of fairness, cannot be ruled out. For the purpose in hand—the recovery of the general trend behind the incident in John—the question is not essential.

[95] *t. Sot.* 14:2.

[96] Deut 21:1–9; *t. Sot.* 14:1. The latter paragraph comes from Johanan ben Zaccai. He is widely deemed the author of 14:2 as well (e.g. by H. L. Strack and P. Billerbeck, *op. cit.* vol. 3, 106 ff.; J. Neusner, *A Life of Rabban Yohannan Ben Zakkai,* 61); and as the disappearance of the ordeal is here placed in the past, sometimes the conclusion is drawn that its demise was due, not to him, but to a prior process of which he only registered the outcome (e.g. J. Neusner, *loc. cit., Encyclopaedia Judaica,* vol. 10, art. "Johanan ben Zakkai"). Once again an argument not affecting the gist of my presentation. It is however unconvincing. For one thing, the Mishnah is generally a safer historical guide than the Tosephta. For another, the main assertion of the former is not contradicted by the latter at all: ben Zaccai is not mentioned in 14:2 and we are free to ascribe it to a later sage. The real conflict, not noticed by the views here combated, is between the motives for the ending of the test given in the two sources. Surely, the position consonant with Hosea smacks of ben Zaccai, whereas it would hardly be cherished by Hiyya.

[97] Eccl 7:26; *b. Yeb.* 63a. Other texts where such criticism is absent or at least toned down: *y. Sot.* 24a; *b. Sot.* 47b.

they draw his attention in so many words? As on other occasions,[98] he proves of superior skill and squares the circle. The Rabbis had established that the Pentateuch itself, on careful search, turns out to contain a momentous *caveat* as to proceedings against a wife: the accuser must be "clear from iniquity."[99] This construction Jesus adopts. The area, I have already pointed out, was not a recondite one; the arguments voiced must have been widely disseminated. So when he alludes to this Old Testament clause, his public—and the readers of the episode—would have no difficulty in comprehending. He refutes the other side's stand on Scripture by showing that it is his teaching which Scripture, as understood by the sages, supports. His appeal to the assembly's conscience, that is, is based, not just on general decency (that would not get him off), but on the law.

To be sure, the case before him—an adulteress caught *in flagranti*—goes somewhat beyond that in the Talmudic texts adduced—a wife suspected of adultery by her husband. But the gap, though undeniably existing, is not too wide. As mentioned above, in so far as the question of paternity is concerned, the latter situation is more serious than the former. Moreover, Johanan ben Zaccai's injunction is quite radical in that he does not merely grant relief in a particular emergency but gets rid, totally, of a time-hallowed institution;[100] and, of course, the realistic effect of curtailing or renouncing the ordeal is to let many an adulteress go unscathed. Nor should we forget that the passage from Hosea which figures so prominently in those discussions in its primary sense does contemplate, not a wife under suspicion, but actual, clear adultery and the like. This prophet,[101] indeed, at least in portraying God's marriage with Israel, glorifies the reacceptance of even the most scandalously unfaithful wife; and no matter exactly how we hear what he tells us of his own marital experiences, a precedent set by God is usually calculated to influence life in this world.

Actually, Johanan ben Zaccai, in a parable about the Tablets of the Law,[102] does extend the vision to human marriage—though not to an ordinary one but one of a king; the wife, however, is a commoner, indeed, brought up in poverty and misery. The first two Tablets of the Law are described by the Bible as the work of God;[103] when the people worshipped the golden calf, God declared he would no longer lead them and Moses smashed the Tablets;[104] yet he then entreated God to change his mind,[105] and God consented and bade him hew fresh Tablets.[106] Why, Johanan wonders, had the second pair to be cut by Moses? One may compare a king taking a wife and supplying the writing-

[98] Matt 19:3–9; Mark 10:2–9.

[99] Num 5:31, on the basis of the division explained above.

[100] Or, should the critics of the account in the Mishnah be right (see above, n. 96), puts the seal of his authority on that institution's exit.

[101] Hosea 1–3.

[102] *t. B. K.* 7:4, *Deut. Rab.* 3 towards the end on 10:1, Midrash Tanhuma (S. Buber, ed.), vol. 2, 117, Ki Thissa 27 on Exod 34:27, Midrash Tanhuma (C. Sundel, ed.) or Zundel (Enoch Sundel ben Joseph), 125b, Ki Thissa 30 on Exod 34:1.

[103] Exod 32:16; Deut 9:10.

[104] Exod 32:10, 19; Deut 9:14, 17.

[105] Exod 32:31 ff.; Deut 9:25 ff.

[106] Exod 34:1; Deut 10:1.

material for the document and the witnesses: just so, God himself cut the first Tablets. Now the wife commits adultery—as the Israelites worshipped the golden calf—and the king divorces her—as God disowned the sinful nation. But good friends plead on her behalf that, considering the lowly environment from which she comes, the king expects too much of her: this corresponds to Moses's prayers. The king agrees to re-marry her—as God re-accepted the people. None the less, this time, the woman must make the arrangements: here lies the explanation why the second Tablets were not provided by God.

The specific issue of discrimination is not raised in this little tract. It extols true love, which is not brought to an end by the beloved's wickedness but looks for data that lessen the blame—such as the influence of a harmful milieu. (The history of this excuse still awaits exploration.) Yet the simile is highly important in the present context: it evinces a striking disregard for the austere customs then in force in the event of a wife's lapse.[107] Significantly, the sources transmitting it keep softening it—just as many commentators on the *pericope de adultera* try to reduce its implications. The great French-Jewish eleventh-century exegete Rashi adopts a version where the wife is innocent and arraigned without cause,[108] which obviously makes the parable pretty pointless.

The would-be avengers, unable to contradict Jesus, depart, "the elder ones first," it is noted. When the Sanhedrin voted on a capital case, it did so in reverse order of seniority: the junior member started off, the senior one came last.[109] The purpose was that the juniors should feel unpressured: which would favour the accused, since it was assumed that they were readier to acquit than the seniors. This story, however, involves no session of a tribunal. In general, it is up to the old ones to set a good example, up to the youngsters to follow it. That is what happens here.

When Jesus joins the others in refraining from condemnation, the range of his message expands. The mere fact that, the crowd having left, a stoning is no longer feasible produces an evident change in atmosphere. His clemency does not, of course, ground in a sense of his own culpability. Neither, however, is it as vague or boundless as commonly held.[110] After all, he is never represented as addressing such a comforting statement to, say, a false witness who engineered the death of an orphan after embezzling his property. In the context, "neither do I condemn you" means, above all, that, in a society which takes licentiousness on the part of men for granted, the right to punish a woman straying from the path is gone: an attitude reminiscent of Johanan ben Zaccai's when putting an absolute stop to the old ordeal.

No Rabbi ever looked on a wife's unfaithfulness as anything but a sin. It is that also in Jesus's final "sin no more." The distinction between sin and punishable deed, often neglected today, was familiar to Judaism from early on. There were indeed many

[107] E.g. *m. Sot.* 5:1.

[108] Rashi on Exod 34:1.

[109] *m. Sanh.* 4:2.

[110] B. Lindars, *The Gospel of John*, 312, makes it too vague: "Jesus's remark merely shows that he, too, dismisses the case, so that she is free to depart." C. K. Barrett, *op. cit.* 493, makes it too general: "Jesus has come to save not to condemn" (3:17). He does add, however: "Yet his very presence has the effect of judging the self-righteous bystanders."

nuances of it, and research into them would probably come up with results of considerable practical value.[111]

The sad tale of the non-follow-up, in medieval and modern theology and law, of the pioneering efforts of the first two or three centuries I have neither the time nor the competence to unfold. Instead, let me in conclusion glance at a detail of no particular relevance to my theme. At first, when asked for his opinion, Jesus "stooped down and with his finger wrote on the ground." It was only when the questioners persisted that he spoke out. And then, once again, he repeated the curious action, till they had dispersed.

It can do little harm to add yet another guess to the large number in existence; it will not be the last. That writing on the ground occurred at the time we know from other sources.[112] The peculiar mode in which Jesus writes on the ground may have been the appropriate posture for a great sage in the face of unworthy interference: he is not readily distracted from drafting his thoughts—religious, philosophical, mathematical. Valerius Maximus, in a work dedicated to the Emperor Tiberius, has a chapter on "study and application." In it, he describes the death of Archimedes. The Roman general who conquered Syracuse gave orders that his life be spared. But when a soldier storming into his house asked him his name while he, "with his mind and eyes fixed on the ground was tracing designs, so strong was his passion for inquiry" that he could not reply. Instead, he urged the soldier to be careful of the drawing: and he was slain.[113]

[111] B. Lindars, *loc. cit.*, believes the exhortation to be tacked on to the original narrative. Even should this be so, there is no reason to doubt that Jesus shares the Rabbinic position. But the argument that the phrase is not found in Syriac Didascalia 7 is weak. This version is extremely summary and, furthermore, the author's aim is to inculcate the duty of welcoming penitent sinners. Hence the omission of "sin no more" is to be expected. It cannot outweigh the united evidence of all MSS. Lindars describes the clause as "missing from the Syriac Didascalia (and likewise the Apostolic Constitutions)." These are not, of course, two independent witnesses, the latter work being based on the former.

[112] *m. Shab.* 12:5, concerning the prohibition of writing on the Sabbath.

[113] Valerius Maximus, *Memorable Deeds and Sayings* 8.7.7. The Latin is: "*studium et industria; dum animo et oculis in terram defixis formam describit, propter nimiam cupiditatem investigandi.*"

Precept and Example

The Rabbis marked off *halakha*, matters of law, from *haggadha*, matters which, though of religious importance, do not affect the law. The exegesis of a Scriptural passage would proceed on different lines according as it was undertaken with a view to the former or the latter. This division has left many marks on the New Testament. One interesting aspect is its relation to the question whether precept or example should be a man's guide. Let us look at a few pericopes from this angle.

A. The Sabbath

The first dispute about the Sabbath is caused by the disciples of Jesus plucking corn. According to Mark and Luke,[1] Jesus in defence refers to David and his band who, as they felt hungry, ate the showbread reserved for the priests. According to Matthew,[2] Jesus, in addition to this argument, mentions the priests breaking the Sabbath for the sake of the temple service—for instance, by slaughtering animals for sacrifice or by burning the sheaf of firstfruits—and remarks that something greater than the temple is now concerned. (The Pharisees held that the sheaf must be offered on the second day of Passover even if it falls on a Sabbath. The reaping in this case involves additional ceremony: the person about to cut it asks three times whether he may do the act "on this Sabbath" and is told three times that he may.[3] Matthew's readers, then, knew of at least one occasion on which the plucking of corn on a Sabbath was permissible and even enjoined.)

It is agreed on all hands that the argument given by Matthew alone, and not by Mark and Luke, is an addition. We may leave open the question whether or not the addition is authentic in the sense that it was at one time introduced by Jesus himself. Nor, for that matter, need we decide whether or not the original argument, to be found in all three Synoptics, actually goes back to him. There appears to be no reason why it should not. But, for the present purpose, it suffices to distinguish between two stages of the dispute, an earlier—represented by Mark and Luke—where the defence invokes the action of David, and a later—represented by Matthew—where it invokes the action of David plus the rules concerning the temple service. What is the meaning of this development?

The original argument—from David's conduct—was of a spontaneous, popular kind, but it was anything but conclusive from the scholarly, legal point of view. For one

[1] Mark 2:23 ff.; Luke 6:1 ff.

[2] Matt 12:1 ff.

[3] *m. Men.* 10:3, 9.

thing, in the case of David, it had not been a question of the Sabbath at all. David, when hungry, had eaten of the showbread; which was no proof, technically, that you might, in a similar situation, break the Sabbath. But an even more serious objection was that what Jesus adduced was the conduct of a historical figure, instead of a law. He quoted a narrative saying that David had acted in a certain way, but not a provision allowing you to act in this way. It was not so much that David might conceivably have been wrong: the Rabbis no less than Jesus assumed that, for one reason or another, his action had been justified.[4] The flaw in the argumentation was more fundamental than that.

It was of the essence of the Rabbinic system that any detailed rule, any *halakha*, must rest, directly or indirectly, on an actual precept promulgated in Scripture. It must rest on it directly or indirectly: that is to say, there was no need for a *halakha* to be laid down in so many words, so long as it could be derived from some precept by means of the recognized norms of hermeneutics. One of these norms, for example, was the inference *a fortiori*, or as the Rabbis termed it, *qal waḥomer*, "the light and weighty." If a man knowingly kept a dangerous animal and it killed a person, Scripture allowed the guilty owner to escape the death penalty on payment of a fine: "then he shall give for the ransom of his life whatsoever is laid upon him."[5] The Rabbis concluded that, *a fortiori*, the place of "eye for eye, tooth for tooth" etc., lesser penalties than death, should be taken by monetary damages.[6] However, even here, be it noted, the *halakha* was ultimately based on a real precept, an express permission, "then he may give for a ransom whatsoever is laid upon him," not on a mere historical datum. Historical data belonged to the province of *haggadha*. They might serve to inculcate moral lessons, general religious truths, wisdom; they might also serve to illustrate and corroborate a *halakha*. But they could not form its primary source.

To be sure, the principle in question was the result of a long and slow evolution. But by the middle of the 1st cent. A.D., notwithstanding certain vestiges of a less rigorous attitude, it was, if not firmly established, at least rapidly gaining ground. On the whole, what a patriarch or a pious king—or, as we shall see, even God—had done on a particular occasion was considered all-important as far as *derekh 'ereṣ*, the good life in general, was concerned; the Rabbis constantly reminded people of Abraham's hospitality to strangers or the meekness of Moses. Given certain conditions, it was also regarded as helpful to a more accurate understanding of a *halakha*, a detailed law. But it was not by itself an adequate basis for a *halakha*. Laws must be ordained, their character as commands, prohibitions or concessions must be clearly recognizable.

It may be worth remarking on the technical expressions "thou findest" and "we have found" which are frequent in Tannaitic literature. They refer *inter alia* to historical occurrences,[7] and particularly to such as might seem to invite imitation. But it is significant that the moral drawn is nearly always *haggadhic*: he who maligns a fellow-

[4] E.g. *b. Men.* 95b.

[5] Exod 21:30.

[6] *Mek.* on Exod 21:24.

[7] We are not here concerned with the entirely different case where an expression of this kind introduces an established *halakhic* doctrine, in order that further conclusions may be drawn; as e.g. in *m. Men.* 12:5, "We find that wine may be offered in a certain way, therefore oil may be offered in that way."

man may deserve heavier punishment than he who commits a straightforward assault, or the patriarchs and prophets were willing to lay down their lives for Israel.[8] Where "thou findest" or "we have found" occurs in the domain of *halakha*, normally, the argument merely supports a conclusion arrived at on the ground of precept,[9] or it survives in connection with a problem of a highly theoretical nature: the problem, for instance, whether, though in general none may marry the widow of a king, a king may do so.[10]

Another technical phrase is illuminating. A Rabbi advocating a doctrine may say of a Biblical passage that "though it supplies no proof (*ra'aya*), yet it does supply a suggestion (*zekher*)." This phrase is not uncommonly used by Tannaites when they can rest a *halakha* only on a historical example but not on an actual precept. We are told that if a couple are married for ten years without having children, the husband should take another wife (not a strict *halakha*, it is true); and, it is added, "though there is no proof, yet there is a suggestion" in Abraham's taking Hagar.[11] The author fully realizes that a precedent like this has not the force of a commandment.[12]

Again, the arguments introduced by the phrase *minnayin*, "Whence?," "From what Scriptural passage do we know?," are of interest. The passage supplied in the answer does not always contain a precept; it sometimes contains an example. Occasionally this may be due to the survival of laxer methods of proof—where example was as good as precept. Moreover, the question often concerns *haggadha*; for instance, "Whence do we know that the Israelites in the desert refrained from unchastity and tale-bearing?"[13] In such a case, of course, no reference to a precept is needed. But even where the question concerns *halakha*, it may be about a detail or definition rather than the actual rule. There is a rule that a circumcised child may be bathed even if this involves a breaking of the Sabbath. How long does this rule apply? It is certainly valid, the Rabbis hold,[14] as long as three days. "Whence do we know that the child may be bathed on the third? Because it is written,[15] And on the third day when they were sore." The Biblical example merely serves to render the *halakha* clearer or more precise.

As a technical argument, then, the mention of the temple service on a Sabbath to be found in Matthew is far superior to that of David's appropriation of the showbread to be found in Mark and Luke as well. Not only does the temple service provide a correct parallel to the action of the disciples, in that it really has to do with the Sabbath—or, more precisely, with the problem under what circumstances its observance must give way to other considerations. What is of almost greater importance is that the argument

[8] *m. Arak.* 3:5; *Mek.* on Exod 12:1.

[9] *Mek.* on Exod 12:22—though the rule to begin and end a journey in daytime is really *haggadhic* rather than *halakhic.*

[10] *m. Sanh.* 2:1.

[11] *t. Yeb.* 8:4, referring to Gen 16:3.

[12] Which does not mean that a precedent constantly used to support a *halakha* may not gradually acquire the status of a true proof. Abraham's action is treated as such by Simeon ben Lakish in the 3rd cent. A.D.; see *y. Yeb.* 7c.

[13] *Mek.* on Exod 12:6.

[14] *m. Shab.* 9:3; cf. 19:3, which represents Eleazar ben Azariah (about A.D. 100) as making use of the passage from Genesis.

[15] Gen 34:25.

from the temple service on a Sabbath rests on a definite precept. That offerings should be brought even on a Sabbath, in other words, that in this sense the temple service should take precedence over the observance of the Sabbath, is expressly laid down in Scripture:[16] "And on the sabbath day two lambs of the first year without spot, the burnt offering of every sabbath, beside the continual burnt offering."

Possibly the fact that this second argument is introduced by "Or have ye not read in the law" is significant. The words "in the law" are not used in introducing the first argument, from David's conduct. They may be intended to draw attention to the distinctive nature of the addition. At any rate, the scholarly, strictly Rabbinic character of the addition is underlined by the employment of a hermeneutic norm to which we have already adverted, the inference *a fortiori*, the *qal waḥomer*. Scripture—thus the argument in Matthew runs—ordains that the observance of the Sabbath must yield to the temple service; *a fortiori* it must yield in the present case, where something greater than the temple demands consideration. There is nothing *haggadhic* about this. The argument is of a kind which no student of *halakha* could lightly dismiss.

B. DIVORCE

There is one other pericope in the gospels, about divorce,[17] where two different Old Testament texts are cited in support of the same decision, and the development seems to have been similar—from proof by reference to an example to proof by reference to a precept. This time, however, the addition must definitely have been made at a fairly early date. Mark as well as Matthew gives both the texts. The second one must, therefore, have been added either prior to Mark or, at the latest, by Mark himself. As Matthew's version of this pericope differs in important respects from Mark's, we shall begin by analysing the latter. It will emerge from our discussion that, where Matthew differs, he has changed the Markan account.

1. *Mark*

Let us, then, inquire into Mark. As the first argument in support of Jesus's attitude to divorce, we are told what God did on the sixth day: "From the beginning of the creation, male and female created he them." The words "male and female created he them" are a quotation from Genesis.[18] At one stage, as we propose to demonstrate presently, this argument stood alone. The other quotation, "For this cause shall a man leave his father and mother" etc.,[19] had not yet been added.

The question arises—and we may point out that it would arise even if there had been the two quotations from the outset: What is the precise force of this argument, "male and female created he them?" At first sight it looks quite irrelevant, speaking neither in favour nor against divorce; or perhaps rather in favour, seeing that God created two independent beings. Modern commentaries incline to slur over the difficulty.

[16] Num 28:9 f.

[17] Matt 19:3 ff.; Mark 10:2 ff.

[18] Gen 1:27, 5:2.

[19] Gen 2:24.

The true explanation lies in the fact that, for the Rabbis, this verse contained the doctrine—familiar to readers of Plato[20]—of the ideal, androgynous man, the doctrine that when God first created man, he created him as both man and woman in one.[21]

The reasons why the Rabbis connected the doctrine with just this verse are two. For one thing, they had to harmonize this verse, "male and female created he them," with the narrative[22] according to which Adam came first and Eve was only subsequently formed from one of his ribs. A plausible solution was to maintain that the original Adam was a composite being, and that this was the meaning of the verse in question. For another thing, the Hebrew text wavers between singular and plural. It starts by using the singular "man"—"God created man in his image"—and then goes on to put the plural "them"—"male and female created he them." What sort of being might it be, the Rabbis asked themselves, of whom one could equally well speak in the singular or plural? Again the answer was that the verse must refer to the androgynous man.

That this interpretation of the verse goes back to New Testament times is certain. Philo has it.[23] It occurs in many different Rabbinic sources. Moreover, the Rabbis inform us that the authors of the LXX, for the enlightenment of their gentile public, slightly altered the verse "male and female created he them": they translated "a male with his female parts created he them," or "male and female created he him"—"him" in the singular. Now admittedly, the LXX in the form it has come down to us does not contain these modifications. But there is every reason to believe that the Rabbis did find them in some Greek versions. We shall presently point out a similar modification of another verse,[24] still preserved in the LXX as we have it. Even if the Rabbis did not find those variants, such a tradition concerning the authors of the LXX could never have grown up had the teaching to which it refers, i.e. of the androgynous Adam, not been of very considerable age. Exactly how the myth reached the Rabbis we need not here decide. Probably it came to them from Plato, though we must bear in mind that Plato himself no doubt had it from the Orient. It does not give the impression of a native Greek product; and, quite possibly, by putting it into the mouth of Aristophanes, Plato means to suggest that he does not want it taken too seriously.

Obviously, understood in this sense, the statement that "from the beginning male and female created he them" was a powerful argument against divorce. God had made the ideal man androgynous, man and woman forming one inseparable being. That was an example of even greater authority than, say, the conduct of a figure like David: it was an example set by God himself in creating the world. The exhortation "What therefore God hath joined together, let not man put asunder" now becomes intelligible. In the present text, it follows the second quotation, "For this cause shall a man leave his father and mother," with which it has no logical connection. But, originally, it came directly after "From the beginning, male and female created he them." God made man and woman in one. That example should be heeded: man is not entitled to break up a unity which God,

[20] *Symposium* 189C ff.

[21] *Gen. Rab.* on Gen 1:26 f.; *Mek.* on Exod 12:40.

[22] Gen 2:18 ff.

[23] *Op.* 24.76.

[24] Gen 2:24.

by proceeding as he did in creating the world, showed to be the perfect state of things.

The exhortation confirms not only our explanation of the whole discussion by reference to the teaching of the androgynous Adam—the words "what therefore God hath joined together" and so on will make sense on no other basis—but also our thesis that at one stage, the argument rested solely on the first quotation from the Old Testament, "From the beginning" and so on. The second quotation, "For this cause" and so on, separates the first from the conclusion drawn from it, it comes abruptly between "From the beginning male and female created he them" and "What therefore God hath joined together let not man put asunder." The second quotation, that is, bears every sign of being an insertion—be it Mark's work or earlier than Mark.

A linguistic detail respecting the verbs συνζευγνύειν, "to join together," and χωρίζειν, "to put asunder," may be noticed. Their choice in this context was almost certainly favoured by the fact that they are reminiscent of ζεύγνυσθαι, in the sense of "to marry," and χωρίζεσθαι, in the sense of "to leave one's husband or wife." In other words, while the usual translation "What therefore God hath joined together, let not man put asunder" is perfectly correct, as a secondary meaning at least something more specific seems to have been intended: "What therefore God hath married into one"—the prefix συν may well express the idea "into one," and in the Matthean parallel Codex Bezae and Itala actually add εἰς ἕν [into one]—"let not man divorce." In support, we may recall the Rabbinic *ziwwegh* or *zawwegh*, a verb going back to the Greek ζεῦγος. It may denote "to join things together" in any way, but it is often used of God's "joining together husband and wife" and, in the form *hizdawwegh* or *'izdawwagh*, signifies "to be married." According to the Jerusalemite Targum,[25] for example, "God taught us to marry [here *barzegh* is employed, the second part of which also derives from ζεῦγος] bridegrooms and brides by his marrying—*zawwegh*, from ζεῦγος—Eve to Adam."

Pursuing our inquiry, we may observe that the pronouncement "From the beginning male and female created he them," alluding as it did to the androgynous Adam, would simply puzzle the unlearned, and even the learned might not immediately see the deeper implications. In other words, it was a pronouncement deliberately obscure, hinting at the truth, but not stating it in plain language.

It cannot be accidental that Philo, in commenting on the verse from Genesis, should remark that the androgynous nature of the original man may be perceived "by those who have the faculty of keen vision"; or that Paul, whom also we shall find making use of the myth, should add on one occasion[26] that "this is a great mystery." It is true that Paul may be describing as a mystery less the teaching of the androgynous Adam as such than its application to the relation between Christ and the church. Evidently, however, that teaching counted as esoteric, a secret the full understanding of which was reserved for the initiated. Moreover, we shall see, when we discuss the form which may be characterized as public retort and private explanation, that this Markan pericope is not the only instance in the gospels where Jesus is represented as answering his opponents by a saying difficult to grasp, which he later expounds to his disciples.

[25] Deut 34:6

[26] Eph 5:32.

About the explanation given to the disciples in the present case, a few words must here be said: it provides yet further evidence that the entire pericope must be understood against the background of the myth of the androgynous man. Jesus declares that it is adultery for a man or woman to re-marry after divorce.[27] Now as far as the woman is concerned, this might be regarded as merely a consequence of the rejection of divorce. That is to say, if marriage is indissoluble, if divorce makes no difference, then a wife remains married to her husband even after divorce, and clearly commits adultery by cohabiting with another man. The same, however, is not true of a man who re-marries after divorce. Certainly, he also, if divorce is not recognized, is still married to his first wife. But, so long as the law allows polygamy, it cannot be adultery if he takes a second one—be it before or after separation from the first. Yet Jesus does here speak of adultery even where it is the husband who re-marries.

The point is that the doctrine on which his decision is based involves the rejection, not only of divorce, but also of polygamy. It does so because it sees in marriage an imitation of the ideal, androgynous state of man. Once marriage is conceived of in this fashion, it becomes just as criminal for a husband to take a second wife while the first lives as for a wife to take a second husband while the first lives. The ideal state is disrupted in the former no less than in the latter case.

It is significant that the pronouncement declaring the husband's re-marriage adultery recurs only in two other passages of the New Testament: in the parallel chapter of Matthew to which we shall come back, and in Luke.[28] Luke, we shall submit in a different chapter (on Violence to the Kingdom), seems to show traces of a context where the androgynous man played a part; in any case this evangelist came from a society which had long ceased to countenance polygamy. Paul probably also looks upon a husband's re-marriage during his wife's lifetime as in principle adulterous. He writes[29] that only if an unbelieving wife or husband dissolves the union, the believing "brother or sister is not under bondage." Surely, the implication is that, except for this case, re-marriage would be illicit—and no less so for a brother than for a sister.

By contrast, in the sermon on the mount, Matthew appears deliberately to avoid the notion of adultery by the husband.[30] There is no reflection on polygamy in the proposition that "whosoever shall put away his wife causeth her to commit adultery." It means that, since marriage is indissoluble, a woman who re-marries after divorce is an adulteress; but the husband who divorced her, thus encouraging her to feel free, bears the moral responsibility. We must remember that the essential words in a bill of divorce were: "Lo, thou art permitted to any man."[31] If there was a stage at which the saying did not contain the proviso "saving for the cause of fornication," the original import may

[27] The prevalent reading of Mark 10:12 refers to "a wife putting away her husband," another to "a wife departing from her husband." The problem will be discussed below, 281 ff., under Terms for Divorce; it has no bearing on the thesis here submitted.

[28] Luke 16:18.

[29] 1 Cor 7:15. [See, however, Pauline Contributions to a Pluralistic Culture, 537 ff.]

[30] Matt 5:32.

[31] *m. Gitt.* 9:3. As we shall see under Terms for Divorce [281], Josephus in *Ant.* 15.7.10.259, speaks of a man divorcing his wife as "conceding," "permitting," her, ἐφιέναι.

conceivably have been similar to that of a saying by Simeon ben Azzai (first half of the 2nd cent. A.D.). He compares a husband who hates his wife to a murderer, for such a man will institute proceedings even against an innocent woman and not rest till she is sentenced to death.[32] He will, that is, represent her as having committed misconduct—which in Greek might be expressed by ποιεῖ αὐτήν μοιχευθῆνα.

One thing is clear: nothing is said or implied in this verse about a second marriage by a husband after divorce—or, for that matter, before. Again, it is generally admitted that 1 Timothy[33] and Titus[34] take polygamy for granted.

It follows, then, that there is in the New Testament no opposition to polygamy but that based on the teaching of the androgynous Adam. Moreover, there was a tendency among Jewish New Testament authors—i.e. a tendency not shared by Luke—to suppress this opposition as they forgot about, or came to disapprove of, its basis.

However, we must return to the argument from "male and female created he them." Profound as it was, it again suffered from a major flaw if it was to be used in serious, scholarly controversy with the Rabbis: like the argument from David's conduct, it invoked an example instead of a precept, it adduced what God had done on a particular occasion instead of what God had said should or should not be done.

Certainly, no example from history could have more weight than one set by God. What is more, of the examples set by God, none could have more weight than those he set in creating the world. To approach the original, ideal creation as God had planned it was a great aim in the eyes of the Rabbis. Nevertheless, even an example set by God in ordering the world essentially belonged to the domain of *haggadha*, and supplied no adequate foundation for a specific *halakha* such as the prohibition and non-recognition of divorce. The Rabbis would appeal to God's example in enunciating general rules of religious, moral or prudent conduct, *derekh 'ereṣ*; they would also appeal to it in elucidating a *halakha* already established on other, proper grounds. But further they would not go.

To illustrate this. The Rabbis, we said, would appeal to God's example in enunciating rules of religious, moral or prudent conduct. Thus in the *Testament of Zebulon*, the nation is warned against putting up two rival leaders—the reference probably is to the terrible conflict between Hyrcanus II and Aristobulus II:[35] "Be not ye, therefore, divided into two heads, for everything which the Lord made hath but one head." Manifestly we are in the realm of *haggadha*, in this case political advice. Again, Job, we learn from R. Judah ben Bathyra, of the first third of the 2nd cent. A.D., decided never to have more than one wife at a time, because he considered that "if it had been fitting for Adam to have ten wives, God would have given him ten, but he gave him only one."[36] Such a consideration would be quite in order from the Rabbinic point of view. It would lead, not to a *halakha* which you must follow, but to a recommendation, far from binding, of the course most fitting for man, i.e. most in accordance with *derekh 'ereṣ*. It is significant that

[32] *Derekh Eretz* 11.

[33] 1 Tim 3:2.

[34] Tit 1:6.

[35] Testament of Zebulon 9:4.

[36] *Ab. de R.N.* 2:5a; the Biblical basis for this Midrash is Job 31:1.

the Rabbi simply refers to God giving Adam one wife, without specifying a particular verse. There is no need to be so exact in a matter of *haggadha*.

It is not, indeed, unlikely that Judah ben Bathyra consciously mitigated an earlier doctrine. In other words, he—or his source—may have been acquainted with a decision of the kind to be met with in the New Testament, a decision put forward by some circles as a binding *halakha* in favour of monogamy and rested by them on the interpretation of certain verses from Genesis as speaking of the androgynous being. But, while recognizing monogamy as the more desirable practice, he did not agree that it was the law; so he advocated it in a vaguer manner, as forming part of the code of *derekh 'ereṣ*. If this is the history behind his comment, it becomes all the more evident what enormous importance the Rabbis attached to the distinction between *halakha* and *haggadha*.

The Rabbis would also appeal to God's example in elucidating a *halakha* already established on other, proper grounds. Here we may mention that the verse "male and female created he them" played a part in the discussion[37] as to how many children a man ought to have and whether or not he had done his duty if they were all of one sex. But two things should be noted. First, the primary *halakha* laying down the duty of procreation was based by the Rabbis on an actual precept—or rather, on what they considered an actual precept since, grammatically, it was an imperative—namely, the words:[38] "Be fruitful and multiply." The verse "male and female created he them" was introduced only as a help to a more exact understanding of this *halakha*. Secondly, it is very doubtful whether, in the Talmudic period, the duty of procreation was a *halakha* in the strict sense at all. It may well have been nearer a moral duty, a duty falling under *derekh 'ereṣ*, the behaviour expected of a good man. Ben Azzai, in the first third of the 2nd cent., openly admitted that he preferred to remain unmarried in order to devote all his time to the study of the Torah. He could hardly have dismissed in this manner, say, the duty to eat unleavened bread and bitter herbs in the first night of Passover.

Apparently, as time went on, the argument from example was found less and less satisfactory. So an argument from precept was added, just as in the case of the dispute about the Sabbath: "For this cause shall a man leave his father and mother, and they twain shall be one flesh; so then they are no more twain, but one flesh."

It is important to realize that the motif of the androgynous Adam is here still present. We accept, of course, the shorter variant, which quotes only part of the Old Testament verse. The longer variant, which completes the quotation by adding "and he shall cleave to his wife," is a palpable assimilation to Matthew—but Matthew we shall consider later. For the moment, we proceed from Mark's "For this cause shall a man leave his father and mother, and they twain shall be one flesh."

Whoever inserted this verse interpreted it as meaning that, in marriage, the two separated halves of the original composite being meet again and, having done so, should stay re-united. It is only if it is taken in this way that the verse, though deprived of the clause "and he shall cleave to his wife," yet decrees the indissolubility of marriage. In fact, that clause is cut out precisely in order to retain the esoteric character of the reply.

[37] *m. Yeb.* 6:6; *t. Yeb.* 8:4; *b. Yeb.* 62a.
[38] Gen 1:28.

If the words "and he shall cleave to his wife" were included, there would be an open injunction in plain language declaring marriage indissoluble. Without these words, what remains is "they twain shall be one flesh"—a commandment fully intelligible only to those who have the key.

At this stage of the controversy, Jesus is still made to ward off his antagonists by a mysterious saying, an allusion to the ideal being that is man and woman in one. The only real difference between the original argument, from "male and female created he them," and the additional one, from "they twain shall be one flesh," is that the former appeals to an example—God created the ideal man androgynous—while the latter appeals to a precept—it is one of God's commandments that the two divided halves should join again for good.

2. *Confirmatory Evidence*

Eight points may be mentioned as corroborating our conclusions. First, the quotation from the Old Testament, "For this cause shall a man leave his father and mother and they twain shall be one flesh," is followed by a brief comment: "so that they are no more twain, but one flesh." The similarity to Plato, where he introduces the theory of love as the craving for one another of the two separated halves of a composite being, is striking:[39] "If such is your desire," the god says to two lovers, "I propose to fuse and weld you into a single piece, so that from being two you may become one."

Secondly, Philo, we saw, adopts the myth of the androgynous Adam. He also adopts the notion of love we have just outlined, and, significantly, he seems to associate it with the verse "For this cause" etc.[40] According to the Bible, God brought all animals before Adam to name them; then he created Eve, whom Adam acknowledged as a true companion; it is at this point that we find the verse "For this cause shall a man leave his father and mother and they twain shall be one flesh." According to Philo, God brought the animals before Adam to name them; then he created Eve, a true companion; then "love supervenes, and brings together and fits into one the divided halves, as it were, of one being." Surely this is a paraphrase of "and they twain shall be one flesh."

Thirdly, Paul twice adduces the verse from Genesis, and both times he is influenced by its interpretation as meaning that, through sexual intercourse, a man and woman actually become one being. In 1 Corinthians[41] he quotes only the words "and they twain shall be one flesh"; and he uses them to support his argument that if a Christian, whose body is a member of Christ, associates with a harlot, he is making a member of Christ into a member of a harlot since he and the harlot become one body, ἕν σῶμα. In Ephesians[42] he quotes the words "For this cause shall a man leave his father and mother and they twain shall be one flesh." In all probability, like Mark, he deliberately suppresses "and he shall cleave to his wife," in order to concentrate on the mysterious, esoteric teaching contained in the ending of the verse, "and they twain shall be

[39] *Symposium* 192E. If there are traces of an analogous theory in Plutarch, *Coniugalia Praecepta* 33, in *Mor.* 142E, they are very faint indeed.

[40] *Leg. All.* 2.49.

[41] 1 Cor 6:16.

[42] Eph 5:31.

one flesh." The quotation, it will be remembered, is followed by the remark: "This is a great mystery." Admittedly, most *codices* do include the part "and he shall cleave to his wife." But Origen affirms in so many words that it is not to be found in Paul; in fact he cites this passage from Ephesians as an example of the freedom with which New Testament writers modify Old Testament texts. The conclusion, therefore, seems justified that the clause, omitted by Paul, was inserted at an early date, by way of assimilation to Matthew and the full Old Testament text. Be this as it may, the verse, for Paul, provides a Scriptural basis for a husband's duty to love his wife "as his own body" or "as his own flesh." Their union approaches the state of the original, androgynous Adam. And it corresponds to the union between Christ and his church.

Fourthly, in the Gospel according to the Egyptians, we are told that Jesus, asked by Salome when his kingdom would finally arrive, replied: "When ye have trampled on the garment of shame, and when the two become one and the male with the female is neither male nor female." "The two become one" may well be a reference to the verse from Genesis; and it is clearly taken to signify the coming into existence of the ideal, androgynous being and the disappearance of the distinction between the sexes—and of their passions. 2 Clement[43] quotes the fragment under notice—with slight modifications—and comments on it. But it considerably rationalizes its source when it explains that the words "the male with the female is neither male nor female" mean: "A brother, when he sees a sister, does not think of the woman in her, nor she of the man in him." It is worth noting that, according to Paul,[44] once people are baptized into Christ, "there is neither Jew nor Greek, neither bond nor free, neither male nor female."

Fifthly, the quotation in Mark follows the LXX. So does the Matthean parallel, and so does Paul both in 1 Corinthians and Ephesians. The Hebrew text—supported by the Targum and the Book of Jubilees[45]—has not "and they twain shall be one flesh," but "and they shall be one flesh." It looks as if the LXX (supported, it is true, by the Samaritan Pentateuch) had inserted "twain" in order to enjoin monogamy, considered as the more civilized practice by the Greeks; and as if this verse had been deemed the appropriate place for such an injunction because commentators already read into it the meeting in marriage of the two halves of the androgynous being. We have already noted Rabbinic reports to the effect that the LXX introduced the androgynous Adam into another verse.[46] Even if it should be held, however, that the LXX preserves the original reading and that the word "twain" has been eliminated from the Massoretic Hebrew,[47] the difference remains important. The word must have been eliminated for some reason, which can only have been that some circles interpreted "twain" as ordaining monogamy. The interpretation, if we take this line, would have to go back to a time prior to the Book of Jubilees, since this work, in agreement with the Hebrew text, omits "twain."

[43] 2 Clement 12:2.

[44] Gal 3:28.

[45] Jub 3:7.

[46] Gen 1:27, 5:2.

[47] This view is taken by R. Kittel, *Biblia Hebraica,* 2nd ed. (1912); but he seems to have overlooked Jubilees.

The next few points are particularly interesting—the Rabbinic treatment of the verse. Sixthly, then, the Rabbis recognized both divorce and polygamy. Consequently, they were driven to an entirely different exegesis. The prevalent view among them was[48] that the injunction was addressed not only to the Jews but also to the gentiles; it was a "Noachian commandment," valid for all mankind, and forbidding unnatural intercourse. More precisely, the first clause, "a man shall leave his father," in the opinion of the Rabbis, was directed against marrying one's father's widow even if she was not one's mother; the next, "a man shall leave his mother," was directed against marrying one's mother; "he shall cleave to his wife" was directed against homosexuality and adultery, both the noun "wife" and the possessive pronoun "his" being emphasized; finally, "and they shall be one flesh" was directed against intercourse with beasts. Now the remarkable thing is that this interpretation of "and they shall be one flesh," however unlike Mark's, Philo's or Paul's in its result, does also presuppose the concept of marriage as the re-union of the divided halves of an original whole. R. Akiba—of the first third of the 2nd cent.—tells us how the Rabbis come to understand the words in that peculiar way, as a prohibition of intercourse with beasts. He explains that, by putting "and they shall be one flesh," Scripture means to restrict a man to such intercourse as really makes him and his partner into one—which is not the case where he comes together with a beast. It emerges that if the verse in Mark has reference to the fusion of man and woman into the perfect composite being, this is quite consistent with the ideas current in the Rabbinic circles of the time. That they persisted in subsequent centuries may be seen from a remark by R. Asi, of about A.D. 300.[49]

Seventhly, there are even traces in Rabbinic literature of a doctrine which made "and they shall be one flesh" into the basis for, if not a prohibition, at least a disapprobation of divorce. The admonition in Isaiah,[50] "Hide not thyself from thy flesh," is occasionally interpreted as enjoining kindness to one's divorced wife.[51] Clearly she is still part of him who was her husband.

Lastly, of one Rabbi at least, Simeon ben Johai, about the middle of the 2nd cent. A.D., we know that, though he could not declare divorce illegal, he strongly disapproved of it; and his disapproval seems to have been linked with, on the one hand, the notion of husband and wife approaching the ideal, androgynous being and, on the other, the notion of Solomon's Song allegorically depicting God's relation with Israel. Simeon[52] commented on the fact that the Old Testament provisions concerning divorce open with the clause "When a man hath taken a wife"[53] instead of with "When a wife hath caused

[48] *b. Sanh.* 58a.

[49] *Gen. Rab.* on 2:24 at the end.

[50] Isa 58:7.

[51] *Lev. Rab.* on 25:39.

[52] *b. Kidd.* 2b. In *b. Nidd.* 31b the interpretation is ascribed to Dosethai ben Jannai, of the end of the 2nd cent. No doubt Dosethai took over Simeon's teaching.

[53] Deut 24:1. It is universally held (see e.g. the standard edition of the Babylonian Talmud and W. Bacher, *Die Agada der Tannaiten*, vol. 2 [(1890)], 104) that the Rabbi refers to Deut 22:13, where the same clause occurs. But, obviously, this is to deprive his remarks of their very point. Maybe the transfer of his interpretation from 24:1 to 22:13 was deliberately undertaken by medieval authorities, who recognized its dangerous implications in its original setting.

herself to be taken to a man." His explanation was that, in marrying, it is the man who seeks what he has lost—the rib. That the Rabbi should have read an allusion to restoration of the androgynous state by marriage precisely into the Biblical permission of divorce must be regarded as a very bold expression of his feelings on the matter. To this we have to add the famous story[54] of the couple who had remained childless for ten years and came to Simeon to be divorced. He advised them to separate with a banquet just as they had married with a banquet. After the feast the husband said to his wife that, when she returned to her father's house, she should take with her whatever she liked best. While he was asleep, she had him carried to her father's house, since there was nothing she liked better than him. The Rabbi then prayed for them and they did get a child. The anecdote ends with the moral that, if a wife who prizes her husband more than anything else will be blessed, how much more will Israel be blessed for prizing God above anything else and exclaiming—in the words of Solomon's Song—"We will be glad and rejoice in thee."[55] In some indirect way, the idea that a marital union ought never to be dissolved is brought into connection with the bond between God and Israel.

3. *Matthew*

When we turn to Matthew, we find that he—or one of his sources—completes the second quotation from the Old Testament, adding "and he shall cleave to his wife." Presumably he no longer connects the verse with the teaching that marriage means a reunion. So the words "and they twain shall be one flesh" are not, for him, of sufficient force; he needs the clause which may be interpreted as a direct, open rejection of divorce—"and he shall cleave to his wife." In other words, according to Matthew, Jesus's argument against divorce is not veiled but intended to be intelligible to all.

As a corollary, whereas in Mark the ultimate consequences of the decision—namely, "Whosoever shall put away his wife and marry another committeth adultery" and so on—are entrusted to the disciples only, in Matthew they are explained to the Pharisees as well. There is no mystery about divorce. The subsequent private discussion between Jesus and his disciples, in Matthew, does not concern divorce or polygamy at all, but the question whether marriage as such is a good thing.

In Matthew, the androgynous Adam is abandoned. The quotation "male and female created he them" has become almost devoid of meaning. All emphasis is now on the precept, "For this cause shall a man" etc.

It might be asked why, though giving up the teaching concerning the androgynous man, Matthew nevertheless retains one of its implications: namely, the rejection of polygamy, or more particularly, the view that even the husband who re-marries after divorce is guilty of adultery. As we saw, this would not follow from a mere prohibition of divorce; it follows only where divorce is prohibited because marriage is looked upon as a re-union of the composite being—here a husband re-marrying breaks up the ideal unity no less than a wife re-marrying. Matthew, who no longer accepts the premise, should logically have dropped the inference. He does not do so in this pericope.

[54] *Song of Songs Rab.* on 1:4.

[55] Cant 1:4.

Probably, the explanation is quite simple: we cannot expect perfect logical consistency. Very likely, the wording of the pronouncement in this context was too firmly established to be changed. As we had occasion to observe before, Matthew does modify it in the sermon on the mount. There it is taken out of the discussion with the Pharisees and placed into a different series of sayings. Hence the evangelist is less reluctant to adjust it to a polygamous milieu.

However, though Matthew himself is presumably no longer influenced by the notion of an androgynous being, there is reason to believe that it played a part in that source from which he took the private reflections of Jesus and his disciples concerning marriage as such: "It is not good to marry, There be eunuchs for the kingdom's sake." More precisely, that source may well have argued on these lines: by marrying a woman, a man unites with her so that they become one body; instead of exclusively belonging to Christ, he makes himself part of another human being; marriage therefore is not worthy of the perfect Christian.

Paul, in 1 Corinthians,[56] argues thus: a Christian's body is a member of Christ; he must not, therefore, associate with a harlot, for by doing so his body and hers would become one—according to the verse "they twain shall be one flesh"—and thus a member of Christ would be defiled; in fact, it is best not to touch any woman whatever—*scil.* but to belong entirely to Christ; however, a decent marriage is far preferable to fornication; and once concluded, marriage is indissoluble. That Paul's teaching rests on the myth of the androgynous being is beyond question. And his teaching is just of the type we are postulating for Matthew's source: since a man's marriage means his merging in a composite being, it also means his withdrawing his body from exclusive union with Christ—hence he had better remain single.

The term αἰτία in the clause "If the case of the man be so with his wife, it is not good to marry" is an old crux. Its normal meanings are "imputation" and "cause," neither of which is really suitable. With all due reservation—for such points can rarely be more than conjectural—let us note that, in Hebrew and Aramaic, the words "*illa*," "pretext" or "cause," and "*il'a*," "rib," are so near in sound that occasionally, it seems, one is spelt—or misspelt, like the other.[57] The latter is used by the Targum in the story of Eve's creation. Conceivably, at an Aramaic stage of the tradition, the clause under discussion contained a direct reference to Genesis.

It should be added that in Matthew the argument from the example of God or the natural world governed by him is by no means uncommon.[58] But it is used to support general rules of nobility and piety—goodness to enemies, trust in God, in short, *haggadha*,

4. *The Zadokite Fragments*

It is instructive to compare with the New Testament development the not dissimilar one to be found in the *Zadokite Fragments*.[59] In this work, there is a paragraph directed against polygamy, and probably also against divorce.

[56] 1 Cor 6:15 ff.

[57] See the dictionaries.

[58] Matt 5:45 ff., 6:26 ff.

[59] *Zadokite Fragments* 7:1 ff.

Three Biblical texts are quoted. The first is "male and female created he them"; this is called "a fundamental principle of the creation." No doubt when this text was first adduced, it was interpreted as referring to the ideal, original creation of the androgynous Adam.

The second text is that which tells us that the animals "went in two by two."[60] This may be a later addition, made at a time when the myth concerning the androgynous man had ceased to play a part in this context. On the other hand, it may be as old as the first quotation. Whichever it is—with its emphatic "two and two," it was not too bad a proof of the universal validity of the "fundamental principle of the creation": the latter applied even to animals.

The third text is the law enjoining that the king "shall not multiply wives to himself."[61] This is almost certainly an addition. In a way, it was not a good text at all. It had nothing to do with any "principle of the creation." It clearly referred to the ruler only, but not to ordinary persons. It was of a far less inclusive scope than the first two texts. But it was added because it was superior to them in containing a precept and not merely an example.

In strictness, neither the way God created the first man nor the way he dealt with the animals when he ordered the world a second time, in the ark, furnished a sufficient basis for a *halakha*, a detailed rule binding on people. To establish a *halakha*, an actual commandment was required; and one confined to the king was better than none. One could always argue that everybody should live up to the highest standard, or that all Jews were equal to kings. In the course of expounding a verse from Amos, "I will raise up the tabernacle of David,"[62] the *Zadokite Fragments* claim[63] that "the king" means "the congregation"; and Simeon ben Johai, of the middle of the 2nd cent. A.D., in a *halakhic* discussion opines that all Israelites are to be considered "kings' children."[64]

C. The Hellenistic Background

We have now presented two controversies between Jesus and the Pharisees—a dispute about the Sabbath and the dispute about divorce—as well as a paragraph about divorce from the *Zadokite Fragments* where an argument invoking an example from history was supplemented by one invoking a precept. It is safe to assume that, in all three cases, the addition was undertaken with a view to satisfying the Rabbinic requirements of a proper *halakha*, as distinct from *haggadha*. Before leaving this topic, we may point out that, if we wish fully to appreciate the Rabbinic attitude in this matter, it is not enough to study the Jewish sources in isolation. To be sure, the principal factors contributing to the Rabbinic system were of native origin. But it looks as if, in the detailed and minute elaboration of the system, the Rabbis had drawn on ideas which, while ultimately going back to Greece, were in Hellenistic times taught by the rhetorical schools throughout the Mediterranean world.

[60] Gen 7:9.

[61] Deut 17:17.

[62] Amos 9:11.

[63] *Zadokite Fragments* 9:7.

[64] *m. Shab.* 14:4.

Here we can only indicate some of the speculations that seem to have influenced their thought. As is well known, Aristotle holds that philosophical theories are powerless to stimulate the mass to moral nobility; the mass needs legal precepts imposing penalties on the disobedient.[65] Philo[66] praises Moses for combining the two methods. In Seneca and Quintilian, however, the antithesis is not between philosophical theories and legal precepts, but between philosophical theories and examples.[67]

This was, of course, the more popular view. We must remember, however, that it inspired not only writers of anecdotes and fables—Phaedrus says: "*exemplis discimus*"[68] ["we learn from examples"]—but also serious historians like Thucydides. That the good historian's work must be a κτῆμα εἰς ἀεί ["a possession for all time"], or, conversely, that people should turn to it for guidance, was a commonplace demand, as may be seen from Aristotle, Cicero, Lucian and many others.[69]

Again, that particular kind of example, the model conduct and pronouncements of a sage whose company you are enjoying, was cultivated by high and low, by the disciples of Socrates, Zeno, R. Johanan ben Zaccai or Jesus[70] no less than by those of many a worthless charlatan. Indeed, taking the wise man's conduct and pronouncements as an example, one may within this example again distinguish between his conduct, which supplies examples in the narrower sense, and his pronouncements, which supply philosophical theories. Thus we are told how Socrates educated his disciples "by word and his own practice":[71] and for Philo[72] he who attains virtue by being taught fixes his attention on what is said by a wise person [hence Abraham "hearkened to the voice of Sarah," not simply "to Sarah"[73]], while he who attains virtue by practice fixes his attention on what a wise person does [hence Jacob "hearkened to his father and mother," not "to their voice"[74]].

When we are told in the *Letter of Aristeas*[75] that it is safer "to hear" about the provisions of the Torah from a wise man than "to read" them, this is a deliberate combination of two elements: full recognition of the Scriptural precepts on the one hand, and

[65] *Nic. E.* 10.9.3 ff.

[66] *Op.* 1.1 ff.

[67] Seneca, *Ep.* 6.5; Quintilian, *I.O.* 12.2.29 ff.

[68] Phaedrus 2.2.2. Cf. Frontinus, *Strat.* 1 *pr.*: "*ita enim consilii quoque et providentiae exemplis succincti duces erunt unde illis excogitandi generandique similia facultas nutriatur.*" ["For in this way commanders will be furnished with specimens of wisdom and foresight, which will serve to foster their own power of conceiving and excecuting like deeds."]

[69] Thucydides 1.22.4; Aristotle *Rhet.* 2.20.8; Cicero, *De Or.* 2.9.36; Lucian, *Quomodo Historia Scribenda Sit* 42, 53—also Frontinus, in the passage quoted in the preceding footnote.

[70] E.g. Xenophon, *Memorabilia* 4.1.1; *Cyropaedia* 8.1.21 ff.; Seneca, *Ep.* 6.5 f., also *Digest* 40.2.5.

[71] Xenophon, *Memorabilia* 4.3.18, 4.4.25 (λέγων τε καὶ αὐτὸς ποιῶν, λέγων τε καὶ πράττων); cp. also 1.2.17 and *Cyropaedia* 1.2.8. In the introductory letter to *Rhet. to Alexander* it is said that the king's subjects will take as example his "life and reason"—his practice and principles. By contrast, self-governing states will follow the law as example. (The law itself can be called example since, in the view of the author, it is reason defined by common agreement.)

[72] *Preliminary Studies* 69 f.

[73] Gen 16:2.

[74] Gen 28:7.

[75] *Letter of Aristeas* 127.

praise of the living example of the sage as the only true way towards the goal on the other.

In the same work there is a further relevant passage:[76] "Our lawgiver first of all laid down the principles of piety and righteousness and inculcated them point by point, not only by prohibitions but also by the use of examples, demonstrating the injurious effects of sin." This is a statement characteristic of the more enlightened Rabbinic schools. The ultimate aims of religion are piety and righteousness; the detailed prohibitions to be found in Scripture keep man from wandering from these aims; and the narrative portions of Scripture are designed to illustrate the soundness of the prohibitions. As far as the relation between detailed prohibitions and narrative portions is concerned, the former are definitely assigned primacy: the precepts are binding as leading to the end, the examples merely help you to see their purpose.

Philo, on the other hand, inclines to accord primacy to the narrative portions. He describes the holy men of the Bible as "unwritten laws" of which the enacted laws are copies.[77] At the same time, we also find him expressing the view which occurs in the *Letter of Aristeas*—that the stories of these men are recounted in order to prove the compatibility of the enacted laws with nature.[78]

Josephus[79] says that young Jews must learn to read the holy books, in order to become familiar with the laws and never to transgress them even from ignorance, and with the deeds of their forefathers, which they should imitate. But, significantly, the duty of thus following both precept and example is represented by him as resting on a commandment of the lawgiver, in Deuteronomy.[80] Precept is the ultimate guide.

However, good Rabbinic doctrine as all this is, it is hardly accidental that the rhetoricians conceive of the respective roles of precept and example in a similar way. Certain of Aristotle's remarks on deductive and inductive reasoning are in point.[81] He opposes proof consisting in an enthymeme to proof consisting in examples. The former, he holds, is objectively far preferable, since it proceeds from universals. But the latter makes a stronger appeal to an audience, since the ordinary man feels more at home with particulars than with universals. Therefore, what a really good orator ought to do is to furnish proof consisting in an enthymeme, and then add an example by way of confirmatory evidence.

In Quintilian, we come across a less philosophical and narrower variation of the theme;[82] but its bearing on the question of the authentic basis of *halakha* is all the clearer. He points out that if you advocate a certain decision of a dispute, you may refer to the example of another court which on a previous occasion dealt with a similar problem, or even with exactly the same problem. (In the latter case, Quintilian would assume

[76] *Letter of Aristeas* 131.

[77] *Abr.* 1.3 f., *Mos.* 1.162.

[78] *Abr.* 1.5. But even here he concludes that, properly, the enacted laws are nothing but memorials of the lives of virtuous men.

[79] *Contra Apionem* 2.25.204.

[80] Deut 6:7, 11:19.

[81] *Rhet.* 1.2.8 ff., 2.20.1 ff., 3.17.5; *Problems* 18.3; *Prior Analytics* 2.24.

[82] *I.O.* 5.2.1 ff.; cp. 5.11.1 ff.

an example only in a loose sense,[83] but we need not here pursue the distinction.) Your argument from such a decision will then be open to several counter-arguments, among them, that circumstances have changed since the previous occasion so that the present dispute must be judged differently, or that quite generally it is wrong to adhere to precedent instead of dealing with each dispute according to its merits. However—Quintilian goes on—if you invoke, not just the decision of an ordinary court, but that of the senate or emperor, these counter-arguments will not be possible. Decisions by the senate or emperor have the force of law, they are not mere precedents, mere examples, but precepts, binding for good. With this kind of problem ventilated in the rhetorical schools, it is easy to imagine that the Rabbis found there much to interest and help them.

This is not the place to examine the relation of precept and example to another proof invariably listed by the rhetoricians, namely, authority, i.e. the opinion of a nation, a great man or a god.[84] Nor can we inquire how far the recognition of example influenced, and was influenced by, such concepts as tradition, *mos maiorum* [custom of the ancestors] and so on. The special position of the example set by a god or by God, the special position of the ideal creation as it first came from his hands—these and allied problems would lead us too far afield. But it may not be amiss to repeat that an investigation of the wider background of Talmudic teaching, that is to say, of the more important Hellenistic views about precept and example, would throw much light on the Rabbinic treatment of the Torah—as also on the efforts of those who had to erect and defend a fresh, rival system.

[83] Cp. 5.2.1 with 5.11.36.

[84] Aristotle, *Rhet.* 2.23.12; Cicero, *Top.* 2.8, 4.24; Quintilian 5.11.36; "the authority of examples" is mentioned, e.g., in Cicero, *De Inv.* 1.30.49; Quintilian 5:11.1.

Violence to the Kingdom

Matthew and Luke[1] preserve a saying about the kingdom suffering violence and being taken by force, or its being preached and everybody pressing into it, the import of which is highly controversial. Let us concede at the outset that all interpretations to be found in modern literature, and quite a few not to be found, are reconcilable with a Jewish milieu. In fact the Rabbinic texts do not enable us to arbitrate. Nevertheless it may be useful to draw attention to a few points which, though relevant to the discussion, are generally neglected. While we cannot clear up the meaning of the saying, we can find out a little more than appears to be known about the possible ideas behind it and the material with which it was traditionally combined.

A. The Saying

1. *General*

First, a preliminary remark regarding its authenticity. We are not here concerned with this question. However, one argument occasionally advanced[2] is weak: that the saying cannot go back to Jesus because he survived John only for a short time and ἀπὸ τῶν ἡμερῶν or ἀπὸ τότε, "since the days" or "since then," presupposes a longish interval. It is difficult to see why the interval must be longish. Moreover, the argument seems to assume that "since John" necessarily signifies "since the death of John." Yet ἀπὸ and—if we think of a Hebrew or Aramaic form of the saying—*min* may be inclusive. That is to say, "since John" may signify "since John began his activity." In Thucydides[3] ἀπὸ παλαιοῦ, "from the earliest times," means "from the beginning"; it does not mean "since the earliest times were passed." "I have walked before you from my youth unto this day," says the old Samuel;[4] "O house of Jacob," we read in Isaiah,[5] "which are carried by me from the womb"; and of David we are told that he had not displeased Adonijah "at any time," literally, "from his days."[6] In all these cases *min* is clearly inclusive.[7] In Rabbinic writings, incidentally, we sometimes have the choice between the readings "since the days of" (*mime-*) and "in the days of" (*bime-*), the sense remaining the same whichever we prefer.

[1] Matt 11:12; Luke 16:16.

[2] E.g. by R. Knopf, *Einführung in das Neue Testament*, 2nd ed. (1923), 259.

[3] Thucydides 1.2.6.

[4] 1 Sam 12:2.

[5] Isa 46:3 f.

[6] 1 Kgs 1:6.

[7] Strangely, in Gesenius' *Handwörterbuch*, 16th ed., by F. Buhl (1915), 433, only the last-mentioned instance is classed under the inclusive usage.

The saying under notice distinguishes between three periods: that up to John's activity or death, that from John till now, and a future one. There may be good reasons for making the period from John till now start at his death rather than at his first public appearance. There may also be good reasons for denying the authenticity of the saying. All that we maintain is that the clause "since the days" or "since then" does not prove what some critics think it does.

2. "βία" *and* "ἁρπάζω" *in Matthew*

Now for Matthew. It is often said, rightly, that, as a rule, when βία and ἁρπάζω—or derivatives of these words—appear together, they denote some wrong. Josephus records[8] that two relatives of King Agrippa were "violent (βίαιοι) and bent on plundering (ἁρπάζω) the goods of the weaker." Unfortunately this statistical consideration gives little help: there is no evidence that the saying in question uses the words in their most frequent sense. We may recall the passage "How can one spoil a strong man's goods except he first bind him?"[9] This refers to a legitimate plundering, ἁρπάζω or διαρπάζω. True, the term βία does not occur. But it would make no difference if it did, if mention were made of an overpowering of the strong by force.

3. *The Kingdom Breaks Through*

Those who regard βιάζομαι as a middle and translate "the kingdom forces its way," "breaks through," may assume some form of *beza'*, *baqa'*, *baraḥ*, *beraḥ*, *giaḥ*, *paraṣ* or *peraṣ* at the Hebrew or Aramaic stage. As for *paraṣ*, the LXX several times renders it by βιάζομαι. A verse from Micah[10]—where the LXX, it is true, has not βιάζομαι—runs: "The breaker is come up before them, they have broken up, and their king shall pass before them and the Lord on the head of them." This, an anonymous Midrash explains,[11] is a description of the way "God will reveal his kingdom." Ἁρπάζω, for the advocates of this interpretation, may correspond to *lakhadh* or *lekhadh*. The verb occurs in the clause "So Saul took the kingdom over Israel,"[12] and the LXX translates it by ἁρπάζω in Amos.[13] But many other verbs are equally suitable: *'aḥaz, 'aḥadh, taphaś* and so on.

4. *Suppression of the Message*

One possibility, however remote, is that the saying is concerned—or at one time was concerned—with suppression, misinterpretation or repudiation of the message of the kingdom. *Kabhash* or *kebhash* is a reasonable Jewish equivalent of βιάζομαι. It is used of a prophet who "does violence to" his message, suppressing it as Jonah tried to do;[14] also of a Rabbi who "does violence to" the *halakha*, misinterpreting or repudiating it. R. Jose (middle of the 2nd cent. A.D.), when a colleague was going to act con-

[8] *Ant.* 20.9.4.214.

[9] Matt 12:29; Mark 3:27.

[10] Micah 2:13.

[11] *P.R.* 161a.

[12] 1 Sam 14:47.

[13] Amos 3:4.

[14] *m. Sanh.* 11:15.

trary to a decision of his in his presence, quoted from the Book of Esther:[15] "Wilt thou force [*kabhash*, βιάζομαι in the LXX] the queen before me in my house?" "The queen" is made to stand for "the law." *Paraq* or *peraq* ought perhaps to be mentioned, because of the phrase "to cast off, tear asunder, the yoke of the kingdom of heaven." Nehunia ben Ha-kanah (about the time of the destruction of the Temple) said that "he who throws off the yoke of the Law, on him shall be laid the yoke of the worldly kingdom and worldly affairs"; and judges who give preferential treatment to the great are described as "throwing off the yoke of heaven and acknowledging a king of flesh and blood."[16]

The suppression of a message may be justified or unjustified. In the case of Jonah it was the latter. When we are warned, "Give not that which is holy unto the dogs,"[17] or not to entrust the secrets of the Law to the young,[18] or when we hear that since the bold ones became numerous the Divine Name was confided only to the discreet in the priesthood and they let it be drowned in the chant of their colleagues[19]—the suppression is from the unworthy and commendable. By contrast, misinterpretation and repudiation of the kingdom are always blameful.

If we proceed from legitimate suppression, the Hebrew or Aramaic behind ἁρπάζω must be a word which, besides "to seize," "snatch," may signify "to hold fast," "withhold": perhaps *taqaph, teqaph* or *ḥasan*. If we proceed from illegitimate suppression, misinterpretation or repudiation, a verb like *ḥaṭaph* deserves consideration. In the Targum, it often represents ἁρπάζω. But it also occurs in Ezekiel's charge:[20] "Her priests have despoiled [Hebrew *ḥameṣu*, violated, LXX ἀθετέω] my law, neither have they showed difference between the unclean and the clean, and have hid their eyes from my sabbaths."

5. *Persecution*

The view that the saying refers to persecution of the Christian sect is supported by many familiar Rabbinic utterances where the oppression of Israel or the pious counts among the signs heralding the end. Several Hebrew and Aramaic verbs—such as *'anas, shadhadh*—denote "to do violence to," "oppress," at the same time as "to seize by force," "rob." (God will not arise, says R. Phinehas ben Hama,[21] till the poor are "oppressed" or "robbed.") It is conceivable, therefore, that the same verb—perhaps in different conjugations, say, *Qal* and *Piel*—underlies βιάζομαι and ἁρπάζω. If so, the original version of the saying would have been somewhat poetic, of a style not uncommon in gnomic literature.[22] The Gospel according to the Nazarenes reads διαρπάζεται instead of βιάζεται, apparently employing the same verb in both halves of the saying.

An apostate may be guilty of persecution of his former brethren as well as misinterpretation and repudiation of the true faith. *Paraṣ* or *peraṣ*, which may have preceded

[15] Esther 7:8; see *t. Ber.* 5:2.
[16] *m. Ab.* 3:5 (our modern problems in a nutshell), *t. Sot.* 14:1.
[17] Matt 7:6.
[18] *Song of Songs Rab.* on 1:2.
[19] *b. Kidd.* 71a.
[20] Ezek 22:26.
[21] *Gen. Rab.* on 32:2, with reference to Ps 12:6.
[22] Prov 11:7; Sir 11:10, 25.

βιάζομαι, is comprehensive enough to express both. In a 3rd-century exposition of the Psalmist's prayer "that there be no breaking in," *pereṣ*,[23] Ahithophel, who took part in Absalom's revolt, is paired off with Jesus, who publicly disgraced[24] the teaching he had received.

Rabbinic terms corresponding to βιασταί would be *'aneshe zero'a* and *ba'ale zero'a*. Phinehas ben Jair, towards the end of the 2nd cent., complained that "when the Temple was destroyed, men of violence and loud tongue prevailed."[25]

6. *Political Hotheads*

The use of ἁρπάζω by John[26] where he speaks of the popular attempt "to seize" Jesus in order to make him king may be invoked by those who interpret the saying as dealing with political impetuosity. Most of the Hebrew and Aramaic verbs already mentioned as equivalents of βιάζομαι and ἁρπάζω would be reconcilable with this theory. The text from Micah quoted—"The breaker is come"—would also suit it. As it contains *paraṣ*, it is from early Tannaitic times brought into connection with the birth of Pharez, who overtook his twin and whom the midwife addressed, "How hast thou broken forth."[27] Actually in the eyes of some Rabbis, it provides evidence that the Messiah will be a descendant of Pharez. One opinion seems to distinguish between (a) a number of people breaking in or through, (b) the king, i.e. the Messiah, and (c) the Lord, i.e. God. The coupling in the saying of *paraṣ*, "to break in, through" with ἁρπάζω would be far from unique. There is a proverb:[28] "A breach attracts the thief." However, we may repeat that the original form of the saying possibly had the same root for βιάζομαι and ἁρπάζω: *'anas, shadhadh, baraḥ, beraḥ*.

7. *Forcing the End*

There is nothing to show whether political impetuosity is approved or deplored. Nor can we decide whether the saying is intended to praise or condemn if it should allude to a forcing of the end—which might indeed overlap with political impetuosity.

In Rabbinic writings it is frequently stressed that God, who knew exactly beforehand when he would deliver the Hebrews from Egypt, also knows the exact date of the final redemption. (The idea is implied in the section of the Passover-eve Haggadah opening: "Blessed is he who keeps his promise to Israel.") He alone knows. It is a mystery beyond the grasp of mortals, asserts R. Nathan (end of the 2nd cent. A.D.), on the basis of a passage from Habakkuk;[29] the same passage which, in the recently discovered ancient Commentary, is taken to mean that, though God revealed to the prophet the things to come about in the last generation, he did not reveal to him "the consummation of time."[30] We

[23] Ps 144:14; *b. Ber.* 17b.

[24] This is how the Rabbis interpret the last word of the verse: "in our streets."

[25] *m. Sot.* 9:15; *b. B. M.* 118a; *b. Sanh.* 58b. Cp. Job 22:8.

[26] John 6:15.

[27] *Gen. Rab.* on 38:29, Jer. Targum.

[28] *b. Sukk.* 26a.

[29] Hab 2:3, *b. Sanh.* 97b.

[30] Dupont-Somer, *op. cit.*, 41.

are told that not even Elijah knows about that moment. In fact it is sinful for a man to calculate the end. Nor may he do anything to hasten it, or, for that matter, to delay it. He must do his duty and wait. "All the times of God arrive in their due seasons," says the Commentary on Habakkuk.[31] The general formulation, "all the times," is deliberate. In the Talmud, too, we meet with the warning that you should refrain from forcing any event, not only the ultimate deliverance.[32] The Sectarian Manual enjoins "not to take a single step outside any of the works of God in their times, not to anticipate their times and not to be late for any of their feasts."[33]

But the opposite attitude is also represented. Indeed we ought not to think of it as strictly separate from that just outlined. The same Rabbi, for example, might on one occasion admonish his public to submit to God's eternal design and on another to move him by repentance and good deeds. In any case we hear of saints and sages who did obtain, or try to obtain, insight into the end; of a shortening or lengthening by God of the period of waiting originally fixed; of the desirability of man's influencing by his action both his individual fate and the fate of the world. Sin may delay redemption, holiness may hasten it—though God may hasten it also freely, from mercy. Again, from a certain moment the people—or some people, like Elijah—are entitled to press forward towards the goal.

As for prayer, some Rabbis favour short prayers, others long ones and others again short or long ones according to the need of the situation. (Eliezer ben Hyrcanus, about A.D. 100, said: "There is a time to abbreviate and a time to prolong."[34]) Here we are interested in the power widely attributed to insistent prayer. You may "conquer" (*naṣaḥ, neṣaḥ*) God by it;[35] it is almost as if you "seized hold" (*taphas, tephas*) of him and did not let him go till your request was granted;[36] "impudence" (*ḥuṣpa'*) prevails against heaven;[37] "the impudent" (*ḥaṣipha'*) conquers the wicked one, how much more the Good One of the World.[38] This last-mentioned adage, incidentally, which is cited by Simeon ben Halaphta (second half of 2nd cent. A.D.), is clearly used in Luke.[39] Still, such remarks about prayer rarely have a specific application to the arrival of the Messiah. They are of a general character, valid at all times. Certainly, a forcing of the end would as a rule involve more than prayer, however earnest and unceasing.

This is not the place to investigate the numerous traces of the notions just sketched throughout the New Testament. Confining ourselves to the saying under discussion, we may point out that, if it refers to a forcing of the end, then, in addition to some of the verbs already listed, two deserve closer attention: *gudh* and *daḥaq* or *deḥaq*.

31 42.

32 *b. Ber.* 64a.

33 Col. 1, Dupont-Somer, 47.

34 *Mek.* on Exod 15:25.

35 *P. de R. K.* 161a.

36 *b. Ber.* 32a.

37 *b. Sanh.* 105a.

38 *P. de R. K.* 161a.

39 Luke 18:6 f. It is debatable whether the fact that these two verses are an adaptation of a proverb speaks for or against Jülicher's thesis that they did not from the outset belong to the main body of the parable, 18:1-5. I am inclined to think that it speaks against him.

The former is rare. It occurs, however, in Jacob's blessing: "Gad, a troop shall overcome, harass, him [πειρατεύω in the LXX] but he shall overcome, harass, their heel," or "at the last." According to the Rabbis,[40] Jacob is thinking of Elijah, a descendant of Gad, "who shall overcome, harass, the end," or "at the end"; and in support they adduce Malachi's assurance,[41] "Behold, I will send Elijah, before the day of the Lord." If, as is not unlikely, *gudh* in this Midrash implies the use of violence, it is plainly of a legitimate kind. From a certain date, Elijah at least is entitled to force.

Daḥaq or *deḥaq* is more important. It is used in the general warning, referred to above, against "pushing one's hour."[42] It recurs in the suggestion by Helbo (middle of the 4th cent.) that "I charge you, O daughters of Jerusalem, that you stir not up my love till he please" is an adjuration by God not to force the end;[43] and further, in Joshua ben Levi's exposition of the verse from Isaiah, "Say to them that are of a fearful heart."[44] Joshua ascribes to *nimhar* the sense "impetuous," "hasty," instead of "fearful."[45] He infers that those who are forcing the end are meant.

What is noteworthy is that this verse introduces the prophecy of the blind who shall see and so on which, in Matthew, is declared fulfilled a few verses before the saying about violence to the kingdom. In other words, the message sent by Jesus to John is the paragraph addressed, according to Joshua, to those who force the end—only that, for Isaiah and Joshua the signs lie in the future whereas Jesus speaks of them as now come about. It is probable, though not certain, that Joshua's intention is to discourage a forcing of the end: he tells the impatient ones that God will indubitably act at the proper time. He lived in the first half of the 3rd cent.; but he often preserves traditions of his teacher Phinehas ben Jair, a Tannaite of Essene leanings. On the other hand, as he had discussions with Jewish converts to Christianity, we must reckon with the possibility of Christian influence.

Perhaps the Old Testament passage most likely to have been in the mind of the author of the saying is that where God, immediately before the revelation at mount Sinai, though allowing Moses to ascend, twice commands that the people may not "break through."[46] The Hebrew has *haras*, Onkelos *peghar* (*Pael*), the Jerusalemite Targum *kun* (*Pael*), and the LXX once ἐγγίζω and once βιάζομαι. The Mekhilta equates *haras* with *daḥaq*, "to force," "to push." It explains that even a single person might by his over-eagerness "impair (*ma'aṭ* in *Piel*) the entire community" or, according to an alternative reading, "prevent," "delay" (*'akhabh* in *Piel*)—it is not said what, but deliverance is the object to be supplied. There are numerous texts in which the *Piel* of *'akhabh* signifies "to delay the exodus, redemption, from Egypt"[47] or "to delay the final

[40] *Gen. Rab.* on 49:19.
[41] Mal 3:23.
[42] *b. Ber.* 64a.
[43] *Song of Songs Rab.* on 2:7.
[44] Isa 34:4; *Lev. Rab.* on 15:25.
[45] In Hab 1:6 it does mean "impetuous" or "hasty."
[46] Exod 19:21, 24.
[47] E.g. *Mek.* on Exod 13:19, in Moses's address to the dead Joseph.

redemption."[48] Possibly *mi'eṭ*, too, means not just "to impair" but "to retard the deliverance for a short time"—on the strength of Haggai's vision,[49] "Yet once, it is a little while [*me'aṭ*], and I will shake the heavens."

Two further points should be observed. First, the Mekhilta dwells on the distinction between different groups with different rights as regards the approach to God: Moses is in a division by himself, the priests form another, less privileged division and the rest of the people a third. Such a precedent may have been of some effect on speculations in New Testament times. Secondly, a "breaking through" or "forcing" in connection with the Sinaitic revelation is obviously unlawful. Yet even if the New Testament saying here discussed is inspired by this section, it would be rash to deduce that it must equally frown on impetuosity. It may well do so. But it is quite conceivable that it intends to establish a contrast with the events at mount Sinai: then a "forcing" had been condemned, now—at the close of history—it is commendable.

8. *"The kingdom is preached" in Luke*

When we go on to Luke, it seems agreed that "the kingdom is preached" is substituted for the more obscure Matthean "it suffereth violence" or "it forceth its way." The word εὐαγγελίζομαι, however, suggests that Luke, or whoever substituted it, found in Q a connection still extant in Matthew: namely, between the saying and the message to the Baptist that the time of glad tidings had arrived. In Matthew, this message comes almost directly before the saying,[50] though in Luke it is placed many chapters previously.[51]

9. *"To press into the kingdom"*

Luke's "to press into the kingdom," εἰς αὐτὴν βιάζεται, if we treat it as translated from the Hebrew or Aramaic, may—though it need not—go back to an original which meant the same as Matthew's "to violate the kingdom" or "to take it by force." Of the Hebrew and Aramaic verbs denoting "to violate" or "to take by force," most (such as *kabhash, kebhash*) can be construed with the prepositions, *be*, *le* or *'al* just as well as with the mere accusative. In other words, εἰς, "into," might be due to an over-literal rendering, perhaps a rendering intentionally over-literal, designed to alter the original meaning.

10. *"Every man presseth into it"*

As has long been realized, the emphasis on "everybody" pressing into the kingdom is consistent with Luke's universalistic tendency. All the same it may derive from a less personal, conventional stock of ideas.

For one thing, the two great qualities of the Law, permanence and attractiveness for all, are eulogized side by side in earlier literature, Philo, for instance.[52] In Luke the

[48] *b. Sanh.* 97b.

[49] Hag 2:6 (7). Cp. on the one hand Heb 12:26, following the LXX, and on the other Akiba's interpretation in *b. Sanh.* 97b.

[50] Εὐαγγελίζομαι occurs at the end of Matt 11:5.

[51] Luke 7:22.

[52] *Mos.* 2.3.14 ff.

sequence is reversed: attractiveness of the kingdom for all and permanence of the Law. But this difference is not very serious.

For another thing, we may read in the Talmud that with the approach of the Messiah "all [gentiles] will become proselytes dragged along," "proselytes attaching themselves by foul means like the Gibeonites when Joshua proved victorious."[53] Eliezer ben Hyrcanus (second half of the 1st cent. A.D.) detects confirmation in Zephaniah:[54] "Then will I turn to the people a pure language, that they may all call upon the Lord." Most Rabbis, to be sure, think little of these last-minute converts and predict that they will desert again before the ultimate consummation.[55] Still, at some moment near the end people will come in flocks to accept Judaism. The term by which they are designated, *gerurim*, is closely analogous to ἑλκόμενοι.[56] But βιαζόμενοι, or even ἁρπαζομενόι, might do as a translation.

B. THE CONTEXT

1. *General*

It is arguable that the Matthean version of the saying reflects an earlier stage than the Lukan. On the other hand, the original context would seem to have left stronger traces in Luke than in Matthew. It is the far greater obscurity of the Lukan sequence of ideas—the bringing together of violence with the retention of the Law, for example, or of the retention of the Law with the exclusion of divorce—which tempts one to assign it priority and, indeed, to seek its roots in an ancient layer of the development crystallized in our documents. If it is a sound rule to prefer the *lectio difficilior*, we ought to apply it also to the *connexio difficilior*.

2. *Inclusiveness and Lastingness*

The first impression is confirmed by closer inspection. We have already noted that the association in Luke between the notion of "every man pressing into the kingdom" and that of "its being easier for heaven and earth to pass away than the law" is not altogether new. Philo writes that the Mosaic institutions will remain "so long as sun and moon and the heaven and universe exist," but that the true marvel is that "they attract all, barbarians, Greeks, the whole inhabited world."

3. *Preaching the Gospel and Violence*

We also suggested that somehow the preaching of the gospel and the exercise of violence must have been coupled in Q. In Matthew, Jesus's message to John that the time of glad tidings has come almost immediately precedes the saying concerning violence to the

[53] Joshua 9.

[54] Zeph 3:9; *b. A. Zar.* 24a.

[55] Maybe we ought to render *b. A. Zar.* 24a not "all [gentiles] will become proselytes attaching themselves by unfair means," but "all [proselytes coming over as late as that] will be proselytes attaching themselves by unfair means," i.e. will belong to the worthless class of bandwagon proselytes.

[56] Cf. Hab 1:15. To the ordinary New Testament instances of ἕλκω should be added οἱ ἕλκοντες ἡμᾶς in the Gospel according to the Hebrews. Unfortunately none of the reconstructions of this paragraph is more than guesswork.

kingdom. In Luke, the message is recorded in a different chapter. But the preaching of the gospel figures in the saying about violence itself. Joshua ben Levi, we may recall, holds that Isaiah's vision of the return to God, the opening of the eyes of the blind and the unstopping of the ears of the deaf is addressed to those who would speed up the end.

4. *The Advent of John and Violence*

There are other points of interest. That the law and prophets contemplated the advent of John, and that his advent is followed by violence, must have been mentioned side by side in Q. Matthew puts the reference to violence first and Luke that to the law and prophets. Moreover, Matthew speaks of "the prophets and law," Luke of "the law and prophets." But these are minor differences. By "the law," incidentally, seems to be meant the prediction in Deuteronomy[57] of a leader the peer of Moses.

The Fourth Gospel[58] apparently looks on Jesus as the prophet predicted in Deuteronomy. It is remarkable that the attempt of the people to crown him by force is recorded immediately after the identification. It looks as if here also there were a connection between the advent of this prophet and violence.

In Acts[59] the passage from Deuteronomy is quoted as applying to Jesus, and we are told that Moses—i.e. the law—and the prophets contemplated these days. There is no allusion to violence. However, as in Matthew and Luke, the period ushered in by the advent of the promised leader is provisional: in Matthew and Luke it lies between John and the future, in Acts between Jesus's death and his return.

5. *The Advent of John and the Law*

In Luke, the reference to John, the preaching of the gospel and violence leads to an emphatic declaration that the Law must stand. This combination is so strange that he must have found it in his source. It is easy to understand why Matthew transferred the declaration to the sermon on the mount, at the head of the re-interpretation of some fundamental Old Testament provisions.[60] Certain vestiges of the old context may still be noticed. In the sermon on the mount, as in Luke, the declaration follows an acknowledgment of "the law and the prophets"—though the exact import of the acknowledgment is different in the two cases. Further, in the sermon on the mount the declaration is followed by a revaluation of the conditions for smallness and greatness in the kingdom (he who breaks a single law will be the smallest, he who observes all the greatest). In Luke, a revaluation—though with a different point—comes just before the acknowledgment of the law and prophets (what enjoys esteem among men is rejected by God); and similarly the Matthean remark on violence is preceded by a revaluation—again with a different point (the least in the kingdom is greater than John). Lastly, Luke deals with an intermediate period, between John and the definitive completion of God's plan. So in the sermon on the mount the Law must stand "till all be fulfilled."

[57] Deut 18:15.
[58] John 6:14 f.
[59] Acts 3:22 ff.
[60] Matt 5:18.

How are we to explain the original combination? It may well be that the identification of John with Elijah, expressly made by Matthew in connection with the saying about violence, played a part from the beginning. More precisely, it may well go back to the common tradition underlying both Matthew and Luke. Now Elijah, according to a Rabbinic view, is the prophet promised in Deuteronomy, "like unto me, unto him ye shall hearken."[61] In any case, we saw that both Matthew and Luke probably regard John as the prophet of Deuteronomy. But this prophet has extraordinary powers. From the clause "unto him ye shall hearken" the Rabbis infer that he must be obeyed even if he orders a transgression of a Scriptural commandment. The Bible relates that Elijah brought a sacrifice on mount Carmel, that is to say, outside the Temple, at an illicit place.[62] According to the doctrine under notice he was entitled to do so, and he will be entitled to act contrary to the Law again when he reappears in the future. Obviously, this is a very early comment. As time went on, and as Pauline Christianity became a factor to be reckoned with, the idea of a prophet having the right to abrogate an established law was more and more disliked by the Jews. In fact, the existence of this comment on the passage from Deuteronomy is surely the principal reason why the latter is so rarely quoted in Rabbinic literature: it was too embarrassing.

We may assume, then, that in the New Testament era the introduction of John as Elijah, or as the prophet promised in Deuteronomy, would evoke the thought of an abolition of the Law, or of part of it. Hence the importance of making it clear that, for the time being at least, the Law must be respected: although Elijah, or the prophet of Deuteronomy, has come and enormous changes are taking place in consequence, yet the Law is still valid.

6. *The Law and Divorce*

What have the permanence of the Law and the rejection of divorce to do with one another? Their association must be pre-Lukan: it is so abrupt.

Three explanations are feasible. First, we may fill in any gaps in the argument by drawing on the sermon on the mount. The result would be as follows: the Law stands and, indeed, ought to be kept in a fuller way than so far; thus, whereas formerly divorce was recognized provided the wife was given a bill, from now it will have no legal effect at all.

No doubt this is the simplest answer, and modern scholars are perhaps rightly satisfied with it.[63] We confess to grave misgivings. Why is nothing said in Luke about a "fulfilment," a greater perfection, of the Law? If the evangelist had reasons for suppressing this aspect, would he not have replaced it by something else to smooth the transition from the statement about the Law to that about divorce? Why, of all the examples of "fulfilment" enumerated in the sermon on the mount, should Luke—or Q—contain just divorce? Is it methodically proper to transfer from the sermon on the mount to Luke an argument of a very peculiar nature?

[61] *Siphre* on Deut 18:15.

[62] 1 Kgs 18:30 ff.

[63] E.g. Creed, *op. cit.*, 206.

Another tenable explanation is this. From long before New Testament times it was expected that Elijah, when returning to proclaim the Messianic age, would concern himself with the purity of the nation. He would make known who were descended from legitimate unions and who from illegitimate ones; and he would restore to the nation families removed by force, *zero'a*,[64] and remove from it families introduced by force.[65] The saying about violence may proceed from this tradition, its meaning being—or having once been—that, paradoxically, since the days of John, i.e. Elijah come back, the influx into Israel of such as use force is greater than ever. Yet (thus the argument may run) the Law will ultimately triumph. Above all, the purity of the nation will not be neglected. Therefore, it is essential to heed the prohibition of adultery, and especially the stricter prohibition imposed on the new sect.

However, this line is too far-fetched to carry conviction. We incline to a different solution.

The sanctity of every jot of the Law and the condemnation of polygamy are intimately linked in the teaching of heterodox Jewish groups of the New Testament epoch, a teaching which, in a modified shape, was adopted by leading Tannaites.

Let us begin with Simeon ben Johai's story (about the middle of the 2nd cent. A.D.) of the Book of Deuteronomy, which went up to heaven to charge Solomon with annulling a *yodh* in the precepts respecting the king. Instead of *l' yrbh* (with vowels *lo' yarbe*), "he shall not multiply wives to himself,"[66] this ruler—the Book of Deuteronomy pleaded—read *l' rbh* (*le' arbe*), "to a multitude of wives for himself." Such a cancellation of a *yodh* in a way amounted to a cancellation of the entire Law. God, however, assured the complainant: "Solomon and a thousand like him will perish, but a word of thee will not perish."[67]

In addition to the obvious points of contact with Luke, there are quite a few which, while less obvious, are equally relevant. As regards formulation, the pronouncement "Solomon and a thousand such" and so on is fairly close to "It is easier for heaven and earth to pass" and so on. It is closer to it than to the Matthean "Till heaven and earth shall pass, one jot or tittle shall in no wise pass from the law." Matthew has a straightforward, temporal clause; he does not compare a higher and a lower degree of durability. Again, though it is the *yodh* which accuses Solomon, several versions represent God as replying that not "a tittle," a *qoṣe*, will be dropped. Matthew mentions both "jot" and "tittle," Luke the latter only—no doubt because his public would be puzzled by the former.

As regards substance, it would be wrong to treat Simeon's story as an isolated, fanciful speculation about Solomon. This Rabbi was a strong opponent of divorce as well as polygamy. He could not, without cutting himself off from orthodox Judaism, declare the institutions illegal. But even in a case where a couple remained childless he was in favour neither of divorce nor of the husband's taking an additional wife.[68] Moreover, he

[64] Above, under A5, we remarked that βιασταί might represent *'aneshe zero'a* or *ba'ale zero'a*.

[65] *m. Eduy.* 8:7; *b. Kidd.* 70a f. From the Mishnah it is evident that by the time of Johanan ben Zaccai, who lived during the destruction of the Temple, this tradition was of long standing.

[66] Deut 17:17.

[67] *y. Sanh.* 20c; *Exod. Rab.* on 6:2.

[68] *Song of Songs Rab.* on 1:4.

accepted the view that the union between husband and wife made them into one being, and he actually contended that this mystery was hinted at in the Deuteronomic regulation of divorce—a very bold method of combating divorce. The opening words of that regulation, he claimed, "When a man taketh a wife," referred to the man's seeking the portion of his body he had lost.[69] It should also be remembered that, while according to other Rabbis none but the children of kings might use rose-oil to anoint a wound on a Sabbath, Simeon permitted it generally, on the ground that "all Israelites are children of kings."[70] The same argument would lead him to consider as generally binding the law that "the king shall not multiply wives to himself."

In the *Zadokite Fragments*, in the section directed against polygamy, and almost certainly against remarriage after divorce,[71] the Scriptural texts adduced are "Male and female created he them," "There went in two and two into the ark" and—"He shall not multiply wives to himself." Moreover, we learn that David did not consult the Book of the Law, hence his transgressions of this prohibition. But the latter is treated as obligatory on any pious person, not only the king—maybe from the consideration, which is propounded in another part of the *Fragments*, that "the king" means "the congregation."[72]

At any rate, it is clear that the rule "He shall not multiply wives to himself" was used in the struggle to ban polygamy and divorce before Simeon ben Johai. The idea that the rule had suffered neglect, and that this neglect in a sense affected the entire Law, also evidently antedates him: David, who was polygamous, is said to have been altogether ignorant of the Law. It would not be surprising if the emphasis on the role of the *yodh* in the field of divorce belonged to the same ancient stratum. Simeon ben Johai's achievement lay in giving the traditional material dramatic expression, in personifying the *yodh*, in representing it as an accuser, and so on.

Luke's statement about divorce implies a condemnation of polygamy; otherwise a second marriage by the husband could never be adultery. In fact it is based on the assumption of husband and wife becoming one indissoluble being. This statement is preceded by the declaration that the universe will cease to exist rather than a particle of the Law. Most probably we have before us a connection similar to that in the *Zadokite Fragments* and Simeon's story—between the sanctity of the precept "He shall not multiply wives to himself," or rather, the *yodh* in it, and the rejection of polygamy and divorce.

May we go even further? The commandment "He shall not multiply wives" is in strictness meant for the king only. Yet the Zadokites, Simeon ben Johai and—if we are right—Q ascribe to it universal validity. As we saw, Simeon thought of all Israelites as children of kings; and the Zadokite reasoning may well have been identical. Possibly, in Q or prior to Q, the reference to the commandment in question was deliberately intro-

[69] Deut 24:1; *b. Kidd.* 2b.

[70] *m. Shab.* 14:4.

[71] *Zadokite Fragments* 7:1 ff.

[72] *Zadokite Fragments* 9:7.

duced after the proclamation of the approaching kingdom—it does not here matter whether the kingdom was represented as victorious or suffering. The new community are all children of a king and must conduct themselves as such.

7. *Conclusion*

To sum up, it must be admitted that, both in Matthew and Luke, the saying concerning violence to the kingdom with the area surrounding it is a *Trümmerfeld*, a heap of ruins; which indicates that there was here matter the Church preferred to omit. Any suggestion as to the original structure is bound to be conjectural. With all due reservation, something like the following line of thought appears likely:

John is Elijah and the prophet promised in Deuteronomy. Miracles are performed (by Jesus), the gospel is being preached, the age foretold in the Scriptures is dawning. The old values are changing; what was great will be small and the small will be great. At this transitional stage, however, much violence is still done to the kingdom. Yet nothing has occurred that would cancel the duty to go on observing the Law, which attracts everybody and will endure longer than this world endures. John, whatever his powers may be, has not abrogated the Law. The faithful will not disregard even the *yodh* in the precept "He shall not multiply wives to himself." It is a precept for royalty, but the true members of the kingdom will cherish it the more on this account. Man and woman by sexual union return to, or re-approach, the ideal androgynous state. A husband remarrying after divorce, or a man marrying a divorced wife, commits adultery.

Terms for Divorce

A. Paul

Let us begin with Paul, whose terminology distinctly reflects the Rabbinic attitude. In his remarks on divorce he uses χωρίζεσθαι and ἀφιέναι. Both are good technical terms. Yet it is clear, on the one hand, that ἀφιέναι is a much better rendering of what a Jewish husband does when he "expels," "dismisses" or "lets go away" his wife, namely, of *gerash*, *shillaḥ* or *hoṣi'* (or, in Aramaic, *tarekh* or *peṭar*); and, on the other hand, that a Jewish wife under Jewish law cannot ἀφιέναι her husband but only "go away" or "separate" from him, *halakh*, *yaṣa'*, *parash* (*nephaq*, *perash*). "To separate," incidentally, may denote the same as "to go away," i.e. actual departure from the common domicile, or merely avoidance of intercourse. Strictly, only the husband can dissolve the marriage. The woman may run away or refuse compliance, which has no legal effect whatever. As Josephus puts it,[1] though she may "separate by her own decision," διαχωρίζεσθαι καθ' αὐτήν, yet she cannot marry another man unless her husband first "concedes" her, ἐφιέναι, or, to go by the less likely reading, "dismisses" her, ἀφιέναι. It is true that given certain conditions—for example, if the husband practises the craft of a coppersmith or tanner, or is afflicted with boils—she may institute proceedings culminating in his being compelled to divorce her. But even then it is the husband who dissolves the bond, though against his will. Of her, it would still be said that she "separates," "goes away" or "is let go away."[2]

Accordingly, in the first two verses,[3] with reference to a marriage where both parties are believers, Paul uses the intransitive χωρίζεσθαι of the wife who "separates," but the transitive ἀφιέναι of the husband who "dismisses" his wife. This is in perfect agreement with the Jewish ideas on the subject. In the next two verses,[4] with reference to a marriage where only one party is a believer, he uses the transitive ἀφιέναι both of the dissolution of the marriage by the husband and of its dissolution by the wife. The latter application of ἀφιέναι is justified since the procedure he has in mind is a non-Jewish one, Roman or Greek. Again, a little further on[5] he uses χωρίζεσθαι of the dissolution of the marriage by an unbelieving partner, husband or wife. No special justification is here needed, the verb being a proper term of divorce. We ought perhaps to add the noun

[1] *Ant.* 15.7.10.259.
[2] E.g. *m. Ned.* 11:12.
[3] 1 Cor 7:10 f.
[4] 1 Cor 7:12 f.
[5] 1 Cor 7:15.

λύσις, "release," a somewhat untechnical word for divorce by the husband—Jewish or gentile—in the admonition:[6] "Art thou bound unto a wife? seek not release."

In confirmation of this analysis it may be pointed out that, in Rabbinic literature, the transitive *gerash*, "to expel," is used once and once only of the wife divorcing her husband, and that it is in a discussion of gentile divorce. The Rabbis observe[7] that in some gentile nations the wife may "expel" her husband. This is a close parallel to the way in which Paul uses ἀφιέναι of the action of the wife under gentile law. To be sure, divorce by mutual agreement—common throughout the Hellenistic world—may be described as "expelling one another" whether the couple is gentile or Jewish.[8] As far as Jewish divorce is concerned, this expression is somewhat loose, seeing that the technical dismissal even here is the doing of the husband alone. But it is easy to understand how the phrase came into existence. Moreover, the earlier Rabbis may well have preferred the more exact "leaving one another," "being left by one another," or "separate from one another":[9] *'azabh* and *parash* (*shabheq* and *perash* in Aramaic), "to leave," are terms no less correct for a Jewish wife's part in divorce than for a husband's.

As regards Paul's "Aryan" followers at Corinth, presumably most of them were either under Roman or Greek law. In the Roman law of the time, that kind of marriage by which the wife came into the *manus* of her husband (that is to say, passed out of her father's family and came under her husband's rule, *filiae loco*) could be dissolved only by the husband; while the other kind, without *manus*, could be dissolved by either party. The latter kind, without *manus*, was no doubt the more frequent by the 1st cent. A.D. As for Greek law, under the old Attic law a husband could divorce his wife, but a wife could dissolve the marriage only with the help of the Archon—a system not unlike the Jewish. She had to produce valid reasons, and the later writers of comedies were fond of this situation.[10] When we consider the Talmudic discussions of the question on what grounds a woman may claim release from marriage—a few of the recognized grounds have been mentioned above—we can well believe that here was material for the comedists. Nevertheless in some Greek states the women from early times seem to have enjoyed the same rights in regard to divorce as the men.[11] At any rate in the Greek law of the papyri, of particular importance in this connection, as a rule either party might dissolve the union.

It is, however, noteworthy that if a husband divorces his wife, the Roman sources regularly speak of *expellere*, *dimittere*, *exigere* and the papyri of ἐκβάλλειν, ἀποπέμπειν and the like, whereas if a wife divorces her husband, they speak of *abire*, *discedere*, ἀπαλλάττεσθαι, ἀποζεύγνυσθαι, ἀπολείπειν, ἐξέρχεσθαι, χωρίζεσθαι, and so on.[12] Diodorus Siculus, about the middle of the 1st cent. B.C., employs ἀπολύειν with refer-

[6] 1 Cor 7:27.

[7] *Gen. Rab.* on 2:24; *y. Kidd.* 58c.

[8] *Gen. Rab.* on 2:24; *y. Kidd.* 58c (gentile divorce); *Gen. Rab.* on 2:21 (Jewish divorce).

[9] *Song of Songs Rab.* on 1:4.

[10] Lipsius, *Das Attische Recht*, vol. 2, pt. 2, 485 ff.

[11] To this extent, Diodorus Siculus 12.18 probably deserves credit.

[12] See, besides the dictionaries, Mitteis and Wilcken, *Grundzüge der Papyruskunde*, vol. 2 (1912), 1, 216 f., and E. Levy, *Der Hergang der römischen Ehescheidung* (1925), 4 ff., 106 ff.

ence to a wife divorcing her husband,[13] but for several centuries he appears to have had little following among non-Jewish writers. Two factors may account for this usage. For one thing, ordinarily, the husband would be the owner of the conjugal residence. Therefore, irrespective of any equality of rights in respect of divorce as such, dissolution of the marriage by him would involve eviction of his wife, while dissolution of the marriage by her would not involve eviction of her husband; it is still she who would have to depart. For another thing, even in the systems under notice, quite likely there was a stage when a wife either had not, or very rarely exercised, the legal power to end the marriage. Language is always conservative. It continued reflecting that stage even when it was a matter of the remote past. It was left to Paul and the Rabbis, who looked at the gentile practice from without, analysing it and comparing it with their own, to call it by its proper name. They saw, and said, that a gentile wife could "expel"—ἀφιέναι, *gerash*—her husband.

It may be added that *gara'* (*mena'*), ἀποστερέω, "to withhold," "to reduce," does not mean a definite refusal of marital companionship, a separation like *parash*, still less a termination of marriage, but rather a grudging of intercourse. An ancient law in Exodus[14] provides that if a man buys another's daughter, lives with her and later takes a second wife, he many not "diminish" the first one's due. Paul no doubt uses the verb in the same sense when he admonishes married couples[15] to fulfil their mutual obligations and not to "defraud" one another.

B. "And if a Woman shall put away her Husband"

Of all the synoptic passages concerning divorce, Mark 10:12 is the only one to contemplate an ending of the companionship by the wife. This in itself would constitute no serious difficulty. Even a Jewish wife could run away from her husband. Actually, in Paul, the warning that she ought not to do so precedes the warning that a husband must not divorce his wife.[16] The problem is that whereas Paul, in the rules referring to Jewish couples, speaks of the wife "departing," "separating," from her husband, Mark 10:12 uses the transitive ἀπολύειν, "to dismiss." This sounds quite un-Rabbinic.

There are two possible solutions: the un-Rabbinic formulation may or may not go back to Mark. It may go back to Mark because, though Jewish law did not allow a woman to divorce her husband, there were circles in which this occurred. Salome, we learn from Josephus,[17] did send her husband a bill of divorce, "dissolving the marriage contrary to the laws of the Jews"; and the verb is ἀπολύεσθαι (middle)—ἀπολυομένη τὸν γάμον—though admittedly "to dissolve the marriage" is not quite so strong as the Markan "to dismiss the husband." Again there was Herodias. Formally, she went less far. She did not, that is, write her husband a bill of divorce but simply "separated"—

[13] Diodorus Siculus 12.18.1.
[14] Exod 21:10.
[15] 1 Cor 7:3 ff.
[16] 1 Cor 7:10 f.
[17] *Ant.* 15.7.10.259.

διαστᾶσα.[18] Yet she married again while he was still alive. Moreover, such criticism as has come down to us seems directed against her marrying her husband's brother rather than against her remarrying as such. It is, of course, possible that the crime of incest was considered so monstrous that little mention was made of other weak points about her second marriage; or again, her first husband may have divorced her when she left him. But it remains a remarkable affair.[19]

It should also be noted that from two papyri of the 5th cent. B.C. it looks as if at Elephantine at least a Jewish wife could legally terminate the union by "disliking and leaving" (*śene' unephaq*) her husband or by a public declaration of "dislike" (*śene'*).[20] The association of the term "dislike" with divorce is old.[21] It has been maintained[22] that these texts refer, not to the wife's divorcing her husband, but to her compelling him to divorce her. But considering that one of them describes dissolution of the marriage by the husband in exactly the same words as its dissolution by the wife—"standing up in the congregation and saying, I dislike my partner"—the probability is that there were regions where the women had gained a stronger position than the Bible or Talmud accords them.

Despite these considerations, there is much to be said for the other alternative, namely, that ἀπολύειν in Mark 10:12 is not genuine. The point is that in Codex Bezae (D), the Koridethianus (Θ) and some *codices* of the Itala there may be found a variant reading, fully compatible with Jewish law and Paul's way of looking at the matter: not "and if a woman shall put away her husband, ἀπολύειν, but "and if a woman shall depart from her husband," ἐξέρχομαι, *exire*, *discedere*. According to Nestle's apparatus, the *codices* of the Itala supporting D and Θ are only few.[23] Strictly speaking this is correct. But in addition to those having *exire* or *discedere*, there are others (MSS. Bob., Colb. and Holm.) giving *relinquere*. From the legal point of view, there is no difference between "departing from the husband" and "leaving him." Either was open to a Jewish wife under Jewish law. It is only *dimittere* which she could not do.

In fact the existence of the *codices* with *relinquere* should preclude any attempt that might be made to declare all the part of the Itala which is consistent with Jewish law as descended from the Greek represented by D, and then to declare D as for some reason or other irrelevant. *Relinquere* presupposes ἀπολείπειν or the like. We must reckon, that is, with at least two Greek forms of the saying possible in a Rabbinic environment: one using ἐξέρχομαι (*exire*, *discedere*) and one using ἀπολείπειν (*relinquere*).

It would not be difficult to explain why, if Mark wrote ἐξέρχομαι or ἀπολείπειν, this was almost completely ousted by ἀπολύειν, and at an early date too. For one thing, the sentence immediately preceding is directed against a husband "dismissing" (ἀπολύειν)

[18] Josephus, *Ant.* 18.5.4.136.

[19] F. C. Burkitt, indeed, in his *The Gospel History and Its Transmission*, 100 f., takes the saying in Mark as directly referring to the action of Herodias.

[20] Cowley, *Aramaic Papyri* (1923), 26 ff., 45 ff.

[21] See the dictionaries and, on the technical meaning of the excuse given by Samson's father-in-law (Judg 15:2: "I thought that thou hadst hated her"), Daube, ["Error and Accident in the Bible"] *RIDA*, 2 (1949), 193 f.

[22] L. M. Epstein, *Jewish Marriage Contract*, 202.

[23] E. Nestle, *Novum Testamentum Graece*, 13th ed. (1923), 113: "*pc* it."

his wife. So indeed are all remaining synoptic passages dealing with the subject.[24] Mark 10:12 may have been assimilated to them; it may have been made to refer, like them, to divorcing one's partner instead of to running away from him. For another thing, in the Graeco Roman world divorce of the husband by his wife was permissible and frequent. We have seen that the practice even spread to certain Jewish groups. Consequently as soon as Mark 10:12 fell into Hellenistic hands, it would be natural to substitute "to dismiss" for "to walk out."

If we regard ἀπολύειν as original, we shall have to assume that D, Θ and the versions of the Itala avoiding *dimittere* got their text from a source—or rather, from sources—in which the saying had been Judaised. This is by no means unthinkable. On the whole, however, the opposite evolution, the Hellenizing of an expression of a Rabbinic character, is more likely.

Brief mention only need be made of two further ways of dealing with Mark 10:12. One is to say that an original "to depart" was replaced by "to dismiss," or an original "to dismiss" by "to depart," through carelessness, and not under the influence of any Rabbinic or Hellenistic ideas. This seems incredible. The other is to attribute the un-Rabbinic "to dismiss" to a mistranslation from a hypothetical Aramaic, which latter did agree with the orthodox Jewish attitude to divorce.[25] But quite apart from the more general objections to such an explanation, it makes the development unnecessarily complicated. The original Aramaic saying would have been based on sound Rabbinic doctrine; then it was mistranslated; finally it was re-Judaised again, in some versions by the introduction of "to depart," in others by that of "to leave." Surely if the saying originally accorded with the Rabbinic view, it is much more plausible to conclude that the *codices* reading or presupposing "to depart" or "to leave" have preserved it intact; and that the substitution of "to dismiss" took place, not in the course of translation, but during its life in Greek.

C. "What therefore God hath joined together, let not Man put asunder"

We have already considered in a previous lecture (under Precept and Example) the import of this saying[26] against the background of Rabbinic speculations concerning an androgynous Adam. Here it is sufficient to recall that the verbs seem to be used each in two senses, a general, untechnical one and a more specific, technical one. More precisely, the primary meaning of the saying is doubtless that brought out by the current translation, with συνζευγνύειν denoting "to join together" and χωρίζειν "to put asunder" in a general way. But it is hardly a mere coincidence that the former verb is reminiscent of ζεύγνυσθαι, "to marry," and the latter of χωρίζεσθαι, "to separate from husband or wife." In other words, the saying is intended to convey a narrower meaning as well: "What therefore God hath married into one, let not man divorce."

[24] Matt 5:32, 19:9; Luke 16:18.

[25] This is the view taken by C. C. Torrey, *The Four Gospels*, 91, 302, *Our Translated Gospels*, 93 ff.

[26] Matt 19:6; Mark 10:9.

Significantly, the Rabbinic *ziwwegh* or *zawwegh*, which goes back to the Greek ζεῦγος, while it may mean "to join together two things" in any way, is often used of God's "joining together husband and wife"[27] and, in the form *'izdawwagh*, means "to marry." A good Rabbinic equivalent of χωρίζειν is *parash* (*perash*), which may signify "to put asunder" or "to separate" (transitive) in a general sense and "to separate" (intransitive) in the sense of "to depart from husband or wife" or "to avoid intercourse." The Greek word, applied in a general sense, occurs in an admonition not so dissimilar to that here discussed, in the *Testament of Zebulon*:[28] "Be not ye, therefore, divided—μὴ οὖν χωρισθῆτε—into two heads, for everything which the Lord made hath but one head." It is true that the particular division against which Zebulun warns his children is not that between husband and wife but political conflict.

Incidentally, the Shekhinah's presence throughout married life is assumed by many Rabbis. Akiba points out[29] that if husband and wife are worthy (or fortunate—the Hebrew may mean either), God is included in their union: the words for "man" and "woman," combined, contain the letters *yodh* and *he*, signifying "Lord." But if they are unworthy (or unfortunate), fire consumes them: without *yodh* and *he*, there remains the word *'esh*, "fire." Akiba held that a husband might divorce his wife even in order to marry another fairer than she.[30] Maybe he thought divorce preferable to burning—and the way Paul expresses his view regarding celibacy and marriage[31] may derive from a Rabbinic argument.

D. LXX, PHILO AND JOSEPHUS

The LXX renders "to divorce a wife" by ἐκβάλλειν where the Hebrew is *gerash*, by ἐξαποστέλλειν or ἀποστέλλειν where it is *shillaḥ*. Perhaps we ought to add ἀφιστάναι and ἀφιέναι, since βίβλιον ἀποστασίου stands for *sepher kerithuth*, "bill of divorce," and ἄφεσις for *shilluḥim*, "dismissal," in the story of Jethro who "took Zipporah, Moses's wife, after his dismissal of her [to lead her back to him]."[32] It is far from certain, however, that the authors of the LXX thought of Moses's action as a divorce.

Be this as it may, it is curious that the Synoptics as well as Paul avoid both ἐκβάλλειν and (ἐξ)αποστέλλειν. The Synoptics keep βίβλιον ἀποστασίου for "bill of divorce"; and they introduce χωρίζειν for "to put asunder" with the connotation of "to divorce." But the two commonest verbs of the LXX are not used even where the Old Testament is quoted.[33] Invariably ἀπολύειν is preferred.[34] It is all the more striking as D and Θ, where they speak of a wife who "departs" from her husband, do use a term ap-

[27] Deut 34:6 in Jer. *Targum*; *Gen. Rab.* on 28:10; *b. Sot.* 2a.

[28] Testament of Zebulon 9:4.

[29] *b. Sot.* 17a. For the departure of the Shekhinah from uncleanness, cp. e.g. *Siphre* on Deut 23:15 (14). The Hebrew for "unclean thing" in this verse is the same as in 24:1, about the ground of divorce.

[30] *m. Gitt.* 9:10.

[31] 1 Cor 7:9.

[32] Exod 18:2.

[33] As in Matt 19:7; Mark 10:4; cp. Deut 24:1.

[34] Matt 1:19 is of course an example of this usage.

plied by the LXX to the wife who is put away, ἐξέρχομαι.[35] As for Paul, he, as we have seen, employs ἀφιέναι and χωρίζεσθαι.

The explanation seems to be this. The LXX renders *gerash*, "to expel," by ἐκβάλλειν. This is a good, literal translation. But it appears that, in general, the Greek verb was used only where the husband proceeded with some vehemence or particular inconsiderateness. (The Hebrew verb was not so restricted.) It is frequent, for example, in the speech against Neaera, the author of which affirms that Neaera was a slave and prostitute, that nevertheless she twice gave her daughter Phano in marriage to Athenian citizens—a serious crime—and that both husbands, on realizing the truth, did what the law demanded, i.e. "expelled," "threw out," Phano.[36] Josephus uses the word in describing that article of the compact between Herodias and her brother-in-law which provided that the latter, on marrying her (incestuously), would "throw out" his present wife, the daughter of King Aretas of Petraea.[37] Obviously, such a term was not suitable for the detached, general discussions of divorce in the New Testament. Neither, however, was (ἐξ)αποστέλλειν. This is a good, literal translation of *shillaḥ*, "to send away." But in ordinary Greek it was not used with reference to divorce. The New Testament writers, then, had to find other verbs. It is a clear case of deliberate rejection of the terminology of the LXX in order to avoid misunderstandings and bring the language up to date.

Philo also has neither ἐκβάλλειν or (ἐξ)αποστέλλειν. He uses ἀπαλλάττεσθαι of the wife who "leaves" her husband—be it because he dismisses her or be it because they have agreed to part company—as also of the wife who, falsely accused by her husband of not having come to him as virgin, may "leave" him whether he wishes her to or not.[38] This liberty of the falsely accused, incidentally, is neither Biblical nor Rabbinic. Philo may have been influenced by ethical considerations, by gentile practice and by the analogous right of a seduced maiden to marry or refuse the ravisher.[39] In the latter case, there is Rabbinic support for his view.[40] Probably παραιτεῖσθαι in one passage[41] means "to divorce a wife"; and another verb to be noted is διαζευγνύειν, occurring in his exposition of the law[42] that a man who has illicit intercourse with a virgin must marry her and can never divorce her—nothing but death "will dissolve [διαζεύξει] the marriage."

His nouns are διάζευξις and ἀπαλλαγή, both referring to divorce effected by the husband.[43]

As we have seen, Josephus once does employ ἐκβάλλειν, where he mentions Herod's intention of "expelling" his wife, the daughter of Aretas.

Of his own first wife, Josephus tells us[44] that "she did not remain long with me but

[35] Exod 21:11; elsewhere in the LXX usually ἀπέρχομαι.

[36] See Lipsius, *op. cit.*, 487 n. 55.

[37] *Ant.* 18.5.1.110.

[38] *De spec. leg.* 1.9.105, 3.5.30, 3.14.82.

[39] *De spec. leg.* 3.11.71.

[40] *b. Ket.* 39b.

[41] *De spec. leg.* 3.11.70.

[42] *De spec. leg.* 3.11.70.

[43] *De spec. leg.* 3.14.80.

[44] *Vita* 75.415.

left," ἀπηλλάγη. It is clear that it was she who wanted and effected the separation; in fact she stayed behind in Palestine when he followed Vespasian to Egypt. Whether he put a formal end to the marriage by giving her a bill of divorce remains uncertain, but no doubt he did.

Elsewhere he speaks of a husband "dismissing" his wife, ἀποπέμπεσθαι (middle), once indeed in recounting his second divorce.[45] His remark that he was "dissatisfied with her behaviour" confirms what might be inferred from his exposition of the rules respecting divorce[46]—that he adhered to the liberal, Hillelite interpretation of the Old Testament reference to divorce "because a man hath found some uncleanness in his wife."[47]

Again, he puts the case of one who wishes to "part from his wife," διαζεύγνυσθαι, and who must "affirm in writing that he will no longer live together with her," γράμμασι περὶ τοῦ μηδέποτε συνελθεῖν ἰσχυρίζεσθαι;[48] and he emphasizes the requirement of a husband's "conceding," "permitting," his wife, ἐφιέναι,[49] for a full, legal divorce.

The latter term is interesting, being a rendering of the Hebrew *hittir*. (He is in this paragraph explaining the Jewish practice to his readers.) The essential words in a bill of divorce were: "Behold, thou art permitted, conceded (*muttereth*), to any man."[50] We find here a clear expression of the idea that the divorcing husband renders possible a remarriage of his wife. In Matthew,[51] where the marriage bond is regarded as indissoluble, this leads to the warning that "whosoever shall put away his wife causeth her to commit adultery."

To return to Josephus, what Herodias did when she left her husband was διαστῆναι (aorist 2 of διαστάναι), "to separate from him."[52] Salome[53] went as far as πέμπειν γραμμάτιον ἀπολυομένη τὸν γάμον, "to send a document, by which she dissolved the marriage," and προαπαγορεύειν την συμβίωσιν, "to renounce the union." Such a measure, Josephus remarks, would be recognized only if taken by the husband. From the point of view of the law, her action was no more than a διαχωρίζεσθαι (passive) καθ' αὑτήν, a "separating by her own decision," a walking out. It is noteworthy that, according to Josephus, when she explained her step to Herod, she used the expression ἀποστῆναι (aorist 2 of ἀφιστάναι), "to part from her husband." Maybe Josephus thought it unlikely that she herself would draw attention to the gross illegality of her procedure. "To part from a husband," being intransitive, does not necessarily imply a dissolution of marriage by a bill of divorce; it may just signify a wife's running away.

[45] *Ant.* 4.8.23.247, 16.7.3.198, *Vita* 76.426.
[46] *Ant.* 4.8.23.253.
[47] Deut 24:1.
[48] *Ant.* 4.8.23.253.
[49] *Ant.* 15.7.10.259.
[50] *m. Gitt.* 9:3.
[51] Matt 5:32.
[52] *Ant.* 18.5.4.136.
[53] *Ant.* 15.7.10.259 f.

Basic Commandments

A. The Credo

The Synoptics tell us[1] how a Pharisee wanted to know from Jesus the fundamental principle of a good life. We shall see (in Four Types of Question) that, in Mark, the question corresponds to one in the Passover Haggadah, put by the *tam*, the man of simple piety, who is interested in *derekh 'ereṣ*, the general rules of decent conduct. In Matthew, the connection with the liturgy of Passover eve is less noticeable, in Luke it is completely absent. Luke has abandoned also another narrowly Jewish feature: whereas in Matthew and Mark the scribe asks which is the greatest commandment, in Luke he asks what to do to inherit eternal life.

Jesus's answer—which Luke puts into the mouth of the questioner—is that two things are essential: the love of God and the love of man. These are coupled as basic requirements already in pre-Christian Judaism. There is pre-Christian evidence.[2] But even without it, the conclusion would be unavoidable, in view of numerous passages from Philo and early 2nd cent. Tannaites.[3]

The first part of Jesus's reply, however, where the love of God is emphasized, creates a problem. In Matthew and Luke, Jesus quotes only the verse "And thou shalt love the Lord," whereas in Mark he quotes also the preceding one: "Hear, o Israel, the Lord is one." Which quotation did Jesus give, or to put it differently, which was attributed to him by the earliest tradition: the shorter or the longer?

At first sight, one might perhaps argue in favour of the shorter. We have just referred to ancient Jewish sources where the duties to love God and to love man are combined. The actual credo, "The Lord is one," occurs in none of them. This appears to support Matthew and Luke, without the credo; and on this basis we should have to assume that Mark added it. In fact, he must have thought the addition highly important, since the scribe, when expressing his agreement with Jesus, comes back to the unity of God.

However, while this view is tenable, we incline to assign priority to the longer quotation. Long before the New Testament period, the section from Deuteronomy beginning "Hear, o Israel" had acquired a central position in Jewish life and worship. Nor was the

[1] Matt 22:34 ff.; Mark 12:28 ff.; Luke 10:25 ff.

[2] Testament of XII Patriarchs, Issachar 5:2, 7:5, Dan 5:3—not to mention Micah 6:8.

[3] Philo, *Sept.* 6.63.282, *Decal.* 22.108 ff., *Siphra* on Lev 19:18. The last-mentioned text records a difference between Akiba and Ben Azzai. Akiba ascribed cardinal importance to "Thou shalt love thy neighbour as thyself." Ben Azzai preferred Gen 5:1, according to which passage every man is akin to God: for Ben Azzai, that is, the love of man rested, or should rest, on the love of God.

opening verse any less prominent than the rest. On the contrary, it was because of this verse that the recital of the whole section was looked upon as an acknowledgment of the one God's rule, as "a taking upon oneself of the kingdom of heaven."[4] Akiba died a martyr's death with the word "one" on his lips—the last word of the opening verse.[5]

Why is it omitted in Matthew and Luke? It probably suffices to inquire why it is omitted in Matthew. For it is hardly to be supposed that the two evangelists cut out the credo each independently of the other. It seems that the Lukan text has suffered assimilation to Matthew in one or two other points. For instance, in its present form, Luke, like Matthew, speaks of the Pharisee "tempting" Jesus. That Luke has been assimilated to Matthew and not Matthew to Luke follows from the consideration that the "tempting" does not really fit Luke's story, where the questioner—in answer to a counter-question—himself provides the correct reply, stressing the love of God and man. It may well have been assimilated in the matter of the credo too.

There is indeed a further possibility, however remote. The credo may have been given up by a stratum of the tradition common to Matthew and Luke. (It need not be what is ordinarily labelled as Q.) But it would make little difference to our discussion; only what we shall say of Matthew would apply, not to Matthew, but to that earlier stratum.

Let us ask, then: why did Matthew dispense with "Hear, o Israel"? Surely not just for the sake of brevity. He did occasionally shorten a narrative or saying. But there must have been a better reason for dropping a verse of such significance. Was it that the Jews found in the verse ammunition against the Christian concept of the nature of God? Considering the early date this is unlikely, and a different solution may be preferable.

In a previous chapter (Precept and Example) we pointed out that Matthew was careful to base religious observances on Old Testament precepts, on imperative pronouncements—of course, we include in this class not only the imperative "do," but also forms like "thou shalt do"—in contradistinction to Old Testament examples. This suggests that his notion, or his opponents' notion, of what constituted a precept was rather technical. The Pharisee requests Jesus to name the greatest "commandment," ἐντολή, *miṣwa* (though, as remarked above, Luke makes him seek the road to eternal life). Presumably Matthew felt that the actual credo, "Hear, o Israel, the Lord is one," did not, in strictness, fall under this category. It might be called "a comprehensive maxim," *kelal*, "an essential part of the Torah," *guph*—but not "a commandment." It was only "Thou shalt love the Lord" that was a precept in the full sense. This verse alone, in the view of Matthew or those he had to convince, ought to figure in a statement concerning the greatest "commandment."

As is well known, the exact division of the Decalogue may well have been controversial as early as in New Testament times; and it is possible that many experts even then considered the verse "I am the Lord, which have brought thee out of the house of bondage" to be one of the ten portions forming the whole.[6] This does not, however, affect our thesis respecting Matthew's notion of "a precept." It should be remembered that the

[4] *m. Ber.* 2:2, 5.

[5] *b. Ber.* 61b.

[6] See the Jer. *Targum*, *Mek.* on Exod 20:16; *b. Makk.* 24a.

Rabbinic term for "Decalogue" is "the Ten Words," *'aśereth haddibberoth*, not "the Ten Commandments." The Old Testament, to be sure, refers to "the covenant which he commanded you to do, the ten words."[7] But this does not mean that the Rabbis of the New Testament era did not distinguish between "words" and "commandments." Again, it is true that, in course of time, even the subtlest Rabbinic teachers classed as "commandments" some utterances showing no imperative form—chief among them "I am the Lord which have brought thee out" and "the Lord is one." But this development is post-Tannaitic.

In the *Letter of Aristeas*,[8] one of the wise men remarks: "God has given us a very great commandment concerning the honouring of one's parents; in the next place he reckons the attitude between friends, speaking of a friend which is as thine own soul." It may not be accidental that the term "commandment" (and, as in the gospels, it is a question of "a very great commandment") is applied only to a precept in the strict sense: "Honour thy father and thy mother." It is not applied to the passage from Deuteronomy[9] which, though it refers to a good friend, does not actually enjoin the honouring of one's friends.

The upshot seems to be that a quotation spontaneously and naïvely used by Jesus was curtailed by Matthew—or someone prior to him—so as to suit meticulous Rabbinic scholarship.

B. A Jewish Prayer

It is relevant to note that, in Matthew, the ending of Jesus's reply is couched in far more erudite terms than it is in either Mark or Luke: "on these two commandments hang all the law and the prophets." *Tala*, "to hang," "to depend on," "to follow from," "to be derivable or intelligible from," is a technical term of Rabbinic exegesis. In the Bible we read that the injunctions enumerated in Leviticus 19—of which "Thou shalt love thy neighbour as thyself" is one—are to be proclaimed by Moses, not just "to the children of Israel," but "to all the congregation of the children of Israel." According to the Tannaites[10] this means they had to be proclaimed in a solemn assembly, the reason being that "the majority of the essentials of the Torah hang on them," i.e. are derivable from them. For Bar Kappara (beginning of the 3rd cent. A.D.), "all essentials of the Torah hang on a tiny section," namely, on a verse from Proverbs:[11] "In all thy ways acknowledge him."

The idea of many conclusions following from one or two premises was applied by the Rabbis also to the way they elaborated their legal system. On the few Biblical laws concerning the Sabbath, they rested a host of detailed regulations: the latter were said (towards the end of the 1st cent. A.D.[12]) to be "like mountains hanging on a hair." In the province of *haggadha*, non-legal exposition, the Tannaites found that often "a great

[7] Deut 4:13.
[8] *Letter of Aristeas* 228.
[9] Deut 13:6. The quotation is from LXX.
[10] *Siphra* on Lev 19:2.
[11] Prov 3:6, see *b. Ber.* 63a.
[12] *m. Hag.* 1:8; *t. Hag.* 1:9; *t. Erub.* 11:23 f.

matter was made by Scripture to hang on a smaller one."[13] That is to say, a great matter might be compared to a smaller one—God's speech to the roar of a lion[14]—in order that it should become intelligible.

However, though by the time of Jesus most Rabbis held that the entire religion was implied in a small number of first principles, or even in a single one (Hillel received into the fold a pagan who recognized only the rule "What is hateful to you, do not do to your fellow"),[15] yet they never ceased to insist on the absolute and independent validity of each particular commandment. That at least certain Christian circles shared this view is obvious from such New Testament passages as "one jot shall in no wise pass from the law." As Christianity—and other sects—gradually concentrated on the principles, to the exclusion of minor regulations, Judaism reacted by various measures, for example, the abrogation of the daily recital of the Decalogue in synagogues.[16]

One development is interesting since it resulted in a prayer—still widely used—which contains a clause very reminiscent of the Matthean ending of Jesus's reply or Bar Kappara's proposition, yet expressive of the opposite approach.

The interdependence of all precepts, their fundamental equality, the importance of even the minor ones, or apparently minor ones, because of their association with the weightiest—these were common themes among the Tannaites. When Ben Azzai (first third of the 2nd cent. A.D.) taught that "you should run to do the lightest duty, for one duty draws another after it, and the reward of a duty is a duty,"[17] he was only summing up, and giving a deeper meaning to, the prevalent doctrine. Nevertheless, in the case of some minor commandments, the Rabbis deemed it either particularly needful or particularly easy to prove their connection with further commandments.

The Bible lays down[18] that a garment ought to be provided with fringes. The Rabbis maintained that whoever observed this commandment was considered by God as if he had observed all; and they pointed out that the numerical value of the letters of *ṣiṣith*, "fringe," was 600, so that, if one added the eight threads and five knots of a correct fringe, one obtained 613—the total number (in their opinion) of Biblical precepts.[19] The Biblical basis for these reflections was, of course, the verse: "It shall be unto you for a fringe, that ye may look upon it and remember all the commandments." This verse does make the fringes into a sign of submission to the entire Torah. Moreover, the Rabbis argued that the word "all," at first sight superfluous (the Bible might have said, "that ye may remember the commandments," without "all"), must be intended to equate the performance of this duty with that of all.

Several prayer-books under the Ashkenazi rite include the following meditation, to be recited on putting on an under-garment or prayer-cloak with the prescribed fringes at its four corners: "May it be thy will, o Lord, that the observance of this commandment

[13] The 14th rule of interpretation of Eliezer ben Jose Ha-gelili.

[14] Amos 3:8.

[15] *b. Shab.* 31a; *Ab. de R. N.* 15.

[16] *b. Ber.* 12a.

[17] *m. Ab.* 4:2.

[18] Num 15:38 ff.; Deut 22:12.

[19] *Siphre* on Num 15:39; *Num. Rab.* on 15:38.

be accounted as though I had fulfilled it in all its details and particulars and intentions, and the 613 commandments that hang on it." The same prayer is said on putting on the phylacteries, and the history is much the same as in the case of the fringes. Among the Biblical portions contained in the phylacteries is:[20] "Hear, o Israel, the Lord is one: and thou shalt love him with all thine heart; and these words which I command thee shall be in thine heart; and thou shalt talk of them when thou sittest, and when thou walkest, and when thou liest down; and thou shalt bind them for a sign upon thine hand." No wonder Eliezer ben Hyrcanus (towards the end of the 1st cent. A.D.) claimed[21] that whoever fulfilled the duty of wearing the phylacteries was considered by God as if he had occupied himself with the Torah day and night.

What is more remarkable is the extension of the prayer to the swinging of the Lulab on the Feast of Tabernacles. True, Abba bar Kahana (of the beginning of the 4th cent. A.D.) emphasized that the precept concerning the Lulab involved many others:[22] he may have thought of the rules that the Lulab must be used together with a citron, that it must be your own, not a borrowed one, and the like. Still, the prayer in question assumes, not that many commandments are involved, but that "the 613 hang on this one." The difference is far from negligible. It is indeed taken into account of in a similar meditation, also recited on the Feast of Tabernacles, on entering the Sukkah, the booth. Here the text runs: "May it be thy will that the observance of this commandment be accounted as though I had fulfilled all the commandments that hang on it." It is not claimed that the entire 613 commandments are implied in that concerning the booth.

The prayer under discussion is not ancient. In fact, it hardly antedates the 16th or 17th century. The idea that the wearing of fringes or phylacteries in a way means the fulfilment of the whole Torah has, we saw, its roots in early Rabbinic theology. The extension of the idea to the swinging of the Lulab no doubt rests on the doctrine that any duty of whatever kind is performed with a view to hallowing the name of the one God and doing his unfathomable will in its entirety. Naturally, this notion is given greater prominence in the case of a duty which looks irrational—like the swinging of the Lulab—than in that of a duty consonant with human reason—say, the giving of charity.[23]

In any case, the prayer uses the language of sayings like those of Jesus (in Matthew) and Bar Kappara, in order to express the opposite, almost a paradox: on a single precept of no obvious importance depend all the others. We have already mentioned that the Christian tendency to recognize first principles only may have contributed to the working out by Judaism of the contrary approach. It remains to add that, in Singer's English *Prayer Book* for Jews,[24] as in numerous others, the clause in question is not to be met with at all. No doubt some authorities find it altogether too sophisticated or one-sided.

[20] Deut 6:4 ff.

[21] *Midrash Psalms* on 1:2.

[22] *Lev. Rab.* on 23:40.

[23] Akiba once said that so long as a man observed one of the great duties—abstention from oppression, honesty and so on—he would be saved; and a somewhat pedantic interpreter added that such a man would count as having observed all great duties (*b. Sanh.* 81a; *Midrash Psalms* on 15:5). But the idea here is not that one duty implies, contains in itself, all the rest.

[24] Pp. 14 f., 218, 232.

Haustafeln

A. Participles of the Correct Practice

There is a post-Biblical form of legislation where the action enjoined, allowed or prohibited is expressed by a participle. The Mishnah[1] lays down that "On the first days of the months—which are half festivals—women may sing dirges for the dead, but they may not wail; after the corpse has been buried, they may not even sing dirges." In the original, the directions are all in the participle: "On the first days of the months, women are singing dirges for the dead but they are not wailing; after the burial, they are not singing dirges." Or quite literally: "On the first days of the months, women singing dirges for the dead but not wailing; after the burial, not singing dirges." Another rule ordains:[2] "The proselyte may bring the first-fruits, but he may not take the Avowal,[3] I profess that I am come unto the country which the Lord sware unto our Fathers for to give us." Literally, this runs: "The proselyte (is) bringing the first-fruits, but (he is) not making the Avowal." Or again:[4] "When the month of Ab comes in—in which the temple was destroyed—one has to reduce gladness." Literally: "When Ab comes in, (they are) reducing gladness."

What are we to make of this form? It occurs not a single time in the Old Testament. Nor, apparently, is it to be found in any of the non-Jewish Semitic systems. Yet in the earlier part of Talmudic literature, in Mishnah, Tosephta and Baraitha, it is more frequent than any other form: a counting might well show four-fifths of the Tannaitic Law, religious or secular, to be given in this form. It is used in permissions, positive precepts, prohibitions. "On the first days of the months, women are singing dirges but they are not wailing"—here we have a permission and a prohibition; "When the month of Ab comes in, they are reducing gladness"—here we have a positive precept. It is used where there is one addressee—"The proselyte is bringing the first-fruits"—and where there are more—"Women are singing dirges"—and in precepts speaking quite generally—"In the month of Ab they, that is to say, everybody, are reducing gladness."

To repeat, this form, to be met with neither in the Old Testament nor in other Semitic systems, dominates the earlier post-Biblical codifications. Here is a nice test for form criticism. If the principles of form criticism are right, these participles must be rooted in a specific experience and need affecting the Jewish people in the first few centuries after the completion of the canon. We submit that this is in fact the case.

[1] *m. M. Kat.* 3:9

[2] *m. Bikk.* 1:4.

[3] Deut 26:3.

[4] *m. Taan.* 4:6.

The distinctive feature of the situation in that period was that, according to Rabbinic doctrine, the age of authoritative revelation was closed and that all further legislation bore the character of interpretation and stabilization of custom. Certainly, there were circles still prepared to acknowledge prophecy: the group responsible for the *Zadokite Fragments,* for example, or the followers of John the Baptist and Jesus, even, apparently, some of the more popular shades of Pharisaism. (In the story of Susannah, Daniel, who advocates a Pharisaic innovation, does so as a messenger of God.[5] It may have been this element rather than minor points which caused the Rabbis to reject the work.) But as for the main stream of Rabbinic Judaism, the position was as just described: direct revelation no longer took place. It is this setting in life which accounts for the form under notice, the participles as a means of injunction, permission or prohibition. More precisely, the form reflects the Rabbinic view of the secondary, derivative, less absolute nature of post-Biblical rules.

To substantiate this explanation, let us examine the form as such, apart from the literary data mentioned. As we said, in this form of legislation the action enjoined, allowed or prohibited is expressed by a participle. The Hebrew participle, as is well known, often stands for our present tense: it is, in fact, the nearest equivalent possible. In particular, however, it stands for our present tense as referring to a habitual event, action or omission. Where the English version has "One generation passeth away and another cometh,"[6] the original has "One generation (is) passing away and another (is) coming."

Now in many languages that mood of the verb which denotes habitual action or omission can also be used, more specifically, to denote a habit that is desirable, required by custom. The English phrase "It is not done" signifies "It is not, by general consent, regarded as desirable, it ought not to be done"; and I might tell my child that "A boy gets up in a bus when a grown-up looks for a seat," meaning, "A boy should get up, is expected to get up." In France, notices like *"On ne fume pas dans cette allée"* are more usual than straightforward prohibitions like "Smoking prohibited"; and even in Germany, where authoritative commands are not entirely unknown, you might find *"Hier wird nicht geraucht."*

It is in this function, as an expression of the course to be taken in accordance with proper interpretation and custom, that the participle became the typically Rabbinic form of legislation. If we want to give it a name, we should call it, not imperatival participle or participial imperative, but rather advisory, didactic participle or perhaps best, participle stating the correct practice. There was a wide gulf between the Bible, the direct word of God, and Rabbinic elaboration and systematization; and the Rabbis, conscious of it, evolved their own form, significantly different from the forceful imperatives and imperfects of the Old Testament. It is the interpreter, the learned student of the holy text, who speaks in a rule like "The proselyte is bringing the first-fruits, but he is not making the Avowal, I profess that I am come unto the country which the Lord has promised unto our Fathers." It is the guardian of custom, the codifier of ritual in every sphere

[5] See the writer's remarks ["Error and Accident in the Bible"] in *RIDA,* 2 (1949), 201.

[6] Eccl 1:4.

of life, who speaks in a rule like "On the first days of the months, women are singing dirges but they are not wailing," or "When the month of Ab comes in, one is reducing gladness."

We shall have to emphasize when we proceed to the discussion of Rabbinic Authority (585 ff.) that the further back we go in Rabbinic history, the freer we find the Rabbis in their decisions. Uniformity came relatively late. In the three centuries preceding the destruction of the Second Temple, different classes, schools and individuals held different views even on important questions. But those warring parties never considered one another as outside Judaism. They all based themselves on the Pentateuch: that made them belong to one religion. The task now was to establish the right meaning of Biblical law and to collect and fix the manifold traditions governing the practice of the people.

In the earlier phase of this process at least, it would have been quite out of place to dictate. A Rabbi would state his decision, or rather opinion, not as on a level with the supreme and absolute revelation of the Bible, not as an unavoidable, fundamental principle, but in this pedestrian, scholarly, didactic participle-form, corresponding to our "One does this or that." Even a regulation like that of the High Priest John Hyrcanus (of the second half of the 2nd cent. B.C.), concerning Tithes, seems to have employed this form—if indeed we may rely on the version preserved in the Gemara.[7] That ruling attempted a solution of the problem of Tithes at once satisfying the scrupulous and not imposing too heavy a burden: "He who buys produce from an *Am-Haaretz*, an Uninstructed, is separating from it the Heave-offering of the first Tithe" and so on. Though a decree of the High Priest, it was a matter, not of divine command, but of working out the correct thing to do.

In a way, the transition from the powerful imperative commandments of the Pentateuch to the participle of the correct practice represents the same development in the field of legislation as does the transition from Psalm to Benediction in the field of liturgy. The Psalm is a form typical of the prophetic age; it is characterized by a bold immediacy of vision. The Benediction, *berakha*, is typical of early Tannaitic piety; it blesses God for qualities and deeds attributed to him in Scripture. The Rabbis, while making use of Biblical Psalms in temple and synagogue, refrained from composing new ones. (Here also, we find exceptions in one or two of the extremer sects.) The form they created and cultivated was the Benediction, more theological and less spontaneous than the Psalm. Just so, in the field of legislation, they preferred the sober, pious participle of the correct practice.

At this point, however, the question arises wherein lies the obligatory element of this form? There is no direct command, "Do" or "You shall do." There is not even any express reference to a requirement such as "It is needful to do so." (Precepts introduced by "It is needful" may occasionally be found in Tannaitic works.[8] In medieval codifications—Maimonides and so on—they are no less frequent than the participles.) The correct practice is simply represented as a fact, "Women are singing dirges but are not

[7] *b. Sot.* 48a.

[8] E.g. *m. Shab.* 2:7.

wailing"; or in English, "It is not done," "A boy gets up." How can a statement of fact impose a duty or grant a privilege?

The answer is that the teacher or lawgiver employing this form addresses an élite among whom the right thing, provided only it is known, is done—or at least is supposed to be done—as a matter of course. There is no need of exhortation or warning. He appeals to the self-respect of his public. In English, "It is not done" more often than not implies "In a decent society like ours, it is not done," and "A boy gets up when an elderly person looks for a seat" means something like "One belonging to that fine class of beings, namely, boys, gets up." These precepts formulated as objective descriptions of customs have a flavour of exclusiveness which other forms, "Do," "You shall do," "It is needful," have not.

I remember a scene in a French park when a man, who thought himself particularly subtle, smoked despite the notice *"On ne fume pas dans cette allée,"* and on being reprimanded by the attendant, replied: *"Mais vous voyez que l'on fume."* The attendant did not know how to counter this argument. In point of fact, however, the smoker, by advancing it, had excluded himself from the civilized public for whom the notice was intended. That public would require no prohibition; it would require only information as to the recognized practice of the place.

This form appeals to the self-respect of a superior group: it must be found suitable, for example, for the constitution of a body like the boy scouts—"A boy scout helps anyone in need." Clearly, it would accord with the attitude of the early Pharisees: they were the *perushim*, "those who kept apart."[9] With some exaggeration, we might paraphrase the provision quoted: "In our exemplary community, as opposed to lesser ones, women are singing dirges but are not wailing, the proselyte is bringing the first-fruits" and so on.

No doubt the form gradually became stereotyped and more and more similar in import to other forms of legislation. The author of the particular precept "Women are singing dirges but are not wailing," for instance, may no longer have had in mind anything else than "Women may sing dirges but they must not wail." Nevertheless it is safe to conclude that, in its "ideal," original application, the participle was designed to guide a superior type of person anxious to follow the right path. On this basis we can also understand why post-Tannaitic authors show far less predilection for the participle: Pharisaism was now the orthodox doctrine, it had ceased to be the affair of an élite among Jewry.

It is demonstrable that several Rabbinic rules which in the course of time became generally accepted at first were not even intended to be binding on the whole people, but represented the convention of a special select group only. An example is furnished precisely by the law respecting Tithes, the regulation of which by John Hyrcanus we have just mentioned. There was the sect of the *Habherim*, the Associates, who undertook to observe the minutiae of Tithes and levitical cleanness. We possess what appears to have been part of their constitution in the time of the Second Temple. One paragraph says:[10]

[9] This is not to say that T. W. Manson must be wrong in asserting ("Sadducee and Pharisee," *BJRULM*, 22 [1938], 12 ff.) that the name originally signified "those holding Persian beliefs."

[10] *m. Dem.* 2:3.

"An Associate is not selling produce to an Uninstructed, and is not visiting an Uninstructed and is not receiving an Uninstructed in his own raiment." Manifestly this code embodied the practice of a select community, not a law universally valid.

In such provisions the participle ought definitely not to be taken in its fully developed legislative sense: "An Associate may not receive an Uninstructed." It is almost used in the ordinary fashion, for making a detached observation, "An Associate does not receive, is not accustomed to receive, an Uninstructed"—except that there is that implicit appeal to pride of which we have spoken. Indeed, we are not yet here very far from the Biblical "A wise man is departing from evil, but the fool is raging":[11] the proper conduct is set down, even set down in a manner leaving no doubt as to the desirability of adopting it, extolled, depicted with all its advantages, but it is not actually enjoined. In tracing the rise of the participle-form in Tannaitic legislation, this background of conventions of special groups must not be overlooked.

Once the setting in life, the original function, of the participle in Rabbinic codifications is appreciated, some curious details become intelligible. On the one hand, in countless Rabbinic provisions, the participle certainly has the value of an imperative or imperfect. "On the first days of the months women are not wailing" does closely approach "They must not wail." It is worth noting that imperative and imperfect, coming down from the Biblical period, live on in Tannaitic law, though occupying a modest place only in comparison with the participle; and that sometimes the participle and one of the older forms are used side by side in the same paragraph of a code—obviously equivalent in that context. To quote such a precept:[12] "The schoolmaster is supervising [participle] the reading of the children on Friday evening, but he himself may not read [imperfect] lest he forget about the commencement of the Sabbath."

On the other hand, there are at least three points showing that the participle never acquired full imperative force in all connections, that it always retained something of its character as an expression of the customary, the agreed, the proper, as distinct from the authoritative, the revealed, the absolute. First, the participle never occurs in a specific demand on a specific occasion. It never stands for an imperative or imperfect of the kind "Leave this room" or "Today is the first of the month of Nissan, so these women should not wail." It is used only in general demands, in rules. We found it in a paragraph laying down that "On the first days of the months, women are not wailing." This is different from "They must stop wailing now."

Secondly, even in rules the participle is never employed where a basic, absolute, unquestionable principle is to be enunciated. The plain prohibition of murder could not be expressed by a participle, just as an English catechism would not say, "One does not murder." In these matters, the authoritative forms alone are adequate. It is when we come to a law such as that one may not kill a man who is about to profane the Sabbath (whereas one may kill one who is about to kill somebody else) that the participle becomes possible.[13] There is something secondary, derivative, debatable about this provision.

[11] Prov 14:16.
[12] *m. Shab.* 1:3.
[13] *m. Sanh.* 8:7.

Thirdly, the participle is avoided where a teacher gives—or is represented as giving—personal advice to his disciples. Quite apart from the influence of Biblical models—mainly in the Wisdom Literature, in Proverbs, Ecclesiastes and so on—the participle, as it refers to the customary, is too impersonal, too cold, for this purpose. A teacher giving personal advice prefers the warmer "Be friendly" to the distant "One is friendly." In the Mishnic tractate Aboth there is not a single participle of the correct practice.

This form of legislation is a result of the change from revelation to interpretation and stabilization of custom, from prophet to scholar and compiler. Its limitations are no less revealing than the fact of its sudden predominance in the earlier Rabbinic codes.

B. HALAKHAH

From early Tannaitic times, the principal term for a binding rule was *halakhah*, literally, "the walking." To be sure, even the Old Testament is rich in expressions like "to walk in the ways of the Lord," "to walk righteously" and so forth. But there is no noun from the verb in this sense; the laws given by God are called "judgments," "statutes," "commandments" or the like.

The Rabbis did not feel entitled to lay down "judgments," "statutes" or "commandments." Leaving out of account the *taqqana* (in Aramaic *taqqanta'*), the "putting straight," "amendment," "reform in an emergency," their main task was a subordinate one: to interpret, elaborate, protect by a "fence" and order the traditional material—chiefly material contained in the Pentateuch, but also usages that had grown up without any such basis. In other words, they had carefully to work out the proper course to take in any set of circumstances, the *halakhah*, the walking expected of a man who desired to do the right thing. It is easy to see that this is exactly the milieu, the setting in life, which we postulated for the participles of the correct practice. They are the form of legislation corresponding to the notion of *halakhah*.

It is only natural that now and then attempts were made to put the *halakhah* on the same level as the laws of the Pentateuch. That does not alter its essential character—certainly not for the ancient Tannaitic period. Moreover it should be noted that the limitations of the participle-form which we outlined above apply also to the notion of *halakhah*, and apply to it up to this day. First, a *halakhah* invariably denotes a general rule, never an isolated order. A Rabbi might inform me that the *halakhah* is to recite the Eighteen Benedictions at a certain hour: but if, when the time comes, he tells me to recite them, this is not a *halakhah*. Secondly, a basic, absolute principle like the duty to honour father and mother or the prohibition of murder is never described as a *halakhah*. Indeed the term is rarely used of any law belonging to the written Torah. The commonest Rabbinic word to denote a written law is *miṣwa*, "commandment," from *ṣiwwa*, "to command." *Halakhah* signifies something less fundamental; not the directly revealed law but the correct practice. The gentiles, while bound by the seven Noachian "commandments," are not bound by any *halakhah*. Thirdly, *halakhah* is different from personal advice. It is objective, meant for all members of the community.

There are quite a few terms related to *halakhah*. One playing a prominent part in New Testament times is *derekh* (*'oraḥ*), "way." To some extent it overlaps with the other:

a *halakhah* indicates the proper *derekh* to go, or at least part of it. But there is this difference, that a *halakhah*, "the correct walking," refers to a conscious human action. *Derekh*, "the proper way," refers to an external phenomenon, something that exists irrespective of human action; it has a wider range.

In consequence *halakhah* became the term for a rule prescribing what a Jew should or should not do, a rule stating the correct walking under the Law. *Derekh* might signify not only the proper way for men but also the proper way of things: the natural growth of a tree, for instance, or the ordinary symptoms of life and death, the "Two Ways." With regard to men, it is not only the good ones who have their typical way, but also the bad ones. Again, while the proper way of a Jew would certainly imply observance of all the *halakhoth*, all the rules concerned with the Law, it would include much more than that—pure sentiments, good manners, prudent behaviour and so on. It might indeed vary according to rank and education. The way of a *talmidh ḥakham*, a scholar, must be different from that of a plain citizen. Of the two tractates on *derekh 'ereṣ*, "the manner of the land," "the conduct of a normal, cultured person," one (Derekh Eretz Zuta) is more specially composed for the use of scholars. Actually, in some respects, each person has his own, individual way, and similarly each thing. Gentiles, though not at all bound by the *halakhah*, might yet follow a proper way, i.e. live a decent, civilized life.[14] No doubt it is partly owing to the strongly universal and ethical character of *derekh* that, in the tractates on *derekh 'ereṣ* just mentioned, the dry, precise participles of the correct practice are far outnumbered by other forms of guidance.

A term of some interest is *serekh*, "a clinging to something," "imitation," "habit," "rule." In the *Zadokite Fragments* it signifies "the regulation" binding on the sect.[15] The secondary, derivative character, however, is far less pronounced than in the case of *halakhah*. True, like the Rabbis, the "lawgiver" (*meḥoqeq*) of the sect only "expounded" (*darash*) the existing Torah; he did not introduce a novel one as Moses had done. Nevertheless he was looked upon as a prophet, as a messenger of God, in a way in which the Rabbis were not. In the eyes of the Zadokites, that is, the era of revelation was not over. Hence the forms of legislation to be found in the *Fragments* in the main follow the Biblical pattern: "And on the Sabbath day, no man shall utter (imperfect) a word of folly or vanity"[16] and so on.

Another factor probably contributed to this result. The provisions enunciated by the "lawgiver" seem to have been conceived of in much the same fashion as the Sadducees conceived of theirs, *scil.* as mere restatements of the written law: hence the phrases *serekh hattora*, "the regulation of the Torah," and *serekh ha'areṣ 'asher miqqedhem*, "the regulation of the land that prevailed of old."[17] There were, in principle, nei-

[14] For some further observations on the notion of *derekh* see the writer's article ["Negligence in the Early Talmudic Law of Contract (*Peši'ah*)"] in, *Festschrift Schulz*, vol. 1 (1951), 140 ff. [See *Talmudic Law*, 324 ff.]

[15] *Zadokite Fragments* 9:1, 11:1, 15:1, 4, 16:1, 17:1; cp. also *Aramaic and Greek Fragments of an Original Source of the Test. of Levi and Jub.*, vv. 29 f.

[16] *Zadokite Fragments* 13:2.

[17] The latter phrase seems to refer in particular to the Biblical rules (e.g. Num 1:1 ff.) concerning the way the people should camp or, having reached Palestine, arrange their settlements. Among the Rabbis, too, we meet with the doctrine that the Pentateuchic regulation of this matter applies also to Jerusalem (*b. Zeb.*

ther elaborations nor inferences nor additions nor changes. This may well have favoured the retention of the old imperative style. In theory at least, the ordinances laid down by the "lawgiver" were nothing but clearer repetitions of the Biblical ones.

Here may be the place to insert a remark—a very conjectural one—on the *sepher hahaghu* which occurs three times in the *Zadokite Fragments.*[18] Charles hesitatingly suggests that the words are corrupt and that the original may have spoken of a work circulating under Haggai's name, *sepher ḥaggay*. But perhaps we ought to translate the phrase as it stands: "the Book of the Study," "the Book of Meditation." *Haghu* might be an Aramaic noun derived from *hagha'*, as *galu* and *galutha'*, "exile," derive from *gela'*, *zenu* and *zenutha'*, "unchastity," from *zena'*, *ḥezu* and *ḥazutha'*, "vision," from *ḥaza'*, etc. The verb *hagha'*—or in Hebrew *hagha*—means "to recite" or "to meditate."

In the history of Pharisaism it plays an important role. "Meditating on Scripture," for the Pharisees, became largely identical with "deducing further laws from the written ones"; and, in coining the terms "written Torah" and "Torah by mouth," they probably had in mind a passage from Joshua:[19] "This book of the Torah shall not depart out of thy mouth, but thou shalt meditate [*hagha*] therein day and night, that thou mayest do according to all that is written therein." One of Job's friends mentions "the sound [*heghe*] that goeth out of God's mouth."[20] R. Judah b. Elai, a pupil of Akiba, explained[21] that *heghe* must mean Torah in the sense of rulings, *halakhoth*, made known by God in the heavenly court.

The sect responsible for the *Zadokite Fragments* had a different attitude: the duty of their leaders was not to elaborate the written Torah, but on the contrary to preserve it absolutely intact. But "meditating" on Scripture was no less necessary for this task than for that undertaken by the Pharisees. It is noteworthy that every time the *sepher hahaghu* is mentioned, the reference is to "those who have insight into it" or "are able to interpret it." Actually a sentiment of the kind to be found in the first Psalm, "Blessed is the man whose delight is in the Torah of the Lord and who meditates [*hagha*] in his Torah day and night," might well have been the slogan of this sect who called themselves "the House of the Torah."

It might perhaps be objected that the Aramaic form *haghu* is not consistent with the fairly (though not completely) pure Hebrew of the *Zadokite Fragments.* But the term may have been technical and therefore been taken over by the author without change. This would also account for the Hebrew article, *hahaghu*, "the *haghu*," "the Meditation," which does not really fit an Aramaic form of noun. The word, being technical and familiar, was treated as Hebrew.

116b): "As was the camp in the wilderness, so should be the camp in Jerusalem; from Jerusalem to the mountain of the House should be the camp of the Israelites, from the mountain of the House to the gate of Nicanor should be the camp of the Levites, and from thenceforward should be the camp of the Divine Presence." Cp. also Heb 13:11.

[18] *Zadokite Fragments* 11:2, 15:5, 17:5.

[19] Josh 1:8. See the writer's article ["Rabbinic Methods of Interpretation and Hellenistic Rhetoric"] in *HUCA*, 22 (1949), 258 f. [See *Talmudic Law,* 350 f.]

[20] Job 37:2.

[21] *Gen. Rab.* on 18:7.

Serekh recurs in the recently discovered *Sectarian Manual of Discipline,*[22] and here once more Biblical, imperative forms of legislation predominate: prophetic revelation was still possible. It is not accidental that, in the same circle, the form of the Psalm also continued to flourish. The hymns of this sect that have come to light are of great beauty. The Rabbis no longer ventured to compose fresh Psalms, and their legislative form was the participle.

However, the participle of the correct practice too appears in the *Sectarian Manual.* All I have seen so far of the document is a reproduction, smaller than the original, of column 1;[23] but luckily, the second half contains a few instances. The reception of converts, we are told, is to be accompanied by the following ceremonies:[24] "And the priests are narrating the exploits of God and are proclaiming his grace for Israel, and the Levites are narrating the iniquities of the children of Israel, and those who enter into the Covenant are confessing after them, We have been perverse, we have rebelled."

Five points are worth mention. In the first place, the participles are used in a section which cannot possibly have been considered as going back to the Bible, a section dealing with the initiation of persons prepared to obey the *serekh hayyaḥadh,* "the regulation of the community."[25] Even if this "regulation" itself was thought of as representing the true Biblical law, the initiation of those desiring to return to it was clearly on a different level, a less fundamental, newer custom, no part of the old revelation. As in Rabbinic codes, that is, the participle expresses the secondary character of a rule.

In the second place, the participles of the *Sectarian Manual* are still descriptive rather than fully legislative. They sound like an account of the ritual given by an enthusiastic spectator rather than injunctions in the strict sense. The author takes it for granted that the addressees will act upon his rules without being expressly told to do so.

In the third place, we evidently have before us the constitution of a very select body—comparable to the Associates referred to above. It is the conventions of a holy band which are formulated by means of the participle.

In the fourth place, just as in the Rabbinic codes, the participle-form alternates with other forms coming down from the Bible. In fact, as we have just seen, the Biblical forms are the rule in the *Manual,* while the participle is the exception. Thus the very first duty of priests and Levites on the occasion of a reception of converts is[26] that "they shall be [imperfect] blessing the God of salvations."

In the last place, there is preserved a Tannaitic summary of the procedure to be adopted for proselyte baptism.[27] The participle-form is used throughout, and its legislative quality is rather more in evidence than in the *Sectarian Manual.* None the less the two cases are essentially parallel. In the *Manual* we read "And the priests are narrating the exploits of God and the Levites are narrating the iniquities of Israel and those who enter are confessing after them"; similarly among the Rabbinic rules we find "And

[22] *Sectarian Manual,* col. 11.16.

[23] In Dupont-Sommer, *The Dead Sea Scrolls,* transl. by E. M. Rowley (1952), 45.

[24] *Sectarian Manual,* ll. 21 ff.

[25] *Sectarian Manual,* l. 16.

[26] *Sectarian Manual,* ll. 18 f.

[27] *b. Yeb.* 47a f.

two Scholars are standing by him and are telling him some of the lighter commandments and some of the weightier commandments."

C. Haustafeln

To turn to the New Testament, it has long been seen that in various epistles the unattached participle sometimes stands for an admonition. "Abhorring that which is evil, in honour preferring one another," says Paul,[28] meaning by it, "Christians should abhor the evil, should honour one another." "The servants subjecting themselves to their masters," says 1 Peter,[29] meaning by it, "Christian servants should subject themselves."

Moulton attempted to prove that this usage was common in the vernacular Greek of the time, but his evidence, taken from closing formulas of letters, is quite unconvincing. Not the remotest trace of the usage is discernible in any of the Hellenistic Haustafeln, such as *Epictetus* 2.10.

The most probable explanation of these strange participles in the epistles is that they are literally taken over from the Hebrew. "Abhorring that which is evil, in honour preferring one another, the servants subjecting themselves to their masters"—all this would be perfectly regular in Rabbinic teaching. It may be recalled—as we have already pointed out—that the auxiliary verb "to be" is always omitted in Hebrew in this connection. The Hebrew, that is, would always be "Abhorring the evil," not "They are abhorring," and "The servants subjecting themselves," not "The servants are subjecting themselves." What strikes us as atrocious in the Greek was excellent in the underlying source.

In other respects also the participles are used exactly as they are used in Tannaitic codes. They appear, not in basic injunctions like the prohibition of murder, but in directions as to the proper behaviour of members of the new Christian society; they appeal to the pride of those addressed—"that ye walk worthy of the vocation wherewith ye are called;"[30] they are meant for a small group only, for the elect; and they occur side by side with other forms of exhortation, such as imperatives and infinitives. Everything points to the existence of early Christian codes of duties in Hebrew, from which the participles of the correct practice crept into the Greek of the epistles. Freedom in the spirit did not relieve the Church of the necessity of insisting on a definite moral order.

Once this is recognized, various difficulties disappear. A minor one, concerning a point from Romans, we shall have occasion to speak about when we discuss Missionary Maxims (565 ff.). Here we may mention two of some importance. First, the unattached participles are to be met with only in certain epistles of the New Testament, and even there only in a single context, in the so-called Haustafeln, dealing with the conduct of Christians in their families, their communities and the state. If the form had been a genuine Hellenistic, vernacular development, why should its usage be restricted in this way? The view here advocated, however, gives a sufficient answer. The passages in

[28] Rom 12:9 f.

[29] 1 Pet 2:18.

[30] Eph 4:1.

question come from the Hebrew, and, in Rabbinic Hebrew, the participle was the normal form for such rules.

Again, it is the Haustafeln which 1 Peter is widely supposed to have borrowed from Paul. This would be curious in itself, and there is an additional problem, namely, that 1 Peter, with a Greek generally far better than Paul's, at least twice has the unattached participle where Paul has not.[31] It is now possible to assume that 1 Peter did not borrow from Paul, but that both of them drew on those Hebrew codes of the primitive Christian community. Incidentally, if this is right, one of the arguments against the authenticity of 1 Peter, its alleged Pauline character, loses much of its force.

We have still to ask what was the nature of the code or codes of which the writers of the New Testament epistles availed themselves. Several years ago I suggested that "when we combine Demai [the constitution of the Associates in which their special obligations respecting Tithes and cleanness are laid down by means of the participle], Aboth [a collection of sayings concerning the right mode of living, where, however, the participle does not occur but only the more intimate forms of personal advice and the traditional forms of the Wisdom Literature] and Derekh Eretz [systems of social duties where the participle is occasionally used but, in the main, preference is given to the same forms as in Aboth], we may be able to form some idea of what the codes behind Romans and so on looked like. It should be borne in mind that, if those codes said nothing of ritual obligations and barriers, in this respect more like the gentler Aboth and Derekh Eretz than Demai, the idea of chosenness, not being and acting like the others, must none the less have played a prominent part in them."[32] The *Sectarian Manual of Discipline*—if, as is likely, it dates from the period between the second century B.C. and the second century A.D.—comes fairly near the picture I tried to draw. Whether a little earlier or later than the epistles in question, it shows the kind of thing possible at that time in Judaism and, consequently, in primitive Christianity. It is a constitution like that of the Associates and definitely meant for a separatist group. But far greater emphasis than in Demai is laid on the social duties of the members towards one another, on missionary aims and on eschatological hope. And the participles of the correct practice are there.

D. A Passage from the Didache

Professor C. Moule most kindly draws my attention to chapter 5 of the Didache[33] which I ought to have considered when, in a note appended to Dr. E. G. Selwyn's commentary on 1 Peter, I investigated the unattached participles of the New Testament: "But the Way of Death is this—it is evil, murders, adulteries, persecutors [διῶκται, noun denoting persons] of the good, hating [μισοῦντες, participle denoting persons] truth, loving [ἀγαπῶντες, participle denoting persons] lies" and so on.

Maybe the whole part from "murders" should be construed as elliptic, exclamatory descriptions of what is to be seen on the Way of Death. On this basis, the nouns and

[31] (1) 1 Pet 3:1 against Eph 5:22 and Col 3:18; (2) 1 Pet 2:18 against Eph 6:5 and Col 1:22.

[32] "Participle and Imperative in 1 Peter," ed. E. G. Selwyn (1946), 487.

[33] Equals Ep. of Barnabas 20.

participles denoting persons, though far from elegant, are not very extraordinary; and the structure is parallel, say, to the opening of Derekh Eretz Zuta, a guide for the use of Scholars: "The ways of Scholars are—meek and humble in spirit, oppressed, beloved by every man, fearing sin" and so on.[34]

It is equally possible, however, that the section from "persecutors" stands in the same line of descent as the participles of the correct practice. To be sure, there is here no trace of an admonitory meaning: on the contrary, this is a list of doings to be avoided. But we may have before us the kind of observation frequent in the Wisdom Literature and such tractates as Mishnah Aboth, i.e. that observation which, since it refers to a habit, easily assumes an admonitory meaning where the habit concerned is a desirable one. Above we quoted from Proverbs: "A wise man (is) departing from evil, but a fool (is) raging." As the ending shows, we cannot here substitute "he should act thus" for "he is acting thus." But it is clear that, in a different context, the first half—"A wise man is departing from evil"—might come to signify "he should depart." The same is true of *Aboth* 5:7: "There are seven marks of the clod and seven of the wise man; the wise man (is) not speaking before one greater in wisdom, and (is) not breaking in upon the speech of his fellow . . . and the opposites of these are the marks of the clod." In an appropriate context, an observation like "A wise man is not speaking before one greater in wisdom" would mean "he should not speak." The passage from the Didache, then, may be explained as going back to a Hebrew source which said: "(They are) persecuting the good, (they are) hating truth, (they are) loving lies."

It is worth noting that the section discussed is reminiscent of, if not dependent on, a verse in Romans,[35] where we find the unattached participle in an admonitory sense: "Abhorring—one should abhor—that which is evil, cleaving—one should cleave—to that which is good." The enumeration of vices in the Didache includes: "Not cleaving to that which is good, being watchful not for that which is good but for that which is evil."

The actual injunctions of the Didache, incidentally, are all given in the warmer, direct address, and several times to "my child," e.g. 3:1 and 5:2: "My child, flee from all that is evil," or "May ye be preserved, children, from all these (vices)."

[34] Cp. Hippocrates, Decorum 3.
[35] Rom 12:9.

Public Retort and Private Explanation

We have already remarked that the way in which Mark describes the controversy about divorce represents a specific Rabbinic form—public retort and private explanation. Let us now consider this form, which is attested in Jewish sources from the 1st cent. A.D. onwards. One of our results will be that it may be advisable to adopt a somewhat more conservative estimate of certain pericopes of the gospels than is prevalent among the leading modern authorities.

To start from the Rabbinic side, a pagan asked R. Johanan ben Zaccai (middle and second half of the 1st cent.) whether it was not sheer sorcery to purify a person who had been in contact with a corpse by means of water containing the ashes of a red heifer.[1] The Rabbi, by his reply, induced his questioner to conclude that the "water of separation" had the same efficacy as those roots which pagans were accustomed to burn in order to cast out an evil spirit that had entered into a man. After the pagan had left, however, the disciples remarked: "Rabbi, him you pushed away with a fragile reed; what will you answer us?" Whereupon the real solution was propounded: neither—Johanan ben Zaccai said—was uncleanness caused by a corpse nor cleanness by the "water of separation," but the statute of the red heifer was one of those which had to be accepted as the will of God though no rational basis could be discerned.

The episode may be divided into four parts: (1) the question put by an opponent; (2) the public retort, mysterious if not misleading, sufficient to silence the questioner but not stating the truth in plain language—actually, in this case, the pagan is led to think that the Rabbi believes in the virtue of magic; (3) when the opponent has gone, a demand by the followers for proper elucidation; and (4) the private explanation, the real answer clearly expressed—in this case, a rejection of any magic and an interpretation of rites apparently magical as expressing submission to God's command.

In determining the setting in life of this form, we must pay particular attention to two points. In the first place, the form reflects a severe division, and indeed enmity, between the outside world, to be "pushed away with a fragile reed," not deserving full enlightenment, and the elect, who are to be entrusted with it. In the second place, it is the outsiders who are attacking and the elect who are on the defensive: part (1), the hostile question, proceeds from the former.

It is worth observing that, from the 3rd cent., quite a few controversies between the Rabbis and Minim, i.e. Jews converted to Christianity, are clothed in this form by Talmud and Midrash. For example, R. Simlai (middle of the 3rd cent.), we are told,[2] was

[1] *Num. Rab.* on 19:2; *P. de R. K.* 40a f.

[2] *Gen. Rab.* on 1:26; *y. Ber.* 12d f.

asked by the Minim how he accounted for the plural in the verse from Genesis: "Let us make man in our image." He replied that this was rectified by the singular in the verse immediately following: "So God created man in his image." The Minim having left, the disciples desired fuller information. Then the Rabbi explained that, by using the plural, God meant to indicate that while he alone would make Adam of earth and Eve of one of Adam's ribs, any further procreation would have to take place through husband, wife and the Divine Presence together. (Note that this interpretation, like the Christian interpretation to which it is opposed, sees in the plural a reference to three persons; only it is not the three persons of the Trinity.)

Once again, we find (1) a question by an outsider, (2) a retort good enough for him but not revealing the deeper truth, (3) the request of the disciples, and (4) the full explanation in private.

A close New Testament parallel to the anecdote of Johanan ben Zaccai is furnished by the discussion concerning the washing of hands preserved in Matthew and Mark.[3] (1) The Pharisees ask Jesus why his disciples omit to wash their hands before meals, thus defiling the food. The subject, that is, is opened by the outsiders putting a hostile question. (2) Jesus, after some general reflections on the behaviour of his opponents, declares: "There is nothing from without a man that entering into him can defile him, but the things which come out of him, those are they that defile a man." This is a correct statement of his position, but it is deliberately obscure. In fact, to the public at large, the uninitiated, it must sound like an allusion to some strange piece of magic. (3) At home, the disciples ask to have the saying explained. (4) The explanation is given them. No relevance, Jesus tells them, attaches to food, which enters and leaves a man without affecting his heart; it is only his vicious leanings which can defile him. In other words, the notion of mechanical defilement is rejected, a person is clean or unclean according to his moral attitude.

Professor Dodd regards parts (3) and (4) as later accretions.[4] Even if they were, whoever added them might have followed the Rabbinic model. We have just pointed out that the form is fairly frequent in Jewish sources where controversies dating from the first few centuries A.D. are recorded.

But Dodd's criticism is hardly convincing. The pericope in question is so similar to the story about Johanan ben Zaccai which we have quoted—similar in structure, setting and substance—that it is difficult to doubt its essential unity. In all probability, parts (1) and (2) never stood by themselves, the four parts formed one whole from the outset—that is to say, from the moment that the incident was recounted in any literary form at all. This does not, of course, mean that none of the details now to be met with in this pericope may be secondary.

The Markan description of the dispute concerning divorce is another illustration of the same form. There are four parts: (1) The Pharisees, in whose opinion divorce is permissible, begin the dispute by putting a hostile question. (2) Jesus gives them a mysterious reply, alluding to the creation of the androgynous Adam ("male and female") and

[3] Matt 15:1 ff.; Mark 7:1 ff.

[4] *The Parables of the Kingdom* (1935), 61, n. 1.

to marriage as the re-union of two halves that once belonged together ("they twain shall be one flesh"). The public may or may not guess at the myth referred to; certain it is that they are not supposed to grasp its full implications. (3) At home, the disciples ask for further information. (4) They receive a clear answer: there can be no valid divorce and, indeed, it is adultery even for a man to remarry after dismissing his first wife—such is the strength of a union making of husband and wife one composite being.

We may note that, as far as this pericope is concerned, Professor Dodd does not seem to claim a growth in two stages; and, in fact, it is clear that we have to do with a single whole. But if the unity of the entire pericope is granted in this case, there is no reason for denying it in the case of the dispute about the true nature of defilement. From the point of view of form, the two cases are exactly the same.

A minor feature may be mentioned. Part (2), the reply in public, falls itself into two sections. In (2a), Jesus puts a counter-question: "What did Moses command you?" This leads to an answer by which his antagonists become vulnerable: "Moses suffered to write a bill of divorcement and put her away." He only "suffered" it (ἐπέτρεψεν), it was a concession. We need not decide why the Pharisees admit this. Either they proceed from the view—often expressed in the Talmud[5]—that divorce is morally undesirable. Or (less probably) they assume that divorce is in principle illegal and sanctioned only for the Israelites.[6] Or (more probably) they construe the law in Deuteronomy[7] not, as, say, Josephus,[8] "When a man's wife find no favour, then let him write her a bill of divorcement" etc., but: "When a man's wife find no favour and he write a bill of divorcement and she go and be another man's wife and the latter write her a bill of divorcement, then her former husband may not take her again." That is to say, divorce is merely tolerated as an established custom, but no express approval is given. The main thing is that the Pharisees do speak of divorce as a concession. In (2b), Jesus uses their answer as the starting-point for his retort: "For the hardness of your heart he wrote you this precept, but from the beginning" etc.

Very possibly, in the controversy about defilement also, (2a) at one time consisted of counter-question and inadequate answer. Matthew still has a counter-question:[9] "Why do ye also transgress the tradition of the elders?"

At any rate, when we go into the Rabbinic examples of the form public retort—private explanation, we find quite a few where part (2) is composed in this peculiar mode.

To take, for instance, the story about Johanan ben Zaccai, part (1) gives the question of the heathen, who looks on the use of the "water of separation" as mere witchcraft. In part (2a), Johanan ben Zaccai puts a counter-question: "What does one do for a man possessed by an evil spirit?" And the heathen is forced to say: "One burns roots" etc. This makes it possible for the Rabbi, in part (2b), to declare that the "water of separation" has the same effect as those roots.

[5] How Simeon ben Johai (about A.D. 150) prevented a divorce is told in *Song of Songs Rab.* on 1:4.

[6] From the 3rd cent. A.D. onwards this opinion occasionally appears; see *y. Kidd.* 58c.

[7] Deut 24:1 ff.

[8] *Ant.* 4.8.23.253.

[9] Matt 15:3.

The same subdivision of part (2) occurs in an episode recorded of R. Joshua ben Karha, of the middle of the 2nd cent. A.D.[10] (1) A gentile asked him why the Jews did not join the more numerous pagans, seeing that, according to Rabbinic doctrine itself, decisions about religious observances were to be made by the majority. (2a) The Rabbi put a counter-question: "What about your children?" And the heathen had to admit that each of them worshipped a different god from the other. (2b) It was now easy to tell him that, before attempting to get the Jews to join him, he ought to bring about unity in his own family. (3) After the gentile had left, the disciples asked for elucidation. (4) So R. Joshua pointed out to them that whereas the Bible used the plural "souls" of Esau's small family, it used the singular "soul" of Jacob's large one[11]—an indication that paganism, with its many conflicting deities, was not to be considered a united majority as compared with Israel, serving the one God.

Again, Hadrian is said[12] to have remarked to Joshua ben Hananiah (who was very old when Hadrian became emperor, but they seem to have met) that whereas in each of the first five of the Ten Commandments—according to the Jewish numbering—the name of God was mentioned, in order to threaten any transgressor with punishment,[13] it was never mentioned in the second half; since the second half alone applied also to the gentiles (no murder, adultery, theft, false witness, coveting), they had an advantage, they were not threatened with punishment. This is part (1), the attack. The Rabbi took Hadrian for a walk through the city, and images of the emperor were everywhere except in lavatories. Joshua asked why none were to be found there; to which no reply was possible but that it would be no honour for the ruler to be linked with such places. This is part (2a), the counter-question compelling the attacker to lay himself open to refutation. Now Joshua declared that it would be no honour for God to have his name linked with the crimes listed in the second half of the Decalogue, murder etc. This is part (2b), the retort. It sufficed to discomfit the attacker, though it was only on his level, implying some crude notions both as regards the unclean character of lavatories and as regards the avoidance of any reference to God in connection with certain matters. At home, however, his disciples wanted from the Rabbi the real reason why the name of God appeared only in the first five commandments: part (3). So he explained that it was because the Law was first offered to the gentiles, but they refused it. Israel alone accepted it. Thus the responsibility Israel undertook beyond the universal obligations occurring in the second half meant a distinction, it brought Israel closer to God. This is part (4), the true solution on a high level.

What renders this case particularly interesting is that W. Bacher, some seventy years ago, suggested that parts (3) and (4) might be additions[14]—a remarkable anticipation of Dodd's attitude. Bacher, however, did not generalize. He had a special reason

[10] *Lev. Rab.* on 4:1 f.

[11] Gen 36:6; Exod 1:5.

[12] *Pesiqta Rabbathi* 21.

[13] Such is the Rabbinic interpretation of "I am the Lord thy God," "I the Lord thy God am a jealous God," "for the Lord will not hold him guiltless," "it is the sabbath day of the Lord thy God," "the land which the Lord thy God giveth thee."

[14] *Die Agada der Tannaiten*, vol. 1 (1844), 180, n. 2.

for considering just this one anecdote as expanded: the idea that the Torah was first offered to the gentiles, he noted, recurred independently of this story in other sources.

But surely, the more plausible conclusion is that Joshua made use of a popular idea to account for a feature of the Decalogue. That it was a popular idea prior to Joshua is practically certain,[15] and we know that other Rabbis used it to explain other Scriptural passages.[16] Even, however, if Joshua was the first to conceive the idea, he might have done so in tackling a particular problem of the Decalogue, and it might subsequently have gained currency in its own right.

Be this as it may, the Talmudic parallels strongly support the thesis here advocated. Obviously, the controversy about divorce as depicted in Mark shows a highly elaborate form, a form made up of four parts, of which the second again contains two sections. Such a structure cannot be the work of several hands; we cannot explain it by assuming an original, brief report, supplemented by haphazard additions. The unity of the pericope is in fact beyond question.

In Matthew's treatment of the controversy, the form is no longer intact. We have already observed that, in his account, part (2), the reply to the Pharisees, is no longer veiled but quite open. It includes, that is, the explanation—"Whosoever shall put away his wife" and so on—which, in Mark, comes in part (4), where the disciples alone are addressed. All further changes are largely the result of this fundamental one.

It may suffice to deal with the most significant of them. In the first place, the private talk between Jesus and his disciples which follows the public discussion must now be about a subject other than divorce. On divorce, everything has been said in public. If the disciples are to receive a special teaching in private, it must concern a different question—according to Matthew, it is the question of marriage as such.

In the second place, the disciples open the private talk, not by a straightforward question, but by a comment—though possibly a comment in an inquiring tone: "If this is so, it is not good to marry." As the question of divorce has been completely cleared up in public, they cannot, as in Mark, "ask him again of the same matter." What they do is to widen the theme, to proceed to the problem of marriage as such. That at one time this problem also may have been considered in relation to the myth of the androgynous being, we have already seen; but Matthew hardly any longer recognizes the connection.

In the third place, in Matthew, whereas the Pharisees are given a clear answer, it is the disciples to whom Jesus speaks in riddles: "For there are some eunuchs. . . . He that is able to receive it, let him receive it." This is a similitude, presented as if the addressees were "those outside," who are not meant easily to understand. Evidently, we have moved far away from the original form. Matthew still has four parts, but they are of a very different kind from the original ones and, above all, no longer constitute a purposeful, coherent structure. Instead of (1) question by enemies, (2) retort, (3) question by disciples, (4) explanation, Matthew gives (1) question by enemies, (2) explanation, (3) comment by disciples, (4) retort.

[15] For numerous references see Strack-Billerbeck, vol. 3, 38 ff. Add, e.g., 4 Ezra 7:72.

[16] E.g. *Tanhuma* on Exod 6:2.

Lastly, as for the subdivision of part (2)—we found that in Mark, as in several Rabbinic stories of this type, (2a) consists of a counter-question, answered in a way that makes possible (2b), the actual retort. As Matthew includes in part (2) the full explanation which, according to Mark, is entrusted only to the disciples, he is forced to alter the retort ("male and female" etc.); then he gives, in the shape of a further question on the part of the Pharisees, what, in Mark, appears as their answer to Jesus's counter-question ("why then did Moses command to write a bill of divorcement?"); and it is Jesus's reply to this further question which he makes to culminate in the full explanation, part (4) in Mark ("whosoever shall put away his wife" etc.).

One or two smaller modifications are to be accounted for in the same way: for example, in Matthew, the Pharisees do not refer to Moses "suffering" divorce, but Jesus, in his final reply, introduces the notion of divorce having been a concession. Enough has been said to show that Matthew is secondary, and that his treatment of the material represents a disintegration of the form we are discussing.

It remains to add three reservations. First, even in those pericopes of the gospels where the Rabbinic form is preserved best—i.e. in the Matthean and Markan sections about defilement and the Markan one about divorce—there is one little detail in which the New Testament diverges from its model. In the Rabbinic stories, the opponent in part (1) visits the Rabbi to question him, and the disciples in part (3) put their request for further information after the opponent has left. In the gospels, Jesus in part (1) is thought of as being in a public place where it is easy to approach him, and the disciples in part (3) put their request after he and they have reached home. The Rabbi, that is, throughout sits with his disciples in the house of study; Jesus, as the scene opens, is among the people and only later withdraws. Apparently, some slight adaptation of the Rabbinic form was unavoidable if it was to fit the altered setting, i.e. the conditions of Jesus's ministry as opposed to those of the typical Rabbi's profession. The difference is small but highly revealing.

That we are not overrating it may be seen from a Midrash designed to illustrate the meticulous justice of God.[17] When Moses wished to hear God, he had to go to the tabernacle; whereas in the case of Samuel, God visited him.[18] Why this discrimination? Because—the Rabbis explain—"Moses sat to judge the people,"[19] i.e. he made them come before him; whereas "Samuel went in circuit to Bethel and Gilgal and Mizpeh and judged Israel in all those places."[20] So God made Moses come before him, while he sought out Samuel. Evidently, people in Talmudic times were only too conscious of the difference between a great man who lets himself be approached and a great man who makes an effort to meet you. This consciousness is reflected in the deviation of the Matthean and Markan form from its Rabbinic model.

Secondly, we do not deny the existence, in New Testament times, of simpler forms, such as (1) aggressive question, (2) retort, without a subsequent conversation with an inner circle, i.e. without (3) request by the inner circle for elucidation and (4) the high-

[17] *Exod. Rab.* on 12:21.

[18] 1 Sam 3:10.

[19] Exod 18:13.

[20] 1 Sam 7:16.

er truth; or (1) aggressive question, (2a) counter-question and reply which renders the refutation easy, (2b) the refutation—again without parts (3) and (4). Indeed, we shall say something about the latter type in the next chapter. The point, however, is that there was also a more elaborate form which included (3) and (4), and which should not be criticized away.

Thirdly, we have tried to demonstrate the unity of the discussion respecting defilement as depicted by Matthew and Mark, and of the discussion respecting divorce as depicted by the latter: the Rabbinic parallels militate decisively against the view that parts (3) and (4) are accretions. Our conclusion, however, does not apply to the parables of the Sower and the Tares.[21] Here Dodd is doubtless right in regarding the private interpretation of the public utterance as a later addition.[22]

It is, indeed, probable that the early theologian responsible for these additions was familiar with the form public retort—private explanation. For one thing, he arranges the private talk in exactly the same manner: first a request of the disciples for explanation, then the explanation. For another, the whole which he produces, i.e. the parable together with the private talk appended to it, involves the same division as the original form between the outside world, destined to grope in the dark, and the elect, alone worthy of enlightenment.

Actually, he makes Jesus dwell on this division in the harshest terms: the outside world, Jesus says, is spoken to in riddles "in order that they may see and not perceive, and hear and not understand."[23] There is no justification for mitigating this statement by declaring ἵνα due to a mistranslation from the Aramaic, as is done, for example, by T. W. Manson.[24] From the beginning, the form in question is anything but universalistic. The author who used it when he supplied the parables of the Sower and the Tares with interpretations may have over-emphasized the exclusion of "those without" from knowledge and salvation; but, essentially, the idea had always been implicit in the form.

Nevertheless, that these parables, unlike the pericopes about defilement and divorce or the Rabbinic episodes adduced, did not from the outset show this form is clear from a number of points. Above all, the form public retort—private explanation, we saw, consists of four parts: (1) hostile question by outsiders, (2) retort, (3) question by disciples, (4) explanation. But in the parables mentioned part (1) is not to be found. Jesus addresses the public not in reply to a question, by way of defence, but unasked, spontaneously. Furthermore, when we pass from the form of teaching to its substance, we notice a great change. In the pericopes concerning the washing of hands and divorce, as in the Rabbinic stories, the point is invariably the misunderstanding by the outsiders, and the true understanding by the master and his circle, of Scripture or the Law. In those concerning the Sower and the Tares, it is not Scripture or the Law, but the nature of the new community, the kingdom, insight into which is withheld from the public at large but vouchsafed to the disciples.

[21] Matt 13:1 ff.; Mark 4:1 ff.

[22] *Op. cit.*, 13, 180 ff.

[23] Mark 4:12.

[24] *The Teaching of Jesus* (1931), 76 ff.

These differences alone would be enough to suggest that we have not before us, in these two parables, a genuine application of the form under notice. The proof, however, is completed by a definite incongruity in the present structure. Jesus begins by addressing the people spontaneously, on the theme of the kingdom; in other words, he calls them. Then comes the private talk, according to which he did not call them but, on the contrary, addressed them in order to reject them for ever. Evidently, this confirms Dodd's proposition that the private talk is the work of a later hand.

We are, of course, concerned solely with the literary growth of these chapters; the ultimate authorship of the interpretations—i.e. whether in some form or other they go back to Jesus—is a different question, not here to be decided.

Socratic Interrogation

In the last chapter we discussed the form public retort—private explanation. It has four essential parts: (1) hostile question by an outsider, (2) reply sufficient to defeat him, (3) request by the inner circle for the true reply and (4) the true reply. We saw, however, that in the New Testament as well as in Rabbinic writings part (2) is occasionally subdivided. It may consist, that is, of (2a), a counter-question by answering which the enemy becomes vulnerable, and (2b), the triumphant conclusion from the enemy's answer. We also mentioned that, besides this intricate form, there is, as one would expect, a simpler one which, though it contains (1) the attack, (2a) the counter-question compelling the inadequate answer, and (2b) the refutation, lacks parts (3) and (4), the subsequent conversation with an inner circle. We propose to make some comments on this simpler form; and we shall call the question by the enemy part (1), the counter-question part (2), the answer which the enemy is forced to make part (3), and the refutation which thereby becomes possible part (4).

First, for the Rabbis. Tineius Rufus, who was governor of Judaea when Bar Kokhba's revolt broke out in A.D. 132, mockingly asked R. Akiba what might be the difference between the seventh day and the others—part (1). Akiba put the counter-question what might be the difference between Rufus and other men—part (2). Rufus answered that his master, the Emperor, wanted the distinction—part (3). Just so, Akiba rejoined, his master, God, wanted the distinction with regard to the Sabbath—part (4).[1]

Now for the New Testament. All three Synoptics use this form in the report about the controversy between Jesus and the authorities regarding his credentials.[2] If we discount certain elaborations, the main scheme is as follows: (1) Whence do you derive your authority? Hostile question. (2) Whence was the baptism of John? Counter-question. (3) We do not know, an admission that they dare not challenge the claims of the Baptist. This answer enables Jesus to proceed to (4), the rejoinder: Neither shall I tell you. His opponents are refuted, the implication being that his authority is no less valid than the Baptist's claims.

In some commentaries[3] it is considered remarkable that no emphasis is laid on the officials making themselves ridiculous by pleading ignorance as to the nature of John's baptism. It is, however, remarkable only as long as the form of the story is not appreciated. Part (3), the enemy's answer, is merely a means to an end, and it is a means to a particular end: part (4), the repulse of the attack and the successful establishing of one's

[1] *b. Sanh.* 65b.

[2] Matt 21:23 ff.; Mark 11:27 ff.; Luke 20:1 ff.

[3] E.g. E. Klostermann, *Das Markusevangelium*, 4th ed. (1950), 120.

own proposition—in this case, that Jesus's authority is more securely founded than his opponents thought when they started questioning him.

Two more examples may be found in Luke. One is a narrative about Jesus healing a sick man on the Sabbath.[4] Jesus's antagonists watch whether he will heal him despite its being a Sabbath—a hostile question, though not an open one: part (1). Jesus asks whether one may do good or evil on the Sabbath: part (2). His adversaries keep silence (though this is merely implied in the description of Jesus as "looking round about upon them all"), since they cannot reject his premise: part (3). Jesus—by performing the cure—points out the result, namely, that one should heal: part (4). The other instance is the scene where Jesus is anointed by a sinful woman.[5] His host objects, though again not openly: part (1). Jesus puts a counter-question, part (2): which of two debtors would love his creditor more, he who had a large debt remitted or he who had a small one remitted? Simon answers that it would be the former: part (3). Thereupon Jesus draws the conclusion, culminating in the words "Her sins, which are many, are forgiven, for she loved much": part (4).

The pattern accords with a Greek rhetorical rule. Aristotle writes:[6] "You may employ interrogation of your opponent when one point is self-evident, as following from another which he will grant you on being questioned. Yet, when you have obtained your first premise by asking him to admit it, you must not put what is self-evident in the form of a further question, but simply state the conclusion yourself."

In the cases just adduced, Akiba interrogates Rufus as to a point which the latter will grant—his rank being willed by the Emperor—and Jesus employs the same method—his opponents must admit that John's baptism cannot be dismissed as worthless, that one may do good but no evil on a Sabbath, that a debtor let off a large sum will love his creditor best. Further, from the narrator's point of view at least, the next, principal point is obvious once the first is settled: the seventh day, set apart by God, deserves no less respect than a Roman governor, Jesus's authority cannot be impugned if John's baptism is not, seeing that one may do only good on a Sabbath one ought to heal, a great sinner will be particularly faithful if accepted in mercy.

What is highly significant is that, in accordance with Aristotle's rule, no second question is put in any of the cases. Akiba does not ask Rufus whether the seventh day, set apart by God, is of less account than a governor appointed by the Emperor; he just states the conclusion. Jesus's procedure is analogous.

The chief reason for the advice that, when your premise is obtained, you should not ask concerning the result but yourself declare it is, of course, that your opponent might prove obstinate: he might refuse to see that the conclusion follows. Indeed, Aristotle warns the person interrogated to be on his guard from the outset, i.e. even when replying to the first question which apparently admits only of one answer:[7] "You must meet ambiguous questions by drawing a distinction, and not too concisely; questions likely

[4] Luke 6:6 ff.
[5] Luke 7:36 ff.
[6] *Rhet.* 3.18.2.
[7] *Rhet.* 3.18.5.

to make you contradict yourself you should solve immediately, before the interrogator has time to ask the next one or draw the conclusion, for it is not difficult to notice the drift of his argument." Rufus, instead of referring to his master's decree, ought at once to have exclaimed that an imaginary God was not comparable to a powerful Emperor, the Pharisees ought at once to have asserted that, though one should do good on a Sabbath, healing—except where a man's life was in danger—was prohibited for special reasons, and so on.

There is abundant evidence that the rhetoricians of the 1st cent. A.D. had not forgotten about the pattern. It may suffice to quote from Quintilian:[8] "The method of argument chiefly used by Socrates was this: when he had asked about a number of things to which his adversary could only agree, he finally drew the principal conclusion, as analogous to the points already conceded." Like Aristotle, Quintilian enjoins the greatest caution in answering these "Socratic," paradigmatic questions.[9]

In general, Socrates cultivated this interrogation for the purpose, not of meeting an attack, but of working out a thesis. In other words, his scheme would not be (1) question by an ill-wisher, (2) counter-question, (3) answer and (4) the refutation made possible by the answer; but part (1) would normally be absent. He would start interrogating a person—part (2); that person would give an answer by which he became vulnerable—part (3); and Socrates would draw the inference—part (4). The inference might indeed take the form of a new interrogation, a new part (2), bringing about a new part (3), and so on. Quintilian primarily thinks of this dialectic, philosophical scheme, despite a reference to its usefulness for the examination of witnesses in court. He recommends not a dramatic single question but "the asking about a number of things," and the examples he cites confirm the impression:[10] "What is the finest fruit? The best. The finest horse? The best. Who, then, is the finest type of man?" or again, "If the woman next door has finer ornaments than yours, which do you prefer? Hers. If she has a more valuable dress? Hers. What if she has a better husband?"

This is not to deny that, in a sense, even here there is part (1), namely, the popular misconception which the philosopher sets out to put right. But it remains latent, unexpressed. Formally, part (1) is lacking. The setting in life of philosophical interrogation is spontaneous inquiry, it is study not provoked by aggression.

Aristotle, on the other hand, has in mind what we may term the forensic variety of the pattern. He seems to speak of the putting of one or two decisive questions only. Above all, part (1) is definitely present. The setting in life of the forensic pattern involves attack. You are attacked, part (1); you put a well-chosen question, part (2); you receive the desired answer, part (3); and from it you deduce the point that squashes the attack, part (4).

It is noteworthy that though Aristotle also connects the form with Socrates, the example he cites is from Socrates's defence.[11] Meletus accuses Socrates of not believing

[8] *I.O.* 5.11.3.

[9] *I.O.* 5.11.27.

[10] *I.O.* 5.11.4, 5.11.27 f.; cp. Cicero, *De. Inv.* 1.31.51.

[11] Cp. Plato, *Apology* 15.27A ff.

in gods—part (1). Socrates asks whether he, Socrates, never mentioned "something divine"—part (2). Meletus admits he did mention it—part (3). Socrates asks again whether divine beings must not be children of gods—another counter-question, another part (2). Meletus admits they must—another part (3). Now Socrates states the conclusion that nobody could believe in children of gods without believing in gods—part (4).

Whether, in ancient Greece, the philosophical variety of the form preceded the forensic or the forensic preceded the philosophical, we need not here decide. What matters is that, in all probability, the Rabbis adopted the forensic variety from Hellenistic rhetoric. (Interestingly enough, they made little use of the philosophical variety.) It might perhaps be objected that the form is so natural that we need assume no borrowing. But, in the first place, it was precisely because Hellenistic rhetoric was "natural," i.e. useful and sound, that it achieved its tremendous popularity. In the second place, it is plain that in the last few centuries B.C., the Rabbis drew on Hellenistic rhetoric in many fields.[12] In the third place, the form is not so natural that it would be successfully handled by anybody and anywhere—it does not occur in the Old Testament—or that it would be the only possible form in any given case.

The last-mentioned point is easily illustrated. The section in John which, in some ways, corresponds to the Synoptic report about the nature of Jesus's authority,[13] is quite dissimilar in form: (1) demand of the Jews for a sign, (2) offer by Jesus of an apparently impossible miracle (were the Temple destroyed, he could rebuild it in three days), (3) expression of disbelief on the part of the Jews, (4) narrator's explanation that the offer had not the meaning it appeared to have and that the miracle was performed (Jesus alluded to his body).

Luke's narrative about healing to which we have drawn attention is closely parallel to a Markan one.[14] But the latter does not comply with the form under notice to the same extent. We do not get (1) watching by the enemies, (2) question, (3) silence admitting the premise, (4) conclusion; but (1) watching by the enemies, (2) question, (3) silence (Mark indeed states in so many words that the Pharisees kept silent), (3a) Jesus "grieving for the hardness of their hearts," (4) conclusion. The conclusion does not follow the silence as the victorious termination of the dispute. It is separated from it by the remark about Jesus's sorrow and thus appears as a more independent action. Mark may have expanded his source, or Luke may have made the narrative suit a stricter pattern. In either case Mark proves that the form in question is not inevitable.

As for the remaining stories about healing on a Sabbath, they are given in entirely different forms. In Matthew,[15] the Pharisees also begin the dispute and Jesus also counters by a paradigmatic question—whether they would not rescue one of their sheep out of a pit on the Sabbath. But then he simply proceeds to explain his meaning by an inference *a minori ad maius*—"how much then is a man better than a sheep"—draws the

[12] See my studies on "Rabbinic Methods of Interpretation and Hellenistic Rhetoric," in *HUCA*, 22 (1949), 239 ff., and "Alexandrian Methods of Interpretation and the Rabbis," in *Festschrift Hans Lewald* (1953), 27 ff. [*Talmudic Law* 333 ff.]

[13] John 2:18 ff.

[14] Mark 3:1 ff.

[15] Matt 12:9 ff.

conclusion and cures the sick man. After their opening of the argument, the Pharisees take no more active part, as they do, by their silence, in the narratives investigated above. Their opening, that is, leads to a *halakhic* lecture by Jesus, which is crowned by the action, the cure; it does not lead to that dramatic interrogation convicting the opponent. Again, in Luke 13,[16] a form is employed which we shall go into below: revolutionary action—protest—silencing of the remonstrants. Jesus performs the cure before he asks the question justifying his conduct—whether one does not lead one's cattle to the watering place on a Sabbath. In Luke 14,[17] the controversy is opened by Jesus himself asking whether one may heal on a Sabbath. He receives no answer, performs the cure and then puts the question to be found in Matthew—whether any of his antagonists would hesitate to save one of his animals that had fallen into a pit on a Sabbath.

To go on to the anointing of Jesus by a woman, none of the versions we meet with in Matthew, Mark and John[18] shows Luke's form, (1) criticism, (2) counter-question, (3) answer, (4) refutation of the criticism by using the answer. In all of them, the form is (1) criticism, (2) explanation.

Manifestly, Socratic interrogation, however natural a form, is not so common as to render unlikely the Hellenistic descent of its applications in Rabbinic and New Testament writings.

It remains to guard against a misunderstanding. In contending that this form comes from Hellenistic rhetoric, we do not claim that a New Testament narrative told in it goes back to a Hellenistic rather than a Jewish milieu. In that period, much of Hellenistic rhetoric was the common property of the civilized Mediterranean world. Its effects are hardly less noticeable in Rabbinic literature than in Greek or Roman. As regards the particular form here in question, we have given a good, Rabbinic example at the beginning of this chapter; and we may repeat that, in a previous chapter, we found this form embedded within a more complicated one, for instance, in a story about Johanan ben Zaccai, who lived at the time of the destruction of the Temple, and in a very similar one about Jesus—both stories dealing with the concept of defilement.

To be sure, the fact that Luke offers more instances of the form than the other evangelists is conceivably due to his stronger Greek contacts: he was perhaps more inclined to give traditional material this shape. But the material may well be Jewish even in these cases. Certainly, it would be quite wrong to doubt the Jewish background of the controversy between Jesus and the officials about his authority, a controversy appearing in all Synoptics. There is every reason to suppose not only that it is in the main historical, but also that it had its present form from the start.

[16] Luke 13:10 ff.

[17] Luke 14:1 ff.

[18] Matt 26:6 ff.; Mark 14:3 ff.; John 12:1 ff.

The Last Beatitude

At first sight a consideration of form might lead to the conclusion that the last beatitude in Matthew and Luke[1] did not originally belong to the same series as the preceding ones, but was added to them by Q. It is strikingly different—broadly speaking, longer and more comprehensive. Moreover, in Matthew, all the preceding beatitudes are of the type "Blessed are the poor," "Blessed are the mourners," and the last only is of the type "Blessed are ye when men shall revile you." In Luke, it is true, the direct address is employed from the beginning.

It is very doubtful, however, whether the argument outlined would be tenable. If the last beatitude is inconsistent, from the formal point of view, with the preceding ones, why did Q add it? It might perhaps be replied that Q did not see the inconsistency. But, then, why should the original author have done so?

In fact, it appears that, in declaring the last beatitude inconsistent—formally—with the preceding ones, we should be prejudiced by a rather narrow, modern definition of sound form and paying too little attention to ancient views. For at the bottom of the argument lies the requirement that, in a series, each member must be of more or less the same length as the other. It is clear, however, that a series with the last member extended is frequent in ancient literature, and may well have struck writers at the period of the New Testament as a pleasant and effective pattern.

It recurs even in modern literature, especially in nursery rhymes. The black sheep's three bags are:

One for the master,
One for the dame,
and one for the little boy that lives down the lane.

In the Old Testament the pattern is common. Take the last five of the ten commandments, for instance. Admittedly, the final, lengthy, prohibition of the tenth may be later than the rest. But if so, at least he who added it seems to have had in mind an accepted form of series, the main feature of which is the comparative length of the last member.

Two examples from Jewish liturgy may be instructive. There is a primitive hymn:[2]

(1) None is like our God, none is like our Lord, none is like our King, none is like our Saviour.

(2) Who is like our God, who is like our Lord, who is like our King, who is like our Saviour?

[1] Matt 5:11 f.; Luke 6:22 f.

[2] Singer's *Prayer Book*, 15th ed., 167.

(3) We thank our God, we thank our Lord, we thank our King, we thank our Saviour.

(4) Blessed is our God, blessed is our Lord, blessed is our King, blessed is our Saviour.

(5) Thou art our God, thou art our Lord, thou art our King, thou art our Saviour, thou art he unto whom our fathers burnt the incense of spices.

Here the last member is not only longer than all others but also the only one to introduce the direct address: while all others speak of God in the third person, in the last "he" becomes "thou." To be sure, the additional length of the last member—from "thou art he unto whom"—may be due to an interpolation.[3] But for one thing, this is far less certain than is ordinarily assumed. For though the reference to incense must be spurious, there is reason to believe that it takes the place of a promise of salvation for Zion which did belong to the original hymn. For another thing, there still remains the direct address, and this cannot be easily explained away. The hymn, as it stands at any rate, is an acrostic, the initial letters of the five members making *'mn b'*, "Verily, he is coming" or "Verily, he is come" or "Verily, come."[4] Obviously, that the last member should contain the direct address, *'atta*, "thou art," thus opening with an *'aleph*, is essential. It has been maintained that the acrostic order is not the original, since there are sources in which the lines are arranged differently.[5] But even in these sources, our last member, with the direct address, always remains the last.[6] Moreover, the probability is that the non-acrostic order is the result of deliberate disarrangement, directed against the eschatological mood of the hymn—highly reminiscent of early Christian utterances: "Maranatha [our Lord is come]; the grace of our Lord Jesus Christ be with you," "Let grace come and this world pass away; Hosanna to the God of David; Maranatha; Amen," or "He which testifieth these things saith, Surely, I come quickly; Amen, come, Lord Jesus."[7] After all the first traces, or rudiments, of the hymns are to be found in works of Essene origin.[8]

Here is another hymn that was in common use in the oldest Gaonic period and probably dates from Talmudic times:[9]

(1) Blessed be he who spake and the world existed, blessed be he.
(2) Blessed be he who was the maker of the world in the beginning.
(3) Blessed be he who speaketh and doeth.
(4) Blessed be he who decreeth and performeth.
(5) Blessed be he who hath mercy upon the earth.
(6) Blessed be he who hath mercy upon his creatures.
(7) Blessed be he who payeth a good reward to them that fear him.
(8) Blessed be he who liveth for ever and endureth to eternity.

[3] See *Jewish Encyclopedia*, vol. 5 (1903), 154, *s.v. En Kelohenu.*

[4] First seen by Schiller-Szinessy; see C. Taylor, *The Teaching of the Twelve Apostles*, 78 f.

[5] Schechter, *JQR*, 4 (1892), 253.

[6] See Frumkin, *Siddur Tefillah* and *Seder Rab Amram, qnṭ* and 334.

[7] 1 Cor 16:22 f.; Didache 10 at the end; Rev 22:20.

[8] Jellinek, *Beth Ha-Midrash*, vol. 2, 47, vol. 3, 86.

[9] Singer's *Prayer Book*, 16 f.; *Jewish Encyclopedia*, vol. 2 (1902), 564, *s.v. Baruk She-Amar.*

(9) Blessed be he who redeemeth and delivereth, blessed be his name.

(10) Blessed art thou, O Lord our God, King of the universe, O God and merciful Father, praised by the mouth of people, lauded and glorified by the tongue of the loving ones and thy servants. We will praise thee, O Lord our God, with songs of David thy servant. O King, praised and glorified be thy great name for ever and ever. Blessed art thou, O Lord, a King extolled with praises.

Once again the last member is longer than the others, and there is a switching over from referring to God in the third person to addressing him directly.

It would lead too far afield to go into the origin of this form. One may speculate whether, in early worship, long before the Rabbinic era, there were hymns at the end of which the singers, who had so far looked in another direction, turned to face the deity; or at the end of which the deity was supposed to appear. But the form need not be of liturgical origin at all, or at any rate not exclusively so. To give the last member of a series a strikingly different form from the others is a plausible course to take wherever it is to contain a summary of the whole, or wherever it is meant as the climax. Greater length must be a usual feature of these cases. A change from the quieter third person to the more vivid direct address may be another device. Be this as it may, it can hardly be doubted that there existed in ancient literature—and there still exists in some branches of modern—a recognized pattern of a series which involves making the last member longer than, and/or otherwise different from, the preceding members.

Isaiah, incidentally, in a part where he recalls God's intimate guidance of Israel in the past and looks forward to a renewal of this relationship, and Sirach, in his chapters on Solomon and Elijah,[10] provide remarkable examples of a change from the third person to the direct address. The change, it is true, does not occur at the end (though, in Isaiah, it may at one time have introduced the close of a prophecy). But it is none the less significant as evidence that Hebrew writers of various periods were acquainted with this mode of expressing a heightening of fervour.

Isaiah begins by referring to God in the third person: "I will mention the lovingkindness of the Lord." He continues like this for some time. Then he switches over to the second person: "So didst thou lead thy people. Look down from heaven. Where is thy zeal and thy strength?" This is conscious art.

In Sirach, the section about Solomon begins calmly: "And there stood up after him a wise son, Solomon, and God gave him rest and he prepared a house for his name." After this, the main part uses the direct address: "How wise was thou in thy youth" and so on.

Similarly, the section about Elijah opens: "There arose a prophet like fire." It goes on in this way for several lines. Then the author is carried away: "How terrible was thou, o Elijah" and so on. Actually, there is in this case yet a further underlining of the rise in pitch: the first verse to use "thou" is also the first to introduce the name "Elijah." Up to this point, Sirach has spoken of "the prophet" (at least according to the Hebrew text, preferable in this respect; in the Greek, which has "And the prophet Elijah arose,"

[10] Isa 63:7 ff.; Sir 47:12 ff., 48:1 ff.

"Elijah" is manifestly a gloss). Now he both addresses him directly and calls him by his name: "How terrible wast thou, o Elijah, who didst raise up a man from death."

To return to the beatitudes, there is no reason why, so far as form is concerned, we should boggle at a series in which all members are of fairly equal length, except the last, which is longer than the others. From the standpoint of form, the last beatitude may be regarded as having been connected with, and formed the conclusion of, the shorter preceding ones from the outset. How many there were of the shorter preceding ones in the original series is here of no relevance.

In fact, applying a somewhat expanded principle of the *lectio difficilior*, we may even say that Matthew's transition from the minor key of the third person to the major of the direct address looks more original than Luke's smoother version. In other words, the original series quite possibly consisted of a number of members of equal length and referring to the blessed in the third person—"Blessed are the poor"—followed by a final member of greater length and addressing the blessed directly—"Blessed are ye." On this view, Luke's aim in using the direct address throughout would have been greater evenness of style. We must not forget that passages like the beatitudes were not intended by their authors as dull, academic lists, but as inspiring programmes of a new faith. In those circumstances, to finish an enumeration of "Blessed are the poor," "Blessed are the mourners," by a flourish of trumpets, "Blessed are ye," may well have appeared highly appropriate.

The pattern here postulated is by no means rare in the New Testament. A section from Luke may be adduced:[11]

Judge not and ye shall not be judged.

Condemn not and ye shall not be condemned.

Forgive and ye shall be forgiven.

Give and it shall be given unto you; good measure, pressed down, and shaken together, and running over, shall men give into your bosom. For with the same measure that ye mete withal it shall be measured to you again.

Certainly Matthew's version of this is very different. But the passage does show that the pattern in question was used in the period of the New Testament, and a great many other instances might be added.

Of particular interest is the song of Zacharias.[12] God is throughout spoken of in the third person. But the second part opens with a prophecy directly addressed to the child: "And thou, child, shalt be called the prophet of the Highest." Since Gunkel it is widely held that the second part is an addition, more precisely a Christian addition, to a Jewish psalm. That may be true. Only it is wrong to invoke the form in support of this opinion. As regards the form, the song of Zacharias could easily be one whole. The sudden turning to the child after a lengthy thanksgiving does not indicate a fresh hand. It is a deliberate, artistic device of the time.

To conclude, the problem of the last beatitude is similar to that of the song of Zacharias. A number of authorities think that the contents of the last beatitude are

[11] Luke 6:37 ff.

[12] Luke 1:68 ff.

incompatible with those of the preceding ones. Whether this view is correct need not here be examined. It is, however, submitted that any assumption of interpolation should be based exclusively on the substance of these verses and that the argument from form should be renounced. The form of the last beatitude is quite in order.

4

The Passover Haggadah and the New Testament

This section argues that the Jewish Passover Haggadah, in the form in which it existed in the first century, illuminates ideas in the Gospels and influences the way in which the ideas are presented.

The Earliest Structure Of The Gospels*

Probably there is no single answer to the question what was the structure of the earliest coherent accounts of Jesus's life. It can be shown, however, that the Passover eve expositions of the exodus current at the time exercised a decisive influence.[1]

This is indeed likely from *a priori* considerations. In the Pentateuch it is ordained that on the 14th of Nisan, in memory of the deliverance from Egypt, a lamb should be slaughtered for each family and that it should be eaten, with unleavened bread and bitter herbs, after nightfall, when the 15th begins; and there is the further command to instruct the youth in the story of the deliverance and the meaning of the sacrifice and meal. By New Testament times a number of specific rites had grown up; also there had accumulated a fair amount of traditional material used in instruction. The latter now took place during the meal, and it was no longer only instruction of youth but also discussion and praise-giving in which everyone took part—though even now at each meal company one person, the most distinguished, presided over and conducted the proceedings. Outside Jerusalem, at celebrations in the family, it would be the father, while in Jerusalem, where many a meal company consisted of pilgrims who had come up together, it might be a man chosen for his age, piety or learning, or even a master surrounded by his disciples. The meal started with wine and hors d'oeuvre; then came the main course, which took hours, because at this stage questions about the festival—its obvious meaning and its deeper one—were asked and answered at length. The narrative of the exodus was retold, details of the biblical account were explained, added to, rearranged, other mighty deeds of God for Israel were compared, the past was used to illumine the future. After the meal a series of psalms, called the *Hallel* or ὕμνος, were sung. It is *a priori* incredible that the expositions of the great events recited on this occasion in an atmosphere of gratitude and fervent hope should not have stimulated in Christian circles the growth of parallels concerning the new exodus.

Imagine the Jews who adhered to Jesus celebrating the Passover in the years following the crucifixion. We know that they went on celebrating it—fully, since the Temple was not yet destroyed. As such a group—a family outside Jerusalem, a band of pilgrims in the city—assembled in the evening to dwell on the rescue from Egypt, the pattern of divine intervention and salvation, is it conceivable that they confined themselves to the customary tales, reflections and prayers, without introducing what was for them the ful-

* Paper read at the International New Testament Congress at Strasbourg, 1958. I should like to thank Professor C. H. Dodd for his helpful criticisms.

[1] See the writer's *The New Testament and Rabbinic Judaism* (1956) [repr. 1973], 158 ff., 183 ff., 278 ff., 412 ff. [343 ff., 399 ff., 383 ff., 416 ff.].

filment of it all? Surely not; and this conclusion is quite independent of whether the last supper was in fact a Passover meal or not. Even if it was not, once Jesus was believed the Messiah, the new deliverance must have ranked at least equally with the old. In fact, if it was not a Passover meal, the Passover features conferred on it by New Testament writers would testify the more strikingly to the influence of this ceremony. Among recent suggestions as to the models on which the various gospels were shaped are biblical books, a proto-Mishnah, the Eighteen Benedictions, Hellenistic works and internal Church products. As far as the completed gospels as we have them are concerned, one or the other of these theories may be plausible. But none is remotely plausible for the beginnings, for the first planned literary or near-literary treatments of Jesus's ministry. It is the Passover eve discourses which were the main factor determining their structure.[2]

The kind of thing that happened is illustrated by the Jewish liturgy itself. The first part of the *Hallel*, immediately preceding the second cup, is concluded by a benediction designated "redemption,"[3] it is one of the great moments of the evening. According to R. Tarphon the "redemption" runs: "Blessed art thou, O Lord our God, King of the Universe, who redeemed us and redeemed our fathers from Egypt and brought us to this night to eat therein unleavened bread and bitter herbs." To this R. Akiba, who thought the advent of the Kingdom was imminent—he was a follower of Bar Kokhba—added this section: "Thus, O Lord our God and God of our fathers, may he bring us to other feasts and festivals which are coming to meet us in peace while we rejoice in the building-up of thy city and delight in thy worship; and may we eat there of the sacrifices and of the Passover-offerings whose blood has reached with acceptance the wall of thy altar; and may we thank thee for our redemption. Blessed art thou, O Lord—he has redeemed Israel." The insertion, made when the glorious end seemed near, has been retained in the service despite defeat and disappointment. There can be no doubt that the earliest Christians dealt with the service exactly as Akiba did. Only their Messianism was less short-lived, and they had years in which to supplement the traditional pieces, both praise-givings and narratives.

In proving our thesis in detail, we cannot, of course, derive support from the mere presence of Passover ideas in a gospel, not even if they are prominent in the Passover eve celebration. The use by an evangelist of ideas associated with the Sabbath or Tabernacles does not mean that he arranged his work so as to follow the lines of the liturgy of those days. What we have to demonstrate is that major, composite chapters of a gospel are fashioned after the Passover eve expositions; or that a pericope inspired by one occurring in the Passover eve celebration occupies a corresponding position. In neither of the two cases is it necessary that there should be any obvious Passover ideas at all.

Another question requiring some care is date.[4] The Passover eve liturgy in its present form is the result of a long evolution. Some of it is pre-Christian, some is later. With

[2] The merely annual character of Passover was no hindrance: in those times, the liturgy would not be forgotten about during the year, to be rediscovered, as a surprise, when the festival came round again.

[3] See E. D. Goldschmidt, *Die Pessach-Haggada* (1936), 68 f. Not all his emendations, however, seem inevitable.

[4] Nearly everything controversial. L. Finkelstein, *HTR* 31 (1938), 291 ff.; 35 (1942), 291 ff.; 36 (1943), 1 ff., favours very early datings, S. Stein, *JJS*, 8 (1957), 15, very late ones. While some of the former's con-

the destruction of the Temple the sacrifice disappeared, yet the meal remained, with unleavened bread, bitter herbs and long hours of exposition and thanksgiving. It was now always a family meal, as indeed it had been before Passover became a festival of pilgrimage. Gradually, in the first seven centuries, just as law and ritual were stabilized by the rabbis, so was the liturgy of this evening. In the end it was redacted in a little work called Haggadah, which may be translated "proclamation," "tale" or "interpretation," and probably signifies all three things. There are a few medieval and modern additions, easily recognizable. Now clearly, any argument concerning the structure of the gospels, to be valid, must be based on pre-Christian parts of the Haggadah. Luckily, important parts are beyond doubt of the requisite age. Besides, the very fact that certain sections of the gospels can be explained in no other way than by assuming dependence on the Haggadah is evidence that the relevant items in the latter were in existence at the time. Just as, for example, the comparison of wine with blood to be found in the New Testament proves the existence at the time of the custom of using red wine on Passover eve—not mentioned in rabbinic sources prior to the fourth century.[5]

An important point to remember is that we are deprived of the greater part of our potential evidence. From the historian's angle the redaction of the Haggadah, like all such undertakings, was both fortunate and unfortunate. Fortunate in that it preserved one version of the Passover eve liturgy, unfortunate in that it entailed the loss of others that must have existed—less orthodox ones. In New Testament times there had been an even greater variety. The ceremonies themselves were not yet finally fixed. For instance, the duty of partaking of the Passover lamb, unleavened bread and bitter herbs was normally carried out by serving the three one after another. Hillel, however, took them together; and it became a rite (whether at his bidding or not we do not know) to take them in his way, in remembrance—"Thus did Hillel. He used to wrap together the Passover, unleavened bread and bitter herbs and eat them in one." The New Testament records the introduction of a not dissimilar memorial rite. The liturgy was still open.[6] This is

---

clusions are precarious, especially when he tries to be too precise, the latter's argument is from silence—extremely weak. Does Philo give a detailed account of the philosophical importance of, say, baptismal catechisms or the Eighteen Benedictions? Stein would leave far too little time for the complicated developments which must have preceded what we find in Mishnah, Tosephta, Mekhilta and Siphre. A great deal, of course, depends on what we understand by a "literary" fixing of the liturgy, which he makes late. One can agree that in New Testament times there was no written liturgy, and not even a single authoritative oral one, without denying that certain orders of service had become traditional—identical only as to a few essential, otherwise different in different regions and groups, with constant interchange between them and much fluidity even within each. Stein himself admits that "*Kiddush*, *Hallel* and some very elementary questions and answers in connection with the rites of the festival" were established long before the New Testament period. In view of the evidence of the gospels, it would be impossible to concede less: but does Finkelstein assume so much more? Incidentally, Stein's principal thesis, that the Passover eve liturgy is indebted to the Symposia literature, gains in plausibility—in fact, is plausible only—if that influence can have been exerted in pre-Christian centuries.

[5] See L. Strack and P. Billerbeck, *Kommentar zum Neuen Testament aus Talmud und Midrasch*, 4 (1928), pt. 1, 61.

[6] See the important article by J. J. Petuchowski, *JBL*, 76 (1957), 293 ff.; Goldschmidt, 21, 70 f.; Strack and Billerbeck, 70 f. The final compromise—reached between the second and fourth century A.D.—is first to take bread and herbs separately (the Passover having dropped out) and with blessings, and then to take them

even truer of the questions asked, the explanations offered and the praises recited. Even in the service as finally redacted we hear of questions other than the four standard ones accepted as the starting-point: we shall see below, for example, that a wise son or disciple was expected to inquire in a different manner from a wicked one. Similarly, even the service as we have it, if it is analysed and attention is paid to variant readings and the like, bears witness to the freedom with which the answers to the questions, the explanatory, narrative, laudatory and promissory portions were once handled. Akiba's innovation has already been mentioned, and of various modes of presenting the history of deliverance favoured by various schools we shall speak presently. There are plainly anti-Gnostic and anti-Christian bits. In one variant, an old teaching that in the exodus God acted himself, not through a messenger, is provided with the continuation "nor through the Word." Again, "not through a messenger" frequently becomes "not through the messenger"—Jesus.[7] The absolute silence of the Haggadah on the role played by Moses is surely a reaction against the deification of the Messiah.[8] And it must be with a view to

together, according to Hillel, but without blessings. No doubt in Hillel's circle the Passover, bread and herbs had been taken only in his way, and with blessings, as a memorial rite. At that stage, the designation of the rite must have been *zekher lehillel*, "in remembrance of Hillel," and the formula must have run as quoted in the text. Though this mode spread, however, the traditional mode—the separate taking—remained prevalent and came to be regarded as more correct by the majority of scholars. How early they arrived at this decision is not clear from *b. Pes.* 115a; hardly in Hillel's lifetime or even before the destruction of the Temple. At any rate, from the destruction, there was a strong, new consideration against Hillel: the bitter herbs—which the Bible mentions only in connexion with the Passover, now gone—assumed the character of a mere rabbinic duty, whereas the unleavened bread—which the Bible mentions also independently of the Passover—continued as a scriptural duty. Hence, in the final compromise, the separate taking plays the major role. Hence also, the title of the memorial rite is expanded into *zekher lammiqdash kehillel*, "in remembrance of the Temple according to Hillel": strangely involved, but the reference to the Temple is considered necessary to make it clear that it was only then that the combined taking was a proper fulfillment of the law, all three duties being still scriptural. Similarly, a few words are added to the opening of the formula: "Thus did Hillel—in the time when the Temple was standing." (The same addition—*pace* Stein, 42—in an interpretation of the Passover going back to Gamaliel I: Goldschmidt, 63 f.) One more remark. The fact that Hillel, in the usual manner, invokes a verse for his peculiar way of taking the three foods does not mean that he did not choose that way because it had a certain significance. Exactly what the combined taking signified it would lead too far afield here to inquire.

[7] See *The New Testament and Rabbinic Judaism*, 326 f. [372 f.]; Goldschmidt, 54 f.

[8] Cf. Petuchowski, 259 f., who says that there must be no human protagonist—God himself being the hero of this drama. In Finkelstein's opinion, *HTR* 35 (1942), 329; *HTR* 36 (1943), 6, Moses is left out because the high priests were against exalting a non-priestly Levite (and Aaron is left out as a non-Zadokite); this seems far-fetched. We think it probable that versions mentioning Moses once existed but fell victim to the trend which culminated in the substitution (already referred to) of "not through the messenger" for "not through a messenger." Many questions of detail are unsettled. Finkelstein, *HTR* 36 (1943), 3, draws attention to a eulogy recounting a series of benefits: according to the Haggadah they were conferred on Israel by God (*maqom*, Place), according to Midrash Siphre on Deuteronomy they—or most of them—were conferred by Moses. Haggadah (Goldschmidt, 60 ff.): "God who brought us forth from Egypt and executed judgment against them . . . and gave us the manna to eat," Siphre: "Moses, the man that brought us forth from Egypt . . . and brought us down the manna." The Midrash, Finkelstein infers, protests against the high-priestly, anti-Mosaic group responsible for the Haggadah. But he himself points out, 4 f., that the eulogy is based on biblical forerunners like Neh 9:6 ff.; Ps 135 f. As in these God is the benefactor, surely the natural conclusion is that the Haggadah simply follows them, without any political bias; and that the Midrash represents a sort of popular variety, in which "God brought us forth" would readily become "Moses brought us forth." That no such pop-

guarding against dangerous deviations in ritual and interpretation that the standard questions concerning the meaning of the Passover eve ceremonies are assigned to the illogical position prior to the performance of the ceremonies: from the description of the service in the Mishnah it is certain that about A.D. 200 the natural sequence, with the questions following the ceremonies, was still prevalent.[9]

Clearly, the New Testament writers had very much more to draw on than what has come down in the Haggadah. Quite a few fragments of alternative passover eve expositions may be scattered throughout rabbinic literature, if only we could identify them; but the bulk must be lost forever. The anecdotes of scholars of the early second century spending the entire Passover night in discussion of the exodus and the Passover laws[10] are hardly exaggerated. They make one realize what a tiny fraction of the material is preserved in the slim volume of the Haggadah. The implication is that, if we can prove certain stretches of the gospels to be composed in analogy to Passover eve expositions, the likelihood is that the same is the case with some of the others as to which, owing to the loss of the original, we have no means of proof.

The rabbis formulated a principle which was to govern the Passover eve expositions of the exodus: one ought to move from disgrace to glory.[11] If this sounds somewhat obvious, we should none the less take note of the fact that they were conscious of and reflected on the structure of their narratives; and if it is rather general, that only underlines what we have just observed concerning the scope for variation. In fact we can trace in the Haggadah at least three different modes—all of them old—in which the principle was carried into effect.[12]

One scheme was attached to the simple statement from Deuteronomy:[13] "Slaves were we unto Pharaoh in Egypt, and the Lord our God brought us out thence with a mighty hand and with an outstretched arm." From oppression by a tyrant in a foreign land to freedom—there is a revolutionary and nationalist flavour about this presentation, however much ennobled by the idea of an exchange of service to man for service to God. Another was based on the declaration, also in Deuteronomy,[14] which was prescribed for a person offering his first-fruits in the Temple: "A Syrian was destroying my father,[15] and he went down into Egypt and sojourned there with a few and became there

ular variety is preserved in our Haggadah is, indeed, significant; it is due to the gradual elimination of anything smacking of a godlike Messiah. What place, if any, is to be assigned to John 6:32 in all this ("Moses gave you not that bread from heaven, but my Father giveth you the true bread from heaven") we shall not here try to decide. Finkelstein, incidentally, *HTR* 36 (1943), 35 f., appears to regard the two versions of the eulogy given in the Haggadah as equally old. There is something to be said, perhaps, for the prose version being earlier than the poem. It is the last words of the former—"to atone for all our transgressions"—which speak decisively for a date prior to the destruction of the Temple.

9 See *The New Testament and Rabbinic Judaism*, 192 ff. [406 ff.].

10 See Goldschmidt, 37.

11 *m. Pes.* 10:4; see *The New Testament and Rabbinic Judaism*, 413 ff. [417 ff.].

12 See *The New Testament and Rabbinic Judaism, loc. cit.* and 279 ff. [383 ff.].

13 Deut 6:21 (roughly); see Goldschmidt, 36 f.

14 Deut 26:5 ff.; see Goldschmidt, 46 ff.

15 The biblical text reads *'obhedh*, "A Syrian ready to perish was my father." The Haggadah, however, understands the word as if it were vocalized *'ibbedh*. This daring reinterpretation, Finkelstein rightly holds,

a nation great, strong and populous, and the Egyptians ill-treated us and afflicted us and laid upon us hard service, and we cried unto the Lord God of our fathers, and the Lord heard our voice and looked on our affliction and our labour and our oppression, and the Lord brought us out of Egypt with a mighty hand and with an outstretched arm and with great terribleness and with signs and with wonders, and he has brought us into this place and has given us this land, a land that floweth with milk and honey."[16] Here the saga begins with the persecution of a lonely family, it goes on to trials, seekings of God and miraculous rescues, and it culminates in the gift of the promised land: from smallness, nothingness, to life as a settled people. The underlying motif is historical election and guidance by God, and response on the faithfuls' part. The third plan opens with the summary,[17] "At the beginning our fathers were servants of idolatrous service, and now the Place [*maqom*, a designation of God] has brought us near unto his service"; and as authority Joshua's farewell speech is invoked,[18] "On the other side of the river dwelt your fathers in old time, Terah the father of Abraham, and the father of Nachor, and they served other gods, and I took your father Abraham from the other side of the river and led him throughout all the land of Canaan and multiplied his seed and gave him Isaac, and I gave unto Isaac Jacob and Esau, and I gave unto Esau mount Seir to possess it, and Jacob and his children went down into Egypt. . . ." In this exposition the spiritual element predominates. The transition from disgrace to glory means above all a change of masters: God himself has turned the servants of idols into servants of his own.

Such outlines of Jewish experience might, of course, be given on occasions other than the Passover festival. For this reason we shall not here enlarge on the traces they have left in the New Testament. (That they have left traces, both in the gospels and other writings, is beyond question.)[19] It would be too difficult an undertaking to isolate those cases which must derive from the Passover eve celebration. Let us rather take the elaborate section Mark 12:1–37, modelled, we submit, on a particular section of the Haggadah.[20]

After a parable concerning a vineyard, which for the moment we disregard, four questions are raised: (1) Is it lawful to pay tribute to Caesar? Asked by Pharisees and Herodians. (2) If a man dies without issue, his brother marries the widow—as is his duty according to Jewish law—he also dies and the next brother marries her, and so forth till she has been married to seven, whose wife will she be on resurrection? Asked by the Sadducees. (3) Which is the first commandment? Asked by a scribe, and (4) How

HTR 31 (1938), 300, must date either from the Maccabean era or from an even earlier one, when Palestine was under Egyptian suzerainty and it was advisable to denounce Syria. He argues in favour of the latter alternative; we much prefer the former.

[16] The last verse, "and he has brought us into this place…," was removed after the destruction of the Temple; see Goldschmidt, 9.

[17] See Goldschmidt, 46 f.

[18] Josh 24:2 ff.

[19] On some points concerning a change of master see *The New Testament and Rabbinic Judaism*, 278 ff. [383 ff.]. The Matthean Passion-narrative certainly ends with glory, Matt 28:18: "All power is given unto me"; in the others the pattern is perhaps a little obscured by the details of the Christophanies. The provenance of some speeches in Acts—7:1 ff. and the like—is worth investigating.

[20] See *The New Testament and Rabbinic Judaism*, 158 ff. [343 ff.].

can the Messiah be David's son, seeing that David in the Psalms[21] calls him his Lord? Asked by Jesus.

There is no logical or historical connexion between these questions. However, the rabbis knew a classification of questions into four types; it is evidenced in an anecdote involving a leading scholar of the half-century following the destruction of the Temple,[22] and it is used in an early section of the Haggadah.[23] (1) "Questions of wisdom," about points of law; (2) "questions of vulgarity," mocking questions, principally about bodily resurrection, by which the questioner cuts himself off from the community—will the dead need sprinkling when they rise, having been in contact with corpses?; (3) "questions of the proper way of the land," about the basis of simple piety; and (4) "questions of interpretation," about apparent contradictions in Scripture—one passage saying that God has chosen Zion, another that he has rejected it. Manifestly the four questions in Mark represent the four types: (1) law, tribute to Caesar, (2) mockery, the widow of seven, (3) simple piety, the first commandment, (4) contradictions, the Messiah David's son and Lord.

If this were all, it might be objected that we have proved only the combination of the Markan questions in conformity with rabbinic categories, but not their direct provenance from the Passover eve liturgy. But there is more. For one thing, it is only in that liturgy that the four types appear in this particular sequence.[24] What clinches the matter is this. The injunction to instruct the youth in regard to Passover recurs four times in the Pentateuch.[25] The rabbis (who could admit no empty repetition) ingeniously connected this phenomenon with their classification. The different injunctions, they

[21] Ps 110 (LXX: 109):1; David's son, for example in Isa 11:1, 10; Jer 23:5.

[22] Joshua ben Hananiah, *b. Nidd.* 69b ff.

[23] The famous Midrash of the four sons; Goldschmidt 39 ff. Commentators, not realizing the classification on which the Midrash is based, have had recourse to artificial explanations and critical remedies; see, for example, Goldschmidt's reason, 44, why the reply the Haggadah has for the wise son is more suitable for and must be transferred to the simple. Finkelstein, *HTR* 36 (1943), 8 ff., is driven to postulate a highly composite character. Even if this were correct, our thesis would stand: the composition would have been undertaken (in its final stages at least) with a view to achieving a whole in conformity with the classification. But more probably the Midrash is not composite at all. (In trying to make out his case, Finkelstein introduces several arbitrary assumptions, such as that a Midrash, when it employs a question put in the Bible—say, Exod 12:26, "What mean ye by this service?"—must also employ the reply provided there—in this case, "It is the sacrifice" and so on; and that if it does not do so, we have proof of subsequent interference. Goldschmidt, 41, 43, approaches the same position. But this is to allow the Midrash—certainly the early Midrash—far too little freedom.) Stein, 35 f., draws attention to Philo's four types of children: that obedient to both father, reason, and mother, worldly education, that obedient to the father only (Philo sometimes seems to regard the former as the best, sometimes the latter), that obedient to the mother only and (the worst) that obedient to neither. But Stein himself recognizes that there could only be the faintest alliance with the four of the Haggadah: the wise, the wicked, the simply pious and the one who does not know how to ask. Perhaps a fourfold division was generally popular. Perhaps some division like Philo's, current before, had encouraged the author of the Midrash to create one of his own.

[24] In the anecdote of R. Joshua the sequence is wisdom, interpretation, vulgarity, way of the land. Even in the version of the Passover eve Midrash offered by the Mekhilta the second and third questions are switched round—and, incidentally, both in this version and that of the Palestinian Talmud (*y. Pes.* 37d) the son of simple piety is ununderstandingly turned into a half-wit.

[25] Exod 12:26 f., 13:8, 13:14; Deut 6:20 f.

claimed, envisaged different types of youth, each to receive the teaching appropriate to his character. And as three of the passages run, "And when thy son asketh [thy children ask], thou shalt say," while one omits the inquiry and simply runs, "And thou shalt shew thy son,"[26] the Haggadah introduces (1) a wise son—or disciple—who asks concerning the manifold Passover laws, (2) a wicked son, who asks in a fashion calculated to show that he excludes himself from the community, (3) a son of simple piety, who just asks what the festival means, and (4) a son who does not know how to ask: in his case, the Haggadah tells us, the father—or master—himself has to open the discourse. Of the questions in Mark three are put to Jesus, the fourth is put by him. This is too singular a feature of the Haggadah to be due to accident. Whoever brought the Markan questions together did not merely adopt the rabbinic categories in general; he adopted the specific application of these categories occurring on Passover eve.

Actually, recognition of the original throws unexpected light on the Christian parallel. For instance, as to a textual point—the third question is put by an honest man, who agrees with Jesus' emphasis on love and is said by Jesus to be not far from the Kingdom. Nevertheless modern editors print as the conclusion of this exchange the remark, "And no man after that durst ask him"—a surprising reaction to a commendation—and they commence the fourth question by "And Jesus answered and said" (there follows the question about the Messiah). In the Haggadah, however, the fourth question begins thus: "And he who does not know how to ask, open thou the discourse for him." Surely, in Mark, we must end the third question with the commendation; and the fourth commences, in exact analogy to the Haggadah, "And no man after that durst ask him, and Jesus answered and said." This not only relieves us of the illogical reaction to Jesus' encouraging words, but also accords with medieval divisions, excellent authority.[27]

Or to take the problem of the import of Jesus's question respecting the Messiah. When we examine the fourth rabbinic category, the question about an apparent contradiction in Scripture, we find that the solution always consists in distinguishing between the two verses concerned so that each has its own range of validity and both, therefore, can be upheld: for example, God chose Zion when it was faithful but rejected it when it

[26] Exod 13:8. In *The New Testament and Rabbinic Judaism*, 165 [348], I thought that the author of the Midrash, forced by the biblical material on which he worked, had to sacrifice the category of contradiction and substitute the person who cannot ask. It now seems to me that, while introducing the person who cannot ask—because Exod 13:8, in contrast with the other three passages, contains no question—he managed to retain contradiction. The teaching of the verse, "Because of that which the Lord did unto me when I came forth out of Egypt," is one of the most difficult ones (from the rabbinic point of view) when confronted with other references to this event. It speaks of "me," whereas elsewhere we find "us" (for example, Deut 26:8) or even "your fathers" (for example, Josh 24:6). The careful formulation of the "redemption" quoted above (Goldschmidt, 68) is significant: "Blessed art thou, who redeemed us and redeemed our fathers from Egypt." The relation between "I" and "we" and "our fathers" and indeed "our children" is dealt with in many sections of the Haggadah; cf. for example the rationalizing solution, "and if the Holy one had not brought out our fathers, we and our children and their children would still be enslaved to Pharaoh" (Goldschmidt, 36 f.). No doubt Exod 13:8 was a familiar example of apparent contradiction, to be solved by assigning to each statement its appropriate domain.

[27] Professor Kingsley Barrett kindly suggests to me that the figure of the disciple who does not ask, yet receives the appropriate instruction, may have been made use of by John 16:5, 30.

deserted him. On this basis, Jesus is not absolutely condemning the notion of the Messiah being David's son. He is both David's son and Lord, the former in one respect, or at one stage of history, the latter in another respect or at another stage.

The case of the four Markan questions is especially instructive as from beginning to end we meet no obvious Passover ideas: yet the composition derives from the Passover eve liturgy. The point is that, in Christian circles celebrating the festival, as the traditional pieces referring to the old exodus were recited, analogous ones referring to the new exodus were added. This does indeed presuppose a fundamental and close correspondence between the two events, and just how fundamental and close it was in the eyes of early Christians we shall not understand unless we pay attention to this very process. But the analogy of a particular piece concerning the old one might be seen in a detail only remotely connected with the significant elements of Passover. It might indeed be seen, as here, in a certain way of arranging questions and instruction. At this stage, the process is almost mechanical; the material is not yet subordinated to theological or, for that matter, literary considerations—there is, for instance, no ascending or descending line discernible in these questions.

This is perhaps the place to point out that the fact of a Christian exposition following the Passover eve liturgy does not diminish its historical value; rather the contrary. The liturgy would be responsible for the selection and grouping of the material, for certain details of its presentation and even, to some extent, for its interpretation. There is no justification for doubting, on this ground, the happenings and sayings recorded: the absence of Passover ideas from the questions just analysed shows that the influence of the liturgy might be severely limited. In any case, as remarked above, these sections are the oldest accounts of Jesus's life meant to last. It cannot have been for long that the believers in telling about him leaned on the Haggadah; soon they must have struck out on their own, with more theological and literary ambition. Admittedly, even these oldest sections may not have escaped subsequent revision. But, precisely in so far as they reflect the structure of the Haggadah, we are in touch with the Passover eve celebrations among Christians in the first decades after the crucifixion. It is the Haggadah which explains how an elaborate chapter like the four questions could come into existence at so early a date; and, we repeat, there is no other kind of composite chapter, no non-Haggadic chapter, in the New Testament for which a similar age can be established or even made likely. These sections are very close to the origins of Christianity.

It remains to glance at the parable of the vineyard. In the Haggadah the discourse concerning the four types of sons or disciples is preceded by a benediction:[28] "Blessed is the Place [*maqom* again], blessed is he, blessed is he who gave the Torah to his people Israel." It is not certain whether this benediction is of the same age as the discourse, still less whether it was already firmly attached to it in pre-Christian times. Not certain, but by no means unlikely. If it was, it may well account for the position of the parable as an introduction to the four questions—otherwise hard to understand. The thanksgiving—humble and proud at the same time—for the bestowal of the Torah on Israel would provide a natural opportunity for Christians to insert a parable known to them, which

[28] See Goldschmidt, 39 f.

starts off with the careful planting and equipping by God of a vineyard, his people, which goes on to his sending out one servant, prophet, after another to remind the husbandmen, the leaders, of their duty, and which culminates in the story of Jesus. The parable (on this assumption) would be placed here as a counterpart of the traditional benediction. (It has been said that it once ended with the discomfiture of the husbandmen: the exaltation of Jesus, implied in the quotation from the *Hallel*—"The stone which the builders rejected is become the head of the corner, this was the Lord's doing"—is without motivation in the rest. But it certainly fits if we think of the blessing for the gift of the Torah.) In this case, despite the descent of the pericope, or rather of its position, from the Haggadah, there would be no specific Passover ideas either in the Christian supplement[29] or in the original piece which suggested the addition: another instance of the primitive, "mechanical" manner of fitting in the material relating to the new exodus.

We now pass to the Massacre of the Innocents, Matt 2:13–18, a striking parallel to a Passover eve exposition.[30] Once again, we are not pronouncing on the historicity of the incident; our sole concern is with the way it is presented and placed. If we are right, the story belongs to the very earliest of the near-literary accounts of Jesus' life; and it is interesting that just recently fresh arguments have been advanced in favour of a historical nucleus.[31]

The Massacre is often considered to be influenced partly by Pharaoh's ordinance to drown the new-born Hebrew boys (which, the rabbis maintained, he issued because he had been told that a deliverer was about to be born),[32] partly by Moses's flight after killing an Egyptian. But the former assumption is only a half-truth, the latter quite incorrect.[33] Apart from the strangeness of the combination of Pharaoh's ordinance and Moses's flight, there are vital discrepancies. Pharaoh's measure is definitely confined to male offspring, Herod's is not. (It is true that the Revised Version translates τοὺς παῖδας by "the male children"; this might be tenable were it not that Rachel is weeping for her τέκνα, clearly including both sexes—we shall return to the point.) Moses escapes of his own will, while Joseph escapes at God's behest. Moses escapes to Midian, to return to Egypt, while Joseph escapes to Egypt, to return to the holy land. Moses escapes alone, and for his own sake, while Joseph escapes with his family, for the sake of a member of it, Jesus. Finally, the sentence from Hosea,[34] "Out of Egypt have I called my son," refers to Israel, not Moses, both in the Bible and in rabbinic exegesis.

All these difficulties disappear as soon as the connexion of the Massacre with the Haggadah is realized. As mentioned above, one Passover scheme of Jewish history took as its starting-point the persecution of Jacob by Laban.[35] This was of course elaborated,

[29] Unless we count the fruit of the vine.

[30] See *The New Testament and Rabbinic Judaism*, 189 ff. [404 ff.].

[31] See E. Stauffer, *Jesus* (1957), 36 ff., 153 f.

[32] Josephus, *Ant.* 2.9.2.205; *Exod. Rab.* on 1:22.

[33] What has contributed to the misinterpretation is the pericope Matt 2:19 ff., which does allude to the episode of Moses. But it has not the same history as the report of the Massacre.

[34] Hos 11:1.

[35] See Goldschmidt, 47 f.

and Laban, "the deceiver," "the cheater,"[36] the Aramean, doubly hated because only a half-foreigner, was unfavourably compared with Pharaoh. He was identified with Balaam, who saw that a Star would come out of Jacob.[37] In order to prevent this happening, worse than Pharaoh, he tried to destroy not only the males but all. Jacob, however, fled into Egypt with his family, bidden to do so by the Word in a dream. In this dream, too, God assured him that "I will go down with thee into Egypt and I will also surely bring thee up again,"[38] a promise, according to the rabbis, both of deliverance from Egypt and of ultimate deliverance (the Hebrew for "I" being the emphatic *'anokhi*, and the second half literally reading "and I will bring thee up, also bring up").[39] The sojourn abroad would be for a time only; and the family now fleeing was destined to produce the Messiah. Thus Laban's plan was vitiated.

If we compare the Massacre of the Innocents—Herod, in his opponents' eyes, was an adept in deceit[40] (so was his son Antipas, "the fox")[41] and, above all, a hated half-foreigner, like Laban; he was an Idumean. (In unvocalized Hebrew script the difference between Aramean and Idumean is small,[42] and there would be nothing surprising in a punning interchange. But it would only support the similarity in substance.) Like Laban, from fear of the messianic king, he attempted to destroy all. Like Jacob, Joseph escaped to Egypt with his family, warned to do so by an angel in a dream. His stay there would be only temporary, "until I bring thee word," but by it the life of the Saviour would be preserved. Thus Herod's plan came to nought. "Out of Egypt have I called my son" is perfectly appropriate in this context: the final deliverance no less than that from Egypt was in fulfilment of God's promise to Jacob.

Other details of the gospel story now become intelligible. The figure of Rachel is not introduced by haphazard: she is Jacob's wife, and Herod, another Laban, is persecuting her children. Again, that Laban should try to wipe out all offspring of Jacob, male and female, is logical: the Messiah is not due for hundreds or thousands of years, and a female survivor might be his ancestress. But Herod, like Pharaoh, ought logically to do away with the males only, since the deliverer whom he fears belongs to this generation. Yet his decree includes all—which renders the analogy with Laban the more distinct. Here we come back to the use of τέκνα in "Rachel weeping for her children." The Hebrew (it is a quotation from Jeremiah)[43] has *banim*, the Septuagint υἱοί: "sons." The substitution of τέκνα has a purpose—to underline the indiscriminateness of Herod's cruelty.

The Massacre, then, is influenced by Pharaoh's ordinance only at a remove—that is, only in so far as that ordinance inspired the Haggadah legend of Laban. It is with the

[36] For example, *Gen. Rab.* on 25:20.

[37] *Jer. Targum* on Num 22:5. Balaam occurs also in the farewell speech of Josh 24:9, which is part of the third scheme noted above. In our present Haggadah, only *vv.* 2–4 are quoted, but the full scheme requires the continuation at least as far as *v.* 13 (Goldschmidt, 11 n. 2).

[38] Gen 46:4.

[39] See, for example, *Exod. Rab.* on 3:12.

[40] For example, Josephus, *Ant.* 14.11.2.274, 15.2.3.20 f.

[41] Luke 13:32.

[42] *'rmi–'dmi*: ר–ד.

[43] Jer 31 (LXX: 38) :15.

latter that the Massacre is in direct touch. The genealogy is, first, the biblical picture of Pharaoh, second, its rabbinic elaboration, third, the transfer in the Haggadah of the elaborated picture, darkened, to Laban, and fourth, the Massacre. As for Moses' flight, that is not alluded to at all in Matt 2:13–18. The allusions are exclusively to Jacob's flight, as represented in the Haggadah.

Have we proved more than that the Massacre draws on a Passover eve exposition? Have we proved that the structure of early gospels is indebted to the Haggadah? It is relevant to note that—if we disregard some introductory matter—Herod's criminal plan comes right at the beginning of Matthew, just as does Laban's plan in the Haggadah scheme in question. The argument is admittedly far from conclusive: in both cases, and especially in Matthew, the position is so natural that no external cause is needed to explain it. (This could not be said of the four questions in Mark, examined above.) Still, our impression is that this is another instance of a narrative concerning Jesus having been formulated at a Christian Passover eve celebration in the first decades after the crucifixion, and having been formulated as part of a general and natural tendency to attach the "tale," "proclamation," "interpretation" of the new redemption to the traditional Haggadah of the old.[44]

Considering the examples submitted, it seems generally advisable, where a pericope or series of pericopes in the gospels depicts the recent events in terms of the exodus from Egypt, to bear in mind the possibility that the immediate stimulus comes neither from the Old Testament nor from some ordinary rabbinic source, but from the Haggadah. (The ten miracles following the Sermon on the Mount in Matthew are conceivably a case in point.[45]) There are further conclusions to be drawn. The earliest accounts of Jesus' ministry formed part, we have seen, of a liturgy, and a most peculiar liturgy at that. Dominated by the certainty, the actuality, of Israel's redemption, it involved ceremonial, worship and instruction, a union of past history and eschatological anticipation, discourses on God's purposes, his favours, his judgments, his means of action, his demands. Here lies at least a partial solution to the great problem of what was the main channel of transmission by which information about Jesus was handed down in the primitive Christian community. And equally we shall be able to appreciate the curious mixture of diverse elements in the gospels which seems to be of their very essence, the interlocking of deeds and sayings, of liturgical, narrative, catechetical and other factors determining the movement. However little may be left of the original

[44] As most components of the Passover eve liturgy are mentioned also in sources other than the Haggadah—Mishnah, Mekhilta and so forth—it might be asked whether the gospel parallels may not derive from the general pool of rabbinic material rather than directly from the service. Suffice it to say, as for the Markan questions, that not only is their dramatization by an evangelist on the basis of an ordinary Midrash improbable in the extreme, but—as indicated above (n. 24)—the versions of the Midrash of the four sons to be found in Mekhilta and Palestinian Talmud are both of them less close to the gospels than is the Haggadah; and as for the Massacre, that the full story of Laban and Jacob is given exclusively in the Haggadah—Siphre on Deuteronomy omits the comparison with Pharaoh, and even in the portion it does not omit notes only deviations, taking it for granted that the reader is familiar with the Passover eve exposition (see Goldschmidt, 11).

[45] Our Haggadah dwells on the ten plagues; Goldschmidt, 57 ff. Other versions presumably related ten miracles: cf. *m. Ab.* 5:4.

nucleus, however much it may be overlaid by fresh material freshly organized, it is evident that the structure of the earliest gospels, in line with the Haggadah, was anything but simple. As time went on, new and varied developments were bound to occur—a mere comparison between the three Synpotics, and again, between them and the Fourth Gospel, shows to what far-reaching differences they led. None the less the roots of the complexity were there from the outset, inherent in the Haggadah, the matrix of gospel tradition.

Four Types of Question

We may now go on to another case where Rabbinic categories like *halakha*, "teaching about law," and *haggadha*, "teaching about non-legal matters," have influenced the New Testament material.

A. A Fourfold Scheme

In Matthew and Mark,[1] four questions are discussed in one section: (1) Is it lawful to give tribute unto Caesar? (2) If a man dies without issue and his brother, in fulfilment of the religious duty of the levirate, marries the widow, the second husband also dies and the next brother marries her, and so on until seven brothers have had her, whose wife will she be at the resurrection? (3) Which is the most important commandment? and (4) How can the Messiah be the son of David, seeing that David in one of his Psalms[2] calls him his Lord?

That the four questions in fact date from the same historical occasion is highly improbable. Matthew alone coincides with Mark in putting them together, whereas Luke puts together questions (1), (2) and (4) only, giving (3) in a different connection.[3] Moreover, both in Matthew and Mark—though admittedly not in Luke—question (4) begins by a fresh description of audience or place: "while the Pharisees were gathered together" and "while he taught in the temple." Which suggests that this question was originally independent of the others.

If this is correct, we must ask ourselves how the questions came to be united. The answer is that whoever united them followed a fourfold scheme with which the first-century Rabbis were familiar. More precisely, he regarded these questions as representative of four different types of question distinguished by the early Rabbis.

The Talmud reports the Alexandrians to have put to R. Joshua ben Hananiah—a leading Rabbi in the half-century following the destruction of the Temple—twelve questions of four kinds, i.e. three of each kind.[4] They put three questions of *ḥokhma*, "wisdom." These are *halakhic* questions, concerning points of law. For example, is a priest, who ought to observe special marriage restrictions,[5] allowed to marry the daughter of a woman who, after being divorced, remarried and, divorced again, returned to her first husband despite the Biblical prohibition of such a return?[6] Evidently a legal problem.

[1] Matt 22:15 ff.; Mark 12:13 ff.

[2] Ps 110:1.

[3] Luke 20:21 ff., 10:25 ff.

[4] *b. Nidd.* 69b ff.

[5] Lev 21:7.

[6] Deut 24:4.

Next they put three questions of *haggadha*, with no bearing on the law. These questions concern apparent contradictions between different verses from Scripture. For example, Ezekiel's "I have no pleasure in the death of him that dieth"[7] seems to conflict with the notice in 1 Samuel,[8] "It pleased the Lord to slay the sons of Eli." Or the verse from Psalms,[9] "The Lord hath chosen Zion," seems to conflict with Jeremiah's "This city hath been to me as a provocation of mine anger that I should remove it from before my face."[10]

Next they put three questions of *boruth*, "vulgarity." They are mocking questions, designed to ridicule a belief of the Rabbi. And they are all directed against the same belief, namely, belief in resurrection. For example, did the child brought back to life by Elisha convey uncleanness, as a corpse? Or on resurrection, will the dead need sprinkling, having been in contact with corpses?

Finally, the Alexandrians asked three questions of *derekh 'ereṣ*, "principles of moral and successful life." What shall a man do to become wise? to become rich? To obtain male children? R. Joshua explained that, ultimately, there was only one answer: Seek the mercy of him who alone can give wisdom (for this, he invoked a line from Proverbs[11]), wealth (for this he invoked Haggai[12]), and sons (this he proved by a Psalm[13]). The same path leads to all three goals.

The four questions in Matthew and Mark can easily be brought under the headings just listed. Question (1), about tribute to Caesar, falls under *ḥokhma*. It is *halakhic*, it has regard to a point of law. It should be noted that the motive of the questioners, which is to "catch Jesus in his words," does not alter the character of the question itself, i.e. it does not turn the question into one of "vulgarity." There are numerous examples in the Talmud of *halakhic* questions asked with a view to "catching" an opponent. The question asked by Jesus about the nature of the Messiah, though calculated to embarrass his adversaries, is far from "vulgar." So is his question, in another chapter, about the baptism of John,[14] where the kind of dilemma in which his antagonists find themselves is very similar indeed to that in which they hoped to place him by the question about tribute to Caesar. But a question of "vulgarity" is different. It is one which could not be put in any other spirit than that of rude mockery.

Question (2), about the seven husbands, is clearly of this sort. It falls under *boruth*. It is designed to ridicule a belief held by Jesus; and significantly, the particular belief attacked in this manner is that which forms the target also in the illustrations of "vulgarity" quoted by the Talmud.

Question (3), about the most important commandment, falls under *derekh 'ereṣ*. It

[7] Ezek 18:32.

[8] 1 Sam 2:25.

[9] Ps 132:13.

[10] Jer 32:31.

[11] Prov 2:6.

[12] Hag 2:8. The Delphic oracle had given a different answer to the question how to get rich: "If thou acquirest what lieth between Corinth and Sicyon" (Athenaeus, *Deipn.* 5.219a).

[13] Ps 127:3.

[14] Matt 21:24 ff.; Mark 11:29 ff.; Luke 20:3 ff.

is concerned with the fundamental principles on which to base one's conduct, as opposed to detailed ritual.

Question (4) falls under *haggadha*. Unlike (1), it has no reference to any point of law. It draws attention to a verse from the Psalms in disagreement with the current teaching of the scribes respecting the Messiah—which teaching, of course, also rests on Scriptural evidence.[15] That is to say, the problem consists in a conflict between various passages from the Bible.

Certainly, there are differences between the Talmudic episode and the New Testament parallel. First, the Talmud has twelve questions, the New Testament only four. No doubt, in a sense, both numbers are artificial. It would, for instance, have been easy, both for the author of the Talmudic episode and that of the New Testament section under notice, to introduce additional questions regarding *derekh 'ereṣ*, "principles." The higher number in the Talmud suggests that the author either had more material at his disposal or permitted himself greater freedom in supplementing questions actually submitted to R. Joshua by others similar in nature but not in fact submitted to him.

Secondly, the Talmudic episode is considerably more stylized than the corresponding New Testament section. (We are disregarding the comments by Rabbis later than Joshua which are appended to the third question of *ḥokhma* and the first of *derekh 'ereṣ*.) There is not so much historical detail, individualization of the settings of the various questions. Once again, we must conclude that either the Alexandrians really arranged a formal test of Joshua and themselves grouped their questions for the occasion in a systematic fashion, or it is the Talmudic author who has sacrificed detail and variety to regularity of arrangement. Whichever may be true, it is interesting that the Talmud starts from the four categories of questions: the several questions are adduced to illustrate the categories. The New Testament starts from the several questions; the fourfold scheme is responsible for no more than their being placed side by side as forming one series.

Thirdly, the order in the Talmud is points of law (*ḥokhma*), contradictions between passages from Scripture (*haggadha*), vulgarity (*boruth*), principles of conduct (*derekh 'ereṣ*), the order in the New Testament is points of law, vulgarity, principles of conduct, contradictions between passages from Scripture. Maybe there was no fixed order. If there was one, it was probably that of the Talmud. The New Testament sequence is perhaps to be accounted for by the assumption that, at some stage of the tradition, questions (1) and (2) stood together without questions (3) and (4), or questions (1), (2) and (3) stood together without question (4); and that (3) and (4), or (4), were added precisely in order to complete the fourfold scheme. However, even if we suppose that the New Testament questions were all collected at the same time by an author acquainted with the fourfold scheme, the deviation from the Talmud is understandable. The question asked by Jesus himself would naturally be placed at the end, as the climax of the series. With that exception, the order is indeed that of the Talmud: law, vulgarity, principles.

This brings us to one more difference worth noting. In the Talmud, all questions are put by the Alexandrians to R. Joshua. In the New Testament, the first three are put by one side, the adversaries or admirers of Jesus, but the fourth by the other, Jesus him-

[15] Isa 11:1, 10; Jer 23:5.

self. Let us postpone for the moment discussion of this divergency; we shall come back to it.

There are indications that the fourfold scheme of questions is of Greek origin. For one thing, in the Talmudic episode, it is the Alexandrians who are the questioners. This is significant no matter whether the report is historical or not—and considering that Joshua, in A.D. 130, as an old man, followed Hadrian to Egypt, it would be rash to assert that it cannot be historical.

Further, the use of the word *ḥokhma*, "wisdom," for what is ordinarily described as *halakha*, "legal points," also suggests a Greek background. Much later, in the 3rd and 4th cents., Eleazar b. Pedath and Raba used *ḥokhma* in this sense;[16] the former was a fervent advocate of Jewish missionary efforts,[17] the latter lived at Mahuza on the Tigris, in a community rich in proselytes. The term *haggadha*, too, is employed in a special sense in the story of Joshua and the Alexandrians. Whereas, generally, it denotes any exegesis of no immediate bearing on the law, here it is confined to the problem of "antinomy," the apparent conflict between two verses.

Again, the appearance of *derekh 'ereṣ*, "principles of moral and successful life," as one of the four cardinal types of question, points in the direction of Hellenism, where this branch of philosophy was greatly cultivated. The questions which, according to the *Letter of Aristeas,* King Ptolemy put to the seventy-two Jewish sages all concern *derekh 'ereṣ*: Which is the highest good in life? How can one attain wealth? Wisdom? Justice?

Similarly, the scorn poured on the belief in resurrection reflects an attitude widespread among Hellenized Jews. Elsewhere in the Talmud,[18] Queen Cleopatra is represented as wondering whether the dead will rise clothed or naked. This was the sort of thing expected of Alexandrians; they are here represented by Queen Cleopatra because the ambiguous flavour of the question suits her character. As for the New Testament, the question concerning resurrection breathes the same spirit as those to be found in the Talmud; and Herodians and Sadducees figure among the questioners.

It might be worth while to search Hellenistic writings on rhetoric for a parallel to, or rather the model of, the fourfold scheme.

At any rate, whoever collected the New Testament questions acted on a definite, artistic plan. Was it Mark or a pre-Markan narrator? Nothing seems to speak against the former alternative. It might perhaps be objected that, if the classification is Greek in origin, it must have been imposed on the New Testament material by a pre-Markan, Hellenistic editor. But this does not follow at all. By the age of Mark, the classification was surely known to the most Jewish of Palestinian Rabbis. It would be used by them wherever it appeared suitable. It was not the only form of Greek origin they used. There is no reason why Mark should not be the author of the grouping to be met with in his and Matthew's gospels.

[16] *b. Shab.* 113b, 31a. In the story of the end of Eliezer ben Hyrcanus, *y. Shab.* 5b, the word seems to signify, not (as is maintained by Strack-Billerbeck., vol. 4 (1928), pt. 1, 316, n. 1) *halakha,* but "wisdom," "intelligence," as opposed to disorder of the mind from which a dying person may suffer.

[17] *b. Pes.* 87b: God scattered Israel in order that they should convert the Gentiles to Judaism.

[18] *b. Sanh.* 90b.

It is, of course, doubtful to what extent we may rely on the Talmudic pattern for filling in details in Matthew and Mark. Still, it should be observed that, where the Alexandrians put questions of *haggadha*, about apparent contradictions between passages from Scripture, the answer is invariably a "distinction." Both passages, that is, are upheld, each being assigned its proper field of application. For example, Ezekiel says that God "has no pleasure" in a sinner's death; yet according to 1 Samuel, "it pleased him" to kill the sons of Eli. Both verses, R. Joshua explains, speak the truth. The antinomy is to be solved by referring that from Ezekiel to the death of such as repent, that from 1 Samuel to the death of the impenitent. Similarly, "the Lord chose Zion" before Solomon married a daughter of the Pharaoh, i.e. so long as the people kept away from foreign idols, but "the city provoked his fury" from that marriage onwards.

If the New Testament question of *haggadha*, concerning the contradictory notions of the Messiah contained in Scripture, is closely analogous—as it may well be at least in Mark and Matthew, where the fourfold scheme is introduced—then the answer implied is not that one notion is right and the other wrong, but that both are right in different contexts. Say, the Messiah is David's son up to a certain moment in history, but his Lord from then; or—this would mean that we have before us an adumbration of Paul's teaching in Romans[19]—he is David's son according to the flesh, but his Lord according to the spirit.

B. The Passover Haggadah

The results we have reached are fully confirmed by a section from the Passover Haggadah, the traditional Jewish service on Passover eve.

The Bible four times ordains that children should be taught the significance of the exodus from Egypt. In the Haggadah of the Seder, the service on Passover eve, these passages are taken to allude to four different types of sons. (1) The *ḥakham*, the wise son, puts a question showing that he wishes to know about all the various laws concerning Passover: "And when thy son asketh thee, What mean the testimonies, and the statutes, and the judgments, which the Lord our God hath commanded us? Then thou shalt say" etc.[20] This is a question of *ḥokhma*, "wisdom," in the sense of "points of law," *halakha*. The latter term (*hilekhoth happesaḥ*, "detailed laws respecting the Passover") actually occurs in the reply the Passover Haggadah declares suitable for the wise son's question.

(2) The *rasha'*, the wicked son, puts a scoffing question by which he rudely dissociates himself from the worshipping community: "And when your children shall say unto you, What mean ye by this service? Ye shall say" etc.[21] In Rabbinic interpretation, the contemptuous "What mean ye?" instead of "What mean we?" indicates a question of *boruth*, "vulgarity." It is noteworthy that though it is not specifically directed against resurrection—the Rabbis could not insert an express reference to it into the Biblical

[19] Rom 1:3 f.

[20] Deut 6:20 f. On the reading "commanded us," instead of the usual "commanded you," we shall make a few remarks presently.

[21] Exod 12:26 f.

text—yet in Talmudic theology to dissociate oneself from the community and to deny resurrection are very similar sins, marks of the same vicious disposition, one of them almost necessarily involving the other. For example, among those consigned to eternal damnation are "atheists who repudiate the Law and deny the resurrection and separate themselves from the ways of the congregation."[22]

(3) The *tam*, the son of plain piety, puts a simple question about the meaning of the festival in general: "And when thy son asketh thee, What is this? Thou shalt say" etc.[23] He is not interested in details, only in the essential significance of things: "What is this?"—the nearest to a question concerning *derekh 'ereṣ*, "principles of life,"—that the Rabbis were able to find in these Biblical injunctions as to instruction of children.

(4) The fourth type of son is he *she'eno yodhe'a lish'ol*, "who does not know how to ask," and whose father, therefore, must take the initiative in opening the instruction: "And thou shalt show thy son in that day, saying" etc.[24] In this case the Bible does not say "And when thy son asketh thee," but at once states the duty to teach, "And thou shalt show thy son." So the Rabbis conclude that the passage must speak about a son incapable of questioning.

Evidently, the author of this Midrash works on the basis of the fourfold scheme of questions we have been considering, his aim being to impose it on his Biblical material. He succeeds in identifying three questions occurring in the Pentateuch with three types occurring in the scheme: law, vulgarity, and principles. One type only he is compelled to abandon—contradictions in Scripture—because the fourth Biblical passage mentions no question. He has to substitute the person who cannot ask: with such a one it is incumbent on you to take the first step. The sequence in which he gives the types, it may be observed, is the same as in the Talmud, except that, very naturally, the son who cannot ask comes at the end. Hence, while the Talmudic order is law, contradictions in Scripture, vulgarity, principles, that in the Passover Haggadah is law, vulgarity, principles, he who does not know how to ask.

This piece of liturgy, then, testifies to the popularity of the fourfold classification of questions with the early Rabbis. The Midrash of the four sons is very old. It is preserved not only in the Passover Haggadah, but also, with certain variations, in the Mekhilta and the Palestinian Talmud.[25]

It supports, too, our opinion that, if there was a fixed order in which the four types used to be listed, it was that followed in the anecdote of Joshua and the Alexandrians. The order in the Passover Haggadah is best accounted for as derived from this one.

Furthermore, there is here additional evidence for our suggestion that this classification is a Hellenistic growth. For, surely, the Midrash under notice is Alexandrian. Quite apart from the significant use of *ḥakham*, "wise," in the sense of "interested in points of law, *halakha*"—we have already called attention to the corresponding use of the noun *ḥokhma*, "wisdom," in the story of R. Joshua—it is clear that the Midrash proceeds, not from the Massoretic text of the Pentateuch, but either from the LXX itself or

[22] Thus the School of Hillel; see *b. R. Sh.* 16b f.

[23] Exod 13:14.

[24] Exod 13:8.

[25] *Mek.* on Exod 13:8, 14; *y. Pes.* 37d; also *Yalqut* on Exod 13:14.

from a Hebrew text underlying the LXX. We have seen that the wicked son dissociates himself from the congregation by asking "What mean ye?" instead of "What mean we?" However, in the Massoretic text, the question which the Midrash assigns to the wise son is little different in this respect; Deut 6:20 runs, "What mean the testimonies, and the statutes, and the judgments, which the Lord our God hath commanded you"—*'ethkhem*, "commanded you," not, as we should expect, "commanded us." It is only the LXX which has the latter: ἐνετείλατο ἡμῖν. That, in Greek or Hebrew, is what the author of the Midrash must have had before him when he gave this question to the wise son.

Actually, the old editions of the Passover Haggadah as well as the versions of the Midrash extant in the Mekhilta and Palestinian Talmud do all read *'othanu*, "us." That modern editions assimilate the question to the recognized Massoretic text and put *'ethkhem*, "you,"[26] is not surprising. But the reading "us" alone makes sense from the point of view of the Midrash, with its emphasis on the contrast between the wicked son who defies the community and the wise son who regards himself as a member of it. And this reading "us" points to Egypt.

It would be quite wrong to infer that the Midrash did not form part of the Palestinian liturgy in the New Testament period. There is, on the contrary, every reason to think that it did, considering its occurrence in the various sources mentioned. As far as the Passover Haggadah is concerned, it ought to be added that it is found in all rites without exception. The most Jewish circles of Palestine were by that time open to Alexandrian influence.

C. The Haggadah and the Gospels

In fact, it looks as if we might draw from this Midrash one or two far-reaching conclusions as to the exact treatment of the fourfold scheme by Mark or his authority. Matthew and Mark have the four types of question distinguished in the story of Joshua and the Alexandrians. But there is a difference which so far we have only noticed but not explained: in the story of Joshua, all questions are put by one side, in Matthew and Mark three are put by various people to Jesus, but the fourth by Jesus to the people. This division of the questions into three by the others and one by Jesus is not so natural that any narrator would try to compose a chapter on such a plan. Mark or his authority here followed the Midrash of the four sons, only three of them ask, whereas in the case of the fourth his father must make the beginning.

The Markan introduction to the fourth question, that by Jesus, is:[27] "And no man after that durst ask him; and Jesus answered and said while he taught in the temple." This is an unmistakable reference to the Passover Haggadah, which says: "And he who does not know how to ask, thou open [the instruction] for him."

To be sure, most editions of the New Testament print "And no man after that durst ask him," not as leading up to the fourth question, but as describing the effect produced by Jesus's answer to the third. However, for one thing it does not fit in this part. The third question is a genuine, reasonable one—"which is the first commandment?"—and

[26] The same is true of some editions of the Mekhilta.

[27] Mark 12:34 f.

the discussion following it ends with the assurance by Jesus: "Thou art not far from the kingdom of God." This should have had an encouraging rather than a deterrent effect. For another thing, there is excellent ancient authority—rightly accepted by Weiss—for connecting the clause with the fourth question.[28]

Of course, readers and copyists unaware of the model, i.e. the Midrash of the four sons, would be tempted to treat it as an appendix to the third, despite its not really fitting there. Already Matthew and Luke failed to see its real point. Matthew placed it right at the end of the entire section, after the fourth question put by Jesus.[29] That this version is secondary compared with Mark is proved, not only by the Passover liturgy, but also by Luke, where the clause still, as in Mark, precedes Jesus's question concerning the Messiah.[30] But even Luke misunderstood its original function. Instead of regarding it as the introduction to Jesus's question—"And no man after that durst ask him, and Jesus answered and said"—he regarded it as giving the reason (γάρ) for the praise extended to Jesus by the scribes after his refutation of the Sadducees: "Then certain of the scribes said, Master, thou hast well said, for after that they durst not ask him anything." These different attempts to rationalize the clause serve only to underline its peculiar role in Mark.

In Mark, it may be repeated, it belongs to the question put by Jesus. Mark—or an earlier narrator—in accordance with a current scheme collected four questions of *ḥokhma, boruth, derek 'ereṣ* and *haggadha*. But his division of these into three put by the people and one put by Jesus to them who do not dare to ask can be explained only as directly dependent on the Passover Haggadah. We are here in touch with an author—no reason why it should not be Mark—who still spent Passover eve with his family or friends reciting the Haggadah.

General considerations render it probable that portions of the gospels grew up in the form of additions to the traditional Passover liturgy made in Jewish-Christian circles. While in former times this liturgy had centred exclusively on the exodus from Egypt, now, where Christians assembled to observe Passover eve, the new redemption also was celebrated. The Markan section discussed furnishes definite proof that matters took this course. It betrays the immediate influence of the Passover-eve recital. Very likely, it first came into existence, or at any rate was published, on the occasion of a Jewish-Christian Seder.

If this is granted, we may bc ablc to understand that passage in Mark, so puzzling at first sight, where the scribe expresses his full agreement with Jesus as to the love of God and man and is told, "Thou art not far from the kingdom of God." No corresponding passage is supplied by Matthew and Luke. Indeed, they regard even the question about *derek 'ereṣ* as designed to ensnare Jesus. For Mark, it is put in good faith, just like the question of the son who is *tam*, "a man of plain piety," in the Passover Haggadah; and it is a characteristic of the *tam* readily to accept good advice—hence the emphat-

[28] See the apparatus in Eberhard Nestle's *Novum Testamentum Graece*, 13th ed. by Erwin Nestle (1927), 122, and J. Weiss, *Die drei älteren Evangelien*, 3rd ed. (1917), *ad loc.*

[29] Matt 22:46.

[30] Luke 20:40 f.

ic assent of the scribe, which Matthew and Luke would no longer appreciate. In Solomon's Song, the woman is called *tammathi*, generally translated "my undefiled." The Rabbis[31] hold that the reference is to Israel, who at mount Sinai showed plain piety by the unreserved promise "All that the Lord hath said will we do and be obedient."[32]

A problem is created by the fact that, in Matthew, the vulgar, wicked questioners—the Sadducees—are "put to silence," "muzzled," whereas Mark and Luke use a milder expression: Jesus "answers them well" or "says well." The Passover Haggadah declares that your reply to the wicked son's question should be such as "to make his teeth blunt." "To muzzle a person"—*ḥasam*—is not quite the same as "to blunt a person's teeth"—*hiqha shinnayim*—but it is clearly far closer to it than is "to answer well" or "to say well." Unless we assume that Matthew introduced the stronger term for reasons of his own (and one could think of such reasons), it looks as if he had here drawn on a variant older than what we find in the present form of Mark or Luke.

It remains to add that the Midrash of the four sons, in the course of its transmission, suffered no fewer alterations than its Markan counterpart. For example, in the Palestinian Talmud and Mekhilta, the son who asks a simple, general question is no longer labelled as *tam*, "of plain piety," but as *ṭippesh*, "stupid." The significance of the former type—the Biblical basis for which had been Jacob, the "plain man," *'ish tam*[33]—is forgotten; *derekh 'ereṣ* has dropped out.

This change brings with it another regarding the order of the types. The original order, preserved in the story of Joshua and the Alexandrians, is: (1) *ḥokhma* (in the sense of *halakha*), (2) *haggadha* (contradiction between verses with no bearing on law), (3) *boruth*, (4) *derekh 'ereṣ*. As we saw, the Passover Midrash, owing to the nature of the Scriptural passages it uses, must abandon *haggadha* and substitute spontaneous instruction, instruction without question. This instruction without question is put at the end, so that the order now is: (1) *ḥokhma* (*halakha*), (2) *boruth*, (3) *derekh 'ereṣ*, (4) instruction of one unable to ask. It is the same order as that in Matthew and Mark (except that in Matthew and Mark number 4 is instruction in *haggadha* of one unable to ask).

On the whole, the version of the Midrash given by the Passover Haggadah proves the least corrupt. It is easier to introduce major changes into a work studied by scholars—Mekhilta or Palestinian Talmud—than into a piece of liturgy in universal use. Certainly, there are exceptions. One we have discussed at some length: modern editions of the Haggadah assimilate the quotation of Deut 6:20 to the Massoretic text, printing "commanded you" in the place of the "commanded us" of the ancient editions. But this is really no more than an adjustment of the Passover liturgy to an even more important branch of liturgy—the reading of the law.

[31] *Song of Songs Rab.* on 5:2.

[32] Exod 24:7.

[33] Gen 25:27. Cp. also in Talmudic language the antithesis between *tam* and *mu'adh*, things normally harmless and things likely to cause injury: e.g. *m. B. K.* 1:4 f.

Zukunftsmusik: Some Desirable Lines Of Exploration In The New Testament Field*

Never before have I been officially encouraged to indulge in this pastime and I appreciate the privilege.[1]

I.

A dictionary like Kittel's,[2] specialising in theological themes, needs constant updating—even if we leave aside certain pervasive simplifications in the area of semantics which have lately come under attack.[3] The scant article on the Land, *ge*, for example,[4] must be completely redone in view of W. D. Davies's pioneering work.[5] A more general desideratum is the inclusion of quite a few concepts at first sight not qualifying. In fact, just because the theology is in these cases implied, part of an overall attitude, rather than explicit, *ad hoc*, we may come here upon clues to deeper strata. *Phimoo*, "to muzzle," to be adverted to below (under V) has no entry. I published both a lecture and a little book on the Scriptural use of "sudden" and a number of particles denoting "at once."[6] Since, as quite often, I did not spell out my major intent, I was apparently misunderstood as being interested in nothing but philological exactitude. But I meant more. "Sudden" is apt to reflect an inner experience clearly reaching into the numinous: "and suddenly there was a multitude of the heavenly host."[7] But even the innocuous-seeming "at once" can be far from religiously neutral. Two examples:

(1) Mark employs *euthys* 40 to 50 times against 15 to 20 in Matthew, 17 in Luke cum Acts, 6 in John. Even though the literal sense "at once" is not seldom present, the sense "duly"—OED: "in due manner, order, form or season"—is never absent and at times the only one. Jesus at Capernaum taught as one having authority "and *euthys* there was in their synagogue a man with an unclean spirit."[8] "Duly" and nothing else. It is Mark's way of conveying his fundamental estimate of these events: they take place

* To Geza and Pamela Vermes

[1] Read at the Symposium de Interrelatione Evangeliorum, Pascha 1984, Jerusalem. I am grateful to William David Davies for his criticism and encouragement.

[2] G. Kittel set it up, editing *Theologisches Wörterbuch zum Neuen Testament*, vol. 1, in 1933.

[3] Spearheaded by J. Barr, *The Semantics of Biblical Language* (1961).

[4] Sasse, in vol. 1, 676 ff.

[5] It will suffice to name *The Gospel and the Land* (1974).

[6] *Suddenness and Awe in Scripture* (1964), and *The Sudden in the Scriptures* (1964) [683 ff.]

[7] Luke 2:13.

[8] Mark 1:23.

one after another in a planful (*planmässig*), inevitable unfolding. Three stretches are lacking the significant connective: the day of questions, the apocalypse and the passion. These he took over from elsewhere without bringing them into line. To the first I shall return below (under IV).

It may be worth adding that the shading-off of *euthys* into "duly" does not originate with Mark; it is met with, e.g., in Aristotle.[9] The root meaning of the word is "straight," and English "straight" or "straightways" also occasionally veers towards "duly."

(2) *Parachrema*, which we may translate "forthwith" in order to keep it apart from *euthys*, occurs in one Matthean pericope, never in Mark, 16 times in Luke cum Acts, never in John. Luke's predilection for the word is explicable by its frequency in medical literature. However, in the New Testament it invariably refers to the immediate, miraculous actualisation of a decision from on high, mostly of Jesus. He takes Jairus's daughter by the hand and tells her to arise "and her spirit came again and she arose forthwith."[10] Peter, in his name, commands a lame man to walk and takes him by the hand "and forthwith his feet received strength."[11] Again, Peter tells Sapphira that she is doomed to instant death "and she fell down forthwith."[12] The quick success of a wonder-worker's intervention is, of course, a widespread phenomenon: in Lucian, a magician assembles all reptiles of a farm and blows on them "and they were instantly—*autika*—burned."[13] On a vulgar level, the illusionist's "presto" belongs here. Yet there are also those in touch with powers that will cure or destroy over time. I guess this delayed-action prodigy is a later growth; for one thing, the evidence is so much less evident. But it, too, goes back to long before New Testament times.[14] At any rate, Luke's *parachrema* does tell us something about his thoughts concerning the effect of a divine or divinely-sanctioned verdict. In one Matthean pericope with *parachrema*, incidentally, the fig-tree cursed by Jesus withers "forthwith" while Mark has the disciples find it withered a day later.[15]

II.

It so happens that a passage containing *euthys* furnishes what I regard as conclusive proof that Matthew draws on Mark, our written Mark.[16] Let me at the outset reassure upholders of the former's priority that I shall eventually meet them a quarter of the way (under V).

To start with Matthew: "Having been baptized, Jesus at once came up out of the water; and behold, the heavens were rent and he saw God descending." "He at once came up out of the water"—this is passing strange. Why ever should he have stayed

[9] Aristotle, *Metaphysics* 4.2.6.10.1004a.

[10] Luke 8:55.

[11] Acts 3:7.

[12] Acts 5:10.

[13] Lucian, *The Lover of Lies*, 13 i.f.

[14] The two kinds of miracles represent a dichotomy met in practically all areas of life. In a forthcoming paper, "The Moment and the Flow of Time," I give other examples.

[15] Matt 21:19 f.; Mark 11:13 ff.

[16] Matt 3:16; Mark 1:10.

down? Now look at Mark. Jesus was baptized "and at once, having come up out of the water, he saw the heavens rent and the Spirit descending." To put "at once" in front, next to a participle not linked to it, and only then the verb which it does qualify is a favourite Marcan device: Jesus is sending two disciples to a certain village "and at once, having entered into it, you will find a colt tied."[17] The statement "and at once, having come up out of the water, he saw" etc. is tremendously meaningful. *Euthys* here signifies "and directly" as well as "and duly." It is at the moment of his emerging from baptism that a proselyte to Judaism's transmutation takes place: "He immerses and comes up, behold, he is like an Israelite in all respects."[18] Matthew makes two sentences of Mark's one, changing the participle into a finite mood. The result ought to be: "Jesus came up and at once the heavens were rent." But he mispunctuates his source, joins the adverb to the participle and reads "and at once having come up, he saw the heavens rent." Hence the absurd ring to his presentation. It is readily explained in this way and I do not think it can be in any other. Luke, not surprisingly, cuts out the coming up altogether; it is on Jesus's praying that the heavens open.[19]

III.

My inference from this episode would hold even without the Jewish pattern behind Mark. Even without it, that is, he would make sense while Matthew would be intelligible only as proceeding from his account. At this juncture, however, I confess that time and again I find Mark preserving more accurately the conditions of Jesus's ministry, both as to basic, popularly-shared Jewish life and beliefs and as to peculiar traits of the protagonist's circle. Such an impression, of course, is not reached without close attention to extra-Biblical material shedding light on the contemporary situation, Midrash and Talmud *inter alia*.

Take the battle between precept and example as man's guide. I shall be brief about it, since I have said enough elsewhere.[20] The main trend of the period, spreading from Sadducees to other groups, was to confine fully-binding force to precept alone. The *Zadokite Fragments*,[21] combating polygamy and probably also divorce, adduce three verses from the Pentateuch: "Male and female created he them," at the time understood to describe the ideal, androgynous *Ur*-Adam,[22] "The animals went in two by two"[23] and "The king shall not multiply wives to himself."[24] The first two offer examples, the third is a precept. It is safe to assume that the third—not really a good text for general con-

[17] Mark 11:2.

[18] *b. Yeb.* 47b.

[19] Luke 3:21.

[20] *The New Testament and Rabbinic Judaism* (1956, repr. 1973), 67 ff. [249 ff.], "Responsibilities of Master and Disciples in the Gospels," in *NTS*, 19 (1972), 4 ff. [752 ff.], and *The Old Testament in the New: a Jewish Perspective,* section III [51].

[21] *Zadokite Fragments* 7.1 ff.

[22] Gen 1:27, 5:2; *Gen. Rab.* on 1:26 f.; *Mek.* on Exod 12:40; Philo, *Op.* 24.76; *Leg. All.* 2.4.13; *Her.* 33.164.

[23] Gen 7:9.

[24] Deut 17:17.

sumption—was appended in response to the movement just mentioned. Similarly, both Matthew[25] and Mark,[26] in the controversy about divorce, begin with "Male and female created he them" and then add "And the twain shall be one flesh."[27] No doubt in this case, too, the example once stood by itself but was gradually found inadequate in debate with opponents.

When we go on from here to the Sabbath dispute caused by the disciples plucking corn, Mark[28]—followed by Luke[29]—is content with the example of David and his band who, as they were hungry, ate of the shewbread reserved for the priests.[30] Matthew[31] provides supplementary defence based on precept; according to the Book of Numbers[32] the Temple service overrides the Sabbath restrictions—*a fortiori* (yes, the text needs a highly-refined extensive interpretation by the method "light and weighty" to be applicable) the present, greater task will do so. The reverse development is out of the question: had Mark had the more cogent argument available, he would not have dropped it. It should be remembered that at Rome also, by the 1st century, example no longer sufficed in matters of licit or illicit.[33]

Another problem I need not enlarge on is denial of one's faith under duress.[34] The Marcan account of Peter's conduct, when suspected of association with Jesus,[35] precisely reflects the position of the sages, in essence going back to the Old Testament era. His first reply is to one person only, the High Priest's maid, and the formulation is evasive, "I do not understand." According to majority doctrine, a renunciation in private was less terrible than one in public, and equivocation less terrible than outright disavowal.[36] The second reply is to the maid amidst bystanders: in public, though still oblique. Then the bystanders press him and he swears: "I know not the man." In public and direct: the extreme betrayal. None of the parallels in the other three gospels[37] is equally pristine.

It may be worth pointing out that there is nothing academic about the distinctions here operative. Any member of an embattled minority would be familiar with them. They are indeed a sort of natural law, apt to recur wherever certain conditions exist. In Europe, in the 1930s and 1940s, I suppose there was hardly a state or group that did

[25] Matt 19:3 ff.

[26] Mark 10:2 ff.

[27] Gen 2:24.

[28] Mark 2:23 ff.

[29] Luke 6:1 ff.

[30] 1 Sam 21:3 ff.

[31] Matt 12:1 ff.

[32] Num 28:9 f.

[33] A related illustration may be found in my "The Three Quotations from Homer in *Digest* 18.1.1.1," in *CLJ*, 10 (1949), 215.

[34] See "Limitations on Self-Sacrifice in Jewish Law and Tradition," in *Theology*, 72 (1969), 291 ff. [*Talmudic Law*, 45 ff.]

[35] Mark 14:66 ff.

[36] E.g. *Gen. Rab.* on 35:17, referring to the disguise of students of Joshua ben Hananiah in a persecution around A.D. 100, *Tanhuma* on Num 20:12, as for the publicity of Moses's disbelief, *Esth. Rab.* on 2:20, as for the queen's tacit concealment of her religion.

[37] Matt 26:69 ff.; Luke 22:55 ff.; John 18:16 ff.

not at some stage or other arrive at the norm—often felt rather than spelled out—that, while to save your neck by a concession in private and/or ambiguous might be venial, a public, unqualified abandonment of your cause would not: its effect would be so much more devastating.

IV.

About my next item I discover one or two new facets each time I return to it.[38] It is in any case particularly relevant to this conference's endeavour. It may be observed at once that it, too, involves a matter which, though most present-day students will find it recondite, was anything but that for the nuclear Christian sect: the Passover-eve recital, the Haggadah.

This time I begin with Mark. Four questions are considered in succession: Is it lawful to pay tribute to Caesar? Asked by Pharisees and Herodians. If a woman goes through a number of levirate marriages, whose wife will she be on resurrection? Asked by Sadducees. Which is the foremost commandment? Asked by a scribe admiring Jesus's stand. How can the Messiah be David's son (in accordance with numerous texts—at least as understood at the time[39]) seeing that David (in the Psalter[40]) calls him his Lord? Asked by Jesus. As there is no logical or historical link between these matters, their compilation has been looked on as relatively late and artificial. In reality, what we have before us is the earliest composite chapter in the gospels.

There is first-century evidence in the Talmud[41] of a division of questions into four types: "of wisdom," about points of law; "of vulgar mockery," such as whether the child Elisha brought back to life[42] conveyed uncleanness, as a corpse; "of the proper way of the land," about practical piety; and "of interpretation," about inconsistencies in the Bible, as when one verse speaks of God's choice of Zion, another of his rejection.[43] The New Testament questions manifestly fall under this schema: the inquiry concerning the permissibility of tribute, the gibe at resurrection, the wish for an overall direction, the puzzle of contradiction. It can be shown, however, that they are put together, not from any scholastic bent, but in analogy to a section of the Haggadah.[44] In it, the four Pentateuchic admonitions to instruct the youth in the subject of the exodus are taken to represent the categories under notice. The passage mentioning "the testimonies, statutes and judgments which the Lord has commanded us"[45] represents legal exploration. That where the youth asks "What mean you by this service?"[46]—"you" instead

[38] Matt 22:15 ff.; Mark 12:13 ff.; Luke 10:25 ff., 20:20 ff. See my *New Testament and Rabbinic Judaism*, 158 ff. [343 ff.], "The Earliest Structure of the Gospels," in *NTS*, 5 (1959), 180 ff. [334 ff.], and *He That Cometh* (1966), 8 ff. [432 ff.].

[39] 2 Sam 7:12 f.; Isa 11:1, 10; Jer 23:5; Ps 89:4 f., 132:11 etc.

[40] Ps 110:1.

[41] *b. Nidd.* 69b ff.

[42] 2 Kgs 4:18 ff.

[43] Ps 132:13; Jer 32:31.

[44] In the first, pre-meal half, beginning: "With regard to four sons, disciples, speaks the Torah."

[45] Deut 6:20 f.

[46] Exod 12:26 f.

of "we"—represents contemptuous disavowal of communion. That with the general "What is this?"[47] represents honest, open search. That where the instruction refers to "what the Lord did unto me when I came forth from Egypt"[48] is at variance with other statements according to which the Lord rescued not "me" but "us," "your fathers," etc.[49]

The dependence of the Marcan piece on the Seder is beyond doubt. The four classes appear in the same sequence, different from the Talmudic one. The answer to the juridical problem is cryptic in both cases. (When those out to inflame the Romans against Jesus speak of an absolute prohibition of tribute,[50] they are misrepresenting him.) While these and other, similar data might be held inconclusive, what clinches the argument is that both in the Haggadah and in Mark—and not in the Talmudic paradigms—the final question is put by the instructor. Moreover, as if to underline its singularity, in both—and not in the Talmud—it is left unanswered. Why? The authors of the Passover liturgy noticed that the first three of their quotes respecting instruction employ some phrasing like "and when your son asks you in time to come, you shall say"; whereas the fourth one, omitting the son's initiative, starts right off "and you shall show your son in that day, saying." Whence they inferred that Scripture distinguishes between the following four characters among sons or disciples: the wise one, asking about law, the wicked one, asking in order to jeer, the simply pious one, asking for plain guidance—these three are pretty obvious—and, far less obvious, the one who refrains from asking. He is to be stimulated by father or master, who will cite him a text controverted elsewhere. To add the solution would defeat the aim, which is the encouragement of participation. Jesus's closing riddle is intelligible only—but also fully—against the background of the Haggadah.

Indeed, it is more faithful to its model than most current editions and translations make it look. In the Haggadah, the fourth category is introduced thus: "And he who does not know how to ask, you [father or master] open for him [i.e. open the discourse for him by posing a text to be elucidated[51]]." In precise conformity, Mark introduces it "And no one any further dared to ask him, and commencing the discourse Jesus said." Ordinarily, the section "And no man any further dared to ask him" is treated, not as leading up to the fourth question, by Jesus, but as depicting the effect of his reaction to the third. But that reaction is the opposite of intimidating; his concluding words are "You are not far from the kingdom." Besides, my paragraphing is supported by excellent medieval authority.[52] The New English Bible accepts it.[53] But it still omits the initial "and"; and it substitutes the elegant "and Jesus went on to say" for the heavy "and

[47] Exod 13:14.

[48] Exod 13:8.

[49] E.g. Deut 26:8; Josh 24:6.

[50] Luke 23:2.

[51] On this sense of *pathaḥ*, "to open," see W. Bacher, *Die Bibelexegetische Terminologie der Tannaiten* (1899), 162 f.

[52] See J. Weiss, *Die drei älteren Evangelien*, 3rd ed. (1917).

[53] *New Testament* (1961), 81.

commencing the discourse Jesus said." Yet, while "to commence and say"[54] is often eroded, denoting little more than "to speak," in the present instance it has its full value: emphatically, the master makes the beginning. I am not saying that, had I been on the Dodd committee, I might not, in deference to the less pedantic reader—the "simply pious"—have voted for the smoother expression.

The day of questions allows us a moving glimpse of the kind of Seder celebrated by the believers in the very first decades after the crucifixion: in the main traditional, with the customary elaborations of the Mosaic exodus supplemented and slowly replaced by parallels from the more recent one. They had not so far developed their own literary structures, the new wine was as yet poured into old bottles. One result, by the way, is that (except for minor adjustments) the material of the supplements must be extremely near in date to the events; in other words, there is the strongest presumption in favour of the historicity (on the whole) of the four incidents here assembled. However, to pursue this line would take me too far from the central topic.

Very likely the chapter is one of those reported by Eusebius[55]—who quotes Papias, who quotes yet prior testimony—to have reached Mark from Peter. Let us go again through the four portions. The problem of tribute to Caesar is closely related to that of temple tax, brought up in Matthew, with Peter a prominent figure. I have suggested elsewhere that the episode is more significant than commonly thought.[56] An intriguing feature may be added: Jesus does not wait for Peter to ask—he might never have done so—but "anticipates" him[57] and himself raises the question, about law this time. As for Jesus's rebuttal of the denial of resurrection, in a lecture just published I remark on Peter, in Acts, distinctly harking back to it.[58] Brotherly love appears in 1 Peter[59] but, admittedly, no extensive apostolic communication would be without some such maxim and in any case the authorship of the Epistle is uncertain. What is striking, however, is Peter's intense engagement in question 4, the son of David—Lord of David discrepancy, in his Pentecostal address,[60] with echoes later on.[61] It was taken for granted, of course, that, as Scripture cannot err, every conflict between two (or more) passages

[54] *Apokrinomai kai lego*, in Hebrew *'ana we'amar*; e.g. Deut 21:7; Job 3.2. In old-fashioned German Bibles, one often finds *anheben und sagen*, more satisfactory than the scrupulous "to answer and say" or *antworten und sagen*. Though, come to think of it, it does obscure the ultimate provenance of the phrase. So does *das Wort nehmen und sagen*, to which E. Klostermann resorts. *Das Markus-Evangelium* (4th ed., 1950), 128. But it gets the meaning absolutely.

[55] *Eccl. Hist.* 3.39.15.

[56] Matt 17:24 ff.; see ["Responsibilities of Master and Disciples in the Gospels"] *NTS*, 19 (1972), 13 ff. [760 ff.].

[57] A concept worth studying. It recurs, e.g., in Jonah 4:2; 1 Thes 4:15; Josephus, *Ant.* 1. Proem 3.12; *Vita*, 315; *y. Meg.* 74a. See my *Typologie im Werk des Flavius Josephus*, vol. 6 of Sitzungsberichte der Bayerischen Akademie der Wissenschaften, Phil.-Hist. Klasse (1977), 4 f. (repr. in *Freiburger Rundbrief*, 31 [1979], 60, English translation in *JJS*, 31 (1980), 19 f.), and "Jonah: a Reminiscence" in *JJS*, 35 (1984), 39.

[58] Acts 3:13 ff., 5:30; see *The Old Testament in the New*, section II [44], German translation by W. Schuller, vol. 10 of *Xenia*, 14 ff.

[59] 1 Peter 3:9.

[60] Acts 2:25 ff.

[61] Acts 5:31.

must, on careful probing, turn out to be merely apparent: the passages, it will emerge, cover different ground, each of them having its own range of validity. In the Talmudic paradigm adduced above, the line "God has chosen Zion"—from the Psalter, i.e. David—is regarded as applying to the time before Solomon married the daughter of Pharaoh,[62] the line "the city has been a provocation of my anger"—from Jeremiah—to the time after. From the answer to the wicked questioner in the Haggadah, it can be seen that one way of reconciling the statement "the Lord freed me from Egypt" with references to the freeing of "us," "your fathers" or the like, was to assign to the former the message that deliverance took place only for the sake of him who trusts in God and not for his scoffing adversary. Peter (if I may give a deplorably rough summary) explains that, while David cherished the promise that the Messiah would be a descendant of his, he also foresaw that that personage would be far superior to him, in being raised from Hades to a seat at the right hand of God without experiencing corruption.

Quite apart from these details—if Mark received this Seder collage from Peter, it would chime in exactly with what we find in Eusebius: Peter "shaped his teachings in accordance with the demands of any occasion, instead of purporting to make an orderly presentation of the Lord's sayings; so that Mark did nothing wrong in thus writing down some pieces as he remembered them." An explicit apology, required at a time when it was still feasible directly to compare, or contrast, the actual sequence, etc. of the incidents with that adjusted to novel requirements—to the revised Passover-eve recital, for instance. Suppose, as an example, that the clash with the Sadducees, question 2, in reality took place before that with the Pharisees and Herodians, question 1, Peter, we are given to understand, switched them around so as to fit into the customary Seder; and Mark, in adopting his order, acted only as a loyal transmitter whom it would be unfair to censure. Let us recall at this juncture the conspicuous absence of the Marcan *euthys*. No "and duly there were the Sadducees" or the like. This chapter is not part of the *planmässige* course of events: it is structured so as to satisfy a *chreia*, a particular want.

When I appealed to ancient Church tradition about thirty years ago, the reaction was so cool that in the first draft of this paper I still felt I had to defend myself. To judge by the present symposium, however, respect for that witness is increasing. At any rate, a major reason for spurning it is surely that it has not seemed possible to make sense, real, concrete sense, of Eusebius's text (except by doing violence to it, one way or another). Well, it is possible: the shaping of the material with a view to the demands of the Seder worship is a case—there may be others—perfectly according with what we are told. Here may be the place to stress that there would scarcely be a greater communal need around, say, A.D. 40, than for guidance on just those issues (the sequence being determined by the Haggadah model): (1) What did the group owe to the foreign government and the native priesthood, an unholy alliance between which had just contrived the horrid death of its head? (2) What about resurrection, linchpin of the group's hope? (3) What, beyond all minutiae, did the group's head expect of members and would-be members big or small, near or far? (4) What about the strangely miraculous Messiahship

[62] 1 Kgs 11:1.

of the group's head? Peter, or whoever amplified the recital expounding the old redemption with parallels from the new, chose well.

In passing—the Haggadah introduces one "who does not know how to ask" whereas Mark has "no one dare to ask." The character under review is met in Philo, as "not daring."[63] (Generally, this root is quite rare in his work.[64]) The perfect man, we are told, ought to teach "those of the young who are willing; and if a less daring one hesitates through awe—or shame—and is slow to come forward and learn, he himself ought to go and pour out guidance." "Not to know how to" and "not to dare to" are near enough; psychology will find countless ties; either, for example, may cause or result from the other. Still, they are not identical. My hunch is that "not to dare to" would be more readily used of a disciple's position *vis-à-vis* the master, a Socrates, an Apollonius, a Hillel, "not to know how to" of an as yet untrained son's *vis-à-vis* his father. The former has more of an aura of formal distance about it. Even while the Temple stood, only a fraction of Jewry made the Passover pilgrimage. Since A.D. 70, the Jewish Seder has become largely confined to the family. Largely, never absolutely; and especially in the immediate post-destruction phase, approximations to the past were sought—witness an illustrious gathering at Lydda, under Gamaliel II, mentioned in the Tosephta,[65] and one at Bene-Berak, under Eliezer ben Hyrcanus, Joshua ben Hananiah, Eleazar ben Azariah, Akiba and Tarphon, which actually came to be commemorated in the Haggadah itself. But with no more groups of devotees going up to Jerusalem under a revered leader, the dice were loaded in favour of a family affair. It is not surprising, therefore, that "not to know how to" alone survives in the liturgy.[66]

When we now proceed to Matthew and Luke, their versions are plainly due to incomprehension of the original scheme. The straightforward, pious seeker has become a decoy—though an inquiry concerning the most basic commandment is hardly a promising trap. Luke, in addition, transfers this section to a totally different context which, it has been noticed, it does not fit;[67] while the questioner, despite his bad faith, still earns Jesus's approval. As for the lack of daring, Matthew gives it what seems to him a more plausible place at the end of the entire chapter: nobody could answer Jesus's question and that stopped people asking him. In Luke, the clause still precedes Jesus's question. But from forming the introduction—"and no one dared and Jesus commenced"—it is turned into the reason some scribes admire his refutation of the Sadducees: they admire it, that is, "because [*gar*] no one any further dared to ask him

[63] Philo, *De spec. leg.* 4.26.140.

[64] See Fitzer, *tolmao,* in *Theologisches Wörterbuch,* 8 (ed. G. Friedrich. 1969), 184.

[65] *t. Pes.* 10:12.

[66] C. K. Barrett points out to me that the disciple who does not ask yet receives the appropriate instruction may be in John's mind in several verses of ch. 16. Perhaps 4:33 f. is a further instance: much as in 16:19 f., Jesus replies to a question the disciples put, not to him, but to each other. Complex problems are raised by 21:12: none of the disciples "dares to examine Jesus" as, risen, he shows himself a third time. Whoever authored this pericope just conceivably preferred "to examine" to "to ask" in order to indicate that what still puzzles the disciples, by now clear as to the identity of their visitor, is his precise nature in this state, no longer with the dead but not yet ascended. Nor shall I inspect an occasion when the disciples "fear to ask Jesus" about a particularly frightening matter, Mark 9:32; Luke 9:45.

[67] Luke 10:25 ff. See J. M. Creed, *The Gospel According to St. Luke* (1930), 151.

anything." The Midrash of the four sons or disciples is shattered and scattered. Far be it from me to deny that, in the process, valuable new perspectives have been introduced.

How, one may wonder, could somebody as close to Jewish practice as Matthew deal with the material in this insensitive fashion? The answer is that, once the chapter was transmitted by itself, no longer embedded in the regular Passover service, it was easy to miss the connection. After all, it has taken till the mid-twentieth century to rediscover it. We must bear in mind that the exchanges presented, though they were no longer of such acute concern in his day as in Peter's, were still important enough. Right to the present their weight has seemed to scholars adequate ground for their being placed together by evangelical redaction.[68] It is only natural, therefore, that, unschooled in higher criticism, he did not go behind the compendium at hand: strong corroboration, once again, of his coming in the wake of Mark, removed from the original setting by a decisive step.

It may be worth noting that divergencies independent of the overall scheme confirm Mark's antiquity. In the debate about resurrection, in Mark, Jesus appeals to "the Book of Moses, at the Bush." "The Bush" is the Rabbinic appellation of the relevant portion. Matthew—though not Luke—drops this detail. In my lecture just adverted to [n. 58], I attach importance also to Mark's mention of "the power of God"—dropped by Luke though not by Matthew—as well as to his use, once, of "to be waked" instead of "to be raised" or "to rise"—met in neither of the other two. In the summary advice, Mark alone quotes "Hear, O Israel, the Lord our God is the only Lord." Moreover, the scrupulous repetition of Jesus's advice to the questioner, culminating in an expansion, is consonant with a method of study then prevailing: but I cannot here dwell on it.[69] Neither Matthew nor Luke reproduces it (understandably: it sounds *de trop* [too much]) except that the latter, under its influence, assigns the whole answer to the questioner—which renders the *mala fide* [bad faith] motivation all the more incongruous.

Two objections to the foregoing exposé have been communicated to me. One is that the Pharisaic-Herodian question about tax concerns political controversy, and hence falls outside the law. This presupposes a fairyland where the two provinces are kept apart. It does not exist anywhere today—think, in the U.S.A., of conscription, desegregation, restrictions on trade with Cuba—and it did not then. Rabbinic decisions on fiercely debated public issues are legion. Quite a few are alluded to in the New Testament: e.g. re the Samaritans[70] and re litigation against a fellow-Jew before a heathen court.[71] As for tax to the Romans, Judas of Galilee condemned it as recognition of their sovereignty in the place of God's.[72] The evolution culminating in the slogan "The law of the State is the law"[73] is beset by difficulties with tax; and Paul, preaching sub-

[68] See K. H. Rengstorf, *Das Evangelium nach Lukas* (9th ed.), 225 ff., seeing in the first three sections Jesus's separation from the various religious parties and in the fourth a counter-attack on the scribes.

[69] Much relevant material is offered by S. Krauss, *Talmudische Archäologie*, 3 (1912, repr. 1960), 231 ff. The notions Mishnah and Tannaite owe something to this method.

[70] Matt 10:5; Luke 10:29 ff.; John 4:7 ff.

[71] 1 Cor 6:1.

[72] Acts 5:37; Josephus, *Bell.* 2.8.1.118, 2.17.8.433; *Ant.* 18.1.1.4 f.

[73] *b. B. K.* 113a.

mission, singles out this item.[74] While a Mishnaic provision treats murderers, robbers and tax-collectors as equally deserving to be misled, the part regarding tax-collectors is toned down in the Gemara: a political change.[75] That already Old Testament laws often deal with topics involving acute political tensions is well known: the position of slaves,[76] naturalization,[77] limitations on the monarchy,[78] mixed marriage.[79] Nor should it be thought that this class has come to an end. It never will. The period of terror 1933–1946 and again the building up of Israel have produced a large number of opinions having to do with politics, affected by it and trying to affect it.[80] Note: "Permissible," *exestin*, occurs six more times in Mark, invariably respecting a legal, halakhic point.[81]

The other objection is that, contrary to my assumption, the *Ur*-Christians may not have had a Passover service at all. I shall not submit detailed evidence. It is so unlikely: an abandonment, at one blow, nation-wide, of the cherished institution. It may, however, be useful to expand slightly on the scenario. To begin with the sizable part of the population not journeying to the capital but spending the festival at home. Some families would consist entirely of unbelievers, some entirely of believers, and some of both. (A simplification, since it leaves out degrees of belief or unbelief.) In the third—no doubt fairly numerous—group, an abrupt, concerted opting out of the believers would have meant foregoing a unique opportunity for propagating the good news. As for the pilgrims—more engaged theologically, on the whole, than those staying behind—believers would tend to join together. Thus a growing proportion of Passover-eve companies at Jerusalem was fervently dedicated to the new faith. It was here, above all, that reports and reflections about the recent, ultimate salvation were appended to those about the preparatory one, gradually linked together and in the end given decisive prominence. Certainly, before long, as other occasions for formulating end-time history developed—the daily sacred meal assemblies, for example[82]—and as gentile converts played an increasing role, this Christian Seder lost in importance. Still, it ought to be granted ten to fifteen years, ten to fifteen most intense, most productive years.

V.

A reservation is none the less called for. In Mark and Luke, Jesus "answers well" or "says well" when challenged by the Sadducees, in Matthew he "muzzles" them, *phi-*

[74] Rom 13:1 ff.

[75] *m. Ned.* 3:4; *b. Ned.* 28a.

[76] E.g. Exod 21:2 ff., 20 f., 26 f.

[77] E.g. Deut 23:4 ff.

[78] E.g. Deut 17:14 ff.

[79] E.g. Ezra 9; Neh 13:23 ff.

[80] It would be interesting to search the Rabbinic sources for rulings the political component of which is submerged. W. G. Braude (*Jewish Proselyting* [1940], 52) rightly affixes the attribute "aristocratic" to the circles opposing the abolition of the Biblical anti-Ammonite and anti-Moabite paragraphs. Again, one could imagine that when Akiba, an admirer of Bar-Kochba, had the Shophar blown after the New Year's benedictions acknowledging God as King, this Halakhah was expressing defiance of Roman domination; see my "Johanan ben Beroqa and Women's Rights," *ZSS*, 99 (1982), Roman. Abt., 23 [*Talmudic Law*, 144].

[81] Mark 2:24, 26 (twice), 3:4, 6:18, 10:2.

[82] See J. Jeremias, *Die Abendmahlsworte Jesu* (3rd ed., 1960), 60 f.

moo. It is not unthinkable that Matthew, independently of any other source, wants a more forceful expression. But I wonder. It is a most uncommon one. Elsewhere in the gospels it is confined to the defeat of a subhuman aggressor: an unclean spirit in one Marcan pericope—where Luke follows suit[83]—a raging storm in another—with neither Matthew nor Luke conforming.[84] In the Epistles (if we disregard references to the Old Testament prohibition of muzzling an ox while threshing[85]) it occurs once only, in 1 Peter. Here, indeed, it is employed much as in the dispute with the Sadducees: the apostle—or his amanuensis—writes that Christians should by their goodness "muzzle the ignorance of foolish men."[86] What chiefly deserves attention is the Haggadah's use of a comparable term: the reply to the scoffer is "to blunt his teeth." (A fairly literal application is met, for example, in the comment that Esau kissed Jacob in order to bite him but the latter's neck turned into marble, so the former's teeth became blunt;[87] the transferred one in the prediction that Shiloh, the Messianic king, will blunt the teeth of the nations.[88]) Maybe—but this is not essential to my argument—a variant of the liturgy once contained the very term "to muzzle," *ḥasam*, quite fitting: the Targum to the Psalter has every liar's mouth "muzzled."[89] We should bear in mind the fluidity, even within literal muzzling, between different shades. Thus Paul, in quoting the law about the ox, puts the cruder *kimoo*, to which quite a few copyists prefer the Septuagintal *phimoo*.[90] Anyhow, I suspect that Matthew in this passage enshrines a Haggadah tradition equal in antiquity with Mark's and, who knows?, supplied by the proto-Matthew in Hebrew we hear of from Eusebius. By the way, Hebrew rather than Aramaic (which is regularly substituted nowadays) would be the natural choice for an evangelist in direct touch with the primitive Christian Seder celebrations, dominated by Hebrew.

Am I making too much of a single phrase? It does not, however, stand alone. I have already furnished grounds for deriving the Massacre of the Innocents from the Seder. In this case, Matthew passes on a fully-fledged *Ur*-Christian parallel to the Passover-eve exegesis of a kind of Credo from Deuteronomy. The first story Matthew tells of Jesus, that is, corresponds to the first story in the Haggadah.[91]

I find nothing of the sort in Luke.

VI.

The Third Gospel, in fact, not unexpectedly offers a contrast to the first two, being far less closely tied to the traditional Judaism of the time. Its author's dissociation from

[83] Mark 1:25; Luke 4:36.

[84] Mark 4:39; Matt 8:26; Luke 8:24.

[85] Deut 25:4; 1 Cor 9:9 (see below); 1 Tim 5:18.

[86] 1 Peter 2:15. See E. G. Selwyn, *The First Epistle of St. Peter* (1946), 173.

[87] *Gen. Rab.* on 33:4.

[88] *Gen. Rab.* on 49:10.

[89] Ps 107:42. On the other hand, in Ps 39:2, the sufferer puts a muzzle on his own mouth when irked by the wicked.

[90] See H. Lietzmann, *An Die Korinther I/II* (4th ed., by W. G. Kümmel, 1949), 41.

[91] Matthew 2. See *The New Testament and Rabbinic Judaism*, 189 ff. [404 ff.], and ["The Earliest Structure of the Gospels"] *NTS*, 5 [1959], 194 ff. [338 ff.].

it becomes manifest when we look, say, at his report in Acts of the installation of seven servers of tables.[92] Throughout his writings, he attaches particular relevance to the concept of Jesus as the new Moses, the final prophet predicted by Deuteronomy, mighty in deed and word, and delivering his people despite their rejection of him[93]—perhaps partly because, for him, Jesus, like Moses, is "the founder of a religion."[94] In this report, then, he makes the Mosaic pattern continue in the Church, the new holy community which, he realizes, must be prepared for a long march. With outstanding artistry he alludes to the appointment of Joshua as well as three other Old Testament chapters where Moses delegates some of his burdens: the creation of judges for routine disputes, the promotion of seventy elders to assist him and the creation of officers of the tribes. In none of all this, however, can he be shown to draw on Rabbinic interpretations of or legends built up around those texts.

We may obtain help from here for assessing certain passages in his Gospel: reflections rooted in Rabbinic teaching do not presumably originate with him. Take the Parable of the Unjust Steward.[95] Its basic message is to emulate, in the ultimate crisis that has arrived, the tycoon's henchman who in the nick of time undoes some of his cruel work by lightening the load of the debtors. An excursus represents him as dubiously motivated—afraid of shameful poverty, intent on providing himself with grateful supporters—and emphasizes that even so he receives praise from Jesus.[96] This expresses the pragmatic standpoint versus the perfectionist in a debate dividing the Rabbis. It is worth noting that the pragmatists took the description in Genesis of Noah as virtuous "in his generation" in the sense of "compared with others in that inferior epoch": such relative superiority, we hear from Philo and Judah ben Ilai, sufficed for his salvation though he would not have passed in a godly age.[97] Just so, Jesus explains that those belonging to the pre-redemption aeon, when they behave like the steward, rank as wiser "for their generation," "considering their surroundings," than would the sons of the light, the redeemed ones. It is safe to regard the whole of this as a pre-Lucan elaboration: a conclusion corroborated by the attempt in the following verses to mitigate the effect and veer towards perfectionism.

[92] Acts 6:1 ff. See my "Neglected Nuances of Exposition in Luke-Acts," pt. 2, "A Reform in Acts and its Models," in *Aufstieg und Niedergang der Römischen Welt*, ed. H. Temporini and W. Haase, Vol. II. 25.3 (1985), 2346 ff. [831 ff.].

[93] Deut 18:15 ff., 34:12; Luke 7:16, 39, 13:33, 24:19; Acts 3:22 f., 7:20 ff. See my review of G. Vermes, *Jesus the Jew*, 1973, in *JJS*, 25 (1974), 333.

[94] See C. K. Barrett, *Luke the Historian in Recent Study* (1961), 58.

[95] Luke 16:1 ff. See my "Shame Culture in Luke," in *Paul and Paulinism, Essays in honour of C. K. Barrett* (ed. M. D. Hooker and S. G. Wilson, 1982), 360 f. [822 ff.], "Neglected Nuances," pt. 1, "Encomium Prudentiae," 2234 ff. [861 ff.], and *The Old Testament in the New*, section VI [56], German translation by W. Schuller, vol. 10 of *Xenia*, 24 ff. For me, Luke 16:8 has become something of an advertisement of the rule of thumb in favour of the troublesome sense (allied to *lectio difficilior*). When, about forty years ago,—see "Concerning the Reconstruction of the 'Aramaic Gospels,'" in *BJRULM*, 29 (1945–46), 71 [66]—I differed from C. C. Torrey and expressed preference for the text as it stands "just because it is so inconvenient," I had no inkling that some day I might hit on an explanation.

[96] "The lord" with the definite article must refer to him.

[97] Gen 6:9; Philo, *Abr.*, 7:36 ff.; *Gen. Rab.* on 6:9.

On the other hand, when the original ending of the episode of the young Jesus abandoning his parents for a debate in the Temple is toned down, *entschärft*, by the assurance that he "subjected himself to them,"[98] quite possibly we have to do with an amendment by Luke. By this time, the sect was consolidated; and whereas, earlier on, the young were to break away from their stubborn elders for a radically fresh start, what was now needed for an orderly development was respectful submission.

VII.

My inclination is obviously against speculative, absolutist theories and in favour of flexible ones, re-tested again and again. The proof of the pudding is in the eating thereof. No case, no line, no particle is so trivial that it may not require modification or even scrapping of the most logically argued, magnificent general proposition. Which leaning does not prevent me from seeing the value of the opposite.

No doubt the progress of mathematical machinery will be of colossal help to synoptic research. I regret that I am too set in my ways to take the big step from disputation to computation. Let me end up, then, by indicating an inadequately tapped potential of a different kind.

A hope, however faint, I am prey to is that more earnest attention will be paid in future to the Jewish material. With some notable exceptions such as G. Vermes's *Jesus the Jew*,[99] New Testament research is satisfied with scratching the surface, i.e. a dutiful acknowledgment of Strack-Billerbeck or the like. Few texts omitted there are ever inspected. As if—I am exaggerating, though not overmuch and in a good cause—as if classical specialists in Socrates were content to analyze Dr. Adams's *Religious Teachers of Greece*, supplemented by the Oxford *Companion*, but never went into the writings of his age and in his language. Whereas, naturally, they are expected to talk and write in fifth-century B.C. Greek better than those who lived then: Ionic, Doric, Laconian, lapidary, tragic, colloquial. Hardly any probers into Christian origins are fluent—really fluent—in the tongue Jesus spoke. Recently, working in a splendid academic theological library, I needed a Passover Haggadah. They had one poor old copy in a remote corner amidst low-ranking fringe liturgy. I asked around a little among the students present—admittedly no scientific poll—and not one of them had ever thought of looking up the little volume, be it even for a glance at the vernacular. Yet that is where it all started. How are we to account for this amazing situation?

Before trying an answer, I ought to clarify my approach in two respects. Firstly, I do not subscribe to the rigid doctrine that the insider alone understands, that only a Jew, a Christian, a black, an Aryan, a woman, a man, can appreciate the experience and thinking of the group.[100] No doubt part of it is inaccessible. But a great deal is not, and part is actually easier for non-members to be aware of, as proved by Shakespeare on Othello and Shylock, de Toqueville on the Americans, Ruth Fulton Benedict on the

[98] Luke 2:41 ff. See my *Civil Disobedience in Antiquity* (1972), 47 ff.

[99] (1973, repr. 1981).

[100] Cf. the penetrating and ranging discussion by W. D. Davies in "Reflections in Retrospect, 1950-1980," *Bulletin of Duke Divinity School* (Oct. 1982), 33 ff.

Japanese. Nor, indeed, are such ectogenous insights confined to sympathizers. As love may make blind, hate may make seeing. Just remember the grains, or lumps, of truth about the enemy unearthed in sectarian polemics. Folk wisdom agrees with me, applying to the individual what I am here saying about groups. A seeker for advice is told, on one occasion, that there is nothing for it but to look into his own heart, on another, that he should make an effort to stand outside himself. Often the latter position has its advantages.

As for the capacity of a literary product to be comprehended beyond its original circle, it is futile to deny it in the face of Aesop's fables, the Thousand-and-One-Nights, the stories of Helen of Troy or Heracles or Parsifal, the teachings of Confucius or Buddha, the Bible itself. Granted that some points will be missed in the transition, a large number will come through and, once again, the foreign recipient may make contributions enriching the native interpretation. Simple, basic features may be discovered or re-discovered—the "parallelism of members" in Hebrew poetry, for instance, described by Bishop Lowth of the eighteenth century. (A little like the disclosure to M. Jourdain in *Le Bourgeois Gentilhomme* that he has talked prose all his life.) Or profound implications: the Oedipus complex, the Hebrew monarchy as the exemplar of institutions flawed yet divinely sanctioned in order to prevent worse, "for the hardness of your heart."

Secondly, I do not believe in scholarship as the sole key to a great work. A reader or listener genuinely attuned needs none of the philologist's equipment to enter into the author's world. He may find treasures old and new in a translation of a translation of a translation. Schopenhauer became acquainted with the Upanishads through a Latin rendering of a Persian rendering; Philo relied chiefly on the Septuagint. In fact, many an intuition arrived at outside academia has proved valuable inside. (Which does not mean that others must be of lesser worth.) Hunches of long ago, such as that the tale of Noah and Ham alludes to castration, or that there is a point in Esther not revealing her lineage rather than telling a falsehood about it,[101] tend to be taken up by modern exegesis. To be sure, a wealth of information of a certain kind is open only to the savant: how Israelite prophecy relates to Canaanite, or Pauline oratory to Hellenistic. But certain other kinds are probably rendered harder of attainment by his very mindset. An analphabet in a "backward" region may hear more than a professor in "the stars in their courses fought with Sisera" or "not what I will but what thou wilt."

My observations, then, have regard only to our peculiar fraternity, pledged by the meticulous application of agreed methods over time to build up a, by and large, dependable body of knowledge, ever growing in breadth, depth and refinement—despite its intrinsic, never quite eradicable, shortcomings. It is within this context only that the neglect of a cluster of sources manifestly of first-rate importance calls for an explanation.

Two reasons one occasionally comes across—I say, occasionally, because in the main the phenomenon is not faced—do certainly play a role. One is the inordinate difficulty of the documents in question. Much of the discussion baffles even a student with perfect Hebrew and Aramaic, so idiosyncratic are its logic and formulation; in fact, the

[101] See above, n. 36.

majority of present-day Rabbis leave huge chunks alone. Moreover, the dating of utterances and of what they are about not seldom raises problems. And so on. To brush aside something one cannot cope with as irrelevant is a common and, up to a point, sound defence mechanism. I have elsewhere confessed to my shelving away a textbook on Roman law in Bulgarian sent me from Sofia, persuading myself that it was unlikely to prove of substantial aid. Still, there must be more to the general, persistent shelving away under notice. After all, in other provinces—say, cuneiform or Homeric studies—similar obstacles have acted as a worthwhile challenge rather than a keep-off sign.[102] Hittite fragments are exploited to the full though the language is beset with riddles. In my own lifetime, the Babylonian and Assyrian laws and Hammurabi himself, as well as the Iliad and Odyssey and their constituent parts, have been assigned to considerably varying epochs; yet the experts soldier on, conscious of the price of letting go.

The other reason given here and there is anti-semitism. Since this emotion, like its counterpart anti-gentilism, operates in untold guises, from the most direct and brutal to the most oblique and rarefied, far be it from me to make light of it. None the less, I wonder whether a third factor is not at work, in addition to these two: a reluctance unreservedly to humanize Jesus—his human side, that is—to place him right in, not above, his historical and social milieu. For the safeguarding of reverential distance, it is better not to know too much. In an entirely different connection, several decades ago, I commented on the cosmetic apparatus of theologians to Father Corbishley. "O yes," he replied, "they are all monophysites." It is an instinctive attitude, avowed neither to the world nor to the self, hence the more compulsive. Being brought up in that stern, orthodox branch of Judaism where God is the wholly other, I have every sympathy with it.

In the 'fifties and 'sixties, as the Dead Sea Scrolls became a popular sensation, there was a moment of suspense. That a valid, scholarly appraisal of the New Testament presupposes familiarity with the surrounding evidence—familiarity as easy as that of the Socrates scholar with Plato, Aristophanes, Thucydides—loomed as an inescapable conclusion; and a few enthusiasts indeed believed that henceforth thorough immersion in the Jewish sources would be *de rigueur* in the pertinent Departments. Significantly, too, I heard of two Jewish converts to Christianity who were so bowled over as to consider going back on their conversion. They had, plainly, been unrealistic before—otherwise the finds would have made no difference one way or the other. (It may not be accidental that they were Protestants, less comfortable, it would seem, with the divinity of Jesus than Catholics and in consequence keener on eliminating the other side. Corbishley is a Catholic. True, J. A. T Robinson, who, in *The Human Face of God*,[103] movingly pleads against monophysitism, is an Anglican, C. K. Barrett, who in *Jesus and*

[102] Here is a relatively simple shot at sorting out different strata in the Haggadah—admitting that the result may be proved wrong by superior reconsideration or fresh evidence. Twice a series of divine benefactions is enumerated, once in verse and once in prose. It is only the latter version which characterizes the Temple as built "to atone for all our transgressions." Which suggests a date for it from before A.D. 70 and a later one for the poetic list. A turning of prose into poetry is in any case more likely than the reverse. See ["The Earliest Structure of the Gospels" in] *NTS*, 5 [1959], 176 [331].

[103] (1973).

the Gospel Tradition[104] can write that "the suffering was more acute than the human Jesus had foreseen," a Methodist.) By now, however, the flurry is over and things are pretty much back to normal.

Support for my guess may be gleaned from many other spheres of Western culture, but I shall restrict myself to one illustration. When I came to England before World War II, under the Lord Chamberlain's rules—since dropped—it was permissible to bring God on the stage, but not Jesus. Whatever the official argumentation, the true aim of this at first sight, to a Jew at least, staggering arrangement was protection of Jesus's divinity. God has no need of such a measure. It matters not what you do to him: he may break into a guffaw, sneeze, show sexual interest, perform a handstand—he remains God. Jesus's divine side, the rules imply, is too precarious, so the safer course is to suppress the human one altogether.[105]

To expand the quest in the direction I am advocating would require not only tremendous, confident openness but also much bureaucratic, unselfish labour. For, if serious, lasting gains are desired, to begin with, a considerable number of young graduands or graduates must be sent out for long, intensive training; not, that is, to get a smattering, but to become masters. The reward of their seniors would consist in watching the new, ampler inquiries take root and bear fruit. Who can say it will not happen? "*'Omnam lo' ka'asher yir'e ha'adham 'abhal lakkol zeman we'eth lekhol ḥepheṣ taḥath hashshamayim,*" "Indeed, not as man sees; but for everything there is a moment, and a time for all business under heaven." Thus, Wessely, in 1782, calling on the Austrian Jews to respond to Joseph II's Edict of Tolerance and add a broad education in German to the traditional, exclusive concern with Torah.

[104] (1967), 108.

[105] A little comparable to the blockage in the New Testament field is that in medieval Roman and Canon Law, whose exponents are not at home, by proper standards, in Islamic (or, for that matter, medieval Jewish) Law. The next fundamental breakthrough will come through a generation seriously exploring the mutual influence between West and East. In this case, too, the difficulty of the task is not the only obstacle. Among the others are a time-hallowed feeling of superiority and the fear of what may emerge. *Experto crede* [believe the expert]! While a Director of the Robbins Library at U.C. Berkeley School of Law, I had ample opportunity of watching the feeding and starving of different interests—the starving often from non-remembrance or, if memory was jolted, relieved by the expression of unspecified good intentions for the future.

The "I Am" of the Messianic Presence

At the foundation meeting of the *Studiorum Novi Testamenti Societas*, a few years ago, Professor T. W. Manson read a paper in which he discussed the New Testament use of ἐγώ εἰμι, literally "I am," in the sense of "The Messiah is present." It is prominent in John. At the end of the conversation between Jesus and the Samaritan woman, for example, the woman says "I know that Messias cometh, he will tell us all things," and Jesus replies "I am"—meaning "the Messiah is here"; or in the account of his arrest we are told that "as soon then as he had said unto them, I am, they went backwards and fell to the ground."[1] But in Mark and Luke also there occurs an utterance like "Many shall come in my name, saying, I am,"[2] where "I am" must be an announcement of the second coming of the Messiah: "he is here." Matthew, who writes "I am the Christ,"[3] obviously no longer understands the exact, original sense of the expression.

It is submitted that the evangelists are following a Rabbinic model, though this has been preserved in one source only, the Passover Haggadah. As pointed out already, the nucleus of the Haggadah consists in the exposition of some verses from Deuteronomy, referring to Israel's deliverance from Egypt.[4] It is in the course of this exposition that the words "I am" are used to denote the personal presence of the redeeming God on that occasion.

Before quoting the paragraph in question, let us recall that as early as in the Pentateuch we come across two conceptions of the exodus, one according to which God himself rescued the nation and another represented by statements such as that "he sent an angel and hath brought us forth out of Egypt."[5] The opposition between these different schools of thought continues throughout Biblical and Rabbinic times. Isaiah says "the angel of his face saved them," but the LXX translates "neither a messenger nor an angel but he himself saved them";[6] and Exodus Rabba[7] observes that "some say he smote the Egyptians through an angel, and some say the Holy one did it himself." Considering the whole atmosphere of the Jewish Passover-eve service, it is only natural that the prevalent doctrine should here be that of God's direct intervention.

The Credo from Deuteronomy contains the declaration: "And the Lord heard our voice, and the Lord brought us forth out of Egypt with a mighty hand and with an out-

[1] John 4:25 f., 18:6. Other relevant texts are 8:24, 28, 58, 9:9, 13:19, 18:5, 8.

[2] Mark 13:6; Luke 21:8.

[3] Matt 24:5.

[4] Deut 26:5 ff.

[5] Num 20:16. See E. D. Goldschmidt, *op. cit.*, 54 n. 1.

[6] Isa 63:9.

[7] *Exod. Rab.* on 12:23.

stretched arm and with great terribleness and with signs and with wonders." The authors of the Passover Haggadah see in the repetition of "the Lord"—"the Lord heard our voice and the Lord brought us forth" instead of simply "and he brought us forth"—an indication of God's personal activity; and, as usual, they support their contention by other texts from Scripture. This is what they say by way of comment: "Not through an angel, and not through a seraph, and not through a messenger, but the Holy one in his glory and himself; as it is written [in Exodus[8]], For I will pass through the land of Egypt this night, and I will smite all the firstborn, and against all the gods of Egypt I will execute judgment, I the Lord." Then they go on to explain that each of the four clauses of the supporting text is intended to announce the carrying out of these deeds by God himself:[9] "For I will pass through Egypt—this means, I and not an angel; and I will smite all the firstborn—this means, I and not a seraph; and I will execute judgment—this means, I and not the messenger, I the Lord—this means, I am and no other."

It will be noted that, whereas the first part of the Midrash has "not through an angel, and not through a seraph, and not through a messenger," the second speaks of "the messenger," not "a messenger": "I and not the messenger." This way of putting the matter may well have arisen when Christianity had to be combated: "the messenger" probably is Jesus.[10] There are versions of the Midrash with more anti-Christian or anti-gnostic interpolations, such as the addition "and not through the Word."[11]

The point here to be made is that in the last few words of the Midrash, "I am and no other," we have before us the model for that ἐγώ εἰμι. Usually these words are taken as meaning "I am he, *scil.* the Lord who does all these things, and no other." But such an interpretation suffers from two flaws. First, *'ani hu'* can hardly signify "I am this or that," referring back to some previous attribute. In the Old Testament it appears in the sense of "I am the Absolute" or the like,[12] and this application certainly prepared the ground for the ἐγώ εἰμι of the Messianic Presence. But neither in the Old Testament nor in Rabbinic language is it used as denoting "I am this or that." To translate "I am he who does it all" would be carrying modern usage into Rabbinic language.

Secondly—and this is decisive—the purpose of the Passover Midrash is to prove that, in the deliverance from Egypt, God acted himself. The Rabbis, that is, are compelled to explain "I the Lord" as emphasizing God's personal intervention. Consequently, when they say it means *'ani hu' welo' 'aḥer*, we must translate "I am and no other," in the sense of "God's own person will be present and no other." This is the ἐγώ εἰμι of that particular value: "the Divine Presence, the Divine Redeemer, is here."

[8] Exod 12:12.

[9] E. D. Goldschmidt, *op. cit.*, 54 f., holds that this explanation does not belong to the original stratum of the Haggadah. But, for one thing, he may well be wrong. He says that it adds nothing of importance to the preceding part—an untenable view as soon as the particular force of *'ani hu'*, "I am," is recognized. For another thing, even if he were right, it would not affect our principal argument. The passage would still show that the manner in which the New Testament employs "I am" is Rabbinic.

[10] This is following up a remark by Abrahams, *JQR*, 10 (1898), 49 n. 2. On the role of the article in Rabbinic exegesis, see below, under The Abomination of Desolation, A [661 ff.].

[11] Abrahams, *op. cit.*, 41, 45 ff., 51.

[12] Deut 32:39; Isa 43:10, 13 etc.

Any other rendering would miss the point of the Rabbinic argument. In fact the special force of the two words must have been firmly established by the time the Midrash was composed. The authors take it for granted that their paraphrase—"I am and no other"—will express the idea of God's personal appearance more clearly than the Scriptural "I the Lord."

It is interesting that the passage from the Haggadah discussed seems to be the only Rabbinic text extant where this application of *'ani hu'* is to be met with. Presumably there was a time when it was not so rare, but the Rabbis found it dangerous and were afraid of abuse. (The Mekhilta, among other things, says this about "I the Lord" in Exodus: "What flesh and blood cannot possibly say." This is manifestly directed against Christianity.) They eliminated the expression as far as possible. But in liturgy, in the Passover-eve service, it withstood the pressure: liturgy is difficult to expurgate. Even here, however, we know of attempts to suppress the "I am." Certain medieval authorities—Zedekiah ben Abraham, for instance[13]—forbade the recital of the portion containing the phrase. Obviously they were still familiar with its implications. To be sure, there do exist allied phrases, such as "I and He." But they are not quite the same, and even they have mainly survived in liturgy, for example, in the service of Hoshanna Rabba.

It should be added that the continuation of the exegesis of the Deuteronomic Credo to be found in the Haggadah fully bears out the view here advanced. For we learn there that in the course of the exodus there took place a *gilluy shekhina*, "an uncovering, a baring, of the Divine Presence." This is a technical term suggesting precisely that milieu where we should expect the curious use of "I am."

According to Deuteronomy, God delivered Israel "with a mighty hand and with an outstretched arm and with great terribleness and with signs and with wonders." The Haggadah—and it may be repeated that we are concerned with a very early section—specifies the meaning of each of these adverbial phrases, adducing other texts for confirmation. Thus "a mighty hand" is claimed to signify pestilence; "an outstretched arm" the sword; "signs" the rod; "wonders" the blood. The comment on "great terribleness" runs as follows: "This means the baring of the Divine Presence; as it is written [in another passage from Deuteronomy],[14] Or hath God assayed to come to take him a nation from the midst of another nation with great terrors." The supporting text, it should be remarked, also speaks of "great terrors" (the plural of "great terribleness"); and, for the Rabbis, the proof that this implies the actual descent of God lies in the words saying that "he came to take people"—instead of merely "he took the people." Onkelos translates *le'ithgela'a lemiphraq*, "to uncover himself to redeem," a distinct reference to the Divine Presence in the act of redemption or, we might now say, to "I am."

To conclude, it has long been seen that the association of terribleness or terrors with the manifestation of the Divine Presence must have been favoured by the similarity in sound between the Hebrew words *mora'*, "terribleness," and *mar'e*, "appearance."

[13] In his *Shibbole ha-Leqet*.

[14] Deut 4:34.

The LXX, in the verses from Deuteronomy quoted,[15] renders "with great terribleness [terrors]" by ἐν ὁράμασι μεγάλοις, and Onkelos by *ubheḥizwana' rabba'* (*ubheḥizwanin rabhrebhin*), "with great sights." It may be worth bearing this in mind when dealing with passages like that mentioned at the beginning of this discussion, "as soon then as he had said unto them, I am, they fell to the ground"; or even, perhaps, when inquiring into the report, towards the end of the Markan gospel,[16] that the women, on finding the grave empty and being informed that they would soon see the risen Jesus, fled and dared not speak about it for fear.

[15] Deut 26:8, 4:34.
[16] Mark 16:4 ff.

Redemption

A. General

The two most prominent Hebrew terms for "to redeem" are *ga'al* and *padha.* The former primarily signifies "to recover a man or thing that had once belonged to you or your family but had got lost," the latter "to ransom a man or thing whose fate would otherwise be destruction, consecration or slavery." Thus *ga'al* suggests the return of men or things into their old, legitimate place, *padha* the deliverance of men or things from their doom. Whereas men, animate things and inanimate things may be the object of *ga'al,* since any of these are capable of being "recovered," there appears to be no case of an inanimate thing being the object of *padha*: only men and beasts can be "ransomed from a doom."

Admittedly, the two terms are often interchangeable. If the owner of a firstborn animal, which is God's, pays the priests its value instead, the transaction may be called a "recovering" or a "ransoming"; and a prophet may speak of God "recovering" or "ransoming" Israel. But the difference remains; and it accounts for the fact, surprising at first sight, that in Old Testament and Rabbinic utterances concerning deliverance through God, *ga'al,* "to recover," occupies a more conspicuous place than *padha,* "to ransom." The point is that the notion of *ga'al* is central to the social legislation of Old Testament times—regarding the recovery of a relative enslaved, of family property alienated, of the blood of a murdered relative, of the childless widow of a relative—and that the social legislation has exercised an enormous influence on the religious concept of redemption.

The social legislation of Old Testament times was largely designed to safeguard the integrity of a family. Accordingly, if one of your relatives had had to sell himself into slavery, if you had had to sell part or all of your ancestral land, if one of your relatives had been murdered or if one of them died leaving a childless widow, it was your right and duty to "recover," *ga'al,* the enslaved relative, your land, your murdered relative's blood (by slaying the murderer) or the widow (by marrying her—given certain conditions). In the Pentateuch, these and other social laws are founded on the exodus: "And thou shalt remember that thou wast a bondman in Egypt and the Lord redeemed thee," or "Unto me the children of Israel are servants, they are my servants whom I brought forth out of Egypt."[1] But it is clear that the exodus itself is depicted in terms taken from social legislation—in fact from social laws which, though not completely identical with those preserved in the Pentateuch, yet must have been very similar.

[1] Deut 15:15; Lev 25:55.

In the exodus, God acts as a father demanding back his son from the tyrant who has enslaved him—"Israel is my son, let my son go"[2]—as a mighty person regaining an impoverished relative or his legitimate property from the hands of a stranger—"thy people which thou has acquired, thou shalt plant them in the mountain of thy inheritance"[3]—or as the revenger of blood—"I have heard the groanings of the children of Israel, and I will bring you out from under the burdens of the Egyptians and I will redeem you with a stretched out arm and great judgments."[4] Nor must we forget that the verb *yaṣa'*, "to go out," so frequent in the story of the exodus, the "going out"—"The selfsame day the hosts of the Lord went out from Egypt"[5]—is technically used of a slave "going out free" under the social legislation.[6] The Hiphil of this verb, *hoṣi'*, "to bring out," may connote a "bringing out from slavery to freedom" in more passages than would appear at first sight. The connotation is plain in a verse like "I am the Lord thy God which have brought thee out of Egypt, the house of bondage." But it may also be present, say, in the clause "for by strength of hand the Lord brought us forth out of Egypt."[7]

We have before us, then, a development in three stages. There were social laws more primitive than, though similar to, those extant in the Pentateuch. These determined the whole way in which the exodus was thought of and described. And the narratives of the exodus in turn influenced, on the one hand, the further history of the social laws and, on the other, the direction which the ideas about God's intervention on behalf of his people or man in general were to take.

That the exodus was construed as an application, on a higher plane, of the social laws is hardly surprising, in view of the particular genius of Hebrew priests and prophets. The Israelites had actually been subjected in Egypt to the most oppressive slavery, and no human kinsmen or former owners with a stronger right had come to the rescue. Yet they were freed: it was, the religious concluded, God who had stepped in and enforced the demands of social justice.

Once that deliverance was interpreted in this fashion, the significance of the social laws even as operating here on earth necessarily increased a thousandfold. Ought not the Israelite to be mindful of the example set by God in putting them into practice? Ought he not to be mindful of his wretched past and miraculous salvation, and ought not this memory to affect his ordinary, daily dealings with his fellow? And ought he not to see in each of his brethren a special protégé of God? Moreover, this tremendous fact at the beginning of the national history—the exodus thought of as an application of the social laws—inspired a firm expectation that, whenever Israel was in distress and no human aid was available, God would act as redeemer again and again. "Then he remembered the days of old, Moses and his people, That led them by the right hand of

[2] Exod 4:22 f.

[3] Exod 15:16 f.

[4] Exod 6:5 f.

[5] Exod 12:41. The noun *yeṣi'a*, "exodus," "the going out," is post-Biblical; in Rabbinic literature the phrase *yeṣi'ath miṣrayim*, "the going out from Egypt," is extremely common.

[6] E.g. Exod 21:7; Lev 25:54.

[7] Exod 13:16.

Moses, dividing the water before them. Look down from heaven. Where is thy zeal and thy strength? are they restrained? Thou, O Lord, art our father, our redeemer."[8]

It was not only the nation as a whole, but also the individual that would look to God for redress if none could be obtained elsewhere. As is natural, the social legislation of the Old Testament was not always strictly observed. The weak did not receive their due. Occasionally, no doubt, the hope was expressed that a great king would remedy this state of affairs: "He shall redeem the needy people's soul from deceit and violence, and precious shall their blood be in his sight."[9] But in general it was realized that the only one who would never desert the poor and who was incomparably stronger than any worldly power was God: "Remove not the old landmark, and enter not into the fields of the fatherless; for their redeemer is mighty."[10]

Let us note that, from the first, the liberation from Egypt meant much more than a liberation from physical sufferings. From the first, the exodus included mount Sinai. It meant, therefore, salvation both in the physical and the spiritual sense.

This element remains attached to divine redemption throughout. Whenever Hebrew priests or prophets represent God as redeemer—be it of his people or of an individual, be it that they speak of deeds he performed in the past or of deeds he will perform in the future—they have in mind redemption not only from material misfortunes but also, in a greater or lesser degree, from impurity, sin and error. Both aspects are clearly noticeable in passages like "No lion shall be there, but the redeemed shall walk there, and the ransomed of the Lord shall come to Zion with songs, they shall obtain joy and gladness," or again, "I know that my redeemer liveth, and that he shall stand up at the latter day upon the earth."[11] But even where the spiritual side alone is referred to, there is no break with the original concept; the most refined notion of redemption by God is descended from the old construction of the exodus. The assurance "I will ransom them from the power of the grave, I will redeem them from death" occurs in the same group of sayings as the verse "Yet I am thy God from the land of Egypt."[12]

So far we have considered certain nuances of redemption in the Old Testament. They all, however, live on in Rabbinism, as may be seen from the comments, Tannaitic and Amoraic, on the relevant Old Testament passages: and it is mainly the features outlined which distinguish the Jewish—and Christian—view of salvation from that of the surrounding Hellenistic and Oriental world. That world was full of hope and speculation as to final deliverance. Yet nowhere but in Judaism—and Christianity—was final deliverance guaranteed by having its ultimate basis in the social laws: God would, in fact, he must, "recover" those who were his property, his children, friends or slaves. Nowhere but in these religions was final deliverance guaranteed by an undisputed historical precedent, the exodus, of which, in a sense, it would be a repetition, though an infinitely superior one and one that would end all history. It is evident that, with this

[8] Isa 63:11 ff.

[9] Ps 72:14.

[10] Prov 23:10 f.

[11] Isa 35:9 f.; Job 19:25.

[12] Hos 13:14, 4.

setting, "recovery," *ge'ulla*, by God must be widely different from say, σωτηρία, and that it could never for any length of time share the nebulous, vague and eccentric character pertaining to not a few elaborations of the Greek idea.

Moreover, while the Jewish—and Christian—image of redemption, "recovery," had its roots in the social laws and their miraculous application in the exodus, and indeed never ceased to be in rejuvenating contact with these sources—at the same time the social conscience of Judaism was constantly stimulated by the religious image. Nowhere but in Judaism—and Christianity—did divine salvation involve such emphasis on the establishment of social justice and (this is the point) lead to such an insistent appeal to man to assist, anticipate and emulate God by doing justice here and now. If Jesus dealt with the world in charity, and if both his deeds and his teaching impressed on his followers the need of taking the same course, this was only in line with the traditional nature and role of redemptive activity in Judaism.

It is sometimes contended that the aspect of the New Testament here contemplated is due to a revolutionary spirit that had got hold of the suppressed masses of the time. Should this be the case, the spokesmen of the revolution would none the less have moved within a framework coming down from the generation who had experienced the deliverance from Egypt as it is set down in the Pentateuch and thought of by priests, prophets and Rabbis.

B. A CHANGE OF MASTER

1. *The Old Testament*

In many parts of the Old Testament we come across the notion that it was through the liberation from Egypt that Israel became God's people: "And I will take you to me for a people, and I will be to you a God, and ye shall know that I am the Lord your God, which bringeth you out from under the burdens of the Egyptians."[13] Actually we are so accustomed to the notion that it seems quite natural to us. But it is not. It is unique, and it calls for an explanation. The explanation lies in the fact we tried to bring out above—that the exodus is construed as an application of the social laws, as a "recovery" by God of an enslaved son, relation or friend or of property fallen into the hands of strangers.

Under the social regime of Old Testament times, an enslaved son, relative or friend who was redeemed, "recovered," by the person nearest to him came into the power of the redeemer; and similarly, family land redeemed by a member of the family became the redeemer's property.[14] (We disregard the effects of the Seventh Year or the Jubilee. We also disregard modern interpretations[15] according to which a slave redeemed did not become the redeemer's subject but acquired full freedom, and family property redeemed went to the former owner or his heir even if another member of the family had redeemed it. These interpretations are in conflict with the texts. Even if they were right, it would still remain true that the actual redeemer of a slave or of family property must be the one to gain effective control, no matter where control might reside in theory: as

[13] Exod 6:7.

[14] E.g. Jer 32:6 ff.

[15] My rejection of them in *Studies in Biblical Law* (1947), 51 f., 73, was too half-hearted.

he proved able to recover what had got lost, it is he who would continue being looked up to as the real protector.) Just so, in the view of the Old Testament writers, the Hebrews, as a result of their redemption from thraldom by God, became his subjects—as sons or slaves—or his property: "They are my servants whom I brought forth [or we may translate: freed] out of the land of Egypt," "Thy people pass over, O Lord, which thou hast purchased" and so on.[16]

This notion is extended from the exodus to any acts of deliverance God may perform for Israel in the course of history, and also to the final deliverance which will end all history: "Fear not, I have redeemed thee, thou art mine."[17] Liberation by God, in analogy to "recovery" prescribed by the social laws, means, not liberation pure and simple, but a change of master. It means a passage from a distressing, foreign and arbitrary yoke to contentment and security under the rightful authority.

As is to be expected, usually no strict distinction is drawn between the different types of "recovery." In other words, it is not usually specified whether God redeemed, or will redeem, Israel as his son, relation, slave or property. The main idea is always the same: God exercises his right of "recovery" and the Hebrews, previously under the rule of alien tyrants, return into the hands of their true sovereign.

Admittedly, in some passages one of the various nuances may definitely predominate. Admittedly, too, some Old Testament writers do see a tension—unresolved and maybe incapable of being resolved—between the various nuances, say, between Israel the son and Israel the slave. But in most cases God simply acts as the "recoverer" in general; and occasionally we find several types of redemption put side by side in the most unsophisticated manner, as in the request "Israel is my firstborn son, Let my son go that he may serve me."[18] Here God appears as father and as master at the same time. It is true that, at a certain stage of civilization, the position of a son while his father lives and that of a slave would not be so very dissimilar. Again, the verb *'abhadh*, "to serve," means not only "to serve as slave," but also "to serve as labourer," "to worship," "to honour," "to cultivate," "to work." In a text like that just quoted one or two of the milder senses may play a part. We must also remember that to be "the slave of the Lord" may be a distinction as great as to be "his son."

Another tension often alluded to is that between God's being the father, friend or owner of the Hebrews for ever and his none the less ceding temporary power over them to their enemies. The reason for his doing so is generally found in the people's sinfulness: "O that they were wise. How should one chase a thousand except their Rock had sold them?," "And the anger of the Lord was hot, and he sold them into the hands of their enemies."[19] But the oppressors are not on this ground justified: "Ye have been sold for nought and ye shall be redeemed without money."[20] This last passage again makes direct reference to the laws concerning "recovery."

[16] Lev 25:55; Exod 15:16.

[17] Isa 43:1.

[18] Exod 4:22 f.

[19] Deut 32:29 f.; Judg 2:14.

[20] Isa 52:3.

Significantly, where it is a question of Israel abandoned and accepted again, we sometimes meet with the term *hikkir*, a term which, in technical usage, denotes the formal, binding "acknowledgment" of a fact of legal relevance. In the story of Judah and Tamar, Judah "acknowledged" the signet, bracelets and staff to be his.[21] The fact to be "acknowledged" may, of course, be a personal status or relationship. There is a provision insisting that though a man's firstborn son was borne to him by the less beloved of two wives, yet he must "acknowledge" his position and give him the larger share which is his due.[22] The Levites, when fighting the worshippers of the golden calf, "did not acknowledge their brethren."[23]

This usage of *hikkir* must be borne in mind in interpreting passages like "Doubtless thou art our father though Jacob acknowledge us not: thy name from everlasting is our redeemer."[24] God, who for a while has turned away from the nation, will one day "acknowledge" the relationship which all others, even the patriarchs, might repudiate. However desperate the momentary situation, God is the reliable, eternal "recoverer" of his own, the redeemer "from everlasting." Thus we read: "I will acknowledge them that are carried away captive of Judah, and they shall be my people and I will be their God."[25] Once more, "acknowledgment" and "recovery" clearly imply not liberation in the crude sense, but a change of master: the redeemed ones become the subjects of the redeemer. The same confidence, incidentally, is expressed in the same terminology by the individual in distress: "There was for me no one," says the Psalmist,[26] "to acknowledge me, refuge failed me; I cried unto thee, O Lord, save me from my persecutors, bring my soul out of prison."

2. *Rabbinic Sources*

The Old Testament ideas and phrases are taken over by the Rabbis, though, inevitably, there is addition, elaboration and a greater awareness of the problems and conflicts involved.

As for the fundamental notion that the exodus was a "recovery," by which the people automatically came under the rule of God, their father, master or owner—a glance at the Rabbinic comments of the relevant Biblical texts will show that it retains all its weight. (We shall find ample confirmation of this when we come to the Passover ritual as practised in the Tannaitic era.) As already remarked, in the Pentateuch the laws for the protection of bondmen are supported by the reminder: "they are my servants whom I brought forth out of Egypt." The Rabbis make God say: "my bill is older [than any which could be drawn up now]."[27] By freeing the nation from strange despots, God acquired it as one acquires a slave: the Mishnah lays down[28] that "A Hebrew slave is

[21] Gen 38:25 f.

[22] Deut 21:17.

[23] Deut 33:9; cp. Exod 32:27 ff.

[24] Isa 63:16.

[25] Jer 24:5 ff.

[26] Ps 142:5 (4) ff.

[27] *Siphra* on Lev 25:42, 55.

[28] *m. Kidd.* 1:2.

acquired by money or by a bill." The Rabbis are fully conscious of the meaning of the reminder. The emphasis they place on it, incidentally, is proof that, even at that time, this concept of the exodus as a divine model of "recovery" still helped to stimulate the social sense in everyday dealings.

A few examples of somewhat different versions of the idea may be of interest.

The rules concerning clean and unclean animals in Leviticus end with the warning, "For I am the Lord that hath brought you up out of Egypt to be your God; ye shall therefore be holy"; and a similar warning follows the prohibition of usury, "I am the Lord which brought you forth out of Egypt to be your God." In both cases the Rabbis explain that God delivered the people on condition that they would receive the yoke of his commandments; and that he who denies the commandments denies the deliverance.[29] Here, strictly speaking, there is no automatic passage from service in Egypt to the service of God. The service of God is voluntarily agreed to, accepted, by the people on being liberated—and if they go back on this compact, they also give up the privileges flowing from it. Possibly this construction is influenced by a custom widespread in antiquity: a master about to manumit his slave exacted from him an undertaking to perform certain offices once he was freed. At any rate, despite the fresh nuance introduced, manifestly the exodus still means a change of master.

Again, the Rabbis raise the question[30] why the exodus is mentioned in connection with so many commandments. The matter, they reply, may be compared to the ransoming of a king—God—of the captive son of a friend—Abraham. The king, however, ransoms the prisoner not to treat him as free or as a son, but to make him his own slave. That is why the commandments are accompanied by references to the ransoming from Egypt: the Israelites, having become slaves of God, may not protest against any burdens imposed on them. In this parable, too, the passage from service in Egypt to the service of God is not regarded as the only conceivable possibility: the king, God, had he wished so, might have granted the people absolute freedom. Of course, in actual life also, a "recoverer" might, if he liked, refrain from asserting his right over the person or property "recovered." But God did not do so; he claimed the people as his own, as his slaves. We shall see below that, in a deeper sense, to be God's slave, to be God's son and to be truly free were held to mean the same thing by the Rabbis.

As in the Old Testament, in general, the Israelites are described as "God's slaves" or "God's sons" without much thought being given to the precise choice of epithet. It is of course as great an honour to be "the slave [servant] of the Lord" in the way Isaiah understands this role as to be "God's son." Frequently, however, the phrase "slaves of God" implies an emphasis on the duties owed. A saying of Antigonos of Soko (of the 3rd cent. B.C.) was:[31] "Be not like slaves who minister to the master for the sake of a reward." At other times, the Rabbis do place slavery and sonship into opposition. The clause "Is not he thy father, thy owner [purchaser, acquirer]?"[32] is interpreted as indi-

[29] *Siphra* on Lev 11:45, 25:38.
[30] *Siphra* on Lev 15:41.
[31] *m. Ab.* 1:3.
[32] Deut 32:6.

cating that when the Israelites do God's will, he deals with them as with sons, but when they do not, he deals with them as with slaves.[33]

Ultimately, I suppose, while our world continues, the conflict between these two expressions of man's relationship with God is unavoidable, just like other conflicts in the region approaching the limits of our understanding—those between grace and merit, predestination and free will and so on. Let us note that, in evaluating particular texts, great care is required, since so many complicating factors must be taken into account. For instance, some Tannaites hold that a slave may be ordered to take off his master's outdoor shoes and put on his indoor ones or to carry his things to the bathhouse; others that a slave need not perform these services, but that a son or disciple must—in the case of a son or disciple they cannot be degrading.[34] The Baptist certainly shares the view that a disciple may show his respect by doing them.[35]

The old tension between God's everlasting reign over Israel and his temporary desertion of them also recurs in Rabbinic theology and—what is important in this connection—is often illustrated by comparisons with affairs based on social laws or, more particularly, the laws respecting slavery. The Israelites are represented as arguing that they need not observe God's will: they have passed out of his power since he himself sold them to foreign nations. But the argument, the Rabbis declare (and prove by a passage from Ezekiel), is fallacious. God sold them only for a time. There is a proviso attached to the sale that after a while they will fall back into his ownership.[36] In the end, God will assert his superior claim.

One change, small in itself but relevant—as we shall see—to the correct exegesis of New Testament texts is that *hikkir*, "to acknowledge," appears to be no longer employed by the Rabbis as a term of art to signify the acknowledgment of kinship by him who exercises the right of redemption. Already in the Old Testament it is sometimes paired off with *yadha'*, "to know," which verb has a wider range and cannot be said to be in technical legal use. In the Rabbinic sources, *hikkir* and *yadha'*, when referring to God's attitude to his people or to the pious, are quite synonymous and mean "to know" in the sense of "to choose," "to care for," "to be intimate with."

It is almost superfluous to observe that the Rabbis are aware that subjection to God is identical with freedom in the highest sense. No doubt when Joshua ben Levi, about the middle of the 3rd cent. A.D., preaches that "thou findest no freeman but him who occupies himself with the study of the Law,"[37] this particular dictum may be directed against, and therefore dependent on, the Christian view of freedom, which implied an abandonment—a partial one at least—of the Law. But the principal insight inspiring the saying can be shown to be extremely ancient. We need only mention these points. One is the constant description of the passing into God's service as a ransoming, a redemption or the like; we have seen enough instances of this. The second is the effect

[33] *Exod. Rab.* on 15:22.

[34] *Siphre* on Num 15:41; *Mek.* on Exod 21:2.

[35] Matt 3:11; Mark 1:7; Luke 3:16; John 1:27; Acts 13:25. See The Offices of a Disciple [747].

[36] *Siphre* on Num 15:41.

[37] *m. Ab.* 6:2.

[38] *Mek.* on Exod 21:2.

of this notion on the social consciousness. This also we have sufficiently illustrated. But we may add that in the opinion of the Tannaites, when the Bible speaks of a Hebrew slave, it does so "against its will."[38] It tolerates slavery reluctantly: he who is a son or slave of God ought to be no man's property even in appearance. Thirdly, there is the testimony of the New Testament itself. John tells us[39] how the Jews answered Jesus: "We are Abraham's seed and were never in bondage to anyone." Abraham's selection by God and his acceptance of it spelled freedom. This is not the place to go into the misinterpretations, misunderstandings and controversies to which the idea necessarily gave rise wherever it took root.

3. *The Haggadah and the New Testament*

In the New Testament, the teaching that redemption through Jesus means a change of master is stressed on a number of occasions and implied far more commonly than is obvious at first sight. Even if we confine ourselves to the passages where it is distinctly set forth—principally in John, in the epistles of Paul and in 1 Peter—there will remain no doubt that it is fairly central. It is a teaching which in many respects separates Christianity from the pagan religions and philosophies surrounding it. Dr. Selwyn observes, apropos of Peter's remark that Christians are free not to do evil but to be slaves of God: "The connection of freedom with virtue was well established in antiquity. But Christian freedom rests not on escape from service but on a change of master."[40] This early Christian concept which, if we disregard Judaism, is unique, comes directly from Old Testament and Rabbinic theology.

Deliverance by God is "recovery." The notion goes back to ancient social legislation. It was transferred to the exodus, which in turn gave a new impetus to the social laws. It was applied to later deeds of God for his people. It was also applied to the rescue by God of the faithful individual and to his final salvation of his own at the end of days. In the New Testament it is applied to the redemption through Jesus.

It is worth pointing out that the notion occurs in the New Testament in many various nuances. God may be represented as the Christian's father or as his master; the Christian's release may be from enslavement to men[41] or from enslavement to sin;[42] and so forth.

For a proper appreciation of the New Testament texts we should remember, what I have hardly touched on so far, that both before and after the destruction of the Temple, the exodus, construed as a "recovery," played a prominent part in the Passover celebration.

In the Haggadah, in the Passover-eve liturgy, the recital of the miracles performed by God opens: "We were slaves unto Pharaoh in Egypt, and our God brought us out [freed us] from there." This is a quotation from Deuteronomy.[43] In Deuteronomy, the fol-

[39] John 8:33.
[40] *The First Epistle of St. Peter* (1946), 174.
[41] E.g. 1 Cor 7:21 ff.
[42] E.g. Rom 6:18.
[43] Deut 6:21.
[44] *m. Pes.* 10:1.

lowing verses make it clear that the giving of the commandments formed the climax of the deliverance. The idea in the Haggadah is the same. God redeemed his people; from being slaves of men, they have become slaves of God.

Naturally, the tension between the external situation of the Jews, sinful and oppressed, and their real, internal freedom as belonging to God, finds full expression in the liturgy. An Aramaic portion of the Haggadah, which was composed in Babylonia before or shortly after the destruction of the Temple, contains this wish: "This year here, the next year in the land of Israel: this year slaves, the next free men." The emphasis lies on the external situation; and, as usual, the prayer is for spiritual as well as political restoration—the two cannot be kept strictly apart.

On the other hand, the real freedom of the Jews as God's people comes out, for instance, in the provision of the Mishnah[44] that for the Passover supper "even the poorest in Israel must recline [on a couch]"; a provision the significance of which becomes intelligible when we consider that in Hellenistic times free men took their meals in this fashion, while slaves ate sitting. In fact, one of the questions traditionally put on Passover eve in order to provoke in reply a recital of God's deeds for Israel is why, at this meal, all participants assume a recumbent position. To this day it is usual for the participants in the Seder, the Passover-eve ceremony, to lean on a cushion placed on one's left side, as did the free men in antiquity. (The right hand must be disengaged to handle food and drink.)

That this custom dates from the New Testament epoch would be plain from its nature, even if there were no allusion to it in Mark and Luke: "He will show you a room furnished with cushions."[45] The Passover supper is taken by those already free, since they are already "recovered" by God: the first part of the Hallel, the "hymn," concludes with a praisegiving for his salvation.[46]

On the whole, the true freedom of God's people, irrespective of the external situation, receives more prominence on Passover eve than usual—the ceremony is largely a re-enactment of the exodus and, so to speak, a "pre-enactment" of the final deliverance. But we saw above that it was not only on Passover that the consciousness of never having been anyone's slave since Abraham was strong among the Jews of the New Testament era.

Again, the Hallel, consisting of Psalms 113–18, forms part of the Passover-eve liturgy. We know that this was so in New Testament times. This group of psalms is sometimes called *himnon*, ὕμνος, by the Rabbis, and from Matthew and Mark we hear[47] that those taking part in the last supper "sung an hymn." Moreover, while the Temple stood, it was these psalms that were sung during the slaughtering of the Passover lambs.[48] Now the first of them begins: "Praise ye the Lord, O servants of the Lord." According to Raba[49] the antithesis implied is "servants of the Lord—not servants of Pharaoh."

[45] Mark 14:15; Luke 22:12. Cp. κλίνη ἐστρωμένη in Ezek 23:41, LXX.

[46] *m. Pes.* 10:6.

[47] Matt 26:30; Mark 14:26.

[48] *m. Pes.* 5:7.

[49] *b. Meg.* 14a.

Admittedly, Raba lived in the first half of the 4th cent. A.D. But as he takes this interpretation for granted and, indeed, uses it to prove another point, it must be considerably older. Anyhow, once more we have before us the idea that through their liberation from Egypt the Hebrews, up to then slaves to men, turned into slaves to God.

There is, incidentally, a Midrash on "I am thy God which have brought thee out of the house of bondage," which must be very old and which insists that the Hebrews in Egypt were slaves, not to slaves, but to kings.[50] It is difficult to decide what motive or motives may underlie it: to establish a contrast between Israel and Canaan who is condemned to be "a slave to slaves,"[51] to make the past less degrading, to suggest that God is strong enough to defeat the mightiest among humans, to bring the oppression in Egypt into line with what in fact often happened to the nation when it was laid under tribute by foreign rulers ("Behold, we are servants this day and the land that thou gavest unto our fathers yieldeth increase unto the kings whom thou hast set over us because of our sins"[52]). What is highly probable is that the exchange of earthly kingship for divine kingship, so conspicuous a theme in the Haggadah, is in the author's mind.

If divine "recovery" may mean a liberation from human sovereigns to pass under the sovereignty of God, it may also mean a liberation from the service of false gods to pass into that of the true one. A section of the Haggadah—which, some Rabbis held, ought to open the recital rather than the opening mentioned above ("We were slaves unto Pharaoh and God freed us")—begins thus: "Originally our fathers were slaves of strange slavery [or: worshippers of strange worship—the technical designation of idolaters], but now God hath brought us near to his slavery [worship]."

The context shows that here, where the antithesis is between slaves to false gods and slaves to the true God, the change of master is thought of as having commenced long before the actual exodus, namely, when God called Abraham. The whole process from that call to the deliverance from Egypt and revelation at mount Sinai is one: an undoing of the chains of idolatry by the rightful lord. It is interesting that the verb "to bring near," occurring in the clause "he hath brought us near to his worship," is technical in Tannaitic language of conversion. "Hillel used to say: Be of the disciples of Aaron, loving mankind and bringing them near to the Law."[53]

We have just quoted a Midrash according to which "I am thy God which have brought thee out of the house of bondage" refers to God's liberation of the Hebrews from earthly kings. Earthly kingship was exchanged for divine kingship. It should now be added that an alternative interpretation was that God liberated the Hebrews from enslavement to idols, or from life among slaves of idols, idolaters.[54] Enslavement to idols was exchanged for enslavement to God.

It is surely against the background of the Jewish concept of redemption, "recovery," and in particular against that dominating the Passover-eve liturgy, that the New Testament references to a change of master acquire their full meaning: John's asser-

[50] *Mek.* on Exod 20:2.

[51] Gen 9:25.

[52] Neh 9:36 f.

[53] *m. Ab.* 1:12; see also e.g. *y. Kidd.* 65b.

[54] *Mek.* on Exod 20:2.

tion[55] that the truth, or the Son, would cause to be free, or to be sons, those who are slaves to sin; Paul's discourse in Romans[56] on the way the slaves of sin, by becoming free of sin, turn into slaves of righteousness; his explanation in 1 Corinthians[57] that those bought to be slaves of Jesus are free from men (and that those free as regards their civil status are yet slaves of Jesus); his warning in Galatians[58] that release by Jesus from the Law and sin involves enslavement to one's fellow-men in love; and 1 Peter's teaching that the Christians are free from men, whatever their worldly position may be, but that they are free only to be slaves of God.

Each of these passages represents some version or versions of the Jewish notion of deliverance. To none of them can we do justice without paying attention to the role the Jewish notion played both generally, and more specifically in regard to Passover. The traditional contrasts between subjection to men and freedom in the hands of God, and between subjection to idols and freedom in the hands of God; the basic connection between divine redemption and brotherly love on earth; the perennial tension and harmony between being God's sons and being his slaves; the different shades of the term "to serve" ("to serve as a slave," "to serve as a son," "to serve as a free labourer," "to worship," "to cultivate")—they all have contributed to the New Testament texts in question.

Occasionally, salvation is equated with "being known by God."[59] To some extent we must reckon with the influence of Hellenistic mysticism. But it has long been seen that there is also a Hebrew root: as already remarked, when the Old Testament or a Rabbi speaks of God "knowing" his people or the faithful, the meaning is that he has chosen and cares for them. A remarkable feature, however, is that Paul, in Galatians, uses, γιγνώσκω, "to know," *yadha'*, in much the way in which ἐπιγιγνώσκω, "to acknowledge," *hikkir*, is used in the Old Testament—but hardly in Rabbinic literature—of one who legally, effectively, recognizes a relative and redeems him from a strange master: "When ye knew not God, ye were in bondage to them which are no gods; but now after that ye have known God, rather are known of God, how turn ye to the weak elements whereunto ye desire again to be in bondage?"

Paul's discourse in Romans deserves special mention, since it has been somewhat harshly treated by modern commentators. He combats the view that those living under grace need not be afraid to sin, and he combats it by affirming that slavery to sin has been replaced by slavery to righteousness.

Dodd, who is highly critical of this section, begins by saying[60] that, as the misconception of grace is already dealt with in the previous section, there is no advance in principle. This may be correct. But even if there is no advance in principle, it is only here that Paul introduces the old notion of a change of master. In the previous section, he spoke of baptism, and of dying and rising with Jesus, as eliminating sin. Now he dwells on the passage from the service of sin to that of righteousness. For himself, and

[55] John 8:32 ff.
[56] Rom 6:16 ff.
[57] 1 Cor 7:20 ff.
[58] Gal 5:1, 13 ff.
[59] E.g. 1 Cor 8:3, 14:38; Gal 4:8 f.
[60] "The Epistle of Paul to the Romans," in *The Moffat New Testament Commentary* (1932), 96.

no doubt for a large part of the recipients of the letter, the historical and religious setting of that notion, and above all its association with Passover, would amply justify the place and importance he assigns to it at this stage.

Another objection proferred is that Paul contrasts with enslavement to sin, not sonship to God, but enslavement to God. The latter idea, Dodd remarks,[61] will later have to be corrected into the more adequate one of sonship. This also seems a little one-sided. As we saw above, though, from a certain point of view, there is a conflict between being God's sons and being his slaves, yet both relations (and several more) are necessary: they not only conflict with, but also supplement, one another, and it depends on the particular situation, on the experience and purpose at a given moment, which may be in the foreground. Here Paul is concerned with the need of obedience; hence it is natural to refer to service.

There is indeed a third criticism which is less easily met. Paul contrasts with enslavement to sin, not only enslavement to God, but also enslavement to righteousness. "Ye were servants of sin, but ye have obeyed that doctrine which was delivered you; being then made free from sin, ye became the servants of righteousness." And again, "As ye have yielded your members slaves to iniquity, so now yield them slaves to righteousness." This, Dodd says,[62] is rather sub-Christian: conversion is represented as simply the acceptance of the ethical teachings of a rule of faith.

What makes the matter really problematic, however, is that the expression is not only "sub-Christian," but also "sub-Jewish." There is not a single Old Testament or Rabbinic text with the phrase "slaves of righteousness" or anything like it—say, "slaves of the Law" or "slaves of good deeds." The faithful are "slaves of God"; they could be slaves to no one and nothing else.

Paul himself is aware that his language—only his language, not his thought—is bold in the extreme, bordering on the blasphemous, and he apologizes in words which he uses on other similar occasions, and which were doubtless technical for this purpose in Jewish circles:[63] "I speak after the manner of men." He apologizes not, as Dodd thinks, because his illustration is "sub-Christian" or because it is not going well in general, but because it is "sub-Jewish." The exhortation to be "slaves to righteousness," unless qualified by this apology, i.e. unless declared to be a mere metaphor, would scandalize the good Jews.

The question, then, arises: Why does Paul use the term "slaves of righteousness"? Why is he not satisfied with the orthodox "slaves to God"?

The answer is that, as already stated, he is trying to refute the argument that, since grace is free and the Law has ceased to be valid, sin need not be shunned and holiness need not be sought, and that, indeed, it may be desirable to sin. His aim is to impress on the addressees of the letter that they must none the less do good. His very insistence on life under grace and without the Law, plus the misinterpretation put on it by radical

[61] P. 99.

[62] P. 98.

[63] *Pace* Strack-Billerbeck, vol. 3 (1926), 136. For a full discussion see below ["I Speak after the Manner of Men," 651 ff.].

antinomians, drives him to use a term which the Rabbis, who held fast to the Law, had no need to use.

The Rabbis had no need to require the people to be "slaves to righteousness." Everything they wanted was implied in the requirement to be "slaves to God." Paul, preaching life under grace and without the Law, but at the same time opposing antinomianism, feels compelled to demand that Christians should be "slaves to righteousness"—though he does not fail to add an apology proving him loyal to the Jewish tenet that, fundamentally, what is demanded is to be "slaves to God."

Two Tripartite Forms

A. Revolutionary Action—Protest—Silencing of the Remonstrants

The Synoptics record at least[1] seven incidents taking this course: (1) Jesus or his disciples perform a revolutionary action, (2) the Pharisees remonstrate with him—or, on occasion, merely "marvel"—and (3) he makes a pronouncement by which they are silenced.

The actions in question are: he forgives a sick person's sins[2] (the place of the pronouncement, the verbal argument, is in this case taken by a further action—the person is made to walk and carry his bed—but from the point of view of the present discussion the difference is irrelevant), he sits at table with publicans,[3] the disciples pluck corn on a Sabbath,[4] he restores a man previously blind and dumb,[5] he or his disciples do not wash their hands before a meal,[6] he heals on a Sabbath,[7] and children call out "Hosanna to the son of David."[8] There are quite a few other pericopes more or less closely approaching this form—e.g. those about the disciples not fasting,[9] Jesus preaching in his home town,[10] and Jesus acting and teaching in the temple,[11] also, in Acts,[12] the episode of Peter's preaching in defiance of the council's prohibition.

Stories told in this way are, of course, to be found in all literatures. A Rabbinic example is that of R. Judah the Prince,[13] who once reversed a ruling on which his father, grandfather and so on—all of them leading scholars—had insisted (revolutionary action). His family objected (protest). But he replied that Asa and Jehosaphat, when they removed the idols from the land,[14] spared the brazen serpent in order that

[1] The following enumeration may well be incomplete.

[2] Matt 9:1 ff.; Mark 2:1 ff.; Luke 5:17 ff.

[3] Matt 9:9 ff.; Mark 2:15 ff.; Luke 5:27 ff.

[4] Matt 12:1 ff.; Mark 2:23 ff.; Luke 6:1 ff.

[5] Matt 12:22 ff.; Luke 11:14 ff.; but Mark 3:22 ff. is different.

[6] Luke 11:37 ff.; in Mark 7:1 ff. part (1) is slightly weakened, in Matt 15:1 ff. it is entirely merged in part (2).

[7] Luke 13:10 ff.; but the form is not employed in Matt 12:9 ff.; Mark 3:1 ff.; Luke 6:6 ff., 14:1 ff.

[8] Matt 21:15 ff., with part (1) weakened just as in Mark 7:1 ff.

[9] Matt 9:14 ff.; Mark 2:19 ff.; Luke 5:35 ff.

[10] Matt 13:53 ff.; Mark 6:1 ff.; Luke 4:15 ff.

[11] Matt 21:23 ff.; Mark 11:27 ff.; Luke 20:1 ff.

[12] Acts 5:25 ff.

[13] *b. Hull.* 6b f.

[14] 1 Kgs 15:12 f., 22:43.

Hezekiah should have the merit of breaking it;[15] just so, his own ancestors had left him room to distinguish himself by a novel decision (silencing of the remonstrants). Any newspaper may report: "Mrs. X refused to fill in the census-paper, an official went to see her, but she told him that as she had kept her age a secret from her husband, she was not going to divulge it to Mr. Attlee."

Manifestly, the situation reflected in this structure constantly occurs in everyday life. It is indeed a special case of what must be one of the oldest, simplest and most frequent types of conversation: unusual conduct—question—explanation. An employee comes home at 6 p.m. instead of 6:30, his wife enquires "You are early today?" and he replies "Yes, the office closed sooner for cleaning."

However, if we ask why this form—revolutionary action, protest, silencing of the remonstrants—is so prominent in the Synoptics, to say that it is a natural form would not be an adequate answer. It is precisely this fact which needs to be investigated: what do we mean by declaring it natural, what is the setting in life of which it appears the only fitting expression, in what situation would it be so popular as to be used again and again?

We must not forget that there were other forms at the disposal of the evangelists (or their precursors). They might, for instance, have employed a more academic style. Regarding the association with publicans, they might have written: Jesus believed that the Pharisees showed too little consideration for sinners, who, sick men, badly needed the physician, therefore he went into their houses, ate with them and called them to repentance. But even if they stuck to the immediate, dramatic presentation, there was a large choice.

As a matter of fact, the Synoptics five times describe a cure performed by Jesus on a Sabbath, but only once in the form under discussion. (As for John, he mentions two healings on a Sabbath,[16] employing a style quite different from the Synoptic.) In Luke 13, we find Jesus healing a crippled woman, the ruler of the synagogue protesting, and Jesus retorting: "Doth not each one of you on the sabbath day loose his ox and lead him away to the watering? And ought not this woman, being a daughter of Abraham, be loosed?" This sequence is revolutionary action—protest—silencing of the remonstrants. But in Matthew 12, Mark 3 and Luke 6, the Pharisees question or watch Jesus, then he explains his attitude, and the action, the cure, comes at the end; while Luke 14 seems a conflation of the two forms—the Pharisees watch Jesus, then he explains his attitude, then he performs the cure, and finally he makes a second pronouncement to refute the opponents.

Luke 14, as a conflation, may perhaps be disregarded. So may the particular structure of Luke 6, which we discussed above, under Socratic Interrogation: the Pharisees watch, Jesus puts a question, they cannot answer, and he draws the conclusion by performing the cure. This is a somewhat elaborate structure. There remains, however, a

[15] 1 Kgs 15:14, 22:44; 2 Kgs 18:4.

[16] John 5:1 ff. and 9:1 ff.

perfectly good and simple form—the enemies on the watch for a certain action, pronouncement, the action—which was known to the evangelists and which they could have used much more often than they did in the place of the form we are considering. Clearly, we are justified in inquiring into the special significance of the form they preferred.

The following points may be relevant. First, the direct, dramatic presentation of revolutionary action, protest and silencing of the remonstrants—as opposed, say, to a more detached, academic record of events—is no doubt meant for a public still in a state of active, lively controversy with the Pharisees, and strongly feeling the need of refuting the troublesome enemy.

Secondly, by placing the revolutionary action at the head, emphasis is laid on the novel, startling character of the kingdom. We have just mentioned an alternative form—used to describe a cure on a Sabbath in Matthew 12, Mark 3 and Luke 6—where Jesus first explains and then acts. Clearly, the action will here cause less surprise to his antagonists, or the public for whom the narrative is composed. Needless to say, this form also has its distinctive purpose, but we are not here concerned with it.

We modern readers, when we come to an incident commencing "At that time Jesus went on the sabbath day through the corn, and his disciples were an hungred and began to pluck and eat," are not particularly excited: we are too habituated to such practice. In New Testament times, however, the effect must have been comparable to that a Lutheran author would intend by starting a life of his hero thus: "On the 20th of December 1520, Martin Luther publicly consigned to the flames a Papal Bull condemning his errors." The narrative opens with a shock. It is a special case of a very ancient device of story-tellers, namely, the device of putting the result at the beginning and the causes leading up to it second. (Gen 12:10 ff. informs us first of Abraham's reasons for introducing Sarah as his sister, and then of what occurred when she was so introduced. But Gen 20:1 ff. starts by recording his action—he introduced Sarah as his sister—and we are kept wondering why till nearly the end of the story, in v. 11. Kleist excelled in this art. In the first paragraph of *Michael Kohlhaas* we are told that this good man became a bandit and murderer, and in the first paragraph of *Die Marquise von O...* that this lady, a widow and mother of untainted reputation, put an advertisement in the papers saying that she had become pregnant without her knowledge, and would the man come forward in order that she might marry him.)

Thirdly, the action is invariably one performed on a single, definite occasion; not "Jesus used to sit at meat in the houses of publicans," but "on a certain day, Jesus ate in the house of a certain publican."[17] This point is connected with that just considered. The kingdom—such is the idea behind the form—manifested itself, broke in, step by step as Jesus and those around him fulfilled their task.

[17] Matt 15:1 ff., unlike Luke 11:37 ff. and Mark 7:1 ff., does not refer to a specific occasion; the failure of the disciples to wash their hands before a meal is represented as a practice. But, then, as remarked above (note 6), the tripartite form in question is here altogether abandoned. The incident falls into question and retort, there is no separate part for the action.

Certainly, underlying these specific actions there were general ideas, and the believers are obliged to pay heed to them; we shall presently see that they are given full expression in the pronouncements ending the encounters. Nevertheless, in this form, things are set in motion by single, datable actions. Which means that the general ideas first became reality in, and will derive their ultimate sanction from, deeds done by Jesus and his followers at particular moments of their activity.

Fourthly, yet another feature points the same way: the action is always an action in the narrow sense, i.e. never a statement. For example, it is easy to imagine the following structure: (1) Jesus declared, "It is praiseworthy to eat with publicans and sinners," (2) protest by the Pharisees, (3) repartee by Jesus. This, however, would be an ordinary disputation, such as might from beginning to end be conducted before a learned audience; and however convincing the final repartee might be, the form as such would not show whether the revolutionary view remained a theory or was once at least put into practice.

By contrast, the structure of which the first member is an action in the strict sense—Jesus ate with publicans and sinners—indicates that the revolutionary programme was carried out, that the kingdom had in fact arrived. To this, the forgiving of sins[18] is, of course, no exception. It is a proper action, indeed, a serious crime according to the Pharisees. A mere statement would be: "Jesus said, I could forgive this man his sins."

Fifthly, the middle part of the form, the protest, sometimes consists in a direct accusation—"He blasphemeth," "He doth not cast out devils but by Beelzebub"—and sometimes in a challenge to justify the objectionable conduct—"Why eateth your Master with publicans and sinners?" for instance. In both cases the remonstrants assume that Jesus and his followers ought to behave as they themselves would behave. Jesus and his followers, that is, are judged as essentially belonging to the same camp as the remonstrants; it is precisely for this reason that their conduct appears as a revolution. Complete outsiders, however strange their actions, would not be called to account in this manner.

Sixthly, the third member of the form, the silencing of the remonstrants, confirms the observation just made. Jesus justifies the action impugned by adducing a piece of teaching which his opponents also recognize as valid: a wise saying ("they that are whole have no need of the physician"), a passage from Scripture ("David did eat the showbread," "Out of the mouth of babes thou has perfected praise"), an established ordinance ("Doth not each one of you on the sabbath loose his ox?"). In other words, he starts from the same basis as his antagonists. If he did not, if he quoted doctrines not accepted by them, it would not put them to silence.

Where he differs from them is as to the interpretation of the teaching adduced. From the maxim that the sick ones only need the physician, he infers—whereas his opponents do not—that it is his duty to sit at table with publicans and sinners; from

[18] Matt 9:1 ff.; Mark 2:1 ff.; Luke 5:17 ff.

David's conduct he infers—whereas his opponents do not—that his hungry disciples have the right to pluck corn on the Sabbath; the verse "Out of the mouth of babes" in his view—but not that of his opponents—is applicable to the Hosanna by which the children greet him; the law allowing that animals may be led to watering on the Sabbath in his view—but not in that of his opponents—shows that one may certainly heal a Jewish person on the Sabbath. The relationship between the two parties is not dissimilar to that expressed by "Ye have heard—but I say unto you," except that "Ye have heard—but I say" is concerned only with the proper understanding of Scripture, while the third member of the form under discussion may refer to any teaching the proper understanding of which is relevant to life in the kingdom.

Seventhly, the third member describes the defeat of the Pharisees on their own ground, by an argument resting on a basis they themselves acknowledge. Here we come back to point one, but we can now be a little more precise: the form dates from a time when it was vital to defend the ways of the new community—revolutionary actions—in a technical, scholarly, Pharisaic manner.

Comparison with a different form may make this clearer. As already mentioned, the gospels several times describe a cure on a Sabbath in the following way: (1) the Pharisees watch whether Jesus will heal the sick person, (2) Jesus explains his attitude, (3) he performs the cure. In this form, which culminates in the cure, the final emphasis is on fearlessness: despite the hostility surrounding him, Jesus acts as he thinks he ought to act. The setting in life must be sought in a milieu where it was dangerous openly to practise the new religion. Evidently, it is different where we are told (1) how Jesus performed the cure, (2) the Pharisees remonstrated, and (3) he refuted them. The final emphasis here lies on the successful vindication of the revolutionary conduct.

Finally, the tripartite form as a whole may owe something to the forensic scheme: action—charge—defence, or successful defence. After all, this scheme, which might be used by any author, must have appeared particularly appropriate to those who recounted Jesus's deeds after his death. They were resuming the trial, they were appealing against the original decision.

B. Odd Gesture—Question—Pronouncement

This form also is a special case of the elementary triad: unusual conduct (the husband comes home at 6 p.m.)—question (his wife asks him why he is so early)—explanation (the office is being cleaned). It is, however, of a rather sophisticated nature. Part (1), the gesture—which may be an action in the narrow sense or an utterance—is performed, not so much for its own sake, as in order to provoke part (2), the question, and thus to furnish an opportunity for what really matters, namely, part (3), the pronouncement.

1. *Odd gesture*

The fool in King Lear offers Kent his cap: part (1). This action is intended to astonish Lear and Kent, who ask him what he means: part (2). It is only now, in part (3), that he makes the statement to which (1) and (2) have been leading up: he points out, what he realizes even at this early stage, that Kent is entering the service of one who is doomed. Till Eulenspiegel used to laugh when faced by a steep ascent and to weep when the road was downhill: part (1). His companions asked him about his strange conduct: part (2). Whereupon he explained—part (3)—that, going uphill, he rejoiced at the prospect of the comfortable walk that would follow, whereas, going downhill, the thought of having to climb up again later made him sad.

He had a forerunner in R. Akiba. Once he and his friends heard the noise of a Roman festivity, and while the others wept, he laughed. The others asked him how he could feel happy at such a moment. To which he replied that if sinful Rome was so fortunate, how glorious must be the future of obedient Israel. Similarly, when they came to the desecrated ruins of the Temple, the others wept but he laughed. Asked again, he replied that as God had so strictly fulfilled the prophecies of destruction, one could be quite confident that he would equally fulfil the prophecies of restoration.[19] (In both stories of Akiba, the form is expanded. It is not, however, necessary here to pursue this point. The main, tripartite framework—which alone we are presenting—is clearly perceptible.)

Another Rabbinic example of this form is a story about R. Johanan ben Zaccai.[20] The dying Rabbi, on beholding his disciples who came to visit him, began to sob: part (1). They inquired why he, the lamp of Israel, should do so: (2). His answer was that he would be frightened if he had to appear before a weak, earthly tribunal; should he not be frightened now that he must appear before a judge who might condemn him to everlasting death? And as a last blessing for his disciples he prayed that their fear of Heaven might always be as great as (it need not be greater than) their fear of flesh and blood: part (3).

It is not always easy to distinguish this form from other cases of unusual conduct—question—explanation, and as we shall see, there is much overlapping. Still, as a rule, we can notice where part (1) is merely, or chiefly, a means of bringing about parts (2) and (3). For instance, in the anecdote of Johanan ben Zaccai, it is significant that he sobbed "on beholding his disciples." They did not come and find him sobbing; he began to sob when they came. Manifestly, the action was addressed to them rather than God. Its main purpose was to elicit the question in reply to which an important teaching might be conveyed.

It is safe to assume that this procedure—i.e. the startling of one's prospective public by an odd gesture in order to be able to deliver the message in reply to a genuine question—is one of the oldest ways of securing attention. Its psychological genesis is clear. Experience shows that a man who behaves in an unusual fashion is likely to be questioned (unusual conduct—question—explanation): consequently, if you wish to be questioned, you behave in an unusual fashion. Eve may well have moped for a few days,

[19] *b. Makk.* 24b.
[20] *b. Ber.* 28b.

waiting for Adam to ask her what was the matter, when she could tell him that she wanted a new apron. In Terence's *Eunuch*,[21] the sly maidservant Pythias pretends to be unaware of Parmeno's presence (thus preventing any doubts on his part as to the reality of her terror) but takes good care that he should hear her muttering: "Oh horrible deed, oh that wicked Parmeno who has brought such misfortune on the young gentleman." Parmeno anxiously inquires what has happened, whereupon Pythias relates the fearful story she wants him to believe. This scene is quite life-like.

There need be no inner connection between the gesture and the pronouncement; the former may consist in any action that will rouse the curiosity of the public. A friend of mine, son of a Prussian colonel, was about five years old when, on coming down to breakfast one morning in midwinter, he found himself seized by his father who, without any apparent reason, gave him a terrific thrashing. The boy shouted: "Let go of me! What have I done?" At last the colonel released him and said: "The time has come for you to be told that the 28th of January is *Kaisers Geburtstag*. I am sure you will never forget it."

2. *Significant gesture*

However, normally, the introductory gesture does give a hint of the pronouncement to come. In all the cases mentioned above—that of the fool offering Kent his cap, that of Eulenspiegel or Akiba laughing when others weep and *vice versa*, that of Johanan ben Zaccai sobbing on his death-bed, that of Eve moping because of her frock and that of Pythias uttering horrified exclamations—the gesture is not merely odd so that any other oddity would do just as well. Any other oddity would have done just as well for my friend's father: he might, for example, have thrown the milk jug against the ceiling. In all the other cases, however, once the teaching is conveyed, the gesture turns out to have been perfectly logical on that basis.

In other words, the gesture appears odd only because and so long as the final message is not known. In reality, it has a definite though hidden meaning, which the pronouncement will bring out. Therefore, instead of speaking of odd gesture—question—pronouncement, we should rather describe the usual sequence as significant but mystifying conduct—question—interpretation of the conduct.

Let us confine ourselves to this commoner type. What is its setting in life? No doubt it will flourish primarily where there is a master surrounded by his circle. If a negligible person performed the gesture, people would pay no heed; whereas a master's circle assembles precisely in order to watch his every movement and be enlightened as to its import. This is not to deny that occasionally a negligible person may get into a position where an odd gesture of his will be effective: the scene from Terence, where a maidservant frightens a valet, may be recalled. But we are here concerned with the problem against what background the tripartite sequence discussed would become a customary narrative form. To this the answer is: a master and his circle. It is in this situation that

[21] *Eunuch* 5.4.943 ff.

gestures worth inquiring about, actions strange at first sight but on interpretation seen to be full of wisdom, will be the rule.

Moreover, it is in this situation that actions full of wisdom will be performed, not for their own sake, but for the purpose of instruction, as gestures. That peculiar feature, the showing off, the addressing of the action to a public, the sobbing "on beholding his visitors," though it may occur anywhere, has its most natural place where guidance is habitually sought and given. Only it should be borne in mind that the term "master" in this connection has a very wide sense. It may mean a sage or a jester (like Eulenspiegel or the fool in King Lear), a prophet or a madman (a certain kind of prophecy and a certain kind of madness were quite close); in short, anyone to whom some circle would look for the disclosing of deeper truths.

The analysis can be carried a little further. A master might, and often does, explain first and act afterwards. In the form we are inspecting, however, the action precedes the explanation: mystifying conduct—question—interpretation. This arrangement corresponds to an attitude to education widespread in antiquity; a man who wished to learn did not attend impersonal, set lectures, but attached himself to a superior mind, lived with or near him, observed his behaviour from day to day and listened to such expositions as might be vouchsafed.

In this scheme, the master's conduct comes first, is noted first, while the theory behind it is only gradually revealed. We had occasion before (in discussing Precept and Example) to advert to the contrast made in Greek literature between two modes of instruction—example and theory. That the example furnished by the master's behaviour forms the beginning of education, to be followed by theoretical exposition, is stated by a writer like Xenophon:[22] "I see that all teachers show their pupils how they themselves practise what they teach, and lead them on by explanation." Evidently, he is speaking from experience, this was how the sage ordinarily taught those around him. The form under notice, which is very much older than Xenophon, reflects this manner.

In Xenophon, incidentally, we come across some rather elaborate specimens of the form. He reports, for instance,[23] that though the indictment had been drawn, Socrates talked to a friend without once referring to his defence: part 1, mystifying conduct. His friend commented upon it: part 2, question. (To be quite accurate, his friend reminded him that he ought to think about his defence. But, essentially, this is nothing but a question concerning his unusual behaviour; we must allow for a little variety of expression when we come to such an advanced class of writing.) Socrates answered that he had prepared for his defence all his life: part 3, interpretation of the odd conduct. However, part 3 again puzzles the audience, the answer itself is difficult to understand. Accordingly, this same part 3 constitutes part 1 of a fresh tripartite sequence; it is another mystifying action, or rather statement. Xenophon goes on to tell us how Socrates's friend inquired what he meant: part 2, question. To which Socrates replied that he had prepared for his

[22] *Memorabilia* 1.2.17.

[23] *Memorabilia* 4.8.4 ff.

defence by always doing right: part 3, interpretation. This, too, sounds queer, since everybody knows that innocence alone, unsupported by effective argument, is no guarantee against condemnation. Therefore, this is a further part 1. We next learn that the friend expressed his doubts: part 2. Whereupon Socrates said that when he did try to work out an argument, the deity resisted: part 3. But once more part 3 is intended, not only to explain, but also to cause renewed bewilderment; that is to say, once more it is at the same time part 3 of one triad and part 1 of the next. His friend now exclaimed, "You speak strangely" (θαυμαστὰ λέγεις): part 2. Here part 1 is expressly described as "strange," "something that causes one to wonder." This time at last Socrates gave a full and intelligible exposition of his attitude.

The way the successive groups of three are interlocked in this chapter is presumably an application of the dialectic method favoured by Socrates and his admirers. It is a curious adaptation of an old popular form to the fashionable requirements of logic.

One reason why, in the opinion of Hellenistic thinkers, it is preferable to learn from the practice of a master rather than from theoretical discourses is that this is the quicker way, or in more philosophical language, that an ordinary person finds it less difficult to assimilate particulars than universals.[24] Needless to say, the ancient master-circle relationship is earlier than any reasons given for it in literature. Still, it is true that, as a rule, people's curiosity is roused more easily by an unusual action than by a lecture or treatise. An unadorned dry pronouncement might fall on deaf ears where one introduced by a mystifying gesture will be received with eager attention. It is worth noting that the first part of the form in question, the gesture, is often deliberately provocative, its queerness is accentuated as much as possible. The master tries to make his audience "sit up and take notice."

Conversely, it seems that if an audience were of the highest intellectual and moral standard, alive to the problems that matter and ever thirsting after knowledge, the mystifying gesture must be superfluous; there would be no need for any special effort to gain a hearing. The form mystifying gesture—question—interpretation, then, essentially presupposes an audience that requires shaking, awakening. To rouse his disciples from lethargy of the spirit and direct their minds to unexpected things, to fields beyond those familiar to them, are the foremost tasks of a true master.

As remarked above, the mystifying gesture may be an action or an utterance. However, if it is correct to hold that the form owes something to the ancient mode of learning—to wit, by attaching oneself to a master—we may perhaps conclude that, originally, there must be an action in the narrow sense: the disciple watches his master's practice, and it is by acting in an unusual fashion that the latter induces the former to question him. When, in the chapter from Xenophon, the mystifying conduct several times[25] consists in a strange utterance, in the master's talking to his disciple in riddles, this may well represent a later development of the form. But there is, of course, no certainty.

[24] Seneca, *Epistles* 6.5; Aristotle, *Rhet.* 1.2.8 ff.; *Prior Analytics* 2.24.

[25] Not always. Socrates's refraining from any mention of his defence is an action—or inaction—in the strict sense.

3. *John*

Turning to the New Testament, one thing we have to remark is that the tripartite form we discussed first—revolutionary action, protest, silencing of the remonstrants—may occasionally show elements of that which we are now concerned with—mystifying gesture, question, interpretation. The mere fact of a revolutionary action being done in public though it could be done in private gives it a little of the nature of a mystifying gesture, a means to an end—the end being the justification of the action. We know that Jesus at one time did perform cures in secret.[26] When, then, we hear of the healing of a dumb person in public, followed by a charge and its refutation,[27] it is arguable that, as seen by the author of this pericope, one aim of the action was to provoke opposition in order that it might be demolished. Similar considerations apply, for example, to the healing of a crippled woman on a Sabbath—in the synagogue, where this must necessarily produce a clash.[28]

However, while so much may be admitted, the essential character of the form revolutionary action—protest—silencing of the remonstrants remains unaffected, and plainly different from mystifying gesture—question—interpretation. The principal purpose even of these public cures is, not the ensuing controversies, but the cures, the realization of the Kingdom "where the blind receive their sight and the lame walk." To put it differently, the cure is in the first place addressed to the sick, and only second (if at all) to the public. True, as the Kingdom is to be made manifest, the action must be open; and as there are enemies, there must be controversy. This does not imply that the primary object of the action is the controversy. We must beware of laying too much stress on the latter. To modern readers, the healing of a person on a Sabbath or the plucking of corn on a Sabbath seems a small affair; whereas they are still impressed by the argument that if one may take an animal to watering one may surely help a man, or "that in this place is one greater than the temple."[29] But at the same time, those actions, far from irrelevant, were striking, unheard of, a new way of life.

There is a simple test. In all cases we have labelled as revolutionary action—protest—silencing of the remonstrants, the first member alone would make a complete story. It would be a complete story to record that Jesus forgave a sick person's sins (without any controversy following), that he ate with publicans, that he healed on a Sabbath and so on. The action can always stand on its own feet. In contradistinction, it would not do if we were told that Eulenspiegel or Akiba laughed when others wept, or that Johanan ben Zaccai sobbed on beholding his visitors, but were not told why, and so forth. The action in these cases receives its *raison d'être* from the interpretation, it is nothing by itself.

[26] Matt 8:2 ff., 9:27 ff.; Mark 1:40 ff., 7:32 ff.; Luke 5:12 ff.
[27] Matt 12:22 ff.; Luke 11:14 ff.
[28] Luke 13:10 ff.
[29] Luke 13:10 ff.; Matt 12:1 ff.; Mark 2:23 ff.; Luke 6:1 ff.

In fact there is in the New Testament only one pericope distinctly approaching the form mystifying gesture—question—interpretation, namely, John's account[30] of how Jesus washed the feet of his disciples, how they were perplexed and how he explained the teaching to be inferred from his conduct: "If I then, your Lord, have washed your feet, ye also ought to wash one another's feet."

Here the opening action is performed, less for its own sake, than as a gesture, like Johanan's sobbing on his death-bed, in order to bring about question and interpretation. From the outset it is the latter, the message, with a view to which everything is done—just as Johanan from the outset intended to admonish his disciples to fear Heaven. Though the narrative contains many complications—John is an accomplished writer—the tripartite framework and the setting we have ascribed to it are quite plain. A master is surrounded by his circle. The former deliberately acts in a way for the moment unintelligible to the latter, in a way that must seem paradoxical, though its significance will ultimately be made clear: "What I do thou knowest not now; but thou shalt know hereafter." And once the significance is revealed, the master's practice turns out to have been right and worth imitating: "For I have given you an example, that ye should do as I have done to you." Even the term "example" (ὑπόδειγμα) occurs.

That the form should be employed solely in the fourth gospel is no accident. There is nothing in the Synoptics equivalent to Jesus's farewell speeches to his disciples which we find in John, and the atmosphere of which is that of the traditional master-circle relationship. It is interesting that the washing of the disciples' feet by Jesus comes not long before those speeches.

4. *Ceremonies*

Nevertheless it would be wrong to think that the whole importance of this form for the New Testament lies in its having influenced one pericope in John. On the contrary, it may well be that the first coherent accounts of Jesus's deeds, the *Ur*-gospels, came into existence as the third parts of such tripartite sequences, as explanations given in answer to inquiries about significant gestures. To substantiate this, we must investigate some further applications of the form, and above all its role in the ancient Jewish service on Passover eve.

It may occur that an unusual action, though not originally meant as a gesture, as a mere basis for question and interpretation, yet by some literary device or as a result of a change in outlook comes to be represented as such. Let us compare a few cases.

The ending of the Book of Jonah is definitely an example of significant gesture—question—interpretation.[31] (Once again, as is to be expected in an elaborate literary work, the form is not preserved in its purity but affected by the requirements of the larger composition.) God prepares a gourd for Jonah and then takes it away again: a strange action and one, be it noted, that would make no complete story if left unexpounded.

[30] John 13:2 ff.

[31] Jonah 4:6 ff.

Jonah is bewildered and, indeed, wishes to die. And then the lesson is imparted: "Thou hast pity on the gourd, and should not I spare Nineveh?"

But take David's behaviour when his child died. Having fasted during the boy's illness, he now ate; and to the servants who wondered he explained that so long as the child was alive he fasted in the hope that God might be merciful, but now "can I bring him back again?"[32] Here the position is complicated. Probably the author thinks of David as having broken his fast without any didactic purpose. His conduct, that is, was no gesture. Only it happened to strike the servants, so he was asked about it and had to explain. From this point of view, therefore, we have to do with a simple case of unusual action—question—explanation. On the other hand, for the author himself, no doubt the episode is worth recording mainly because of the teaching in which it culminated—that death must be accepted as an irrevocable fact. On this basis, the action is little more than a means of causing us to wonder and thus preparing us for the interpretation, which alone matters.

Similar oscillations are frequent in plays. Suppose the hero of a drama, a statesman, burns the photograph of the woman he loves; a friend surprises him and asks for the reason; the statesman declares that no one in these times is justified in tying another person's fate to his own. Within the drama, the hero's action is anything but a gesture. He had no intention of conveying a teaching; he did not even expect to be watched. It is an ordinary instance of unusual conduct—question—explanation. But the playwright does want to convey a teaching. And we may regard him, or his hero, as the master; and the public in the theatre as the disciples, whose mouth-piece is the hero's friend when he inquires what the action may mean. Considered from this angle, the burning of the photograph is a mere gesture, the object of which is to bring about the question and, through it, the message. We have already referred to the tendency among modern readers to regard as merely "significant" some of Jesus's actions which the evangelists depict as "revolutionary": thus the omission to wash his hands before a meal[33] becomes a means of being able to preach about the respective importance of various duties.

Religious ceremonies and customs are of particular interest in this connection. Many of them are obviously free from didactic intentions. The scapegoat is sent into the wilderness, laden with the sins of the people;[34] according to some Rabbis, one ought to put on the right shoe before the left.[35] These practices are not designed to convey a teaching—at least not at the outset. They may indeed be re-interpreted as implying a message. Modern orthodox writers who adopt the rule that one should begin with the right shoe ascribe to it the object of impressing upon you the pre-eminence of justice, the right side symbolizing this virtue.[36]

[32] 2 Sam 12:20 ff.

[33] Luke 11:37 ff.; Mark 7:1 ff.

[34] Lev 16:22.

[35] *b. Shab.* 61a; *Derekh Eretz* 10.

[36] L. Jacobs, *Chayenu*, 20 (1952), p. 2. The author very kindly points out to me that the rudiments of his explanation are already to be found in medieval and Renaissance commentaries.

There are, however, observances inherently of a didactic nature. Where, for instance, prospective converts are to be attracted, symbolic rites may be performed which allude to holy secrets; their ultimate aim is instruction. (Of course, even a practice not essentially representing a message may be used for proselytizing and thereby acquire a didactic character. A flagellant who scourges himself in private is performing an act of contrition; one who does it in the streets may intend to warn people of the approaching judgment.) Feasts or ceremonies of commemoration are plainly didactic: their principal object is to put you in mind of an important person or event. According to one version of the Ten Commandments the Sabbath is to recall God's resting from his creation.[37] The Feast of Tabernacles must be observed "that your generations may know that I made the children of Israel to dwell in booths."[38] Frequently the commemorative purpose is superimposed on an earlier, different meaning. But we need not go into this complication. It is clear that, by the time of the New Testament, the Jews had for many centuries been accustomed to rites performed in memory of turning-points in their or the world's history.

The historical event most commemorated was the exodus from Egypt. Some passages in the Old Testament betray a tendency to consider the entire religion, "the testimonies and the statutes and the judgments," as designed to commemorate the exodus;[39] and it would lead too far afield here to enumerate the particular ceremonies to which this purpose is attributed. The second version of the Ten Commandments makes the Sabbath a commemoration of the exodus.[40] Naturally, the rules concerning the first-born of man and beast are brought into connection with the slaying of the first-born in Egypt.[41] But, as is well known, the chief commemoration of the exodus takes place on Passover eve: the sacrificing of the lamb and its eating with unleavened bread and bitter herbs.[42]

Now there is a strong affinity between ceremonies aiming at instruction and the form under discussion: significant action—question—interpretation. The setting of such ceremonies is very much like that which we postulated for this form. There is a master—the priest in possession of secrets which the prospective converts do not know, the elders of the people in possession of the tradition to be perpetuated—and a circle—the prospective converts, the younger or more ignorant among the people. The latter's interest must be roused by mystifying rites; and these will then be explained by reference to the great message.

Admittedly all didactic ceremonies need not take the form in question. There are so many factors which may cause deflection. Above all, very few rites are exclusively didactic. The Passover lamb, though professedly sacrificed in memory of the exodus, yet

[37] Exod 20:11.
[38] Lev 23:43.
[39] E.g. Deut 6:20 ff.
[40] Deut 5:15.
[41] Exod 13:14 ff.
[42] E.g. Exod 12:1 ff.

is not a mere reminder: even scholars living in a closed community, where no one was likely to forget about that miracle, would have to offer it.

None the less we do come across adumbrations of the tripartite form in several Old Testament passages dealing with commemorative ceremonies. One text,[43] where all religious practice is interpreted as glorifying the God who led the nation out of Egypt, runs: "And when thy son asketh thee, What mean the testimonies and the statutes and the judgments? Thou shalt say, We were Pharaoh's bondmen in Egypt and the Lord brought us out with a mighty hand." Again, the rules concerning the first-born are followed by this injunction:[44] "And when thy son asketh thee, What is this? Thou shalt say, When Pharaoh would hardly let us go, the Lord slew all the first-born in Egypt." Finally, there is a passage[45] specifically referring to the Passover ritual in which the sequence ritual—question—message is assumed: "And when your children shall say, What mean you by this service? Ye shall say, It is the Lord's passover, who passed over the houses of the children of Israel when he smote the Egyptians."

5. *The Passover-eve supper*

At any rate, the Passover-eve service, the Seder, as it existed in the time of Jesus was arranged within this tripartite framework. We shall presently have to discuss a fundamental change it underwent in a later period. In New Testament times, this service—which has never been analysed from a form-critical point of view—took the following course: (1) There was the meal, distinguished by special features, the most important of them the roasted lamb, the unleavened bread and the bitter herbs. (2) The youngest member of the company—the son if it was a family—had to ask what the strange ceremonies meant. (3) The leader of the company—the father if it was a family—had in answer to recount God's mighty deeds for Israel, beginning with shame (the heathen past and the slavery in Egypt) and ending with praise (the exodus, Sinai, the holy land and the Messianic future).

Manifestly, in this service, the commemorative rites are treated as mystifying gestures, intended to provoke inquiries into their significance on the part of the young or less learned. The latter do put the expected questions, and in reply the master reveals the message implied in the ceremonies.

It may be observed that neither part (2), the questions, nor part (3), the recital of God's deeds, was fully stereotyped by the time of the New Testament. The question would normally refer at least to the three prominent dishes we mentioned, roasted lamb, unleavened bread, bitter herbs; so would the reply—a R. Gamaliel (probably I, before the destruction of the Temple, possibly II, about A.D. 90) indeed declared it a duty to speak of these three. We also know that the reply from early times contained an exegesis of some verses from Deuteronomy,[46] outlining the miraculous history of Israel, a short Credo.

[43] Deut 6:20 f.

[44] Exod 13:14.

[45] Exod 12:26 f.

[46] Deut 26:5-9.

But that in New Testament times, and for centuries after, there was room for variety in detail is evident, in the first place, from the fragments of ancient Passover-eve liturgies discovered in the Cairo Genizah; in the second place, from Talmudic passages which show that the traditional questions and the traditional answers were freely added to or altered;[47] and in the third place, from the Midrash of the four sons, already considered in another connection (under Four Types of Question), which presupposes the possibility of different types of children asking different questions and receiving different answers. To repeat: the form of the service was odd gestures—questions—interpretation of the gestures. But the wording of the questions and interpretation was not strictly fixed.

In the Haggadah as we have it, incidentally, there comes first a comprehensive question, "Wherein is this night different from all other nights?" and then references to the particular oddities: "For in all other nights we eat leavened food and unleavened food, this night only unleavened food," etc. A very similar formula recurs in a Rabbinic comment[48] on the story of how God gave the Israelites twice the usual amount of manna on Friday, how they informed Moses and how they were told that this was so in order that they should do no work on the following day, the Sabbath. (The incident is supposed to have taken place before the Sinaitic legislation concerning the Sabbath, so the people could not yet know.) The Midrash says that they came to Moses asking, "Our teacher Moses, wherein is this day different from all other days?" Maybe the formula was technical where a question was to be put about the meaning of days or nights set apart for special religious purposes; or again, the authors of the Midrash about the manna and Sabbath may deliberately imitate the old Passover question.

What is relevant is that here the question forms part (2) of the tripartite sequence we are discussing. For the Midrash, the extra ration is a mystifying incident, calculated to arouse curiosity and ultimately lead to the first teaching about the Sabbath: (1) God gives the people double the ordinary amount of manna, a strange happening, (2) they inquire what special significance this day may have, and (3) their master ("our teacher Moses" they address him) tells them of the Sabbath.

No doubt the earliest gospels, the earliest coherent accounts of Jesus's activity, came into existence on the Passover eves following the crucifixion. We need not here decide whether or not the last supper was a Passover-eve meal. For whichever view one may take, the fact remains that, for several decades at least after Jesus's death, his followers, like all other Jews, assembled every year on Passover eve to celebrate the liturgy which culminated in the solemn recital of God's deeds for Israel. We have seen that this recital was not yet then stereotyped. Is it even conceivable that the Jewish Christian

[47] E.g. *b. Pes.* 115b f.; Josephus (*Ant.* 2.9.3.212 ff.), for the speech by which God comforts Amram, clearly draws on his Passover Haggadah. The wanderings of the patriarchs under divine guidance, the division of their inheritance, the rapid increase of the nation, the quotation of "Thy fathers went down into Egypt with three score and ten persons" (Deut 10:22)—all come in the same sequence in the Haggadah used today. But there are also numerous, significant differences.

[48] *Mek.* on Exod 12:22.

groups did not add to the traditional account one of the deliverance freshly achieved? Or that they did not do so from the first Passover after the crucifixion?

In fact, the entire service, not only part (3), must have been affected. It is safe to assume that parts (1) and (2), the ceremonies and questions, also received striking modifications calculated to draw attention to the new redemption; while part (3), the interpretation of the ceremonies, the narrative, was crowned by an exposition of the recent great events. Herein lies the real relevance to an understanding of the New Testament of the form (1) significant gesture (2) question (3) message: the *Ur*-gospels originated as parts (3) of such sequences.

A few points may be worth mention. First, the Passion, on which narrators surely bestowed particular attention from the outset, would perfectly satisfy the requirement, adverted to above, that the account of God's guidance of his people must begin with shame and end with praise.

Secondly, we have already pointed out (in considering Four Types of Question) that at least one section in Matthew and Mark[49]—namely, where tribute unto Caesar, a woman who married seven brothers, the greatest commandment and the Messiah are discussed—was composed in direct dependence on, as a deliberate parallel to, the Midrash of the four sons which figures in the Passover-eve liturgy.

Thirdly, it is perhaps possible to detect further cases of this kind. For example, as already observed, the Midrashic exegesis of a certain portion from Deuteronomy, an ancient Credo, belongs to the oldest parts of the reply to be given to the questioning youth. This portion begins thus, with shame: "An Aramaean ready to perish was my father and he went down into Egypt." For the Midrash, this means: "An Aramaean, namely, Laban, wished to destroy my father, namely, Jacob—and Laban was even worse than Pharaoh, since whereas Pharaoh wanted to kill only the males, Laban wanted to kill all—and my father went down into Egypt, compelled to do so by the word of God." Exactly how Laban's hostility caused Jacob's emigration to Egypt the Passover Midrash does not say. Maybe the escape from Laban is simply considered as the first and therefore decisive move in a series ultimately leading to emigration. Or there may at one time have been a more elaborate tale—now lost—in which Laban continued the struggle even after they had parted.[50]

At any rate it is tempting to assume that the first story Matthew tells us of Jesus, his escape from Herod, is intended as an analogy to this first story of the Passover Midrash. Herod, an Idumean, an Aramaean in a sense, in any case closely resembling Laban in being at the same time an alien and a relation, wishes to kill Jesus and does kill the children of Bethlehem; and Joseph takes Jesus to Egypt, warned to do so by an angel.

Certainly there are details in Matthew reminiscent of the narrative of the exodus rather than that of Jacob and Laban: after all the Passover Midrash itself connects the

[49] Matt 22:15 ff.; Mark 12:13 ff.

[50] A remnant may be seen, for instance, in the view transmitted by the medieval Sepher Hayyashar that, when Jacob had got free from Laban, the latter counselled Esau to take over the task of undoing the enemy.

two narratives. Herod consults the high priests, scribes and magi concerning the Messiah, just as according to the Rabbis Pharaoh had consulted his astrologers.[51] And the command given to Joseph after Herod's death—"go into the land of Israel, for they are dead which sought the young child's life"—distinctly echoes the command to Moses in Midian—"return into Egypt, for all the men are dead which sought thy life."[52]

However, the latter allusion hardly counts in this connection. It occurs in a pericope which there is good reason to regard as a separate story—namely, about the journey to Nazareth. That Jesus stayed in Egypt only till the death of Herod is recorded already in a previous passage,[53] so that this information is not required to complete the account of the escape.

Quite apart from this, the narrative of Jacob and Laban—or more precisely, that narrative in the dress in which it appears in the Passover recital—seems more relevant than any other. So far we have only mentioned the general similarity between it and the Matthean story. Let us note some additional points of contact.

(a) Laban resembled Herod not only in being a hated half-foreigner, but also in fearing and persecuting the future Messiah. In the view of the Rabbis, he was identical with Balaam, who, well aware that there would "come a Star out of Jacob,"[54] tried to "swallow the people, the house of Israel" (*bela' 'amma'*).[55]

(b) Laban's usual designation, "the Aramaean," was regarded by the Rabbis as referring not only to his origin but also to his character as "the deceiver," *rammay*;[56] and there are numerous descriptions of him stressing the same characteristic. Herod was "a fox."[57]

(c) Moses, unlike Jesus, escaped to Midian and, his persecutors dead, returned to Egypt. It was Jacob who—if we follow the Passover legend—escaped to Egypt and, as a nation, returned to the holy land. In a sense he returned even in person, since his body was buried there.[58]

(d) Jacob received the advice to go to Egypt from God in a dream, a feature absent from the narrative of Moses's flight but recurring (with modifications) in Matthew.[59]

(e) The passage "I will go down with thee into Egypt, and I will also surely bring thee up again" was interpreted by the Rabbis as foreshadowing not only the redemption

[51] Josephus, *Ant.* 2.9.2.205; *Exod. Rab.* on 1:22. Exodus Rabba mentions no earlier scholar than Jose b. Hanina, of the second half of the 3rd cent. A.D. Were it not for Josephus, we should have no proof that the Rabbinic tradition goes back to New Testament times.

[52] Matt 2:20; Exod 4:19.

[53] Matt 2:15.

[54] Num 24:17.

[55] *Jer. Targum* translates Num 22:5, "he sent messengers unto Balaam," by "unto Laban the Aramaean, called Balaam because he wanted to swallow the people, the house of Israel." Joshua b. Levi, of the first half of the 3rd cent., also identified him with Kemuel (*Gen. Rab.* on 22:21) because "he stood up against the people of God," *qam keneghedh 'ummatho shel 'el.*

[56] *Gen. Rab.* on 25:20.

[57] Luke 13:32.

[58] Gen 50:12 f.

[59] Gen 46:2 ff.; Matt 2:13.

from Egypt but also the final redemption—one of their proofs lying in the repeated use of the fuller form for "I," *'anokhi*, instead of *'ani*.[60]

(f) Matthew applies to Jesus's return the words of Hosea: "Out of Egypt have I called my son."[61] It is relevant to note that "my son" in this verse signifies not Moses but Israel; and that this is not only the natural meaning of the phrase in its original context but also that given it by the LXX, the Targum and the Rabbinic exegetes.[62] The calling of Israel out of Egypt was the fulfilment of the promise made to Jacob.

(g) The reference to "Rachel weeping for her children"[63] may well be an original component of the Christian Seder Midrash here postulated. Rachel was Jacob's wife: she would therefore come in by an association of ideas.

(h) Matthew has "her children," τέκνα, whereas Jeremiah has "her sons," *baneha*, in the LXX υἱοί. The difference may be accidental. On the other hand, when we consider that, according to the Passover Midrash, Laban, more cruel than Pharaoh, was out to destroy all, not only the males, the reading τέκνα may be intended to bring out the affinity between the old Laban and his modern counterpart. In the body of the episode the word used is παῖς, also fairly general: Herod slaughtered πάντας τοὺς παῖδας—there is no clear restriction to male children.[64]

We are not pronouncing on the historicity of the massacre of the Innocents. We are only suggesting that, as placed in the *Ur*-gospels of the first Passover eves after Jesus's death, the tale may well have corresponded to that of Laban, more wicked than Pharaoh, and Jacob, sent to Egypt by the divine word.

The way Jewish Christians dealt with the Passover-eve celebration may furnish the explanation of a most puzzling thing that Judaism did to this liturgy. In New Testament times, we saw, there was (1) the meal distinguished by strange rites, (2) the questions, (3) the interpretation of the rites in the form of an account of God's deeds for Israel. The Midrash still has this natural sequence. The Gemara, however, places (1) after (2) and (3). Ever since then, what happens on a Jewish Seder is that the questions are asked before the ceremonies to which they refer are performed; for example, the child asks "Why do we eat only unleavened bread tonight?" before anything has been eaten at all, leavened or unleavened. The questions are followed by the reply, the narrative of God's mighty works. And then at last the decisive ceremonies are gone through, the eating of unleavened bread and bitter herbs (the sacrifice of the lamb having ceased with the destruction of the Temple).[65]

Strack-Billerbeck[66] transfer the arrangement of the Gemara and modern Jewish liturgy back into the Mishnah, with queer results. Three examples may suffice. (1) In

[60] E.g. *Exod. Rab.* on 3:12.

[61] Matt 2:15; Hos 11:1.

[62] E.g. *Deut. Rab.* on 16:18.

[63] Matt 2:18; Jer 31:15, in LXX 38:15.

[64] Matt 2:16. In Homer, *Il.* 2.289, παῖδες νοαροί means "little children" of either sex; Plato, *Philebus* 65C, says that our pleasures are like children, παῖδες, in being devoid of any reasoning power.

[65] See E.D. Goldschmidt, *Die Pessach-Haggada* (1936), pp. 8 ff., with references to literature.

[66] *Op. cit.*, vol. 4 (1928), pt. 1, pp. 63 ff.

the Mishnah[67] it is ordained that when unleavened bread and bitter herbs have been served (the lamb was eaten only while the Temple stood), and a second cup of wine has been mixed, the son should put his questions. Which clearly means that he should put them during the meal, expressing his astonishment at the curious dishes. But Strack-Billerbeck, misled by the later re-arrangement, remark[68]—without justifying their statement—that the meal did not start until after the questions and, indeed, the recital given in answer to them. (2) In one paragraph of the Mishnah[69] the problem is treated exactly how to divide the Hallel, the "hymn," Psalms 113-18, in two parts; and the next paragraph[70] deals with grace after the meal, to be followed by the second part of the Hallel. Which clearly implies that its first part is to be sung before grace, towards the end of the meal. But Strack-Billerbeck remark[71]—without giving any reasons—that the first part belongs before the commencement of the meal. (3) From the Mishnah[72] we learn that according to R. Tarphon (about A.D. 100) the first part of the Hallel should be concluded with the following blessing: "Blessed be thou who has let us reach this night to eat in it unleavened bread and bitter herbs." To this R. Akiba, who expected the early restoration of the temple service through Bar-Kochba, added: "So, our Lord, let us reach other festivals that are coming towards us, when we may rejoice in the building of thy city and in thy cult; and there we shall eat again of the sacrifices and passover lambs." All this is most appropriate at the close of a meal where unleavened bread and bitter herbs have been taken but from which the sacrificial lamb has been missing—Akiba looks forward to Passover meals of the ancient kind in the near future. Yet Strack-Billerbeck[73] place it before the washing of the hands for the meal.

In point of fact, the change round makes nonsense of the questions and indeed of the whole structure of the service. It seems to have taken place about the end of the 2nd or beginning of the 3rd century.

It is one of the most tantalizing riddles in the history of Jewish liturgy. A widely accepted solution is that an orderly putting of the questions and an orderly giving of the reply may have proved difficult after a meal which included wine; hence the meal with its ceremonies was placed at the end.[74]

But this is quite unconvincing. For one thing, had drunkenness constituted a problem, the simplest way to deal with it would have been to decree that no wine might be taken but what was required by the ritual itself. That would have made two cups (one for the blessing of the day and one to go with the meal) for the whole time from the beginning of the service to the completion of the reply: hardly an excessive amount. It

[67] *m. Pes.* 10:3 f.
[68] P. 67 under 4a.
[69] *m. Pes.* 10:6.
[70] *m. Pes.* 10:7.
[71] P. 69, in their translation of *m. Pes.* 10:6.
[72] *m. Pes.* 10:6.
[73] Pp. 69 f. under 6b.
[74] Goldschmidt, *op. cit.*, p. 10, n. 1, with some hesitation adopts this view.

is noteworthy that this method of restriction was actually adopted by the Rabbis for the part of the service coming after the meal.[75] For another thing, on the basis of the solution under notice it becomes inexplicable why the second part of the Hallel,[76] the "hymn" as it is called in the gospels,[77] was not also placed before the meal. But it was not; it is still sung afterwards, as it was in the period of the New Testament[78] and in that of the Mishnah.[79] Was it considered right to recite these psalms under the table? Above all, why, if it was drunkenness which rendered necessary the placing of (1) after (2) and (3), are our sources absolutely silent upon this change? It was an enormous change; we should expect plenty of discussion about it; but we hear nothing.

It is much more likely that the transposition was undertaken in defence against Jewish Christian abuses. In the original arrangement—(1) ceremonial meal, (2) questions, (3) interpretation of the ceremonies—the nature of (2) and (3), the questions and the interpretation, must be largely determined by that of (1), the ceremonial meal. It is part (1), the performance of the unusual gestures, that sets in motion and decides the direction of all that follows. (Here may be the place to refer to Luke's report[80] that the disciples knew the risen Jesus "in the breaking of the bread." Most probably Luke means that Jesus repeated the pronouncement he had made at the Last Supper, "This is my body"—of course, without prefacing it by "The Lord Jesus took bread and gave thanks and said" or other words to the same effect. It was the direct "This is my body" which caused the disciples to recognize Jesus.) In Jewish Christian circles part (1), the meal, was certainly transformed in such a manner that the emphasis from the outset lay on the new deliverance; and parts (2) and (3), the questions and recital, would proceed along the lines thus laid down.

By relegating part (1), the meal, to the end, the Rabbis took the life, or at least any undue vitality, out of it. The service now opened with some formal, orthodox questions; so formal that they referred to rites which had not yet even taken place. To these questions, an orthodox narrative would be given as reply. And the meal with unleavened bread and bitter herbs came at the end, as the fulfilment of a Scriptural precept. The sequence mystifying gestures—questions—interpretation was replaced by the sequence formal questions—reply—fulfilment of prescribed ceremonies. The danger of the service being set on a wrong course was eliminated.

None of the objections we raised against the prevalent explanation applies to that just advanced. The change round was a very clever means of preventing any fundamentally new significance being attached to the meal—whereas it would have been

[75] *m. Pes.* 10:7; *y. Pes.* 37d. It is possible, however, that the prohibition of drinking between the third and fourth cups antedates the reason given for it—to prevent drunkenness; the original reason may have been quite different.

[76] Pss 113-18; the second part 114-18 or 115-18.

[77] Matt 26:30; Mark 14:26.

[78] See the passages quoted in the preceding footnote.

[79] *m. Pes.* 10:7.

[80] Luke 24:31, 35.

unnecessary had the aim been to prevent drunkenness. Again, we can now understand why the Rabbis, when making the transposition, left the second part of the Hallel in its original place after the meal: these psalms were innocuous, there was no real risk of any revolutionary innovation here. But had the transposition been caused by fear of drunkenness, these psalms also would have had to come before the meal. Finally, the silence of our sources on the affair ceases to be unintelligible. For one reason or another, the Rabbis were frequently reticent about measures taken to check the influence of heretical sects or to stress the separation from them.

Chronology

A. The Problem

According to Matthew[1] the devil tempts Jesus first by asking him whether he can turn stone into bread, next by leading him to Jerusalem and asking him whether he can cast himself down from the temple unhurt, and finally by taking him up to a mountain and offering him all kingdoms of the world. In Luke,[2] the first temptation is the same. But Matthew's third comes second—and there is no mention of a mountain—while Matthew's second comes third.

Creed[3] thinks Matthew has the original sequence: Luke altered it in order to avoid a second change of scene. In Luke, the temptations to turn stone into bread and to accept worldly rule take place in the same locality, and only that to leap from the temple takes place at Jerusalem; in Matthew, the temptation to turn stone into bread takes place in the desert, that to leap from the temple at Jerusalem and that to accept worldly dominion on a mountain. T.W. Manson, on the other hand, prefers the Lukan sequence.[4] Matthew's narrative, he argues, works up to an exciting climax: the devil tells Jesus to perform a sign, he tells him to perform a greater sign, he promises to make him ruler of the earth. Had Luke had this sequence before him, he would not have interfered with it. It is Matthew who rendered the original story more dramatic.

The writer inclines to Manson's view. But no matter how we account for the difference between the two versions, few modern scholars would maintain that an evangelist was incapable of regrouping incidents or sayings with a view to a more pleasing or stronger effect. The wider aims of an author—to retain the attention of his public, to impress certain points on them or to elaborate an important thesis—on occasion took precedence over adherence to strict chronology. In the Fourth Gospel, in particular, the order in which some matters are presented becomes intelligible only if we suppose that to exercise considerable freedom as to dates, to abandon a traditional sequence, to repeat the same thing twice or three times and so on, were not reckoned unforgivable sins.

How is this attitude to be explained? We are not concerned with changes resulting from carelessness; nor with those introduced because an evangelist—rightly or wrongly—believes that the order by which he replaces that handed down to him is the true, historical one, that he is restoring the original order. Certainly such cases are frequent.

[1] Matt 4:1 ff.

[2] Luke 4:1 ff.

[3] *The Gospel according to St. Luke* (1930), 63.

[4] Major, Manson and Wright, *The Mission and Message of Jesus*, 334 ff.

But here we are interested in those alterations which an author deliberately makes although he has no reason to doubt the accuracy of his source. Whether Luke rearranged the temptations in order to avoid a second change of scene, or whether Matthew rearranged them in order to render them more dramatic—there was a deviation from the traditional chronology for a reason other than that the chronology was deemed wrong. In the Synoptics, the temple is cleansed towards the end of Jesus's activity, in John near its commencement. The incident was redated—no matter by whom—in order to enhance its significance. Nowadays we constantly assume alterations of this sort, but we do not ever seem to inquire where an evangelist (or his precursor) might find his justification for them.

Perhaps, before attempting an answer, we ought to make a distinction. I may narrate events in a non-chronological order and yet convey the exact order in which they occurred. I may say, for example, that Churchill became First Lord of the Admiralty in 1911 and had been Home Secretary in 1910. This would be only a formal deviation from the historical sequence. The latter would not be materially upset unless I said that Churchill first served at the Admiralty and then became Home Secretary. It should, however, be borne in mind that if events are narrated in a non-chronological order, the chance of a listener or reader receiving a wrong impression of their actual relation is usually rather strong. If I say that Churchill, in the course of his career, was First Lord of the Admiralty and Home Secretary, giving no dates, my public may easily conclude that he started being First Lord and was Home Secretary later. We shall come back to this question. For the moment it suffices to observe that, in general, where an evangelist arranges incidents or sayings in a non-chronological way without dating them, we may treat the case as a material deviation from the historical order.

B. "There is no before and after in Scripture"

Among the factors which contributed to the attitude of the evangelists the most important may well have been a principle of interpretation we know to have been applied by R. Ishmael's school in dealing with *haggadhic*, non-legal, points of the Old Testament: "There is no before and after in Scripture." The Bible, that is, frequently puts a later event before an earlier event; the order of events in reality is not always reflected in the order of events in the Bible.

The Mekhilta sees an illustration in a verse from the Song of Moses:[5] "The enemy said, I will pursue." This verse refers to something—the decision of the Egyptians to destroy the Israelites[6]—that happened before what is referred to in the opening lines of the Song[7]—the drowning of the Egyptians.[8] It would be more exact, chronologically, the Mekhilta holds, if the verse in question formed the beginning of the chapter and all mention of the drowning came after it. However, the Biblical arrangement is accounted for by the rule "There is no before and after in Scripture." Another Midrash, Siphre on

[5] Exod 15:9.
[6] Exod 14:5 ff.
[7] Exod 15:1–8.
[8] Exod 14:23 ff.

Numbers, makes use of the rule in commenting on the provisions, relating to Passover, which were made known to Moses "in the first month of the second year after they were come out of Egypt."[9] Nine chapters before, the Midrash notes, we are told about an event that must have occurred a month or so later, namely, God's request to Moses to take the sum of the children of Israel, a request made "on the first day of the second month, in the second year after they were come out of Egypt."[10]

It might be argued that in both these cases the Bible deviates from the historical order in a formal sense only, not in a material one. Every reader will know that the drowning of the Egyptians was later than their wicked scheming, and the incidents recorded in Numbers are provided with full dates. So let us add two more examples, one again from the Mekhilta. The first chapter of Ezekiel depicts a strange vision, the second his call. According to the Mekhilta, historically, the call preceded the vision. Now this is a proposition far from self-evident, and at any rate the text as it stands does convey the impression that the vision preceded the call. Yet the Rabbis felt entitled to postulate the opposite sequence, since "There is no before and after in Scripture." The prophet, from theological motives, redated the actual events.

Similarly, R. Ishmael (first third of the 2nd cent. A.D.) and R. Joshua ben Levi (middle of 3rd cent.) contended that only the first two of the Ten Commandments ("I am the Lord" and "Thou shalt have no other gods") were given to the Israelites directly by God. Their thesis was attacked on the ground that, according to the plain sense of the Biblical account, it was not till all Ten Commandments had been promulgated that the people asked Moses: "Speak thou with us, but let not God speak with us, lest we die."[11] But Joshua ben Levi made light of the objection, invoking the maxim "There is no before and after": the people's request was made immediately after the Second Commandment.[12]

In a slightly modified form, the rule is to be found among the 32 Middoth, principles of interpretation, compiled by Eliezer ben Jose Ha-gelili for *haggadhic* exposition. It is the last Middah, and it runs: "The before that comes after in the Biblical sections," or "The after comes before in the Biblical sections." Earlier and later periods in history are not necessarily dealt with in earlier and later sections of Scripture; many a section refers to an earlier period than a section preceding it.

Two illustrations are given in Eliezer's compilation. The seventh chapter of Numbers describes the ceremonies accompanying the setting up of the tabernacle. In reality, these took place—the Rabbis say—before the events recounted in the preceding chapters; they took place, that is, immediately after the events recounted towards the end of Exodus,[13] where it is stated that "Moses reared up the tabernacle and fastened its sockets." The other illustration may be more interesting in this connection since it concerns a chronological problem of a kind well known from the Fourth Gospel.

[9] Num 9:1.
[10] Num 1:1.
[11] Exod 20:19.
[12] *b. Hor.* 8a; *Song of Songs Rab.* on 1:2.
[13] Exod 40:17 ff.

In Genesis 12,[14] when Abraham leaves Haran for Canaan, he is said to be seventy-five years old. In Genesis 15,[15] when God announces to him what will befall his descendants, his age is not mentioned; but he cannot be older than seventy if the various dates referring to him in the Pentateuch are to be harmonized.[16] There is no difficulty in this for the Rabbis: the announcement recorded in chapter 15 was made to him before his immigration into Canaan recorded in 12. It is simply a case of "The before that comes after in the Biblical sections."

As for the age of this mode of interpretation, the instances adduced are most of them from the earliest Tannaitic Midrashim preserved to us. This in itself would not, perhaps, take us back farther than, say, A.D. 150. But there are two reasons at least for assuming a far earlier origin. First, the principle under notice appears in those Midrashim as firmly established. Even if none of the particular cases where we find it applied were older than R. Ishmael—an unlikely hypothesis—the rule as such must have grown up before. Of course, its exact formulation may have differed from that with which we are familiar. Secondly, an exegesis of the Old Testament stories and sayings on the supposition that there is minute historical arrangement, with no anticipation, no turning back, no repetition, is a glaring impossibility. It strikes any cursory reader. It must have struck the Rabbis, who spent their lives studying the Scriptures, from the outset. Nowadays discrepancies are eliminated by the methods of modern criticism, postulating different sources, ascribing mistakes to the writers of the Bible, and so on. None of these solutions was open to the Rabbis. The principle "There is no before and after in Scripture," in one form or another, was the only and the obvious solution to adopt.

C. "SERES"

It may be worth calling attention to another method of interpretation, also favoured by Ishmael's school, *seres*: a verse or section at first sight illogical might be made logical by turning round its several components.

This method was not only used to establish a plausible chronology. For example, the assurance "In any place where I allow my name to be mentioned I will come unto thee"[17] was considered by some expounders as reversing what was really meant. The

[14] Gen 12:4.

[15] Gen 15:7–21.

[16] The calculation is as follows (*S.O.* 3). In Gen 15:13, God says that the Israelites will be enslaved during 400 years. According to the Rabbis, this covers not only the time in Egypt (which, on the basis of other Biblical dates, must have been far briefer) but the whole period from Isaac's birth to the exodus. But in Exod 12:40, we are told that the Israelites were slaves for 430 years. How is Exod 12:40 to be reconciled with Gen 15:13? The answer is that, while Gen 15:13 takes as the beginning of the slavery Isaac's birth—400 years between then and the exodus—Exod 12:40 takes the time when God announced to Abraham the future of his descendants, the very incident, that is, recounted in Gen 15:7–21—430 years between then and the exodus. It follows that this incident, the announcement of what would befall the Israelites, occurred thirty years before Isaac's birth. As Abraham was 100 years old when Isaac was born, he was seventy when God made with him the covenant of Gen 15:7–21.

[17] Exod 20:24.

real meaning, they asserted, was: "In any place where I come unto thee [*scil.* in the tabernacle and temple] I will allow my name to be mentioned."[18] This has nothing to do with dates.

Still, as a rule, *seres* was resorted to where the Biblical chronology could not be accepted at its face value. The Bible tells us[19] that a number of men brought a problem "before Moses and before Aaron," that Moses transmitted it to God and that God informed him of the solution. Rabbinic commentators claimed that the men must have approached Aaron first, and when he did not know they went on to Moses who had access to God. The real meaning, then, was that the problem was brought "before Aaron and before Moses." The Bible, for special reasons, deviated from strict chronology.[20] Similarly, from the text as it stands we learn that Jacob in a dream saw a ladder reaching to heaven and received a promise of divine help; then, on waking up, he vowed an altar if God should help him.[21] Some Rabbis argued that, had he already received that promise, he would no longer have used the conditional "If God will be with me, this stone shall be his house." They concluded that the vow in reality preceded the vision. The Biblical narrative, for a theological purpose, rejected the historical order, placing the vision first and the vow second.[22]

Interpretation by transposition, *seres*, was founded on the belief that the Bible, and in particular the Pentateuch, was inspired by God. Any passage might therefore contain various layers of meaning, one beneath the other (the words "Then sang Moses," in the opinion of the Rabbis, referred to what happened in the past, after the destruction of the Egyptians, but also to what would happen in the future, after the resurrection of the dead, when a similar song would be recited),[23] or it might even convey theological or moral instruction if read as it stood and a historical point if read in a different order.

The verb *haphakh* sometimes figures as synonymous with *seres*.[24] *Haphakh* is the term which, in a saying by Hillel or one of his proselytes,[25] of the last half-century B.C., denotes the constant "turning round" of each Scriptural passage, with a view to discovering ever deeper revelations. It is here not, indeed, confined to the method of *seres*, but embraces all methods by which a fuller understanding of God's word may be gained—or, as we moderns should put it, by which the text may be made to yield fresh insights. "Turn it round and turn it round, for everything is in it." Clearly, for scholars who proceeded from this conception of the nature of Scripture, *seres* was no more absurd a method than a division into sources is for us today.

[18] *b. Sot.* 38a.

[19] Num 9:6 ff.

[20] *Siphre* on Num 9:6.

[21] Gen 28:12 ff.

[22] *Gen. Rab.* on 28:20.

[23] *Mek.* on Exod 15:1, stressing the fact that the Hebrew for "sang" is not the perfect *shar* but the imperfect *yashir*.

[24] *Tanhuma* on Gen 49:4.

[25] *m. Ab.* 5:22; *Ab. de R. N.* 12.

D. THE EVANGELISTS

It is not improbable, we suggest, that the writers of the gospels, or some of them, were influenced by a rule of the type "There is no before and after in Scripture." At least it will be granted that, if this is so, many puzzles of long standing should prove less disquieting. (Needless to say, the explanation here advocated does not supply a panacea, and it will always remain necessary to take careful note of the special circumstances of each single case of rearrangement.) Those writers played the game when they disregarded dates, arranged and repeated incidents or pronouncements as they deemed best, combined several narratives or divided one. The readers were not supposed to look for a meticulous chronological order in their works.

A possible objection might be that the adage "There is no before and after in Scripture" is a rule of interpretation, not one of writing. There is a difference, it might be argued, between recognizing that "there is no before and after in Scripture" and writing oneself with little respect to the actual sequence of events; and the evangelists, though acquainted with deviations from the historical order in the Old Testament, would not, on that account, have dared to deviate from the historical order in presenting their own material.

There is, however, a reply to this. We may admit that the rule discussed was introduced by interpreters of a holy text, who were forced to reconcile conflicting dates. At the same time it is easy to imagine that it was gradually taken advantage of by authors as well, in particular by such of them as took the holy text as their model. These would not necessarily think of themselves as replacing or supplementing the Mosaic revelation. As we have seen, the principle "There is no before and after in Scripture" was applied by the Rabbis not only to the Pentateuch but also to other books of the Old Testament, the prophets, the psalms and so forth. It is unlikely that an exactitude which was considered to be absent from the Old Testament, and to be slighted, for example, by Ezekiel for the sake of a higher message he had to convey, was eagerly striven after by the religious story-tellers of the Talmudic era. The evangelists must have wished for much freedom in the matter of chronological arrangement, in order to emphasize ideas of greater importance in their eyes; and their licence was warranted by tradition. Elsewhere[26] I have tried to show that the Alexandrian model of *seres*, namely, ἀναστροφή, developed from a method of interpretation into a famous type of writing—the cento.

Here may be the place to refer to the Jewish liturgy of Passover eve. For hundreds of years before the New Testament it had included, as it still includes, an account of the redemption from Egypt. Certain portions of the gospels no doubt came into existence when the early followers of Jesus inserted into, or paralleled, this account by one of the new, greater redemption. It is, therefore, relevant to note that the traditional Jewish narrative does not list events in a rigidly chronological manner.

True, we do not know the precise age of the structure as we have it before us (even leaving on one side obviously medieval additions). But there is evidence that the 3rd- or 4th-century Rabbis at least, in fixing the arrangement, were not bent on accurate

[26] ["Alexandrian Methods of Interpretation and the Rabbis"] *Festschrift Hans Lewald* (1953), 27 ff. [*Talmudic Law*, 357 ff.]

progress, step by step, from one period to the next. The Mishnah, in a provision certainly going back to New Testament times, lays down[27] that the recital "should begin with the disgrace and end with the glory." This in itself is not a historical plan in the narrow sense, for it means at least the omission of the ideal world before Adam's fall—the recital must open with "disgrace"—and of any lapses after the acceptance of the Law at mount Sinai—the recital must end with "glory." It is, however, a controversy recorded in the Gemara about the precise import of the Mishnah which sheds more light on the Rabbinic attitude to chronology.[28]

In the opinion of Rab (first half of the 3rd cent. A.D.), we should begin with the paragraph "Originally our ancestors were idolators"; whereas according to Raba (middle of the 4th cent.),[29] we should begin with the paragraph "We were slaves to Pharaoh," and recite the other section later. (It is widely held that the two parties each rejected the other's recital entirely—an improbable assumption.) There is no need to examine which of the two, if either, gives the right interpretation of the Mishnah. The point is that the question of chronological arrangement does not arise at all. The Rabbis were interested only in the problem when was that shameful past of the nation from which the Mishnah says we should start: was it when we were pagans or was it when we were slaves? In fact, Raba's view has prevailed in Judaism, because supported by R. Nahman (apparently bar Isaac, second half of the 4th cent.). The recital in use up to this day opens with the paragraph "We were slaves to Pharaoh" and then only turns back to the earlier period, "Originally our ancestors were idolators." Admittedly, a company celebrating the Passover is expected to know the actual sequence of events despite any rearrangement—or at least the adult members are expected to know. The case accordingly falls under the category of formal rather than material deviation from the true dates. The fact remains that the order is here determined not by "the before and after" in history, but by theological considerations.

A very ancient part of the Passover-eve narrative expounds the verse from Deuteronomy:[30] "The Lord looked on our affliction and our trouble and our oppression." We are told that "our affliction" means the abstention of the Israelite husbands from intercourse with their wives, "our trouble" Pharaoh's threat to their male babies, and "our oppression" the toil imposed on the Israelites by their masters. Clearly, the verse is not credited with any chronological order; otherwise we should expect (1) the toil imposed on the Israelites, (2) the threat to their male offspring and (3) their abstention in order to have no offspring for Pharaoh to kill. In this case, an ordinary, unlearned participant in the Passover-eve ceremony might not immediately be able to substitute the historical order. There is a certain degree of material deviation from the actual sequence of events. The latter was of secondary importance for the authors of the narrative.

In a previous chapter (on Four Types of Question) we tried to show that the four questions posed in Matthew 22 and Mark 12—is it lawful to give tribute unto Caesar?

[27] *m. Pes.* 10:4.

[28] *b. Pes.* 116a.

[29] An alternative reading is Samuel (a contemporary of Rab) instead of Raba. If this is accepted, the R. Nahman mentioned would be bar Jacob (first half of the 4th cent.).

[30] Deut 26:7.

etc.—were put together by the evangelists as corresponding to the questions which are quoted in the Passover-eve liturgy as suitable for different kinds of children. Matthew and Mark, as they stand, both convey the impression that the four questions were posed one after the other on the same day. We may confidently assume that they were not. But we should also realize that, when the evangelists dated them in the way they did, they were only adopting a Rabbinic convention: there were claims overriding those of chronology.

E. HELLENISTIC INFLUENCE

So far we have considered the Rabbinic evidence in isolation. It is necessary, however, to remember that the Rabbinic principles of interpretation and story-telling are not a little indebted to Hellenistic thought. This is not to deny that the early students of the Old Testament noticed discrepancies, and were driven to postulate deviations from the historical order of events, independently of outside aid; nor that Jewish religious story-tellers—like others—might make up their own, unhistorical arrangement long before coming into contact with Greek theories. Nevertheless the latter, when they did make their way to the East, must have played a major part in causing what had been done in a more or less haphazard, unconscious fashion to become a proper art.

In an article referred to above[31] I have submitted that the method of *seres*, interpretation by transposition, was taken over by the Rabbis from Alexandria, and that the term *seres* itself is nothing but a rendering of ἀναστροφή. The formulation of a principle like "There is no before and after in Scripture," though the fact it expresses had probably been realized for centuries, may also be a result of Hellenistic teaching. It follows that, indirectly at any rate, the attitude of the evangelists is connected with contemporary Hellenistic practice. We do not mean to rule out direct Hellenistic influence on one or the other of them or their precursors, but this is a question which we may leave undecided.

That the Iliad opens in the middle of the war against Troy instead of at the beginning was a feature much commented on by the ancient scholars.[32] Thucydides considered it important to bring out the exact historical sequence of events not only in matter but also in form: a historian must not only give the right dates—he reproached a predecessor for not doing so[33]—but also present the facts in the order in which they occurred.[34]

There were, however, others who considered this procedure as dull. Dionysius of Halicarnassus blamed Thucydides on this ground.[35] The notion—common in Hellenistic times—that primitive historians composed bare annals may also originally have implied some disparagement of a mechanical, chronological scheme.[36] Certainly,

[31] ["Alexandrian Methods of Interpretation and the Rabbis"] *Festschrift Hans Lewald*, 27 ff. [*Talmudic Law*, 357 ff.]

[32] E.g. Quintillian, *I.O.* 7.10.11.

[33] Thucydides 1.97.2.

[34] Thucydides 2.1, 5.26.1.

[35] *De Thuc.* 9, 335 ff.

[36] Cicero, *De Or.* 2.15.51 ff. But Cicero thinks very highly of Thucydides.

as regards non-historical literature—eulogies, forensic speeches and so forth—the general view was that chronological arrangement was only one of many possibilities. It might make for clarity, but not necessarily; and an author might legitimately prefer to proceed from the less weighty to the weightier (or vice versa), or from the simple to the complex (or vice versa), or indeed to divide up his narrative into sections and treat a separate topic from beginning to end in each of them.[37]

The question arises: were there Hellenistic doctrines allowing a historian to redate events in order to impress a certain moral on his public? There were. History was often classed as belonging to epideictic writing, i.e. writing designed to please the reader, to exhort the reader, to praise a person or the like.[38] In epideictic writing, it was permissible to twist the facts. (This liberty, of course, extended beyond chronology, to facts of any kind.) Quite a few authorities disagreed with this assessment of history and insisted on truthfulness. In one of his works[39] Cicero puts this point of view and, significantly, requires chronological arrangement. Frequently we come across what may be regarded as a compromise, a sensible one, though rarely worked out with any thoroughness: on the one hand, a historian should keep to the truth, on the other, he need not tell the whole truth—uninteresting or useless details might be omitted—and his work should be a vehicle for imparting philosophical ideas, ethical teaching, good advice.[40] Much of the discussion on the subject shows traces of Aristotle's distinction[41] between the poet, concerned with universal truth, i.e. what might or ought to be the facts, and the historian, concerned with particular truths, i.e. the facts as they are.

Speculations of this kind undoubtedly reached the Rabbis, who tried to find in the Scriptures both "universal truths" and "particular truths."

As for the evangelists, let us add a reservation. To be sure, they only followed a convention in regrouping scenes and pronouncements with a view to a theological or literary effect. But we must not forget that there were limits to their freedom. They did want to put down what had actually happened as well as what it signified. They did want to report facts as well as to proclaim a religious message and glorify the person of Jesus. It is not, however, within the scope of this lecture to inquire just what were the restrictions on a New Testament writer's liberty to alter his sources and, in particular, their chronology.

F. Papias

Papias declares[42] that the Hebrew gospel of Matthew—whatever may be meant by this work—consisted of an ordered collection of the sayings of Jesus (συνετάξατο). It is probable, though not certain, that the order he has in mind is chronological: Matthew, according to Papias, arranged the sayings in the order in which they were uttered. By

[37] Aristotle, *Rhet.* 3.16.1 f., Cicero, *Part. Or.* 4.12 ff., *De Inv.* 1.20.29, 1.21.30, Quintillian, *I.O.* 7.10.11.

[38] E.g. Cicero, *De Or.* 11.37.

[39] *De Or.* 2.15.62 f.

[40] E.g. Lucian, *Quomodo Historia Scribenda Sit.*

[41] *Poetics* 9.

[42] *Eusebius* 3.39.16.

contrast, of Mark we are told[43] that "he wrote accurately, though not in any order (οὐ τάξει), what he remembered of the sayings and deeds of the Lord." Again the order referred to—and referred to as absent—seems to be of a chronological character.

Mark's excuse, in the view of Papias, is that he was not a direct disciple of Jesus. He only followed Peter; but Peter had never composed an ordered collection (σύνταξις) of the sayings of Jesus, he had simply taught as the moment demanded it. So the best Mark could do was to write down the single points (ἔνια) as he had heard them.

Two things are clear. First, Papias recognizes that the Markan order cannot always be regarded as reflecting the historical order—especially if Matthew should be treated as reflecting it. Secondly, this would be to Mark's discredit but for the defence just outlined. That is to say, Papias for one does not accord an evangelist any liberty in the matter of chronology; he demands strict adherence to the actual dates.

[43] *Eusebius* 3.39.15.

A Supernatural Birth*

The first, though not capable of proof, may deserve consideration even as a possibility; there seems to be a trace of a Jewish legend of a conception without a human father, and the child in question may well be Moses. This would not be a virgin birth—both Miriam and Aaron were older than Moses. But it would be close enough to be of interest.[1]

Long before the time of the New Testament it had become usual to recall on Passover eve the mighty deeds of God for Israel; and the Midrashic exposition of a certain portion of Deuteronomy[2] preserved in the Haggadah, the service for Passover eve, forms the nucleus of the recital.[3] That portion is a brief Credo, originally for use by a person offering the first-fruits in the temple; it is a solemn proclamation stating that the nation was enslaved in Egypt, that God delivered it with signs and wonders, and that he has now brought it into the promised land. The Hebrew word employed in this pericope for "to proclaim" is *higgidh.*[4] The very term by which the recital of Passover eve is designated, "Haggadah," is taken from it.

The Midrash, in the typically Rabbinic manner, attributes a very specific meaning to every detail in these verses, and, wherever possible, attempts to prove it by reference to other Scriptural passages. Thus one verse in Deuteronomy[5] reads: "And he saw our affliction, and our distress, and our oppression." Of "our distress" the Midrash remarks: "This means the sons, as it is written [in Exodus[6]], Every son that is born ye shall cast into the river." This, in its way, is a reasonable exegesis. In the eyes of the Rabbis, of all causes for distress that the Israelites had in Egypt, the destruction of the male children was the most terrible, and Josephus, for example, thinks the same.[7] Yet that order of Pharaoh was followed by the miraculous rescue of Moses. Accordingly (the Rabbis

* This section comes from the discussion of Messianic Types (119 ff.). It began: "There are numerous unmistakable references to Moses [by the New Testament writers]—for example, the command to Joseph, after the death of Herod, to 'go into the land of Israel, for they are dead which sought the young child's life,' which echoes the command to Moses in Midian to 'return into Egypt, for all the men are dead which sought thy life' [Matt 2:20; Exod 4:19]. No purpose would be served by enumerating the well-known parallels. It may suffice to draw attention to three points." The first follows.

[1] [See now the evidence put forward by Dale Allison, *The New Moses: A Matthean Typology* (Minneapolis, 1993), 146–50].

[2] Deut 26:5 ff.

[3] See *m. Pes.* 10:4.

[4] Deut 26:3.

[5] Deut 26:7, second half.

[6] Exod 1:22.

[7] *Ant.* 2.9.2.208.

argue) the meaning of "he saw our distress" is to be inferred from "Every son that is born ye shall cast into the river."

Similarly, "our oppression" is explained by the Midrash as follows: "This means the coercion—the cruel tasks laid upon them—as it is written [in Exodus again[8]], And I have also seen the oppression wherewith the Egyptians oppress them." Here the connection is quite obvious, in sense and in wording: "oppression" is common to the verse from Deuteronomy and that from Exodus.

Difficulties arise, however, when we come to the comment on "our affliction." The Midrash declares: "This means the abstention from sexual intercourse, as it is written [in Exodus[9]], And God saw the children of Israel, and God knew."

The view that at some stage in Egypt marital union did not take place appears in several Rabbinic sources.[10] Some Rabbis contemplate enforced abstention decreed by Pharaoh, some voluntary abstention for the purpose of atonement, and some voluntary abstention undertaken because of the threat to any male offspring. The last-mentioned idea is probably the oldest: it would naturally occur to ancient Jewish interpreters of the Biblical narrative. Now it is indeed quite intelligible why "our affliction" was associated by the Rabbis with this episode. The verb "to afflict" occurs in those statutes which enjoin fasting and—at least in Rabbinic interpretation—abstention from sexual intercourse: "Ye shall afflict your souls."[11] But it is far from clear how they came to regard the notice "And God saw the children of Israel, and God knew" as supporting this exegesis.

The only satisfactory explanation seems to be that the author of the Midrash took "to know" in the sexual sense. The Israelites abstained from marital relations. God saw their affliction, and he "knew." In other words, it may well be that, for the author of this Midrash, as natural propagation was impossible, the women—or perhaps only the mother of Moses[12]—conceived from God himself. After all, once the Rabbis had formed the opinion that in consequence of Pharaoh's decision to kill any newborn sons the Israelites refrained from intercourse, they had to find some answer to the question how Moses nevertheless came to be born in that period.

One or two orthodox solutions are still extant. For example, when Pharaoh promulgated his decree and Amram, because of this threat to any male offspring, divorced Jochebed, she was already in the third month of pregnancy. But the relative lateness of this explanation is obvious. First, the narrative of the separation of Amram and Jochebed is preserved in two sources; yet only one of these contains the notice that she was already with child.[13] Secondly, if she was already with child, how could her husband hope to thwart Pharaoh's plan by divorcing her? Clearly, in the original version of

[8] Exod 3:9.

[9] Exod 2:25.

[10] *Exod. Rab.* on 1:15 and 2:25 at the end; *b. Yom.* 74b; *b. Sot.* 11b f. Cp. *b. B. B.* 60b at the end.

[11] Lev 16:29, 31, 23:27, 32.

[12] This possibility is by no means ruled out by the position of Exod 2:25 ("and God knew") after the narrative of Moses's birth and flight to Midian, 2:1 ff. The Rabbis were quite capable of regrouping the texts when it suited them and, in fact, formulated a principle—"There is no before and after in the Torah"—allowing much freedom in matters not affecting the *halakha,* the law. See above, 412, under Chronology.

[13] Only *Exod. Rab.* on 1:15 and 2:2, not *b. Sot.* 12a.

the narrative she was not pregnant.

It is worth recalling that according to the Rabbis the death of Moses was caused, not by the angel of death, but by a kiss of God. Later the legend was extended to include his brother Aaron, later still to include his sister Miriam as well, and in the end to include all pious men.[14] But when the idea was first propounded, with reference to Moses alone, it was hardly less bold than, and may have corresponded to, the idea of a direct intervention of God at Moses's birth.

Again, that the verb "to know" in the verse concerned should have given rise to speculations is not surprising. It has no object, either express or implied, and this is highly unusual. Modern critics have long suspected that the object may have dropped out.[15] The LXX has καὶ ἐγνώσθη αὐτοῖς, "and he became known to them," be it in order to avoid the bare "and God knew" or be it in order to combat the interpretation of the words as alluding to a virgin birth.[16]

Anyhow, on the basis outlined, the verse "And God saw the children of Israel, and God knew" would indeed fit very well where it comes in the recital of Passover eve.

The question of date arises. Certainly, even if the legend came into existence after the New Testament, it would not be without relevance: it would still show that the notion of a supernatural or virgin birth was not absolutely alien to the Jewish mind. There can be little doubt, however, that, if there was such a legend, it is older than the New Testament. For one thing, as already pointed out, the section of the Haggadah in which it is contained is among the earliest. For another, when once the Christian heresy had sprung up, the tendency must have been to suppress rather than to work out ideas of this nature.

This brings us to a final point. There do exist indications that the Midrash under notice was disliked, and this would of course speak in favour of the suggestion advanced. We have already seen that, possibly, the rendering of the LXX—"he became known to them" instead of "God knew"—was directed against a dangerous interpretation. Onkelos radically alters the whole verse. He translates: "And the servitude of the children of Israel was revealed before the Lord, and the Lord said he would deliver them." This is very striking and does look like another illustration of Onkelos's aversion from any anthropomorphisms. The connection of the verse with sexual abstention is def-

[14] *Jer. Targum* ascribes this end only to Moses; it translated Deut 34:5, "Moses died according to the word [*pe*, mouth] of the Lord," by "through the kiss of the Lord." Of Aaron, Num 33:38 tells us that "he went up into the mount according to the word of the Lord, and died there." Though in strictness the clause "according to the mouth of the Lord" qualifies the going up and not the dying, *b. B. B.* 17a shows that as early as in the Tannaitic era it was regarded as indicating that Aaron died in the same manner as Moses. The further extension to Miriam had also taken place by the time of *b. B. B.* 17a. But it obviously created difficulties, there being no Scriptural passage on which to rest it. It was only R. Eleazar (second half of 3rd cent.) who discovered a way in which even Miriam's supernatural death might be derived from the Bible; see also *b. M. Kat.* 28a. In *Song of Songs Rab.* on 1:2, "Let him kiss me with the kisses of his mouth" is treated as evidence that all pious men die as Moses did.

[15] Dillmann, *Die Bücher Exodus und Leviticus*, 2nd ed. (1890), 21. In Exod 3:7 there is an object: "I know their sorrows."

[16] The rendering presupposes only a small change in the vowels of the Hebrew: *wayyiwwadha' 'alehem* instead of *wayyedha' 'elohim.*

initely rejected, and the verb "to know" is avoided. He must have had a strong reason for such thorough rewriting. The Jerusalemite Targum also introduces enough changes to eliminate any conceivable allusion to a virgin birth: "And the Lord saw the trouble of the servitude of the children of Israel, and the repentance which they practised in secret was revealed before the Lord, for they did not know of one another [i.e. of one another's repentance]." No mention is made of sexual abstention. The cryptic phrase "and God knew" is interpreted as expressing the commonplace idea that God takes note of a sinner's change of heart even if no one else does. And, significantly, as in Onkelos, the verb "to know" is not used of God: the conduct of the Israelites "was revealed before him." The verb is indeed retained, but it refers to the Israelites and has its usual meaning, "they did not know of one another's repentance."

No less suggestive than these translations is the attitude of Midrash Rabba to the verse in question. With one exception, none of the comments preserved makes use of the notion of sexual abstention. (As is to be expected, one interpretation is similar to that we find in Onkelos, and one to that in the Jerusalemite Targum.) The exception runs as follows: "And God saw—this means, he saw their abstention; and God knew—this means, he knew that the time had come which he had fixed to Abraham [for the redemption of his descendants]." Here the verse is associated with the episode of the abstention just as in the Haggadah. Only the "knowing" has nothing to do with it, and is given an innocent meaning. The result is that the reader is left wondering what may be the justification for connecting the verse with that episode. Why should his observation of the conduct of the Israelites have reminded God that the date foretold to Abraham had arrived?

Perhaps we may here add that, in the Gospel according to the Hebrews, Mary is not a human woman. She is Michael or a power or the Holy Ghost.

It was, then, only in the Haggadah that the objectionable legend survived without being explained away; we do not meet with it anywhere else, though we do meet with what seem to be signs of suppression. The Haggadah is a piece of liturgy, and it is more difficult to expurgate liturgy than almost any other kind of literature.

If the foregoing argument is tenable, it furnishes support for the view—which appears to be increasingly favoured by modern scholars on other grounds—that the narrative of Jesus's birth originated in a properly Jewish rather than Hellenized milieu.

The Significance of the *Afikoman*

Jeremiah, we are told, in order to indicate the impending subjection to Babylonian rule which God had decreed, put a yoke on his neck.[1] Suppose he had waved his cap instead. Far from supporting his message, the gesture would have made his public doubt his rationality. The yoke was readily seen as a symbol of serfdom. What was new, and impressive, was only its application to the international situation of the time. A waving of the cap would have conveyed no meaning in that context.

Yet it is conduct of this kind which is universally attributed to Jesus on the occasion of the Last Supper. If there was no previously established symbolism relating to the unleavened bread, then what were his disciples to make of it when he "gave to them and said, Take, eat, this is my body"[2]? Nowadays we are so accustomed to this declaration that we no longer wonder how it struck the original hearers. But, evidently, had it come out of the blue, it would have been no better than if Jeremiah had waved his cap—an empty, indeed absurd, action.

A Traditional Symbol

However, it did not come out of the blue. There were already circles whose fervent expectation of redemption fastened on the observances of Passover eve. For them, the unleavened bread stood for the people of Israel, and a fragment was eaten solemnly as corresponding to the vital part missing for the ultimate deliverance—the Messiah. The novelty of Jesus's pronouncement, therefore, consisted merely in the identification: whereas before, the fragment had signified the Messiah in the abstract, promised but not yet a reality, now, Jesus explained, he had arrived concretely in his own person—"this is my body." His disciples had no more difficulty in understanding his meaning than Jeremiah's public had in regard to the yoke. They were familiar with the ceremony of distributing a piece of unleavened bread which represented the Messiah, and when Jesus gave it the specific reference to himself, it was not a waving of the cap, it was simply the use of a traditional symbol to reveal his claim.

The old Messianic ritual which he applied in this way is still extant in our Jewish Seder. It is the *Afikoman*. The word is Greek: *aphikomenos*, "the coming one," in Hebrew *habba'*, clearly referring to the Messiah. Though by now deliberately played down, the once tremendous role of this observance may be gathered from two facts.

[1] Jer 27:2.

[2] Mark 14:22. In the Aramaic it may well have been "this is me." For the order to commemorate, see Luke 22:19; 1 Cor 11:24.

First, it spans the entire meal: prior to the main recital and supper the person conducting the Seder breaks off and puts aside a piece of unleavened bread, which much later he brings back and divides among the company as the very last food for the night. Secondly, there is the Midrash of the four sons, or disciples, in the *Haggadah*: it is a statement (an obscure, mysterious one) concerning the Afikoman by which, in reply to the wise son's question, is summed up the import of all the manifold provisions associated with the keeping of Passover.

WHY DO WE HIDE IT?

Today in many parts of the world the children playfully hide the fragment lying aside, so that the person conducting the celebration, when he needs it at the end of the supper, at first cannot find it; alternatively, the leader himself may hide it and the children search for it. At its inception the game may have been of a more serious character, an allusion to the Messiah who, though existing, is in concealment, guarded by God until the appropriate hour. After all, at the latest from the Middle Ages, the Afikoman is described as *tzafun*, which may denote both "that which is preserved" and "that which is hidden:" a suitable designation for the Messiah waiting in the wings to be summoned to his task.

From early on, varied and at times daring interpretations were placed on the unleavened bread (and no doubt, while the sacrificial cult continued, on the lamb as well;) and they were apt to be formally proclaimed in the course of the Passover eve liturgy. One Talmudic text considers it of the essence of the unleavened bread that "they make solemn declaration over it."[3] We still recite, for example, an interpretation by Rabbi Gamaliel I, to the effect that the unleavened bread is to remind us of the speed with which, in the end, salvation came in Egypt; and another, of slightly later date, laying the stress on the wretchedness of the food—"This is the afflicted bread which our fathers ate."[4] It follows that, when Jesus made his own pronouncement, that by itself was no fresh departure.

"THUS DID HILLEL..."

In fact, even the commemoration of his action by the Church was not without precedent (or, who knows?, precedents.) The great Hillel had eaten the unleavened bread in a highly individualistic manner, apparently hinting at an ideal end-time unity. To this day, in remembrance of him, in addition to the orthodox rite, we also perpetuate his, with the words "Thus did Hillel, he wrapped together" and so forth. To begin with, presumably, it was only his closer followers who paid this tribute: and though it was soon taken over by Jewry at large, its non-conformist provenance even now comes out in the fact that it is performed without a blessing.

[3] *b. Pes.* 36a, 115b. The addition of "many" in a variant—"they recite many things over it"—is an easier reading, from a period when the original definition was no longer appreciated.

[4] Note the personification of the unleavened bread, called "afflicted bread," not, as in Deut 16:3, "bread of affliction."

The Afikoman is certainly of sectarian origin, owing its rise to particularly zealous, Messiah-oriented groups. Significantly this ceremony, too, is provided with no blessing, either when the fragment is first broken off or when it is distributed and consumed last thing. Its demotion over the past 1500 years or so to a series of acts totally devoid of sense (indeed, it is almost bad form to enquire into their sense) is due to (1) a general distrust of Messianic speculation and symbolism and (2) an abhorrence of what post-New Testament (not New Testament) Christianity made of the Last Supper.

These factors have exercised an enormous influence on the Passover eve service, both on specific passages and on wider features. Take the declaration over the unleavened bread quoted above: "This is the afflicted bread which our fathers ate." Some medieval Rabbis feared that this phrasing might evoke the notion of transformation, the idea that the bread on the table had become the bread of Egypt. So they substituted: "Like this was the bread which our fathers ate."[5] To what lengths the transmitters of the liturgy went in eliminating anything that might smack of a human mediator is shown by the complete suppression of the name of Moses. What a *tour de force*: to weave legends, prayers, hymns around the Exodus without once making mention of the figure that dominates the biblical account. It is arguable that, while the anti-Messianic or a-Messianic trend wards off certain grave dangers, it also stifles some genuine, imaginative piety.

PAST, PRESENT OR FUTURE?

A concluding word about tense. The Hebrew *habba'* may refer to past, present or future; indeed it may cover the three or two of the three at once. The Greek *aphikomenos*, being what in Greek grammar is termed an aorist, denotes "he that came" or "has come" rather than "he that comes" or "shall come." To understand why this rendering was chosen it would be necessary to probe into the Messianic time scale of the translators. The *Haggadah* itself contains intricate overlaps of periods. Here and there it is the contemporary community we belong to who were enslaved in Egypt and liberated: "We were slaves unto Pharaoh in Egypt, and the Lord brought us forth." Even the individual may have taken part in those events: "That which the Lord did for me when I came forth"—a bold conception which is rationalised, and in a way weakened, in a precept introducing an "as if:" "In each generation a man is obliged to regard himself as if he himself had gone forth from Egypt."

The benediction following the *Hallel* and called "redemption" is particularly relevant. Rabbi Akiba who, acclaiming Bar-Kochba, believed the end of history imminent, inserted a prayer into this "redemption" for the advent of peaceful festivals in a rebuilt Jerusalem and with a restored Temple cult; and he concluded: "Blessed are You, O Lord—he has redeemed Israel." The structure of this blessing is extraordinary; analogy with other blessings would demand either "who has redeemed Israel" or "redeemer of Israel." Moreover, modern commentators point out, a prayer for the future cannot logically lead up to "he has redeemed" in the past. Hence some of them emend, normalise the text, bring it into line. But, at the latest from the fourth century, the abrupt "he has"

[5] The prevalent reading is still without "like," however.

figures also in the benediction "redemption" after the *Shema* in the daily morning service; and similarly, the past tense is already remarked on by Raba who lived in that century.[6] There are, it appears, violent moments when tomorrow is seized today.[7]

[6] *b. Pes.* 117b.

[7] Literature: Eisler, *ZNW* 24, 1925, 161 ff. Lietzmann, same *Zeitschrift* 25, 1926, 1 ff. Marmorstein, same volume, 249 ff. Petuchowski, *JBL* 76, 1957, 293 ff. Daube, *NTS*, 5, 1958/9, 174 f. [329 f.], and *He That Cometh*, St. Paul's Lecture (London Diocesan Council for Christian-Jewish Understanding) 1966, 6 ff. [429 ff.]. Goldschmidt, *Die Pessach-Haggada*, 1937, 68 f.

He That Cometh*

I now proceed to my second topic. I am under strict instructions not to go beyond ten minutes to seven. It is good to be firm with a speaker. I shall never forget the occasion when I arrived very late for a lecture. It was a crowded lecture and I asked the man nearest the door: "Has he finished?" To which the answer was: "Yes, he has finished, but he doesn't stop."

So let me take up the institution of the Eucharist. In the Jewish Passover eve liturgy, almost at the start, prior to the supper, a portion of the unleavened bread on the table is broken off and laid aside, to be brought back after the meal, when it is distributed among the company by the master conducting the celebration and is taken as the last bit of food that night. In the traditional list setting out the successive numbers of this service and going back at least to the Middle Ages,[1] the breaking off is called *yahas*, "let him divide," while the broken off piece brought back at the end of the meal and taken as the final food is called *saphun*. This word has several meanings: it means both "that which is preserved" and "that which is hidden." The ritual bridges the entire Passover eve supper, the breaking off and putting aside of a piece of unleavened bread taking place before it, the eating of that which is preserved or hidden forming its conclusion. It occupies two out of the traditional fourteen numbers of the liturgy of the evening. It is a universal rite, found in all versions of the Passover eve liturgy, so must be considered very old.

Forty years ago the basically correct understanding of this ritual was furnished by a scholar—or shall I say madman? he was both—named Robert Eisler, who noticed that it was a Messianic ceremony. The Messiah is a broken off portion of the Jewish people, existing but as yet concealed, and his coming at the end of this Passover supper will make the people complete, whole.[2] The reaction, however, to this thesis was of extreme violence, from both sides, the Christian and the Jewish. Lietzmann, a leading Christian scholar, and Marmorstein, a leading Jewish one, came down on poor Eisler in a fearful

* Lecture given October 1966 in the crypt of St. Paul's Cathedral, London. This is the second part of the lecture "He That Cometh" (see 157 ff. for the first part). The lecture began, "I wish to make two points tonight, which is two points more than I usually make in a lecture. First I should like to draw attention to the influence that the Old Testament figure of Hezekiah has had on New Testament thought, and then I should like to say something about the background of the institution of the Eucharist."

[1] See E. D. Goldschmidt, *Die Pesach-Haggada* (1937), 18.

[2] *ZNW*, 24 (1925), 161 ff.

pincer movement and just crushed him.[3] There were three reasons at least for being annoyed with him. First, he did include in his argumentation a good deal that was speculative or even wild. Secondly, I have already indicated that he was impossible. But, thirdly, the principal motivation for the fierceness of the assault (whatever its merits in substance), I am sure, lay far deeper. I wonder whether it is time[4] to have a calmer look at things.

The usual explanations for the ritual are palpably forced. For example, the prevalent orthodox Jewish one is that this piece of unleavened bread must be laid aside in order that it should not be inadvertently eaten up during the meal.[5] But surely this begs the question, takes for granted what we want accounted for: some very peculiar value attaching to this fragment. Why should it not be eaten up? What is so special about it? (Let alone other objections such as that a practical device of this kind would never have led to a separate number in the service, or that if the ceremony had been introduced with that purpose in mind, it would be most unsuitable seeing that the putting aside certainly involves the risk of the piece getting lost.[6]) Nowadays in many regions a children's prank is added to the rite: after the fragment has been removed from the table by the master, the children—with his connivance—get hold of it and hide it from him, to give it up for a little reward when it is needed at the end of the supper. Maybe this play grew up after the old meaning was forgotten or suppressed; it may indeed be modelled on the hiding of the Easter eggs (which itself, it should be remembered, enshrines a deeper symbolism). It is possible, however, that even this children's prank is a remnant of the ancient, more serious role played by this rite.

Anyhow, it is no longer necessary to dwell on the enormous importance in New Testament times of the concept of the hidden Messiah: I am content to refer to Sjöberg's book on the subject.[7] The comparison of the nation with a cake goes back to the Old Testament[8] and for the period here relevant I need only remind you of Paul's admonition, couched, be it noted, in Passover language: "Purge out, therefore, the old leaven that ye may be a new lump."[9] The unleavened bread of Passover is personified, for example, in the Jerusalemite Targum, one of the old Jewish translations of the Pentateuch into Aramaic, where what in the Hebrew appears as "the bread of poverty,

[3] Lietzmann, *ZNW*, 25 (1962), 1 ff., Marmorstein, same volume, 249 ff. An explanation by Lietzmann—then editor of the Zeitschrift—why he was refusing to publish Eisler's rejoinder may be found in the following volume, 26 (1927), 96.

[4] Perhaps it is not. The situation has changed, but not all that much. For instance, in Goldschmidt's *Pesach-Haggada*, a scholarly work, cited above, note 1, no mention, absolutely no mention, is made of any of the New Testament references to Passover eve customs, despite the fact that for some of them the New Testament provides the earliest extant evidence.

[5] See Goldschmidt, *l.c.*, 20.

[6] See Goldschmidt, *l.c.*, on a misadventure of this sort which did happen to the admired eleventh century scholar Rashi.

[7] *Der verborgene Menschensohn in den Evangelien* (1955). The Targum, incidentally, in its version of Mic 4:8 speaks of the preserved, hidden Messiah as *tamir*, an Aramaic equivalent of *saphun*.

[8] Hos 7:8.

[9] 1 Cor 5:7.

affliction" is rendered as "the poor, afflicted bread."[10] The *Zohar*, the famous Kabbalistic work, by the way, explains the term as denoting "the bread of the poor one" and identifies "the poor one" with King David; so the unleavened bread of Passover is to be taken as the bread of King David in his humiliation.[11] However, as this is a medieval compilation, liable to Christian influence, I am not invoking it in support.

At the present day, three cakes of unleavened bread are used for the Passover eve celebration, named after the three divisions of the Jewish people: Priest, Levite, Israelite. The ritual here in question concerns the middle cake, the Levite; it is from this cake that a portion is broken off before the meal begins, to be brought back and to serve as the last food that night.[12] Which suggests in the background a belief in the Messiah from Levi, the Messiah from the same tribe as the first deliverer, Moses; this expectation was fairly common in ancient Judaism.[13] However, the three cakes are not met in the early sources, still less their designation as Priest, Levite and Israelite; and it is chiefly on this ground that Marmorstein condemned the entire thesis of Eisler.

The thesis does not, however, depend on these details. The Talmudic sources do attest the taking of unleavened bread at the close of the Passover supper, the purpose being, we are told, that the feeling of satiety should be caused by this food and that its taste should remain with one.[14] This strongly suggests a Messianic interpretation of this food. Similarly, they do attest the use on Passover eve of a broken-off, fragmentary cake of unleavened bread, associated with the Biblical expression "the bread of poverty, affliction."[15] It is true that this is taken as the supper commences, but then, it would be a mistake to postulate for that epoch an absolute uniformity of custom. Thus the decisive framework for a Messianic ritual is there, in the early sources.

This is not to assert that a ritual of this description was universally practised in New Testament times: I think it was not, it was still confined to certain groups. Again, we cannot say how elaborate it was in that period: I guess it varied in different circles. These and similar questions of a minor nature may be left open. The dismissal of Eisler

[10] Deut 16:3, Hebrew *lehem 'oni*, Jer. Targ. *lahma' 'anya'*. The Septuagint has *artos kakoseos*, following the Hebrew. Onkelos, another still earlier Aramaic translation, leaves the Hebrew phrase untranslated—no doubt in order to allow of any of the various interpretations then current: a rendering would have had to choose between them. So Levy, *Chaldäisches Wörterbuch über die Targumim* (1867), 228. Levy is right in connecting the Jerusalemite Targum's rendering with the first of the two interpretations recorded by *Siphre* on Deut 16:5. What he does not see is that, underlying that interpretation in the *Siphre* itself, is a personification of the unleavened bread.

[11] Section *Vayetse* 157a. The interpretation "of the poor one" involves a slight change in the puctuation of the Hebrew: *'ani* instead of *'oni*. The identification with King David is based on Ps 76:1: "Bow down thine ear, O Lord, and hear me: for I am poor and needy."

[12] Goldschmidt, *l.c.*, 14, 20 f., 32, 71.

[13] Eisler, *l.c.*, 177 f., supplies references. The Dead Sea Scrolls are interesting in this connection.

[14] *b. Pes.* 119b.

[15] *b. Pes.* 115b f., *b. Ber.* 39b. The latter discussion preserves a remark by R. Papa (middle of the fourth century A.D.) which, in addition to presupposing a long established use of a whole cake and a fragmentary one, informs us *expressis verbis* [in express terms] of complete agreement among the Rabbis as to the duty of placing the fragmentary one underneath the whole one (or, I suppose, one might interpret his words as meaning that the fragmentary one is somehow made to appear as part of the whole one, *hinniah perusa bethokh shelema*).

was not only excessively hasty but also rather hard, seeing that he himself had observed, first, that originally the ritual may well have been simpler, involving a single cake only to symbolize the nation,[16] and, secondly, that no matter when the three cakes became established, their naming after the three estates may well be a secondary stage.[17] In any case, granted the likelihood that the triplication of the cakes and their naming after the three estates are of medieval provenance, both are plainly developments of an initial, simpler rite—which already contained the representation of the people and its Messiah by the unleavened bread ceremoniously eaten at this supper.

In the course of the Jewish Passover eve service, then, whether at the conclusion of the supper (the practice which has carried the day) or at its commencement (as according to some Talmudic practice at least), a piece of unleavened bread is taken as the Messiah by the company. The traditional designation of this fragment is *Aphiqoman*. The word is neither Hebrew nor Aramaic. Medieval Jewish commentators give fanciful etymologies.[18] Modern scholars realize that the word is Greek, yet for once their etymologies are even more whimsical than those of the Rabbis. They do not even disdain made-up formations for which there is no evidence whatever in the whole of Greek literature.[19] Lietzmann, in his article putting down Eisler,[20] improving upon an idea of Jastrow's, claims that the word stands for *epi komon*, in German *auf den Bummel!*, "off to a crawl!" Eisler, however, was right: *Aphiqoman* is the Greek *aphikomenos* or *ephikomenos*, "The Coming One," "He that Cometh," Hebrew *habba'*, Aramaic *'athe*. But for the theological and historical consequences that follow, it is hard to believe that this obvious, philologically easiest, *naheliegendste* derivation would have been overlooked in favour of the most far-fetched, tortuous ones. Eisler's replique to Lietzmann was denied publication.[21]

Admittedly there are difficulties, plenty of them—how could there not be in such a matter? The earliest occurrence of the term *Aphiqoman* is in the section of the Passover eve liturgy introducing four types of sons, or rather disciples, and recommending the appropriate kind of instruction for each.[22] The four types are the wise disciple interested in the laws, the viciously scornful one, the simply pious and sensible

[16] *L.c.*, 168. He did, it is true, incline to date the three cakes back to the New Testament era, 163 f., but the point is quite inessential to his main conclusion.

[17] *L.c.*, 164.

[18] See Zobel, art. "*Afikomon*," in *Encyclopaedia Judaica*, vol. 1 (1928), 930, and Marcus, art. "*Afikomen*," in *The Universal Jewish Encyclopedia*, vol. 1 (1939), 106.

[19] E.g. *epikomon*; see Eisler's comments, *l.c.*, 174.

[20] *L.c.*, 4.

[21] See above, note 3. The reason Jewish scholars find a thesis like Eisler's too monstrous even to debate is, of course, that the bread of the Eucharist no longer merely symbolizes the Messiah, but that the Christian eats God. The revulsion engendered by this aspect is further increased by the often very concrete interpretation placed on the eating of Christ. (Heine makes fun of it when, in the *Disputation*, he makes the monk affirm: *Denn in mir ist Jesus Christus, Habe seinen Leib genossen. Christus ist mein Leibgericht* [Inside me is Jesus Christ, I have enjoyed his body. Christ is my favorite dish] This was written towards the end of his life, when he had grave doubts about his conversion of twenty-five years before.)

[22] Goldschmidt, *l.c.*, 39 ff.

one and, lastly, in contrast to these three who will ask the master about Passover in ways revealing their characters, the one who does not know how to ask. The section is pre-Christian; indeed there is modelled on it the chapter in Mark with Jesus asked three questions, the first by a person interested in the lawfulness of tribute, the second a mocking one about resurrection, the third by a person of simple piety and good sense, and with those not daring to ask forming a last, fourth category.[23] It is in the reply the master is advised to give the wise disciple that the term *Aphiqoman* is found: this disciple in answer to his question is to be told of an injunction concerning the *Aphiqoman*. The injunction recurs in other Tannaitic—early Talmudic—sources.[24] But it is untranslatable. It may mean that one should not finish up after the Passover lamb with the *Aphiqoman*, or on the contrary that one should not dismiss the *Aphiqoman* after the Passover lamb, or goodness knows what. However we interpret it, it is contrary to regular Hebrew-Aramaic syntax. No attempt to translate it as it stands can be said to have succeeded, and none could have: this is an arcane pronouncement, the very fact that it is addressed to the wise disciple is significant, it refers to the mystery of this evening. It is even conceivable that once it was more intelligible but has been mutilated.

That to grasp the point of the passage we must proceed along these lines is confirmed by another strange feature. It has long been noticed that, apparently, the injunction concerning the *Aphiqoman* is totally unsuitable as an answer to the wise disciple's question. If you read the section, you will find that he wishes to be illuminated as to the meaning of all the testimonies, statutes and regulations enjoined by God in connection with Passover. This desire is to be met—by what? By—if we do not see through it—the quotation of a single, most trifling little meal custom; it is almost like making fun of his meritorious ambition. This is so obviously unsatisfactory that orthodox Jewish commentators, not normally given to interference with the text, have resorted to open emendation, with the object of making the text say that the master should supply a thorough exposition of the Passover rules to the wise disciple. But apart from the fact that even the emended text does not really say what it ought to,[25] it is wrong, unnecessary, to emend. As soon as you realize that the injunction has regard to "The Coming One," the great secret of this celebration, the arrival of the Messiah, it is clear why it is addressed to the wise disciple, and why it is a full answer to his enquiry: it is this one point which enshrines, sums up, the meaning of all the rulings and observances attached by God to this festival.[26]

[23] Mark 12:13 ff., cp. Matt 22:15 ff., Luke 10:25 ff., 20:21 ff.; see Daube, *l.c.*, 158 ff. [343 ff.], and *NTS* 5 (1958/9), 180 ff. [334 ff.]. To my delight I have come across the fourth type, who will not ask and is none the less to be instructed, in Philo: *Leg. Spec.* 4.26.140. I shall not here enlarge, except to call attention to a terminological point of special interest: while the Passover eve liturgy speaks of a disciple "who does not know how to ask," *she'eno yodhea' lish'ol*, Philo, like the Synoptics, speaks of one "who does not dare," *tolmao*.

[24] E.g. *m. Pes.* 10:8.

[25] See Goldschmidt, *l.c.*, 42.

[26] Jesus's answer to the question of law, "Render unto Caesar" etc., though not (or only very indirectly) concerned with the Messianic expectation, is definitely a riddle which only the initiated can solve. Let him who doubts this contemplate the uses to which the saying has been put in the course of nineteen hundred years.

The Talmudic interpretations of the word *Aphiqoman* are wide off the mark—maybe deliberately so.[27] The injunction as a whole is explained in diverse ways, more or less close to what may have been the original sense. One explanation I have already adverted to: some unleavened bread should be eaten at the close of the supper, in order that satiety should be produced by this food and that the taste of the food should linger. A complication is that, according to a different teaching, it is the Passover lamb a piece of which should be eaten last thing. Actually, in the Sephardi tradition, to this day the *Aphiqoman*, though consisting in a fragment from the cake called Levite, is understood as representing a piece of the Passover lamb: if it were not for the destruction of the Temple bringing with it the cessation of sacrifice, it is the Passover lamb which would figure in this ceremony.[28]

It is indeed arguable that, in its inception, the ritual under discussion was associated with the lamb rather than the bread. Surely, as a result of the lamb dropping out from the Passover celebration in A.D. 70, we must have lost a substantial amount of ancient reflection and observances built up around it. (In the century or so prior to A.D. 70, as it became usual for sizeable bands of pilgrims to celebrate Passover at Jerusalem, each company having one lamb only, the lamb ceased to be the main dish of the meal.[29] The main dish now was the festal offering, of which one could have as much as one liked, while the lamb more and more acquired the character of merely ceremonious, religious food: a development, one would think, of some consequence.) This does not mean, however, that, long before the destruction of the Temple, ideas attaching to the lamb might not equally attach to the bread, or be extended to it. The oscillation between bread and lamb is familiar enough from the New Testament. The two are close in Paul's exhortation I cited earlier on: "Purge out therefore the old leaven that ye may be a new lump, for even Christ our passover is sacrificed for us."[30] In the Didache, the taking of the Eucharist, wine and bread, "sates" the taker,[31] just as, in the Talmud, satiety is caused either by the final piece of Passover lamb or by the final piece of unleavened bread. I shall presently adduce a symbolical action of Hillel, the great Rabbi of around 15 B.C., involving at the same time the lamb, the bread and, indeed, the bitter herbs which are also prescribed by the Bible for this supper. In New Testament times, the Passover eve service was still in a state of flux. There was room for much variability in observances[32] and—just as important—in the meanings ascribed to observances. It would be rash to assume that the exact history of the rite of "The Coming One" is restorable.

[27] *t. Pes.* 10:11;, *b. Pes.* 119;, *y. Pes.* 37d.

[28] Goldschmidt, *l.c.*, 71.

[29] See Strack and Billerbeck, *op. cit.*, vol. 4, pt. 1 (1928), 46.

[30] 1 Cor 5:7.

[31] Didache 10:1.

[32] This applies to the lamb as well as to the bread. It may be relevant to point out that the piece of lamb which, according to some authorities, is to be taken at the close of the supper is sometimes the piece taken in fulfilment of the Biblical commandment, e.g. in *t. Pes.* 5:3, sometimes an additional one while the Biblical commandment is fulfilled towards the commencement of the supper, e.g. in *b. Pes.* 119d f. The latter practice is presupposed also in *m. Pes.* 10:9; see Strack and Billerbeck, *op. cit.*, 46, 66.

Perhaps too little attention has been paid by writers on the background of the New Testament to the differences between a passover at Jerusalem and one outside; the latter is generally treated as of little relevance, but *non constat* [it is not apparent] that it did not contribute ideas and certainly it would evolve its own nuances. After all, the vast majority always celebrated Passover outside Jerusalem. As regards the relation of the Passover lamb and the unleavened bread—even while the Temple stood the former figured only at Jerusalem, the latter also elsewhere. That would produce different emphases at least, and we need not wait for the destruction of the Temple to get interest, speculation, symbolism centering on the bread in large and influential groups. The word *Aphiqoman,* a Greek word, on any interpretation points to a somewhat Hellenized setting of the reply to the wise disciple. Accordingly, a non-Jerusalemite or even non-Palestinian origin, though far from certain, is at least not unlikely.

Hellenistic colouring is indeed a mark of the entire section concerned with the four types of disciples: the designation *Aphiqoman* is not the only straw in the wind. The four-fold scheme as such may well stem from Alexandria.[33] Moreover, the noun "wisdom" is employed in the sense of "points of law," and the adjective "wise" in the sense of "interested in points of law"[34]: unusual terminology, confined, it would seem, to Greek-influenced environment. Most strikingly, the wise disciple's question, a quotation from Scripture, is based on the reading of the Septuagint over against the Massoretic Hebrew text.[35]

However we account for these items, the ritual in question looks like being sectarian in origin. The Passover eve liturgy contains a number of esoteric elements. There is the "I am" of the Divine Presence, the phrase "I am" in the sense of "The Divine Majesty itself is here"[36]—a usage known from the gospels but, as far as Jewish sources are concerned, to be found solely in this liturgy.[37] There is the dissolution of the Passover eve company by its members falling asleep: a feature essential to an appreciation of the scene at Gethsemane.[38] As for sectaririan eating rites, we know of one in particular, still surviving, a commemoration coming down from a generation or so prior to the last supper of the New Testament. The famous Hillel, whom I have mentioned several times already, instead of conforming to the established manner of taking the three principal ingredients of the Passover supper—the Passover lamb, the unleavened bread and the

[33] To the considerations I advanced in *The New Testament and Rabbinic Judaism*, 161 ff. [345 ff.], may now be added the appearance of the non-daring disciple in Philo; see above, note 23.

[34] Hebrew *hokhma*, "wisdom," *hakham*, "wise," *halakhoth*, "points of law."

[35] Whereas the wicked disciple asks the question of Exod 12:26. "What mean ye by this service?," and, by saying "you" instead of "we," excludes himself from the community, the wise disciple asks the question of Deut 6:20, "What mean the testimonies and the statutes and the judgments which the Lord our God hath commanded us?" The Massoretic Hebrew text, however, has "commanded you," *'ethkhem*. It is the Septuagint which reads "commanded us," *hemin*.

[36] Goldschmidt, *l.c.*, 54.

[37] See Daube, *l.c.*, 325 ff. [371 ff.] (where it is pointed out that the formula "I and He" is different). On p. 325, Professor T .W. Manson is erroneously named instead of Professor William Manson. Both are dead. William was charming on the occasion, not in the least cut up about the credit going to T. W.

[38] *m. Pes.* 10:8; see Daube, *l.c.*, 332 ff. [442 ff.]. This portion of the Mishnah is omitted (represented by dots), as of no interest, from the translation by Strack and Billerbeck, *op. cit.*, 73.

bitter herbs—namely, one by one, separately, made of them a single united dish. He did so, incidentally, at the commencement of the celebration, this was how he fulfilled the Scriptural ordinance prescribing these foods.[39] Precisely what kind of union his action was intended to allude to I shall not here enquire.[40] What is of moment here is that a memorial ritual grew up among his disciples, who would take the three foods in just the way he had done, performing the ceremony expressly "in remembrance of Hillel," and prefacing it with the words: "Thus did Hillel—He wrapped together the Passover lamb, the unleavened bread and the bitter herbs and ate them in union." The affinity both in substance and in form with Paul's reference to the last supper is unmistakable.[41]

Here, then, you have a circle commemorating the significant way in which the master ate the Passover supper around 15 B.C., the master who, incidentally, was himself looked on as a descendant of David; and, just as the once esoteric memorial meal of the circle of Jesus spread and became universal, so, in Judaism, the Hillelite commemoration soon gained general acceptance. It now forms part of all versions of this liturgy—though, on closer scrutiny, we may discern that it is still marked off as, *au fond*, irregular. Whereas Hillel pronounced over the united dish the benedictions ordinarily applicable to these foods, in the traditional Passover eve liturgy no benediction accompanies the taking of the dish in his remembrance. So there is still a trace of the sectarian character of the rite. Similarly, no matter what may have been the practice, or practices, in

[39] Goldschmidt, *l.c.*, 21, 70 f. His textual authority was Num 9:11: "They shall eat it [the Passover lamb] with unleavened bread and bitter herbs." Which, if pressed, can be taken to mean that the three should be combined.

[40] The two key terms associated with this rite and important for its implications are *karakh*, "to wrap together," and *beyahadh*, "in union." Let me note, in passing, that there are signs that Hillel aimed at pushing the Passover lamb in the direction of "a sacrifice of the community," *qorban sibbur*, as opposed to a "sacrifice of an individual" *qorban yahidh*. If it should be this Hillel and not the later one who declared that there will be no Messiah for Israel since they already enjoyed—"ate"—him in the days of Hezekiah (see 158), exploration in further directions is manifestly indicated.

[41] 1 Cor 11:23 ff. See Petuchowski, *JBL*, 76 (1957), 293 ff., Daube, ["The Earliest Structure of the Gospels"] *NTS*, 5 (1958/9), 177 f. [331 f.]. It is conceivable that Hillel's unified dish was not his habitual mode of celebrating the supper, but a demonstration on a specific occasion. After "Thus did Hillel," the words *haya korekh we'okhel*, literally, "he was wrapping together and eating," need not mean "he used to wrap together and eat," but could mean "on the occasion in question he wrapped together and ate." Actually, even without the introduction "Thus did Hillel," I wonder whether the phrase quoted must refer to a habit. It is true that *haya* followed by a participle is invariably translated by "he used to do so and so." But while this is often correct, maybe sometimes a different interpretation, missed by the grammars, is preferable. It has recently been shewn (Honoré, *Gaius* [1962], xv f.) that the Latin imperfect may be used for oral transmission of the statement of a master, be it by one who heard him in person, be it by one who learnt about it within the school; *dicebat*, for instance, need not mean "he used to say," frequently it is to be paraphrased "I remember him saying on a certain occasion" or "our tradition has it that he said on a certain occasion." *Haya* with the participle might well here and there have the same function—for example, in quite a few paragraphs of Mishnah Aboth, as also in the commemoration of the Hillelite Passover. Such usage of *haya* would be one more illustration of the international character of much that went on in the academic and semi-academic establishments of the time; see Daube, ["Rabbinic Methods of Interpretation and Hellenistic Rhetoric"] *HUCA*, 22 (1949), 239 ff., and ["Alexandrian Methods of Interpretation and the Rabbis"] *Festschrift Lewald* (1953), 27 ff. [*Talmudic Law*, 333–376]. However, I shall rest no conclusions on this possibility.

the Talmudic era, in the traditional Passover eve service no benediction accompanies either of the two numbers, "let him divide," the breaking off of a piece of unleavened bread, or "that which is preserved or hidden," the eating of the *Aphiqoman*. Indeed the two numbers are carefully arranged in such a fashion that the broken off piece, the *Aphiqoman*, is excluded from the benediction pronounced this evening over the unleavened bread: the *Aphiqoman* is removed from the table before that benediction. Both numbers, the breaking off and the eating of the fragment, in fact take place in complete silence: the role of silence in ceremonies with sectarian antecedents is a phenomenon that might repay investigation.

All this fluidity must be borne in mind when we consider the relation of the ritual involving the *Aphiqoman*, "The Coming One," to the institution of the Eucharist. We must not look for an exact parallel. Eisler tried too hard to do just this. Yet the essence is there in the New Testament. Clearly, Jesus's action took place at the beginning of the meal, like Hillel's and like some practice I adduced from the Talmud.[42] In the ritual involving "The Coming One," only the breaking off a fragment and its removal occur at the beginning, the eating at the very end. The alternative, that the Jewish rite derives from the Christian,[43] is ruled out not only by the date of the evidence—it is enough to recall the section about the four sons or disciples—but also because the whole trend of the Jewish Passover eve service is the other way, towards dissociation from what Christianity made of it. Christian potentialities are suppressed.

Let me cite two glaring examples. In the Passover eve liturgy as depicted in the early parts of the Talmud, the striking ceremonies of that night elicit questions by members of the company (such as those asked by various types of disciples), and these questions in turn provide the opportunity for instruction and discourses by the master. At some date after A.D. 300, however, a re-arrangement was decided on, and ever since then, in all versions of the liturgy, a number of stereotyped questions expressing surprise about the ceremonies are put, senselessly, before the ceremonies have been performed.[44] Only the gravest reasons could have warranted so drastic a change, which ruins the whole structure of the celebration. It was done in order to forestall attempts to divert the exposition from its safe, recognized path into a heretical one—towards Christianity.[45] Again, the figure of Moses, dominating the Biblical narrative of the exodus from Egypt and, naturally, at one time prominent, too, in the celebration of the deliverance on Passover eve, is radically eliminated: in the Passover eve liturgy as it

[42] See above, note 15; cp. also note 32. I ought to make it clear that I am expressing no view as to whether the last supper was in fact a Passover eve supper. The evidence seems to me to be in the balance.

[43] Independent developments? This strikes me as implausible in the extreme.

[44] Goldschmidt, *l.c.*, 33.

[45] See Daube, *The New Testament and Rabbinic Judaism*, 192 ff. [406 ff.]. The discussion in *b. Pes.* 116a at the end shews that in the time of R. Nahman, who died A.D. 320, the questions were still live ones. In a very different area, that of Talmudic studies, what is more discouraged than anything else by the orthodox method is fresh ways of asking. This is pointed out by Gershfield, *Conservative Judaism* 21 (1966), 51: "What is dangerous and intolerable is for the students to *ask a new question*, one that has not been offered by the commentators, and thus by indirection to cast doubt upon the whole structure of the previous interpretive tradition."

stands, his name is not mentioned once in any of the prayers and recitals woven around the Biblical record, and, more than that, no Biblical passage mentioning it is quoted. It is a fantastic *tour de force*. Think what it means. It is as if one were to spend annually a night commemorating Britain's rescue in the Second World War, rehearsing the main course of events as well as telling elaborate stories about them—without once mentioning Churchill. A fantastic *tour de force*: but there must be no human Mediator.[46]

There is, however, further evidence that the Eucharist was modelled on, made use of, an earlier Jewish rite. In my opinion it is in fact the best evidence, which Eisler unfortunately missed; it is, so to speak, internal evidence, from the New Testament account itself. What I mean is that the institution of the Eucharist as recorded in the New Testament of necessity presupposes a ritual essentially (not in details, to be sure, but essentially) like that of "The Coming One." Jesus could not at the same time have introduced both the general idea of eating a cake of unleavened bread as the Messiah and the specific identification of that cake with himself. This is just not how rites come into being. The ceremony—some ceremony—of eating a piece of unleavened bread as the Messiah must have been practised before; the new thing was the identification, the self-revelation, the proclamation that the Messiah had now found bodily, human presence—"This is my body" (or even, at an Aramaic stage, "This is me"). When Jeremiah was commissioned by God to put a yoke around his neck in public in order to impress upon the people the imminent and inevitable doom of foreign rule,[47] the idea that a yoke symbolized enslavement was there, familiar to all. (It is present in English "subjugation.") What was new was the application of the idea to the situation. Just so, the rite of eating a broken off fragment of unleavened bread as the Messiah was there, the novelty—a tremendous one—was the application to the situation, the identification of the bread with Jesus.

We are so used to Jesus's action on that occasion that we no longer wonder about its peculiar character, take it as, in the circumstances, the most natural thing in the world. A moment's reflection, however, will expose the untenability of this attitude. Let me put it this way: had no ritual of the kind preserved in the Jewish Passover eve service existed, and had Jesus suddenly distributed a cake of unleavened bread and said of

[46] Petuchowski, *l.c.*, 295 f., Daube, ["The Earliest Structure of the Gospels"] *NTS*, 5 (1958/9), 178 [332]. The quotation of Exod 12:31 (Goldschmidt, *l.c.*, 58) looks an exception, but even this one exception is more apparent than real. The verse is quoted as proving that there were fifty plagues, not ten. To this proof the second half naming Moses makes no contribution, it might just as well be omitted and, in fact, the apparatus suggests that it is an intrusion. Goldschmidt puts it in brackets. Not all attempts to shed whatever might smack of Christianity were successful. An old Aramaic proclamation over the unleavened bread begins (Goldschmidt, *l.c.*, 32): "This is the poor, afflicted bread that our fathers ate in the land of Egypt." Some medieval Rabbis felt that the phrasing might encourage the notion of transformation, the notion that the bread on the table was actually the same as had figured during the exodus. (Whether the phrasing was in fact chosen with a view to this interpretation I leave undecided. It will be noticed that we find here the personified bread of the *Jer. Targum* Deut 16:3; see above, note 10.) They introduced a slight change, so slight as in the Aramaic to consist in one additional letter, *ke*, "like," and thereby obtained: "Like this was the poor, afflicted bread that our fathers ate. . . ." Their innovation, however, did not prevail, the common reading is still "This is."

[47] Jer 27:2.

it, "This is my body," his disciples—to put it mildly—would have been perplexed. With such a ritual referring to "The Coming One" in existence, the self-revelation made sense. Up to then, the fragment of unleavened bread was, so to speak, the Messiah in the abstract, the unknown Messiah; now he was known. The ritual of eating "The Coming One"—whether at the commencement of the supper or at its close or at any other stage—must precede the institution of the Eucharist, the decisive point of which was the identification: the ancient expectation was now fulfilled. If we did not find such a ritual in the Jewish background, we should have to invent it. As it does occur, the reasonable course seems to be to accept it for what it is.[48]

There is no lack of corroboration. In the Didache, we meet the prayer: "As this broken bread was scattered on the mountains and, being gathered together, became one, so may thy Church be gathered together."[49] This is very reminiscent of the major implications inherent in the ritual of "The Coming One." The meal here ends with the invocation "Maranatha," "Our Lord cometh."[50] Another passage worth comparing occurs in Paul: "The bread which we break, is it not the communion of the body of Christ? For we being many are one bread and one body."[51] A little further on, there is mention of the coming: "For as often as ye eat this bread and drink this cup, ye do shew the Lord's death till he come."[52] But—I reiterate: open questions and, worse, inconsistencies abound.

One question I ought perhaps to say something about in conclusion. That *Aphiqoman* represents Greek *aphikomenos* or *ephikomenos*—meaning "The Coming One," *habba'* in Hebrew, *'athe* in Aramaic—is, I think, certain. But why, it may be asked, did they not choose the far commoner designation *erchomenos*? It should be observed, at the outset, that, apart from this matter of frequency of usage, either *aphikomenos* or *ephikomenos* is perfectly suitable to denote "The Coming One." The former verb often signifies the arrival of a welcome guest. Both verbs have eschatological or apocalyptic potentialities. The Septuagint employs *aphikneomai* in a line from Proverbs, "when your fear cometh as desolation," and, interestingly, *pareimi* and *erchomai* are paired off with it as synonyms[53]; and *ephikneomai* is used in the Sybilline Oracles of the rise of Alexander the Great as a conquering beast.[54] The answer to the

[48] Suppose Jer 27:2 told us that, to indicate impending foreign rule, Jeremiah drank a glass of water (instead of carrying a yoke), we could not rest till, somewhere in the Oriental material, we had discovered the drinking of water symbolizing subjection; and if the material remained obdurate, we should postulate that symbol regardless. The case of the bread symbol at the last supper is exactly of this nature—only the material is willing.

[49] Didache 9:3. For a recent analysis, see Riesenfeld, *Eranos*, 54 (1956), 142 ff. The picture of dispersal "on the mountains" may be indebted to Manna mythology; see e.g. the exposition of Gen 7:20, "and the mountains were covered," by R. Eleazar of Modiim (time of Hadrianic war) in *b. Yom.* 76a.

[50] Didache 10:6.

[51] 1 Cor 10:16 f.

[52] Didache 11:26.

[53] Prov 1:27: "When your fear cometh as desolation [Hebrew *ba'*, Greek *aphikneomai*] and your destruction cometh as a whirlwind [Hebrew *'atha*, Greek *pareimi*], when distress and anguish cometh upon you [Hebrew *ba'*, Greek *erchomai*]."

[54] *Syb. Or.* 11:25: "For on thee [Babylon] shall come a dreadful lion, a flesh-eating beast, wild, strange to justice, wearing on his shoulders a mantle."

question, then, is that *Aphiqoman* is an apt designation. And as for *erchomenos* being commoner—we have no right to expect the commoner word, not in general and most certainly not in the province of sectarian, arcane wisdom.

If this answer does not satisfy you immediately, may I remind you that idiosyncrasy of precisely this sort can be illustrated from the New Testament. As is well known, John alone of the evangelists uses *heko* just like *erchomai* as an expression of epiphany.[55] Above all, take the word *epiousios* which occurs in "Our Father." Whatever its meaning—it is usually rendered as "daily"—no word could be more exceptional. If we discount literature dependent on "Our Father," it is unique, a *hapax legomenon*, known from not a single other text.[56] What is more, it is another term for *Aphiqoman, habba', 'athe*. The usual rendering, as just remarked, is "Give us this day our daily bread." But once again, the by far most satisfactory philological derivation is from *epeimi*, and the by far most satisfactory translation is "coming." It is an eschatological usage, exactly the same as *aphikomenos* or *ephikomenos*. The sentence must be rendered: "Give us this day our coming bread" (or possibly, at an earlier Semitic stage, it was "Give us this day the bread of The Coming One"). Some ancient versions do in fact translate this way or in a way that is not too distant, "our coming bread," "our bread of tomorrow"; and in Rabbinic literature "the bread of The World That Cometh" and "the bread of The Kingdom" are familiar concepts, and attested in the first century A.D.[57] The request for such bread "this day" is reminiscent of the frequent Jewish prayer for final redemption "speedily, in our days."[58] But even the direct "this day" is evidenced in Jewish eschatological hope. It occurs, for instance, in the legend of R. Joshua ben Levi and the leprous Messiah at Rome, where, alas, the latter's promise of advent "this day" is conditioned in the sense of the words of the Psalmist: "This day if ye hearken unto his [God's] voice."[59]

I have not treated the problem of the wine. On this, I differ fundamentally from Eisler.[60] But if you wish to have my views, you will have to ask me another time. This evening my time is up; and more than two points would really be too much for one lecture.

[55] Schneider, art. "*heko*," in *Theologisches Wörterbuch zum Neuen Testament*, vol. 2 (1935), ed. Kittel, 930.

[56] *Pace* Bauer, *Wörterbuch zum Neuen Testament*, 4th ed. (1952), 537, Origen was right. But even if he was not, it does not materially alter the position. For literature, see the commentaries and dictionaries, e.g. Foerster, art. "*epiousios*", in *Theologisches Wörterbuch zum Neuen Testament*, vol. 2, 587 ff. Eisler discusses *epiousios*, *l.c.*, 190 ff.

[57] In a statement by R. Joshua ben Hananiah, *Gen. Rab.* 82 on 35:17 (Prov 28:19); see Strack and Billerbeck, *op. cit.*, vol. 2, 484, vol. 4, pt. 2 (1928), 840. This Rabbi is the one to whom the Alexandrians put four types of questions: see above, note 33. "The bread of The Kingdom" occurs in *Ruth Rabba* on 2:14, on which passage cp. Daube, *The New Testament and Rabbinic Judaism*, 47 [153].

[58] E.g. *m. Ab.* 5:20.

[59] *b. Sanh.* 98a; Ps 95:7. R. Joshua ben Levi flourished in the first half of the third century A.D. See Strack and Billerbeck, *op. cit.*, vol. 2, 286, vol. 4, pt. 2, 993.

[60] *ZNW*, 25 (1926), 5 ff.

Two Incidents after the Last Supper

A. The Omission of the Fourth Cup

1. *The Omission of the Fourth Cup*

Of the four cups of wine prescribed for the Passover-eve service, the third, over which grace is said, is to be taken immediately after the supper.[1] In technical language it appears as "the cup of blessing," *kos shel berakha, kasa' debhirketha'*.[2] According to the Synoptics and Paul, this third cup is the cup of the New Covenant. Paul actually adopts its technical designation.[3]

There is, however, in Matthew and Mark a reference also to the fourth and last cup of the Passover liturgy. It is contained in the words:[4] "I will not drink henceforth of this fruit of the vine until I drink it new in my father's kingdom" or "in the kingdom of God." The meaning is that the fourth cup will not be taken, as would be the normal thing, at a subsequent stage of this service; it will be postponed till the kingdom is fully established.

Four points may be mentioned in support of this interpretation.

First, from the phrase "fruit of the vine" it is clear that Jesus, or whoever the author of the saying may be, has in mind a drinking after a further, formal benediction: "Blessed art thou, O Lord, who createst the fruit of the vine." Normally, on Passover eve, that would be the fourth cup.

Secondly, whereas under Jewish law additional, non-liturgical drinking is permissible between the first and second cups and between the second and third cups of the service, it is not permissible between the third and fourth.[5] Jesus's announcement, therefore, that he will drink no more from now, i.e. from after the third cup, till the next formal, liturgical drinking is in accordance with the Rabbinic rules concerning the interval between the third cup of the Passover-eve service and the last.

Thirdly, we have seen that the third cup, the "cup of blessing," is taken immediately after supper. Normally, on Passover eve, over the fourth cup (if we disregard accretions later than the New Testament era) there is completed a group of psalms called the Hallel or "hymn" and there is recited "the blessing of the song," *birkath hashshir*, consisting in an acknowledgment of the universal reign of God. It is doubtful whether the earliest "blessing of the song" is the piece beginning with "All thy works shall praise thee" (*yehalelukha*) or that beginning with "The breath of every living being shall bless

[1] *m. Pes.* 10:7.
[2] *b. Ber.* 51a.
[3] 1 Cor 10:16.
[4] Matt 26:29; Mark 14:25.
[5] *m. Pes.* 10:7.

thy name" (*nishmath kol ḥay*). (The glorification of Jesus in Phil 2:6 ff. shows striking affinities with the latter.) The question does not, however, affect our argument. In both of them we find the clause "and they shall assign kingship to thy name, our King" (*weyamlikhu 'eth shimekha malkenu*), giving expression to the principal theme. The fourth and last cup of the Passover-eve service, then, is taken to celebrate God's kingdom. When Jesus says that he will drink no more till he can drink in the kingdom, he is only substituting the real, perfect, final kingdom for that which is still to a large extent a matter of belief and hope. But he is evidently referring to the fourth cup.

Fourthly, the notice that "when they had sung a hymn they went out into the mount of Olives" now acquires a fuller sense. The implication is that they go out directly after the "hymn," without drinking the fourth cup and probably also without reciting the "blessing of the song." This portion of the liturgy is postponed till the arrival of the actual, final kingdom.

We do not intend here to discuss the Lukan version, except to say that it is far less technically Rabbinic than Matthew and Mark.

2. *"Only one kid"*

Perhaps a note may be added about "Only one kid" which, in some regions, is the last of the poems recited after the fourth cup. It does not seem to antedate the 15th century. Yet it is not inconceivable that it replaces a far earlier piece—maybe a less poetic one—the main idea of which was the same. The lack of direct evidence to prove the existence of a predecessor may be due to the fact that, like "Only one kid," it was of a somewhat esoteric character and, in consequence, never gained universal recognition but remained confined to one or two rites.

"Only one kid" is a story about a kid which was bought by "my father" for two coins, and devoured by a cat. The cat was killed by a dog. The dog was slain by a stick. The stick was burnt by fire. The fire was extinguished by water. The water was drunk up by an ox. The ox was slaughtered by a slaughterer. The slaughterer was slaughtered by the angel of death. The angel of death was slaughtered by the Holy one, blessed be he.

This is strangely reminiscent of Paul's declaration in 1 Corinthians[6] that, in the end, Jesus will destroy "all rule and authority and power"—which phrase clearly includes both human and non-human forces—and that the last enemy to be destroyed will be death. As is well known, 1 Corinthians is rich in references to Passover. (T.W. Manson thinks it was written shortly before that festival.[7]) The passage in question could be an allusion to a predecessor of "Only one kid." It is far from certain, but it would be rash to consider it as impossible.

B. The Sleeping Companions

According to Matthew and Mark, when Jesus and his disciples came to Gethsemane, they still formed a *ḥabhura*, a company united for the celebration of the Passover. To be sure, the Bible ordains that "in one house shall the passover be eaten."

[6] 1 Cor 15:23 ff.
[7] *JTS*, 46 (1945), 8.

But for one thing, the phrase "in one house" was from early times taken by the Rabbis to signify "in one company"; under Rabbinic law, therefore, a company was perfectly entitled to commence the meal in one place and continue it in another.[8] For another thing, Jesus and his disciples may well have finished the actual meal indoors, yet gone on with the service—prayers, recounting the deeds of God for Israel, praise of God—on the Mount of Olives; that would be enough to leave the *ḥabhura* intact. The Jewish Passover Haggadah, the liturgy used on Passover eve, contains a story about some Rabbis of the early 2nd cent. A.D., who spent the whole Passover night discussing the exodus from Egypt, until their disciples reminded them that it was dawning and the time had come to recite the morning prayer. We need not conclude that these scholars kept eating all the time: the *ḥabhura* remained in existence through the continued occupation with the great theme of the festival.

At Gethsemane, then, Jesus asked his disciples, the members of his company, to stay awake while he was saying a prayer by himself. He returned and discovered that they had not stayed awake. He admonished them, or Peter in particular, and prayed again. But again, when he returned, he found them asleep, and indeed, in a deeper slumber—it seems—than before. We are told that "their eyes were heavy"; Mark even states that "neither wist they what to answer him," which presumably means that, on being spoken to, they were able to reply at random only. Once more Jesus prayed, but now they fell into a proper sleep, as may be gathered from the emphatic καθεύδετε καὶ ἀναπαύεσθε, a reference to sleep as a complete rest (no matter whether we ascribe to the clause an imperative, an interrogative or any other sense). This time Jesus said, "It is enough, the hour is come, the Son of Man is betrayed" and so on.

It is generally held that Jesus requested his disciples to stay awake because he wanted to feel that they shared in his struggle. They failed to do so, however, thus leaving him alone.

This explanation is no doubt correct, only it is not the full explanation. If it were, one could understand the view of those scholars who regard the scene as legendary, as artificially composed in order to illustrate a theological truth. For it would be difficult to refute the argument that, first, Jesus's request to his disciples lacked a sufficiently specific motivation, and secondly, that their very natural sleepiness was treated as more significant than would seem warranted—except in the province of legend.

For a proper understanding of the scene, it is necessary to consider a rule transmitted by Jose ben Halaphta,[9] to the effect that if some members of a Passover company doze, the meal may be resumed again, but if they fall into deep sleep, it may not be resumed again.

Five points may be noted. First of all, R. Jose, though he lived about the middle of the 2nd cent. A.D., frequently preserves earlier traditions. The presumption is that the rule quoted, or a similar one, goes back to the New Testament era. (A remark in the Mekhilta[10] suggests that the rule may originally have been rested on the verse from

[8] *Mek.* on Exod 12:46; *Targum* Onk. and Jer. *Targum* (both translating "in one house" by "in one *ḥabhura*").

[9] *m. Pes.* 10:8.

[10] The concluding remark on Exod 12:42.

Exodus which refers to the Passover night as "the night of watchfulness." But we need not here settle this question.) Secondly, in the Mishnah, the rule occurs in a paragraph dealing with the stage of the celebration after the ceremonial eating of the prescribed portion of the Passover lamb. The case contemplated is that of members of the company getting tired during this later stage of the service. The rule, that is, applies to precisely that part of the celebration which Jesus and his disciples had reached when they came to Gethsemane. Thirdly, there are Talmudic precepts[11] designed to ensure that even children taking part in the service should stay awake at least until the completion of the essential ceremony—which, after the destruction of the Temple, was the eating of unleavened bread. (From the fall of the Temple, the lamb, like all sacrifices, ceased to be offered.) Modern writers are apt to miss the point of these warnings: they must have originated in circles where it would have been a grave matter if any members of the company had fallen asleep during the first part of the evening. Fourthly, R. Ashi, at the beginning of the 5th cent., defines the meaning of "a doze," which does not bring about a dissolution of the *ḥabhura*, as opposed to "a proper sleep," which does. A man, he says, merely dozes "if, when addressed, he replies but does not know how to answer sensibly."[12] This late comment is curiously reminiscent of Mark's description of the state in which the disciples were when Jesus returned the second time: "neither wist they what to answer him." There is, however, nothing surprising in the coincidence. As soon as any relevance is attached to the distinction between dozing and sleeping, some criterion like that recognized by Mark and R. Ashi is bound to be set up. Fifthly, in the Sectarian Manual of Discipline discovered a few years ago, falling asleep in the assembly is considered a major breach of discipline, punishable by exclusion from the assembly for thirty days.[13]

We may conclude that, though Jesus asked his disciples to stay awake because he wanted to feel they were with him, yet his request had also a more specific meaning: they should not let the *ḥabhura* come to an early close. Similarly, while the giving in of the disciples to their natural desire for rest did leave him alone, it left him alone not only in a general sense but also in the sense that the Passover union was ended.

Luke has abandoned all reference to the Rabbinic law concerning the Passover *ḥabhura*. Jesus does not ask his disciples to stay awake: he tells them to pray. The distinction between slumber and sleep plays no part. Jesus prays and returns only once. The disciples fall asleep, not from natural fatigue, but from sorrow. Jesus's final remark is not "It is enough" and so on, implying that from now he must go forward without them, but a repetition of the command to pray.

Luke almost certainly depends on the longer account. We need not decide whether he did not understand the Rabbinic provisions or whether he thought his readers might not understand them. What is interesting is that he has not turned the narrative into a legend, but has left it its historical, factual character. If the scene is dissociated from

[11] *t. Pes.* 10:9; *b. Pes.* 109a.

[12] *b. Pes.* 120b.

[13] See J. Hempel, *Die Funde in der Wüste, Almanach auf das Jahr des Herrn* (1954), 13. No such serious view, however, seems to be taken of the offence in Acts 20:9 ff.

the Rabbinic law concerning a *ḥabhura*, then a request to the disciples to stay awake, or the attribution of a profound significance to their sleep, assumes the colour of legend. Luke, however, when he dropped the allusions to Rabbinic law, also dropped both the request to stay awake and the interpretation of the sleep of the companions as placing Jesus apart.

The omission of the scene from John is part of a wider problem, into which it is not intended here to inquire.

A Prayer Pattern in Judaism

Mark[1] attributes to Jesus in the garden of Gethsemane this prayer: "Abba, Father, all things are possible unto thee: take away this cup from me; nevertheless not what I will but what thou wilt." Substantially this is confirmed by both Matthew and Luke. Matthew[2] has: "Father if it be possible"—this corresponds to "all things are possible unto thee"—"let this cup pass from me"—Mark's "take away this cup from me"—"nevertheless not as I will but as thou wilt"—just as in Mark. Again Luke:[3] "Father, if thou be willing"—meaning "all things are possible unto thee"—"remove this cup from me, nevertheless not my will but thine be done."

RGG[4] calls this combination of desire and self-dedication the *Urspannung*, the fundamental tension, of all prayer; and Heiler,[5] following Hoffding, speaks of "the highest moment in the history of prayer." He puts this prayer above those occurring in Jeremiah because it expresses not only trust but surrender. Precisely if one agrees with these views, it may be interesting to find out whether the prayer has a traditional setting, and if so, of what nature. However, for this purpose, we must not simplify, as these scholars do, who (understandably, from their theological standpoint) concentrate on the antithesis wish–surrender. The structure of the prayer is not twofold, wish–surrender, but threefold, acknowledgment ("Father, all things are possible unto thee"), wish ("take away this cup"), surrender ("not what I will but what thou wilt"). It is true that in Matthew and Luke the first part is somewhat weakened. (Many commentators have, of course, noticed this part. Lohmeyer[6] draws attention to it. Allen[7] considers it rather unsuitable here.)

Now we need only look up Singer's Prayer-Book,[8] used throughout the British Empire, to see that the prayer of a Jew on his death-bed opens thus: "I acknowledge before thee, O Lord, that my cure and my death are in thy hands. May it be thy will to send me a perfect healing. Yet if my death be fully determined by thee, I will in love accept it at thy hand, and may my death be an atonement for all my sins," etc. Here then we have the exact structure of Jesus's prayer: "I acknowledge, O Lord, that my cure

[1] Mark 14:35 f.

[2] Matt 26:39.

[3] Luke 22:42.

[4] Schmitz, in *Die Religion in Geschichte und Gegenwart*, 2nd ed. (1928), 881, s.v. Gebet: III A. Im NT.

[5] Prayer, transl. from the German by McComb (1923), 123.

[6] *Das Evangelium des Markus* (1937), 315.

[7] *The Gospel according to S. Matthew*, 3rd ed. (1912), 279.

[8] *The Authorised Daily Prayer Book of the United Hebrew Congregations*, with a new translation by Singer, 9th ed. (1912), 317.

and my death are in thy hands"—"Father, all things are possible unto thee." "May it be thy will to send me healing"—"take away this cup from me." "Yet if my death be determined, I will in love accept it and may my death be an atonement" etc.—"nevertheless not what I will but what thou wilt." Needless to say, there are differences in contents. In Jesus's prayer it is not a question of disease and recovery and, above all, the concluding part does not refer to any sins committed by him. In the Jewish prayer, essentially a confession or associated with one, this reference is appropriate.

The version in Singer's Prayer-Book is due to Hermann Adler, Chief Rabbi towards the end of the last century.[9] He took most of it from the Spanish-Jewish scholar Naḥmanides,[10] of the first half and middle of the 13th century—except that in Naḥmanides the mention of atonement comes first and that of love second, in a fresh paragraph: "I acknowledge, O Lord, that my cure and my death are in thy hands. May it be thy will to send me a perfect healing. Yet if I die may my death be an atonement.... Lord of the World, behold I am receiving death in truth and joy, and make me worthy to testify to the unity of the name of thy holiness in abundant love." Still, while such is the declaration according to Naḥmanides given in *Siddur 'Oṣar Hattephilloth*,[11] in his *Torath Ha'adham*[12] the portion commencing "Lord of the World" is not to be found at all (nor in Jacob ben Asher in the first half of the 14th century).[13] The confession here runs: "I acknowledge" etc. "May it be thy will" etc. "Yet if I die may my death be an atonement ... and give me a share in the garden of Eden" etc. Probably the paragraph "Lord of the World" was added to Naḥmanides's prayer by later editors; in itself it may be quite old—there are many Talmudic passages breathing its spirit.[14] The important point is always the same, and indeed comes out the more clearly the shorter the version: acknowledgment, wish, surrender.

Naḥmanides intimates that the prayer has long been in use: "We have received it thus from pious men." There is no reason for doubting that, in outline, it existed in New Testament times. We know from Tannaitic sources[15] that it was the practice to make confession on the death-bed. Moreover, the words "May my death be an atonement for all my sins" are prescribed by the Mishnah[16] where a criminal sentenced to death is unable to confess in detail. And that, in general, these words counterbalance a petition for rescue may be gathered from the interesting prayer (in which, obviously, they cannot have

[9] *Prayer Book*, Preface, VII.

[10] Abrahams, *Annotated Edition of the Authorised Daily Prayer Book* (1914), CCXXV f., note on 317. I am grateful for additional advice received from Dr. A. Altmann of Manchester.

[11] New York (1946), vol. 2, *sedher widduy*, towards the end of the volume.

[12] I have consulted the editions Constantinople (1518), 7a f., and Venice (1595), 14b.

[13] *Turim*, vol. 2 (*Yore Dhe'a*), 338, 2.

[14] Ps 101:1, "I will sing of judgment and mercy," is interpreted as meaning "I will sing to thee whether thou dealest with me in mercy or in judgment" (*Midrash Psalms ad loc.*, *y. Ber.* 14b); for R. Akiba, Deut 6:5, "Thou shalt love the Lord with all thy soul," means "even if he take thy soul" (*b. Ber.* 61b); Isa 53:10, "Yet it pleased the Lord to bruise him ... when thou shalt make his soul an offering, he shall see his seed," according to R. Huna means that "God crushes him in whom he delights, but only if the suffering is received in love" (*b. Ber.* 5a).

[15] *b. Shab.* 32a.

[16] *m. Sanh.* 6:2.

this function for the first time) to be said on entering a bath-house:[17] "May it be thy will, O Lord, to deliver me from this ... and let no sin befall me. Yet if I fall into sin may my death be an atonement for all my sins."

Of the combination wish-surrender, we have indeed other early testimony, in circumstances not dissimilar to those of Jesus's or Naḥmanides's prayer. (We are not concerned with wish or surrender by itself. Naturally, there are plenty of instances of the former, "Save now,"[18] "Remember how I have walked before thee,"[19] but also some of the latter, from Eli's acceptance of his house's doom onwards.[20]) R. Eliezer the Great, of the end of the 1st and beginning of the 2nd century, recommends this "short prayer" in a place of danger:[21] "Do thy will in heaven above; grant tranquillity of spirit to those who fear thee below, and do that which is good in thy sight; blessed art thou, O Lord, who hearkenest unto prayer." There is something reminiscent of the antithesis under discussion in the pair "grant tranquillity of mind—do that which is good in thy sight."

But in fact the antithesis goes right back to the Old Testament. When King David has to leave Jerusalem because of Absalom's revolt, the priest Zadok brings the ark out of the city to him. Whereupon David says:[22] "Carry back the ark.... If I shall find favour in the eyes of the Lord, he will bring me back again and shew me the city and his habitation; but if he thus say, I have no delight in thee, behold, here am I, let him do to me as seemeth good unto him."

At this juncture I ought of course to go into the wider question whether we may class an utterance like this with prayer. From the point of view of form criticism, does David's pronouncement of wish and surrender fall under prayer, or at least is there an affinity? I have time only to claim that the answer is in the affirmative. I would just point out that, for instance, David's answer to the prophet Gad[23] has become part of the Jewish daily liturgy, under the name of *taḥanun*, "petition for grace,"[24] and figures as a prayer already in Sirach.[25] (The prophet gave David the choice between various punishments. "And David said unto Gad, I am in a great strait; let us fall now into the hands of the Lord, for his mercies are great; and let me not fall into the hand of man.")

Actually, in my opinion, a general's last word on the eve of battle is also relevant. Joab orders his brother to take on the Ammonites in the rear while he is fighting the Syrians in front, and adds:[26] "Be strong and let us be valiant for our people; and the Lord do that which seemeth him good." That this application of the pattern, encouragement involving a wish-surrender to God's decision, lived on in Judaism is shewn

[17] *b. Ber.* 60a.

[18] Ps 118:25.

[19] 2 Kgs 20:3.

[20] 1 Sam 3:18.

[21] *t. Ber.* 3:7.

[22] 2 Sam 15:25 f.

[23] 2 Sam 24:14.

[24] *Prayer Book*, 62; Abrahams, LXXVI.

[25] Sir 2:18. For the present discussion the verse retains its interest even if it should be a secondary insertion.

[26] 2 Sam 10:12; 1 Chr 19:13.

by its recurrence, in an expanded form, in 1 Maccabees.[27] Judas addresses his men in these words: "Gird yourselves and be valiant men and be ready on the morrow to fight against these Gentiles, for it is better to die in battle than to look upon the evils of our people and the Holy Place. Nevertheless, as may be the will in Heaven so shall he do."

I would venture an explanation why we find earlier evidence for the twofold structure, wish-surrender, than the threefold, acknowledgment-wish-surrender. The twofold structure is indeed expressive of the *Urspannung*. The situation is so elemental that, as observed above, scholars dealing with Jesus's prayer have almost overlooked the introductory acknowledgment. This acknowledgment, I suspect, belongs to a more formalized stage, namely, to the solemn confession expected of a Jew preparing for death. Here we get more than the spontaneous pair wish-surrender; we get first acknowledgment of God's free action and judgment, very important where, in a way, the course of events must appear inevitable, and then only wish and surrender, the latter implying the hope of expiation. This is not to maintain that the opening by acknowledgment is artificial. Jeremiah[28] prays, "Heal me, O Lord, for thou art my praise," and Sirach[29] exhorts his reader, "My son, in sickness pray unto God, for he can heal." (The eighth of the Eighteen Benedictions[30] is very close to these two passages: "Heal us, O Lord, for thou art our praise; vouchsafe a perfect healing, for thou art God, King, a faithful and merciful healer.") From the latter especially it is not a far cry to "Thou canst heal, save me." None the less there is something ceremonious about a weighty acknowledgment prefacing wish and surrender.

It should perhaps be noted that in Matthew and Mark (though not in Luke) Jesus prays three times: often these formal prayers are customarily repeated. Codex Bezae and Itala may well be inferior in Mark 14:39 to the majority reading, which adds specifically, on the second occasion, that "he spake the same words." At any rate, Matthew clearly assumes repetition. But it is again significant that he quotes the full, formal prayer, with the acknowledgment at the beginning, only the first time; the second time he has only wish and surrender, the more natural, spontaneous parts; and the third time he is content with telling us that "he spake the same words." The fact that, in Mark, on the first occasion, a summary of the prayer in a dependent statement—"he prayed that the hour might pass"—is followed by a direct, full quotation—"he said, Abba, Father..."—seems another indication of the prayer being thought of as something like a ritual; and the address "Abba, Father" points the same way.

A good many problems remain—the psychological and religious background of the combination wish and surrender, the relation between the Synoptic prayer and the parallel in John,[31] the relation between both and an allusion in Hebrews,[32] the connection between the tripartite prayer here analysed and certain Rabbinic views about the proper arrangement of a prayer, and so forth. (R. Simlai, of the 3rd century, favoured the

[27] 1 Mac 3:58–60.
[28] Jer 17:14.
[29] Sir 38:9.
[30] *Prayer Book*, 47.
[31] John 12:27 f.
[32] Heb 5:7 f.

sequence praise-request,[33] basing himself on a prayer of Moses:[34] "O Lord, thou hast begun to shew thy greatness, for what God can do according to thy works? I pray thee, let me go over." R. Hanina, of the 4th century, explained[35] that in the first section of the Eighteen Benedictions the person praying was comparable to a servant eulogizing his master, in the second to one requesting largesse, in the third to one giving thanks for largesse received.) There is no time for them now. May I, however, mention that if my suggestion is correct, an old crux disappears. It is sometimes asked—a little pedantically, no doubt—how, as Jesus prayed at some distance from the disciples and, in addition, these were dozing or asleep, the contents of his prayer could be known. This question can now be answered, at least as far as the general structure is concerned. Jesus's prayer follows an established Jewish pattern; he chose that hour to make the traditional declaration, accepting death in love.[36]

[33] *b. Ber.* 32a; *A. Zar.* 7b.

[34] Deut 3:24 f.

[35] *b. Ber.* 34a.

[36] I am indebted to Professor W. D. Davies of Princeton University for his criticisms.

Wine in the Bible*

To go on to my second subject—towards the end of the last century Harnack contended that, though at the farewell meal Jesus shared with his disciples the drink which he associated with his destiny happened to be wine, that was not essential; and for a considerable time it was open to believers to commemorate the Last Supper with water.[1] This proposition was at once attacked by Zahn[2] and Jülicher[3] and has found little acceptance. Nevertheless a number of scholars today go further and hold that, in the primitive Church, the commemoration required neither wine nor water. If wine was available, all the better: its addition to the bread would make the theological meaning clearer. But the only ingredient needed was bread.[4] Lietzmann distinguishes between a first stage, when the disciples after their master's death relived the daily meal companionship with him, with bread only, and a second stage, when the farewell meal was singled out, with bread and wine.[5] One wonders whether, if the matter were not of such deep religious concern (Jülicher speaks of "bulwarks of preconceived opinions"[6]), a yet more radical thesis would not command a strong following, to wit, that Jesus himself assigned no special implication to the drink.

On balance, the evidence does not warrant so negative a conclusion. Still, it is worth while to go through the pointers in that direction. Before continuing, however, I would plead once for all that while I, conservatively, speak of Jesus doing or not doing

* Martin Sullivan, Dean of St. Paul's Cathedral, London, wrote of the publication *Wine in the Bible,* dedicated to Charles Kingsley and Margaret Barrett, "Professor Daube gave the St. Paul's Lecture in 1966. This was subsequently published under the title "He that Cometh" and enjoyed a wide sale both here and in the U.S.A. Copies were also ordered from many parts of the world and the Lecture was quoted by Father Corbishley in his Lent Book for 1974. Towards the end of that Lecture Professor Daube said 'I have not treated the problem of the wine … if you wish to hear my views, you will have to ask me another time.' Acting on this hint the London Diocesan Council for Christian-Jewish Understanding invited him to give the thirteenth lecture in 1974. We were delighted that he was able to accept despite the fact that he is now resident in California and no longer at All Souls, Oxford. The Lecture made a profound impression on those who heard it in the Çrypt of St. Paul's on September 10th, 1974, and we are confident it will arouse much interest in its published form." The first part of the lecture was devoted to the topic of Drunkenness in the Bible (To appear in Vol. 3).

[1] A. v. Harnack, "Uber das Gnostische Buch Pistis-Sophia. Brod und Wasser," in *Texte und Untersuchungen*, vol. 7, pt. 2 (1891), 115 ff.

[2] T. v. Zahn, *Brot und Wasser im Abendmahl der alten Kirche* (1892).

[3] A. Julicher, "Zur Geschichte der Abendmahlsfeier," in *Theologische Abhandlungen Carl von Weizsacker gewidmet* (1892), 215 ff.

[4] C. K. Barrett, *The First Epistle to the Corinthians* (1968), 266 ff.

[5] H. Lietzmann, *Messe und Herrenmahl*, 3rd ed. (1955), 211 ff.

[6] A. Julicher *op. cit.*, 235: *Bollwerke von Vorurtheilen.*

so-and-so, the more critical school that judges it futile to reconstruct his true words or acts should have no difficulty in going along with my argumentation, by simply substituting Jesus doing or not doing so-and-so "in the earliest preaching of the community."

For a start, then, let us note the textual situation. With regard to the bread, there is a nucleus of a proclamation which is the same in Mark,[7] Matthew,[8] Luke,[9] and Paul's First Epistle to the Corinthians,[10] namely, "This is my body." In my previous Lecture in this Cathedral I maintained that these words were indeed Jesus's decisive self-revelation.[11] The Passover eve company used to eat a piece of unleavened bread—in some groups perhaps a piece of the lamb—thought to represent the longed for Messiah and called *Aphiqoman*, "the Coming One." By stating "This is my body" (possibly, at an Aramaic stage, "This is me"), Jesus announced that the Messiah had now arrived in his person. No such stable nucleus exists with regard to the wine. Mark[12] and Matthew[13] offer "This is my blood of the testament" or "of the covenant." Luke has come down to us in two variants. One reads "This cup is the new testament—or the new covenant—in my blood,"[14] agreeing with 1 Corinthians,[15] the other contains no explanation of the wine at all. This discrepancy between the two elements is striking.

Next, the view, adverted to above, that in ancient Christian celebrations the drink was optional is certainly correct. Luke and 1 Corinthians depict Jesus as asking for future re-enactments of the Last Supper. However, in Luke, the commandment "Do this as my memorial" is attached solely to the bread, with no parallel for the wine[16]; and Paul has Jesus say of the bread, "Do this as my memorial," but of the cup, "Do this, as often as you drink, as my memorial."[17] "As often as you drink"—so there were occasions without this part. The apostle, it should be observed, is reminding his charges of the ultimate, authoritative model of their holy gatherings, hence no doubt formulating carefully. Here may be the place to remark that if, as is most likely, Rabbinic terminology underlies the clause with which he introduces his account of the Last Supper—"For I received from the Lord that which I also handed on to you"[18]—the receiving must have involved the same immediacy as the handing on.[19] The apostle, that is, considers himself to have this account directly from Jesus. Nor is it necessary, as Lietzmann assumes,[20] to think of the meeting on the road to Damascus as the only possible oppor-

[7] Mark 14:22.

[8] Matt 26:26.

[9] Luke 22:19.

[10] 1 Cor 11:24.

[11] *He That Cometh* (1965), 6 ff. [429 ff.]; see also "The Significance of the *Afikoman*," in *Pointer*, 3 (1968), 4 f. [425 ff.].

[12] Mark 14:24.

[13] Matt 26:28.

[14] Luke 22:20.

[15] 1 Cor 11:25.

[16] Luke 22:19 f.

[17] 1 Cor 11:24 f.

[18] 1 Cor 11:23.

[19] See W. D. Davies, *Paul and Rabbinic Judaism* (1948), 248 f.

[20] H. Lietzmann, *An die Korinther I und II*, 4th ed. by W. G. Kummel (1949), 57.

tunity: there is reason to believe that he had visions after this one.[21] Cullmann indeed submits that since, for Paul, the exalted Lord lived on in Church tradition, even what was gathered from the latter might be boldly labelled as gathered from the former[22]—possible, if somewhat speculative.

Again, as is well known, the early sources contain many references to bread only. The Pentecostal community of Acts "devoted themselves to the breaking of bread and the prayers,"[23] and "day by day, attending the temple and breaking bread in their homes, they partook of food with gladness."[24] We are told how "on the first day of the week, when the disciples came together to break bread, Paul preached";[25] and during his perilous voyage as a prisoner, he urged his companions to take a meal with him, "took bread and, giving thanks to God in the presence of all, broke it and began to eat."[26] The Didache lays down, "When you assemble on the Lord's Day, break the bread and give thanks,"[27] which may well come from a different stratum than another chapter with a bread and wine Eucharist.[28] No doubt in some such passages the bread can be interpreted as shorthand for bread and wine, in some as belonging to Lietzmann's daily meal companionship as distinct from the commemoration of the Last Supper. Still, it is cumulative evidence of some weight.

Of particular relevance is the description in Luke of Jesus's appearance at Emmaus after his crucifixion. At first his disciples did not recognize him; but when "he took the bread and blessed and broke it and gave it to them,"[29] they did, and later on, at Jerusalem, they reported "how he was known to them in the breaking of the bread."[30] There can be little doubt that what enlightened them was his repetition—maybe slightly modified—of the self-revelation "This is my body." Surprising support is furnished by the Gospel according to the Hebrews. James had vowed not to eat till he had seen the resurrected Lord. The latter appeared to him and some others and said: "Bring a table and bread." He then "took the bread, blessed and gave it to James the Just and said to him, My brother, eat your bread, for the son of man is risen from them that sleep."[31] Here the self-revelation in the breaking of the bread is spelled out. (I shall not go into a further, remarkable affinity between Luke and this Gospel: in both, the disciples to whom Jesus showed himself had not, if we go by the mainstream of the tradition, been present at the Last Supper.)

However, despite these data, the notion that Jesus endowed the drink, too, with a novel symbolism is so firmly embedded in the oldest accessible records that it would be

[21] See e.g. Acts 22:17, 26:16; 2 Cor 12:1 ff.

[22] O. Cullmann, *The Early Church*, translated by A. J. B. Higgins (1956), 59 ff. I owe this reference to Professor C. K. Barrett who kindly read the typescript of the Lecture.

[23] Acts 2:42.

[24] Acts 2:46.

[25] Acts 20:7.

[26] Acts 27:35.

[27] Didache 14:1.

[28] Didache 9:1 ff.

[29] Luke 24:30.

[30] Luke 24:35.

[31] Gospel according to the Hebrews 8.

rash to dismiss it. A better way of coming to terms with the secondary role of this element is by bearing in mind its lesser standing in the Passover eve liturgy.

The unleavened bread belonged to the three distinctive Passover foods—the other two being the lamb and bitter herbs[32]—which, we learn from Rabbi Gamaliel I (Paul's teacher), must be specifically explained in the course of the service.[33] Wine was prescribed also on the Sabbath and other festivals, though not four cups as on Passover eve;[34] and, above all, there was no duty to enunciate a solemn explanation of the wine. This difference alone is of no little consequence. On the Passover eves following the crucifixion, when the believers would add items from the new exodus to those concerning the one from Egypt, there was a definite place for a pronouncement respecting the bread, but none for the wine. Considering that some of the *Grundstock*, the core fabric, of the gospels must have crystallized in that fashion, by supplementing the established ceremonial,[35] a degree of uncertainty as to the wine should be expected.

But the Passover wine ranked behind the bread not only in this formal respect but also in substantive import: the latter feature was indeed the cause of the former. For the purpose in hand, it is enough to observe that nothing like "the Coming One" was ever seen in the wine. So again, an utterance of Jesus's about the wine could be longer taking root in the celebration and be subject to more varied treatment.

At this juncture, attention may be called to an apparent paradox: while, as observed above, the archaic sources are more expansive about the bread than the wine, Jesus at the Last Supper could be briefer—and in Mark,[36] Matthew[37] and the shorter Luke[38] is represented as briefer—about it. (This Lucan variant has no proclamation over the wine at all.) The point is that the same recognized, weighty bread symbolism which accounts for the general prominence of this element also rendered his tersest comment upon it meaningful. "This is my body," said of the piece standing for "the Coming One," was a full disclosure of his Messiahship. An analogous assertion concerning the drink would have conveyed nothing. It had to be at least something like "This is my blood of the testament," as in Mark[39] and Matthew,[40] or "This cup is the new testament in my blood," as in the longer variant of Luke[41] and 1 Corinthians.[42] In fact, Mark and Matthew append "which is shed for many"—Matthew going on "for the remission of sins"—and the longer Luke "which is shed for you."

At one time I considered whether "which is shed for many or you" must not necessarily date from before the crucifixion. Crucifixion, unlike, say, being cut into pieces

[32] Exod 12:8; Num 9:11.

[33] *m. Pes.* 10:5; Passover Eve Service—see E. D. Goldschmidt, *Die Pessach-Haggada* (1936), 62.

[34] *m. Pes.* 10:1.

[35] See my "The Earliest Structure of the Gospels," in *NTS*, 5 (1959), 174 ff. [329 ff.].

[36] Mark 14:22.

[37] Matt 26:26.

[38] Luke 22:19.

[39] Mark 14:24.

[40] Matt 26:28.

[41] Luke 22:20.

[42] 1 Cor 11:25.

in battle, involves no shedding of blood in the narrowest sense. So I wondered whether those words must not reflect an anticipation of something like death in a violent disturbance. However, this would be to press the text too much. As early as in the Book of Numbers, "to shed blood" embraces any killing,[43] and when the Psalmist asks God to revenge "the blood of your servants which is shed,"[44] he is not excluding people innocently hanged or pressed to death. In the Fourth Gospel, blood does actually flow.[45]

The declaration "This is my body," it may be reiterated, is accompanied by no elucidating clause either in Mark, Matthew or the shorter Luke. Its message, unlike that about the wine, was intelligible from the familiar rite of "the Coming One." The longer variant of Luke affixes "which is given for you." This is palpably an interpretation of Paul's "which is for you." Already in several ancient manuscripts we find it, or similar interpretations, intruding into 1 Corinthians;[46] and all the authorities are agreed that it is, in essence, correct—from which basis, understandably, they proceed to look on Paul's formulation as clumsy.[47] In reality, the latter just does not equal "which is given for you." Admittedly, his Greek is deficient; but if he had wished to express this—from the linguistic point of view—not too complicated idea, somehow he would have managed.

The idea he does express is significantly different, and it ought to be respected. Roughly, "which is for you" amounts to "which is for your good." This preliminary paraphrase, however, can be provided with more precision. Paul makes much use of *hyper*, "for," where it is a question of action in a person's interest or concern about him.[48] The words in their position here have a Semitic ring: one is reminded of Hebrew *'asher ba'adhkhem* or *shellakhem*. Probably the best-known sentence in the New Testament where somebody is "for," *hyper*, somebody is the saying: "He that is not against us is for us."[49] Quite a few pertinent lines occur in the Psalms: "My enemies shall turn back; this I know for God is for me, *li*,"[50] "If it had not been the Lord who was for us, *lanu*, they had swallowed us up quick,"[51] "The Lord is for me, *li*, I will not fear."[52] The Septuagint does not feel compelled to translate over-literally. The last-quoted verse runs "The Lord is my helper and I will not fear," and it figures thus in the Epistle to the Hebrews.[53] Naturally, this expression "to be for somebody" continues in post-Biblical speech. Hillel, around 15 B.C., exclaimed, " If I am not for myself, *li*, who is for me,

[43] Num 35:33; cp. Deut 21:27.

[44] Ps 79:10. Cp. also passages like Ezek 22:3, 27; Joel 4:19; Prov 6:17.

[45] John 19:34.

[46] See the apparatus ad 1 Cor 11:24.

[47] C. K. Barrett *op. cit.*, 266.

[48] F. Blass and A. Debrunner, *A Greek Grammar of the New Testament*, based on 9th–10th German edition, trsl. by R. W. Funk (1961), 121.

[49] Mark 9:40; Luke 9:50. In the opposite maxim, Matt 12:39 and Luke 11:23, *meta* is employed.

[50] Ps 56:10. Septuagint: "for you are my God."

[51] Ps 124:1. Septuagint: *en*.

[52] Ps 118:6. A curious coincidence may be noted. The medieval hymn *Adon Olam*, "Lord of the Universe" (Singer's *Authorised Daily Prayer Book* [1890], 3) concludes with these words but, like the Septuagint, it adds the conjunction "and": "and I will not fear." However, there is no dependence on the Septuagint—the addition is necessitated by the metre.

[53] Heb 13:6.

li?";[54] and incidentally, it is not impossible that this motto includes an esoteric sense, "If the Lord is not for me, who is for me"?[55] The upshot is that "This is my body which is for you" (or "This is me who am for you") in 1 Corinthians means "This is my body which is your help, your salvation" (or "This is me who am your helper, your saviour"). The distortion in the longer Luke is readily explicable. For one thing, it must have been extremely tempting to obtain a perfect parallel to the blood "which is shed for you," and that would lead to the body "which is given for you."

By "This is my body," then, Jesus identified himself as Messiah, without—if we discount the longer variant of Luke—any reference to his death. This is not to deny that the approaching end may have been greatly in his and his entourage's minds as he made this pronouncement; but the pronouncement as such neither predicted nor even hinted at it. By contrast, his statement concerning the wine did indicate that he was about to lay down his life.

The fact that a solemn explanation of the drink was not obligatory in the Passover eve celebration does not mean that it was never discussed. From third-century Rabbis we hear[56] that the four cups prescribed for this service correspond to four terms for redemption: a suggestion of this kind would be a very suitable contribution to the festivity. At any rate, Jesus linked the "cup of blessing"[57] taken directly after the meal—the third of the four Passover eve cups[58]—with his testament or covenant sealed, so to speak, by his blood. A momentous proclamation, yet on a different level from, subsidiary to, the Messianic claim "This is my body."

Of the two versions, "This is my blood of the testament" in Mark[59] and Matthew[60] (Matthew depending on Mark) and "This cup is the new testament in my blood" in the longer Luke[61] and 1 Corinthians[62] (Luke depending on Corinthians), the latter is likely to be the original. (Except that the epithet "new" may be due to Paul's preoccupation with this concept.[63]) First, it was not the wine which was peculiar to the Passover eve celebration but the four cups of it.[64] Hence any discourse respecting the drink was apt to focus on, speak of, the cups: the Rabbinic exposition just adduced, which connects the four cups with various terms for redemption, is typical. Secondly, the stark "This is my blood," evoking the idea of a drinking of blood, can hardly go back to a thoroughly Jewish milieu.[65] Thirdly, the route from the other version to this one is easy to trace. From the outset there would be some tendency to assimilate "This cup is the [new] testament in my blood" to the more central "This is my body." It must have enormously

[54] *m. Ab.* 1:14.
[55] Cp. Rashi ad *b. Sukk.* 53a.
[56] *y. Pes.* 37b.
[57] 1 Cor 10:16; *b. Ber.* 51a.
[58] *m. Pes.* 10:7; Passover Eve Service—E. D. Goldschmidt *op. cit.*, 78.
[59] Mark 14:24.
[60] Matt 26:28.
[61] Luke 22:20.
[62] 1 Cor 11:25.
[63] Ce.g. 2 Cor 5:17.
[64] *m. Pes.* 10:1.
[65] See W. D. Davies, *Paul and Rabbinic Judaism* (1948), 244 ff., C. K. Barrett *op. cit.*, 268.

gained in strength as the original significance of the latter utterance was forgotten and, from self-revelation, it became a prediction of self-surrender. The sensible thing now was to employ the same simple structure for both statements: "This is my body—this is my blood." We have already seen that, conversely, the longer variant of Luke assimilates the pronouncement over the bread to that over the wine, by putting "which is given for you" in analogy to "which is shed for you."

It would lead too far afield to inquire into the function of the blood. The preposition *en* in "This cup is the new testament in, *en*, my blood" may denote "in," "through," "for the sake of," "at the price of" or any combination of these. Nor is the problem eased if we start from "This is my blood of the testament."

What is important here is that the comparison as such, the likening of wine to blood, would be readily understood by the meal company. Wine can be styled in Hebrew "blood of the grape [or grapes]."[66] Moreover, the Passover eve wine was red. This is indeed one of the cases bringing out the difficulties of dating. The earliest extant Talmudic mention of the rule to use red wine belongs to the first half of the fourth century A.D.[67] Had we no other evidence, we might deduce that the custom grew up in that period and no doubt we should find plausible causes. Yet the report of the Last Supper shows that it goes back considerably farther.

To sum up, Jesus's revolutionary explanations of the bread and the wine emanated from portions of the liturgy of very different character. "This is my body" had regard to the piece named "the Coming One" and meant that the Messiah was no longer hidden but actually there in person. "This cup is the [new] testament in my blood," or, if you prefer, "This is my blood of the testament," by likening the wine to his blood, looked forward to his death as initiating a better aeon. The incongruities listed at the beginning are largely the result of a growing together of these related yet, in a way, disparate pronouncements. In substance, the former, fundamental one was assimilated to the latter, that is to say, was taken as another reference to the supreme sacrifice. In form, it was chiefly the latter one which was assimilated to the former, except for the longer Luke's "which is given for you."

An old crux in the final understanding, the non-Jewish pairing off of body and blood as the two constituents of a person, now proves tractable. In Jesus's declarations as he intended them, this antithesis played no part. When he informed his disciples, about to eat a piece of unleavened bread as "the Coming One," "This is my body [or me]," he was referring to himself as an entire being, not to a part marked off from blood. "The Coming One" was come. Again, when, as they reached the third cup, he said "This cup is the [new] testament in my blood" or "This is my blood of the testament," he was speaking of his blood dedicated for the new dispensation, without opposing it to a second part of him, the body. He would sacrifice his life. It is the subsequent turning of "This is my body" into another forecast of tragedy, practically an equivalent of the statement about the wine, which produced the inauthentic pair body and blood.

[66] Gen 49:11; Deut 32:14; Sir 39:26.
[67] Rabbi Jeremiah in *y. Pes.* 37c.

Once the initial relation of the two utterances is appreciated, it will be found to have left numerous traces in New Testament writings. A concept as influential as that of the believers as the body—not the blood—of Christ belongs here.[68] I am not, of course, saying that a host of other factors have not contributed to its history. But I refrain from pursuing this vast topic.

Rather, in conclusion, some reflections on two relatively peripheral matters.

First, as to a detail concerning the manner of communal drinking. In general,[69] the participants in a Sabbath or festival meal had each his own cup before him, and this practice prevailed also on Passover.[70] In a third-century fantasy about the Messianic banquet, however, it seems to be assumed that King David's cup will make the round among the company.[71] It is possible, therefore, that when Mark and Matthew stress that at the Last Supper all drank from the cup over which Jesus predicted his death, that is designed to underline the Messianic nature of this celebration.[72]

Second, according to Mark[73] and Matthew,[74] Jesus, after his proclamation regarding the wine, vowed to drink no more till he would drink in God's Kingdom. The message was plainly that the ultimate resolution was at hand. However, I have argued elsewhere[75] that it may well have had a more specific, situational content, anchored in the Passover eve service. "The cup of blessing," we have seen, was the third of the four cups of that ceremony; and whereas additional, non-liturgical drinking was permitted between the first and second cups and between the second and third ones, it was not between the third and fourth ones.[76] So Jesus was pointing forward to the last cup: he would drink no more in this age, ready to drink the fourth cup in the next. The full import of these words, understood thus, will be clear when it is remembered that the fourth cup was traditionally associated with an acknowledgment of God's universal reign. All creation, a song recited over it ran,[77] "assigns kingship to you, our King." Jesus indicated that, presently, what had so far been to a large extent a matter of hope and trust would be reality; he delayed the fourth cup till the new world was truly established.

At any rate, the vow is surely relevant to the notice in Mark[78] that Jesus declined the spiced wine tendered to him before his crucifixion. The custom of relieving by this means the anguish of criminals about to be executed is attested in the Rabbinic sources.[79] Mark does not explain the negative response: how could readers forget the pregnant words "I will drink no more" and so on. Even at that terrible moment at the

[68] 1 Cor 10:17; Didache 9:4.

[69] On what follows, see H. L. Strack and P. Billerbeck, *Kommentar zum Neuen Testament aus Talmud und Midrasch,* vol. 4 (1928), pt. 1, 58, pt. 2, 1147, 1164 f.

[70] *m. Pes.* 10:2, 4, 7; cp. Luke 22:17.

[71] *Midrash Psalms* on 23:6, citing Rab.

[72] Mark 14:23; Matt 26:27.

[73] Mark 14:25.

[74] Matt 26:29.

[75] *The New Testament and Rabbinic Judaism* (1956) (repr. 1973), 330 f. [441 ff.].

[76] *m. Pes.* 10:7.

[77] *b. Pes.* 118a; Passover Eve Service—E. D. Goldschmidt *op. cit.*, 84, 86 ff.

[78] Mark 15:23.

[79] *b. Sanh.* 43a; see Strack and Billerbeck *op. cit.*, vol. 1 (1922), 1037.

start of the execution, Jesus was certain of the drink awaiting him in the Kingdom. (This does not rule out the possibility of a further motive—to experience the suffering in full consciousness.) In a way, the confident refusal stands in contrast to the later cry of despair, "My God, why has thou forsaken me?"[80] It was the latter (misconstrued as a calling on Elijah) which caused a bystander, no doubt remembering the refusal, to hold up to Jesus a sponge soaked with vinegar.[81] Whether the introduction of vinegar owes something to a Psalm[82] in which an innocent man is given gall and vinegar by his persecutors may be left open.[83]

The Psalm is unquestionably in Matthew's mind.[84] For him, already the first offer was malicious, "wine mixed with gall," and it was for this reason that Jesus, "having tasted it, would not drink." There is no connection with the vow. In fact, the incident is depicted as a mere double of the second one—as to which Matthew follows Mark fairly closely.[85] It is not, indeed, from Matthew's point of view, an empty double: both the vinegar and the gall of the Psalm are now represented in the Passion.[86] But the Marcan account, as usual, appears to be the primary one.

Luke,[87] like the other Synoptics, has Jesus forswear the fruit of the vine this side of the Kingdom. But he did so at an earlier point in the service, that is to say, as the company were having the second cup, prior to the meal. No mention is made of spiced wine presented and rejected before the crucifixion; and the vinegar is a brief item exemplifying the cruel behaviour of the soldiers.[88] All three differences may be supposed to have been brought about by Luke revising his material. Since, however, the shorter variant contains no pronouncement "This is" with respect to the wine, let us once again take up the question posed at the beginning: was there perhaps no such pronouncement? More precisely, could it be that the vow—foretelling his imminent exaltation—was all Jesus said about the wine, and that even the earliest "This is"-statement about it derives from this vow, being coined under the spell of "This is my body"?[89] I feel this would be too extreme a position. As noticed above, the wine was less prominent than the bread both in the customary Passover eve discourse and in Jesus's proclamations. When we consider, in addition, that the primitive Christian commemoration of the Last Supper must have been highly flexible (as was, indeed, the Passover eve liturgy of the time), the omission from the shorter Luke of a "This is" over the wine is not too hard to understand.

This leaves John. That he, with no parallel to the Synoptic Last Supper, has no parallel to the vow is to be expected. We hear of no spiced wine before the execution.

[80] Mark 15:34; Matt 27:46.

[81] Mark 15:36.

[82] Ps 69:22.

[83] See e.g. K. Klostermann, *Das Markus - Evangelium*, 4th ed. (1950), 167.

[84] Matt 27:34.

[85] Matt 27:48.

[86] See S. E. Johnson, "The Gospel according to St. Matthew," in *The Interpreter's Bible*, vol. 7 (1951), 602 f.

[87] Luke 22:18, cp. 16.

[88] Luke 23:36.

[89] A line of thought suggested to me by Professor C. K. Barrett, in the letter giving his reactions to my typescript.

Vinegar, however, was tendered to and accepted by Jesus on the cross, after he exclaimed "I thirst."[90] Even at this last moment of his ministry, John writes, Scripture had to be fulfilled. This is evidently an allusion to the Psalm already adduced, from which John, the greatest artist among the evangelists, quotes another verse towards the beginning of the ministry:[91] "The zeal of your house has eaten me up."

[90] John 19:28 ff.
[91] John 2:17; Ps 69:10.

5

Conversion

This section explores conversion to Judaism and to early Christianity.

Conversion to Judaism and Early Christianity

I.

To begin with, two general remarks.

First, Jewish religion and Jewish peoplehood are co-extensive, having their common root in Abraham's response to the divine call.[1] Conversion, therefore, means naturalization and vice versa. This has not changed from the era of the patriarchs to this day; and attempts since the nineteenth century to split up the two have remained confined to the fringe. To be sure, one aspect or the other may be more conspicuous in different epochs or settings.

As King Ahab's wife, Queen Jezebel is an Israelitess—despite her never-wavering adherence to her Zidonian idolatry. Actually, the latter now renders her doubly guilty.[2] Conversely, though someone adopts the Jewish faith and customs, or their essentials at any rate, he or she is not Jewish so long as they continue aside from the nation. Jethro, Moses's father-in-law, while acknowledging God, remains a Midianite in Midian.[3] The Midianite Hobab becomes a resident alien in Moses's camp, but still not a Hebrew.[4] Rahab of Jericho, who harbours Joshua's spies, acknowledges God and, when Jericho is sacked, is spared with her kinsfolk to stay on as resident aliens.[5] The Syrian commander Naaman, cured of leprosy by Elisha, acknowledges God and, indeed, decides even when back in his country to sacrifice to him only; yet even he is merely a god-fearing gentile.[6] So are the Kings Nebuchadnezzar and Darius who, moved by the insight of Jewish counsellors and the miraculous survival of Jews in a furnace and a lion's den, acknowledge God, going as far as to order their subjects to worship him.[7]

In Rabbinic literature, most of these worthies are represented as proselytes proper.[8] But, then, the assumption is that they do more than is recorded in the Bible and fulfil all conditions for becoming Jewish—both religiously and nationally. In the case of Rahab, this interpretation as well as legends depicting heaven's reward for her assistance to the Hebrews[9] are demonstrably B.C.: she ranks as an ancestress of Jesus in

[1] Genesis 12 ff.
[2] 1 Kings 16 ff.
[3] Exod 18:11, 27.
[4] Num 10:29 ff.
[5] Josh 2:11, 6:25.
[6] 2 Kgs 5:15, 17 ff.
[7] Dan 2:46 f., 3:28 f., 6:26 ff.
[8] E.g. *Mek.* on Exod 18:1.
[9] E.g. *Siphre* on Num 10:29; *b. Meg.* 14b.

Matthew.[10] The Rabbinic exegesis, while anachronistic, supports rather than contradicts my thesis: conversion inevitably brings you into the religion and people at the same time.

My second reflection is this. From the earliest times, the procedure of becoming a Jew is dominated by a distinction between the sexes: the chief requirement for males is circumcision, inapplicable to females. Hence the step is incomparably easier for the latter than the former. (This is no longer so true of the better classes in Britain and British America, where circumcision of babies has become widespread. But my general argument is not thereby affected. The practice, by the way, doubtless originated, partly at least, under Scriptural influence.) It is not accidental that Jesus's genealogy in Matthew[11] includes two female converts—Rahab and Ruth—but, unless we count Abraham, no male one. That, historically, as just observed, Rahab does not qualify is immaterial: the evangelist, resting on Rabbinic tradition, sees her in the same light as Ruth. There is no male counterpart.

If it were the other way round, if things were vastly more convenient for males than females, surely the spokespersons of women's liberation would treat it as flagrant discrimination. To this, they might perhaps reply that the motive behind the advantageous position of females is not respect for them but, on the contrary, contempt. However, for one thing, this is definitely not the whole explanation: a, so far at least, intractable physical difference, for instance, also plays a part. For another, in areas where women are put down, very wisely the protesters will no longer accept alibis in the form of "it is meant for their good." Sauce for the gander, please: the fact is that, for whatever reasons, in the matter of becoming Jewish, females are spared a formidable obstacle.

Its role is illumined in a dramatic fashion by the division between Judaism and Christianity. Had the apostles not abolished the requirement of circumcision there would today be no Christianity separate from Judaism. This measure of theirs facilitated the coming over *en masse* of males as well as females; with the result that the open branch, those for whom Jesus was the Messiah, grew into a world religion, while the other one, those who did not share this belief, remained a self-contained, small group. It is, incidentally, the compactness of Judaism which has helped to preserve the primitive identity of conversion and naturalization which I have been stressing.

II.

Now for a survey of the evolution of the procedure, or rather, the main currents. There is throughout, I would caution, far more fluidity than may appear from my summary.

The fundamental division is between the period before the Babylonian exile and that from the exile onwards. In the pre-exilic era, a man becomes Jewish by circumcision. A woman's description follows her father's or husband's. As a rule, therefore, she becomes Jewish by marriage—as, in many modern states still, a foreign woman marry-

[10] Matt 1:5.

[11] Matt 1:1 ff.

ing a citizen by that fact obtains citizenship. It may, however, also happen when she lives in the paternal home or when she is the wife of a gentile, by her father or husband becoming Jewish. This will be an extremely rare occurrence. Yet what is, in a sense, the prototype of conversion shows the principle at work: the circumcision of Abraham and the males among his household brings into the fold the females, without further ado.[12]

Another episode in the Book of Genesis belongs here.[13] Jacob's sons propose to the Hivites of Shechem a tribal merger, really a joining of Jacob's family by the Hivites. True, they do so in bad faith, indeed, with murderous intent, but this is not here relevant. If all Hivite males, they declare, undergo circumcision, "we will give our daughters to you and take your daughters to us, and we will dwell with you and we will become one people."[14] Evidently, no ceremony is necessary for the Shechemite females. They automatically participate in their men's change of status.

A man, then, while having to take a hurdle a woman need not fear, once he does achieve naturalization pulls his female establishment along with him; and if the men of a tribe convert *en bloc*, the tribe, men and women, becomes Hebrew. A woman's naturalization affects no one else: at this stage, it is just an aspect of her subordination. The point always to remember is that the hurdle is enormous. There is this proviso, too, that, even in a patriarchy, a woman may have some say as to whom she is going to marry—a number of stories illustrate different degrees of such power[15]—so a switch of peoplehood would not be against her will.

Naturalization by marriage is contemplated by a Deuteronomic statute[16] concerning a prisoner of war. "You shall bring her into your house, and she shall shave her head and pare her nails and put her raiment of captivity from off her and stay in your house and bewail her father and mother a full month; and after that you shall possess her and she shall be to wife to you." The rites all symbolize separation, be it from her origin, be it from her prisoner's condition. None symbolizes incorporation: marriage does that. In this case, plainly, she is not asked.

Marrying a heathen is frequently branded as evil—Deuteronomy itself warns against it[17]—and heathen women figure much more prominently in these and allied texts than heathen men.[18] Nevertheless the marriage with a heathen woman is valid, the offspring fully legitimate. The two tribes of Ephraim and Manasseh descend from Joseph's union with the daughter of an Egyptian priest.[19] Moses's father-in-law is a Midianite priest.[20] Rehoboam is a son of Solomon and an Ammonitess, Ahaziah and

[12] Gen 17:9 ff.

[13] Gen 34:1 ff.

[14] Gen 34:16.

[15] Gen 24:15 ff.; 1 Samuel 25.

[16] Deut 21:10 ff.

[17] Deut 7:3; cp. Judg 3:6.

[18] Gen 24:3, 26:35, 27:46, 28:1; Exod 34:16; Num 12:1, 25:1 ff.; 1 Kgs 11:2, 16:31. On Ezra and Nehemiah, see below, 469 ff.

[19] Gen 41:50 ff.

[20] Exod 2:21; cp. Num 12:1.

Jehoram are sons of Ahab and the Zidonian Jezebel. All three succeed to the throne without any difficulty on account of the mother's provenance.[21] It is significant that, while quite a few Biblical names refer to the father, Abigail for example, none refers to the mother. This matter, however, I shall not pursue.

A reservation is called for: we must not make the rules too rigid. Apart from the existence of various types of marriage, with various legal effects—if a foreign woman marries a Jew or, for that matter, if a Jewess marries out, her husband dies or divorces her and there is no offspring, she may re-acquire her original nationality. We shall presently find this exemplified in the Book of Ruth. A parallel is provided by a priest's daughter who, on marrying a layman, ceases to be entitled to sanctified food, but regains fitness if she returns under her father's roof, childless, after termination of the marriage.[22] (The situation of Judah's daughter-in-law Tamar at a certain stage[23] shows how complicated things can be; I shall not here go into it.) The conduct of the son of an Egyptian living among the Israelites and an Israelitess gives rise, we learn in the Pentateuch,[24] to legislation about blasphemy. He shares his father's status, and the law promulgated expressly threatens "as well the stranger as the home-born."[25] The same status would attach to his mother. By contrast, Bathsheba, who bears no child to her Hittite husband Uriah, on his death can marry David as a Jewess. The marriage would have re-naturalized her in any case.[26]

In the Book of Ruth,[27] Elimelech, a Judean, because of a famine, goes to live for a while in Moab, with his wife Naomi and their two sons Sickly and Weakly. He dies. His sons marry natives, Orpah and Ruth, who automatically enter the family.

However, the young men, too, now die, without children. For the moment, Naomi is more or less head of the house and, the famine having ended, she resolves to move back to Judah. Orpah—I quote—"returns to her people and to her gods," thereby reassuming her native Moabite status. Ruth follows Naomi: "Your people is my people and your God is my God."[28] No doubt she remains part of the group. Incidentally, the unity of nation and religion could not be expressed more clearly.

To be sure, in the narrative, the epithet "the Moabitess" sticks to her.[29] At one time, I thought it might not mean much more than when my colleagues call me a German. But it does: there is the implication of a very special loyalty on the part of that lady from abroad. To recapitulate: in this epoch, a woman's religion is determined by her father's or husband's—except where she got into the group by marriage and the marriage ends without children. In these, obviously most uncommon, circumstances, she decides. A mere woman, she may opt for her present affiliation or her former one. That is dramat-

[21] 1 Kgs 14:21; 2 Chr 12:13; 1 Kgs 16:31, 22:40, 52 f.; 2 Kgs 3:1 f.
[22] Lev 22:12 f.
[23] Gen 38:11.
[24] Lev 24:10 ff.
[25] Lev 24:16.
[26] 2 Samuel 11.
[27] See Excursus [489 ff.].
[28] Ruth 1:15 f.
[29] Ruth 1:22, 2:2, 6, 21, 4:5, 10.

ic enough, but Ruth's choice is all the more so since, up to now, she never set foot outside the country of her birth. Rebekkah journeys into a distant land in order to marry Isaac,[30] and Israel follows the Lord, her bridegroom, into the wilderness.[31] Here a stranger married to an Israelite even after his death accompanies his mother into the, to her, quite unknown Judah. The Moabitess who has freely, trustingly, preferred her new allegiance—that is what the attribute conveys. It is anything but an empty phrase.

On the other hand, it in no way suggests that she is not Jewish. At her first meeting in Judah with Sickly's and Weakly's sturdier relation Boaz, Pillar, he congratulates her on "leaving your father and mother and the land of your nativity and coming unto a people which you did not know heretofore," and blesses her, "a full reward be given you of the Lord God of Israel under whose wings you are come to trust"—again, note, people and God figuring equally. In fact, he ends by marrying her as belonging to Elimelech's estate which he redeems, i.e. saves from falling into the hands of outsiders.[32]

Throughout the story, no rite of reception is alluded to. A woman is received through marriage. If widowed and childless, retention or loss of her acquired nationality depends on whether she stays or returns to her kin. Certainly, the Rabbis, as mentioned already, take compliance with their requirements for granted, but this is to transfer them back into a different system.

It is in fact highly remarkable that they admit to finding no Scriptural indication of baptism of female converts. Otherwise so adept in interpreting the old writings their way, here they concede. They do, of course, none the less manage to prove its early existence: it is demonstrable, we are assured, by logic, nearly as good as a text. The precise reasoning offered is the rather desperate one from *reductio ad absurdum*: in the absence of such a ceremony, there would have been, they claim, no means of gathering in the female part of the people when the Sinaitic community was founded—a conclusion impossible to contemplate.[33]

During a brief visit with the Samaritans at Nablus, I enquired about their regulations and was informed that marriage is, and has always been, enough to incorporate a woman. I was delighted for, if correct, it is of manifest relevance.

III.

In the exile, the archaic regime proves inadequate; and above all, the part of it relating to females. Jewry is a tiny band on alien soil, in the midst of a grand pagan civilisation, to assimilate to which is a constant temptation. In these conditions, when a Jew marries a gentile woman, quite likely, far from her joining his set, he will do his best to go over to hers and be lost to his own. You will not need my help to think of modern parallels. Marriage itself, therefore, can no longer be deemed to incorporate a woman in the fold. To achieve this effect, a special act is required that brings her over

[30] Gen 24:58.

[31] Jer 2:2.

[32] Ruth 3:10 ff., 4:1 ff.

[33] *b. Yeb.* 46a. On the nature of *reductio*, see my *Roman Law* (1969), 176 ff.

as a person, on the basis of a decision: baptism. How far the choice of this rite is due to the Biblical instances of immersion, how far to Babylonian cults, I shall not here inquire.

My explanation of the development is strongly supported by the fact that, as soon as resettlement in the holy land gets under way, the laxer method comes to the fore again and women from the local tribes are introduced into the community by marriage. There is no longer the all-pervasive fear of being swallowed up by the surrounding culture. Ezra and Nehemiah, however, both having grown up and reached eminence in Persia, on taking charge of affairs in the land voice the most intransigent opposition.[34] The men are given the choice between dismissing their wives, together with any children, and being excluded themselves from the new-founded state. This dismissal is not by a regular bill of divorce,[35] which presupposes a valid marriage and mentions the woman's freedom to conclude a fresh one. Ezra and Nehemiah recognize no tie with these women and none, in consequence, with the children. Something of an analogy is furnished by the contrast between the unwillingness of the pre-world-war II German and British Rabbinates to receive converts and the relaxed attitude in Israel.[36] I daresay the diehards I knew at Frankfurt am Main and London, if they could take over at Jerusalem and Tel-Aviv today, might carry out a few evictions.

Anyhow, a corollary of the new dispensation is that a woman can convert on her own, without marriage. Before then, it is marriage or her father's or husband's conversion that naturalizes her. Henceforth, at least one who is not under a man's *potestas*—say, a widow whose father is dead—may make up her mind to embrace Judaism and be baptized. That this must profoundly change the entire atmosphere of conversion stands to reason. Conviction will often be the dominant factor, the emphasis shifting from change of peoplehood to change of religion—only the emphasis: both are still firmly linked. Furthermore, it is a landmark in the advance of women towards influence and power. Under the old system, we have seen, about the only situation where a woman can independently document her faith is that of Ruth; and her saga shows with what gratitude adherence—not, in strictness, conversion, but adherence—to the Hebrew side is appreciated. From now, there is far more opportunity for women to take a stand.

Before long, the requirement of baptism is extended to males, added to circumcision. Presumably the idea of regeneration attaching to baptism acquires such weight that confinement to one sex is intolerable. At any rate, the factors that bring about a reception rite for women affect also the conversion of males: increasingly, attention focuses on its religious element, and in particular, on submission to the commandments. In the midst of a foreign environment, their observance becomes absolutely essential to the preservation of the group. That their centrality is upheld after the return is due to the efforts of Ezra and Nehemiah.[37] Even so, re-settlement in time permits a good deal of

[34] Ezra 9 f.; Neh 13:23 ff.

[35] See my "Pauline Contributions to a Pluralistic Culture: Re-Creation and Beyond," *Jesus and Man's Hope*, 2 (1971), 244 n. 71 [549], and *Civil Disobedience in Antiquity* (1972), 16 n. 4.

[36] Since writing this, I have found confirmation in a review by E. L. Ehrlich of J. R. Rosenbloom, *Conversion to Judaism* (1978), in *Freiburger Rundbrief*, 31 (1979), 141.

[37] Nehemiah 8.

laxity until the loss of statehood in A.D. 70 produces a renewed concentration on strict practice. Once more, the contemporary scene is illuminating: it is easier to go for an outing in your car on the Day of Atonement and remain a Jew in Israel than in Britain.

It is during the exile, then, that naturalization comes to mean entry not only into the Abrahamic covenant but also into the Sinaitic one. Abraham goes on being "the father of proselytes." [38] Even in our day, a male convert's Hebrew name describes him, not as "son of John or Henry," his physical father, but as "son of Abraham," and traditionally a female convert is called "daughter of Abraham." [39] (Though "daughter of Sarah" seems to be making headway.[40]) At the same time, the requirements of conversion are based by the Rabbis on what, in their belief (or that of a majority), had been demanded of the people assembled at Sinai: as for the males, circumcision, baptism and a sacrifice, as for the females, the latter two. For the purpose in hand, it does not matter that this doctrine involves much tortuous reasoning as well as forced interpretation of the Biblical record. The sacrifice, of course, drops out with the destruction of the second Temple.[41]

In the preparation of a would-be convert, the Torah coming from Sinai now plays a conspicuous part. The initial link of this component with the introduction of baptism—both called forth by the exigencies of exile and reconstruction under Ezra and Nehemiah—leaves permanent traces. A representative sample of the commandments, for instance, is to be recited, the Rabbis lay down,[42] during the actual immersion. This may be the place to add that the Talmudic regulation[43] that baptism must take place before witnesses or even a court looks like another consequence of the situation in exile, when the community needs to be assured in this way where the person stands. Previously, there is in general no problem about clarity.

By New Testament times, proselyte baptism for both sexes has gone on for centuries. It is so established an institution that John the Baptist can transfer it to the inner mission, the call to Jews to become true, end-time Jews, aimed at men at least as much as women. This proselytizing of those already within is the novel feature of his activity (which does not exclude earlier adumbrations, say, among the Dead Sea monks) accounting for the epithet "Baptizer" or "Baptist" bestowed on him. An agent noun tends to be employed where the action indicated by the verb is performed in an extraordinary fashion.[44] We all dream, but it is when you are absent-minded during an important meeting or absorbed in thought in the middle of a busy road that you are called "a dreamer." Nothing remarkable in baptizing a gentile entering Judaism. But John proclaims that even the Jews must enter: "Think not, We have Abraham to father,"[45] i.e., you must acquire him just like strangers. It is when he baptizes even Jews that he becomes "the Baptizer," "the Baptist."

[38] *Midrash Tanhuma* on Gen 14:1. Cp. Matt 3:9 to be quoted presently.

[39] Cp. *b. Ket.* 72b; *b. Gitt.* 89a; Luke 13:16.

[40] See C. G. Montefiore and H. Loewe, *A Rabbinic Anthology* (1938, repr. 1974), 574.

[41] *b. Ker.* 9a; *b. Yeb.* 46a f.

[42] *b. Yeb.* 47b.

[43] *b. Yeb.* 46b f.

[44] See my *Roman Law* (1969), 2 ff.

[45] Matt 3:9.

The nature of his baptism as proselyte baptism comes out in details.[46] The precise moment at which a gentile becomes Jewish is when emerging from the water: "He immerses and comes out—behold, he is like an Israelite in all respects."[47] Accordingly, Mark,[48] in reporting Jesus's baptism by John, tells us: "And at once, coming out of the water, he saw the heavens rent and the Spirit descending." In passing, Josephus relates[49] that John exhorted the Jews to practise righteousness and undergo baptism, and that Herod became alarmed "when others gathered with them." Who these others may have been is a longstanding puzzle. Could it be gentiles? Luke[50] seems to assume that some joined the crowd—though, considering his pronounced inclination to universalism, this is not the strongest evidence.

IV.

By the opening of the current era, Judaism exercises a strong attraction. The possession of the Old Testament may well be a major factor. It is consistent with this explanation that Jewish-Christian preaching has had scant success in the East—India, China—with comprehensive religious Scriptures of its own. (In my opinion, the predominance of Roman law from the Middle Ages on owes more to its availability in a written corpus than to quality. "*Denn was man schwarz auf weiss besitzt*," ["For what we possess in black on white"] Goethe has a trusting young student believe,[51] "*Kann man getrost nach Hause tragen*." ["We can take home and keep for good"]) Anyhow there are many women converts[52] and many god-fearing men, men who, short of circumcision, conduct themselves as Jews.[53] For Schürer, the numerical superiority of full proselytesses over full proselytes bespeaks the female heart's susceptibility to religious movements.[54] Something in this, no doubt. But I wonder whether the statistics would not look a bit different if a woman wishing to be received had, say, to turn into an Amazon.[55] An article by Pope presents a sound picture.[56]

[46] See my *New Testament and Rabbinic Judaism*, 111 f. [505 f.], and *The Sudden in the Scriptures* (1964), 46 f. [718 f.]

[47] *b. Yeb.* 47b.

[48] Mark 1:10.

[49] Josephus, *Ant.* 18.5.2.117 f.

[50] Luke 3:14. "Nothing to show whether the soldiers are Jewish soldiers of Antipas or Romans under the Procurator": J. M. Creed, *The Gospel according to St. Luke* (1930), 53. But even Antipas's soldiers would most probably include non-Jews: K. H. Rengstorf, *Das Evangelium nach Lukas*, 9th ed. (1962), 57, with reference to Josephus, *Ant.* 17.8.3.198.

[51] Goethe, *Faust*, Part 1, Schülerszene.

[52] E.g. Josephus, *Bell.* 2.20.2.560.

[53] E.g. Josephus, *Ant.* 14.7.2.110.

[54] See E. Schürer, *Geschichte des Jüdischen Volkes im Zeitalter Jesu Christe*, 2nd ed., pt. 2 (1886), 561: "*Am meisten erwiesen sich auch hier, wie bei jeder religiösen Bewegung, die Frauenherzen empfänglich.*"

[55] Cp. Kleist, *Penthesilea*, Scene 15: "*Doch als die feige Regung um sich griff, Riss sie die rechte Brust sich ab und taufte Die Frauen, die den Bogen spannen würden, Und sank zusammen, eh' sie noch vollendet: Die Amazonen oder Busenlosen!—Hierauf ward ihr die Krone aufgesetzt.*" ["But as base fear began to sweep the people, she tore away her own right breast, baptizing thus all these women who would wield the bow—herself, ere she had finished, swooned away—the Amazons, that is: the breastless ones!"]

[56] See M. H. Pope, in *The Interpreter's Dictionary of the Bible*, 3 (1962), 928.

In a culture where surgical instruments are crude by our standards and there is neither anaesthesis nor antisepsis, circumcision is a gruesome prospect for an adult. The Pentateuch itself, in the narrative about Shechem,[57] regards ill-effects as common. "And it came to pass on the third day, when they were suffering, that" and so on;[58] the suffering is referred to in a subordinate clause, it is not an extraordinary result that would deserve a main one. In Matthew,[59] the scribes and Pharisees are said to "compass sea and land to make one proselyte." This testifies to intense missionary longings but not, as often thought,[60] to signal success. On the contrary, one senses a note of despair in respect of the chances of winning male converts. The very occasional break—and we do hear of several[61]—is such a triumph that no effort is too great. (I am discounting enforced conversions which did happen, though rarely.[62] Josephus disapproves.[63]) Billy Graham need not fly from one continent to the other to gain one soul. A friend of mine does it: he is looking for supporters of an Institute of Ancient Jewish Law to be founded—and funded.

From Josephus we learn[64] that a prince of Commagene, betrothed to Drusilla, daughter of Agrippa I, in the end withdrew, unwilling to convert; whereupon she was given to the king of Emeza "who had consented to be circumcised." Apparently, circumcision more than anything else was the stumbling-block. Drusilla finished up as the procurator Felix's wife.[65]

When the apostles decree[66] that baptism suffices for men no less than women, mass proselytization becomes feasible. A man need no longer be in dread of that operation. Even women will find the step more comfortable: previously, quite a few inclined to take it would hold back since their husbands could not—or not easily—join them.

To some extent at least, it must be under the impact of Christianity's enviable progress that the Hillelite sage Joshua ben Hananiah, around A.D. 100, takes up the same position: a male gentile, like a female one, is Jewish as soon as baptized. Yet not quite the same: whereas in Christianity circumcision is definitely abandoned, for Joshua it does remain an inescapable duty. A proselyte not circumcised in the course of coming over is obliged to get circumcised after. If he is remiss, then, though he is a Jew—or precisely because he is one—he is committing a terrible sin.

Joshua's suggestion is allowed a fair trial run. This is reflected in a paragraph in the Talmud representing—implausibly—his more rigid colleague Eliezer ben Hyrcanus

[57] See above, 467.

[58] Gen 34:25.

[59] Matt 23:15.

[60] See E. Schürer, *op. cit.*, 558.

[61] King Izates of Adiabene, Josephus, *Ant.* 20.2.4.46; Onkelos; *b. Gitt.* 56b f., etc.

[62] E.g. Josephus, *Ant.* 13.11.3.318.

[63] Josephus, *Vita* 23.113. That routine circumcision—or baptism—of children or youngsters within the group is enforced was not then realized; it is barely beginning to be realized today. To be clear about it does not, of course, necessarily mean rejection. For some comments of mine on unwanted salvation, see *Humanities in Society*, 2 (1979), 74 ff.

[64] Josephus, *Ant.* 20.7.1.139.

[65] Acts 24:24.

[66] Acts 15.

as agreeing; a preceding summary shows him in his usual role. The concession however, is much too limited to restore the balance. By the end of the second century, the majority has decisively turned against it, insisting on circumcision as indispensable to conversion.[67] If "the fountain" in Juvenal's antisemitic lines alludes to baptism, he is depicting the early, uncompromising stand: Moses, he says, commanded "to conduct to the fountain solely the circumcised."[68]

More and more, the purest dedication to God and his Torah is expected of a candidate. A woman's intent to wed a Jew is listed by the Rabbis among the inadequate stimuli: ironical, considering that, prior to exile, marriage is the regular route by which she enters the nation. R. Nehemiah, a survivor of the Hadrianic persecution, voices the extreme view that not only should a person prompted by love not be accepted, but if, despite this bar, the procedure is gone through—circumcision and baptism in the case of a man, baptism in that of a woman—it is invalid.[69]

The motive of *'ahabha*, by the way, passes through revealing stages. Basically, the word signifies "love"; but as in the present context it refers to non-sexual emotions—non-sexual as viewed by the Rabbis, unacquainted with Freud—we had better speak of "friendship" or "affection." (The Mishnah contrasts the object-oriented *'ahabha* between Amnon and Tamar with the pure one between David and Jonathan.[70]) In the Palestinian Talmud, friendship with a Jew or Jewess figures side by side with intent to marry as an improper ground for conversion.[71] The Babylonian Talmud omits it.[72] Not, surely, because of a more favourable assessment, but because it no longer belongs to the world of experience. In the post-Talmudic tractate on Proselytes[73] it is paired off as unsatisfactory, not with intent to marry, but with fear of the Jews, of which the Book of Esther supplies the chief precedent.[74] A. Cohen rightly concludes that what is envisaged is not personal friendship, but appreciation of the Jews at large. The tractate puts it as a foil to fear—both, of course, by this time quite academic. Apparently, however, Cohen cannot bear even the theoretical rejection of a gentile with a genuine enthusiasm for Jewry. So he adds that he is "perhaps deriving material advantage from his conversion."[75]

V.

As hinted above,[76] with baptism comes in the notion of conversion as rebirth.[77] Rebirth is chic nowadays—and skindeep. When brought about by Jewish baptism, it is

[67] *b. Yeb.* 56a f. Cp. L. H. Feldman, in The Loeb Classical Library's *Josephus*, 9 (1965), 410 f.

[68] Juvenal, *Satires* 14.104.

[69] *b. Yeb.* 24b.

[70] *m. Ab.* 5:16; 2 Samuel 13; 1 Samuel 18 ff.

[71] *y. Kidd.* 65b.

[72] *b. Yeb.* 24b.

[73] *Gerim* 1.7.

[74] Esth 8:17.

[75] See A. Cohen, *Soncino edition of Minor Tractates of the Talmud*, 2 (1965), 604.

[76] See above, 469 f.

[77] *b. Yeb.* 48b.

serious, creating a fresh child. Its effects on family are specially notable. For example, the bond between a couple who convert is dissolved: they are now different persons. To be sure, it is readily restorable by cohabitation—at least before the Rabbis, from the third century on, become more and more hostile to marriage by intercourse.[78] Again, a mother and a son who convert may marry: they are no longer related. With regard to this type of case, already in the pre-Christian epoch the sages introduce a proviso: no union must be contracted which is repudiated by the surrounding heathen society. It is in this modified form that the early Church takes over the practice. Paul[79] condemns the marriage between a stepson and stepmother among his Corinthian flock because this, he explains, "does not pass even among the gentiles."

The reason for the restriction transmitted in the sources is that a convert allowed to marry someone that would not be allowed under heathen law might believe Judaism to be lax in such matters and generally slip back into licentious habits. Doubtless the Rabbis also fear the impression on outsiders. As is well known, total neglect of the usual barriers is a widespread charge in antiquity against Jews and Christians. "They abstain," Tacitus reports of the former, "from taking foreign women; but among themselves nothing is illicit."[80] A number of the latter are convicted of "Oedipodean intercourse" at Lyons and Vienne in the second century.[81] It is universally assumed, without discussion, that it is all sheer calumny. Conrat's treatment is typical: "It need hardly be mentioned that these accusations were groundless."[82] But they are not—not entirely. From whom would gentiles—including relatively objective students among them—get firsthand information about the two faiths? Mainly from converts, a cousin, an aunt, who had become Jewish or Christian. And these would tell them of their freedom. Paul's Corinthian community are "puffed up" by, proud of, their standing above the ordinary curbs between close relations—relations no longer as a result of baptism.[83] To an outsider, unappreciative of the miracle, incest is incest. Plainly, the indictment does not spring up *ex nihilo*, and counter-measures such as the one discouraging the most offensive ties are to be expected.

Conceivably, the influx of slaves also plays a part. A Roman master might breed slaves as we do terriers: the incest taboos do not apply, often a slave would have no idea of the identity of father, mother, son, daughter and so on, alliances between otherwise forbidden degrees are unavoidable and instinctive aversion to them cannot but be greatly reduced. However, this is at most a minor factor in the growth of the misunderstanding. The hostile writers definitely connect the Jews' and Christians' immorality with their religion. So it is the convert's treatment as a new being which must be chiefly responsible.

Generally speaking, propaganda against a collective cannot be successfully based on a one-hundred-percent lie; you want a grain of truth, however microscopic. If Hitler

[78] *m. Kidd.* 1:1; *b. Kidd.* 12b.

[79] 1 Cor 5:1.

[80] Tacitus, *Histories* 5.5.

[81] Eusebius, *Eccl. Hist.* 5.1.14.

[82] See M. Conrat, *Die Christenverfolgungen im Römischen Reiche* (1897), 31.

[83] 1 Cor 5:2.

had contended that every Jew has an eye at the back of his head enabling him to watch what goes on behind him, it would not have worked. His assertion that there is no financial scandal not caused by a Jew did impress. Some smoke is needed to shout "Fire!" with effect; and I think that the familiar, gross pagan anti-Jewish and anti-Christian aspersions are none of them devoid of a minimum factual input. To work this out would be interesting from more than one point of view, but this is not the place for it.

There is absolute agreement in literature that Jewish proselyte baptism does not possess sacramental character. I do not like disputing about nomenclature. But I would be curious to hear a definition of "sacramental" excluding an act so powerful as this one. Christianity, as it spreads outward, forgets about and sheds the full implications of re-creation. Judaism still acknowledges them. When I was young, Jewish scholarship rather avoided dealing with them. They could by no manner of rationalization be reconciled with, made palatable to, the then prevalent climate of Western theology. Things move fast. Some ten years ago, preparing a book that never appeared, I wrote: "If there were an isolated part of the globe where, for instance, marriage between brother and sister were tolerated, and a gentile family adopted the Jewish faith, such a marriage would be in order even today." We need no longer be so hypothetical. Sweden may soon provide the Rabbinate with a case testing the doctrine. It is, of course, not a reawakened Norse belief in true renewal but a devaluation of kinship that makes it easier for us to come out of the closet.

Paul, I have just pointed out, still goes along with the Jewish scheme. A remarkable illustration is furnished by the problem of a convert whose spouse does not join in.[84] The marriage, he teaches, is terminated: the convert is a new person. None the less, if the unbeliever is content to stay on, that ought to be accepted. Cohabitation will "consecrate" him or her, will bring about a fresh marriage—preferable to a casting off. Not surprisingly, from the early Middle Ages on, the argument, proceeding as it does from the Rabbinic estimate of rebirth, has been totally misunderstood, the outcome being the so-called Pauline privilege.

In support of his advice not to oust the unbeliever, Paul names two motives: peace and the hope that, ultimately, he or she may be won over. This involves a fundamental question. A convert is "in the position of a child just born," the Rabbis hold,[85] the result of "a new creation," in Paul's language.[86] "The old things have gone," the latter exclaims, "new things have come into being." The trouble is that, in living reality, the miracle is less thorough. The whole issue of legislation enacting an impossibility arises in this connection[87] though I shall confine myself to a few conundrums from conversion.

In the sphere of law, secular or religious, it is relatively easiest to make a fresh start. Marriage dissolved. Blood ties severed, hence no forbidden degrees, as also no

[84] 1 Cor 7:12 ff.

[85] *b. Yeb.* 48b; cp. John 3:3.

[86] 2 Cor 5:17; Gal 6:15.

[87] See my *Pope John XXIII Lecture* ["The Marriage of Justinian and Theodora: Legal and Theological Reflections"] in *CUALR*, 16 (1967), 386 ff., and my *Natural Law Lecture* ["Greek and Roman Reflections on Impossible Laws"] in *NLF*, 12 (1967), 1 ff.

claims to inheritance. And so on. But even here, difficulties crop up. Are debts cancelled? Is a slave convert free? (Needless to say, whatever the Jewish or early Christian answers, gentiles would not allow them to work to their disadvantage—which is a further complication.) Is a prostitute convert a virgin? Do children born before conversion count towards fulfilment of the duty of propagation?[88] If a proselyte who had a son before has sons again, is the new firstborn entitled to a double share of the estate?[89] May a convert recite the Avowal speaking of the land "which the Lord swore to our Fathers for to give us?"[90] The opposite of the legal domain is the physical, where the old things will persist most stubbornly. A one-armed person remains one-armed. Milieu, in a way, belongs to the grace-resistant, physical world. A water-carrier continues a water-carrier. A Jew is suspected of an affair with a gentile woman and she converts: is marriage permissible even though it must lend colour to the rumour?[91]

In between is the area of morality in the widest sense. The two considerations advanced by Paul, peace and hope of winning another convert, pertain to milieu—public policy, to be precise. Plainly, however, he feels that, apart from them, the converting spouse does not get rid of all responsibility for the non-converting one: witness the warm directness of his appeal, "For how do you know, O wife, if you may not save your husband, or how do you know, O husband, if you may not save your wife?" The Rabbis[92] are exercised by the sufferings of proselytes: for what sins could they be inflicted? One solution refers to violation of the Noachian duties—natural morality—in pre-conversion life. This implies full continuation of the moral personality. Many, however, will not admit this. So another explanation is that proselytes tend to comply with the commandments from fear of God rather than love, or they tend to be negligent in details—hence deserve punishment. An answer with a long history[93] places the cause in the transitional period between discovery of God and actual conversion: the sin consists in prolonged hesitation after seeing the light. Somehow, for the purpose of basic moral accountability, rebirth is pre-dated to that moment.

VI.

The main phases of the baptismal instruction recommended in the Talmud[94] date from the pre-Christian period. One piece of evidence is their recurrence in the earliest Christian catechisms. This applies to both form and substance, that is to say, to both the arrangement of topics and the ideas.

The arrangement comprises five parts: test, commandments, charity, penalties, reward and world to come. Test: is the candidate suitable? Commandments: an outline of what is expected of a Jew. Charity: obligations to the poor of the community.

[88] *b. Yeb.* 62a.
[89] *Ibid.*
[90] Deut 26:3; *m. Bikk.* 1:4.
[91] *m. Yeb.* 2:8.
[92] *b. Yeb.* 48b.
[93] Cp. Josephus, *Ant.* 20.2.4.45.
[94] *b. Yeb.* 47a f.

Penalties: the responsibility incurred by a sinful Jew. Reward and world to come: the bliss in store for the righteous.

The test may look simple; it is actually of extraordinary subtlety. The applicant is to be asked: "What have you seen that you have come in order to convert? Do you not know that Israel at this time are broken down, pushed about, driven about and tossed about, and that sufferings befall them?" If he replies "I know and am not worthy," no further proofs are needed. Mere willingness to conform is not enough: it must spring from the right disposition. Once that is present, on the other hand, everything will be alright.

It is quite usual for an outsider wishing to be let inside to have to prove his fitness. Rituals of initiation when a tribe or a fraternity admits a stranger or a freshman, or when the adults of a tribe admit those coming of age, are relevant; but also the long questionnaires an alien seeking naturalization must fill in and his oath of allegiance. The Essenes and the Qumran band were notoriously difficult to join.[95] Two qualifications above all tend to be looked for: earnestness of the desire to join and useful attributes. A community has little interest in creating unreliable or unprofitable members. Often one test will establish both requirements. If you wanted to settle for good in medieval Podersdorf, you had to carry a huge dog through the village. This, besides being an occasion for merriment, showed you at once really determined to live just there and endowed with strength and courage.[96]

In the case of a man, circumcision is an initiatory rite placing firmness of intent beyond the shadow of a doubt. The test here inspected, which takes place before circumcision, is of much later origin and, as already noted, highly sophisticated. It is applicable to men and women alike; and it is designed to make sure not only of the keenness of intent but also of the most important attributes a member of the faith can have—a true understanding of Israel's destiny.

One feature deserves special notice. Many groups, with a view to discouraging undesirables, make entrance hard. But this test goes further. The petitioner is reminded that the very result of conversion would be unpleasant: even should all the obstacles in the way of entrance be overcome—the test itself being one of them—or precisely then, he would find himself in a miserable position, far worse off than now. The interesting point about such cautioning is that, of really serious candidates, though some may be put off by it, more will be spurred on. In fact, this line pays off in other provinces of life—as any Don Juan knows: do not let yourself in with me, I am a good-for-nothing, unfaithful, doomed, bringing sorrow wherever I step; and promptly she falls for him. Or Churchill's summons to nothing but blood, sweat and tears.

A number of factors explain the seductive effect of this kind of warning. Masochism is a widespread phenomenon. So is guilt, assuaged by sharing the fate of the underdog. So is eagerness to take up a challenge: there is an enormous genetic premium on it (so long as it is not excessive). A would-be Jew, in particular, is likely to feel that a religion whose followers are so loyal to it despite all the drawbacks advertised must be wonder-

[95] Josephus, *Bell.* 2.8.7.137 ff.; *Manual of Discipline* 6.13 ff.

[96] See H. Fehr, *Der Humor im Recht* (1946), 12 f.

ful. From the warner's standpoint, it may be added, there are advantages extending to after he has gained his main object. Those won over through such negative propaganda may be inspired to disprove it and demonstrate the possibility of happiness in their new state. Again, should things go wrong, he can meet reproaches by "I told you so."

Yet, on a deeper level, what at first sight appears to be a self-deprecatory statement is exactly the opposite: a proud reference to Israel's glory. Their afflictions are a sign of God's nearness to them: "his name rests upon him whom chastisements befall."[97] Moreover, the saintly individual who suffers may be sure of inheriting the world to come;[98] while the nation's woes presage the final deliverance. "Israel at this time are broken down": at this time, which will presently give way to a new aeon. The ideal catechumen is to understand all this. Given due intimation of the terrible things awaiting him, he responds: "I know and am not worthy."

One could look on the test as exemplifying the Rabbinic dictum that "ever the left hand should thrust away and the right hand draw near."[99] The right hand, of course, is the stronger one. A beautiful adumbration of the design is supplied by Naomi's speeches to her widowed daughters-in-law as they have to choose between returning to their original kinsfolk and cleaving to her. One, in the end, heeds her grim predictions and leaves—and there is not the slightest adverse comment made on it. As the other proves "absolutely steadfast," Naomi desists from further dissuasion and takes her with her to Judah. This one becomes the ancestress of the house of David.[100]

VII.

On the remaining heads of the catechism I have so little to add to what I have said elsewhere that I shall not waste your time over them. Instead, let me append a note as to my dating of the material. Far from being comprehensive, it will be confined to two points often neglected. My reason for bringing them up is that they answer, I trust, two questions raised by my friend Morton Smith in a letter concerning a previous publication of mine.[101]

Point one is loosely connected with the famous criterion of the *lectio difficilior*: we must pay attention to the greater or lesser attractiveness of an idea as time goes on. More precisely, if an idea is in conformity with "progress," we want strong evidence before being sure it is old; whereas the opposite presumption applies to an idea that is awkward to accommodate. Smith asks me why I take the exemption of a convert to Judaism from the normal laws of incest to be of early origin. My reply is that—quite apart from other indications such as the Pauline epistles I have quoted and the cultural background of the Talmudic cases—this admission of what to any unlearned onlooker must seem the ghastliest perversity cannot but come down from a remote epoch. Already for the Tannaites, it becomes palpably more and more difficult to take. It would

[97] *Mek.* on Exod 20:23.

[98] *b. Kidd.* 40b; Syriac Apocalypse of Baruch 52:6.

[99] *b. Sot.* 47a.

[100] Ruth 1:8 ff., 4:17.

[101] "Pauline Contributions to a Pluralistic Culture: Re-Creation and Beyond," *Jesus and Man's Hope*, 2 (1971) (ed. D. G. Miller and D. Y. Hadidian), 223 ff. [537 ff.]

not have been set going, say, any time A.D. It goes back to B.C., and the Rabbis are busy watering it down. As a parallel—even if we looked at nothing but twentieth-century evidence, it would be safe to conclude that the ceremony of Halizah[102] was not a modern invention: the discomfort with it is so marked.

Point two: we must distinguish between the—relatively—stable essentials of a piece as our chief guidance and the variable incidentals that may come from any moment in the course of its transmission. Towards the end of the *Odyssey*, the hero is said to have come though he has come late. The same is said in Schiller's *Die Piccolomini* of Count Isolan. The gist of the remark remains due to Homer even after the substitution of a different person and different circumstances.[103] In discussing relations with outsiders, I have maintained that primitive Christianity inherits from Judaism a combination of two aims: that of harmony with them and that of eliciting their admiration or even winning them over. As a Jewish model I cite the conduct of Simeon ben Shetah, of the first half of the first century B.C., who, though not strictly obliged to do so, returns to a heathen a pearl mistakenly delivered, because "he prefers hearing the Saracene say, Blessed be the God of the Jews, to all the gain of this world."[104] But, Smith objects, Saracenes figure in Greek sources from the third century A.D. only: so can this anecdote be older? Yes, it can, and considering what we know about its protagonist and his milieu, it may safely be treated as, on the whole, reliable—indeed, it fits no other period half as well. Only a Saracene is substituted for some other foreigner in prior versions: such a change keeps a story alive, up to date. Wherever possible, in regaling my class at Boalt Hall with legends I heard long ago about Cambridge or Oxford dons, I replace them by my present confrères; yet the Camford character of the quips is scarcely affected.

Basically, Plautus's *Comedy of Asses* is, as he says, a play by Demophilos, though many of the witticisms are Plautine. When I worked on fables, I was amused by the transformation of animals in the course of migration. The longbeaked bird that removes a bone from the wolf's throat is a heron, a waterfowl, in Babrius's Greek version, a crane in Phaedrus's Latin one, a stork in La Fontaine. Joshua ben Hananiah speaks of an Egyptian partridge; and the wolf becomes a lion—symbolizing Rome or the Emperor Hadrian.[105] None the less the body of the paradigm stays the same throughout. This is not to deny that, when we trace the career of a doctrine or a tale, the slightest modification may be immensely significant. For correct and full use, however, it must be set

[102] Deut 25:9.

[103] Homer, *Od.* 23.7; Schiller, *Die Piccolomini* 1.1; see G. Büchmann, *Geflügelte Worte*, 26th ed. by B. Krieger (1920), 188.

[104] *y. B. M.* 8c.

[105] *Gen. Rab.* on 26:29; see my *Ancient Hebrew Fables* (1973), 13. J. Levy, *Wörterbuch über die Talmudim und Midraschim*, 2nd ed. (1924), translates *qore'* in the fable by *Rebhuhn*, "partridge," twice: in vol. 2, 476, s.v. *laghlegh*, and vol. 3, 220, s.v. *maqqora'*. (To which may be added J. Levy, *Wörterbuch über die Targumim* (1867), 383, s.v. *qore'a, qora'a, qore'*.) However, in the principal entry of the word, vol. 4, 275, we are told that, while "partridge" is its usual meaning, this fable employs it in the sense of *Rabe*, "raven"—though the raven has no particularly long beak. The argument offered is that "the well-known fable of the lion and raven is being recited." There must be some lapse here.

precisely against the original, main part. What is truly Plautine about the *Comedy of Asses* cannot possibly be seen if the entire work is given the date of the latest jokes.

One day in the future, a Columbia professor will be represented as having complained, in the nineteen-seventies, about a dull-witted Martian colleague's flimsy chronology. The Martian will have superseded a Californian in this account, but the Columbia historian's views about the problem will still be recoverable.

VIII.

In view of the inseparability of religion and peoplehood in Judaism, it may be worth while to subjoin a discussion on the child of a Jewess and a gentile. Today it is considered Jewish, on virtually the same level as where both parents are Jews.[106] But the rule is post-Biblical, slowly evolving from the second century A.D. onwards and approaching victory only around A.D. 400. Behind it lies a sad tale of human tragedies—relieved by the compassionateness of the Rabbis.

We have seen[107] that, before the Babylonian exile, a gentile woman marrying a Jew automatically became a Jewess; accordingly, there was no problem about the offspring. From then on, however, a ritual of conversion was required, in the absence of which she was not deemed Jewish—and neither was the offspring. Ezra and Nehemiah saw to it that the new practice was strictly carried on after the return.

It is important to realize that the change did not affect the case of a Jewess marrying a gentile. Now as before she was lost to the nation. If anything, this would henceforth be insisted on more strongly: there was conscious determination to cut off one who went over to the heathen camp.

The finally prevailing canon by which we are now guided is found in no Tannaitic work. While a movement towards it is noticeable from the beginning of the second century A.D., in quite a few texts, Tannaitic and Amoraic, it is assumed that the child of a Jewess and a gentile is a gentile. In a number of others, it is classed as a bastard, *mamzer*. Evidently, the older standpoints were not definitely superseded till near the time of the redaction of the Talmud.

Before filling in details, it is advisable to dispose of an episode involving Herod Agrippa I—grandson of Herod the Great—which has been badly misconstrued.[108] Already his Edomite great-great-grandfather or great-great-great-grandfather had converted to Judaism. Nevertheless many people would resent a king not of pure lineage, and especially a descendant of Edomites who, even after conversion, were entitled to free intermarriage within Jewry only from the third generation on.[109] On a certain festival, when he was publicly reciting the paragraph of the king from Deuteronomy, on reaching the exhortation "You may not put a foreigner over you who is not your brother,"[110] he

[106] See R. Posner, art. "Jew," *Encyclopedia Judaica*, 10 (1971), 23.

[107] See above, 466 ff.

[108] *m. Sot.* 7:8; *t. Sot.* 7:16.

[109] Deut 23:8 f., as understood by the Rabbis: *m. Yeb.* 8:3.

[110] Deut 17:5. For the original point of this interdiction, see my article ["One from among Your Brethren Shall You Set King over You"] in *JBL*, 90 (1971), 480 f.

burst into tears. Whereupon the sages reassured him: "Fear not, you are our brother." In fact, they said "you are our brother" three times, a formal acknowledgement.

Obviously, they were alluding to the provision concerning Edom just mentioned: "You shall not abhor an Edomite, for he is your brother; the children of the third generation may enter into the assembly of the Lord." Beyond this fact, not much can be said with confidence about their legal and political motives. R. Nathan of the second century A.D. charged them with sinful flattery. (According to Josephus, it is in order to flatter Herod the Great that the historian Nicolas of Damascus replaces his Edomite origin by a Babylonian Jewish one.[111]) What is erroneous is the idea, entertained in modern literature,[112] that the report proves adherence as early as in Temple days to the principle that the child of a Jewess and a gentile is Jewish. It simply does not envisage a union of this nature. It is noteworthy that, however much the late Rabbis may have wished for a precedent from that date, nowhere in Talmud or Midrash do we meet this mix-up.

Now for some passages treating the offspring of a Jewess and a gentile as a gentile; and first, the Mishnic provision[113] that a proselyte with a Jewish mother may praise "the God of our fathers." No doubt this puts him above one with a gentile mother. Yet it still leaves him a proselyte. But for his conversion, that is, he would not be a Jew.

Similarly, the Bible tells us of "the going forth of the son of an Israelite woman, who was the son of an Egyptian man, in the midst of the children of Israel."[114] In Siphra,[115] the clause, "in the midst" and so on is declared "to teach that he had converted to Judaism." So a Jewish mother is not enough to make a man a Jew. Perhaps it should be added that the interpretation is unhistorical. The original narrator is not thinking of conversion; what he means is that the man, though sharing his father's status as a kind of resident alien,[116] went right among the full Israelites. Just so, Dinah "went forth" among the full Shechemitesses.[117] For the present purpose, the difference is irrelevant: the point is that Siphra here no less than the Bible looks on the child of a Jewess and a gentile as a gentile.

Again, we hear of scholars of the third and fourth centuries allowing a proselyte with a Jewish mother to be a judge.[118] The breakthrough occurred when such a proselyte ran for town manager and his rival, an established scholar, demanded his exclusion before R. Joseph. The proselyte, however, had a Rabbinical friend, Adda bar Ahaba, who persuaded R. Joseph to lay down that a proselyte with a Jewish mother is "from among your brethren."[119] Joseph's pupil Raba adopted the opinion. By the way, the scholar was not left without comfort: a man like him, Joseph explained, had best devote himself to higher, "heavenly" concerns, while the other one engaged in the more mun-

[111] Josephus, *Ant.* 14.1.3.9.

[112] See e.g. L. M. Epstein, *Marriage Laws in the Bible and Talmud* (1942), 196.

[113] *m. Bikk.* 1:4.

[114] Lev 24:10.

[115] *Siphra* on Lev 24:10.

[116] See above, 468.

[117] Gen 34:1.

[118] *b. Yeb.* 102a; *b. Kidd.* 76b.

[119] Deut 17:15.

dane city affairs. One is reminded of the division of labour between Mary and Martha envisaged by Jesus.[120]

It is not impossible that the case of the king-judge Agrippa I, though essentially quite different, plays a certain part: his distinguished Jewish ancestry on his mother's side was in his favour, a consideration which may conceivably have been generalised. At any rate, R. Joseph's verdict is a notable concession. Nevertheless, it definitely does treat the man as a proselyte, not as a native Jew. This is underlined by the reservation that a convert with a Jewish mother, even when installed as judge, may not act in questions respecting levirate marriage. Judgment here may determine a party's "name in Israel,"[121] and a proselyte comes from outside—even one whose mother is a Jewess.

According to the Acts of the Apostles,[122] Timothy had a Jewish-Christian mother and a Greek father. Paul, wishing to appoint him his assistant-missionary, circumcised him in deference to the Jews of the region, "for they all knew that his father was a Greek." The natural meaning is that they knew him to be a gentile: hence, if his mission was to have any chance with them, he had to be incorporated by circumcision.

Commentators, anachronistically carrying back into this period the principle that the child of a Jewess is always Jewish,[123] get into difficulties with "for they all knew" and so on. What did it matter? One way out taken by some[124] is to regard Luke as ignorant of the Jewish position. But this is not a recondite, sophisticated detail. It is a matter as to which anybody with the remotest contact with Judaism would be informed. Another line attempted[125] is to postulate that the words in question are not to be taken in their natural sense. The Jews knew, Luke intends to convey, that Timothy, though one of them on account of his mother, was unlikely to be circumcised since his father was a gentile. However, why, if this is what Luke wants to say, he does not say it, remains unexplained. Also, it makes the Jews even worse jumpers to conclusions than they are. Had it been the law that such offspring was Jewish, it is difficult to see why circumcision on the eighth day should have been uncommon. Of Timothy, we know that he was very much brought up by his mother.[126]

Whether Paul, despite his rejection of proselyte circumcision, did in fact proceed as Luke relates, we need not decide; still less whether—within the framework of this tradition—he would have proceeded thus had both parents been gentiles. (I have little doubt that the account in Acts is true: his task takes precedence over consistency with doctrine. There are quite a few other examples.[127]) What matters in the present context is that the incident—historical or not—presupposes, indeed, is valuable evidence for, the old system under which a Jewess married to a gentile produces gentile progeny.

[120] Luke 10:38 ff.

[121] Deut 25:10.

[122] Acts 16:1 ff.

[123] Most of them rely on H. L. Strack and P. Billerbeck, *Kommentar zum Neuen Testament aus Talmud und Midrasch*, 2 (1924), 741.

[124] See e.g. H. Conzelmann, *Die Apostelgeschichte* (1963), 89.

[125] See e.g. E. Haenchen, *Die Apostelgeschichte*, 13th ed. (1961), 420; J. Munck, *The Acts of the Apostles* (1967), 155.

[126] 2 Tim 1:5.

[127] Some are quoted in my "Pauline Contributions," 227 ff. [541 ff.]

The earliest authority represented as deviating is Simeon of Teman, of the second century A.D., for whom the child was Jewish, though of the most inferior category: a bastard, *mamzer*. Within a very short time, Simeon ben Johai pronounced it legitimate, *kasher*.[128] The considered formulation of Mishnah,[129] Tosephta[130] and Siphra[131] opts for bastardy, though the Tosephta also notes the more generous line of Simeon ben Eleazar. Evidently, the portions in these sources presupposing that the child is a gentile are relics not brought up to date.

Among the followers of Simeon of Teman in the same century were Aqiba, Ishmael and Meir, in the third Johanan bar Nappaha, Hanina bar Hama, Ammi, Resh Laqish, Eleazar ben Pedath and Hiyya II bar Abba, and in the fourth Rabba bar Bar Hana and Dimi. Among the followers of Simeon ben Johai in the same century were Simeon ben Judah and Simeon ben Eleazar, in the third Bar Kappara, Jonathan ben Eleazar, Joshua ben Levi, Zeira and Mattena, in the fourth Rabin and in the fifth Rabina, Ameemar and Aha bar Raba. Judah the Prince and, it seems, Samuel too are variously assigned to one or the other faction.[132] My guess is that they in fact belonged to the former, being subsequently transferred to the latter as it was gaining in strength. As far as Judah the Prince is concerned, the Mishnah's official line—the child is a bastard—makes this a near-certainty. We shall find the same tendency at work in respect of Rab Judah bar Ezekiel and Raba.[133]

How did it come to recognition, be it as bastard, be it as legitimate? Nothing points to foreign inspiration. For one thing, in second-century Roman law, the offspring of a Roman woman married to an alien shared the latter's nationality.[134] It must be an internal development. But what accounts for it seeing that, in general, the Talmudic trend was towards ever greater strictness in this area? More particularly, what made it start in an age of extreme hostility to, and terrible suffering at the hands of, the occupying power? And why was the earliest advocate of full acceptance, legitimacy (at least the earliest named in the sources) Simeon ben Johai, a foremost opponent of assimilation and for years outlawed by the government?[135]

It is precisely the paradoxical aspect of the reform which furnishes the clue. In that fearful period, abuse of Jewish women by the enemy was common. Significantly, the Talmud barely distinguishes between cruelties of this kind in Maccabean times and Hadrianic ones.[136] Rabbinical circles were not, of course, spared. The daughter of the martyred Hananiah ben Teradion was carried off to a brothel from where, we are told (with, perhaps, some embellishments), R. Meir, her brother-in-law, eventually bought her back.[137]

[128] *y. Yeb.* 6b f.; *y. Kidd.* 64c f.; *b. Yeb.* 16a f., 44b ff., 99a, 102a; *b. Kidd.* 68b, 75b ff.; *b. A. Zar.* 59a.

[129] *m. Yeb.* 7:5.

[130] *t. Kidd.* 4:16.

[131] *Siphra* on Lev 22:13.

[132] Judah the Prince: *b. Yeb.* 45a; Samuel: *b. Yeb.* 45a, *y. Yeb.* 6c.

[133] See below, 486 f.

[134] Gaius, *Institutes* 1.78; Ulpian, *Regulae* 5.8.

[135] How bitter he could be may be seen from *y. Kidd.* 66b.

[136] *b. Gitt.* 57b.

[137] *b. A. Zar.* 18a f.

Imagine a place after a week's devastation by the soldateska. Here were pious wives and daughters of pious parents, raped. Suppose they gave birth to gentiles, that must cause not only much personal anguish but also, as the children grew up, tensions a critically enfeebled community could not afford. A reform of the traditional system was highly desirable. What made it possible was an integral element in the situation: the father against whom it was directed was absent, did not care one way or the other.

It may be asked why, if this is how the new regulation came about, it was carried on even when things became more peaceful. Part of the answer is that assault on women in one form or another never ceased being a real threat. We learn, for instance, of the ransoming towards the end of the third century of a Jewess who had become pregnant in captivity.[138] I do think, however, that the measure's chance of success would have been far less if it had not been sponsored by a man like Simeon ben Johai, generally the most adamant purist. (His stand against extradition of a fellow-Jew in any circumstances is typical.[139])

Simeon ben Teman held the child to be a bastard. From a modern point of view, his solution may look like having made matters worse. While a gentile can convert, thereby becoming more or less the equal of a born Jew, a bastard is virtually unable to rise, hence will never be a suitable marriage partner for an unblemished person. But this is not how they felt then. A bastard was at least one of them, inside, a Jew—and that was an immense improvement: it consoled the families afflicted and it averted the danger of rearing a fifth column. We should bear in mind that, during Hadrian's terror regime and often afterwards, the pagan authorities would make conversion a very risky affair. Anyhow, legitimacy began to replace bastardy quite soon.

Naturally, any measure giving relief in these heartbreak conditions had to be extended to marriage of a Jewess and a gentile. Most texts dealing with the topic employ a term which primarily designates an irregular union—a gentile "comes upon," *ba' 'al*, a Jewess[140]—which gives further support to my thesis. (Its first occurrence is in the complaint by Lot's elder daughter to the younger, after the destruction of Sodom, that "there is no man on earth to come upon us."[141]) The considered ruling of Mishnah and Siphra, however, speaks of a Jewess "married to," *niśśe'th le*, a gentile.[142] Such a marriage might indeed be contracted in error as to his status: say, he gets circumcised but neither he nor his Jewish bride are aware that baptism is equally essential for conversion. I shall come back to this case[143] where, clearly, treatment of the offspring as Jewish would be called for on humanitarian and political grounds much as in the violent situations described above. Still, the new principle could not be applied selectively: it must cover any progeny of a Jewess.

[138] *b. Yeb.* 45a.

[139] See my *Collaboration with Tyranny in Rabbinic Law* (1965), 28 ff.; but also ["Jewish Law in the Hellenistic World"] *JLA*, Suppl. 2 (1980), 45, 59 [*Talmudic Law*, 83 ff., 213, 227]

[140] E.g. *t. Kidd.* 4:16.

[141] Gen 19:31.

[142] *m. Yeb.* 7:5; *Siphra* on Lev 22:13.

[143] *b. Yeb.* 46a; cp. *y. Kidd.* 64c; see below, 486 f.

A striking adumbration of the Rabbis' concessions regarding the status of offspring is contained in Paul's teaching, already adverted to,[144] about conversion of one of two spouses. As the convert is a new being, the marriage is ended; but if they stay together—which the apostle recommends—intercourse establishes a fresh marriage. This implies two momentous deviations from traditional practice: admission of marriage with a heathen and, since the fresh marriage comes about even where the convert is a woman, admission of a woman's capacity to "consecrate," *qiddesh*, a man. Paul's argument for recognition is: "else were your children unclean."[145] True, the situation he deals with involves no violence; indeed, in a way, it is the opposite of that the Rabbis are facing. The latter, in response to the desperate losses suffered by their flock, try to mitigate such further disruption as they can. Paul's aim is to enhance the growth of an already growing Church. Yet, though coming from such different places—fear of utter ruin, hope for ever more glorious advance—or indeed, because of this, they are both led to basically the same concern.

Once the setting of the problem is seen, much that is otherwise puzzling falls into place. First, the enormous span of opinion: total exclusion of the child at one end, bastardy in the middle, legitimacy at the other end. Actually, it is even more extreme than might be thought: for the sponsors of the third, ultimately prevailing view, the child is legitimate—not a bastard—even if the mother is properly married to a Jew at the time.[146] If she had a child from another Jew, it would be a bastard. Surely, this dispensation could have originated only in the dire dilemma I am assuming. I am aware of the argumentation since built up so as to fit everything into a neat, logical structure.

Secondly, the long struggle between these various attitudes: some three hundred years. Even of as late an authority as Rabina, the Gemara finds it necessary to prove that he did not rank the child as a bastard.[147] This feature, too, is explained by the evolution here outlined, with rooted tenets being challenged by social exigencies. This usually makes for a tough conflict.

A third item is closely connected with the second: the ambivalence of quite a few sages confronted by the problem. Hiyya II, when visiting Gebal, noticed that Jewesses there married, and conceived from, gentiles who, having undergone circumcision, counted as proselytes though baptism had been omitted. He kept silent till ordered by his teacher Johanan to announce to them that their children were bastards.[148]

Also in the late third century, Judah bar Ezekiel counselled the son of a Jewess and a gentile either to marry "a woman of his kind"—a bastard was permitted only to marry another bastard—or to conceal his antecedents so that he might marry into legitimate stock. Raba, in the fourth century, gave similar advice, to marry "a woman of his kind" or go abroad.[149] The Gemara, to be sure, infers that these scholars deemed the ques-

[144] See above, 476 ff.
[145] 1 Cor 7:14.
[146] *b. Yeb.* 45b.
[147] *b. Kidd.* 68b.
[148] *b. Yeb.* 46a; *b. A. Zar.* 59a.
[149] *b. Yeb.* 45a.

tioner legitimate. They would not have suggested deceit for the purpose of wrongful marriage: they suggested it because a number of colleagues still stuck to the less favourable judgment and, also, because even if their benign ruling was accepted, the man would not be welcome everywhere. However, this is most probably another instance of adherents to the stricter doctrine being re-classed.[150] Raba, as I pointed out,[151] at some stage or in some contexts at least, looked on such a person as not even a bastard but a gentile—as a proselyte if converted. The point is that the Rabbis were torn between time-hallowed principle on the one hand and gentleness and expediency on the other. I wonder whether, even in this century, it might not have been better in many cases if courts having to allow or disallow a marriage had asked fewer questions.

This is not to deny that, especially in the upper stratum of society, even with legitimacy granted, there would indeed be prejudice against admitting a person of inferior description into one's family. Rab,[152] approached by the son of a Jewess and a gentile, decided in favour of legitimacy, yet when the man asked him for his daughter's hand, declined. A younger confrère, Shimi bar Hiyya (elsewhere, too, in controversy with him[153]), quoted a proverb (in the manner of Rab[154]), "In Shangri-la a camel will dance on a table,"[155] adding: "Here is the table, the camel and Shangri-la, but no dancing." That is to say: your decision—he is legitimate—created a fairyland setting and we were all agog to watch the corresponding performance—his becoming your son-in-law—but it does not materialize. Rab retorted that he would not budge even if the suitor were like Moses's successor Joshua.[156] To which Shimi replied that, if he were like Joshua, he could easily find himself another wife despite Rab's rebuff; but as it was, other fathers would now be suspicious and reject him. As the man refused to leave, Rab fixed his eyes on him and he died.[157] (The sage was famous for his mastery of esoteric knowledge.[158] Earth from his grave was used to cure fever.[159]) He belonged to the aristocracy; and it may well be that daughter of his who subsequently married into the Exilarch's house.[160]

Isaiah, according to legend,[161] in a remotely comparable quandary, behaved differently from Rab. He had reproved King Hezekiah for remaining unmarried, and when the latter gave as his reason a vision that any children of his would be grave sinners, had rejected this as irrelevant: a man ought to do his duty and leave the rest to God. Hezekiah repented—and asked the prophet to let him have his daughter to wife. Isaiah agreed.

[150] See above, 484.
[151] See above, 482.
[152] *b. Yeb.* 45a.
[153] E.g. *b. Yeb.* 47a; *b. Yom.* 28b.
[154] E.g. *b. Sanh.* 106a. See W. Bacher, *Die Agada der Babylonischen Amoräer* (1878), 32.
[155] Literally, "In Media, a camel dances on a *qab*." A *qab* is about 2000 cubic centimeters.
[156] Cp. *b. Hull.* 124a towards the end.
[157] Cp. Acts 5:5, 10.
[158] See W. Bacher, *op. cit.*, 16 ff.
[159] *b. Sanh.* 47b.
[160] *b. Hull.* 92a.
[161] *b. Ber.* 10a; see my *Medical and Genetic Ethics: Three Historical Vignettes* (1976), 8 ff.

Incongruities in the determination of status are not unknown in modern systems. It so happened that, while I was sketching the foregoing history of the Jewish approach a few years ago, the International Social Service was fighting for some four thousand children born during the occupation of Japanese women married to Americans. Under present Japanese law they are aliens, and under American law their citizenship lapses unless they reside continuously for two years in the States between the ages of 14 and 28. No need to worry about a child of a Japanese woman and an American not married to one another: it is recognized as Japanese on the mother's entering it into the family register.

EXCURSUS

The following material is culled from lectures and writings of mine in the period 1961–73. It may be of moderate interest even though much will be judged shallow or redundant now that we have available Calum Carmichael's chapter on Ruth in his great, I am tempted to say magical, book *Women, Law and the Genesis Traditions*.[162]

The book of Ruth is the *Winter's Tale* of the Bible: vain search for prosperity and fearful losses at first, mature reconciliation of the survivors and the promise of a new generation in the end. The family's head, Elimelech, "God is King," and both his heirs, Mahlon and Qilyon, "Sickly" and "Weakly," die abroad, and one of his Moabite daughters-in-law, Orpah, "the Turner-back," re-enters her native community. But the other, Ruth, "the Friend," follows his widow, Naomi, "the Pleasant one," to Elimelech's home at Bethlehem—though at this stage Naomi re-christens herself Marah, "the Bitter-fated"; maybe there is here an echo of Tamar, who is cited in the Book as an old-time model for the two women and who also went through long years of suffering.[163] After a period of trial, they, joined by a relative of Elimelech's, Boaz, "the Pillar"—a descendant of Judah and Tamar[164]—re-establish, and indeed ensure a glorious future for, the seemingly ruined house. (My translations of the names may not all stand up to scholarly etymology. What matters here is that they convey, I think, the narrator's understanding.) With a purposive and caring deity keeping watch, it is the loyalty, patience and wisdom of the protagonists that bring about the happy conclusion. Of Greek writers, Sophocles alone in his two dramas about Oedipus treats of the healing power of time in comparable fashion.[165]

Arguably, we ought to speak of the Book of Naomi. The story begins with her, is dominated by her and terminates with her. It is she who emigrates with husband and sons, who returns solitary except for Ruth's devoted attendance and who is eventually recognized as, in an ultimate sense, the mother of the son born by the latter and destined to be the ancestor of King David. When the entire family is brought low, the Lord has testified "against her," and when it prospers, to her the felicitations are tendered.[166] Every single step of Ruth is taken under her direction. By a curious coincidence, the road to expiation, peace and hope in *The Winter's Tale* is mapped out by one of the queen's friends not herself a participant in the main exchanges of love and hate.[167]

I shall occupy myself with a few facets to which, as a rule, it does not seem that justice is being done: the relation of youth and age (1), female friendship (2), the obstacle in the way of "redemption" and the means of surmounting it suggested by Naomi (3), the following out of her design by Boaz (4), the counterpoint to the Book of Ruth supplied by that of Esther (5) and the nature of the Book (6).

[162] (1979), 74 ff.

[163] Ruth 4:12; Genesis 38, on which latter episode see my *The Duty of Procreation* (1977), 4 f.

[164] Ruth 4:18 ff.

[165] See my article ["Greek Forerunners of Simenon"] in *CLRev*, 68 (1980), 310. The role of time in Shakespeare's last plays is inspiringly discussed by Gustav Landauer, *Shakespeare*, vol. 2, (1922), 240 ff., 280 ff. The work is among those edited by Martin Buber after the author's murder by right-wing extremists.

[166] Ruth 1:21, 4:14 f.

[167] See G. Landauer, *op. cit.*, 256.

1. Youth and age. To start with Boaz—he is fiftyish, about twice as old as Ruth. From their first encounter he addresses her as "my daughter."[168] He is "a mighty man of wealth."[169] His speech is dignified, almost solemn, his position and actions those of a respected, getting-on citizen. Though single, he engages in no amatory pursuits: obviously Naomi, when she encourages Ruth to visit him in the barn where he will lie down after a merry-making, is sure he will be alone.[170] As Ruth approaches him, offering to become his wife, he thanks her—"my daughter" again—for her kindness in not preferring somebody younger. No intercourse takes place: far from being an impetuous lover, he displays the utmost restraint. She suggestively occupies the place of a spouse—we must remember that, though by much his junior, she is a widow, not a trembling virgin. But that nothing happens beyond this is quite clear from his reflections on a kinsman with a better title who will have to be dealt with before they can go ahead. It would be too risky to anticipate success in disposing of this prior claim. Indeed, Ruth leaves before dawn in order that their intimate meeting should not become public; otherwise suspicion would be aroused and they would be putting themselves very much in the wrong. A further, more specific motive for secrecy will emerge in due course. A little remark by Naomi provides corroboration. Having received Ruth's report, she assures her that they will not now have to wait long: "the man will not sit still until he have finished the thing this day."[171] There has been no fulfilment; but he is stirred. The shrewd lady knows the effect it will have—was it not all her doing?

It should be added that Tamar also conceived from a man belonging to the previous generation, Judah, her father-in-law. She also favoured him above a highly eligible younger option, his surviving third son. She also was far from inexperienced and threw herself in the boldest manner at the worthy to be won, as he was, like Boaz, alone after a festivity. Lastly, once enlightened as to where he stood, he, like Boaz, was fully capable of keeping his impulses in check.[172] Whether or not the earlier narrative finds the difference in age interesting, it would not escape the author of Ruth.

As for Naomi—her matronliness receives enormous emphasis and is in fact far more important than Boaz's seniority. As Ruth's mother-in-law, we would assume her to be roughly his contemporary. This may be checked. Her sons married while in Moab. Say, they were then around twenty, she around forty. We are told[173] that about ten years elapsed before they died and she returned—fiftyish. Two passages, however, add greatly to the picture. Early on, we learn in circumstantial language that she is virtually past childbearing;[174] and towards the close of the Book, her neighbours wish her joy because the babe "will be a nourisher of your old age"[175]—the kind of felicitation suitable only for a woman with no more active aspirations.

[168] Ruth 2:8, 3:10 f.

[169] Ruth 2:1.

[170] Ruth 3:4.

[171] Ruth 3:18.

[172] Gen 38:36.

[173] Ruth 1:4.

[174] Ruth 1:12 f.

[175] Ruth 4:15.

2. Friendship. The Book has in common with a remarkable number of Old Testament plots involving succession that the major decisions are made by brave and resourceful women—even though, essentially, in behalf of their men who have to be trapped into their good fortune. Tamar, of course, comes to mind; Sarah, Rebekkah and Bathsheba are other examples.[176] But nowhere else do we find an attachment between two women as here, genuine, for better or worse, person to person. There is a trusting sharing of father-husband between Lot's daughters, deprived of any other human communication;[177] but it remains a single, if moving, episode. (Maybe there is a civilisatory dilution of a theme in the sequel: a child from the father for Lot's daughters, from the father-in-law for Tamar, from a senior kinsman for Ruth and Naomi.) Ruth accompanies Naomi into a country unknown to her, where they are likely to live in poverty and isolation. The latter in turn forgoes in favour of the former her own chances of gaining a "redeemer" a new husband—at least as that role is normally understood. In deeper reality, as we shall see, theirs also is a sharing, though of a more refined sort than in the primeval legend, and just as in that legend, the elder one takes the initiative and lends encouragement to the younger one. Ruth "loves" Naomi and to Naomi, who has lost her children, Ruth "is better than seven sons"—as the barren Hannah's husband hopes to be to his wife.[178] The narrator takes pains to impress on us the extraordinary level attained by the two: Orpah aspired to it, at first intending, like Ruth, to journey with her mother-in-law, but finally she had not the courage. We must not forget that both Ruth and Orpah already in Moab chose an unusual path, by attaching themselves wholeheartedly to Judean refugees.[179] Ruth goes it to the end.

Actually, as far as I can make out, the alliance is unique in ancient literature. There are many parallels to David and Jonathan or Nisus and Euryalus,[180] male comrades risking their lives for one another. Stith Thompson contains dozens of such entries under Friendship[181]—not a single remotely corresponding one about women. The only approximation that occurs to me is in Sophocles: Ismene would like to die together with her sister Antigone. The relationship, however, is marred because, earlier on, she had not had the spirit to join Antigone in contravening the royal decree, so the latter now spurns her request. In a way, Orpah is reminiscent of Ismene.

Of the reasons for this lacuna in the sources it must suffice to name three, interconnected. One: our informants are mostly male, interested in women only insofar as their doings affect the male world. If any of Queen Vashti's ladies shared exile or the gallows with her,[182] we cannot expect to hear of it. (Not one dream of a Jewish woman is recorded by either the Old Testament or the New. A glance at Helen's Note-Books will reveal the incongruity of this.) Two: the heroic mode of mutual self-sacrifice popular with the bards—in battle, in political conspiracy—is on the whole outside the range of

[176] Genesis 21, 27; 2 Kings 1.

[177] Gen 19:30 ff.

[178] Ruth 4:15; 1 Sam 1:8 (ten sons).

[179] Ruth 1:8.

[180] Virgil, *Aeneid* 9.176 ff.

[181] *Motif-Index of Folk-Literature*, 5 (1957), 163 ff.

[182] Esther 1; see below, 497.

female activity. There is blood-brotherhood, no blood-sisterhood. Women serve in other ways. Three: to the extent that men mastered the art of *divide et impera*, an unbreakable bond between two women would in fact be a relatively rare achievement.[183] What a beautiful paradox. An extraordinary conflux of circumstances accounts for the commemoration of this pair. Yet it is Ruth's oath of allegiance to Naomi—"Whither you go I will go, the Lord do so to me if aught but death part you and me"[184]—that to this day is quoted as expressing the highest level of dedication, irrespective of sex; it figures in marriage celebrations; it has been set to music over and over again.

3. The marital problem: the scheme. Naomi, back at Bethlehem, is in control of what remains of Elimelech's realm, Ruth and the land. As regards the latter, this chimes with a pericope in the Second Book of Kings,[185] where a widow (with a son under age) resides on the estate, moves abroad during a famine, on her return finds herself dispossessed and is reinstated at the king's behest; she is even reimbursed for the fruits the intruders took in her absence.[186] Still, it is a sad existence: apart from the lack of a man, there is so little food that Ruth must procure some by gleaning. Boaz admires the high-minded couple, being particularly taken by Ruth—indeed, he says so to her.[187] Moreover, he appreciates their need and makes it as easy as possible for them to get enough to eat from his fields. For all that, he is studiously cautious, takes not steps to accomplish a real change in their situation. He first meets Ruth at the beginning of the barley harvest: both it and the wheat harvest go by and he still is just supportive, tender—distant.

What more could he do? A great deal. If an impoverished owner of land has sold it or is about to sell it, his agnatic relations, in order of proximity, have the right, and a moral duty, to "redeem" it, to buy it back or pre-empt it.[188] A clan's territory ought to be kept intact. Jeremiah, even while imprisoned by the authorities, "redeems" a cousin's property, even while it is occupied by the Babylonian army.[189] Boaz could put it to Naomi that, should no closer relation come forward, he would be a generous purchaser. However, there is a snag. Under the system prevailing in this epoch, if the land belongs to a childless widow, a "redeemer" must take her to wife and the firstborn will always be her original husband's heir. In these special conditions, "redemption" has strong affinity with levirate—best known from Tamar's romance. The Biblical levirate operates within the nuclear family, primarily where—as in the saga of Tamar—a married son dies childless in his father's lifetime: the widow, without change of family, goes to a brother and their firstborn will count as begotten by the deceased. (There is one extend-

[183] A reminder from modern times is furnished by Mörike's *Zwei Schwestern*, made into a duet by Brahms.

[184] Ruth 1:16 f.

[185] 2 Kgs 8:1 ff.

[186] Cp. *Digest* 13.7.22.2, Ulpian XXX *ad edictum*: *A praedone enim fructus et vindicari extantes possunt et consumpti condici* [For surviving fruits can be claimed from an usurper by a (*vindicatio*), and those consumed by a (*condictio*)].

[187] Ruth 2:11 ff.

[188] Lev 25:25 ff.

[189] Jer 32:6 ff.

ed application:[190] if, after the father's death, his sons stay together on the undivided estate[191] and one of them, married, dies childless, again, the widow is taken over by a brother and the first son ranks as the deceased's.) To be sure, the purpose of this institution is not to avert any loss of land but to provide a luckless family member with the line he hoped for.[192] Nevertheless, in the peculiar "redemption" case involving a childless widow, once the agnate qualified steps forward, he must show the same concern for the deceased member of his clan—a very major point of contact. At any rate, this is what holds Boaz back: the requirement to marry the dowager. It will soon become apparent that it is not a mere matter of carnal appetites—though I am the last person to pooh-pooh them.

Naomi has made up her mind that he would be the ideal protector. She is aware of his ground of hesitation. She also knows how to interpret his dealings with Ruth, reticent and tactful as they are. She decides to show him a way out of the impasse. She sends him Ruth, attired as for a wedding. He gets the message: he can do his duty by Naomi by taking charge of Ruth—who is very willing to fall in with the plan. At this juncture, there commences a phantasmagoria which will go on right to the finish, a series of scenes with the parties appearing in different masks and each mask itself being ambivalent. It is not, however, a play but a real-life struggle for high stakes. For the moment let us recall that Judah did his duty by Tamar, the respectable widow, by having intercourse with Tamar, posing—masked in the literal sense—as a whore. She thus, basically, acted both roles, of Naomi and of Ruth, at the same time. I cannot resist mentioning that *The Winter's Tale* culminates in a mummery (a sacred one, in a chapel[193]): the wronged queen is restored to her husband who has done penance for sixteen years, but first she is shown him as if she were a statue.

4. The marital problem: the execution. Boaz now is galvanized into action. He indicates to Naomi that he understands: while retaining Ruth as his bedfellow throughout the night—although without sexual commerce—in the morning he bids her take a bridal present, the *Morgengabe*, *pretium pudicitiae*, to Naomi.[194] In strict law, it is she who has been with him, as whose "redeemer" he proceeds. The same day he sets out to tackle his potential rival, and the ingenuity by dint of which he eliminates him proves him worthy of being Naomi's choice. Before a quorum of elders, he asks him whether he wishes to "redeem," purchase, Elimelech's land, up for sale; otherwise he, Boaz, will do so. The first answer, plainly anticipated, is yes. Then he goes on:[195] "What day you buy

[190] Deut 25:5 ff. See my comments ["Consortium in Roman and Hebrew Law"] in *JR*, 62 (1950), 71 ff.

[191] Cp. Gaius, *Institutes* 3.154a: *Olim enim, mortuo patre familias, inter suos heredes quaedam erat legitima simul et naturalis societas quae appellabatur ercto non cito, id est dominio non diviso* [For once upon a time, when the male head of a family was dead there was among his descendants who had become free from his power at the same time both a statutory and a natural partnership that was called (*erecto non cito*), that is to say "with the ownership not divided."].

[192] An arresting modern levirate, in James Purdy's *Mourners Below* (1981), comes my way as this book is going to print.

[193] Mozart uses church music for the Count's pardon by the Countess in the last act of *Le Nozze di Figaro*.

[194] Ruth 3:15, 17. Cp. Gen 24:22, 47, 53, 34:12.

[195] Ruth 4:5.

the field from the hand of Naomi and from Ruth the Moabitess, you have bought the wife of the dead to raise up the name of the dead upon his inheritance." The childless widow is part of the estate; and immediately the answer turns into no. The point is that Boaz, though by now he knows better, formulates in such a way that the other one can envisage only marriage with Naomi. Literally, "the wife of the dead" may describe either her or Ruth, both being childless widows; and this is of no small moment since Boaz must not be guilty of a straight falsehood. But as the phrase occurs in a statement about Elimelech's land, anyone trusting fair play is bound to think of Naomi. Boaz himself had been alerted to the possibility of a substitution only the night before. We have to do with a mode of deception familiar from the Jacob cycle, for instance.[196]

The transaction is not so comprehended by most scholars that they revise the text in order to get rid of the ambiguity: "what day you buy the field from the hand of Naomi, you have bought Ruth the Moabitess, the wife of the dead."[197] Ruining everything—like many an emendation.[198] It destroys the artful web woven by the three heroes in cooperation; it represents Boaz as leaving the outcome entirely to chance, or worse, to his opponent's discretion; and it makes the latter's emphatic refusal most uncomplimentary to Ruth. It is indeed possible that the words "and from Ruth the Moabitess" are an interpolation, dating from a time when the figure of Naomi lost in prominence and the subtleties of the plot began to be less fully grasped. They are not included in Boaz's final declaration of "redemption."[199] Be this as it may, on no account should we tamper with the deliberately misleading concentration on marriage with Naomi. The dangerous candidate withdraws because that is not what he wants—just as Boaz had not wanted it.

All this is illumined by the reason he gives, "lest I spoil my own inheritance."[200] No passage in this work has produced more headaches. How could "redemption" marriage—whether or not Naomi or with Ruth—interfere with his own patrimony? The firstborn would obtain Elimelech's, but nothing else, nothing from his physical begetter. What does he fear? Commentators mostly resort to evasion.[201] The very replacement of the forceful "to spoil," "to destroy," "to wipe out," by a vague "to mar" in English versions is revealing. Well, the explanation is that he has Naomi in mind, unlikely to have any more children. So for a few year's enjoyment of Elimelech's riches, he would leave his own heirless. But could he not marry a younger woman in addition? No. It is evidently assumed that he cannot. Which means either that the events take place in an interregnum of monogamy—not unimaginable—or, at least, that where it is your duty to see to the revival of a dead relation's name, you may not take another wife before you have satisfied it. Near Eastern documents offer several cases in which no second wife is allowed; and Jacob binds himself by treaty to refrain from further conquests.[202]

[196] See my *Studies in Biblical Law* (1947) (repr. 1969), 191 ff.

[197] See e.g. E. Würthwein, *Ruth*, in *Die Fünf Megilloth, Handbuch zum Alten Testament*, 18 (1969), 19 f.

[198] E.g. the treatment of *'o nishba* as a dittography of *'o nishbar* in Exod 22:9.

[199] Ruth 4:9.

[200] Ruth 4:6.

[201] Here is a desperate non-lawyer's projection: "The storyteller, of course, was not interested in the legal points." L. P. Smith, *The Book of Ruth*, in *The Interpreter's Bible*, 2 (1953), 849.

[202] Gen 31:50. See R. Yaron, *Introduction to the Law of the Aramic Papyri* (1961), 60.

Considering that both Tamar's story and an extensive regulation in Deuteronomy dwell on the faithlessness of levirs,[203] it will not be surprising if the law debars a "redeemer" of a childless widow's estate from similar conduct. The temptation to play false would be gigantic. It is relevant to note that Deuteronomy itself, while admitting that a delinquent levir may perpetuate his own name, makes the perpetuation worthless: the name will be stained for ever.[204]

Boaz, I maintained above, was unenthusiastic about marriage with Naomi from motives transcending sex-appeal. It can now be said that he, too, dreaded the extinction of his own name. This does not, it should be stressed, put him on the same level: his sustained solicitude for the two returnees testifies to his dependable, unselfish side. Again, I hinted at a specific object of his in not permitting Ruth's nocturnal call to transpire. This also is now clear. Had it become known, his competitor might well have sensed that a stratagem was afoot, perhaps even guessed its drift. As it is, he is thoroughly fooled. It should be observed, however, that even when he has expressed his disinterest, the circumspect, steady Boaz does not immediately come out with the truth. If he did that, the other one would change his mind and, especially since he has been tricked, would have little difficulty in getting an informal refusal held void. Hence Boaz calmly waits till the surrender of title is ratified by a solemnity that puts it above any attack, renders it absolute, "confirms" it.[205] (Jacob's extraction of an oath after Esau has already informally ceded his birthright is analogous.[206]) It is only then that he triumphantly announces: "You are witnesses that I have bought all that was Elimelech's and Qilyon's and Mahlon's. Moreover—the climax—Ruth the Moabitess, wife of Mahlon, have I bought to be my wife, to raise up the name of the dead upon his inheritance." So Ruth the desirable, thirty-year-old, fertile one is "the wife to the dead" whom the nearer kinsman renounced. Boaz, not at all a passive recipient of good luck, has skilfully carried out the operation the women entrusted to him. The ancient audience of the epic would share their happiness and laugh at their victim.

The Tamar precedent plays a considerable part in this scene at the city gate. The rival "will not spoil" his own domain for the sake of the dead Elimelech. Onan "spoilt" his semen in order not to lose a portion of the patrimony for the sake of his dead brother.[207] The moral: in a sense, here is a repetition of Onan's betrayal, this kinsman, too, withholds his semen from the bereaved widow. Yet it is not a simple identification. With superb craftsmanship we are given to understand that, blind as he is, he "spoils" precisely while intent on "not spoiling." There is more. Under the Deuteronomic ordinance

[203] Genesis 38; Deut 25:5 ff.

[204] Deut 25:10.

[205] Ruth 4:7, *qiyyem; negotium conficere* in Cicero's terminology—see next footnote.

[206] Gen 25:33; see my *Studies in Biblical Law*, 196. Cicero, *De Officiis* 3.14.58 f., tells of the owner of a lakeshore villa who, while entertaining a prospective buyer, got a large number of retainers to row about pretending to be catching fish. The guest offered a high price. But a simple, informal sale would not have been good enough since in the resultant *bonae fidei* proceedings the judge would take account of fraud. Accordingly, the vendor got his visitor to confirm the sale by a formal "literal contract," leading to strict proceedings with, at that time, no allowance for misrepresentation.

[207] Ruth 4:6, *hishḥith*, Hiphil, Gen 38:9, *shiḥeth*, Piel.

already averted to, one who, roughly speaking, acts like Onan is publicly shamed: he has his shoe taken off by the woman he abandons in front of the elders.[208] The potential contender, by way of releasing his lien, in front of the elders takes his shoe off himself.[209] True, he does so in compliance with a ritual customary for certain major transactions. But, surely, the author wishes us to see him at the same time as a dupe, suffering self-inflicted disgrace. Yet a further allusion should be listed. Onan is killed by God. So, on a certain level, is the outwitted relative. While Judah and Boaz are among the ancestors of David, he is forgotten by history. This is brought out dramatically by the fact that, in contrast to the other persons who have speaking names, names indicating their character and destiny, he has no name whatever. Boaz addresses him as "such a one,"[210] a unique usage in Scripture. His greed did him no good. It made him obtuse, and for the things temporal he lost the things eternal.

The dazzling alternation of roles goes on after his defeat. Boaz marries Ruth and the people hope his house will be blessed like that of Pharez, the offspring of Judah and Tamar. Yet when, in due course, they have a son, it is Naomi who receives congratulations on successful "redemption," who formally takes up the heir and places him in her lap, and whose neighbours exclaim, "There is a son born to Naomi," and call him Obed, "Servant (of God)," doubtless in memory of Elimelech, "God is King."[211] Here we must remind ourselves that several wives of patriarchs, when unable to conceive, lent female slaves or quasi-slaves of theirs to their husbands, with a view to the progeny being credited to them.[212] It is manifestly this arrangement on which that devised by Naomi is patterned. In legal construction, through Ruth, she is vicariously cohabiting with Boaz. And inevitably, just as in the tales about the patriarchs, there is a constant to and fro between construction and material actuality. The latter prevails in the genealogy appended in the last four verses of the last chapter: Obed here figures as Boaz's son, not Elimelech's.

5. Esther. From the foregoing discussion, it is certain that there is in Ruth a persistent harking back to the Tamar incident. In turn, as I have set out elsewhere,[213] the Book has helped to shape the account of the Feeding of the Multitude in all four gospels and that of the Annunciation in Luke. The question I would raise now is whether it has influenced Esther.

If, with Goethe, we dub the Book of Ruth the loveliest idyll coming down from antiquity, that of Esther is definitely the greatest thriller. I know of no work Eastern, Greek or Roman rivalling it as to construction, tension, flow of events, denouement. How such a perfect specimen of its genre came to be produced we shall probably never find out.

In Ruth, salvation is wrought by a foreign woman brought in, in Esther, by a Jewish woman being sent out. Both selflessly leave their native base. But Ruth, of Moabite provenance, is to become an ancestress of David, Esther, related to the family of Saul,

[208] See my article ["The Culture of Deuteronomy"] in *Orita*, 3 (1969), 35 ff.

[209] Ruth 4:2 ff.

[210] Ruth 4:1.

[211] Ruth 4:12 ff.

[212] Gen 16:2; 30:2, 9.

[213] See my *The New Testament and Rabbinic Judaism* (1956) (repr. 1973), 27 ff. [137 ff.]

relinquishes any hope of being a link in her people's continuation. In Biblical times, a child's nationality follows the father's. When Mordecai tells her that, if she dissociates herself from the beleaguered Jewish community, it will be rescued in some other way but "she and her father's house will perish,"[214] the warning carries an overtone of pathos: her glory cannot be transmitted to any descendants. Significantly, whereas generally in the Old Testament motherhood or barrenness is recorded in respect of far lesser figures, here not a word. The silence is deafening: whether or not she had children does not matter. Buber somewhere admires Abraham for offering up on mount Moriah not just the present but hope. Esther, and also Mordecai, her adoptive father, otherwise progenyless, are equally devout and there is no angel from heaven intervening at the last moment. The tragic component of this tale is tremendous. (We should assign to it also the court-Jew quality of Mordecai's and Esther's final position.[215]) They do, of course, by their sacrifice deliver Jewry—and the world. German-Jewish orthodoxy, in whose midst I grew up, despised anyone marrying out—but far less if the gentile partner was high-placed. (Other sins too were rendered more venial by success: Heine and Disraeli could be mentioned.) This was not, as I then thought, sheer worship of the golden calf or the like. There was also the feeling that important well-wishers outside were badly needed for the embattled minority's survival. The exemplar of Esther might have been a consolation to many a traditionalist family with a straying member.

The Book of Ruth, I said above, might be entitled the Book of Naomi. Just so, the Book of Esther might be entitled the Book of Mordecai. He is introduced at the beginning of the main part, he plans the decisive steps and he receives the final eulogy. Instead of a woman, however, there is a man at the helm. This drama is set in a milieu of machismo. In its defence, the court indeed resorts to strong measures;[216] and it is the banishment of proud Queen Vashti in the opening scene which makes possible Esther's rise—a bit as the extinction of Naomi's closest ones except Ruth makes possible the latter's union with Boaz. Not surprisingly, insistence on male supremacy in Esther does not render female charms and ruses any less effective than they are in Ruth.

Both heroines are bereft of parents, yet both are granted wonderful replacement. Ruth adopts Naomi as her mother—though the term "to foster," "to rear," which one might expect, is reserved for the finale where Naomi becomes the adoptive mother of Ruth's son.[217] Mordecai adopts Esther as his daughter and "fosters" her.[218] Both heroines must undertake dubious, risky enterprises, requiring perseverance at once and boldness at the right moment; and both scrupulously obey their respective guides.[219] Naomi advises Ruth how to enhance her attractiveness for Boaz,[220] Mordecai enquires

[214] Esth 4:14.

[215] See my *Typologie im Werk des Flavius Josephus*, no. 6 of *Sitzungsberichte der Bayerischen Akademie der Wissenschaften*, Phil.-Hist. Klasse (1977), 24 ff., English translation ["Typology in Josephus"] in *JJS*, 31 (1980), 33 ff.

[216] Esth 1:16 ff.

[217] Ruth 4:16.

[218] Esth 2:7, 20.

[219] Ruth 3:5; Esth 2:10, 20.

[220] Ruth 3:3.

every day as Esther is being prepared for her first meeting with the King.[221] In both recitals, the turning point from peril to deliverance occurs at night.[222] At a time of distress, Naomi calls herself "the Bitter one,"[223] and Mordecai "cries with a loud and bitter cry."[224] What Naomi seeks for her widowed daughters-in-law is "rest"; at first she recommends they find it through re-marriage in Moab, afterwards she procures it, perfectly, for Ruth.[225] Haman urges the King "not to let the Jews rest" but in the end, having triumphed, "they rest from their enemies."[226]

In both Books, there is much disguise and ambiguity. I have dwelled sufficiently on the masks in Ruth; Esther's concealment of her roots is, of course, crucial. As for utterances inviting misinterpretation, Elimelech's nearest agnate thinks, reasonably but wrongly, that the "widow of the dead" offered in marriage is Naomi; by declining, he loses out and enables Boaz to win. Haman things, reasonably but wrongly, that he is the man for whom the King devises a special honour; by counselling on this basis, he brings about humiliation for himself, aggrandisement for Mordecai.[227] The element of literalism noticeable in these cases comes into full play in connection with the edicts determining the fate of Jewry. The first one allows the populace to crush it out. A royal edict cannot be revoked. So the second one, in substance a revocation, is worded as an encouragement of the intended victims to arm themselves and resist. With the result that it is their assailants who are decimated.[228]

In all likelihood, none of these agreements and disagreements is due to contact. Nevertheless, the following line may be defensible.

The Book of Esther has been explained as, essentially, a heathen myth—be it in celebration of spring, be it in celebration of the Babylonian gods Ishtar and Marduk over Elam. It has been explained as referring to a historical persecution, under one regime or another. It has been explained as an allegory of wisdom in action. I suspect there is truth in all these theories: the story has gone through many stages. I have myself contributed yet a further twist: the final editor presents a political program, impressing on government which hosts Jews that the proper course is not to annihilate them but to profit by their commercial and diplomatic skills.[229] Such an accumulation of layers is far from unique. Think of the road from Hero and Leander via Romeo and Juliet to West Side Story. Just conceivably, one of those through whose hands the work passed was acquainted with Ruth and touched up some passages so as to evoke that precedent. If I had to single out one instance—to Naomi's daring proposal that Ruth visit Boaz at night, the latter replies: "All that you say I will do." Then she does "according to all that her mother-in-law bade her." As Esther is taken to the palace among the candidates for

[221] Esth 2:11.
[222] Ruth 2:8 ff.; Esth 6:1 ff.
[223] Ruth 1:20.
[224] Esth 4:1.
[225] Ruth 1:9, 3:1.
[226] Esth 3:8, 9:16, 17, 18, 22.
[227] Ruth 4:5 ff.; Esth 6:6 ff.
[228] Esth 8:8 ff.
[229] See ["The Last Chapter of Esther"] *JQR*, 37 (1946), 139 ff.

queenship, she daringly keeps silent as to her origin, "for Mordecai had bidden her not to reveal it"; and once again, as she wins the crown, we are told of her silence "as Mordecai had bidden her, for she did the saying of Mordecai, since he was fostering her."[230] Admittedly, reiteration of striking points is a characteristic of Esther, so we must not make too much of this aspect of the parallel; it is pretty impressive anyhow.

6. Nature of the work. That Ruth conveys profound messages in a number of areas—religious, moral, social, political, international—is universally recognized. What has not been ventilated is the possibility that, in addition to other aims, it advocates a legal reform, is a *Rechtslegende*, like, say, the account of the rescue of Susannah.[231] This virtuous woman, we read, was sentenced to death after two elders had testified against her in the traditional, collective manner; but when, at an inspired young sage's insistence, they were examined in one another's absence, their contradictions proved her innocent. It has long been seen that a major purpose of the story is to secure acceptance of the up-to-date Pharisaic method of hearing witnesses. I have little doubt that, similarly, the Book of Ruth intends to recommend a relaxation in the province of "redemption": there is to be an acknowledged proviso that, should the childless widow owner be above a certain age, a junior dependent may be substituted.

We should remember that complications of this kind were then quite important. By the Talmudic era, "redemption" had long been theoretical, so a large amount of ancient detail has dropped out. But comparable problems affecting the levirate are indeed debated in considerable depth. In the matter of virility, for example, a distinction is drawn between a man congenitally impotent and one impotent in consequence of castration or old age: the former is totally excluded from this marriage, the latter is not, in principle, but even he must avoid it by extending the refusal which Deuteronomy, thinking of a healthy levir, treats as unforgivable[232]—all of it mitigating the rigour of the law.

However, I shall not enlarge. This excursus is too long already. I am reminded of an occasion ages ago, when I delivered a lecture before the Cambridge University Jewish Society and the then Chief Rabbi was asked to open the discussion. He spoke longer than I, there was no time for any further input and the student-President immediately rose to propose the vote of thanks. That cheeky guy thanked the Chief Rabbi for his address, introduced by Dr. Daube.

[230] Ruth 3:5 f.; Esth 2:10, 20.

[231] See my remarks ["Error and Accident in the Bible"] in *RIDA*, 2 (1949), 200 f.; and ["Texts and Interpretation in Roman and Jewish Law"] *JJSOC*, 3 (1961), 12 ff. [*Talmudic Law*, 187 ff.]

[232] *t. Yeb.* 2:6.

A Baptismal Catechism

A. General

In recent writings—notably those of Archbishop Carrington,[1] Dr. Selwyn[2] and Professor Davies[3]—much attention has been devoted to the pattern of the earliest Christian catechisms. It may be useful, therefore, to say something about the arrangement of that baptismal instruction which the Tannaites in the Talmud[4] recommend should be given to candidates for admission to Judaism.

The term "baptismal instruction" may at first sight look strange, since it contains no reference to the other rites of entry into Judaism, circumcision and sacrifice. But, first, it has the advantage of brevity. Secondly, the instruction was in fact given by way of preparation for baptism. We shall see that its central part was repeated during the act of immersion. Thirdly, the sacrifice was never as essential as circumcision or baptism, and its cessation when the Temple was destroyed created no major problem. In all probability, it was widely understood to be the convert's first act of worship as a Jew. Fourthly, as for circumcision, it was of course required only in the case of a man. In that of a woman, even Judaism regarded baptism as the only indispensable rite of reception—a point not always given its due weight by those interested in the origins of the Christian ceremony. It is often claimed that Jewish baptism, in contradistinction to Christian, was crudely purificatory rather than moral, spiritual and sacramental; it had no higher significance—that was confined to circumcision. But if this were correct, we should be left with no actual rite of entry for female converts, no rite by which they were brought into the covenant. Yet they were more numerous than male converts.

We shall come back to this question of the nature of Jewish proselyte baptism. But as it is not our main concern—we are primarily concerned with the pattern of instruction given to candidates for admission to Judaism—some preliminary remarks may be made in order to avoid repetition.

Those who think of Jewish proselyte baptism as levitical in the sense of quasi-physical rely almost exclusively on indirect, comparative, folkloristic evidence. But this has little bearing on the Judaism of New Testament times, an advanced religion. Even rites which were still largely purificatory had been sublimated to a greater or less degree.

Johanan ben Zaccai explained that neither did a person become really unclean by a corpse nor did he become really clean by the "water of separation," but that the rele-

[1] *The Primitive Christian Catechism* (1940).

[2] *The First Epistle of St. Peter* (1946).

[3] *Paul and Rabbinic Judaism* (1948).

[4] *b. Yeb.* 47a f.; cp. *Gerim* 1.

vant provisions must be observed because it was the will of God.[5] A reader of the Mishnic tractate Mikwaoth ("Immersion-pools") might easily decide that the authors were dominated by notions of taboo. But the Mishnah is a code of laws and rarely indicates the ideas underlying them. As it happens, in another tractate[6] we learn that R. Akiba said: "Blessed are ye, O Israel. Before whom are ye made clean and who makes you clean? Your Father in heaven. As it is written,[7] And I will sprinkle clean water upon you and ye shall be clean. And again it says,[8] O Lord, the hope, *miqwe* (which may also signify "immersion-pool"), of Israel: as the *miqwe* cleanses the unclean, so does the Holy One cleanse Israel." This hymn concludes the tractate Yoma ("Day of Atonement")—which would be impossible if spiritual elements had not penetrated any kind of immersion, i.e. even immersion other than baptism of a proselyte. Proselyte baptism, however, was essentially quite outside the levitical sphere: pagans were not susceptible of levitical uncleanness, so in principle there was simply no room for purification.[9]

To be sure, a few Rabbinic passages apparently favour the opposite view. The one receiving most emphasis in modern treatises[10] occurs in Mishnah Pesahim,[11] where the problem from what moment a convert may share in the Passover is discussed side by side with that of unclean Israelites. But the connection is dictated by the strict Biblical prohibition of pagan participation in the Passover.[12] It was just as necessary to determine exactly who was excluded on this ground as who was excluded on the ground of uncleanness. The following chapter of the Mishnah deals with the second Passover,[13] to be celebrated four weeks after the first by those who missed the first—persons who were unclean at the time, persons who were away on a journey, persons who became converts too late. It is very rash to draw inferences as to the meaning of baptism from this treatment of the subject in the Mishnah. If modern—or ancient—election law refuses a vote to foreigners, absentees and lunatics, this does not mean that naturalization or return to one's domicile is deemed to be a step from insanity to sanity.

A significant fact, usually overlooked, is that the same problem—i.e. from what moment a convert may share in the Passover—recurs in Mishnah Eduyoth[14] in an entirely different context. Here it figures among the matters in regard to which the School of Hillel took a more stringent line than that of Shammai. In Pesahim, then, the association of conversion with cleanness is the result of the peculiar Scriptural regulations about the Passover meal. In Eduyoth, conversion is associated with certain subjects for a historical reason concerning the two Schools. Neither case justifies the con-

[5] *Num. Rab.* on 19:2; *P. de R. K.* 40a f.

[6] *m. Yom.* 8:9.

[7] Ezek 36:25.

[8] Jer 17:13.

[9] *y. Pes.* 36b; *m. Neg.* 7:1.

[10] E.g. Strack-Billerbeck, vol. 1, 103 f., followed by Flemington, *The New Testament Doctrine of Baptism* (1948), 5 ff.

[11] *m. Pes.* 8:8.

[12] Exod 12:43 ff.

[13] Cp. Num 9:9 ff.

[14] *m. Eduy.* 5:2.

clusion that the topics put together had any fundamental affinity with one another.

The conflict between the two Schools is worth closer inspection. That of Shammai held that a pagan being converted on the eve of Passover might at once take part in the celebration; that of Hillel denied it, since "he who separates himself from the uncircumcision is like one who separates himself from the grave." In other words, according to the School of Hillel, he must wait for the second Passover, as one defiled by burial.

This dispute is attested in a number of sources. Moreover, the elder Eliezer ben Jacob (who survived the destruction of the Temple and, together with Hillelites of the type of Johanan ben Zaccai, helped to adapt Judaism to the new conditions) reports that on one occasion pagan soldiers fighting on the Jewish side became converts on the eve of Passover and were immediately admitted to the supper—in accordance with the Shammaite practice.[15] Hence there is direct proof that the conservative Shammaites at least did not look on the rites of entry as purificatory. It is the progressive Hillelites who brought a levitical concept into conversion. Indeed, of the elder Eliezer ben Jacob, just mentioned, we know that he attached much importance to its full and consistent application.[16] How is this to be explained?

In general, the Hillelites were more lenient than the Shammaites. Even in cases where they are said to have been stricter, we sometimes find that their strictness was superficial whereas, in reality, theirs was the more liberal attitude. For example, we are told that, though for the Shammaites the Book of Ecclesiastes did not render the hands unclean, the Hillelites insisted that it did.[17] The implication, however, is that the Shammaites refused to recognize this work as canonical, whereas the Hillelites recognized it.

It is, therefore, advisable to pay careful attention to the motives of the Hillelites wherever they advocated a more rigorous doctrine than the Shammaites; doubly advisable if they did so in a question respecting conversion. Hillel himself was famous—or notorious—for his readiness to facilitate conversion.[18] He admitted a pagan, for instance, who would acknowledge only a single ethical rule, "What is hateful unto thee do not do unto a fellow-man." (True, after the pagan had become a Jew, Hillel undertook to show him that the Law was binding since it was nothing but a logical elaboration of the golden rule.) One of Hillel's maxims was: "Love mankind and bring them nigh unto the Law."[19] Towards the end of the 1st cent. A.D., leading Hillelites—above all, Joshua ben Hananiah—claimed that baptism alone was sufficient to make even a male gentile Jewish.[20] They did not go quite so far as Paul: they did not deny that it was the duty of a male convert to be circumcised. But they did consider him fully Jewish as soon as he was baptized. It is interesting that their argument was that baptism was the decisive rite in the case of a woman, so it should be the same in that of a man.

[15] *y. Pes.* 36b; *t. Pes.* 7:13.
[16] *m. Ker.* 2:1; *b. Ker.* 8b.
[17] *m. Eduy.* 5:3.
[18] *b. Shab.* 31a.
[19] *m. Ab.* 1:2.
[20] *b. Yeb.* 46a.

Such, then, was the position of Hillel and his School as represented by the Talmud and Midrash; and we must consider that it is certainly toned down in these works, which were redacted much later than the Hillelite period. Judaism in the meantime had become more rigid and Hillel's universalism was now regarded as dangerous. Obviously, it would be a mistake to suppose that, in their conflict with the Shammaites, the Hillelites stood for a primitive view of conversion. On the contrary, their decision that "he who separates himself from the uncircumcision is like him who separates himself from the grave" followed from the profound thought—doubtless earlier than Hillel[21]—that conversion meant a passage from death to life. We have before us an instructive example of the way in which, at a certain stage in the religious evolution, the introduction of ritual may reflect, not a belief in taboo, but a highly spiritual attitude.

There are various points confirming our argument. For one thing, the parallelism in form between the two parts of the maxim—"he who separates himself from the uncircumcision is like him who separates himself from the grave"—is striking: it suggests a parallelism in substance, an actual comparing of him who rises above heathenism to one who rises from the dead. The language is remarkable in another respect. Had the Hillelites thought in crude levitical terms, the natural thing to say would have been that a convert was "like one who has touched a corpse."[22] The phrase "like one who separates himself from the grave" indicates that their starting-point was the idea that, spiritually, heathenism equalled existence in a tomb. The levitical element was only used to give this idea clear and forceful expression.

It should be noted that the term "uncircumcision" in the maxim discussed has the metaphorical sense of "heathenism." We are expressly told that the Hillelites applied the maxim to female converts as well as male ones:[23] the former also "separated themselves from the uncircumcision" and, accordingly, were treated as "separating themselves from the grave."

The figurative use of the word "dead" to denote an unenlightened person or a sinner is to be met with in most languages. It is adumbrated in the Old Testament[24] and existed in New Testament times: "Let the dead bury their dead."[25] But the Hillelite concept of conversion as resurrection was, of course, something far more specific.

Its influence may be seen in many utterances and incidents. There is, for example, an anonymous (and, therefore, undatable) comment on the verse from Ecclesiastes: "So I saw the wicked ones buried, and they came." This is interpreted by the Rabbis as referring to the proselytes: proselytes are people who have risen from their graves.[26] Again, the Rabbis assumed that the Israelites with whom the Sinaitic covenant was con-

[21] Below we shall quote *b. Taan.* 32a, giving a conversation between Alexander the Great and "the Elders of the South." Though legendary, it does reflect views current among Egyptian Jews in the two or three centuries preceding our era.

[22] Num 19:16. Cf. e.g. *m. Ohol.* 1:1: "If a man touches a corpse, he contracts seven-day uncleanness."

[23] *t. Pes.* 7:13.

[24] E.g. Ps 106:28.

[25] Matt 8:22; Luke 9:60.

[26] *Eccl. Rab.* on 8:10.

cluded were circumcised. Two passages are quoted by way of evidence:[27] one from the Book of Joshua,[28] "Now all that came out of Egypt were circumcised," and one from Ezekiel,[29] "And when I passed by thee and saw thee polluted in thy blood, I said, In thy blood live, in thy blood live." The repetition of the exclamation is found significant by the Rabbis: the first imperative is held to allude to the blood of circumcision, the second to that of the Passover lamb. The whole proof from Ezekiel, however, is distinctly more artificial than that from Joshua. No doubt it was added by the Hillelites, when they worked out the idea of conversion as a transition from death to life. At one time the passage from Ezekiel formed part of the Passover Haggadah, the narrative of God's redemption of Israel recited on Passover eve; presumably it was removed from fear of the blood accusation.

Very likely, some of the mocking questions which the opponents of the belief in bodily resurrection liked to put to the Pharisees were suggested by the Hillelite interpretation of conversion as a rising from the dead. The Alexandrians asked Joshua ben Ḥananiah (about A.D. 100) whether, on resurrection, the dead would need sprinkling, having been in contact with tombs: a clever way of ridiculing a Rabbi who taught that a convert, since he had risen from the grave, fell under the provisions respecting corpse-uncleanness.[30]

Enough of the conflict between the Schools. Let us remember that, for both of them, the decisive moment in proselyte baptism was the "going up" or "coming up"—no doubt because of its symbolical value. The relevant Tannaitic provision—which, we shall see presently, is alluded to in the New Testament—runs: "When he has undergone baptism and come up, *ṭabhal we'ala*, he is like an Israelite in all respects."[31] How easily such a detail is overlooked once its role is no longer appreciated may be seen from the fact that even scholars like Montefiore and Loewe, in translating the provision,[32] simply cut out *we'ala*. Their rendering is: "When he has been baptized, he is regarded in all respects as an Israelite." Yet it is a detail of the highest importance. The "coming up" was the decisive moment because of its symbolic meaning, and once such symbolism was established, it could always be used in new ways.

It is, for example, conceivable that among the reasons why the Baptist chose to baptize in the Jordan was that he saw in the "coming up" a new entry into the Promised Land. The usual verb for "to go up to Palestine from abroad" is *'ala*. Moreover, it figures prominently in the scene where Joshua crosses the Jordan dry-shod:[33] "On that day the Lord magnified Joshua. And he spake, saying, Command the priests that they come up out of Jordan. Joshua therefore commanded the priests, saying, Come ye up. And when the priests were come up, the waters of Jordan returned. And the people came up

[27] *b. Ker.* 8a.
[28] Josh 5:5.
[29] Ezek 16:6.
[30] *b. Nidd.* 69b ff.
[31] *b. Yeb.* 47b.
[32] *Rabbinic Anthology* (1938), 579.
[33] Josh 4:14 ff.

out of Jordan on the tenth day of the first month." Josephus records[34] that Theudas, who claimed to be a prophet—he is mentioned in Acts[35] and no doubt claimed to be "the prophet like unto Moses"[36]—declared he was capable of dividing the Jordan. As for Hillel's interpretation of proselyte baptism as a passage from death to life—*'ala* may denote "to rise from the grave."[37]

In fact, the "coming up" is expressly noticed in the narrative of Jesus's baptism as told by Matthew and Mark;[38] conclusive evidence—if any were still needed—that Christian baptism originated in Jewish proselyte baptism. The notice makes sense only if we regard it as alluding to the provision quoted above. The "coming up" is the decisive moment—it is at this moment that Jesus sees the heavens opened and the Spirit descending. Luke and John[39] omit the reference. Luke or his public no longer understood the Jewish ritual. John, unlike the Synoptics, does not purport to give a full account of the event; indeed, he does not speak of an actual baptism of Jesus at all. So we cannot expect him to mention the "coming up." But he was surely familiar with the Jewish law on the matter. In any case, that law was far from levitical in a primitive sense.

One more principle may be advanced which was generally recognized by the Rabbis of the New Testament period, and which would be quite incompatible with the notion of baptism as a merely purificatory act: a convert—and even a female one, received by baptism alone—had the status of a new-born child.[40] Had this doctrine been the basis only for such teachings as that a proselyte's former sins are forgiven,[41] it might be argued that it was just an academic whim. But it influenced important legal decisions.

In principle, a proselyte, being newly born, could marry any of his relatives even if the relative, too, had become a Jew. It was only in order to prevent a convert from gaining the impression that he had passed "from a weightier sanctity into a lighter sanctity" that the Rabbis enacted limitations to the principle. One group of Rabbis excluded those unions which were contrary even to gentile, Noachian morality.[42] (Paul adopted this standard when he condemned the marriage of a convert with his widowed stepmother as "fornication that is not so much as named among the Gentiles."[43]) There was no objection, however, to, say, a proselyte marrying his paternal half-sister or a proselytess marrying her paternal half-brother, even after both had become Jewish. No blem-

[34] *Ant.* 20.5.1.97 ff.

[35] Acts 5:36.

[36] Deut 18:15.

[37] E.g. *m. Sanh.* 10:3: "The company of Korah shall not rise up."

[38] Matt 3:16; Mark 1:10.

[39] Luke 3:21; John 1:32.

[40] *b. Yeb.* 48b, quoting Rabbis of the 1st and 2nd cents.

[41] E.g. *Eccl. Rab.* on 1:8, quoting Joshua ben Hananiah. According to *y. Bikk.* 65c f., R. Zeira, at the beginning of the 4th cent., hesitated to accept ordination but finally consented because, on ordination, his previous sins would be wiped out. This effect of ordination had, of course, been established long before his time. The proof for it was seen in the forgiveness of sins extended to proselytes. The belief that a proselyte's sins are forgiven must, therefore, be even older.

[42] *b. Yeb.* 22a; *b. Sanh.* 58a ff.; *b. Kidd.* 77a ff.

[43] 1 Cor 5:1. That some Rabbis considered marriage with a widowed stepmother as permissible under Noachian law is irrelevant. Paul sided with those like Akiba (*b. Sanh.* 58b) who did not so consider it.

ish of any kind attached to the offspring of such a union—they might marry into priestly families. It is obvious that the notion of a new birth was taken seriously; more seriously (a strange thought) than it seems to be taken by modern Christianity. And we may note again that in the majority of conversions—namely, in conversions of women—the new birth was effected by baptism alone.

B. The Pattern of Instruction

1. *The Test*

When we analyse the baptismal instruction recommended in the Talmud, five divisions emerge, of which the first is in the nature of a test. The person wishing to become a Jew "at this time" should be asked whether he does not know that "Israel at this time is broken down, pushed about, driven about and tossed about, and that sufferings befall them." If he replies "I know and am not worthy," no further tests are needed, but he should at once be admitted as a candidate and be taught.

The first thing to be noticed is that, in strictness, the question and reply here envisaged do not form part of the prospective convert's preparation: they precede it. It is the gentile who approaches the Jews, not the Jews that approach the gentile; and the Rabbis lay down that, before his proper initiation can even begin, he must have grasped the fundamentals of the faith—he must recognize even that Israel's humiliation in this age means exaltation.

No doubt it would all be resumed and elaborated in the course of his instruction; and Israel's sufferings in particular might form not only the final subject of the preliminary negotiations, but also the introductory one of the lessons. But for the present it is important to realize that, in the Rabbinic system before us, the main place of the elements of the faith is prior to the actual catechism. The candidate must have familiarized himself with them beforehand. This accords with several reports regarding conversions in New Testament times. Three gentiles wanted to be received into the Jewish fold on special terms—terms rejected by Shammai but agreed to by Hillel.[44] One would recognize only the written Law but not the oral; another required that he should be taught the entire Law while he could stand on one foot; and a third demanded to be made High Priest. We need not here consider the exact significance of these stories. What is relevant is that by the time the preparation of these men began, they had already decided that Judaism was best.

The scheme reflects the normal attitude of the Tannaites to proselytizing. (In reality, on occasion, matters might take a very different course. There might even be compulsory conversion. Josephus tells us[45] how a mob proposed to place before two pagan noblemen who had deserted from Agrippa the alternative between undergoing circumcision and facing death or expulsion. But the circumstances were exceptional, and at any rate the plan of the mob was diametrically opposed to the prevalent Rabbinic teaching.) They did desire converts. But in general they refrained from persuasion, since a gentile complying with the seven Noachian commandments, the elementary principles of moral-

[44] *b. Shab.* 31a.

[45] *Vita* 23.113, 31.149 ff.

ity, was preferable to a Jew spurning any one of the numerous regulations of the Law.

Moreover, some of these regulations—the law of circumcision, for instance—were of such a nature as to render mass proselytizing impossible. Matthew,[46] where he speaks of the missionary zeal of the Pharisees, distinctly contemplates the proselytizing of individuals. It is against this background that we must see the provisions respecting baptismal teaching. They refer to the case of a gentile—a single gentile—asking to be received, and he is expected to know about the essence of Judaism even at this stage.

Nevertheless there were Rabbis who considered it all-important to win over fresh adherents and did not hesitate to make occasional concessions. Hillel belonged to this wing; while circles somewhat removed from Rabbinic orthodoxy went even further in relaxing the Law with a view to gaining converts or, indeed, half-converts. It is well known that in the Hellenistic era not a few pagans lived on the fringe of Judaism: without formally joining it, they had adopted some of its dogmas and customs. In this connection it should be recalled that two kinds of propaganda were favoured by all Jewish parties: they all wished to convince the gentiles of the validity of the Noachian commandments, the simplest demands of morality, and they all wished the heathen world at least to respect the Jewish religion. Evidently, where the latter aim was pursued, apologetic motives were at work as well as missionary ones.

It is not surprising, therefore, to find plans of instruction very different from that just described, namely, plans where the instruction starts practically "from scratch." Josephus in his defence of Judaism begins by demonstrating the antiquity of the nation, then he dwells on its contribution to civilization, then he goes on to explain its conception of God and his worship—Strabo too had learned about this[47]—and finally he discusses its laws. In works like this, the author would normally address himself to the gentile masses, not merely to one or two exceptional individuals.

There was indeed another kind of mass proselytizing which should not be overlooked: the inner mission, and above all, the attempts of certain sects to convince their fellow Jews of the superiority of their particular doctrines. The problem of circumcision did not here arise. A Jewish propagandist could not hope to cause large numbers of gentiles to submit to the Law. But, say, a good Essene preacher or writer might well attract large numbers of Pharisees. Of John the Baptist we hear that he had a considerable following.[48]

In such cases, naturally, the teaching would be more or less confined to features peculiar to the sect, items as to which it differed from the Judaism surrounding it. But the same sect might have several catechisms. For one thing, just as there were Jews and people half-converted to Judaism, so some of the sects consisted of an inner circle, the initiated, and several other outer circles, those on the way to full membership. Three years were the minimum period between application for admission to the order of the Essenes and final reception.[49] The instruction of a candidate doubtless varied according to the state he had attained.

46 Matt 23:15.

47 Strabo 16.2.35.

48 Matt 3:5; Mark 1:5; Luke 3:7; Josephus, *Ant.* 18.5.2.118.

49 Josephus, *Bell.* 2.8.7.137 ff.

The presumption is that the different kinds of Jewish missionary teaching all had their counterparts in the early Christian Church, and that they all have left traces in the New Testament. Peter at Pentecost,[50] like the Baptist, appealed to his fellow Jews at large, of whom three thousand are said to have undergone baptism; and his sermon dealt exclusively with the Messiahship of Jesus, the great distinctive tenet of his group. As the conditions of reception were revised—first unofficially and later officially—mass proselytizing of gentiles also became feasible. Henceforth, however, missionaries frequently had to concentrate on matters which, in addressing Jews, they could take for granted. The belief in salvation through Jesus might take root among a set approving of incestuous relations. A situation of this sort would necessitate something like the Tannaitic scheme of preparation: the teacher's task would be, not so much to convince his public of a fundamental dogma, as to impress on them its implications and the practical consequences to be drawn. Again, one plan might be suitable for a gathering of vague sympathizers and another for candidates already knowing a good deal and resolved to join the new religion.

It is widely held that not a few sections of the Epistles repeat, or allude to, baptismal teaching. If one looks at the pattern suggested by the authorities named at the beginning of this chapter, one receives the impression that, as a rule, early Christian catechists, like the Tannaites, expected their pupils to be acquainted with the essence of the creed.

The catechisms they used were in the main intended for such as had already heard—and accepted—the gospel. There is little sign of a complete exposition and argumentation such as would be required for inducing outsiders to come over. The emphasis lies on affirmation, clarification and rules of conduct. (The *Haustafeln* [295 ff.] in particular, far from placing at the head a description of the proper attitude to God, are silent on the subject: the addressees are supposed to know about it.) What remained to do once actual preparation for baptism began was, first, to make clear to candidates the deeper significance of the revelation they acknowledged, and secondly, to give them directions as to the life they ought to lead in future.

Let us now inspect more closely the nature of the test which the Tannaites impose on a candidate before instruction may commence. He must, we are told, show a proper understanding of the sufferings of Israel. This means that a mere declaration of willingness to live under the Law is not enough. It might be dictated by unworthy or inadequate motives: fear of enemies, desire for advancement, love of a Jewess or the like.[51] But, as Josephus puts it, only that proselyte is welcome who takes the step from προαίρεσις, and not ἐκ παρέργου, from deliberate choice and not incidentally, while in reality pursuing a different object.[52] So the purity of his intentions must be proved—by his attitude to Israel's fate.

[50] Acts 2:14 ff.

[51] *b. Yeb.* 24a.

[52] *Contra Apionem* 2.28.209 f. Cp. 2.39.284, about the Law conquering mankind without the bait of pleasure.

There is reason to believe that early Christian catechisms usually opened by a reference to affliction and temptation.[53] Carrington rightly stresses its traditional character, adducing the beginning of the second chapter of Sirach. When he goes on to say, however,[54] that it was only Christianity which added the idea of rejoicing or boasting in adversity, we must dissent. According to the Tannaites, the prospective convert, on having his attention drawn to the sufferings of Israel, is supposed to reply: "I know and am not worthy." Whether we interpret the answer as meaning "I am not worthy to share these sufferings" or "I am not worthy to bend my neck under the yoke of him who spake and the world came into being,"[55] it is more than a resigned acceptance of an evil. Israel's sufferings are here looked upon as resulting from a special relationship to God; and from this point of view, they are Israel's hidden glory.

The associations of the phrase "sufferings befall them" are relevant. In the verse[56] "As a man chasteneth [makes to suffer] his son, so the Lord thy God chasteneth [makes to suffer] thee," the Rabbis maintain[57] that the apposition "thy God" is not superfluous: it means that the Lord is in a special sense the God of him who suffers—"the name of God rests upon him whom sufferings befall." The expression "sufferings are beloved, precious" occurs again and again, in the earliest and latest parts of the Talmud. Paul's word "we glory in tribulations" is thoroughly Jewish.[58] Nor should we forget about a particular quality the Rabbis ascribe to sufferings: sufferings help a man to inherit the World to Come. R. Eleazar ben Zadok, who flourished about A.D. 100, declared this to be the reason why God "let sufferings befall the pious."[59]

In fact, the Syriac Apocalypse of Baruch contains the admonition:[60] "Rejoice in the suffering which ye now suffer, and prepare your souls for the reward which is laid up for you." There is no reason to assume that this passage was inspired by Christian models. It is Jewish.

Here is the place to remark on another suggestive feature of the Tannaitic plan: the eschatological undertone of the introductory point. The repetition of the words "at this time" is striking: if a gentile asks to be received "at this time," the Rabbis hold, Israel's sufferings "at this time" should be emphasized. "At this time" signifies "while Israel is oppressed"—a state which roughly covers the entire period between the reigns of David and Solomon in the past and the Messianic reign in the future.[61] Certainly, even nowadays there may be occasional periods when Israel prospers and God betrays his preference for his people. But R. Nehemiah, about A.D. 150, says that persons who join Israel at one of these moments cannot be considered genuine until they give proof of their loyalty "at this time," i.e. in the face of persecution; or at least, if they have no opportuni-

[53] E.g. Rom 5:3; 1 Thes 1:6; 1 Pet 1:6; Jas 1:2.

[54] Pp. 22, 59.

[55] The former interpretation is given by Rashi on *b. Yeb.* 47a, the latter in *Gerim* 1.

[56] Deut 8:5.

[57] *Mek.* on Exod 20:23.

[58] See Strack-Billerbeck.

[59] *b. Kidd.* 40b.

[60] Apoc Bar 52:6.

[61] *b. Yeb.* 24a; *b. A. Zar.* 3b.

ty of documenting their faith in this way, their motives ought to be as sincere as if they were converts "at this time," i.e. as if there were persecution.

We shall presently see that eschatology is the principal theme of the concluding part of the Tannaitic catechism; and the notion "at this time" recurs there, being opposed to "the World to Come." Manifestly eschatology plays a role even at the opening stage. "At this time" means an interlude evoking reminiscences of a happier past but also, and even primarily, the expectation of a glorious future.

The eschatological setting of John's baptism and early Christian baptism turns out to be inherited from Judaism. Certainly both John and the early Christians accorded greater prominence to this element. But it was there before John. John, believing the kingdom of heaven imminent, preached the baptism of repentance. A Rabbi like Eliezer ben Hyrcanus, about A.D. 100, predicted[62] that at the approach of the Messiah the gentiles would come in flocks to be received. Eliezer would never have applied proselyte baptism to people already Jewish. It was because John did so[63] that he was called "the Baptist." Yet the eschatological character of his and early Christian baptism was Jewish. Some rebukes administered to Pharisees and Sadducees according to Matthew and Luke[64] closely correspond to an opinion, held by many Rabbis,[65] that people seeking admission in the days of the Messiah were not to be trusted.

As for Christian baptism, since, in a way, the kingdom had arrived, the rite, in a way, symbolized entry into the kingdom. Yet in this case also it is easy to exaggerate the difference from Jewish proselyte baptism. Flemington[66] deserves credit for stressing that, even for the early Church, all the eschatology was not "realized." There was still to be a future consummation, and this expectation affected baptismal teaching. At any rate, in the Tannaitic system, the gentile is asked whether he is not aware of Israel's humiliation "at this time," and he replies: "I know and am not worthy." In 1 Peter we read: "You who are kept through faith unto salvation in the last time, wherein ye rejoice though now for a season ye are in heaviness through manifold temptations, that the trials, being more precious than gold, might be found unto praise and glory at the appearing of Jesus Christ." The Tannaitic influence is unmistakable.

2. *The Commandments*

The actual preparation of the catechumen should begin by making known to him some of the lighter and some of the weightier commandments—at least if we follow the prevalent translation. It is certainly the most likely one. R. Judah the Prince gave the advice:[67] "Be heedful of a light commandment as of a weighty one, for thou knowest not the reward for each." The terms "small" and "great" may replace "light" and "weighty."[68] Just so, we find Matthew speaking of judgment, mercy and faith as "the

[62] *b. A. Zar.* 24a.

[63] And not because of any distinctive form of this baptism—that would not account for the designation.

[64] E.g. Luke 13:25.

[65] *b. A. Zar.* 3b.

[66] *Op. cit.*, 74.

[67] *m. Ab.* 2:1.

[68] *Deut. Rab.* on 22:6.

weightiest" commandments;[69] we find Matthew and Mark speaking of the love of God and the love of one's neighbour as the "greatest" commandments;[70] and we find Matthew condemning the abolition of even the "smallest" commandment.[71]

However, a different rendering is just possible. The word *qal* may denote not only "light" but also "easy," and *ḥamur* not only "weighty" but also "burdensome." Gamaliel and Simeon ben Azzai, about A.D. 100, considered[72] the prohibition of blood one of the "easiest" (though definitely not one of the "lightest") commandments, because man had no natural craving for the taste of blood. They taught that the special warning—"Only be steadfast"—prefixed by the Bible to this easy commandment must all the more be taken to heart in connection with burdensome ones. Josephus says[73] that even those practices which the Jews find "the easiest"—working with one's own hands, observing restrictions as regards to diet, sexual relations and extravagance, and resting on the Sabbaths—others would not put up with. Again, a Rabbi might *heqel* or *heḥemir*, interpret a law (whether it was "light" or "weighty") in an "easy," lenient, way, or in a "burdensome," restrictive, way. According to Matthew, the scribes incline to do the latter, to "bind heavy burdens."[74] So the provision discussed conceivably means that a catechumen should be told about some of the easier and some of the more burdensome commandments.

Whichever translation we adopt—and maybe we ought to adopt both, since the authors of the plan may not have strictly distinguished between the various nuances of *qal* and *ḥamur*—the instruction appears to be, not simply in the chief duties, but in the general atmosphere of the new life. This part of the catechism, therefore, would be the most important.

The conclusion is confirmed by the fact that this part alone recurs at a subsequent stage of the procedure: during the act of baptism, during immersion, we learn, two Scholars are to stand by—in the case of a woman they are to stand outside but within hearing—in order to communicate to the proselyte some lighter and some weightier commandments. We may regard this as another sign that, by the Tannaitic epoch at least, proselyte baptism was no purificatory rite but had a moral and spiritual significance: instruction in the commandments would not be a fitting accompaniment of a primitively levitical ceremony. It should also be observed that not one commandment dealing with levitical purity is singled out for mention.

Actually, we may go as far as to assert that, in listening to the commandments during baptism, the proselyte stood at mount Sinai. From the beginning of the 1st cent. A.D. down to our day the ceremonies of reception into Judaism have been based on the same principle:[75] they must be identical with those by which the Israelites were

[69] Matt 23:23. Luke 11:42 omits the technical description.

[70] Matt 22:35 ff.; Mark 12:28 ff.. Luke 10:25 ff. again avoids the term and re-writes the question put to Jesus, with the result that it is of a type less technically Rabbinic and more adapted to the understanding of a non-Jewish public.

[71] Matt 5:19.

[72] *Siphre* on Deut 12:23 f., in conjunction with *b. Makk.* 23b.

[73] *Contra Apionem* 2.32.334.

[74] Matt 23:4. Cp. Luke 11:46, where, however, the technical term is not used.

[75] See *y. Pes.* 36b; *b. Yeb.* 46a; *b. Ker.* 9a; *Siphre* on Num 15:14, citing the Schools of Hillel and Shammai, R. Eliezer ben Hyrcanus and R. Joshua ben Hananiah.

received into the Sinaitic covenant. According to the Rabbis—or most of them, at any rate—the Israelites were received through circumcision, baptism and sacrifice. The texts by which they support this assumption are, for circumcision, "All the people that came out of Egypt were circumcised" and "When I passed by thee, I said, In thy blood live, in thy blood live";[76] for baptism, "Sanctify the people and let them wash their clothes" and "Moses sprinkled the blood of the covenant on the people";[77] and for the sacrifice, "Moses sent young men which offered burnt offerings."[78] That to us some of these texts may seem inconclusive does not matter; we are concerned with the ideas current in New Testament times.

Like the Israelites, the proselyte must enter by circumcision, baptism and sacrifice. We have already mentioned that the sacrifice was less essential a requirement than the other two; and that circumcision was necessarily confined to male converts—the minority. In any case, the entire procedure, far from being levitical in a quasi-physical sense, was conceived of as a re-enactment of the exodus and the pilgrimage ensuing on it, with the gift of the Torah as the climax.

In a previous chapter [167 ff.]—on "Ye have heard, but I say unto you"—we referred to the formula "I might hear, understand," used in the old Midrash to introduce interpretations of Scripture which, though conceivable, are not to be approved; and we pointed out that the bringing up and rejecting of such interpretations is frequently no academic game, but a very serious measure—those interpretations being actually believed in by some earlier or rival school. It is, then, of interest to note the Midrash on the provision: "And when a stranger shall sojourn with thee and will keep the passover, let all his males be circumcised." The Rabbis start by saying:[79] "I might understand that as soon as a person has been converted he should celebrate the Passover." (We must remember that the identification of "stranger" with "proselyte" and of "to sojourn" with "to be a convert" is common in Rabbinic exegesis.)

The special point of the interpretation here mentioned as conceivable is that, at a pinch, the Hebrew could be translated: "And when a stranger—proselyte—shall sojourn—be a convert—with thee, then at once let him keep a Passover; and let his males be circumcised." This interpretation is then refuted with the help of another verse. What emerges as likely, however, is that there was an ancient school according to which a gentile, on attaching himself to Judaism, had actually to bring a paschal offering to symbolize his conversion.

To return to baptismal teaching, it is designed to bring out the general atmosphere of Jewish life. Significantly, it is to deal with the "commandments," *miṣwoth*; an exposition of the learned and subtle Rabbinic directions, the *halakhoth*, is not prescribed. (That an instructor might take for granted some familiarity with the fundamentals of the faith we pointed out above.) The candidate must hear about the kind of things God has told the Jews to do or not to do. He need not—as yet—concern himself with the exact manner in which the Rabbis hold that those precepts should be carried out.

[76] Josh 5:5; Ezek 16:6.
[77] Exod 19:10, 24:8.
[78] Exod 24:5.
[79] *Mek.* on Exod 12:48.

To be sure, an instructor cannot help presenting the Law in the light of that Rabbinic interpretation to which he is used; besides, he will be neither able nor willing to refrain from enlarging on one point or the other and introducing some results of pious exegesis and moral reflection. But, if he is true to the plan, he will concentrate on basic obligations. He will, for instance, inculcate the duties of loving God with all one's heart, soul and might, and of commemorating the exodus every year, without necessarily going into the precise implications of each of the three terms, "heart," "soul" and "might,"[80] or into the proper order of the Passover-eve service.

The decision exactly which commandments may suit a given case is left to the teacher, whose choice would depend partly on his own bias and partly on the needs of his audience. Presumably certain collections became traditional. As a Jewish catechist, however, would normally have to do, not with a large class, but with one person, and a rather extraordinary one at that, the greatest attention must have been paid to individual requirements.

What may an anthology of precepts have looked like? In the Song of Solomon there occurs the exclamation "Thou art fair, my love." For the Rabbis[81] it is addressed to Israel and means: "Thou art fair through the commandments and loving deeds; through the commandments both positive and negative; through the commandments concerning the house, through heave-offerings and tithes; through the commandments concerning the field, through gleanings, the forgotten sheaf, the corner, the second tithe and property renounced; through mixed seeds, the show-fringes, the first-fruits, the fourth year of planting; through circumcision, the uncovering of the corona, prayer, the reading of the Shema [confession of the unity of God], the door-posts, the phylacteries, the Lulab and Ethrog [to be used on the Feast of Tabernacles]; through repentance and good works; thou art fair in this world and in the World to Come." This list would have been in order for baptismal instruction, though there is no saying whether it was ever put to such use.

Occasionally, however, we come across a selection indubitably reflecting catechetical teaching. For instance, we are told[82] that when the Israelites reached the desert, God began to announce "some of the lighter and some of the weightier commandments, such as those concerning the Sabbath, incestuous unions, the show-fringes and the phylacteries." We have just shown that, in New Testament times, a convert to Judaism was thought of as passing through the experience of Israel rescued from Egypt. In this legend, the Israelites, just rescued from heathen surroundings, are represented as converts. They are introduced to the general character of Jewish life as one would introduce a candidate for baptism. The phrase "some of the lighter and some of the weightier commandments" is a direct reference to the rules respecting the instruction of proselytes.

Similarly, it is probable that remarks on passages from the Book of Ruth sometimes contain clues as to the way candidates were taught. Ruth, after all, was one of the out-

[80] For conclusions drawn by the Rabbis from this accumulation, see the Targumim, *m. Ber.* 9:5 and *b. Ber.* 61b.

[81] *Song of Songs Rab.* on 1:15.

[82] *Siphre* on Num 15:41.

standing converts of the Bible. One example may suffice.[83] When Ruth said to Naomi, "Whither thou goest I will go," that, the Rabbis claim, was in reply to Naomi's observation that Jews were forbidden to move outside a limited area on the Sabbath. When she went on, "And where thou lodgest I will lodge," it was in reply to Naomi's pointing out to her that a Jewess was forbidden to meet in private any man but her husband. "Thy people shall be my people" was in reply to the warning that there were 613 commandments; and "Thy God shall be my God" in reply to the warning that no idolatry was permitted. We must remember that Naomi gave these illustrations of lighter and weightier laws after Ruth had begged for permission to accompany her and share her poverty. The part on commandments, that is, follows the gentile's approach "at this time," while Israel is forsaken—the real test.

Levitical regulations are rarely, if ever, conspicuous in Tannaitic comments of this kind. By contrast, prominence is often accorded to the ethical aspect of the Law. Josephus maintains[84] that the Jewish laws are calculated to instil the virtues of justice, love, liberality, industry, courage and so on—all of them, he says, facets of piety, reverence for God, εὐσέβεια.

Nor was he out of step with the practice of some Rabbis. Many no doubt would have thought his emphasis wrong; even of those who did not, many would have drawn up a different catalogue of virtues. But, fundamentally, Hillel would have been on his side. To the gentile who demanded to be taught the entire Law while he could stand on one foot, he said "What is hateful unto thee, do not to a fellow creature"; and he added that all the detailed provisions of the Law had no purpose but to ensure the observance of this maxim. Let us also note that, where Josephus enumerates as the essentials of Jewish religion justice, temperance, fortitude and complete harmony between all members of the community,[85] it is only the first three of these qualities which coincide with the demands of the Platonic School. The fourth, harmony, replaces the Platonic wisdom—surely a most revealing change.

This is not to deny that the catechisms of some sects may have insisted more strongly on levitical rules: the community which has left us the *Zadokite Fragments* probably tended this way. Again, the concept of priesthood must have played a greater part than might appear from our Talmudic sources—most of them dating from after the destruction of the Temple. The gentile who approached Hillel with the request to be made High Priest was attracted by the splendour of that office. That this was not an isolated occurence is shown by a number of Rabbinic utterances to the effect[86] that the descendant of a proselyte may in fact become High Priest. Evidently, that was an important consideration for many a prospective convert.

The different lines a catechist might take come out in the different expositions of the Biblical verse "The Lord loveth the stranger in giving him food and raiment."[87] The

[83] *b. Yeb.* 47b; *Ruth Rab.* on 1:16 f.

[84] *Contra Apionem* 2.16.170, 2.14.146, 2.41.291 f.

[85] *Contra Apionem* 2.16.170.

[86] *Gen. Rab.* on 28:20; *Exod. Rab.* on 12:43.

[87] Deut 10:18.

Rabbis[88] identify the stranger with the proselyte; and whereas according to some "food" means the Torah and "raiment" the *ṭallith*, the resplendent coat of men distinguished by piety and scholarship (it is mentioned in Mark and Luke),[89] according to others "food" means the showbread reserved for priests and "raiment" the priestly robes. The latter interpretation obviously antedates the fall of the Temple, the former was adopted about A.D. 100 by Joshua ben Hananiah, on being questioned concerning the status of converts by the convert Aquila who translated the Bible into Greek. Doubtless in most cases an instructor tried somehow to do justice to all branches of the religion; but some measure of preference for one or the other would be unavoidable.

When we compare early Christian catechisms we see that they also appear to have attempted, not so much to give a systematic account of dogmas and duties, or even of the major dogmas and duties, as to convey an impression of the atmosphere of the new life. Lighter and weightier matters, easier and more burdensome duties, stand side by side. The candidate was very gradually led towards the goal, at first hearing only about "some of the commandments": he was given milk before he could receive strong nourishment,[90] just like the Israelites in the desert or the converts to Judaism. Mass proselytizing enabled a greater degree of standardization than Judaism had known. But there are enough variations to show that no rigidly fixed syllabus was followed. Different teachers still emphasized different aspects. There never was a single *Ur*-catechism.

On the whole, then, the Jewish scheme was taken over. Support for this view is furnished by parallels in detail. For example, in the Jewish scheme, part (2), the commandments, must have included large tracts in an impersonal form: "One may pray only in a sober mood," "One must maintain the poor non-Jews with the poor Jews," "The proselyte should bring the first-fruits."[91] Literally translated, these provisions run: "Praying only in a sober mood," "Maintaining the poor non-Jews with the poor Jews," "The proselyte bringing the first-fruits." This use of the participle, which we discussed above [295 ff.], under *Haustafeln*, was common in Tannaitic rules. But, as we shall see when we come to part (4), the catechumen was also directly addressed: "Know that conversion involves such and such risks," and so on. Primitive Christian catechisms in Hebrew seem to have alternated in the same way. In 1 Peter[92] we find the clause "The servants being subject to their masters." It means "They should be subject" and is clearly an over-literal rendering of a Hebrew rule which employed the participle. This impersonal rule, however, may well go back to the same code as its explanation, "For even hereunto were ye called," or the admonitions "Honour all men, fear God"[93]—all in direct address.

Again, the Jewish character of much of the Christian catechetical vocabulary and imagery has long been realized. A careful search would reveal an even closer continu-

[88] *Gen. Rab.* on 28:20.

[89] Mark 12:38; Luke 20:46.

[90] 1 Cor 3:2; 1 Pet 2:2; Heb 5:12 f., also 6:1 f.

[91] *m. Ber.* 5:1; *b. Gitt.* 61a; *m. Bikk.* 1:4.

[92] 1 Pet 2:18.

[93] 1 Pet 2:21, 17.

ity than is commonly assumed. As we have seen, the exodus and the events that followed it were at the heart of pre-Christian baptismal teaching. One source of Paul's predilection for ἐνδύειν, "to put on,"[94] surely was the allegorical interpretation of the verse "The Lord loveth the stranger—the proselyte—in giving him food and raiment." Or when he says[95] that a covetous man is an idolater—not merely "like an idolater" but "an idolater"—we are reminded of the Rabbinic dictum that "he who multiplieth his wealth by usury is Esau the wicked."[96] Josephus[97] mentions wars for the satisfaction of covetousness among the evils against which the Jewish laws are directed. Nor should his remark be dismissed as purely Hellenistic. The list in which it occurs, while using terminology palatable to a gentile public, distinctly represents Jewish and early Christian ethics.

3. *Charity*

Next the candidate is to be told of the guilt incurred by a Jew who fails to give away the gleanings, the forgotten sheaf, the corner and the poor man's tithe.[98] These are imposts, not in favour of the Temple, but in favour of the poor. Evidently, it is not sufficient to advert to them in the course of part (3), the commandments in general. A separate section of the baptismal catechism must be devoted to them. It may be remarked that this insistence on charity can hardly depend on Christian models. If it did, one would expect references to less specific and more impressive demands, such as "Thou shalt love thy neighbour as thyself."[99]

In principle, the four duties applied only within the Jewish community. Admittedly, "for the sake of the ways of peace," if a gentile came to reap the gleanings, the forgotten sheaf or the corner, he must not be prevented.[100] (The same rule was not necessary in the case of the poor man's tithe: This was not left in the open for anyone to take, but distributed on the threshing-floor or in the house.) The Rabbinic codes contain many concessions of this kind—i.e. "for the sake of peace"—both with regard to relations between Jews and gentiles and with regard to relations among Jews; and Paul occasionally adopts the idea, for example, in discussing dietary questions (which bear on the relations among Christians) or the dissolution of a marriage by the non-believing partner (where the relations between a Christian and a non-Christian are affected).[101] Nevertheless, essentially, the gleanings, the forgotten sheaf, the corner and the poor man's tithe were intended to benefit fellow Jews.

[94] Rom 13:12; Eph 4:24; Col 3:10; 1 Thes 5:8.

[95] Eph 5:5.

[96] *Exod. Rab.* on 22:26. This is the reference which Schöttgen had in mind and which Strack-Billerbeck, vol. 2 (1924), 607, confess themselves unable to find. True, Schöttgen put "idolater" instead of "Esau the wicked." But there is little difference in the sense. He may have committed a slip under the influence of Eph 5:5, or he may have had before him an edition which did read "idolater."

[97] *Contra Apionem* 2.41.291 f.

[98] Lev 19:9 f., 23:22; Deut 24:19 ff., 14:28 f.

[99] Lev 19:18.

[100] *m. Gitt.* 5:8.

[101] Rom 14:17 ff.; 1 Cor 7:15; see also Rom 12:18.

Why are these examples of charity singled out? Certainly, a teacher might add others. But it is obvious that, in the eyes of the authors of the scheme, these are of particular relevance.

There are various reasons. First, the honest fulfilment of these commandments involved much self-abnegation. According to the Talmud, a poor man might live on gleanings: R. Johanan ben Nuri, at the beginning of the 2nd cent. A.D., did so.[102] That this is no exaggeration may be seen from ancient works on agriculture. Varro writes[103] that normally, the harvest being over, a landowner should sell the gleanings.

Secondly, the Bible, in prescribing these imposts, expressly mentions "the stranger"—"the proselyte" according to Rabbinic interpretation—as entitled along with the poor. We have observed that the assurance that God gives the stranger "food and raiment" is referred by the Rabbis to spiritual nourishment. But they do not, on this account, deny its implications on the material sphere: a proselyte in need has the same right to be looked after as a home-born.[104] This principle did not remain a dead letter: the expectation to become a recipient of alms is sometimes enumerated by the Rabbis among the unworthy motives for conversion.[105] In some of the Biblical provisions in question the stranger is actually named first, and once a reminder is added that the home-born himself was not always in his privileged position: the tax "shall be for the stranger, the fatherless and the widow, and thou shalt remember that thou was a bondman in Egypt." When, in addition, we remember the way Boaz treated the proselytess Ruth as she came to glean in his field, we can understand the suitability of this and similar obligations for a baptismal catechism.

For wealthy gentiles, incidentally, the prospect of alms cannot have meant a great deal; and if poor ones were attracted by it too much, rich ones may have been attracted too little. A story about the proselyte Aquila—about A.D. 100—part of which we have already recounted, seems to reflect this problem. Aquila found the promise of "food and raiment" far from grand. Joshua ben Hananiah, we saw, explained to him that the phrase signified "Torah and *ṭallith*." But R. Eliezer was less accommodating. He angrily pointed out that the patriarch Jacob himself had prayed for no more than that God "will give me food to eat and raiment to put on."[106] The story makes it probable that the warning

[102] *y. Peah* 20d.

[103] *De Re Rustica* 1.53; cf. *Digest* 50.16.30.1, 18.1.40.3.

[104] *Gen. Rab.* on 28:20—quoting a retort of R. Eliezer to the proselyte Aquila which we shall consider in detail presently. There are many similar cases of the Rabbis insisting on the material aspect of an institution in addition to the spiritual. A section of the Haggadah composed in Babylonia before or shortly after the destruction of the Temple requests "all that are hungry to come and eat, all that are needy to come and celebrate the Passover." This is primarily a genuine invitation—or at least the formalized reflection of a genuine invitation—to the meal. It may be recalled that while the Temple stood the inhabitants of Jerusalem were under an obligation to give free hospitality to the pilgrims (*m. Ab.* 5:5; *Ab. de R. N.* 35; *b. Yom.* 12a; Matt 26:18; Mark 14:13 f.; Luke 22:10 ff.). Certainly it is also an offer of the divine food of the religion; it is even a summons to outsiders to join the true faith (this may explain the odd form *weyiphsaḥ*, "and celebrate the Passover" or "and leap over"). But the primary, material sense is not sacrificed to the spiritual one.

[105] *Yalqut* 1.645 on Lev 23:22.

[106] Gen 28:20.

against greed in 1 Timothy—"having food and raiment let us be therewith content"[107]—derives from Jewish catechetical teaching.

It is interesting that a candidate should be reminded, not just of the importance of charity, but of the guilt incurred through neglect of it. From Josephus we know[108] that the practice of charity was one of the things sympathizers with Judaism imitated; and we are told in Acts[109] how the gentile Cornelius, even before he became a Christian, "gave much alms to the people." The task of a Jewish catechist was to impress on his pupil that, from his reception, charity was no longer voluntary, an "extra," but a definite duty.

No doubt this is a further reason why the authors of the plan choose such specific, clear-cut orders as those concerning gleanings and so on rather than vaguer exhortations—"Thou shalt not shut thine hand from thy poor brother"[110] or the like. Charity, for a Jew, was a definite duty. It was to be exercised in honour of God,[111] and though ordinary, human tribunals could do nothing in such matters, God would punish him who was remiss. A few of the Biblical commandments end with the exclamation "I am the Lord, your God," by which, in the view of the Rabbis,[112] God promised to reward those who did their share and threatened to take revenge on those who did not.

That in early Christian catechisms a section was set apart for charity within the community is strongly suggested by certain tracts in the Epistles, for instance, in Romans and 1 Peter.[113] It would be quite in keeping with Jewish precedents. Equally so is the concept of charity as practised for the sake of God, or Jesus, a concept permeating all Christian teaching on the topic. Again, when a series of exhortations is followed by an announcement of reward in case of obedience and divine punishment in case of disobedience—"The eyes of the Lord are over the righteous, but his face is against them that do evil"[114]—this plainly corresponds to Tannaitic proselyte instruction.

No special mention is made in the Tannaitic scheme of humility and subordination. This does not indeed mean that Jewish catechists were silent on these subjects. The treatise Derekh Eretz Zuta opens: "The ways of Scholars are, Meek and humble in spirit." We have just quoted a clause from 1 Peter, "The servants being subject to their masters," which is certainly derived from a code in Hebrew and may well have originated in Judaism.

Antigonos of Soko, in the 3rd cent. B.C., distinguished[115] between slaves ministering for the sake of reward and slaves ministering from no such motive. He demanded that one should be like the latter, urging his audience "to let the fear of Heaven be upon

[107] 1 Tim 6:8.
[108] *Contra Apionem* 2.39.283.
[109] Acts 10:2.
[110] Deut 15:7
[111] *y. Peah* 15d; *b. B. B.* 10a.
[112] *Siphra* on Lev 19:10, 23:22, also on 18:2.
[113] Rom 12:1–13; 1 Pet 3:8–12.
[114] 1 Pet 3:12.
[115] *m. Ab.* 1:3.

you." It looks as if the association in early Christian catechisms of the notion of "fear" with the duty of subjection[116] were Jewish. For that pronouncement of Antigonos is not isolated. We have already adduced—in discussing some Lukan allusions to the young Samuel—a favourite saying af Abaye's [first third of the 4th cent. A.D.], extolling the value of humility [123]. It may now be added that here also a reference to "fear" is introduced: "A man should always be wise in fear, a soft answer turneth away wrath [this is taken from Proverbs],[117] and he should increase peace with everybody, including gentiles, in order to be beloved by God and men."[118] In the same connection we mentioned a passage from the *Letter of Aristeas*:[119] "God accepts the humble, and the human race loves those willing to subject themselves." Both the *Letter*, a piece of pre-Christian Jewish propaganda, and Abaye, much later, contain the idea—also frequent in early Christian catechetical material—that if you humble yourself before others you will be approved by God and men.

Again, an Essene neophyte had to take an oath:[120] "To keep faith towards all, in particular the rulers, since there is no government but through God, and should he [the neophyte] himself come to govern, never to boast of his power or to outdo those subject to him by his garments or ornaments." This coupling of the duty to respect your superiors with that to be considerate to inferiors recurs in several Epistles: "The elders I exhort, Feed the flock not as being lords but being examples; likewise ye younger, submit yourselves unto the elder."[121]

The fact remains that the particular Tannaitic plan under notice, while assigning a place of its own to charity, says nothing on humility and subordination. There is here some support for Dr. Selwyn's conclusion,[122] reached by an entirely different route, that early Christian catechists evolved one pattern with love or benevolence as the chief virtue and another or others where humility and subordination were equally prominent.

4. *The Penalties*

Now the candidate is to be instructed in the penalties for transgressions; and the difference between his former state, when he could eat forbidden fat or violate the Sabbath without incurring extirpation or stoning, and his new state, when he cannot,[123] is to be impressed on him. The warning is in the direct address: "Know that before thou camest unto this dispensation thou couldst eat suet," etc. This part provides further evidence of the antiquity of the scheme: the death penalty by stoning for desecration of the Sabbath is still in force—otherwise there would be little point in the warning.

The section deals not—or not primarily—with minor slips, but with serious crimes: the penalties of extirpation and stoning applied solely to sins committed with full intent

[116] Eph 5:21, 33, 6:5; Col 3.22; 1 Pet 2:18, 3:2; Didache 4:11.
[117] Prov 15:1.
[118] *b. Ber.* 17a.
[119] *Letter of Aristeas* 257.
[120] Josephus, *Bell.* 2.8.7.140.
[121] 1 Pet 5:1 ff.; cp. 3:1 ff., Eph 5:22 ff.; Col. 3:18 ff.
[122] Pp. 374, 414 f., 460.
[123] Lev 7:23 ff.; Exod 35:2; Num 15:32 ff.

or even in a spirit of defiance, apostasy. Once we realize this, the arrangement appears perfectly natural. Having been informed of the nature of the life he is about to enter, a candidate must be cautioned as to what will happen should he later repudiate his undertakings.

Persons joining the Essenes, the Zadokites or the band who composed the *Sectarian Manual* were also threatened with dire consequences should they fall away.[124] Possibly, in the catechisms of these sects, the warnings occupied the same place as in the Tannaitic system—after the duties.

At any rate, as pointed out above, certain Rabbinic comments on the first dialogue between Ruth and Naomi reflect catechetical practice. There we do find the sequence from "some lighter and some weightier commandments" to "penalties for transgressions." Naomi (the Rabbis explain) told Ruth that, as a Jewess, she could not move beyond a fixed limit on the Sabbath, and Ruth replied "Whither thou goest I will go." Naomi told her that, as a Jewess, she must meet no man in private but her husband, and Ruth replied, "Where thou lodgest I will lodge." Naomi told her that there were as many as 613 commandments, and Ruth replied, "Thy people shall be my people." Naomi told her that idolatry was prohibited, and Ruth replied, "Thy God shall be my God." So far the commandments. Then Naomi asked Ruth to remember the various modes of capital punishment the courts might inflict, but Ruth replied, "Where thou diest will I die"; and when Naomi mentioned the plots used for the burial of persons executed, Ruth replied, "And there [where thou art buried] will I be buried." Clearly, this agrees with the Tannaitic plan.

How skillfully the plan is drawn up may be seen from the way part (4) hangs together with part (3). In the first place, even in part (3), on charity, reference is made to the culpability of whoever disregards the laws concerning gleanings and so on. Part (4) takes up this theme and works it out in a more general fashion, for all departments of the Law. In the second place, the punishment envisaged in part (3), for uncharitableness, is in the hands of God. So part (4) begins with extirpation, a penalty inflicted by the heavenly tribunal. Only then does it go on to stoning, carried out by man. In the third place, like part (3), part (4) starts from such provisions as were often followed by semi-converts. In the same chapter where Josephus remarks on the imitation by pagans of Jewish charity, he mentions their adoption of the dietary rules and the Sabbath. In Rabbinic writings,[125] among the inadequate motives for joining Judaism, we meet with the desire to exchange the nasty, unclean food of the heathen table for the decent Jewish food and to participate in the pleasant Sabbaths and festivals. So in this part, as in (3), emphasis is placed on the fact that observances which, before conversion, were voluntary and might be given up at will, would henceforth be compulsory and might never be shaken off.

In one respect, part (4) is meant as an antithesis to (3). Whereas part (3) is devoted to good deeds within the community, part (4) dwells on opposition to the outside

[124] Josephus, *Bell.* 2.8.8.143, *Zadokite Fragments* 9.28 ff., *Sectarian Manual* col. 2, according to Dupont-Somer, *op. cit.*, 49.

[125] *T. de Be El.* 146.

world. It is hardly accidental that the two institutions singled out, the dietary laws and the Sabbath, are those which then as today most effectively separated the Jew from his non-Jewish neighbour. Tacitus describes the Jews as "taking their meals apart," Rutilius Namatianus speaks of "humanis animal dissociale cibis" ["an animal hostile to food of humans"] and Juvenal ridicules the half-convert "for whom every seventh day is removed from any contact with life."[126] The proselyte enters into the congregation of the Lord, a holy brotherhood. But he must pay a price. He must renounce his former life and the unholy world around him; and he will look back at his peril.

It seems that early Christian catechisms normally contained a similar section or sections, where the previous or outside life, "according to the former lusts in your ignorance," was contrasted with life in the Christian Church, and where the wrath of God, "who judgeth according to every man's work,"[127] was called down upon whoever would relapse into sin. Moreover, there are indications that warnings of this kind often followed the proclamation of duties.[128] The penalties are as a rule such as God would carry out—which is natural, considering the circumstances of the Church about the middle and towards the end of the 1st cent. But, occasionally,[129] separation from or excommunication of the sinner is enjoined.

In respect of arrangement of matter, maybe even portions of Christian catechisms not dealing with penalties are indebted to parts (3) and (4) of the Tannaitic scheme. Chapter 12 of Romans is in point. Its first half is concerned with charity towards fellow-Christians, the second with the attitude of Christians to non-believers. This structure may well derive from Tannaitic baptismal teaching, with its transition from part (3), on gleanings and similar obligations, i.e. the duties of brotherhood, to part (4), on dietary rules and the Sabbath, i.e. isolation from the gentiles.

5. *The Reward and the World to Come*

Finally, the catechist should draw attention to the reward of keeping the commandments. The World to Come is made only for the sake of the righteous. "At this time" Israel can receive neither the greater part of the good nor the greater part of the retribution it deserves. But—the Tannaites add—a catechist should give no long or detailed exposition of these matters.

This part, then, contains the promise offered by the religion, taking up the theme of part (1) on a different level. At the opening stage, the applicant must humbly and half-blindly admit that Israel's sufferings are Israel's glory. Now he receives explicit assurance that it is so, and that those doing their duty in the face of present affliction—and only those—will be exalted when history comes to an end. "According to the suffering, so is the reward" was the favourite saying of one of the pagans whom Hillel had converted.[130] The resumption of the concept "at this time" is significant. It occurs twice

[126] *Hist.* 5, *De Reditu Suo* 1.384, *Satires* 14.105 f.

[127] 1 Pet 1:14 ff.

[128] Matt 7:24 ff.; Gal 6:7 f.; Eph 5:5 ff.; Phil 3:18 ff.; Col 3:25; 1 Thes 4:5 ff.; Heb 6:4 ff., 10:26 ff., 13:4; 1 Pet 3:12.

[129] Matt 18:15 ff.; Rom 16:17 ff.; 1 Cor 5:11 ff.; Tit 3:10 f.

[130] *m. Ab.* 5:23.

in the introductory part, and it recurs here, in the concluding part—where "the World to Come" is contrasted with it. The entire catechism is thus set in an eschatological framework. It is instruction as to man's purpose, task and hope in the passing phase that is this world.

A closer analysis, however, will show that the part under discussion is itself subdivided. It seems to begin, not with any eschatological prospects, but with rewards God may grant you on this earth. In other words, it starts—soberly enough—by counter-balancing the penalties announced in part (4). Just as he who spurns the commandments is liable to penalties—inflicted by God or by human courts—so he who fulfils them may be rewarded—by God alone, of course. As far as this antithesis is concerned, the rewards thought of are no doubt of this world: long life, children and the like.

The Bible lays down[131] that if you take the young of a bird you should let the dam escape, "that it may be well with thee and thou mayest prolong thy days." The Rabbis[132] declare that a promise given for the fulfilment of such a "light commandment" must *a fortiori* be valid for the "weighty commandments." This comment may well have originated in baptismal teaching. Similarly, to the prohibition of blood[133] the Bible adds: "that it may go well with thee and thy children after thee." The Rabbis conclude[134] that if such a reward is bestowed on him who abstains from blood, which man does not crave for (so that the prohibition is light in the sense of "easy to observe"), it must *a fortiori* be bestowed on him who abstains from dishonest gain and unchastity, towards which our evil instincts do draw us.

From this point onwards, however, eschatology is in the foreground. It is noteworthy that here again, as in the section warning the candidate of the risks he faces, the intimate form of the direct address appears: "Know that the World to Come is made only for the sake of the righteous ones." In a sense, this supplements the references to rewards in this age. It is a common experience that, in this age, just as a sin is not inevitably followed by failure, so piety does not always lead to success. The Tannaites held[135] that matters would be put right in a future aeon. God is just.

Now we reach the last phase of the teaching: Israel "at this time" can receive only some of the favours and some of the retribution due to it. The catechism here proceeds from the question of individual fortunes to that of the corporate destiny. Part (1), it may be recalled, opens by a reference to the present status of Israel as a whole. Part (5) closes by one to its future status. The proselyte must know that, as a Jew, though he will have his personal task to perform and may expect punishment and reward according to his efforts, yet his fate is inextricably bound up with that of the people to whom he belongs. He shares their humiliation—and exaltation—now; he will also share what is in store for them in the World to Come.

It is in consequence of this transition from individual to corporate destiny that the motif of punishment is introduced once more. As far as the individual is concerned, the

[131] Deut 22:7.

[132] *m. Hull.* 12:5.

[133] Deut 12:25.

[134] *b. Makk.* 23b.

[135] E.g. *m. Ab.* 2:16, a saying of R. Tarphon, of the first half of the 2nd cent. A.D.

penalties are dealt with in part (4), so that part (5) may be devoted to rewards. But the mention of the corporate destiny entails a further allusion to punishment, or rather, since the word used is *pur'anuth*, to "solution," "payment," "disaster." For when this age comes to a close, Israel, though in a sense assured of salvation, will none the less be judged by a severe God.[136] The main idea of this section, incidentally, was incorporated in a prayer for rain by Honi the circle-drawer, a miracle worker of the last century B.C., who is mentioned by Josephus.[137] He wanted neither too much rain nor too little, since "Israel can bear neither too much good nor too much retribution."

The Tannaites direct that a catechist should not dwell unduly on these matters. Some commentators are of opinion that this mandate covers all parts of the catechism (which would mean that catechisms must be short), others that it forbids a catechist to exercise either overmuch persuasion or overmuch dissuasion. But the natural sense of the clause is that the eschatological part should be kept down. At least in the 3rd cent. A.D., it appears to have been still understood in this way. Eleazar ben Pedath tried to find Scriptural support for it, and he adduced the verse from the Book of Ruth:[138] "When Naomi saw that Ruth was steadfastly minded to go with her, she left speaking to her." For the Rabbis, we saw, Naomi's decision to accept Ruth followed a proper baptismal instruction. On this basis, clearly, "she left speaking," i.e. she became reticent, when she reached the concluding part of the catechism—eschatology.

Very possibly, this recommendation of brevity is later than the main body of the catechetical scheme. It may be anti-Christian; that is to say, it may have been appended at a time when speculation about eschatology was dangerous because it might lead to inquiry into or even acceptance of the Christian tenets. Still, one school of Rabbis always discouraged excessive occupation with problems of this sort, and certainly any discussion of them with, or in the presence of, immature or unlearned persons. Be this as it may, the warning shows that, left to their own devices, Jewish catechists were prone to enlarge on the subject.

To come back again to the Rabbinic elaboration of the scene between Ruth and Naomi, we found reflected in it the test, i.e. the eagerness of the candidate to share Israel's sufferings, the commandments—Naomi explained to Ruth some light and some weighty duties—and the penalties—Naomi told Ruth of the different kinds of capital punishment and the graves for criminals. The exposition has come down to us in two versions. It is significant that only in one of them[139] are any eschatological hints preserved, and even they seem to be mutilated. When Ruth said. "The Lord do so to me and more also," Naomi admonished her to be tireless in the fulfilment of commandments and the doing of good deeds in this world, since as for the World to Come—"death will part thee and me." This is enough to prove that part (5) was represented. But, manifestly, the tendency was to suppress or shorten utterances about this topic.

[136] E.g. Testament of Benjamin 10:8: "And the Lord shall judge Israel first, for their unrighteousness; and then shall he judge all the Gentiles."

[137] *b. Taan.* 23a; *Ant.* 14.2.1.22 ff.

[138] *b. Yeb.* 47b; Ruth 1:18.

[139] *Ruth Rab.* on 1:16 f.

In the *Zadokite Fragments,* the promise of pardon for the faithful[140] succeeds the threats of punishment for the treacherous. In the *Sectarian Manual of Discipline,* to go by the brief description of Dupont-Somer,[141] the opposite sequence is to be found. We cannot, of course, be sure about the arrangement adopted by these groups in their catechisms. It is, however, interesting that the promises and threats of the Zadokites contain distinctly eschatological elements.

That early Christian catechisms finished by a section on eschatology is agreed. It must have differed in important respects from the corresponding Jewish section. Yet, fundamentally, there was no break. There was the promise of ultimate reward for the good, there was the warning that the godless would not share in it, there was the expectation that even the believers would be judged—"and if the righteous scarcely be saved, where shall the sinner appear?"[142]—and there was also the recognition of the corporate character of the Christian band, the common fate of those within as opposed to those without.

Dr. Selwyn[143] distinguishes between two patterns of Christian eschatological teaching: a primitive one, where eschatology was used as an incentive to conduct befitting the baptized, and a later one, where it served to inculcate the correct attitude to a persecution. The phrase "at this time" which occurs in the final part of the Tannaitic plan, and which refers to this age in which "Israel is broken down and sufferings befall it," suggests that, in Jewish proselyte instruction, the discussion of eschatology normally touched on the theme of persecution. But, naturally, the degree of emphasis accorded to it would vary with the times, and we are far from claiming that Dr. Selwyn's thesis is seriously affected.

The Christian eschatological vocabulary is to a large extent traditional. A word like καρτερία [perseverance]—the Hebrew equivalents are *'amaṣ* and *ḥazaq*, the Aramaic ones *ṭeqaph* and *'alem*—would be worth investigating. (It plays a prominent part in Josephus's *Contra Apionem.*[144]) Again, we have referred to the Rabbinic notions of conversion as a rising from death to life, a new birth and a liberation from former sins. It is safe to suppose that catechists discussed these notions partly in the introductory section, but chiefly in the final one, concerning the reward and the World to Come. The effect of these ideas on early Christianity can hardly be overrated. The believer is thought of as "begotten again," "a newborn babe," "a new man," "a new creation."[145] "He who separates himself from the uncircumcision is like one who separates himself from the grave" was a principle of the School of Hillel. Paul says:[146] "And you, being dead in the uncircumcision of your flesh, hath he quickened."

There is an Old Talmudic legend[147] according to which Alexander the Great asked

[140] *Zadokite Fragments* 9.50 ff.

[141] *Sectarian Manual,* 49.

[142] 1 Pet 4:18.

[143] Pp. 375 ff., 439 ff.

[144] E.g. *Contra Apionem* 2.16.170, 2.39.283.

[145] E.g. 1 Pet 1:3, 2:2; Col 3:10; 2 Cor 5:17.

[146] Col 2:13.

[147] *b. Taan.* 32a.

the Elders of Africa, "What shall a man do that he may live?" They answered: "Let him kill himself." Then the King asked, "And what shall a man do that he may die?," to which the Elders replied: "Let him keep himself alive." Some New Testament allusions to the true convert dying and rising with Jesus are very similar—for example, "He that loveth his life shall lose it, and he that hateth his life in this world shall keep it unto life eternal."[148] Even the doctrine that baptism, as it means a rising from the dead in a moral and spiritual sense, also means a dying to the sinful world,[149] has its roots in Jewish teaching. Joshua ben Hananiah, towards the end of the 1st cent. A.D., received a gentile woman into Judaism though she confessed that her eldest son was the father of her youngest—that is to say, she had transgressed the most elementary of the Noachian laws. But the Rabbi justified his attitude by saying that "as soon as she resolved to become a proselyte, she no longer lived to the world."[150]

It would lead too far afield to give further illustrations of the Jewish influence in this domain. Perhaps we may say, in conclusion, that the frequency with which the phrases "we know," "ye know," "know ye not," occur in the Epistles—and not only in eschatological pronouncements—will appear less strange if we assume that in the catechisms to which they often refer back, just as in the Tannaitic one, fresh paragraphs were occasionally opened by "Know": "Know that before thou camest unto this dispensation, thou couldst eat suet without incurring extirpation, but now" etc., or "Know that the World to Come is made only for the righteous."

C. JOSEPHUS

From the point of view of form, the Tannaitic catechism falls into five parts: (1) the test, (2) the commandments, (3) charity, (4) the penalties, (5) the reward and the World to Come. There is a lengthy section in Josephus's *Contra Apionem*[151] the structure of which is strikingly similar. The two main differences are these. One, there is no reference to a test. But this must be expected, since Josephus is not dealing with an actual applicant for admission to Judaism; his concern is to defend and explain his religion to the world at large. Two, instead of a special part on charity within the community, he has one on humanity to aliens, enemies and even beasts. Charity within the community is relegated to a subordinate place in the part on commandments. This deviation also is easily understandable. The work is directed against those many antisemites who accuse the Jews of being haters of all the rest of mankind. The sequence, then, is: commandments, humanity (instead of charity), penalties, reward.

It might perhaps be argued that the sequence is so inevitable that the agreement—such as it is—with the Talmudic catechism means nothing. But this is hardly convincing. An exposition of Judaism would be conceivable with humanity coming first, for example, or penalties last, or with penalties not mentioned at all. Moreover, the fact that, though the *Contra Apionem* was composed a considerable time after the fall of the

[148] John 12:24 f.; Matt 10:39; Luke 9:24, 17:33.

[149] E.g. Rom 8:6 ff.; Eph 2:1 ff.; Col 2:11 ff.

[150] *Eccl. Rab.* on 1:8.

[151] *Contra Apionem* 2.22.190 ff.

temple, Josephus writes as if it still stood and as if the cult still continued, suggests dependence on earlier models. The agreement does seem significant; and the points of difference only confirm, what we observed already, that even where several authors or teachers used more or less the same scheme of instruction, each would adapt it to his particular requirements.

Josephus begins by stating that he will say something about the commandments, positive and negative. (The reading ἀπαγορεύσεις [prohibitions] is no doubt the right one: the distinction was current in Rabbinic Judaism.) He lists easy and difficult precepts, light and important ones. He speaks about the one God, whose form it would be sinful to conjecture, but who is manifest by his works and lovingkindness. He goes on to the one temple—one, like God—its priests, worship and sacrifices. Then he outlines the marriage laws, mentioning the prohibitions of unchastity, of paying any attention to dowry in taking a wife and of killing any offspring, born or not yet born. He makes reference to certain purificatory rites. He emphasizes the duties of properly educating one's children, of piously observing the traditional funeral ceremonies, of honouring one's parents, of showing respect to one's elders, and of being loyal to one's friends, incorruptible as judge, charitable to those in need and honest. Clearly, an attempt to convey a general impression—a favourable one, of course—of life under the Law.

Now follows the chapter concerning the attitude to non-Jews. Any of them who elects to become a Jew may be sure of a genuine welcome. Those who do not wish to join cannot be admitted to much intimacy, since that might lead to corruption of Jewish conduct. Nevertheless, all must be treated with friendliness, and even enemies and beasts are entitled to mercy.

The penalties for transgressions of the laws are declared by Josephus to be heavier than among other nations, and he gives illustrations. It is interesting that the Tannaitic catechism mentions only two very serious punishments: extirpation and stoning.

The last part deals with the reward of the pious. It is no crown of olive or such-like worldly distinction, but the gift of a better life in a new aeon. It is because of this conviction, Josephus adds, that Jews prefer to endure the most terrible sufferings rather than abjure their faith. As in the Tannaitic catechism, the promise of exaltation in the future is closely linked with the theme of persecution in the present. It is also linked, very naturally, as in many New Testament passages, with the idea of steadfastness in the face of dangers. And in accordance with the Rabbinic warning discussed above, Josephus refrains from giving any details about resurrection; in fact he is remarkably brief.

The Burdened Convert*

Paul deems a convert a new creation. What, then, are we to make of his searing self-reproach for what he did to the Christians before joining them? "I am not meet to be called an apostle because I persecuted the church of God."[1] It is an anguish that never abates, attested in Acts as well as his own writings.

I.

The easy reply that the newness is mainly metaphorical will not do. For the Rabbis of his time, conversion—by circumcision and baptism in the case of males, baptism alone in that of females—was a true, miraculous rebirth, and he is no less serious about it. In his view as in theirs, a convert's entire past is gone: all connections good or bad, rights, duties, sins. A shying away from this extremism, plus unfamiliarity with the Jewish model, have produced odd puzzles and distortions in studies of the Epistles, 1 Corinthians in particular. As instances of major consequence I single out (a) the convert and his or her original family, (b) the convert and his or her original marriage.[2]

To begin with, as for the Jewish structure.[3] (a) Nothing links a convert to the original family—obviously, seeing he or she has just come into existence. One result is that if, say, a heathen household convert en bloc, incest prohibitions no longer apply and the closest relations—relations no longer—may intermarry. However, it was found that this freedom gave rise to misunderstandings among the unthinking: they might gain the impression that Judaism took incest lightly. The sages, therefore, ordained that proselytes must abstain from such unions as were illicit in the surrounding culture. This did not, let us note, encroach on the principle. For example, notwithstanding the restriction, a brother and sister both of whom convert and then marry still become husband and wife—only if they act from defiance, they will be excommunicated, and if from igno-

* To Eric and Tina

1 1 Cor 15:9.

2 See my following writings: *The New Testament and Rabbinic Judaism (*1956, rept. 1975), 113 [506 f.]; "Pauline Contributions to a Pluralistic Culture: Re-Creation and Beyond," in *Jesus and Man's Hope,* ed. D. G. Miller and D. Y. Hadidian (1971), vol. 2, 223 ff. [537 ff.]; "Biblical Landmarks in the Struggle for Women's Rights," in *JR*, 90, n.s. 23 (1978), 184 ff. [236 ff.]; "Historical Aspects of Informal Marriage," in *RIDA*, 25 (1978), 95 ff. [*Talmudic Law*, 153 ff.]; *Ancient Jewish Law: Three Inaugural Lectures* (1981), 14 ff. [474 ff.]; and "Onesimos," in *Christians among Jews and Gentiles: Essays in Honor of Krister Stendahl*, ed. G. W .E. Nickelsburg and G. W. MacRae (1986), 40 ff. [553 ff.]

3 Principal texts *m. Kidd.* 1:1; *m. Nidd.* 5:4; *y. Yeb.* 12a; *b. Yeb.* 22a, 48b, 62a, 98b; *b. Sanh.* 58a ff.; *b. Kidd.* 77a ff.; *Gen. Rab.* on 12:2.

rance, he will be bidden to divorce her. (b) The pre-conversion marriage survives as little as the pre-conversion family: the convert is simply a different person from the one that was married. In practice, it is true, the impact is often less traumatic than might be supposed at first blush. In the New Testament period, the commonest mode of marrying is by intercourse. (It still figures in the Mishnah as number 3, behind money and writ.) Hence if a couple convert both of them and stay together, they are validly married again through that very togetherness. It is indeed "married again," not "married still," but mostly the transition will be smooth. I shall not go into exceptional complications.

1 Corinthians 5 must be read with (a) in mind. A member of the flock lives with his stepmother, his father's widow. It is plainly done, not in the spirit of moral nihilism then prevalent in some segments of society, but from rapturous delight in the absolutely fresh start: the whole community is "puffed up,"[4] elated, in sympathy with him—a reaction the current commentaries cannot appreciate. Paul condemns it. It goes counter to the cautionary rule to avoid a degree like this, "in no way among the gentiles,"[5] abominated by them—this reference to their standard is also pretty pointless except against the background of the Rabbinic canons. Marvellous as the new creature's opportunities are, Paul insists, he must subordinate them to the welfare of the growing church and not be carried away by self-centered arrogance.

Chapter 7 deals with conversion of one spouse only, and here (b) is relevant. Paul leaves no doubt that the convert is released. Good Rabbinic doctrine: the married person he or she was has ceased to be. At the same time, if the unconverted spouse continues living with the convert, this cohabitation, in Paul's analysis, makes them into a couple again—in accordance with the above-quoted norms as to the conclusion of marriage.

Two observations should be added. One, regarding the termination of the pre-conversion bond. In the traditional opinion, Paul is thereby infringing Jesus's stand on the indissolubility of marriage. But he is not; it is surely inconceivable that he should be. He adheres to the Rabbinic position, so "to be a new creation" is more than a trope. The convert is just not identical with the previous incarnation: that is the ground for his or her release. It is much later exegetes who, cut off from their roots and oblivious therefore of the genuine import, substituted divorce. They thus had a deviant teaching on their hands which they defensively titled "the Pauline Privilege." My second remark concerns the new marriage if the converted spouse stays on. In this matter, Paul is characteristically and daringly more liberal than the Rabbis. For one thing, he recognizes the union even if the unconverted partner is a heathen. (Adumbrations of this occur in earlier fringe groups.[6]) For another, it is not only a male convert who can "sanctify,"[7] make into a spouse, an unconverted woman, but also a female convert who can "sanctify" an unconverted man. This directive, I suggest, has a claim to attention whenever Paul's attitude to women is being inspected.

Philemon is another illustration of his sharing the Rabbis' belief in a realistic, supernatural effect of conversion. It has long been noticed that, though not asking

[4] 1 Cor 5:2.

[5] 1 Cor 5:1.

[6] Testament of Levi 14:6.

Philemon to manumit Onesimos, yet he does ask him to receive him not as a slave but as a brother. The explanation is that a manumission would be superfluous if not offensive. The baptized Onesimos, by virtue of the baptism, is no longer he that was owned by Philemon. The latter, himself guided into the faith by Paul, would understand.

Both Jews and early Christians were denounced by the pagans as practising incest,[8] an accusation historians brush aside as sheer calumny. Unfair. Pagans would derive most of their information about those religions from someone, or the acquaintance of someone, who had gone over and reported back. He or she was bound to dwell on the awesome emergence as another being; and indeed, if belonging to a circle of enthusiasts such as we come across at Corinth, on privileges which, to outsiders, must be indicative of a general, despicable perversion. The sages, we have seen, were alive to the likelihood of misconceptions here. The indictment in question is in fact weighty evidence in support of the picture I am drawing.

As the church became de-Judaized, conversion, once a tornado, changed into a breeze. Above all, it was tamed so as to turn around the inner life only but not life in its totality. While there was still cleansing from fault and granting of spiritual faculties, such worldly things as civic status, relationships, monetary affairs were no longer touched. Probably, even apart from the non-Jewish influence, the development was inevitable when Christianity rose to be the dominant creed. So long as the number of converts was relatively small—as in Jewry and *Ur*-Christianity—a problem like the extinction of inherited blood-ties was manageable. With masses involved, to hold on to the pristine treatment of it would have been too undermining of the established order. A pessimist might class this as yet another case of religion buying security and prosperity by leaving the material, social scene to the powers that be. An optimist will plead that we have to do with one of the prudent concessions—not the same as surrenders—necessary day in, day out, in an imperfect universe.

The Jewish law of conversion has undergone no major reform since the Pauline days. Suppose, as is by no means impossible, fifty years from now marriage between half-brother and half-sister were legitimized in the Western hemisphere, such a pair of proselytes would be entitled to wed. Still, one cannot help sensing a certain reserve in this field among modern Jewish scholars, as if they were a little ashamed. Hardly surprising: in the climate of rational propriety dominating academia during the two centuries prior to the two world wars, to spell out the magical detachment of a convert from the mightiest taboos was to risk feeding into very popular proofs of Talmudic inferiority. Quite likely, it is largely due to this near-silence that the native basis of Paul's design has remained unrecognized until recently. For its Rabbinic material, New Testament research is dependent on Jewish experts, hence apt to break down when these default. Future exploration will no doubt be far less timid, for two curiously disparate reasons: respect for, or at least interest in, thorough renewal from on high is on the increase and, owing to the melting down of the family, the age-old, instinctive horror of incest is lessening.

[7] 1 Cor 7:14.

[8] Tacitus, *Histories* 5.5; Athenagoras, *Plea for the Christians* 31.1; Eusebius, *Eccl. Hist.* 5.1.14.

II.

So I come back to Paul's guilt—which, at a cursory glance, almost makes it look as if, in contrast to subsequent generations, he was having more difficulty with the heaven-wrought supersession of the inner man than that of outer conditions. The key to the riddle may lie in a combination of two factors.

First, logic is not everything: it is only natural that, whatever the strict implications of his system, sorrow and, indeed, remorse for fearful evil perpetrated should endure in his heart. Yet this cannot be the whole answer. It might satisfy if these feelings were barely discernible here and there. But they receive the clearest public expression and, moreover, are never relieved by any hint that baptism has made the crooked straight. He is too mindful of his responsibility as instructor to give free rein to wayward sentiments where so momentous a subject is involved. There must be something that renders them appropriate, maybe even the bearers of a lesson for his particular audiences. Secondly, then, he seems to follow a Rabbinic view that what is not wiped out by conversion is the wrong in delaying it once the truth has been taken in.

Josephus reports[9] that the King of Adiabene, though adopting the Jewish faith and devoting himself to the study of Scripture, yet, for a while, with his mentor's approval, did not undergo circumcision—which might provoke a revolt of the populace. What merits attention is that, in principle, to refrain from the act at this stage counts as a dereliction, only because of the extraordinary risks, "God will grant pardon." After some time, however, Josephus goes on, another, less accommodating master intervened, charging the king with impiety in reading the Law without following it out. "How long will you continue to be uncircumcised?" For this rigorist, no excuse is good enough. Both agree on the essential: that he who has clearly heard the summons is henceforth accountable for failing to pay heed.

In the Talmud, the idea is met in a discussion among sages flourishing from towards the end of the first century A.D.[10] They are exercised by the problem that proselytes commonly suffer oppression—hated by those they have left—though, unlike the bulk of the Jews, they do not deserve it, being "children just born," their past vanished, no blame on their shoulders. One solution is that they lingered over the final decision: that stubbornness does enter into the new state.[11] Nor have we to do here with an extravaganza. Around 300, Abbahu (or his son Hanina) discovers textual support for this justification of the hardship in store for proselytes—to wit, in the saga of one who did not lag and, accordingly, fared well. Ruth, the model convert in Rabbinic eyes, showed supreme eagerness to be allowed into the fold; and when Boaz blessed her, "May your reward be

[9] *Ant.* 20.2.4.38 ff.

[10] *b. Yeb.* 48b.

[11] The verb for "to linger," *shahah,* has the same range as its English equivalent, including culpable passivity. Tax evasion by means of delay occurs in *b. Meg.* 13b. *Num. Rab.* on 4:19 contains an exegesis of Moses's order to Aaron in Num 17:11: "Take your fire-pan and carry it quickly unto the congregation." Why, the Midrash asks, had it to be done quickly? Moses saw the angel of death about to strike, hence called out "Quickly—why do you stand and tarry?"

complete, *shelema*,"[12] he meant just this—that in her case the renewal from above would be perfect, unmarred by hesitation. Abbahu, it may be recalled, often disputes with Christians.[13]

Possibly, note should be taken of other homilies which appear to assign a special place to a gentile unerringly pursuing conversion. Ruth's appeal to Naomi not to reject her is interpreted as an appeal "not to sin over her."[14] Again, the Bible has Naomi realize that "Ruth was steadfastly minded to go with her." The phrase "to go with her," Judah ben Simon holds, indicates that from the moment of her resolve Ruth was Naomi's equal.[15]

The baptismal catechism preserved in the Talmud recommends that a would-be proselyte be warned not to take the step rashly: it will bring him into a wounded nation and burden him with commandments violation of which entails heavy penalties.[16] Is this inconsistent with the notion of culpable delay? Not necessarily. Frivolous chase after novelty is one thing, genuine insight into a higher world that offers is another. It makes sense to discourage the former, diversion rather than conversion, while considering it a duty to bow to the latter. There is, besides, a fundamental datum: in areas like this, encompassing the mysteries of conscience, choice of path, receptivity to the Lord's bidding, extent of liability, we ought to reckon with an enormous diversity of opinion. Josephus's tale itself supplies an example. The first counsellor admitted a concession (even he, it is true, merely since principled conduct was singularly perilous), the second "came from Galilee, reputed to be exceedingly strict about the traditions."

As for Paul, it may be expected that, of all standards feasible, he would prefer the most demanding one—applying it to himself at least if not universally. Nor must we overlook the uniqueness of his experience, adding immeasurably to the gravity of his shortcoming. As he must see his pre-conversion life, he not only kept battling the gospel when fully acquainted with it and its worth but also, in so doing, spurned "God's separation of him from his mother's womb."[17]

Two passages in Acts and a third in 1 Corinthians concerning blameworthy slowness are reminiscent of the Rabbinic attitude outlined. In Acts 26:14, Jesus addresses him who is still Saul: "Why do you persecute me? Hard for you to kick against the pricks." The opening (recorded also in two previous chapters)[18] is a rhetorical question,

[12] Ruth 2:12.

[13] See W. Bacher, *Die Agada der Palästinensischen Amoräer* (1896), vol. 2, 115 ff.

[14] *Ruth Rab.* on 1:16.

[15] *Ruth Rab.* on 1:18. A good illustration of the diverse uses which can be made of the same idiom. Judah ben Ilai sees in the notice, Gen 6:9, that "Noah went with God" an allusion, not to his equality, but to his imperfection: he resembles a toddler dependent on the parent. By contrast, Abraham was told by God, Gen 17:1, "Go before me": like an adult (*Gen. Rab.* on 6:9). See my "Neglected Nuances of Exposition in Luke-Acts," in *Aufstieg und Niedergang der Römischen Welt*, ed. H. Temporini and W. Haase, 1985, pt. II, Principat 25, Religion 3, 2338. [865.]

[16] See my *New Testament and Rabbinic Judaism*, 113 ff. [507 ff.], and *Ancient Jewish Law*, 18 ff. [477 ff.].

[17] Gal 1:15.

[18] Acts 9:4, 22:7.

really an emphatic pointing out of the senselessness of Saul's warfare. *Skleros,* "hard," and several words containing the root often refer to obduracy; doubtless this meaning plays a part here. Most revealing is the expression "to kick against the pricks." Conjuring up an unruly horse's fate, it always denotes the fruitless, self-maiming insubordination of the subject of an all-powerful ruler, man versus God in Pindar and Euripides, citizen versus monarch in Aeschylus.[19] Thus Saul is not approached as a complete outsider yet to be brought into the fellowship. To some degree at least he is indentured already and reminded of the severe lasting damage he is doing himself by his defiance.[20]

Acts 22:16 tells us how, as soon as his sight was restored, his instructor exhorted him: "And now, why do you tarry? Arise and be baptized." To take the first clause as a mere jovial encouragement cannot be right, considering the overwhelming significance of the situation. It must be a condemnation of the slightest traces of holding off. While the circumstance could not be more different from those relating to the King of Adiabene, it is less remote from "How long will you continue uncircumcised?" than might appear at first sight.

1 Cor 15:8 brings out the point more strongly. "But last of all he was seen also of me, as of one born out of due time."[21]

Of the three Septuagintal occurrences of *ektroma,* two need not detain us. The stricken Job wishes never to have lived, to be like "an untimely birth coming out of the womb, infants who never saw the light"; and Ecclesiastes laments that, however blessed a man may be with children and long life, if he cannot enjoy it, "an untimely birth is better than he, for it comes in vain and goes in darkness and has not seen the sun."[22] In the straits here contemplated, to be "an untimely birth" is a good thing whereas normally, and in 1 Corinthians, it is about the worst. The third text is all the more important. It is from the Pentateuch, from Numbers[23] part of an amazing interlude—amazing at least to readers two thousand years or so ago. Miriam is struck with leprosy for maligning Moses, and Aaron, her accomplice, asks Moses to get her healed: "May she

[19] Pindar, *Pythian Odes* 2.95; Euripides, *Bacchanals* 795; Aeschylus, *Agamemnon* 1624. In Psalms of Solomon 16:4, God steers man away from the wrong path by pricking him as a rider does his horse: a very different thing.

[20] According to J. Munck, *Acts of the Apostles,* rev. W. F. Albright and C. S. Mann (1967), 242, the clause deals with the future: "from now on it will be difficult for you to kick against the goad," "the call of Christ will from now on constrain you." This sounds too abrupt after "Why do you persecute me?," which is about the past and present. Again, future recalcitrance is so out of the question that there is no need to enlarge on its futility. Lastly—a decisive objection—the text ought to contain some pointer at least to "from now on" if we were intended to take it that way.

[21] I gratefully borrow from the literature, in particular J. D. Schneider, art. "*ektroma,*" in *Theologisches Wörterbuch zum Neuen Testament,* ed. G. Kittel (1935), vol. 2, 463 ff.; H. Lietzmann, *An die Korinther I/II,* 4th ed. by W. G. Kümmel (1979), 7, 192; C. K. Barrett, *The First Epistle to the Corinthians* (1968), 343 ff.; W. F. Orr and J. A. Walther, *I Corinthians* (1976), 318, 322 f.; G. K. E. Nickelsburg, "An *ektroma,* Though Appointed from the Womb: Paul's Apostolic Self-Description in 1 Corinthians 15 and Galatians 1," in *Essays in Honor of Krister Stendahl,* 198 ff. All of these authors mention other important contributions.

[22] Job 3:16; Eccl 6:3. See my "Black Hole," in *RJ,* 2 (1983), 182 ff.

[23] Num 12:12.

not be as something equal to death, as an untimely birth coming out of the mother's womb, and it consumes half of her flesh." It is this precedent on which Paul bases and which would occur to such recipients of his letter as were at all in touch with Scripture.

To get an idea of the speculation the episode engendered, we need only survey the ancient versions and expositions of this very line. The underlying Hebrew includes no noun "untimely birth" at all and, indeed, is altogether much plainer: "May she not be as the dead one that, when he comes out of his mother's womb, half of his flesh is consumed." What led to the Greek is far from obvious. Perhaps, in the translator's judgment, the crass likening of Miriam to a corpse sounded implausible or even irreligious. He resorted to elaboration, thereby introducing the rare term—by which he may understand a live monsterbirth. This does not, however, account for a switch at the end: while the Hebrew speaks of the dead child's devastation, the Septuagint speaks of the mother's, "half of her flesh." No doubt the child's is taken for granted; even so, the addition of the mother remains baffling. Philo, incidentally, in his *Allegorical Interpretation*[24] takes over *ektroma* and follows the Greek also in assuming harm to the mother. One certainty that emerges is that already in the epoch of the Septuagint this incident was eagerly studied.

To proceed to Aramaic, Onkelos eliminates anything smacking of a person's death, be it fetus or adult. "May she not be removed from our midst [the camp] since she is our sister; pray now over this dead flesh being in her and she will be healed." By contrast, the Jerusalemite Targum describes her as a leper "unclean in her tent as one dead" and at great length compares her to a child that completes nine months in the womb and perishes as the mother is sitting down on the travailing chair: Miriam went with the rest through the trials of Egypt and the desert but, unless restored, is to be banished now that they are approaching their land.

Like the Septuagint, the Siphre interferes with "his flesh." It does not, of course, alter the wording but it argues that its real meaning is "our flesh," in the sense of "our sister"; and by similarly interpreting "his mother" as "our mother," it achieves a result close to Onkelos. Aaron's plea to Moses, that is, must be understood thus: "May she not be unclean like one dead, she who came out of the womb of our mother, so that [if nothing is done about it] half of our sister is consumed."[25]

It would lead too far afield to set forth, however summarily, the mighty and subtle thoughts massed in this brief narrative, all of them again and again drawn on by future Biblical authors.[26] Here are the features which explain why Paul has recourse to it. Its bête noir is a prophetess who badly falls down on her vocation, inveighing against the God-appointed leader, in fact, the precursor of the Messiah to come. No one deserves such an attack less: he is "very meek, above all the men that are on the face of the

[24] *Leg. All.* 1.24.76.

[25] Needless to say, the Siphre feels justified in redirecting the pronoun: Aaron is displaying such reverence towards Moses that he will not dare to say "our," as if they were comrades. See K. G. Kuhn, *Sifre zu Numeri* (1933–1934), 224, 275.

[26] An inter-testamental quotation: Sir 45:4, "For his faithfulness and meekness he chose him out of all flesh." A New Testament one: Heb 3:2, "As also Moses was faithful in all his house."

earth." This, though he far surpasses the ordinary prophet: "My servant Moses, in all my house he is trusted, mouth to mouth will I speak with him." When the Lord threatens her with condign horrendous punishment, with for ever being "as an *ektroma*," it is her innocent victim whose prayer saves her. Not from some discipline: she has to bear with shameful seclusion for a period. But even this is lightened by the people patiently waiting for her instead of marching on; lightened and at the same time rendered more deplorable, since the communal goal will be reached that much later. That Paul would detect in this drama an anticipation of his destiny is small wonder—on the presupposition that, despite baptism, he continues answerable for his extended, bitter fight against it.

Not a few questions I shall leave open. For instance, when he confesses to "having persecuted the church of God," is this an echo—in part—of the hurt to the mother in the Septuagint and Philo? Again, does *ektroma* in his Epistle denote a fetus miscarried—the usual sense of the noun—or one stillborn—the case envisaged in the Jerusalemite Targum—or a live monsterbirth—possibly alluded to by the Septuagint? Maybe one should not even try to pin him down. Yet harder is the following: is he distressed chiefly by his No to the task laid on him from conception or to that he learned about from those like Stephen sent to enlighten him? Whichever line we take, the designation from Numbers, where it brings out the abject fate of the leper, evokes a child gruesomely disfigured as it emerges from the mother. Paul is that child. He, "the last," missed being around the human Jesus or finding his way into the church at its dawn. Instead, those lost years were exceptionally unfortunate, marked not merely by a holding back but by the grossest misdeeds. Such contumacy towards his deeper, better knowledge leaves him mutilated and penitent even now.

In conclusion, I retract what I said above about his never hinting that baptism has made the crooked straight. Paradoxically and providentially, it is just the hellish attribute he owns up to which implies relief. Miriam, his predecessor, obtained forgiveness through the mediation of the holy one whom she had persecuted. Not without having to expiate by accepting pain and disgrace—but still, full forgiveness in the end. So it will be with him. His identifying with her, by the way, is yet another item that should weigh in assessing the place of women in his anthropology. It would not, indeed, be surprising if she were in his mind in another section of the same Epistle, equally dealing with a legend from Numbers—the Israelites drinking of the rock that accompanied them. The Rabbis call this rock "Miriam's well."[27]

[27] 1 Cor 10:4; Num 20:7 ff., 21:16 ff. The first named Rabbi mentioning it is Hiyya, around A.D. 200, *y. Kil.* 32c. But that he is not coining a novel concept may be inferred both from the way he speaks and from first-century statements like Joshua's, *Mek.* on Exod 16:35, and Pseudo-Philo's *Antiquities* 21A. For more texts, see H. L. Strack and P. Billerbeck, *Kommentar zum Neuen Testament aus Talmud und Midrasch*, 4 vols. (1924–1929, rpt. 1969), passim.

Pauline Contributions to a Pluralistic Culture: Re-Creation and Beyond

As my paper will culminate in a rejection of the accepted thinking concerning the "Pauline privilege," *privilegium Paulinum*, let me remind you that, under this head, a convert to Christianity has the right to divorce a partner who remains unconverted. It is universally believed that Paul in 1 Corinthians 7 in this case relaxed Jesus's teaching of the indissolubility of marriage in the lifetime of the spouses—hence the name of the institution. "There is little evidence of its exercise in the earliest times," says the *Oxford Dictionary of the Christian Church.*[1] No wonder. What Paul advised is pretty much the opposite, really something quite different.

In 1 Cor 5:1 ff.[2] Paul orders the excommunication of a convert who has married his stepmother—no doubt after his father had died or divorced her.[3] My starting-point is the apostle's emphatic remark (vs. 1) that this kind of incest is avoided even by the heathen.

To appreciate his meaning we must remember the Rabbinic teaching that a proselyte is as a newborn child. Hence he has no relations from before; and as far as his pre-conversion ties are concerned, in principle the rules of incest do not apply; in principle he may marry his stepmother or indeed his own mother—neither is related to him, a new man.[4] However, the Rabbis feared that a thorough following-out of this doctrine might cause a proselyte to stumble. Suppose he grew up in a culture where marriage with the mother or sister is prohibited. If he finds that his new religion allows him to marry her, he might conclude that it is lax in these matters, that "he has come from a weightier sanctity into a lighter sanctity"; and he might slip back generally into that promiscuity and licentiousness which characterize pagan life. The Rabbis, therefore,

[1] "Pauline Privilege" in *The Oxford Dictionary of the Christian Church*, ed. F. L. Cross (London, 1957), 1035.

[2] See David Daube, *The New Testament and Rabbinic Judaism* (London, 1956), 113 [506 f.]

[3] Paul speaks of "his father's wife," technical of incest apart from adultery ever since Lev 18:8, 20:10 f. Cf. the analysis propounded by Gaius 1.63: "I may not marry one who once was my stepmother. We say, who once was, since if the marriage producing that alliance were still continuing, I should be precluded from marrying her on another ground."

[4] Entry into Judaism, with such far-reaching consequences, is effected, in the case of males, by circumcision and baptism, in that of females, by baptism alone. For obvious reasons, female proselytes far outnumbered male ones. Even in the case of the latter, the precise moment of entry is that of coming up from the water. How, in the face of these facts, many scholars go on labelling Jewish proselyte baptism as of a purely levitical character, is difficult to understand. See Daube, *The Sudden in the Scriptures* (Leiden, 1964), 47. [718 f.]

modified the principle to this extent that a convert, though really having no preconversion relations, yet must refrain from such degrees as are prohibited by pagan law.[5]

The primitive church, or at all events Paul, took over this scheme *in toto*. In 2 Cor 5:17 the apostle speaks of a Christian as "a new creation"; and in 1 Cor 6:15 he affirms that a convert's body has become a member of Christ.[6] The case he is dealing with in 5:1 ff. is damnable because, in his judgment, it involves a degree banned even by pagan law: Roman as well as Jewish law repudiates marriage with the stepmother.[7] The person disregarding this prohibition is guilty of a grave and dangerous crime. If, as is possible,[8] there were subcultures in the Hellenistic world of the time admitting the union, Paul takes no notice of them. He could hardly have taken the same stand had a convert married, for example, his half-sister from the same father: this marriage was too common to be classed as repugnant to gentiles.[9]

That Paul's handling of the incident must be understood in this way is clear not only from the Rabbinic sources but also from internal evidence. Sheer, gross incest would not have been openly condoned by the Corinthian Christians, bad as they were. By contrast, this affair they did not just tolerate: they were proud of it, "puffed up" (vs. 2), "glorying" (vs. 6). There is all the difference between being wicked—cheating, fornicating—and elevating what is normally considered wicked into a fine thing.[10] In this case they seriously claimed that what was being done was their privilege as new creations.

"To be puffed up," *physioomai*, occurs exclusively in Paul and in no other New Testament writer. He uses it seven times,[11] six times in this Epistle, once in Colossians. It always signifies the misguided reliance on an imaginary special knowledge. (It may signify much the same in the Testament of Levi 14:7, fulminating against those "puffed up because of their priesthood."[12]) In Colossians Paul warns against Gnostic secrets.[13] In 1 Cor 4:6 he asks the competing factions—his own followers, those of Apollos, those of Cephas—not to rank each of them its specific instruction above the others. Similarly, in 4:18 and 19 he denounces the assumption of his opponents that he considers himself inferior to their teachers and will not dare to appear in person. In 8:1 he questions the certainty of those who declare food offered to idols to be permissible in all circum-

[5] *b. Yeb.* 22a, 48b, 62a, 98b; *Gen. Rab.* on 12:2. I shall not here go into possible, unavowed motivations favoring the regulation.

[6] Cf. 1 Cor 11:3, 12:12 ff. Chapter 15, as is well known, culminates in the description of a second, final resurrection at the end of days. See Daube, *The New Testament and Rabbinic Judaism*, 137, 443. [525, 681.]

[7] Gaius 1.63, though see also Cicero, *Pro Clu.* 5.14, 6.15; Lev 18:8, 20:11.

[8] See Cicero, cited in the preceding footnote; also R. Eliezer's exegesis of Gen 2:24 (second half of first century A.D.), transmitted in *b. Sanh.* 58a.

[9] Though it, too, is contrary to both Jewish and Roman law: Gaius 1.61; Lev 20:17. In early biblical law it had been permissible: see Daube, *Studies in Biblical Law* (Cambridge, England, 1947), 78 ff.

[10] Below, 542 shall submit that the sinners reproached in 6:8 ff. probably did not regard their doings as admirable.

[11] Eight if we add the noun formed from it, and found in 2 Cor 12:20, as one of a number of sins Paul fears are rife at Corinth. Doubtless the meaning corresponds to that of the verb.

[12] That they pretend to special privileges and knowledge is suggested, for instance, by verse 6, where they are said to marry gentile women, "purifying them with an unlawful purification."

[13] Col 2:18. This passage, then, is an argument—though not, admittedly, a conclusive one—in favor of the authenticity of Colossians.

stances. In 13:4 he points out that, however superior a person may be in ecstatic speech, prophecy, surrender of his possessions or even his body, it means little if he is not truly loving. Evidently, in 5:2 the reference is to the conviction of his addressees that their status entitles them to contract the union in question.

In 2 Cor 2:5 ff. Paul asks that a certain offender, having accepted his punishment, should be restored to his place in the community, forgiven and comforted. This may well be the sinner of 1 Corinthians 5. If so, there is here a further indication that it was a matter not of simple, vulgar immorality but of immorality thought to be justified: the kind of concern shown by Paul strongly points in this direction. We cannot, however, be completely sure about the identity of the man.[14]

The Rabbis, I remarked, restricted a proselyte's freedom in order that he should not draw the wrong conclusions and relapse into heathen vice. That is what Paul has in mind when he bids his flock "purge out the old leaven" (vs. 7). "Leaven" is a Rabbinic term for the convert's previous, evil state, ever luring him back. For Eliezer ben Hyrcanus (second half of the first century A.D.) the reason the Pentateuch so many times requests consideration to the convert is to prevent him from "reverting to his leaven." In his actual dealings, this Rabbi was less patient than his contemporary Joshua ben Hananiah: the proselyte Aquila, we are told, was treated harshly by Eliezer and "would have reverted to his leaven" but for Joshua's extreme gentleness.[15]

There is indeed a nuance in Paul arising out of his particular situation. The Rabbis were interested in the individual proselyte. The apostle, hoping for a flourishing church at Corinth, pure in the midst of impurity, stresses the possible effect of the wrongdoer's conduct on his fellows: the entire community may go astray—"a little leaven leavens the whole lump" (vs. 6). To use two verbs of his, the Rabbis forbade a convert certain degrees because, though in principle legitimate, they would be the opposite of beneficial, *sympbero*, to him. Paul forbids them both for this reason and because they would be the opposite of upbuilding, *oikodomeo*, for the church.[16] It will soon emerge[17] that, in other contexts, the Rabbis, too, weighed up the wider repercussions to be expected from a decision.[18]

[14] That he is the one arraigned in 1 Corinthians is perhaps still the prevalent view; and I see no force in the objection that "of such a situation Paul could not have written (2 Cor 2:9) that his only interest was in obedience to himself," Clarence T. Craig, "The First Epistle to the Corinthians," *The Interpreter's Bible*, vol. 10 (New York, 1953), 294. First, why could he not? Secondly, he does not in fact write this.

[15] *Mek.* on Exod 22:20; *Gen. Rab.* on 28:20. See Bacher, *Die Agada der Tannaiten*, vol. 1, 2nd ed. (Strassburg, 1903), 106 f., 182; Daube, *The New Testament and Rabbinic Judaism*, 128 [518].

[16] For the sake of compactness, throughout this study, except for an occasional allusion (e.g., below, nos. 28, 29), I refrain from inquiring at what point Paul might assume sin apart from the non-beneficial and non-upbuilding.

[17] See below, 542, 543 f., 544 f., 545 f.

[18] Verses 6–8 are, of course, permeated by Passover ideas, in particular, the obligation, prior to the festival, of cleansing the house of all leaven. (Indeed, 6 is among the best evidence we have that the Rabbinic insistence on removal of even the smallest particle goes back at least to the era of Paul.) As for the role, in this context, of the comparison of the community to "a lump," a cake of unleavened bread, see Daube, *He That Cometh* (London, 1966), 7, 10 [431, 434]; and as for the background of the term "to purge out," *ekkatheiro*, see Daube, ["The Culture of Deuteronomy"] *Orita*, 3 (1969), 49 f.

I am aware that *symphero* (or the noun belonging to it) may cover what is beneficial to others and *oikodomeo* what is upbuilding for yourself. In 10:33 Paul depicts himself as adjusting to various milieus "not seeking my own benefit but that of many, that they may be saved"; and in 14:4 he holds that "he that speaks in a tongue upbuilds himself, but he that prophesies upbuilds the church." Still, mostly where he distinguishes between the permissible in the abstract or the second-best and elevated Christian choice, he defines the latter as involving *symphero*, your own spiritual welfare, and *oikodomeo*, your contribution to society.

The Hebrew behind *symphero* is *tobh*, "good." In Sirach we read: "Not everything is good for everyone."[19] Among many feasible courses you must elect that most suited to your individual condition. In 6:12 Paul explains that though in strictness any action is licit—adultery, theft, drunkenness—not any will benefit you. In 7:35 he observes that celibacy, though far from a commandment, is beneficial to a person—at least in certain circumstances.[20] *Symphero* is also met in the Matthean section on the subject: "If the case be so with his wife, it is not beneficial to marry."[21] Here, too, by beneficial is meant what will most advance a man—abstention—in contrast to what he is free to do—marrying.[22] 10:23, towards the end of a disquisition on food offered to idols, opposes to the licit both the beneficial and the upbuilding: we shall see that, according to Paul, it is indeed a man's own salvation and his thought for his fellows which should guide him in this question.

As for *oikodomeo*—in Hebrew *bana*[23]—it occurs in 8:1 and 10:23 in connection with food offered to idols: you must always remember to upbuild the other members of the community.[24] In 14:3 f. and 17 Paul finds less merit in the public speech in ecstasy, since it does not upbuild the listeners, than in prophecy, which does.[25]

It is not, then, quite accurate to describe the attitude of those rebuked in chapter 5 as antinomianism. They may, of course, have been antinomians; but in this affair they contended only that their preconversion ties had gone as a result of re-creation. Where

[19] Sir 37:28; *tobh* in Hebrew, *symphero* in Greek.

[20] According to Miss Ford, *A Trilogy on Wisdom and Celibacy* (Notre Dame, 1967), 82 ff., the passage contemplates solely widowers and widows.

[21] Matt 19:10. This statement in turn harks back to, and in a way boldly contradicts, Gen 2:18: "It is not good that the man should be alone." In the latter passage, the Greek for "good" is *kalon*; and *kalon* recurs in 1 Cor 7:1, "It is good for a man not to touch a woman"—cp. 7:8 f., 26, 37 f.

[22] In 1 Cor 7:35 *symphero* really has both senses: that which is beneficial to yourself and that which is beneficial to your fellows. I point out in the text that, just as in Matt 19:10, it designates a man's highest destiny by comparison with the second-best. At the same time, this benefit, seen from the viewpoint of the apostle in relation to his addressees, is the benefit of others: his words are, "I speak for your own benefit"—distinctly reminiscent of 10:33, "not seeking my own benefit but that of many."

[23] *Pesiqta Rabbathi* 43:4 contains an interesting application. The Midrash is puzzled by the plural in Gen 21:7, where Sarah gives suck "to children." The solution is that the gentiles brought their children to her to give them suck. Indeed, those who were brought in sincerity converted, "they were built in Israel" or "they built themselves in Israel"—and there seems to be a pun, for we are probably meant to understand also "they became children in Israel" *(nithbanu)*.

[24] An ironical twist in 8:10: if you act selfishly, you may "upbuild" others so as to relapse into idolatry.

[25] As noted above, 14:4 says that by ecstatic speech you upbuild yourself only.

they went wrong was in insisting on this principle absolutely, without heeding the harm likely to ensue if it was carried out beyond a certain point.

Once the true nature of this case is grasped,[26] the Epistle gains hugely in thematic unity. Again and again, as here, what Paul is anxious to stop is the making of a fetish of some in itself praiseworthy notion, and especially one peculiar to Christians. That would bring about a rigidity not much better than that he had found entailed by a strict observance of the old Law. There is no doctrine (even that of re-creation, for instance) so unconditionally valid that, in practising it, you should not ask at each step whether it is beneficial to yourself and, above all, upbuilding for others or the church as a whole. This overriding importance of the consequences for those around you is summed up in the requirement of constant exercise of *agape*, "love," "charity"—maybe in this area we had better translate "consideration," "considerateness" or "caring for."

The discussion in 8:1 ff. of food offered to idols is closely allied in structure to that of incest. The Christian is not fettered by specific dietary regulations; in principle it does not matter what he eats.[27] Does it follow that he may buy from a pagan, or accept in a pagan home, food which has been, or may have been, dedicated to their gods? Even more extremely, may he take part in temple feasts?

A number of Corinthians said, Yes. A sophisticated Christian would realize that idols were nothings—so the food remained the same whatever heathen invocation had been uttered and at whatever place. However, the advocates of this position, Paul urges, superior though they look, forget about the two limitations to any doctrine. They forget about benefit (9:24–10:23, *symphero* being employed in the last verse). Even the finest mind, if courting temptation, may in the end succumb, find himself back in the mire from which he once escaped.[28] And they forgot about upbuilding, care (8:1–9, 10:23–28, *oikodomeo* appearing in 10:23). To many a simple soul, if he sees his fellow-believer, and especially a highly educated one, take food avowedly dedicated to idols, it will not be clear that this implies utter contempt for them; but, on the contrary, he will infer that there must, after all, be some sense in pagan rites and he will join in to his perdition.

[26] Strack and Billerbeck, *Kommentar zum Neuen Testament*, vol. 3 (München, 1926), 353 ff. are most unsatisfactory. They fail properly to bring out the *rationale* of the relevant Rabbinic decisions and confuse quite different ideas which played a part. (No need here to disentangle them.) Moreover their bias gets in the way. The mitigation introduced to prevent a proselyte from believing to have fallen into a lighter sanctity they call "opportunism." R. Eliezer (second half of first century A.D.) appears to have regarded marriage with the stepmother as consistent with pagan custom, so that a proselyte would be entitled to this marriage (see above, n. 8): which shows, Strack and Billerbeck say (p. 358), "how totally irrelevant Jewish teaching had become to the apostle Paul, who had grown up in Rabbinism, when he had to deal with great moral issues." No wonder the *Kommentar* is helplessly silent on 7:12 ff., which I shall go into at the end of this study, 545 ff.

[27] Mark 7:15.

[28] The stretch 10:14–23 is part of this argument: the most enlightened man may be corrupted, and participation in temple feasts betokens corruption. Whatever logic may tell us as to the total insignificance of idols, sacrificial fellowship with heathens remains evil, irreconcilable with participation in Christian worship. A Christian generally unmoved by dedication to idols rightly regards himself as "stronger," further advanced in faith, than "a weak one" who thinks dedication does something. But if he arrogates the right to participate in temple feasts, contrary to God's warning not to provoke his jealousy (e.g., Deut 32:21, "they have moved me to jealousy with a non-god, they have provoked me to anger with their vanities"), he is claiming to be "stronger" than God.

As in chapter 5, the target of the apostle's criticism is a stiff, proud standing on sham knowledge: "We know that we all have knowledge. Knowledge puffs up. . . . If any man imagines that he knows anything, he knows nothing as he ought to know" (8:1 f.). Freedom mechanically, soullessly exercised can be as deadly as the old Law. As in chapter 5, he is worried not only about the risk to the individual proselyte but also about that which his example spells to others. And as in chapter 5, those he admonishes were not necessarily antinomians *tout court*. All they maintained was that, in view of the utter nothingness of an idol, there was no wrong ever in this particular act, the eating of food devoted to it.

To be sure, the case is not one hundred percent parallel to that of incest. In the matter of food Paul leaves no doubt that, essentially, it would be desirable to recognize no shackles whatever,[29] to be firm enough in faith not to bother, say, when buying goods in the market, what ceremonies they may have been subjected to. Those to whom such externals matter have not yet reached the heights. If he nevertheless hopes that the "strong" believer will abstain from eating wherever it might be misconstrued by a "weak" one, this is a yielding to the second-best: the latter, in a higher interest, becomes the thing to do. Concession to frailty plays a considerable part in the Rabbinic system.[30] Since the destruction of the Temple, R. Ishmael asserts (first half of the second century A.D.), by rights meat and wine should be banned, but as the majority could not endure this hardship, it will not be imposed.[31]

A fundamental difference between Paul's task from the Rabbinic one which is revealed by this discussion results from his abandonment of the old Law. For the Rabbis, the problem how far a person may go if normal legal restraints are removed arose only within a narrow compass: a convert is as newborn, hence with regard to his previous relations the rules of incest—and a few others affected by the doctrine, inheritance for example—are basically non-operative. Paul faces the problem on a much larger scale. In fact, for him, there is no group and no department of life untouched by it. It is fascinating how in this Epistle, in developing his solutions, he leans on the Rabbinic miniature model. It is partly the pervasive influence of this precedent which accounts for the distinctive flavor of 1 Corinthians as compared with Romans.[32]

There are numerous variations on the main theme. In 6:8 ff., Paul attacks antinomianism proper which would deem wrongdoing irrelevant. He counters it with the same slogan he uses in his discussion of food: "All things are lawful unto me, but not all things are beneficial [*symphero*]." There is no evidence, however, that any Corinthian party actually felt authorized to commit the vices listed. From the tone of the section it is more likely that much objectionable behavior in fact went on and the offenders complacently relied on the saving power of their new religion.

In this warning against immorality, the argument refers only to the individual's sal-

[29] Except for temple feasts, to be shunned under the new dispensation as under the old; see the preceding footnote.

[30] See Daube, ["Concessions to Sinfulness in Jewish Law"] *JJS*, 10 (1959), 1 ff. [*Talmudic Law*, 1–13].

[31] *b. B. B.* 60b; see Daube, *op. cit.*, 8 f [8 f.].

[32] See in particular Rom 14:1–15:3.

vation; there is no mention of the effect of his actions on others.[33] Conversely, in 14:1 ff., the emphasis is heavily on the latter aspect: while ecstatic speech is classed as a great gift, it is rather discouraged in favor of prophecy, which alone of the two upbuilds (*oikodomeo*) the believers and indeed (vss. 23 25) will induce non-believers to join.

The preceding chapter 13 contains the famous praise of *agape*. It is sometimes regarded as an earlier, independent composition by Paul which he decided to insert at this point.[34] In reality, as should be obvious by now, it describes that disposition which, far above the old Law and any new doctrine, furnishes the highest standard for Christian conduct, a standard consistently invoked in this Epistle. (Verse 4, we saw above, employs *physioomai*, recurring five more times in the Epistle: any excellence, if not imbued with love, is empty, "puffs up.") Why does the hymn come just here? In chapter 12 Paul exhorts those with special gifts each to cultivate his variety, at the same time respecting all the others. It would be harsh to go on directly to place one gift, ecstatic speech, below another, prophecy. We must remember that, in this portion of his missive, he has to do with the most zealous, single-minded, valuable members of his church, whose feelings he would strain to spare; and also that possibly in their heathen background ecstatic speech enjoyed particular esteem. To preface chapter 14 by a full exposition of what the truly enlightened Christian—the "man," not the "babe" (vs. 11)—is guided by is an arrangement worthy of the author; in fact, like many another subtlety in the Epistle, an expression of his *agape* towards his flock.

Another instance of inculcation of conduct founded on meekness rather than on right is met in 6:7, where the apostle upbraids his charges for going to law against one another instead of putting up with injury. In 11:33, altruism, it seems, stands in contrast to selfish piety. Paul urges the participants in the Eucharist to wait for one another. Their ruthless haste—mentioned in verse 21—was partly at least, I suppose, not just vulgar discourtesy but motivated by eagerness for the sacred food: over-eagerness in the circumstances, since lacking in care. *m. Yom.* 2:2 appears to be somewhat comparable. If there were several priests, we learn, desirous to remove the ashes from the altar, they used to race for it; but the system was given up because it led to trouble. On one occasion, when two were even, one pushed the other so that he fell and broke a leg.[35]

Paul himself constantly forgoes his due for the sake of his own spiritual welfare as well as the advance of the church and the gaining of converts. 9:1–23 stands in the middle of his advice on food and is intended to illustrate the basic ideas from his own practice. An apostle has the right to material support: yet Paul renounces it since to preach the gospel is his God-imposed task (vs. 16) and acceptance of remuneration might be an obstacle to progress (vs. 12). Indeed (vss. 19–23) though free from all, in order to win over as many as possible he makes himself a servant to all and accommodates himself to the Jews, to those under the Law, to those outside the Law, to the "weak."[36]

[33] If he were addressing serious antinomians, we should probably hear of the danger to upbuilding.

[34] Craig, *op. cit.*, 165, rightly rejects this view.

[35] A fatal case is recorded in *b. Yom.* 23a f.

[36] For details of the Jewish background of sentiment and vocabulary, see Daube, *The New Testament and Rabbinic Judaism*, 336 ff., 352 ff. [561 ff., 575 ff.]

It is noteworthy that the Corinthians themselves at one time experienced his indulgence with the immature when, as he recalls in 3:1 f., he preached to them as to "babes in Christ: I fed you with milk and not with meat."[37] With this adaptation of instruction to the limited capacity of the recipient, we may compare not only the familiar stories of Hillel and his converts[38] (latter half of the first century B.C.), but also Rabbinic practice outside the missionary field. R. Ishmael, I noted above,[39] was of opinion that by rights the Jews ought to submit to severe asceticism, only in deference to the majority's character this course was not to be adopted. What is here of interest is that he would not even have the people informed of the ideal: "It is better they should transgress in ignorance than wittingly."

The dialectic between the licit, the beneficial and the upbuilding reaches its climax in the discourse about marriage, chapter 7. First, marriage as such. Marriage is lawful, not a sin (vss. 28, 36). None the less, ideally, a person should remain celibate (vss. 1, 8, 26 f., 37, 40):[40] this is his most beneficial state (*symphero* figures in verse 35). Yet again, for those—doubtless the bulk of the community—who if celibate would succumb to fornication, marriage is definitely the path to choose (vss. 2, 9, 28, 39): "It is better to marry than to burn" (vs. 9).[41] Even in this area the ideal must not become a fetish.

The recommendation of the *pis aller* [second best] is couched in the form current in Rabbinic exposition: "It is better they should transgress in ignorance than wittingly" Ishmael, "It is better to marry than to burn" Paul. Interestingly, Paul concentrates on the individual's welfare: genuine celibacy will enhance it, but sham celibacy will undermine it and is therefore greatly inferior to marriage. R. Ishmael, when considering a decree against intercourse, gave equal prominence to the communal factor. By rights, he observed, as the Roman government prevented circumcision and the study of the Torah, Jews ought to refrain from begetting children. But not only would the majority not comply (thus falling into willful sin) but such a course would threaten the existence of the nation.[42] Presumably Paul's conviction that "time is short" (vs. 29) renders the latter peril of less account.

Second, within marriage (vss. 2–5). Marriage is a second-best, though better than the best for the average, fallible mortal. Once married, it is your duty to be agreeable to your spouse. Abstention is to be practised only by consent, for temporary devotion to prayer: undue prolongation might end in recourse to immoral outlets. You must act, that is, in a manner conducive to your own contentment and virtue as well as your partner's.

[37] Now they are "men": see 13:11, cited above, 543. See Daube, *op. cit.*, 125 [516].

[38] *b. Shab.* 31a. See Daube, *op. cit.*, 336 f. [561 f.].

[39] 542.

[40] In verse 1, it is true, the ideal is quoted by Paul from a letter the Corinthians had sent him; but he does fall in with it, in verse 2, as an ideal. See also Matt 19:10.

[41] Cp. Matt 19:10 ff. Ford, *op. cit.*, 70 ff., 82 ff., argues that in 8 f. and 25 ff. Paul thinks of widowers and widows only, in the former section of middle-aged and old ones, in the latter of young ones.

[42] Some branches of the Essenes put up with marriage strictly insofar as it served procreation: Josephus, *Bell.* 2.8.13.160 f. See Daube, ["Concessions to Sinfulness in Jewish Law"] *JJS*, 10 (1959), 6, 8 f. [*Talmudic Law*, 6, 8].

The beneficial and the upbuilding are here inextricably combined.

Paul goes on (vs. 6): "I speak this by way of *syggnome*—permission, indulgence, concession, Hebrew *reshuth*—not by way of *epitage*—commandment, duty, Hebrew *miswa* or *hobha*." A technical reference to a class of rulings, not infrequent in Rabbinism, which make allowance for human weakness but are not binding on the elite.[43] Exactly what Paul is saying is not clear. He may be reminding his public that, celibacy being the ideal, the entire section on marital life is concessive.[44] Or he may be labelling as a concession his advice against prolongation of continence: a couple spiritual enough not to have to fear fleshly urges are at liberty to go on.[45] Chapter 7 presents quite a few ambiguities and obscurities; and it may be that this reflects some particular involvement on the author's part, resulting in unease, ambivalence, indecision.[46]

I conclude with a third problem tackled in this chapter: a convert whose spouse remains an "unbeliever" (vss. 12–16). The Greek is *apistos*, presumably covering an unbelieving Jew as well as a heathen: the mention of circumcised Christians in the section directly following, vss. 17 f., makes this impression into a near-certainty.[47] How does Paul's approach—the so-called Pauline Privilege, *privilegium Paulinum*—chime with that to incest in chapter 5 which latter, in my contention, implies the treatment of a convert as a new creation?[48] It chimes perfectly. Indeed, it becomes intelligible precisely and only if we bear in mind that strange doctrine. The interpretations so far given are all defective, and the traditional construction of the Privilege will have to be revised.

If one of two spouses converts, the bond, according to Paul, ceases to operate (vs. 15). This cannot possibly, as is generally held, be an indulgence granted by the apostle. Jesus himself had declared marriage indissoluble in the lifetime of one of the partners,[49] a regulation repeated by Paul in the two verses (vss. 10 f.) immediately preceding those under review, and, what is more, marked off as the Lord's authoritative charge in contradistinction to his own directions. A contradicting of that charge is unthink-

[43] See Daube, *op. cit.*, 12 [*Talmudic Law*, 12]. For an example from an entirely different sphere—extradition under duress of a member of the community—see Daube, *Collaboration with Tyranny in Rabbinic Law* (London, 1965), 12 f. [*Talmudic Law*, 72 f.]

[44] Thus e.g., Craig, *op. cit.*, 77.

[45] Thus Daube, *op. cit.*, 12. Ford, *op. cit.*, 68 f., thinks that it is a married couple's continence of which Paul remarks that he is merely tolerating it. I find it difficult to believe that he would have looked on agreed, temporary abstention, with the purpose of prayer, as a concession, a thing that had better be avoided.

[46] This is not to deny other factors, such as the manner in which the community had formulated certain questions which the chapter is intended to answer.

[47] There is no need, however, here to decide the point. The *New English Bible* (1961) is clearly rash in substituting "heathen" for the accurate "unbelieving" or "unbeliever" of earlier versions. Ford, *op. cit.*, 73 ff., suggests that Paul is dealing with an esoteric, inner-Jewish complication: marriage between a person from a recognized Pharisaic family and one of doubtful stock. This seems hardly tenable. Why, for example, should a partner of doubtful stock wish to break away?

[48] It was this question, put to me by my friend John T. Noonan, which caused me to have another good look at 1 Corinthians.

[49] Matt 5:31 f., 19:3 ff., Mark 10:2 ff., Luke 16:18; cp. also 1 Cor 7:39. See Daube, *The New Testament and Rabbinic Judaism*, 75. [255].

able.[50] What accounts for Paul's position must be something fully within the Jesuanic conception of marriage; it is the nature of conversion as re-creation. The convert is simply not the same person as the preconversion one. Hence his marriage is dissolved; and if the unbeliever goes off, that is that.

In passing—there is much controversy in the literature around this text as to the precise effects on a convert's standing if the partner leaves. Above all, in Paul's opinion, may the convert remarry? The doubts are due entirely to the mistaken assumption that we have before us some discretionary concession of Paul's. There is no real difficulty: of course the believer is free to remarry, "under no bondage"—his previous marriage no longer exists.

However, if the unbeliever is content to stay, you ought not, Paul lays down, to part with him (vss. 12 f.). Why not? For one thing, for the sake of peace (vs. 15 at the end). This motive, *mippene darke shalom*, "on account of the ways of peace," is common in Rabbinic extensions to less worthy people within Jewry or to gentiles of privileges to which in strictness only worthy people or Jews are entitled. "A woman may lend a fan or a sieve to another woman though she is suspected of not observing the Sabbatical Year... on account of the ways of peace."[51] "The poor of the heathen are supported along with the poor of Israel, the sick of the heathen are visited along with the sick of Israel, on account of the ways of peace."[52] Two passages from Romans are in point. In one, about food, it is a question of accommodation to the "weak" members of the community: "Let us therefore follow after the things which make for peace and things wherewith one may upbuild one another."[53] In the other, Paul is concerned with the behavior of Christians to non-Christians: "As much as lies in you, live peaceably with all men."[54]

In early Rabbinic thought, not surprisingly, the aim of peace with gentiles is often interchangeable with that of eliciting their admiration for the Jewish religion or even winning them over. Simeon ben Shetach (first half of the first century B.C.), though not strictly obliged to do so, returned to a pagan a pearl mistakenly delivered, because "he preferred hearing the Saracene say, Blessed be the God of the Jews, to all the gain of this world."[55] The two ideas of deference for the sake of peace and deference in order

[50] In reply to a query in the course of the Pittsburgh discussion, I should perhaps point out that Paul's teaching in the first half of 7:11 is fully consistent with that of Jesus. Though a wife may at a pinch take up a domicile of her own, she must go on respecting the marriage bond, i.e., she may not marry anyone else. Cp. Daube, *op. cit.*, 362 f. [281 f.]. Similarly, when, as mentioned above, 543, despite Jesus's instruction that the preacher of the gospel should live by it (9:14), Paul declines support, this is, of course, not an abrogation of that instruction. On the contrary, he firmly insists on its validity, as also e.g. in 2 Thes 3:9. Otherwise, indeed, his renunciation would not be worth dwelling on. The point is that the obligation deriving from the principle falls on the community, not on the preacher. There are countless cases of this type. It is a Scriptural law that the poor be given alms or that a creditor be paid what is rightfully owing to him. But this never meant that a poor man must become a beggar or that a creditor might not let off his debtor.

[51] *m. Gitt.* 5:9.

[52] *b. Gitt.* 61a. See Daube, *op. cit.*, 127 [517].

[53] Rom 14:19.

[54] Rom 12:18.

[55] *y. B. M.* 8c.

to acquire converts are similarly close in first-century Christianity. Paul's injunction in Romans to "live peaceably with all men" is preceded by the recommendation of honesty as a means of attracting unbelievers: "Provide things honest in the sight of all men."[56] In the present case, the motive of peace (vs. 15 at the end) is followed by that of missionizing: by continuing with the unbeliever, you may be the means of saving him (vs. 16). The special influence one member of a family can exercise on another in matters of religious attachment is already known to the Old Testament—where it is mentioned in connection with seduction to idolatry.[57] 1 Peter expects Christian wives to be so exemplary in their conduct that their non-Christian husbands may join the faith.[58]

It is usual nowadays to see in the clause "God has called us (you) to peace" Paul's reason for allowing the marriage to end. That this would entail sanction of divorce for any deeply divided or even inordinately quarrelsome couple has not escaped notice. It is unnecessary to inspect the tortuous ways in which some commentators have tried to avoid the conclusion, or others have tried to evolve from here a liberal divorce regime. As we have seen, it is not Paul who allows the marriage to end: the marriage is ended because the converted spouse is a new creation. The clause gives Paul's reason for advising against breaking with the unbeliever if he will stay.[59]

Again, the hope Paul expresses in the following verse, that by living on together with the unbeliever you may guide him towards the light, is turned by the prevalent interpretation into its very opposite: let him go since you have no certainty of changing him. This negative attitude to the chance of bringing about a fellow-being's (indeed, in this case, your closest companion's) salvation is grotesquely out of keeping with all that Paul, or any of the leading New Testament figures, stands for. It discourages any extra effort, it advocates callous indifference. I can think of no parallel anywhere in the pertinent sources (whereas the coupling of peace and proselytizing influence, I have just pointed out, is firmly rooted in the missionary thinking of the time).[60] The proper paraphrase is: "For who knows, O wife, you may yet save your husband. Or who knows, O man, you may yet save your wife."

[56] Rom 12:17. See Daube, *op. cit.*, 342 [565 f.]. For some further aspects of impressing the outside world, see Daube ["Limitations on Self-Sacrifice in Jewish Law and Tradition"] *Theology*, 72 (1969), 292 ff. [*Talmudic Law*, 46 ff].

[57] Deut 13:6: "If thy brother, the son of thy mother, or thy son or thy daughter or the wife of thy bosom or thy friend which is as thine own soul, entice thee. . . ." There are several illustrations in the narrative parts.

[58] 1 Pet 3:1. In Tit 2:5 the result hoped for is more modest: that the non-Christian husbands will not come to disrespect the faith.

[59] The interpretation here combated has to make light of the "but," *de*, in the clause in question. The principal part of verse 15 explains that if the unbeliever goes off, there is nothing to be done: let him go off, the convert is free. Then Paul goes on: "But God has called us to peace." If this were the reason for doing nothing, for letting the unbeliever go off, it should be "for," not "but"; and indeed, some translations—the RSV, for example—do put "for." The text, however, has "but"—meaning that the preferable outcome would be to continue with the unbeliever. I am not maintaining that in an involved argumentation like Paul's *de* cannot conceivably play the role ascribed to it by the prevalent interpretation. Still, taken at its face value, it is on my side.

[60] If (possible though doubtful) 7:39 warns a widow against marrying outside the community, that is surely no analogy. 2 Cor 6:14 ff. too is designed for entirely different situations.

The structure, then, of this little tract is: As a convert you are not to cast off a spouse who remains an unbeliever (vss. 12–14). If he will not stay, that is a different matter: let him go, you are not tied to him (major part of vs. 15). But it is more consonant with God's call if you live on with him, in the hope of saving him (end of vs. 15 and vs. 16). Once more, Paul acknowledges, and wishes his charges to acknowledge, the supremacy of *agape*. Strictly, the convert's marriage is ended, and ended by a supernatural event of the highest order, re-creation, which might easily make him who experiences it proud, unbending, privilege-conscious. Yet he must look further, he must do what upbuilds; which means, if the unbeliever desires that there be no change, that desire is to be respected, even welcomed. It is in the nature of such consideration that its recipient is improved: an unbeliever so treated may attain belief. Paul's self-abnegation with a view to gaining converts will be recalled,[61] as also his preference for prophecy which, unlike ecstatic speech, is adapted to the listener's understanding and, he says, may move gentiles to see the truth.[62] The problem of a mixed marriage, or rather a marriage which becomes mixed, is solved in the spirit pervading the entire Epistle.

Obviously a very major question remains: what kind of union is it in which the convert is to live on with the unbeliever? Their original marriage is gone—so what kind of union is this?

Paul proffers a thorough explanation (vs. 14): by the couple's continuing cohabitation the marriage is re-constituted, or better, a fresh marriage is constituted—indeed, one essentially conforming, he holds, to Jewish requirements.[63] This is the force of "consecrated," more specifically, of the unbeliever being consecrated by the convert. The verb—*hagiazo*—is used in a pregnant sense, not by way of a vague or fanciful speculation. (New Testament scholars have enormous difficulty infusing a measure of meaning into it. The various conjectures often then become bases for more general theories about Paul's concept of holiness.[64] All this must be jettisoned.) Hebrew *qiddesh* signifies "to consecrate to wife." To this day, throughout the world, the Jewish wedding formula spoken by the groom is: "Behold thou art consecrated unto me by this ring according to the law of Moses and Israel."[65] The ring, however, is not inevitable. A dime or any object worth about that will do. What is of decisive importance in the present connection is that the giving of value is not the only mode of contracting a marriage. The Mishnah lists three: by money, by document, by intercourse.[66] It is the third which Paul assumes to make a recognized marriage of the union in question.

[61] 1 Cor 9:22, 10:33.

[62] 1 Cor 14:25. No doubt missionary fervor underlies 1 Cor 5:10 where he stresses that he does not mean Christians to avoid contact with even the vilest heathens.

[63] Two deviations will be pointed out below, at the close of my discussion, 551 f.

[64] E.g., Craig, *op. cit.*, 79; Procksch, art. "*hagiazo,*" in *Theologisches Wörterbuch zum Neuen Testament*, ed. Kittel, vol. 1 (1933), 114. The *New English Bible* says the unbeliever ("heathen" it calls him) "belongs to God": similarly, "otherwise your children would not belong to God." Earlier versions are more historical when using "sanctified" or "consecrated" and—of the children—"unclean."

[65] *Authorized Daily Prayer Book*, transl. Singer (1891), 298.

[66] *m. Kidd.* 1:1. The verb here is *qana,* "to acquire." "A woman is acquired *(niqneth)* in three ways. . . ." See below, n. 79.

I refrain from details, such as that in general the woman or her father must consent,[67] or that in general the man must perform intercourse with intent to make the woman his wife.[68] It may be helpful, however, to adduce a Talmudic case for comparison.[69]

A heathen converts together with his two wives, who are mother and daughter or sisters. The ruling, it will be seen, implies that the marriages are now extinct, that neither woman is related to the other, and that continuing cohabitation will bring about a fresh marriage. This is what the Rabbis ordain: (a) he should keep one and dismiss the other; (b) once he has had intercourse after conversion with one, this is his wife; and (c) if he has had intercourse after conversion with both, both are his wives. The *rationale* of the decision is as follows. Jewish law prohibits marriage with a woman and her daughter or sister.[70] However, owing to conversion, neither of these women is any longer related to the other. In principle, therefore, there is no objection to marriage with both. Nonetheless, according to (a), one ought to be discarded, because otherwise Judaism might look like a lighter sanctity: even heathens do not customarily marry mother and daughter or sisters, though as the present case shows it does happen. Which of the two is to go is up to the man; and it is worth noting that the verb in the text, *hosi*ʾ, "to lead out," may refer not only to dissolution of a marriage but also to dismissal where there is no room for divorce proper—e.g. to Halitzah.[71] For, again, owing to conversion, the marriages are ended. He simply bids one of them leave. With the one he keeps, a fresh marriage is constituted by continuing cohabitation. This is evident from (b) where it is provided that once he has cohabited with one, he has lost his free choice: she has become his wife. It is confirmed by (c): by cohabiting with both, however undesirable it may be, he has made both his wives. It seems that the Rabbis do not even insist that he now divorce one of the two: the risk of giving the impression of a lighter sanctity is not in this case so overwhelmingly grave as to call for further measures once he has remarried both—heathens do occasionally contract this union.

Paul adds that, but for this consecration, the children henceforth born would be "unclean," *akathartos*, whereas the consecration causes them to be "sacred," "holy," *hagios*. Such is indeed the stark alternative—and it corroborates my thesis that he regards the original marriage as extinct. Unless there were a fresh marriage, the children would not only not be members of the community but would be spurious, born out of wedlock, "unclean." By contrast, as the offspring of a fresh marriage properly contracted they are legitimate, they are full members of the community—"sacred." There

[67] In the case of a minor, the father's consent alone is relevant. *b. Kidd.* 2b, 3b.

[68] *t. Kidd.* 1:3. R. Eleazar (third century A.D.) goes as far as to hold that in the absence of this intent, the man renders the woman a *zona*, "prostitute"; this opinion was not accepted: *b. Yeb.* 61b. Strack and Billerbeck, *op. cit.*, 343, attribute the opinion to R. Eliezer (first century), but the reading Eleazar is better attested and historical considerations also are in its favor.

[69] *y. Yeb.* 12a.

[70] Lev 18:17 f., 20:14.

[71] *m. Yeb.* 3:5; *m. Eduy.* 4:9. The first occurrence of *hosi'* in this area is in Ezra 10:3, 19: surely not a regular divorce by bill, which would mention the women's freedom to conclude a fresh marriage. In 10:3 the children are "led out" together with the wives.

are numerous Rabbinic texts distinguishing between a heathen's child conceived or born "not in sanctity" and a convert's child conceived or born "in sanctity."[72]

The children's fate were it not for the fresh marriage is advanced by Paul as proof that a fresh marriage must have come into being. The unbeliever, he asserts, is consecrated—validly taken to spouse—by the convert: "else were your children unclean." It is a *reductio ad absurdum*: the hypothetical consequence if the assertion were rejected is so utterly unacceptable that it demonstrates the correctness of the assertion. Modern jurisprudence would call the argumentation result-oriented: the apostle wants the couple to carry on together and he wants their offspring within the church, that is why he fastens on circumstances and considerations rendering everything in order. This is perfectly true, but it in no way detracts from the cogency of his reasoning. I have elsewhere written on the popularity of the *reductio* among first-century Roman jurists; it was cherished no less by the Rabbis.[73]

One reason verse 14 has not so far been understood is that, in most dictionaries, *qiddesh* figures only for espousal, betrothal, by money (or some object, a ring).[74] This, however, is to suppress the early history of the verb, and the nouns deriving from it or belonging to it.[75] At one time it denoted actual marriage, not only betrothal,[76] and it covered all three modes equally, money, document, intercourse. In the Mishnah the title of the tractate concerning marriage is *qiddushin*, "consecrations," very likely dating from that period. (It is in the ideas underlying this ancient usage that we have to seek for the ultimate origins of the Christian view of marriage as a sacrament.) The word's contraction in scope is due to two interlocking developments: first, an increasing technical differen-tiation between betrothal and actual marriage,[77] and secondly, an increasing aversion to marriage by intercourse. In the early third century A.D. Rab imposed the penalty of stripes on a man resorting to this mode,[78] and nowadays I doubt whether a Jewish court would uphold it except in dire circumstances. *Qiddesh* thus came to be restricted, more or less, to the sense recorded in the dictionaries.[79]

[72] *m. Ket.* 4:3; *t. Yeb.* 12:2; *b. Sanh.* 57b etc.

[73] See Daube, *Roman Law* (Edinburgh, 1969), 193 f.

[74] See e.g., Levy, *Neuhebräisches und Chaldäisches Wörterbuch über die Talmudim und Midraschim*, vol. 4 (1889), 250 (nothing relevant in the 2nd ed. by Goldschmidt and Fleischer [1924]). Ben Yehuda, *Milon Ha-Lashon Ha-Ivrit (A Complete Dictionary of Ancient and Modern Hebrew)*, vol. 12, ed. Torczyner (1959), 5781 f., is wide enough. He quotes an anecdote from *b. Sanh.* 11a. A woman appeared in R. Meir's academy (middle of second century A.D.) and said: "One of you has consecrated me by intercourse." The Rabbi, anxious both to remedy her situation and to save the culprit from disgrace, there and then wrote her a bill of divorce, followed by all his disciples.

[75] Among the latter is *qedusha*, "sanctity." We have seen, 537 f. 549, that observance of forbidden degrees constitutes "sanctity"; and that only those born within the fold are born "in sanctity."

[76] Even betrothal, it should be noted, is far more than the term might suggest to a Western ear. In fact it is almost equivalent to marriage proper; for example, it would need a divorce to be undone.

[77] This is too intricate a subject here to pursue.

[78] *b. Kidd.* 12b.

[79] On the relation of *qiddesh*, "to consecrate," to *qana*, "to acquire," I shall say no more than that *qana* is surely the older term in this area, going back to the remote past. By New Testament times *qiddesh* had become very popular, however. From, say, the late second century A.D. *qana* again ousted *qiddesh* in references to marriage by intercourse.

Anyhow *m. Nidd.* 5:4, manifestly of great age (and inconvenient to later generations) provides: "A girl can be consecrated *mithqaddesheth*, by intercourse from age three."[80] The very text which reports Rab's intervention says that he imposed flogging on *meqaddesh*, "one who consecrates," in certain objectionable—though valid—ways, such as without previous negotiations, by money or document in the street, through intercourse.

Intercourse, interestingly, does persist long after Rab as the mode in which a levir takes to wife his dead brother's widow. In fact it is here the only mode: money and document have no place since the fresh marriage so to speak resumes the former one.[81] The levir steps into his dead brother's shoes. The idea of resumption is so powerful that, according to the Rabbis, cohabitation brings the fresh marriage into being even if the levir has no intent to make the woman his wife, indeed, even if he mistakes her identity; nor is her consent required.[82] The case has some affinity with that Paul is concerned with: in the latter, too, the fresh marriage to all intents and purposes resumes the original one. At any rate it is this cultural milieu, however alien to the modern mind, which we must comprehend to do justice to Paul. Incidentally, the fact that, in his time, marriage was still often concluded by the simple mode of intercourse goes a long way towards explaining his language in 6:16, where he speaks of the association with a prostitute almost as if it were marriage: "He who cleaves to a harlot is one body, for the two, he says, shall be one flesh." The reference is to God's pronouncement in Gen 2:24.[83]

There are, however, two deviations from Jewish practice in vss. 12–14. One is the admission of marriage with a heathen. In these special circumstances, where one spouse converts and the other does not, the convert may, rather should, hold on to the other. Their union is marriage by intercourse—and this is so even if the other is a gentile. For the Rabbis, Paul would be on a par with those priests of whom the Testament of Levi says that they marry gentile women, "purifying them with an unlawful purification."[84]

The second deviation has regard to the role of women. In Judaism, it is invariably the woman who is consecrated to spouse by the man. Paul deems it immaterial whether the convert is a man or a woman. Even if it is a woman, the unbeliever is consecrated to spouse by her. This is in line with, in the spirit of, the reformed view of marriage proclaimed by Jesus: neither spouse can divorce the other, the husband is as indissolubly tied to the wife as she is to him.[85] Paul's statement in 7:4—"The wife has not power over her body, but the husband; and likewise also, the husband has not power over his body, but his wife"—is not irreconcilable with Jewish tradition though the formulation is peculiarly strong.[86] His extension of consecration is totally untraditional.

[80] Often quoted in Rabbinic debate, e.g., *b. Kidd.* 10a; *b. Yeb.* 57b; *b. Sanh.* 55b.

[81] *b. Yeb.* 52a, 53b; *b. Kidd.* 2a.

[82] *m. Yeb.* 6:1 and many other texts, e.g., *b. Kidd.* 4b. The verb is *qana:* "he acquires her by intercourse."

[83] Cp. Matt 19:5; Eph 5:31.

[84] Testament of Levi 14:7. See above, n. 12.

[85] See above, n. 49. On the connection of this teaching with the myth of an ideal, androgynous Adam, see Daube, *The New Testament and Rabbinic Judaism,* 71 ff., 143 ff., 418, 442 [252 ff., 308 f., 661, 680].

[86] Cp. e.g., *m. Ket.* 5:7, cited by Strack and Billerbeck, *op. cit.*, 369.

We must not indeed assign to it too far-reaching implications. Other passages in this very Epistle show that he is not fighting for equality of the sexes.[87] Like his recognition of marriage with a heathen, his recognition of consecration by the woman is meant (in the first place at least) for the special situation on which he is pronouncing. Even so it is a momentous *novum* [innovation]. He is, of course, conscious of it; probably that is why he finds it necessary so painstakingly to put everything he has to say twice, once for the man, once for the woman: "If any brother has a wife... let him not put her away. And the woman who has a husband... let her not leave him. For the unbelieving husband is consecrated by the wife. And the unbelieving wife is consecrated by the husband.... For what know you, O wife.... Or what know you, O man."

This section has a very personally Pauline flavor. It combines the most refined legal analysis with the most imaginative daring—and both are governed by his one great passionately held aim.

Its subsequent history, however, is paradoxical. Christianity soon gave up, and forgot about, that vital presupposition of his teaching: belief in conversion as a real re-creation. As a result of this and a few other developments, the apostle, who had encouraged and justified the staying united with an unbeliever, was understood to introduce the possibility of dissolving a mixed marriage—the Pauline Privilege. Judaism, by adhering to its Law, has preserved the concept of a proselyte as a newborn child, with all its consequences: it is as much part of the Jewish system today as it was at the time of 1 Corinthians.

[87] See 1 Cor 11:3 ff., 14:34 ff.

Onesimos

When Paul deems conversion to imply a "new creation," he is in line with the Jewish tenet—valid to this day—which assigns a convert the position of a "child just born."[1] One consequence is that a pagan family coming over *en bloc* is in principle unaffected by incest taboos: they are no longer related. Still, the Rabbis, lest the unthinking might conclude that incest was being taken lightly, impose a restriction, pragmatic and variable—banning such unions as are illicit in the surrounding culture. Along with the maxim, Paul also adopts this proviso: he tells the Corinthians that their pride in their novel state must not lead to marriage with a stepmother, "fornication not found among the gentiles" (1 Cor 5:1). No tenet, he urges, not even one so fundamental, so cherished, as that of re-creation, is to be turned into a fetish. Glory becomes vainglory when the resultant actions are the opposite of beneficial to the individual, the opposite of upbuilding for the church. I am going to suggest that some passages in his Epistle to Philemon may have to be read bearing in mind the same counterpointal interplay: on the one hand, a radical concept of conversion; on the other, moderation from considerateness as an individual as well as from dedication to the church's welfare.

All writers on the Epistle observe that Paul does not ask Philemon to manumit Onesimos, yet does ask him to receive him not as a slave but as a brother. The explanation is that the man baptized by Paul is no longer the man that was owned by Philemon. Paul actually speaks of him as "my child whom I have begot": echo of the rabbinic idiom mentioned above, and let us recall the dictum—applied to Abraham, prototype of proselytizers—that "anyone who brings a gentile near is as though he had created him."[2] Philemon, of course, himself guided into the faith by Paul, will understand this well. Possibly, the remark that Onesimos, now a beloved brother to Paul, should be this "all the more to Philemon, both in the flesh and in the Lord," is intended to emphasize the completeness of the change. The very body that was once subject to Philemon is no more; the present Onesimos is a different being in every respect. In any case, the main part of the letter opens with the reminder that Paul could simply direct Philemon in Christ to

[1] *b. Yeb.* 22a; 2 Cor 5:17. For details, see my following works: *The New Testament and Rabbinic Judaism* (London: University of London, Athlone Press, 1956; reprinted New York: Arno, 1973) 113 [506 f.]; "Pauline Contributions to a Pluralistic Culture: Re-creation and Beyond," in Donald G. Miller and D. Y. Hadidian, eds., *Jesus and Man's Hope* (Pittsburgh: Pittsburgh Theological Seminary, 1971) 2. 223 ff. [537 ff.]: "Biblical Landmarks in the Struggle for Women's Rights," *Juridicial Review* 90 n.s. 23 (1978) 184 ff. [236]; and *Ancient Jewish Law: Three Inaugural Lectures* (Leiden: Brill, 1981) 8, 14 ff. [470, 474 ff.].

[2] *Gen. Rab.* on 12:6. The biblical text puzzlingly reports a "making" of souls. For the midrash, this is an allusion to a gathering in of heathens which, indeed, equals a making, a giving life.

renounce his hold. Surely, what is envisaged here is not an arbitrary demand but one that would be fully warranted by the transformation that has occurred.

So much for the principle. There is, however, a great deal in mitigation. For one thing, Paul clearly expects Onesimos patiently to accept whatever decision Philemon will make. Though free—and also, it should be added, not accountable for wrongs of the former Onesimos—if Philemon cannot let go, he is to submit. For another thing, movingly, the apostle himself, in this matter of great concern to him, sets an example of self-restraint. He beseeches instead of ordering. He appeals to love and partnership. He will be content with what is tendered willingly rather than exact the utmost. In fact, should Philemon feel strongly about it, he volunteers to bind up the breach and make good any loss. To be sure, throughout, he leaves no doubt as to what he hopes will be Philemon's response. But this does not detract from the genuineness of his approach. Philemon has a choice. If he makes the wrong one, no irreparable harm is done and Paul will go on trying. If, as is likely, the right one, the positive effects will be enormous all around. From Col. 4:7 it would appear that Philemon did come through.

A brief return to 1 Corinthians may be helpful. I have already adverted to the section on "incest"—in inverted commas—between converts. Another one (1 Cor 7:12–16) deals with converts whose spouses do not join them. Since the convert is a new person, the marriage is dissolved and he or she is at liberty to wed someone else. (This proposition, when its roots were forgotten, came to be mistaken for an infringement on Jesus's teaching and was named *privilegium Paulinum.*) Nevertheless, once again, the principle is not carried to extremes. If the unbeliever is prepared to stay on, that is to be welcomed. Cohabitation will bring about a fresh marriage, preferable to a casting off, in the interest both of peace and of the chance that, ultimately, the unbeliever will be won over. There follows a disquisition on the basic irrelevance of external callings: circumcision or uncircumcision, slavery or freedom. Commentators are distinctly uneasy about a lack of connection with what precedes: the designation "excursus" is common. But the meaning, the proper understanding, of re-creation is a very substantial link. The child just born need not, should not, trouble about whether he is circumcised or not. Moreover, even if in his preconversion existence he was a slave, he is that no longer, though circumstances may be such—yet another instance of adjustment—that he ought to put up with being kept in servitude. In a previous publication[3] I claimed that 1 Corinthians has far greater thematic unity than is generally recognized. This "excursus" provides further support. And it is in perfect agreement with the doctrine of the Epistle to Philemon.

How widely shared this construction was, how long it persisted, will not here be investigated. I confine myself to pointing out that in a number of the other Epistles, while they contain nothing irreconcilable with re-creation in its fullest sense, the weight is all on the conduct worthy of the holy community. Both slave and master are exhorted to it in Ephesians and Colossians, the former alone in 1 Timothy, Titus, and 1 Peter.[4]

[3] "Pauline Contributions," 227 [541].

[4] Eph 6:5–9; Col 3:22–4:1; 1 Tim 6:1–2; Tit 2:9–10; 1 Pet 2:18. Similarly, whereas the duties of both spouses are outlined in Ephesians, Colossians, and 1 Peter, only the wife's are in 1 Timothy and Titus; see Edward Gordon Selwyn, *The First Epistle of St. Peter* (London: Macmillan, 1946), 182.

Two thoughts in conclusion. First, if my view is correct, any lingering scruples as to the authenticity of the Epistle to Philemon may safely be dismissed. The mix is so unique. Second, one could imagine that Paul's extraordinary preoccupation with the miraculous power of conversion has to do with his own extraordinary experience. In both 1 Cor 15:8 and Gal 1:15, short as the accounts are, they contain references, couched in intense language, to his natural birth and his higher one. It may be asked why, starting out afresh, he should feel as contrite as he does about his previous stubbornness. But logic has its limitations. He was very special to God from his mother's womb, yet went to fearful lengths in denying his election. Some Rabbis are exercised by the sufferings of proselytes who have not yet had time to sin in their new life. An old answer is that what counts against them is a too long hesitation to embrace the truth after becoming aware of it.[5] Near enough. In Acts 9:8 there is no mention of birth but, instead, of blindness and starvation for three days, reminiscent of the tomb.

I am profoundly grateful for the opportunity of offering this note to Krister Stendhal, whose generosity and warmth will never allow the growth of a fetish.

[5] *b. Yeb.* 48b; Josephus *Ant.* 2.2.4; see Daube, *Ancient Jewish Law*, 17–18 [476 f.].

The History of Proselytising

Recently some publications have appeared intended to introduce into Judaism a freer and more spiritual attitude towards proselytising than has been prevalent in the past few centuries. This is certainly a most welcome tendency. But those who represent it ought to be careful not to let their historical judgment be clouded by the desire to find authority in the sources for their aims. There is enough without trying to rectify the evidence. I am thinking mainly of a valuable contribution to the problem made by William G. Braude, a Lecturer at Brown University. In his *Jewish Proselyting in the First Five Centuries of the Common Era*,[1] he depicts the Rabbis as enthusiastic missionaries, and denies the slightest wavering throughout the Talmudic period.

I would recommend anyone who still imagines that the Rabbis ever abandoned the belief in universalism and the idea of proselytising to read this treatise, which will thoroughly undeceive him. None the less, it must be said that the author occasionally goes too far. R. Helbo's remark that "proselytes are as troublesome as the itch" Mr. Braude considers to be directed not against proselytes, but against the government, which imposed penalties on proselytising. The arguments he advances for this interpretation, however, are far from convincing. In fact, the very reference to "the itch," the skin disease mentioned in Lev 13:2, makes it probable that R. Helbo did regard proselytes as irritating, dangerous boils on the body of the nation. He clearly was not the only one to think so. A statement like "Marry not a proselytess" cannot be got rid of by declaring it to be "no practical precept" or a "witticism." Even of Jethro, that model of a proselyte, the Mekhilta on Exod 18:9, not quoted by Mr. Braude, records that he was grieved to hear of Egypt's downfall (which incident, it may be remembered, is used to illustrate the wisdom of the rule not to talk disparagingly of gentiles in the presence of a convert). Mr. Braude contends that the Rabbis one after the other bettered the position of the proselytes. In support, he contrasts passages putting the convert below bastard and temple slave with others granting him a higher standing. The reasoning would be sound if we knew that the former passages date from an earlier time than the latter. Mr. Braude concludes that they do, his argument being that there was a constant evolution in favour of proselytes; he concludes that there was this evolution, his argument being that we find cases like the passage contrasted. This obviously is arguing in a circle.

Again, we know that at least from the third century a proselyte whose mother was a Jewess could hold certain public offices. The author asserts that originally he could

[1] Cp. my review in *JTS* (1942), 127 f.

not, but there are no texts to confirm this thesis. If it is true, the Rabbis raised the status not of proselytes as such, but of proselytes with Jewish mothers, a very different matter. The law concerning marriage with an Ammonite or a Moabite creates difficult problems. The Talmud interprets the Biblical prohibition in a narrow sense as referring only to an Ammonite, not an Ammonitess, only a Moabite, not a Moabitess. It is widely held that this interpretation was chosen in view of David's descent from Ruth, a Moabitess. Mr. Braude disagrees. He thinks that if such had been the motive of this interpretation, no actual law would have been based on it; the motive must have been to extend the hand of friendship to proselytes. This opinion, however, appears hardly tenable when we look more closely at the law in question. Admittedly, it is declared legitimate to marry Ammonite or Moabite women. But this, in the Talmudic era, was an entirely academic proposition, for both Ammonites and Moabites had ceased to be identifiable races. It is highly significant that few Rabbis applied the same narrow interpretation to, say, the provisions respecting Edomites, among whom there had been no Ruth; and that several forbade marriage with Palmyrene proselytes, which was an innovation, since no Palmyrenes occur in the Pentateuch, and an innovation far from academic.

It is dangerous to press Haggadic statements. When a Rabbi observes of a certain town that its inhabitants must be foolish because "no proselytes come from their midst," it by no means follows that he deems other towns less foolish, and no far-reaching conclusions ought to be drawn. Even graver doubts arise as to whether it is wise unquestioningly to take elaborations of Biblical narratives and injunctions as reflecting actual practice. True, the Rabbis have much to say about Abraham as a missionary and converts like Jethro. But I am not so sure that some of these tales are not mere visions of a golden past or future. They are certainly no more in the eyes of the average orthodox person of the present day. The story of how the fair treatment of the Gibeonites by the Jews led to the conversion of thousands of heathens might have made the author more cautious. For he himself admits that the Rabbis made no efforts to bring about mass conversions. That story, therefore, is a plain instance of idealising. From the province of Halakhah Mr. Braude adduces the Rabbinic exegesis of Deut 23:16. According to the Rabbis, this provision means that no runaway slave, whether Jewish or heathen, may be returned to a heathen master. Mr. Braude believes that the desire for converts played some part. In point of fact, the Rabbinic rule must have been extremely hard to carry into practice: to act on it would in many cases have meant risking serious punishment under the law of Rome.

In brief, I submit that even if the chief propositions put forward by Mr. Braude are correct (as they may well be), the Talmudic attitude was far less uniform than he makes it out to have been. There were ups and downs, and even individual bias may here and there have influenced a decision. There are, however, three points at least of a rather more fundamental character to which Mr. Braude does not seem to pay sufficient attention. First, only very few passages exist in Rabbinic literature that directly advocate proselytising. The author is aware of the fact, but does not go into it. Yet I cannot help feeling that it is a matter of some relevance. Secondly, the Rabbis embarked on no mass proselytising. Of this also Mr. Braude is aware, but again he attempts no explanation. He might perhaps reply that the reason is obvious: it would have been hopeless to ask entire cities or states to accept the Law. But this does not prove, thus he might argue, that the Rabbis would not have welcomed mass conversions had they been at all practicable.

There is, however, another side to the case. Paul gave up the Law when he found that it was an obstacle in the way of mass proselytising. The Rabbis, or at any rate the ultimately dominant group, did not. They preferred to retain the Law rather than be able, without the Law, to undertake mass proselytising. Is this not a most suggestive difference? Thirdly and finally, there are the Noachian commandments. Mr. Braude does not mention them at all. This is to be deplored, for it is probably an examination of their history and their place in the Jewish system that would provide the best basis for a satisfactory answer to the question: What was the Rabbinic attitude towards proselytising? One factor contributing to the rise of the doctrine of the Noachian commandments may well have been the realisation that it would be impossible, this side of the Messianic age, to convert large numbers. Considered from this point of view, the Noachian commandments may be said to be a sign of resignation. On the other hand, a religion according to which anyone, Greek or barbarian, submitting to the seven most elementary principles of human morality is certain of salvation, cannot be accused of narrowness. It is truly universal in the sense that it makes God's love embrace all mankind. It might be argued that this religion, which imposes the yoke of the Law on a very small group only while admitting every living being into the presence of God, does not need to proselytise. It has solved the problem raised by the existence of different creeds by taking seriously its faith that God is the Father of all, that (as R. Simeon ben Azzai formulated it) the greatest principle in the Torah is the verse: "This is the book of the generations of Adam. In the day that God created man, in the likeness of God made He him."

Missionary Maxims in Paul

The purpose of the following remarks is to suggest that two striking ideas about missionary methods are taken over by Paul from Jewish teaching on the subject: the idea that you must adopt the customs and mood of the person you wish to win over, and the idea that, to be a successful maker of proselytes, you must become a servant of men and humble yourself.

A. Accommodation

1. *1 Corinthians*

First, for the idea of accommodation. Let us start from a passage in 1 Corinthians:[1] "Unto the Jews I became as a Jew, that I might gain the Jews; to them that are under the law, as under the law, that I might gain them that are under the law; to them that are without law, as without law, that I might gain them that are without law; to the weak became I as weak, that I might gain the weak; I am made all things to all men, that I might by all means save some."

This attitude had formed part of Jewish missionary practice long before Paul. Two Talmudic illustrations of Hillel's work are relevant:[2] he accepted into the fold a gentile who refused to acknowledge the oral Law, and he accepted another who refused to acknowledge any Law beyond the most fundamental ethical principle. True, he admitted them in order subsequently to instruct them and get them to see the absurdity of adhering to the written Law only, and the importance of rendering ethics practicable by means of a detailed code. But the fact remains that, at the decisive moment of conversion, he fell in with the notions of the applicant and declared himself satisfied with recognition of the written Law or a single, basic moral precept.

It is worth noting that the incidents are preserved in two versions, of which one, manifestly secondary, normalizes Hillel's method by making the detailed instruction precede the initiation. Whereas according to the older version—in the tractate Shabbath—Hillel "received the candidate into the faith" on the candidate's terms and then led him into a better understanding, according to the secondary version—in Aboth de Rabbi Nathan—he merely invited the candidate "to sit down" to study and then led him to a better understanding. According to the secondary version, that is, Hillel's generosity consisted only in not showing the unenlightened applicant the door; according to the original version, he immediately accepted him as a Jew. The medieval commen-

[1] 1 Cor 9:20 ff.

[2] *b. Shab.* 31a; *Ab. de R. N.* 15.

tator Rashi, too, finds it necessary, and not a little difficult, to justify the procedure described in the tractate Shabbath. Evidently, its dangerous implications were fully realized by later authorities, who attempted to get rid of them. Hillel, we might put it, was made all things to all men, that he might by all means save some.

Did he, or other Rabbis, formulate any maxim to express this method? His saying "Keep not aloof from the congregation"[3] clearly contemplates life within the community. But there is another, which may chiefly contemplate relations with outsiders:[4] "Do not appear naked, do not appear dressed, do not appear laughing, do not appear weeping—as it is said,[5] A time to weep and a time to laugh, a time to embrace and a time to refrain from embracing."

To be sure, the place of the saying in the Tosephta shows that those who incorporated it in that compilation regarded it as a rule of seemly conduct, enjoining polite compliance with the habits of your company. It is possible, however, that, when first enunciated by Hillel, it was meant as a piece of advice for intercourse with prospective proselytes. There was in those centuries a constant two-way traffic between principles of morality or courtesy represented as of absolute validity and principles represented as useful for the treatment of such as might be converted to one's faith or prevented from leaving it.

On the one hand, many rules belonging to the former class were taken over into the latter. Both Jewish and Christian circles which were desirous of proselytes, in approaching heathens, deliberately stressed the precepts concerning decency and good manners at the expense of levitical and theological ones. Hillel, we have just seen, admitted a man who undertook to observe a single injunction: "What is hateful to you, do not do to your fellow man." Naturally some precepts of this type proved more effective, from the missionary point of view, than others, and as a result acquired prominence. When Simeon ben Shatah (of the first half of the 1st cent. B.C.) gave as reason for dealing honestly with an Arab that "he preferred hearing the Arab say, Blessed be the God of the Jews, to all gain of this world,"[6] he was turning an absolute ethical rule into one useful in the missionary field. Exactly the same is done by 1 Peter,[7] admonishing the faithful to "have your conversation honest among Gentiles, that they may by your good works glorify God." Honesty—and not only to Arabs or gentiles—was an established virtue before Simeon ben Shatah or 1 Peter. In the passages cited, it becomes a missionary instrument.

Quite generally, the favourable or unfavourable impression of good or bad deeds on onlookers, and in particular onlookers from a different camp, was considered of enormous importance. To impress them favourably meant a sanctification or magnification of God's name, to impress them unfavourably a profanation. "If ye work that which is good," we read in the Testament of Naphtali,[8] "God shall be glorifed among the Gentiles

[3] *m. Ab.* 2:5.
[4] *t. Ber.* 2:24.
[5] Eccl 3:4 f.
[6] *y. B. M.* 8c.
[7] 1 Pet 2:12.
[8] Testament of Naphtali 8:4 ff.

through you, but through him that doeth not that which is good God shall be dishonoured." We may compare the exhortation in the sermon on the mount:[9] "Let your light so shine before men that they may see your good works and glorify your Father."

On the other hand, it happened that rules originally having regard to missionary activities in course of time lost their specific character. In Judaism, this must have been almost the normal development. As missionary zeal gave way to exclusiveness and rigid insistence on every detail of the Law, written or oral, those sayings were no longer suitable in their proselytizing sense. Some were discarded as heretical, others were reinterpreted as innocuous principles of proper conduct in general.

The phenomenon, however, occurs in Christianity also. There also the missionary setting of an utterance was occasionally lost sight of or eliminated. In the *Letter of Aristeas*[10] we find the argument that, though most people are generous to their friends, it is more important to be generous to your opponents, in order to make them realize what is right. The sermon on the mount also emphasizes the importance of loving your enemies,[11] but the missionary motive is far less pronounced; while in Paul's Epistle to the Romans,[12] that motive does come in again.

Suppose (we cannot be certain) that Hillel's saying referred to proselytizing, it would not be surprising that the Tosephta, composed at least two hundred years later, when concessions of the kind made by him had ceased to be tolerated, should treat it as a mere demand of politeness. We pointed out above an analogous alteration suffered by the stories of how he received into the community gentiles who did not recognize the Torah as understood by the Rabbis. According to the revised text—in Aboth de Rabbi Nathan—Hillel did not really yield to these candidates, not even temporarily; he did not receive them and then instruct them. He was merely patient with them; instead of sending them away, he instructed them and then received them.

It is, however, in any case likely that, behind Hillel's missionary maxim (if it was one), there had stood a general rule of etiquette; just as a general rule underlies Simeon ben Shatah's and 1 Peter's exhortation to honesty with a view to conversions. R. Meir (of the middle of the 2nd cent. A.D.) quotes the proverb:[13] "If you come into a city, do according to their customs." There is no sign of this proverb, similar in substance to Hillel's advice and, maybe, as old or older, originated in missionary circles. Hillel may have known it. If not, he knew others little different. The point is that he seems to have given the idea a new turn; he seems to have realized its value for the achievement of his great aim of "bringing the creatures nigh to the Law."[14]

In the treatises Derek Eretz Rabba and Derek Eretz Zuta,[15] we meet with descendants of Hillel's maxim. The former contains this paragraph: "A man should not be joyful among the weeping, nor weep among the joyful, nor wake among the sleeping, nor

[9] Matt 5:16.

[10] *Letter of Aristeas* 227.

[11] Matt 5:43 ff.; cf. Luke 6:32 ff.

[12] Rom 12:14, 20 f.

[13] *Gen. Rab.* on 18:8; *Exod. Rab.* on 34:28.

[14] *m. Ab.* 1:12.

[15] *Derek Eretz Rab.* 8:4; *Derek Eretz Zuta* 5:5.

sleep among the waking, nor stand among the sitting, nor sit among the standing—the principle of the matter is, A man should not make different his mind from that of his fellows and the sons of men." The passage from Derek Eretz Zuta is substantially the same, with two exceptions: there is a further pair of warnings, "nor should he read Scripture among those reading Mishnah, nor Mishnah among those reading Scripture," while the summing up runs, "A man should not differ from the usage of the creatures."

These paragraphs are evidence that Hillel's idea was taken up by others and lived on. Moreover, the changes in Derek Eretz Zuta may be regarded as illuminating the process already mentioned: missionary maxims showing some laxity are turned into general rules of seemly conduct in strict harmony with the legalistic attitude. The version of Derek Eretz Rabba might still come down direct from a missionary setting, where it meant: "Accommodate yourself to any type of people, in order to convert them." Derek Eretz Zuta, on the contrary, includes technical details of a definitely Jewish nature, the additional pair of warnings concerning Scripture and Mishnah; and its summing up makes it quite clear that you are expected to adapt yourself only in matters of "usage," social habits. It can only mean: "Good manners require a certain degree of accommodation."

Like Hillel's counsel in the Tosephta, the paragraphs discussed are both placed side by side with principles of courtesy. No wonder seeing that the treatises in which they occur were put together even later than the Tosephta. It should, however, be remembered that a growing number of scholars incline to the view that much of the material of these treatises goes back to a section of Judaism of strongly proselytizing tendencies.

Two further points may be noticed. For one thing, rules about courtesy to strangers were apt to interest missionaries and become part of their programme. To be with strangers—whether they come to you or you to them—frequently means to be with persons whose creed differs from yours: they should be won over. For the Rabbis, the first great maker of proselytes was Abraham, who was hospitable to strange visitors. A text like "The stranger would not lodge in the street, I would open my door to the traveller"[16] was widely interpreted as meaning that any gentile is welcome to God as a proselyte.[17] According to Matthew,[18] scribes and Pharisees would go out to distant countries in order to convert people. When Jesus appointed the first missionaries,[19] he gave them precise instructions as to the proper conduct in strange cities. As for the particular virtue of accommodation, in Greek literature and proverbs, for example, it is recommended mainly to travellers; and it is recommended not as an absolute virtue, but as a means to an end. By adapting themselves to their hosts, they will obtain what they want.[20] All this renders it rather probable that Hillel did intend his maxim, which refers to behaviour among strangers, for use in missionary activity.

[16] Job 31:32.

[17] *Exod. Rab.* on 12:43.

[18] Matt 23:15.

[19] Matt 10:1 ff.; Mark 6:7 ff.; Luke 9:1 ff.

[20] Athenaeus, *Deipn.* 7.317a, 12.513b ff.

For another thing, in establishing the Jewish antecedents of Paul's plan, we need not rely exclusively on Hillel and sayings derived from his. In the *Letter of Aristeas*,[21] the king asks how he might meet with acceptance when travelling abroad; and the answer opens, "By becoming equal to all," πᾶσιν ἴσος γινόμενος. As it stands, it is advice for a traveller—a traveller who wishes to find favour with his hosts. Moreover, the term "equal" has a political sense: the traveller is a king, and he is advised to make light of his rank. None the less it may be assumed that, as early as the time the *Letter* was composed, this was also a slogan of proselyte-makers. The author of the *Letter* himself was a Jewish propagandist.

Paul, when he wrote the passage from 1 Corinthians quoted at the beginning, was drawing on a living element in Jewish religion.

2. *Romans*

We must now turn to Romans:[22] "Rejoice with them that do rejoice, and weep with them that weep; be of the same mind one toward another." At least that is how the verses are usually translated.

That they are reminiscent of the rules in Derek Eretz Rabba and Derek Eretz Zuta has long been recognized; though, curiously, the older saying by Hillel is never adduced in this connection. But it is universally held that Paul has here in mind, not the missionary problem, not relations between Christians and outsiders, but life within the Christian society. This interpretation is not intrinsically untenable. There is no reason why the same principle of morality or etiquette should not be employed once with regard to missionary work and another time with regard to conduct within the community or even as of absolute validity; no reason why Paul should not have recommended accommodation as useful for proselytizers in 1 Corinthians and as a virtue within his flock in Romans.

As a matter of fact, however, the probability is that in Romans, too, he is dealing with relations between Christians and outsiders. This could not, of course, be realized so long as the missionary setting—or at least the potential use for missionary purposes—of Hillel's maxim and its descendants was unsuspected. Once it is realized, a troublesome difficulty about the passage disappears.

The difficulty concerns the position of the passage in the structure of chapter 12. A series of demands are addressed to the new community. Verses 1 to 13 speak of conduct within the community, ending with an exhortation to hospitality. In view of what we said above about rules respecting the treatment of strangers, it is significant that, immediately after this exhortation, Paul goes on to relations with those outside: verse 14 runs, "Bless them which persecute you, bless and curse not." It is at this juncture that confusion appears to set in. According to the current interpretation, the next two verses, i.e. 15 f., "Rejoice with them that do rejoice" etc., return to conduct within the community. Verses 17 to 21 again speak of conduct to outsiders, beginning with: "Recompense

[21] *Letter of Aristeas* 257.

[22] Rom 12:15 f.

to no man evil for evil, provide things honest in the sight of all men." (The latter half of this verse enjoins honesty as a means of attracting unbelievers, on the same lines as Simeon ben Shatah and 1 Peter.) The awkwardness of this arrangement has not escaped modern commentators.[23]

In reality, the arrangement is in order. Verses 1 to 13 are devoted to conduct within the community, and 14 to 21 to conduct to those outside, or more precisely, individuals outside. Chapter 13, on the attitude to the Roman state, forms a logical continuation. The theme of conduct to individuals outside is far from interrupted by 15 f., "Rejoice" etc. In these two verses Paul takes up the concept of accommodation we meet with in the *Letter of Aristeas* and, in a more elaborate form, in Hillel and the treatises from Derek Eretz.

His way of putting it is nearest Derek Eretz Rabba, but there are two notable differences. First, he has only one antithesis, rejoicing and weeping, whereas the Talmudic treatise has three. Hillel, it may be recalled, has two.

Secondly, the maxim in Derek Eretz Rabba is negative, but Paul's is positive. Instead of "A man should not be joyful among the weeping, nor weep among the joyful, a man should not make different his mind from that of his fellows," in Paul we find: "Rejoice with them that do rejoice, and weep with them that weep, be of the same mind one toward another." That the deviation is due to Paul is not, however, likely. There were no doubt positive versions prior to him. The proverb cited above is positive: "When you come into a city, do according to their customs." It has no reference to proselytizing, but we saw that general rules of this sort often formed the basis for specifically missionary ones; and in the *Letter of Aristeas* there is the positive injunction "to become equal to all."

The question is similar to that concerning the Golden Rule. In that case also both negative and positive formulations were known in pre-Christian times. Aristeas[24] combines the negative, not to do to another what you would not have done to yourself, with the positive, to let others partake of all the good of which you would want to partake. Alexander the Great, we hear in the Talmud, asked the Elders of the South: "What should a man do to find favour with the creatures?" To which they replied: "Let him hate kingship and power." But he retorted: "My thought is better than yours; I say, Let him love kingship and power, and do good to the sons of men."[25] Whether historical or not, the anecdote is certainly very old. The Psalmist demands:[26] "Keep thy lips from speaking guile, depart from evil and do good." 1 Peter[27] quotes the negative beginning and the positive conclusion, and a 3rd cent. Rabbi expressly draws attention to the importance of "not indulging in sleep" after observing the negative.[28] Eliezer ben Hyrcanus (about A.D. 90) says:[29] "Let the honour of thy fellow be dear to thee as thine own."

[23] E.g. C. H. Dodd, *The Epistle to the Romans* (1932), 198.

[24] *Letter of Aristeas* 207.

[25] *b. Tam.* 32a.

[26] Ps 34:14 f.

[27] 1 Pet 3:10 f.

[28] R. Alexander, in *b. A. Zar.* 19b.

[29] *m. Ab.* 2:10.

When an author preferred a prohibition to a positive precept or vice versa is a problem calling for a careful, impartial study. The Old Testament warns us:[30] "If thine enemy be hungry, give him bread to eat, and the Lord shall reward thee." This remains an important rule for the Rabbis, who declare the final clause to signify "and the Lord shall make him a friend to thee."[31] No doubt Paul accepts this interpretation when he replaces[32] "and the Lord shall reward thee" by "be not overcome of evil but overcome evil with good." In the sermon on the mount,[33] we are admonished to "bless them that curse you, pray for them which despitefully use you." R. Meir (middle of the 2nd cent. A.D.) did pray for his enemies and saw that this was always the right course to take.[34] A more passive attitude is reflected in a meditation composed by Mar bar Rabina (beginning of the 5th cent. A.D.).[35] It is still recited by Jews three times a day, after the Eighteen Benedictions: "To such as curse me let my soul be dumb, yea, let my soul be unto all as the dust." Paul in Romans combines the positive and the negative: "Bless and curse not."

Verse 16 deserves special mention. "Be of the same mind one toward another" must be misleading, i.e. must appear as concerned with behaviour within the community, unless we take account of the fact that it simply corresponds to the ending of the Jewish maxim: "A man should not make different his mind from that of his fellows." The negative injunction is replaced by a positive one, of the kind occurring in the *Letter of Aristeas*: "Become equal to all." That is the only change, which, plainly, does not detract from the missionary point of the rule; if anything, it renders it more intense in this context.

Admittedly, "to be of the same mind" refers to unanimity within the community in other Pauline utterances.[36] But this is to be expected since, as repeatedly observed, accommodation was a recognized virtue before being made into a missionary method; and, of course, it always continued to rank among the forces holding a society together. Just so, the exhortations to honest dealings with outsiders do not mean that honesty has ceased to be a virtue within the community. It goes on to appear in the latter role.[37] Hillel, who went to such lengths in meeting prospective proselytes half-way, attached no less value to tolerance within Judaism: "Keep not aloof from the congregation." Again, the phrase "one band," normally denoting a united Israel,[38] in a prayer prescribed for the New Year and Day of Atonement[39] includes the gentile world: "O Lord, impose thine awe upon all thy works, that all creatures may prostrate themselves before thee and may all form one band to do thy will with a perfect heart." There is nothing strange in Paul applying the notion "to be of the same mind" to different situations.

[30] Prov 25:21 f.

[31] Targum: *nashlimeh* instead of *neshallemhe*.

[32] Rom 12:21.

[33] Matt 5:44; cp. Luke 6:28.

[34] *b. Ber.* 10a.

[35] *b. Ber.* 17a, Singer's *Prayer Book*, 54.

[36] Rom 15:5; 2 Cor 13:11; Phil 2:2, 4:2.

[37] E.g. Jas 3:13.

[38] *Lev. Rab.* on 23:40, *Tanhuma* ed. Buber, *Debharim* 24b f., on Deut 29:9.

[39] Singer's *Prayer Book*, 239.

It may be worth comparing two passages in Josephus's *Contra Apionem*,[40] where he praises mutual agreement, using ἀλλήλων or ἀλλήλους, "one another." In one of them he definitely thinks of the inner life of the nation alone. After listing a large number of laws, he explains that it is these which "keep together our association with one another," τὴν πρὸς ἀλλήλους ἡμῶν συνέχει κοινωνίαν. The other observation is of a more general character, not essentially confined to relations between Jews. Identity of religious belief, he says, and "to differ from one another in nothing regarding life and habits will bring about a wonderful harmony in the natures of men," τῷ βίῳ μηδὲν ἀλλήλων διαφέρειν καλλίστην ἐν ἤθεσιν ἀνθρώπων συμφωνίαν ἀποτελεῖ.

The principal cause of the prevalent misinterpretation of verses 15 f., "Rejoice," as contemplating life within the community is undoubtedly the fact that, for many centuries, translators have done scant justice to the original. It is verse 16 which has suffered most. The maxim to be found in Derek Eretz is impersonal: "A man should not make different his mind from that of his fellows." In Romans, modern versions of the Bible—such as the English—put an imperative, a direct command addressed to the recipients of the letter: "Be of the same mind one toward another." Thus the impression is conveyed that the rule, far from being universal, has regard to internal conditions only. That is to say, "one toward another" becomes equivalent to "one of you toward another of you." Yet the Greek has τὸ αὐτὸ εἰς ἀλλήλους φρονοῦντες, "Being of the same mind one toward another." In the chapter on *Haustafeln* [295 ff.], we suggested that this constitutes an over-literal rendering of a Hebrew rule using the participle. The meaning is impersonal, and a closer translation would be: "One should be of the same mind one toward another." The Vulgate, incidentally, still retains the participle, "*idipsum invicem sentientes*."

When we consider that verse 15, in the Greek, is also impersonal, with two infinitives—still kept in the Vulgate, "*gaudere cum gaudentibus, flere cum flentibus*"—the true connection with verse 14 becomes apparent. We must interpret thus: "Bless them which persecute you; bless, and curse not. It is proper to rejoice with them that rejoice and weep with them that weep. One should be of the same mind one toward another." There is here no break in the argument—unless we disregard the formulation of the original. It all concerns the attitude to those outside. It all has a missionary flavour.

We may perhaps add that, in the history of Christian mission, accommodation has often proved highly effective. It seems agreed that, if the Jesuits achieved greater things in China than the Franciscans, they did so because they paid more attention to the method in question.

B. SERVICE AND HUMILITY

1. *Paul*

The second part of Romans 12:16, so far left out of consideration, reads: "Mind not high things, but condescend to low ones; be not wise in your conceits." (The translation "condescend to low ones," in the sense of "undertake humble service," is preferable to

[40] *Contra Apionem* 2.27.208, 2.19.179; cp. 2.16.170, 2.38.281, 2.39.283, 2.41.294.

"condescend to men of low estate.") In 1 Corinthians[41] the author declares that he has faithfully kept to his course: "For though I be free from all men, yet have I made myself servant unto all, that I might gain the more." We submit that this idea also is adopted by Paul from traditional Jewish teaching.

In Romans, the injunction "Mind not high things" immediately follows "Rejoice with them that rejoice." In 1 Corinthians, the verse "I have made myself servant unto all" immediately precedes "And to the Jews I became as a Jew." The intimate association of the duty of humble service with that of accommodation is indeed obvious.

Roughly, the latter duty—discussed above—may be said to follow from the former, which is wider: service demands many things, among them accommodation. The men Hillel had converted by falling in with their views met, we are told, and agreed: "The meekness of Hillel brought us under the wings of the Shekhina." Here, we find meekness as a missionary method traced back to Hillel, and we find it as closely connected with acceptance of the candidate's mood and customs as in Paul—meekness manifesting itself in acceptance of the other party's standpoint.

Hillel, however, was always meek, not only when he was out to gain a proselyte; and, of course, the general moral demand of meekness existed long before him—and not in Judaism alone. Even the notion that humility rather than self-assertion leads to greatness, success and the acquisition of friends considerably antedates Hillel, and it, too, is fairly universal, to be found all over the world. That you may have to "stoop to conquer" was explained by Goldsmith neither under the influence of Hillel nor under that of Paul. (The idea may assume many different nuances. For instance, references to the conquest of an enemy by doing him good, "*beneficiis vincere*," are no less frequent in pagan literature than in Jewish.[42]) It follows that, when men like Hillel introduced that specifically missionary twist, "Stoop to conquer unbelievers," they were doing what was shown above to have been a common thing: they recognized the particular value of an ethical principle as a help in proselytizing.

In the Talmud and Midrash we come across a number of sayings by Hillel which express the idea that self-abasement is the road to glory as a general rule of morality, wisdom or good manners. It is quite conceivable that some of them were originally applied by him to the more specific question of the enlisting of new members of the faith. Take the statement "My humility is my exaltation, and my exaltation is my humility." In one source,[43] it is brought into connection with David's and Moses's humility before God, for which David obtained his victories and Moses the privilege of divine revelation. In another,[44] it is introduced as concerning humility before men, taking the lower seats, which conduct can only bring honour; and illustrations are taken from Moses's humility before God. Hillel himself may well have offered success in winning over unbelievers as further confirmation; or to put it differently, his saying may well have been meant to cover this province.

[41] 1 Cor 9:19.

[42] Sallust, *Bellum Jugurthinum* 9.3; Apuleius, *Apologia* 99.557.

[43] *Exod. Rab.* on 33:12.

[44] *Lev. Rab.* on 1:1.

How freely the idea under notice passed from the domain of proper behaviour in general to that of behaviour to heathens and back again, may be seen from an anecdote[45] about a banquet provided by Gamaliel II (end of the 1st cent. A.D.). The venerable Rabbi stood to wait on his fellow-scholars. So far, this is just an example of humility in general. Some of the guests thought it wrong to accept the honour, but R. Joshua observed that Abraham had done the same for the angels though he took them for idolatrous Arabs (the Scriptural basis being the words "and he stood by them under the tree").[46] There can be little doubt that Abraham's standing to wait on the "Arabs" at one time figured among the many illustrations of his proselytizing activity, implying the maxim "Stoop to conquer unbelievers." In the anecdote, however, the missionary element has become irrelevant: his conduct simply means lowliness in general. But this is not the end. R. Zadok, the story goes on, was able to cap Joshua's quotation. He reminded the company that God himself served the creatures, sustaining the good and the bad, and even the worshippers of idols. Here we seem again to approach the universalistic, missionary side of the argument.

Pseudo-Phocylides[47] recommends sober persuasion of the wicked; he does not, like Hillel or Paul, go so far as to recommend humility. In the *Letter of Aristeas* we find three passages which bear on the matter in hand. The first says that one should persuade one's opponent in an attitude of subjection.[48] In the second,[49] the king asks how he might meet with acceptance when travelling abroad; and he is told "to become equal to all and to behave rather as inferior than as superior to his hosts." In the third,[50] he asks how to avoid pride; and he is told to bear in mind the virtue of equality, since God puts down the proud and exalts the humble. It is interesting that the two last-mentioned passages associate accommodation and humility, just as we find them associated in Paul and the stories about Hillel. True, in Aristeas, as far as accommodation is concerned, it is of a political rather than a social and theological character. The sequence in the *Letter of Aristeas* is the same as in Romans and the Rabbinic stories: accommodation—humility. In 1 Corinthians, we saw, it is humility—accommodation.

A closer examination of the grammar and vocabulary of the Pauline texts corroborates our thesis that he is working on an established Jewish missionary pattern. The exhortation "Mind not high things but condescend to low ones," in Romans, like the first part of the verse ("Be of the same mind"), is framed in that curious way—by means of absolute participles—which must be explained as an over-literal rendering from Hebrew codes: μὴ φρονοῦντες ἀλλὰ συναπαγόμενοι, "Not minding but condescending."

As for 1 Corinthians, Paul here uses κερδαίνω for "to win over an unbeliever." In the next chapter we shall try to demonstrate that this application of the verb must be accounted for by reference to the Hebrew root *śkr* or its Aramaic equivalent *'gr*, and more particularly by reference to the use of *hiśtakker*. This term, with the primary mean-

[45] *Mek.* on Exod 18:12.

[46] Gen 18:8.

[47] *Pseudo-Phocylides* 76 f.

[48] *Letter of Aristeas* 266.

[49] *Letter of Aristeas* 257.

[50] *Letter of Aristeas* 262 f.

ing "to profit," is employed by the Rabbis in the sense of "to win over unbelievers or sinners." There is a series of texts in which *hištakker* is so employed, and in which we find precisely the idea of making oneself servant that one might gain the more. It is, in fact, God who proceeds in this manner, who lets himself be conquered—i.e. induced to forgive—in order to gain the masses. So Paul, free from all men, serves all that he might gain the more. The similarity in thought and expression is too specific to make coincidence an acceptable solution.

The problem of date might perhaps be raised. In the Rabbinic texts, the earliest authority named is Ishmael ben Jose, who flourished towards the end of the 3rd cent. A.D. But, for one thing, various authorities base the idea on various sections in Scripture. This indicates that the idea as such is older than these authorities, who apply it each in his own way. For another thing, it is impossible to assume that the Rabbis drew on Paul's epistles in this matter. Quite apart from other arguments, the passage from 1 Corinthians was far too remote from and unimportant for them. Paul drew on a Rabbinic tradition. His background must be reconstructed by means of the texts containing *hištakker*—and, of course, those referring to Hillel and Abraham and the passages we have quoted from Aristeas and Pseudo-Phocylides. In all these latter cases, the question of date creates no difficulty at all; some are pre-Pauline and some roughly contemporary with Paul.

A further point deserves attention. When we go through the New Testament texts where κερδαίνω is used as denoting "to win over," a remarkable result emerges: they all represent humility as an instrument of conversion, however different may be the particular situations contemplated and the degrees of intensity with which the notion is set forth.

Enough has been said about 1 Corinthians, where κερδαίνω appears five times in four successive verses. The first of them refers to the wider duty of serving in order to attract, the others to the duty of accommodation following from it.

1 Peter[51] urges wives to "be in subjection to your husband, that if any obey not the word, they may be won by the conversation of the wives." There is the absolute participle, αἱ γυναῖκες ὑποτασσόμεναι, "the wives being in subjection to their husbands." And there are good reasons for supposing that already in the source on which the author of the epistle drew, the demand of subordination was followed by a final clause giving conversion as the aim to be achieved in this way.[52]

Lastly, Matthew[53] contains an exhortation to self-restraint when you are wronged, in order to win over the offender: "If thy brother shall trespass against thee, tell him his fault between thee and him alone, and if he shall hear thee, thou hast gained thy brother."

The most satisfactory mode of explaining this position is to postulate a missionary maxim—serve and be humble to gain those far from you—earlier than the codes underlying Paul, earlier than the source of 1 Peter and earlier than Matthew. This maxim in

[51] 1 Pet 3:1.

[52] E. G. Selwyn, *The First Epistle of St. Peter* (1946), 434.

[53] Matt 18:15.

course of time was put to use in the most various domains. (Its absence from a section of Luke corresponding to that of Matthew here considered[54] may be due to Luke's unfamiliarity with the traditional way in which this maxim was expressed.) With this inference from internal evidence of the New Testament, the conclusion reached above on a comparative basis is in fullest harmony: that maxim was of Jewish origin.

2. *The Gospels*

We have just seen that one rule of conduct in Matthew at least is affected by our result. When we consider the range of application of the maxim in question in the Jewish sources—a king who travels should assume an attitude of lowliness if he wishes to find favour, an opponent will be more readily led to understanding if treated with deference, God lets himself be conquered in order to gain the masses, Abraham waits at table when dealing with prospective proselytes, Hillel remains submissive in the face of stupidity and arrogance on the part of candidates—it would not be surprising if it has influenced not only Paul and one exhortation in Matthew, but also some other pericopes in the gospels, both such as concern the activity of Jesus himself and such as concern the activity required of his followers. Furthermore, one would expect that difficulties of interpretation might occasionally be removed once we take due account of the fact that this and similar maxims had their roots in morality or wisdom in general, and that even after attaining particular, missionary significance, they were apt at any moment to become quite general again.

Mark offers one possible example.[55] The disciples wondered which of them was the greatest, whereupon Jesus exclaimed: "If any man desire to be the first, the same shall be the last of all, and servant of all." The text goes on: "And he took a child and set him in the midst of them; and when he had taken him in his arms, he said, Whosoever shall receive one of such children in my name, receiveth me."

Of the latter verses Klostermann remarks:[56] "They take over the motive of the blessing of children in 10:13–16, though it does not fit here. Where does the child of verse 36 come from? Why is it one only, against several in verse 37? Why is it being embraced?"

This criticism may be justified as far as it goes. None the less the association of the verses with what precedes appears less arbitrary if we suppose that it was effected by one for whom—rightly or wrongly, as far as the original sense of the saying is concerned—the phrase "servant of all" was a missionary slogan, and the embracing of children symbolized the welcoming of converts. On this basis, the present place of the following verses, 38–40, which Klostermann finds even queerer, also becomes intelligible. For this section too, culminating as it does in Jesus's exhortation to tolerance towards those only loosely and unofficially bound to the new religion, contains an important principle as to the proper treatment of outsiders. Actually, the principle is similar in spirit to that discussed above, the principle of accommodation. Whoever made this

[54] Luke 17:3.

[55] Mark 9:33 ff. Cp. Matt 18:1 ff.; Luke 9:46 ff.

[56] *Das Markusevangelium*, 2nd ed. (1926), 105.

arrangement would have looked on verse 41 as a suitable continuation: anyone showing kindness to Christians will be saved, even though he may not be a full member of the community. And verse 42 also was capable of being regarded as dealing with the same theme, namely, as a warning not to offend newcomers to the faith.

It is worth noting that the parallel section in Matthew is directly followed by the precept of reproving in private and thus winning over—κερδαίνω—one who has wronged you.

A Missionary Term

It is generally held[1] that κερδαίνω in the sense of "to win over an unbeliever to your faith"[2] or "to win back a sinner to the way of life required by his and your faith"[3] is an "*echter terminus technicus der Missionssprache* [genuine technical term of missionary language]," with no precedent in either Hellenistic or Rabbinic language. This view is not correct. Admittedly, the sense is un-Greek. In Greek, κερδαίνω denotes "to profit," "to derive advantage," "to traffic," but not "to win over somebody." The latter meaning would be more naturally expressed, say, by μετάγω or λαμβάνω, both occurring in the *Letter of Aristeas*,[4] or by (συν)αναπείθω, used by Josephus.[5] We may also grant that no Rabbinic parallels have so far been adduced. The most familiar Rabbinic words for "to proselytize" are not to the point. *Qibbel* signifies "to receive," not "to gain," and there is no missionary fervour about it; while *hiqribh* is more fervent, but its proper meaning is "to bring near," very different from κερδαίνω. Nevertheless the usage in question, though it may reflect a specifically Christian trend, is in the main determined by the Rabbinic vocabulary.

Three terms deserve consideration.

A. "Kanas" (or "kenas," "kenash"), "to gather"

In the Old Testament, this verb means "to gather wealth": "I gathered me silver and gold," or "a time to cast away stones and a time to gather stones."[6] It also means "to gather men," and some of the passages are suggestive, speaking as they do of the bringing back of the diaspora: "I caused them to be led into captivity but I have gathered them again," or "The Lord gathereth together the outcasts of Israel."[7]

In Rabbinic literature the verb continues to signify both "to gather goods"—the Targum uses *kenash* in the text just cited, "I gathered silver"—and "to gather men." There are the derivatives *kenesiyya*, "a gathering of people," *beth hakkeneseth*, meaning on the one hand "a storehouse for goods" (such as wood), on the other "a synagogue," *keneseth yiśra'el*, "the congregation of Israel," "Ecclesia," *keneseth haggedhola*, "the

[1] J. Weiss, *Der erste Korintherbrief*, 9th ed., 10th impr. (1925), 243; A. Schlier, *s.v.* κέρδος, κερδαίνω, in *Theologisches Wörterbuch zum Neuen Testament*, ed. G. Kittel, vol. 3 (1938), 672.

[2] 1 Cor 9:19 ff.; 1 Pet 3:1.

[3] Matt 18:15.

[4] *Letter of Aristeas* 227, 266.

[5] *Ant.* 20.2.3.35.

[6] Eccl 2:8, 3:5. In both texts the Qal is used.

[7] Ezek 39:28; Ps 147:2. Piel in both texts.

Great Synagogue."[8] (The Aramaic forms are *kenisha'*, *kenishta'*.) It is noteworthy that the verb also retains the sense of "to gather the diaspora." The Targum employs it in the verse from Psalms, "He will gather the dispersed of Israel";[9] and the Midrash explains that this line refers to the restoration of the diaspora, of the Ten Tribes, or of those excommunicated—people like Korah and his followers.[10] We are told that "the diaspora will be gathered only as a reward of faith,"[11] and that "when he gathers them again, he will gather them only by means of clouds."[12]

The term is used of "the receiving, gathering in, of travellers." The Jerusalemite Targum[13] makes Abraham say, "I shall receive the passers-by." *Hakhnasath 'oreḥim* "the reception of travellers," "hospitality," is a frequent expression.[14]

"To gather the diaspora," "the excommunicated ones," "the travellers"—to these uses must be added the blessing which a father had, and still has, to recite at his son's circumcision: "Blessed art thou who has commanded us to gather him into the covenant of Abraham." The bystanders take up just this word and respond: "As he has been gathered into the covenant, so may he be gathered into the Torah, nuptial canopy and good deeds."[15]

But the verb is even directly used of "the winning of proselytes." For one thing, the well-known phrase "to bring under the wings of the Shekhina," though as a rule a rendering of *hiqribh* or *qerebh*, "to bring near," occasionally stands for a form of *kanas*, "to gather."[16] In Genesis[17] it is recorded that "Abraham took all the souls that they had gotten." The Hebrew is *'aśu*, the souls they had "made." The Midrash[18] accounts for the curious expression by asserting that Abraham took the souls "they had gathered under the wings of the Shekhina." The verb recurs in the famous utterance of Eleazar ben Pedath (of the second half of the 3rd cent. A.D. The text names Eliezer ben Hyrcanus, about A.D. 100, but this is universally considered to be a corruption. I am not entirely convinced. Eliezer's hostile remarks on proselytes as they are in reality do not prove that he may not have taken up a fundamentally positive attitude): "God scattered Israel only in order that proselytes should be added; for Hosea says,[19] And I will sow her in the earth; does any man sow a small measure unless in order to gather many big ones?" This is a good illustration of the scope of the verb, which, in the phrase "to gather big measures," denotes "to win riches," yet alludes to "the winning of converts" at the same time.

[8] *m. Ab.* 4:11; *y. B. B.* 14c; *m. Meg.* 3:1; *Song of Songs Rab.* on 1:4; *m. Ab.* 1:1.
[9] *Targum* on Ps 147:2, Qal or Piel.
[10] Cp. *Midrash Psalms* on 70:1 f.; Piel and Pual.
[11] *Mek.* on Exod 14:21; Hithpael.
[12] *Mek.* on Exod 14:24; Piel.
[13] Jer. *Targum* on Gen 18:3, Qal.
[14] *b. Shab.* 127a.
[15] *b. Shab.* 137b; Hiphil and Niphal.
[16] Qal, Piel or Hiphil.
[17] Gen 12:5.
[18] *Siphre* on Deut 6:5; cp. *Lev. Rab.* on 1:2.
[19] Hos 2:25.

Finally, there is in the New Testament a close association between κερδανίω in the sense of "to win over" or "to win back" and σῴζω, "to save."[20] This is to be expected. But it is interesting that in Rabbinic language, too, *kanas*, "to gather," may be synonymous with *hiṣṣil*, "to save":[21] "Isaiah says,[22] Then Hezekiah (desperately ill) turned to the wall and prayed; according to Joshua ben Levi (first half of the 3rd cent. A.D.) he turned to the wall of Rahab, saying, Lord of the universe, Rahab saved only two souls for thee, *hiṣṣil* (the spies she helped to escape), and how many souls has thou saved for her, *hiṣṣil* (all her family were spared);[23] my fathers gathered for thee all the proselytes, *kanas*, how much the more shouldest thou spare me!"

B. "QANA" (OR "QENE")

This is the usual verb, both in the Old Testament and in Rabbinic writings, for "to buy," "to acquire," though when God is the subject, it may also mean "to found," "to create." It refers to "the winning of men," for instance, in Sirach,[24] "If thou gainest a friend, gain him by trial," and in the Mishnah,[25] "Joshua ben Perahyah (second half of the 2nd cent. B.C.) says, Gain thee a fellow-disciple."

It occurs in a maxim somewhat similar to that which we find in the Synoptics,[26] emphasizing the disappointment of a man "if he shall gain, κερδαίνω, the whole world and lose his soul." We are informed:[27] "In Palestine they say, If a man has gained knowledge, what does he lack? If he has not gained that, what has he gained?"

It is doubtful, however, whether the verb ever has the sense of "to proselytize." Perhaps we ought to mention a Rabbinic comment[28] on Melchizedek's greeting of Abraham: "Blessed be thou of the most high God, creator—possessor, acquirer, *qone*—of heaven and earth." R. Isaac (of the second half of the 3rd cent. A.D.) takes "creator" as an attribute of Abraham: as he converted people to monotheism, God regarded him as his partner in the creation. *Qone*, then, is here interpreted as "creator," but there may be a pun on the sense of "gainer," "converter." The same pun may underlie a remark to the effect that Abraham, in Melchizedek's greeting, appears as a special possession of God: God "possesses," or, if this pun is intended, "converts," Abraham. That Abraham was the first proselyte is a favourite idea of the Rabbis.[29] Possibly, an illusion to proselytizing is contained also in the words addressed by God to Gabriel, *qene lekha ʿedha*, "found—or, gain—thee a congregation."[30] But if so, it is remote, and in any case the

[20] 1 Cor 9:22; 1 Cor 7:16 in conjunction with 1 Pet 3:1; Jas 5:20 with Matt 18:15.

[21] *Eccl. Rab.* on 5:6.

[22] Isa 38:2.

[23] Josh 2, 6:25.

[24] Sir 6:7.

[25] *m. Ab.* 1:6; cp. 4:11.

[26] Matt 16:26; Mark 8:36; Luke 9:25.

[27] *b. Ned.* 41a.

[28] *Gen. Rab.* on 14:19.

[29] *b. Sukk.* 49b.

[30] *b. Pes.* 118b.

passage is obscure. On the other hand, there are texts which certainly do not belong here, since it is the proselyte who "gains God," not God or the faithful who gains the proselyte. For example, Jethro, the Midrash affirms,[31] is called a Kenite "because he gained, *qana*, heaven and earth." We have already quoted a maxim about the importance of "gaining knowledge"—a similar usage of the verb; and we may add Hillel's saying (of the last cent. B.C.):[32] "If a man has gained words of the Law, he has gained life in the world to come."

C. "ŚAKHAR"

So far we have seen that the verbs *kanas* and *qana* signified both "to acquire wealth" and "to gain men"; and *kanas* at least was definitely a missionary term. Yet they do not fully account for the use of κερδαίνω in the manner indicated. Had they alone influenced the writers in Greek, surely the choice would have fallen on a Greek verb with the same basic sense as *kanas*, namely, "to gather," or with the same basic sense as *qana*, "to buy," "to acquire." Therefore, while *kanas* and *qana* no doubt helped to prepare the ground, we consider a third verb as the one of which κερδαίνω is an immediate translation: *śakhar* or, in the forms more common in the relevant texts, *niṣkar* and *hiśtakker*. We may admit at the outset that there is a slight gap in our evidence, which we shall point out. At any rate, here are the principal arguments.

First, the general range of the Rabbinic term, and the way in which it can be applied, are highly reminiscent of κερδαίνω. The noun *śakhar* denotes "wages," "profit," "advantage," "*lucrum*"; it can be used exactly like κέρδος. The Mishnah lays down[33] that "none may set up a shopkeeper on the condition of receiving half the profit." In the spiritual sphere the Torah, Wisdom, Life to come, fulfilment of a commandment or martyrdom may be the *śakhar* of the pious.[34] So the Christian's κέρδος Christ.[35] The Mishnah distinguishes various characters.[36] Of one, easy to provoke and easy to appease, it is said that "his loss is cancelled by his gain." The regular opposite of *śakhar*, "profit," is *hephsedh*, "loss." It occurs in this saying, and it corresponds to ζημία, the regular opposite of κέρδος. Just so, the regular opposite of the verb *niṣkar* or *hiśtakker*, "to profit," is *hiphsidh* or *niphsadh*, "to suffer loss," corresponding to ζημιοῦμαι, the opposite of κερδαίνω. "But what things were gains, κέρδος, to me," Paul writes,[37] "I counted loss, ζημία; I count all things loss, ζημία, for Christ, for whom I have lost all things, ζημιοῦμαι, that I may win Christ, κερδαίνω." Philo[38] gives as a reason for the Seventh Year: "Do not be entirely under the power of lucre, κέρδος, but submit to some loss, ζημία." To quote a few more examples from the Rabbis—Judah the Prince says:[39] "Reckon the loss

[31] *Siphre* on Num 10:29.
[32] *m. Ab.* 2:7.
[33] *m. B. M.* 5:4.
[34] E.g. *Gen. Rab.* on 6:3; *m. Ab.* 4:2; *b. Men.* 29b.
[35] Phil 3:7 f.
[36] *m. Ab.* 5:11.
[37] Phil 3:7 f., just adduced.
[38] *De spec. leg.* 2.19.87.
[39] *m. Ab.* 2:1.

(material loss) resulting from a precept against its reward (from God), and the reward (material) from a transgression against its loss (from God)." Another epigram is:[40] "Some are industrious and gain—namely, those working all the week but not on the eve of the Sabbath—and some are industrious and lose—those working also on the eve of the Sabbath." According to Admon (of the 1st cent. A.D.), a son who gets no inheritance because his father leaves just enough to maintain the daughters may complain: "Must I suffer loss because I am a male?" Ben Nanos (of the first half of the 2nd cent. A.D.) disagrees with the view that, if a man is survived by several wives, only the one he married last may receive her jointure without taking an oath: "Should she profit because she is the last?"[41] Instead of *śakhar*, sometimes its Aramaic equivalent, *'aghar*, *'aghra'*, is contrasted with *hephsedh*: "A bond was issued against the children of R. Ilish, stipulating half profits and half loss."[42]

Secondly, as for the verb, *niṣkar* or *hiśtakker*, quite apart from its relation to *hiphsidh*, *niphsadh*, ζημιοῦμαι, just discussed, it might be rendered by κερδαίνω in a great many cases. It means "to be at an advantage" in a decision by R. Meir (middle of the 2nd cent. A.D.)[43] that if an ox gores several oxen, the claim of the owner of the last takes precedence: the owner of the last "is at an advantage." A principle frequently operating is that the law must be formulated in such a way that a sinner or dishonest person should not "profit," "be at an advantage." If dough becomes unclean, only a very small proportion need be given up as dough-offering; but should a woman intentionally render the dough unclean, the normal proportion is due, in order that the sinner "shall not profit."[44] Here also, the opposite *hiphsidh* occurs: R. Jose (middle of the 2nd cent. A.D.) rejects certain opinions because, if they were law, "what loss would the deceiver suffer?"[45] This reasoning is clearly allied with that according to which a sinner "must make no profit." Again, the verb means "to benefit by a thing." Jacob, the Midrash says,[46] "benefited by," "derived advantage from," his flock, getting the milk and wool. The Talmud states[47] that "no man knows by which enterprise he will profit." It may even signify, like κερδαίνω, "to deal in," "to traffic." R. Ishmael (of the first half of the 2nd cent. A.D.) held that with the surplus of the Shekel-chamber wine and the like should be bought, that it should be resold to those wishing to bring a private offering, and that "the profit," *śakhar*, should go to the Temple: while Akiba (his contemporary) was of opinion that "one should not traffic" with what belongs to the Temple.[48] In popular, modern dictionaries,[49] *niṣkar* and

[40] *b. Pes.* 50b.

[41] *m. Ket.* 13:3, 10:5.

[42] *b. B. M.* 68b.

[43] *m. B. K.* 4:1.

[44] *m. Hall.* 2:7. Cp. *m. Shebi.* 9:9; *b. Yeb.* 92b.

[45] *m. B. M.* 3:4 f.

[46] *Tanhuma Wayyeshebh* 13 on Gen 38:1.

[47] *b. Pes.* 54b. Cp. also *m. Erub.* 3:6.

[48] *m. Shek.* 4:3. Cp. *b. B. B.* 91a.

[49] E.g. I. Raffalovitch, *Anglo-Hebrew Modern Dictionary*, *s.vv.* "earn" and "profit"; I. Elfros, J. Ibn-Shmuel Kaufman and B. Silk, *English-Hebrew Dictionary*, *s.vv.* "earn" and "profit"; M. D. Gross, *Hammillon Hashshalem*, pt. I (Hebrew-German), *s.v. śakhar*.

hiśtakker are listed as denoting "to earn," "to profit," or, in German, "*verdienen*," "*profitieren*"—values precisely equivalent to κερδαίνω.

Thirdly, we have already adduced a Rabbinic saying comparable to the Synoptic one about him who "gains the whole world and loses his soul"; in that saying *qana* is used. But we also find one where *hiśtakker* takes the place of κερδαίνω. Simeon II ben Gamaliel II, Judah and Jose (all of the middle of the 2nd cent. A.D.) reproached a man who did not pay his tithes properly:[50] "Thou hast gained money but destroyed—or lost, *'ibbedh*—souls." It is easy to see why, in this connection, *'ibbedh*, "to destroy," "to lose," may be opposed to *hiśtakker*: its meaning is here no different from that of the normal opposite of *hiśtakker*, i.e. *hiphsidh*. However, *hiphsidh* itself occurs in an older version of the saying. Eleazar ben Azariah (of the first third of the 2nd cent. A.D.), combating the exemption of certain groups from certain tithes, exclaimed to his antagonist: "Lo, thou wouldest make them enjoy worldly riches (*mamon*, our "mammon"), yet thou wouldest but lose souls."[51] (That this is the older version follows not only from the date of Eleazar but also from the fact that the plural, "souls," fits his statement better than that of Simeon II, Judah and Jose: Eleazar contemplates whole sections failing to pay their tithes, the other Rabbis address one individual only.) It is also worth noting that just as *hiphsidh* is replaceable by *'ibbedh*, so is ζημιοῦμαι by ἀπόλλυμι. In the Testament of Judah we read that a fornicator "suffers loss," ζημιοῦμαι, in that of Reuben that fornication "destroys," ἀπόλλυμι.[52]

Fourthly, Symmachus has κέρδος for *śakhar* in the verse:[53] "Two are better than one, because they have a good reward for their labor." The LXX, it may be observed, does not use κερδαίνω and κέρδος at all: it normally renders *śakhar* by μισθός. The reason is not far to seek. In the Old Testament, *śakhar* and its derivatives have not yet attained the range of κερδαίνω; μισθός and μισθοῦμαι more or less cover the ground; nor is there any other synonym of κερδαίνω. How far the development had gone by the time of the LXX, it is impossible to say. When Symmachus wrote, it was undoubtedly completed: *śakhar* had all the meanings to which we have referred. Its translation by κέρδος, in a verse where it plainly does not signify μισθός in the narrow sense, must now have appeared quite natural.

Fifthly and lastly, there is a series of texts of particular interest where *hiśtakker* denotes "to win men." The Psalmist says, "He will not always chide."[54] The Hebrew for "always," *laneṣaḥ*, is interpreted by the Rabbis as meaning "for conquest," so that they obtain: "He will not chide for conquest." God, the Midrash explains, reflects thus: "Did I not conquer the generation of the Flood and I suffered loss (*hiphsidh*, ζημιοῦμαι)? But when Moses conquered me (obtaining forgiveness for the people after they had made the Golden Calf) I profited (*hiśtakker*, κερδαίνω) in my world. Hence, He will not chide for conquest." Resh Lakish (of the middle of the 3rd cent. A.D.) gives the

[50] *t. M. Sh.* 3:18.
[51] *m. Yad.* 4:3.
[52] Testament of Judah 15:1; Testament of Reuben 4:7.
[53] Eccl 4:9.
[54] Ps 103:9.

main idea in a more general form:[55] God says, When I conquer I suffer loss (*hiphsidh*), but when I am conquered I gain (*hiśtakker*). I conquered dealing with the generation of the Flood, but I lost (*hiphsidh*), for I destroyed all those masses (*'okhloza'*, the Greek ὄχλος). But when the Golden Calf was made, Moses conquered me and I gained (*hiśtakker*) all those masses." In another passage the idea is propounded in connection with the verse from Isaiah:[56] "For he will not be wroth for conquest"—*laneṣah* being taken in this sense instead of its real meaning of "always." In support, the Midrash adduces the opening of a Psalm,[57] "To the chief musician," *lamenaṣṣeah*, which phrase is declared to mean: "To him that rejoices when they conquer him." Traces of this exegesis may be found in a remark attributed to Ishmael ben Jose, a contemporary of Judah the Prince.[58]

We submit that *niṣkar* or *hiśtakker*, used of "the making of a profit" and of "the gaining by God of men whom he had cast away," accounts for the role of κερδαίνω as a missionary term in the New Testament. Admittedly, we have come across no texts where the Rabbinic term denotes "to convert"; and this particular nuance, therefore, may still be Christian, though we do not think so. This is the gap in our argument, which we announced at the beginning. The masses which God "gains" in the series of texts just examined are Israelites condemned and reprieved, "won back," not gentiles "won over." But it is not a serious gap, as three considerations will show.

In the first place, in Matthew at least,[59] κερδαίνω signifies, not "to win over proselytes," but "to win back a sinner," just like the Rabbinic term. For this application, then, the evidence leaves nothing to be desired.

In the second place, in one ancient saying, the Aramaic equivalent of *śakhar*, to which we referred before, namely, *'aghar*, is employed in a manner all but positive proof that proselytes proper, won over from another faith, might be described by this word. Simeon ben Shatah (of the first half of the 1st cent. B.C.) refused to regard as his own a pearl found on an ass which had been bought for him from an Arab, declaring[60] that he was no *barbari*, barbarian, and that he preferred hearing the Arab say "Blessed be the God of the Jews"—*scil.* whose followers are honest—to all *'aghar*, "gain," of this world. Surely, where such an expression was possible, it was also possible to "gain a proselyte." In an age when one might be recognized as belonging to a faith though very loosely attached to it, causing a gentile to praise God did constitute a kind of proselytizing. The New Testament contains suggestive passages like "Let your light shine before men that they may see your good works and glorify your Father."[61] In chapter 2 of 1 Peter there is the admonition, "Having your conversation honest among gentiles, that they may by your good works, which they shall behold, glorify God," in chapter 3, "Ye wives,

[55] *Pesiqta Rabbathi* 166b.
[56] Isa 57:16; see *Pesiqta Rabbathi* 32b–33a.
[57] Ps 4:1.
[58] *b. Pes.* 119a.
[59] Matt 18:15.
[60] *y. B. M.* 8c.
[61] Matt 5:16.

be in subjection to your husbands that if any obey not the word, they may be won while they behold your chaste conversation."[62] The latter verse has κερδαίνω.

This leads to the third consideration. Nowadays we distinguish rather sharply between mission proper, the "winning over" of unbelievers, and *innere Mission*, the "winning back" of lax and sinning members of the faith. Certainly the difference existed, was seen and had practical consequences even in the earliest Rabbinic period. But when we recall, what we just adverted to, that there were various degrees of membership of faith, some in closer, some in vaguer contact with the centre; further, that there must have been a constant fluctuation between them; and that the organization of a faith was quite generally not too rigid, we shall hardly expect two separate vocabularies for the two types of mission. Even nowadays we speak of "the conversion of a sinner" as well as "the conversion of a pagan."

In other words, it is most unlikely that a writer using κερδαίνω of the "winning back of a sinner," as it is used in Matthew, would have hesitated to use it, as it is used in Paul and 1 Peter, of actual "proselytizing." Nor can we think of any reason why the Rabbis, who used *niṣkar* and *hiśtakker* of the "winning back of sinning and doomed Israelites," should have avoided the term in speaking of "missionizing" proper. However, even if we proceed from the former, narrower application, it is clear that when κερδαίνω became a missionary term in early Christianity, it was far from unsuitable. As a rendering of *niṣkar* or *hiśtakker*, it was a good choice.

In the last chapter (Missionary Maxims) we saw that the passages in the Epistles where κερδαίνω occurs in the sense of "to win over to one's faith" are altogether modelled on Jewish missionary schemes—which corroborates our thesis regarding the origin of the usage of this verb.

[62] 1 Pet 2:12, 3:1 f.

6

Concepts and Conventions

This section describes concepts and conventions found in Rabbinic sources that explain puzzling or surprising features of the New Testament.

Rabbinic Authority

It would be surprising if the question of Jesus's Rabbinic authority had played no part in the course of his activity. For, though not ordained, he certainly claimed the status of a Rabbi. As a matter of fact, the gospels record two incidents at least which must be understood against the background of this problem.

A. "A New Teaching with Authority"

Mark tells us[1] how the first time Jesus appeared in public—in the synagogue of Capernaum—the people "were astonished at this teaching, for he taught as one having authority and not as the scribes." Moreover, on the same occasion he expelled a demon from one of the persons present, and they "were amazed insomuch that they questioned among themselves, What thing is this? A new teaching with authority, and he commandeth the unclean spirits."

What is the meaning of "authority" in this pericope? Once Jesus was recognized as the Messiah, the term, when used to describe his standing, almost invariably denoted something like "divine authority" or even "almightiness." It is quite possible that Mark here employs it in this sense. His intention may be to indicate that the absolute supremacy of Jesus was acknowledged from the outset. But if this were the original point of the episode, it would strike one as a legend rather than as history.

Yet there are indications that it is in the main historical, or at any rate deriving from a sober, oral report. In the first place, the popular reaction is depicted not only in the usual, detached fashion—"they were astonished," etc.—but also by quoting a comment of the people themselves—"they said, What thing," etc. This should not lightly be treated as made up after the event. In the second place, the people "questioned," "disputed." There was no enthusiastic agreement of the kind to be expected in a legend. In the third place, there are incongruities—or apparent incongruities—which an evangelist freely composing might have avoided. The contrast between "to teach with authority" and "to teach like the scribes" is a crux up to this day: the scribes—if we identify them with the leading Rabbis of the time—were held in the highest esteem. Again, the amazement at Jesus's teaching is mentioned twice, once after the notice that he taught and another time after the expulsion of the demon. The repetition smacks of a version prior to any written source. What is particularly remarkable is that the emphatic reference to "a new teaching" follows the exorcism, not the notice that Jesus taught.

[1] Mark 1:21 ff.

We shall see below that Matthew and Luke smooth out much of this. The fact, however, that they do so in different ways confirms the superiority of Mark. His account, then, ought to be capable of being explained as the product of a very early date.

If this is correct, "authority" cannot always have signified "almightiness." The equivalent in Hebrew or Aramaic is *reshuth* or *reshutha'*, denoting *inter alia* Rabbinic authority. We may assume that, originally, "authority" had this meaning. The people were surprised that Jesus should teach like one ordained.

Two further re-interpretations now become necessary. First, the word "scribes"—*sopherim* or *saphrayya'*—in this narrative signified not the learned Rabbis but, on the contrary, the ordinary teachers without the right to proclaim decisions. It can be shown that the term was current in this sense in New Testament times. Jesus, the people noted, taught as if possessing Rabbinic authority and not like the ordinary teachers. Secondly, the expression "a new teaching with authority" is far more specific than might at first sight be supposed. It refers to the privilege, enjoyed only by a proper Rabbi, of introducing novel doctrines.

The difficulties listed above can all be solved on this basis. The text distinguishes not between "to teach with authority" and "to teach like the venerable Rabbis," but between "to teach with Rabbinic authority" and "to teach like those not ordained." Further, the association by the crowd of authoritative new teaching with power over demons becomes intelligible. A great Rabbi was expected to be prominent in both fields, or rather, the two fields were not kept strictly separate. Johanan ben Zaccai (who died about A.D. 80), a pupil of Hillel, received praise distinctly reminiscent of the passage under discussion. He was familiar, his admirers remarked, with "Scripture and Mishnah, Talmud, *halakhoth* and *haggadhoth*, the subtleties of the Torah and those of the old scholars, the inferences *a fortiori* and those from analogy (i.e. the methods by which fresh laws, new teaching, might be derived from Scripture), astronomy and geometry, the conversations of angels and those of evil spirits" and so on.[2] It should be observed that, according to Matthew and Mark,[3] when Jesus taught at Nazareth, his listeners were taken aback both by his "wisdom" and by his "powers"; and in this case too we are not simply informed that it was so—"they were taken aback"—but are given the comment they made—"they said" etc. In Acts[4] we learn that Paul brought "the word of God" to a deputy of the country. A sorcerer, who tried to turn the deputy from his faith, was punished with blindness: "then the deputy believed, being astonished at the teaching of the Lord." "The teaching of the Lord" includes both Paul's instruction and the miracle wrought or announced by him.

We can now also appreciate the "questioning" or "disputing." That a person not ordained should preach and act in the manner of one ordained must have evoked misgivings. His appearance at Capernaum would be all the more bewildering as, in that period, the general standard of learning in Galilee was low.[5]

[2] *b. Sukk.* 28a.

[3] Matt 13:54; Mark 6:2.

[4] Acts 13:6 ff.

[5] Cp. John 1:46, 7:41, 52.

To substantiate our thesis we must say a few words (1) about the institution of *reshuth*, "Rabbinic authority," in the time of Jesus; (2) about the designation of inferior teachers, as opposed to scholars, by the name of *sopherim*, "scribes"; and (3) about such concepts as "a new teaching with authority" in Tannaitic utterances.

1. *Reshuth*

First, then, for *reshuth*. While authorization apparently never required much ceremony in Babylonia, in Palestine a solemn rite used to be performed up to some date in the 3rd cent. A.D.[6] The Rabbi who conferred authority "leaned"—*samakh*—his hands on the candidate's head. Palestinian ordination was therefore *semikha*, "a leaning on." The master communicated his personality, his status, to the disciple, who thus became a Rabbi with *reshuth*, "authority," himself: henceforth he shared in that wisdom and power which, as was believed, ultimately descended from Moses.

For the Tannaites, Joshua's installation by Moses was the prototype of ordination, and since then each generation of spiritual leaders had been linked to the preceding one by the same mode. We read in the Bible that Moses "leaned" his hands on Joshua, in order to bestow on him part of his glory. The Midrash explains that Joshua was thereby permitted to enunciate teachings, deliver judgments and sit on a special chair like Moses—obviously the privileges resulting from ordination in New Testament times. References to "sitting on Moses's chair" occur in the New Testament as well as in Rabbinic writings;[7] and the continuity of tradition from Moses down to the Tannaitic age is stressed in the opening paragraph of the Sayings of the Fathers, "Moses received the Law from Sinai and committed it to Joshua, and Joshua to the Elders, and the Elders to the Prophets," etc.[8] Incidentally, so long as an uninterrupted transfer of authority was assumed, this in itself would imply the possibility of a Rabbi being not only an inspired interpreter of the Law, but also something of a prophet and miracle-worker. We have already pointed out that in the period of Jesus these components of Rabbinic authority were not yet quite suppressed.

Semikha was designed to communicate Rabbinic authority, *reshuth*, and in principle it was the only means of communicating it. Once the chain was allowed to break, there would never be authority in the full sense—unless God restored it in some exceptional way. Hence the enormous importance attributed in the Talmud to a step taken by Judah ben Baba (who died about A.D. 135).[9] He was the only Rabbi to survive the Hadrianic war, and Hadrian had prohibited any further ordinations. In defiance of this decree Judah ordained several pupils of Akiba: the latter was already dead. The Romans slew him for his offence, but the traditional authority lived on—for a time.

In the New Testament epoch, any man who was authorized himself, and only a man who was authorized himself, could authorize others.[10] Johanan ben Zaccai, for instance,

[6] *Siphre* on Num 27:18 ff.

[7] Matt 23:2, *P. de R. K.* 7b (Pisqa 1 on Num 7:2 f. and 1 Kgs 10:19).

[8] *m. Ab.* 1:1.

[9] *b. Sanh.* 13b f.

[10] *y. Sanh.* 19a.

ordained Eliezer ben Hyrcanus and Joshua ben Hananiah. We have just adverted to the ordination by Judah ben Baba of some of Akiba's pupils. *Semikha* meant the pouring of one man's wisdom and powers into another man. In a way, the man receiving authority became a new being: some Tannaites contend[11] that sins committed prior to ordination are forgiven, like sins committed prior to election as King or Patriarch, to marriage or to conversion to Judaism. Admittedly, there may be an element of hyperbole in such statements; nor is it certain that they were universally approved. Nevertheless they do shed light on the character of *semikha*.

In the latter half of the 2nd cent. A.D. the right to ordain became the exclusive right of the Patriarch and his court, largely for the sake of greater uniformity of doctrine. But the "leaning on" now lost most of its original significance. Instead of being a conveyance of the master's personality to his disciple, it was no more than a formal appointment. Still, even in later times, when the "leaning on" was entirely dispensed with, scholars valued their "pedigree" and on occasion based far-reaching claims on it. Rabbah bar Rab Huna (at the beginning of the 4th cent. A.D.) maintained[12] that, though living in Babylonia, he was not compelled to accept the views of the Exilarch, his authority having originated in Palestine: "I obtained *reshutha'* from my father, he from Rab, Rab from R. Hiyya and R. Hiyya from R. Judah the Prince."

In the time of Jesus, if we disregard the sacrificial cult and the case of a criminal to be stoned on whose head witnesses and judges must "lean" their hands, the rite *semikha*, "leaning on," was confined to the grant of complete Rabbinic authority. It was not used for appointing minor officials or representatives. It was too sacred for that, its supernatural effects too weighty. The early Church took over the Jewish application of *semikha*: a bishop might ordain his successor in this manner.[13] However, the first Christians, convinced of a renewal of immediate, divine guidance in all affairs pertaining to their community, boldly extended the scope of the ceremony. A "leaning on" of hands, in order to transfer one's qualities, took place not only where a Rabbi—or bishop—ordained his disciple, but also where the religious leaders wished to consecrate some of their number as special missionaries, where a congregation chose a few men to be distributors of charity, or where an apostle imparted the Holy Ghost. We shall discuss these cases in the next chapter (on The Laying on of Hands). In Judaism, it was not till after A.D. 200 that *semikha* might serve to give limited, well-defined rights as distinct from full Rabbinic authority.[14] But the reason for this development, far from being a religious revival, was the change in the nature of *semikha* mentioned above: it no longer signified one man's pouring his personality into another, it was simply a form of appointment.

How much authority, *reshuth*, meant in Jesus's time and for the next hundred years or so may be gathered from the existence of those numerous parties and schools—the Pharisees, the Sadducees, the Essenes, the Hillelites, the Shammaites, the Schools of

[11] *y. Bikk.* 65c.

[12] *b. Sanh.* 5a.

[13] 1 Tim 4:14, 5:22; 2 Tim 1:6.

[14] For examples, see Strack-Billerbeck, vol. 2 (1924), 656 f.

Akiba, Ishmael, Tarphon and so forth. They would have been impossible but for an extraordinary degree of independence on the part of each Rabbi. In fact, the further back we go in Talmudic history, the freer we find the Rabbis in their approach to the Law. Uniformity came by very gradual steps. It is revealing that the earlier of the ordained Tannaites often dealt with major cases only, whilst minor ones were submitted to their disciples. But under Judah the Prince (about A.D. 200) it was laid down[15] that even minor cases might be settled by a person not yet authorized only if he had received special permission from his Rabbi. A master who refused to concern himself with petty questions was no longer tolerated; and teaching of any sort must be under central control. There is no doubt that the standing of a man with "authority" in the New Testament era was incomparably higher than that of such a man three or four centuries later.

2. *Scribes*

We must now consider the term "scribes." It is true that in the New Testament it normally denotes "the learned theologians," as it often does in Rabbinic sources. But there are other meanings. Let us remember, above all, that in general the application just mentioned is far commoner in the last five centuries B.C.—the best-known example being "Ezra the Scribe"—than later, when appellations such as *ḥakham*, "Sage," *zaqen*, "Elder," *mumḥe*, "Expert," are preferred.[16] From the 1st cent. A.D., in Talmudic literature, "scribe," *sopher*, frequently distinguishes "the Rabbi of the olden time" from contemporary Rabbis. We may recall the eulogy, quoted above, on Johanan ben Zaccai, who "was familiar with the subtleties of the old scholars": the Hebrew for "old scholars" is *sopherim*. Actually, the New Testament is the latest work extant in which "scribe" regularly means "a learned man." Even here one passage is to be found[17] where it means "a keeper of records," "a town-clerk." Philo and Josephus both employ it almost exclusively in the sense of "copyist," "keeper of records." In the Mishnah also it may signify "a writer of documents,"[18] and a post-Talmudic tractate is entitled "Tractate for *sopherim*," since it states the rules for "copyists," *scil.* of the Scriptures.

It follows that, when translating γραμματεύς or *sopher*, we can arrive at the exact nuance only by an examination of the context. Now in addition to the meanings enumerated, *sopher* has yet another, namely, that of "elementary teacher" or "Bible teacher" in contradistinction to the superior Rabbi. It is this meaning which γραμματεύς must originally have had in the narrative discussed. The "scribes" are here manifestly opposed, and considered inferior, to those having "authority." The teaching with "authority" is something exceptional and exciting; it is, as the Galilean crowd remarks, quite unlike the everyday instruction of the "scribes," the "elementary teachers"—of whom there were certainly more than enough in any Palestinian village.

Examples of this use of "scribe" in Tannaitic utterances abound, and not a few are

[15] *b. Sanh.* 5b.

[16] See J. Jeremias, γραμματεύς, in *Theologisches Wörterbuch zum Neuen Testament*, ed. by G. Kittel, vol. 1, 740 ff.

[17] Acts 19:35.

[18] *m. Gitt.* 8:8.

very early. A *sopher*, "Bible teacher," we learn,[19] may explain in his simple, ordinary way even those portions—as, for instance, the priestly blessing and the story of David and Bathsheba[20]—which as a rule must be left untranslated. The pair *sopherim umashnim* is constantly to be met with: the *sopherim*, "scribes," merely teach the Bible while the *mashnim* are expounders of the Mishnah. In a conversation in the house of R. Tarphon (about A.D. 100) the question was asked[21] to what kind of people the Psalmist referred in the verse,[22] "Blessed is he that doeth righteousness at all times"; and the answer was that he referred not to "the Bible teachers and Mishnah teachers" but to those adopting an orphan as Mordecai had done. An Amoraic dictum[23] brings out well the difference between *sopherim* and *mashnim*: R. Asi and R. Ammi (about A.D. 300) declare them to be the best watchmen of a town because they recite (the *sopherim*) and expound (the *mashnim*) and thus guard the Torah day and night.

A lament—in Aramaic—of Eliezer ben Hyrcanus (about A.D. 90) contains precisely the antithesis which, if we are right, was the original point of Mark's narrative.[24] As stated above, a proper Rabbi is often described as *ḥakham*, "a Sage." In commenting on the election of seventy elders recorded in Numbers, the Midrash enumerates the qualities a man must have to be made a *ḥakham*, i.e. to be ordained;[25] similarly, *ḥakham* occurs in that passage which refers to atonement through ordination. With these *ḥakhamim*, "the Sages," "the proper Rabbis," we find the *sopherim*, "the teachers of lower standing," contrasted on many occasions. It may suffice to quote Eliezer's saying that since the destruction of the Temple the *ḥakkimayya'*, "the Sages," have become mere *saphrayya'*, "scribes," "inferior teachers." The ordained Rabbis, that is, are now of the standard previously attained by the mass of ordinary teachers, "scribes." He concludes by asking, "On whom can we now rely?"; which means that nobody now is really able to apply and develop the Law and do the great things that the scholars used to do in former times. Clearly, here lies the clue to an understanding of the assertion that "Jesus taught as having authority, and not like the scribes."

3. *"A new teaching with authority"*

As regards a "new teaching with authority," this may mean a new rule, *halakha ḥadhasha* or *halakha 'aḥereth*, which only an ordained Rabbi was entitled to lay down.

Rengstorf[26] says that διδαχή is always synonymous with *talmudh*. This is an oversimplification. No doubt it often does correspond to *talmudh*. It unquestionably does so in certain sayings[27] derived from Isaiah 29:13, "taught (*melummadha*) by the precept of men." It may do so even in the Markan pericope with which we are concerned, and we

[19] *t. Meg.* 4:41.
[20] Num 6:23 ff., 2 Sam 11.
[21] *Esth. Rab.* on 2:4.
[22] Ps 106:3.
[23] *Lam. Rab.*, Introduction, 2.
[24] *m. Sot.* 9:15.
[25] *Siphre* on Num 11:16.
[26] *S.v.* διδαχή in *Theologisches Wörterbuch zum Neuen Testament*, ed. G. Kittel, vol. 2, 166.
[27] Matt 15:9; Mark 7:7; Col 2:22.

shall presently consider this possibility. But it is no more than a possibility; and there are many cases where διδαχή definitely reflects some other Hebrew or Aramaic term. In the LXX, διδάσκω stands not only for *limmedh* but also for *hora* and *'illeph*.

Jesus did deliver decisions classifiable as "new rules," "new *halakhoth*," as when he defended his disciples who had plucked corn on a Sabbath. Even the type of argument he used—from a precedent set by David—is by no means foreign to the Talmud (though we have tried to demonstrate, in Precept and Example [249 ff.], that just about that time it gradually ceased to be treated as conclusive). The concept "a new rule" occurs in a legend concerning Ruth.[28] Ruth is here identified with a woman of the name of Hodesh who appears in 1 Chronicles.[29] Hodesh is connected with *ḥadhash*, "new." It was Ruth's cognomen, we are told, because by her marriage with Boaz she created a new rule, or, more literally, "the *halakha* was renewed." According to a law in Deuteronomy[30] no Moabite may be received as a member of the community. Ruth, however, realized that this excluded Moabite men only, but not Moabite women. In this legend, Ruth figures as endowed with prophetic and Rabbinic vision, whereas Boaz is "dumb respecting the words of the Torah."[31]

If the phrase "a new teaching" refers to Jesus's *halakhic* activity, it may also stand for *horaya ḥadhasha*. *Halakha* and *horaya* are often synonymous. But the former is derived from *halakh*, "to walk," and essentially means the proper way to take in life; it is therefore mostly used of a general rule covering a set of facts wherever and whenever they may present themselves, or even of the entire system of law worked out by the Rabbis. The latter derived from *hora*, "to guide," "to instruct," and is mostly used of a decision regarding only a particular case. The difference comes out in a provision to the effect that the pronouncement of a disciple not yet ordained is not a true *horaya*, "decision," "teaching," even if in perfect agreement with the *halakha*, "the recognized rule."[32] Strictly, Jesus's opinion when his disciples had plucked corn was of the nature of a *horaya*, concerning a particular case, while his opinion in the matter of healing on a Sabbath was more like a *halakha*, a general rule. However, just as *halakha* sometimes denotes a decision about a specific case, so *horaya* sometimes denotes the Law as a whole. (The place where Abraham was tested is called "Moriah," a commentator says,[33] because from there the *horaya*, "the Law," took its rise.) At any rate, it is quite conceivable that the people in Mark wondered at Jesus's delivering "a new *horaya* to all appearances founded on authority."

On the whole, it seems more likely that "a new teaching" in this narrative has a wider sense, comprising Jesus's views about faith, ethics, the right mode of living and so on as well as about *halakhic*, i.e. legal or ritual questions. Matthew, we shall see, places the reference to his teaching with authority after the sermon on the mount,[34]

[28] *y. Yeb.* 9c.

[29] 1 Chron 8:9.

[30] Deut 23:4.

[31] A pun on *'almoni*, "such a one," in Ruth 4:1—*'illem* signifying "dumb."

[32] *y. Shebi.* 36c.

[33] *Gen. Rab.* on 22:2.

[34] Matt 7:29.

which is anything but restricted to *halakhoth* and *horayoth*. On this basis, the underlying Hebrew or Aramaic might be *tora ḥadhasha ('aḥereth)*, *'ulephan ḥadhath ('aḥaraya')*, *'orayetha' ḥadhatta' ('aḥaritti)*, *dath ḥadhasha ('aḥereth)*, or *talmudh ḥadhash ('aḥer)*. With the exception of *dath*, the nouns are all connected with roots signifying "to teach."

Tora ḥadhasha, "a new Law"—equated by the Rabbis with *ḥiddush tora*, "a renewal of the Law"—and *'ulephan ḥadhath*, meaning much the same, have come down to us only in references to the Messianic age. Isaiah's promise "Ye shall draw water out of the wells of salvation" is rendered by the Targum as: "Ye shall receive a new Law from those chosen in righteousness."[35] The Leviathan, an Amoraic scholar affirms, will not need to be slaughtered in the ritual fashion for the Messianic feast, because "a new Law" will reign.[36] One might perhaps incline to conclude that, before Jesus was acknowledged as the Messiah, "a new Law" could not be ascribed to him. But it looks as if, in the Tannaitic era, the expressions under notice had been used far more loosely than the extant applications would suggest. We find the Tannaites complaining of the fact that owing to the arrogance of some followers of Hillel and Shammai, the original Torah has become *kishete toroth*, "like two Torahs."[37] Evidently, "Torah" did not necessarily signify the unique ideal Law of God, it might signify the Law as understood by a particular group. Jesus's audience, then, may well have exclaimed that he was adding another Torah, propounding a new kind of understanding the Law.

Frequently, *'orayetha'* is indistinguishable from *tora*, "the Law." In the famous consultation of a Christian philosopher by the wife of Eliezer ben Hyrcanus (about A.D. 90), "the Law of Moses" is opposed to the Gospel, *'orayetha' 'aḥaritti*, "another Law."[38] (There are, it is true, variant readings like *'awen gillayon*, "falsehood of blank paper"—a pun on εὐαγγέλιον—which may be older.) That *'orayetha'* need not always denote the Law of Moses is clear also from the Aramaic translation of Psalm 144.[39] The clause "Their right hand is a hand of falsehood" appears in the Targum as "Their Law—*scil.* the Law of the gentile nations—it is a false Law." Moreover, *'orayetha'* may mean a teaching in the sense of "interpretation of the Law" or "interpretation of a portion of the Law"; and a scholar may be expected to bring with him *'oraya' ḥadhatta'*, "a novel inter-pretation."[40] Accordingly, it may be *'orayetha' ḥadhatta'* or *'aḥaritti* which underlies "a new teaching" in Mark.

Dath ḥadhasha or *'aḥereth* is a remote possibility. The Rabbis distinguish between "the Law of Moses," ordinances found in or inferred from Scripture, and "the Jewish Law," customs observed because of the special decency and piety required of Jews—for example, that a woman should not have her head uncovered.[41] *Dath* may even approach the sense of "religion": *hemir dath* means "to change the religion," "to

[35] Isa 12:3: *'ulephan ḥadhath*.

[36] *Lev. Rab.* on 11:1: *tora ḥadhasha*.

[37] *t. Sot.* 14:9.

[38] *b. Shab.* 116b.

[39] Ps 144:8, 11.

[40] *y. Shek.* 47c.

[41] *m. Ket.* 7:6; cp. 1 Cor 11:5.

become an apostate."[42] *Dath ḥadhasha*, therefore, might be used of a new doctrine embracing not only legal matters but all conduct. So, finally, might *talmudh ḥadhash*. *Talmudh* might signify an opinion about a particular point, *halakhic* or other (we hear of "a firm opinion expressed by R. Johanan"—who lived in the 3rd cent. A.D.);[43] or the entire teaching or knowledge of a man (Judah ben Elai, about A.D. 150, holds that you are the disciple of him from whom you have acquired "the greater part of your knowledge");[44] or that branch of scholarship which consists in the deduction of rules—usually *halakhic* ones—from other rules already established (Johanan ben Zaccai, we saw, was famous for his mastery of "Scripture, Mishnah, Talmud" and so on).[45]

While it would be rash to reconstruct the exact Hebrew or Aramaic behind the Greek, it is safe to say that the concept we find in Mark, "a new teaching with authority," would naturally occur to a Jewish audience in Jesus's age.

When we turn to the other Synoptics, we find in Luke[46] a pericope parallel to Mark's. Of the differences, the following ones are here relevant. First, the contrast between "to teach with authority" and "to teach like the scribes" does not recur in Luke. The people "were astonished at his teaching, for his word was with authority." Mark's more difficult version is plainly older. It is interesting that Luke shows himself aware of the unsoundness of opposing a "teaching with authority" to a "teaching like the leading scholars." We have submitted "scribes" in this narrative originally referred to unordained, lesser instructors. Secondly, the somewhat technical expression "a teaching with authority" is avoided. Thus a further trace of the original point of the incident had disappeared. In fact, if it were not for Mark, we might no longer guess that at one time it had to do with the problem of Jesus's Rabbinic authority. Thirdly, there is no "questioning" or "disputing." The people "spake among themselves." Jesus, that is, earns nothing but applause: the problem of Rabbinic authority does not come in.

What Luke has not entirely abandoned is the mixing up of teaching and miracle-working. Having witnessed the expulsion of the demon, the people "spake, What a word is this? for with authority and power he commandeth the unclean spirits." This may be more ambiguous than Mark, where the people exclaim "A new teaching, and he commandeth." But the introduction of the term "word," used a few verses before of Jesus's teaching, still links the two kinds of authoritative activity. (At Emmaus the disciples speak of Jesus as having been "mighty in deed and word";[47] and the opening verse of Acts refers to "the former treatise of all that Jesus began both to do and teach.")

No analogous section occurs in Matthew. He does, however, find a place for the notice that the people "were astonished at his teaching, for he taught as one having authority and not as the scribes." Only he puts it after the sermon on the mount.[48] Teaching and exorcism are not combined, the teaching stands by itself; and, as in Luke,

[42] *b. Sukk.* 56b; *b. Pes.* 96a.
[43] *b. Shebi.* 40b.
[44] *t. B. M.* 2:30.
[45] *b. Sukk.* 28a.
[46] Luke 4:31 ff.
[47] Luke 24:19.
[48] Matt 7:28 f.

no mention is made either of "a new teaching"—Matthew may have a special motive for omitting the phrase in a context where he draws attention to the upholding of the Law by Jesus—or of any "questioning," "disputing." There are indeed other passages in Matthew, Luke and John where the people are represented as taken aback by Jesus's teaching alone.[49] But as far as his activity at Capernaum is concerned, the earliest version indubitably placed equal emphasis on teaching and power over demons.

This is not to claim that the whole of Mark's narrative must go back to a pre-literary stratum. The final remark—that Jesus's fame spread[50]—may well have been added when the story was given its definite shape within a larger work. There may, of course, be other modifications. Still, the upshot seems to be that, according to the oral tradition, Jesus's lack of Rabbinic authority became an issue from the moment he commenced his task.

B. "By What Authority Doest Thou These Things?"

Presumably Jesus's disciples from the beginning considered his authority to be unique, not inferior but superior to that conferred by the usual ordination. Jesus himself also must have shared this feeling. But his antagonists would not. The clash between their view that, to do the things he did, he ought to have Rabbinic authority of the recognized type and the belief of Jesus and his circle that he possessed all the authority of a Rabbi and more is preserved in a report of his questioning by Jewish officials towards the end of his activity. This report, substantially the same in the three Synoptics,[51] is all the more interesting as we may see from it how easily, according to a person's assessment of Jesus's position, the notion of "Rabbinic authority" might pass into that of "divine authority" or "almightiness."

Jesus, we learn, was asked: "By what authority doest thou these things? and who gave thee this authority?" Whatever incident may have been the immediate occasion of the attack—and we shall go into this problem below—the cause was that Jesus acted like a Rabbi without being ordained. In fact, if there should be any doubts, this pericope proves that neither Jesus nor the Baptist was ever technically ordained. In the passage just cited "authority" can mean only *reshuth* in the sense of Rabbinic authority. Jesus is requested to produce his license. In New Testament times any Rabbi was entitled to create other Rabbis. Hence the general and somewhat rhetorical question, "By what authority doest thou these things?" is followed by the specific one: "Who gave thee this authority?" He ought to name the Rabbi from whom he derives his status.

It is equally clear that in the proud answer, "Neither tell I you by what authority I do these things," *reshuth*, "authority," acquires a very different sense. Here it alludes to a supreme title far above the common Rabbinic one. We need only consider that, before ending the dispute in this way, Jesus embarrasses his adversaries by the mention of the Baptist, whom "all counted that he was a prophet"—a prophet, not just a Rabbi. If, as is probable, the major part of the pericope comes from the oral tradition—indeed,

[49] Matt 22:33; Luke 4:22; John 7:15.

[50] Mark 1:28; Luke 4:37; it is taken over also by Matthew, in 4:24.

[51] Matt 21:23 ff.; Mark 11:27 ff.; Luke 20:1 ff.

there is no reason to doubt its historicity—then this may be the earliest instance of "authority," *reshuth*, referring to Jesus's "divine authority" or "almightiness." In the narrative concerning his appearance at Capernaum, we saw, the term originally meant no more than "Rabbinic authority." In other words, it is possible that the entire use of it to denote something like "almightiness" has its root in the reply given by Jesus to the officials.

To understand why *reshuth* might so readily shade off from one meaning into the other, we must bear in mind that the word often refers to the domain of God or even to God himself. When Elisha ben Abuya (about A.D. 100), the great heretic, saw the chief angel Metatron, he thought: "Perhaps there are two *reshuyoth*, governments of the universe."[52] R. Isaac (in the second half of the 3rd cent. A.D.) explains[53] that the apparent plural word *'elohim*, "God," is construed with the singular—"God creates," not "create"—in order to refute dualism and make it quite clear that the world is not due to "two governments." Sometimes the distinction is made between the fallible "earthly government," *reshuth shel maṭṭan*, and the infallible "heavenly government," *reshuth shel ma'alan*.[54]

After all, Rabbinic authority and divine right have an essential feature in common: legitimacy. The Greek in the narrative about the reception at Capernaum as well as in that about the interrogation by the officials has ἐξουσία. In Hellenistic literature, words like κράτος, ἰσχύς, δύναμις usually mean "strength," "control," "ascendancy," "power," irrespective of the legal or moral side of the matter, that is to say, whether the power in question is justifiable or not. It is the fact that ἐξουσία signifies power lawfully exercised within an organized community which made the term specially suitable for describing both Rabbinic authority and the superior mandate of Jesus. (Foerster[55] draws attention to another pericope,[56] where the enemies of Jesus exclaim: "Who is capable, δύναται, of forgiving sins but God?" Jesus in reply does not use the same term: he says that "the Son of Man has authority, is entitled, ἐξουσίαν ἔχει, to forgive sins.") Roughly, it may be said that the concept of Jesus's ἐξουσία always, or for a long time at least, remained in touch with *reshuth* as Rabbinic authority; only that through his mighty works and Messianic message it also implied a higher title, namely *reshuth* as supreme government or sphere of God.

A further point is of importance. We have already adduced the opening lines of the Sayings of the Fathers: "Moses received the Law from Sinai and committed it to Joshua and Joshua to the Elders and the Elders to the Prophets" etc. This refers not only to the instruction but also to the authorization of each generation of leaders by the preceding one. The first ordination, in the eyes of the Tannaites, had been that of Joshua; and since then there had been no break in the passing on of authority. However, Moses himself had, of course, not been ordained. He had received the Law—and his authority—"from

[52] *y. Hag.* 15a.
[53] *Gen. Rab.* on 1:1.
[54] *y. Sanh.* 23d f.
[55] *S.v.* ἔξεστιν in *Theologisches Wörterbuch*, vol. 2, 563 ff.
[56] Mark 2:7, 10; Luke 5:21, 24.

Sinai," a circumlocation meaning "from God (at Sinai)." When Jesus claimed, in scarcely veiled language, that his authority, like John's baptism, was "from heaven," another circumlocation meaning "from God (in heaven)," he was applying to himself a doctrine which all Jews admitted at least in the case of Moses, and many no doubt in the case of a few other prophets too, namely, that, in very exceptional circumstances, authority could originate even in the absence of ordination, directly from God.

It is obvious that the aim of Jesus's questioners was not, as is widely believed,[57] to convict him of being "an Elder that rebels against the court." That would have presupposed recognition of his Rabbinic authority, the very thing they were determined to refuse. The Mishnah provides that not even the disciple of an Elder is liable to this charge, since he is not yet ordained.[58] The aim of Jesus's questioners must have been to convict him of teaching without any justification or, possibly, of being a false prophet.

A strange opinion held by some modern authorities is that the form of the narrative as it stands is not Jewish-Rabbinic. The counter-question by Jesus, it is claimed, must originally have been the end, the rest being secondary.[59] But this is certainly not correct. In the chapter on Socratic Interrogation (315 ff.) we observed that the Tannaites were perfectly familiar with the form (1) hostile question, (2) counter-question, (3) answer by which the enemy becomes vulnerable, (4) refutation stated by way of inference from the answer. The form is evidenced from the 1st cent. A.D. onwards. Nor is this the only pericope in the New Testament where it is used. Admittedly, the narrative before us may contain a few additions and modifications as compared with its oral predecessor. As far as form is concerned, for example, the "reasoning among themselves" of the enemies is not an essential part. But the main structure must have constituted a unit from the outset.

The same critics maintain that the intervention of the officials could not, as Mark appears to assume, have been produced by the cleansing of the Temple: the latter, they think, was not an appropriate occasion for a debate concerning Jesus's authority. But it was. Its importance lay not in the breach of peace. If, for example, some ruffians had driven out the merchants and upset the tables, it would have been an ordinary row: nobody would have dreamt of asking them by what authority they had proceeded. It was the deeper meaning of the action that put it on a different level. Nor does it matter whether Jesus condemned a specific abuse of the Temple only (so that we might speak of a *halakha* in the narrower sense) or at the same time the whole mistaken attitude behind it (so that he would proclaim a *halakha* in the wider sense or even a *tora*). Mark informs us expressly not only that Jesus accompanied his action by teaching, but also that it was the teaching implied in and accompanying the action which astonished the crowd; it was not the external disturbance as such.

[57] Strack-Billerbeck, vol. 1 (1922), 860 ff., E. Klostermann, *Das Markusevangelium*, 4th ed. (1950), 119.

[58] *m. Sanh.* 11:2.

[59] Bultmann seems to be responsible for this proposition. J. M. Creed, in *The Gospel according to St. Luke* (1930), 244, accepts the premise (that the form is not Jewish-Rabbinic) though he is not convinced of the conclusion (that the counter-question was the original ending). E. Klostermann, *op. cit.*, 119, is equally undecided.

In fact, the succession of ideas is closely analogous to that in the narrative about his first appearance at Capernaum; there is even verbal similarity. At Capernaum, the people were amazed by Jesus's teaching and wondered on what authority it might rest. In Jerusalem, the people were amazed by his teaching and the administration inquired on what authority it rested. Moreover, we saw that at Capernaum also the teaching is intimately associated with an action, though of a slightly different kind—the expulsion of a demon.

That the controversy was brought about by something more than mere teaching is suggested by the question itself: "By what authority doest (ποιεῖς) thou these things?" Certainly it is not impossible for a phrase like "thou doest these things" to refer to teaching and nothing else; the scope of the verb "to do" is almost unlimited. But in Hebrew and Aramaic as well as Greek and English it would as a rule be used of undertakings not purely academic.

The question, it may be noted, recurs in Matthew and Luke, though both clearly consider it as having regard to teaching only and divorce it from the cleansing of the Temple. But in Matthew, this treatment strikes one as artificial. "And when he was come into the temple, the chief priests came unto him, who was teaching, and said" etc. The word διδάσκοντι, "who was teaching," looks as if deliberately inserted by the evangelist in order to represent this activity as the immediate reason of the interrogation. Luke is far smoother. "And on one of those days, as he taught in the temple and preached the gospel, the chief priests spake unto him." On the whole, Mark, with that mixing up of a purposeful action and teaching which would characterize a great Rabbi or a prophet, seems superior to Matthew and Luke.

Finally a word about John. There is no official inquiry into Jesus's Rabbinic authority, *reshuth*. Nevertheless we find an incident corresponding to it,[60] where the Jews—the ordinary people, not the authorities—ask: "What sign shewest thou unto us, that thou doest these things?"

Various points are of interest. First, as in Mark, it is the cleansing of the Temple which leads to a demand for credentials. This strongly supports Mark over against Matthew and Luke. Secondly, the people want a sign, not any proof of ordination. Rabbinic authority of the normal type does not matter; the doubt is whether Jesus can give evidence of a special, divine call as a prophet or the Messiah. Thirdly, it is in consequence of this different approach that any express mention of teaching is dropped. Jesus through his action purports to bring about the Messianic era. Hence the question does not concern his teaching and his authorization to propound it, but his action and his mission to perform it.

However, we must not establish too sharp a contrast between John and the Synoptics. To begin with, in New Testament times, as pointed out above, Rabbinic authority still included a prophetic element; and the greater a Rabbi, the more boldly he would not only teach but also act. Even in the Synoptics the question put to Jesus has regard to "doing": "By what authority doest thou these things?" It is significant that there was no need for John to alter the part about "doing these things." In fact it would

[60] John 2:18 ff.

be quite feasible to uphold the historicity of both the Synoptics and John, by supposing that while the former concentrate on the reaction of the authorities (if you are not ordained, either your doctrines and actions are ridiculous or you may be a false prophet), John concentrates on that of a section of the common folk—those half-convinced of the uniqueness of these events (if you show us a sign, we shall acknowledge you as a prophet or the Messiah). This is not to minimize the difference between the theological preoccupations of the Synoptics and of John; it is only to warn against exaggerating them.

Let us also note that distinct adumbrations of the Johannine standpoint may be found in the Synoptics. We have already seen that in all three the term "authority," as used in Jesus's reply, means much more than a technical Rabbinic privilege. It means a higher mandate and indeed something like almightiness. Jesus invokes the precedent of the Baptist, whom "they counted that he was a prophet." Moreover, in Matthew and Luke—though not in Mark—the pronouncement by which Jesus accompanies the cleansing is not called "a teaching." This brings them nearer to John. The pronouncement becomes a more integral part of the cleansing, the emphasis lies on the prophetic action which consists in cleansing plus pronouncement. Again, in Matthew—though not in Mark and Luke—the cleansing is followed by miraculous cures and the shout of the children, "Hosanna to the son of David"—a Messianic acclamation.

The cures referred to by Matthew in this chapter deserve special attention. According to John, the people after the cleansing of the Temple required a sign. Miraculous cures would be a sign. True, Matthew, at first sight, stands alone among the Synoptics. But, for one thing, at Capernaum, Mark and Luke connect what might be regarded as a sign—the expulsion of an evil spirit—with authoritative teaching. For another, the cleansing of the Temple and some sign go together not only in Matthew but also in Mark: both of them place the story of the blasting of a fig-tree next to that of the cleansing. Actually, in Mark, the cursing of the tree immediately precedes the cleansing and the effect of the curse immediately follows it. This combination of the two stories is so strange that we ought probably to attribute it to an early, oral version. (It is absent from Luke, who may well have found it intolerable.) The original idea seems to have been essentially similar to John's: Jesus must show a sign and does so.

To sum up, the story of how the authorities called Jesus to account because he was not ordained and how he and his circle relied on a higher title certainly belongs to a very early stratum; and it may well be right to assign to the same stratum the report that it was the cleansing of the Temple which occasioned the official inquiry as well as demands for a sign. We may add that these matters would be of practical interest precisely among the first Christians. It was not only Jesus (and the Baptist) who had not been ordained—that was a difficult enough problem—but the same was true of his immediate disciples. Jesus's followers did perform *semikha*, "a leaning on," the apostles did, the bishops did. But, as far as we can judge, Jesus himself did not. His immediate disciples were called in a different way. Which made it all the more important for the early Church to be assured that full authority to teach and act might be conveyed without the traditional rite.

The Laying on of Hands

A. The Old Testament

There is a widespread confusion regarding this matter. Robertson Smith says[1] that only in the case of the scapegoat was the laying on of hands interpreted as a transfer of the sins of the people.[2] By contrast, in the case of ordinary burnt-offerings and sin-offerings, no such transfer was thought of. Here, he maintains, the idea was the same as in acts of blessing and consecration,[3] namely, a general identification, by means of physical contact, of the person imposing his hands with the person or animal on whose head he imposed them. Other writers[4] agree that, on the whole, there was no difference in respect of the imposition of hands between an offering, a blessing and a consecration.

The weakness of this view is that it throws together ceremonies described in Hebrew by different terms signifying different things. Where an offering or a consecration is concerned, the texts invariably employ *samakh*, "to lean one's hands upon somebody or something"; but where a blessing is concerned, the verbs used are *śim* or *shith*, "to place one's hands." Unfortunately the LXX translates both *samakh* and *śim* by ἐπιτίθημι and *shith* by ἐπιβάλλω; and in English we do not distinguish at all, speaking indiscriminately of a laying on, putting on or imposition of hands no matter which of the three Hebrew verbs is in question. No doubt the reason why the LXX did not render *samakh* literally, i.e. by ἐρείδω, was that the rite of leaning one's hands upon a being would have struck a Hellenistic public as very outlandish. It is *au fond* the same reason which accounts for our refusal to translate the verb by "to lean." However, if we wish to establish the original nature of the various ceremonies, we must surely pay attention to the technical vocabulary of the Hebrew sources.

Let us begin by a summary comparison of *samakh*, "to lean," and *śim* or *shith*, "to place." The latter two verbs, incidentally, may be treated as synonymous in this connection. Jacob, on his death-bed,[5] "laid his right hand upon Ephraim's head," *shith*, whereupon Joseph told him: "This—Manasseh—is the firstborn; put thy right hand upon his head," *śim*. We have, then, *samakh* on the one side and *śim* and *shith* on the other.

Samakh signifies "to lean." A person who is exhausted, for example, may "lean his hands upon the wall."[6] The rite of "leaning one's hands upon somebody or something"

[1] *Religion of the Semites* (1889), 401 f., taken over without substantial changes by S. A. Cook, in the 3rd ed. of 1927, 422 f.

[2] Lev 16:21.

[3] Gen 48:14; Num 8:10; Deut 34:9.

[4] E.g. M. Grunwald, art. "Hand," in *Jewish Encyclopedia*, 6 (1904), 211 f.

[5] Gen 48:14 ff.

[6] Amos 5:19.

involves the exercise of some force, and the force is concentrated at the base of the hand, near the joint. The attitude is familiar to travellers trying to close trunks into which they have packed too much. (A similar analogy occurred to the Rabbis.[7]) It is not the typical attitude of one pronouncing a blessing. What may have been the import of the ceremony in Old Testament times? In all probability, by leaning your hands upon somebody or something, by pressing in this way upon a person or animal, you were pouring your personality into him or it (the simile of pouring also may be found in Rabbinic literature[8]); or in other words, you were making him or it into your substitute.

Śim or *shith*, on the other hand, signifies "to place." The verbs have a far wider range, are far less specific, than *samakh*. The rite of "placing one's hands upon somebody" will as a rule be of a gentler character than the rite of *samakh*. Vigorous pressure is not essential. Possibly there are occasions when it is enough to use the fingers. The main element of the ceremony is the touch. The idea no doubt was that, by placing your hands on a person, some magic attaching to them took effect upon him. At a later stage, maybe your hands were conceived of as transmitting an influence from above, one might almost say, like conductors.

So far we have argued more or less in the abstract. We must now test the result by inspecting the several applications of the terms under discussion in the Old Testament.

Samakh occurs some twenty times in the sense of "to lean one's hands on an animal to be sacrificed." With regard to the scapegoat, the context[9] makes it obvious that the ceremony meant loading it with the sins of the people: "And Aaron shall lean both his hands upon the head of the goat and confess over him all the iniquities of the children of Israel and put them upon the head of the goat." This is quite consistent with the basic idea of the rite here postulated—pouring your personality into the animal.

We must remember that in any religion, but particularly in an ancient one, an idea of this kind is capable of a good deal of adaptation to varying circumstances. In the case of the scapegoat, the sins of the people, their undesirable attributes, were transferred; the people *qua* sinners were replaced by the animal. The same clearly happened, say, when King Hezekiah abolished the idolatrous institutions of his father and when he and the congregation pressed their hands on the seven goats brought as a sin-offering.[10] But this does not exclude the possibility that, in other cases, the positive, beneficial qualities of a person were passed on. This aspect would predominate, for instance, where men leaned their hands on a peace-offering which symbolized the solidarity between the participants among themselves and between the participants and God. No need to dwell on the numerous nuances possible. It may safely be affirmed that all the passages where *samakh* is used in connection with a sacrifice are explicable by reference to the same fundamental notion.

We may next consider the use of *samakh* in a pericope telling us about the formal consecration of the Levites, in the course of which "the children of Israel shall lean

[7] See *Siphre* on Num 27:23, to be discussed below.

[8] *Num. Rab.* on 27:20 will be quoted below.

[9] Lev 16:21.

[10] 2 Chr 29:23.

their hands upon them."[11] Once more the idea must have been that the rest of the people merged in the Levites, made the Levites into their representatives, into their other selves. The Bible explicitly states that the Levites are to stand for the firstborn of the people: "For they are wholly given unto me from among the children of Israel; instead of the firstborn of all the children of Israel have I taken them unto me." In a way the case is very close to sacrifice. Only the basic idea again assumes a form modified in accordance with the special occasion.

Samakh three times describes the act of Moses who, when ordaining his successor Joshua, "leaned his hands" on him.[12] Nor are we left in any doubt as to the meaning. "And thou shalt put of thine honour upon him," God commands Moses: and in the chapter recording Moses's death we read that "Joshua was full of the spirit of wisdom, for Moses had leaned his hands upon him." Joshua, that is, became a second Moses. (We must not expect pedantic consistency: for the authors of the Bible there was no irreconcilable conflict between the view that Moses had conveyed his personality to Joshua and the view that "there arose not a prophet since like unto Moses.") This has nothing to do with sacrifice, of course, yet the ceremony has the same effect: the creation of a substitute.

Finally, there is the narrative of a blasphemer, concerning whom God told Moses:[13] "Let all that heard him press their hands upon his head and let all the congregation stone him." It must be admitted that this episode is rather problematic. Maybe the rite served to assimilate the death penalty to a sacrifice. But it is equally possible that the witnesses were regarded as themselves tainted by the crime and needing to throw back on to the actual culprit the guilt he had brought upon them. Or the whole community was tainted and the witnesses acted on its behalf. Or, maybe, the witnesses by anticipation threw back on the criminal the blood-guiltiness which would rest on them as a result of his execution. On any hypothesis, however, the basic idea seems to have been the same as in all other instances.

It should be noted, incidentally, that if—as is practically certain—Susannah is translated from a Hebrew original, the latter must have contained *samakh*:[14] "Then the two elders stood up and leaned their hands upon her head," *scil.* testifying against her. The LXX as usual has ἐπιτίθημι, and Theodotion τίθημι.

This completes the list of applications of the rite of *samakh* in the Old Testament. *Śim* and *shith* we have already met in the story of Jacob's death. It was clearly an act of blessing that was accompanied by his "placing his hand" on the head of the person concerned: "And Israel placed his right hand upon Ephraim's head and his left hand upon Manasseh's, and he blessed Joseph and said, The angel bless the lads." And again, after Joseph had asked him to "place his right hand" on the head of Manasseh, the Bible tells us how "his father refused and said, He also shall be great, but his younger brother shall be greater, and he blessed them that day."

[11] Num 8:10.

[12] Num 27:18, 23; Deut 34:9.

[13] Lev 24:14.

[14] Susannah 34.

Evidently, the physical attitude in a case of *śim* and *shith* is quite unlike that in a case of *samakh*: the word *samakh* implies the exercise of pressure, but there is no question of this at the moment of blessing. For one thing, Jacob was in bed and dying. For another, the very position of his grandsons at the moment of *śim* or *shith* would have made physical pressure extremely difficult. Joseph, it may be recalled, had led Manasseh towards Jacob's right hand and Ephraim towards his left. Jacob had to cross his hands in order to place his right one on the younger. Had the ceremony consisted in "leaning the hand," in *samakh*, he could hardly have been satisfied with this arrangement.

In view of the striking external difference between *samakh*, "a leaning of the hands," and *śim* or *shith*, "a placing of the hands," it would be odd if the two rites had had the same meaning. There is in fact no sign in the narrative of Jacob and his grandsons of the rite of *śim* or *shith* involving a merging of one personality in another. We may conclude that, by such contact, some beneficial virtue inherent in the hand of the blessing party would produce its results in the party blessed. It may be worth remembering that, when Aaron blessed the people, he merely "lifted up (*naśa'*) his hands towards them."[15]

A few words may be added about healing. In this case, just as in that of blessing, the notion of conveying one's personality in the sense of creating a substitute would be completely out of place. Accordingly, the term *samakh* never appears in this field.

Two instances deserve mention, though they are resurrections rather than healings. First, a dead man was buried in Elisha's sepulchre and when he touched (*nagha'*) the bones of the prophet, he revived.[16] Manifestly, the essential thing was the contact. It should be observed that it was not the prophet who deliberately touched the dead man, but the latter who by accident touched the bones of the prophet. Secondly, while Elisha was still alive, he once raised a child from the dead by lying on and bending over him (*shakhabh* and *gahar*).[17] He was following the example of Elijah[18] who had "stretched himself," "measured himself" (*hithmodhedh*) over a dead child to restore him. But even here there was no *samakh*, no "leaning"; and another important difference is that whereas in the rite of "leaning" the hands were always leaned on the head, in the cases under consideration the whole body was dealt with. Elisha, we learn, "placed (*śim*) his mouth upon the child's mouth, and his eyes upon his eyes and his palms upon his palms." There certainly flowed a vital force from the prophet to the dead child. But the meaning was not, as it was where a man leaned his hands upon the head of another being, a transfer of spiritual and moral qualities.

The upshot is that we must keep apart two different kinds of laying on of hands: (1) that which is described by the word *samakh*, (2) that which is described by either of the words *śim* or *shith*. The first kind of imposition is applied to certain offerings, to Levites at their consecration (which was in the nature of an offering by the people), to Joshua at his ordination by Moses and to a criminal convicted of a capital offence. It indicates,

[15] Lev 9:22; Sir 50:20.

[16] 2 Kgs 13:21.

[17] 2 Kgs 4:34.

[18] 1 Kgs 17:21.

we suggest, the pouring of one's personality into another being, the creation of a representative or substitute. It is for this kind of imposition of hands that we propose to use the term *samakh*. The second kind of imposition is applied in blessing and, to some extent, in healing. It indicates the transference of something other than, or less than, the personality; it means the employment of a special, supernatural faculty of one's hands. For this kind of imposition of hands we propose to use the words *śim* and *shith*.

As remarked above, the latter words are far less technical than *samakh*; their range is very wide, and we cannot here go into all applications. Perhaps we ought to advert to Job's complaint about the inequality between him and God:[19] "Neither is there any daysman betwixt us that might lay (*shith*) his hand upon us both." Very likely the reference is to an arbiter to whom both Job and God would owe obedience and who might "lay his hands upon both," *scil.* as a sign of sovereignty.

B. Rabbinic Literature

When we come to the Rabbinic position in New Testament times, there is one change: the occasions on which *samakh* is performed have become fewer. The rite itself, as we shall see, is not altered, but it is practically restricted to two uses—the sacrificial cult and the ordination of a Rabbi. This is remarkable.

We should have expected its range of application to have increased. There are in the Rabbinic era so many new kinds of representation: the *shaliaḥ*, the delegate, of a private person, of a congregation (the precentor), of the Court (of the Beth-Din), of a district that must be represented at the daily offering in the Temple, the "Seven of a City" and so forth.[20] Moreover, the nature of representation is fully realized; again and again the governing principle is repeated that "the delegate of a man is as if he were the man himself" or "the Seven of a City are as if they were the city itself." Yet the appointment of these agents is never effected by means of a "leaning on of hands." One cannot help feeling that, in the eyes of the Rabbis, "leaning on" is a ceremony which they are not entitled to extend. It must remain confined to those cases where it has direct Mosaic sanction. This in itself suggests that *samakh* is still of a significance which does not attach to a mere *śim* or *shith*.

Actually, as already indicated, its scope has contracted. We find nothing corresponding to the consecration of the Levites by the rest of the people, nor is there any *samakh* on the part of witnesses at the moment of accusation. It might perhaps be argued that there could be no parallel to the former event, which had taken place in unique circumstances. But the New Testament shows—we shall have to go into this—that a community experiencing another age of revelation was quite capable of reviving the ceremony for what they felt to be similar purposes.

As for the disappearance of *samakh* from accusation, this is indeed due to special reasons. Since the beginning of the last century B.C. the Pharisees had opposed the ceremonial, collective testifying of witnesses against an accused, so easily misused for throwing dust in the eyes of the judges, and they had advocated instead an informal,

[19] Job 9:33.

[20] *m. Gitt.* 4:1; *m. Ber.* 5:5; *m. Yom.* 1:5; *m. Taan.* 4:2; *t. Taan.* 4:2 f.; *y. Meg.* 74a.

cool cross-examination of each witness in the absence of the other. It was one of the principal aims of the Book of Susannah to demonstrate the superiority of the rational, modern method: as we have just seen, but for Daniel's intervention, Susannah's innocence would not have helped her once the wicked elders, taking advantage of the old procedure, had solemnly "leaned their hands" on her head and proclaimed her guilty.[21] By the time of the New Testament, the Pharisaic innovation is widely adopted. It is the new method through which, if we go by Mark,[22] the attempt to get Jesus convicted for his utterance concerning the destruction of the Temple breaks down. At any rate, in Rabbinic writings, *samakh* is ousted from this area.

In the case of stoning, to be sure, the witnesses—and the judges—still perform *samakh*.[23] But they do so after the verdict is given, when the execution commences. The act is designed to throw back on the person to be stoned the blood-guiltiness which his violent death will bring on witnesses and judges, for the Rabbis explain that those "leaning their hands" on the criminals should speak: "Thy blood be on thy head for thou has caused this." *Samakh*, then, retains its original meaning: the pouring of one's personality—in this case, of one's personality weighed down by blood-guiltiness—into another man.

Apart from this application, the rite continues only in connection with sacrifice and ordination, and here too it is never described by any other term than *samakh*: *śim* or *shith* occurs not a single time. Philo, in his discussion of sacrifice,[24] in addition to ἐπιτίθημι, which goes back to the LXX, uses ἐπιφέρω. This is a stronger term, suggesting that he correctly thinks of a true "leaning" of the hands on the animal. But there is direct evidence that this "leaning" is still vastly different from a "placing." We know of a controversy which started in the 2nd cent. B.C. and went on even after the death of Hillel and Shammai, in their Schools, as to whether leaning one's hands on an animal to be slaughtered was permissible on a festival.[25] One party took the view that, as it is performed by a man "with all his strength" (*bekhol koḥo*), he is causing the animal to bear his burden; and to use an animal on a festival is prohibited.[26]

It is inconceivable that such a controversy could ever have arisen with regard to blessings. Actually, up to this day it is precisely on Sabbaths and festivals that Rabbis and parents are accustomed to "place" (*śim*) their hands on the children's heads and bless them; while the priestly blessing is still accompanied by a mere "lifting" (*naśa'*) of the priest's hands.[27]

Similarly, in the case of ordination, it can be clearly shown that, at least up to the first half of the 2nd cent. A.D., the rite is executed in the original manner and with the

[21] See Daube, ["Error and Accident in the Bible"] *RIDA*, 2 (1949), 200 f.

[22] Mark 14:59.

[23] *Siphra* on Lev 24:14.

[24] *De spec. leg.* 1.37.198 ff.

[25] *m. Betz.* 2:4; *m. Hag.* 2:2 f.; *b. Betz.* 20a; *b. Hag.* 16b.

[26] J. Levy is of opinion (*Wörterbuch über die Talmudim und Midraschim*, 3, 2nd ed. [1924], 545) that the dispute originally was about a different point. Even if he is right, the Talmudic description of *samakh* as performed "with a man's whole strength" remains—enough for our purpose.

[27] E.g. *m. Tam.* 7:2.

original intent: it involves a real "leaning on" as opposed to a gentle "placing," and its object is the pouring of the ordaining scholar's personality into the scholar to be ordained. The Bible says that Moses "leaned his hands on Joshua."[28] This clause the Midrash Siphre, which goes back to the School of R. Ishmael, interprets as meaning: "He pressed on him as one presses on a vessel already full to overflowing (Joshua having been endowed with the Spirit even before his ordination[29]) in order to stuff even more into it." (Such is the sense of the Siphre's comment.[30] The prevalent rendering[31] is slightly incorrect, but it would furnish even stronger support for the thesis here advanced: "Moses pressed on Joshua in order to make him like a vessel full to overflowing.") Since for the Siphre Joshua's appointment is simply the first Rabbinic ordination on which all further ones are modelled, it is plain that the rite of *samakh*, by this time, has lost nothing of its specific character.

It is significant that in the Tosephta[32] "leaning" for the purpose of ordination and "leaning" for the purpose of bringing a communal sacrifice[33] appear side by side. We may also mention two similes which the Rabbis introduce again and again: though Moses "leaned his hands on Joshua," he did not lose his own faculties because he was "like one kindling a light with a light"; and when he "put of his honour upon him," he was "like one pouring from vessel to vessel."[34]

From the latter half of the 2nd cent. A.D., far-reaching reforms were introduced into the institution of Rabbinic ordination. Above all, whereas before that time any scholar himself authorized could confer authority on others, now the right to ordain became the exclusive right of the Patriarch and his court. About the middle of the 3rd cent. at the latest the ceremony of *samakh* itself was abandoned. The centralization of ordination at the Patriarch's court may have contributed to this result. For one thing, it was certainly a factor making for the ordination of absent candidates, in which case the rite was physically impossible; for another, once it was no longer the teacher who ordained his own disciple, the notion of the creation of a second self would naturally lose ground. Again, the practices of the Patriarch Judah II, who seems on occasion to have sold the Rabbinic authority for money, doubtless helped to diminish the importance of the ceremony: a *samakh* performed by such a man cannot have been regarded as a sacred act. Another reason for giving it up[35] probably was the increasing role played by the imposition of hands in the Christian religion.

Anyhow, henceforth ordination took place without any "leaning of the hands" on the candidate's head. The Midrash Siphre Zuta is from the School of Akiba and generally represents a later stage of the tradition than the Midrash Siphre from which we quoted above. It explains that when God ordered Moses "Lean thine hands upon

[28] Num 27:23.

[29] According to Num 27:18: "Take Joshua, a man in whom is the spirit, and lean thine hands upon him."

[30] See Kuhn, *Rabbinische Texte*, 2nd ser., *Tannaitische Midraschim*, 2, 577, n. 12.

[31] Adopted e.g. by Strack-Billerbeck, 2 (1924), 648.

[32] *t. Sanh.* 1:1.

[33] As prescribed by Lev 14:15.

[34] *Num. Rab.* on 27:18, 20.

[35] Suggested by Bacher and accepted, for example, by Strack-Billerbeck, 2 (1924), 655 f.

Joshua,"[36] he did so "that thy disciple may be blessed through thee." Here the ceremony of *samakh* is no longer strictly distinguished from that performed in a case of blessing, though even now the term would hardly be interchangeable with *śim* or *shith*. The comment must date from a period when the rite of *samakh* was in decline, if not obsolete.

As for healings, while some Rabbis are credited with the power of healing or even raising a person from the dead, there is never any imposition of the hands or touching. Mostly the result is achieved by fervent prayer. Thus Hanina ben Dosa, of the 1st cent. A.D., successfully invoked God's mercy for the sick children of Johanan ben Zaccai and Gamaliel II.[37] Sometimes we come across a sort of command. A pupil of Judah the Prince, of the second half of the 2nd cent., restored a dying servant of the Roman emperor by saying: "Why doest thou lie and thy master standeth on his feet?"[38] The command "Arise from thy flux" was commonly used—i.e. not only by Rabbis—when giving medicaments to a woman suffering from an issue of blood.[39] Also in common use was anointing with or without prayer or incantation.[40]

C. The New Testament

From the foregoing considerations it follows that, in the earliest Jewish Christian community, the ceremonies in which the imposition of hands is described by the words ἐπιτίθημι or τίθημι in the New Testament cannot all have had either the same form or the same import. Modern authorities speak of a single rite of "the laying on of hands," though, to be sure, they admit that it served various purposes. Strack-Billerbeck, for instance,[41] after discussing blessings pronounced over children, go on to say: "On the laying on of hands in connection with ordination, see below," etc. The implication is that there is no fundamental distinction. Foakes Jackson and Kirsopp Lake[42] are guilty of the same error. So is Flemington[43] who puts together, as far as Jewish sources are concerned, blessings, sacrifices, the consecration of the Levites, the installation of Joshua and the ordination of Rabbis; and as far as the New Testament is concerned, blessings pronounced over children, healings and the giving of the Spirit. But it is evidently necessary to discriminate between *samakh* and *śim* or *shith*.

To take the easier part first, when Jesus blessed the children, we have to assume *śim* or *shith*, a gentle "placing of the hands."[44] The touch is the main element of the ceremony. It is noteworthy that, while according to Matthew he was asked to "place his hands on them" and did so, according to Mark and Luke he was asked to "touch them," *nagha'*, and, in compliance with the request, "placed his hands on them."[45] There are

[36] Num 27:18.

[37] *b. Ber.* 34b; *y. Ber.* 9d.

[38] *Lev. Rab.* on 8:2.

[39] *b. Shab.* 110a; see Strack-Billerbeck, 1 (1922), 520, 2 (1924), 10.

[40] *y. M. Sh.* 53b; see Strack-Billerbeck, 1 (1922), 429.

[41] 1 (1922), 807 f.

[42] *The Beginnings of Christianity*, pt. 1, *The Acts of the Apostles* (1933), 137.

[43] *The New Testament Doctrine of Baptism* (1948), 44.

[44] Matt 19:13 ff.; Mark 10:15 ff.; Luke 18:15 ff.

[45] Luke omits to mention the action.

several examples in Rabbinic literature of the belief that the hands of a saintly person might be possessed of a beneficent virtue. In a previous lecture we mentioned a legend according to which Ruth ate her fill and left some of her food even though Boaz had given her only a little; and we found the Rabbis discussing the question whether a special blessing rested within her or on his fingers [137 ff.].

Towards the end of Luke,[46] incidentally, Jesus blesses his disciples by "lifting up," *naśa'*, his hands. This, we have seen, was the gesture prescribed for the priestly blessing. Its introduction here may have something to do with the fact that Luke, at the close of the gospel, takes his readers back to the Temple where his story began. He may wish to indicate that, for the believers, the service from now had a new meaning.

Śim or *shith* would be the appropriate expression also where healings are concerned. (We leave out of account for the moment the restoration of Paul's sight by Ananias.) A "laying on of hands" is mentioned in connection with the revival of a girl believed to be dying or dead (Jesus is asked to "place his hands on her,"[47] though what he actually does is to take her by the hand[48]); the curing of sick people in general;[49] the curing of a deaf-mute;[50] the curing of a blind man;[51] and the curing of a man suffering from fever and a flux of blood.[52]

That *samakh*, a "leaning," is out of the question is obvious. One does not "lean one's hands on a blind man's eyes," one only "places them there." Moreover, as in acts of blessing, it is the touch which is of primary relevance. In the case of the deaf-mute, Jesus is asked to "place his hands on him"; what he does—clearly in accordance with what he is expected to do—is to "put his fingers in his ears," to "touch his tongue" and so on. (In addition he pronounces a command: "Be opened.") Conversely, in the case of the blind man, he is asked to "touch him"; and what he does is to "place his hands on him," to "place his hands on his eyes" and so on. As is well known, there are cures where we hear only of Jesus "touching," *nagha'*, the sick and nothing of a "laying on of hands": they concern a leper,[53] blind people[54] and the high priest's servant wounded in the course of Jesus's arrest,[55] and we may add the raising of a young man from the dead by touching his bier and a command "Arise."[56] Again, here and there we meet with the Old Testament notion, or more precisely, with extended applications of it, that a cure may take place even if—instead of the miracle-worker taking action—the person in need touches the miracle-worker or something belonging to him: the story of a woman

[46] Luke 24:50.

[47] Matt 9:18; Mark 5:23. In Luke 8:41 he is simply asked to come.

[48] This mode of healing recurs in Matt 8:15; Mark 1:30; Matt 9:25; Mark 5:41; Luke 8:54 and Acts 3:7.

[49] Mark 6:5, 16:18; Luke 4:40, probably Acts 28:9 (in conjunction with the preceding verse), possibly Acts 5:12, 14:3, 19:11.

[50] Mark 7:32 f.

[51] Mark 8:22 ff.

[52] Acts 28:8.

[53] Matt 8:2 ff.; Mark 1:40 ff.; Luke 5:12 ff.

[54] Matt 9:29, 20:34. In Mark 10:52 and Luke 18:24 the word of Jesus alone suffices.

[55] Luke 22:51.

[56] Luke 7:14.

with an issue of blood is recounted in detail,[57] and there are notices about many sick persons healed in this way.[58]

Incidentally, when cures were expected if "the shadow of Peter would overshadow the sick,"[59] this manner of healing may well have been a modified imitation of what Elijah and Elisha had done: the former had "measured himself" over a dead boy, the latter "lain and bent" over one. Peter was one of the apostles; according to the Rabbis[60] Elijah and Elisha, when restoring the children, acted as *sheliḥim*, delegates of God, literally, as "envoys," "apostles."

It is interesting that the Epistles contain not a single reference to healing by a "laying on of hands." As it appears from Mark and Acts[61] that such healing was practised in the early Church, this may be accidental. But it is quite possible that some writers found themselves in a situation in which, while far from opposing the practice, they did not want to encourage it.

As a matter of fact, the question of healing is brought up in only two Epistles, in 1 Corinthians and James.[62] In the former nothing is said about the procedure except that it must be "in the one Spirit." In the latter, a normal Jewish procedure is enjoined: prayer and unction. True, to go by the prevalent reading, the anointing is to be performed "in the name of the Lord," and "the Lord" certainly means not God in the Jewish sense, but Jesus. To this extent Christian influence is noticeable. But it is rather doubtful whether the words "of the Lord" are genuine.[63] If we omit them, there remains anointing "in the (divine) name," i.e. invoking or thinking of God, which would be perfectly in order in Jewish circles.[64]

So much for *śim* or *shith*, "to place one's hands," an act suitable for blessing and healing. When we go on to ordination and suchlike matters, we enter the department of *samakh*, "to lean one's hands," a rite quite unlike *śim* or *shith* in form as well as meaning. Before inspecting the texts alluding to it, we may put forward an argument which is none the less strong for being drawn from silence. Nowhere in the whole of the New Testament does Jesus commission a disciple by means of an imposition of hands. There is the call, "Follow me"; there is the appointment to a task, "And as ye go, preach, heal the sick, cast out devils"; there is the grant of powers, "Whatsoever thou shalt bind on earth shall be bound in heaven," and so on. But none of these injunctions or promises is ever accompanied by a laying on of hands. Why not?

Hardly because under Rabbinic law Jesus, having no Rabbinic authority himself, had no right to confer it on others (though even if this were the reason, it would bring out the radical difference between *samakh* and *śim* or *shith*: no formal authorization was needed for a laying on of hands to bless or heal). His followers considered his authori-

[57] Matt 9:20 ff.; Mark 5:27 ff.; Luke 8:44 ff.

[58] Matt 14:36; Mark 6:56; Luke 6:19; Acts 19:12.

[59] Acts 5:15.

[60] *Midrash Psalms* on 78:29; *b. Sanh.* 113a.

[61] Mark 16:18; Acts 28:8 f., 9:10 ff. The question of the provenance of Mark 16:9 ff. is not here relevant.

[62] 1 Cor 12:9, 28 f.; James 5:14.

[63] See the apparatus.

[64] For an appeal for mercy "in the name" (*bashshem*) see *m. Yom.* 6:2; *y. Yom.* 40d ff.

ty fully equal to that of a Rabbi.[65] The point is that a laying on of hands for such a purpose would be not *śim* or *shith*, but *samakh*; and *samakh*, in contradistinction to *śim* or *shith*, implies the pouring of one's personality into another being. Joshua, on whom Moses had "leaned" his hands, had thereby become a second, if in many respects inferior, Moses. In the view of the New Testament writers, there could be no second Jesus. A *śim* or *shith* on his part was possible; a *samakh* was not.

Among the first Christians, however, the ceremony enjoyed a striking revival. In Rabbinic Judaism, we saw, it was confined to the sacrificial cult, for which it was prescribed by the Bible, and the ordination of a Rabbi, the passing on by a master to his disciple of the wisdom and authority which he in turn had received from his master and which ultimately went back to Joshua, ordained by Moses. But "the Seven of a City," for example, were installed without any *samakh*. It was customary for the Jewish inhabitants of a Palestinian city to choose seven worthies to look after the common affairs, and these administrators had full power of representation: "the Seven of a City are as if they were the city itself." Yet as it was not ordination in the sense outlined above, the rite of *samakh* was not performed.

When the Christians of Jerusalem decided to appoint seven distributors of charity[66]—no doubt on the model of "the Seven of a City"—they did use the ceremony. *Samakh* was a sacred means of creating a substitute. In this case a few members of the community were to stand for all in a matter of great religious importance. So, when the people had elected them, they "set them before the apostles," thus formally demonstrating their confidence in these men and recommending them to the apostles, and they "leaned their hands on them," thus making them into their representatives, their extended selves, *vis-à-vis* the apostles. The distribution of charity was now in the hands of the community—the community living in its deputies.

It is true that the verse just quoted is generally interpreted in a different way, namely, as meaning that, while it was the people who presented those elected to the apostles, it was the latter who imposed their hands. Even on this basis, *samakh* would involve the passing on of one's personality, only now the distributors of charity would become "extensions" of the apostles and not of the people. Our main thesis, that is, would remain unaffected. But the interpretation is artificial. If we follow the natural sense of the Greek, the subject of the verb "they set"—in the clause "whom they set before the apostles"—is also the subject of the following verbs—in the clause "and having prayed, they leaned their hands on them." There is one subject: the people. It might perhaps be objected that, when first proposing the scheme, the apostles speak of men "whom we may appoint over this business." But "we" here most probably includes those whom they address; it means "we, the Christians of Jerusalem," not, "we, the apostles"; it says nothing about the mode of installation. The correct view seems to be that the appointment was made jointly by the apostles and the rest in the sense that the former suggested the new office; that the rest of the community elected the holders and accredited them to the apostles, i.e. presented them and, by "leaning" their hands on them, made them into their representa-

[65] Mark 1:22, 27; Luke 4:32; Matt 21:23 ff.; Mark 11:27 ff.; Luke 20:1 ff.

[66] Acts 6:1 ff.

tives; and that the apostles agreed with the choice. It is relevant to note that Paul's companion appointed to help him administer the funds collected[67] appears as a delegate of the Macedonian churches at large, not of any apostles. Indeed his office would serve little purpose if he represented the leaders instead of the people.

Codex Bezae, to be sure, favors the orthodox opinion. It has a reading making it quite clear that the "leaning on" was done by the apostles. But the reading is surely secondary. Its introduction is in fact evidence for rather than against the original meaning here advocated: it goes back to someone who no longer approved of the idea of the community participating to such a degree in the installation of officers. Whether he already desired to make of the incident the prototype of apostolic succession may be left undecided. The author of Acts certainly has no such thing in mind. For one thing, the office in question, the office of a deacon, though highly important, is inferior to that of an apostle; therefore, what is said about the appointment of deacons does not really bear on that of apostles or the successors of apostles. For another, taken as the prototype of apostolic succession, or even delegation in a wider sense, the incident would not show at all that a single apostle has power of ordaining. In any case we ought to reject not only the reading of Codex Bezae but also its meaning; and adhere strictly not only to the *lectio difficilior* [more difficult reading] of the other codices but also to their *sensus difficilior* [more difficult meaning].

How do we know that it was a "leaning," *samakh*, and not a mere *śim* or *shith* that took place? Apart from general considerations, there are distinct allusions in this pericope to the appointment of Joshua. He had been fit for his office because he was already endowed with the spirit: "Take thee Joshua, a man in whom is the spirit."[68] So are the distributors of charity: "Look ye out seven men of honest report, full of the Holy Ghost and wisdom, and they chose Stephen, a man full of faith and the Holy Ghost" and so on.[69] Again, in the case of Joshua, Moses had presented him to the people and publicly made him into his substitute: "And Moses set him before Eleazar the priest and all the congregation, and he leaned his hands upon him."[70] So, in the case of the distributors of charity, the community presents them to the apostles and publicly makes them into its substitutes: "And the multitude chose Stephen and Philip etc., whom they set before the apostle, and having prayed they leaned their hands on them."

This taking over of language from Joshua's appointment not only proves that there was *samakh*, but also underlines a feature referred to above: the self-confidence of the first Christians. The appointment of the distributors of charity was no Rabbinic ordination (not even if we accept the variants of Codex Bezae). Their task was more closely circumscribed than a Rabbi's, their authority narrower. None the less the first Christians regarded a major step in the development of their organization as of sufficient moment to be linked with that outstanding event in Old Testament history.

67 2 Cor 8:19 f.

68 Num 27:18.

69 The addition of "wisdom" in Acts may be due to Deut 34:9: "And Joshua was full of the spirit of wisdom, for Moses had leaned his hands on him." But it need not be: the same addition is to be found in Luke 2:40, 52, as compared with 1 Sam 2:26.

70 Num 27:22 f.

Let us proceed to the consecration of Paul and Barnabas as missionaries, when, at the bidding of the Holy Ghost, their fellow prophets and teachers at Antioch appointed them by "leaning their hands" on them.[71]

It is hardly necessary to point out that this also was not Rabbinic ordination. We are expressly told that Paul and Barnabas belonged to that group of prophets and teachers. They were not students to be promoted. They were equals—indeed, leading figures—to be detailed for an exceptional task. Still, their installation took the form of *samakh*. The earliest Christians did not hesitate to apply this rite outside its traditional field where a man's personality was to be conveyed to another under divine guidance. Here, then, the idea was that the two should carry out their special duties on behalf of all. They were sent out as representatives of the whole group. The others made them into their extended selves.

This interpretation—that the rite took the form of *samakh* and that it meant making Paul and Barnabas into representatives of the group—is confirmed by the language used, which echoes that of the Old Testament in the chapter dealing with the consecration of the Levites. "Take the Levites from among the children of Israel" and "Thus shalt thou separate the Levites," God had commanded Moses.[72] "Separate me Barnabas and Saul" is the bidding of the Holy Ghost. The LXX uses διαστέλλω for "to separate," whereas in Acts we find ἀφορίζω; but the meaning is the same, the Hebrew *hibhdil*. The special work for which the separation is required is called ἔργον both in the LXX[73] and Acts. Clearly, the ceremony performed at Antioch is a "leaning on" of hands, and it still serves to create a substitute. As the Israelites had delegated the Levites by this means, so the prophets and teachers of Antioch delegate Paul and Barnabas.

As observed above, the Levites had, in a sense, been an offering brought by the Israelites: God had accepted them in lieu of the firstborn. This particular nuance, it seems, no longer plays any part in the New Testament episode. But the connection established with the consecration of the Levites is not purely formal. The two missionaries are thought of as entrusted with a service analogous to that of the Levites of old; and they are in a fuller sense than their fellows "wholly given unto the Lord."

We cannot here go into the implications of this concept; nor into its possible role in other passages; nor into the question how far its growth may have been stimulated by certain practices of the Levites in New Testament times. It may suffice to say that the notion of the "separation" of the missionary which occurs in Acts is not a freak. As is well known, Paul twice refers to his being singled out, "separated," for missionary work in addition to being an apostle, in Romans and Galatians;[74] and both times he uses ἀφορίζω.

Whether he is in exact agreement with Acts as to the nature of this separation is a different matter. In Galatians he emphasizes that it was God who separated him "from my mother's womb" (drawing on similar utterances by Isaiah and Jeremiah,[75] but, significantly, neither of these has ἀφορίζω, *hibhdil*). This by itself would not conflict with

[71] Acts 13:1 ff.

[72] Num 8:6, 14.

[73] Num 8:11, 15.

[74] Rom 1:1; Gal 1:15.

[75] Isa 49:1; Jer 1:5.

the record of Acts; even according to Acts, Paul and Barnabas were "sent forth by the Holy Ghost."[76] The further remark, however, that he passed many years as a missionary without having consulted any of the other leaders—except, on one occasion during that period, Peter and James—raises a serious problem. Possibly one of the factors responsible for his attitude—we are far from denying that there were others as well—was uneasiness about the increased use of *samakh* in the early Church, the extension of the rite to fresh cases; an uneasiness he need not always have felt; and one due not only to his Rabbinic background but also, and even primarily, to the fear lest this transfer of qualities might to some extent disguise the free and direct bestowal of gifts by God.

We must now say something on the communication of the Spirit. Still postponing the discussion of the case of Paul and Ananias, we have to consider the story of the Samaritans to whom, after they were baptized, the apostles sent Peter and John in order to impart the Spirit to them, which they did by a laying on of hands; the story of the Ephesians who, baptized unto John's baptism, were baptized once more by Paul in the name of Jesus and invested with the Spirit by a laying on of hands; and the enumeration of the laying on of hands, side by side with the doctrine of baptisms, among the Christian fundamentals in Hebrews.[77]

A negative statement can at once be made: the imparting of the Spirit was not Rabbinic ordination. In the first place, it was far more freely granted, it was granted to any converts, it was not reserved for a few as an exceptional privilege. In the second place, at the time of the New Testament, a Rabbi ordained himself was entitled to ordain others. But the story of the conferment of the Spirit at Samaria shows that not everybody who had received the Spirit could pass it on: Simon Magus asked the apostles to sell him their special faculty of being able to do so.

Unfortunately, as regards the question whether the laying on of hands consisted in *samakh* or a mere *śim* or *shith*, there is nothing in the texts pointing one way or the other. However, there can be no doubt that it consisted in the former, and that the idea, as in the other instances of *samakh*, was the pouring of one man's personality into another.

This is not to deny that, in certain circumstances or in certain circles or at certain times, this idea might be quite absent and the gift of the Spirit be looked upon as coming direct from heaven without any laying on of hands—whether spontaneously, as at Pentecost, or as the result of repentance and baptism, listening to the gospel or the like. All we mean to say is that, where there was imposition of hands, it was a *samakh*. The communication of the Spirit is too near those other cases to be connected with *śim* or *shith*. (Carrington's proposition[78] that the laying on of hands in the course of baptism "would harmonize well with counsels to humble oneself and be subordinate" is, therefore, untenable for the New Testament period. A laying on of hands by way of symbolizing authority and subjection would be *śim* or *shith*. Above we cited a probable example from Job.[79]) That the basic idea of the ceremony—the creation of a second self—

[76] Acts 13:4.

[77] Acts 8:14 ff., 19:1 ff.; Heb 6:2.

[78] *The Primitive Christian Catechism* (1940), 84.

[79] Job 9:33.

underwent modificatins so as to suit the nature of each case we have mentioned already. Here a particular gift was conveyed, a gift, however, which affected the whole life of him who possessed it.

The account, in Acts,[80] of the restoration of Paul's sight by Ananias presents difficulties, but they are not insuperable. Paul, deprived of his sight, had a vision of Ananias laying his hands on him in order that he might see again. Ananias in turn had a vision in which he was informed of this and sent to Paul. He went and laid his hands on him in order that he might see again and—here comes the crux—be filled with the Spirit. Paul immediately did see again and received baptism.

The laying on of hands for the purpose of healing was a gentle act, a placing of the hands, *śim* or *shith*. It is this act which we must assume Ananias to have performed. Yet he was sure that it would not only cure Paul physically but also bring him the Spirit. How can this be reconciled with our view that the laying on of hands for the purpose of imparting the Spirit took the form of leaning, *samakh*?

The answer seems to be that this was not a communication of the Spirit by one person to another at all. More precisely, Ananias did not confer the Spirit on Paul in the way Peter and John conferred it on the Samaritans or Paul himself on the Ephesians. What Ananias was ordered to do and did was to restore Paul's sight. As this marked the last phase of a change of heart, he knew it would be followed by the gift of the Spirit. The Spirit was not, however, thought of as transferred by Ananias but as falling upon Paul direct from heaven. In this respect, that is, the case is parallel to the descent of the Spirit at Pentecost, or as a result of baptism or listening to the word of God—with no human intervention, no laying on of hands. There was, in short no *samakh* because it was not Ananias who bestowed the Spirit on Paul. After all, the triumph of faith, or baptism as its expression, is often enough described as a passing from darkness to light. In this case, a regaining of sight was considered a triumph of faith; and it was the latter which, as in the parallel instances just referred to, led to the gift of the Spirit.

In Paul's epistles no mention is made of imposition of hands on converts, whether before or after baptism. This silence need not be significant. On the other hand it may be. Flemington holds[81] that there was no need for him specially to refer to the rite since for those with a Jewish background it was such an obvious custom. But that is precisely what it was not. In Judaism, *samakh* was restricted to the sacrificial cult and Rabbinic ordination. There was no *samakh*—nor, for that matter, any *śim* or *shith*—in connection with the reception of proselytes. The widening of the scope of this ceremony is a distinctive and suggestive feature of early Christianity. Neither is there much force in the argument that, in one passage,[82] Paul appears to distinguish the grant of the Spirit from baptism. It is difficult to see why this should necessarily imply an imposition of hands.

In the narrative of Jesus's baptism the distinction is clearly made. First comes the actual baptism, completed as Jesus comes up. (On the significance of "coming up" we remarked above in A Baptismal Catechism [505].) Then the Spirit descends on him.

[80] Acts 9:10 ff.
[81] *Op. cit.*, 44.
[82] 2 Cor 1:21 f.

These are two different things, however closely linked. But, manifestly, no laying on of hands takes place. In fact, as far as Mark is concerned, the word "straightway" very likely qualifies "he saw," not "coming up" ("and straightway, coming up, he saw the heavens opened," not "and straightway coming up, he saw the heavens opened"); and its sense may be less vague than usual; that is to say, it may be intended definitely to exclude any thought of John having imposed his hands on Jesus.

To repeat, Paul's silence need not be significant, but it may be. So once again the question arises—we first put it in discussing his "separation" as a missionary—whether, from a certain moment at least, he may not have had scruples about the imparting of the Spirit by means of *samakh*. Quite apart from the austere Rabbinic attitude in this matter, he may have felt uneasy at the suggestion of human intervention implicit in this passing on of the Spirit from one person to another, and have preferred the notion of a direct flow from heaven.

It remains to inspect three passages from the Epistles to Timothy.[83] In the first, the writer admonishes Timothy not to neglect "the gift that is in thee, which was given thee by prophecy, with the laying on of hands of the presbytery." The conclusion generally drawn is that Timothy was made bishop by an imposition of hands on the part of the presbytery. It may be correct, but it is difficult to reconcile with the second passage, where Timothy is warned to "lay hands suddenly on no man." This, at first sight at least, seems to assume that the imposition of hands is performed by the bishop, not by the presbytery; or in other words, that a bishop is appointed by a previous bishop. There are, of course, several ways of harmonizing the texts. We may, for example, regard the second passage as speaking not of the appointment of a further bishop, but of the bestowal of the Spirit on a convert.

The problem becomes almost insoluble, however, when we add the third passage, from 2 Timothy, where the writer admonishes Timothy to stir up "the gift of God which is in thee by the laying on of my hands." Here the only natural interpretation is that Timothy was installed by the writer and no one else. To say, as is usually said, that "the laying on of my hands" means "the laying on of my hands—together with the presbytery" is reading a great deal into the text; not to mention the fact that even so the conflict is not quite resolved, unless we take a further step and say that, in the first passage, "the laying on of the hands of the presbytery" means "the laying on of the hands of the presbytery—together with me."

However, such is the prevalent view, and it may be right. If so, it is impossible to decide whether the ceremony still consisted in *samakh* and still involved the idea of creating a representative, an extended self, or whether it had lost its original form and meaning and become a *śim* or *shith*, with the touch as the principal element.

We incline to a different solution. The clue seems to lie in the first passage. The phrase ἐπίθεσις τῶν χειρῶν τοῦ πρεσβυτερίου looks like a rendering of the technical term *semikhath zeqenim*,[84] literally, "the leaning on of elders"; its meaning being "the leaning on of hands on persons in order to make elders, Rabbis, of them," or briefly,

[83] 1 Tim 4:14, 5:22; 2 Tim 1:6.

[84] E.g. *b. Sanh.* 13b.

"Rabbinic ordination." In the only two other New Testament texts where πρεσβυτέριον occurs,[85] it stands for *zeqenim*, "elders"; and the most likely reason why the collective noun is put instead of πρεσβύτεροι is that the reference is not to individual Rabbis, but to the Sanhedrin as a body. Surely, as *semikhath zeqenim* denotes not the ordination of specified individuals, not the appointment of certain men as elders, but the rite of ordination in general, πρεσβυτέριον is here the proper equivalent of *zeqenim*. On this basis we ought to translate: "Neglect not the gift which was given thee by prophecy, with *semikhath zeqenim*, due ordination, ordination conferring full authority."

The difficulties with which the current interpretation has to contend are now removed. Rabbinic ordination in the New Testament era took the form of *samakh*, "a leaning on of hands": the master would lean his hands on his disciple's head, thus passing on the wisdom and authority which Moses had passed on to Joshua, Joshua to his successors and so on. In the passage under discussion, the installation of a bishop is likened to Rabbinic ordination, indeed, is supposed to be the corresponding Christian practice.

It follows that Timothy must have been ordained by his master alone, and that is exactly what is implied in the similar exhortation in the Second Epistle: "Stir up the gift of God which is in thee by the laying on of my hands." Again, at the time any Rabbi himself authorized was entitled to authorize others. But there are many stories in the Talmud showing that great care was exercised to ordain only such as deserved it; and as a rule a candidate must be forty years old.[86] It is, therefore, open to us to connect the rule "Lay hands suddenly on no man" with ordination. It is a warning that might have been given by any Rabbi to a younger colleague.

The result is curious. The installation of the seven distributors of charity, normally treated as an adumbration, if not the prototype, of apostolic succession or delegation, was no such thing. Those officers were the delegation of the ordinary people who had leaned their hands on them. Conversely, the passage in 1 Timothy, commonly interpreted as speaking of a democratic installation of a bishop by the presbytery, turns out to be the earliest reference to apostolic succession, i.e. the creation of a bishop by a *samakh* on the part of one who is bishop already—on the model of Rabbinic ordination.

So once again a question concerning the silence of our sources arises, the last one: why do we not hear of an equivalent of Rabbinic ordination—of a disciple being invested with full authority by a master leaning his hands on him—prior to the Epistles to Timothy? (If the translation of ἐπίθεσις τῶν χειρῶν τοῦ πρεσβυτερίου here suggested is rejected, then even these Epistles offer no certain instance of this kind of succession.) As nearly always, the silence may be accidental. But in all probability it is not. One can think of various reasons why some time should have elapsed before *semikhath zeqenim* was definitively taken over by the Church for the appointment of bishops.

First, Jesus himself had been without Rabbinic authority: he had, indeed, been attacked on this ground.[87] Secondly, the attitude expressed in the words "The scribes

[85] Luke 22:66; Acts 22:5.

[86] See the comment of R. Judah ben Elai (middle of the 2nd cent. A.D.) in *Exod. Rab.* on 2:14; cf. also *m. Sanh.* 4:4, reflecting the attitude of the Mishnic period.

[87] Matt 21:23 ff.; Mark 11:27 ff.; Luke 20:1 ff.

and Pharisees sit in Moses's seat" may have delayed the adoption of the Rabbinic practice. (In the Rabbinic writings preserved, "the seat of Moses," *qathedhra' demoshe*, does not occur before the 4th cent. A.D.:[88] a striking illustration of the fact that an institution or idea may be early even though mentioned only by the later Rabbis.) Thirdly, the working out of the principles of church government was an enormous task. Even when the principles were agreed on, such details as the way in which to ordain a bishop need not have been immediately obvious. Jesus, we have seen, had never used the rite of *samakh*, "leaning on," for commissioning his disciples; they had been called and given power as Moses had been—by the word alone. When it came to the appointment of successors, the exact mode of installation may well have presented a problem.

This does not mean that Rabbinic ordination cannot have been applied to bishops before the Epistles of Timothy, even, perhaps, in the time of the apostles. The description of the installation of a bishop as *semikhath zeqenim* must in any case go back to a fairly early date, when Jewish Christians were still in close and living contact with the Synagogue. Only, from the silence of the earlier portions of the New Testament, as well as from general considerations, it does seem likely that a few decades at least were needed for Rabbinic ordination to find its lasting place in Christianity.

The later development, when "leaning" became confused with "placing," lies outside the scope of our inquiry.

[88] R. Aha of Lydda, *P. de R. K.* 7b.

Disgrace

A. "Niwwul"

The term *niwwul* and other words from the same root are used in various interesting senses by the Tannaites. Like αἰσχύνη or ἀτιμία, they may signify "disgrace" in general. Since the judges took to accepting bribes, the Rabbis complain, vulgar people were raised and exalted ones degraded, so that the government "fell into contempt."[1] Paul says: "Ye are honourable, we are despised"; "we minister by honour and dishonour"; "hath not the potter power to make one vessel unto honour and another unto dishonour?" And he contrasts "less honourable" or "shameful" parts of the body with others.[2] Again, an unchaste woman is called "dishonoured" in the Talmud, and indeed considered as "dishonouring" all her sex; idols are described as "disgraceful"; and in figurative speech, "the disgraceful one" may stand for the evil inclination, the tempter.[3] So Paul speaks of men's "vile affections" by which they "dishonour their bodies."[4]

It is far from certain that Paul in these texts thinks of *niwwul*. There are other Hebrew and Aramaic words with a similar meaning, for example *bizzayon*. He may not be influenced by Hebrew or Aramaic at all. What is clear, however, is that αἰσχύνη, ἀτιμία, and *niwwul* are roughly synonymous.

Frequently, *niwwul* refers to disgrace attaching to a person's appearance. A man letting the hair grow too long, or a woman shaving it off, is termed "undignified"; while a woman who, suspected of adultery, must undergo the ordeal of the bitter water, "is rendered despicable" by having her head uncovered, her hair loosened and so on.[5] In the latter case, needless to say, the disgrace is brought about not only by the appearance as such—the uncovered head, the dishevelment—but also by the circumstances, the fact that it had to come to a trial of this kind. Moral disgrace and physical disgrace are here not strictly distinguished. Paul says that "every man praying, having his head covered, dishonoureth his head, but every woman that prayeth with her head covered honoureth her head," and again, "if a man have long hair, it is a shame unto him, but if a woman have long hair, it is a glory to her."[6] The passage quoted above, where he con-

[1] *b. Sot.* 47b.

[2] 1 Cor 4:10; 2 Cor 6:8; Rom 9:21 (cp. 2 Tim 2:20); 1 Cor 12:23.

[3] *t. Sot.* 2:3; *Siphre* on Deut 22:21 (with reference to the Scriptural *nebhala*, "folly" or "outrage"); *Song of Songs Rab.* on 1:9; *b. Kidd.* 30b.

[4] Rom 1:24 ff.

[5] *y. M. Kat.* 81c; *Num. Rab.* on 16:6; *Siphre* on Deut 21:12; *b. Yeb.* 48a; *b. Sot.* 8b (cf. Num 5:18).

[6] 1 Cor 11:4 ff.

demns those who, by giving in to "vile affections dishonour their bodies," furnishes an example of moral disgrace involving physical disgrace.

The desecration of a corpse also constitutes *niwwul*. Under Rabbinic law, if the validity of transactions into which a person entered shortly before his death depends on whether or not he had attained maturity, it is none the less forbidden to exhume and strip the corpse and perform an autopsy: that would be *niwwul*. For the same reason, if a man is killed by another, you may not examine the body in order in see whether there might have been a fatal disease which would in any case have resulted in death at the moment of murder.[7] Mark tells us that one of the servants sent out by the owner of a vineyard to receive the fruits from the lessees was "dishonoured" by them. The meaning may be that they showed disrespect by beating him, or that they ill-treated him in a manner producing disfigurement, or that they stoned him to death and desecrated the body. It should be noted that according to Mark (here again Matthew and Luke differ) the owner's son was killed and his body thrown out of the vineyard. Evidently they left him unburied, a flagrant case of *niwwul*—whether or not the author of the pericope has in mind the actual term.[8]

Perhaps the gravest kind of *niwwul* is that disfigurement of a person, alive or dead, which may have an adverse effect on resurrection. In New Testament times it was widely—though by no means universally—held that the dead would rise in the shape in which they were buried. God might subsequently heal any wounds, abolish any flaws; but to begin with, the original figures would reappear.[9] Moreover, in popular belief at least, the bones played a particular part: a person whose skeleton was damaged might not be able to rise at all. The curse "may his bones be ground" must be understood on this basis,[10] maybe also the death of Judas according to Acts—by "bursting asunder."[11] Again, death by the sword "disgraces," whereas death from hunger does not.[12]

Of course, most Rabbis stood above such superstitions. For them, God simply had the power to bring the dead back to life. In fact, a man, precisely by dying a "disgraceful" death, by being tortured, beheaded, left unburied, might contribute to the wiping out of sins committed by himself or others; and if he suffered martyrdom for the sake of God, the reward would be all the greater.[13] Still, the problem was not easy. We come across compromise solutions, such as that by Joshua ben Hananiah—about A.D. 100—who held that a tiny part of the spine was indestructible and would be used by God for raising the dead.[14] Paul felt it necessary to explain to the Corinthian community how "it

[7] *b. B. B.* 154a f.; *b. Hull.* 11b.

[8] Mark 12:4 ff.; Matt 21:35 ff.; Luke 20:11 ff.

[9] Apoc. Bar. 50:1 ff.; *Gen. Rab.* on 46:28. Cp. Constance's speech in *King John*, after her son's arrest: "Oh father Cardinal, I have heard you say That we shall see and know our friends in heav'n. If that be, I shall see my boy again. But now will canker-sorrow eat my bud, And he will look hollow as a ghost, And so he'll die; and rising so again, When I shall meet him in the court of heav'n, I shall not know him." For a different view see e.g. *Gen. Rab.* on 2:7.

[10] *Gen. Rab.* on 32:26; *Lev. Rab.* on 19:23; cp. Dan 6:25.

[11] Acts 1:18.

[12] *b. B. B.* 8b.

[13] 2 Mac 12:43 f., 7:10 f.; *Gen. Rab.* on 2:7; *Siphre* on Num 15:31; *b. Ber.* 61b.

[14] *Lev. Rab.* on 15:1.

was sown in dishonour, and raised in glory."[15] The analogy of the grain has long been recognized as Rabbinic.[16] The allusion to the disfigurement of a decaying corpse suggests that the addressees were worried by some of the popular ideas just indicated.

B. Criminal Law

In criminal procedure, *niwwul* might on occasion be not only admissible but even enjoined. We have already mentioned the woman suspected of adultery who, in the course of the ordeal of the bitter water, suffers the disgrace of having her head uncovered by the priest and so forth. Another notable instance is the burial of executed criminals in a plot kept by the court, without the usual ceremonies—or as Josephus puts it, "dishonourably, by night."[17]

Certain forms of capital punishment dating from the pre-Christian era would involve a disfigurement serious enough to create difficulties for the early believers in resurrection. The Old Testament, when it imposes stoning, means the putting to death of a criminal by hurling stones at him. Yet if this is done, he is bound to suffer fractures, some of them very visible. Similarly, where the burning of a criminal is ordained, if the precept is really followed, the body will be turned into ashes.

Regarding a murderer, the Old Testament demands that he should be killed. No doubt for a long time, whoever was charged with carrying out the penalty—mostly the nearest relation of the person murdered—slew the offender as best he could. As the court undertook the task, maybe there were groups in favour of precise talion: the murderer ought, as far as possible, to be despatched in the fashion in which he had despatched the victim. But there is no proof that this system was ever advocated. Those scholars who think it was normally rely on passages from the Book of Jubilees, 2 Maccabees and Philo. But in Jubilees and 2 Maccabees it is God who inflicts retaliation.[18] (Charles[19] also adduces a passage[20] where we learn that Nicanor's head, and his hand "which had stretched out against the house of the Almighty," are shown to the people. This, however, is not talion at all. It is punishment of the member through which the sin was perpetrated, "mirroring" punishment.) As for Philo, he observes[21] that a murderer must suffer the same as he whom he murdered. This need not refer to the manner of execution. It probably means nothing but that the murderer, having killed, is to be killed in his turn. Another custom is much better evidenced: it seems to have been usual at one time to execute a murderer by means of an axe, that is to say, exactly as, according to a section in Deuteronomy, if a murderer remains undetected, a heifer is to be slaughtered in expiation of the deed.[22] However, whether the murdered person's rela-

[15] 1 Cor 15:43.

[16] Strack-Billerbeck, vol. 3 (1926), 475.

[17] *m. Sanh.* 6:5 f.; *Ant.* 4.8.6.202, 4.8.24.264, 5.1.14.44.

[18] Jubilees 4:32; 2 Mac 5:10.

[19] In commenting on Jubilees 4:31 f. (*Apocrypha and Pseudepigrapha of the Old Testament*, vol. 2 [1913], 19).

[20] 2 Mac 15:32.

[21] *De spec. leg.* 3.15.84, 3.19.106.

[22] *m. Sanh.* 7:3; *t. Sanh.* 9:11; *Mek.* on Exod 21:12; *b. Sanh.* 52b; cp. Deut 21:1 ff.

tion kills the culprit as best he can, whether exact talion is inflicted, or whether the axe is used—damage to the murderer's bones must almost invariably result.

Between about 100 B.C. and A.D. 100 a far-reaching reform of the modes of execution was effected by the Pharisees.[23] First, stoning, they decided, was to be performed, not by pelting the criminal to death, but by pushing him down from a moderate height; if this did not suffice, one stone was to be dropped on his heart; and only if he stayed alive even then, stoning proper was to take place. This reformed mode of stoning—which appears, for example, in the story of Susanna as given by the LXX[24]—is obviously designed to avoid a breaking of the skull, chest, legs and so on. Secondly, burning, in the Pharisaic opinion, was to be performed, not by burning the criminal at the stake, but by forcing material set on fire down his throat. This, too, will exclude any destruction of the skeleton. Thirdly, wherever the Bible did not specify the form of execution, the Pharisees insisted on strangling "by a towel of coarse stuff within one of soft stuff":[25] in this case no mark whatever will be left on the body.

Decapitation of a murderer remained even in the reformed Pharisaic code. The axe was replaced by the sword; which entailed the further change that, whereas formerly the person condemned was stretched out face downwards, with his head resting on a block, and the blow fell from behind, now he knelt, with his head inclined backwards, and the blow came from the front. A few Rabbis took exception to the introduction of the sword, regarding it as a "disgraceful" Roman method. But the majority considered the ancient procedure, where the murderer was treated like the heifer from Deuteronomy, to be "the most disgraceful way of all."[26]

We need not here inquire why, in the case of murder, the disfiguring punishment was retained. Let us note, however, that there are traces of attempts—unsuccessful attempts—to extend the reform even to this field. It looks as if certain Rabbis had suggested the substitution of strangulation for decapitation; and as if others had made use of the verse "Whoso sheddeth man's blood, by man shall his blood be shed,"[27] and argued that a murderer should not be beheaded but be bled to death—his skeleton thus remaining intact.[28] As they stand in the Midrash, these views sound purely academic. But, as pointed out above [170] under "Ye have heard but I say unto you," many points which, in the Rabbinic discussions preserved to us, appear to be made only for argument's sake were once seriously maintained by one school or another.

Now we must not conceive of the reform of the Pharisees as a single effort, with no antecedents or vacillations and devoted to one purpose only. Two at least of the modes of execution which they favoured are very ancient indeed, though not figuring among those prescribed by the Old Testament: the pushing down of a criminal from a height,

[23] For references see A. Büchler, *Monatsschrift für Geschichte und Wissenschaft des Judentums*, vol. 50, 550 ff., 683 ff., and 704 ff.

[24] Susannah 62.

[25] *m. Sanh.* 7:3.

[26] *m. Sanh.* 7:3.

[27] Gen 9:6.

[28] *Mek.* on Exod 21:12.

by which they replaced stoning, and strangulation, which they applied where no other mode was specified in the Bible.

Further, it seems that the original method of stoning—pelting a person to death—was on occasion resorted to even in New Testament times.[29] It would naturally happen where there was an element of lynching. Josephus tells us[30] how he feared being stoned by the mob. (As we know from Luke,[31] even lynching might take the form of hurling from a rock.) But it might also occur by way of an official execution—though perhaps only if the court was under the direction of Sadducees.[32]

Again, there were influential Pharisaic groups who considered it more important that a man sentenced to death should suffer as little as possible than that his skeleton should be preserved. From their standpoint, some of the changes we have outlined were far from commendable; and decapitation, for instance, would be a less severe mode of execution than strangulation.[33] ("O Ping Siang, select the most agreeable manner and weapon for your end—By your side this person perceives a sword, his only request is that the blow shall be a sufficiently well-directed one."[34]) In other words, we must reckon with Sadducean opposition, with a good deal of wavering among the Pharisees, with local differences and so on.

Lastly, strangulation may have been given preference over other modes not only because it left the body intact, but also because it required little machinery and ceremony. It was, therefore, suitable even in periods when, in principle, the Romans alone exercised capital jurisdiction. Origen's remark[35] that Jewish courts inflict the death penalty "neither quite openly nor keeping it secret from the government" is significant. So is the fact that adultery, which according to the Old Testament as well as the early Tannaites was as a rule punishable by stoning ("He that is without sin, let him first cast a stone at her"),[36] from the 1st cent. A.D. gradually became punishable by strangulation. Origen tells us[37] that a Jewish court "*homicidam punire non potest nec adulteram lapidare, haec enim sibi vindicat Romanorum potentia*" ["For it cannot punish a murderer nor stone an adulteress, for the Roman power claims these rights for itself"]. In

[29] We need only refer to passages like John 8:1 ff., 8:59, 10:31 ff.; Acts 7:56 ff.; Josephus, *Ant.* 4.8.23.248, 20.9.1.199 f.

[30] *Vita* 13.76.

[31] Luke 4:29.

[32] Cp. Josephus, *Ant.*, *loc. cit.*

[33] *m. Sanh.* 7:1; *t. Sanh.* 9:11. Cp. Tertullian, *Apol.* 9.7, "ferro enim mori optaverit" ["For he chose to die by the sword"].

[34] E. Bramah, "The Vengeance of Tung Fel" (in *The Wallet of Kai Lung*).

[35] *Ad Africanum* 14.

[36] John 8:7. Strack-Billerbeck, vol. 2 (1924), 520, claim that the woman can have been engaged only, not married, since in the Rabbinic sources an adulterous married woman is liable to strangulation. But these sources reflect an innovation not yet universally recognized when the episode recorded in John took place or was written down. Ezek 16:40 refers to stoning; and similarly, according to the LXX, Susanna, had she not been saved by Daniel, would have been stoned (v. 62)—though in the reformed, Pharisaic manner, i.e. she would have been pushed down from a height.

[37] In his *Commentary on Romans*, according to Rufinus's version. l.6. c.7.

the case of murder, where the Pharisees retained beheading, the Roman intervention created no great problem: a murderer would be beheaded by the Romans, instead of by the Jews. In the case of adultery, however, the Romans in the first few centuries A.D. would only rarely inflict the death penalty; on the other hand, they did not allow the Jews to stone the guilty parties. This may well have been an additional motive for substituting strangulation, a punishment attracting less notice.

Nevertheless, when all necessary reservations are made, it remains true that between about 100 B.C. and A.D. 100 the Pharisees carried through a radical reform of the traditional modes of execution; a reform so radical that it would be inexplicable but against the background of a momentous religious movement. It was the movement which stressed the bodily resurrection of the dead.

We have already pointed out that, for most Rabbis, God's power to raise a man from the dead did not depend on the integrity of the skeleton. Even the opinion that the dead would in the first instance come to life in the form they had possessed when last on earth was never shared by all. Why, then, did the majority support the reform in question? Principally, we may assume, in order to strengthen the belief in physical resurrection among the masses: the masses would accept the dogma more readily if the religious leaders did everything to emphasize the importance of the body, everything to save the most durable parts, the bones, from destruction. This seems to be the object also of the warning against dissection in the Pseudo-Phocylidean poem: "not to break up the structure of a human body, because we hope the remains of the departed will again come forth from the earth."[38] The hostility to cremation shown up to our day by orthodox Judaism[39] and several branches of Christianity offers something of a parallel.

C. THE CRUCIFIXION

It has recently been argued that it was not the suffering of Jesus as such, but the abject form it took, which the Jewish antagonists found "scandalous."[40] Certainly, about A.D. 130, R. Ishmael, when facing martyrdom, is said to have exclaimed: "Do I weep because we are to be slain? No, but because we are to be slain like murderers and desecrators of the Sabbath."[41] The Jew Tryphon is represented by Justin as remarking on the "disgraceful" death of Jesus.[42]

Be this as it may, John at least is concerned to deny that Jesus underwent a particular kind of *niwwul*, namely, that disfigurement which—in popular thought—might stand in the way of resurrection. He records that Jesus's legs were not broken.[43] He also informs us that it was the Jews who, since they wanted the bodies taken down before the Sabbath, proposed the breaking of the legs. This suggests that the anti-Christian party used the disfigurement as an argument against the resurrection of Jesus. John is warding off an attack,

[38] Pseudo-Phocylides 101 ff.

[39] Tacitus was angry about it with the Judaism of his time: *Histories* 5.5.

[40] 1 Cor 1:23; Gal 5:11; see W. D. Davies, *Paul and Rabbinic Judaism*, 283 f.

[41] *Sem.* 8.

[42] *Dial.* 32, 89.

[43] John 19:31 ff.

he asserts that things did not happen as his opponents imagine and wish them to have happened. That is also why he adds so emphatically that it is his version which gives the truth. It may indeed be one of his motives (though one can think of others which are perfectly adequate) for omitting the institution of the Eucharist: hostile readers might misinterpret the breaking of the bread as hinting at a breaking of Jesus's body. No direct mention of a breaking of bread is made in chapter 6, where there is a discourse about the significance of the Eucharist;[44] and though in chapter 2 the phrase "to destroy the Temple" is explained as referring to the destruction of Jesus's body,[45] the expression λύω, "to destroy," "to undo," is too general to be suggestive of a breaking of bones.

It should be recalled that John insists more strongly than even Luke on the appearance of the risen Jesus in the precise form he had when last alive. In Luke, Jesus says: "Behold my hands and feet, handle me and see." Neither of the two other Synoptics mentions this. John, however, in addition to an analogous passage, has the detailed narrative about Thomas.[46] Incidentally, ideas concerning resurrection may well play a similar part in the *Martyrdom of Polycarp*.[47] The Jews, we are told, were very keen on burning him, but as the fire refused to kill him, an executioner had to stab him to death. Thereupon the Jews interceded with the magistrate not to give up the corpse to the martyr's friends, and the corpse was burned. Yet even now the bones remained and were gathered by the faithful.

According to John, Jesus's body remained intact "that the scripture should be fulfilled, A bone of him shall not be broken." A number of modern critics hold that the reference to the Passover lamb came first, and the story of how a breaking of the legs was avoided second. John, they maintain, wrote the story in order to assimilate Jesus to the lamb. But surely, this purpose could have been achieved in a less complicated manner. From the foregoing discussion it is clear that priority belongs to the story: it was essential to rule out *niwwul* in the sense of destruction of the bones. The reference to the Passover lamb is added by way of interpretation. Nor was the quotation inappropriate. When we consider that a verse like "The Lord keepeth all the bones of the righteous, not one of them is broken"[48] occurs in an ancient Jewish prayer for the dead, or that Ezekiel's vision of the revival of the dried up bones[49] forms the prophetic lesson on the mid-festival Sabbath of Passover, it appears probable that, even before John, the inviolability of the bones of the Passover lamb was widely regarded as symbolizing the individual's hope of resurrection as well as the nation's of a glorious future.

John's exclusion of a disfiguring *niwwul* is adumbrated in Matthew and Luke. Mark speaks of Jesus's dead body as πτῶμα, which, as has long been seen, is more primitive than σῶμα, employed by Matthew, Luke and John.[50] The usual explanation of the change

[44] John 6:48 ff.

[45] John 2:19 ff.

[46] Luke 24:39; John 20:20 (cp. 1 John 1:1), 20:24 ff.

[47] *Martyrdom of Polycarp*, 13 ff.

[48] Ps 34:21.

[49] Ezek 37:1 ff.

[50] Mark 15:43, 45; Matt 27:58; Luke 23:52; John 19:38, 40. Even in Mark 15:43 σῶμα has ousted πτῶμα in a number of MSS.

is that σῶμα was found more respectful in a general way than πτῶμα. There may indeed be some truth in this. But the main factor must have been the consideration that πτῶμα was particularly suitable for describing a mutilated corpse, and thus a corpse mutilated in the course of an execution. (The word corresponds to *pegher* in Hebrew, *peghar* or *pigra'* in Aramaic. Isaiah says:[51] "But thou art cast out of thy grave like an abominable branch, and as the raiment of them that are slain, thrust through with a sword, that go down to the pit, as a carcase trodden under feet." "Carcase" represents *pegher* in the Hebrew, *peghar* in the Targum.) In the New Testament itself πτῶμα occurs where the beheaded Baptist is buried.[52] As applied to Jesus, there was danger of the term suggesting that his legs were crushed. But it is John alone who expressly denies this *niwwul*, by giving a circumstantial account of how it was avoided.

D. Jesus's Grave

As stated above, Rabbinic law contained provisions respecting the burial of a person who had been executed. While nothing was to be done that might impede resurrection, most of the customary ceremonies in honour of the deceased must be omitted. One rule which involved "disgrace" was that executed persons might not at once be buried in the family grave. The court kept two plots for their provisional burial by relatives or officials. It was only after a year or so that the bones were gathered and transferred to the family burying place.

Quite possibly this was another—though less serious—allegation of *niwwul* made by the anti-Christian party: the burial of Jesus in one of the public plots. To be sure, even if he was buried there, his followers could have argued that it constituted part of his suffering for the sake of the Kingdom. They could have referred to as early a case as that of the true prophet whom Jehoiakim "slew with the sword and cast his dead body into the graves of the common people," or to the prophecy about the servant of the Lord, whose "grave was made with the wicked."[53] But the enemies would have disagreed with this interpretation. At any rate, the gospels reveal an inclination in some Christian circles to deny the existence of this *niwwul*.

According to Mark, Jesus was buried in "a sepulchre"—which may mean any grave, even a public one for criminals; it clearly does not mean the grave of Jesus's family. According to Luke, however, he was buried in "a sepulchre wherein never man before was laid." John concurs; indeed he adds the attribute "new," it was "a new sepulchre." Luke and John intended to rule out burial in a grave previously used for other executed persons. They do not say that the grave did not belong to the court—John's remark that it was near the place of crucifixion might be taken as an indication that it did—but they do say that it had never been desecrated by the corpse of a sinner. Matthew states that it was the family grave of Joseph of Arimathaea, newly built. That is to say, it was definitely not a public one, nor had it ever been used either for sinner or for saint.[54]

[51] Isa 14:19.

[52] Matt 14:12; Mark 6:29. In Matthew the Koine reading is σῶμα, clearly secondary.

[53] Jer 26:20 ff.; Isa 53:9.

[54] Mark 15:46; Luke 23:53; John 19:41; Matt 27:60.

The accounts are not necessarily contradictory as far as historical events are concerned. It is possible that Mark, Luke and John no less than Matthew are thinking of Joseph's family grave; and there are other ways of reconciling the facts related by the evangelists. (Incidentally, as Jesus was executed by the Romans, it is doubtful whether, under the Jewish law of the time, he ought to have been buried in a plot for criminals. The question is complicated by his having been found guilty of blasphemy by the Sanhedrin.) For our purpose it suffices to bring out the concern of three at least of the four definitely to mitigate or exclude "disgrace."

In the Tosephta[55] it is laid down that "even if the criminal were a king of kings, he may not be buried in the grave of his fathers, but only in that prepared by the court." The term "king of kings" designates the king of the Persians, the Roman emperor or the like. Its use here seems to be figurative, since a Jewish court was never likely to pronounce sentence of death on a foreign ruler of such rank. Probably the provision simply means that, however highly placed, a criminal executed must suffer the "disgrace" of a criminal's burial. It is, however, conceivable that the rule contains an anti-Christian point. The hyperbole may have been introduced in order to show that Jesus could not have escaped being buried in a public grave. The paragraph under discussion ends by quoting a verse from Psalms: "Gather not my soul with sinners."[56] According to the Tosephta, David here implores God not to be buried as a criminal.

E. Jesus's Burial Clothes

Normally, in New Testament times, funerals were conducted with great luxury, and even the poorest felt obliged to bury relatives or friends in valuable burial clothes. It was Gamaliel II, about A.D. 90, who, in order to relieve poor people of this burden, had himself buried in a plain linen cloth.[57] Before that reform, a plain cloth chosen without care would be used only for a criminal or at best a person despised by everyone. It would be a sign of shame.

It is interesting, then, that whereas according to Luke and John, Jesus was wrapped in "a linen cloth," Matthew and Mark make it clear—in different ways—that it was a new cloth.[58] The historicity of the latter view need not be doubted. But the presumption is that Luke and John are closer to the original tradition. The emphasis on the freshness of the cloth which we find in Matthew and Mark springs from the desire to eliminate any suggestion of *niwwul* marking the burial.

The presumption is confirmed by the manner in which Matthew and Mark refer to the quality of Jesus's burial clothes, a manner which proves these references to be intrusions into the earlier account. Mark tells us that Joseph of Arimathaea, having obtained permission to bury Jesus, "bought a linen cloth"—the implication being that he did not just use any cloth that was to hand. But this buying of cloth on the first day of Passover—and for Mark at least that was the date—constitutes an old crux. Jewish law

[55] *t. Sanh.* 9:8.

[56] Ps 26:9.

[57] *b. Ket.* 8b. Tacitus, *Histories* 5.5, remarks on the care bestowed by the Jews on the bodies of the dead.

[58] Luke 23:53; John 19:40; Matt 27:59; Mark 15:46.

forbade buying on a festival day. Some modern authorities indeed argue that the Greek of Mark may be due to a mistranslation of an Aramaic word which did not signify "to buy."[59] But we need not accept this counsel of despair. The most likely solution is that Mark, or his source, when introducing the point as to the quality of the burial clothes, went too far and, by some oversight, spoke of a purchase on the first day of Passover.

Matthew seems to have noticed the difficulty. He omits the purchase, and simply makes "a clean linen cloth" of the "linen cloth" to be found in the other evangelists. The effect as regards the problem of *niwwul* is the same as in Mark: there was no "disgrace." But the transgression of the rules about the observance of festival days is avoided.

F. The Anointing at Bethany

Preoccupation with the question of *niwwul* may well have been a major factor in the growth of the narrative of the anointing at Bethany. In other words, the different versions[60] seem to reflect so many different explanations of the treatment of Jesus's body at the time of his burial.

1. *Mark and John: the Main Distinction*

The fundamental difference between Mark and John is that in Mark the woman anticipates, i.e. here and now performs, the burial rite of anointing, whereas in John she does not. In Mark, Jesus says of her that "she is come aforehand to anoint my body to the burial." The import of this ought not to be watered down: her act is boldly declared a valid, though proleptic, anointing of the body for burial. Jurists would call the statement a legal fiction, an authoritative interpretation of facts as something which, but for that interpretation, they would not be. On the basis of the interpretation in Mark, the burial rite of anointing has now taken place. The sources show that the Rabbis were quite familiar with acts of this sort—acts with immediate legal or religious effect though, in reality, an essential element is still to come. (The equivalent of προλαμβάνειν in the relevant texts is *qadham* or *hiqdim*. You can reward a service in advance; a *prosbul* made out in anticipation of a loan to be given is valid; if I send you a gift in order that you should make me a loan, this is interest paid in advance and therefore prohibited.[61])

In contradistinction, in John, if we accept—as we must[62]—the reading "let her alone, that she may keep it against the day of my burial," no such fiction is established. No assertion is made that a burial ceremony has been performed, but the burial is thought of, quite naturally, as entirely belonging to the future. It is relevant to notice that Jesus speaks, not as in Mark of "the burial," which may in a sense be celebrated now, but of "the day of the burial"—a reference to a distinct point in time, a future date.

To understand the difference, it is necessary to consider the treatment which the two evangelists assume Jesus's body received after his death. According to Mark who has a burial ceremony by way of anticipation, Joseph of Arimathaea did not anoint the

[59] E.g. Strack-Billerbeck, vol. 2 (1924), 833.

[60] Matt 26:6 ff.; Mark 14:3 ff.; Luke 7:36 ff.; John 12:1 ff.

[61] *y. Sot.* 22d; *m. Shebi.* 10:5; *m. B. M.* 5:10.

[62] The Koine reading τετήρηκεν is an assimilation to Matthew and Mark.

body, and the women who intended to do so came too late. According to John, who has no burial ceremony by way of anticipation, Joseph and Nicodemus anointed the body with a hundred pounds of spices.[63] The position cannot be the result of a series of coincidences. Both Mark and John take care to point out that the burial rite of anointing was performed. For Mark, it was performed at Bethany—by virtue of a fiction—and nothing was done after Jesus's death. For John, Jesus's body was actually anointed after his death, and the action at Bethany is not represented as performance of the rite.

Very probably, the earliest tradition was that Jesus had been buried unanointed, like a common criminal, "dishonourably, by night."[64] This tradition was unbearable to the believers. We have already remarked on the luxury practised in that period even by the poorest when it came to burying a relative or friend. Moreover, the Jewish unbelievers doubtless seized on this additional *niwwul*, as a confirmation of the "scandal" of the crucifixion. If it was the form of Jesus's suffering rather than his suffering as such which constituted the "scandal," the omission of anointing would be an integral part of the charge. Mark gives one reply: Jesus's body was anointed in advance. John gives another: his body was anointed by Joseph and Nicodemus.

This does not imply that John's report is historically worthless. John may have had access to information which Mark lacked. It would be far from surprising since, if his report is true, it is to be supposed that Joseph and Nicodemus did everything to avoid publicity. Nor would it be right to deny that the way Mark understood the incident at Bethany had some basis in historical reality. But these questions are beyond the scope of our investigation. We are concerned less with what happened than with the ideas that influenced the New Testament writers. It does look as if they had been exercised by the problem of "disgrace" that would be produced if Jesus's body was left unanointed. Mark found the solution in the episode at Bethany, John in the action of Joseph and Nicodemus.

It is noteworthy that John—and John alone of all evangelists—lays emphasis on an actual absence of *niwwul*, on a regular anointing after death. As we saw above, he alone expressly testifies to the intactness of Jesus's body, the failure of the soldiers to break his legs. Surely his attitude to the two matters is dictated by the same fundamental considerations.

2. *Mark and John: Continuation*

Four details may be added.

First, in Mark's version of the anointing at Bethany, since a burial rite here and now is contemplated, the box is broken and the entire ointment poured over Jesus's head. No doubt we are meant to infer that the ointment covered him; this is borne out by his own words, "to anoint my body." In any case, it is not the way in which one would ordinarily anoint a guest or teacher. In John, as no present burial rite is contemplated, the box is not broken, and it is Jesus's feet that are anointed, presumably with the hand. No anointing of the body is implied in Jesus's words, "let her alone" etc. The Talmud men-

[63] Mark 15:42 ff.; John 19:39 f.

[64] *m. Sanh.* 6:5 f.; Josephus, *Ant.* 4.8.6.202, 4.8.24.264, 5.1.14.44.

tions superstitious scruples entertained by people about anointing themselves, not with the hand, but direct from a flask.[65] Very likely these fears had their root in the association of the latter method with funerals.

Secondly, in Mark, the argument is as follows. Some contend that the value of the ointment ought to have been spent on almsgiving. Jesus's reply is in three parts, forming an ascending line. He begins by saying that the woman has done "a good work." This is a technical term. It means almsgiving, putting up strangers, visiting the sick, burying the dead or the like.[66] (According to R. Simlai, of the second half of the 3rd cent. A.D., the Torah opens with "a good work," God clothing the naked, and concludes with one, God burying Moses.[67]) So the first part of the reply is intended to mystify the audience: Jesus affirms that the woman's action is "a good work" just as much as almsgiving. Exactly what kind of "good work" he means he does not yet explain, and his hearers can hardly be expected to guess. Next he adds that "ye have the poor always... but me ye have not always." This is reminiscent of the Rabbinic doctrine[68] that almsgiving is less praiseworthy than the other "good works," one reason being that the former can be done only for the living whereas the latter extend also to the dead. Here, then, he commences to specify the "good work" he has in mind: it is superior to almsgiving, superior because done to one—and that one Jesus—whom "ye have not always." There follows the culmination, the revelation to which the first two parts of the reply have been leading up: the woman has performed the burial rite of anointing.

Now in John, all this is different. The first part is completely missing. The woman's action is not called "a good work." It could not be: the anointing does not constitute a burial rite. The reply begins with "let her alone" etc., corresponding to the third part in Mark, but, as pointed out above, quite unlike in substance. There is no assertion of a present burial ceremony, but a reference to the future day of burial. The clause "for the poor always ye have with you" etc., coming second in Mark, to prepare the revelation that this is the anointing for the burial, comes last in John. As no burial rite here and now is in question, it must not precede the allusion to the future day of burial. If the impression of abruptness is to be avoided, it must be introduced as an afterthought to, a fuller explanation of, that allusion.

Thirdly, in Mark, the incident takes place after the entry into Jerusalem and very near Passover—as near the actual burial as possible. In John, it takes place before the entry and not quite so near.

Fourthly, John emphasizes that Joseph and Nicodemus dealt with the body "as the manner of the Jews is to bury." This does sound as if directed against disparaging talk on the part of Jewish opponents. John flatly denies any basis in fact for their charge. There is no mere reinterpreting of some other action as standing for the rite. The rite was really performed in the correct, indeed, in a particularly splendid, fashion. The presence of Nicodemus, which at first sight looks somewhat unmotivated, may well be stressed as

[65] *b. Sanh.* 101a.

[66] For numerous references see Strack-Billerbeck, vol. 4 (1928), pt. 1, 536 ff. and 559 ff.

[67] *b. Sot.* 14a.

[68] *t. Peah* 4:19; *b. Sukk.* 49b.

guaranteeing the proper observance of the ritual: he was a respected Pharisee.[69]

As for dependence, it is obvious even at this stage that Mark was ignorant of an actual anointing after death. Otherwise he would not have dropped it in favour of anointing by anticipation. A fiction, however good a substitute for fact, is still a substitute. Unbelievers would not readily accept it, and even a believer, unless trained in such matters, might feel uneasy. (This is not to judge—let it be repeated—about the historical value of Mark's interpretation.) Neither, however, is it likely that John used Mark. There would have been no reason for replacing the anointing of the head by one of the feet. Certainly, John did not need an anointing of the head—and body—since, in his eyes, the woman was not there and then performing the burial rite. But it is difficult to think of any objection he might have had against this mode of anointing had he been following Mark. (The breaking of the box is a different matter. That he might have rejected as peculiar to the anointing of a corpse.) Another change would be even more inexplicable: in John, the woman wipes the anointed feet with her hair. If John was following Mark, why should he have inserted this unnatural feature?[70]

We shall submit a conjecture as to the growth of the narrative at the end of our inquiry.

3. *"That she may keep it"*

So far we have not gone into the precise meaning of this phrase which occurs in John. Our main thesis is indeed unaffected by the question; nevertheless it may be worth while to draw attention to a few points.

(1) The usual—probably the correct—way in which it is understood is: "that she may keep the ointment." In John, it should be recalled, there is no breaking of the box and pouring out of the entire contents, as at burial. The woman anoints Jesus's feet. So some ointment may be left.

But what is the purpose of keeping it? It is to be kept "against the day of my burial." It is tempting to see here a trace of the tradition represented in Mark and Luke, though not in John (nor in Matthew), that after Jesus's death several women planned to anoint the dead body. The identification in John of the woman of Bethany with Mary—not to be found in the Synoptics—points in the same direction: according to Mark and Luke, Mary was among the women that hoped to anoint the body. If this is so, the phrase under discussion means that she ought to keep the ointment for that anointing. As John, however, does not report the attempt of the women to anoint the dead body, it would follow that he cannot be the original author of the phrase. He must have taken it over from a source which still did report, and attach great importance to, the women's plan. We should have before us, that is, a pre-Johannine nuance of Jesus's remark, which, in John, has lost its point.

Mary, then, is to keep it for that subsequent occasion. Her present gesture of reverence adumbrates what she will do, or attempt to do, when Jesus is dead. Here we may

[69] John 3:1.

[70] Wagner, however, in his *Parsifal*, adopts it: Kundry, having washed the hero's feet, anoints them and only then dries them with her hair.

come back to that very strange feature in John's version that, having anointed Jesus's feet, she dries the ointment with her hair. It will appear less strange if the version grew out of another, in fact out of one like that preserved in Luke, where a penitent woman washed his feet with her tears, dried them with her hair and then anointed them. In John, the washing is omitted, in order to achieve a closer foreshadowing of the anointing after death. Only the drying is still retained, illogically and with a disturbing result.

(2) However, there is a well-known difficulty about the interpretation "that she may keep the ointment": one would expect the text to speak of "the rest," τὸ περισσεῦον, or the like. So perhaps we should paraphrase "that she may treasure up the act."[71] It would be reading a great deal into the pronoun αὐτό, "it" ("that she may keep it"), but it cannot be ruled out. The sense would be that Mary should treasure up the act for the day when she and others would wish, but be unable, to anoint the dead body. In other words, we should have to do, not yet with a definite proleptic burial rite as in Mark, but with something coming rather near it. Treasuring up an act for a future occasion is not quite the same as performing here and now an act strictly appropriate only to the future, but it contains the germ of the latter idea.

Once again, as John does not report the plan of the women to anoint the dead body, we must assume—if we accept this rendering—that he took the clause from his source. That the source had not yet, like Mark, fully reached the idea of a burial ceremony by anticipation is confirmed by various significant differences. In Mark, the head is anointed; in the version before John, it was still the feet. In Mark, there is no drying of the ointment with the hair; in the version before John, it still occurred. The version before John had not yet, like Mark, shed the vestiges of an earlier stage, when the narrative simply concerned a penitent woman paying homage to Jesus.

(3) The verb τηρέω, "to keep," sometimes denotes "to keep in one's memory," "to remember." The phrase in question could be translated: "that she may remember it"—*scil.* the ointment she has used, or (but this again would probably be giving αὐτό too much weight) this incident, this act. We do not regard this meaning as likely. But it is just conceivable, and the difficulty attaching to the interpretation "that she may keep the ointment that is left" does not arise. The woman is to remember the ointment with which she anointed Jesus's feet, or the entire incident; so no reference to "the rest," τὸ περισσεῦον, is wanted.

Three other passages with derivatives of τηρέω come to mind: two from Luke—Mary "kept in her heart" what the shepherds had said and how the young Jesus had taught in the Temple—and one from Genesis—Jacob "retained in his memory" Joseph's dreams.[72] In all these cases, the event remembered adumbrates, provides the understanding one with a foretaste of, the real thing to come. Joseph's dreams point forward to his exaltation in Egypt, the testimony of the shepherds to the worship of the Church, the young Jesus's discourse amidst the doctors to the message of the mature Jesus. Presumably—if we take τηρέω in this sense—the ointment used at Bethany is to be

[71] This was very kindly suggested to me by Professor C. Moule of Cambridge, but I hasten to add that he does not subscribe to my conclusions.

[72] Luke 2:19, 51; Gen 37:11.

remembered as foreshadowing the costlier one used by Joseph and Nicodemus in the most tragic and yet most glorious circumstances.

Should this be the meaning of John, there are three possibilities. Either John drew on a version of the narrative with no reference to Jesus's burial whatever—a version of the kind we find in Luke—and he himself turned the incident into one foreshadowing the final anointing by Joseph and Nicodemus. That is to say, he himself suppressed the woman's contrition and tears—with the awkward result that she dries the ointment with her hair—and introduced the clause "Let her alone that she may remember..." and "For the poor always...." This solution, however, is extremely improbable. Once it was established that Jesus's body was actually anointed after his death in the proper mode, there was no need for violent interference with an entirely different type of anointing during his life.

Or John drew on a version which, like Mark, saw in the anointing at Bethany a present, proleptic performance of the burial rite. As John taught that Jesus was in fact anointed after his death, he did not want this rite to be anticipated. Consequently, he eliminated the fiction of a present burial, he changed the performance in advance into adumbration, he cut out the description of the woman's action as "a good work" and toned down the expression "she has come aforehand" into "that she may remember it against the day when Joseph and Nicodemus will actually observe the ritual."

Or, finally, the version before John used "to keep" in the sense of "to treasure up an act," and regarded the anointing at Bethany as an adumbration of the women's later, unsuccessful plan to anoint the dead Jesus. John made no verbal alteration, but he regarded the action as adumbrating the real anointing by Joseph and Nicodemus, he used "to keep" in the sense of "to keep in memory an event apparently unimportant and incomplete, yet prefiguring a great fulfilment in the future."

It may be repeated that the account John knew can at most have been like Mark's—namely, in insisting on a burial rite in advance, or in treating Mary's action as foreshadowing her subsequent attempt to anoint the dead body—but it cannot have been the Markan account itself. In the version before John, it was still the feet that are anointed, and the woman still dried the ointment with her hair. In other words, though that version may already have contained the fiction of a burial rite here and now, or something approaching this fiction, it had not yet drawn out all the consequences. It was a "proto-Markan" version, and John gave up any allusion to the performance of a burial rite by Mary in favour of an adumbration—to be remembered—of the true anointing by Joseph and Nicodemus.

4. *Matthew*

Matthew is fairly close to Mark. As in Mark, the incident takes place after the entry into Jerusalem, very near Passover. True, the box is not broken. But the ointment is poured over Jesus's head and also, quite clearly, over his body: "for in that she hath poured this ointment on my body," Jesus says. Further, as in Mark, Jesus's reply consists of three parts, and is designed to prove the superiority of the woman's action, as constituting a burial ceremony, over almsgiving—in accordance with Rabbinic doctrine. As for the statement "she hath done it for my burying," it expresses the performance of the burial rite here and now even more strongly than Mark's "she is come aforehand to anoint." Accordingly—the most significant fact from the point of view of the thesis here advocated—Matthew, like Mark, has no real anointing after death.

Where they differ, Matthew as a rule appears secondary. Let us take a few examples.

In the first place, "she is come aforehand to anoint to the burial," in Mark, is the formulation of somebody still wrestling with the problem, somebody who must explain how an anointing of the living Jesus could stand for one after his death. Matthew has the much simpler declaration "she hath done it to my burying"—which indicates that the Markan solution of the problem has been fully accepted. She has performed the burial rite: the fact that it is done by anticipation, the element of fiction, is no longer even hinted at.

The substitution by Matthew of the verb, "to bury me," for Mark's noun, "to the burial," also follows from this perfect assurance that the burying takes place at this moment. "To the burial"—Mark—is still slightly more formal, less concrete, than "to bury me"—Matthew.

Again, in Mark, that the ointment poured over Jesus's head covered his body is only indirectly conveyed, implied, in the interpretation of the action: "she is come aforehand to anoint my body." In Matthew also it comes in the interpretation, but quite explicitly: "for in that she hath poured this ointment on my body."

There is another sign that Mark is not yet comfortable: the clause "she hath done what she could," which is absent from Matthew. Mark is still conscious that the burial rite at Bethany is a second best, an "as if." Matthew no longer shares this feeling.

How completely satisfied Matthew is may be inferred from his omitting the attempt of the women to anoint the dead Jesus, which is still extant in Mark. The omission is striking. Matthew doubtless held that such an attempt was not only superfluous after the performance of the rite at Bethany, but even apt to weaken the definitive "she hath done it to my burying."

5. *Luke: the Growth of the Narrative*

The clue to the different versions of the anointing at Bethany lies in the recognition that the development of the narrative was determined by the tendency to free Jesus's burial from any *niwwul*—a tendency understandable in itself, but in all probability intensified by the Jewish attitude to the "scandal" of Jesus's end.

Surely we must start from Luke. He knows nothing of the anointing by Joseph and Nicodemus, and the women came too late. Neither, however, is there any allusion to Jesus's death in the chapter about the sinful woman who anoints him while he lives. We do not meet with the phrase "good work," which could fit so well if it had the vague sense of any fine deed. Its absence confirms the technical interpretation we have put on it in Mark and Matthew; but in Luke there is no thought of the performance of a funeral rite. The incident—not yet located at Bethany—is right outside the passion cycle, and the woman does not pour ointment over Jesus's head, but washes with her tears, dries with her hair and anoints Jesus's feet. While there may be secondary elements,

Luke on the whole stands nearest the original tradition. It is noteworthy that, in depicting the action of the woman, John is close to Luke, except for the omission of her tears in favour of an exclusive stress on the anointing of the feet. Of course, John has the complaint about the waste and the reply "Let her alone" and so on—both foreign to Luke.

The following stages in the evolution of the tradition regarding Jesus's burial are suggested.

(1) A woman washed with her tears, dried with her hair and anointed Jesus's feet while he lived. After his death, nobody anointed or attempted to anoint his body. This stage is not preserved in any of our sources.

(2) The "disgrace" was mitigated by introducing an attempt of some women to anoint the corpse (which may be perfectly historical). They could not carry out their plan because, in the meantime, Jesus had risen. This was a justification of their failure more than sufficient for the faithful. But why had they not come earlier? Because "they rested on the sabbath day according to the commandment." This ought to silence the Jewish questioners. They could say nothing against strict compliance with the Law, which prohibited any buying—and therefore the buying of any spices—on a Sabbath. Curiously, Luke—though not Mark—assumes that the act of anointing itself was forbidden on a Sabbath, and not, or not only, the purchase of spices. It would be rash to deny that some Rabbis may have held this view in New Testament times. But the Mishnah allows the anointing of a corpse,[73] while buying would be a grave transgression of the rules. Mark agrees with the Mishnic doctrine; so it is possible that Luke misunderstood the matter.

However, apart from this detail, the stage of the tradition just outlined is preserved in Luke. Its distinctive mark is that the non-observance of the rite of anointing is still admitted. Only it is claimed that it resulted not from a treatment of the body as that of a criminal, but from keeping the Sabbath and the resurrection immediately afterwards. The non-observance of the rite is explained, but not yet explained away, still less flatly denied.

(3a) One possibility is that the incident at Bethany was now made into an adumbration of the women's attempt to anoint the dead body—perhaps in order to endow that attempt with greater weight. It had, after all, failed. This might explain the account in John, if we paraphrase the clause "that she may keep it" either by "that she may keep the ointment" or by "that she may treasure up the act." The naming of Mary as well as the omission of the woman's tears, with the strange result that what she dries with her hair is the ointment, would fit: these features can be ascribed to a desire to effect a closer foreshadowing of the plan to anoint the dead Jesus.

However, the development, though it produced the account in John, would have to be pre-Johannine. For John himself discards the attempt of the women, asserting that there was successful anointing by Joseph and Nicodemus. So he himself would not have connected the anointing at Bethany with that attempt. He himself simply denies that there was any neglect at the time of Jesus's burial.

(3b) If we take "that she may keep it" in the sense of "that she may remember it against the day when Joseph and Nicodemus will anoint the body," there is a remote

[73] *m. Shab.* 23:5.

possibility that John himself turned a contrite washing and anointing of the feet into an adumbration of the final anointing by two faithful men. The omission of the tears, with its awkward consequence, and the formulation of the saying "Let her alone" etc. would be due to himself.

(3c) However, should this interpretation of the clause be tenable at all, it is better to suppose that John proceeded from a more advanced stage than that represented by Luke; namely, from a stage where the anointing at Bethany was already thought of as anticipating the burial rite, as constituting an anointing for burial here and now, or at least as adumbrating Mary's later attempt to perform the rite. To be sure, in the version before John it is still the feet that are anointed, and there is still drying with her hair; we are midway, that is, between Luke and Mark. As John had the actual rite after death, he changed performance in advance ("she is come aforehand") or adumbration of Mary's unsuccessful attempt ("that she may treasure up the act") into adumbration of the actual rite ("that she may remember it against the day Joseph and Nicodemus will do it"); and, accordingly, he dropped the reference to Mary's "good work on me." For him, an event of apparent insignificance prophetically pointed towards a great fulfilment.

If John drew on a "proto-Markan" account, incidentally, it may have included some eulogy similar to that occurring in Mark, "wherever this gospel shall be preached, this also shall be spoken of"; and the corresponding passage in John may be the remark that "the house was filled with the odour of the ointment." Admittedly, it is perhaps fanciful to credit the latter clause with a deeper meaning. The ancients liked strong scent, and a description of this kind need contain no symbolism. "Were Hera's perfume shaken in the palace of Zeus," Homer says,[74] "its savour would reach unto earth and heaven." Still, it may be recalled that the Rabbis liken Abraham before he went out to preach to a flask of perfume stowed away so that its odour cannot spread; and that, in their view, "precious ointment spreads from the bedchamber to the dining-room, but a good name spreads from one end of the world to the other."[75]

(4) Mark, who does not know the anointing by Joseph and Nicodemus, far from giving up performance by anticipation—"she is come aforehand"—and the "good work," follows out some further implications of the idea of a present burial rite. He puts the story after the entry into Jerusalem, immediately before the crucifixion; replaces the anointing of the feet by a breaking of the box and pouring of the ointment over Jesus's head—and body; and suppresses the drying. At the same time, he still retains the attempt of the women after Jesus's death; and there are other indications—such as "she hath done what she could"—that he is aware that his account, *au fond*, constitutes an explaining away of such facts as have been handed to him.

(5) Matthew, finally, takes over the Markan solution, but with far more confidence. Its problematic nature is no longer felt, as is shown, for instance, by the omission of "she hath done what she could" and by the straightforward "she did so" in the place of "she is come aforehand to do so." The most notable innovation in this respect is the abandonment of the attempt of the women to anoint the corpse as superfluous.

[74] *Il.* 14.173, commented on by Athenaeus, *Deipn.* 1.17b.

[75] *Gen. Rab.* on 12:1; *Eccl. Rab.* on 1:3, 7:1.

Samaritan Women

A. The Decree of A.D. 65/6

When Jesus asked the Samaritan woman to give him to drink, John tells us,[1] she was surprised by his kindness. Why? Surely, for an unsophisticated mind, as a rule, it is the offer of a drink, not the request for one, which expresses love.

To appreciate the story, it is necessary to assume a technical Rabbinic background. A regulation of A.D. 65 or 66 laid down that, from the point of view of the laws of purity, "the daughters of the Samaritans are menstruants from their cradle."[2] This decree was much talked about in the first decades of its existence. For it was enacted in highly dramatic circumstances, on the eve of the revolt against Rome, by that famous synod of Hillelites and Shammaites where the extreme zealots among the latter were in the majority and, overawing the opposition, passed a large number of chauvinistic measures.[3] As late as the end of the century, bitter words could be exchanged between followers of the various parties about this episode and its consequences; and as the moderates gained the upper hand, the day when the synod had met came to be regarded as a day of calamity for the nation.[4]

The formal justification of the decree was, of course, that according to strict Pharisaic principles, as the Samaritan provisions concerning purity differed in some respects from the Pharisaic, there was always at least the possibility of a Samaritan woman being in a state of uncleanness. It is indeed very likely that, in the more rigid circles, this view had been prevalent, and acted upon, long before it was given full legal force. The point is of importance for the question of the historicity of the incident under notice. There is no reason to doubt that it may have occurred when John says it did, though, obviously, the interest in it must have been much intensified by the events of 65/6.

The woman Jesus met was deemed unclean, like a menstruant, and her uncleanness was conveyed to the vessel she held.[5] (We need not consider special cases where contamination might be avoidable.) If it was a vessel from which she used to drink, the case was particularly serious: the spittle of a menstruant was contaminating in a very high degree. In any case, a 2nd-century Rabbi praises the good old times when it was

[1] John 4:7 ff.
[2] *m. Nidd.* 4:1.
[3] *b. Shab.* 16b.
[4] *y. Shab.* 3c.
[5] *m. Kel.* 1:1 ff.

a matter of course for one in a state of purity not to eat together with a menstruant.[6] By asking the woman to give him to drink, Jesus showed himself ready to disregard that hostile presumption respecting Samaritan women for the sake of a more inclusive fellowship.

Maybe he already acted on the same principle when he let his disciples purchase food in the city near-by. Presumably they bought from Samaritans. But as certain dry food-stuffs were not regarded as susceptible to uncleanness, the question must be left open. The disciples may have confined themselves to these. Among the decrees of the synod referred to were some prohibiting the use of several important kinds of food obtained from pagans. Apparently, however, the Samaritans were not here mentioned.

We are told that the woman, when she went back into the city in order to call her friends, "left her waterpot." Bauer remarks[7] that he is unable to discover the significance of this detail. But for one thing, it helps to round off the story. Jesus had asked the woman for a drink, he himself having "nothing to draw with, and the well was deep." A conversation ensued, and now she placed the vessel at his disposal, to use it for getting water and drinking. This is indeed how the words have always been understood. (Towards the end of the Second Part of Goethe's *Faust*, the Mulier Samaritana invokes the Mater gloriosa's mercy "*bei dem Eimer, der dem Heiland kühl die Lippe durft berühren* [by the pail that was permitted once to cool the Saviour's lips].") What has not been seen is that his drinking from that pitcher was an act comparable to, and indeed more serious than, dealings involving contact with an Am-Haaretz, a Jew careless about the rules of cleanness. Clearly, for bringing out this aspect of the matter, a note like that in question is indispensable.

B. THE MEANING OF συγχράομαι

So far, to be sure, the argument might appear somewhat conjectural. But there is support in the clause οὐ γὰρ συγχρῶνται Ἰουδαῖοι Σαμαρίταις.[8] Literally, of course, συγχράομαι means "to use together," though sometimes it is employed in the more general sense of "to use." The natural interpretation is: Jews do not use—*scil.* vessels—together with Samaritans. This would confirm the thesis advanced; and in all probability, had the point of the incident been recognized, nobody would ever have thought of any other rendering.

That Samaritans in general are named, not only Samaritan women, may be explained in various ways. The author may have thought that the restriction to women was sufficiently implied by the context. ("Thou askest drink of me, which am a woman of Samaria?") Or he may have committed a slight mistranslation from the Semitic. Or—perhaps the most plausible solution—he did refer to a group of Pharisees that avoided contact of the kind contemplated not only with Samaritan women but also with the men. Logically, once the women were presumed to be menstruants, their husbands must be presumed to be defiled by them. Sadducean women received treatment not dissimilar to

[6] *t. Shab.* 1:14.

[7] *Das Johannesevangelium*, 2nd ed. (1925), 68 f.

[8] John 4:9.

that of Samaritan women; and the Talmud records[9] that "it happened that a [male] Sadducee was talking to a high priest in the market and spittle issued from his mouth and fell upon the clothes of the high priest; whereupon the face of the high priest turned pale and he went to see the other's wife [to inquire whether she had practised the proper, Pharisaic precepts]."

However, the point of the story has not hitherto been recognized, and it is now universally believed that, in the passage quoted, συγχράομαι means "to associate on friendly terms," "to be familiar": Jews do not associate on friendly terms with Samaritans. Certainly, this translation is just possible. The simple verb χράομαι, besides "to use," can signify "to be intimate"; συγχράομαι, besides "to use together," can signify "to use"; since it may have one of the meanings of the simple verb, namely, "to use," there is no *a priori* reason why it should not have another, namely, "to be intimate." Nevertheless there is one objection, not conclusive, but quite serious enough: the absence of any evidence, apart from the present text, of συγχράομαι in the sense of "to be intimate." Some dictionaries say such evidence exists, but on closer examination the ultimate authority invariably turns out to be—the present text itself. (It should be observed that the allied meaning "to have commercial dealings with" also is more than doubtful.)

Preisigke does not note the unusual sense at all. In former editions of Liddell and Scott, only this text was adduced for it. The latest edition adds a passage from Diogenes Oenoandensis,[10] following Moulton and Milligan; but we shall see that there is no justification for doing so. Moulton and Milligan, it is true, refer to three passages as analogous: one from Epictetus,[11] one from the *Epistle of Ignatius to the Magnesians*[12] and one from Diogenes Oenoandensis. But there is little doubt that, had it not been for the current interpretation of the clause from the Fourth Gospel, none of them would ever have been considered as containing the extraordinary usage.

In Epictetus, it is a question of "using" certain criteria for deciding a problem: ταῖς τῶν ἐκτὸς ἀξίαις συγχρώμεθα. Oldfather translates:[13] "But for determining the rational and the irrational, we employ not only our estimates of the value of external things, but also the criterion of that which is in keeping with one's character." There is no trace here of the meaning required for the orthodox explanation of the passage from John, "to associate on friendly terms," "to be familiar."

According to the view here combated, Epictetus is speaking of a criterion commonly employed. Then the equation is made: "commonly employed" equals "familiarly employed," which equals "to be familiar," which equals "to associate on friendly terms." Evidently, all this is twisting an innocent word for the purpose of obtaining a parallel to John. For Epictetus, the word means "to employ" or, perhaps "commonly to employ"; but definitely no more. Moulton and Milligan, in adducing this text, rely on J. B. Lightfoot, on whose position we shall presently have to say a few words.

[9] *t. Nidd.* 5:3; *b. Nidd.* 33b.

[10] Diogenes Oenoandensis 64.

[11] Epictetus 1.2.7.

[12] *Epistle of Ignatius to the Magnesians* 3.

[13] Epictetus (in The Loeb Classical Library) (1926), 1, 17.

Let us go on to the *Epistle of Ignatius to the Magnesians*. He exhorts the recipients μὴ συγχρᾶσθαι τῃ ἡλικίᾳ τοῦ ἐπισκόπου ἀλλὰ πᾶσαν ἐντ ροπὴν αὐτῷ ἀπονέμειν, "not to take advantage of the youth of the bishop, but to show him all respect." Or if we credit συγχράομαι with its full force, we may translate "not to take advantage together," "not to combine to take advantage." The Anglo-Latin version of the 13th century has *couti* [to use together], though, admittedly, as it is always punctiliously literal, this is of little significance.

It might perhaps be argued that the author means to discourage undue familiarity. Even if that were granted, συγχράομαι would still denote "to use" or "to use together," not "to be familiar." Ignatius does not write μὴ συγχρᾶσθαιτῷ ἐπισκόπῳ which might justify the rendering "not to be familiar with the bishop"; he writes μη συγχρᾶσθαι τῇ ἡλικίᾳ τοῦ ἐπισκόπου, which can only be rendered by "not to exploit (together) the age of the bishop"—whether the exploitation consisted in undue familiarity or not. As a matter of fact the continuation of the letter shows that the danger lay, not in undue familiarity, but in insubordination.[14] Ignatius goes on to cite the praiseworthy example of the presbyters, whom he describes as "not making use (προσειληφότας) of his manifest youth but yielding to him"; and he adds that it is necessary "to obey without any hypocrisy." Thus there is no conceivable basis for the rendering "to be familiar."

It was J. B. Lightfoot[15] who first thought that here was a parallel to John—to John misunderstood, we should say—and suggested that συγχράομαι ought to be translated by "to presume upon," "to treat lightly" (which, even if correct, would still not be quite the same as "to be familiar" or "to be friendly"). He, too, cited Epictetus as another illustration of the usage; we have already dealt with this passage. Lake's translation,[16] "Now it becomes you not to presume on the youth of the bishop," and Srawley's translation,[17] "You too should not treat lightly the youth of your bishop," are obviously based on Lightfoot. Others are more accurate, such as Bauer,[18] "*Für euch aber schickt es sich, euch das jugendliche Alter des Bischofs nicht zu nutze zu machen* [It is not fitting for you to exploit the Bishop's youth]" ("to exploit"), and Hennecke,[19] "*Es ziemt euch aber, das jugendliche Alter eures Bischofs nicht zu missbrauchen* [It is not seemly for you to abuse the Bishop's youth]" ("to abuse"). At any rate, this is decidedly no case of συγχράομαι in any special sense.

There remains a fragment of Diogenes Oenoandensis, which now figures in Liddell and Scott. Towards the end, we find the passage οὐκοῦν ἑκάτερον ὑμῶν ἰδία δεῖ βαρεῖσθαι δί ἡμᾶς, συγχρῆσθαι δὲ τῷ ἑτέρῳ τὸν... The rest of the text is lost, and though it is safe to assume that the word ἕτερον followed,[20] we do not know how the sentence ended. Consequently it would be rash indeed to pronounce on the exact meaning of συγχράο-

[14] 1 Tim 4:12, "let no man despise thy youth," and Tit 2:15, "let no man despise thee," may refer to the same danger. In the latter text, the words immediately preceding are: "rebuke with all authority."

[15] *The Apostolic Fathers*, 2nd ed., pt. 2 (1889), 112.

[16] *The Apostolic Fathers* (in The Loeb Classical Library) (1945), 1, 199.

[17] *The Epistles of St. Ignatius*, 2nd ed. (1919), 54.

[18] *Die Apostolischen Väter* (1923), 221.

[19] *Neutestamentliche Apokryphen*, 2nd ed. (1924), 524.

[20] See J. William, *Diogenes Oenoandensis* (1907), 60.

μαι in this context. How, then, do Moulton and Milligan—the source of Liddell and Scott—come to take it as denoting "to be familiar"?

This interpretation goes back to J. William. He, in the Preface to his edition of Diogenes Oenoandensis,[21] contended that the fragment could not, as had been suggested by previous commentators, be part of a letter written by Epicurus himself. The authorship of Epicurus, he maintained, was ruled out by the language, which must date from a subsequent period. And among the points proving the language late, he mentioned the use of συγχράομαι in the sense of "to be familiar." Here is the source of Moulton and Milligan.

Three things are to be said on this. First, William quite naturally was rather eager to detect late nuances in the fragment. Secondly, the sole evidence in view of which he felt it possible to attribute to συγχράομαι in Diogenes Oenoandensis the sense of "to be familiar" is—the clause from the Fourth Gospel here under discussion. Thirdly, if, despite the fact that the sentence breaks off in the middle, we venture guesses as to its meaning, the most satisfactory results are obtained by proceeding from the properly established values of the verb, "to use together" or "to use." In the passage immediately preceding, the author of the letter has referred to money sent him by his father and other friends. Now he says: "It is not right that each of you should be burdened with his own share in my support,[22] but each should use together with the other"—and we may suppose that there came something like "such extra sums as he is able to spend," "such resources as are available." The dative ἑτέρῳ, that is, if we translate "to use together," would be connected, not with the main body of the verb, χράομαι, but with the prefix συν: "to use together one with the other," not "to use one another." Again, if we translate "to use," we get: "It is not right that each of you should be burdened with his own share in my support, but each should make use of the other." He means that they should ask one another to assist. This also makes much better sense than "each should be familiar with the other." No doubt other guesses are possible. But it is idle to speculate further. We do not know what the lost portion contained. What emerges is that there is no good reason why we should translate συγχράομαι here by "to be familiar," "to associate on friendly terms."

The conclusion is obvious. Unless John applies the verb in a way recurring nowhere else—it may be repeated that this is just possible—it must signify either "to use together with another person," or "to use two things together" (this sense is less frequent than the others, but Preisigke is surely right, against Moulton and Milligan, in finding it in a papyrus[23] with the phrase συγχράομαι, "to use both force and stubbornness," and we may compare Polybius[24] where he speaks of Hannibal ἅμα δὲ συγχρησαμένου συναγωνιστῇ τῷ ποταμῷ καὶ τοῖς θηρίοις, "using as fellow-combatants at the same time both the river and the elephants"), or simply "to use something." The meaning "to use two things together," rare in any case, does not fit. Neither does the

[21] William, *Diogenes Oenoandensis*, XXVIII.

[22] The author constantly refers to himself as ἡμεῖς.

[23] BGU IV, 1187.22.

[24] Polybius 3.14.5.

simple "to use something." A statement to the effect that Jews do not make use of Samaritans would be neither true nor—and this is decisive—to the purpose in this particular context: the woman must be referring to some plain unkindness on the part of the Jews. It should be observed, incidentally, that even if this argument is not accepted, we arrive only at "to use," not at "to associate on friendly terms." The result is that, in all probability, the prefix is stressed, the verb denoting "to use something together with another person": Jews do not use vessels together with Samaritans, most definitely not with Samaritan women. True, there is no clear case where the dative after συγχράομαι depends on the συν. Diogenes Oenoandensis is too problematic. But that is doubtless accidental. The possibility of this construction must have existed.

It may be worth adding that the Hebrew verb *hishtammesh*, "to use," naturally occurs in Rabbinic discussions about clean and unclean vessels. According to the School of Shammai,[25] for example, "it is forbidden to use—*lehishtammesh*—a vessel the outside of which has been rendered unclean by a liquid."

C. THE SYRIAC VERSION

The clause here analysed, οὐ γὰρ συγχρῶνται and so on, is missing in the Sinaiticus, the Codex Bezae and some representatives of the Itala (א D *a b d e*). The question therefore arises whether it goes back to the evangelist. If not, we must assume that the Gospel, after being completed, fell into the hands of an expert in Rabbinic lore. This is perhaps not inconceivable. Yet the easier explanation seems to be that we have before us a comment by John himself. As remarked above, that anti-Samaritan decree of A.D. 65 or 66 formed part of a famous, or rather notorious, legislation. The reason for the absence of the clause from the manuscripts named probably is that it was no longer understood when they were written. We ought to remember that, if the thesis submitted is correct, the interpretation of συγχράομαι as meaning "to associate on friendly terms" was not known to ancient editors and scribes. So the passage must have sounded very queer to them.

Or did this interpretation spring up already at an early date? The Vulgate certainly is not acquainted with it: *non enim coutuntur Judaei Samaritanis* [for Jews do not use together with Samaritans]. (*Couti* [to use together], we saw, stands for συγχράομαι also in the Anglo-Latin version of *Ignatius to the Magnesians*.) But, to judge by modern translations, the Syriac version has it. A. L. Smith,[26] for instance, renders the Syriac of the passage from John thus: "For the Jews have no dealings with the Samaritans." Modern dictionaries agree, alleging that the relevant Syriac verb is here employed in the sense of "to have dealings or intercourse with."[27]

In point of fact, however, the Syriac version is as free from this error (error—on the

[25] *b. Ber.* 52b.

[26] *A Translation of the Four Gospels from the Syriac* (1894), 169, and *Some Pages retranscribed from the Sinaitic Palimpsest with a Translation of the Whole Text* (1896), 88.

[27] J. Payne Smith, *Syriac Dictionary* (1903), 162, R. Payne Smith, *Thesaurus Syriacus*, 1 (1879), 1399 ("nullo commercio utuntur cum" ["They have no dealings with"]), and W. Jennings, *Lexicon to the Syriac of the New Testament*, revised by U. Gautillon (1925), 83.

basis of the view here advocated) as the Vulgate. This is not saying that the story was still properly understood at that time; it only means that it was not yet rewritten. The modern treatment of the Syriac version is due to the same lack of insight into the Rabbinic background which has already led to, first, the assignment of an exceptional sense to συγχράομαι in the Greek text and, secondly, the "discovery" of this sense in Epictetus, Ignatius and Diogenes Oenoandensis. As there is now, thirdly, an unwarranted rendering of a Syriac verb, one wonders whether this avalanche will ever come to a halt.

The Syriac verb appearing in the passage concerned is the Ethpa'al of *ḥashaḥ*. It occurs in five other passages.

(1) Acts 27:3. The Greek has φιλανθρώπως τε ὁ Ἰούλιος τῷ Παύλῳ χρησάμενος, "Julius used Paul kindly." In the Syriac version, what Julius used was, not Paul, but kindness: "The centurion used mercy (*bimeraḥamenutha'*) towards (*lewath*) Paul." The verb means "to use." Accordingly, the lexicographers are wrong in singling out this passage for the sense "*tractare*" or "to behave self toward, to treat."[28] Presumably their attitude is yet another indirect effect of the current interpretation of John. The next step would be to assert that Acts 27:3 provides a second example of the Syriac verb denoting "to associate on friendly terms." It is worth noting that there is a passage in Bar-Hebraeus[29] closely analogous to Acts 27:3—except that *'im*, "with," is put instead of *lewath*, "towards"—which is apparently destined to become the next victim. R. Payne Smith still gave the unprejudiced translation "*misericordia usus est erga incolas*" ["He used pity towards the natives"]. In J. Payne Smith, this has become "he behaved mercifully towards the inhabitants," and the text is placed next to that from the Fourth Gospel. That is to say, we are given to understand that the meaning here approaches "to associate on friendly terms." But the verb unambiguously signifies "to use."

(2) 1 Corinthians 7:31, "And they that use this world," χρώμενοι. Again, clearly "to use."

(3) 1 Corinthians 9:12, "We have not used this power," ἐχρησάμεθα. The same.

(4) 1 Corinthians 9:15, "But I have used none of these things," κέχρημαι. The same.

(5) 1 Thessalonians 2:5. The Greek has οὐ γάρ ποτε ἐν λόγῳ κολακείας ἐγενήθημεν. The English version gives "For neither at any time used we flattering words," and this is exactly what we find in the Syriac. Again, "to use."

It follows that the Ethpa'al of *ḥashaḥ* must be rendered by "to use" and nothing else. (The Old Testament application of the root is consistent with this result. The root occurs—though never in the Ethpa'al—three times[30] and always refers to what is needful.) It must be so rendered also in John. And it is desirable that this text should be deprived of its separate position in Greek and Syriac dictionaries, though as to Greek a slight doubt may remain. *A fortiori* all those passages pressed into service with a view to justifying that special position should be given back their original, innocent meaning.

We do not propose here to inquire exactly when the traditional misinterpretation of

[28] R. Payne Smith, *loc. cit.*, Jennings, *loc. cit.*

[29] *Chronicon Syriacum* 80.347.

[30] Dan 3:16; Ezek 6:9, 7:20.

the clause under discussion came into being. By Luther's time it was established—"*Denn die Juden haben keine Gemeinschaft mit den Samaritanern* [For the Jews have no association with the Samaritans]"—but it is no doubt much older. We have already mentioned that the original point of the narrative of Jesus and the Samaritan woman must soon have become unintelligible to Christian readers. Once that had happened, it was easy to assimilate it to passages like that in Acts:[31] "Ye know how that it is an unlawful thing for a Jew to keep company (κολλᾶσθαι) or to come unto (προσέρχεσθαι) one of another nation; but God hath shewed me that I should not call any man common or unclean."

[31] Acts 10:28.

Two Aramaisms

A. "Multitude" and "Width"

Mark and Luke,[1] as commonly understood, tell us that Jesus preached in a house at Capernaum; that a paralytic was to be brought to him in order to be healed; that the people who carried him could not enter the house δια τὸν ὄχλον, "because of the crowd" besieging it; and that in consequence they uncovered the roof and let the bed down that way.

This interpretation is not quite satisfactory. For one thing, would the crowd not willingly have made room if a miracle was expected? For another, once the way to the door was barred, how did the people who carried the sick man succeed in taking the more difficult route across the roof? It has been suggested that, on beholding the crowd, they turned and ascended the roof from behind the house. Apart from the complete lack of textual evidence, however, if this was what happened, most members of the crowd would not have seen the paralytic. Their astonishment, therefore, when he was cured, would be hard to understand. In the second Philippic,[2] Cicero accuses Antonius of having had immoral relations with Curio. The latter's father, he says, set watchmen in order that Antonius might not cross his threshold; but Antonius at night was let down through the tiles. This certainly must have happened from a side of the house other than the front, which was guarded. But, then, the object of Antonius in entering via the roof was precisely to remain unnoticed by the watchmen. By contrast, the paralytic ought to have been discerned by all, or as many as possible.

We may admit that the problems here raised about the clause "because of the crowd" are not very serious. Perhaps we should be content with noting them. Yet it is tempting to get rid of them by assuming a slight mistranslation of a Hebrew or Aramaic word. It is true that this particular mode of solving the difficulties involves us in a further drawback: we are conscious that to maintain a mistranslation in the New Testament is nearly always wrong and never clearly right.

One of the Hebrew equivalents of "multitude" is *shiph'a*. The Bible uses it of a multitude of camels, horses or warriors.[3] In the last-cited case, "he spied the crowd of Jehu" is rendered thus by the Complutensian Polyglot: εἶδεν τὸν ὄχλον Εἰού. In Rabbinic literature, however, the nouns *shiph'a* and *shippua'* (Aramaic *shiph'a'* and *shippu'a'*) as well as the verb *shapha'* (Aramaic *shepha'*) refer not only to the numerical

[1] Mark 2:1 ff.; Luke 5:17 ff.

[2] *Philippic* 2.18.45.

[3] Isa 60:6; Exod 26:10; 2 Kgs 9:17.

size of a collective but also to the extent in space of a particular object. In other words, they signify not only "multitude" or "to be numerous," but also "great length or breadth" or "to be wide." The primary meaning of the root seems to be "to flow abundantly," "to overflow":[4] it is easy to see how its range might have been enlarged in various directions.

He who has a *qora shopha'ath*, a "strong, huge joist," we hear,[5] will place it in the centre of the room. Again, the Biblical provision "and any overhanging part [of the curtains] thou shalt make to hang over [the backside of the tabernacle]" in the Jerusalemite Targum reads *weshippua' tashpa'*; and in the following verse "it shall hang over" appears as *yehe' meshuppa'*.[6] Finally, the Mishnah deals with tents smaller at the bottom than at the top. As regards uncleanness, it is laid down[7] that everything lying under the upper, wider part of such a tent, even though actually outside the tent itself, shares the fate of the objects which are inside, and vice versa. The text runs as follows: "All protruding parts of a tent, *shippu'e 'oholin*, count as the tent itself. In the case of a tent that protrudes, *shehu' shophea'*, at the top, slopes down and is but one finger-breadth at the bottom, if there is uncleanness inside the tent, vessels under the protruding part, *hashshippua'*, are also unclean. If there is uncleanness under the protruding part, *hashshippua'*, vessels inside the tent are also unclean."

These examples could be multiplied. It is noteworthy that in the Jerusalemite Targum and the Mishnic rule *shippua'* does not simply denote "hugeness." It denotes, in a more specific sense, that portion of a thing by which it is bigger than another: the remaining part of longer curtains as compared with shorter curtains in the Targum, the wider part of a tent as compared with the smaller in the Mishnah.

Supposing, then, that ὄχλος in the narrative under discussion stands for *shiph'a* or *shippua'* (*shiph'a'* and *shippu'a'*), the reason, in the original version, why the paralytic could not be brought through the door may well have been that the bed was too large, the door too small. This would at least avoid the weakness of the reason that is given in the present version. According to Mark, it was four men who carried the bed—a fact very possibly mentioned in order to indicate how big the bed was. The vernacular behind διὰ τον ὄχλον would have meant "for the hugeness," *scil.* of the bed, or even, if *shiph'a* was employed in its more technical signification, "for the protruding" of the bed.

How *shiph'a* came to be represented by ὄχλος may be left undecided. Seeing that the Rabbinic word does frequently denote "a multitude," it was, perhaps, just a slip, committed when the Aramaic form of the story was turned into Greek. Whoever first told it in Greek may have been influenced by the mention, towards the beginning, of a great many people come to listen to Jesus.[8] On the other hand, this remark towards the beginning is quite possibly editorial, itself the result of ὄχλος occurring further on. However, there are so many other pericopes introducing a crowd that it would not be surprising if some narrator had taken *shiph'a* in this sense even where, for once, it meant something different.

[4] Cp. the application of the nouns *shepha'* in Deut 33:19 and *shiph'a* in Job 22:11, 38:34.

[5] *Gen. Rab.* on 2:7.

[6] Exod 26:12 f.

[7] *m. Ohol.* 7:2.

[8] Mark 2:2; Luke 5:17 (somewhat divergent).

If the theory suggested is correct, a Talmudic anecdote provides a much closer parallel than hitherto supposed. When Rab Huna died, his bed was too large to be brought out through the door. His disciples therefore began to remove the roof. Rab Hisda, however, pointed out to them that this procedure would be incompatible with the respect due to a deceased Rabbi. The disciples then proposed laying him on another, smaller bed. Again Rab Hisda intervened and observed that a great man like Rab Huna must be carried on his own bed. In the end they resorted to a rather rigorous course: they widened the entrance by destroying parts of the wall itself.[9]

It might perhaps be asked how the Rabbi's bed, if it was so broad, had originally been conveyed into the house. But, of course, no difficulty exists when there is no one lying on a bed, since one can then turn it round. This accounts also for the ending of the narrative of the paralytic,[10] where we read that, after being cured, he took up his bed and walked home. Actually, it is not improbable that the miracle partly consisted in the very fact that he was able to carry without assistance a bed of large dimensions.

B. "To Beguile" and "To Shake"

Paul writes to the Thessalonians[11] that he sent them Timothy, "to establish you and comfort you concerning your faith, that no man should be moved in these afflictions." The Greek for "to move" is here σαίνω. In general, it may be used of a dog "wagging" his tail, of an animal or person "fawning" on somebody. The last-mentioned sense is no doubt in Paul's mind. A little further on he says that he was afraid "the tempter might have tempted" his flock. The words "that no man should be moved," we may suppose, refer to the importance of no one being "beguiled," "deceived," by Satan and his instruments.

Nevertheless, while admitting that the primary meaning of σαίνω in this passage is "to beguile," we should expect it to have the connotation of "to shake." Timothy's task was to steady such as might have been caused to waver. The trouble is that no Greek author employs σαίνω in the sense of "to shake." It has been maintained[12] that Diogenes Laertius offers an example. But this claim is of the kind we came across in the previous chapter (on Samaritan Women, where we discussed συγχράομαι): in order to parallel a New Testament usage, real or imaginary, a word in some non-Christian, Greek source is interpreted in an artificial manner. Diogenes Laertius tells us[13] how Pythagoras lived in a cave and his mother secretly kept sending him notes of all that went on in the world; at last he reappeared again, looking like a skeleton, declared that he had visited Hades and read out to the people—of course, from his mother's notes—what had occurred in his absence. His hearers were σαινόμενοι, wept and looked on him

[9] *b. M. K.* 25a. *Midrash Psalms* on 24:7 also seems to suggest that the case of a door being too small for any big furniture to be brought in or out was not infrequent.

[10] Mark 2:12; Luke 5:25; also Matt 9:7.

[11] 1 Thes 3:3.

[12] M. Dibelius, "An die Thessalonicher," in *Handbuch zum Neuen Testament*, vol. 11, 3rd ed. (1937), 17.

[13] Diogenes Laertius 8.1.41.

as divine. Clearly, σαινόμενοι signifies "beguiled," "deceived." If it were not for Paul's use of the verb, nobody would ever have thought of suggesting the translation "shaken."

Either, then, σαίνω in Paul has not the connotation of "to shake," however much we may expect it. Or—the better view, we think—it has this connotation, in which case the likeliest explanation is that Paul is under the influence of the corresponding Hebrew or Aramaic, *kishkesh* or *kashkesh*. This verb is used of an animal "wagging" its tail, of an animal "striking about" with its tail (so as to do damage, for example), of a person "patting," "soothing," another person or an animal, and of a person "shaking" an object (nuts, for instance, for a child's entertainment, or jars, in the course of washing up).

Of particular interest is a Rabbinic utterance to the effect that the evil impulse *mekhashkesh* the creatures, i.e. "pats" or "shakes" them in order to turn them from the proper path.[14] Salomon Buber[15] was of opinion that we ought to emend the text and substitute *meśakhśekh* or *mesakhsekh*: the evil impulse "ensnares." But apart from the fact that no emendation is necessary, there is not even convincing evidence that either of the two verbs recommended might signify "to ensnare." However, Jastrow in his dictionary carried the idea further. He postulated a verb, attested nowhere else, *kaśkeś*, which he regarded as a transposition of *śakhśekh*, and to which he attributed the meanings "to entangle," "to catch," "to confound." In Levy's dictionary, these conjectures are not adopted; they are in fact unwarranted. Paul uses σαίνω in the sense of "to beguile"—as we saw above, a remark on the tempter follows—yet the nuance "to shake" is also there. The Rabbis use *kishkesh* or *kashkesh* as denoting something between "to soothe in order to seduce" and "to shake in order to seduce." It may be said that the passage from 1 Thessalonians and the Midrash throw light on, and support, one another.

[14] *Eccl. Rab.* on 4:14, *Midrash Psalms* on 9:2.

[15] *Midrasch Tehillim* (Wilna, 1891), 82, par. 37.

Amen

In the sermon on the mount[1] we come across for the first time that curious use of "Amen" in the sense of "verily"; i.e. as a particle, not confirming a previous statement, but opening a statement and emphasizing its truth and importance. It is universally held that "Amen" was not so used before Jesus, and that there is no Rabbinic analogy.[2] The explanation most widely accepted seems to be that of Dalman:[3] Jesus was opposed to swearing, consequently he put "Amen" in the place of an oath.

The difficulty is that if, in Jesus's view, "whatever is more than Yea, yea or Nay, nay cometh of evil," it is hardly credible that he sought a device to evade this teaching. It is chiefly dodges, be it remembered, such as swearing by heaven instead of by God himself, which he is represented as attacking. "Amen" surely would be a dodge of just this kind.

However, we do not intend here to pursue this problem, but a different, more pedestrian one. Whoever introduced the "Amen" under discussion, be it in order to have an oath that was not an oath, or be it for other reasons, must have relied on some support in contemporary speech or in a special tradition. He could not have brought in the new use of "Amen," as it were, *ex nihilo*. If he had, it would have produced no effect.

One tradition which may have been of influence is that going back to Isaiah who, where he speaks of the creation of a new heaven and earth, says that in those days "he that sweareth shall swear by the God of Amen."[4] That many modern critics think the original text had *'omen*, "faith," instead of the present *'amen*, is irrelevant: in the New Testament epoch, we may assume, *'amen* was already established. The "Amen" of the New Testament may be intended as a fulfilment of this prophecy. It is used only by Jesus himself and mostly, if not exclusively, where the advent of the true kingdom is concerned.

There may, however, be also a few roots in actual Hebrew speech. It is worth mention that in the Old Testament the particle *'omnam*, "verily," which is etymologically connected with *'amen*, does occur at the beginning of a statement, like the New Testament "Amen"; for instance, "Verily, the kings of Assyria have destroyed the nations."[5] But it is rare even in the Old Testament, non-existent in Rabbinic language, and in any case not identical with *'amen*, however closely allied. So no great importance can be attached to it.

[1] Matt 5:18.

[2] Strack-Billerbeck, 1 (1922), 243 f.; *Jewish Encyclopedia*, vol. 1, *s.v.* Amen.

[3] *Die Worte Jesu*, 186.

[4] Isa 65:16.

[5] 2 Kgs 19:17; Isa 37:18.

Yet some points suggest that, if there is no complete parallel of the New Testament "Amen" in Jewish works preserved to us, it may none the less have been current at that time in certain circles.

For one thing, it is easy to imagine how the use in question might have come into existence. The "Amen" confirming a previous statement is often expanded. This happened as early as the period of the Old Testament. Jeremiah replied to a rival who contradicted his terrible forecasts and maintained that Judah would flourish: "Amen, the Lord do so."[6] In Jewish liturgy combinations like "Amen, praise the Lord," "Amen, let his great name be blessed for ever" or "Amen, my help is from the Lord" are frequent.[7] In all these cases, it is true, the "Amen" signifies acceptance of a preceding wish or prayer. Still one has only to think of it in connection with its appendix to come fairly near the meaning of "verily." In other words, as soon as the expanded "Amen" is thought of as a more or less independent phrase, a translation would have to be: "Verily, the Lord will do so" or "Verily, my help is from the Lord."

How easily the particle confirming a previous statement may become a particle opening and emphasizing a fresh one is illustrated by a repartee in Longfellow's *John Endicott*.[8] Norton, the Calvinist minister, exclaims: "Anathema maranatha! The Lord cometh!" To which Edith, a Quaker, retorts: "Yea, verily he cometh, and shall judge the shepherds of Israel." This in Hebrew might well be *'amen ba' weshaphaṭ 'eth r'oe yiśra'el*.

However this may be, there are at least two examples in Jewish literature of an "Amen" almost corresponding to that of the New Testament. According to the Ashkenazi rite, if a man recites by himself the Credo, the *Shema'*, the confession of the unity of God followed by some Scriptural portions, he ought to prefix the words *'el melekh ne'eman*, "God, faithful King."[9] This is an acrostic, the initial letters making "Amen." Indeed, the acrostic is particularly clever, seeing that the last letters of the last word also make "Amen." (Manifestly, the clause derives from the Eighteen Benedictions,[10] where, however, no acrostic is formed of it.)

It may be noted, first, that according to a Talmudic explanation "Amen" itself is a Notarikon, i.e. an abbreviation standing for "God, faithful King";[11] and secondly, that in the old prayer-books of Saadia and Amram and in the Mahzor Vitry, there is still left the proper "Amen" before the Credo instead of the acrostic.[12] Here, then, we find "Amen" introducing the solemn acknowledgment of the unity of God.

Another case is more interesting. Some seventy years ago a primitive hymn, "None is like our God," still popular in Jewish liturgy,[13] was shown by Schiller-Szinessy to be an acrostic giving *'amen b'*. As far as the consonants are concerned, *b'* may mean either

[6] Jer 28:6.

[7] *Num. Rab.* on 4:16; Singer's *Prayer Book*, 75 f.

[8] *John Endicott*, Act 1, Scene 1.

[9] Singer's *Prayer Book*, 40.

[10] Singer's *Prayer Book*, 47.

[11] *b. Shab.* 119b; *b. Sanh.* 111a.

[12] *Encyclopaedia Judaica*, *s.v.* Amen.

[13] Singer's *Prayer Book*, 167.

"he is coming," "he is come" or "come!" Schiller-Szinessy indeed discovered a manuscript in which the initials of the lines were written in the place of the hymn and the two words thus formed are provided with vowels: *'amen ba'*.[14] On the basis of this pointing we should have to render "Verily, he is coming" or "Verily, he is come," while the imperative "come" would be excluded. But the pointing need not, of course, represent the original one, which may have been *'amen bo'*, "Amen, come."

In any case, the hymn takes us to the mood of passages like "Our Lord is come. The grace of our Lord be with you" (though Paul also may think of the imperative, "Our Lord, come"—if we divide *marana tha* instead of *maran atha*), "Let grace come and this world pass away. Hosanna to the God of David. Our Lord is come. Amen" (here again we could divide so as to obtain "Our Lord, come"), and "He which testifieth these things saith, Surely I come quickly. Amen, come, Lord Jesus."[15] It may be remarked that the hymn seems to have been designed as the final hymn of certain services; and most rites still place it at the end of those services for which it is used.[16]

Here a reservation must be made. It is possible that, originally, both these "Amens" had the character of normal, concluding "Amens." The "Amen" before the *Shema'*, the Credo, may have been meant, not to open the Credo, but to confirm the benedictions preceding it. This is strongly suggested by the fact that medieval scholars like Rashi and Hananel declare the benediction immediately preceding to be one of the few to which even a person praying by himself may add an "Amen." As a rule you may say "Amen" only after a benediction recited by the precentor. The words "God, faithful King," with which an Ashkenazi, when he prays alone, now begins the Credo, may simply derive from that "Amen" referring to a previous benediction.[17] Similarly, the author of "None is like our God" may have had in mind the preceding service, to which his "Amen" should constitute the conclusion. In fact if we point *bo'*, so as to get the imperative "come," no other explanation is possible. We must have before us the ordinary, if expanded, "Amen"; we cannot translate "Verily, come!" but we must—on this pointing—assume that the author had the same intention that is found at the close of Revelation (and, if we divide *marana tha*, also in 1 Corinthians and the Didache). There the addressees receive the promise "Surely, I come quickly," to which they reply, "Amen, come, Lord Jesus"—the ordinary, though expanded, "Amen."[18] Just so, the author of "None is like our God" would have composed his hymn for a service leading up to an assurance of salvation and the reply, in the form of an acrostic, "Amen, come."

The case of the hymn is complicated by two further points. First, it is not absolutely certain (though I have no doubt) that the hymn was an acrostic from the outset. There are sources in which the lines are arranged differently.[19] Secondly, Rashi—whom we

[14] C. Taylor, *The Teaching of the Twelve Apostles*, 78 f.

[15] 1 Cor 16:22 f.; Didache 10:6; Rev 22:20.

[16] *Jewish Encyclopedia*, vol. 5 (1903), 154, *s.v.* En Kelohenu.

[17] *Encyclopaedia Judaica*, *s.v.* Amen.

[18] Curiously, one Armenian version presupposes ἦλθε instead of ἔρχου (Hoskier, *The Text of the Apocalypse*, vol. 2, 646), i.e. it has "Verily, he is come." The version is worthless, it seems. Nevertheless it shows with what freedom "Amen" was treated.

[19] See Schechter, *JQR*, 4, 253.

have already mentioned in connection with the "Amen" before the *Shema'*—deciphers the acrostic not as *'amen ba'*, but as *'amen barukh' atta*, "Verily, blessed be thou." This is a conceivable, though extremely artificial solution. It means that while we have to take the initial letters of the first three lines of the hymn, we have to take the entire initial words of the following two lines.

I do not think the significance of the two examples is essentially diminished by these difficulties. At the most cautious estimate, we may see from the instances adduced how what were at first ordinary "Amens" in the course of time became "Amens" closely resembling the introductory "Amens" of the New Testament. For whatever its origin, the "Amen" before the Credo is now connected, not with the benediction that it follows, but with the Credo itself—though, admittedly, in the dress of *'el melekh ne'eman*, "God, faithful King." Whatever its history, the hymn "None is like our God" now makes *'amen ba'* with no reference to any previous prayer; and, as observed already, in one manuscript at least, it is represented by the pointed words *'amen ba'*, which can be rendered only by "Verily, he is coming" or "Verily, he is come." At the most cautious estimate, therefore, the cases discussed are evidence that the development from the normal "Amen" to something very much like the "Amen" in the sense of "verily" is feasible, and has taken place, in Hebrew, outside the New Testament. Whoever introduced the New Testament "Amen," that is, did not go beyond the natural possibilities of actual Hebrew speech.

In fact, it may well be that the difficulties outlined contain the key to a full understanding of the position. It looks as if the introductory "Amen" had been disliked by the Rabbis. Supposing the "Amen" in the sense of "verily" was mainly employed in, roughly speaking, eschatological utterances. That would explain its frequency in the New Testament and its almost complete suppression in Jewish literature.

We might then argue that the "Amen" before the Credo did start as an opening; and that, if the Sephardim dropped it entirely, the Ashkenazim disguised it as "God, faithful King" and some Rabbis—Rashi among them—made it the ending of the benedictions preceding the Credo, thus turning it into an ordinary "Amen," these were all different attempts to eliminate the dangerous "verily." Similarly, as for the hymn "None is like our God," the acrostic order would have come first and a deliberate disarrangement would have followed later. Indeed, the acrostic form itself may have been chosen as a less open version of "Verily, he is coming" or "Verily, he is come." Rashi's deciphering of the acrostic as *'amen barukh 'atta* would be an ingenious method of replacing "Verily, he is coming" or "Verily, he is come" by "Amen, blessed be thou"; which latter clause, for synagogue-goers, would be merely one of the expanded "Amens" described above—such as "Amen, let his great name be blessed for ever." Maybe it is no coincidence that the first traces, or rudiments, of this hymn are to be found in works of at least partly Essene origin.[20]

[20] Jellinek, *Beth Ha-Midrash*, vol. 2, 47, vol. 3, 86.

"I Speak After the Manner of Men"

A. Paul

Paul uses this phrase, or one very like it, four times. Strack-Billerbeck[1] maintain that it has a different meaning each time, and that it is not of a technical character. However, though there are slight differences—naturally, since no phrase has exactly the same meaning twice—the essential import is invariably the same, and the phrase must be regarded as technical. One suspects that it may have been the difficulty of linking it up with any technical phrase in Rabbinic literature which was a subconscious factor contributing to Strack-Billerbeck's conclusion: it drove them to deny its technical nature in Paul and to exaggerate the differences between the four passages where it occurs.

The phrase is an apology for a bold statement which, without such an apology, might be considered near-blasphemous—be it because it is too anthropomorphic or be it because it sounds otherwise lacking in reverence for God or an established religious idea.

Let us look at the four texts. In Romans 3:5 Paul apologizes for framing the hypothesis that God may be unrighteous. Of course he refutes the hypothesis. But the mere fact that he puts it, unless accompanied by this apology, might be judged blasphemous by a Jewish public.

In Romans 6:19 he apologizes for admonishing the recipients of the letter to become "slaves to righteousness." In a previous chapter (on Redemption [375 ff.]) we pointed out that the Old Testament and the Rabbis never describe the faithful as slaves of anyone or anything but God. Paul's term is not only, as Dodd remarks, "sub-Christian," it is above all "sub-Jewish." He has recourse to it in order to impress on antinomian doctrinaires that, just as formerly they were eager to sin, so now they should be eager to do good, to live saintly lives. Nevertheless the apology is needed since, without it, in the eyes of good Jews, his exhortation would be objectionable.

In Galatians 3:15 he compares a disposition made by God with one made by a man, and besides he considers the question whether it is subject to repeal or change. However vigorously he denies this possibility, the mere hypothesis requires an apology. The case is similar to Romans 3:5.

I have left 1 Corinthians 9:8 to the last, the matter being a little more complicated. But even here there is no doubt as to the meaning of the phrase.

[1] Vol. 3 (1926), 136.

Paul contends that an apostle is entitled to support from his congregations, as a shepherd takes milk from his flock; and he adds that he does not intend to apologize, i.e. he is not "speaking after the manner of men." Obviously he assumes that some of the recipients of the letter will expect this apology here. They will expect him to indicate that his words are not to be taken literally, that they are a bold metaphor which, without the apology, might be deemed wanting in reverence for God or an accepted religious custom.

Now in New Testament times the Rabbis were agreed that the word of God must be taught gratuitously. Hillel (about 30 B.C.) said, "He who makes use of the crown [the Torah] will perish," and Zadok (about A.D. 50), "Make not the words of the Torah a spade wherewith to dig."[2] A few concessions were made in the case of elementary instruction of children; but even they seem to have been introduced at a later date. It is, then, the Jewish traditionalists among his addressees to whom Paul declares that there is to be no apology to mitigate his assertion. This assertion, that apostles are entitled to support, must be taken literally, and if it causes offence it cannot be helped.

That he anticipates opposition of the kind we outlined is confirmed by the manner he argues. Having made his assertion, he does not simply refer to the pronouncement by which Jesus authorized his messengers to live by their office. On the contrary, he begins by adducing a passage from the Law, from Deuteronomy—"Thou shalt not muzzle the mouth of the ox that treadeth out the corn"—and this he interprets most freely with a view to extracting from it the proof he needs. But even when he goes on to Jesus's pronouncement, he represents it as a mere extension by analogy of Old Testament regulations: "They which minister about holy things live of the temple—even so hath the Lord ordained that they which preach the gospel should live of it." Neither in Matthew nor in Luke[3] is Jesus's pronouncement rested on Old Testament authority (though, significantly, in Matthew it appears in a far more restrained version than in Luke: Matthew mentions a right to meat only, Luke one to hire). 1 Timothy also,[4] though like 1 Corinthians it quotes first the Deuteronomic law—"Thou shalt not muzzle" and so on—and only then Jesus's pronouncement, does not connect the latter with Old Testament rules.

Paul in 1 Corinthians has to deal with the charge that the right he claims for apostles is contrary to a hallowed religious principle. Despite the charge he insists on the right, explaining that he does not here "speak after the manner of men."

The evidence bears out what we said at the beginning. The phrase "I speak after the manner of men" has one definite meaning. It constitutes an apology for a statement which, but for the apology, would be too bold, almost blasphemous. The author by this phrase emphasizes that he is speaking with all due reserve. He is using the words apologized for only because he sees no other way of bringing out his point. But his words ought not to be pressed, no irreverence is intended.

The phrase occurs four times in Paul. This alone is sufficient to prove it technical. In what circles was it technical? Clearly in Rabbinic ones—no matter whether or not

[2] *m. Ab.* 1:13, 4:5.

[3] Matt 10:10; Luke 10:7.

[4] 1 Tim 5:18.

we can discover it in Jewish sources. For one thing, the attitude reflected in it is Rabbinic. It is an attitude of humility towards God and religious institutions: man's language is not always capable of doing justice to them. (This distinguishes the phrase from, say, "*sit venia verbo*" ["Let there be forgiveness for the word"], which has no such background; in Pliny[5] "*venia sit verbo*" ["Let there be forgiveness for what was said"] corresponds to our "touch wood.") For another thing, every time Paul employs—or expressly refuses to employ—the phrase, he does so in defence against what strict Jews might have to say. Which shows that he regards them as familiar with it.

B. Jewish Sources

The Jewish sources, however, pose a neat riddle. In Tannaitic literature the technical apology for an overbold statement is *kibheyakhol*, "as if one could (say so)."[6] Johanan ben Zaccai (who lived at the time of the destruction of the Temple) tries to explain why a thief, who steals in secret, must pay double, whereas an open robber need only repay the principal. He claims that the thief—in contradistinction to the robber—fears man more than God: "as if one could say so, he thinks the Eye above will not see."[7] The mere hypothesis that God might not see, even though the Rabbi ascribes it to a criminal, must be accompanied by this excuse. Another example is the saying that "whenever Israel is enslaved, the Shekinah—as if one could say so—is enslaved with them."[8] Without the apology, the statement would be too anthropomorphic.

Kibheyakhol, then, as far as sense is concerned, is very near Paul's "I speak after the manner of men." But it is manifestly another expression. Paul's phrase is not a rendering of it.

Yet from the late 9th century, we find anthropomorphisms occurring in the Bible justified by the maxim: "the Torah speaks after the language of the sons of men."[9] According to Judah ibn Koreish, Tobia ben Eliezer, Maimonides and so on, whenever the Bible refers to God sitting, standing, talking or the like, it is a concession to the human mind. We could not understand God's perfection were it not that "the Torah speaks after the language of men."

This phrase is highly reminiscent of Paul's; it is almost identical with it. There is only one material difference which, it is true, is of such importance that it greatly affects sense and application. Whereas Paul's phrase is an apology for a daring statement made by a human person, "I speak so and so," the medieval phrase serves as an explanation and mitigation of an anthropomorphism to be found in Scripture itself, "the Torah speaks so and so."

The problem is complicated, but perhaps ultimately brought nearer a solution, by a further factor. The maxim "the Torah speaks after the language of the sons of men" occurs already in Tannaitic literature; it is advocated by R. Ishmael, of the first half of

[5] *Ep.* 5.6.46.

[6] Bacher, *Die älteste Terminologie der Jüdischen Schriftauslegung* (1899), 72 f.

[7] *Mek.* on Exod 22:6 (5).

[8] *Mek.* on Exod 12:41.

[9] Bacher, *op. cit.*, 98.

the 2nd cent. A.D. Only its meaning is not the same as in the Middle Ages. It is of a far narrower scope, concerned with the philology of the Bible.

More precisely, Akiba and Ishmael disagree as to the proper method of interpreting the Bible. The former and his School hold that the Bible chooses its expressions with incomparably greater care than would be applied to any human document. Hence *haggadhic* and *halakhic* conclusions may be derived from pleonasms, from an infinitive preceding the finite verb and the like. The latter and his School maintain that these phenomena, as they are common in daily speech, should not be made the basis for special deductions.

For instance, the Bible lays down that whoever despises the word of the Lord "shall utterly be cut off." The Hebrew text does not contain the word "utterly." Instead there is an infinitive before the finite verb: "to be cut off, he shall be cut off." Akiba sees in the twofold mention of "to be cut off" evidence that the sinner in question is to be cut off from this world and the next. (His view goes back to New Testament times, in whatever way it may then have been supported; this may be gathered from Matthew:[10] "Whoever speaketh against the Holy Ghost, it shall not be forgiven him, neither in this world, neither in the world to come.") Ishmael refuses to accept Akiba's evidence. (He inclines to leniency in any case.) An infinitive preceding the finite verb is a feature of ordinary speech. It is used for emphasis, and Ishmael denies that it has any other purpose in Scripture. Consequently, in his opinion, the person is to be cut off only from this world: "the Torah speaks after the manner of men."[11]

C. PAUL AND THE JEWISH SOURCES

We now have the following data.

First, Paul avails himself of a phrase, which must have been technical in the Rabbinic Judaism of his epoch, to explain that an expression of his, though it might at first sight appear irreverent, is not to be pressed; he uses it in order to be understood by the ordinary public. No analogous phrase, however, is to be met with in extant contemporary Jewish utterances.

Secondly, Ishmael, in the first half of the 2nd cent. A.D., avails himself of a similar phrase to explain that an expression occurring in the Pentateuch, though some exegetes will draw far-reaching conclusions from it, should not be pressed; it is used in the way an ordinary author would use it.

Thirdly, from the 9th century, Jewish writers avail themselves of Ishmael's phrase to explain that an expression occurring in the Bible, though it may at first sight appear anthropomorphic, should not be pressed; it is used in order that the ordinary public may understand.

The most plausible inference is that when Paul wrote, it was quite usual for a strict Jew to excuse an overbold statement by adding "I speak after the language of men." Ishmael transferred the phrase to Biblical philology; i.e. he and his followers took the view—against Akiba and his followers—that, on the whole, the Bible should be read

[10] Matt 12:32.

[11] *Siphre* on Num 15:31.

like a human document, and syntactic and stylistic features which would pass as normal in daily speech should not be pressed merely because they occurred in the Bible. So he declared that "the Torah speaks after the language of men." It is this application of the phrase which, I believe, drove out the original one, "I speak after the language of men." At least it drove it out from official literature. As soon as there was a principle that "the Torah speaks after the language of men," it would have sounded presumptuous if a person said of himself "I speak after the language of men." This is the reason why in Jewish sources only the *kibheyakhol*, "as if one could say so," remained to express what, before Ishmael, could also be expressed by "I speak after the language of men." In other words, this is the reason why Paul's phrase, though a technical Rabbinic phrase, cannot be paralleled from Rabbinic writings.

When in the 9th century the scope of Ishmael's maxim expanded so as to cover Biblical anthropomorphisms, this may have been just a natural process: originally it had been directed against undue insistence on certain philological points, now it was also directed against undue insistence on certain statements about God. It is, however, possible that the phrase "I speak after the language of men," in the sense of *kibheyakhol*, "as if one could say so," though Ishmael's maxim had caused its disappearance from official sources, had lived on all the time in unrecorded usage. It would not be the only instance of an expression being eliminated from orthodox literature and yet continuing to be employed where people talk off their guard. If so, this phrase, "I speak after the language of men," in the sense of "as if one could say so," may well have helped to bring about the new application of Ishmael's maxim in the 9th century. That is to say, this new application to Biblical anthropomorphisms would have two roots: not only Ishmael's maxim respecting the philology of the Bible, but also the old Rabbinic phrase which we come across in Paul, which lived on in unofficial speech among Jews even after Ishmael and which was an apology for daring statements. It would be from these two roots that sprang the medieval principle "the Torah speaks after the language of men" as an explanation of those passages where God is represented as sitting, standing or the like.

One might perhaps think of a third influence on the medieval role of this maxim: Paul's epistles themselves, or more precisely, those verses where he professes to "speak after the manner of men" (or declares that he does not do so). However, that they should have directly contributed to the 9th-century extension of Ishmael's maxim seems to me unlikely in the extreme.

Two Symbols

A. A Symbol of Ezekiel in Revelation

In a vision Ezekiel sees his people punished.[1] But—in accordance with his doctrine that the just must not suffer with the wicked—those who are innocent have their foreheads marked at God's express command, and the destroyers are told not to come near them.

The procedure is of a kind common in antiquity when a fugitive, a ἱκέτης, was granted asylum. He might be marked as the property of his protector. If the protector was credited with superhuman power, the mark presumably had the additional purpose of exercising an apotropaeic effect, of averting evil.

The Hebrew word for "mark" in the passage under discussion is *taw*, that for "to mark" *tawa*. Probably *taw* acquired the meaning of "mark," "signature,"[2] because, for one thing, it was the last letter of the Hebrew alphabet and, for another, in ancient script it looked more or less like an oblique cross, like x. But that Ezekiel represents it as the signature conferring protection may well have a further reason. In Egypt a fugitive to a sanctuary was marked with two crosses on the forehead, like the priests.[3] Ezekiel, of priestly stock himself, must have been familiar with such rites.

It is indeed possible that *taw*, the cross, was employed in a similar fashion long before him. We are told how David fled from Saul to Achish, the king of Gath. As he feared the latter's jealousy, he acted the madman—the inviolable madman:[4] "And he feigned himself mad in their hands and made *taws* on the doors of the gate and let his spittle fall down upon his beard."

Versions and commentaries invariably try to explain away *wayethaw*, here translated by "and he made *taws*." Yet there is good evidence, on the one hand, that at least by the time of Ahab Israelite prophets bore marks on the forehead;[5] and, on the other, that the custom of protecting a house by signing the door-posts is very ancient—we need only recall the narrative of the exodus.[6] Here again, incidentally, Egyptian influence may play a part. When we remember in addition the sign of Cain and the frontlets, the *ṭoṭaphoth*, also first mentioned in connection with the rescue from Egypt,[7] and later

[1] Ezek 9:2 ff.

[2] Cp. Job 31:35.

[3] K. Latte, *Heiliges Recht* (1920), 107 f.

[4] 1 Sam 21:14 (13).

[5] 1 Kgs 20:38, 41.

[6] E.g. Exod 12:7 ff.

[7] Exod 13:16.

called *tephillin*, "prayer-capsules," or phylacteries, it seems unnecessary to boggle at the appearance of *tawa* in the story of David.

The mark survives throughout the centuries. There is a figure of a priest of Isis dating from the Rome of the 1st cent. A.D., with the two crosses on his forehead.[8] To go by a Tannaitic report, the priests of the Temple were anointed in the form of the letter x.[9] Whether or not this is correct does not matter. Even if it is not, the fact remains that the Rabbis were acquainted with the use of this sign for consecration.

In Ezekiel, however, it is highly doubtful whether they still associated *taw* with the cross. The old script, where *taw* was written in that form, had long gone out of fashion. Even the LXX renders the word simply by σημεῖον, "sign," without specifying the shape. To be sure, some circles may have preserved a tradition giving the original form. But it is not probable.

Yet in Revelation, at the approach of the end, before the earth and sea are hurt, those of the children of Israel who are slaves of God are sealed on their foreheads with "the seal of the living God"[10]—a scene unquestionably inspired by the Old Testament model: as in Ezekiel, some who are to escape the general ruin are to be visibly marked. The author of Revelation no doubt alludes to baptism. We may assume that by his time, when a person was baptized, he was signed on the forehead with a cross. It follows that the form of the saving mark is the same as that to which Ezekiel referred.

The problem is whether there is a direct line from Ezekiel to Revelation. In all likelihood there is not. The author of Revelation arrived at this form solely by proceeding from the Christian cross. His agreement with Ezekiel is just an odd coincidence.

We know, however, that he inclined to provide established symbols with a new significance. Accordingly, we cannot rule out the possibility of his having in mind also the prevalent mark used for granting asylum (note that those to be signed are called "the slaves of God," i.e. God's property); the Rabbinic theory concerning the anointing of Jewish priests (God and the Lamb, according to Revelation,[11] are the true Temple); and even the identification, which may still have lingered on in certain sects, of Ezekiel's *taw* with a cross. In other words, he may have interpreted one or two or all of these old symbols as the cross figuring at baptism. He may have seen in them the cross of Christ, "the Father's name," "the name of my God and the new Jerusalem," "the name of God and the Lamb."[12] His thought, of course, is focused on the Christian cross. But it is conceivable that he knew of the pre-Christian uses of this sign—his interests in general speak rather in favour of this assumption—and that his knowledge had some influence on the chapter here in question.

Naturally, in later times, Christian exegetes all ascribed to the mark occurring in Ezekiel the form of a cross: they looked on the Old Testament vision in the light of the

[8] Wolters, K. *Glyptothek und Skulpturensammlung des Staates*, Archäelogischer Anzeiger (1910), cols. 470 ff.

[9] *b. Hor.* 12a.

[10] Rev 7:2 ff.

[11] Rev 21:22.

[12] Rev 14:1, 3:12, 22:4.

scene from Revelation. What is more remarkable is[13] that the Christian view influenced not a few Cabbalists; and that in several medieval Jewish mystic works Ezekiel's *taw* is declared to be the cruciform Tree of Life, the source of all salvation.

B. "Arepo" in the Sator Square

Since its discovery at Pompeii, the magic square, which can be read in different directions, is once again the object of much interest. Its better-known form is: "The Sower Arepo holds with care the wheels." Probably the other form is older: "The wheels with care holds Arepo the Sower." Here are both:

(1)	S A T O R	(2)	R O T A S
	A R E P O		O P E R A
	T E N E T		T E N E T
	O P E R A		A R E P O
	R O T A S		S A T O R

The difference is irrelevant for our purpose. Either version, as is widely accepted, is made up of PATERNOSTER twice over, and necessarily arranged as a cross (since the middle letter, N, appears only once in the square), plus the symbolic characters A and O twice over. That is to say, either version is a cryptogram of:

```
            A
            P
            A
            T
            E
            R
A P A T E R N O S T E R O
            O
            S
            T
            E
            R
            O
```

One word in the square is still unexplained: "Arepo." Many derivations have been attempted—the most recent from Celtic—but none is at all convincing. There is, however, a simple solution: it is a Hebrew or Aramaic rendering of ἄλφα ὦ, the epithet of God we find in Revelation;[14] and be it noted that wherever it occurs in Revelation, it occurs as ἄλφα ὦ, not say, as ἀ ὦ—hence something like "Arepo" may be expected.

As just remarked, the square consists of the symbolic characters A and O twice over in addition to PATERNOSTER twice over. The author, that is, knew the epithet in question. Indeed he treated it as of fundamental importance—though, for obvious reasons, in choosing the letters with which to build the square, he proceeded from the shorter form, A O or ἀ ὦ. Clearly, if it can be shown that he intended ἄλφα ὦ as the name

[13] Zöckler, *Das Kreuz Christi* (1875), 31 f., 475 ff.

[14] Rev 1:8, 21:6, 22:13.

of the "Sower," his square will make fairly good sense and sense in harmony with the constituent letters: "The Sower Alpha O holds with care the wheels."

Normally, ἄλφα ὦ, in Hebrew or Aramaic, would give "alep o." Here it is "arep o." Why? In both these languages, *l* and *r* are very close indeed. That writers from early times were conscious of the fact may be gathered from a pun by Micah:[15] *rekhesh—lakhish* ("horses"—"Lachish"). In other languages also, such as Greek, *l* sometimes becomes *r*. The author manifestly put "arepo" as the nearest thing to "alepo" he was able to attain. "Arepo" followed from PATERNOSTER and, read backwards, supplied a suitable word, "opera"; "alepo" did neither; so "arepo" it had to be. ("His name was not Bun but Wood, but Wood would not rhyme with gun but Bun would.") Considering the enormous difficulty of constructing such a square, he did not do too badly.

However, it is possible that a slight twist of this kind was even desired. The modified forms of the tetragrammaton in use among Jews, or the spelling "Eloqim" for "Elohim," may be recalled. "Alep o" certainly enjoyed some degree of sanctity. We must reckon with a good deal of reverence, and no doubt also with a little superstition.

The view that "Arepo" means "alep o," standing for ἄλφα ὦ, has a bearing on the provenance of the square. We do not propose here to go into it, beyond observing, first, that a Jewish-Christian origin might account for several features which have puzzled scholars; and secondly, that it is unintelligible to me why so many historians, in investigating the Sator Square, proceed from the premise that no Christians, or Jewish Christians, can have lived in Pompeii prior to A.D. 79. I think some may have lived there from the middle of the century—whether they professed their faith or kept it to themselves. The Sator Square, incidentally, if affixed to a house, might serve as a secret mark of recognition among the initiated.

[15] Micah 1:13.

The Abomination of Desolation

A. A Construction "Ad Sensum"

In his oracle concerning "the abomination of desolation standing where it ought not," Mark[1] defines the neuter noun, βδέλυγμα, "abomination," by a masculine participle, ἑστηκότα, "who will stand"—no doubt with a view to conveying information as to the actual nature of the abomination. Famous as the text is, the question has never been raised what was the technical background of this exploitation of a grammatical irregularity. Yet the point is not without interest. For one thing, it is not enough to say, as is always said, that we have before us a construction *ad sensum*. Normally Mark, like every other writer, follows the rules of grammar, not of sense. If he deliberately deviates from them in one passage, there must have been some literary convention enabling him to do so. Otherwise, he would not have been understood. For another thing, as we shall see, there are grounds for suspecting that his device may have had its root in a pre-Greek phase of speculations about the "abomination of desolation." In fact he seems to follow as closely as possible an old Rabbinic analysis of the Hebrew term behind the Greek one.

The Rabbinic expounders of Scripture were ever ready to draw conclusions from any peculiarity of grammar therein. One example is their mode of dealing with irregularities concerning the singular or plural number of words. In the account of man's creation[2] there is a wavering between singular and plural. "God created man in his image, in the image of God created he him [singular], male and female created he them [plural]," and so on. That was taken as basis for the view that the first man was androgynous.[3] We have seen [Precept and Example, 252 ff.] that this interpretation of the verse contributed to its use in the New Testament as an argument against divorce: husband and wife are near the ideal state as it was at the beginning—they must not undo it by separation. Or take the passage where God says to Cain:[4] "The voice of thy brother's blood which is shed crieth unto me." Literally translated, the Hebrew gives: "The voice of thy brother's bloods cry unto me." The Samaritan Pentateuch substitutes the singular: "crieth unto me." The Rabbis, to explain the emphasized plural, say[5] some that Cain had destroyed not only Abel but also his potential offspring, others that Abel's blood was cast over trees and stones. The point is that they noted and found significance in the grammatical incongruity.

[1] Mark 13:14.

[2] Gen 1:27, 5:1 f.

[3] *Gen. Rab.* on 1:27.

[4] Gen 4:10.

[5] *m. Sanh.* 4:5.

The Hebrew for "abomination of desolation" occurs three times in Daniel, but only once[6] in a form which is grammatically correct: *shiqquṣ shomem*, "the abomination which devastates" or "the abomination of a devastator." It has long been seen that the expression was intended to suggest *shiqquṣ shamayim*, "the abomination of heaven"—Zeus Ouranios.

In the two other passages, however, there are grammatical difficulties. In one[7] we find the phrase *shiqquṣim meshomem*. However we may nowadays construe it, or emend it (both Kittel's *Biblia Hebraica*[8] and the latest edition of Gesenius's *Handwörterbuch*[9] make the somewhat facile proposal to turn the plural into a singular, *shiqquṣ*), to a Rabbi it must have seemed a noun in the plural, accompanied by a participle in the singular: something like "abominations which renders desolate." It ought to be noted that, if there is corruption, it is old enough for our purposes: the LXX read a plural, βδέλυγμα τῶν ἐρημώσεων. There can be little doubt that this passage gave rise to much ingenious interpretation. In fact a specimen is preserved in the Talmud.[10]

But the meaning of the passage[11] appears even more pertinent in the present connection. It has *hashshiqquṣ meshomem*, the article in "the abomination" striking one as very odd. If the meaning intended by the author is "the abomination of a devastator," we should expect the so-called construct state, "abomination" without "the." In this case also emendations have been attempted (Kittel restores the syntax by reading *hashshiqquṣ hashshomem*). But whether they are justified or not, it looks as if Theodotion at any rate had read the strange article. For that may well be the reason he translates here, not βδέλυγμα ἐρημώσεως, but βδέλυγμα ἠφανισμένον: he, or some precursor, found it impossible to regard the Hebrew as a construct state.

Now it was an established method of Rabbinic exegesis to read some meaning into any article, and in particular, of course, into any article that looked superfluous. Frequently such an article was interpreted as drawing attention to a specific, prominent person, thing or event. There is a law in Deuteronomy:[12] "When ye come nigh unto the battle, the priest shall approach." "The priest," according to the Rabbis,[13] means, not any priest, but the priest anointed for the battle. The Psalmist exclaims:[14] "The ungodly shall not stand in the judgment." According to the Rabbis,[15] "the judgment," with the article, means "the Last Judgment." It is hardly too rash to suggest that *hashshiqquṣ meshomem*, with its extraordinary article, must very early have been taken as a deliberate reference to something or somebody special. Quite possibly successive genera-

[6] Dan 12:11.
[7] Dan 9:27.
[8] 2nd ed. (1925).
[9] 16th ed. by Buhl (1915).
[10] *b. Taan.* 28b.
[11] Dan 11:31.
[12] Deut 20:2.
[13] *m. Sot.* 8:1.
[14] Ps 1:5.
[15] *m. Sanh.* 10:3. Above, 518–19 [372], we drew attention to a Passover Midrash where "the messenger," instead of "a messenger," signifies Jesus.

tions used the phrase in different ways. What emerges as probable is that behind Mark's Greek stands this passage from Daniel, with the article in Midrashic fashion interpreted as singling out a particular individual—the Antichrist, a heathen god, the Emperor or his statue, or whoever else it might be. In Greek, the implication could best be rendered by making the attribute of βδέλυγμα masculine instead of neuter.

Mark could be sure that the erudite part of his public would grasp the meaning: the Rabbis were used to attributing special significance not only to any strange article or any discrepancy between singular and plural, but also to any discrepancy in gender. It would be a worth-while task to collect all these deductions from grammatical irregularities, with a view to bringing out the Rabbinic notions of regular grammar.[16] It is clear, for instance, that the Rabbis were fully conscious of the main principles concerning agreement in gender. In God's warning to Cain,[17] "the sin crouches at the door," "sin" is feminine (*ḥaṭṭa'th*), "crouches" masculine (*robheṣ*). The prevalent modern solution is that originally there was a reference to a demon, "the croucher is at the door"; later the word "sin" was clumsily interpolated. The Rabbis assumed that the discrepancy was deliberate. There is a catena of explanations,[18] the first apparently being that evil inclination begins by being weak as a woman and ends by being strong as a man.

As is well known, the LXX had little difficulty in copying in Greek a pun occurring in the Hebrew original.[19] What is more important: in the Aramaic Targum we may find many cases of renderings carefully chosen so as to guide readers familiar with Rabbinic methods towards certain conclusions.[20] According to the Hebrew text, Abraham said of Sarah:[21] "And also, indeed, she is my sister, the daughter of my father." Most Rabbis found this utterance inconvenient and tried to prove that "sister" was here used in the sense of "niece" only. Onkelos shares this view, and conveys it to his readers by a subtle modification. He translates "and also" (*wegham*) by "and yet" (*ubheram*). The particle "yet" (Hebrew *'akh*, Aramaic *beram*), according to a recognized hermeneutic rule, was looked upon as restricting a statement. Onkelos, by putting it, indicates that Abraham's declaration must not be taken at its face value.

A very relevant parallel to Mark is Onkelos's treatment of the verse[22] in which we are told how a certain proposal of Jacob concerning his wages was accepted by Laban: "Behold, I would it might be according to thy words." For here, as in Mark, an interpretation gained by the Rabbis with the help of one method seems to be brought out by the translation with the help of another, better suited to the language of the translation. To go by the plain meaning of the Biblical narrative, Jacob, while observing the letter

[16] A beginning has been made, and further monographs have been promised, by S. Rosenblatt, *The Interpretation of the Bible in the Mishnah* (1935). See also the present writer's observations on the history of the hermeneutic rules of *Ribbui* and *Mi'ut*, in ["Concerning the Reconstruction of 'The Aramaic Gospels'"] *BJRULM*, 29 (1945), 89 f. [78 ff.].

[17] Gen 4:7.

[18] *Gen. Rab. ad loc.*

[19] E.g. Judg 10:4; see Kay's note on Susanna 54–9 in Charles's edition.

[20] See the writer's remarks *op. cit.*, 93 ff. [80 ff.].

[21] Gen 20:12.

[22] Gen 30:34.

of the agreement (to keep the brown goats separate from the spotted ones), quite disregarded its spirit (he placed coloured rods before the brown goats). In fact he cheated Laban. The Rabbis, loath to admit this, detected in the verse just quoted evidence that Laban was the first to tear up the treaty. They equated the Hebrew *hen*, "behold," with the Aramaic *hen*, "yes"; and they read *lu*, "I would," as *lo*, "no." They maintained, that is, that what Laban had said was: "It might be (yes)—it might not be (no) according to thy words." Onkelos accepts the Rabbinic teaching; and he introduces it into his translation by taking advantage of precisely that rule concerning the restricting force of *beram*, "yet," which we mentioned already. He translates: "Yet (*beram*) I would it might be according to thy words"—apparently a smooth sentence. But any reader familiar with Rabbinic exegesis would see the implication of "yet"; Laban withdrew his consent even while giving it. It was he who started the double-dealing.

It looks, then, as if Mark, when writing τὸ βδέλυγμα ἑστηκότα, was imitating as best he could *hashshiqquṣ meshomem* in Daniel, a Hebrew phrase for "abomination of desolation" with a grammatical flaw—the article—which was traditionally explained as designed to suggest a certain person or his image. Even if it should be held, however, that this part of our thesis is going too far, even if it should be held that, in this particular case, Mark was following no model but that it was his own idea to enlighten us as to the nature of the βδέλυγμα by supplying it with a masculine attribute, the fact remains that the technique he employed was good Rabbinic technique. In other words, this much may be considered as certain, that the kind of construction *ad sensum* to be met with in this passage sprang from, and was intended for, a milieu thinking in Rabbinic terms and reading through Rabbinic spectacles.

B. "LET HIM THAT READETH UNDERSTAND"

1. *A problem of punctuation*

It is universally assumed that, in Mark and Matthew,[23] "let him that readeth understand" is a parenthesis advising us to find out exactly who or what is meant by the "abomination of desolation." Accordingly the sentence in which it occurs is supposed to consist of the following three parts: (1) protasis, "When ye shall see the abomination of desolation," (2) apodosis, "then let them that be in Judaea flee," and between these (3) parenthesis, "let him that readeth understand." On this basis, the passage differs widely from the Lukan parallel, both in form and substance. This parallel runs:[24] (1) protasis "When ye shall see Jerusalem compassed with armies," (2) apodosis, "then know that the desolation thereof is nigh," and (3) a further admonition, "then let them which be in Judaea flee." Dodd has recently mentioned the point among his proofs[25] that Luke in this section was not merely re-editing Mark, but drew on an independent tradition as well.

Very likely the prevalent view is correct. It should be borne in mind, however, that there is another possibility. We could construe Mark and Matthew thus: (1) protasis,

[23] Mark 13:14; Matt 24:15.

[24] Luke 21:20 f.

[25] "The Fall of Jerusalem and the 'Abomination of Desolation,'" *JRS*, 37 (1947), 48.

"When ye shall see the abomination of desolation," (2) apodosis, "let him that readeth understand"—in the sense of "let him pay heed to it and take the necessary steps," and (3) a further admonition, "then let them which be in Judaea flee." Taken in this way, the general pattern at least would be much the same as in Luke. The main difference in form would be that where Mark and Matthew have "let the reader pay heed to it," Luke has the direct address, "know that the desolation is nigh." This might be due to Luke's bringing the clause into closer agreement with the protasis, "when ye shall see."

Several points may be noted. First, ever since Homer, the two verbs ἰδεῖν, "to see," and νοεῖν "to understand" in the sense of "to mark what one sees," form a pair—a fact unquestionably speaking in favour of the interpretation "When ye shall see the abomination, let the reader mark it." The antithesis "to see"—"to mark" gets lost if we cut off "let the reader understand" from the rest and treat it as a parenthesis.

Secondly, it might perhaps be objected that Mark and Matthew simply write "let the reader understand," not "let the reader understand it"; and that the addition of "it" would be necessary if the meaning were to be "let the reader mark it—i.e. the abomination—and take the requisite steps." But again, as early as in Homer, we come across a sentence like this:[26] "To the daughter of Zeus alone he brought no offerings, whether he forgot or whether he paid no heed"—without any pronoun specifying the exact object of his neglect.

Thirdly, according to the present division of the gospels into verses, in Mark, "when ye shall see the abomination—let the reader understand—then let them in Judaea flee" forms one verse; which supports the view that "let the reader understand" is a parenthesis. In Matthew, there is a full stop after "understand." We are given two verses, that is one "when ye shall see the abomination—let the reader understand," and the next "then let them in Judaea flee"; which supports the treatment of "let the reader understand" as the apodosis to "when ye shall see the abomination." Of particular interest, however, is the fact that, as the apparatus shows, there is ancient authority for a full stop after "understand" even in Mark.

Nevertheless, as stated above, the prevalent construction of "let the reader understand" as a parenthesis is probably justified. For one thing, whereas Luke has "then (τότε) know," so that the character of the clause as apodosis is unmistakable, Mark and Matthew have "let the reader understand" without "then"; it is only the following part which opens with "then"—"then let them flee." That in Matthew, and at one time also in Mark, the scholars who fixed the verses made a whole verse of "when ye shall see the abomination, let the reader understand" may well be owing to their having been influenced by the Lukan parallel: they assimilated the other gospels to Luke. It may not be without interest to note that the Rabbis were familiar with the nature of a parenthesis. Indeed they had a technical term: "the before which, as regards subject-matter, should come after."[27] One of their illustrations was this passage:[28] "And the lamp of God had not yet gone out—Samuel being asleep—in the temple of the Lord."

[26] *Il.* 9.536 f.

[27] The 31st of Eliezer ben Jose Ha-gelili's 32 rules of hermeneutics.

[28] 1 Sam 3:3.

We shall take it, then, that "let him that readeth understand" is a parenthesis, intended to call attention to the cryptic βδέλυγηα ἐρημώσεως ἑστηκότα.

2. *The Reader*

If the parenthesis goes back to Jesus, or anyone else who preached but did not write, then "he who readeth" cannot mean the reader of this oracle: a preacher referring to his public would have spoken of "him who heareth." Consequently, if the parenthesis dates from the oral stage of the transmission, "he who readeth" must be interpreted as "he who habitually reads the Scriptures," "the student of Scripture." It must be the Biblical scholar who is exhorted to look carefully into the cryptic expression—so as to discover its connection with Daniel and, presumably, the traditional interpretations of Daniel.

However, to translate ὁ ἀναγινώσκων by "the student of Scripture" is to credit the Greek verb with a sense not to be found in any other text. Nor does the Hebrew equivalent, *qore'*, standing by itself, signify "Biblical scholar." There is indeed a Hebrew and Aramaic noun from the same root, and having exactly the same consonants, *qara'*, which does mean "Biblical scholar." It is possible to argue that the parenthesis was originally in Aramaic; that *qara'* was used; and that it was somewhat clumsily rendered as "he that readeth."

On the whole it is more plausible to ascribe the parenthesis to Mark or whoever wrote down the oracle before him. That is to say, "the reader" means the reader of this—written—apocalypse.[29] He is asked to interest himself in the deeper meaning of the passage. Codex Bezae, supported by a small group of the Itala, contains an addition which, if it were genuine, would put the matter beyond doubt: the clause here is worded "let the reader understand what he reads." In this form, the request can only be addressed to the reader of the present oracle. Unfortunately the additional phrase—"what he reads"—is almost certainly spurious. Still, it seems to be consistent with the original meaning of the exhortation.

3. *"Let him that readeth understand"*

When Spinoza rejected the authenticity of certain portions of the Old Testament, he was indebted to Ibn Ezra, the Spanish Jewish scholar of the first half of the 12th century. (Attempts on the part of hyper-fundamentalists to exonerate Ibn Ezra from the charge of critical insight into the sources[30] have proved complete failures, one is glad to think.) Ibn Ezra, however, had only hinted in veiled language at what Spinoza openly proclaimed. It is noteworthy that while Spinoza was excommunicated by his Amsterdam congregation, Ibn Ezra is still honoured and studied by the very strictest Jews. As Spinoza put it:[31] "*Aben Hezra... qui primus omnium quos legi hoc praeiudici-*

[29] Dodd, *op. cit.*, 54, appears to hold, on the one hand, that the note is due to Mark, and on the other, that it means "let the student of Scripture understand." But ὁ ἀναγινώσκων, in ordinary Greek, signifies "the reader," not "the student of Scripture."

[30] E.g. M. Friedlaender, in *Publications of the Society of Hebrew Literature*, ser. 2, vol. 4 (1877), 60 ff.

[31] *Tractatus Theologico-Politicus* 8.

um animadvertit non ausus est mentem suam aperte explicare, sed rem obscurioribus verbis tantum indicare" ["Ibn Ezra... who was the first person I read to detect this opinion did not dare to speak his mind openly, but only to advert to the matter in rather obscure words"].

Perhaps Ibn Ezra's favourite method of conveying his opinion without too boldly expressing it was to remark that the text in hand contained a mystery, and to add: "and let him that discerneth keep silence," "and let him that understandeth keep silence," or "and let him that discerneth understand." Among the passages he calls attention to in this way are one from Genesis,[32] "And the Canaanite was then in the land," and one from Isaiah,[33] "Kings shall see and arise." The former, he implies, can hardly go back to Moses, in whose time the population was still Canaanite: he would not have written that it was Canaanite "then," i.e. in the time of Abraham. Similarly, the latter, Ibn Ezra holds, refers to the termination of the Babylonian exile under Cyrus: how could it be the work of Isaiah, who lived some 150 years before?

One of the phrases quoted at least, "let him that discerneth understand," is strongly reminiscent of "let him that readeth understand." It is most unlikely that Ibn Ezra was the first exegete to use it, and the others, in the fashion described, *scil.* as indicating the presence of a secret better not talked about (though, before him, the secret hardly ever consisted in higher criticism). For one thing, the phrases occur so often that one has the impression of a well-established method. However, it would lead too far afield to trace them back through early medieval literature; nor is it even certain that we should find them in such material as is preserved. Nevertheless it seems possible to arrive at the position in the age of the New Testament by a short cut. Let it be said at once that the precise words "let him that readeth understand" are not extant in Talmudic writings. There are, however, a sufficient number of significant phenomena to show that the clause, if it was not current among the Rabbis, at least is in perfect harmony with their mode of thinking. In other words, it would be natural for a Rabbi to call attention in this way to a cryptogram, and particularly, it appears, to one of the nature of Mark's.

The general idea may, indeed, be met with in any civilized language. In Terence's *Phormio*,[34] the following dialogue takes place:

ANTIPHO: You must find the necessary money.

GETA (slave of Antipho's father): I should love to: but tell me where?

ANTIPHO: My father is back in town.

GETA: I know; but what follows?

ANTIPHO: Ah, a word is enough for the wise (*verbum sapienti sat est*).

Quintillian[35] discusses a class of figure "whereby we excite suspicion that there is another, hidden meaning which the hearer may discover"; and he adds that it is used "where it is not quite safe to speak openly." Plutarch's explanation of the obscurity of

[32] Gen 12:6.

[33] Isa 49:7.

[34] *Phormio* 3.3.8; cp. already, Plautus, *Persa* 4.7.19.

[35] *I.O.* 9.2.65 f.

the Delphic oracle may be compared.[36]

To establish the Rabbinic background of "let him that readeth understand," we want more specific evidence than evidence of this kind. We propose to demonstrate, first, that the words are adumbrated in the Old Testament; secondly, that some Rabbinic contrasts between the outward aspect and deeper meaning of a text come fairly close to them; thirdly, that the root *bin*, "to understand," which may be taken to underlie Mark's νοείτω,[37] is employed by the Rabbis preferably where the deeper meaning in question is of a secret, dangerous character; and fourthly, that the Rabbinic terminology accounting for "let him that readeth understand" has influenced other passages in the New Testament as well.

(1) The clause under consideration is foreshadowed in the Old Testament. Two of Ibn Ezra's phrases come straight from there: one from Amos,[38] "Therefore let him that discerneth keep silence, for it is an evil time," the other—the more important one for us—from Daniel,[39] "The words are closed up, but the discerning shall understand," or "but let them that discern understand." It is worth pointing out that the next verse goes on to the "abomination of desolation."

In the story of Belshazzar's feast, the antithesis "reading—explaining" (*qera'—peshar*) is repeatedly put; for instance, "But they could not read the writing nor make known the explanation thereof."[40]

There are frequent exhortations throughout the Old Testament to "understand," *bin*, i.e. see the real significance of, historical events, "Would they were wise, that they discerned this, that they understood their latter end";[41] or the nature of God, "Have ye not known? have ye not heard? have ye not understood from the foundations of the earth?";[42] or the prophet's teaching or a wise man's utterance, "Who is wise that he understand these things? understanding that he knows them?,"[43] "Hear ye indeed but understand not; make their ears heavy, lest they hear with their ears and their heart understand,"[44] and "My words are plain to him that understandeth";[45] or a vision or revelation, "I am come to inform thee, therefore, be understanding in the vision."[46]

The root *bin* appears as meaning "to understand," "to be able to interpret," a foreign language:[47] "Thou [the righteous] shalt not see a people of deeper speech than thou canst hear, of a stammering tongue of which thou hast no understanding." (Of David we

[36] *P.O.* 26, in *Mor.* 407E.

[37] *Hiśkil* is also conceivable, though less likely. Some of the following arguments would apply to this term as well; see below, n. 50, n. 72 and n. 80.

[38] Amos 5:13; cp. also the less relevant texts Prov 11:12 and 10:19.

[39] Dan 12:9 f.

[40] Dan 5:8; also 5:7, 15–17.

[41] Deut 32:29; cp. Jer 9:11; Ps 107:43.

[42] Isa 40:21; cp. 1:2 f., 43:10, 44:18.

[43] Hos 14:10—the concluding sentence of the Book.

[44] Isa 6:9 f.—applied in the New Testament to the parables of Jesus.

[45] Prov 8:9; cp. 4:1, 5:1, 8:1 ff., 20:5; Job 34:16.

[46] Dan 9:23; cp. 8:15, 17, 10:1.

[47] Isa 33:19.

are told[48] that when he saw his servants whispering, he "understood," "interpreted this as indicating," that his child had died.) More immediately interesting are two other passages. One says[49] that Daniel "understood in the books the number of years whereof the word of the Lord had come to Jeremiah": *bin* here denotes "to get to the bottom of allusions made in the sacred books." In the other, which depicts the first ceremonial reading of the Law by Ezra, a distinction is made between "reading" Scripture and "understanding" or "discerning" it: "So they read in the Book in the Law of God distinctly, and applying discernment, and they showed understanding in the reading. And on the second day were gathered the chief of the fathers unto Ezra the scribe, even to discern the words of the Law."[50] It is not enough to "read"; you must perceive the import of a text.

(2) Here are some suggestive Rabbinic distinctions between the outward aspect of a text and its deeper meaning. What the text "says," *'amar*, or what is "written" in it, *kathubh*, is constantly opposed to what it "tells," you, *higgidh*. "Thou citest [*'atta 'omer*], In the beginning God created the heaven and earth [first chapter of Genesis]. I might take it that the heaven came first. But there is a teaching in the words, In the day that the Lord God made the earth and heaven [second chapter]. This tells you [*maggidh*] that both came simultaneously."[51] The term "Haggadah," from *higgidh*, signifies these implied pieces of information.

Frequently the contrast is between what the text "says" or what is "written" in it and what it "teaches," *limmedh*, or what you may "learn," *lamadh*. The words "Then sang Moses"[52] are translatable also by "Then Moses will sing." R. Judah the Prince commented:[53] "It is not written [*kethibh*] sang but will sing: thus we may learn, infer [*lemedhin*], the resurrection of the dead from the Torah." The term *talmudh lomar*, "there is a teaching in what the text says," is old and common. It may be found, for example, in the discussion of the creation quoted above: "there is a teaching in what the text says, In the day that the Lord God made the earth and heaven." Equally usual is *ba' hakkathubh lelammedh*, "what is written comes to teach." The provision "Thou shalt take him [the murderer] from mine altar that he may die" is said "to come to teach that the Temple service [in contradistinction to the Sabbath] may not be set aside to save a human life."[54] On the other hand, when a text must be taken literally, the Rabbis declare that there is "no teaching in what it says," but "matters are according to their writing," *debharim kikhethabham*.[55]

[48] 2 Sam 12:19.

[49] Dan 9:2.

[50] Neh 8:8, 13; cp. Ps 119:27, 34, 73, 95, 100, 104, 125, 130, 144, 169 (*bin*), 99 (*hiśkil*), 45, 155; Ezek 7:10; 1 Chr 28:8 (*darash*). It should be observed, in connection with the remark made above, n. 37, that *hiśkil*, or some word from this root, is paired off with *bin* in several of the texts quoted: Dan 12:9 f.; Deut 32:29; Isa 44:18; Neh 8:8, 13. Cp. also Dan 9:22, 25, with 9:23, and Ps 119:99 with the verses using *bin*. In Prov 10:19 *hiśkil* alone appears. One of the qualities ascribed to Daniel in the story of Belshazzar's feast is *śakhlethanu*, Dan 5:11 f., 14.

[51] *Mek.* on Exod 12:1.

[52] Exod 15:1.

[53] *Mek. ad loc.*

[54] *Mek.* on Exod 21:14.

[55] *b. Kidd.* 17b, Eleazar ben Azariah, about A.D. 100.

Similarly, what is "written" may be contrasted with what you "derive by interpretation," *darash*. Eliezer ben Hyrkanos (about A.D. 100) was reproached for going too far: "Thou sayest to what is written, Be quiet while I interpret."[56]

The "distinct," *mephorash*, is opposed to the "concealed," *sathum*. "Thou shalt not steal" is a "concealed" commandment, since it does not specify whether it refers to theft of persons, a capital crime,[57] or theft of property, less serious; whereas the two commandments allied with it, prohibiting murder and adultery, are "distinct."[58] (Bacher[59] is wrong, an extremely rare occurrence with him. The two "distinct" commandments must be Exodus 20:13 and 14, since it is only from them that the Rabbis could deduce—what they wanted to deduce—that 20:15 also was concerned with a capital offence, theft of a person. Of the two passages given as "distinct" by Bacher, one, Leviticus 19:11, in the opinion of the Rabbis, referred to a monetary, private delict only.)

There are several further pairs of this kind. It may suffice to present three more, in all of which one of the opposites is "reading" Scripture, *qara'*. The first two are "reading" Scripture and "interpreting" it, *darash*, and "reading" Scripture and "making it distinct," *peresh*. The Ecclesiast says:[60] "The dead know not anything." R. Jonathan (at the beginning of the 3rd cent.) took this literally. R. Hiyya, however, told him: "Thou knowest to read, but thou does not know to interpret," and he adduced a verse from Deuteronomy:[61] "This is the land which I sware unto Abraham, saying." Here the Rabbis found "a teaching in what the text says," to the effect that God speaks of the dead patriarchs as living.[62] Of a passage in Leviticus,[63] R. Johanan ben Zaccai claimed[64] that "the priests interpreted this text—or, this reading, *miqra' ze*— to their advantage." Sometimes, if two Rabbis disagreed about the meaning of a text, one would upbraid the other: "If thou hast read it, thou hast not done it twice, and if twice, not three times, and if three times, they have not made it distinct to thee."[65]

The remaining pair is the most significant. Not only is here "reading," *qara'*, distinguished from "understanding," *bin*, as in Mark, but also, as in Mark, "understanding" means penetrating beneath the surface by seeing through a grammatical irregularity—in fact, an ambiguity regarding the grammatical connection of a word with the rest of the sentence. A word, that is, may be explained as attached to what precedes it or to what follows it. We have already quoted the report about Ezra's reading of the Law: "So they read in the Book and showed understanding in the reading." One Rabbinic view is[66] that "they showed understanding in the reading" means: they understood the pas-

[56] *Siphra* on Lev 13:49.
[57] Exod 21:16; Deut 24:7.
[58] *Mek.* on Exod 20:15.
[59] *Die älteste Terminologie der Jüdischen Schriftauslegung* (1889), p 137.
[60] Eccl 9:5.
[61] Deut 34:4.
[62] *y. Ber.* 4d; cp. Matt 22:32; Mark 12:26; Luke 20:37.
[63] Lev 6:16.
[64] *m. Shek.* 1:4.
[65] *b. M. K.* 16b; *b. Ber.* 18a.
[66] *Gen. Rab.* on 9:26.

sages lacking "weighing down of the scale," a "turning of the scales," an "adjudication," *hekhrea'*. This is a happy term to designate syntactic accuracy in the sense of clarity as to the relative place of a word, clarity as to whether a word is attached to what precedes it or what follows it. I have suggested elsewhere that the working out of the concept may owe something to the Hellenistic grammarians, for whom the case of a sentence which might be divided in several ways came under the heading of σύνθεσις and διαίρεσις.[67]

R. Isi ben Judah held[68] that there were five such ambiguous passages in the Pentateuch. Let us mention two. In God's warning to Cain,[69] the Rabbi said, the word *śe'eth*, "pardon," might be construed as belonging to the portion preceding it or to that following it; so that we might interpret, in the natural way, "Why is thy countenance fallen? Shall there not, if thou doest well, be pardon?," but might also get a deeper sense, a reference to Cain's ultimate reprieve, "Why is thy countenance fallen? Surely it will not be if thou doest well. But pardon shall take place even if thou doest not well."[70]

Another example given by Isi ben Judah was a verse from Deuteronomy,[71] where he declared *weqam*, "and arise," to be connectible with what follows it, as a perfect, or with what precedes it, as a participle. If the former construction, the natural one, be adopted, we should translate: "Behold, thou shalt sleep with thy fathers; and this people will rise up and go after the gods of the strangers." If the latter, the text would provide proof of resurrection: "Thou shalt sleep with thy fathers and rise up; as for this people, it will go after the gods of the strangers." The latter construction, it may be recalled, was relied on by Gamaliel of Jabneh, about A.D. 90, in a controversy with the Sadducees.[72]

Obviously, where "they showed understanding in the reading" might denote the gaining of insight into the deeper meaning of a text by taking note of a deliberate ambiguity in syntax—and we must never forget that, for the Rabbis, when a sentence in Scripture lacked a "weighing down of the scale," when the relative position of a word was undecided, that was necessarily deliberate, a subtle hint on the part of the author—we are very near the precise use of "let him that readeth understand" in Mark.

(3) The term *bin*, "to understand," is favoured by the Rabbis where the message

[67] ["Alexandrian Methods of Interpretation and the Rabbis"] *Festschrift Hans Lewald*, 34 ff. [*Talmudic Law*, 364–76]. For an instructive example, see Athenaeus, *Deipn.* 1.12a f., about *Il.* 24.476.

[68] *Mek.* on Exod 17:9.

[69] Gen 4:6 f.

[70] The point of this alternative, deeper (and highly artificial) interpretation seems never to have been appreciated. Strack-Billerbeck, vol. 3 (1926), 26, do not see it. L. Blau, "*Massoretische Studien*," *JQR*, 9 (1896–97), 139 n. 2, remarks: "I must confess I cannot understand how a Tanna could have had any doubt whether in Genesis 4:7 *śe'eth we'im lo' theṭibh* was to be read. The matter is very obscure." Yet a glance at Onkelos will show what Isi ben Judah was driving at. Onkelos gives an unusually long paraphrase in order to convey both the natural meaning, forgiveness if Cain does well, and the deeper one, forgiveness even if he does not: "If thou doest well, thou shalt be pardoned; but if thou doest not well, for the day of judgment the sin is laid up if thou dost not repent; but if thou repentest, thou shalt be pardoned."

[71] Deut 31:16.

[72] *b. Sanh.* 19b. As regards *hiśkil* (see above, n. 37), the words "and applying discernment" in Neh 8:8 are taken in *Gen. Rab.* on 9:26 as indicating that, when the Law was read on that occasion, the divisions within the verses, the *ṭe'amim*, were properly observed.

behind a text is of a particularly secret, dangerous nature.[73] The Mishnah lays down[74] that "no one may interpret the Chariot[75] except a Sage who understands of his own knowledge," *mebhin midda'to*. Johanan ben Zaccai praised Eleazar ben Arak for "showing understanding in, searching into and interpreting" this section, *lehabhin welaḥqor welidrosh*.[76]

The root is prominent in this sense as early as in the Old Testament. Some of the passages from Daniel quoted above come to mind,[77] and we may compare others: only the prophet "understands" the manner in which God reveals himself;[78] few "understand" the tremendous powers of God;[79] God "understands" all secrets.[80]

(4) It remains to point out that the Rabbinic terminology here held to account for "let him that readeth understand" is reflected in other places. To begin with, a verse in Revelation[81] bids the reader ponder on a number supplied by the text: "Here is wisdom. Let him that hath understanding, ὁ ἔχων νοῦν, count the number of the beast, for it is the number of a man." He that "understands" is not expressly opposed to him that merely "reads," but the contrast seems implied.[82] (This is not to deny that the possession of νοῦς in Revelation may involve being a *Pneumatiker* [a person endowed with the Spirit, sometimes ecstatic and sometimes enthusiastic or both].) It is interesting that the standard illustration which the Rabbis give of exegesis on the basis of the numerical value of letters[83] is the reference to Abraham's household in Genesis,[84] with 318 taken as the number of a man, namely, Eliezer, Abraham's trusted servant. According to the *Epistle of Barnabas*,[85] the figure represents IH = 18 = Jesus, plus T = 300 = Cross.

Possibly exhortations like "Who hath ears to hear, let him hear"[86] are also intended to draw attention to a hidden meaning, though they might simply mean "This is important, so listen." Old Testament and Rabbinic usage would warrant either interpretation. The former one, however, was adopted by at least those versions of Mark which add "and let him that hath understanding understand," ὁ συνίων συνιέτω. We may further note the remark that "the Pharisees knew that he had spoken the parables against them."[87]

One section from an early Christian tract outside the New Testament, the *Epistle of*

[73] See Bacher, *Die Agada der Tannaiten*, 1, 2nd ed. (1903), 70 n. 42.
[74] *m. Hag.* 2:1.
[75] Ezekiel 1 and 10.
[76] *b. Hag.* 14b.
[77] Dan 9:2, 10:1, 12:9 f.; see also 12:8, 8:27.
[78] 1 Sam 3:8; 2 Chr 26:5.
[79] Job 13:1, 26:14.
[80] Prov 24:12; Sir 42:18. Of these texts, only Dan 12:10 contains *hiśkil* as well: see above, n. 37.
[81] Rev 13:18.
[82] Cp. Dan 9:2, quoted above: "I understood in the books the number of years."
[83] *Gema reya'*, the 29th of Eliezer ben Jose Ha-gelili's hermeneutic rules.
[84] Gen 14:14.
[85] *Epistle of Barnabus* 9:8.
[86] Matt 13:9; Mark 4:9; Luke 8:8.
[87] Matt 21:45; Mark 12:12; Luke 20:19.

Barnabas,[88] deserves consideration. Its close affinity to the Markan "let him that readeth understand" is manifest. The author quotes Daniel's vision of "the fourth beast, dreadful and terrible."[89] He has in mind the Roman emperor. But, too prudent to state the application openly, he tells his readers to look for the true meaning behind the text: "Now you must understand."

So far we have dealt with passages speaking of "understanding" in a way that suggests a contrast with mere "reading." There is also a group speaking of "reading" in a way that suggests a contrast with "understanding," namely, the rhetorical questions put into Jesus's mouth: "Have ye not read this or that text?" It is conceivable that these should be paraphrased: "Surely you have read this or that text, so you ought to understand its import," or "but you do not seem to understand its import." They occur in (a) Matthew 12:3, 5, Mark 2:25, Luke 6:3; (b) Matthew 19:4; (c) Matthew 21:16; (d) Matthew 21:42, Mark 12:10; (e) Matthew 22:31, Mark 12:26; and (f) Luke 10:26, with some slight modification.

In favour of this paraphrase speaks the fact that in each case Jesus does propound, or indicate, an interpretation going beyond the literal meaning. Moreover, as for (a), in Matthew at least[90] it is plainly stated that "knowing" a text is what matters: "But if ye had known what this is, I will have mercy." In another chapter of Matthew we find the formulation:[91] "But go ye and learn what it is, I will have mercy." We have already discussed *lamadh* in the sense of "to learn," "to infer," something from Scripture; and the phrase *ṡe'ulemadh*, "go out and learn," *scil.* this or that from the text, is technical in Rabbinic debate.[92] Regarding (e), the Sadducees who deny resurrection are described as "erring," to which Matthew adds that they do not "know," "grasp," the Scriptures. One is reminded of the antithesis in Isaiah:[93] "They that erred in spirit shall know understanding." According to Matthew,[94] the multitude was struck by Jesus's διδαχή, here presumably corresponding to *talmudh* or *midrash*, "teaching" or "exposition."[95] Luke in this controversy with the Sadducees makes Jesus use the highly technical term *remez*, signifying "a hint," "a slight covert indication," contained in a text:[96] "That the dead are raised Moses hinted (ἐμήνυσεν or ἐδήλωσεν) when he calleth the Lord the God of Abraham, Isaac and Jacob." We saw above that a Rabbi not aware of the "teaching" of Deuteronomy 34:4 "This is the land which I sware unto Abraham, saying," was considered as "able to read but not to interpret."[97] But we even meet with *remez* in this connection. Another verse from Deuteronomy,[98] "I kill and I make alive," is claimed to be one of four Biblical passages in which "a hint at the resurrection of the dead was given to the Israelites." (The

[88] *Epistle of Barnabus* 4:5 f.
[89] Dan 7:7 f.
[90] Matt 12:7.
[91] Matt 9:13.
[92] See Bacher, *Die älteste Terminologie der Jüdischen Schriftauslegung* (1899), 75.
[93] Isa 29:24.
[94] Matt 22:33.
[95] On various possible translations of the word, see above, under Rabbinic Authority [590 ff.].
[96] See Bacher, 182 f.
[97] *y. Ber.* 4d.
[98] Deut 32:39; see *Siphre* on 32:34.

same term, incidentally, underlies the *Epistle of Barnabas* where, as already mentioned, it is concerned with the 318 members of Abraham's household:[99] the Lord, we are told, δηλοῖ "hints at," "gives a *remez* for," Jesus and the Cross.) Lastly, with (f) we might perhaps connect Mark 12:34. A man properly appreciating the most important commandments[100] is here praised as talking νουνεχῶς, "with understanding."[101]

The author of Revelation begins by an admonition[102] to heed the prophecies; and very possibly, when he says that "hearing" and "keeping" or "guarding" them is necessary in addition to "reading," he may include careful interpretation. We have seen that an exclamation like "Who hath ears to hear let him hear"[103] may signify something between "This is important" and "This calls for further inquiry if the deeper significance is to be grasped."

However, a number of passages in Acts and Paul's epistles provide illustrations of an express opposition of "reading" and "understanding" Scripture. The Queen of Ethiopia's treasurer was asked by Philip[104] whether he "knew," "grasped," what he was "reading." That we have to give the distinction its full Rabbinic force is plain from the continuation: "Then Philip opened his mouth and, beginning at the same text [from Isaiah], preached unto him Jesus." In Rabbinic language, "to open one's mouth," *pathaḥ piw*, as a rule shortened into "to open," frequently denotes "to open a lecture on Scripture" or even "to lecture on Scripture." (The history of the phrase postulated by Bacher is not convincing.[105] This is not the place to discuss the question, especially as it does not affect our main argument. It may suffice to point out that the section under consideration alone, Acts 8:30 ff., which he entirely overlooks, seems to disprove his theory.) R. Johanan ben Zaccai asked Eliezer ben Hyrcanus:[106] "Open and expound," *pethaḥ udherosh*. Again, "to begin at a certain text" sounds quite genuine. The Mishnah ordains[107] that, when commemorating the exodus on Passover eve, "one should begin with the disgrace and end with the glory, and expound from the verse in Deuteronomy,[108] A Syrian ready to perish was my father."

According to a report in Acts,[109] Paul accused the Jews of "not knowing him [Jesus or, just conceivably, the Baptist] and the voices of the prophets" (or of "not understanding the writings of the prophets") "which are read every sabbath day." They "read" Scripture, he complained, but did not "know," "grasp," it. Whatever one may think of the origin of this speech, it is certain that Paul did formulate charges like this. In 2 Corinthians[110] he writes: "But their understanding, νοήματα, was blinded, for until this

[99] *Epistle of Barnabus* 9:8.

[100] Deut 6:5; Lev 19:18.

[101] Cp. Rev 13:18, cited above, ὁ ἔχων νοῦν.

[102] Rev 1:3.

[103] Matt 13:9; Mark 4:9; Luke 8:8.

[104] Acts 8:30.

[105] *Die Exegetische Terminologie der Jüdischen Traditionsliteratur*, 2 (1905), 174 ff., and *Die Pröomien der Alten Jüdischen Homilie* (1913), 27 f.

[106] *Ab. de R. N.* 8.

[107] *m. Pes.* 10:5.

[108] Deut 26:5.

[109] Acts 13:27.

day remaineth the veil untaken away in the reading, ἀναγνώσει, of the Old Testament."[111]

It is remarkable that Paul appears to transfer this terminology from Scripture to his own writings. In Ephesians[112] he says that those "reading" his letter will be able to "understand" the mystery it is his task to communicate. The idea seems to be that his message contains no secrets accessible only to the most learned. The recipients, if they will trouble to peruse it, may be sure of acquiring the full substance.

That there is no discrepancy between the outward aspect of his words and their real significance when he speaks about his own person and plans, he feels compelled to emphasize in 2 Corinthians:[113] "For we write none other things than what ye read and also acknowledge, ἀναγινώσκετε ἢ καὶ ἐπιγινώσκετε; and I trust ye shall acknowledge even to the end, as ye have already acknowledged us in part." He continues his defence against the imputation of ambiguity in the following sentences, alluding to Jesus's saying concerning "Yea, yea" and "Nay, nay."

In the next chapter,[114] the pair γινωσκομένη και ἀναγινωσκομένη at first sight looks like an empty, stereotyped jingle, the "knowing" preceding the "reading." For one thing, however, this part of the epistle reflects great strain and excitement, and there are several illogicalities. For another, conceivably, we are here moving in a completely different province from that considered above. Paul may not be thinking of a surface meaning and a deeper meaning at all. His point may be that his followers are recognized as such and, being recognized, are read as such—i.e. read as letters of commendation and letters of Christ.

It is evident that a large proportion of the New Testament passages making, or proceeding from, a distinction between "reading" and "understanding" Scripture refer to "understanding" in the sense mentioned above, as often expressed by *bin*, namely, in the sense of understanding a particularly secret or dangerous meaning beneath the text. Revelation 13:18, Barnabas 4:5 f., Matthew 21:42, Mark 12:10, Matthew 22:31, Mark 12:26, Acts 8:30, 2 Corinthians 3:14, all tend in this direction.

Another detail is in harmony with the proper Rabbinic character of the whole complex. From the Rabbinic illustrations submitted it is clear that "reading" might be opposed to "understanding" whether it was private reading or reading the Sabbatic lesson. When a Rabbi told his colleague, "Thou knowest to read but not to interpret," obviously, he was referring to private reading. On the other hand, a verse from Nehemiah[115] was declared to show that the people listening to Ezra's recital of the Law comprehended the passages lacking "a turning of the scales." Just so, in the story of the Ethiopian treasurer, the "reading" is private, whereas in the charges preferred by Paul against the Jews it is liturgical.

[110] 2 Cor 3:14.
[111] Cp. also the following verse, 2 Cor 3:15.
[112] Eph 3:4.
[113] 2 Cor 1:13 f.
[114] 2 Cor 3:2.
[115] Neh 8:8.

C. A PARALLEL FROM PHILO

Dr. Wilfred Knox, of ever-cherished memory, pointed out to me that a section from Philo[116] furnished support of the view here taken of the manner in which Mark deals with the "abomination of desolation." Philo comments on the notice in Genesis[117] that "all flesh had corrupted its way"—in Greek: κατέφθειρε πᾶσα σὰρξ τὴν ὁδὸν αὐτοῦ. He observes that the masculine αὐτοῦ, "his way," is used with reference to the feminine σάρξ, "flesh"; and he explains that this need be no grammatical blunder but may be put on purpose to indicate a second meaning. The first, apparent meaning is that the flesh corrupted its own way. But the deeper meaning, he says, may be that it sought to mar the way of God—and for this, we do want the masculine, "his way." Then Philo adds the remark: "Know that this is wisdom, for through it the understanding (ὁ νοῦς) reaches the goal."

Dr. Knox suggested that the words "Know that this is wisdom" might here signify, not so much "Know that this way to God which the people of the flood marred is wisdom," as "Pay attention to this piece of wisdom conveyed by the grammatical irregularity in the Biblical verse." In Revelation,[118] we saw, the information conveyed by a number is described as "wisdom," accessible to "him that hath understanding." However, quite apart from this clause, we clearly have before us a case of a disagreement in gender being used as basis for a teaching. And it is a disagreement to be found only in the Greek version, not in the Hebrew original. In Hebrew, *baśar*, "flesh," is masculine, so that there is no discrepancy between it and *darko*, "his way." (Of course, it is quite possible that even before Philo, and on the basis of the Hebrew text, some Rabbis had interpreted "his way" as "the way of God.") If Philo was capable of adopting this kind of method, undoubtedly Mark and the circles from which he sprang were.

One may wonder whether R. Johanan (of the generation after Judah the Prince) also had in mind the incongruity in the Greek text when he inferred from this passage that the flood came because tame beasts cohabited with wild ones, men with animals, males with males and females with females.[119] The "wrong" gender in grammar might have suggested to him the wrong sex in reality. True, there are other elements in the verse which would sufficiently account for his exegesis, especially the associations of *hishḥith*, "to ruin," "to pervert," and *derekh*, "way," "sexual intercourse." Nor can we be even certain that he was the first to propose it. Still, his is the earliest name we come across in this connection. Besides, was it not he who gave permission to instruct girls in Greek[120] because a knowledge of that language would be an adornment to them? Surely, he must have been well acquainted with the LXX.

[116] *Quod Deus Immutabilis Sit* 30.141 ff.

[117] Gen 6:12.

[118] Rev 13:8.

[119] *b. Sanh.* 108a.

[120] See Bacher, *Die Agada der Palästinensischen Amoräer*, 1 (1892), 257.

The Interpretation of a Generic Singular

Paul's Rabbinic scholarship sometimes manifests itself more clearly in the manner of his argument than in the matter. In Galatians[1] he cites a verse where the holy land is promised "to Abraham and to his seed." He identifies "the seed" with Jesus, taking the generic singular "and to thy seed" as a proper, specific singular: "He saith not, And to thy seeds, as of many, but as of one, And to thy seed, which is Christ."

Before adducing any Rabbinic models he may have in mind, we ought perhaps to justify the assertion that he is dealing with a verse where the land is promised and not, as some authorities seem to hold,[2] with one saying that Abraham's offspring will be a blessing for the world. First, in the latter case, the Old Testament simply does not contain the clause commented on by Paul. The expression used is "in thy seed," not "to thy seed"; the Hebrew as well as the LXX read "there shall be blessed in thy seed all the nations."[3] It is only in promises of the land that "and to thy seed" may be found—twice in the Hebrew,[4] three times in LXX:[5] "to thee will I give it (have I given it) and to thy seed." This is the phrase Paul quotes. Secondly, we shall see below that it was in connection with a promise of the land that the Rabbis resorted to an interpretation of "seed" with which Paul's has much in common. Thirdly, Paul in Galatians counts 430 years from the event of which he thinks to the giving of the Law. The Rabbis[6] counted this number of years from the covenant "between the pieces" in Genesis 15, where the land is promised, to the giving of the Law. To be sure, in this chapter, the land is promised not "to thee and to thy seed," but merely "to thy seed."[7] But for one thing, this chapter, with its mention of an affliction for 400 years and a return after four generations, formed the general basis for chronological speculations as to the interval between Abraham and Moses. For another, from the LXX[8] and Josephus[9] it appears that, in New Testament times, no strict distinction was made between the promise of the land Abraham received "between the pieces" and promises of the land he received on other occasions. For the LXX and Josephus, 430 years elapsed between Abraham's arrival in

[1] Gal 3:16.

[2] Even Strack-Billerbeck, 3 (1926), 553, refer not only to Gen 13:15 and 17:8, but also to 22:18. On the other hand, they omit 15:18 which, as will presently be shown, is undoubtedly of some relevance.

[3] Gen 22:18.

[4] Gen 13:15, 17:8.

[5] Gen 13:15, 17:8, 24:7.

[6] *Seder Olam Rab.* 3.

[7] Gen 15:18.

[8] Exod 12:40.

[9] *Ant.* 2.15.2.318. We need not go into other datings he gives.

Canaan—when there was a promise of the land "to thee and to thy seed"[10]—and the exodus. Clearly, Paul takes the same line.

This is not to deny that, in the eyes of both Paul and the Rabbis, the promise of the land and that of becoming a blessing to all the earth are frequently one and the same thing. They are obviously one and the same thing in Galatians. Still, the actual verse Paul invokes is one where the land is promised.

To go on to the background of his argument, it is correctly observed by Strack-Billerbeck[11] that "the interpretation of the number in which a word appears plays a certain part even in *halakhic* exegesis." But Paul is not here concerned with *halakha*. No wonder that the Talmudic example supplied by Strack-Billerbeck, though it does show that the Rabbis paid attention to the number of a word, and though it has to do with the word "seed," yet is without particular bearing on Paul's thesis. "Whence do we know"—the example runs[12]—"that despite the prohibition of mingling diverse seeds,[13] five kinds of seeds may be sown in a bed six handbreadths square, four on the sides and one in the middle? Because it is written,[14] As the garden causeth its seeds to spring forth. It is not written, its seed, but its seeds." Nobody would maintain a direct connection between this piece of teaching and that in Galatians. One might even object that the word "seed" is here employed in a generic sense throughout. The singular is not, as in Paul, treated as specific. Even if the garden brought forth "its seed," not "its seeds," one might object, it would still be one sort of seed; it would still not be, as it ought to be if the reasoning were really parallel to Paul's, a single plant. A further criticism might be made: the word for "seed" decisive in this Talmudic provision, *zerua'*, is slightly different from that to be met with in God's promise to Abraham's *zera'*.

As a matter of fact, there are two early *haggadhic* teachings the direct influence of one of which on Paul is certain, and the direct influence of the other not improbable.

When God concluded with Abraham the covenant "between the pieces," he foretold: "Thy seed shall be a stranger in a land not theirs, and they shall serve them and they shall afflict them four hundred years."[15] The 400 years created a problem for the Rabbis, since according to the story of the exodus "the sojourning in Egypt was four hundred and thirty years."[16] Their solution—adopted by the LXX and Josephus—was (if we disregard the more subtle datings) that, on the one hand, the time between the covenant with Abraham and the exodus was 430 years: "the sojourning in Egypt" included the wanderings of the patriarchs in Canaan. On the other hand, the covenant with Abraham was made thirty years before Isaac's birth—hence God predicted only 400 years of trouble for Abraham's descendants.[17]

[10] Gen 13:15.
[11] 3 (1926), 553.
[12] *m. Shab.* 9:2.
[13] Lev 19:19; Deut 22:9.
[14] Isa 61:11.
[15] Gen 15:13.
[16] Exod 12:40.
[17] *Seder Olam Rab.* 3.

It is the Rabbinic analysis of this prediction which Paul unquestionably follows. The Rabbis argued that "thy seed shall be a stranger" signified "Isaac shall be a stranger," i.e. Canaan would not yet definitively belong to him; "in a land not theirs" signified the wanderings of Isaac and Jacob; "and they shall serve them and they shall afflict them" signified the stay of the Israelites in Egypt; "four hundred years" covered the whole period from Isaac's birth to the exodus. The point is that "thy seed" was understood by the Rabbis to be a specific singular. It alluded to one person: Isaac. In support, they referred to the prophecy, "For in Isaac shall thy seed be called."[18] It is relevant to note, however, that though they felt it necessary to establish a scrupulously accurate chronology of the pre-Sinaitic era, yet they were convinced that the promise of salvation after sufferings which God gave to Abraham "between the pieces" was valid not only up to the exodus but for the entire future history of Israel. This extension is demonstrably old: it occupies a prominent place in an early section of the Jewish liturgy for Passover eve ("And this is the promise that has held good for our ancestors and ourselves" etc.). Some Rabbis rested it on the expression "and also" in God's assurance: "And also that nation whom they shall serve will I judge, and afterwards shall they come out with great substance."[19] God said "and also," instead of just "also," in order to include later oppressors of his people.

When we consider that Paul is proceeding from a verse in which Abraham receives a promise of the land, that he expressly introduces the Rabbinic chronology, that like the Rabbis he emphasizes the eternal validity of the promise, that the generic singular he makes into a specific one is "seed," and that Isaac is regarded by the early Christians as prefiguring the Messiah in more than one way, we may confidently assume that the Midrash outlined is a source of Paul's argument. In fact, it is quite possible that he believes some at least of the recipients of his letter to be acquainted with it, and that he deliberately furnishes them with a deeper application.

In a *haggadha* about the creation of man, too, the Rabbis turned a generic singular into a specific one. The interpretation was famous in the Talmudic era, and quite conceivably Paul is drawing on it also.

The Bible tells us[20] that "God created man in his image, in the image of God created he him, male and female created he them," and again, "In the day that God created man, in the likeness of God made he him, male and female created he them and called their name Adam." An ordinary reader would ascribe a generic sense to "man" and "he," the sense of "a man and a woman," or maybe even that of "mankind." The Rabbis could not have admitted this, since if they had there would have been a conflict with the story of Eve's formation from a rib of Adam. In consequence they emphasized the curious wavering in the verses quoted between the singular and the plural: God created "man" and "him," yet at the same time he created "them" male and female and called "their" name Adam. This wavering was declared to prove—what was traditionally assumed anyhow—that the first, ideal man was androgynous. That is to say, the plu-

[18] Gen 21:12.
[19] *Gen. Rab.* on 15:14.
[20] Gen 1:27, 5:1 f.

ral, it was held, indicated not several beings, but one composite being; and the singular was not of a generic character, it did not denote mankind, but it was a specific singular, it denoted one human being only, the first bisexual one, out of whom Eve was subsequently taken.

That this explanation is ancient would be probable, even if there were no other evidence, from the consideration that the two accounts of man's creation in chapters 1 and 2 of Genesis must have called for a harmonization from the moment the canon was treated as a faultless whole. (Indeed, a tendency to harmonize is perhaps noticeable in the Biblical accounts themselves, but those early efforts would mean a rewriting, not a re-interpretation.) Fortunately, evidence is not lacking. According to a tradition preserved in numerous sources—among them the Mekhilta[21]—the clause "male and female created he them" was one of the passages altered by the authors of the LXX in order to prevent misunderstanding on the part of King Ptolemy: they translated "a male with his female parts created he them," or "male and female [i.e. bisexual] created he him [singular, and plainly specific singular]." Whether or not the tradition is historical—and it is difficult to believe that no Greek renderings of the kind described were in circulation—it could not have arisen unless the teaching which it presupposes, the androgynous Adam, had been of considerable age. Actually, as we tried to show above (under Precept and Example [252 ff.]), the interpretation of "male and female created he them" as alluding to the ideal, androgynous man occurs in the gospels as well as in Philo; and Paul himself in 1 Corinthians and Ephesians not only adopts the doctrine that sexual intercourse restores man and woman into an androgynous state, but even uses a verse from Genesis 2 in support.

The Rabbis, then, contended that the Bible, when speaking of "man," did not mean "man and woman," still less "mankind," but the original, ideal Adam alone. A generic singular was given the force of a specific one. It is very possible that this *haggadha* as well as that about Isaac is in Paul's mind where he, in Galatians, avails himself of this method of exegesis. Needless to say, he does not think of an androgynous Jesus. Yet the sentence "There is neither Jew nor Greek, neither bond nor free, neither male nor female"[22] may contain a trace of the myth respecting the first man. Again, it must be admitted that the Rabbinic Midrash concerning Adam and Paul's Midrash concerning Jesus are due to very different circumstances. The Rabbis wished to prove that all human beings, including Eve, were descended from the first man—in accordance with chapter 2 of Genesis—and they had to explain away inconvenient texts—like those referring to a creation of "male and female." Paul wishes to prove that what was promised to Abraham's offspring was promised to Jesus only, and he has to read an indication of this into the text itself. But there are elements common to the two cases, above all, the insistence on the ultimate unity of mankind. As the Rabbis laid stress on the oneness of Adam, father of all, so Paul lays stress on the oneness of Jesus who, on the strength of the old promise, gathers up in himself all those redeemed.

[21] On Exod 12:40; cp. *Gen. Rab.* on 1:27.

[22] Gal 3:28.

[23] Rom 5:14.

We must not forget that Paul sees in Jesus the last Adam, and in the original Adam "the figure of him that was to come."[23] The absence from Galatians of any explicit reference to this notion does not necessarily mean that it plays no part. After all, Paul in this epistle does describe him who is in Jesus as "a new creature,"[24] which suggests a contrast with the first creation.

Three remarks in conclusion. First, Paul is given to emphasizing the oneness of Jesus, of the community, of Jesus with the community, of the events connected with Jesus and so on. One wonders whether quite a few passages containing this idea[25] may not reflect *haggadhoth* involving the method here discussed—the pressing of a singular. Of course, the *haggadhoth* need not have regard to Isaac or Adam, they may relate to entirely different figures or events. Philo[26] says that "since God is one, there may be only one temple." Similarly, in his *Antiquities*,[27] Josephus explains that "there may be only one temple since God is one and the Hebrew race is one." In his *Contra Apionem*[28] he mitigates the argument from the singularity of the nation and speaks of "one temple for the one God, since like is ever the friend of like, and [here comes the part replacing the outspoken reference to the Jewish race] the temple must be common to all, belonging to God who is common to all." Now these statements show distinct traces of popular philosophy. That "like is the friend of like" was proverbial long before Aristotle.[29] Nevertheless even here, we cannot rule out the influence of certain traditional interpretations of Scripture. We know, for example, that many Rabbis saw an apparent contradiction between the promise that God would choose his dwelling-place "out of all your tribes" (which in the opinion of these Rabbis, must mean that somehow all tribes would have a share in it) and the promise that he would choose it "in one of thy tribes."[30] There may well have been solutions of the difficulty accounting for Philo's and Josephus's views.

Secondly, we come across Rabbinic comments on the unity of God or mankind or both which, though they contain no explicit reference to an important singular in Scripture, yet are unquestionably based on such a singular. For example, the question is raised[31] why man was created as one, and among the answers are these: in order that the *Minim*, the Christians, might have no ground for maintaining that there are several powers in heaven, or in order that the pious people might not claim a different ancestry from the wicked. Behind these affirmations there clearly stands the exegesis discussed above, according to which "man" in the story of the creation is a specific singular.

Thirdly, it should be noted that, in Hebrew as in English, the word "seed," "issue," now and then refers to an individual even apart from any artificial interpretation. To be sure, the generic meaning is invariably present by way of connotation: if you call your

[24] Gal 6:15, cp. 2 Cor 5:17.

[25] Such as Gal 3:20; Eph 2:14 ff.

[26] *De spec. leg.* 1.12.67.

[27] *Ant.* 4.8.5.200 f.

[28] *Contra Apionem* 2.23.193.

[29] *Nic. E.* 9.3.3; cp. 8.1.6; Sir 13:15, 27:9.

[30] *Siphre* on Deut 12:5, 14.

[31] *b. Sanh.* 38a.

son "your seed," "your offspring," the idea of the family, the line, as a whole is somehow brought in. Nevertheless, that "seed" may be used in this way, of an individual, renders the Rabbinic and Pauline arguments less inappropriate. (Similarly, the Rabbis would not have taken "man" as a specific singular in those passages from the story of the creation had the word not been capable of this meaning in ordinary language.) An example of "seed" denoting an individual occurs in the remark by which Eve greeted Seth:[32] "God hath appointed me another seed instead of Abel, whom Cain slew." The passage is of some interest in this connection since at least from the 3rd cent. A.D., but probably long before, the Rabbis claimed that "another seed" alluded to the King Messiah who, Eve foresaw, would come "from another place," from a strange place, namely, from Ruth, a Moabite woman, or even directly from God.[33] (That the striking phrase from Ruth, "the seed which the Lord shall give thee," may have played a part in this legend was pointed out in a previous chapter.[34]) If Paul is familiar with this or a similar Midrash, his choice of argument in Galatians becomes even more understandable.

[32] Gen 4:25.

[33] *Gen. Rab.* on 4:25.

[34] Ruth and Boaz, [141 ff.]; see Ruth 4:12.

The Sudden in the Scriptures

Chapter One
The Old Testament and Rabbinic Literature*

1. *Pith'om* and *petha'*

a) *General*

There are two words in Old Testament Hebrew exclusively used in the sense of "suddenly," *pith'om* and *petha'*. They are synonymous, and in four texts they are joined as a double expression, "very suddenly."[1] With one or two questionable exceptions,[2] they always occur in connection with disaster. They would be out of place in the Song of Solomon.

The bias is largely explicable on realistic grounds. As we look at objects and beings, destruction is in fact likely to be swifter than creation. It takes time to build a house, but it may collapse in a moment. Human birth follows a pregnancy of nine months, but an apoplexy comes out of the blue. Furthermore, it is the unexpected that hits, gives you a jolt, which is called "sudden"; and the unexpected that hits you is more often than not of an unpleasant nature—if only because we incline to take the pleasurable (or the absence of the unpleasant) for granted. We are more forcibly struck by the abrupt onset of a headache than its abrupt disappearance. There is indeed, for many people, something worrying in the unexpected as such: one might hear a man declare, "I do not like surprises" (*ich liebe keine Überraschungen*), expressing an indiscriminate aversion to what is not planned, even though beneficial. That dangers are easier to meet if mentally prepared for is stated by Aristotle: "It is the mark of a braver man to be fearless in sudden (*aiphnidios*) fears than in those anticipated; what is anticipated one may face by reasoning, the sudden (*exaiphnes*) according to character."[3] In insecure times—among which for the present purpose we may include the entire Old Testament period—distrust of the unforeseen is bound to be greater than in times of comparative security. That (in addition to normal wear and tear) is behind the gradual relaxation of the meaning of *pith'om* and *petha'*: in post-Biblical Hebrew, we shall see, they are no longer tied to misfortune.

* N.B. Some aspects of the subject are elaborated in *Suddenness and Awe in Scripture*, Tenth (1963) Robert Waley Cohen Memorial Lecture (London, 1964).

[1] Num 6:9; Isa 29:5, 30:13; Sir 11:21.

[2] 2 Chr 29:36; Sir 11:21; see below, 687 ff.

[3] *Nic. E.* 3.8.15.

The foregoing considerations are admittedly of so general a character that they ought to be valid for other languages as well. They are, *mutatis mutandis.* In fact, the evidence from other languages confirms that the development in Hebrew is not due to some accident of transmission. In the Latin *subitus,* for instance, the *sub* indicates a disagreeable, uncanny element (though possibly the idea of one thing following upon another is also present). In Italian, the adverb *subito* means no more than "directly," while "suddenly" nowadays has its nearest equivalent in *improvvisamente* or the like; in Spanish, on the other hand, *subito* still means "suddenly." German *plötzlich* has to do with *platzen,* "explosion" (related to *plaudere*), *Blitz, auf dem Platz,* all originally uncomfortable things. In modern English we can certainly say "suddenly I noticed my girl," "the solution of the problem came to me by a sudden revelation," as well as "he died a sudden death," "suddenly he fell," "suddenly the alarm rang out." But a glance through the quotations in the Oxford Dictionary will shew that the word starts in association with terror and gradually becomes neutral. (The case of "stroke" comes to mind. We speak of "a stroke of luck," but when this phrase was coined—in the 19th century—it was no doubt a paradox.) Even today, if one looked for "sudden" in titles of books, one would have a better chance with the green Penguin series than the red one.

However, we are not claiming that this realistic background alone accounts for the restriction of *pith'om* and *petha'* to the sphere of evil. There are additional factors of which the most important is familiar from many comparable cases: it will emerge that, once the two words had been prominently employed in certain contexts, that fact itself made for continued usage along the same lines, at the expense of other potentialities. (The tension between this tendency and what we described above as wear and tear is a common phenomenon.) Especially in literary style, a traditional prevalence of "sudden" in, say, invocations of evil on one's enemies or in warnings concerning the last judgment, might well contribute to a narrowing of the range.

Etymological considerations we shall leave on one side, if only because there is too little certainty. Are *pith'om* and *petha'* from the same root? Accadian *pitta, pittimma, ina pitta* and so on—"instant," "instantly" or "suddenly"—may well be related and would be worth comparing; but the relevant volume of the Chicago Dictionary is not yet available. The root *b't,* expressing the seizure of a man by some terror, is claimed to be identical, originally, with *petha'.*[4] This would greatly strengthen our case. An out-of-date derivation by Gesenius will be mentioned at the end of this essay.[5]

b) *The Texts*

Let us inspect the evidence. From the Pentateuch only three passages are to be listed, all in Numbers. A Nazarite may not come into contact with a corpse; and "if any man die very suddenly by him," he must bring a sacrifice.[6] Another law is designed to mitigate vengeance where a man killed another man unwittingly, "thrust him suddenly, without enmity."[7]

[4] Professor T. H. Gaster kindly drew my attention to this point.

[5] See below, 742.

[6] Num 6:9, with the double expression *bephetha' pith'om.*

[7] Num 35:22.

Thirdly, as Aaron and Miriam rebelled against Moses, "the Lord spake suddenly unto Moses and Aaron and Miriam, Come out ye three."[8] God appeared as judge, the summons was a threat; so the term has its usual implications. But we find here, what we shall find again and again, that where it is a question of opposing parties, a certain ambiguity tends to creep in: what is dreadful for one may be welcome to the other. *Dem einen sein Tod ist dem andern sein Brot* [What is death to one is food to another]. Moses on the present occasion was vindicated by God. By making the latter speak "suddenly," the narrative emphasizes the effect of the intervention on the guilty brother and sister; and, of course, at this moment Moses himself does not yet know what is to happen. It remains none the less true that this "sudden" intervention brought him deliverance.

Two passages in Joshua. Joshua made a forced night march against the Amorite kings and "came upon them suddenly";[9] and similarly, in the case of the king of Hazor and his allies, "Joshua and all the people of war with him came upon them suddenly and fell upon them."[10] Again, the "suddenly" looks at it from the point of view of the victim. These affairs were anything but fearful for Joshua.

Isaiah predicts the overthrow of Sennacherib in one gruesome night: "The multitude of thy terrible ones shall be a chaff that passeth away, yea it shall be very suddenly."[11] Here, too, the reference is primarily to the impact on the enemy—his discomfiture, however, is Jerusalem's salvation. It is interesting that, in giving warning of Sennacherib's forthcoming incursion, Isaiah also uses the term, this time from the point of view of Jerusalem: "Therefore this iniquity shall be to you as a breach ready to fall, swelling out in a high wall, whose breaking cometh very suddenly."[12]

Babylon's defeat at the hand of Cyrus is announced in Deutero-Isaiah: "Mischief shall fall upon thee, and desolation shall come upon thee suddenly, thou shalt not know."[13] Very likely it is this event which is recalled in the passage: "I declared the former things from the beginning, and out of my mouth they went forth and I shewed them; suddenly I did them and they came."[14]

Jeremiah warns his people: "Breaking upon breaking is cried, suddenly my tents are spoiled and my curtains in a moment."[15] "The spoiler shall suddenly come upon us."[16] "I have caused a spoiler to come to them, upon the mother of the young men, at noonday; I have caused him to fall upon her suddenly."[17] "Let a cry be heard from their houses when thou shalt cause a troop to come upon them suddenly."[18] The word also occurs in a prophecy of doubtful authorship, against Babylon: "Babylon is suddenly

[8] Num 12:4.
[9] Josh 10:9.
[10] Josh 11:7.
[11] Isa 29:5, *lephetha' pith'om.*
[12] Isa 30:13, *pith'om lephetha'.*
[13] Isa 47:11.
[14] Isa 48:3.
[15] Jer 4:20.
[16] Jer 6:26.
[17] Jer 15:8.
[18] Jer 18:22.

fallen and broken."[19] In all these cases the "sudden" ruin of one party coincides with the triumph of the other—not to mention the role of God, standing above both.

Retribution will overtake the ruthless, according to Habakkuk: "Shall they not rise up suddenly that shall bite thee?"[20] Malachi's proclamation of the judgment is famous: "And the Lord, whom ye seek, shall suddenly come to his temple."[21] The clause "whom ye seek" is ironical, the idea being that of Amos: "Woe unto you that desire the day of the Lord; the day of the Lord is darkness and not light."[22] The very use of "suddenly" points this way, but we need only read on to find it confirmed. For Malachi continues: "And who may abide the day of his coming? and who shall stand when he appeareth?"[23] However, the ambiguity to which we have repeatedly adverted is not absent: the judgment, "sudden" and terrible as it is for the haughty sinners, will at the same time vindicate those oppressed by them, the fatherless, the widows, the strangers.

In Psalm 64, while the wicked ones use calumny as arrows against the author—who is good—and "suddenly shoot at him," God "shall shoot at them with a sudden arrow."[24] Here it is very evident how what for one party is a blow, "sudden," is welcome to the other. The Psalm ends: "The righteous shall rejoice in the Lord" and so on.[25]

Proverbs contains several relevant passages. The wise disciple may be confident: "Be not afraid of sudden terror, neither of the desolation of the wicked when it cometh."[26] As for the false man, "suddenly shall come his calamity, suddenly shall he be broken without remedy."[27] Of two unreliable types of men we are told: "For suddenly shall rise up their calamity, and the ruin of them both who shall know?"[28] Again, "he that hardeneth his neck shall suddenly be broken, and that without remedy."[29]

In a last text from Proverbs,[30] *pith'om* is a different word from that under review. More precisely, it belongs to *patha* or *pethi*, "compliant," "simple," and is either an exceptionally formed adverb or in need of slight emendation. (The LXX assumes *patha* or *pethi* instead of *pith'om* in two texts besides the present one,[31] and we shall presently suggest an emendation along these lines for a passage from Chronicles.[32] In the

[19] Jer 51:8.

[20] Hab 2:7.

[21] Mal 3:1.

[22] Amos 5:18.

[23] Mal 3:2.

[24] Ps 64:5, 8. The latter verse is hardly intact, but the general sense is clear.

[25] Ps 64:11.

[26] Prov 3:25. The verse is alluded to at the end of 1 Pet 3:6: good women need not fear. Quite possibly the author here is still thinking of Sarah. In the first half of 3:6 she is held up as a model because she called her husband "lord" (Gen 18:12). But on the same occasion she committed a wrong (laughing at the annunciation of a son) which, challenged, she feared to admit (Gen 18:15). The end of 3:6 may well mean: "whose children ye are, doing good only, however, and therefore not fearing with any scare."

[27] Prov 6:15.

[28] Prov 24:22; hardly intact.

[29] Prov 29:1.

[30] Prov 7:22; see commentaries and dictionaries.

[31] See below, 691 f.

[32] 2 Chr 29:36; see below, 687 f.

Zadokite Fragments such an emendation is widely accepted.[33]) The section deals with a young man's seduction by a loose woman: "He goeth after her in his simplicity, as an ox goeth to the slaughter." In any case, in the view of the author, the young man is in for disaster—so the text suits our general thesis with or without emendation. We must, however, append a reservation. Though the original reference is to "simple-mindedness," in course of time, as "suddenly" was losing its fearful connotation, readers might think of this adverb in interpreting the text.[34] This tendency would be encouraged by the picture—also dating from a period when the term had become less sinister—of the fool as one who acts "suddenly," in an erratic, abrupt fashion.[35] To be sure, even the fool's "suddenness" is ultimately ruinous in the literature in question.

One of Job's friends, Eliphaz, says: "I have seen the foolish taking root, but suddenly I cursed his habitation."[36] That this envisages a dramatic fall is clear. Possibly we should translate "I found his habitation cursed," "I had to declare, call, his habitation cursed"; the opposite of *'ishsher,* "to praise, call, happy." Eliphaz also tells Job that it is for his moral shortcomings that "sudden terror troubleth thee."[37] Job himself sees God equally thwarting the good and the bad: "If the scourge slay suddenly, he will laugh at the trial of the innocent."[38]

For Ecclesiastes, too, things happen without rhyme or reason: "The race is not to the swift nor the battle to the strong neither yet the bread to the wise. For man also knoweth not his time: as the fishes that are taken in an evil net, so are the sons of men snared in an evil time when it falleth suddenly upon them."[39] In Job, the complaint is about God's indifference to ethics: the good is treated no better than the bad. In Ecclesiastes, it is about fate making nonsense of human faculties. This does not indeed mean that the ethical problem is foreign to Ecclesiastes. It is just a little below the surface—as in the song from the Dreigroschenoper: "*Ja mach nur einen Plan, sei nur ein grosses Licht, und mach noch einen zweiten Plan—gehn tun sie beide nicht* [Well, make a plan, be just a shining light, then make another plan–neither of them will work]."

This leaves a single text in the canonical Old Testament[40] where "suddenly" is associated with a happy event: the Chronicler, after describing the rededication of the Temple by Hezekiah, adds, "And Hezekiah rejoiced and all the people over what God had prepared for the people, for the thing took place suddenly." To be sure, the rededication involved elimination and destruction of impure objects,[41] but this aspect is not in the foreground in the jubilant concluding remark quoted. A possible explanation is that, by the time of Chronicles, the word had become neutral enough to be suitable for

[33] *Zadokite Fragments* 14.2; see below, 698 f.

[34] See below, 692, 698, on the renderings of Aquila, Symmachus and, above all, the Targum.

[35] See below, 692 f., 700 f., on the variant *aphno* in the LXX, Eccl 10:3, on *exapina* in Lev 21:4, Num 4:20, and on Rabbinic disquisitions concerning the sudden (*pith'om*) entry of a house.

[36] Job 5:3.

[37] Job 22:10.

[38] Job 9:23.

[39] Eccl 9:11 f.

[40] 2 Chr 29:36; on Sirach, see presently, 688.

[41] 2 Chr 29:16.

any striking, unexpected, fast-occurring incident. But there is room for doubt. The form *bephith'om* (with the particle *be*, "in," "with") is unique in the Old Testament and very rare even in post-Biblical literature.[42] It is probably, however, unobjectionable: *bephetha'*, after all, occurs three times.[43] What is of greater weight is that it is far from obvious how to understand "suddenly": does it refer to the unexpected change of policy after Ahaz?, or to the fact that Hezekiah undertook the reform immediately on accession?, or to the speed with which it was carried through?, or to what? Maybe recourse should be had to an emendation similar to that mentioned above:[44] we might read *bappetha'im* or *biphetha'im*—which would touch none of the consonants, only the vocalisation. "For the thing took place among (the) simple ones."[45] In doctrine, the passage would be allied to others where God grants special protection and enlightenment to "the simple," to those who, however weak, liable to error, inadequate, are eager to do his will.[46] It should be observed that, in verses directly preceding the concluding remark under discussion, we learn that as the ritual could not be performed exactly as it ought to have been (because there were not enough priests), it was performed in the nearest possible fashion.[47]

It is universally assumed that *pith'om* and *petha'* have a pleasant sense also in Sirach. *Pith'om* occurs three times, twice plainly of disaster: as a sinner, do not (Sirach warns you) delay repentance, "for suddenly doth his wrath come forth";[48] and ill-gotten gain or its owner "shall suddenly perish for ever."[49] But there is another maxim, to the effect that God may "very suddenly make a poor man rich."[50] Box and Oesterley adopt Edersheim's verdict, that "the moral of this verse can scarcely be considered elevated."[51] But though the Greek does give this text, the Hebrew is defective: the portion "make a poor man rich" is not there. The presence of "suddenly" rather militates against this reconstruction.

That Sirach adheres to the archaic restriction of the term is suggested by his warning against the unannounced, inconsiderate entering of a house. Whereas a Talmudic allusion to it has *pith'om,* a more reliable quotation in a Midrashic work has "hastily," "soon," *mehera*: "The foot of a fool is soon into a house."[52] The Talmudic passage con-

[42] It is met, e.g., in *b. Shab.* 153a, to be discussed below, 700, but even here the Munich MS at least has *pith'om.*

[43] Num 6:9, 35:22; Sir 11:21; in the first and third of these *bephetha' pith'om.*

[44] In connection with Prov 7:22; see 686.

[45] The form *bappetha'yim* occurs in Prov 7:7, concerning a young man's seduction: "And I beheld among the simple ones a young man void of understanding."

[46] Pss 116:6, 119:30. Ezek 45:20 prescribes an annual cleansing of the Temple "from a man that erreth and from a simple one." Cp., possibly, from the Dead Sea Scrolls, Hab 12:4 f., where "the beasts" of the original (Hab 2:17) are interpreted as "the simple ones of Judah, the doers of the Torah."

[47] 2 Chr 29:34 f. Cp. 2 Chr 30:17 f., a very similar situation at Hezekiah's Passover.

[48] Sir 5:7.

[49] Sir 40:14.

[50] Sir 11:21, with the double *bephetha' pith'om.*

[51] Charles, *Apocrypha and Pseudepigrapha,* vol. 1 (1913), 355.

[52] Sir 21:22; Greek *tachys.* See *b. Nid.* 16b, Pirqa deRabenu Haqadosh, Baba deShisha 4, ed. Schönblum (1877), 14a. Schönblum, however, did not spot the provenance of the quotation: that was discovered later.

tains matter plainly not represented in Sirach; the Midrashic version is superior. It may be worth adding, in view of Rabbinic sayings to be mentioned below,[53] that Sirach is thinking of entering somebody else's house, not one's own.

2. Regha'

Besides *pith'om* and *petha'*, it is necessary to look at *regha'*, "moment," or *keregha'*, "as a moment," which in prophecy and poetry sometimes denotes "suddenly." How the noun comes to denote "moment" is not our concern, but we shall mention, and criticize, the prevalent view at the end of this essay.[54] From "moment" to "suddenly" is an easy transition, considering the swiftness of the sudden event: it takes you unawares, it comes like a thunderclap, "in a moment." Anyhow, whenever used in this sense, like the other two words, *regha'* has regard to disaster.

In Deutero-Isaiah, in the section announcing Babylon's defeat, two verses before that quoted above as containing *pith'om*,[55] we find *regha'* in the same sense: "And these two things shall come to thee in a moment in one day, the loss of children and widowhood, they shall come upon thee in their perfection."[56] Jeremiah has *regha'* in the same line as *pith'om*: "Suddenly my tents are spoiled and my curtains in a moment."[57] The Psalmist prays: "Let all mine enemies be ashamed and confounded, let them return and be ashamed in a moment."[58] As in numerous cases of *pith'om* and *petha'*, the ruin "in a moment" of one side will mean triumph to the other, but the immediate reference of the expression is to misfortune. Elihu, one of Job's friends, urges that high and low are equally at God's mercy: "In a moment shall they die, and at midnight shall the people be troubled."[59] Here there is no victorious party, unless it be God.

In several texts it is doubtful whether the sense is "suddenly" or, less frightening, "quickly," "in an instant." The *Handwörterbuch* favours the former—and we incline to agree—but Koehler the latter.[60] In Numbers, twice God tells Moses and Aaron to leave a guilty community "and I shall consume them in a moment."[61] Of the wicked, the Psalmist says: "How are they become a desolation in moment."[62] In Lamentations we read: "The iniquity of the daughter of my people is greater than the sin of Sodom, that was overthrown in a moment."[63]

In a passage from Exodus, the choice lies between "suddenly" (*Handwörterbuch*) and "for a short while" (Koehler), and it matters rather more than in the other cases. It

[53] See 700 ff.

[54] See below, 742.

[55] See 685.

[56] Isa 47:9.

[57] Jer 4:20; see above, 685.

[58] Ps 6:11.

[59] Job 34:20.

[60] Gesenius's *Handwörterbuch über das Alte Testament*, 16th ed. by Buhl (1915), 745; Koehler, *Lexicon in Veteris Testamenti Libros* (1935), 874.

[61] Num 16:21, 17:10.

[62] Ps 73:19.

[63] Lam 4:6.

is either "Ye are a stiffnecked people, I will come up into the midst of thee in one moment and consume thee," or alternatively, "If I came up into the midst of thee for one moment I would consume thee."[64] The *Handwörterbuch* also brings under "suddenly" a text from Sirach where, however, the meaning is plainly "for a short while." The section depicts the woes of man, leaving him no peace even at night: "For a little, vainly, for a moment, he reposeth, and then is disturbed by dreams."[65]

The verb *hirgia'* may signify "to act suddenly" in a line which occurs twice in Jeremiah.[66] "I will suddenly make him run away from her." In Proverbs we read: "The lip of truth shall be established for ever, and a lying tongue"—and now we may render "as long as I give rest," "for a moment," or "until I act suddenly."[67] Finally, a prophecy of Deutero-Isaiah: "I will make my judgment to rest for a light of the people; my righteousness is near."[68] On the basis of minor or major emendations of commentators, we might obtain "in a short time my righteousness shall approach" or "suddenly I bring near my righteousness." If the latter interpretation is chosen, the prophet would here be stressing the menace of the judgment. But the text is too obscure to count.

3. ASSOCIATED WORDS

Looking back over the texts with "suddenly," we notice that characteristic notions are apt to recur in them or their immediate neighbourhood. The "sudden" event is "an evil,"[69] "death,"[70] "blow," "wound," "smiting,"[71] "breaking,"[72] "desolation,"[73] "calamity,"[74] "fall,"[75] "spoiling,"[76] "consuming."[77]

These things "come" or "come upon a man,"[78] or "fall upon a man"[79] or "among men."[80] Even in the law concerning the unwitting homicide, one of the cases listed is where he accidentally "causes a stone to fall upon a man";[81] and the preposition "on" is employed in the law requiring a Nazarite to bring a sacrifice "if any man die very suddenly by him"—literally "on him," *'alaw*.[82] (In English, "on" may connote "so as to

[64] Exod 33:5.

[65] Sir 40:6; text not intact, but general drift clear. For a similar mistranslation of *hereph 'ayin* by Strack-Billerbeck, see below, n. 682.

[66] Jer 49:19, 50:44; Rudolph, *Jeremia* (1947), 248, 264, assumes a corruption.

[67] Prov 12:19.

[68] Isa 51:4 f.

[69] Isa 47:11; Eccl 9:12.

[70] Num 6:9, 35:22 f.; Josh 10:9 ff.; Jer 18:21 f.; Job 9:23, 34:20.

[71] Josh 10:9 f., 11:7 f.; Jer 18:21 f.; Ps 64:8.

[72] Isa 30:13; Jer 4:20, 51:8; Prov 6:15, 29:1.

[73] *Sho'a* in Isa 47:11; Prov 3:25; *mashshu'a* and *shamma* in Ps 73:18 f.

[74] Prov 6:15, 24:22.

[75] Jer 51:8; Ps 73:18 f.

[76] Jer 4:20, 6:26, 15:8.

[77] Exod 33:5; Num 16:21, 17:10; Job 9:22 f.

[78] Josh 10:9, 11:7; Isa 47:9, 11, 48:3; Jer 6:26, 15:8, 18:22; Mal 3:1; Prov 3:25, 6:15.

[79] Isa 47:11; Jer 15:8; Eccl 9:12.

[80] Josh 11:7.

[81] Num 35:22.

[82] Num 6:9.

cause trouble"; a landlady might say of her lodger that "he fell sick, died, on me.")

Man "does not know" how these things happen.[83] They "confuse" or "terrorise" him.[84] "Night" is their proper time.[85]

Needless to say, the Old Testament is full of sudden events, events thought of as sudden, though the term is not employed; the foregoing evidence is, therefore, very incomplete. Dinah's brothers "came upon" her seducer and his fellow-citizens;[86] Gideon, encouraged by a Midianite's dream in which "a cake came unto the Midianite tent and smote it and it fell," attacked the enemy at night;[87] the Psalmist prays, "Let desolation come to my adversary, he shall not know, let him fall in it"[88]—these and numerous similar texts contemplate sudden disasters. The author, that is, had he been so minded, might well have used *pith'om, petha'* or *regha'*. There are many more cases, however, which, though well within our modern, large concept of "sudden" would not at the time have fallen under any of those terms. In establishing their scope, it is safest to base on those texts where they are actually found.

4. The LXX

a) *Renderings of pith'om, petha' and regha'*

The LXX makes no demonstrable difference between *pith'om, petha' and regha'*. (We consider, of course, only texts where *regha'* means "suddenly."[89]) *Pith'om* is translated *aphno,*[90] *exaisios,*[91] *exaiphnes* or *exapines,*[92] *eperchesthai,*[93] *eutheos,*[94] *parachrema.*[95] In three texts the LXX reads a form of *patha* or *pethi,* "simple," "foolish," instead of the Massoretic *pith'om*; it is certainly right about one of them—concerning a young man going after a woman—where it has *kepphousthai,* "cajoled," "ensnared."[96] In others, it translates *nepios,* "fool,"[97] and *parabainon,* "transgressor."[98] *Petha'* is translated

[83] Isa 47:11; Prov 24:22; Eccl 9:12. Absence of knowledge is implied also in Num 35:22; cp. the description of the unwitting homicide as acting "without knowledge" in Deut 4:42. This is not to deny the significance of the fact that Numbers 35 does not actually use the root "to know"—we cannot go into it here.

[84] The root *hmm* in Josh 10:9; *bhl* in Jer 15:8; Ps 6:11; Job 22:10; *blh* Ps 73:19; *pḥd* Ps 64:2; Job 22:10; Prov 3:25.

[85] Josh 10:9; Job 34:20. In Isa 29:5, about Sennacherib's discomfiture, this is not stated, but the reader is surely expected to remember the details: cp. Isa 17:14, 37:36; 2 Kgs 19:35.

[86] Gen 34:25, 27.

[87] Judg 7:13 ff.

[88] Ps 35:8; cp. e.g. Isa 47:11.

[89] Hence not, e.g., Isa 54:8, where it means "for a moment," though see on this text below, 741.

[90] Josh 10:9; Jer 4:20 (where *regha'* may be included), 18:22, 51:8; Eccl 9:12.

[91] Job 9:23, 22:10.

[92] Josh 11:7; Isa 47:11, 48:3; Jer 6:26, 15:8; Mal 3:1; Ps 64:5; Prov 6:15 (where *petha'* may be included), 24:22; 2 Chr 29:36; Sir 5:7, 11:21.

[93] Prov 3:25.

[94] Job 5:3.

[95] Num 6:9, 12:4; Isa 29:5, 30:13 (where *petha'* is included).

[96] Prov 7:22; see above, 686.

[97] Ps 64:8.

[98] Sir 40:14. This case is not clear; see Box and Oesterley, in Charles, *op. cit.*, 462. In Sir 21:22, as argued above, 688 f., the Hebrew original had *mehera,* not *pith'om:* LXX *tachys.*

exaiphnes or *exapines,*[99] *parachrema,*[100] *stigme,*[101] *dia tachous.*[102] *Regha'* is translated *eisapax,*[103] *aphno,*[104] *exaiphnes* or *exapines,*[105] *spoude,*[106] *dia tachous;*[107] and the verb *hirgia'* appears as *tachys.*[108] In one text *regha'* is not rendered at all,[109] in another the LXX reads *negha',* "plague," and translates *plege.*[110]

Presumably much of the variety is due to laxness or different hands, though in some cases one can think of a reason for the stronger expression—*aphno, exaisios, exaiphnes*—or the less frightening one—*eisapax, eutheos, parachrema, spoude, stigme, tachys.* In a passage from Proverbs, *eperchesthai,* "to come," which we mentioned above as typically associated with "suddenly," actually does service for the latter. "Be not afraid of sudden terror" in Hebrew, LXX "Be not afraid of terror that cometh."[111] Similarly, a variant of the passage from Numbers brings in "lack of knowledge," also, we saw, often coupled with "suddenly." "If any man die very suddenly by him" is explained as *agnoountos,* "without his knowing."[112]

Contrary to the prevalent myth, Aquila is not much tidier than the LXX. In the Hexapla we find noted: *arthroos,*[113] *aphno,*[114] *exaiphnes,*[115] *parachrema.*[116] Symmachus has *aphno,*[117] *aiphnidios,*[118] *exaiphnes.*[119]

b) *Related Texts*

A few words about the remaining use by the LXX of these words, or some of them at least, may be in place.

Aphno recurs in Proverbs where the Hebrew says "when your terror cometh as a desolation."[120] Note the characteristic words "terror," "desolation," "to come."[121] In

[99] Num 6:9, 35:22; Hab 2:7; Prov 6:15 (possibly—see above footnote 92, in connection with *pith'om*), 29:1.

[100] Isa 30:13; see above, footnote 95, in connection with *pith'om.*

[101] Isa 29:5.

[102] Sir 11:21.

[103] Num 16:21, 17:10.

[104] Jer 4:20 (possibly—see above, footnote 90, in connection with *pith'om*).

[105] Isa 47:9; Ps 73:19.

[106] Lam 4:6.

[107] Ps 6:11.

[108] Isa 51:4 f.; Jer 49:19, 50:44; Prov 12:19.

[109] Job 34:20.

[110] Exod 33:5.

[111] Prov 3:25.

[112] Num 6:9.

[113] Ps 6:11; but conceivably his rendering here is *exaiphnes.*

[114] Jer 15:8.

[115] Isa 29:5, and maybe Ps 6:11.

[116] Ps 64:5, 8; Prov 6:15, 7:22; Job 5:3.

[117] Prov 6:15; Job 9:23.

[118] Ps 64:8.

[119] Jer 49:19; Ps 6:11; Prov 7:22; Job 22:10; Lam 4:6.

[120] Prov 1:27.

[121] "Terror," *paḥadh,* "desolation," *sho'a.* Further on in the same verse "calamity," "to come upon a man."

Ecclesiastes, however, in a variant, *aphno* describes the abruptness of a fool. "When the fool walketh" in Hebrew, a variant of the LXX "when he walketh suddenly."[122]

In 1 Maccabees, the word is employed, as in Joshua, of the surprise assault of an army—with "to leap upon, "fall," "to fall upon," "smiting," "night," "to kill."[123] In 2 Maccabees, Heliodorus, about to violate the Temple, is visited by a fearful apparition and "suddenly" drops to the ground; he is enwrapped by "darkness."[124]

Symmachus has *aphno* in Psalms. Hebrew "For it passeth quickly and we fly away"; Symmachus "For suddenly cut off we fly away."[125]

A survey of *aphno* must be supplemented by *aiphnidios*. In Wisdom, during the plague of darkness the Egyptians are haunted by apparitions and "sudden fear came upon them"—with typical words and setting.[126] In Maccabees we hear three times of a "sudden" military attack;[127] also of an army thrown into "sudden consternation."[128]

Symmachus translates *regha'* by *aiphnidios* in Ezekiel's prophecy against Tyrus: the princes of the sea will tremble "at the sudden things"—Hebrew "every moment."[129] Note "fall," "slaughter," "desolation," "terror" in this section.[130] That he uses *aiphnidios* for the "sudden" arrow in Psalms we mentioned above.[131] Another case in Psalms is interesting. The Massoretic text offers two versions, "May desolation be upon them (my persecutors)" or "May death seize upon them."[132] Symmachus has: "May sudden death come upon them." It looks as if he had wished to do justice to both alternatives.

Next, *exaisios*. Several texts in Job. In the first, the Hebrew runs "mine ear received a whisper (?) from him," and the LXX has *exaisia*, "terrible things," for "whisper."[133] The Hebrew consonants are *shmṣ*; maybe the LXX reads a form of *shmm*, "desolation," one of the words often accompanying "suddenly." In the following two verses we find "night" and "terror."[134] Then we meet *exaisios* as an attribute of "calamity," with no equivalent in the Hebrew.[135] "Terror" and "death" in the same section.[136] In another passage, in the Hebrew "the joy of the wicked is short," in the LXX it is "a terrible ruin."[137] Probably the LXX does mean to translate the Hebrew before us, stressing the quick end.

122 Eccl 10:3; the principal reading is *aphron*. As for the "suddenness" of a fool, cp. above, 686 f., in connection with Prov 7:22, and below, 694, and 701, in connection with Lev 21:4, Num 4:20, and the Rabbinic discussions regarding the sudden entry of a house.

123 1 Mac 3:23, 4:2, 5:28; cp. Josh 10:9.

124 2 Mac 3:27.

125 Ps 90:10.

126 Wis 17:15; cp. below, 695, on Wis 18:17, in connection with *parachrema*.

127 2 Mac 5:5, 14:22; 3 Mac 3:24.

128 2 Mac 14:17.

129 Ezek 26:16.

130 "Desolation," *shmm*, "terror," *bhl*.

131 Ps 64:8; see 692.

132 Ps 55:16. The former is "what is written," the latter "what is to be read." The word for "desolation" is related with *shmm*.

133 Job 4:12.

134 Job 4:13 f.; "terror," *paḥadh*.

135 Job 18:12.

136 Job 18:11, 13 f.

137 Job 20:5.

Three times *exaisios* stands for the root *pl'*, "wondrous," "awesome,"[138] and a fourth time it has the meaning without an equivalent in the Hebrew.[139] In these cases there is no allusion to disaster. Yet the "wondrous," even when beneficial, surpasses comfortable understanding, is uncanny, not easy to rely on, to live with. We shall come back to this aspect in the section on the New Testament, where "suddenly," though no longer confined to disaster, is confined to the sphere of the "wondrous"; *exaisios* does not occur.

In Habakkuk, a variant twice has *exaisios* as an attribute of a thunderstorm or waters stirred up by the coming of God:[140] no equivalent in the Hebrew text. Plainly another instance of the sense "wondrous."

Exaiphnes or *exapines* occurs in a Pentateuchic section forbidding a priest to defile himself for any dead except his nearest relations. The Hebrew goes on: "He shall not defile himself, a master among his people."[141] The LXX reads *balla'* for *ba'al,* thus obtaining "suddenly" in the place of "a master." The word, however, approaches here the meaning "thoughtlessly," "without due consideration." In another section we are informed of the arrangements needed before the Kohathites may approach the holiest of holies. The Hebrew goes on: "And they shall not come to see the sanctuary *kebhalla'*, for a moment."[142] The LXX translates again "suddenly," i.e. "thoughtlessly," "without the prescribed arrangements." Below, we shall adduce a Midrash dealing with a provision in Leviticus which debars Aaron from free, informal access to the sanctuary: it is in the course of this discussion that the Midrash quotes Rabbinic utterances against entering a house "suddenly," *pith'om.*[143] There may or may not be a connection between this kind of "suddenness," "thoughtlessness," and the "suddenness" of the fool we touched on in discussing the young man seduced from Proverbs.[144]

Micah threatens the wicked: "And ye shall not walk upright."[145] The LXX adds "suddenly." The word "evil" occurs in this verse, "spoiling" in the next. Daniel repeatedly speaks of a conqueror who succeeds "in security."[146] Apparently he exploits his victim's feeling of security. At any rate, while Theodotion translates *en eutheniai,* the LXX substitutes *exapina.* The associated words "to come" and "breaking" occur in these verses.[147]

To Sirach's condemnation of corrupt children a variant adds that their end will take place "suddenly."[148] We must, however, recall another passage, where "suddenly" refers to the bestowal of riches on a good, pious man.[149] As observed above, we suspect that

[138] Job 5:9, 9:10, 37:16.

[139] Job 34:24.

[140] Hab 3:10, 15.

[141] Lev 21:4; text hardly intact.

[142] Num 4:20; translation dubious.

[143] *Lev. Rab.* on 16:2 f.

[144] Prov 7:22; see above, 686.

[145] Mic 2:3.

[146] Dan 11:21, 24.

[147] "To come" in Dan 11:21, 24, "breaking" in 24. In the latter verse the LXX substitutes "he shall lay waste" for "he shall come"; altogether the LXX aims at clarification of the somewhat dark original.

[148] Sir 13:3.

[149] Sir 11:21; see above, 688.

the Hebrew original was different. At least in the Greek, *exapina* has completely lost its sinister overtones, though, conceivably, the author may mean to convey the element of the "wondrous."

In 1 Maccabees, as in Joshua, the word signifies the surprise assault of an army.[150] Note "to fall upon," "smite," "destroy," "blow." In 3 Maccabees we find destruction "suddenly" decreed against the Jews.[151]

Symmachus, where the Psalmist says "I would hasten my escape," puts "Suddenly I would make my escape."[152]

Parachrema means "straightway," "forthwith," in 2 Samuel. The Hebrew reads "Abner sent messengers on his behalf."[153] The expression "on his behalf," *taḥtaw,* literally "under himself," "for himself," occasionally signifies "at his place."[154] The LXX—as also Theodotion—is proceeding from this usage when it puts "straightway": we may compare "on the spot," *auf der Stelle* or, slightly less close, *sur-le-champ.* Similarly, in Job, "Tread down the wicked *taḥtam*, where they stand,"[155] in the LXX leads to *parachrema,* "straightway"; and an obscure clause in Psalms, something like "and he was exalted *taḥuth,* under, my tongue,"[156] is rendered by Symmachus "and straightway my tongue was exalted."

In two passages *parachrema,* though probably denoting "straightway," has definite ties with "suddenly." The Psalmist asks help against his enemies: "May they be desolate as a reward for their shame."[157] Rendered by the LXX: "May they get as reward *parachrema* for their shame." The reference to "desolation," so often associated with "suddenly,"[158] accounts for this interpretation. This is confirmed by the other case, from Job. Hebrew: "The young ones of the eagle suck up blood, and where the slain are, there is he."[159] The Hebrew for "there" is *sham,* which the LXX takes as a form of "desolation"—hence translating "and where the slain are, *parachrema* they are found."

The particle signifies "suddenly" in Wisdom, in a description of the overthrow of the Egyptians: "Then suddenly apparitions in terrible dreams troubled them"—with characteristic associated terms and in nocturnal setting.[160] In Maccabees, on the other hand, it invariably means "straightway": "and straightway he despatched him,"[161] "straightway he stripped off Andronicus's purple robe,"[162] "had he pressed forward, he would straightway have been turned back,"[163] "the king commanded to heat the pans,

[150] 1 Mac 1:30; cp. Josh 11:7.
[151] 3 Mac 4:2.
[152] Ps 55:9.
[153] 2 Sam 3:12; text possibly corrupt, translation dubious.
[154] E.g. 2 Sam 2:23, "he died in the same place"; LXX *hypokato autou.*
[155] Job 40:12.
[156] Ps 66:17.
[157] Ps 40:16.
[158] The root used in Ps 40:16 is *shmm.*
[159] Job 39:20.
[160] Wis 18:17; cp. 17:15 quoted above, 693, for *aiphnidios.*
[161] 2 Mac 4:34.
[162] 2 Mac 4:38.
[163] 2 Mac 5:18.

and these were straightway heated,"[164] "he straightway took possession,"[165] "send someone straightway,"[166] and finally, the martyrs bravely faced threats to be executed "straightway."[167]

In Tobith, according to the Codex Sinaiticus, Raphael went after the demon and "bound him straightway."[168] The Vaticanus and Alexandrinus do not have the adverb. Either the Sinaiticus has added it, in order to make the deed even more splendid, or its absence from the other recension is due to abbreviation.[169] Comparable divergences in Bel and the Dragon. According to the LXX Habakkuk was miraculously brought back from Babylon to Palestine "on the same day," according to Theodotion "straightway";[170] and Daniel's enemies, thrown into the den, "were devoured" according to the LXX, "were devoured straightway" according to Theodotion.[171]

Symmachus in Psalms seems to use *parachrema* in the sense of "suddenly." Hebrew: "Our steps have now compassed me."[172] Symmachus reads *'ishsheruni,* "they praise me happy," for *'ashshurenu,* "our steps," and renders: "While praising me happy, suddenly they (the wicked ones) compassed me."

We might add that a Greek and, indeed, a Hebrew "suddenly" is to be assumed behind *subito expavescent* in 4 Ezra[173]—the last trumpet striking people with fear. It would be idle to try and be specific as to which of the foregoing terms would be the most likely.

Eperchesthai is too common to be presented in detail. It may suffice to point out that it is practically confined to adverse and "wondrous" things—on which latter we remarked in connection with *exaisios.*

Euthys, on the other hand, is truly neutral; and so is *tachys* which usually corresponds to the Hebrew root *mhr,* "speed," "haste." *Stigme* recurs in 2 Maccabees, where we are told how the pains of Antiochus Epiphanes increased *kata stigmen,* "from moment to moment."

Spoude[174] with which we take *spoudazein,* at first sight neutral, is more often than not associated with disagreeableness. Haste is pleasant when you are making for a joyful occasion. It is unpleasant when you are fleeing a disaster, and also when you are being driven, hurried. The two kinds of unpleasantness may merge: Lot was "hurried" by the angels in order that he should escape the ruin of Sodom,"[175] and in a way the departure of the Israelites from Egypt belongs here—they were "hurried" by their oppressors who were afraid that the slaughter of the firstborn might become a universal

[164] 2 Mac 7:4.
[165] 2 Mac 10:22.
[166] 2 Mac 11:36.
[167] 4 Mac 14:9.
[168] Tob 8:3.
[169] The latter solution would fit in with the evaluation of Simpson, in Charles, *op. cit.,* vol. 1, 175 f.
[170] Bel 39.
[171] Bel 42.
[172] Ps 17:11; text hardly intact.
[173] 4 Ezra 6:23.
[174] 2 Mac 9:11; the intactness of the text has been questioned.
[175] Gen 19:15.

one.[176] Deutero-Isaiah proclaims that, by contrast, the forthcoming second exodus will not be "with hurry (scare, anxious flight)."[177] In the LXX *spoude* and *spoudazein* are in the main unpleasant.

They are so in most texts where the underlying Hebrew is *bhl*, "confusion," "terror," a root referred to above as among those characteristically adjoining suddenness.[178] Two of the texts in question actually do contain *pith'om.*[179] Again, there is one text where the underlying Hebrew is *hmm*, "confusion," another root often accompanying suddenness;[180] one text, just mentioned, about Lot, where the Hebrew is *'uṣ*, "to hurry on";[181] three texts, just mentioned, about the departure from Egypt, in two of which the Hebrew is *ḥippazon*, "hurry," "scare," "anxious flight," represented by *bhl* in the Targum,[182] in the third *miher*, "to hurry on";[183] one text where the Hebrew is *b't*, "terror," a root sometimes alleged to be related to *petha'*, "suddenly";[184] and finally, one text where the Hebrew is *regha'*, "moment," "suddenly."[185] In some passages where it is difficult to say exactly which Hebrew word *spoude* is intended to render, we can at least note that it qualifies fearful happenings.[186]

In the Apocrypha, little remains of this Septuagintal colouring of *spoude*. Occasionally an old tradition comes through. Wisdom of Solomon, explaining the origins of idolatry, remarks on the desire of princes to receive homage even from subjects living afar; these had to make images of the princes, "that by their zeal they might flatter the absent (princes) as if they were present."[187] Here *spoude* means "zeal," "diligence," "striving"—as usually in Hellenistic writings.[188] By contrast, in the description of how the Egyptians "pressed the Israelites to be gone and sent them forth with speed," the unpleasant sense of "driving," "hurrying on," present in the exodus account of the LXX,[189] is adopted.

[176] Exod 12:33.

[177] Isa 52:12, *ḥippazon*, cp. Exod 12:11; Deut 16:3. The LXX translates *tarache* in Isaiah, *spoude* in Exodus and Deuteronomy: we shall presently encounter a similar difference between Jer 14:19 and 8:15.

[178] See 690 f.

[179] Jer 15:8; Job 22:10. The others are: Isa 21:5; Zeph 1:18; Ps 78:33; Job 4:5, 21:6, 23:15 f.; Dan 2:25 (hurry to prevent a disaster; Theodotion has *spoude* also in 3:24, 6:20, in both cases hurry in discomfort). Towards the end of this essay, below, 738 f., we shall touch on *bhl* as denoting "speed" in the service of a king. The LXX has *spoude, spoudazein, speudo* and *epispeudo*: Eccl 8:3; Esth 2:9, 6:14, 8:14; Ezra 4:23; 1 Esdr 2:30 (cp. 6:10). In 1 Sam 21:9 it has *kata spouden* for the king's business which was *naḥuṣ*, "pressed," "pressing."

[180] Ezek 7:11. The Hebrew text is obscure and hardly intact.

[181] Gen 19:15.

[182] Exod 12:11, Deut 16:3.

[183] Exod 12:33.

[184] Jer 8:15; see above, 684. In 14:19 the same Hebrew is rendered *tarache*, "trouble," "confusion": cp. above, footnote 177, concerning the difference between Exod 12:11 and Deut 16:3 on the one hand, Isa 52:12 on the other.

[185] Lam 4:6; see 689 f., 691.

[186] Panicky flight in Judg 5:2, Dan 10:7; punishments and fears of the wicked in Theodotion's version of Dan 9:27, 11:44.

[187] Wis 14:17.

[188] No need to assume a direct link with *bhl* and *spoude* in the specific sense of "haste in the service of a king" to be mentioned below, 738 f.; the relevant texts are already quoted above, footnote 179.

[189] Exod 12:33, see above, 696 f.

5. THE TARGUM

To turn to the Targum—here we do find a difference made between *pith'om* and *petha'* on the one hand and *regha'* on the other. The usual rendering of the former two is *bithekheph.*[190]

In Proverbs *shilya'* is favoured to render "suddenly."[191] Significantly, the word—as a feminine noun—may stand for "desolation."[192] In one passage, where the Hebrew says that the obdurate sinner "shall suddenly be broken," the Targum has *ba'aghala'*, "with speed."[193] The young man following the seductress does so *sheli'ayith.*[194] This may well mean the same as *shilya'*; it is simply an adverbial form. It is, however, conceivable that, by the slight change from the usual, the translator is indicating that we ought to bear in mind another application of the root, namely, "security," "thoughtlessness."[195] As already remarked, the Hebrew must originally have had to do with *patha* or *pethi,* "simple," "foolish," and the LXX translates *kepphousthai.*

In Ecclesiastes, instead of "when evil time falleth suddenly upon them," we get "when evil time falleth upon them *righ'a' ḥadha' mishshemayya'*, in one moment from heaven."[196] It is strange that this is the only occurrence in the Targum of *righ'a'*, etymologically identical with Hebrew *regha'*; yet it is *pith'om,* not *regha'*, which is being thus translated.

Regha' in the texts considered above is represented by *sha'a'*, "a short time," "a moment,"[197] *zeman,* "time," "moment,"[198] or *zeman ḥadha'*, "one moment";[199] the verb *hirgia'* by *zeman,* "moment,"[200] or *'istarhebh,* "hasty."[201]

6. THE DEAD SEA SCROLLS

In the Dead Sea Scrolls, in Habakkuk, *pith'om* replaces the Massoretic *petha'*: no change in sense, it is just a substitution of the commoner term.[202] As will presently be observed,[203] *petha'* is extremely rare in Rabbinic literature.

Pith'om recurs in the *Zadokite Fragments.*[204] The text, which is corrupt,[205] may refer to the wicked being "suddenly" punished; though most authorities emend into

[190] Num 6:9, 12:4, 35:22; Josh 10:9, 11:7; Isa 29:5, 30:13, 47:11, 48:3; Jer 4:20, 6:26, 15:8; 18:22, 51:8; Hab 2:7; Mal 3:1; Ps 64:5, 8; Job 5:3, 9:23, 22:10.

[191] Prov 3:25, 6:15 (for *pith'om* and for *petha'*), 24:22.

[192] E.g. Ps 35:8, Hebrew *sho'a.*

[193] Prov 29:1.

[194] Prov 7:22.

[195] Cp. 2 Sam 3:27.

[196] Eccl 9:12.

[197] Exod 33:5; Num 16:21, 17:10; Ps 6:11, 73:19; Job 34:20; Lam 4:6.

[198] Isa 47:9.

[199] Jer 4:20.

[200] Jer 49:19, 50:44.

[201] Prov 12:19.

[202] Hab 2:7; 8:13 in the Scroll.

[203] See 699.

[204] *Zadokite Fragments* 14.2.

[205] Though see now Kuhn, *Revue de Qumran,* vol. 14 (1963), 220 n. 164a.

petha'im so as to obtain punishment of the "foolish," as in a line which occurs twice in Proverbs.[206] Above we discussed another case in Proverbs where *pith'om* may be substituted for an original *petha'im*.[207] The line here in question indeed means that "the foolish (imprudent) pass on (when evil threatens) and are made to pay for it," while the *Zadokite Fragments* mean, "the foolish (wicked, blind) transgress and are punished." But this re-interpretation is found also among the Rabbis.[208] Actually, we shall see that they somehow associate *pith'om* with it: so there may, after all, be a case for not altering the word in the *Fragments* and yet accepting that they speak of the punishment of the "foolish."

Two passages from the *Hymns*. One, while extremely fragmentary, may confidently be regarded as dealing with the judgment on the wicked.[209] The other at first sight speaks of a blessing: "Suddenly the waters shall gush forth which were hidden in secret." But on closer examination these turn out to be the waters of curse for the damned; and the very use of *pith'om* supports this interpretation—the author is thinking of the judgment.[210]

Regha' in the sense of "suddenly" is not evidenced in the Dead Sea Scrolls. Indeed there is so far only one defective place where the root may possibly be employed.[211]

7. Talmud and Midrash

In Talmud and Midrash, in general, *pith'om* still refers to the terrifying or at least the unwelcome. But only in general: it can now also describe happy occurrences. *Petha'* is hardly used—the Habakkuk Scroll, we saw, turns it into *pith'om*[212]—*regha'* in the sense of "suddenly" not at all. The disappearance of *regha'* is easily accounted for: even the Old Testament never uses it for "suddenly" in prose.

In Mishnah and Tosephta, *pith'om* and *petha'* are not met—hardly surprising in view of the legal character of these collections. It is true that the words occur in two provisions in Numbers, cited above.[213] But by Talmudic times the qualification expressed by them was subsumed under, swallowed up by, wider technical terms such as *sheghagha*, "error," "inadvertence," now the standard characterization of unwitting homicide.[214]

Johanan ben Zaccai, 1st century A.D., compares the end to a meal to which a king invited his servants without fixing a date. Whether the Rabbi has in mind death, or the day of the Lord, or both, is dubious. The probability is that this kind of parable was common in eschatological discourse, where it alluded to the day of the Lord; and that

[206] Prov 22:3, 27:12. The prevalent spelling in 22:3 is *pethayim*, in 27:12 *petha'yim* (with an aleph), so the latter is closer to *pith'om*.

[207] Prov 7:22; see 686 f.

[208] *b. Ker.* 9a, *Num. Rab.* on 6:9; see below, 702.

[209] *Hymns* 17:5; see Licht, *The Thanksgiving Scrolls* (1957), 206 f.

[210] *Hymns* 8:18; cp. Licht, *op. cit.*, 136.

[211] *War Rule* 5:18.

[212] Above, 698.

[213] Num 6:9, 35:22; see 684.

[214] E.g. *m. Makk.* 2:1. As for the Rabbinic treatment of Num 6:9, see below, 701 f.

ben Zaccai is thinking primarily of individual death, i.e. he somewhat changes the application of the simile. Anyhow the foolish servants went about their business, convinced that no meal could start without preparation. They fared badly when the king "suddenly" summoned his guests.[215] We found this usage in the Old Testament: the "sudden" judgment to be feared.[216]

However, we also noticed that frequently what is calamity for one side is triumph for the other. Even the judgment will end in purification and bliss for the righteous. How "suddenly" may acquire a different connotation when the emphasis shifts over to the positive aspect of an event is exemplified by Malachi's prophecy, quoted above: "Behold, I send my messenger and he shall prepare the way before me, and the Lord shall suddenly come to his temple."[217] In the original, a threat. But in a Midrashic discussion of the faithless spies sent out by Moses to explore Canaan, it has become a merely comforting promise: "In this world, as they were messengers of mortals, they did not enter the land; but in the World to Come I send you my messenger suddenly and he (i.e. a messenger, not of mortals, but of God) will prepare the way, as predicted by Malachi."[218] An alternative translation would be "they were mortal messengers," in which case "my messenger" must be conceived of as a supernatural being, an angel or the like. It makes no difference to our argument.

Perhaps we should also note that while in the original text the coming of the Lord is sudden, in the Midrash it is the preparatory sending of the messenger. Two possible explanations. Either, for the Midrash, "the messenger" and "the lord" are identical. That is to say, the two clauses "I send my messenger" and "the lord will come" are regarded as saying more or less the same. Which leads to the interpretation "I send my messenger suddenly," "the messenger—the lord—will come suddenly." Or the "suddenly" is deliberately—we might almost say, arbitrarily—transferred from the coming to the sending, on the strength perhaps of the exegetical method *seres,* in Greek *anastrophe.* The Midrash, that is, prefers to ascribe suddenness to the preparatory cleansing instead of to the subsequent theophany. Whichever explanation we choose, the Midrash's motive was to overcome an apparently serious difficulty in Malachi's formulation; namely, that after preparation by the messenger, the coming should none the less be sudden. The contradiction is seen by Powis Smith,[219] though the majority of modern commentators fail to notice it.[220] In a subsequent paragraph of this study we shall say something on there being room for the sudden within the expected, provided the latter is sufficiently general.[221]

An instance of typical Rabbinic use of *pith'om* is provided by Akiba's maxim (first half of 2nd century A.D.): "Do not enter your house suddenly, still less another

[215] *b. Shab.* 153a.

[216] Mal 3:1, to which we shall come back presently.

[217] Mal 3:1.

[218] *Num. Rab.* on 13:17.

[219] *The Book of Malachi* (1912), 63.

[220] E.g. Horst, *Die Zwölf Kleinen Propheten* (1938), 263.

[221] See below, 739 f.

[222] *b. Pes.* 112a.

man's."[222] It was adopted by his disciple Simeon ben Johai.[223] In the Midrash, the latter's version is ingeniously, though no doubt secondarily, given as a comment on the law in Leviticus that Aaron may enter the sanctuary only with much formality—properly attired and offering the prescribed sacrifice: "he may not enter at all times."[224] It may be recalled that the LXX uses *exapina* in a similar provision in Numbers (concerning the Kohathites' approach to the sanctuary), where the Hebrew has not got "suddenly."[225]

The same section of the Midrash contains an anecdote about another disciple of Akiba's, Hananiah ben Hakinai. He came home "suddenly" after an absence of thirteen years devoted to study. His wife's soul left her and returned only in answer to his prayer.

According to Johanan bar Nappaha, first half of 3rd century A.D., Sirach condemns him "who enters another man's house suddenly"; the Rabbi adds that one's own house should be included.[226] As observed above, Sirach himself here used, not *pith'om,* but the more neutral *mehera,* "hastily."[227] Rab, an older contemporary of bar Nappaha's, supplies an extension of the usual warning: "Do not enter into a city suddenly"—quite possibly directed against surprise official inspection.[228] The maxim may indeed antedate Rab.[229]

In Derek Eretz we are told that the proper conduct of not entering another's home "suddenly" may be learnt from God's example. When he "called unto Adam, where art thou?" he must have stood at the door of the garden: he announced himself before entering.[230]

The Rabbinic discussion of the requirement in Numbers that a Nazarite must bring a sacrifice "if any man die very suddenly by him"[231] involves several artificial interpretations of *pith'om* and *petha'*. But even these are evidence that by now the words are less uncompromisingly sinister.

The Biblical text has the double phrase *bephetha' pith'om.* the Siphre holds[232] that the requirement is thereby extended beyond intentional defilement: *petha'* includes constraint, *pith'om* inadvertence, or vice versa—the former alternative seems to be advocated by Josiah, the latter is advocated by Jonathan. Both were disciples of Ishmael, around the middle of the 2nd century A.D.

According to Numbers Rabba,[233] Jonathan rests his interpretation of *petha'* as inadvertence on the law concerning the unwitting homicide, where the word has this sense,[234] that of *pith'om* as constraint on the presence of the word in God's summons,

[223] *b. Nidd.* 16b; *Lev. Rab.* on 16:2 f.

[224] Lev 16:2 f.

[225] Num 4:20; see above, 694.

[226] *b. Nidd.* 16b. We are told that he saw in Sirach's saying an interpretation of Prov 19:16, "He who is careless of his ways shall die."

[227] Sir 21:22; Greek *tachys.* See above, 688 f., and n. 98.

[228] Jastrow, *A Dictionary of the Targumim, the Talmud and Midrashic Literature* (1926), 1250.

[229] See Bacher, *Die Agada der Tannaiten,* vol. 1, 2nd ed. (1903), 270 f.

[230] Gen 3:9; *Derek Eretz Rab.* 5.

[231] Num 6:9.

[232] *Siphre* on Num 6:9.

[233] *Num. Rab.* on 6:9.

[234] Num 35:22; see above, 684.

"And God spake suddenly to Moses, Aaron and Miriam."[235]

Kuhn suggests that Jonathan did not in fact make use of these texts.[236] But this may be hypercritical. That the texts may not appear sound arguments to us moderns is neither here nor there. It should be noted that they are the only ones in the Pentateuch in which *petha'* and *pith'om* recur again. That is to say, as far as the Pentateuch is concerned, we have to do with *dis legomena* [written but twice]—the importance of which class in early Rabbinic exegesis has been established by Schwarz even though one may not follow him all the way.[237] Our thesis is not affected by the question.

The notion of God's summons as "constraint," *'ones,* is very interesting. It, or something very like it, recurs at least in one more post-Biblical text; namely, in the Passover Haggadah, in an early exposition of a portion of Deuteronomy—more precisely, of the clause "and he (Jacob) went down into Egypt."[238] Perhaps the author of the exposition vocalized *wayyuradh,* "and he was brought down," instead of *wayyeredh,* "and he went down." Anyhow Jacob, he tells us, was "constrained, *'anus,* by the Word": doubtless he is thinking of the vision Jacob received on his way to Egypt at Beersheba.[239]

We also learn from Numbers Rabba that the interpretation—probably Josiah's—of *pith'om* as inadvertence may be based on Proverbs, "The fool believeth every word."[240] Obviously, *pith'om* is here treated as an adverb belonging to *patha, pethi,* "foolish," "simple."[241] Unfortunately we are not informed what text might support *petha'* as referring to constraint. A further possible understanding of *pith'om,* however, is added by the Rabbis at large; namely, as denoting the intentional deed. Proof is found in the passage from Proverbs, "The fools (imprudent ones) pass on," to which the Rabbis (like the *Zadokite Fragments* mentioned above) ascribe the sense, "The fools (wicked ones) transgress."[242]

The subsequent exegesis of the Nazarite's obligation in this source proceeds from the assumption—clearly the one which prevailed—that, while *petha'* designates inadvertence, *pith'om* may be used indiscriminately for intention, constraint or inadvertence.

The Talmudic comments on the matter look like summaries of those in Numbers Rabba. At any rate, they arrive at the same final conclusions.[243]

To repeat, what emerges is that, in Rabbinic usage, *pith'om* and *petha',* while no longer confined to adversity, still mostly qualify happenings not of a joyful character. This is underlined by the almost regular absence of the terms where, otherwise, they might be expected. For example, "Three come," a Tannaitic saying goes, "when

[235] Num 12:4; see above, 685.

[236] *Sifre zu Numeri* (1933), 97.

[237] *Die Hermeneutische Analogie in der Talmudischen Litteratur* (1897), 61 ff.

[238] Deut 26:5, *Die Pessach-Haggada,* ed. Goldschmidt (1936), 48.

[239] Gen 46:2 ff.; *yaradh,* "to go down," both in 46:3 and 4. It is Gen 46:2 ff., incidentally, which Matt 2:13 is designed to parallel; see Daube, ["The Earliest Structure of the Gospels"] *NTS,* 5 (1959), 184 f. [338 ff.].

[240] Prov 14:15.

[241] See above, 686 f., 691, 699.

[242] Prov 22:3, 27:12, *Zadokite Fragments* 14:2; see above, 699 f.

[243] *b. Ker.* 9a; even shorter *y. Naz.* 57a.

thoughts are elsewhere, the Messiah, a find and a scorpion."[244] For R. Zera (beginning of the 4th century A.D.), who transmits the saying, it was indeed convenient that it had this formulation, instead of one with "sudden." He used it to discourage his colleagues from speculation about the date of redemption: such speculation (which, incidentally, was frowned on by many from early times) would delay redemption since their thoughts were not elsewhere.

The following case illustrates even better what, in overall effect, amounts to an avoidance of the terms on pleasant occasions—illustrates it better because, from our point of view, the terms would be so highly appropriate. R. Hiyya the Elder (about A.D. 200) thinks that redemption will begin like the dawn and only by stages attain its full splendour.[245] The reason, according to R. Judan (middle of the 4th century A.D.), is that Israel, deep in sorrows, could not bear deliverance "all at once"; just as, if the sun wheeled up without being preceded by the dawn, the creatures would be blinded.[246] The Rabbis proceed from the experience that even sudden joy or sudden removal of pressure may do harm. But we find neither *pith'om* nor *petha'*. In Judan's statement we find *bebhath 'aḥath,* "all at once," "in one go" (*eisapax, auf ein Mal*).

[244] *b. Sanh.* 97a.

[245] *Song of Songs Rab.* on 6:10; *Esth. Rab.* on 8:15.

[246] *Midrash Psalms* on 18:51. Bacher, *Die Agada der Palästinensischen Amoräer,* vol. 3 (1899), 246, suggests that Judan's resumption of the old idea may have been prompted by Julian's relaxations.

Chapter Two
The New Testament

1. "SUDDEN" AND "SUDDENLY"

The following words are used in the New Testament for "sudden" or "suddenly": *aiphnidios, aphno, exaiphnes, exapina.* They may be described as rare. *Aiphnidios* occurs once in Luke, once in 1 Thessalonians; *aphno* only in Acts, three times; *exaiphnes* five times—once in Mark, twice in Luke, twice in Acts; *exapina* once, in Mark. To be sure, there is an occasional circumlocution.[247] But the general picture is not affected: the notion, we shall see, is confined to a very few areas.

Aiphnidios. "Take heed," says Luke, "lest that day come upon you as a sudden one, as a snare, for it shall come upon all them that dwell on earth."[248] This is the traditional fear of the apocalyptic day, represented in the Old Testament, for example, by Malachi, quoted above,[249] and in Rabbinism by the parable of the summons to the feast—though ben Zaccai, we suggested, possibly reduces its application to the individual's death.[250] The appearance of "to come upon" in this context is significant: from early on this verb is associated with sudden calamity.[251]

In the Marcan parallel the word employed is *exaiphnes,*[252] in Matthew this particular passage is not paralleled. However, both in Matthew and in Luke, in the parable of the servant put in authority, we find a close circumlocution. The arrival at the moment of reckoning, that is, is depicted in a way that might constitute a definition of "suddenness": "The lord shall come in a day when he looketh not and in an hour that he knoweth not."[253] "Not to know," it may be recalled, is from early on associated with the sudden.[254]

According to 1 Thessalonians,[255] "when they shall say, Peace and safety, then sudden destruction cometh upon them, as travail upon a woman with child." Again, the reference is to the last judgment. "Destruction" and "to come upon"[256]—the old typical words connected with suddenness. Among the Old Testament texts in the background we should include those two from Jeremiah where people hope for peace "and behold, *be'atha,* terror"; above we adverted to the possible etymological affinity between *b't* and *petha'*.[257]

[247] See presently on Matt 24:50; Luke 12:46.

[248] Luke 21:34 f.

[249] Mal 3:1; see above, 686.

[250] *b. Shab.* 153a; see above, 700.

[251] See above, 690 f. Luke 21:34 uses *ephistanai* (cp. 1 Thes 5:3 to be quoted presently), 21:35 *epeiserchesthai.* Both *ephistanai* and *eperchesthai* are favourite Lucan words; see Creed, *The Gospel according to St. Luke* (1930), 258. On *eperchesthai* and *epeiserchesthai* in the New Testament see below, 709 f.

[252] See below, 705, on Mark 13:36.

[253] Matt 24:50; Luke 12:46.

[254] See above, 691.

[255] 1 Thes 5:3.

[256] *Ephistanai* as in Luke 21:34, above, this page.

[257] Jer 8:15, 14:19; see above, 684, 697.

In the preceding and following verses in 1 Thessalonians the day of the Lord is compared to "a thief in the night." The comparison recurs several times in the New Testament, but "suddenness" is never introduced. This is hardly accidental. A thief may indeed break in when not expected, the element of "not knowing the hour" is indeed there,[258] but a "sudden" event is in addition striking, stunning, often violent. The onset of pangs of childbirth is "sudden." Admittedly, as time goes on, the simile of the thief gets more and more mixed up with others; so that in the later sources it would not be surprising to find "suddenness" intruding.[259] In fact, however, the intrusion never takes place.

Aphno. On the first Christian Pentecost, "suddenly there came from heaven a sound of a mighty wind," accompanying the descent of the Spirit.[260] When Paul and Silas were praying in jail at midnight, "suddenly there was a great earthquake" opening the doors.[261] Finally, at Malta, a viper fastened on Paul's hand; he shook it off but the barbarians present expected him "to fall down dead suddenly."[262]

At least in the first two passages there is no question of a disaster; this is not, or no longer, the necessary implication of *aphno.* What all three, however, have in common is that they are of an awe-inspiring, supernatural character. They might all be called *exaisios,* "terrible"—a word by which, as we saw, the LXX renders *pith'om,* "suddenly," as well as *pl',* "wondrous," "awesome."[263] In the case of Paul and the viper, it is indeed a disaster that the barbarians feared. But even here it is more probably the "wondrous" element to which *aphno* directs attention. They were enthused, we are told, when nothing *atopon,* "strange," "enormous," happened to Paul.[264] Of traditional associations with suddenness, we may note the nocturnal setting of the earthquake, and the words "to fall" and "dead" in the story of Paul and the viper. We shall come back below[265] to a certain aspect of this story.

Exaiphnes. "Watch, lest coming suddenly he find you sleeping": Mark.[266] In a similar warning Luke, we just saw, has *aiphnidios.*[267] "To come" is traditionally associated with the sudden,[268] and so is the setting which is at night.

[258] Matt 24:43; Luke 12:39; Rev 3:3.

[259] Jesus, it seems, referred to an actual case, a man who had failed to protect his house from thieves; and the moral was that his listeners should be more far-sighted as to the judgment threatening them. Matt 24:43 and Luke 12:39 connect the judgment with the *parousia.* In 1 Thes 5:2, 4 the day of the Lord may overtake people like a thief—we are fast moving away from the concrete basis. In 2 Pet 3:10 the day of the Lord comes like a thief, and the heavens will pass away with great noise. Finally, in Rev 3:3, 16:15 Christ writes that he will come like a thief. See Jeremias, *Die Gleichnisse Jesu,* 6th ed. (1962), 45 ff., and cp. below, 738.

[260] Acts 2:2.

[261] Acts 16:26. On the "immediate" opening of the doors, see below, 716, under *parachrema.*

[262] Acts 28:6.

[263] See above, 693 f.

[264] The New English Bible translates Acts 28:6: "They still expected that any moment he would swell up or drop down dead." This is inexact, first, in toning down "suddenly" and thus losing the particular atmosphere evoked by the word, secondly, in making the adverb cover both the swelling and the dropping dead whereas, in the original, it qualifies only the latter.

[265] See 740.

[266] See Mark 13:36.

[267] Luke 21:34; see above, 704.

[268] Mark here uses *erchesthai.*

In the Lucan birth narrative, "and suddenly there was with the angel a multitude of the heavenly host."[269] No disaster, to be sure, but neither a sweetly comfortable happening, no *gemütliche Weihnachtsabend in der warmen Stube* [no cosy Christmas eve in the warm room]. A few verses previously[270] there is a first vision, of an angel surrounded by the glory of the Lord, which strikes terror into the shepherds. The angel calms them and announces the birth of the Saviour. Now, however, "suddenly," a second vision, of the full heavenly army: surely, no less fearful than the first. (Even their proclamation "Peace among men in whom he is well pleased" implies judgment as well as promise.[271]) The sense of *exaiphnes* is the same as that of *aphno:* the breaking in of the "wondrous." The setting is at night.[272]

The father of an epileptic describes his son's disease: "A spirit taketh him and suddenly crieth out and teareth him that he foameth."[273] Maybe it is the son who "suddenly crieth out"—it makes little difference to the present argument. In the Marcan parallel the spirit shouts, not as it seizes the victim,[274] but as, at Jesus's command, it has to come out—and this shout is, of course, not sudden.[275] Luke's description of the seizure may be influenced by medical idiom.[276] At any rate, the adverb denotes a supernatural, demoniacal, sinister attack; the use is comparable to that of *aphno* in the story of Paul and the viper in Acts.[277] Matthew mentions no shout and, indeed, no spirit.[278]

The adverb occurs in two of the three accounts of Paul's conversion in Acts. The author writes: "and suddenly there shone round him a light out of heaven and he fell upon the earth."[279] Paul, in an address to the Jews of Jerusalem said to have been delivered in Hebrew,[280] declares: "suddenly there shone from heaven a great light round about me, and I fell unto the ground."[281] A supernatural, awe-inspiring event. Admittedly it involves judgment and even temporary blindness, but the point of *exaiphnes* is the unexpected impact of the "wondrous." Note the verb "to fall," often connected with suddenness.

In the third account, where Paul speaks before Agrippa, *exaiphnes* is not found, nor the blindness.[282] It is hardly accidental that, whereas the two first accounts refer direct-

[269] Luke 2:13.

[270] Luke 2:9.

[271] See Lagrange, *L'Evangile selon Saint Luc* (1921), 77.

[272] The New English Bible does less than justice to *exaiphnes* by translating "All at once there was with the angel." Rembrandt brings out splendidly the panic, at the angel's apparition, of shepherds, flocks, trees and earth. It is true that the heavenly host whom, somewhat anticipating, he shews circling the dove consists of attractive little angels.

[273] Luke 9:39.

[274] Mark 9:18, 20. On "at once" in 9:20 see below, 726, under *euthys*.

[275] Mark 9:26.

[276] See Hobart, *The Medical Language of St. Luke* (1882), 19.

[277] Acts 28:6; see above, 705.

[278] Matt 17:15 ff.

[279] Acts 9:3 f.

[280] Acts 21:40.

[281] Acts 22:6.

[282] Acts 26:13.

ly to what the supernatural, the light, did—"there shone round about him (me) a light"—the third concentrates on what Paul did—"I saw a light."

Exapina. According to Mark, Elijah and Moses talk with the transfigured Jesus, an apparition frightening the disciples. Then a cloud overshadows the latter, and a voice declares: "This is my beloved son, hear him." "And suddenly," the text goes on, "having looked round about, they saw no man any more save Jesus only with themselves."[283] Here it is particularly important not to weaken the force of the adverb. For in this version, it is the final sentence—where the disciples see Jesus alone, Elijah and Moses having vanished—which constitutes the climax: it is an awesome revelation to discover him as the one and only one designated by the voice, the Old Testament prophets being "no longer with them." "Suddenly"—a striking, tremendous, "wondrous" event. Mark is indeed somewhat disquieted about the disciples' initial ignorance, reflected in Peter's proposal of three tabernacles. He was so afraid, we are told, that "he wist not what to say": this note is doubtless inserted as an excuse.[284]

In Matthew, it is no longer a revelation that the voice should refer to Jesus and Jesus only. It is taken for granted that it could refer to no one else. So the adverb "suddenly" has no place in the last sentence where the disciples see Jesus alone.[285] The point of the narrative, from a singling out of Jesus, shifts to something in the nature of an epiphany. Moses and Elijah talk with the transfigured Jesus: no mention of fright at this stage. Peter, in proposing three tabernacles, addresses Jesus as "Lord," not, as in Mark, as "Rabbi."[286] There come the cloud and the voice, and it is on hearing the voice that the disciples are frightened and indeed fall on their faces, clearly in worship.[287] From this culmination the line descends. Jesus bids them arise and calms them: no such calming before the final sentence in Mark, far from it. Then: "and having lifted up their eyes they saw no man save Jesus only."[288] The particle "any longer" is dropped: the point here is not the revelation that as the Old Testament prophets are "no longer with them" Jesus alone must be meant by the voice, this ending in Matthew means restoration of the normal relationship after the epiphany. It is quite different from Mark.

Lohmeyer remarks on the Marcan ending: *So ist jetzt auch den Worten nach die alte Verbundenheit wieder hergestellt* [Thus are fulfilled the promises according to the Old Covenant].[289] This is absolutely correct—for the Matthean ending. But where it stands, it constitutes an assimilation of Mark to Matthew. The tendency, as may be expected, started early. D has *euthys,* "at once," "in due course," instead of *exapina,* "suddenly," in Mark.[290] This is not merely substitution of a commoner word; it is also a toning down.

[283] Mark 9:8.

[284] Mark 9:6.

[285] Matt 17:8.

[286] Matt 17:4; Mark 9:5.

[287] For possible influences from Dan 8:17 f., 10:7 ff., and an echo in Rev 1:17, see Lagrange, *L'Evangile selon Saint Marc,* 2nd ed. (1947), 232.

[288] Matt 17:8.

[289] *Das Evangelium des Markus* (1937), 177.

[290] See below, 725, under *euthys.*

Luke agrees with Mark in a vital respect: it is emphasized—not taken for granted—that the voice designates Jesus and no one besides. Only this is conveyed, not in the form of a "wondrous" revelation to the disciples, but in a factual, impersonal style: "and as the voice occurred—or, had occurred—Jesus was found—or, found himself—alone." No room here for "suddenly."[291] The problems raised by Luke's choice of this mode of report—as well as by other peculiarities of his version—lie beyond the scope of this study.

The extent to which Mark stands out can be demonstrated from a different angle. Except for his account of the transfiguration, "suddenly" is never used in the Bible—Old Testament or New—of the disappearance, the ending, of a supernatural display. It is the unlooked for opening which startles, which is "sudden." "And suddenly there was with the angel a multitude of the heavenly host."[292] A supernatural display indeed ends as abruptly as it begins: it is all the more significant that where this is brought out, it is done otherwise than by "suddenly." The vessel shewn to Peter in Acts "was at once received up into heaven," *euthys,* the angel delivering him from prison "at once departed from him," *eutheos.*[293] The Marcan transfiguration is unique—because, for once, it is a disappearance which is the really shocking thing, the disappearance of Moses and Elijah; of course, it coincides with the positive "seeing Jesus only with themselves" as the beloved Son to be heard.

In the whole of the New Testament, then, "sudden" or "suddenly" is met in two areas only. One is eschatology—the last judgment may overtake man in this way. Three passages belong here, one from Mark,[294] one from Luke,[295] and one from 1 Thessalonians.[296] We have also quoted a saying from Matthew and Luke which, though not containing the word, gives as precise a definition as one might ask for;[297] and further approximations, both from the Synoptics and the Epistles, might be added. The other area is that of supernatural, awesome occurrences, with eight passages: one from Mark,[298] two from Luke,[299] and five from Acts.[300]

In the area of eschatology, we conclude, there is a common strand in the Synoptics—with an old Jewish tradition behind it—where the sudden arrival of the supreme moment is stressed. It is a strand which, both in the gospels and in the Jewish sources, is capable of being isolated (more or less), expressing a (more or less) definite attitude and its development. The absence of the notion from John is significant, as is that of, say, the related notion "to watch." (Neither *agrypnein* nor *gregorein* is found.)

[291] Luke 9:36. The translation of the New English Bible, "was seen to be alone," is a fierce assimilation to Matthew and Mark.

[292] Luke 2:13. Or "The Lord spoke suddenly unto Moses and Aaron and Miriam," Num 12:4. See above, 706, 685 and below, 738.

[293] Acts 10:16, 12:10; see below, 736.

[294] Mark 13:36.

[295] Luke 21:34.

[296] 1 Thes 5:3.

[297] Matt 24:50; Luke 12:46.

[298] Mark 9:8, transfiguration.

[299] Luke 2:13, heavenly host, 9:39, epileptic.

[300] Acts 2:2, Pentecost, 9:3, Paul, 16:26, earthquake, 22:6, Paul, 28:6, viper.

John's historical and theological starting-point leads him away from this kind of suddenness.

The use of the terms with reference to "wondrous" events is so rare that little can be said by way of comparison between various writers. Luke is conceivably a little more inclined to this use than the other evangelists (owing to his medical background?). That Mark alone has it in the transfiguration means nothing since there are special reasons for its omission by Matthew and Luke—and John omits the entire pericope.

2. "To come upon"

It may be useful to consider the fate in the New Testament of the more interesting remaining Septuagintal words for "sudden" or "suddenly" though, in the New Testament, they have not this meaning: *eperchesthai* or *epeiserchesthai, parachrema* and *euthys, eutheos. Eisapax* and *exaisios* do not occur in the New Testament;[301] they are infrequent enough in the Old. On *spoude* and *tachys* we have nothing fresh to say; except, with regard to the former, that the New Testament contains no vestige of the unpleasant sense discernible in the LXX and, here and there, in the Apocrypha harking back to it.[302] Luke's *stigme chronou* we shall briefly comment on in the last but one section of this study.[303]

The first of the terms to be discussed, "to come upon," is a Lucan favourite. It is used either in connection with disasters or threats of disasters or in connection with awe-inspiring occurrences. We come across one exception, in Ephesians, in the technical phrase "the coming ages."[304] Even this phrase has its ultimate origin in an eschatological setting.

The verb is found ten times: four times in Luke (including the only passage with *epeiserchesthai*[305]), four times in Acts, once in Ephesians—in the text just cited—and once in James.

In two passages we have to do with a "wondrous" event, in fact, the same event in both—the descent of the Spirit. There is the annunciation, "The Holy Ghost will come upon thee,"[306] and there is the promise to the disciples prior to Pentecost, "But ye shall receive power when the Holy Ghost is come upon you."[307] It may be recalled that, on Pentecost, "suddenly there came from heaven a sound."[308]

In two passages it is a question of attack: in Luke's simile of Jesus's superiority over Satan, "But when a stronger shall come upon him, he taketh from him his armour,"[309] and in a scene in Acts where "the Jews came" to stone Paul.[310] The Matthean and

[301] *Atopos*, however, in the story of Paul and the viper, Acts 28:6, above, 705, is not far from *exaisios*.

[302] See above, 696 f.

[303] Below, 740 f.

[304] Eph 2:7; cp. Hermas, *Vision* 4.3.5.

[305] Luke 21:35.

[306] Luke 1:35.

[307] Acts 1:8.

[308] Acts 2:2; see above, 705.

[309] Luke 11:22.

[310] Acts 14:19.

Marcan parallel to Luke's simile is slightly different and the verb does not occur.[311]

We may here insert a remark on *phthanein epi* employed in this pericope by Matthew and Luke. (The sentence is not in Mark, so it is Q whatever that may mean.) "If I cast out devils, then the kingdom of God is come upon you."[312] In the Greek Old Testament, the expression invariably has an adverse sense;[313] and so it has in the only other New Testament text where it occurs, 1 Thessalonians,[314] "For the wrath is come upon them [the Jews] to the uttermost." It is highly probable that the kingdom in the Beelzebub controversy means in the first place condemnation, defeat, ruin, of the opponents addressed: "has overtaken you" rather than the usual English "is come unto you,"[315] the German *ist zu euch gekommen,* the French *vous est arrivé.* The contact between the controversy and 1 Thessalonians is more than purely verbal.

There remain five passages in all of which *eperchesthai* is used of calamity. One is the request of Simon Magus, cursed by Peter: "Pray for me that none of these things come upon me."[316]

The other four are concerned with eschatology. Luke speaks of "men's hearts failing them for fear and for looking after those things which are coming upon the earth."[317] Note the "fear"—often met, we saw, in this context. The sentence is not paralleled in Matthew or Mark,[318] but it may well be taken from traditional material: "the things which are coming upon the earth" is a Rabbinic phrase.[319]

In the concluding part of this chapter, Luke has the warning with *aiphnidios* discussed above: "lest that day come upon you as a sudden one, as a snare." "To come upon" here *ephistanai.* He goes on: "For it shall come upon all them that dwell on the face of the earth," *epeiserchesthai.*[320] This illustrates well the force of the verb—or at least of the strengthened form *epeiserchesthai*—which, without any further qualification, will convey the threatening, desperate aspect of the happening. "It shall come upon" is quite enough to evoke this sinister element. It is interesting that, instead of "lest that day come upon you suddenly as a snare, for it shall come upon all," some MSS read "lest that day come upon you suddenly, for as a snare it shall come upon all." This is

[311] Matt 12:29; Mark 3:27.

[312] Matt 12:28; Luke 11:20.

[313] Judg 20:34, "they knew not that evil was coming upon them"; 20:42, "and the battle came upon them"; Eccl 8:14, "upon the just there cometh according to the work of the wicked"—significantly, in the second half of the verse, alluding to undeserved prosperity, the preposition is not *epi* but *pros*; Dan (Theodotion) 4:21, "this is a decree of the most High which is come upon my lord the king"; 4:28, "all this came upon the king Nebuchadnezzar."

[314] 1 Thes 2:16.

[315] The New English Bible correctly puts "upon." The thesis here propounded, incidentally, is neither for nor against Aalen's interpretation of *basileia* in *NTS*, 8 (1962), 215 ff.; the present text is discussed on 230.

[316] Acts 8:24.

[317] Luke 21:26.

[318] Matt 24:29 ff.; Mark 13:24 ff.

[319] See Strack-Billerbeck, *Kommentar zum Neuen Testament aus Talmud und Midrasch,* vol. 2 (1924), 255, 358, vol. 4, pt. 2 (1928), 985 etc.

[320] Luke 21:34 f.; see above, 704.

manifestly an "easier reading." The particular force of *epeiserchesthai* is not, or no longer, sufficient. So, in order to make the day not only universal but also menacing, the words "as a snare" are attached to this verb.

According to Acts, Paul preached to the Jews of Antioch: "Beware lest that come upon you which is spoken of in the prophets—Behold ye despisers and wonder and perish, for I work a work in your days which ye shall in no wise believe though a man declare it unto you."[321] The quotation "Behold" etc. is from Habakkuk.[322] In the Dead Sea Commentary on Habakkuk the expression "to come upon" occurs twice in the discussion of this verse: "all that is coming upon the last generation," "all that is coming upon God's people."[323] More than that, the verse is interpreted as directed against those not believing in the words of the Teacher of Righteousness, the New Covenant, the things "coming upon" the world in its final phase.

A third bond between Acts and the Dead Sea Scrolls is worth a mention. The Massoretic Hebrew text of Habakkuk reads "Behold among the nations," *baggoyim,* whereas Acts, "Behold ye despisers," follows the LXX, *hoi kataphronetai*; in Hebrew this would presuppose *habboghedhim* or *boghedhim,* not very remote from the Massoretic. (It should be remembered that vowels are not written.) Now it is clear that the Dead Sea Commentator, if he had not "despisers" before him, at least interpreted what lay before him in just this sense. Three times we find the actual word *(hab)boghedhim*: the quotation from Habakkuk, we are informed, envisages "the despisers with the Man of the Lie," "the despisers of the New Covenant," "the despisers at the end of days."[324] Translators prefer "traitors" or "unfaithful." The argument here advanced is not affected if we adopt this rendering—only it should then also be adopted for Paul's speech in Acts.

There can be no doubt that Paul gives Habakkuk an application—or is represented as giving it an application—the main outline of which was already established; the main outline and, indeed, some detail of importance as well, including the concept of "to come upon."

Lastly, James—"Ye rich, weep and howl for your spoilings that are coming upon you."[325] Note "spoiling," at home, we observed, in the province of suddenness.

It will be noted that *eperchesthai* does not figure in Matthew, Mark or John. However, the passages where it does figure offer too small a basis for comparison. So nothing will be said here as to any possible significance of the concentration in Luke and Acts.

[321] Acts 13:40 f.

[322] Hab 1:5; cp. Isa 29:14.

[323] Commentary on Hab 2:7, 10, in the Scroll, with *ba' 'al* for "to come upon": *kol habba'oth 'al,* "all that is coming upon." The expression recurs in 7:1, where Hab 2:1 f. is discussed: "And God told Habakkuk to write down that which was coming upon the last generation." No reference to the Dead Sea Scrolls is given in the fairly recent commentary on Acts by Haenchen, *Die Apostelgeschichte,* 13th ed. (1961), 355.

[324] Commentary on Hab 2:1, 3, 5, in the Scroll.

[325] Jas 5:1. The New English Bible "descending on you": why?

3. "STRAIGHTWAY"

a) *General*

Parachrema occurs eighteen times in the New Testament: twice in Matthew—though, as both times it refers to the same event in the same pericope,[326] for the purpose of establishing relative frequency we might count this as one emphatic application—apart from this only in Luke—ten times—and Acts—six. Luke evidently has a predilection for it. The word is common in medical treatises.[327] Though this may be an initial cause, it does not fully account for the way Luke uses it, which is far more specialised. In the medical treatises, for example, we find not only that a disease will "straightway" have such and such consequence but also that certain remedies should be applied "straightway."[328] The latter usage is not paralleled in Luke. It is likely that, whatever first determined his choice, his handling of the adverb largely reflects his own theological or stylistic bias.

In the New Testament the word does not mean "suddenly"; it means "straightway," "forthwith." None the less there are some noteworthy connotations linking it loosely to that sphere. Above all, the element of the "wondrous" is present in all eighteen passages. On closer analysis it may be affirmed that, in seventeen out of the eighteen—the exception being the death of Agrippa in Acts[329]—it is a question of immediate miraculous actualisation of an order or prediction of Jesus, or one in Jesus's name, or some influence emanating from Jesus, or the impact of the Spirit.[330]

b) *Matthew*

In the Matthean cursing of the fig-tree, as distinct from the Marcan (no parallel in Luke or John), it is stressed that no interval elapsed between the curse and its effect. Jesus condemned the tree, "and straightway it withered away"; and this feature is mentioned again in the reaction of the disciples, who "marvelled, saying, How is it straightway withered away?"[331] In Mark, Jesus curses the tree, then intervenes the cleansing of the Temple, and it is on the following day that he and the disciples pass again and the latter notice that the tree is destroyed.

The double *parachrema* in Matthew is directed against such a version, whether the Marcan itself or one similar in this respect. The response, for Matthew, was immediate and he is concerned to leave no doubt about it. The rendering "suddenly" would obviously miss the point: the difference between it and *parachrema* is here well illumined.

The problem is how Matthew in this one pericope comes to use a terms otherwise confined to Luke and Acts, where indeed it is frequent in precisely this sense. If elsewhere the term occurred in Luke only, one might argue that it is favoured by Q and that

[326] Matt 21:19 f.

[327] Hobart, *op. cit.*, 96 ff.

[328] Hippocrates, *Opera Omnia*, per Anutium Foesium (1624), Intern. Affect., 551, line 7—among Hobart's quotations.

[329] Acts 12:23; see below, 717 f.

[330] Cp. Lagrange, *L'Evangile selon Saint Luc* (1921), 152.

[331] Matt 21:19 f.; Mark 11:11 ff.

the episode of the fig-tree is Q though not appearing in Luke. But this line is closed owing to the frequency of the term in Acts. So why does Matthew not use *euthys,* as in more than fifteen other cases? The explanation may be that, in the episode of the fig-tree, where he attaches such importance to the immediacy of the response, he chooses *parachrema* because *euthys,* as we shall see, is not quite so unambiguous: we shall see that, though basically signifying "at once," sometimes it means little more than "in due course." It is true that this latter meaning is Marcan rather than Matthean, still *parachrema* is stronger.[332]

c) *Luke*

According to Luke, the angel Gabriel told Zacharias that he would be dumb "until the day that these things shall have come to pass";[333] and in fact, when the son was born and named John, "his mouth was opened straightway."[334] It might perhaps be objected that the angel announced not that, as soon as the things had come about, Zacharias would be able to speak, but that till then he would be unable. But this would be to impose too pedantic an interpretation on the narrative. We shall meet a very similar fulfilment of a prediction, "straightway" at the end of a term, in Luke's version of the cock-crow.[335]

On Jesus's rebuking the fever that had befallen Simon's mother-in-law, "it left her and straightway she got up and ministered unto them."[336] One might just conceivably translate "and straightway, having got up, she ministered." But a comparison with other Lucan pericopes renders this interpretation unlikely.[337] The parallel in Matthew has no such adverb,[338] that in Mark perhaps has *eutheos,* "at once," with "it left her."[339] We shall see that Luke substitutes *parachrema* in several places.[340]

The man sick with palsy, at Jesus's command, "having straightway risen up before them, having taken up that whereon he lay, departed to his house."[341] Again, conceivably, we might translate "straightway, having risen, he departed," but it is implausible. No such adverb in Matthew,[342] *euthys* in Mark:[343] one of the cases where Luke substitutes *parachrema.*[344]

In the story of the woman with an issue of blood *parachrema* occurs twice. She touched Jesus's garment "and straightway her issue stanched." Jesus noticed that some power had emanated from him, upon which the woman proclaimed that she had touched

[332] On *euthys,* see below, 718 ff.
[333] Luke 1:20.
[334] Luke 1:64.
[335] Luke 22:60; see below, 715.
[336] Luke 4:39.
[337] E.g. Luke 8:55, where "straightway" must refer to the getting up, no other verb being there.
[338] Matt 8:15.
[339] Mark 1:31; see below, 720 f.
[340] Luke 5:25, 8:44, 8:55, 18:43, 22:60; see this and the following pages.
[341] Luke 5:25.
[342] Matt 9:7.
[343] Mark 2:12; see below, 721.
[344] See Luke 4:39 just discussed.

him "and was healed straightway."[345] Jesus dismissed her in peace: "Thy faith hath made thee whole."

In Matthew, the woman touches Jesus, he assures her "Thy faith hath made thee whole," and now follows the statement: "And she was made whole from that hour."[346] This or similar phrases are employed in the same sense in other Matthean narratives;[347] and John elaborates the meaning in connection with the healing of the centurion's servant.[348] We shall come across a passage in Acts[349] where "in that hour" and *parachrema* are synonymous.

In Mark, the woman touches Jesus and "at once, *euthys,* her blood was dried up."[350] So Luke's *parachrema* replaces *euthys.*[351] When we come to her confession in Mark, this adverb is not repeated, we are simply informed that "she told him all the truth." There is less emphasis on the point, it seems, than in Luke. There is indeed a second *euthys* in the Marcan version: Jesus "at once" noticed that power had emanated from him. We shall discuss this below.[352]

Jairus's daughter was told to arise; "and her spirit came again and she arose straightway."[353] Matthew has no such adverb,[354] and Mark has *euthys* (followed in the same verse by another *euthys,* "and they were at once astonished").[355] Another Lucan substitution of *parachrema.*[356]

The woman with a spirit of infirmity, when Jesus laid hands on her, "was straightway made straight."[357] No parallels in the other gospels.

Bartimaeus was told "Look up, thy faith hath made thee whole." "And straightway he looked up."[358] In the Matthean parallel we find *eutheos,* in the Marcan *euthys,* "at once."[359] Luke has substituted *parachrema.*

Surely, in the Lucan introduction of the parable of the pounds *parachrema* expresses the same idea as in the texts discussed so far. Jesus seeks and obtains hospitality from Zacchaeus, a publican, which sets people complaining. Yet Jesus says to Zacchaeus: "This day is salvation come to this house, forsomuch as he also is a son of Abraham." That this is intended to be a public proclamation as well as a communication to Zacchaeus is clear from the third person: "he is a son of Abraham."[360] Jesus goes

[345] Luke 8:44, 47.

[346] Matt 9:22.

[347] Matt 8:13, 15:28, 17:18.

[348] John 4:52 f. The response in 19:27 deserves attention.

[349] Acts 16:33; cp. 16:18, 22:13. See below, 716 f. On Acts 22:13 we shall comment at the end of this division of *parachrema*; see below, 717.

[350] Mark 5:29; see below, 723.

[351] Cp. Luke 4:39, above, 713.

[352] See 723.

[353] Luke 8:55.

[354] Matt 9:25.

[355] Mark 5:42; see below, 723 f.

[356] See above, 713 f., in connection with Luke 4:39.

[357] Luke 13:13.

[358] Luke 18:43.

[359] Matt 20:34; Mark 10:52; see below, 726, and n. 545.

[360] See Creed, *op. cit.*, 231.

on: "For the Son of Man is come to seek and save that which was lost." Then he offers a parable "because he was nigh to Jerusalem and because they thought that the kingdom of God should appear straightway."[361] They (whoever they may have been) thought so, that is, in reliance on the power of Jesus's word—"This day" etc. No parallels in the other gospels.

Lagrange translates *sur-le-champ,* interpreting it as *soudainement*; and he does not list this text among the illustrations of the typically Lucan use of *parachrema.*[362] But this is to tear the verse from what precedes it in the evangelist: after Jesus's proclamation, a fulfilment "straightway" was expected. Not a "sudden" one; "straightway" in the Lucan sense of immediate response. The New English Bible errs in the opposite direction, translating "at any moment." This is too non-committal.

In Luke, Jesus's prediction to Peter is: "The cock shall not crow this day before thou shalt thrice deny that thou knowest me."[363] As Peter is making his third denial, "straightway, while he yet spake, the cock crew."[364] Matthew and Mark formulate the prediction a little differently: "This night, before the cock crow (twice, in Mark), thou shalt deny me thrice."[365] (As far as the point here relevant is concerned, John agrees with Luke.[366]) In both Matthew and Mark (as also in John), "at once," *euthys* (*eutheos* in John), "the cock crew" ("the second time," in Mark).[367]

Parachrema, substituted by Luke for *euthys,*[368] has its full, characteristic force. We pointed out above that the pattern is the same as in the story of Zacharias, who was to be dumb till certain things had come about and then "straightway" spoke.[369] This pattern accounts for Luke's formulation of the prediction in the present case: the cock was restrained till the appropriate moment and then "straightway" crew. Whether the formulation of the prediction is Luke's work or whether he chose it from several alternatives already current we shall not attempt to decide, especially as the Johannine problem would be involved.

This exact fulfilment of the prediction is further underlined in Luke by two additions. First, the cock crew "while he yet spake." Secondly, "the Lord turned and looked upon Peter."[370] It is true that from here onwards Luke falls in, in the main, with the other Synoptics—Peter remembers essentially the Matthean and Marcan formulation, "Before the cock crow, thou shalt deny me thrice."[371] This may be simply lack of consistency on Luke's part; but it is not impossible that we have to do with post-Lucan assimilation.[372]

[361] Luke 19:11.

[362] *L'Evangile selon Saint Luc* (1921), 152, 492 f.

[363] Luke 22:34.

[364] Luke 22:60.

[365] Matt 26:34; Mark 14:30.

[366] John 13:38; there are divergences, but the decisive "shall not before" recurs.

[367] Matt 26:74; Mark 14:72; John 18:27. In some MSS a first cock-crow, without "at once," in Mark 14:68.

[368] See above, 713, in connection with Luke 4:39.

[369] Luke 1:64; see above, 713.

[370] Luke 22:61.

[371] Luke 22:61.

[372] Luke 22:62 is widely regarded as assimilated to Matt 26:75; see Rengstorf, *Das Evangelium nach Lukas,* 9th ed. (1962), 259.

d) *Acts*

In Acts, Peter, in the name of Jesus, commands a lame man to walk and lifts him up: "and straightway his feet received strength."[373]

Sapphira is told by Peter that she is doomed to instant death, having tempted the Spirit of the Lord: "and she fell down straightway."[374]

Paul, "filled with the Holy Ghost," tells the sorcerer Elymas that "the hand of the Lord is upon you and thou shalt be blind, and straightway there fell on him a mist."[375] D substitutes the commoner *eutheos,* "at once."[376]

On the other hand, D inserts the double phrase *parachrema eutheos* into a healing at Lystra. Paul told a cripple to stand upright, "and he leaped and walked," D: "and straightway at once he leaped and walked."[377] This pleonasm is classical,[378] but D has clearly imported the adverbs from similar stories. We have not included this text in our statistics of *parachrema* presented above.[379]

In the story of Paul and Silas in prison at Philippi, *parachrema* occurs twice. At midnight, suddenly (*aphno*) there was an earthquake shaking the foundations, "and straightway all the doors were opened and everyone's bands were loosed."[380] The "sudden" earthquake implies action by God or the Spirit. We found a "sudden" sound as of a mighty wind portending the descent of the Spirit on Pentecost,[381] and on another occasion its descent is marked by an earthquake—in fact, and earthquake following the prayer of Peter, John and their company,[382] just as that in Philippi follows the prayer of Peter and Silas. It emerges that *parachrema* here, too, denotes the immediate result of divine intervention. The latter itself is "sudden," and then, "straightway," comes its effect: the difference between the two concepts is here once again neatly illustrated.

The jailer and his family readily listen to Paul's and Silas's preaching; "and he took them the same hour of the night and washed their stripes, and was baptized, he and all his, straightway."[383] Considering the numerous passages we have inspected, it is very plausible that the quick conversion, "the same hour of the night," "straightway," is being represented as taking place under the direct impact of the Spirit, the power revealed in the earthquake and also, maybe, in the staying behind of all prisoners so that the jailer's life is saved. We must not forget that in quite a few cases where a person is "straightway" healed through Jesus's word or influence, belief and acknowledgment are virtually part of the cure.[384] In the case of Simon's mother-in-law, if we punctuated—improbably—"and straightway, having got up, she ministered unto them," the adverb would be direct-

[373] Acts 3:7.

[374] Acts 5:10.

[375] Acts 13:11.

[376] See below, under *euthys,* 736.

[377] Acts 14:10; see below, under *euthys,* 736.

[378] Blass-Debrunner, *Neutestamentliche Grammatik,* 5th ed. (1921), 282.

[379] See 712.

[380] Acts 16:26; see above, 705, for a discussion of *aphno* in this text.

[381] Acts 2:2; see above, 705.

[382] Acts 4:31.

[383] Acts 16:33.

[384] Luke 4:39, 5:25, 8:47, 13:13, 18:43; Acts 3:7 f.; see above, 713, and this page.

ly connected with entry into the service of Jesus.[385] The ministering is indeed not quite unparalleled in the narrative under review: the jailer takes Paul and Silas into his house, washes their stripes, is baptized, gives them food and believes.

"In that hour" and "straightway" are practically synonymous in this narrative. The former phrase is used in this sense in two other passages in Acts.[386] One, concerning Paul's cure from blindness, we shall consider presently.

This cure is mentioned twice. The first time we are told how Ananias, sent by Jesus, lays hands on Paul: "And at once (*eutheos*) there fell from his eyes as it were scales and he looked up."[387] There is a variant reading: "and straightway, *parachrema,* he looked up." Its support, however, is very slight. We may take it that in one line of transmission of the gospel *parachrema* has been added by way of assimilation to narratives like that of Bartimaeus.[388] In the statistics of *parachrema* set out above this text is not included,[389] though it would, of course, make a perfect fourteenth to the thirteen in this division.

Let us note, however, that whoever added *parachrema* probably felt justified by the subsequent second account of the cure: "in that very hour I looked up on him."[390] "In that hour," as just pointed out, is very close to "straightway."

e) *Luke and Acts*

This leaves one passage only in Acts where *parachrema* has not the peculiar meaning found in all the seventeen others; namely, the account of Herod Agrippa's death. He delivered a public oration, and the people declared his voice to be that of a god: "and straightway the angel of the Lord smote him, because he gave not God the glory, and he was eaten of worms and gave up the ghost."[391] Here we are not told that what happened "straightway" happened in response to the divine command or prediction. Indeed the word appears to signify something not remote from "suddenly."

Perhaps the solution lies in the fact that, whereas all the other seventeen texts are concerned with Jesus and his followers, that before us concerns an outsider. It may be taken over from some source without much adaptation of the vocabulary to the rest of Acts.

There is, however, just a possibility that appearances are deceptive and that the sense here is less exceptional than one might believe at first sight. In Josephus[392] the king, having accepted praise belonging only to God, first sees the bird whose coming, he knows, announces his death within five days,[393] then his fatal illness seizes him. If Acts draws on some such version, the *parachrema* might be put under its influence even though—for very understandable reasons—the prediction was suppressed.

It can hardly be denied that *parachrema,* with its pregnant sense, has a definite

[385] Luke 4:39; see above, 713.

[386] Acts 16:18, 22:13. For the gospels, see above, 713 f., in connection with Luke 8:44, 47.

[387] Acts 9:18; see below, 735.

[388] Luke 18:43; see above, 714.

[389] See above, 712.

[390] Acts 22:13; see above, n. 349.

[391] Acts 12:23.

[392] *Ant.* 19.8.2.346.

[393] *Ant.* 18.6.7.200.

place in Lucan theology, is part of a message he wishes to convey. Let us add that the reaction of observers to the result occurring "straightway" is marvel, *thaumazo,*[394] fear, *phobos,*[395] ecstasy, *ekstasis, existemi,*[396] astonishment, *ekplessomai.*[397]

4. "AT ONCE"

a) *Mark*

Euthys or *eutheos* is found between forty and fifty times in Mark, between fifteen and twenty in Matthew, seven times in Luke, six in John, some ten in Acts, and once in each Galatians, James, 3 John and Revelation. The word never means "suddenly." Indeed we shall see that at least in Mark and texts drawing on him, it often means less—or, according as one looks at it, more—than "at once." We begin with Mark.

Jesus was baptized; "and at once, coming out of the water, he saw the heavens rent and the Spirit descending."[398] The adverb here denotes the immediacy of the event: we may recall that in Jewish proselyte baptism, "he immerses and comes up—behold, he is like an Israelite in all respects."[399]

D omits *euthys*. Maybe the scribe mistakenly connected it with "coming up": "and at once coming up, he saw." That seemed queer—why ever should he not come up at once?—so it was simplest to drop the adverb. At any rate Matthew must have divided Mark in this erroneous way, hence: "baptized, Jesus at once came up."[400] (To be sure, Matthew goes on: "and behold (*idou*) the heavens were rent.") The scheme of the Marcan passage, with a participle between "at once" and the verb it qualifies, recurs in over fifteen other texts in Mark, plus, maybe, three times in Matthew independently of Mark; never in Luke, John or Acts.[401]

Luke, besides other changes, omits *euthys* and also the technical reference to the "coming up."[402] John is not really comparable.[403] Let us note in passing first, that all attempts to dissociate New Testament baptism from Jewish proselyte baptism—futile on numerous grounds—break to pieces against this technical term "to come up," '*ala,* having its full force in Mark, a little weaker in Matthew, suppressed by Luke; and secondly, that the Matthean version making Jesus "come up at once," affords conclusive proof of some use at least by Matthew of a written Mark—it cannot be accounted for in any other way.

The baptism ended in divine acknowledgment: "and at once the spirit driveth him

394 Matt 21:20; see above, 712.

395 Luke 1:65; Acts 5:11; see above, 713, 716.

396 Luke 5:26, 8:56; see above, 713 f.

397 Acts 13:12; see above, 716.

398 Mark 1:10.

399 *b. Yeb.* 47b. The New English Bible translates well: "At the moment when he came up, he saw."

400 Matt 3:16; see below, 729, and n. 545.

401 Here are the other cases: Mark 1:18 (where Matt 4:20 again mispunctuates), 1:21, 1:29, 2:8, 2:12, 5:30, 5:36, 6:27, 6:54, 7:25, 8:10, 9:8 in D; 9:15, 9:24, 11:2, 14:43 (more or less), 14:45, 15:1. The three Matthean texts are: Matt 14:31, 25:15 f, 27:48. See this and the following pages.

402 Luke 3:21.

403 John 1:32 ff.

into the wilderness."[404] Here *euthys* cannot be pressed; Matthew does not lose much by substituting "then," *tote*,[405] though there is in *kai euthys* a trace of "in due course," "as had to happen after what preceded," "and so." It is less purely temporary, more theological, than *tote*; it is reminiscent of *oun* in one of its applications. The German *alsbald* is not a bad rendering, the New English Bible translates well "Thereupon the Spirit sent him away." Luke puts the noncommittal connecting particle *de*.[406] No parallel in John.

Jesus bade Simon and Andrew follow him, "and once, leaving their nets, they followed him."[407] Doubtless a tribute to their readiness, but also, more generally, an indication of how things follow one another as they must, "and duly."

Matthew again seems to divide wrongly, "and these, at once leaving their nets, followed him."[408] It is not certain, but a comma after *hoi de* is more natural than after *hoi de eutheos*.[409] The New English Bible takes it in this sense: "They left their nets at once and followed him." Alas, it also assimilates Mark: "And at once they left their nets and followed him." Fortunately in this episode, as opposed to that of the baptism, the sense is not fundamentally affected. In Luke and John the call is told quite differently and *euthys* does not occur.[410]

The role of *euthys* as simply (or not so simply, according as one looks at it) indicating the *planmässige*, steady, blow upon blow succession of events comes out clearly in the next few verses. Soon after gaining Simon and Andrew Jesus saw the sons of Zebedee: "and at once he called them, and, after leaving their father, they went after him."[411] Here the call, not the response to it, occurs "at once." The narrative goes on: "And they go into Capernaum and at once on the sabbath day, entering into the synagogue, he taught."[412] Even more schematically: "And at once there was in the synagogue a man with an unclean spirit."[413]

Matthew, in the call of the sons of Zebedee, gives "at once" a—for him—more meaningful position, namely, the position it has in the call of Simon and Andrew: "and he called them and these, at once leaving, followed him."[414] No parallel in Luke or John. The notices about teaching at Capernaum and the man with the unclean spirit are not paralleled in Matthew or John, and Luke omits "at once" both times.[415]

The New English Bible cuts out "at once" from both the two first Marcan texts: "he called them," "and on the Sabbath he went to the synagogue and began to teach."[416] This is not only to lose the flavour of Mark's style—at least partly based on his theolo-

[404] Mark 1:12.
[405] Matt 4:1.
[406] Luke 4:1.
[407] Mark 1:8.
[408] Matt 4:20; see below, 729.
[409] Cp. Matt 4:22, to be discussed presently, on the same page.
[410] Luke 5:1 ff.; John 1:40 ff.
[411] Mark 1:20.
[412] Mark 1:21.
[413] Mark 1:23.
[414] Matt 4:22; *hoi de eutheos* as in 4:20, just discussed. See also below, n. 545.
[415] Luke 4:31, 33.
[416] Mark 1:20, 21.

gy—but also to obscure the relation between the various gospels. It makes it look as if Matthew, where he says that "they left at once," freely added the "at once."[417] In the third Marcan text the New English Bible actually replaces "and at once" by "now"—"Now there was a man"[418]—thus creating the impression of a break where Mark emphasizes continuity; and, of course, it makes Mark look as smooth as Luke.[419]

As a result of Capernaum, Jesus's fame "went out at once."[420] A bit conventional, but it does stress the immediacy of the effect. Luke omits it.[421] No parallel in Matthew or John.

In the following verse we are told: "And at once, having gone out of the synagogue they went into the house of Simon and Andrew."[422] "At once" is not to be pressed; the meaning approaches "in due course." D omits it. So do Matthew and Luke.[423] No parallel in John.

Simon's mother-in-law was ill, "and at once they tell him about her."[424] Even here, the meaning is perhaps rather "and so," "and as had duly to happen." The notice is not represented in Matthew;[425] it is in Luke but he omits the adverb.[426] No parallel in John.

In the following verse, Jesus raised her up "and the fever left her at once."[427] The adverb here denotes the immediacy of the cure. To be sure, it is missing from important MSS,[428] as also from Matthew.[429] But Luke may well have read it: "And it left her, and straightway (*parachrema*) she arose."[430] The substitution of *parachrema* for *euthys*, we saw, is frequent in Luke; and his transfer of the adverb from "it left her" to "she arose" does not seem inexplicable. No parallel in John.

Jesus told a leper to be clean, "and at once the leprosy departed from him."[431] The cure took place immediately, that is. Matthew and Luke both agree in this respect.[432] No parallel in John.

In the following verse Jesus "at once dismissed him."[433] Whether this stresses the immediacy or approximates "duly" cannot be decided without going into the difficult

[417] Matt 4:22.

[418] Mark 1:23.

[419] Mark 1:23; Luke 4:33.

[420] Mark 1:28. In this case the New English Bible translates *euthys* twice: "The news spread rapidly, and he was soon spoken of."

[421] Luke 4:37.

[422] Mark 1:29. The New English Bible translates correctly: "On leaving the synagogue they went straight to the house of Simon and Andrew." For the structure of the sentence see above, 718 f., in connection with Mark 1:10.

[423] Matt 8:14; Luke 4:38.

[424] Mark 1:30. Strangely the New English Bible here translates literally: "They told him about her at once."

[425] Matt 8:14 ff.

[426] Luke 4:38.

[427] Mark 1:31.

[428] The New English Bible seems to follow the reading without it: "The fever left her."

[429] Matt 8:15.

[430] Luke 4:39; see above, 713.

[431] Mark 1:42. The New English Bible correctly: "The leprosy left him immediately."

[432] Matt 8:3; Luke 5:13; see below, 730, and n. 545.

[433] Mark 1:43. The New English Bible: "Then he dismissed him."

background of the dismissal.[434] The notice is not represented in Matthew or Luke.[435] No parallel in John.

Jesus again went to Capernaum, his presence became known, "and at once many were gathered together."[436] The adverb appears only in some MSS. It denotes the immediacy of the consequence. The notice is not represented in Matthew,[437] nor really in Luke.[438] No parallel in John.

Some scribes thought him a blasphemer, "and at once, as Jesus perceived it in his spirit that they so reasoned, he saith unto them."[439] The immediacy is stressed: Jesus retorted before being expressly challenged. D omits the adverb. So do Matthew and Luke.[440] No parallel in John.

Jesus told a man "Arise, take thy bed and go unto thy house": "and he arose and at once, having taken up the bed, went out before them all."[441] The adverb is half-way between "immediately" and "duly." There is good reason why it comes, not at the beginning of the verse, but only after "and he arose":[442] the majority of the crowd are outside the house, so it is only after "and he arose" that the fully public part of the miracle takes place. Matthew omits the adverb (besides other changes).[443]

Luke, as elsewhere, replaces *euthys* by *parachrema* and places it at the beginning of the verse—but he also introduces full publicity from the first moment: "and straightway having arisen before them, having taken up that whereon he lay, he departed."[444] In John, at Bethesda, Jesus tells a sick man "Arise, take up thy bed and walk"—"and at once the man was made whole and took up his bed and walked."[445] The scene is laid in the open, not in a house; the adverb (*eutheos*), as in Luke, stands at the beginning of the verse.

Jesus gave offence by healing on a Sabbath; "and having gone out, the Pharisees at once took counsel."[446] The meaning is probably half-way between "immediately" and "accordingly," "in due course." D omits the adverb, as do Matthew and Luke.[447] No parallel in John.

434 Cp. Mark 5:18 f.; Luke 8:38.

435 Matt 8:4; Luke 5:14.

436 Mark 2:2, cp. 6:54 f., 7:25.

437 Matt 9:1 ff.

438 Luke 5:17 f.

439 Mark 2:8; cp. Mark 5:30, to be discussed below, 723. The New English Bible suppresses the adverb. for the structure of the sentence see above, 718 f., in connection with Mark 1:10.

440 Matt 9:4; Luke 5:22.

441 Mark 2:12. The New English Bible accepts "at once" but connects it with the wrong verb: "took his stretcher at once and went out." No great matter in this case, but see above, 718 f., in the discussion of Mark 1:10, for the structure of the sentence.

442 See below, 725, for a similar difficulty in Mark 7:35.

443 Matt 9:7.

444 Luke 5:25; see above, 713.

445 John 5:9; see below, 733.

446 Mark 3:6. The New English Bible renders the sense: "but the Pharisees, on leaving the synagogue, began plotting."

447 Matt 12:14; Luke 6:11.

In the parable of the sower, some seed fell on rocky ground, "and at once it sprang up, and when the sun was risen it was scorched."[448] The reference is to quick, ephemeral growth. Matthew agrees,[449] Luke omits it.[450] No parallel in John.

In the interpretation of the parable the adverb occurs three times. First, the parable itself mentions seed dropped by the way side and devoured by birds. This, we learn, means: "When they have heard, at once Satan cometh and taketh away the word."[451] "At once" equals "immediately." This is quite clear from the contrast with the next category of men, in the following verses, who at least initially take note of the word. Matthew omits the adverb,[452] Luke puts *eita,* "then."[453]

In the following verses, then, we are given the interpretation of the fast, ephemeral seed, and here we find *euthys* two more times: "When they have heard the word, at once they receive it with joy; and they have no root, then, when tribulation ariseth, at once they stumble."[454] Easy come, easy go: "at once" refers to superficial haste. The first "at once" is omitted by D. Matthew has the adverb both times,[455] Luke not at all.[456] No parallel in John.

In the parable of the seed growing secretly, the sower is confident and patient; "but when the fruit is ripe, at once he putteth forth the sickle."[457] "At once" means "immediately," emphasizing the contrast between the time of quiet wait and the moment of action. No parallel in other gospels.

The quotation from Joel is met also in Rabbinic eschatology.[458] That might be said to be so natural as to have no relevance. But the Rabbis use it to oppose the period before ripeness to the moment of ripeness, and more than that, they use it to impress the futility of harvesting during the former and the efficiency in seizing the latter: "If a field is reaped before its time, even its straw is no good, if at its time, it is good."

When Jesus went ashore in the country of the Gadarenes, "at once there met him a man with an unclean sprit."[459] The adverb cannot be pressed, it rather means "in due course," "as had to happen at that stage." It is omitted by Matthew and Luke.[460] No parallel in John.

[448] Mark 4:5. The New English Bible correctly: "it sprouted quickly."

[449] Matt 13:5; see below, n. 545.

[450] Luke 8:6.

[451] Mark 4:4, 15. The New English Bible renders the sense: "No sooner have they heard it than Satan comes."

[452] Matt 13:19.

[453] Luke 8:12.

[454] Mark 4:16. The New English Bible renders the sense in the first half, "as soon as they hear, they accept," and translates literally in the second, "they fall away at once."

[455] Matt 13:20 f.; see below, n. 545.

[456] Luke 8:1.

[457] Mark 4:29, quoting Joel 4:13. The New English Bible renders the sense: "but no sooner as the crop is ripe, he sets to work."

[458] *Song of Songs Rab.* on 8:14; see Strack-Billerbeck, *op. cit.*, vol. 1 (1922), 672, vol. 4, pt. 2 (1928), 860.

[459] Mark 5:2. The New English Bible omits the adverb.

[460] Matt 8:28; Luke 8:27.

The devils asked to be sent into the swine, "and Jesus gave them leave at once."[461] However, an alternative reading is "and he gave them leave." To establish the exact import of "at once"—i.e. whether it means "immediately" or "duly"—it would be necessary to analyse the significance of request and response in this problematic episode. The adverb does not appear in Matthew or Luke.[462] No parallel in John.

The woman with an issue of blood touched Jesus's garment from behind, "and at once her blood dried up"[463]—the cure, that is, was immediate, as in other cases.[464] Matthew does not use "at once," but (disregarding major divergences) he does say that the woman was cured "from that hour."[465] Luke (otherwise less divergent) substitutes *parachrema* for *euthys*.[466] No parallel in John.

In the very next verse we read: "And at once, as Jesus perceived that virtue had gone out of him, turning him about he said."[467] Again, emphasis on immediacy: Jesus reacted without being first told. The notice is not represented in Matthew,[468] and Luke, among other change, omits "at once."[469] No parallel in John.

The New English Bible is extraordinarily emphatic as far as the cure is concerned: "And there and then the source dried up." By contrast, it does less than justice to Jesus's immediate discovery: "At the same time Jesus, aware, turned round." This is too smooth an idiom.

Jairus's daughter was reported to have died; "but Jesus at once, overhearing the word spoken, saith, Fear not."[470] The adverb is omitted in many MSS, but as it looks somewhat awkward and as it occupies a characteristically Marcan position,[471] the probability is that it is genuine. Anyhow it denotes immediacy, Jesus gives his assurance without first making enquiries. The incident is not represented in Matthew,[472] and Luke omits "at once."[473] No parallel in John.

Subsequently in this narrative, there are two more occurrences of the adverb. We are told how Jesus bade the girl arise, "and at once she arose."[474] The cure was immediate, as in other cases.[475] Matthew omits "at once,"[476] Luke substitutes *parachrema*.[477] No parallel in John.

461 Mark 5:13. The New English Bible follows the shorter reading, without "at once."

462 Matt 8:32; Luke 8:32.

463 Mark 5:29.

464 E.g. Mark 1:31, 42, above, 720.

465 Matt 9:22; see above, 714.

466 Luke 8:44; see above, 714.

467 Mark 5:30; cp. 2:8, above, 721.

468 Matt 9:22.

469 Luke 8:45 ff.

470 Mark 5:36. The New English Bible follows the reading without "at once."

471 See above, 718 f., in the discussion of Mark 1:10.

472 Matt 9:18 ff.

473 Luke 8:50.

474 Mark 5:42. The New English Bible correctly: "Immediately the girl got up."

475 Cp. Mark 5:29 just discussed.

476 Matt 9:25.

477 Luke 8:55; see above, 714.

The adverb recurs very soon after: "and they were at once astonished with a great astonishment."[478] Here "accordingly," "duly," "in the steady, continuous development of events," seems to be meant. Matthew and Luke omit it.[479] No parallel in John.

Herodias told her daughter to ask the king for the head of the Baptist; "and having come in at once with haste she asked."[480] Whether the meaning is near "immediately"—she came while the king was still at table—or "accordingly—in pursuance of her mother's desire—is hard to say. D omits the adverb. Matthew makes no mention of an exit and re-entry.[481] No parallel in Luke[482] or John.

The story goes on to say that the king was sorry but could not refuse; "and at once, having sent forth a soldier, he commanded to bring his (the Baptist's) head."[483] The action in question here is preceded by reluctance, conflicting feelings, though finally the king decides that he has no choice. The adverb, it is evident, does not signify "immediately"; it signifies "accordingly," "duly," "as had to happen." It is omitted by Matthew.[484] No parallel in Luke or John.

Jesus fed a multitude; "and at once he constrained his disciples to enter into the boat, while he himself sendeth the multitude away."[485] Probably emphasis is laid on the immediacy of the departure of the disciples, as contrasted with the staying behind of Jesus. But it may be the more general Marcan *euthys,* "and so." It is taken over by Matthew;[486] John has *oun* in what may be regarded as the corresponding passage,[487] but this may well have nothing to do with the adverb in Mark.

The disciples, seeing Jesus walk on the sea, think him an apparition; "but he at once spoke with them, Be of good cheer."[488] Probably the word again denotes immediacy—either in the sense that Jesus lost no time in calming them or in that, that he spoke before they could take a wrong step to deal with a demon. D omits the word, and so does John;[489] but Matthew has it.[490] No parallel in Luke.

"And when they were come out of the ship, at once, knowing him, they (the people) ran through that whole region and began to carry the sick."[491] The meaning is

[478] Mark 5:42. The New English Bible approximates the sense by rendering: "At that they were beside themselves."

[479] Matt 9:26; Luke 8:56.

[480] Mark 6:25. The New English Bible correctly "the girl hastened back at once."

[481] Matt 14:8.

[482] Execution of the Baptist is mentioned in Luke 9:9.

[483] Mark 6:27. The New English Bible renders the sense "So the king sent a soldier with orders"; though the peculiarly Marcan attachment of the adverb to "he commanded" gets lost—see above, in connection with Mark 1:10, 718 f.

[484] Matt 14:10.

[485] Mark 6:45, cp. Mark 8:10, below, 725. The New English Bible: "As soon as it was over, he made his disciples embark."

[486] Matt 14:22; see below, n. 545.

[487] John 6:15.

[488] Mark 6:50. The New English Bible here admits "at once."

[489] John 6:20.

[490] Matt 14:27; see below, n. 545.

[491] Mark 6:54 f. The New English Bible correctly puts "immediately" but connects it with the wrong verb: "he was immediately recognized; and the people scoured." For the characteristically Marcan arrangement, see above, 718 f., under Mark 1:10.

"immediately," just as in the narrative of Jesus's return to Capernaum[492] or in the following text.[493] Matthew omits it.[494] No parallel in Luke or John.

Jesus's wish to remain unrecognized was in vain: "but at once, as a woman whose daughter had an unclean spirit had heard of him, she came and fell at his feet."[495] Immediacy, as in the text just discussed.[496] Matthew says nothing about the desire to remain unrecognized and the woman hearing about Jesus; "at once" is omitted, but we do find "behold," *idou*—Matthew starts "and behold a woman came."[497] No parallel in Luke or John.

The New English Bible strangely translates "almost at once." As elsewhere it connects the adverb with the wrong verb: "Almost at once a woman heard of him, came in and fell at his feet." In actual fact "at once" qualifies "she fell at his feet," in the manner explained above.[498]

A man who was deaf and suffered from a speech impediment was told by Jesus "Be opened": "and his ears were opened and at once the bond of his tongue was loosed."[499] The adverb may merely mean "and so," "and at the same time." It is however, possible that it stresses the immediacy of liberation, of free expression, once Jesus's word had been able to penetrate, so that a literal translation would be best. Many MSS omit the awkward word. No parallel in the other gospels.

Jesus fed a multitude (a second time) and sent them away; "and at once, having entered into a ship with his disciples, he came to Dalmanutha."[500] Probably "and in due course," though it is just conceivable that the immediacy of removal from the scene is being emphasized. Certainly no miraculously fast crossing is thought of, as in a Johannine story of a storm at sea to be inspected below.[501] Matthew omits "at once."[502] No parallel in Luke or John.[503]

In the story of the transfiguration, as already observed, in the ending "and suddenly, having looked round, they saw no one save Jesus," D substitutes "and at once," *kai eutheos*.[504] This seems a toning down to the more usual "and in due course," "in accordance with the course things had to take."

492 Mark 2:2; see above, 721.

493 Mark 7:25, to be discussed presently.

494 Matt 14:35.

495 Mark 7:25.

496 Mark 6:54 f.

497 Matt 15:21.

498 See 718 f. in connection with Mark 1:10.

499 Mark 7:35. The New English Bible may be rendering the sense correctly: "and at the same time." Though when it goes on "the impediment was removed," it eliminates important associations evoked by *elythe ho desmos*.

500 Mark 8:10; cp. 6:45, above, 724. The New English Bible connects *euthys* with the wrong verb, "and without delay got into the boat." For the right connection, see the discussion of Mark 1:10, above, 718 f. However, the editor who inserted *euthys* at the end of John 21:3 probably anticipated the misconstruction: see below, 732.

501 John 6:21; see below, 733.

502 Matt 15:39.

503 But see below, 732, on a variant in John 21:3.

504 Mark 9:8; see above, under *exapina*, 707.

Jesus joined his disciples who were surrounded by a crowd: "and at once all the crowd, when they beheld him, were greatly amazed."[505] Half-way between immediacy of effect and steady, necessary succession of events. The notice is not represented in Matthew[506] or Luke, though the latter, in telling how one of the crowd asked help for his son, begins "and behold (*idou*) a man of the company cried out."[507] No parallel in John.

One of the crowd, then, brought his son who was possessed; "and when the spirit saw him, at once he tore him."[508] Half-way between "immediately" and "as would happen." D omits it. The notice is not represented in Matthew.[509] Luke does not depict the seizure as the demon's reaction to the sight of Jesus, and he omits *euthys*. The latter may well, however, have influenced his version: he emphasizes that a seizure took place just as they were bringing the patient, "as he was yet a coming."[510] No parallel in John.

Euthys occurs a third time in this narrative. Jesus encouraged the father to believe; "at once, crying out, he said, I believe."[511] "At once" to be taken literally: the response was immediate. The dialogue is not represented in Matthew and Luke.[512] No parallel in John.

Jesus told Bartimaeus, "Thy faith hath made thee whole": "and at once he received his sight."[513] The cure was immediate, as in other cases.[514] Matthew agrees,[515] Luke substitutes *parachrema*.[516] No parallel in John.

In the preparation of the entry into Jerusalem, *euthys* occurs twice, both times pregnantly in the sense "in due course," "in the appropriate succession of events." Jesus sends two disciples into a village, "and at once, entering, ye shall find a colt."[517] If the emphasis were on immediacy, surely the adverb would be resumed a few verses further on, where the execution of the mission is reported; but it is not.[518] Matthew agrees—though, by ejection of the participle "entering," the typically Marcan structure ("at once"—participle—main verb to which "at once" belongs) is dissolved.[519] Luke omits the adverb.[520] No parallel in John.

[505] Mark 9:15. The New English Bible: "As soon as they saw Jesus, the whole crowd was overcome with awe." For the structure of the sentence, see above, 718 f., in connection with Mark 1:10.

[506] Matt 17:14.

[507] Luke 9:37 f.

[508] Mark 9:20. The New English Bible renders the sense: "And as soon as the spirit saw him, it threw him into convulsions."

[509] Matt 17:14 ff.

[510] Luke 9:42. In Luke 22:60, discussed above, 715, "while he yet spake" is coupled with a *parachrema* taking the place of a Synoptic *euthys*.

[511] Mark 9:24. The New English Bible suppresses the adverb. For the structure of the sentence, see above, 718 f., in connection with Mark 1:10.

[512] Matt 17:18; Luke 9:42.

[513] Mark 10:52. The New English Bible does translate "at once."

[514] E.g. Mark 1:31, 42, above, 720.

[515] Matt 20:34, see below, n. 545.

[516] Luke 18:43; see above, 714 f., 720.

[517] Mark 11:2. The New English Bible "just as you enter"; yet in this case a literal understanding seems inadequate. For the structure of the sentence, see above, under Mark 1:10, 718 f.

[518] Mark 11:4.

[519] Matt 21:2; see below, 729, and n. 545.

[520] Luke 19:30.

Jesus goes on to explain to his disciples that they are to take the colt and, if challenged, to declare: "The Lord hath need of him and at once he will send him again hither."[521] Hardly a promise of direct return, out of keeping with the majestic demand: the meaning must be "in due course." It is perhaps worth remarking that if you borrow without the owner's knowledge (Cambridge undergraduate cyclists, please note!), according to the School of Shammai you are a *gazlan*, "thief," "robber," according to that of Hillel a proper borrower.[522]

Matthew retains the adverb but apparently makes this part of the sentence into a prediction of the challenger's understanding; "again is omitted—so we get "and at once he will send them," i.e. the challenger will allow the animals (in Matthew it is two animals) to be taken.[523] The challenger seems to have become the owner, who can confer the right to use his property. Even so, the sense may well be "duly," as in the preceding verse "at once ye shall find." Luke omits the difficult clause.[524] No parallel in John.

"Behold," said Jesus, "he that betrayeth me is at hand"—"and at once, while he yet spake, cometh Judas."[525] Here emphasis on immediacy—Judas comes the moment Jesus announces him—and emphasis on the blow upon blow, *planmässige*, course of things coincide. The New English Bible is very wrong in introducing a break instead of stressing continuity: "Suddenly Judas appeared." This was anything but "sudden."

D omits the adverb. So do Matthew and Luke, though both, after "while he yet spake," insert "behold," *idou*.[526] In Luke indeed, Jesus does not announce Judas's coming. The account in John differs.[527]

Judas had told those whom he brought that the man he would kiss would be Jesus; "and, having come, at once, having gone up to him, he saith, Master."[528] Half-way between "immediately" and "duly." D omits it. Matthew has it;[529] though, in view of this evangelist's misconstruction of the same syntax in an earlier case,[530] it may well be that he means "and at once having gone up to Jesus, he said"—not, as Mark, "and at once, having gone up, he saith." At any rate the New English Bible, while admitting "at once," connects it with the wrong verb: "he came forward at once."

Luke omits "at once" in pursuance of other changes: he does not say that Judas had pre-arranged the kiss.[531] The incident is not noted in John.[532]

[521] Mark 11:3. The New English Bible "without delay," but once more we prefer the other, typically Marcan sense.

[522] *b. B. M.* 43b, cp. *b. B. B.* 88a.

[523] Matt 21:3; see below, n. 545.

[524] Luke 19:31.

[525] Mark 14:43. The structure of the sentence is similar to that explained above, 718 f., in connection with Mark 1:10.

[526] Matt 26:47; Luke 22:47.

[527] John 18:3. Verse 4 contains a reference to Jesus's foreknowledge.

[528] Mark 14:45.

[529] Matt 26:49; see below, 729, and n. 545.

[530] Matt 3:16 misconstruing Mark 1:10, see above, 718. Cp. also Matt 4:20 very likely misconstruing Mark 1:18; see above, 718.

[531] Luke 22:47. In verse 48, however, such a pre-arrangement is alluded to.

[532] John 18:3 f.

Jesus had predicted to Peter that before the cock would crow twice he would betray him three times; Peter did deny him a first, a second, a third time—"and at once the second time the cock crew."[533] Probably: "in due course," no miracle in the narrow sense, just the inevitable chain of events. Matthew and John also have "at once";[534] whereas Luke substitutes *parachrema* and adds "while he yet spake," more in the nature of a miracle or rather, as shewn above, an immediate compliance with Jesus's prediction.[535]

Finally, "And at once in the morning the chief priests, having consulted, having bound Jesus, carried him away and delivered him to Pilate."[536] "In due course," "accordingly," "as had to happen." Neither Matthew nor Luke nor John has the adverb.[537] Matthew writes *de*, a non-committal particle, John, on the other hand, *oun*, not so remote in sense from the Marcan *kai euthys*. The New English Bible omits "at once," thus assimilating Mark to the other Synoptics.

Weiss noted[538] that *euthys* in Mark frequently defies literal rendering, and that in many of these passages it is absent from a variant reading or the parallel version in other gospels. The conclusion he drew was that the adverb was employed by Mark on a very small number of occasions only, and that everywhere else it is due to later scribes. This goes counter to the—still sound—working hypothesis in favour of the more difficult alternative. Kilpatrick avoids this mistake.[539] But he may be too extreme in another direction. From the fact that in the vast majority of cases *euthys* comes at the beginning of its clause, he infers that it is not in Mark an adverb of time but a mere connecting particle.

However, in not a few texts the literal force of "at once" is clear—in most of those, for example, where Luke substitutes *parachrema*.[540] As for the others, quite likely part of the explanation is that *euthys* at the time may have been widely used in a reduced, worn-out sense, as a connecting particle. But it is only part of the explanation. Its role in Mark is too uniformly a little more than only that; a fact underlined by cases where the position of the particle is rather subtle, certainly not mechanical.[541] Perhaps the proper way of putting it is that Mark had a reason to choose just this connecting particle where he did—the reason being that it does express the inevitable, one-after-the-other succession of events, from the first temptation to the final delivering over to Pilate. There are two or three lengthy stretches without the adverb, notably the day of questions,[542] the Synoptic Apocalypse,[543] the passion.[544] Were these taken over from some source or sources without much modification? Or is it accident?

533 Mark 14:30, 72. The New English Bible, weakly, "Then the cock crew a second time."

534 Matt 26:74; John 18:27; see below, 734, and. n. 545.

535 Luke 22:60; see above, 715.

536 Mark 15:1. For the structure of the sentence, see above, 718 f., in connection with Mark 1:10.

537 Matt 27:1; Luke 22:66; John 18:28.

538 *ZNW*, 11 (1910), 124 ff.

539 *The Bible Translator*, 7 (1958), 2 f.

540 Mark 1:31, 2:12, 5:29, 5:42, 10:52, 14:72.

541 E.g. "and he arose and at once went out before all" in Mark 2:12; above, 721.

542 Mark 12.

543 Mark 13.

544 Mark 15:2 to the end.

b) *Matthew*

In Matthew, the adverb appears less than half as often as in Mark—eighteen times. That may be the reason why it is never, it seems, omitted in variants: it is already suppressed in most of the awkward places. In fourteen texts it appears in Mark as well as Matthew, and we shall not dwell on them.[545] This leaves four.

Peter, walking on the water, cried for help; "and Jesus, at once stretching forth his arm, caught him."[546] The meaning is "immediately." The incident is not recorded in Mark or John,"[547] and there is no parallel in Luke.

That the saviour should respond without delay is natural; a rescue *eutheos* from danger at sea by Serapis is mentioned in a papyrus.[548] What is remarkable is that, at first sight, in this as in two more texts to be inspected presently, we seem to have before us the structure so greatly favoured by Mark: a participle separating "at once" from the verb it qualifies.[549] We might interpret, that is, "and at once Jesus, stretching forth his arm, caught him." But Matthew probably means it the other way. Going through the four texts where Mark has his characteristic structure and *euthys* recurs in the Matthean parallel, we find that Matthew misunderstands the structure—i.e. connects the adverb with the participle—in at least one,[550] very likely two,[551] possibly three;[552] and in the fourth where he correctly connects the adverb with the main verb, he drops the participle.[553] It looks, therefore, as if, formally, in choosing the sequence "at once"—participle—main verb, Matthew might have been influenced by the Marcan style, but that syntactically, there is a difference: in Matthew "at once" does belong to the participle, in Mark it does not. This may be a complicated solution, but, then, the Synoptic relationships are complicated. The alternative would be to invoke some common source behind both Mark and Matthew—not only more complicated but also less plausible on other grounds.

The Synoptic Apocalypse warns of tribulations which will precede the coming of the Son of Man.[554] Then we are given a first description of his coming—it will be like lightning.[555] There follows a second description which starts: "and at once after the tribulation of those days shall the sun be darkened."[556] Meaning: "immediately." In Mark, the first description is not found. We hear of tribulations, then: "but in those days,

[545] Matt 3:16 with Mark 1:10; Matt 4:20, Mark 1:18; Matt 4:22, Mark 1:20; Matt 8:3, Mark 1:42; Matt 13:5, Mark 4:5; Matt 13:20, Mark 4:16; Matt 13:21, Mark 4:17; Matt 14:22, Mark 6:45; Matt 14:27, Mark 6:50; Matt 20:34, Mark 10:52; Matt 21:2, Mark 11:2; Matt 21:3, Mark 11:3; Matt 26:49, Mark 14:45; Matt 26:74, Mark 14:72.

[546] Matt 14:31. The New English Bible correctly "at once."

[547] Mark 6:45 ff.; John 6:15 ff.

[548] *BGU* 423.8 cited by Bauer, *Wörterbuch zum Neuen Testament*, 5th ed. (1958), 633, s.v. *eutheos.*

[549] See above, 718 f., the discussion of Mark 1:10.

[550] Matt 3:16; Mark 1:10, see above, 718.

[551] Matt 4:20; Mark 1:18, see above, 718.

[552] Matt 26:49; Mark 14:45, see above, 727.

[553] Matt 21:2; Mark 11:2, see above, 726.

[554] Matt 24:21 ff.

[555] Matt 24:26 ff.

[556] Matt 24:29. The New English Bible: "As soon as the distress of those days has passed."

after that tribulation the sun shall be darkened."[557] Luke is similar to Mark in this respect.[558] *Eutheos de* in Matthew is inserted, we conclude, in order to regain contact, across the first description of the parousia, with the period of tribulation. No parallel in John.

In the parable of the talents, a man about to travel entrusted various servants with various sums of money; "he who had received the five talents, at once going forth, traded with them."[559] Meaning: "immediately"—the good servant lost no time in setting to work. As in the story about Peter,[560] the structure looks Marcan and we might translate "at once he who had received the five talents, going forth, traded with them." But more likely Matthew connects *eutheos* with the participle.

According to a variant reading, certainly inferior, "at once" belongs to the previous clause, concerning the master: "and he took his journey at once." The meaning would still be "immediately." That is to say, no instructions were given, the servants were left to make their own decisions.

The parallel in Luke is told quite differently.[561] No parallel in Mark or John.

Some of those who witnessed the crucifixion said that Jesus was calling Elijah; "and one of them, at once running and taking a sponge, gave him to drink."[562] The meaning is "immediately": the man acted before the other bystanders expressed their different attitude.[563] The word does not appear in Mark but, then, in Mark the man's action is not followed by an utterance of the others.[564] The accounts of Luke and John are rather different.[565]

Let us note that, as in two of the texts discussed above,[566] we might connect "at once" with the main verb, "gave him to drink." But Matthew hardly intends this structure.

It emerges that where Matthew uses "at once" independently of Mark, a literal interpretation is safest. The same, we shall see, is true of Luke. This is not in conflict with the observation that to emphasize, against Mark, the immediate fulfilment of a curse uttered by Jesus, Matthew uses *parachrema.*[567]

c) *Luke*

In Luke, the adverb occurs seven times; only once in agreement with Mark—"and at once the leprosy departed from him."[568] In one passage (which, if we counted it, would bring the total up to eight), in a saying exclusive to Luke, "at once" is second-

557 Mark 13:24.

558 Luke 21:25.

559 Matt 25:15 f. The New English Bible has "at once."

560 Matt 14:31.

561 Luke 19:12.

562 Matt 27:48. The New English Bible: "at once."

563 Matt 27:49.

564 Mark 15:36.

565 Luke 23:35 ff.; John 19:28 f.

566 Matt 14:31, 25:15 f.

567 Matt 21:19 f.; Mark 11:11 ff.; see above, 712.

568 Luke 5:13; Mark 1:42; see above, 720.

ary: "and no man having drunk old wine at once desireth new."[569] *Eutheos* is not well attested; it is evidently inserted by post-Lucan editors in order to mitigate the—no doubt originally pre-Lucan—saying, which seems to recommend the old regime.[570]

He that hears Jesus but does not act on it is like one building a house without proper foundation, "against which the stream brake and at once it fell in."[571] Meaning "immediately." D omits the word, as does Matthew—but in Matthew it would not be so fitting since he enumerates a series of assaults the house suffers before collapsing: "and the rain descended, and the floods came, and the winds blew and smote upon that house, and it fell."[572] Matthew is near to Ezekiel in this respect.[573] In a simile like this we must indeed allow for freedom in detail. In the Rabbinic models, sometimes we do find *miyyadh,* "at once," sometimes we do not.[574] No parallel in Mark or John. Nowadays, of course, it would be acting without hearing that would be compared to building a house without foundations.

"Be like unto men looking for their lord; that when he cometh and knocketh, they may at once open to him."[575] "Immediately." No direct parallel in the other gospels, but readiness is of course enjoined in Matthew and Mark.[576]

"When ye see a cloud rising in the west, at once ye say, There cometh a shower."[577] "Immediately"—without hesitation, genuine or affected, in contrast to their refusal to appreciate the present crisis. That there is not overmuch emphasis on it is evident from the following verse, where it is not resumed: "and when ye see a south wind blowing, ye say, there will be a scorching heat."[578] In the Matthean parallel the adverb does not appear—no great matter.[579] No parallel in Luke or John.

"Which of you shall have a son (ass?) or an ox fallen into a well, and will not at once draw him up on a sabbath day?"[580] "Immediately"—in much the same application as in the text just considered: no hesitation, genuine or affected, in contrast to the attitude they shew when a sick man is brought before Jesus on a Sabbath. But again, there is not overmuch emphasis, and it is not surprising that "at once" is absent from a parallel rhetorical question in Matthew.[581] In another, generally comparable Lucan pas-

[569] Luke 5:39; absent from Matt 9:16 f.; Mark 2:21 f.

[570] See Lagrange, *L'Evangile selon Saint Luc* (1921), 173.

[571] Luke 6:49; cp. Jas 1:23, below, 737. the New English Bible: "As soon as the river burst upon it, it collapsed."

[572] Matt 7:27.

[573] Ezek 13:11 ff.

[574] Strack-Billerbeck, *op. cit.*, vol. 1 (1922), 469, gives references. *Miyyadh*, e.g., in *Ab. de R. N.* 24:2, 3, 4; not in 22 (equals *m. Ab.* 3:18).

[575] Luke 12:36. The New English Bible: "ready to let him in the moment he arrives."

[576] E.g. Matt 24:43 ff., 25:1 ff.; Mark 13:33 ff.; see above, 704 ff.

[577] Luke 12:54; cp. the next text, Luke 14:5. The New English Bible: "at once."

[578] Luke 12:55.

[579] Matt 16:2 f. The authenticity of these verses is questioned; but there is much to be said for their being genuine, and for the textual position being the result of attempts to overcome difficulties created by them.

[580] Luke 14:5. The New English Bible: "will he hesitate to haul him up?"—a very apt rendering of the sense.

[581] Matt 12:11.

sage, "at once" would indeed be out of place since it is a question, not of reaction to some event, but of regular, customary procedure: "Doth not each one of you on the sabbath loose his ox or ass and lead him away to watering?"[582]

"But who is there of you, having a servant, that will say unto him when he is come in from the field, At once coming up sit down to meat, and will not rather say, Make ready wherewith I may sup, and afterward thou shalt eat?"[583] "Immediately"—in contrast to delay through further work indoors before mealtime.

Whether Luke means to connect "at once" with the participle—in Matthew's way—or with the main verb—in Mark's—make little difference. Lagrange prefers attachment to the participle,[584] as does the New English Bible: "Come along at once and sit down." They may well be right. It is just conceivable—though extremely unlikely—that we ought to connect *eutheos* with the preceding clause: "Who is there that will say at once, Coming up sit down, and will not rather say." The sense would not be greatly affected even then.

Some inferior MSS omit "at once." No parallel in the other gospels.

In the Synoptic Apocalypse, we learn that there will be wars; "for these things must needs come to pass first, but the end is not at once."[585] Again "at once" in the literal sense. In Matthew and Mark the word "first" is not found, and instead of "not at once" we find "not yet."[586] Exactly what the difference implies cannot here be examined.

It is not enough to say that "at once" in Luke always means "immediately." What is equally interesting is that, with a single exception, where it comes from Mark,[587] it never overlaps with *parachrema.* It never, that is, describes the immediate submission to an order by Jesus or the like. Why in that one passage Luke has failed to substitute *parachrema* we cannot say. Plainly, our contention that *parachrema* has a very special meaning is strongly supported by the almost complete denial of this role to *euthys.* Our survey of Acts will lead to a similar result.

d) *John*

John uses *euthys* and *eutheos* sparingly—six times, if we discount a clause in the last chapter: "and they entered into the boat at once."[588] "At once" is weakly attested. The meaning approaches that common in Mark, but found nowhere else in John: "duly." Probably the word was here inserted by an editor under the influence of Mark's style, especially a passage "at once, having entered a boat with his disciples, he came to Dalmanutha"—which the editor in question no doubt understood as "having at once entered the boat, he came."[589]

Jesus told a lame man at Bethesda, "Arise, take up thy bed and walk"—"and at

[582] Luke 13:15.
[583] Luke 17:7 f. The New English Bible: "at once."
[584] *Op. cit.*, 455.
[585] Luke 21:9. The New English Bible correctly: "but the end does not follow immediately."
[586] Matt 24:6; Mark 13:7. There are other divergences looking slight but possibly significant.
[587] Luke 5:13; Mark 1:42, the first text to be discussed in this section; above 730.
[588] John 21:3.
[589] Mark 8:10; see above, 725.

once the man was made whole."[590] Meaning: "immediately." D omits it, as does Matthew in a comparable context.[591] Mark in that context, however, does have *euthys*,[592] Luke *parachrema*.[593]

The disciples, in a boat during a storm, saw Jesus walking on the sea; they were frightened, but Jesus reassured them and they were willing to take him into their boat—"and at once the boat was at the land whither they were going."[594] Meaning: "immediately." This particular miracle is not met in the corresponding pericopes in Matthew and Mark; and there is no parallel in Luke. However, "at once" repeatedly occurs in those pericopes: "and at once he constrained his disciples to enter into the boat,"[595] "he at once spoke with them,[596] "he at once stretched forth his arm and caught him."[597] The latter two passages are, of course, more relevant than the first if we look for a possible source of influence.

In this connection it is also worth recalling that, in Mark, after the second feeding of a multitude, Jesus "at once, having entered into the ship with his disciples, came to Dalmanutha."[598] In John there is only one feeding, and it is after this that the storm and miraculous crossing take place. To be sure, Mark intends no miracle.

"He then having received the sop went out at once."[599] Meaning: "immediately." Whether the prompt departure takes place in obedience to Jesus's request to act quickly,[600] or as a result of the sop's and Satan's entry into Judas—the sop is mentioned four times in this brief episode[601]—or for a variety of causes, we cannot decide.

The New English Bible suppresses "at once." Yet it is anything but a mere connecting particle, nor does it even stand at the beginning of the sentence. Certainly John, as distinct from the Synoptics, wishes to make it unmistakably clear that Judas left at this stage, before the farewell discourses, the glorification. He reiterates the fact in opening the following section: "When therefore he was gone out, Jesus saith."[602] In the Synoptics it remains obscure how and when Judas detached himself.[603] John alone, too, explains how he could find the place where Jesus was arrested.[604]

Towards the beginning of the farewell discourses, Jesus says: "and at once he (God) shall glorify him (the Son of Man)."[605] Meaning: "immediately." It would lead too far

[590] John 5:9. The New English Bible: "The man recovered instantly."
[591] Matt 9:7.
[592] Mark 2:12; see above, 721.
[593] Luke 5:25; see above, 713 f.
[594] John 6:21. The New English Bible: "immediately."
[595] Matt 14:22; Mark 6:45; see above, 724, and n. 545.
[596] Matt 14:27; Mark 6:50; see above, 724 f., and n. 545.
[597] Matt 14:31; see above, 729.
[598] Mark 8:10; see above, 724.
[599] John 13:30.
[600] John 13:27.
[601] John 13:26, twice, 27, 30.
[602] John 13:31.
[603] Matt 26:21 ff.; Mark 14:18 ff.; Luke 22:21 ff.
[604] John 18:2.
[605] John 13:32.

afield to go into the implications of this announcement. One of them may be that the cross, not a subsequent coming, constitutes fulfilment.[606] We shall soon come across another text where immediate fulfilment is stressed.[607] No parallel in other gospels.

The New English Bibles translates: "and he will glorify him now." This would be sound in the abstract, but it is inadequate when held together with the beginning of the speech: "Now (*nyn*) is the Son of Man glorified." John's subtle play on time and tense is lost if different adverbs—rare ones, too—are rendered the same way.

"Peter then denied again, and at once the cock crew."[608] Meaning: "immediately." As pointed out above, both Matthew and Mark also have "at once," whereas Luke turns it into *parachrema*.[609] Actually the Johannine version of the cock-crow is in literal agreement with Matthew (except that John has *eutheos,* Matthew *euthys*); Mark has "a second time," Luke "while he yet spake," and in Luke, moreover, instead of "the cock crew" we find "crew the cock." In the prediction of the incident, John essentially agrees with Luke against the others: "The cock shall not crow till thou hast denied me thrice."[610] However, in John, the prediction takes place in pursuance of the idea that no one can follow Jesus at this stage.[611] This may account for the absence, after the cock-crow, of any remark as to the subjective effect on Peter: the inability to follow has been objectively established and sealed—that is enough.

"But one of the soldiers pierced his side and there came out at once blood and water."[612] Meaning: "immediately." We need not go into the manifold implications. It suffices to say that the miracle consists, not in the flow of blood, but in that of water. The former, if a man barely dead was stabbed, would be taken for granted;[613] the latter would be unheard of. The sequence of word bears out this conclusion: "and water" carries the accent. This is not to deny that there may be a hint at baptism and eucharist—John excels in multivalence—but if that were the primary intention, we should get the "correct" sequence,[614] water and blood. The primary intention goes to the miracle of the flow of water. "There came out at once blood *and water*": the prophecies of Zechariah are realized right at this moment—"In that day there shall a fountain be opened," or "And it shall come to pass in that day that living waters shall go forth from Jerusalem."[615] Salvation, John means to convey, or the offer of it at least, is there. As we have just seen, an earlier passage, at the beginning of the farewell discourses, may be designed to emphasize the concept of the cross as fulfilment.[616]

[606] See Bultmann, *Das Evangelium des Johannes,* 14th ed. (1956), 401.

[607] John 19:34; below.

[608] John 18:27. The New English Bible renders the sense: "and just then a cock crew." But why it is "a cock" here and in Luke 22:60, and "the cock" in Matt 26:74 and Mark 14:72, is a puzzle. The Greek has the article in none of the four texts, nor in any of the four predictions.

[609] Matt 26:74; Mark 14:72; Luke 22:60; see above, 715, 728, and n. 545.

[610] John 13:38; cp. Matt 26:34; Mark 14:30; Luke 22:34; see above, 715, 728.

[611] On the singularity of John in this matter see Daube ["Death as a Release in the Bible"], *NT* 5 (1962), 92 f.

[612] John 19:34. The New English Bible: "at once."

[613] Cp. the Babylonian example adduced by Bauer, *Das Johannesevangelium,* 2nd ed. (1925), 219.

[614] For which Bauer, *op. cit.*, 220, cites 1 John 5:6.

[615] Zech 13:1, 14:8.

[616] John 13:32; see above, 733.

A verse from this part of Zechariah is actually quoted by John in the pericope under review: "They shall look on him whom they pierced."[617] Both prophecies, "In that day" and "And it shall come to pass," as well as others referring to the waters which with the advent of the Messiah will flow from the sanctuary, figure in ancient Rabbinic exegesis.[618] There is an allusion to the second of the two prophecies in Revelation: "And he shewed me a pure river of water of life, proceeding out of the throne of God and of the lamb."[619] The thought of Jesus as Temple may indeed play a part in the Johannine miracle.[620]

In John, in sum, the adverb is used in six vital texts. It is used with deliberation. Its force must not be played down. The healing command of Jesus was at once obeyed.[621] Willing to receive Jesus, the disciples at once arrived at their destination.[622] Judas having received the sop at once departed.[623] Jesus announced that God would at once glorify him.[624] On Peter's third denial, the cock crew at once.[625] On Jesus's death his body was pierced and at once blood and water appeared.[626] The list is a tribute to John's masterly handling of vocabulary, with its apparently most negligible members becoming powerful instruments of his thought.

e) *Acts*

Ten texts in Acts, and the adverb has its literal meaning in all of them, just as in Luke.

Ananias in Jesus's name laid hands in Paul, "and at once there fell from his eyes as it had been scales."[627] "Immediately"—as in the story of Peter telling Aeneas in Jesus's name to arise and make his bed, "and at once he arose."[628] In Luke, it may be recalled, in a passage agreeing with Mark, we found "and at once the leprosy departed from him,"[629] though in general, in cases of this type, the evangelist definitely prefers *parachrema* in the place of *eutheos*. But as argued above this seems due to secondary interference.[630]

The adverb comes again two verses after Paul's cure. He stayed a while at Damascus "and at once he preached Jesus in the synagogues."[631] "Immediately": he lost no time. There is, however, a complication. In Galatians also "at once" occurs in the report about Paul's activity following his conversion, and here it is stated that his

[617] John 19:17; Zech 12:10.

[618] *t. Sukk.* 3:9, in the main quite like dating from New Testament times; cited by Strack-Billerbeck, *op. cit.*, vol. 3 (1926), 854 f.

[619] Rev 22:1; Zech 14:8.

[620] Cp. John 2:21, 4:20 ff.

[621] John 5:9.

[622] John 6:21.

[623] John 13:30.

[624] John 13:32.

[625] John 18:27.

[626] John 19:34.

[627] Acts 9:18. The New English Bible: "immediately."

[628] Acts 9:34.

[629] Luke 5:13; Mark 1:42; see above, 720, 730 f.

[630] See above, 717.

[631] Acts 9:20.

first step was to go to Arabia and only then he returned for a stay at Damascus: "But when it pleased God to reveal his Son in me, that I might preach him among the heathen, at once I conferred not with flesh and blood but went into Arabia and returned again unto Damascus."[632] A slightly different punctuation is just conceivable, but it would not affect the point here of relevance: "that I might preach him among the heathen at once, I conferred not."

There may well be legitimate ways of harmonizing the two accounts. But they ought not to be harmonized by weakening *eutheos* in Acts, i.e. by translating it "at some stage not long afterwards" and reading into this an allusion to an interval spent in Arabia. (Maybe that is what the New English Bible intends with its weak rendering: "soon was proclaiming Jesus." In Galatians, it does accept "at once.") This would be not only to ascribe to the adverb a sense it never has in Luke or Acts—nor even in Mark—but also to credit author and public with a supernatural degree of subtlety.

In a trance Peter saw a vessel descend from heaven filled with unclean beasts and he heard an order to kill and eat. "And this was done thrice, and at once the vessel was received up into heaven."[633] "Immediately"—as in the story of Peter helped out of prison: "and at once the angel departed from him."[634] The sight displayed in a vision and the miraculous deliverer both disappear from one moment to the other: that is the very hallmark of a temporary supernatural intervention of this kind.

In the former case, some inferior MSS omit *euthys,* and this variant has found defenders[635]— for no good reason. The very fact that the text sounds smoother without the adverb speaks in its favour; and so does the very similar application in the episode of Peter's liberation.

When Elymas was condemned by Paul to lose his sight for a time, "straightway there fell on him a mist."[636] An inferior variant replaces *parachrema* by the commoner *eutheos.* A cripple was told by Paul, "Stand upright on thy feet"—"and he leaped up and walked."[637] And inferior variant reads "and at once straightway [*eutheos parachrema*] he leaped up and walked"—no doubt taking over both adverbs from other narratives of this type. We did not include these two occurrences of "at once" above, when speaking of ten texts in Acts.

At Troas, Paul had a vision of a Macedonian asking for help: "and when he had seen the vision, at once we sought to go forth into Macedonia."[638] "Immediately," in obedience to God's call. There is a variant which, in the course of a general rationalization of the account, omits the adverb.

[632] Gal 1:16. On the relation between the two reports, see e.g. Jacquier, *Les Actes des Apôtres,* 2nd ed. (1926), 293 f.

[633] Acts 10:16. The New English Bible: "and then."

[634] Acts 12:10. The New English Bible suppresses the adverb.

[635] Jacquier, *op. cit.*, 319.

[636] Acts 13:11.

[637] Acts 14:10; see above, 716 f.

[638] Acts 16:10. The New English Bible: "at once."

Whether Paul and Silas were in danger at Thessalonica or whether the magistrates ordered them to leave, "the brethren at once by night sent them away unto Beroea."[639] "Immediately." The adverb is omitted in an inferior variant. The Jews at Thessalonica, however, stirred up trouble at Beroea too, "and at once, thereupon, the brethren sent forth Paul."[640] "Immediately."

A crowd dragged Paul out of the Temple "and at once the doors were shut."[641] "Immediately."

Paul, about to be scourged, invoked his Roman citizenship: "at once, then, they which were about to examine him departed from him."[642] "Immediately."

Much as in Luke, "at once" in Acts always means "at once." There are two stories (in Luke there was one) where it is used in the specific sense otherwise represented by *parachrema,* namely, the cures of Paul and Aeneas.[643] Curiously, the two stories are found very close to one another. A third story might at first sight look a candidate for *parachrema,* but it is not. When Paul and his companions, moved by the former's vision at Troas, "at once" resolved to travel to Macedonia, that was not a direct, miraculous consequence of the vision. It was a rational decision, taken by them since they were "assuredly gathering that the Lord has called us."[644] It was taken "at once": they knew no hesitation in accepting the call. But it is not as if the vision had effected it *parachrema. Eutheos* is the right word, from the point of view of usage in Luke and Acts. The case in fact underlines that usage.

f) *Epistles and Revelation*

As for the three passages in the Epistles. We have already mentioned Galatians, apparently insisting that Paul directly after his conversion preached to the gentiles, and thus difficult to reconcile with the account in Acts.[645]

According to James, a man who hears the word but does not act on it is like one who observes his face in a mirror "and goeth his way and at once forgetteth what manner of man he was."[646] The meaning is "immediately"—this passing sight does not stay in the mind at all. (The shadowy character of the image itself may also influence the choice of simile.) What the author wishes to convey is that only by doing is the word kept alive, its impression made lasting.

The author of 3 John finishes by saying that instead of writing he hopes "at once to see thee."[647] Quite apart from the fact that in concluding phrases of letters a good deal of irregular grammar and meaning is apt to creep in—we know too little of the situation

[639] Acts 17:10; see Jacquier, *op. cit.*, 516. The New English Bible: "as soon as darkness fell."

[640] Acts 17:14. The New English Bible: "at once."

[641] Acts 21:30. The New English Bible: "at once."

[642] Acts 22:29. The New English Bible renders the sense correctly: "withdrew hastily."

[643] Acts 9:18, 34; cp. Luke 5:13, above, 730, 732.

[644] Acts 16:10.

[645] Gal 1:16; Acts 9:20; see above, 735 f..

[646] Jas 1:23; cp. Luke 6:49, above, 731. The New English Bible: "very soon." This is a far more responsible, cautious, scholarly statement: but it is not James.

[647] 3 John 14. The New English Bible may well give the correct sense: "very soon."

to decides which is more plausible, a literal interpretation, "immediately," or a vaguer, "shortly," "very soon." Perhaps rather the latter.

Lastly, Revelation. "A door opened in heaven, and the voice as it were of a trumpet talking with me, Come up hither. At once (and at once?) I was in the spirit."[648] "Immediately": a miraculous transposition.

5. MORE DEFINITION

The sudden event is unexpected, swift, startling; we might speak of a striking discontinuity. To take the three attributes in reverse order, we have repeatedly insisted on the third. A supernatural intervention may terminate as swiftly as it begins, but, as pointed out in the discussion of Mark's transfiguration,[649] since in general its beginning takes you aback far more than its termination, it is to the former that the qualification "sudden" normally attaches. A theft may be totally unexpected but, as pointed out in the discussion of a warning in the last judgment in 1 Thessalonians,[650] since it does not startle (though, to be sure, the news of it may), it is not described as "sudden." Speed and suddenness are near enough for the Hebrew noun *regha'*, "moment," to be used in elevated Old Testament speech in the sense of "suddenly." But in English, for example, "in a moment" never quite has that sense. (On the other hand, the noun "start," which may still signify "sudden move," at one time signified also "moment"; how the two uses are related must be left open.) Nor has *regha'* that sense in post-Biblical Hebrew. Nor has the phase "twinkling of an eye" that sense; it will be discussed below.[651] It would not do to curse an enemy, "May he lose health and fortune in the twinkling of an eye."

Speed is allied to suddenness in various ways; three of them may be mentioned. First, if you wish to achieve suddenness, an unexpected stroke, you may have to proceed speedily—otherwise your plan may become known. The Gibeonites, besieged, asked Joshua to their aid "quickly" (Hebrew *mehera,* LXX *tachos*), and his "sudden" attack on their besiegers took place after a night march.[652] Of course, there is no speed of this kind where you do not plan; say, you kill somebody without intent, "suddenly."[653] Nor, by the same token, where impersonal forces produce the suddenness. God indeed need not hurry even if he plans a sudden intervention.[654]

Secondly, in early literature, where the sudden is always a catastrophe, speed may be a consequence of it—you run away in a panic. We observed above that *bhl* is among the roots characteristically in the neighbourhood of suddenness:[655] it signifies "terror" and, in the later sources, "haste." Some texts listed by the dictionaries under the latter sense perhaps still shew a trace of the former: they refer to haste in the service or at the

[648] Rev 4:2. The New English Bible: "at once."

[649] Mark 9:8; see above, 707 f.

[650] 1 Thes 5:3; see above, 704 f.

[651] See 740 f.

[652] Josh 10:6, 9; see above, 685.

[653] Num 35:22; see above, 684.

[654] E.g. Num 6:9; Luke 2:13—the idea of speed of the kind in question is definitely not present; see above, 684, 706.

[655] See 690 f., 697.

word of a king.[656] In one passage the causative *hibhhil* is used of the priests "hurrying out" King Uzziah when, in the act of usurping their functions in the sanctuary, he was smitten with leprosy.[657]

Above all, thirdly, the sudden event itself is swift, altering the situation in no time. One could not say, "In the course of the 20th century the Empire experienced a sudden reversal of fortune," however unexpected and startling the change might have been. The LXX, translating the Psalmist's wish that his enemies be ashamed "in a moment," has *dia tachous*, "quickly."[658] The same phrase is employed in Sirach, with regard to the "sudden" turn for the better to be hoped for by a poor man who is pious.[659] In Lamentations, sinful Sodom is overthrown "as in a moment" in the Hebrew, *hosper spoudei* in the LXX.[660] Luther frequently renders "suddenly" as *schnell*, "quickly"; for example in the Lucan warning lest *komme dieser Tag schnell über euch*.[661] We have already drawn attention to *regha'*, "moment," in the sense of "suddenly."[662]

It might indeed be argued that, as a rule, the outcome, the culmination, of a gradual process may be anticipated; and that accordingly, swiftness and unexpectedness are more or less the same, or two sides of a medal—the former an objective attribute of the event, the latter the subjective state of the person affected. However, there is something to be said for separate headings.

As for unexpectedness, this is essential and its importance, in early times especially but still today, reflects man's awareness of his limitations, his being in the hands of forces he cannot direct. However, the unexpected that is not swift and striking at the same time is not "sudden." If on waking up I find the sun shining, contrary to the pessimistic weather forecast, it is not a case of "suddenness." The unexpected news of Miss X's engagement to Mr Y may or may not be "sudden" according as I have reason to be shocked or no.

Unexpectedness is relative. Within the general scheme of things, any person is liable to die at any moment. Yet that is not how life affects us: the Pentateuch speaks of a Nazarite being with a man and that man "suddenly" dying.[663] What is meant is that, at that particular moment, that contingency had not entered into the Nazarite's calculations. The pious poor is encouraged to trust that God will "suddenly" make him rich.[664] The unexpected "sudden" may be embedded, that is, within a wider framework of expectation; and the framework need not always be so wide as in the case of liability to death or the justice of God. If I tinker with the electric switch, my friends know what will be the result, yet when the lights go out it may strike them as "sudden."

Unless we bear this relative nature of unexpectedness in mind we may find diffi-

656 Eccl 8:33; Esth 2:9, 6:14, 8:14; Ezra 4:23 (equals 1 Esdr 2:30). See above, n. 179.

657 2 Chr 26:20.

658 Ps 6:11; see above, 689, 692.

659 Sir 11:21, only in the Greek; see above, 688, 692.

660 Lam 4:6; see above, 689, 692.

661 Luke 21:34; see above, 704.

662 See 689, 738.

663 Num 6:9; see above, 684, 690.

664 Sir 11:21, in the Greek; see above, 688.

culty where none exists. Malachi preaches: "Behold I will send my messenger and he shall prepare the way, and the Lord shall suddenly come to his temple."[665] We have already cited Rabbinic texts trying to eliminate the contradiction that though the way is prepared, the coming is sudden; of modern commentators Powis Smith notices the problem.[666] The point, however, is that general preparation does not preclude "suddenness" of the coming in the sense that you are seized unawares at the particular moment. In the Synoptics, we are enjoined to watch "at all time":[667] the only way to guard against that threat.

The story of Paul and the viper gains in interest if this aspect is appreciated.[668] When Paul had, as the islanders thought, been bitten by a viper, they "expected, *prodokao,* him to be fated, *mello,* to swell up or suddenly, *aphno,* fall down dead"; and they went on doing so "for a long time," *poly.* The general expectation that something terrible would happen was there; but they were quite prepared (maybe there is here a trace of a suggestion that that would be the way of barbarians) to be startled and accept it as "sudden," at the particular moment and in the particular form it would occur.

6. *Stigme chronou* and *ripe ophthalmou*

Little need be said about *en stigmei chronou* in Luke: according to Luke—though not Matthew—the devil shewed Jesus all kingdoms of the world "in a pinpoint of time."[669] We saw that *stigme* represents *petha'*, "suddenly," in the LXX, in a prophecy of disaster by Isaiah;[670] it will occur in Hebrew *lephetha' pith'om,* in the LXX *hos stigme parachrema.* In Luke, there is nothing sudden about the display. Indeed, a comparison of the two cases is useful in bringing out plainly that what happens in a "pinpoint," moment, may, but need not, be sudden. No suddenness in 2 Maccabees either, where *stigme* is applied in yet a different way: Antiochus's pains increased *kata stigmen,* "every moment."[671]

As the dictionaries shew, Luke's wording is perfectly normal; and there is no indication that he is alluding to, or under the influence of, any particular text or area of doctrine.

There is more specific history behind Paul's assurance that "we shall be changed in a moment, in the twinkling of an eye."[672] Whether or not he might have put "suddenly" is a matter for speculation. Very likely he might, but the fact is, he does not. That is to say, he is here concentrating not on the awe-inspiring aspect, nor on the astonishment experienced at that juncture, but on the hope which will materialize in an instant when God so decrees.

665 Mal 3:1; see above, 686.

666 See above, 700.

667 Luke 21:36.

668 Acts 28:3 ff.; see above, 705.

669 Luke 4:5; Matt 4:8.

670 Isa 29:5; see above, 685, 692.

671 2 Mac 9:11; see above, 696.

672 1 Cor 15:52. Contrast the description in 1 Thes 4:13 ff.

The expression he employs is a double one. The first half, *en atomoi,* is consonant with general Greek usage; in fact Aristotle repeatedly speaks of *atomon* in a discussion of change.[673] At the same time it is safe to assume that Paul has in mind the Hebrew *regha'*, "moment." The phrase *en atomoi* is preserved in only one other Biblical text, namely in Symmachus's translation of Isaiah, and there it renders *regha'*.[674]

The second half, *en ripei ophthalmou,* is a *hapax legomenon,* met nowhere else either in the Bible or any other writing. That it represents a Hebrew phrase *hereph 'ayin,* both in sense and even, to some extent, in sound (*ripe—hereph*), was noticed nearly a hundred years ago by Siegfried and Levy.[675] But what caused Paul's choice of precisely this phrase which, even in Hebrew, is not too common? For one thing, it is relevant to note that the Rabbis define *regha'* as *hereph 'ayin*: "How long is a moment? As a twinkling of an eye."[676] So the two halves of Paul's double expression belong traditionally together.

For another thing, *hereph 'ayin* seems to have had a place in eschatological exposition already before Paul, besides being employed generally where the rapidity of God's power of succour is stressed.[677] A verse from Psalm 46 deserves attention: "Be still (LXX: *scholasate*)—or, desist (Symmachus: *easate*)—and know that I am God."[678] The Rabbis connect the whole psalm with the last things, both because its contents naturally lend themselves to such exegesis and because its authors are the sons of Korah, who did not die, Scripture says,[679] never quite died, according to the Rabbis, and therefore possessed much knowledge not accessible to ordinary mortals. In the opening, "a song upon Alamoth" is variously understood as "a son upon worlds"—i.e. the two worlds assigned in the judgment to the righteous and the wicked.[680] The line "Therefore will we not fear though the earth be removed" is said to imply that, when God renews the world, the righteous ones, resurrected, will received eagle's wings and so forth—they will be changed.[681]

In the verse "Be still" etc., the part "and know that I am God" is invariably considered as envisaging final judgment or deliverance. The first word, "be still" or "desist," in Hebrew is *harpu.* The way it was pronounced—or at least widely pronounced—may be gathered from a transliteration extant in the Hexapla, *uarphu.* The Rabbis see here an allusion to *hereph* and, in their usual manner, credit *harpu* at once

[673] E.g. *Physics* 6.5.235 f. The word for "change," it is true, is *metaballo.*

[674] Isa 54:8. At first sight it looks as if it corresponded to Hebrew *beshṣeph,* but this is deceptive. It corresponds to *regha',* just like Theodotion's *pros oligon*—on which latter see Field, *Originis Hexpla,* vol. 2 (1875), 536 n. 19.

[675] Siegfried, *Analecta Rabbinica ad Novum Testamentum* (1875), 9, Jacob Levy, *Wörterbuch über die Talmudim und Midraschim,* vol. 1 (1876), 495, s.v. *hereph.*

[676] *y. Ber.* 2d; *Lam. Rab.* on 2:19; see Strack-Billerbeck, *op. cit.*, vol. 2 (1924), 156.

[677] *Gen. Rab.* on 24:10; other supernaturally swift actions are also characterized by this phrase, e.g. *Song of Songs Rab.* on 3:6.

[678] Ps 46:11.

[679] Num 26:11.

[680] *Midrash Psalms* on 46:1; Strack-Billerbeck, vol. 4, pt. 2 (1928), 1039.

[681] *b. Sanh.* 92a f.; cp. *Midrash Psalms* on 46:3; see Strack-Billerbeck, vol. 2 (1924), 255, vol. 3 (1926), 481, 845.

with its literal meaning and that of *hereph 'ayin,* "twinkle of an eye." Thus according to one view the verse means "Desist from evildoing and do penitence but for the twinkling of an eye, and redemption will come."[682] That punning interpretations of this sort go back a long way is certain: Aquilas renders *harpu* as *iathete,* "be healed,"[683] presupposing a Hebrew *heraphe'u.*

7. A GHOST

In conclusion we would lay a ghost walking the most reputable dictionaries. In the first half of the last century Gesenius, in his Thesaurus,[684] explained *petha',* "suddenly"—and *pith'om,* treated as an outgrowth of it—as deriving from *pathaḥ,* "to open." The basic meaning was "an opening of the eyes," hence, "a moment of time," "suddenly." He adduced the German *Augenblick* as a parallel. If this were correct, *petha'* would anticipate by about a thousand years the Rabbinic and Pauline "twinkling of an eye" (though this is not, we saw, synonymous with "suddenly"). Nothing *a priori* exceptionable in this; only it just does not happen to be the case.

There are three steps. First, the derivation from *pathaḥ*: implausible. Second (if we grant the first), the assumption that the specific "opening" which via "moment" led to "suddenly" must be of the eyes. But why ever should this be so? Third (if we grant the first two), the parallel *Augenblick. Augenblick,* however, in the sense of "fraction of time," has a very different history. In fact it is on the cards that it was Luther's rather literal translation of Paul's *ripe ophthalmou* by *Augenblick*[685] which stimulated this application of the word in German.

One suspects that Gesenius's theory concerning *petha'* is really due to the influence on him of that use of the German *Augenblick.* Modern authorities no longer pay attention to this theory, presumably because step one, the derivation from *pathaḥ,* is rejected. They do, however, carry on his theory concerning *regha',* which he doubtless equally formulated under the spell of *Augenblick.*

Regha' he derived from *ragha',* "to agitate." Its basic meaning was "nod of an eye," hence "a moment of time." Parallel: *Augenblick.*[686] (The further specialisation to "suddenly" he did not discuss—and it is indeed, as pointed out above,[687] readily intelligible.) This view is generally approved, with the embellishment, apparently, that the Latin *momentum,* from *movere,* is also held to have reached the sense of "fraction of time" via "twinkling of an eye": yet another parallel.[688] Once gain, we are presented with an anticipation of the Rabbinic-Pauline phrase.

[682] *Pesiqta* 163b, *Song of Songs Rab.* on 5:2: Resh (Simon ben) Laqish, middle of 3rd century A.D., and R. Levi, second half of 3rd century. See Strack-Billerbeck, vol. 1 (1922), 163—where, however, the translation *in einem Augenblick,* "in a moment," should be corrected into *einen Augenblick,* "for a moment." For a similar mistranslation of Sir 40:6 by the *Handwörterbuch,* see above, 690.

[683] The variant *ilasthete* is probably a development from this.

[684] Vol. 2, fasc. 2 (1840), 1140 f.

[685] 1 Cor 15:52; cp. *in brahva augins* in the Gothic version.

[686] *Thesaurus,* vol. 3, fasc. 1 (1843), 1264.

[687] See 689.

[688] E.g. *Handwörterbuch,* 744 f., doubtfully, Koehler, 874, firmly.

This time the first step, though far from certain, is not untenable. The chief reason we regard it as uncertain is that *ragha'*, "to agitate," occurs twice only, of God who "agitated the sea and the waves roared": once in Deutero-Isaiah and once in Jeremiah.[689] This is a slender foundation to build on. Not to mention the difficulty of constructing a bridge from "agitation" to "fraction of time," not quite the same as from "movement" to "fraction of time." Still, the derivation is obviously better than that of *petha'* from *pathaḥ*.

The second step is completely arbitrary. Why (granting the first) should the "agitation" accounting for *regha'*, "moment," be of the eye? As for step three, we have already noted that *Augenblick*, far from supplying a parallel, may owe the prevalence of its sense of "moment" to Paul.

The recent, fourth step, the forcing of the Latin word into the same scheme, is amusing. There is no longer any thought for the evidence, readily accessible in the *Thesaurus Linguae Latinae*. The scheme has developed—shall we say—its own momentum.

Certainly, if (as is barely conceivable, despite the lack of any testimony) *ragha'*, "to agitate," was widely employed in the sense of "to move"; and if *regha'*, "moment," evolved from this use; we may, though even then we need not, have before us a development resembling that from *movere* to *momentum* as denoting "a fraction of time." But neither the Hebrew nor the Latin has anything to do with a "twinkling of an eye."

In his *Handwörterbuch*,[690] earlier than his *Thesaurus*, Gesenius ascribed the meaning "to nod with the eye" to the verb *ragha'* itself; the passages in Deutero-Isaiah and Jeremiah he translated "calmed (by his nod) the sea when its waves roared." From this starting-point, we should indeed arrive with ease at *regha'*, "wink," "moment," *Augenblick*. But there is little to be said for the starting-point. In the *Handwörterbuch*, already Gesenius claimed an analogy between the Hebrew and the Latin development, but it does not look as if he had thought it very close, i.e. as if he had considered *momentum* to be a movement of the eye. The dominant inspiration was the German *Augenblick*.

[689] Isa 51:5; Jer 31:55. Job 26:12 may have to be added.
[690] (1828), 763 f.

7

Disciples

This section explores various aspects of the relationship between masters and disciples.

The Offices of a Disciple

According to Matthew, the Baptist considered himself unworthy to carry the shoes (or sandals) of Jesus, according to Mark, Luke, John and Acts to take them off.[1] In Talmudic utterances, whenever a slave's services are illustrated, these two—carrying the master's things before him to the bath-house and taking off his shoes (when he comes home)—are listed together.[2] Let us note, however, that the Baptist was willing to do them for Jesus not as a slave, but as a disciple. It was a general rule that a son or disciple owed the duties of a slave.[3]

Why does Matthew mention one of the two services and Mark, Luke, John and Acts the other? Or supposing the original saying referred to both, why does Matthew omit one and Mark and so on the other? Of course it may be due to an accident of transmission, or we may have to invoke one of the modern theories concerning Q. On the other hand, there may be an altogether different explanation.

R. Joshua ben Levi held that a disciple should do for his teacher anything a slave would do—except take off his shoes.[4] It is true that this Rabbi flourished about A.D. 250. But his principle may be much older. (The earliest datable identification of the Suffering Servant with Israel in Jewish literature is as late as the 12th century. Yet we know from Origen that it was prevalent in certain Jewish circles in his time, some 900 years before.) If the principle had followers in the New Testament epoch, it may account for the difference. Matthew represents the Baptist as having adhered to the principle: he spoke only of carrying the shoes of Jesus, but not of taking them off. The latter is not a disciple's task. The other sources represent the Baptist as eager to perform for Jesus precisely that service which some Rabbis thought too low for one who was free, even if he was a great man's disciple.

In the chapter on Redemption (382) we found that there were Rabbis who imposed heavier duties on a son or disciple than on a slave. Their object was to exempt a slave from degrading services; but they felt that no service was degrading if done by a son or disciple for his father or teacher. An idea like this may also have contributed to the non-Matthean version of the Baptist's saying.

[1] Matt 3:11; Mark 1:7; Luke 3:16; John 1:27; Acts 13:25.

[2] *Mek.* on Exod 21:2; *Siphre* on Num 15:41; *b. Kidd.* 22b.

[3] *b. Ket.* 96a.

[4] *b. Ket.* 96a.

Responsibilities of Master and Disciples in the Gospels

The subject of this paper could include an enormous variety of aspects. The one that probably comes to mind first is the mutual responsibility of a master and his disciples to one another. For example, what kind of promise is implied in Jesus's assurance to those he calls that he will make them fishers of men?[1] Or what degree of obedience or of support do those who accept the call owe him? On this phase of the subject, however, a good deal has been written, though perhaps not much that is truly satisfactory. I shall go into a question which seems to have been totally neglected: namely, what is the responsibility of a master and his disciples in the outside world for one another's conduct? More precisely, how far is Jesus held accountable by the outside world for the conduct of his followers, and how far are the latter held accountable for his conduct?

There is admittedly an overlap. A master may be performing his office to his disciples by offering himself in their stead to those outside that find fault with them; and his disciples may be doing their duty by him in facing the reproaches levelled against him by those outside. None the less the two obligations—to one another, to the outside world for one another—are distinct. I propose to concentrate on the latter, on the obligation imposed by third parties on a master and disciples, on Jesus and his followers, in respect of one another.

We are all acquainted with the problem in modern conditions. Marcuse is blamed for the misbehaviour of his students, or indeed any students somehow influenced by his teaching. Nietzsche is blamed for Hitler. Conversely, a communist may be told: "Look how your great Stalin concluded a pact with the Nazis." Or a Billy-Grahamist may be assailed because of a sermon the preacher delivered at the White House. The instances could be multiplied *ad infinitum.*

The phenomenon is no less common and of no less moment in antiquity. Among the charges preferred against Socrates was that of corruption of the youth of Athens. The excesses of characters like Alcibiades were laid at his door. On the other hand, his admirers—Antisthenes, Plato, Xenophon—vied in writing defences of his life, as if on trial themselves. Socrates himself seems on occasion to have made use of the notion that a master is answerable for what his disciples are doing. While under indictment for corrupting the young—Plato informs us[2]—he asked Euthyphro, who prided himself on full knowledge of religious matters, to take his instruction in hand: this would enable him to tell his accuser, if he still disapproved of his doctrines, to bring to trial Euthyphro for

[1] Matt 4:19; Mark 1:17; Luke 5:10.

[2] *Euthyphro* 5.5A f. See my *Civil Disobedience in Antiquity* (1972), 74.

corrupting the old. That this plan is ironical does not here matter; it does show how the relationship might be viewed.

Fifty years before, Anaxagoras had been charged with the same crime of *aseby*, impiety, possibly also with treasonable correspondence with Persia. According to one version he was sentenced to death, but while he was awaiting his end, Pericles came forward and asked the people whether they could discover any blemish in his own career. They replied that they could not. If so, he retorted, they ought to let off Anaxagoras whose disciple he was. Whereupon they did release him. Alas, he took his indignity badly and committed suicide.[3] In this case, a master is given credit for his disciple's meritorious achievements. It is indeed normal that a master should be complimented on his successful disciples or, for that matter, that his disciples should bask in his reflected glory. This is only the obverse of their answerability for one another's lapses.

The complex under discussion has affinity with other familiar topics. One is the instigation to a crime: a gangster persuades a poor guy to burgle a store. The distinctive feature of the master-disciples association is here missing: the overall guidance by the master and the self-identification with him by the disciples. The instigator is clearly a major cause of the particular offence. But one would not reproach him for other misdeeds of the agent, in the way one imposes a wide-ranging liability on a master. Again, the agent may be a willing instrument in this particular affair, but no one would dream of taunting him at large with what the instigator is up to, as one does the disciples with any weaknesses of their mentor. There is a point in upbraiding a communist for Stalin's pact with Hitler or even for his personal brutality. There is no point in upbraiding the guy induced to burgle for the gangster's lack of morality or drinking habits. Much the same considerations apply to the area of superior orders: a captain orders a private to shoot prisoners. Here, too, as far as the incident is concerned, there is no difficulty in singling out the captain as the effective criminal. But one would not regard him as liable for other unconnected offences of the private; and it would be senseless to blame the private for flaws in the captain's mode of life—more senseless even than to blame the burglar for the instigator's shortcomings. The private lacks not only the disciple's self-identification with his superior, but even the agent's freedom to say No. He shoots not, or not necessarily, because he assents to the captain's decision, but because he is bidden. Even the relation between teacher and pupils is not on the level with that between master and disciples. No doubt if a teacher conveys information in a manner dangerous to his society—say, his biology produces outlandish orgies among his charges—he may lose his job. But his influence is very limited, and certainly his pupils, in so far as they remain pupils and do not become disciples, will never be picked on for his failings. They do not identify themselves with him.

The relationships nearest to that between master and disciples are that between parents and children and that between a community and its members. Parents are, in a sense, masters, and children, in a sense, their disciples. The difference is that this connection is based on nature, whereas that between a master and disciples is based on choice. Hence, in a rational system, such transgressions of the children as are not due

[3] Diogenes Laertius 2.13.

to the parents would not be held against the latter, and once children dissociate themselves from their parents the latter's misbehaviours would no longer be held against the former. Few systems, however, are rational. Similarly, if you belong to a community by nature—you are an American or a German or a Jew or a Catholic by birth, not by naturalization or conversion—rationally, its responsibility for you and yours for it should be narrowly circumscribed. In actual fact, this is not so. For one thing, for the most part, choice confirms nature: your community happily accepts you, and you happily accept it. Anyhow, it is quite usual for outsiders to run down the church if one or two members prove scoundrels, or to challenge an individual Catholic because of an encyclical that appears objectionable. In the case of communities resting on choice, say the Republican party, within certain limits the responsibilities here contemplated are well founded. A master and his disciples can indeed be looked upon as a group of this type.

As far as the law's reaction to undesirable ties is concerned, in some respects it is easier to deal with the more specific one of instigator and agents, captain and private, teacher and pupils, than with the more comprehensive ones of master and disciples, parents and children, community and members. But this does not mean that legal sanctions may not be inflicted on the latter category. A political club may be dissolved because a member has thrown a bomb, the children of a convict may be excluded from public office. Especially wartime regulations are apt to envisage the penalization of a leader for wrongs by those under him or, say, of an occupied city for an act of sabotage by a handful of its inhabitants, as also, on the other hand, the penalization of subordinates for their leader's wickedness or of a member of a guerrilla corps for exploits by the latter in which he had no part. After all, it was in a proper trial that Socrates was linked with the outrages committed by Alcibiades. At any rate, in this study I shall be interested in moral responsibility no less than in legal.

The accountability of false prophets and teachers for the errors practised by their flock is commonplace in the Old Testament, the intertestamental writings, the Dead Sea Scrolls and rabbinic literature. The tractate Horayoth contains a considerable number of rulings on the consequences of a mistaken decision by recognized authority. Far less material in this corpus bears on the accountability of disciples for the errors of the master. The principal reason is that there is no lengthy *ex professo* description of such a group in its day-to-day encounters with the outside world. (Chassidic lore is rich in pertinent tales.) To some extent the gap is filled by material concerning a closely parallel situation. The supreme guide of Jewry is God as represented in the Scriptures; and Talmud and Midrash report many a hostile inquiry put to the Jews as to what their God does or says. "Why is your God jealous of the powerless heathen idols?," "Your God is a thief, taking a rib from the sleeping Adam,"[4] and so forth. The Rabbis must constantly justify the ways of God to men.

[4] *b. A. Zar.* 55a; *b. Sanh.* 39a. The first question is put to and answered by Gamaliel II, the second is put to him and answered by his daughter. Gamaliel's reply shows psychological sensitivity: a woman of worth will feel insulted precisely if her husband takes as second wife one devoid of admirable qualities. His daughter's repartee is very elegant: God acted like a thief who steals a silver jug, leaving a golden one behind.

The evangelists record three instances of a request to Jesus to explain the conduct of his disciples: why do they not fast, why do they pluck corn on a Sabbath, why do they eat with hands unwashed? Essentially similar is a fourth contretemps, caused by the public acclamation of Jesus as Saviour.

According to Mark,[5] the question about fasting is put either by the disciples of the Baptist and the Pharisees, among whom fasting was practised with great zeal, or—more likely—by the ordinary public puzzled by the absence of this practice in a circle otherwise so ardently preparing for the early advent of the final judgment. For Matthew,[6] the questioners are the disciples of the Baptist; for Luke,[7] the Pharisees. It is arguable that, as originally conceived at least, the question implies little criticism, rather mostly curiosity—though we must remember that any deviance from the customary is apt to make people uncomfortable. In Luke, the element of criticism is perhaps somewhat strengthened. Jesus is not here asked, as in Mark and Matthew, why his disciples do not fast but why they eat and drink—a suggestion, possibly, of luxuriousness: "the Son of Man has come eating and drinking, and you say, Behold, a glutton and a drunkard."[8] However this may be, in none of the three gospels does Jesus evince the slightest surprise that the inquiry should be directed to him. This is evidently a natural thing to happen, and he gives the appropriate reply.

The plucking of corn is reproved by the Pharisees in Mark, Matthew and Luke[9]—definitely reproved: they characterize it as not permitted. In Mark and Matthew, they voice their grievances to Jesus. Mark vividly depicts their telling him to declare himself: "Look, why are they doing on a Sabbath what is not permitted?" Matthew makes the phrasing a shade more precise and formal: "Behold, your disciples are doing what is not permitted to do on a Sabbath." The answer, too, is introduced in a somewhat looser style in Mark—"and he said to them"—than in Matthew—"he, however, said to them." The tenor, however, is the same in both: Jesus is responsible for the infringement of the law, all the more since it goes on before his very eyes. There is no trace of any hesitation in approaching him about it or in his taking up the complaint.

The answer brings out the underlying idea with extraordinary boldness, taking great freedom with an Old Testament report. To begin with Mark, Jesus appeals to the example of David during his flight from Saul:[10] as he and those with him were hungry, he ate of the shewbread and distributed it among his companions. Surprisingly, when we look up 1 Samuel 21, we find that David was alone on that occasion and he alone ate of the sacred food. He did make up a story for the benefit of the priest who suspected (rightly) some queer business because he appeared without attendants, to the effect that he was presently meeting with them. But it was a story, and he went happily away with a single sword he begged from the priest (Goliath's sword it was). There were no others

[5] Mark 2:18 ff.

[6] Matt 9:14 ff.

[7] Luke 5:33 ff. I follow there the interpretation of Creed, *The Gospel according to St. Luke* (1930), 82.

[8] Matt 11:19; Luke 7:34.

[9] Mark 2:23 ff.; Matt 12:1 ff.; Luke 6:1 ff.

[10] As for the cogency or otherwise of such an example in establishing the law, see my *The New Testament and Rabbinic Judaism* (1956), 67 ff. [249 ff.]

participating in this affair. The reason they figure in Jesus's answer is that the episode as it stands is not a good enough precedent. The defence that David, when hungry, brushed aside certain regulations, so why should the disciples not do likewise, is too easily countered by—allow me to use a maxim evoking painful memories of my childhood[11]—"*Quod licet Jovi non licet bovi*" ["What is permitted to Jove is not permitted to an ox"]—how can they arrogate his standing? But if David shared his illicit meal with a band of faithful ones this rebuttal is avoided. It is the latter's humble role that the disciples re-enact. For the present study, what is of particular interest is that a positive handing out of bread by David to his men is offered as the model of Jesus's tolerating the plucking of corn by his disciples. So powerful is a master's position that an action he condones may be imputed to him just as much as one he initiates. Seneca's Agamemnon exclaims: "*Qui non vetat peccare com possit iubet,*" "He who forbids not sin when in control commands it."[12]

It may be asked whether perhaps the Rabbis of the New Testament period, or some of them, detect in 1 Samuel a hint at a sharing of the meal by David with a retinue: the reply by Jesus might then proceed from this understanding of the narrative. I know of no such exegesis in the sources. On the contrary, the Rabbis draw attention to David's ravenous appetite which caused him to devour the entire supply at one sitting.[13] Even if—as is conceivable—a rabbinic interpretation no longer extant should have asserted a giving away of part of the bread to others its choice out of several as basis for Jesus's answer would remain significant. We could still infer the prevalent thinking about his accountability for the doings of his followers.

Partly at least the conflict with 1 Samuel may be owing to reliance on memory, without a recheck. Relying on memory, one might easily think of the friends David assures the priest are awaiting him somewhere as actually present or at least near enough for him to bring them food. There is support for this suggestion in the fact, long seen, that Jesus calls the priest Abiathar, whereas in 1 Samuel it is his father Ahimelech—manifestly the kind of error likely if you do not look up your text.

I have a hunch that, in the matter that I am concerned with, the defence at one time did accord with 1 Samuel and mentioned David only. It was just David who was hungry: the words "he and those around him" were not yet there. And all that happened was that he ate of the shewbread: the clause "and he gave also to those who were with him" was not yet there. These bits were added when, in debate with the Pharisees, the point already adverted to was encountered—that a liberty assumed by David furnished no justification for the disciples.

Three considerations in favour of this development are: first, the discrepancy with the Old Testament episode would be easier to explain. Secondly, the references to David's men give the impression of appendices, readily detachable without disturbing

[11] My father used to quote it when my brother or I exceeded the approved limits of *imitatio patris.*

[12] Seneca, *Troades* 290; see my *The Defence of Superior Orders in Roman Law* (1956) [reprinted in *LQR*, 72 (1956)], 15, 20. Cf. 1 Sam 3:13.

[13] *Yalqut* ad 1 Sam 21:5, cited by Strack and Billerbeck, *Kommentar zum Neuen Testament,* 1 (1922), 619.

the rest. Thirdly, they actually produce an awkwardness, not a very serious one, but still an awkwardness. David ate of the hallowed bread and gave of it also to his men: this sounds as if, in the case at hand, Jesus had plucked corn as well as his disciples or even taken the lead. I take it that he did not do so, not only because all three evangelists definitely confine the action to his disciples, but also because, had he been guilty of it, alone or in company, his opponents would have gone for him, not for the lesser fry. It might perhaps be argued that the disciples are singled out simply because, at the time of the writing of the gospel, it is they who are wrestling with the non-believers, the master being dead. But this would be to overlook the more numerous cases where the latter remains the target. Moreover, had there been a tradition that Jesus himself set the pace in this matter, the evangelists would have welcomed such authority.

In the original version (assuming this development), to the Pharisaic attack Jesus retorts that if his disciples, driven by hunger, are human, so was David. No awkwardness here, except that it may be considered presumptuous of them to take a leaf out of that king's book. The version before us, by representing the latter as not only eating himself but also giving his companions to eat, meets this objection: the disciples are now merely imitating the companions. But the improvement in this respect is bought at a price with regard to another. The parallel has become slightly faulty: the disciples now correspond to David's men but Jesus, not having yielded to hunger and plucked corn, does not quite correspond to David.

Matthew presupposes a consultation of the Old Testament chapter. The mistaken name of the priest is erased, with no replacement. The clause "and he gave also to those who were with him," devoid of any warrant in 1 Samuel is also suppressed. Instead, it is simply stated that "they ate"—namely, the king and his entourage. (This distinctive reading of the earliest of manuscripts is universally preferred to "he ate," an assimilation to Mark and Luke prevalent in the later ones.) Understandably, the participation of the men in the meal is not given up; they are too valuable an analogue to the disciples. In fact, by putting "they ate," meaning David and them, Matthew welds them more firmly into the account: we can no longer, as in Mark, remove them by the mere cutting out of a few words. Altogether David and they are more of a unified group here.

Incidentally, Matthew is not content with Mark's notice that the shewbread "is not lawful to eat but for the priests"; the shewbread, he writes, "was not lawful for him [David] to eat neither for those around him, but only for the priests." This elaboration is yet another echo of the continuous battle with the Pharisees. One of the rejoinders to the Davidic example would be that, for special reasons, that particular shewbread was not holy. Quite a few rabbinic discussions are preserved culminating in the proof that David's procedure was licit.[14] They may be relatively late, but similar ones doubtless date from much earlier. Matthew is opposing this way of invalidating Jesus's quotation. On his grappling with a further, more fundamental objection, by subjoining a second, entirely different defence resting on the Pentateuchic provisions concerning Sabbath sacrifices, I have commented elsewhere.[15]

[14] See Strack and Billerbeck, *op. cit.*, 618 ff.

[15] See above, n. 10.

Passing on to Luke, we come upon a striking change. The Pharisees censure, not Jesus, but the disciples: "Why are you doing what is not permitted on a Sabbath?" At first sight, one might conclude that Luke anticipated those Californian students who will resent it if their vices are saddled on their educators. It is humiliating; they are not puppets; their vices are theirs. This is not, however, at all what Luke has in mind. On the contrary, he intends to exalt the figure of the master. Though the Pharisees accuse the disciples, it is still Jesus who replies and indeed, his reply—his intervention, we ought now to call it— is described in solemn language: "but answering to them Jesus spoke."

Here should be mentioned a hitch common where a wrong is committed by subordinates under the direction of a leader. The latter—be it the head of a family, a sect, a gang or a regiment—should it come to a threat of retribution, is apt to back out, leaving his inferiors in front to take the rap.[16] Certainly now and then, we hear of one who, even when not pressured, is eager to sacrifice himself in order to ransom those in trouble for his sake. When the census organized by David was punished by a pestilence sent on the people, he prayed to God: "Lo, I have sinned, but these sheep, what have they done? Let your hand be against me."[17] Piso explained to Tiberius that his son Marcus had been a most reluctant accessory to his misdeeds.[18] But as a rule the opposite happens, and addressing an audience that is acquainted with twentieth-century war crime trials I can dispense with evidence. In Luke, Jesus, himself not challenged, stands up for his disciples who are. At the beginning of this paper I distinguished two kinds of a master's responsibility: one, that to his disciples, the other, that for his disciples vis-à-vis third parties—the latter forming my topic. Both are taken for granted by all three, Mark, Matthew and Luke. It is the former which Luke intensifies. Jesus of his own accord steps in in support of his disciples under attack.

In view of this attitude of Luke's, it is no wonder that while abandoning the erroneous name of the priest, he does retain the prominent role of David. The latter is not, as in Matthew, merged in the group. Luke, like Mark, writes: "He was hungry, he and those around him," and "he ate and gave to those around him." Some slight smoothings-out of the Markan formulation[19] do not affect this major concurrence.

Now for the washing of hands before a meal. Both in Mark and Matthew[20] Pharisees and scribes reprovingly ask Jesus why his followers neglect this tradition of the fathers, and he confounds the questioners. That the criticism should be addressed to him and that he should deal with it is apparently felt to be quite normal in the circumstances.

Luke omits this section. Presumably he regards it as compensated for by one peculiar to him,[21] where Jesus accepts a Pharisee's invitation to a meal, his host wonders at his not washing his hands, and he denounces false ritualism. As no disciples are involved, this incident need not detain us.

[16] See my *The Defence of Superior Orders in Roman Law*, 7 f. (repr. in *LQR*, 72 [1956], 498 f.).

[17] 2 Sam 24:17; 1 Chr 21:17; see my *Studies in Biblical Law* (1947) (repr. 1969), 162.

[18] Tacitus, *Annals* 3.16.

[19] After "and gave" the particle "also" is omitted. The reference to the illicitness of the meal, which in Mark separates "he ate" from "and he gave," is placed at the end.

[20] Matt 15:1 ff.; Mark 7:1 ff.

[21] Luke 11:37 ff.

It may, however, be worth observing that the scene is by general agreement due to Luke and historically improbable.[22] To the arguments found in the literature I would add two. First, had Jesus himself been reputed to eat with his hands unwashed, the Pharisees and scribes of Mark and Matthew would have fastened, not on his disciples, but on him. No more than in the case of the plucking of corn can this be seen as owing merely to the fact that the controversy is written up after Jesus's death, with the disciples alone carrying on the new faith. A tradition ascribing the conduct in dispute to Jesus himself would not have been neglected by any evangelist: in Luke, the wish for such a basis finds dramatic expression. Secondly, Luke's setting reflects a far more advanced stage of Christianity. It is significant that he provides a very similar one on two more occasions, to one of which I shall come back below.[23] There is a huge difference between the followers of a religious innovator flouting some orthodox custom and the innovator flouting the custom while the guest of a member of the establishment. Deviations of the former class are bound to occur almost from the start: there is no reason to doubt the accuracy of the gospels in this respect. An action of the latter class is provocative. It carries the war into the enemy's camp. It reflects a stage where the new community asserts itself, creates outposts and forges ahead here, there and everywhere. (For an agnostic dining *en famille* to dispense with grace is one thing. But I remember an occasion in the Common Room of All Souls when G. D. H. Cole happened to preside as senior Fellow present and, prior to port, instead of getting up and saying *Benedicto benedicatur*, got up and said: "Gentlemen, you may stand for a moment if you like, but I refuse to say grace." That was another thing, more like Luke, except that by the 1950s the issue had long ceased to be a live one.)

All gospels, including the Fourth, know of a triumphal procession to Jerusalem.[24] In Mark and Matthew there is no immediate reaction on the part of the antagonists. Matthew, however, informs us of a second public acclamation,[25] at once pounced on. It occurs in the temple, after the cleansing, as Jesus is healing sick people: the children shout Hosanna. Angrily, the chief priests and scribes ask Jesus whether he hears what they say. He replies in the affirmative and quotes from Psalms "Out of the mouth of babes" and so on.[26]

Here we have to do with a political figure's accountability for the conduct of his partisans. Jesus is reproached for an action, not of his disciples, but of a number of children who salute him as Messiah. They symbolize the best, unspoilt part of the nation, or maybe the converts to join the church: the latter allusion would chime with the Lukan treatment, on which I shall comment presently.

As in the case of the plucking of the corn, his presence at the happening surely makes him more culpable than he would be anyhow. In fact, he may well be perceived as almost directly *particeps criminis* [a participant in the offence]—more so than in the

[22] See e.g. Creed, *op. cit.*, 165.

[23] Luke 7:36, 14:1; on the former, see below, 759 f.

[24] Mark 11:1 ff.; Matt 21:1 ff.; Luke 19:28 ff.; John 12:12 ff.

[25] Matt 21:15 f.

[26] Ps 8:3.

queries concerning his disciples not fasting, plucking corn on a Sabbath, eating with unwashed hands. One would not be surprised if, instead of "Do you hear what these are saying?," he were asked: "Why are you creating this upheaval?" Still, that point is not in fact reached. The structure of the pericope is very much like that Matthew employs for the three other incidents.

Luke has the corresponding section immediately after the first—and, for him as for Mark and John, only—Messianic outburst. According to him, the disciples exclaim "Blessed be the King" and so on. Some Pharisees admonish Jesus to call them to order, but he pleads that if they kept quiet, the stones would cry out.

The political significance is if anything more palpable than in Matthew: Luke has Jesus explicitly hailed as king.[27] Yet at first blush at least, whereas Matthew steps outside the circle of disciples, bringing in the children, Luke remains within, more strictly consistent with the line-up in the debates about fasting and plucking corn. (That about the washing of hands does not, in Luke, have regard to the disciples.) I should point out that this remains true whether the Pharisees who urge Jesus to silence his admirers are hostile or whether—less likely but possible—they want to save him from disaster;[28] and again, whether his reply is designed to vindicate the enthusiasts or whether—less likely but possible—it is in anguished agreement with the critics, confessing his inability to stem the tide.[29] Whichever line we take, responsibility for the demonstration of the disciples is imposed on and accepted by Jesus.

The initial impression that Luke speaks of the disciples only may, however, be misleading. The phase he uses, "the whole multitude of disciples," *hapan to plethos ton matheton,* suggests more than a dozen. It is indeed reminiscent of one of the numerous passages in Acts where he emphasizes the miraculous growth of the community: "In those days, when the number of disciples was multiplied... the twelve called the multitude of disciples," *plethynonton ton matheton... to plethos ton matheton.*[30] It is generally thought[31] that in this chapter of Acts the term "disciples" for the first time signifies "Christians." If, as I incline to assume, Luke sees in the jubilant celebration as Jesus approaches Jerusalem a prefiguement of the victorious church, this wider meaning of "disciples" is up to a point already present here. It would come fairly close to the Matthean "children," should these be converts.

John agrees with Luke in representing the Pharisees as at once upset by the popular applause. Only they do not express their view to Jesus but deplore among themselves his irresistible attraction. This account, therefore, contributes nothing here of relevance.

A few words about the relation of the evangelists may be permissible. John appears to depend on Luke. Like the latter, he records one ovation resented by the Pharisees; no indignation on their part is noticed by Mark. Moreover, just as in Luke Jesus is extolled because of his mighty works, so in John he is because of his raising of

[27] See Creed, *op. cit.*, 24.

[28] See Rengstorf, *Das Evangelium nach Lukas*, 9th ed. (1962), 219.

[29] See Taylor, in *The Interpreter's Bible*, VII (1951), 138.

[30] Acts 6:1 f.

[31] See Munck, *The Acts of the Apostles*, rev. by Albright and Mann (1967), 56.

Lazarus—the greatest of his feats in this gospel. Mark does not in this connection refer to Jesus's deeds. Lastly, Luke's exuberant introduction of a "multitude of disciples" may be behind the realization of John's Pharisees that "the world—*ho kosmos*—has gone after him."

Matthew and Luke draw on the Q stream—or alternatively, Luke may be drawing on Matthew. In both a complaint about the welcomers is addressed, not to the latter, but to Jesus, and he deals with it, dismissing it. There is no trace of this in Mark. Neither does Mark advert to Jesus's deeds in this context, whereas Matthew and Luke both do—though Matthew calls them *thaumasia* [wonderful things] (grudgingly noticed by the antagonists) and Luke *dynameis* [mighty] (for which the disciples praise God). This coincidence would admittedly be of little significance were it not for the major one just outlined. Similarly, without the latter one, no weight would attach to a third agreement, a doubtful one, between Matthew and Luke versus Mark: the new body of believers, the children in Matthew, the multitude of disciples in Luke.[32]

I proceed to the reverse challenge, namely, of disciples on the ground of their master's obnoxiousness. The principal example concerns Jesus's unworthy meal company. All three, Mark, Matthew and Luke,[33] contain a scene where Jesus and his disciples are entertained at a publican's home. In Mark and Matthew, the Pharisaic scribes (Mark) or the Pharisees (Matthew) ask the disciples why Jesus eats with publicans and sinners. Formally, in Mark, it may not be a question; we could translate "they said to his disciples that—*hoti*—he ate with publicans and sinners." In substance, even so, it would be a demand for an explanation. The basis for the demand is brought out with some emphasis by Matthew. Mark writes "why does he eat?," Matthew "why does your master eat?" Discipleship entails that kind of responsibility. Their own attendance at the meal, it may be noted, is discounted, it is merely a corollary of his and very minor compared with it.

Jesus hears the remark or of the remark: the Greek could mean either. That is to say, he may be thought of as overhearing it or as hearing about it from his disciples.[34] At all events, he conducts his own defence: it is the sick, he observes, who need a physician. Just conceivably, the defence is made (or represented by the evangelists as being made) to his disciples. But considering the atmosphere of this and similar episodes, the likelihood is that it is made (or represented as being made) to his detractors. It has always been so understood. As far as Matthew is concerned, we may actually speak of a near-certainty, since the quotation from Hosea he adds, "I desire mercy and not sacrifice,"[35] is added by him also to the dispute about the plucking of corn, where Jesus undeniably confronts the Pharisees.

It is interesting what kind of conduct on Jesus's part his disciples are called on to justify. It is public, habitual and contrary to what the questioners expect of a saintly man. It is not, however, contrary to the law, an important negative which places it in the

[32] As far as the sheer size of the crowd is concerned, Matthew enlarges it already for the first acclamation: compare Matt 21:8 f. with Mark 11:8 f.

[33] Mark 2:15 ff.; Matt 9:10 ff.; Luke 5:29 ff.

[34] In Matt 14:13, for instance, *akouo* can signify only "to hear of": Jesus is informed of the Baptist's fate.

[35] Hos 6:6.

neighbourhood of the disciples' practice of not fasting rather than that of eating with hands unwashed, let alone the plucking of corn on a Sabbath. A further trait deserves attention: it is conduct which, while the questioners deem it incompatible with saintliness, will turn out, paradoxically, when illumined, to be the truly saintly one.

Luke remodels the structure. The Pharisees and their scribes ask the disciples, not why their master sits at table with publicans and sinners, but why they do so. Their attendance, not Jesus's, is focused on; and it is significant that already in the description of the scene, prior to the query, Luke is at pains to slur over Jesus's presence. Mark: "And as he sat at table, many publicans were sitting together with Jesus and his disciples." Luke: "And there was a large company of publicans sitting at table with them." None the less, once the query is advanced, it is still Jesus who replies; and Luke leaves not the shadow of a doubt that the reply is made to the Pharisees.

It will be recalled that in the case of the plucking of corn, Luke modifies Mark and Matthew in having the complaint directed to the disciples who committed the transgression instead of to Jesus. His motive, I argued, is to enhance the standing not of the former but of the latter: Luke's Jesus of his own accord goes out to face the disturbers of his flock. The evangelist's handling of the present incident confirms this analysis. This time, already in Mark and Matthew, the questioners address the disciples; what he does to achieve the same effect as in the other case is to transfer to the disciples the practice worrying the questioners. As a result, here too, the frame is that the disciples are asked concerning an action of theirs, and Jesus freely intervenes on their behalf. Indeed, as in the controversy about the plucking of corn, the intervention is solemnly introduced: "And answering, Jesus spoke to them."

It is consistent with Luke's approach that what in Mark and Matthew is a question with a censorious overtone becomes a definite protest: it is against a definite attack that Jesus defends his disciples. Hence, the Pharisees and their scribes "murmured against the disciples." It may be added that, in this gospel, the complaint is not just about eating in evil company, but about eating and drinking. It is Luke, we have seen, who represents the Pharisees as asking, not why the disciples do not fast, but why they eat and drink. Here as there, it may be that a hint at luxurious living is attributed to the enemies.

Historically, it is easily understandable how Luke can make the disciples into conspicuous friends of publicans and sinners. By his time, active Christian mission among people of the most diverse provenance is in full swing and greatly encouraged. We found an aspect of this development coming out in his story about Jesus not washing his hands when a Pharisee's guest.

However, that Jesus himself set the example of fraternizing with outcasts is too important a matter for Luke to give up, or tone down, without compensation. One of three passages to be adduced derives from Q: the ill-wishers allege that the Son of man is "a glutton and a drunkard, a friend of publican and sinners."[36]

Two others are more significant in this connection, bearing a specifically Lukan imprint. A well-known section,[37] peculiar to Luke as far as the points here relevant are

[36] Matt 11:19; Luke 5:34.

[37] Luke 7:36 ff.

concerned, is devoted to a notorious female sinner washing Jesus's feet with her tears. This takes place as he is eating at the home of a Pharisee, who concludes that he cannot be a prophet, else he would have spotted what sort of woman it was and rejected her. Jesus, of course, had spotted it. He now tells the parable of the two debtors and fiercely condemns his host's cold hospitality and self-righteousness. Essentially, the scene is like that where, having accepted a Pharisee's invitation, he eats with hands unwashed. In a subsequent chapter,[38] not paralleled in the other gospels at all, Jesus assembles publicans and sinners, the Pharisees and scribes "murmur" against his eating with sinners (the publicans are omitted in this verse) and he parries by propounding the parables of the lost sheep, the lost coin and the prodigal son.

The disciples play no part in any of these three pieces, so I need not enlarge.

A story about payment of the temple tax, recounted only by Matthew,[39] furnishes yet another illustration of disciples being treated as responsible for their master's decisions. True, both in form and spirit it greatly differs from the interrogation concerning Jesus's meal company. In a way, however, this makes it all the more valuable: it shows that the phenomenon under discussion is not confined to a narrow corner. The literature seizes on details of the incident but considers the incident as a whole rather pointless. This is a mistake; on closer examination, a profound teaching does emerge.

The collectors ask Peter: "Does not your master pay the tax?" The "your" is a plural in the Greek, *hymon,* so Peter is being addressed as representing the disciples at large. He expresses no surprise at being questioned with regard to Jesus's conduct, and he replies: "Yes."

Apparently, his intention is above all to be rid of, satisfy, the officers; he does not seem to be sure of Jesus's position. On his return, we are told, the latter "anticipates" him; which means he enters upon the problem before Peter has reported the encounter and inquired as to the correct solution.

Jesus's solution is indeed far from a straightforward "Yes."[40] He takes the view that he and his are not liable to the tax any more than the sons of an earthly king would have to offer tribute. Only he does not wish to give offence. The Greek is "lest we should offend them" *skandalizomen*; the "we" must mean either Jesus and his disciples or Jesus and Peter—the latter standing for all. Jesus ends by sending Peter out to cast a hook: the first fish to be caught will have in its mouth the appropriate coin, which Peter is to pay for Jesus and himself. Once again, though the other disciples are not expressly considered, Peter surely represents them in the sense that they, like him, should somehow remain on the right side of the authorities. What is interesting is that Jesus takes responsibility for that: he is in charge, Peter merely follows his directions.

Here, as far as my topic goes, I could leave this story. But as it has hitherto suffered cavalier treatment, I go on to remark that Jesus and Peter at the same time do pay and do not pay. They do by handing the temple the coin. They do not in that the coin is

[38] Luke 15:1 ff.

[39] Matt 17:24 ff.

[40] With my exegesis, contrast e.g. that of Johnson, "The Gospel according to St. Matthew," in *The Interpreter's Bible,* VII, 465: Matthew wished to remind Christians "that they must give free and willing obedience to the state."

not genuinely theirs; it is brought along by the fish for the very purpose that they can get away in this fashion and preserve their freedom. From the formalistically legal point of view, to be sure, Jesus, through Peter, acquires the ownerless property: that is why they can make valid payment with it. But economically and psychologically—or in baby's slang, really, really—they give up nothing of their own, they do not submit.

Dodges of this nature are familiar to the rabbis. On a pagan festival,[41] in order that you may not cause a thanksgiving to an idol, you should neither lend to a pagan nor borrow from him and neither discharge a debt to him nor let him discharge one to you. This regulation prevailed over a milder one which, while prohibiting lending and the making of a payment, would have allowed borrowing and receipt of a payment. Even the latter transactions, the extremists urged, might please the pagan and induce him to praise his idol. Once on such a festival[42] Rabbi Judah II, grandson of Judah the Prince, was sent a gold coin by an idolater,[43] apparently as a present, and asked Resh Laqish who happened to be with him what to do. "If I do accept it, he may render thanks to his idol; if I do not, he will conceive enmity against me." The fear of giving offence is here of a very down-to-earth kind. Resh Laqish advised him to take it but to drop it into a well, as if by accident, a mishap,[44] in front of the messenger who brought it. That would obviate both the objectionable thanksgiving—because the coin was lost—and offence—because it was not refused. Thus Judah did and did not accept the coin. He did by, for a moment, taking it, the minimum gesture to satisfy the donor; and on a narrowly juristic construction, he did acquire it and therefore had the right to dispose of it. Really, really, however, by dropping it into the well the minute he got it, he never made it his own, he did not accept it.

The episode in Matthew, it is agreed,[45] contains some Pauline ideas. The role of Peter admits of a number of explanations, the simplest being that he had been a fisherman. Sometimes his power to bind and loose is quoted in this connection,[46] but I cannot see its relevance. The message Jesus conveys, by his action even more than his exposition, is to do the necessary but, if possible, without doing anything. This group is not bound to the tax. Only, for the sake of avoiding trouble, the translation of the principle into practice must be flexible, devious, subtle, clever. Basically, we are not far from the atmosphere of "Render to Caesar" and so on.[47] This, in the mouth of Jesus, is

[41] And for three days before: *m. A. Zar.* 1:1; *b. A. Zar* 6b.

[42] *b. A. Zar.* 6b, cited by Strack and Billerbeck, *op. cit.*, 885.

[43] *Min* in the original. Whatever precise sect may be contemplated, it must be one celebrating a festival which involves what the Rabbi judges to be idolatry.

[44] *Kile'aḥar yadh.* Strack and Billerbeck's literal, over-literal, translation, "*wie mit der Rückseite der Hand* (*in ungewöhnlicher Weise*)" ["as with the back of one's hand (in an unusual manner)"], fails to bring out this meaning. Goldschmidt, *Der babylonische Talmud,* VII (1903), 815, may have had it in mind though he is highly obscure: "*Ich meine en passant*" ["I mean incidentally"]. Mishcon, Abodah Zarah (*The Babylonian Talmud,* ed. Epstein, Nezikin VII) (1935), 27, gets it wrong: "I mean you should do it by sleight of hand." He would, that is, have the coin thrown away without the messenger noticing. But if he does not notice, he will report to the sender that everything is fine—and the idol will be glorified.

[45] See Johnson, *op. cit.*, 465 f.

[46] See Johnson, *op. cit.*, 465.

[47] Mark 12:17; Matt 22:21; Luke 20:25. On the riddling nature of the saying see my *He That Cometh* (1966), 9, 18. [433, n. 26.]

by no means a counsel of subservience to the state, rather one of minimum performance. It is phrased so evasively that the adversaries are left floundering, with nothing to get their teeth into; yet the wise will understand. That Matthew alone preserves the paragraph about the temple tax may yet turn out to be more revealing than is being held so far.

In conclusion, let me suggest that the evangelists would have understood the subject of this talk. Three indications. First, there is their sophisticated, substantive treatment of the responsibilities in question. Secondly, in not fewer than five cases—fasting, plucking corn, washing hands, Hosanna and meal companions—the same basic shape of the story is discernible, however much it may be adapted by a given writer to his special aims; and this is so though in four cases, originally at least, the master is questioned about his disciples and in the fifth the disciples are questioned about the master. Thirdly, in Mark and Luke,[48] three of the cases form a series; and this again though, originally, in the first the disciples are answerable for their master while in the second and third it is the other way round.[49]

[48] Mark 2:15 ff.; Luke 5:28 ff.

[49] Paper read at the S. N. T. S. meeting at Claremont on 31 August 1972. My thanks are due to Professor Kingsley Barrett for valuable criticism.

The Authority of the Church and Private Judgement*

I.

The problem of the authority of the Church and private judgement is as intricate as any theological problem can be: and the first discovery one makes in considering this problem from the Jewish point of view is rather discouraging. It is the discovery that there exists no fully worked-out solution. Certainly, many great Jewish writers have dealt with the problem, especially in post-Talmudic times. But it is, I think, safe to say that none of them has created a system as clear and coherent as, e.g., the system of the Roman Catholic Church. The question arises: Why is that so? Why is it that the Jews, in particular the ancient Jews, have not laid down a logical and complete set of rules regarding the authority of the Church and private judgement? It seems to me that, broadly speaking, there are two factors accounting for this deficiency.

First of all, as is well-known, one of the notable features of Judaism is the absence of missionary activity. There have been periods, it is true, when even the Jews tried to make proselytes. But, in contradistinction to Christians and Mohammedans, they never regarded this kind of work as a great unavoidable duty. Now, if you preach your religion to the adherents of other creeds, if you wish to make your religion universal, you must state your principles, you must organize the development of dogma, you must establish a general, clear-cut doctrine on the relation of the Church and its individual members. The Jews neither did, nor do, feel this need for an accurate and explicit formulation of doctrine. It is only when Judaism is attacked, by dissentients from within or by rival creeds from without, that they have to take up their position and explain it. But the theories evolved in this manner are counter-theories; however brilliant and convincing, they rarely go further than is required by the attack; and they change according to the nature of the attack. The Jews, since they have no mandate to teach all nations, are not compelled to go and offer non-Jewish communities a perfect, plausible and workable theology. The second reason why the problem under discussion has not been fully elaborated by Jewish philosophers is closely connected with the first: but it is of a more fundamental character. Judaism is not merely a creed. For many centuries Jews were, and to some extent they still are, a national, social and racial community, as well as a religious community. I am no Zionist, but I should be blind were I to deny these extraordinary elements in Judaism.

Where a community is based solely on a creed, and not also held together by subsidiary bonds of a national, social and racial nature, it is essential that the various parts

*An address delivered before the Society of Jews and Christians in London.

of that creed should again and again be examined and confirmed, and, above all, that innovations, or apparent innovations, should be proved authentic. Obviously, disagreement on one or two points of the dogma may break up the community. For the Jews it is not quite so necessary to be clear about the roots and the growth of their religion. Even if certain tenets or customs are of doubtful origin, they can still be accepted by the community as a national, social and racial community. A religion must constantly justify itself: a nation carries on without bothering to do so. Incidentally, the fact that the Jews are more than a religious body appears to me to be one of the main causes of their insisting on forms and practice rather than on dogma and pure faith. Religion is founded on faith. National and social groups are founded chiefly on a common mode of life. National and social forms are observed, even though they may not be believed in or be analysed at all; and so, indeed, are religious forms once they have been adopted by a nation or society as such. Church-going and funeral services remain fashionable long after religion has gone. The Jewish customs do not express only the religious ideas of the people; they also express its national and social unity and, to this extent, are felt to be binding absolutely, on the believing and on the unbelieving.

Admittedly, then, Jewish theology does not provide us with a detailed and final solution of the problem of the authority of the Church and private judgement. It must be observed, however, that the sources, and even the ancient sources, contain a good deal more about this question than one might be inclined to suppose; and, before going on to outline the modern situation, I should like to call attention to a Talmudic tractate which so far has been strangely neglected. I mean the tractate entitled Horayoth—Instructions, Decisions. A large part of this tractate deals with the case where the Sanhedrin, or another court, lays down a rule contrary to the Law. Pastor Windfuhr, joint-editor of a German translation of the Mishnah and a man of great merit, says in his preface to this tractate: "The reader, when he has finished the tractate Horayoth, will gladly put it away as of little profit, just as the translator did. For it has not sprung from the real life of the ancient Jewish people; it never constituted the legal basis for the actual practice in the matters raised, but it owes its existence to the scrupulous care of its authors who would in no circumstances allow any of the commandments revealed in the Torah to disappear from the field of their Law-bound devout studies." The whole of Horayoth, according to Pastor Windfuhr, is an artificial and confused piece of work made up with a view to getting some meaning out of Leviticus 4 and parallel passages.

I am not going here to examine whether Pastor Windfuhr is right in ascribing to the tractate a purely theoretical significance. Supposing he is right, I should say that the tractate is an achievement all the more striking. However academic the discussion, however far-fetched the connexion between the views expressed and the Biblical passages from which the Rabbis claim to derive them, the main ideas that appear in this section of the Talmud are extremely interesting. In fact, it is the subject here under notice—the authority of the Church and private judgement, certain aspects of which are investigated by the Rabbis. As usual, the Rabbis contemplate particular, concrete cases, not the problem as a whole (though there is less casuistry here than in other tractates). But the conclusions which they propose (especially those to be found in the earlier Tannaitic part, upon which I shall concentrate), are suggestive of the tendencies noticeable, or even prevalent, in all branches of Judaism and at all periods of its long history. The very fact that the courts, among them the Great Court, the Sanhedrin at Jerusalem, are considered capable of proclaiming a rule contrary to the Law is significant. There is no definite organ in Judaism recognized as infallible. The Sanhedrin, properly constituted and proceeding in the prescribed fashion, may arrive at a false result.

The next point to be remarked upon is the difference made by the Rabbis between the case where a court gives a wrong instruction unwittingly, and the case where a court wantonly deviates from the Law: in the opinion of the Rabbis, the highest authority may be guilty of heresy. A further distinction is established, partly coinciding with the one I have just mentioned, but more directly relevant to the problem with which we are concerned; the distinction between a decree of the court uprooting an entire "body," an entire principle, an entire complex of the Law, and a decree of the court annulling only a portion of such a complex. The examples given in the Talmud show that "to uproot an entire complex" means to deny or disregard the whole Biblical regulation of a certain matter; while "to annul a portion" means to transgress only a particular rule and one, moreover, which is not expressly set forth in the Bible. For instance, an instruction stating "There is naught in the Law concerning the Sabbath" would be uprooting an entire complex; an instruction stating "The Law treats of the Sabbath, but he who carries a burden on Sabbath from a private domain to the public domain is not culpable" would be annulling only a portion. We might say, if we are not afraid of generalizing, that the distinction before us is between a decree doing away with a whole section of the written Law and a decree inconsistent only with a particular rule belonging to the oral Law, the Law based on interpretation, Rabbinic Law. To maintain that the Law knows no such thing as the Sabbath at all is to deny a commandment clearly enunciated in the Bible: but there is no express prohibition in the Bible of carrying a burden on Sabbath from one's house to the street.

It is worth noting that, according to the Talmud, a decree of a court uprooting an entire complex cannot but be the result of a deliberate, wanton rejection of the Law. A court may come to a wrong decision unwittingly where a particular rule of the oral Law (such as the prohibition of carrying from a private domain to the public domain) is concerned. But no court, the Talmud assumes, can disregard unwittingly an entire complex (e.g., the Sabbath as such). To generalize again, for the Talmud, a court, an assembly of sages, begins to be fallible in the usual narrower sense of the word, in the sense of being liable to commit ordinary errors of judgement, only when it comes to points of oral Law, interpretation, Rabbinic Law.

II.

If we now turn to the critical question of what attitude the Rabbis expect of an individual man in the case of a false instruction, the general rule seems to be that he who acts on a false instruction is free from all responsibility. There are, however, three important exceptions to this rule. First, where a court wantonly abandons the Law, an individual conforming to the decree is not fully excused, even if his personal good faith cannot be questioned. The idea underlying this exception is, I suggest, not so much that anybody ought to feel when a decision constitutes a deliberate repudiation of the Law, as that a court which deliberately teaches heresy puts itself altogether outside the boundaries of Jewish life. The instructions of a court of this kind can be of no weight whatever: the man observing them may be perfectly honest, yet he commits a sin (though only "a sin in error") as if the court had never sat at all. Secondly, the rule as to freedom from responsibility does not apply to one who follows a false instruction, not only knowing that it is false, but positively bent on breaking the Law. The reason for this exception is obvious: if a man performs an unlawful act with intent to defy the Law, the nature of his crime is not altered by the existence of a false instruction declaring that act to be permitted. As part of the whole system of tradition and evolution, this exception is of no small significance. For it means that there is a certain limit beyond which each individual person has to account for his own deeds; and that in the case of a court so corrupt that acceptance of its decrees would amount to active, open participation in the overthrow of the Law, you must choose between making yourself guilty of the gravest offence and resisting the authority.

Finally, the third exception, perhaps the most important one for the purpose of this paper, consists in the special liability placed on a scholar. The Talmud distinguishes between two types of addressees of false instructions: the ordinary layman, and the scholar who is himself able and entitled to teach the Law. It is only the former who, provided he does not act on purpose to defy the Law, incurs no blame by carrying out a false instruction. The latter has to satisfy one more condition: he must not only (as the layman) act without intent to defy the Law: he must act without realizing at all that the instruction is false. A scholar who realizes that the court is wrong and nevertheless complies with the decisions, is liable to a sin-offering even if he does not scorn the Law as such (if he did, he could not, of course, put things right by an offering). This principle—and the Rabbis formulate it as a principle in concise, pregnant words—clearly implies that, even if a decree has been passed by the highest authority, a scholar has not only the right but also the duty to go his own way should he find it contrary to the Law: the position of a scholar, under this régime, is one of great independence and responsibility. I am only looking at the same matter from a different angle when I say that the Rabbis, by excepting the scholar from the general rule, severely restrict the power of the courts. Their decrees may be examined and, if necessary, rejected by any of the spiritual leaders of the community.

The little I have said may suffice to show that the tractate Horayoth is not just so much barren ground. I cannot, within the compass of these brief observations, give even a rough sketch of the history of the problem in Judaism. It is indeed a fascinating history. There existed, it may be recalled, many divergent schools of thought in the period of Jesus and for about a hundred years after His death. To prevent Judaism from disintegrating, to make the Rabbis of different camps give up their private opinions and agree on a common line of teaching, was an urgent task. We have seen that, according to the Talmud, a man learned in the Law is not excused if he consciously submits to a false instruction of the court. There is, however, another side to the matter: the Talmud contains the strictest provisions against "an elder who rebels against the decision of the court." Actually, a scholar who ignores the court's well-founded ruling is to be put to death. In this connexion, I might remark, the Talmud makes a valuable distinction. So long as a scholar confines himself to stating his view, to differing from the court academically, he is exempt from punishment; it is only when he offers positive resistance, by settling actual cases submitted to him in a way disapproved of by the court, that he can be condemned by the earthly authority. This is no negligible step in the direction of freedom of thought, and even of teaching, as opposed to freedom of action. It is highly improbable that any Talmudic scholar suffered the death-penalty for his decisions. But we know that it was quite usual for the president of the Sanhedrin to place his antagonists under an interdict. An incident which occurred under the presidency of Gamaliel II (who flourished at the end of the first century and the beginning of the second) illustrates well this eternal struggle between organization and individual. In the view of Rabbi Joshua, the president had made a mistake in fixing the date of the Day of Atonement. Gamaliel requested Joshua to appear before him on the day which he, Joshua, considered the right Day of Atonement, with staff, bag and purse. Joshua complied. But Gamaliel was later deposed from his office (though only for a short while) for this and other acts of tyranny.

As a matter of fact, most points relating to the problem of the authority of the Church and private judgement were raised, in one way or another, in the tremendous controversies of that time. It was in that time that the Rabbis attempted to solve the question of tradition and interpretation. There was a group laying stress on those teachings which had been handed down by tradition; there was another group inclined to elaborate and develop the Law by interpretation: and a compromise had to be found. It was in that time, too, that they attempted to put in order tradition as such. Tradition had become corrupt, conflicts were innumerable. The Sanhedrin, therefore, summoned persons in possession of old teachings, and made them give evidence as in a trial. Their evidence was examined, possibly recorded, and the Law fixed by a majority vote of the court. It was in that time that the Rabbis had to face the antithesis of the Law revealed and the Law as in the hands of man. During one debate, a voice from Heaven was heard deciding in favour of one of the parties; yet Rabbi Joshua refused to accept the verdict. He maintained that the Law was entrusted to man once for all, and that doubts were to be settled, not by miracles, but by discussion and a vote of the majority. It is interesting to note the prominence of the majority principle (which, by the way, the Rabbis find in the Bible).

From a rational point of view, the majority-principle seems odd in matters of religion. It is sensible enough for individuals in a community, even a religious community, to act and to behave as the majority of the community or as an authoritative body decrees. But the assumption that the resolutions of the majority will express the true content of the religion (or even the assumption that they will do so in the long run, after sporadic failures) is, from a rational point of view, most troublesome. It might be worth while to study how far it was regarded as really leading to the divine Law.

But I have already dwelt too long on the past. I leave the Talmud, and, with a heavy heart, I skip the Middle Ages; no word on the Karaites of the eighth and ninth centuries, who revolted from the Rabbinic system back to Scripture, thereby giving rise to a renewed examination of all the problems of organized religion; no word on the rise of Jewish philosophy culminating in Maimonides. One general point only I should like to mention, because it is not always sufficiently taken into account. In considering the history of the problem of Church and individual, one must not forget that similar problems present themselves in other fields; and that the Churches may well have adopted some of their solutions from elsewhere. The problem of master and slave, or, more precisely, the authority of the master and the judgement of the slave, is distinctly related to that of Church and individual: and ancient lawyers had a good deal to say about the former, for the question was practical in many ways. Even more nearly related is the problem of the authority of the commander, the king, the State, and the judgement of the soldier, the subject, the citizen. In *Henry V* the King, disguised as a private, says to some soldiers: "Methinks I could not die anywhere so contented as in the King's company, his cause being just and his quarrel honourable." One of the soldiers replies: "That's more than we know," and another adds: "Aye, or more than we should seek after: for we know enough if we know we are the King's subjects: if his cause be wrong, our obedience to the King wipes the crime of it out of us." This dialogue would need little modification to be fit for a Guide to the Faithful.

III.

What is the position in Judaism at the present time? As I have to be very brief, I shall begin by stating which sides of the subject I am not going to consider. For a Christian, I suppose, the phrase "private judgement" may denote two different things of fairly equal importance: it may denote the internal disposition, the beliefs of the individual, and it may denote his external acts, his conduct. Now I have shown before that in Judaism, for certain reasons, it is conduct that matters most. Accordingly I shall concentrate upon the problem of the authority of the Church and private conduct, leaving aside (as far as possible) the question of private beliefs. But even in this reduced shape the problem is too vast to be dealt with in the remaining part of this survey. I shall therefore say nothing about the actual organization of contemporary Judaism, about our congregations and the larger unions formed by them, about Rabbis in office and Rabbis not officially appointed, about the lay governors of congregations, and so forth. There exist, of course, a number of rules as to the degree of obedience that the individual must render to the administration. But these rules, which I might call political rules, are of comparatively minor interest if regarded by themselves. Very few or none of them can nowadays be enforced. Judaism probably has less power of compelling observance of its political rules than most other Churches, and it seems to me that, of political rules which have no sanctions attached to them whatever, only the tendency, the theoretical basis, is really worth inquiring into (no offence is meant to international lawyers). In any case, to discuss the place of the individual in the actual political organization of Judaism would be discussing a very secondary matter. The cardinal problem, on the solution of which depends one's attitude to all others, is much deeper. It is this: To what extent ought the individual Jew to conform to what is laid down by the recognized heralds of the Law? Again, to what extent is the Church itself, are the recognized heralds of the Law themselves, affected by the conduct of the individual Jew?

On this great problem the Jews are by no means agreed. The two extreme parties, as is common knowledge, are the orthodox Jews and the liberal Jews. According to the former, God gave Moses two distinct kinds of Law: the written Law, the Pentateuch, and the oral Law, preserved to us in the post-Pentateuchal portions of the Bible, in the Mishnah and in the Babylonian Gemara. In addition, Moses was taught certain principles of interpretation by means of which the oral Law can be deduced from the written Law, from the Pentateuch. For though God revealed to Moses the oral Law itself, He foresaw that in course of time many details would be forgotten or become doubtful; in these cases, the principles of interpretation enabled the authors of the Talmud to find the point in the Bible. The written Law, the oral Law, and the principles of interpretation are all three unalterable. Every Jew must accept them wholly; they rest on the wisdom and will of God, not of man.

Yet there is room for private initiative even under this rigid system. Certainly, the Law as such is complete, is fully contained in the Bible, Mishnah and Babylonian Gemara. But our human knowledge of the Law is not complete, and, in consequence, innovations, sound or unsound, are possible: that which is deemed lawful or illegal today may be deemed the opposite tomorrow. In other words, the decrees of Bible, Mishnah and Babylonian Gemara cannot be changed by any of the Rabbis living after the redaction of the Talmud. But the Rabbis may differ from one another, and correct one another, as far as the explanation, the meaning of these decrees, is concerned. What it actually comes to is that orthodox Judaism moves very slowly indeed, and that fresh ideas usually are received with the utmost distrust. It would, however, be unjust to deny that, given favourable conditions, a great man can make even orthodox Judaism steer a new course, or at least shift the emphasis from one branch of the Law to another: Maimonides is a convincing example.

The liberal doctrine is radically different from the orthodox. Strictly speaking, the liberal Church has no canon. If the Bible and, in a far lesser degree, the Talmud, constitute its main sources of inspiration, it is not because they offer us God's revealed eternal Law (essentially, these books are divine no more and no less than, e.g., Plato and Shakespeare); it is because, for one thing, they symbolize the progress of civilization in the field of religion and ethics, and, for another thing, a good many ideas and feelings expressed in them still belong to our most cherished spiritual possessions. It is clear that the liberal scheme allows the individual an infinitely greater amount of freedom than the orthodox scheme. No binding force attaches to the precepts of Bible and Talmud as such, or, for that matter, to those of any definite Law. In fact, it would be wrong for a person to stick to a code which, in his judgement, has lost its meaning. It is the task of any individual to seek a more perfect way of living, for himself and for his fellow man, than has been reached before him; to shake off such traditions as may impede his efforts; and to keep only those which have proved to be pure gold. Like mathematics and medicine, Law (if this term may be used at all in describing the liberal standpoint) is the work of man: which, needless to mention, does not imply that man can advance without the aid of God. Bible, Talmud and all other legislations are—or at any rate ought to be—mere steps to yet higher achievements.

In short, according to the liberal view, the individual has the right and duty to leave behind him any specific Law if it is no longer reconcilable with his superior knowledge and more refined conscience. Conversely, any specific Law, in addition to its lasting elements, includes rules of an ephemeral character, thus reflecting both the discernment and the weaknesses of the individual who has created or embraced it. What it actually comes to is that liberal Judaism disapproves of most ancient Jewish customs as obsolete or worse, while it continues to preach monotheism, immortality and love. There is, perhaps, little that distinguishes a liberal Jew from a Unitarian. That little, however, even liberal Judaism seems to be eager to preserve, and it is these vague and subtle, yet strong, ties of piety, which the individual is supposed to respect.

The main difficulty about orthodox Judaism is that it makes rather excessive demands on people's faith. That God at Sinai revealed the entire written and oral Law, let alone the principles of interpretation, that He meant every detail to be of eternal validity, that the authors of Mishnah and Babylonian Gemara set down the Law complete and unspoilt—all this is hard (I do not say impossible) to harmonize with the results of modern history and philosophy. The main difficulty about liberal Judaism is that it may gradually lead to disintegration. If it dispenses with any sort of formal discipline, a community of relatively small size spread over the whole world can scarcely go on for long. The individual, enfettered under the orthodox régime, is too unrestrained under the liberal.

I should like to end by saying that there is a group of Jews, midway between Orthodoxy and Liberalism, who, it is to be hoped, will work out a compromise preserving what is most valuable of each of the two conflicting doctrines. The adherents of this third party are rational enough to deal with religion scientifically; they cherish all that is positive in European civilization; they hold that God reveals Himself not only once in history and in one nation, but whenever and wherever He chooses; they require that each individual be prepared to be God's instrument: that is to say, that each individual do his best to bring about a deeper understanding of man's destination. At the same time, they believe that Judaism has a mission to fulfil, that by virtue of its unique experience it is under the obligation to bear witness to God's might, justice and goodness. They also believe that the time has not yet come for dismissing tradition. Many of our ancient customs are conducive to holiness now as they were in the past; many others can be made profitable by reinterpretation. But there exists another, more fundamental reason for upholding them: it is only by accepting the forms that the substance can be saved. It is only by observing these innumerable old rules that the lasting ideals behind them, the love of God and the love of man, are constantly brought to mind, and that the community pledged to these ideals is kept alive and intact. The forms, whether of particular utility in themselves or not, are a wall built round the ideals: so long as they are maintained, the ideals will not easily die.

Temple Tax*

Matthew's four verses about this subject[1] do not rate high in the prevalent opinion, chiefly because the introduction of the fish is uncomprehended—to say the least.[2] A further reason is the neglect of a controversy within Jewry certainly very intense in the thirties but going on right until A.D. 70. The following pages are intended to show that the little section forms a well-constructed whole; that it is definitely part of *Ur*-Christian lore and, indeed, most probably harks back to an actual occurrence; and that the fish makes perfect sense in a directive of eminent practical and spiritual importance for the earliest believers.

The collectors of the Temple tax accost Peter. What they say is translatable in two ways between which it is fortunately not necessary to decide: "Your teacher does not pay the half-shekel" or "Does your teacher not pay the half-shekel?" If we go by the first alternative, they assume resistance; but even the second presupposes suspicion—they would not be surprised by Jesus opting out, they are on the attack. The challenging of a disciple for his master's aberrations is a universal phenomenon. A Jungian is expected to defend Jung's response to the Third Reich, a devotee of EST Werner Erhard's socializing. In the first two Gospels Jesus's disciples are interrogated why he eats with publicans and sinners.[3] Peter's "Yes," however, quickly stops the confrontation. No doubt he thinks that Jesus cannot be remiss, though he may be far from sure about the ins and outs. It is likely, moreover, that his desire to get rid of the officers without ado plays a part in the terse affirmation.

As he returns from the encounter, ere he can report, Jesus divines his perplexity and enlightens him. At first sight, one might infer that we have to do with the type of disciple who does not dare or know to ask and whose interest is to be aroused by the

* Written for the *Festschrift* in honor of William R. Farmer, to be edited by E. P. Sanders. I am deeply grateful to William David Davies for criticizing the first draft of this paper. Whether he is less skeptical about the present one I dare not guess.

[1] Matt 17:24 ff. See my "Responsibilities of Master and Disciples in the Gospels," *NTS*, 19 (1972); 13 ff [see 760 ff.], and "Fraud No. 3," in *The Legal Mind: Essays for Tony Honoré*, ed. N. MacCormick and P. Birks (1986), 15.

[2] It might be worth while, as a contribution to *Wissenschaftsgeschichte* [history of scientific research], to study the diverse methods (including silence) of dealing with this embarrassment. Even authors who, as far as the rest is concerned, come close to the approach of this paper—e.g., G. A. Buttrick, "The Gospel According to St. Matthew: Exposition," *The Interpreter's Bible*, vol. 7 (1951), 465 ff., and E. Schweizer, *Das Evangelium nach Matthäus* (1976), 231 ff.—are at a loss when it comes to the haul.

[3] Matt 9:10 ff.; Mark 2:15 ff., restructure in Luke 5:29 ff. See my "Responsibilities of Master and Disciples," 11 ff. [see 758 ff.]

teacher. This type figures in the ancient Seder, from where it is taken over into Mark's day of questions: "And no one dared any longer ask him, and Jesus, commencing the discourse, said."[4] Yet the set-up before us is not quite the same. For one thing, whereas both in the Seder and in the Marcan analogue, the problem does not enter the disciple's mind till his attention is called to it, in the Temple tax story, he comes upon it himself. Again, whereas both in the Seder and in the Marcan analogue, the master refrains from unravelling the knot—his task being to get the disciple to cogitate—in the Temple tax story, Jesus does so. Lastly, maybe Peter would have asked, only that Jesus "anticipates him," gets in first. This action, as we shall see, is indeed of no mean import. It sets the tone: he has rare powers at his command. We may compare his spontaneous taking up of the dispute among his disciples as to which of them will be the greatest in the kingdom—found in Mark and Luke;[5] also, though it is less close, his precise acquaintance with the home life of the Samaritan woman in John.[6]

The handling of the Temple tax, he explains to Peter, is a far from simple matter and the "Yes" stands in need of a vital qualification. He begins his instruction by setting out the latter: ideally, he and his are not bound at all. He reasons that earthly kings exact tribute from strangers only and not from their sons. By analogy, as he and his are sons—*scil.* of the heavenly King, the Temple's sovereign—they must be free.

The antithesis between son or member of a family and stranger is common both in Greek and in Hebrew. Herodotus[7] tells of a woman whose entire kinsfolk are under sentence of death. Darius, moved by her continual laments (one is reminded of the Lucan judge[8]), allows her to pick one of the lot to live. She names a brother, whereupon he enquires why she chooses one who is "more a stranger than your children." Hosea speaks of bastards as "sons that are strangers,"[9] and the stricken Job is accounted "a stranger" by his own household.[10] Particularly relevant, however, is the attachment in Jewish religion of the label stranger to a non-priest, frequent from Exodus, "a stranger shall not eat thereof,"[11] through Sirach, "but strangers [Korah, Dathan and Abiram] were incensed against him [Aaron],[12] to the Talmud where, indeed, we find a derivative added, an abstract, strangeness, signifying the quality of being a non-priest.[13] Such a

[4] Mark 12:34 f. See my *The New Testament and Rabbinic Judaism*, (1956), 158 ff.; "The Earliest Structure of the Gospels," *NTS* 5 (1959), 180 ff.; *He That Cometh* (1966), 8 ff.; and "Zukunftsmusik," *BJRULM* 68 (1985), 58 ff. [343 ff., 334 ff., 432 f., 357 ff.]

[5] Mark 9:33 f.; Luke 9:46 ff. Not in Matt 18:1 ff.: the display of extraordinary perception in the Temple tax piece suffices. It has long been seen that there is a genetic tie between "And when they were come to Capernaum... and when he [Peter] was come into the house" in Matt 17:24 f. and "And he came to Capernaum and being in the house he said to them" in Mark 9:33. (None of it in Luke.) Which of the two descends from which may here be left open.

[6] John 4:17 ff.

[7] Herodotus, *History* 3.119.

[8] Luke 18:1 ff.

[9] Hos 5:7.

[10] Job 19:15, 17.

[11] Exod 29:33.

[12] Sir 45:18.

[13] E.g. *b. Yeb.* 68b, towards the beginning.

formation testifies to considerable reflection and discussion upon the area. The point here is that, in Jesus's time, the priests insisted on exemption from the Temple tax,[14] doubtless as "belonging" in a fashion incompatible with this obligation on strangers. The reverberations of this issue in fragmentary reports and allusions—several of which will be inspected—give us an idea of just how hotly and widely it was debated. To some degree, it appears, he is casting himself and his followers in a similar role.

Several other groups were immune: women, slaves, minors, gentiles and Samaritans. In all five cases, we have to do with a *privilegium odiosum,* a benefit that is really a degradation.[15] A specimen from our day is the non-conscription of asthmatics and homosexuals. There was, moreover, within the five a division into two ranks. Women, slaves and minors, though under no duty, yet might make payment of their own will; whereas none was accepted from gentiles and Samaritans—they were right outside, with no stake in the community. (No need here to go into fluctuations with respect to Samaritans.) To this, too, there are modern parallels. An asthmatic, not too sick, if offering to serve, will not necessarily be rejected; but the army has no room for a homosexual. The priests' contention was on a radically different level from any of these categories: for a privilege in the proper sense, a mark of excellence. They regarded themselves as intimates of the Revered one at whose feet the levy was laid. They were almost recipients of it, standing apart from, above all the rest, whether payers or non-payers. So essentially tied to their calling, in their eyes, was the exercise of this distinction that they—or at least the extremists among them—declared unenforced payment by a priest to be a sin, an abdication of their special relationship. Persons dispensed from the draft because of their absolutely vital work in thermonuclear development would be something of a present-age counterpart. Or better, in 1914, the young man at Oxford who, unlike most of his contemporaries, did not volunteer. When a patriotic lady, passing him in the street, reproved him, "What are you doing here? Why are you not with your comrades in the trenches, defending civilization against the Huns?," he replied: "Madam, I am civilization."

It is against this background that the reaction of the Pharisees becomes understandable. To them, the attitude summarized was one more instance of unwarranted priestly pretensions—smacking of Sadducean exclusivity. At the academy of Jabneh, one Ben Bukri reported a pre-destruction tradition to the effect that a priest paying voluntarily was committing no sin.[16] Johanan ben Zaccai, the academy's head, now as before advocated an even stronger line: it was sinful for a priest to abstain from paying. The Mishnah's legal ruling, which must have prevailed in the final years of the State whenever the Pharisees had the upper hand, agrees with Johanan, that is, priests ought

[14] *m. Shek.* 1:3 f. See H.L. Strack and P. Billerbeck, *Kommentar zum Neuen Testament aus Talmud und Midrasch,* vol. 1 (1926), 762 f. *Hophshi* and *eleutheros* denote similar freedom already in 1 Sam 17:25.

[15] See my "Enfant Terrible," *HTR* 68 (1975), 371 ff. [see *Talmudic Law*, 137 ff.]; "Johanan ben Beroqa and Women's Rights," in *ZSS,* 99 (1982), Rom. Abt., 27 ff. [see *Talmudic Law*, 148 ff.]; and "Fraud No. 3," 4 ff.

[16] Ben Bukri is known only for this testimony, cited, besides *m. Shek.* 1:4, in *b. Men.* 21b f., 46b; *b. Arak.* 4a.

to pay, nonetheless "one does not compel them, for the sake of the ways of peace."[17] Relaxations in order to avoid ill-feeling are no rarity in Rabbinic—or New Testament—teaching;[18] the very pericope here studied ends up with one, on the part of those who feel unjustly taxed. It is worth noting, however, that, possibly, a variant of the Mishnah's compromise, preserved in the Jerusalemite Talmud, reflects a stage when the priests' aspirations still enjoyed a measure of recognition. Instead of "the ways of peace," we meet here the far less usual term "the ways of honour": indicating, possibly, less a mitigation of a principle than a genuine relief on account of exalted vocation.[19] After all, vestiges of their past glory survive in fairly late statements—e.g. a fourth-century one, that the priests, when officiating, were representatives, not of the congregation before God, but of God before the congregation.[20]

In debate with Johanan ben Zaccai, prior to the catastrophe, the priests appealed to an injunction in Leviticus[21] according to which offerings brought by them for themselves must be totally burnt, without any portion being eaten. Quite a few offerings, their arguments went, as for example the showbread, the ingredients of which the Temple purchases with its revenue,[22] are expressly given over to them as food in the Pentateuch.[23] If they contributed to the revenue, they would be helping purchase these offerings,[24] ergo be bringing them—in part at least—for themselves, ergo be precluded from eating them. Seeing that, on the contrary, they are encouraged to do so, it follows that they must have no hand in the purchase. The conclusion: they may not lawfully participate in the tax. It would be naive to think that the provision in Leviticus and the tortuous ratiocination taking off from it were the actual root of their claim. The latter came first and was perhaps in existence for centuries before being pegged to the Pentateuch.[25] Roughly, from Hillel on, any regulation, to be fully binding, had to be based on a Scriptural law. Mattathias, for instance, and his entourage had allowed their troops to fight on a Sabbath if attacked, after experience showed that, otherwise, the Syrians would simply annihilate them; and there is no indication that they invoked a Mosaic ordinance. Some hundred-and-fifty years later, however, Hillel managed to prove from Deuteronomy that a Jewish army need not interrupt a siege on a Sabbath. This code forbids the use of fruit-bearing trees for siegeworks, adding: "only those not for food, with them you shall build bulwarks against the city until it be subdued." "Until it be sub-

[17] *m. Shek.* 1:3 f. and, consistent with it, 1:6.

[18] See my "Pauline Contributions to a Pluralistic Culture," in *Jesus and Man's Hope*, ed. D.G. Miller and D.Y. Hadidian 2 (1971), 233 ff. [546 ff.]

[19] Such distinctions as that between interrupting one's prayer to greet somebody from fear and doing the same in acknowledgment of his honor are pertinent: *m. Ber.* 2:1 and accompanying Gemara. "The honor of kings" occurs in *b. Ber.* 19a.

[20] *b. Yom.* 19a f.; *b. Kidd.* 23b; *b. Ned.* 35b. See Strack and Billerbeck, *Kommentar*, vol. 3 (1926), 4; vol. 4, pt. 1 (1928), 150.

[21] Lev 6:16.

[22] Confirmed by Josephus, *Ant.* 3.10.7.255.

[23] Lev 24:9.

[24] It would be interesting to examine this construction within a history of legal personality in Jewish law.

[25] The Roman priests who protested against being taxed in 196 B.C.—Livy, *From the Founding of the City* 33.52.4—had no Pentateuch to support them.

dued": that is to say, according to Hillel, without desisting on a Sabbath.[26] An interpretation manifestly superimposed on, not generated by, the original tenor—just like the priests'. Again, when Jesus's disciples pluck corn on a Sabbath, in all three Synoptics he supports them by referring to David and his band who, as they suffered hunger, ate the showbread reserved for the sanctuary. In Matthew, he appends a justification from what may be read "in the law." In the Book of Numbers, the Temple priests are supposed to break the Sabbath, say, for the slaughter of sacrifices. What is now involved, he urges, is greater than the Temple, ergo plainly supersedes those rules. The conclusion: the plucking of the corn is licit. Once more, a highly refined syllogism, employing the technical step *a minori ad maius,* not at all envisaged by the old text.[27] The derivation from the Torah of the prohibition of suicide (subscribed to by Hamlet when he deplores "the Everlasting's canon 'gainst self-slaughter") and the duty of procreation (in the Bible, a blessing) are of the same nature.[28] The number of these cases is large; enormous if we include all the slightly less extreme ones, where the passage resorted to contains some element at least of what is made of it. A systematic exploration would throw much new light on the evolution of the Rabbinic edifice.

The assumption by Jesus and his circle of priestly status of some sort is traceable from early on in so many different strata of the New Testament that—discounting any reinforcement from the Dead Sea Scrolls—its beginnings may safely be ascribed to his lifetime. It is indeed met in this quotation, just adverted to, of the precedent set by David and his retinue who, in an emergency, ate the priests' showbread. The implication is that their overriding task entitled them, even obliged them, to act thus, they were directly engaged in executing God's Messianic plan,[29] and now it is Jesus and his faithful who occupy this place. The additional plea, from precept (the Book of Numbers) instead of from example (David's boldness), puts the notion in more explicit terms: the Sabbath restrictions, suspended for the priests serving in the Temple, must *a fortiori* not stand in the way of a greater service, greater priests. The "cleansing" of the Temple with, in Mark, prominence accorded to a technical detail of the daily priestly business,[30] is another strong piece of evidence.

Jesus is not willing to waive the prerogative: this is the major premise he impresses on Peter. From here, however, he goes on to a formidable complication. A downright

[26] 1 Mac 2:39 ff.; Josephus, *Ant.* 12.6.2.276 ff., 13.1.3.12 f.; Deut 20:20; *t. Erub.* 4:7. See my "Texts and Interpretation in Roman and Jewish Law," *JJSOC* 3 (1961) 9, 15 [*Talmudic Law*, 182, 191.]

[27] Matt 12:1 ff.; Mark 2:33 ff.; Luke 6:1 ff.; 1 Sam 21:1 ff.; Num 28:9 f. See my *New Testament and Rabbinic Judaism,* 67 ff. [249 ff.]

[28] See my, "*Das Alte Testament im Neuen—aus jüdischer Sicht,*" *Xenia*, vol. 10 [1984], 7 (German translation by W. Schuller), "The Old Testament in the New: A Jewish Perspective," [43 ff.], where the reading back of the ban on suicide into the Ten Commandments is noted (in section 1); and my *The Duty of Procreation* (1977), 1 ff., 42.

[29] It would not be surprising if pious scribes of Jesus's era had taken David's declaration in 1 Sam 21:3, "The king has commanded me a business," in the sense not of "Saul has commanded me" but of "God has commanded me." For one thing, on this basis David would not be guilty of deception. That the interpretation is not preserved may be due precisely to the use made of the episode in the gospels. But, of course, one cannot build on this speculation.

[30] Mark 11:16, a provision singled out by the priest Josephus, *Contra Apionem* 2.8.106.

refusal of the administration's demand might put off[31] people not otherwise hostile—interfering with his mission. No doubt there are conditions in which a path must be continued regardless. But the Temple tax does not fall under them, hence creates a dilemma. He solves it by devising a course which formally, in semblance, amounts to perfect compliance, so will avoid any discord while, in reality, they part with nothing that is genuinely their own, so are not subjecting themselves to the impost. The latter is to be satisfied with a coin Peter will take from the mouth of the first fish he catches. Whosever it was in the past, it became ownerless when the fish carried it off, and now it falls to the finder. It can, therefore, be validly employed to discharge a debt and—equally important—no uninitiated will be aware of anything out of the ordinary. Nevertheless, as far as substance is concerned rather than image, no concession is made. Economically and psychologically, the passing on of money coming from nowhere and the group's property for a fleeting moment only, just long enough to fulfill the purpose of appeasing an environment of deficient insight, is not a true contribution on their part.

Dodges of this pattern were familiar in that period. Here is one dating from before the middle of the first century B.C. and going on for hundreds of years.[32] Under the austere Roman reglement of insolvency, infamy befell not only an actual bankrupt but also a debtor who got his creditor to be content with a percentage. A creditor wishing to spare his debtor this punishment would cooperate in the following procedure. Say, the debtor owed 1,200 and all he had was 200. He paid 200 and the creditor immediately returned it, by way of gift. The debtor then paid it again, to get it back again as a gift. And so on—and only the sixth payment was kept by the creditor. Formally, in semblance, the debtor had now paid in full. But 1,000 out of the 1,200 were, so to speak, brought along by a fish, provided to him for just the brief hour of the transaction, economically and psychologically not a true disbursement by him. A Talmudic anecdote,[33] where it is not payment that is simulated but acceptance of a gift, is worth quoting here because the reason for staging the make-believe is to forestall the would-be donor's resentment: reminiscent of Jesus's reason for feigning conformity. On a pagan festival, Jews were to refrain from any dealings that might boost the thanksgiving to idols—such as lending or making a present to a pagan. Some Rabbis worried even about receiving a present since this might make the pagan rejoice and bless his gods. When Judah II (grandson of Judah the Prince) on such a festival was sent a gold piece by a pagan acquaintance, he asked Resh Laqish who happened to be with him: "If I do accept, he may render thanks to his idol, if I do not, he will conceive enmity against me." At Resh Laqish's advice, he took the piece but at once, while the messenger was still there, dropped it into a well as if by accident. Thus the donor, on being told, could not be insulted—since his gift was accepted—but neither would he be moved to praise his

[31] *Skandalizo:* when it has its full weight, "to give offense to somebody leading to his alienation, missing the right way, stumbling"; at times, little more than "to give offense to somebody"—our modern "to scandalize." See G. Stählin, art. "*Skandalon, Skandalizo*," *Theologisches Wörterbuch zum Neuen Testament,* founded G. Kittel, ed. G. Friedrich and others, vol. 7 (1964), 343 ff.

[32] *Digest* 46.3.67, Marcellus XIII *digestorum.* See my *Roman Law* (1969), 93 f., and "Fraud No. 3," 14.

[33] *b. A. Zar* 6a, cited by Strack-Billerbeck, *Kommentar,* vol. 1, 885.

idol—since no sooner was it accepted than lost. It was "accepted" in inverted commas, for a few seconds, so no animosity would ensue.

Modern commentators tend to overlook the fact that Jesus is supplying an illustration, a model, and that it is offered not for literal imitation but for imitation as to its substantive content, its message—namely, that while the position of this special priesthood is inabdicable, it must be exercised gently. *Au fond*, it accords with the counsel: "Be subtle as the serpents and harmless as the doves," which, curiously, like the Temple tax narrative, is preserved only in Matthew.[34] His sending out of Peter for a coin the first fish will present draws on his superior capacity of being informed about odd circumstances, certainly not meant to be reproduced. As noticed above, the session opens by his realizing what has occurred without being told. This is a peculiar knowing of past and present. His mandate regarding the coin actually implies a foreknowing—such as he manifests when he predicts to the disciples preparing his entry into Jerusalem that they will find a colt tied for his use[35] and to those looking for a room for his Passover meal that they will meet a guide.[36] Of course, once he is gone, the community cannot rely on a magical haul. But this does not dispense them from heeding the core of the lesson. They will have to contrive mundane, ever varying ruses enabling them to reconcile the conflicting requirements—to live up to their election at once and not upset the ignorant. It is the master alone who may choose a shortcut bordering on the miraculous for the exemplary precedent. For one thing, in this way, it can be flawless—as even the best-intentioned schemes lacking supernatural assistance seldom are.[37] It should be observed that this mode of instruction is evidenced among the Tannaites. The clearing up of a complex of questions by Gamaliel II, successor of Johanan ben Zaccai as president of Jabneh, involved his astounding identification of a person he had never seen before: "He recognized him through the holy spirit and from his words we learnt three things."[38]

In the most fundamental respect, Jesus's attitude to tribute to Caesar is at one with that just outlined. Caesar does occupy an elevated rank, but when his bidding clashes with God's, God must prevail: in the maxim to pay "what is Caesar's to Caesar and what is God's to God," the emphasis is on the final words. Often, here too, the best course will be to be serpent as well as dove, to get along by means of loopholes.

(Wolfgang Kunkel[39] lived up to it in the Second World War. He was a military judge in the East. In 1943, one captain denounced another one for having listened to the Moscow radio a year previously: a capital crime. What prompted him to come forward

[34] Matt 10:16.

[35] Matt 21:2 ff.; Mark 11:2 ff.; Luke 19:30 ff.

[36] Mark 14:13 ff.; Luke 22:10 ff., considerably reduced in Matt 26:18 f.

[37] Take the one mentioned above, where creditor and debtor colluded to save the latter from infamy. The earlier jurists did not pass it: they decided that, as 1,000 came in effect from the creditor's funds, it remained a case of insolvency. By contrast, even these diehards would have had no complaint about money furnished to the debtor by a god or, for that matter, discovered inside a fish.

[38] *t. Pes* 1:27; *y. A. Zar.* 40a; *b. Erub.* 64b; *Lev. Rab.* on 27:2.

[39] A sketch of his personality by Dieter Nörr may be found in *Gedächtnisschrift für Wolfgang Kunkel*, edd. D. Nörr and D. Simon (1984), 9 ff.

at that moment was that the culprit had just been appointed *Bahnhofskommandant*, i.e., was given charge of a little railstation. Terrifying the degree by which this put him ahead of the accuser was minuscule; and so, of course, was either's life expectancy. Kunkel did not want to pronounce sentence of death. The trouble was that his verdict would have to be approved by higher-ups behind the front, and they were ruthless. It would have been no use, for example, to point to the promotion as proof that the man was doing his duty to the full. Yet he found a way. The decree which ordained the death penalty was issued *für den grossdeutschen Raum*, "for the greater German realm." The area around Moscow was not part of this, but again, to simply state this and acquit would not have sufficed: the Berlin authorities would have rejected it as formalistic and weak-kneed. Kunkel declared the decree inapplicable because the Moscow area was *noch nicht*, "not yet," incorporated in the *grossdeutsche Raum*. By phrasing it thus, he appeared to be absolutely confident of the outcome: it was only a matter of a few clean-up operations. To make doubly sure, and no doubt also to teach the informer a lesson, he added a rider in which he severely censured the latter for waiting so long before bringing so serious an offense to the attention of his superiors. The judgment was duly confirmed.)

Indeed, Jesus's reply itself was "subtle," serpent-like, so framed that while sympathizers will appreciate where priority is placed, no easy pretext for intervention is handed to the government. Significantly, in Mark, this section corresponds to that of the Seder exhibiting the type of disciple concerned about law, and he also receives a cryptic answer.[40] The opacity of the saying is underlined by the contradictory meanings attributed to it already in New Testament times. According to Luke,[41] it was used in Jesus's arraignment before Pilate, distorted into an unambiguous No to Roman taxation. In Romans,[42] it is pretty much the opposite. (Admittedly, juristic acumen can turn around the clearest dictum. A forthright Mishnaic paragraph treats murderers, robbers and excise-gathers as equally deserving to be misled. The Gemara transmits an exegesis of it which, deferring to Caesar like Romans, virtually annuls the part as to the publicans.[43]) Of course, notwithstanding the profound affinity, there are bound to be major dissimilarities between the two cases. One is that, Caesar being a heathen tyrant, whatever may speak against submitting to his tribute, it cannot be his fatherhood; nor can we expect from Jesus a warning against "putting him off." Another, that, in the gospel framework, the question respecting Caesar emanates from hostile outsiders, whereas that respecting the Temple is gone into within the inner circle. As a result, the answer to the former has to remain on a general level, whereas that to the latter follows up the governing principle with specific, practical guidance.

In conclusion, some remarks on setting. Few nowadays deny that the first half of the pericope goes back to before the destruction. After it, the conquerors appropriated

[40] Mark 12:13 ff. See the writings listed in footnote 4.

[41] Luke 23:2, prepared for by 20:20. See J. M. Creed, *The Gospel According to St. Luke* (1930), 247. The historicity or otherwise of the notice is immaterial in the present connection.

[42] Rom 13:6 f.

[43] *m. Ned.* 3:4; *b. Ned.* 28a.

the tax, diverting it to heathen worship.[44] To take the argument as envisaging this *Fiscus Judaicus* will not do. No first-century Christian author can have thought of the saved ones as sons of the Emperor to whom it went, and to be sons of the Highest would be irrelevant if the tax was not his.

The second half is mostly treated as an eccentric appendage. There is a tendency, moreover, to postulate relatively late elements both in it and in the first. If the foregoing exposition is approved, the pre-destruction date holds good for the pericope in toto, including the catch—essential to the complete, down-to-earth teaching. As for the late elements, the arguments are unconvincing. Jesus's repudiation of liability is alleged to evince a disdain for the Temple at variance with his zeal as he "cleanses" it.[45] In reality, his stand founds on the conviction that he and his are its truest priests. The view here combated would mean (unless the comparison he draws is quite off, *hinkend*) that the sons of the earthly kings are left untroubled by the treasury because they despise the throne; whereas, palpably, the reason is their closeness to it, their share in it. It would mean also that, when Jesus, in defence of his disciples, cites the eating of hallowed food by David and his men, he is depicting them as scornful of the sanctuary—not credible. They were, indeed, at this moment its most devoted fighters, precursors of Jesus's group. This is not to exclude the possibility that the preservation (precarious, via Matthew only) of the incident owes something to precisely this misinterpretation of it as documenting contempt. Again, the prominence of Pauline ideas is noted as militating against the first half of the century: the Christian's freedom from the law as a child of God and the yielding in order not to cause the weak to stumble.[46] But it may be Paul who is secondary. The freedom theme in the Temple tax story is far less developed than in his writings; and all the three Synoptics carry strong pronouncements by Jesus against putting off the little ones.[47]

W. D. Davies lists the second half among the Matthean revisions by which a Jesuanic absolute is toned down, to make it livable with; it is akin, as he sees it, to Paul's procedure anent tribute to Caesar.[48] The parallel, however, is illusory. Jesus's saying about the tribute guardedly (since ill-wishers are listening) recommends a bending which, however, must never be such as to detract from the principal allegiance; Paul bids us pay.[49] By contrast, Jesus's saying about Temple tax openly (since he is address-

[44] Josephus, *Bell.* 7.6.6.218; Suetonius, *Lives of the Caesars*, Domitian 12.2; Dio Cassius, *Roman History Epit.* 65.7.2.

[45] See e.g. E. Lohmeyer, *Das Evangelium des Matthäus*, ed. W. Schmauch (1956), 275; F.V. Filson, *A Commentary on the Gospel According to St. Matthew* (1960), 195; G. Stählin, "*Skandalon, Skandalizo*," 350 f. Basically similar is the position of C. H. Dodd, *History and the Gospel* (1938), 90 ff.: The story "of the Coin in the Fish's mouth is pertinent to the question of the payment of the Temple tax by Jewish Christians who no longer felt themselves to be within the Jewish community. That question is hardly likely to have become acute in the stage of Church life represented by the early chapters of Acts, and still less likely during the lifetime of Jesus. The story is suspected, not without good reason, of being a later accretion."

[46] See e.g., S. E. Johnson, "The Gospel according to St. Matthew: Exegesis," *Interpreter's Bible*, vol. 7 (1951), 465 f.

[47] Matt 18:6; Mark 9:42; Luke 17:2.

[48] W. D. Davies, *The Setting of the Sermon on the Mount* (1964), 389 ff.

[49] With a powerful underpinning, so there be no breach.

ing a confidant) denies its bindingness and the practical solution following on it (again, not needing to be veiled) is in line, not with Paul, but with the original, cautious word about the tribute: do make the requisite gesture without, however, any surrender of substance. This latter agreement, already mentioned above, sets the case apart from others where Davies is right. He takes no account of the fish. It may be worth observing that, even if it were due to Matthew, this manner of procuring the tax ought to be credited with the goal here postulated: appeasement but no stepping down. It would still be, not some extravaganza, but a standard for an embattled community to emulate. To this extent, that is, the gist of my thesis would remain unaffected.

A number of traits do strongly favor a very early origin of the whole—the nature of the band in particular. As already pointed out, the collectors expect Peter to account for Jesus's conduct. Furthermore, they speak of "your teacher" with "your" in the plural: any one of the disciples represents all the others. Nor is this all. In expounding the situation, Jesus does not differentiate between himself and his followers: they are all equally of the family of the Temple's Lord. By the same token, the coin he foresees will be a *stater*, a full shekel, to serve in one go on behalf of both himself and Peter;[50] and doubtless, qua recipient of the model advice on how to cope, Peter once more stands for his fellows as well. Such a presentation suggests a time when the group was small and close-knit and before the crucifixion had rendered the master more distant. Perhaps the latter point can be made more concrete by adducing again the Matthean expansion with Jesus's statement[51] that "here is something greater than the Temple." From the sixth century on, we meet the reading "somebody greater." The Temple tax episode is unmistakably conceived in terms of "something greater."

Peter's appearance may have to be taken seriously. If he were singled out just for retrieving a bonus from a fish, that might be brushed aside by reference to his former trade. But he is on stage from the first, when probed by the officials. There is reason to believe that Mark's day of questions derives from a Seder where Peter fitted sayings of Jesus into the pre-established liturgy.[52] The opening topic is tribute to Caesar. Quite possibly, then, Peter heard about the related topic of Temple tax, too, from Jesus. 1 Peter, it should be recalled,[53] contains what sounds like an echo of the scene here ana-

[50] For B. H. Streeter, *The Four Gospels*, new ed. (1930), 504, the *stater* supports an Antiochene provenance of the pericope: it seems that only at Antioch and Damascus was this coin worth exactly two half-shekels. But, first, the evidence is shaky. Secondly, the *stater* is customarily equated with a full shekel, so at any rate near enough. Third, the half-shekel being seldom coined in Jesus's time, it may indeed have been quite usual for two persons to combine and pay with a *stater*: see A. H. McNeile, *The Gospel According to St. Matthew* (1955), 257. Lastly and above all, even if the *stater* hails from Antioch, by itself it proves nothing for the bulk of the narrative. "When I worked on fables, I was amused by the transformation of animals in the course of migration. The longbeaked bird that removes a bone from the wolf's throat is a heron in Babrius, a crane in Phaedrus, a stork in La Fontaine. Joshua ben Hananiah speaks of an Egyptian partridge; and the wolf becomes a lion—symbolizing Rome or the Emperor Hadrian. None the less the body of the paradigm stays the same throughout": see my *Ancient Jewish Law* (1981), 22 [480 f.]. Valuta is at least equally exchangeable. Streeter himself describes the point as of merely "infinitesimal" significance.

[51] Matt 12:6.

[52] See my "Zukunftsmusik," 61 ff. [357 ff.]

[53] 1 Pet 2:4 ff.

lyzed: the Christians are looked upon as the choice Temple and priesthood and as such, indeed (by now Jesus has been crucified and the battle lines are drawn), a rock putting off[54] unbelievers.

At any rate, two basic considerations seem scarcely disputable. One, the Temple tax problem must have been terribly hard, on every level, for Jesus and those around him. Two, whatever Jesuanic tradition existed concerning it is likely to have crystallized, say, around A.D. 40, in those years, that is, when the community would badly want to hear about what it owed to the foreign regime and the native Temple rulers, an unholy alliance between whom had just contrived the death of its head. Even Paul, preaching obedience to the State, still focuses on tax as the ultimate criterion.[55] For one who disagrees with Bill's affirmation of the overall priority of Matthew, it is gratifying to be able to write up for his *Festschrift* an occurrence as authentic as anything in Mark. It is one of very few such instances, leftovers, one imagines, from the Hebrew precursor.

[54] *Petra skandalou.*

[55] Rom 13:1–7.

Judas*

I.

In 1962, I delivered the Edinburgh Gifford Lectures on The Deed and the Doer in the Bible, the tenth and last being entitled The Doer after the Deed. This article presents the case with which I concluded: Judas through whom an unprincipled administration could lay hands on the one they feared. In Matthew[1] it leads to self-punishment, by hanging. In Acts[2] punishment is inflicted from above, he falls and bursts. (Similarly, Papias[3] has him bloated, inflamed, perishing in his filth.) Church tradition, setting out from Matthew, finds here the prototype of the very worst evildoer, adding to his outrage of selling the Saviour the ultimate one of self-slaughter. This has become the dominant interpretation—though a different one from the early third century will be looked at below.[4] A representative German account runs:[5] "*Das Ende des Judas... entspricht jüdischem Empfinden, für welches der Satz gilt (Tobit 12.10), 'Die Frevler sind Feinde ihres eigenen Lebens,'* "The end of Judas... reflects Jewish feeling, in line with the dictum 'The evildoers are enemies of their own life.'" But it is a misreading, it does no justice to Matthew at all. Let us go through the story.

II.

Matthew starts by saying that Judas felt remorse. Right here, the Church-influenced commentators move to get it their way—way out. The verb used, μεταμέλομαι, corresponding to Hebrew נִחַם, "to repent," "to regret," is weaker, they claim, than ἐπιστρέφω, Hebrew שׁוּב, "to return." There is, however, simply no evidence for such an overall ranking.

נִחַם, strictly, is more concerned with motivation, unhappiness about wrong, שׁוּב with result, re-adherence to right. Hence, the former perhaps tends to be more specific, alluding to the peculiar flaws renounced, the latter to concentrate on the general, posi-

* Dedicated to my wonderful friend Reuven Yaron and his family.—Soon after sending it off, I received Bernard S. Jackson's "Brother Daniel: The Construction of Jewish Identity in the Israel Supreme Court," *International Journal for Semiotics of Law*, VI/17 (1993), 115 ff. Something like his semiotic analysis, 135 ff., would certainly be of value in exploring my texts. The first ten paragraphs appear in *CLRev*, 82 (1994), 95 ff., the whole is due to re-appear in a special issue of *ILR* in honour of Reuven Yaron.

[1] Matt 27:3 ff.

[2] Acts 1:16 ff.

[3] See K. Bihlmeyer, *Die apostolischen Väter* (1924), Fragment III.

[4] Ch. VIII on Origen.

[5] E. Lohmeyer and W. Schmauch, *Das Evangelium des Matthäus*, 3rd ed. (1962), 376.

tive outcome. Jeremiah complains that the people "refused to return" and however carefully he listened, "no man repented his wickedness."[6] "Repent and return" Peter admonishes the Jews who helped to bring about Jesus's death.[7] But the scheme is not rigid. In another part of Jeremiah, Israel is forced by God to return like an unteachable bullock and only then repent: "after I returned I repented."[8] In Exodus, God himself, having told Moses of his resolve to annihilate the worshippers of the golden calf and make Moses into a nation instead, is implored by the latter: "return from your fierce wrath and repent of this evil against the people."[9] Alluded to in a psalm, "a prayer of Moses": "return, o Lord, by when?, and repent yourself concerning your servants."[10] Here are three more quotes showing up the futility of down-grading נִחַם. God, according to Jeremiah, confirms an apocalyptic prediction thus: "and I will not repent and I will not return from it."[11] Joel, as a disaster threatens, appeals for a true change of heart so God "may return and repent."[12] And the king of Nineveh hopes: "who knows, God may return and repent."[13] To leave no room for an argument that where נִחַם stands by itself, as in Matthew, it loses in force, here are a few instances, first, of שׁוּב without נִחַם, then of נִחַם without שׁוּב. Deuteronomy assures the nation that its captivity will end when "it returns" to God.[14] Isaiah must proclaim the judgment that the people are too impious "to return."[15] Achior, an Ammonite commander, warns Holofernes against an attack on the Jews who, formerly sinning, "have returned to their God."[16] Luke has Jesus predict at the last supper that Peter, though about to fall prey to Satan, "will return."[17] As for "to repent"—emphasizing the finality of God's rejection of Saul, Samuel adds that he "will not lie nor repent, for he is not a man that he might repent."[18] "The Lord has sworn and will not repent" in Psalms[19] envisages the triumph of "the priest for ever after the order of Malkizedeq." Job's very last words to the Lord are "I repent in dust and

[6] Jer 8:5 f., אֵין אִישׁ נִחָם–מֵאֲנוּ לָשׁוּב. Septuagint: ἐπιστρέφω—μετανοέο, the latter equivalent to μεταμέλομαι. In an entirely non-doctrinal context, a somewhat analogous relation comes through. God led the freed slaves through the desert rather than the nearer Philistine territory "lest they repent when they see war and return to Egypt" (Exod 13:17, נִחַם, μεταμέλομαι—שׁוּב, ἀποστρέφω equivalent to ἐπιστρέφω).

[7] Acts 3:19, μετανοήσατε καὶ ἐπιστρέψατε.

[8] Jer 31:18, אַחֲרֵי שׁוּבִי נִחַמְתִּי. The Septuagint 38:19 simplifies: "after my captivity I repented," ὕστερον αἰχμαλωσίας μου μετενόησα.

[9] Exod 32:12, שׁוּב—וְהִנָּחֵם. The Septuagint simplifies: "cease, παῦσαι, from the wrath of your spirit and become kindly, ἵλεως γενοῦ, about the evil of the people."

[10] Ps 90 (Septuagint 89):13, שׁוּבָה—וְהִנָּחֵם, ἐπίστρεψον… παρακλήθητι. Παρακαλέω in this sense, e.g. Judg 21:6, 15; 2 Sam 24:16.

[11] Jer 4:28, וְלֹא נִחַמְתִּי (μετανοήσω in Septuagint) וְלֹא־אָשׁוּב מִמֶּנָּה (ἀποστρέψω ἀπ' αὐτῆς).

[12] Joel 2:14, נִחַם—שׁוּב, Septuagint ἐπιστρέφω—μετανοέω.

[13] Jonah 3:9, יָשׁוּב וְנִחַם, Septuagint μετανοήσει καὶ ἀποστρέψει.

[14] Deut 30:2, שׁוּב, Septuagint ἐπιστρέφω.

[15] Isa 6:10, שׁוּב, ἐπιστρέφω. Quoted in Matt 13:15.

[16] Jdt 5:19, ἐπιστρέφω.

[17] Luke 22:32, ἐπιστρέφω.

[18] 1 Sam 15:29, נִחַם. The Septuagint reverently substitutes "to return" for "to lie" in the first half: οὐκ ἀποστρέψει οὐδὲ μετανοήσει ὅτι οὐχ ὡς ἄνθρωπός ἐστι τοῦ μετανοῆσαι αὐτός.

[19] Ps 110:4. Septuagint 109:4 οὐ μεταμεληθήσεται.

ashes,"[20] the fullest imaginable confession and renunciation of errancy. The result: Matthew chooses μεταμέλομαι because Judas was horrified by, and wanted to do something about, his particular lapse—for the moment allowing less concentration on the broader theological aspect. It has nothing to do with one being more or less serious than the other; it is the natural choice in the situation.

III.

(Not yet done.)

Here is to follow a paragraph showing that to drop the tendentious treatment of μεταμέλομαι in Matt 27:3 is important not only for my thesis, i.e. the proper understanding of the Judas narrative, but for a much wider territory. Why? The desire to reduce μεταμέλομαι to an inferior standing—quite off—has coloured the treatment of the vocables involved in general and caused misinterpretation in any number of texts, however remote. The distorting effect on "innocent" passages is really amazing. It is carried farthest, of course, in scholarly dictionaries, especially such as are devoted to selected subjects and go into historical detail. These works will need major revisions in quite a few portions to get rid of the fall-out of forced exegesis, all from the one text. No one would have dreamt of such violence to the other passages were it not for the need to assimilate them to the misunderstood Matt 27:3.

IV.

Well, then, Judas repented.[21] He, when Jesus's way grew incomprehensible, had contacted the judges of the Sanhedrin and for a monetary reward enabled his arrest, keeping them informed about his movements and, as their troops came upon him and his at Gethsemane, pointing him out.[22] Now that they pronounced the death sentence on the ground of blasphemy, he once again approached them—to return what he had come to realize was a reward for enabling them to shed the blood of an innocent.

At this juncture, again, reservations are put forward to get over the positive evaluation an ordinary reading will convey. We are advised that his action meant little: he was only complying with a postulate in Jewish law that if you truly repent a wrong you must give up any gain gotten through it. No doubt there was such a postulate, traceable in many places.[23] It is found also of course in Shakespeare, where the King who murdered his predecessor concedes that he cannot really pray because "I am still possessed Of those effects for which I did the murder, My crown, mine own ambition, and my queen."[24] So Judas did certainly intend to satisfy this condition, but there is nothing in

[20] Job 42:6, נִחַם. Mitigated in the Septuagint: ἥγημαι δὲ ἐμαυτὸν γῆν καὶ σποδόν, "I consider myself dust and ashes."

[21] C. H. Dodd, who took to my opinion, translated "was seized with remorse," hinting at extraordinary quality: *The New English Bible, New Testament*, (1961), 52.

[22] Matt 26:14 ff., 45 ff.

[23] E.g. *m. Gitt.* 5:5; *t. B. K.* 10:14; *t. B. M* 8:26.

[24] *Hamlet*, III.iii.53–55.

Matthew to warrant the "only," he was "only" complying, as if formalistic monetary readjustment was all he had in mind.[25] His change of heart was sincere. His acknowledgment "I have sinned" recurs in Luke in the mouth of the prodigal son[26] and from early on in the Hebrew sources may express genuine sorrow over one's straying.[27] Indeed, "Lord," a Midrash exclaims,[28] "doest thou ever require of a man more than that he utter, I have sinned?" The running down of Judas's avowal, incidentally, is far more prominent in German commentaries than English ones. German, in addition to commonplace designations for the confession of an offence, has *beichten* and *Beichte*, the official variety before a priest: and Judas, it is stressed, did not resort to that.[29] Agreed—but (leaving aside *Beichte*'s overall history) neither did the prodigal son or, a thousand years before, Abigail when admitting, taking upon herself and seeking pardon for her husband's miserable conduct.[30] Anyhow, only desperate over-theorizing can turn the apostle's offer into empty ritualism—in total neglect of the reality that, proceeding as he did, he risked, hoped, to be executed instead of, or at least with, his master. A cynic like the present writer might actually be less impressed by a report to an understanding *Beichtvater.*[31]

V.

What he confessed to was the grave misdeed of steering a fellow-Jew into the hands of a power out for his life under its repressive policy. Even the little I know about it would take up too much space.[32] So I just note that its scope varied enormously in different circles and periods. For example, while the hostile regime was usually non-Jewish, now and then it was Jews of an objectionable variety—or, as in this instance, an unholy alliance; or while in general silence was the course to take, now and then it was lying; or yet again, in exceptional situations—say, with an entire group doomed

[25] Even formalistic compliance is of considerable diversity; see my reference to "The Charge of the Light Brigade" in "Three Footnotes on *Civil Disobedience in Antiquity*"; *Humanities in Society*, 2 (1971), 76.

[26] Luke 15:18.

[27] Exemplified by Saul, 1 Sam 15:24, 30, 26:21; by David, 2 Sam 12:13, 24:10, 17; 1 Chr 21:8, 17; by Hezekiah, 1 Kgs 18:14; by Mic 7:9, Pss 41:5, 51:6; Job 7:20. Abimelech, in Gen 20:9, stresses his manifest integrity of intent vis-à-vis Abraham by the rhetorical question "What have I sinned against you?." See also below, footnote 31, on Achan.

[28] On 1 Sam 7:6.

[29] See Lohmeyer and Schmauch, *op. cit.*, 375.

[30] 1 Sam 25:24, 28.

[31] Confession's history is immensely complicated from Genesis 3 on. Joshua is told by God (7:10 ff.) that a military venture miscarried because one of his men appropriated some of the accursed treasures of destroyed Jericho. A magical procedure identifies Achan as the criminal, dooming him and all his family and possessions to extermination. However, he is still needed to reveal exactly where the booty is hidden and at Joshua's behest—addressing him as "my son"—he gives glory to the Lord and cooperates without reserve. By Talmudic times, he thereby gains atonement (*m. Sanh.* 6:2): as he and all his are being put to death, Joshua exclaims "Why has thou troubled us? the Lord shall trouble you this day"—for the Rabbis "this day, but not in the next world."

[32] I shall be reproved, rightly, for not at least citing the Hebrew, Aramaic and Greek terms for the offence. But that would be about two dozen, with major problems never so far tackled. So I let sleeping dogs lie rather than get awake ones to embark on too complicated a truth.

unless a certain member was abandoned—betrayal might be legitimated.[33] Here, Judas, his confidence and loyalty broken down, delivered—in fact, sold—Jesus to the Jewish leaders threatened by the radical preacher and enlisting Roman officials for his elimination. Monstrous. However, the very next morning, by whatever dispensation his spirit recovered. He revoked his charge, pressuring the judges to let him take the place of the pure one whose capture he had engineered or at least to make him share the penalty as equally culpable. In all likelihood, in less singular circumstances, the Sanhedrin would have listened, with whatever outcome. But he not only did not interest them. At this stage, when they were just about to succeed in their plot against Jesus, they could brook absolutely no interference, and they rudely bade him be off. Utterly alone, engulfed by self-reproach, he made over the thirty pieces of silver to the Temple and, without even waiting for Pilate's decision and the crucifixion, killed himself.

This Judas manifestly died in extreme contrition; and to do what has been done now automatically for some seventeen hundred years, i.e. side with his detractors—"what is that to us?" etc.—is like falling in some thirty-five verses further on with "if you are the son of God, come down from the cross."[34] He was a more radical Peter. The latter, when the bulk of disciples fled, stayed around, yet even he, under duress, disavowed the arrested Jesus and wept bitterly about it as the day broke.[35] Within a few hours, Judas, who had gotten him arrested, sought to share his fate and, contemptuously dismissed, hanged himself. As his getting Jesus into the enemy's hands was far, far worse than Peter's denial, so it was paid for more dearly than by tears. There is an unmistakable fundamental cross-reference.

VI.

He is mercilessly demoted in Acts.[36] In Acts: not worthy of having his exit recounted in Luke's gospel. (I take Luke to be the author of both.) Credited with no attempt to undo his treason, buying himself a field for the ill-gotten pay instead of returning it, struck down into an ugly heap by heaven instead of hanging himself, and getting his destiny summed up by two devastating lines from Psalms.[37] To be sure, a reader sharing the long-standing—1700 years—distortion of the profoundly pious suicide in Matthew ought to find the Lukan Judas far less culpable—as if Luke wished him into paradise. Quite irreconcilable, however, with the whole tone in Acts. The explanation is that Matthew had Judas redeem himself by his ending; and that Luke would not grant him this redemption, hence had him felled by what is plainly a damning blow from on high.

Two questions arise at this juncture: one, what was the Jewish attitude to suicide at the time, the other, what made Luke oppose Matthew's re-acceptance of the deserter?

[33] Cp. John 11:50; 18:14. I last discussed this subject in *Appeasement or Resistance*, (1987), 75 ff. [See 95 ff.]

[34] Matt 27:4, 40.

[35] Matt 26:75.

[36] Acts 1:15 ff. The demotion sets in already when, in Luke 22:47 f., his kiss is rejected. Or indeed in 22:22 when the synoptic record is shortened: see below, ch. X n. 63.

[37] Acts 1:20; Pss 69:26, 109:8.

On no. 1, it is enough to recall that neither Testament contains a word against suicide, let alone an ordinance; that in Jewish law to this day it is far from universally rejected; that the Samson of the Book of Judges[38] invoked God when he made the palace collapse on himself together with thousands of Philistines; that old Ahithophel was clearly taking the reasonable, respectable course when, realizing Absalom whom he supported was about to lose out, "he got himself home, put his household in order and hanged himself";[39] that Philo, bravely protesting against the threat of putting up a statue of Caligula in the Temple, explained that a planned mass-suicide of Jews would have to be the response;[40] and that even Josephus[41] did feel at one with the garrison of Masada holding out after the fall of Jerusalem and, when it was to be stormed, killing first the women and children, then one another, and the last survivor himself—the very Josephus whom his special call did not allow to live up, or die up, to such heroism.[42] Certainly there were authorities—he among them—opposed in principle, though hardly any who would not approve in a fair number of dilemmas.

No. 2 is accounted for by Luke's world being well beyond the breakthrough one that had room for the Matthean Judas. In *Ur*-Christianity enthusiasm—and the sheer need for support at any price—favoured admission and re-admission on relatively few tests. As the sect gained in recognition and settled down, a stricter selection developed. The Letter to the Hebrews states in so many words that with the founding years over, a more exacting regime must judge apostasy unforgivable.[43] Just so Luke, while pardoning (up to a point) Peter's lack of courage in a precarious situation, allowed no degree of regret or restitution to make up for a going over to the enemy. The renunciation of life, then, by the Matthean Judas in order to reunite with his victim was refused to the Lucan. He broke up in a mode unmistakably signifying perdition.[44] There are other episodes adapted by Luke to the increased stringency called for as organization advanced. Jesus's parents made a Passover pilgrimage to Jerusalem with the twelve-year-old son. Travelling homewards with their caravan, after a day or two they discovered that he was not, as they had assumed, among the company. They returned to Jerusalem and here comes the main bit, in a standard tripartite form:[45] (1) revolutionary action, Jesus had stayed

[38] Judg 16:27 ff.

[39] 2 Sam 17:22. It is widely held that the Judas episode is influenced by this one; see e.g. Lohmeyer and Schmauch, *op. cit.*, 375. Does not conflict with what I say but strikes me as rather improbable.

[40] *Embassy to Gaius* 234 ff.

[41] *Bell.* 7.8.6.320 ff.

[42] See my "The Linguistics of Suicide," in *PhilPubAffairs*, 1 (1972), 410, repr. in *Suicide and Life-Threatening Behavior*, 7 (1977), 155.

[43] Heb 6:1 ff.; 10:20 ff. In my lifetime, on two or three occasions, when the ruling coalition in Germany was opposed by a radical party, you might join and leave and be welcomed on rejoining the latter. Growth in number, however, diversity and self-confidence were apt to turn a leaving into irremediable desertion.

[44] Why did Luke not retain the suicide and explain that, in this case, because of the preceding desertion, it did not work in Judas's favour? Would have been too complicated, too academic, at that stage. Up to a point, it became the dominant understanding, say, from A.D. 250; see just a little further on, 790.

[45] Ten applications from the gospels are cited in my *The New Testament and Rabbinic Judaism* (1956, repr. 1973), 170 ff. [389 ff.], starting with Matt 9:1 ff.; Mark 2:1 ff.; Luke 5:17 ff. where (1) Jesus declares a paralytic's sins forgiven (2) the scribes declare it a blasphemy (3) he makes the paralytic walk and carry his bed.

behind in the Temple in discussion with the Rabbis, (2) protest, his mother asked how he could do this to his parents, (3) silencing of the remonstrants, did they not know that he had to attend to his heavenly Father. Thus far, obviously old tradition. The continuation, that he went back with them and "subjected himself to them," is no less obviously from Luke, writing when an orderly acknowledgment of boundaries had become a priority respected even by the young Jesus.[46]

VII.

(Like III. not yet done.)

At this point, at the risk of distraction, I plan to call attention to a further factor making for the Lucan position: the growing influence of the more rationalist, Greek-descended culture. To this day, an educated Western public just cannot brook Asian irrationalism. E.g. Cain utterly damned for a monstrous deed in Gen 4:11 f. and fully re-elevated in 15 ff. Intolerable from pretty early on and bringing about to this day far-reaching misinterpretations, *à la* Dillman (distortion of the meaning of מִפְּנֵי, "from"). In this sense, Cain is a precursor of Judas: full pardon intolerable. King David receives similar treatment, maltreatment, though less extreme. If it be objected that they did not, like Judas, abjure God directly, the worshippers of the golden calf did: at first rejected for good, welcomed back immediately after intercession.

It is not accidental that it is the same Luke who, instead of being satisfied with little modifications of the traditional gospel, takes the giant step to a new era: Acts.

Perhaps I should say something about the greater care required in using material. We should not, for example, press phantastic Oriental exaggerations as if they came from a painstaking Western thinker. Say, an exclamation like "it would be good for so-and-so never to have been" ought not automatically to be applied to its fullest logical potentiality. Poor Strack-Billerbeck have to falsify the meaning of "thou sayest" into a definitive "yes" because they cannot bear the less precise or less direct Eastern diction.

To have Acts as a new beginning is not by accident the achievement of the one evangelist with one parent originally non-Jewish. The whole base and exposition become more logical, orderly.

A curious result: it is the New Testament, not the Old, which imposes on a certain sin strict unforgivableness—from about A.D. 300. Still upheld in large portions of the globe. One might almost say: serves them right for their looking down on Old Testament religion as less merciful, whereas in truth, however demanding, it does not, cannot, exclude anyone rigidly from divine fulfilment.

Fortunately, ways around barriers are found in many instances. I was struck by Tolstoy making use of one in Anna Karenina (no doubt this has been noticed before): half a sentence or so, just before she expires, is dedicated to the thought crossing her mind that she would prefer setting out afresh and positively instead of putting an end to herself—repentance saving her from eternal torture as she enters the next world. The

[46] Luke 2:41 ff. "The verb is ὑποτάσσειν, which is technical in the rules of behaviour, the codes of community discipline, fashioned as the primitive Jewish-Christian sect began to crystallize": my *Civil Disobedience in Antiquity* (1972), 48.

view that regretting the act before expiring may make all the difference has, of course, a long history prior to Tolstoy—and after: compare Codex Iuris Canonici 1917, c. 1240, with 1983, c. 1184.

VIII.

As one would expect, the collision of Matthew—where a guilt-laden Judas confidently sought a reconciling death—with Acts—where an outcast Judas was publicly demolished—was resolved by the Church fundamentally in favour of Acts, geared towards its disciplinary needs. The pro-Judas version indeed came to be taken as anti, as describing how, bereft of all hope, he gave himself up to hell. With an effect not dreamt of by the evangelists: the anti-Judas exegesis was re-inforced by seeing here a radical disapproval of suicide as such, stamping it as the route for one beyond redemption. Had there been a trace of this at the time of Luke, he need not have substituted some malefic outer force. With little exaggeration one can say that while for the past 1700 years or so Judas committed suicide because he was beyond the pale, in historical truth suicide, for Christians, got beyond the pale because he resorted to it.

Amazingly, what is almost direct testimony to the authentic position in Matthew has survived. Origen, in his commentary,[47] devotes considerable reflection to Judas who, his loyalty restored, hurried to put things right as far as he could in this world and be in the next before his master, confident of a merciful response. In my Edinburgh presentation I touched on this only in passing, wondering what on earth could have led Origen to so appreciative an attitude. The obvious answer struck me only a few years ago:[48] he was, on the whole, still faithful to the Matthean understanding of the scene. Still faithful, not returning.

Even more recent is my appreciation of the hero's—yes, the hero's—name, "Judas," making him a successor of Jacob's famous son. Whether it was in fact his name in life or only posthumously I leave open. It fits to perfection. The Judas of Genesis, while dissuading his brothers from killing Joseph, maps out his sale to foreign traders which will equally rid them of him—in fact, lead to his end before long—and, above all, will provide them with cash, a rarity so long as you are under a *paterfamilias*. Their father will be shown fake evidence that the youngster has been devoured by a wild beast. Not a glimmer of sympathy for one deprived of the creature dearer to him than any other.[49] Similarly, Matthew's Judas, in horrendous distraction, takes cash for delivering Jesus to his enemies.[50] Years later, the brothers are captives of Joseph whom they do not recognize: he is by now the highest official in Egypt. He does recognize them and, in order to test them, declares that they may all return home save Benjamin, since his brother Joseph's disappearance inordinately treasured by Jacob.[51] This time Judah comes up to the sternest demands of piety. Having caused the loss of Joseph, he cannot

[47] Migne, *Patrologia Graeca*, 13 (1857), 1766 ff.

[48] Shows how long it takes to shake off all the fall-out of a long-entertained major misconception.

[49] Gen 37:26 ff., 31 ff.; 44:18 ff.

[50] Matt 26:15.

[51] Gen 44:14 ff.

see Jacob lose Benjamin too: so he pleads to be enslaved in his stead.[52] The Matthean Judas, too, finds his way back, in fact, within a much shorter time, ready to suffer in the place of or jointly with Jesus.[53] It is his subsequent diabolization by assimilation to the Lucan one which disconnects him from Genesis; might just as well be called Haman. In earnest: the English and German Bibles ought to refer to Judah and Juda in Matthew, to Judas in Luke and Acts.

IX.

If I have not so far convinced you, it does not worry me: my main evidence is only coming now, antedating the New Testament by about two centuries.[54] It concerns the end of a prominent Jew who treacherously helped the occupying power in the annihilation of heaven-dedicated separatists, his saintly uncle the most outstanding. No earthly authority would have exacted retribution but he did so himself and received miraculous pardon.

Yakim (Eliakim, Alcimus), from a distinguished family, was a Hellenizer, an admirer of the Syrians who rewarded him with powerful positions, including the high-priesthood. Of rare political talent—of sorts—he gained the trust of the *Chasidim*, extreme religious idealists on the opposite side—only to arrange an enormous slaughter among them. By contrast, his uncle Jose ben Joezer,[55] leading Rabbi of the period, genuinely stood his ground, refused to cooperate with the administration in anti-traditional measures and was sentenced to die at the cross. While he was up there on the Sabbath, his nephew rode by on his steed, mocking him: "Look at the horse which my sovereign has me ride and at the horse which your sovereign has you ride." To which Jose replied: "If it goes so well with those who anger him, all the better will it go with those who do his will." And when Yakim asked, "Has any human done his will more than you?," Jose warned him: "If so heavy is the lot of those who do his will, all the heavier it must be for those who anger him."[56] Yakim was overcome by penitence, went home and proceeded to a gruesome self-execution, comprising all four Mosaic forms of capital punishment. His uncle, by now barely alive, in a doze saw Yakim fly heavenwards and uttered these last words: "By a short hour he (Yakim) has preceded me (Jose) into the Garden of Eden!"

The similarity in both the setting and the unfolding is impressive. Setting: The superpower—Rome, Syria—capable of rewarding its collaborators, yet firmly resisted by the believers in a higher, if for now sadly held off, order; with the ugliest relations between the two camps, resisters and collaborators, as a result. This is not to overlook

[52] Gen 44:33 f.

[53] Matt 27:3.

[54] *Gen Rab.* 65 on Gen 27:27; *Midrash Psalms* 11:7; 1 Mac 7:9 ff., 9:54 ff.; Josephus, *Ant.* 12.385 f., 391 ff., 413, 20.235.

[55] See on him I. Broydé, *Jewish Encyclopedia* (1907), vol. 7, 242, and on Alcimus A. Büchler, vol. 1, 332 f. Jose has a place among the rare early stars commemorated in the Mishnah's *The Fathers* (1:4). Apparently he is not meant to be forgotten: this tract still figures in the traditional Sabbath afternoon service between Passover and New Year.

[56] I wish I had thought of these two *a fortioris* when I wrote on Rabbinic argumentation.

considerable differences owing to date, to social environment—classier in the early incident[57]—and so forth. Unfolding: One close to the leader of the resisters—Jose's nephew, Jesus's disciple—joins the enemies, in fact, lends decisive support to their unholy measures against him. The divulging of secrets of the resisters naturally ranks high in such a constellation. Judas is the "hander-over," "betrayer," of Jesus, and the first thing we hear about Yakim in Josephus is his communicating to the Syrian king subversive activities of the Maccabean chief.[58] No sooner is the result irreversible, however, than the defector is appalled by his error. So much so that, there being no earthly avenger, he takes his own life—and is restored to eternal grace, in unison with his victim.

Despite the resemblance, I see little reason to doubt the historicity, *cum grano salis* [with a grain of salt], of the this-worldly elements in the two reports. Indeed, caution recommends reticence even in the assessment of direct influence. To this day, once a fundamental idea about how a surprising result may emerge gains acceptance, we apply it very freely: so the Judas picture could have other precedents as well. Nevertheless, one detail surely does go back to the Yakim one, where it fits much better than in the later case. Yakim kills himself as Jose is beyond any this-worldly rescue, Judas when the last word about Jesus's fate has not yet been spoken: there is still to come the presentation before Pilate who would actually prefer to execute Barabbas, not to mention his wife's dream.[59]

This may be the place for a conjecture—it is no more—about the non-suicidal death of Judas in Acts.[60] Non-suicidal but scarcely natural. In fact, it exceeds in frightening strangeness all the ghastly endings commonly offered as parallels.[61] He "falls down on the ground, bursts asunder in the middle, pours out his bowels... on the field of blood." Perhaps lurking behind this termination are the four modes of capital punishment Yakim succeeded in subjecting himself to—with the enormous difference that they are here inflicted by a superior power, it no longer being a suicide.[62] Exactly when and where this combination came up and how long it was appreciated, with consciousness of the allusion to and distancing from the Yakim precedent lasting, I dare not speculate on.

X.

A number of problems arise—such as Jesus's ominous remark to Judas at the Last Supper, in Matthew and Mark: "Woe unto the man by whom the Son of man is betrayed;

[57] Comes out in many ways: e.g. Yakim is the leader's nephew, Judas a disciple, Yakim "sells" him in inverted commas, Judas for cash.

[58] I advisedly keep quiet about his name in the text. The few readers who consult footnotes are hopefully experienced enough not to get too confused by its, too, being Judas. N.B. Neither 1 Maccabees nor Josephus records the drama of Jose and Yakim.

[59] Matt 27:1 ff.

[60] Acts 1:18 f.

[61] The deaths of Agrippa I, Herod the Great and Antiochus Epiphanes, e.g., by J. Munck, *The Acts of the Apostles* (1967), 10, 114 f.

[62] While dubious, then, about the *Verharmlosung* [downplaying], the treatment as amply parallelled, of Judas's death in Acts by commentators like Munck, I am no happier with its dismissal as silly, say, G. Bardy speaking of an *écho de fables assez puériles* [echo of rather childish fables] in *Dictionnaire de Théologie Catholique*, 11:2 (1932), 1946.

it had been good for this man if he had not been born."[63] Does this not exclude salvation, leave the monster to his deserts? The easy escape route would be Yes, it does, and to assign the passage—and maybe one or two similar ones—to a source not sharing the gospel's prevalent positive outlook; left unamended by oversight or a late intrusion. It would be quite wrong. We had better acknowledge the enormous room in Scripture for the unpredictable and, indeed, the contráry.[64] It is not, of course, quite absent from, say, Greek tradition but rarer and rarer as rationalizing trends prevail. In the Bible, it retains its hold from the start to almost the end (almost—definitely loosened in Luke, Acts and some Epistles). A horrendous verdict against Cain is replaced, two verses later, by extravagant protection, the building of the first city, the founding of a long-lasting mighty family.[65] God himself, as the people defect to the golden calf, announces that he will destroy them and start a nation with Moses, to change his mind in no time at the latter's plea.[66] Again, he has Isaiah predict to a sick Hezekiah that he is about to die; when the prophet has left the King prays and God, according to the version in Kings, "before Isaiah has crossed the court," sends him back to promise another fifteen years of happy rule.[67] The "woe" applicable while Judas is benighted has no unshakable validity.

Believers in sober, "Western" unfolding cannot take it. Hence, for example, in the clause "and Cain went out from before the Lord," the preposition מִלִּפְנֵי, "from before," is widely credited with indicating a permanent, punitive barrier, a never mended exclusion of intimacy.[68] Certainly, the word being neutral, it could be used of a regrettable separation—as when Jonah,[69] disobeying God's order to confront the Ninevites, sets out to flee "from before the Lord" or when Aram flees "from before Israel."[70] But there are plenty of instances to the contrary, among them, in fact, most of those involving יָצָא, "to go out." Surely, the closest parallels are Joseph and Mordecai. Joseph, made virtual dictator, "went out from before Pharaoh" to look after the entire realm.[71] Mordecai, appointed Prime Minister in the place of Haman and having secured the King's signature for the pro-Jewish ordinance, "went out from the King" in royal apparel and with a crown of gold.[72] If something like banishment were alluded to, one would expect not מִלִּפְנֵי but מִפְּנֵי, analogous to the phrasing just before,[73] "and from your face I shall be hid."

[63] Matt 26:24; Mark 14:21. Luke 22:2 omits the second half, "it had been…", relegating the main treatment of an evil figure to Acts 1:15 ff.; see above, 787 ff.

[64] Only underlined by its pronounced exclusion at certain junctures, like 1 Sam 15:29: "The Strength of Israel will not lie nor repent, for he is not a man that he should repent." Another proviso ought to be recorded here: superior, guiding factors are even behind the contráry—Cain's reinstatement, for instance, to be cited presently. I might inquire into all this if I were assured of another 15 years; see the next footnote but two. —I am aware that the OED, 2nd ed. (1989), vol. 3, 841, ranks this use of "contráry" as colloquial and dialectical.

[65] Gen 4:10 ff.

[66] Exod 32:9 ff.

[67] 2 Kgs 20:1 ff.; Isa 38:1 ff.

[68] See e.g. A. D. Dillman, *Die Genesis*, 4th ed. (1882), 95.

[69] Jonah 1:3, 10.

[70] 1 Chr 19:18.

[71] Gen 41:46. His father Jacob, too, honourably received by the ruler, departed in this fashion: Gen 47:10.

[72] Esth 8:15—possibly echoing the Joseph elevation.

[73] Gen 4:13.

The futility of making Matthew conceive of Judas as beyond redemption is shown up fully by the far more massive rebuttal he has Jesus administer to Peter: "Get thee behind me, Satan, you are an offence to me, for you see not the things of God but those of men."[74] Does not keep Peter from within a week being one of the three chosen to witness the transfiguration.[75] Commentators try to get rid of Satan by pointing to occasions when the meaning is attenuated. Nothing in the text, however, points to attenuation. It is our discipline that insists on it.

Let me end this paragraph with an observation on "Father, forgive them, for they know not what they do." Confined in the New Testament to Luke,[76] it surely owes its place to the evangelist or his school—with a decisive bearing on its meaning at this juncture. At first sight one might assume a generously pardoning attitude like that at the close of Jonah or in a Socratic teaching: "should I not spare Nineveh . . . with more than sixscore thousand persons that cannot discern between their right hand and their left hand, and much cattle?," "nobody is wittingly evil." But while such a message would be reconcilable with Matthew, the traitor being reinstated on a sincere mending,[77] it is not with Luke, focused on the rational consolidation of a growing community and indeed one which, with its strong foreign admixture, is in special need of discipline. By now a Judas who, one of the Twelve, betrayed Jesus could never rise again. I have already cited the Epistle to the Hebrews' irreversible No to the one who has seriously strayed.[78] The theme plays a greater part throughout Luke-Acts than is generally realized. The fate of Ananias and Sapphira, for instance, makes it clear that downright apostasy is not the only unpardonable crime against this new world: certain machinations within it are no better. This couple take credit, claim privileged status, for a higher financial sacrifice in the community's interest than they made and, charged by Peter, drop down dead.[79] In the Lucan "Father, forgive them...," then, we have before us no idealistic, universal embrace, *carte blanche* for any returnee, but an intercession solely for as yet unenlightened, groping outsiders, Jewish or Roman or what-not. They are welcome however worthless up to now[80] while, once inside under this regime, a serious breach of faith is no longer tolerable. In the history of Christianity, the roles assigned to the prayer in different periods, parts of the world, circles and circumstances to this day are of profound significance.

74 Matt 16:23; Mark 8:33.

75 Matt 17:1 ff.; Mark 9:2 ff.

76 Luke 23:34; cp. above, 788 f. See my *Sin, Ignorance and Forgiveness in the Bible*, Claude Montefiore Lecture (1960), "For they know not what they do" in *Studia Patristica* 4 (1961), 58 ff. [847 ff.], *Ancient Jewish Law* (1981), 49 ff., and "Jonah: a reminiscence," *JJS* 35 (1984), 36 ff.

77 I am not saying that Matthew does have the full argument in mind.

78 See n. 43.

79 Acts 5:1 ff. When J. Munck, *op. cit.*, 40, calls the case of Achan in Josh 7:1 ff. (above, 786 n. 31) "a just parallel," he misses a great gulf between the two.

80 Though over-extended hesitation could be a problem. Paul may have felt guilty of it: see my "Onesimos," in *Christians among Jews and Gentiles: Essays in Honor of Krister Stendahl*, ed. G. W. E. Nickelsburg with G.W. MacRae (1986), 42 f. [555].

XI.

An excursus on H. L. Strack and P. Billerbeck's *Kommentar zum Neuen Testament aus Talmud und Midrasch* may be in order. Of rare learning and nobility, it enjoys the trust of the scholarly world—and it does so even on the, say, two dozen occasions when it bends the evidence to the advantage of treasured convictions. No historian dealing with major issues can avoid this failing. "Failing" from the strict, scholarly point of view. In real life, often, the effect of "misinterpretation" is preferable to what a "correct" reading would produce: for example, in the U.S.A., when a statute assigning a certain right to men is held to include—have included all the time—women.

Their treatment of Jose ben Joezer's faith[81] is a relatively simple illustration.[82] They declare it unlikely that he called the abode of the departed pious ones "the Garden of Eden," as also that he assigned immortality to them; the first Rabbi to sanction these notions, they hold, was Johanan ben Zaccai who died ca. 80 A.D. So when Jesus came upon the scene, ideology in those circles was rather undeveloped. Such is the prestige of these scholars—understandably—that, for instance, the Encyclopaedia Judaica's article *Paradise*[83] by the liberal Rabbi B. J. Bamberger cites Johanan ben Zaccai alone for "Garden of Eden": not a word about Jose. For my main thesis it matters little if the latter expressed himself differently. But the report sounds quite coherent in itself and Strack-Billerbeck offer absolutely no suggestion as to what it contained in the place of their cuts. Besides, Jose is precisely the profound eccentric to stand at the beginning, with Johanan ben Zaccai seeing it through.[84] Above all, the Dead Sea discoveries, from after the death of Strack and Billerbeck, contain enough material to strengthen one's confidence in the Jose tradition. The Community Rule, for instance,[85] assures the just ones of "eternal joy in life without end, a crown of glory and a garment of majesty in unending light."[86]

Here is a distortion not of date but of substance.[87] Three times Jesus answers a question by σὺ εἶπας "you have said (it)," or σὺ λέγεις "you say (it)": (1) to Judas;[88] (2)

[81] See on him above, ch. IX.

[82] Vol. 4 pt. 2 (1924), 1130 f.

[83] Vol. 13, (1973), 831.

[84] Even he reaching back further than a superficial look might indicate: he lived well over 100 years.

[85] 1 QS 4.7 f., see G. Vermes with the collaboration of P. Vermes, *The Dead Sea Scrolls—Qumran in Perspective*, (1971), 137.

[86] I am indebted to the Community Rule in another context. In 1946, E. G. Selwyn, publishing a commentary on the First Epistle of St. Peter, included an Appended Note by me, Participle and Imperative, 467 ff. I argued that "a strange use of the participle in Romans, Ephesians, Colossians, Hebrews and 1 Peter must be the participle of Hebrew rules, of Mishnah, Tosephta and so on." There was strong support but some opposition as well, based on the post-New-Testament date of the final Mishnah and Tosephta. A weak argument seeing that not a few rules in question are truly archaic and, indeed, that this application of the participle becomes much rarer as Tannaism comes to an end around 200. Well, the Community Rule does testify to the pre-New-Testament origin of the phenomenon: "All that enter are saying, Amen... The priests are recounting the just exploits of God... and all that enter are confessing after them," 1.18 ff. See my *Ancient Jewish Law*, 79 ff. [see 192 ff.].

[87] Vol. 1 (1926), 990 f., 1006, 1031.

[88] Matt 26:25, σὺ εἶπας.

to the High Priest[89] or to him and others;[90] and (3) to Pilate.[91] (1) is about the destiny of Judas, (2) and (3) are about his own. According to Strack-Billerbeck, it is a straight confirmation: *du hast recht*, "you are right," *wie du sagst, so ist es*, "as you say, so it is." They do realize that the Hebrew equivalents will not ordinarily carry this sense. Still, they go on, אָמַרְתָּ, "you have said (it)," does in one passage,[92] enough to legitimize their contention. Wishful thinking. Even there, the meaning, far from a clear "yes, correct," is eminently ambiguous.

The passage concerns a dispute between two survivors of the war with Rome as to whether a certain entrance to the Temple had required a washing of hands and feet. Rabbi Simon the Modest, in the presence of Rabbi Eliezer ben Hyrcanus, reports that he entered without washing. Whereupon Eliezer, a giant in learning and piety yet rudely domineering, asked him who was more esteemed, he or the High Priest. Simon kept silent. Eliezer: "You are ashamed to admit that the High Priest's dog was more esteemed than you."[93] Simon: "Rabbi, you have said (it)." Eliezer: "By the Temple service, they would break even the High Priest's head with their clubs [were he to enter unwashed]; what would you do that the guard might not find you?"

To appreciate the scene, we must remember that Eliezer was an extreme adherent to rigorous tradition and so crassly contemptuous of the majority that in the end he was excommunicated. His opinion that the entrance in question was restricted is what one would expect. So is his offensive comment on Simon's worthlessness. The extraordinary bit—no doubt accounting for the anecdote's survival—is the latter's respect for any word of that great man while holding on to the right to go his own way. Actually, in strictness, he was here referring not to the major conflict—washing requisite or not requisite—but to the comparative ranking of himself and the High Priest's dog. He was humble enough to put up even with that, but to read it as an unqualified "you have hit the nail on the head," "laid down the valid route," is quite off. "I respect your stand" comes nearer. It was surely this concession which earned him his surname: he turns up in no other text. Indeed, he pays for his modesty to this day, not figuring in the complete register of Sages added to Strack-Billerbeck by J. Jeremias and K. Adolph.[94] I shall come back to this register again.

A glance at the gospel references. (1) In Matthew, as Jesus predicts betrayal by one of the twelve, they one after the other ask "surely, I am not him, Lord?"[95] Judas's participation in this interlude receives special notice. He asks the question (with "Rabbi" instead of "Lord") after Jesus's threat that it would be better for the traitor not to have

[89] Matt 26:64, σὺ εἶπας.

[90] Luke 22:70, ὑμεῖς λέγετε.

[91] Matt 27:11; Mark 15:2; Luke 23:3; John 18:37, σὺ λέγεις.

[92] *t. B. K.* Kelim 1:6.

[93] Strack-Billerbeck, 990, take it as a rhetorical question: "*Du schämst dich wohl zu sagen, daß (selbst) der Hund des Hohepriesters beliebter ist als du?*," "You are ashamed, are you not, to admit...?" Quite possible. Makes no difference.

[94] *Verzeichnis der Schriftgelehrten* (1961). The Simons are on 139 f.

[95] Μήτι comes near "surely not," for example, in Mark 4:21: "Surely, a candle is not brought to be put under a bushel or under a bed? Is it not [brought] that it may be set on a candlestick?"

been born; and is told "you have said (it)." To work out the complicated role of this response would lead too far afield; it is plainly miles apart from a bare, solid "yes, you will betray me."

(2) Again, in Matthew, as the High Priest adjures Jesus to tell them whether he is the Christ, son of God—an assertion punishable by death—Jesus replies "you have said (it); yet (πλὴν) I say unto you, hereafter you shall see the Son of man sitting at the right hand of power. . . . " He declines to provide the prosecution with an explicit "Yes," comfortable for them. At the same time, the continuation with "yet," to those ready to hear does make of the following pronouncement an implicit arrogation of that rank. The High Priest, ignoring the finesse, reacts as if Jesus had simply admitted the charge. By modern standards, defensible. By the standards of some two thousand years ago, more geared towards literal interpretation, liable to count as overweening. In Luke, the dignitaries asking Jesus whether he is the Christ are refused an answer because they would not believe and were he to ask them they would not answer. From now, he goes on, the Son of man will sit at God's right. As they all ask, "Are you then the Son of God?," he replies "you say (it)"—which they take as relieving them of the need for witnesses, "for we ourselves have heard it." As in Matthew, then, the evasion is ruthlessly rejected.[96]

To come back for a moment to Matthew, Strack-Billerbeck base on their misunderstanding an enormous idealization of the early strugglers: doubtless the urge to do so helped on the faulty process. Jesus's "you have said (it)," let me recall, in answer to whether he is Christ, is far from a definite confirmation. For Strack-Billerbeck, we have seen, it is—and they go even further. As it replies to an adjuration—"I adjure you that you tell us whether thou be the Christ"—it has, they contend, the force of an oath. More than this, it proves that Jesus himself recognized its imposition by the regime in power as a legitimate institution. This is not first century Palestine; this is the disciplined Prussia of the 1920s. I am a Badener.

In the corresponding Marcan pericope,[97] Jesus resorts to no ambiguity. A charge that he boasted of the ability to destroy the Temple and within three days replace it he disdains to attend to; even when admonished by the High Priest, "he kept silent and answered nothing."[98] By contrast, the latter's question whether he is the Christ meets with "I am, and you will see the Son of man sitting on the right hand of power." One need only hold this mighty assertion against the Matthean and Lucan "you have said" or "say" to sense the disparity. Whichever comes first—I think almost certainly Mark, but even if not—the contrast between absolute, militant clarity versus caution, reservation, is tremendous.

[96] J. M. Creed in his *The Gospel according to St. Luke*, 1930 (p. 279), anticipates the essence of my interpretation. While σὺ εἶπας, σὺ λέγεις and ὑμεῖς λέγετε were "understood to imply assent... the personal pronoun, σὺ, ὑμεῖς, must be significant: the statement is yours, i.e. a certain protest against the question is implied." He cites Euripides, *Hippolytus* 352, where Phaedra, Theseus's second wife, is about to reveal to her nurse her love for Hippolytus, Theseus's son from an Amazon. She cannot bring herself to openly name him, so says "whoever haply he is, the Amazon's." The nurse: "You mean Hippolytus?" Phaedra: "From yourself you hear this, not from me." A certain protest against her own confession.

[97] Mark 14:57 ff.

[98] Mark 14:61.

Strack-Billerbeck are inordinately uncommunicative as to this version.[99] Not a word about "I am" in the place of "you have said" or "say," and the most laconic listing of the Talmudic "to keep silent and say nothing";[100] no name associated with it, no hint at the occasion. Such reticence—less than one line—is all the stranger as they find room for generous accommodation of the quote apropos of two parables: the unmerciful servant in Matthew[101] and the forgiving of big debt versus small debt in Luke.[102] And this though what the quote contributes to the two cases is of no major importance.

As for the unmerciful servant—Rabh Saphra, around A.D. 300, cultivated contact with Jewish Christians. One day they challenged him to explain Amos 3:2, "You only have I known of all the families on earth, therefore I will punish you for all your iniquities": should anger be allowed to prevail over friendship? When he could not answer, מְצַעֲרוּ לֵיהּ "they took him by the throat," tormented him. Strack-Billerbeck record the incident because the unmerciful servant in Matthew, himself forgiven a debt of 10,000 talents, none the less ἔπνιγεν, "took by the throat," a poor guy who owed him 150 pence. While it is interesting to be reminded of a Hebrew verb that would fit,[103] no particular light falls thereby on the Matthean simile. An even fuller recital of the Saphra incident is attached to Luke's parable of a creditor who releases two debtors, one owing 500 pence, the other 50: the former will be more thankful. Strack-Billerbeck here add the portion where Saphra's Palestinian sponsor, R. Abbahu, explains to the Christians that they should not expect the former to be an adept at original Biblical exegesis: his base being Babylonian, he needs to be abreast only of post-Scriptural development—whereas Abbahu must cope also with what the Christians appeal to, the ancient text as such, never mind what the Sages made or did not make of it. He, then, can provide the answer: it is from preference that God punishes the Jews more. Suppose you are a lender of money to a friend and to an enemy: you will keep demanding it back *peu à peu* from the friend—the situation in Amos—while having the enemy accumulate his burden to his destruction. Once again, a most interesting piece; but as a comment on the two debtors in Luke, both graciously let off, not in place. No more to the point than any other instance of two debtors.

What one senses is an enormous urge on the part of Strack-Billerbeck to play down Mark. Oversubtle? There is surprising evidence where, in fact, they come out as winners. The register by Jeremias and Adolph lists Saphra as referred to by Strack-Billerbeck on fourteen occasions, Matt 18:28 and Luke 7:41 among them. Unlisted is Mark 14:61 though Strack-Billerbeck direct us to the same Saphraic "keeping silent and replying nothing" (yes, *b. A. Zar.* 4a)—without spelling out his name. They are doing their duty, then, but in a fashion that the generally very painstaking Jeremias and Adolph miss out on it—relegating Mark to a safer distance. There are several analogous

[99] Vol. 2, 51.

[100] *b. A Zar.* 4a. Not the only place where the expression is met but pretty representative.

[101] Matt 18:28, vol. 1, 799.

[102] Luke 7:41, vol. 2, 163.

[103] There are others; חָנַק seems favoured in 19th century translations.

complications in Strack-Billerbeck. How far planned, how far instinctive, may be left open: in a sense tragically, the aim is throughout to serve truth and clarity.

(3) When proceedings have moved before Pilate, in both Matthew and Mark he asks Jesus whether he is the King of the Jews, to be told "you say (it)." A number of charges, not specified, are added by priests and elders. These Jesus ignores nor does he give way even when the governor confesses himself puzzled. In Luke, the crowd leading Jesus to the governor allege that he perverted the nation, forbade tribute to Caesar and declared himself to be Christ, a king. To Pilate's question whether he is the King of the Jews he answers: "You say (it)." Pilate advises the Jewish audience that he finds no culpability in him, upon which they accuse him all the more fiercely of agitation. The charges against which Jesus will not defend himself are transferred by Luke to the occasion (mentioned by no other evangelist) when he is tried before Herod.[104]

In John, notice that we do not find "you say (it)." Manifestly developed from it, however, is "you say that I am a king," at the end of a private interrogation of Jesus by Pilate in the course of which he spells out the otherworldly nature of his office. Pilate honours this right to the end when he has the cross inscribed: "Jesus the Nazarene the King of the Jews"—rejecting the protest of the priests who want "who said, I am King of the Jews."[105] This is an immensely simplified summary—remember that when Jesus, after "you say that I am a king," declares standing up for the truth his task, Pilate leaves with the words: "what is truth?"[106]

[104] Luke 23:9 f.
[105] John 19:19 ff.
[106] John 18:38.

Paul a Hellenistic Schoolmaster?*

In the First Epistle to the Corinthians (4:21) the apostle assures the quarrelsome factions that he will come, and it is up to them whether it will be "with a rod or with love." A few sentences before[1] he contrasts himself, the one father of the Corinthian church, with its thousands of schoolmasters or attendants (παιδαγωγοί). Hence, when he threatens "the rod" he may have in mind either the punishing role that a father must sometimes assume,[2] or the punishing role of a schoolmaster or attendant as opposed to the loving one of a father[3]—or, indeed, as I incline to believe, both and neither, the metaphor being used in a general indeterminate sense. Schneider holds[4] that Paul is referring to a schoolmaster or attendant; and since in Jewish schools (he states) it was not the rod but the strap *(reṣu'ah)* that was employed, he reaches the conclusion that the passage clearly reflects Hellenistic life. It may be worth while entering a protest before this establishes itself as one of the many fanciful arguments surrounding Paul's background and mode of thought.

For his distinction between Jewish and Hellenistic instruments of school discipline Schneider quotes Klostermann.[5] Unless I have overlooked a paragraph or sentence, however, Klostermann does not deal with this question at all. In any case, to start with the Hellenistic schoolroom, we have only to look at vases and other pictorial representations of educational scenes to discover that the rod was far from being the only weapon wielded. As regards literary sources, it is sufficient to draw attention to a piece by Herodas entitled *The Schoolmaster*, in which the teacher is depicted as being in possession of a selection of straps and the pupil as being well acquainted with their respective characteristics. The young miscreant is to suffer the δριμὺ σκῦτος the "sharp leather thong," i.e. a kind of "scorpion" on which bones were strung, also described as βοὸς κέρκος, "the ox-tail," and he begs for the milder kind of punishment without the bones.[6]

* Leon Roth was ever appreciative of the efforts of colleagues less gifted than he, and engaged on work of only indirect relevance to the crucial ethical and spiritual problems to which he devoted his energy. The following short note may, therefore, be acceptable in a volume dedicated to the memory of a great and generous man.

[1] 1 Cor 4:15.

[2] This is how it is taken e.g. by Parry, *The First Epistle to the Corinthians*, Cambridge Greek Testament (1937), 85.

[3] Thus, e.g. Craig, *The First Epistle to the Corinthians*, Interpreter's Bible, 10 (1953), 59.

[4] Art. "ῥαβδος" in *Theologisches Wörterbuch zum Neuen Testament*, ed. Friedrich, 6 (1958), 968.

[5] "Das Schulwesen im alten Israel," in *Theologische Studien*, Zahn Festschrift (1908), 193 ff.

[6] *Didaskolos* 68, 73. See *The Mimes of Herodas*, ed. Nairn (1904), 40, and *Herodas*, ed. Knox (1922), 114 f.

His petition is not granted. It may be noted that our word "belt" is the same as the Latin *balteus*: in Juvenal[7] slaves get it, and there is no reason to suppose that bad boys did not.

How Schneider reaches the view that the rod was unknown in Jewish schools I am unable to guess. (Though it could soon be true of Berkeley.[8]) Possibly it has something to do with Krauss,[9] who in his *ex professo* discussion of punishment in talmudic schools mentions the strap only. In the section dealing with punishment by parents, however, the rod does appear, as it also does in that on the punishment of slaves.[10] Differences of course there are. The slipper, used in the home by the mother, will play no part at school; nor, at the other extreme, will the *maghlabh*, a stick with metal barbs, the mere sight of which made slaves quail. But it is difficult to see why both strap and rod should not have been plied by both father and teacher.

Strack-Billerbeck's commentary[11] rightly treats rod and strap as interchangeable. Of the parallels cited, one is particularly appropriate: according to Rabbi Simeon b. Yoḥai, in the middle of the second century C.E., God gives Israel the choice between bread, if they are obedient, and the rod (*maggel*) if they are not.[12]

Paul's word for "rod" is ῥάβδος. The following occurrences of the word in the Septuagint are here relevant. Exod 21:20 (a master beats his slave); 1 Sam (Kgs) 17:43 (the rod appropriate for subduing a dog); 2 Sam (Kgs) 7:14 (God will chastise Solomon as a father does his son); Job 9:34 (sufferings inflicted by God are described as "His rod"); Ps 89 (88):33, echoing 2 Sam 7:14 (God, whom David calls his father, will chastise David's sons); Prov 10:13 (punishment of a fool); 22:15 (a foolish lad is improved by correction); 23:13 f. (a father procures his son's salvation by timely beating); 26:3 (a fool needs to be beaten); Isa 10:5 (God describes the Assyrian, sent against His people, as "the rod of My anger"); 10:15 and 24 (the rod is an instrument of punishment); Lam 3:1 (punishment inflicted by God is described as "the rod of His wrath"); Ezek 20:37 (God uses the rod by way of punishment and education).

In view of this role of ῥάβδος in the Greek Old Testament, coupled with the fact that the strap—*rᵉṣuʿah*—appears in post-biblical Hebrew literature only, one might almost make out a case for the latter being a Hellenistic addition to the arsenal of the Jewish pedagogue. One of the fundamental weaknesses of a theory like Schneider's is that it takes for granted a clear-cut division between Jewish and Hellenistic institutions which no longer prevailed by the time of Paul. However, to postulate Jewish borrowing in this matter would likewise be rash. For the present, at any rate, we have too little information for any such deductions. What is surely undeniable is that Paul's picture is in good old traditional style. That did not make it unintelligible to a gentile public—the rod is a universal aid to discipline.

[7] *Satires* 9.112.

[8] According to the *San Francisco Chronicle* of 16th June, 1965, 5, the disciplinary manual discussed at a meeting of the Board of Education "approved… strapping, but specifically outlawed… the use of a ruler."

[9] *Talmudische Archäologie*, 3 (1912), 225 f.

[10] *Op. cit.*, 2 (1911), 19 f., 95 f.

[11] *Kommentar zum Neuen Testament aus Talmud und Midrasch*, 3 (1926), 341 f.

[12] *Siphre* on Deut 11:12, ed. L. Finkelstein (1940), 83, 1. 16.

Although there is but a remote connection between corporal correction in the course of education and the official penalty of scourging, it may be of interest here to recall a possible change of instrument for the infliction of the latter—the rod giving way to the strap. Under talmudic law flogging is administered by means of a specifically described *r^e^ṣu'ah,* i.e. a strip of calf-hide with multiple folds.[13] This was very likely the recognised instrument already in New Testament times. The general consensus of opinion, however, seems to be[14] that the regulations laid down in Deut 25:1 ff. for flogging indicate the bastinado, administered with a stick, and that the strap was substituted much later under Greek and Roman influence. There is much to be said for this theory. To be sure, the existence of ancient oriental laws which prescribe the strap for official scourging[15] is an argument against it and in favour of there having been no change between Old Testament times and the Talmud; but it is by no means conclusive. We know that, as far as capital punishment is concerned, the biblical methods of execution were drastically reformed at the beginning of the present era;[16] stoning, for example, in the literal sense was replaced by pushing the condemned person down from a height. This latter method is in itself extremely old, yet within the Jewish penal system—or at any rate within one strand of it—it represents a second and relatively late stage.

[13] *m. Makk.* 3:12, H. Danby's translation, 407.

[14] See S.R. Driver, *Deuteronomy*, ICC (1903), 279; Benzinger, art. "Law and Justice" in *Encyclopaedia Biblica*, ed. Cheyne and Black, 3 (1902), col. 2722; Levesque, art. "Bastonnade" in *Dictionnaire de la Bible*, ed. Vigoroux, 1, part 2 (1912), col. 1500; Buerlier, art. "*Flagellation,*" *ibid.*, 2, part 2 (1912), col. 2281.

[15] E.g. Code of Hammurabi, 202. The Assyrian laws have rods, e.g. 18.

[16] See A. Büchler, *Die Todesstrafen der Bibel und der jüdisch-nach-biblischen Zeit*, in *MGWJ*, 50 (1906), 539 ff., 664 ff.; also Daube, *The New Testament and Rabbinic Judaism* (1956), 304 ff. [see 619 ff.] and "Origen and the Punishment of Adultery in Jewish Law" in *SP*, 2 (= *Texte und Untersuchungen* 64) (1957), 109 f. [*Talmudic Law*, 167 ff.].

8

Studies in Luke-Acts

This section lays out Luke's distinctive ideas and biases.

Inheritance in Two Lukan Pericopes

I.

Luke tells us[1] how Jesus rebuked a man whose brother apparently opposed a division of their joint inheritance, and who requested Jesus to make him consent to a division. It is widely held that only Jesus's refusal to intervene is early, whereas the condemnation of covetousness goes back to the evangelist.[2] This may well be correct. One wonders, however, whether this refusal does not itself imply some disapproval of the petitioner's case—be it because he shews himself covetous or be it for another reason.

As has long been seen, the refusal is couched in language reminiscent of the insult offered to Moses when he attempted to make peace between two Hebrews: "Who made thee a prince and judge over us?"[3] According to Rabbinic legend, the men were the brothers Dathan and Abiram, subsequently to be participants in Korah's revolt.[4] This identification seems to have been known to the tradition behind Luke. In Acts we find Moses reminding the quarrelling pair: "You are men that are brethren."[5] Which is surely an allusion to the words Abraham used to impress on Lot, his brother's son, how wrong they were in falling out: "We are men that are brethren."[6] Underlying Jesus's refusal, then, there may be the idea that while Moses, who tried to re-establish concord between brothers, was spurned as without authority, Jesus, asked to bring about a separation between brothers, declared that he had no authority to do so.

Whether this is acceptable or not, it is difficult to see how Jesus could have declined to help had he fully acknowledged the rightness of the claim. The question arises: Does the man's claim and Jesus's disapproval fit into a Jewish background? The answer is in the affirmative.

From patriarchal times, the remaining together of coheirs—usually brothers—as one family is a recognized institution.[7] The technical term in the Old Testament is *yashabh yaḥadh,* "to dwell together." In Greek, χωρὶς οἰκεῖν signifies the splitting off from the family household of a member to set up on his own. Abraham "dwells together," in the technical sense, with his deceased brother's son Lot until they decide to part,

[1] Luke 12:13 ff.

[2] See Creed, *The Gospel according to St. Luke* (1930), *ad loc.*

[3] Exod 2:14; Acts 7:27.

[4] Num 16:1; *Exod. Rab.* on 2:12.

[5] Acts 7:26. This translation is suggested by Strack-Billerbeck, *Kommentar zum Neuen Testament*, vol. 2 (1924), *ad loc.*, without reference, however, to the legend.

[6] Gen 13:8.

[7] See Daube ["*Consortium* in Roman and Hebrew Law"], *JR* 42 (1950), 71 ff.

and so does Jacob with Esau.[8] In nomadic conditions "to dwell together" is quite consistent with wandering about; the wanderings are undertaken together. At a more advanced stage it usually means to live together on the ancestral estate. In Deuteronomy it is laid down that if one of the brothers who "dwell together"—*scil.* on the ancestral estate—dies, leaving a childless widow, another should marry her in order that her first-born son may take the place of the deceased in the household. Failure to comply with this law would be gross disloyalty and would lead to public denunciation.[9] The institution is idealized by the Psalmist when he speaks of the sweetness of a "dwelling together" of brothers.[10]

Such an arrangement does not always entail absolute communism. To take the examples of Abraham and Lot and of Jacob and Esau, what is primarily owned in common—or, as we have to do with nomads, we should rather say, used in common—is the land; even in respect of the land there may be some apportionment for practical purposes, one brother confining himself to this part and the other to that. At any rate it is clear that each has his own wives, children, slaves and cattle. Indeed, it is their growing wealth in private goods which renders a dissolution of the household imperative. Whether the narrator conceives of this dissolution in terms of a division of the land, or in terms of one brother—Abraham, Jacob—staying on and the other—Lot, Esau—having to seek a new habitation and new pasture ground, we need not here decide.

One point is of interest. While no blame attaches to him who initiates a dissolution—it is Abraham in the case of Abraham and Lot—it is regarded as a sad necessity which calls for justification: the increase in riches, and the economic problems and the frictions resulting from it.

It may be noted that, just as a "dwelling together" is not invariably equivalent to a complete fusion of property, so there may be a sharing of some property between brothers who do not continue as one household. Judah, we learn, while his father was still alive, "went down from his brethren,"[11] i.e. set up on his own, χωρὶς οἰκεῖν. In the eyes of the narrator, presumably he did not thereby lose his prospective part in Jacob's inheritance. Nor would he necessarily have given up his part had he left his brothers only after his father's death, though, in that epoch, co-ownership from a distance must have involved no small problems.

For the Psalmist, a "dwelling together" is definitely preferable to separation. His enthusiasm suggests that separation was frequent at the time. We may compare Aulus Gellius who, about the middle of the second century A.D., wrote longingly of the Roman *consortium* of bygone days.[12] The exact motive of the Psalmist is doubtful. He may simply be keen on harmonious, selfless family life. He may also think of the joint household as most in accordance with the kind of state aimed at by the social laws: the notion he introduces of God "commanding the blessing" occurs in legislation concerning the

[8] Gen 13:1 ff., 36:6 ff.

[9] Deut 25:5 ff.

[10] Ps 133:1.

[11] Gen 38:1

[12] *Attic Nights* 1.9.12.

Seventh Year, in the promise of a plentiful harvest in the sixth.[13] He may even be concerned about political strife, seeing in the arrangement recommended the model of a united people. "Be not divided into two heads," is the advice given to the sons in the Testament of Zebulon—quite possibly directed against the struggle of Hyrcanus II with Aristobulus II.[14]

By the beginning of the Talmudic era, as we may gather from the Mishnah, it was still not unusual for brothers to leave the inheritance undivided, whether they stayed together or not. On the other hand, even brothers who stayed together might divide the property between them, or most of it at least.[15] Josephus observes that among the Essenes all property is owned in common, "as among brothers."[16] He adds that one Essene enters any other's house, even if they have never met, like an intimate friend. Evidently, the description presupposes acquaintance with the extreme type of *consortium* between brothers, where they know no individual ownership and reside together.

Under Talmudic law, brothers living together and/or sharing property may at any moment agree to end the arrangement; and even if only one of them desires separation, separation there will be. However, an action may be legally unimpeachable, yet not in accordance with the highest moral principles. A Rabbinic discussion of the middle of the second century A.D., about a clause from the story of Abraham and Lot, is significant.[17] R. Judah interprets it as meaning that God was angry with Abraham for not cleaving to his brother's son. R. Nehemiah, frequently in controversy with R. Judah, takes the opposite view: the clause indicates that God was angry with Abraham while the unworthy Lot was with him. It is plain that Abraham's conduct in suggesting a separation constituted a problem for these Rabbis. Perhaps their different opinions on *consortium* are related to their opinions on the association between the good and the bad in wider fields. Of the builders of the tower of Babel we are told in Genesis: "The people is one and they have all one language and now nothing will be restrained from them." According to R. Judah, by uniting they had taken the first step towards grace; had they added penitence, nothing would have been refused them. According to R. Nehemiah, on the contrary, their unity was the cause of rebellion; nothing could now keep them in check.[18]

Roman law on more than one occasion was forced to combat the claim of provincials—a claim doubtless based on local custom—that one coheir has no right to insist on division against the will of the other. An imperial rescript of A.D. 294 declares: "*In communionem nemo compellitur invitus detineri; quapropter aditus praeses provinciae ea quae communia tibi sum sorore perspexerit, dividi providebit*" [No one is compelled against his will to remain in community of ownership or partnership. Therefore the governor of the province who has been approached will provide for the division of these

[13] Ps 133:3; Lev 25:21.

[14] Testament of Zebulon 9:4.

[15] *m. B. B.* 8:7, 9:3 f.; *m. Bekh.* 9:3.

[16] *Bell.* 2.8.3.122.

[17] *Gen. Rab.* on 13:14. The clause in question is "after that Lot was separated from him." As it is in strictness superfluous, the Rabbis assume that it must convey a special teaching.

[18] *Gen. Rab.* on 11:6.

things that he regards as common to you with your sister.][19] Obviously, either the petitioner or his sister was averse to a division. To be sure, it is unlikely that they were Jewish. The attitude in question was wide-spread in the East. Even in Rome, the younger Pliny felt at least under a moral obligation to explain why he sold his part of a joint inheritance to an outsider, and very cheaply too.[20]

Still, the evidence as a whole does warrant the conclusion that the incident recounted by Luke was possible and meaningful in a Jewish milieu; possible because both the petitioner's attitude and his brother's can be parallelled from relevant sources, and meaningful because it was not just any claim Jesus refused to support, but a claim not of the highest order. Even the warning against covetousness, though it may be an appendix, is not as unintelligent an appendix as it is generally made out to be. Jesus's reply, it may be added, is no indication of a profound legal training, only of an ordinary familiarity with the traditional ways in which brothers might deal with the goods left to them. It is not proposed here to inquire into the connection between the incident and the more general doctrines about private possessions and litigation to be found in the New Testament.[21]

II.

In the parable of the two sons,[22] the final verses concerning the attitude of the elder of them are sometimes held to be a later addition.[23] Let us first, however, consider the parable as it stands, including these verses. What is the legal position envisaged?

The story begins by the younger requesting his portion of the family goods and the father complying. The implication must be that this child would have no further claims either in the father's lifetime or on his death. Otherwise the subsequent development—his distress at the loss of his goods, his throwing himself on his father's mercy and the father's generosity in responding—becomes unintelligible. Having received his portion, the younger son went abroad. We said something about χωρὶς οἰκεῖν above, under I, citing the case of Judah "who went down from his brethren." Evidently, the younger son cut his personal ties with his kin as well as his proprietary ones. Henceforth he could not even expect, for instance, to be fed and clothed together with the lowest member of the household.

From the continuation of the parable (taking it as it stands) the expression "he divided unto them the goods" looks inexact, though we shall see that it is not necessarily so. It does not look as if the father had divided the goods "unto them." The younger son alone obtained his share, while the elder was content to remain in dependence on his father, without property of his own. The inexactitude, however, if such it is, is far from monstrous in a work not, after all, written by or for jurists. A layman would naturally speak of an arrangement by which one of two sons is paid off and the other retains his status in the family as a division "unto them."

19 *Code* 3.37.5.

20 *Ep.* 7.11, cp. 14.

21 E.g. Luke 12:32 f., 18:22; Acts 2:44 ff., 4:32 ff., 5:1 ff.; 1 Cor 6:1 ff.

22 Luke 15:11 ff.

23 Wellhausen's theory; see Creed, *ad loc.*

In many legal systems a son, on coming of age, may compel his father, or at least put pressure on him, to hand over to him his portion of the estate as his private property. As a rule this will automatically end his prospective title to the inheritance.[24] The arrangement may also be brought about at the father's initiative—for example, in order to ensure that the other children will not after his death have any trouble with the one paid off. The younger son of the parable wanted to manage his affairs and the father consented. The problem is that, at first sight, according to Talmudic law, he would not thereby lose his prospective rights to the inheritance. In fact, what he received on this occasion would simply count as a special gift and, on his father's death, would not even be deducted from his share.[25] But this is not the meaning of Luke. For Luke, he lost his rights.

We have the choice between four explanations. First, the parable may be founded on non-Jewish law—a solution to be accepted only if there is no other. Secondly, the parties entered into complicated, exceptional contracts designed to render the normal law inoperative. The text, however, contains not the slightest hint at such a procedure. Thirdly, the father, at the same time as he paid off his younger son, made a gift of the rest to the elder, keeping back for himself the usufruct and the running of it for life. This transaction, fully recognized in the Talmud,[26] may be alluded to by the phrase "he divided unto them the goods," which, on this premise, would not be inexact at all. The younger son obtained absolute control and enjoyment of his share at once. The elder also was given his share—so that on the father's death there would be nothing left for the younger to inherit—only the elder did not at once obtain control and enjoyment; these, though not ownership, remained with the father while he lived. The division, on this interpretation, was certainly "unto them," and the effect would be in harmony with Luke's meaning: the younger son had no more prospects.

While regarding the explanation as quite satisfactory, I incline to a fourth. The Talmudic law of inheritance, as laid down in Mishnah, Gemara and so on, seems to me to reduce to a rigid uniformity what was at one time a far more varied and flexible body of customs. I think that at the period of the New Testament, and for long afterwards wherever the Talmudic regulation was not strictly enforced, it was possible for a Jewish father to give one of his sons—preferably the younger—some compensation and thereby exclude him from all further claims. There was no need, if he was to be excluded, for any dodges or for making over the rest to the elder son, minus a usufruct for life. A father could simply pay off a son—maybe before witnesses or by means of a document—and thus extinguish his right to the inheritance.

Of Abraham we learn[27] that, when about to die, he bestowed his entire possessions on Isaac; but that earlier on, "while he yet lived," he had settled once for all the claims of the sons of his concubines by making them appropriate gifts. Moreover, "he sent them away from Isaac unto the east country." The paying off, that is, had been combined with

[24] On this point, and on others arising out of the parable, see Rabel, "Elterliche teilung," in *Festschrift zur 49. Versammlung Deutscher Philologen und Schulmänner zu Basel im Jahre 1907*, 521 ff.

[25] *m. B. B.* 8:7.

[26] *Ibid.*

[27] Gen 25:5 f.

dismissal from the family community: the sons of the concubines should χωρὶς οἰκεῖν. The whole arrangement in this case was due to the initiative, not of the sons to be emancipated—they were not as adventurous as the prodigal of the parable—but of Abraham, who wished to secure Isaac from possible rivals. For the present discussion it does not matter if, as is just conceivable, in the eyes of the narrator the bestowal of the possessions on Isaac also took place some time before Abraham's death.

It might perhaps be objected that this is very ancient law and, besides, that the treatment of children of concubines is no evidence for what may be done to children of one's chief wife. But a Rabbinic legend referring to Abraham's dealings deprives this objection of much of its force.[28] The descendants of Ishmael, the Arabs, pleaded before Alexander the Great that Palestine was theirs, on the strength of the provision in Deuteronomy[29] that if a man has two wives—Hagar and Sarah—and hates, or divorces, one—Hagar—then, though his firstborn son should be from this one—Ishmael—he ought to let him have a double portion of the estate. To this the delegate of the Jews replied that a man was free to do with his children as he pleased; that Abraham made use of this freedom; and that according to the Biblical record he bestowed all his possessions on Isaac. The Arabs were not yet satisfied. They demanded to be shewn "the document of sending away which divided the estate between Abraham's sons." Whereupon the Jewish delegate referred them to the verse: "But unto the sons of the concubines Abraham gave gifts and sent them away from Isaac, while he yet lived, unto the east country."

In this legend no importance is attached to the fact that Isaac's mother was a chief wife and Ishmael's a concubine only. The distinction no doubt mattered to the author of Genesis, but the author of the legend does not invoke it. Moreover, in the legend, "the document of sending away" does not appear to concern merely the setting up of a separate household by Ishmael, as does the phrase "to send away the sons of the concubines" in Genesis. It appears to be an instrument by which a father removes a child from the family and puts an end to any legal rights he may have had in it.

It may be argued that the legend goes back to a milieu influenced by Hellenistic or other non-Jewish Eastern notions. But, then, if so, there is no reason why these notions should not have been influential also among first century Palestinian Jewry. Or it may be argued that the Jewish delegate deliberately took a stand not in harmony with Jewish law, but calculated to impress Alexander, a gentile. This is tenable but does not strike me as likely. Or it may be argued that the legend can in fact be harmonised with the Talmudic system. "The document of sending away," it may be said, is not a technical term for the exclusion of a child from his privileges. The legend simply means that Abraham in his lifetime distributed everything between his sons, and as the distribution was very unequal it speaks of the pittance given to Ishmael as a "sending away"—as we might speak of a "disposing of a person." Theoretically, Ishmael would not have lost his status; only when, on Abraham's death, he came to seize his part of the inheritance he would find that no inheritance existed, Abraham having already made Isaac owner of all before he died. It is true that, if we take the legend in this way, there is no

[28] *Gen. Rab.* on 25:6.

[29] Deut 21:17.

discrepancy with Talmudic legal doctrine. But the interpretation is artificial. It is hard to believe that "the document of sending away" should not signify a technical *Abfindung* or *Abschichtung* [final settlement], removing a member from the family.

There are other indications that, in certain periods and regions at least, contrary to orthodox Talmudic law, a Jewish father could transfer a portion of his goods to a son, thereby ending any further claims of the latter. Quite apart from *qonam,* an interdict by vow, or an institution like *qesasah,* "severance," the precise import of which has never been investigated (one of its functions may have been that of *abdicatio* [renunciation])—there is a papyrus of the sixth or seventh century A.D. containing a petition by one Sousneus, who probably thinks in terms of Jewish law.[30] He explains that his father, "while he lived," i.e. not just when about to die, had put a younger son, David, in possession of their mother's land, whereas the other children were still maintained on their father's land. When about to die, he ordered David to receive a small piece of land, saying that was enough for him since he had the mother's land. For three years after the father's death David was content with the mother's land and the small additional piece, but now he demanded also a share in the land of Sousneus. The problem of the case seems to be that the father on his deathbed did not expressly convey the principal part of his estate to Sousneus: had he done so, Sousneus would not fail to mention it in his petition. All the father did was to confirm David in his ownership of the mother's land, to allot to him another field besides, and to declare that sufficient. David therefore contends that the mother's land and the small piece of the father's land left him constitute special gifts, which do not detract from his right to the father's inheritance—a position certainly defensible on the basis of a rigorous application of the Talmudic rules. Sousneus, on the other hand, maintains that this would not agree with the spirit of their father's arrangements: he gave David these gifts in lieu of his right to the inheritance. It is not known how the case was decided. But whether it was decided for Sousneus or for David, we do here again meet with the notion that a Jewish father, by compensating a younger son, may reserve the inheritance as a whole for the elder.

The papyrus dates from some four hundred years after the redaction of the Mishnah. It may be found incredible that an unorthodox notion should survive so long; and the inference may be drawn that the agreement with Genesis, the Lukan parable and the legend about Alexander is a coincidence, and that Sousneus and his father, if not just stupid, imitated a foreign custom. However, the practice of eliminating one of several prospective heirs by giving him a share in advance is so much simpler than the Talmudic regulation under which something approximating this effect can be achieved only if, simultaneously with giving him his share, all the remaining property is made over to the others, the father retaining the usufruct. The simple often remains the popular even when official sanction is withdrawn. I think that if we regard as foreign the opinion of Sousneus and his father, we have to regard as foreign also the law in Luke and in the story of Alexander. There may be something to be said for this solution. But it seems far preferable to explain all three cases by reference to a continuous tradition, adumbrated as early as in Genesis.

[30] Oxy 1.131.

The younger son of the parable wasted his goods, returned and was joyfully welcomed by his father. If we suppose that the father, at the same time as he had paid him off, had conveyed the rest of his estate to the elder, keeping back only the usufruct and running of it, it is highly doubtful whether he could fully reinstall the son returned. He might treat him as an honoured guest, prepare feasts for him, present him with the finest garments, perhaps even accept him permanently into the household again; but he could not restore his title to the estate, which irrevocably belonged to the other son. The text does not in so many words speak of a reinstatement. Indeed, to the elder son's protest the father replied that "all mine is thine"; which sounds like an assurance that the elder would not need to share his rights as owner with the younger.

As already remarked, I incline to assume that the father, when paying off the younger, had not given away the rest of his property to the elder. He had remained owner, and when the younger returned, he replaced him in his old position. Just as a father had power to pay off a son and thereby extinguish his prospects, so he could fully reinstate him. (Of *qesasah* we know that, like *abdicatio* [renunciation], it could be reversed.) The only difficulty, if we adopt this view, is about the father's words to the elder son, "all mine is thine." It is a double difficulty. For one thing, at the moment the father was still owner, whatever might be the son's expectations; and for another, the younger son, too, would now have some title to the inheritance. The words must be used in a loose sense, of the strong community of interests between the father and his elder son.

The elder son's complaint, incidentally, that his father had never given him a kid for a merrymaking with his friends has also legal associations. The Rabbis deal with the question[31] of one of several sons being allowed by his father to send presents to a friend and the friend retaliating after the father's death: does what the friend sends belong to this son alone or does it belong to the inheritance so that he must share it with his brothers?

We must still consider what would be the result should the final verses of the parable, in which the elder's reaction to the younger's welcome is depicted, be secondary. The original story would then be that the father, requested by the younger son to give him his portion, gave a share both to the younger and the elder: "he divided unto them the goods." But he also retained a large part himself. How the elder son fared we are not told (if we disregard the concluding verses). Presumably he did not leave the home and carried on much as before. The younger did leave, he did break off from the joint household, χωρὶς οἰκεῖν. On his return, however, the father received him back into it again.

There is a flaw in this version, however. If we proceed from it, it is not easy to see why either of the sons should have lost his right to inherit in the event of the father's death. But surely, the point of the parable is that the younger at least had abandoned all title in exchange for his immediate portion and that, when he had wasted this, he could be rescued only by his father's love. It appears, therefore, that the elimination of the final section of the parable as a later growth creates more problems than it solves.

[31] *m. B. B.* 9:4.

Whichever line we favour—the prodigal was greeted by his father as one "who was dead and is alive again, who was lost and is found." No doubt these metaphors primarily express his passage from immorality to penitence and obedience. But they may also contain a reference, however subordinate, to the mere fact of re-joining the family. Of a man severed from his family by *qesasah* the Rabbis say that "he got lost from his family."[32] Admittedly, I can recall no Talmudic text equating loss of one's family status with death and restoration with revival. We do, however, come across comparisons not very dissimilar,[33] such as that of a leper, who is cut off from the community, or of a childless person, with one who is dead.[34] [Addendum: Just before publication, Mr. Yaron comes across a passage confirming my suspicion that *Abfindung* or *Abschichtung* was practised in Talmudic times. In *t. B.B.* 2:5 and *b. B.B.* 47a we are told that, while as a rule a son cannot usucape his father's property, a son who has received his share can. This must refer to one definitively independent, with no further claims.]

[32] *Ruth Rab.* on 4:7.

[33] *b. Ned.* 64b.

[34] I am indebted to Mr. R. Yaron, of Jerusalem and Aberdeen Universities, for valuable criticism.

Shame Culture in Luke

To be allowed to contribute to a *Festschrift* for Charles Kingsley Barrett, to whose work—*aere perennius* [more long-lasting than bronze]—students of the New Testament are indebted for a wealth of learned information, for profound new insights and for what can only be called inspiration, is an inestimable honour. It is also, for me, a source of deep, personal joy; for what he and Margaret have given me, generously, unfailingly, in times good and bad, has been among the great blessings of my life. I am sorry I cannot at the moment think of anything worth-while in the Pauline field on which this volume focuses. But in view of the dedicatee's important A. S. Peake Memorial Lecture, my topic may not be quite out of place.[1]

Ruth Benedict's *The Chrysanthemum and the Sword*, of 1946, was an outstanding achievement, spiritually and academically. It drew a respectful, sympathetic picture of Japan at a time when feelings against that country were running high; and it familiarized scholars with the dichotomy between eastern shame culture and western guilt culture. Of course, both traits, attentiveness to appearances and attentiveness to the inner voice, play some part in every society, class and individual (except in California, which seems to be doing without either). Yet more often than not one or the other distinctly prevails. Ceremonial harakiri contrasts with our solitary suicide. Of two budding executives, one may have a liaison beneath his station for a few years and be thoroughly happy so long as there is no scandal, indeed, the memory of it will be a solace to him in old age;[2] while the other will be tortured for the rest of his life by a single night's lapse which cannot possibly ever become known.

It is almost two decades since I noticed that Deuteronomy is considerably more shame-oriented than the remaining four Books of Moses.[3] For example, the army must

[1] Said a Fellow of Boalt: "I've a block/against writing on Paul and his flock./Any mention of law/leaves my nerve-endings raw./It's high time that I turned to a Doc."

[2] Paradoxically (as he likes it), Heine in his early twenties publicizes his participation in this kind of thing:

Blamier' mich nicht, mein schönes Kind,	[Don't embarrass me, my pretty girl,
und grüss' mich nicht unter den Linden.	Don't say hello to me *unter den Linden* ("under the lime trees").
Wenn wir nachher zu Hause sind	When we get home tonight,
wird sich schon alles finden.	Everything will be alright.]

[3] I outlined my thesis in No. 2 of my Edinburgh Gifford Lectures 1963, on Law and Wisdom in the Bible, taped but as yet unpublished. An address, with extensive documentation, which I had delivered before the Institute of Jewish Studies, University College, London, and the Oxford Society of Historical Theology, appeared ["The Culture of Deuteronomy"] in *Orita*, vol. 3 (1969), 27 ff. My connection with this journal I owe to my friend E. Bolaji Idowu, whom, like Charles Kingsley, I first met when he studied at Wesley House, Cambridge. The transfer of a Deuteronomic shame-cultural provision to an international setting in the First

have a spot outside the camp where to relieve oneself, in order that God should see no immodest mark among his protégés; a bastinado inflicted on a wrong-doer may not be excessive, lest he become contemptible: the punishment of one who breaks faith with a dead brother is public degradation, the dead man's widow spitting at him in front of the elders; God himself is anxious about his reputation—he spares the sinful Israelites because their enemies would assign the credit for their downfall to themselves instead of to him.[4] To account for it, I referred to Deuteronomy's affiliation with Wisdom, whose ideal, reaching outward, is to find favour and avoid disgrace.[5] Some three years ago it struck me that just as Deuteronomy stands out for shame-cultural emphasis in the Pentateuch, so does Luke among the Synoptics. More than that: basically, the explanation is very similar.

Here is the material, some two dozen excerpts with a shame-cultural flavour—and Wisdom elements in most of them. I shall follow the order in which we find them. I start with the parables, looking first at three the Gospel shares with Mark or Matthew so that its particular note is clearly revealed.

1. *The Watchmen.* In Luke,[6] if they are vigilant, the returning master will wait on them: a choice of symbol reflecting a fair interest in table etiquette. It is met neither in the corresponding Marcan section nor in the Matthean,[7] but we shall come across it in yet another exclusively Lucan formulation outside the parables.[8] It depicts, of course, a tremendous reversal of the norm—which latter itself, significantly, figures in a parable offered by Luke only.[9]

2. *The Great Supper*. In Matthew,[10] the invitees simply "did not want to come"; even when pressed, they simply, "paid no heed and went off, one to his farm and another to his business." In Luke,[11] they send their regrets: a piece of land or a number of oxen just bought must be inspected, a newly-wed pleads that event. We are in the Berkeley hills. Lady Troubridge recommends "owing to a previous engagement": and if you can specify an urgent one–"I have already undertaken to conduct the youth orchestra"—all the better. These apologies are perfect. A purchaser of land or oxen might incur serious loss by letting the term set for examination expire;[12] the phrasing," I have necessarily to inspect the land," makes the point. A recent marriage—not mentioned in Mark and Matthew—exempts from otherwise inescapable obligation in Deuteronomy as well as Lydio-Greek saga.[13]

Book of Kings will be discussed in the forthcoming issue of the *Juridical Review* ["Ahab and Benhadad: A Municipal Directive in International Relations" (1982), 62-67].

[4] Deut 23:13 ff., 25:1 ff., 25:5 ff., 32:26 f.

[5] Prov 3:4, 34 f.

[6] Luke 12:37.

[7] Mark 13:33 ff; Matt 24:45 ff.

[8] See below, 827, on Luke 22:27.

[9] See below, 822, on Luke 17:7 ff.

[10] Matt 22:1 ff.

[11] Luke 14:16 ff.

[12] Shades of *de modo agri* [on the extent of land], *displicentia* [if dissatisfied], *ad gustum* [that it be tasted] and so forth.

[13] Deut 20:7, 24:5; Herodotus 1.36. See J. M. Creed, *The Gospel according to St. Luke* (1930), 192.

Moreover, the form is no less impeccable than the substance. Both the buyer of land and that of oxen end their messages with the polite, lengthy "I beg you, hold me excused." The newlywed says: "Therefore I cannot come." "I cannot" obviously does not envisage either physical or legal impossibility. However, in many languages, ancient and modern, "I cannot," "you cannot," etc. may mean "cannot in deference to a belief, standard, convention which it would be improper to breach." A behind-the-times father to his son: "You cannot remain seated when a lady enters the room." A professor offered a fortnight at the Villa Serbelloni: "I cannot in all decency ask for special leave here, having joined the faculty only two months ago." It is this shame-cultural usage that we have before us; and we shall indeed encounter a second instance in a parable peculiar to Luke.[14] What is intriguing is that, of all the codes in the Pentateuch, Deuteronomy alone employs the expression. The king ought to be a Hebrew, "you cannot put a foreigner over yourself." If a divorcee has remarried, then after dissolution of her second marriage, "her former husband cannot come back to take her to wife."[15] It is always treated as interchangeable with "you shall not," "he shall not." But whereas the latter is the prophetic injunction or ban of guilt culture,[16] the former implies: that would be out of tune with the model order here designed, in so wonderful a set-up surely that will be out of the question—something of this nature.

3. *The Lost Sheep*. In Matthew,[17] the owner, having it back, simply rejoices. In Luke,[18] he rejoices and collects his acquaintances to rejoice with him. An eager sharing of happiness suits a demonstrative, display-geared ethos. Deuteronomy, it should be recalled, sets much store by communal merry-making on the festivals of pilgrimage.[19] How important such gatherings are for the Third Gospel is shown by their recurrence in two more parables, to be adduced among the next category, parables not paralleled elsewhere.[20]

I proceed, then, to this group.

1. *The Importunate Friend*.[21] Permeated with shame considerations. The neighbour called out at midnight submits an excuse, like the Lucan invitees to a feast. Matthew might have written, "He did not want to get up." It is a good excuse: "The door is shut and my children are with me in bed." No mention of his own comfort; that would not do. He is prevented by his position as *paterfamilias*. Hence, not "I shall, or will, not rise" but "I cannot rise": the "cannot in view of the superior pattern to which we conform." "Considering my responsibilities here, it would be the wrong thing to rise."

So there is he, his children and the bed—*koite* in Greek, often signifying "marriage-bed." As far as I am aware, no commentator has asked: where is the wife? If the

[14] See below on Luke 11:5 ff.

[15] Deut 17:15; see ["The Culture of Deuteronomy"] 41 ff.; also ["Repudium in Deuteronomy"] *Studies in Honour of Matthew Black* (1968), 236; ["To Be Found Doing Wrong"] *Studi in onore di Edoardo Volterra* (1969), vol. 2, 1 ff.; and ["One from among Your Brethren Shall You Set King Over You"] *JBL*, 90 (1971), 480 f.

[16] See my forthcoming *Ancient Jewish Law* (1981), part III, "The Form is the Message," 74 ff [189 ff.].

[17] Matt 18:12 ff.

[18] Luke 15:3 ff.

[19] E.g. Deut 12:12. See ["The Culture of Deuteronomy"], 41.

[20] See below, 821, on Luke 15:8 ff; and 15:11 ff.

[21] Luke 11:5 ff.

scene were laid in this State, there would indeed be no cause for wonder: there has been a divorce and, as he is the more mothering of the two and she has a career, he got custody. But it is Luke. She is omitted from squeamishness: one does not announce, "I am lying with my wife." In this case, as the man stands for God, her inclusion would be doubly offensive. Conceivably, in some version she did figure while the children did not. The closed door sounds like a symbol of the privacy of the marital night which it is indelicate to breach, be it intruding from outside, be it emerging from within.

In the end, he is stirred up into compliance "because of his shamelessness": a straight shame term. It may have regard to the supplicant's insolent stubbornness;[22] or to his own ill-fame if he dismisses a friend in need.[23] Sirach attaches much weight to old friendship; and he lists the turning away of a friend among conduct to be ashamed of.[24] Or to his debasement by being involved in an unpleasant scene or, simply, by watching the caller carry on in a pitiful condition. In analysing a cluster of Deuteronomic directions "not to hide yourself" (one of them "you cannot hide yourself"), I pointed out that, in this milieu, shame may be experienced not only on being discovered in an undignified state but also on discovering somebody else in it.[25] Of the Three Monkeys at Nikko, only one portrays abstention from unbecoming action, "speak no evil," while two portray abstention from unbecoming reception, "see no evil," "hear no evil." Quite likely, we have to reckon with a mixture of the various aspects outlined.

The petitioner, too, is enveloped in embarrassment. He has no victuals in store; and though his guest arrives unannounced and after dark, it would be discreditable to give him nothing to eat. Hospitality to a wanderer at night is an old Wisdom value.[26] What to do? One would never, at this hour, disturb anyone on one's own behalf. But his concern for his good name as a host can be represented as dutifulness to the traveller—just as his neighbour, we saw, makes play with what is owing to his children. Indeed, he is justified in persisting despite his neighbour's initial reluctance. In general, as illustrated by Proverbs and Horace,[27] that would be impudent. But there are exceptions: the Rabbis encourage the penitent sinner to pray and pray—"the impudent one overcomes the All-Good one."[28] At the same time, he scrupulously keeps within the limits of good taste, requesting only the minimum sufficient for a meal. Gentility at this point almost gets the better of the parable's lesson, which is that we ought to ask, seek, knock for mercy—not reticence. In turn, the neighbour, once responding at all, knows what is expected in such circumstances and supplies everything needed. I am reminded of the well-bred games in the old-fashioned Freiburg of my youth. One student to another after class: "I have an appointment with my dentist but left my money in another suit. Can you lend me 5 Pfennige for a tram-ride?" "Oh, but you must have lunch also. Here are 2 Marks."

[22] This is how it is usually taken.

[23] A. Fridrichsen's interpretation, *Symbolae Osloenses*, vol. 13 (1934), 40 ff., quoted by J. Jeremias, *Die Gleichnisse Jesu*, 6th ed. (1962), 157.

[24] Sir. 9:10, 41:21 belonging with 41:16 ff.

[25] Deut 22:1, 3, 4. See ["The Culture of Deuteronomy"], 29 f.

[26] Job 31:32.

[27] Prov 25:17; Horace, *Satires* 1.9.

[28] *y. Taan* 65b.

2. *Humility.*[29] To this piece, it is true, the Western Matthew offers a parallel,[30] so it does not, perhaps, belong here. At any rate, it urges that if, invited to a wedding feast, you place yourself near the head of the table, you will incur "shame" should the host evict you in favour of somebody "more esteemed"; whereas if you choose a lowly spot, you have a good chance of being publicly singled out as "Friend" and promoted, winning "honour in front of all." Straight shame vocabulary again.

Jesus gives this instruction in a distinguished Pharisee's home, as he and his fellow-guests are about to sit down to a Sabbath dinner, the others trying to come out as high as possible. Seating-order is a popular topic of refined hellenistic table talk; and needless to say, the motif of homage and slight plays an enormous part.[31] The main idea, as is well known, already occurs in Proverbs:[32] "Put not forth yourself in the presence of the king. For better it is said unto you, Come up hither, than that you should be put lower in the presence of the prince whom your eyes have seen."

3. *The Cost of Discipleship.*[33] Two similes. First, a man begins building a tower he has not the means to complete; everybody now "mocks" him. For the immediate purpose of the admonition—think twice, the risks of this undertaking are heavy—the latter result is not needed, stark failure is enough. But in a shame environment, it is the ridicule ensuing that hurts most.

Second, a king embarks on a war with vastly inferior forces. He will not simply lose, he will become a joke: long before even sighting the enemy, he must sue for peace. Again, the stress lies on the humiliation.

The advisability of knowing one's limitations and looking before leaping is an established Wisdom theme, and in Proverbs we learn that "any purpose is established by counsel, and with good advice make war."[34] The builder ought to have "sat and calculated the cost," the king "sat and taken counsel." To this day, "to sit" characterizes a person or body deliberating; the only other New Testament passage with "to calculate" contemplates extraordinary sagacity;[35] and "to take counsel" speaks for itself.

4. *The Lost Coin.*[36] Like the owner of the lost sheep, the woman wants everybody around to celebrate the successful outcome of the search with her.

5. *The Prodigal Son.*[37] He is charged, not with any specific sins, but with wasting his goods. This is shameful and foolish, Wisdom warns us,[38] doubly so when it is done in pursuit of whores. What happens to him is predicted in Proverbs:[39] "Strangers will

[29] Luke 14:7 ff.

[30] At Matt 20:28. See below, 829.

[31] Plutarch, *Moralia* 148E ff.; 615C ff.; 644C. See my essay ["King Arthur's Round Table"] in *Gesellschaft, Kultur, Literatur—Beiträge Luitpold Wallach Gewidmet* (1975), 206.

[32] Prov 25:6 f. See J. M. Creed, *op. cit.*, 190.

[33] Luke 14:28 ff.

[34] Sir 32:19, the anonymous *quidquid agis prudenter agas et respice finem* [Whatever you do you must do with care, and look to the end]; Prov 20:18, similarly 24:6.

[35] Rev 13:18.

[36] Luke 15:8 ff.

[37] Luke 15:11 ff.

[38] Prov 5:10 ff., 12:11, 17:2, 21:17, 23:19 ff.

[39] Prov 5:10 ff.

be filled with your wealth and your labour will be in the house of a stranger, and you will mourn at the last, How I have despised reproof." His abject situation as a dependent of a citizen in a foreign country chimes with descriptions by hellenistic philosophers: you might have to eat dog-fashion at your protector's feet what he tosses to you.[40] Finally he returns to his father and declares himself "no longer worthy to be called his son": language that in both Greek and Semitic expresses deep shame. "I am not worthy" no doubt also occurs in formal selfdeprecation. But even here we have to do with shame culture; and there are countless nuances between the formal and the genuine, some of which we shall meet below.[41] So degraded was his recent life that he will gladly occupy the position of a paid hireling—lower than that of an unpaid family member.[42] An even subtler differentiation in status is introduced at the end: a steady, reliable son ranks above one to celebrate whose homecoming after straying the fatted calf is killed.

As for the father, he is not satisfied with intimate happiness but arranges a festivity, with music and dance. Furthermore, his first step, in preparation, is to have the boy clad in gorgeous attire: a spectacular restoration.

6. *The Unjust Steward.*[43] About to be dismissed, he ponders his future. "To dig I am not strong enough": possibly a bit contemptuous of the labouring class who, as Sirach puts it,[44] "shall not be inquired of for public counsel and in the assembly enjoy no precedence." The proverbial Greek, "I cannot dig," seems to have this overtone.[45] Anyhow, shame is the explicit ground for rejecting the second alternative: "To beg I am ashamed." This assessment of begging is commonplace in Wisdom.[46]

What he does is make sure by means of unusual benefactions that there will be people around to take care of him when he is out of office. That you should prepare in good times for hard ones is one of the hoariest Wisdom slogans all over the globe. The ant stores up food in summer for the winter,[47] Joseph laid in corn in the seven plentiful years for the seven lean ones,[48] "Remember the time of famine in the time of fulness," we are warned by Sirach.[49] Jesus lauds such foresight; and the opening of his response virtually proclaims its Wisdom contact—"he had done wisely," "the children of this world are wiser than the children of the light."

7. *The Servant's Reward.*[50] An appeal to meal etiquette in a well-regulated household. The slave, however hard he has worked all day, may not sup before serving his master, nor is he to be specially thanked for it. It may be recalled that, in the eyes of

[40] Athenaeus, *Deipn* 4.152f f., quoting Posidonius.

[41] See below, 826, on Luke 7:1 ff.

[42] Something of an early precedent is discussed by Reuven Yaron and me in ["Jacob's Reception by Laban"] *JSS*, 1 (1956), 60 ff.

[43] Luke 16:1 ff.

[44] Sir 38:33.

[45] Aristophanes, *Birds* 1432.

[46] Sir 40:28 ff. with, in the Greek, the same word for "to beg" as in Luke.

[47] Prov 6:6 ff., 30:25; Babrius, Fable 140.

[48] Genesis 41.

[49] Sir 18:25.

[50] Luke 17:7 ff.

punctilious traditionalists, overmuch affability on the part of a superior is despicable.[51] At certain formal parties—and not only in Britain—the personnel are still to be treated as non-persons.

8. *The Unjust Judge.*[52] He is, *au fond* [at bottom], incorrigible yet does end by listening to the widow who would not be shaken off. As has long been seen, in quite a few societies, ancient and not-so-ancient, obligations—a promise, a Nabob's duty to an aged retainer—are apt to be fulfilled mainly in order to get rid of embarrassing protestations of the claimant.[53] Shame culture. There are striking examples from the judicial sphere. "Opposite the entrance of the court sat the Cadi," relates a nineteenth-century traveller. "The front-hall was crowded with people, each demanding that his case should be heard first. In the meanwhile, a poor woman broke through the orderly proceedings with loud cries for justice. She was sternly bidden to be quiet and reproachfully told that she came every day. 'And so will I do,' she loudly exclaimed, 'until the Cadi hears my case.' Her story was soon told, the case was quickly decided and her patience was rewarded."[54] I have a feeling that the report is influenced by Luke: the author was an ardent divine. Even so it is, on the whole, a dependable parallel.

The reflection prompting the judge to yield deserves examination: *hina me hypopiaze me*. I would take it as it stands: "lest she strike me in the face." A blow in the face is the archetypal shaming insult among Hebrews, Greeks and Romans.[55] In the New Testament, it figures several times: Jesus charges his followers to bear it meekly,[56] and while he himself does so,[57] Paul is less patient when similarly tested.[58] What the fellow is dreading is a desperate assault that would lower him in public esteem. It is widely argued[59] that considerations of Greek grammar militate against one final outbreak, so we ought to assume a mitigated, metaphorical sense: "lest she cause me grave trouble." I suspect the advocates of this interpretation are themselves a little offended by the crudeness of the literal alternative: contemporary shame reflex. Surely, the "grave trouble" must be an escalation comparable to a slap, her visits will have that disgracing effect.

Commentators on the parable call attention to Sirach's trust in God as the rescuer of widows neglected by judges.[60] Equally relevant is his advice to avoid noisy quarrels,[61]

[51] Plutarch, *Aemilius Paulus* 38.3; Cicero, *Letters to Atticus* 1.12, confesses that the loss of his charming young reader affects him more than a slave's death should. See W. Kroll, *Die Kultur der Ciceronischen Zeit* 2 (1933), 86, 114.

[52] Luke 18:1 ff.

[53] See R. C. Thurnwald, art. "Recht," in *Reallexikon der Vorgeschichte*, vol. 11 (1927/8), 60.

[54] See H. B. Tristram, *Eastern Customs in Bible Lands* (1894), 228, quoted by B.T.D. Smith, *The Parables of the Synoptic Gospels* (1937), 150; and J. Jeremias, *op. cit.*, 154.

[55] Isa 50:6. See my *The New Testament and Rabbinic Judaism* (1956, repr. 1973), 259 ff. [See 181 ff.]

[56] Matt 5:39; Luke 6:29.

[57] Mark 14:65, 15:19; Matt 26:67 f., 27:30; Luke 22:63 f.; John 18:22, 19:3.

[58] Acts 23:2 ff. See my *Sin, Ignorance and Forgiveness in the Bible* (1960), 13.

[59] See J. M. Creed, *op. cit.*, 223. K. H. Rengstorf, *Das Evangelium nach Lukas*, 9th ed. (1962), 205, gives a fairly literal rendering: *damit sie nicht mir ins Gesicht fährt.*

[60] Sir 35:14. See J. M. Creed, *op. cit.*, 222; K. H. Rengstorf, *op. cit.*, 206.

[61] Sir 8:3.

which the judge prudently follows. Wisdom accounts, too, for the latter's characterization, given twice: when he is introduced as one who "feared not God nor regarded man," and at the turning-point when he himself subscribes to this portrayal—I must give in "though I fear not God nor regard man."[62] Nor is this vision confined to the Hebrews. In fact, a very close approximation to the Lucan summing-up of the anti-hero is found in Dionysius of Halicarnassus: a gang of Roman conspirators are stigmatized as "neither fearing the wrath of the gods nor regarding the indignation of men."[63]

We must not overlook the widow's shame dilemma, already adverted to in connection with the Importunate Friend: as a rule, forwardness is frowned on, and yet now and then it is in order.

9. *The Pharisee and the Publican.*[64] The former "stands up" visibly to pray: arrogance. We shall see, however, that there can be in this culture a commendable standing up.[65] The latter "stands afar," in the typical position of shame. Nor does he dare to look up. Enoch is asked by the fallen angels to intercede for them, "for they could not lift up their eyes to heaven for shame of their sins."[66] An eighteenth-century variety: "Fixing his eyes on Clara, who modestly dejected hers."[67]

So much for the parables; now for the rest.

1. The barren Elisabeth, miraculously conceiving in old age, like the Rachel of Genesis, thanks God—not for the pregnancy but—for taking away "her reproach among men."[68] The disgrace resulting from childlessness is treated as almost worse than the deprivation itself.

2. During pregnancy she hides herself[69]—plainly shame. No need to enquire here into the exact nuance: was she bashful generally or apprehensive that people might laugh because of her and her husband's age?[70] From the garden of Eden on, shame avoids sight;[71] and above I touched on "hiding oneself" in Deuteronomy.[72] The sexual domain is indeed shame's birthplace and forever and everywhere remains its *point d'appui* [base of operation].[73] Ordinarily, moreover, its presence in this field is looked on as, *au fond*, a blessing. Elsewhere I have argued[74] that the Genesis myth, like the Greek one of the acquisition of fire, commemorates man's rise, notwithstanding its pious reinterpretation as concerned with his fall; and the acquisition of shame, for this Wisdom narrator, is the most desirable achievement, actually represents the basis of all civilization. To be without it is to be animal-like, unenlightened, pitiable.

[62] Prov 3:4.

[63] Dionysius of Halicarnassus, *Roman Antiquities* 10.10.7. See J. M. Creed, *op. cit.*, 222 f.

[64] Luke 18:9 ff.

[65] See below, 827, on Luke 21:36.

[66] 1 Enoch 13:5

[67] *The Woman of Honour* (1768), III 26.

[68] Luke 1:25; Gen 30:23.

[69] Luke 1:24.

[70] Cf. Gen 17:17, 18:12 ff., 21:6.

[71] Gen 3:8, 10.

[72] Not, however, in the Greek.

[73] See ["The Culture of Deuteronomy"], 33, 40.

[74] See my *Civil Disobedience in Antiquity* (1972), 61.

It has been suggested that Elisabeth's retirement is dictated by the plot: the news of her pregnancy is not to reach Mary just yet.[75] I am not excluding this explanation. Even if we proceed from it, her conduct must make sense to the readers, and it does so in a shame milieu.

3. The aspersions non-believers doubtless heaped on Mary are countered with the utmost delicacy. There is no express reference to them. Yet, as I have shown previously, an effective refutation is furnished in the annunciation scene by depicting her as a second Ruth.[76] The latter, the Rabbis insist, despite her pre-marital, nocturnal visit to Boaz, at first sight highly dubious, was the purest of all women.

Matthew is more direct: he does mention Joseph's initial, unworthy suspicions.[77] Here too, by the way, the shame aspect plays a major role: Joseph generously refrains from "making her a public example." As just noted, where sexual matters are involved, the tendency for shame to come to the fore is pretty universal.

4. The child Jesus "grew and became strong, filled with wisdom, and the grace of God was upon him"; the adolescent Jesus "advanced in wisdom and stature and grace with God and men."[78] Similarly—as has long been observed[79]—the young Samuel "went on and was good both with God and with men."[80] The ideal progress of Wisdom's votary: he enjoys the favour of, is in good standing with, not only heaven but also this world. The repeated Lucan insertion of the concept "Wisdom" is significant.

In fact, a measure of importance is attached to bodily appeal: "he became strong," "he advanced in stature." Saul was handsome and "higher than any of the people."[81] There is an old and persistent Wisdom strand with esteem for beauty male as well as female: Joseph, David and Daniel belong here.[82] This does not mean that good looks cannot be inadequate (David's eldest brother)[83] or misused (Absalom and Adonijah)[84] or that the blemish of their lack cannot be compensated by weightier qualities: we shall find a possible allusion to this in the Third Gospel itself.[85]

5. At Nazareth, the audience wonder at Jesus's "words of grace":[86] the same key term as in the verses just cited. The remark does not figure in Mark or Matthew.[87]

6. Immediately after, he guesses that they will confront him with "this proverb, Physician, heal yourself."[88] Not in the other Synoptics. It is a common tag in the ancient world: "Physician, heal your own limp," "A physician of others, himself covered with

[75] See J. M. Creed, *op. cit.*, 12 f.

[76] Luke 1:35, 38. See *The New Testament and Rabbinic Judaism*, 27 ff. [See 137 ff.]

[77] Matt 1:19 ff.

[78] Luke 2:40, 52.

[79] See J. M. Creed, *op. cit.*, 46.

[80] 1 Sam 2:26.

[81] 1 Sam 9:2, 10:23.

[82] Gen 39:6; 1 Sam 16:12; 17:42; Dan 1:4, 15.

[83] 1 Sam 16:7.

[84] 2 Sam 14:25; 1 Kgs 1:6.

[85] See below, 827, on Luke 19:1 ff.

[86] Luke 4:22.

[87] Mark 6:2; Matt 13:54.

[88] Luke 4:23.

festering boils,"[89] holding up its target to derision. The word *parabole*, by the way, when denoting "proverb," seems usually to refer to exposure: "byword of reproach."[90] Of course, proverbs belong to wisdom.

7. Whereas in Matthew,[91] the centurion with a sick slave approaches Jesus in person, in Luke,[92] he despatches Jewish elders who explain that in view of what he has done for the Jews "he is worthy" of special attention. In both accounts, he professes that "he is not worthy" to have Jesus enter under his roof. But in Matthew, he continues speaking to him directly; in Luke, once again, he sends friends to tell him so, as he is approaching his house. There is evidently a certain degree of shame culture even in Matthew: I remarked on "unworthiness" above, in commenting on the Prodigal Son. But the Third Gospel has superimposed a most elaborate etiquette.

Quite likely, this version is designed to allude to later gentile converts who never met Jesus in the flesh.[93] Even so, the man's doings cannot be absurd—else the evangelist's public would be put off. They are perfectly sound in an environment keen on decorum.

8. For the story of the woman with an issue of blood, we also have another Synoptic as a foil. In Mark,[94] she fears only Jesus's reaction to her daring. In Luke,[95] the stress lies on her exposure: "she saw that she was not hidden." In Mark, she confesses to Jesus. In Luke, "she declared in front of all people." As a result, the praise she received from him is represented as private in Mark, as public in Luke.

9. "Go not from house to house,"[96] the seventy are advised—without parallel in Mark and Matthew.[97] Such conduct offends the refined sensibilities. Sirach speaks of "the reproach of wandering" and deems it "an evil life to go from house to house."[98] The "shamelessness" of an uninvited guest is censured in hellenistic literature,[99] and Horace sketches "a parasite at large with no fixed stable."[100]

10. Jesus's opponents, shown up as treating their cattle better than their sick, "are ashamed."[101] Whether or not this effect implies a harking back to Isaiah,[102] neither Mark nor Matthew has it in comparable situations. Who knows?, when the *pericope de adultera* was assigned by some to the Third Gospel,[103] one of the considerations may

[89] *Gen. Rab.* 23, on 4:23; Euripides, Fragment 1071, in A. Nauck, *Tragicorum Graecorum Fragmenta*, 2nd ed. (1889). See J. M. Creed, *op. cit.*, 68.

[90] Wisdom of Solomon 5:3; cf. Ezek 18:2; Ps 44:14, in LXX 43:14.

[91] Matt 8:5 ff.

[92] Luke 7:1 ff.

[93] See J. M. Creed, *op. cit.*, 100.

[94] Mark 5:24 ff.

[95] Luke 8:47 ff.

[96] Luke 10:7.

[97] Mark 6:10; Matt 10:11.

[98] Sir 29:23 f.

[99] Athenaeus, *Deipn.* 1.8b, quoting Archilochos.

[100] Horace, *Ep.* 1.15.28. Maenius, to be sure, has a certain grandeur, having gone through a large inheritance with supreme indifference.

[101] Luke 13:17.

[102] Isa 45:16. See J. M. Creed, *op. cit.*, 183.

[103] After Luke 21:38.

have been the similar experience of the accusers there.[104] I shall presently come back to this.

11. Possibly, the tiny Zacchaeus who has to climb a tree to see Jesus[105] stands for (among other things) those unfortunates who, because of the lack of normal, visible endowments, are apt to be laughed at. That this Gospel is interested in stature, we saw above. Plato thinks an undersized person deserves pity,[106] but that is not all he commonly gets.[107] Randy Newman's splendid song springs from a sensitivity rare even today.[108]

12. The apocalyptic discourse culminates in the exhortation to the disciples so to apply themselves that they can "stand up before the Son of man."[109] Not in Mark and Matthew.[110] It may mean "remain undestroyed."[111] On the other hand, it may be shame-oriented. A sinner like the publican, conscious of his shortcomings, will not "stand up." A self-righteous sinner like the Pharisee will, all the worse for him. The fragment before us may envisage a state in which you have nothing to be ashamed of and are, therefore, able to "stand up" genuinely. Whoever placed the *pericope de adultera* after this chapter perhaps thought along such lines.

13. As Jesus eats with his disciples for the last time, he teaches that while, in general, the diner is greater than he who serves him, he is serving them.[112] An allied saying in Mark and Matthew[113] neither speaks of a waiting at table nor is presented as table talk at the Last—or any other—Supper. In Luke, the choice of symbol we met in the parable of the Watchmen, focusing on the meal conventions of the élite, surfaces again on this solemn occasion.

For a thorough evaluation of the phenomenon here demonstrated, we should have to examine the precise varieties of shame and Wisdom represented in these quotations. Thus, as for Wisdom, we would discover in the parables of the Importunate Friend, Unjust Steward and Unjust Judge traces of a wide-ranging debate whether a good deed remains good even if performed for one's own benefit and at little cost. The Importunate's neighbour and the Judge oblige not from affection or highmindedness but in order to avoid loss of face; and the Steward reduces the debtors' burdens not from kindness but in order to win supporters. Pragmatic and purist ethicists of antiquity fight over the problem. Among the Rabbinic cases are extra courtesy to your lender, a small gift to a poor man which will just bring him up to a total excluding him from such privileges as

[104] Now John 8:9. No shame term, however.

[105] Luke 19:1 ff.

[106] Plato, *Protagoras* 323D. Crito seems not too happy that his elder son is a bit short for his age: *Euthydemus* 271B. (He also worries about his education: 306D.)

[107] Aristophanes, *Frogs* 709.

[108] I am sorry for him. Over here, many people are so literal-minded that they mistook his satire on the brutes for an attack on their victims. Hard to believe but true.

[109] Luke 21:36.

[110] Mark 13; Matthew 24.

[111] Cf. Rev 6:17.

[112] Luke 22:27.

[113] Mark 10:43 ff.; Matt 20:26 ff.

gleaning in your field, abstention from work as the Sabbath approaches from indolence rather than devotion.[114] Notions like *'aram* and *piqqeaḥ*, "subtle," "clever," reminiscent of *phronimos* in the parable of the Unjust Steward, occur in this context.[115] In the early third century A.D., Rabh bridged the gulf between the two camps by pleading that, once you get into the habit of doing good, then, even if to begin with you are out for yourself, you will finish up with the right motivation.[116] His argument has become a canon in Jewish moral instruction. The difficulty theologians have with the three parables[117] would be greatly mitigated if the Wisdom input were appreciated.

However, it would lead too far afield here to pursue this investigation. One reason relatively little has been done in this area by New Testament scholars no doubt lies in Wisdom's concentration on how to succeed on earth with, *prima facie*, scarce thought for things divine. But, in actual fact, for Hebrew Wisdom—and much Gentile Wisdom as well—the latter are an absolute *sine qua non*. The first member in "to find favour in the eyes of God and man"[118] is meant very seriously indeed. Still, I must not enlarge,[119] and shall be brief even on the question of whether the Lucan data are to be linked to hellenization. Hellenization, it is by now agreed, was ubiquitous at the time. But there were degrees—just as in West Germany, there is a difference in intensity of Americanization between Heidelberg and Konstanz or a psychoanalyst and a coalminer. Now by itself, preoccupation with shame and Wisdom is no clue since it has a long, uninterrupted history in Judea as well as Greece. Nevertheless, Jewish shame and Wisdom and Greek shame and Wisdom, so long as not fully amalgamated, are distinct in many respects. It may well be that, on careful probing, the material here collected would come out nearer to Heidelberg. I can remember no Midrash addressing a class where to thank a servant counts as not *comme il faut* [the done thing]; "I cannot dig," we saw, is Greek cliché; and "to fear not God nor regard man" may be derived—directly or indirectly—from Dionysius of Halicarnassus, to whose *Roman Antiquities* Josephus opposed his *Jewish Antiquities*.[120] It may be added that the parables of the Rich Fool and the Cost of Discipleship and a section about inheritance—all peculiar to Luke—contain ideas and rare words met in Dionysius and Josephus.[121] Enough.

It remains to ask to whom the extraordinary shame component is due. It is certainly post-Jesuanic. This needs no proof for statements about him; but even with regard to statements put in his mouth, a glance at the major commentaries will show that, on one

[114] *b. B. M.* 75b; *b. Sot.* 21b; *b. Pes.* 50b.

[115] *b. Sot.* 20a.

[116] *b. Pes.* 50b.

[117] Or such difficulty as remains even on the basis of J. D. M. Derrett's interpretation, *Law in the New Testament* (1970), 48 ff.

[118] Prov 3:4. Cf. the clause from Dionysius of Halicarnassus adduced above.

[119] I have penned the first draft of an *Encomium Prudentiae* [in "Neglected Nuances of Exposition in Luke-Acts," *Aufstieg und Niedergang der Römischen Welt*, II, 25:3 (1985) 2329-2346]. [See 857 ff.]

[120] See my *Typologie im Werk des Flavius Josephus*, No. 6 of *Sitzungsberichte der Bayerischen Akademie der Wissenschaften* (1977), 28 f.; [English translation, "Typology in Josephus"] *JJS*, 31 (1980), 35 f.

[121] Luke 12:16 ff., 14:28 ff. (discussed above), 12:13 ff. See J. M. Creed, *op. cit.*, 173, 194, and my article ["Inheritance in Two Lukan Pericopes"] in *ZSS*, 72 (1955), Roman. Abt., 326 ff. [See 807 ff.]

ground or another, the feature in question is pronounced secondary. Neither, however, is it chiefly the evangelist's work. For one thing, a parable quite similar to that about Humility is included in the Western Matthew.[122] Admittedly, a weak argument: this version may be dependent on Luke. A far stronger one is that, here and there, the evangelist tones down an excessive leaning towards pragmatism, most conspicuously in the parable of the Unjust Steward. The man doing good from selfishness and with somebody else's money is greatly praised to begin with, but then follows denunciation after denunciation of such dishonesty—anticipating the concern of many a later reader. What decides me is that, with one or two possible minor exceptions (such as the fear of those who hear of a capital punishment, *à la* Deuteronomy),[123] I can detect no particular interest of the sort discussed in Acts.

It follows that, on the whole, he found it in his sources, oral or written. It is in any case likely that he was in touch with more sophisticated circles than Mark and Matthew: this legacy is a consequence. He took it over from faithfulness to tradition: its absence from Acts is evidence that his own world view was not deeply affected. It is a complicated situation, but not so hard to grasp. Somebody today might write a life of the founder of Hasidism. This might be distinctly influenced by Martin Buber's tales of him—which, needless to say, comprise much theology alien to eighteenth-century Lithuania: analogous to shame and Wisdom emphasis. The same writer, if going on to describe the revival of Hasidism in the States—Acts—might display hardly any vestiges of Buber's thought.

This is not to maintain that not one of the illustrations I have listed can be owing to Luke. I like to think that "Physician, heal yourself" comes from him. Alas, one indication making it plausible is that it is out of place:[124] it is never alleged by Jesus's opponents that he is himself suffering from the ills he sets out to cure.

[122] At Matt 20:28, as already mentioned.

[123] Acts 5:5, 11 (cf. 19:17); Deut 13:12, 17:13, 19:20, 21:21; see ["The Culture of Deuteronomy"], 40. The "church" of Acts 5:11 may correspond to "Israel" or "the people" of Deut 13:12, 17:13.

[124] See J. M. Creed, *op. cit.*, 68.

A Reform in Acts and Its Models*

It gives me the deepest satisfaction to participate in a *Festschrift* for William David Davies. His and his family's friendship have for many years been among the best things in my life. *Bekhol 'eth 'ohebh harea' we'aḥ leṣara yiwwaledh* [A friend loveth at all times, and a brother is born for adversity (Prov 17:17)]. How much I have learned from him about both Christianity and Judaism in the New Testament period will be apparent in every line of my contribution.

In Luke-Acts the concept of Jesus as the new Moses, the final prophet predicted in Deuteronomy,[1] is distinctly more conspicuous than in Matthew and Mark.[2] It looks as if here and there in Acts the Mosaic pattern were carried on in the Church. Right at the beginning the apostles receive instruction from Jesus for forty days,[3] as Moses had from God.[4] A more elaborate instance is the installation of seven servers of the tables.[5]

Elsewhere I have pointed out the affinity with the appointment of Joshua.[6] God had commanded Moses, "Take thee Joshua, a man in whom is the spirit"; whereupon Moses "set him before Eleazer the priest and before all the congregation and he leaned his hands upon him."[7] The apostles urged the faithful, "Look ye out seven men... full of the spirit and wisdom"; whereupon the people chose Stephen, Philip and so on, "whom they set before the apostles and having prayed [or possibly: and praying][8] they leaned their hands upon them."[9] However, the narrative is influenced also by three other chapters, describing a giving up of some burdens by Moses during his lifetime. The first, Exodus 18, tells of the creation of judges to hear routine disputes; the second, Numbers 11, of the promotion of seventy of the elders to assist him; and the third, Deuteronomy 1, of the creation of officers of the tribes.

* The following reflections formed part of Lecture 7, Reforms of Machinery, of my as yet unpublished Edinburgh Gifford Lectures 1963, on "Law and Wisdom in the Scriptures." They appeared in *Jews, Greeks and Christians: Essays in Honor of William David Davies*, ed. R. Hamerton-Kelly and R. Scroggs (Leiden, 1976), 151 ff. (*Studies in Judaism in Late Antiquity*, vol. 21).

1 Deut 18:15, 18 f.

2 Luke 24:19; Acts 3:22 f.; 7:22, 37. See my review of G. Vermes's *Jesus the Jew* (London, 1973), in *JJS*, 25 (1974), 333.

3 Acts 1:3.

4 Exod 24:18; 34:28.

5 Acts 6:1 ff.

6 Daube, *The New Testament and Rabbinic Judaism* (London, 1956), 237 ff. [see 609 f.].

7 Num 27:18 ff.

8 Cf. Acts 1:24, on which see E. Haenchen, *Die Apostelgeschichte* (13th ed.; Göttingen, 1961), 127.

9 On the translation "they leaned," see excursus below.

The report of Acts commences with a vague "in those days." This is often found in the Old Testament, as is its equivalent "at that time." The relevant section of Deuteronomy 1 starts with the latter.[10]

Next the background is filled in: "those days" are characterized by growth—"as the disciples multiplied." Commentators usually brush this aside as of no moment; even the few who stop to take note declare it a minor factor.[11] But this cannot be the right treatment of the first occasion on which "disciples" signifies "Christians." (The designation is, I believe, anticipated once in Luke,[12] when Jesus, approaching Jerusalem, is welcomed by "the multitude of the disciples"—a prefigurement of what came true in Acts.) Moreover, the opening motif is emphatically resumed not only in the following sentence, about the apostles assembling "the multitude of the disciples," but also at the end of the episode by way of culmination: the process continued, "and the number of the disciples in Jerusalem was multiplied greatly." We have to do with an essential element. As will emerge below, in the Rabbinic exegesis of Exodus 18 and Numbers 11 the winning of proselytes plays an important part, to a considerable extent indeed foreshadowed in the Biblical presentation. Above all, however, in Deuteronomy 1 it is the miraculous increase of the people that renders a reform inevitable: "the Lord your God hath multiplied you and behold, ye are this day as the stars of heaven for multitude."[13]

The word for "multitude" in Acts (and in Luke), *plethos*, is the same as in the Septuagint of Deuteronomy. As the term is rather frequent in Acts generally, this by itself would mean little. But *plethyno*, "to multiply," also common to Acts and Deuteronomy, is much rarer. In Deuteronomy it is transitive: "hath multiplied you." In its first occurrence in Acts it is intransitive: "they multiplied." The second time it occurs it is transitive, if we take *eplethyneto* as passive: "was multiplied"; it might, however, be middle intransitive: "multiplied." There is enough agreement to merit attention.

We learn that there arose "a murmuring," *goggysmos*, definitely not an ordinary term. It recalls the situations in Exodus and Numbers which weary the leader.[14] *Goggyzo*, "to murmur," occurs in the Septuagint in the first verse of Numbers 11: "and the people murmured." Their grievance concerns the provision of food, and so, apparently, does the grievance in Acts. Acts speaks of "a daily service," *diakonia kathemerine*. The Manna causing dissatisfaction in Numbers is to be gathered "for day unto day," *kath' hemeran eis hemeran*.[15]

The Grecians, Acts informs us, felt discriminated against by the Hebrews. Whatever the composition of the two groups, it is evident that the former was the weaker—presumably a more recent arrival within the fold. In Numbers 11, at one stage,[16] the lead in disapproving of the food is taken by "the mixture" or "the admixture" among the

[10] Deut 1:9.

[11] *Nebenumstand*: Haenchen, *Apostelgeschichte*, 213.

[12] Luke 19:37; see Daube, "Responsibilities of Master and Disciples in the Gospels," *NTS*, 19 (1972), 10. [See 757].

[13] Deut 1:10.

[14] Exod 15:24; 16:2, 7, 8, 9, 12; 17:3; Num 14:2, 27, 29, 36; 16:11; 17:6, 20, 25.

[15] Exod 16:5.

[16] Num 11:4.

Israelites, though the latter soon join in. The Hebrew is *'asaphsuph*; *'asaph* denotes "to gather." According to a Midrash,[17] the noun means "those gathered from everywhere," "the proselytes." No doubt in New Testament times a reference to proselytes might be assumed here even by readers not familiar with Rabbinism. The Septuagint translates literally (*epimiktos)*, so we cannot be certain of its interpretation. It is suggestive, however, that in another passage *episynegmenoi* is used in the sense of "proselytes";[18] *episynago* as a rule corresponds to *'asaph*. That there is no basis for the introduction of proselytes in the Hebrew original of this verse is immaterial in the present context.

As for discrimination in Deuteronomy 1, Moses directly after instituting the officers of tribes, reiterates the admonition "to judge righteously between every man and his brother, and the stranger that is with him, and not to respect persons in judgment, but to hear the small as well as the great."[19] A scene towards the end of Numbers 10 also might well be relevant. Moses persuades a Midianite relation-by-marriage to attach himself to Israel; and Moses assures him of equality: "with that same good with which the Lord shall do good unto us, we shall do good unto thee."[20] The Septuagint employs *agathopoieo* and *eu poieo* for "to do good," phrases central in the area of charity.[21]

The answer to the trouble in Acts is a committee. The picture, then, is one of marvellous growth resulting, however, in conflict too great for the apostles to handle. While Numbers 11 mentions neither growth nor conflict, Exodus 18 does mention the latter and Deuteronomy 1 both. In Numbers there are simply too many people—hundreds of thousands[22]—to be controlled by one ruler; in Exodus there are too many to have their disputes adjudicated by him. Deuteronomy stresses the people's wonderful expansion, and it is precisely this which produces the "cumbrance, burden and strife" which a single ruler cannot manage,[23] similar to Acts. Deuteronomy is closest to Acts in a further detail. The complainants of Acts articulate no measure; it is the apostles who do so. Similarly, in none of the three Old Testament chapters do the people advocate innovation. But there are slight differences. In Exodus the idea emanates from Jethro and is accepted by Moses.[24] In Numbers God, entreated by Moses, explains what is to be done.[25] In Deuteronomy Moses himself thinks of the remedy, much as the apostles do.[26]

The apostles propose leaving the smaller, controversial business to the committee, while they would confine themselves to preaching and prayer, preaching possibly being given greater prominence than prayer.[27] In Exodus 18 the judges are to sit in minor dis-

[17] *Siphre* on Num 11:4.

[18] 2 Chr 5:6.

[19] Deut 1:16 f.

[20] Num 10:32.

[21] The latter denotes the performing of "good works" in Mark 14:7; on the former, see G. W. H. Lampe, *A Patristic Greek Lexicon* (Oxford, 1961), 4.

[22] Num 11:21.

[23] Deut 1:12.

[24] Exod 18:19 ff.

[25] Num 11:11 ff.

[26] Deut 1:13 ff.

[27] Preaching appears in Acts 6:2, 4, 7; prayer only in 6:4.

putes, while the major and difficult ones will be submitted to Moses. Altogether he is said to be "for the people God-ward, and thou shalt bring the causes unto God, and shalt teach them ordinances and laws, and shalt show them the way wherein they must walk and the work that they must do."[28] Of the neglect of the principal calling in order to do everything, Acts says, "it is not propitious," *ouk areston estin.* As Jethro sees Moses tiring himself out with negligible matters, he remarks, "Not good is the thing that thou doest";[29] the Septuagint renders, *ouk orthos sy poieis to rema touto.*

The argument, "it is not propitious that, having left the word of God, we should serve tables," is universally supposed to look to the future: "We ought not henceforth to abandon preaching in order henceforth to engage in the distribution of supplies."[30] Throughout the centuries commentators have rejected an alternative interpretation of the passage as a description of the present, unsatisfactory state: "it is no good that, having abandoned preaching, we are engaged in the distribution of supplies." Perhaps, however, this is the correct understanding. The aorist *kataleipsontas*, "having left," slightly favours this interpretation—though it is by no means incompatible with the prevalent view. Again we hear of no functionaries other than the apostles who might have been in charge of charity up to this moment. There is, besides, the precedent of Exodus 18, commencing with Moses spending all day on tasks far beneath those for which he is uniquely qualified; and—yet one more feature of interest—his devotion to these lesser affairs does not even pay off. The system is just as irksome to the people as to him.[31] There must be a change, Jethro counsels, so that "thou shalt be able to endure and all this people shall go to their place in peace."[32]

Further, the apostles advise the community: "Look ye out among you seven men… whom we may appoint over this business." In Exodus it is Moses whom Jethro encourages to pick the judges: "Thou shalt look out of all the people men of worth… and appoint them over them."[33] In Numbers too Moses is to collect his assistants, though from the existing elders.[34] By contrast, the procedure in Deuteronomy is more like that in Acts—Moses tells the people, "Bring ye wise men… and I will appoint them chiefs over you."[35] Linguistically, Acts is a blend of Exodus and Deuteronomy, plus the appointment of Joshua. The structure of Acts 6:3 is reminiscent of the passages in Exodus and Deuteronomy. With regard to vocabulary, *episkeptomai*, seldom employed for "to look out," is fairly near to *skeptomai*, which the Septuagint has in Jethro's scheme. The full *episkeptomai* figures in Moses's request, after learning that he must soon die, that God name a successor: "Let the Lord… look out a man over the congre-

[28] Exod 18:19 ff.

[29] Exod 18:17.

[30] Some who have annotated the passage, to be sure, do not go into this question at all; e.g., cf. Conzelmann, *Die Apostelgeschichte* (Tübingen, 1963), 43 f.

[31] Exod 18:18.

[32] Exod 18:23.

[33] Exod 18:21.

[34] Num 11:16.

[35] Deut 1:13.

gation."[36] *Kathistemi*, "to appoint," recurs both in Jethro's plan[37] and in Deuteronomy.[38]

The committee is to be "of repute, full of the spirit and wisdom." Literally, *martyromenos* signifies "attested," "born witness to." In Numbers God orders Moses to gather seventy men "of the elders of whom thou knowest that they are elders of the people and their officers";[39] and in Deuteronomy Moses bids the people provide men "known to your tribes"[40] (the Septuagint translates *synetoi eis tas phylas hymon*, "perceived [or intelligible] among your tribes"). According to Josephus, the woman who pleaded with the Abelites to dissociate themselves from the rebel Sheba argued that "nobody knows who he is."[41] In addition, the helpers of Deuteronomy ought to be "wise and understanding."[42] It is only in the course of being installed that the elders of Numbers receive "of the spirit" of Moses,[43] as Joshua receives "the spirit of wisdom" towards the end of Deuteronomy.[44] But in the main account of Joshua's appointment to which I have repeatedly adverted, his possession of the spirit is the reason for his elevation: "Take thee Joshua… in whom is the spirit."[45]

The offer of the apostles "pleased" (*aresko*) the hearers. Moses's audience in Deuteronomy reply that "the thing is nice" (*kalon to rema* in the Septuagint).[46] In Acts the community now "selected" Stephen and others (*eklegomai*); *epilego* is applied by the Septuagint of Exodus to Moses "selecting" the judges.[47]

Then the community "set" (*histemi*) Stephen and others before the apostles. As noted at the outset, Moses "set Joshua before Eleazer the priest and all the congregation" (Septuagint, *histemi*).[48] To this the promotion of seventy of the elders must now be added: Moses "set them [*histemi*] round about the tabernacle," that is, before God who is to bestow on them some of Moses's spirit.[49]

"And having prayed," the ceremony continues, "they leaned their hands upon them." The natural construction, I feel, is that it is the people who leaned their hands on the seven. Moses had "set Joshua before Eleazer and all the congregation and he leaned his hands upon him";[50] he, namely Moses, leaned, thus making Joshua his substitute. Just so, the people "set Stephen and six others before the apostles and they leaned their hands upon them"; they, namely the people, leaned, thus making the seven

[36] Num 27:16.
[37] Exod 18:21.
[38] Twice: Deut 1:13, 15.
[39] Num 11:16.
[40] Deut 1:13.
[41] 2 Sam 20:19 ff.; Josephus, *Ant.* 7.11.8.291.
[42] Deut 1:13.
[43] Num 11:17, 25.
[44] Deut 34:9; LXX *pneuma synesoeos*, not *sophias.*
[45] Num 27:8.
[46] Deut 1:14.
[47] Exod 18:25.
[48] Num 27:22; the same verb in 27:19.
[49] Num 11:24.
[50] Num 27:22 f.

their substitutes. Henceforth the serving of tables was to be in the hands of the community itself, represented by its delegates. In the Jewish public law of the time, "the Seven of a City are like the City."[51]

Orthodox opinion has the apostles perform the rite. In support of this opinion, one might perhaps invoke "whom we may appoint" in the proposal for a committee, quoted above. But such language is quite reconcilable with a "leaning on" of hands by the people, in order to offer their choices as extended selves. It was done, after all, in the presence of the apostles and indeed in pursuance of their directions. Alternatively, the expression may be explained by taking the "we" as inclusive, "we and you together." The apostles, that is, may have represented the step as one to be taken jointly by them and their followers whom, it should be observed, the apostles were addressing as "brethren." Codex Bezae, it must be admitted, definitely sides with the current approach. Instead of, "The community chose so-and-so and so-and-so, whom they set before the apostles and, having prayed, they leaned their hands upon them," it reads: "the community chose so-and-so and so-and-so, who were set before the apostles who, having prayed, leaned their hands upon them." Surely, however, this concerned rephrasing speaks for, rather than against my preference; what we have before us is a transfer of the decisive, constitutive act from the people to the authorities. It may be recalled that "they [the apostles or the assembly at large] set up [*histemi*] Joseph and Matthias" as candidates for the vacant place of Judas.[52] In this case few would deny that the reading of Codex Bezae, "he [Peter] set up," has a centralizing purpose.[53]

In any case the new arrangement proved successful; there was sustained preaching and even more vigorous growth than before. In Deuteronomy 1 Moses, fully aware that his problem is caused by the enormously risen numbers, is quick to make it clear that he hopes for and foresees yet greater increase: "the Lord make you a thousand times so many more and bless you as he hath promised you."[54]

Acts appends a mysterious statement: many priests submitted to the faith. Of the various explanations which have been advanced, one or even more than one might well be right. It should nevertheless be remembered that Jethro, the Midianite priest who dominates Exodus 18, exclaims to Moses, "Now I know that the Lord is greater than all gods."[55] Not surprisingly, a Midrash assumes him to have converted on that occasion, and in fact to have returned to his country only because he desired to convert others.[56] The son of Moses's father-in-law, whom we found joining the Israelites in Numbers 10, is, of course, also a priest.

At least two of the servers of tables, Stephen and Philip, went on to excel as missionaries and miracle-workers rather than administrators. Philip actually had daughters

[51] *y. Meg.* 74a; see H. L. Strack and P. Billerbeck, *Kommentar zum Neuen Testament aus Talmud und Midrasch*, 5 vols. (Munich, 1922-56), III, 641.

[52] Acts 1:23.

[53] See Haenchen, *Apostelgeschichte*, 127.

[54] Deut 1:11.

[55] Exod 18:11.

[56] *Mek.* on Exod 18:27.

who "prophesied." Stephen was full of "grace and power" (*charis kai dynamis*). The "men of worth" who become judges in Exodus 18 appear in the Septuagint as *andres dynatoi*.[57] Far more significant, the elders promoted in Numbers 11 "prophesy."[58] In light of the fact that Stephen was falsely accused of blasphemies against Moses and God, the two elders "prophesying" independently of the rest in Numbers are of special interest.[59] They are denounced to Moses as illicit rivals (actually, the Rabbis represent them as predicting Moses's premature death, so that Joshua would lead the people into the promised land).[60] Moses, however, far from stopping them, wishes that everybody were like them. *Eldad and Modat*, a Greek Apocryphon, survives in a quotation of four words,[61] which may be directed to proselytes: "The Lord is near to the converted." To be sure, *epistrephomenoi*, basically "those that turn," could denote "the penitent." Stephen perished at the hands of an enraged crowd. The Rabbis hold that the seventy elders, as they were called, and Moses, took it upon themselves that the people would curse and stone them.[62]

In conclusion let us consider Stephen's angelic appearance. Could this be a still further Mosaic trait, this time from Exodus 34,[63] where Moses's face is depicted as "radiant" (Septuagint, *dedoxasmai*, "endowed with splendor")? Splendor of face is a characteristic of angels.[64] There is curious emphasis on the fact that it is those Stephen encounters who notice his radiance, as if he himself has been oblivious. Moses at first does not know of his distinction.[65]

Not all the Old Testament parallels adduced on the foregoing pages are equally telling. But there are a sufficient number of striking ones to warrant the assertion that this narrative in Acts is composed differently from most others in the book. The Rabbinic analogies, on the other hand, are remarkably unimpressive. We may infer that the author drew directly on the Old Testament or, conceivably, on a fund of exposition accumulated outside Rabbinism. Whether he was Luke himself or only a source of Luke's will be left open here. The message conveyed—all the guidance the Israelites had in the desert the Church enjoys through its inspired preachers—seems in full agreement with Luke's theology.[66] Another question I shall not pursue is the historicity of the events, except to say that the particular mode of composition is no ground for treating them as invented.

Similar data may be described in similar fashion by various writers completely independent of each other. However, there comes a point where indebtedness does appear likely, as, I think, in the case of the story of the servers of tables in relation to

[57] Exod 18:21, 25.
[58] Num 11:25.
[59] Num 11:26 ff.
[60] *Siphre* on Num 11:26.
[61] *Shepherd of Hermas*, Vision 2.3.4.
[62] *Siphre* on Num 11:11 f., 16.
[63] Exod 34:29, 35; cf. 2 Cor 3:7.
[64] E.g., *Targum* on Cant 1:5.
[65] Exod 34:29.
[66] See C. K. Barrett, *Luke the Historian in Recent Study* (London, 1961).

the Pentateuch. It may be useful to show that such a division of labour can be reported in very different language. In 242 B.C. the establishment of a second praetor because of the influx of aliens is commented upon by a Roman jurist: *Post aliquot deinde annos, non sufficiente eo praetore (scil. urbano) quod multa turba etiam peregrinorum in civitatem veniret, creatus est et alius praetor qui peregrinus appellatus est* [Then, after some years, when that praetor (i.e. urban) was not sufficient, because a great crowd of foreigners had come into the state, another praetor was created who was called "peregrine"].[67] A modern scholar says of Diocletian: "*293 schuf er das System der Tetrarchie,... um die übergroße Last der politischen und militärischen Aufgaben aufzuteilen*" ["In 293 he created the political system called "tetrarchy" to distribute the too heavy burden of governmental and military duties"].[68] In 1859, a recent treatise on Austro-Hungary relates, Francis Joseph announced a liberalization: "a 'substantial part' of the duties hitherto carried out by officials was to be transferred to local bodies, 'if possible autonomous'; and after completion of these 'first and most urgent tasks,' bodies representing the Estates (*ständische Vertretungen*) were to be called into being in the various Crown-lands."[69] An illustration from the Old Testament is also pertinent: "But the priests were too few, so that they could not flay all the burnt offerings; wherefore their brethren the Levites did help them."[70] Acts itself states: "Separate me Barnabas and Saul for the work whereunto I have called them."[71]

As a matter of fact, the narrative of the seven servers is far from a perfect copy of its models. In one of my Edinburgh Gifford Lectures, 1962 (as yet unpublished),[72] I detailed the wisdom setting of Exodus 18 and Deuteronomy 1; and I went on to demonstrate that hardly a trace of it remains in Acts. In all probability the absence is not because of any hostility to wisdom, but because of a more fundamental break. Wisdom is simply not grasped; it has no meaning in the present circumstances.

Acts contains two more installations. One, just mentioned, is that of Paul and Barnabas. It is closely patterned on the consecration of the Levites in Numbers 8.[73]

The other is that of Matthias to replace Judas,[74] conceivably alluding to the substitution of David for the rejected Saul. There is undeniable similarity in a fundamental point: it was with the help of divine illumination that Matthias was seen to be the worthier of two worthies, and the same route leads to David's rise above the other sons of Jesse.[75] That whoever wrote this portion of Acts was alive to the coincidence is suggested, in the first placc, by Peter's citation of Psalms 69 and 109: "Let his habitation

[67] *Digest* 1.2.2.28, *Pomponius libro singulari enchiridii.*

[68] F. G. Maier, *Die Verwandlung der Mittelmeerwelt* (Frankfurt, 1968), 32.

[69] C. A. Macartney, *The Habsburg Empire 1790–1918* (London, 1968), 498 f.

[70] 2 Chr 29:34.

[71] Acts 13:2.

[72] Daube, "Reforms of Machinery," Lecture 7, Edinburgh Gifford Lectures—"Law and Wisdom in the Scriptures," 1962.

[73] See Daube, *The New Testament and Rabbinic Judaism*, 239 ff. [see 611 f.].

[74] Acts 1:15 ff.

[75] 1 Sam 16:1 ff.

be desolate" and "his office let another take."[76] An audience, for whom David was the author of Psalms, would readily think of Saul as the original villain of these verses. Their combination seems calculated to strengthen the link. It is reminiscent of Saul's condemnation by Samuel (taken up in a Pauline speech in Acts): "But now thy kingdom shall not continue, the Lord hath sought him a man after his heart."[77] In Psalm 69:2 f. the Rabbis detect a reference to the tribe of Judah obtaining the kingdom,[78] in 69:9 a reference to an incident while David was in flight from Saul.[79] The whole of Psalm 109, in the belief of prominent medieval Jewish scholars,[80] was intoned by David during that flight. The claim, it is true, is not met in Talmud and Midrash, but this is doubtless due either to an accident of transmission or, more likely, to a feeling of regret that David expressed himself in such cruel terms.[81] A further Old Testament reference in Acts may be discernible in the entreaty: "Thou, Lord, which knowest the hearts of all [*kardiagnostes*], show [*anadeiknymi*] which of these two men [Joseph and Matthias] thou hast chosen [*eklegomai*]." God tells Samuel he will "show" him whom to anoint (*gnorizo* in the Septuagint);[82] and it is because God "looketh on the heart" (*opsomai eis kardian*)[83] that David is "chosen" from among his brothers (*eklegomai*).[84]

Of course, in the case of Matthias, the association would not be Mosaic but Samuelic-Davidic. Still, if there is substance in this association, it becomes arguable that Old Testament sanction is sought particularly for the way, or ways, Church offices are conferred. But as I indicated, all this is highly speculative. Such a suggestion would, however, explain why this particular report draws so heavily on the Old Testament: The Scriptures are appealed to to legitimize the transmission of authority in the church.

76 Ps 69:26 (LXX 68:25); 109:8 (LXX 108:8).

77 1 Sam 13:14; cf. Acts 13:22.

78 *t. Ber.* 4:18.

79 *b. Zeb.* 54b.

80 E.g., David Kimhi, around 1200.

81 *b. M. Kat.* 16b, about 2 Samuel 22; Psalm 18.

82 1 Sam 16:3.

83 1 Sam 16:7.

84 1 Sam 16:8, 9, 10.

EXCURSUS

The clause I translate "they leaned their hands upon them" is usually translated "they laid their hands upon them."[85] As I noted long ago, English, following Greek, does not mark off *samakh* from *śim* or *shith*.[86] Yet in dealing with New Testament texts, it is important to establish which rite is meant. *Samakh* signifies "to lean"; it involves the exercise of some force, concentrated at the base of the hand near the joint. *Śim* or *shith* signifies "to place"; it is gentler, indeed, can be done with the fingers only. (Not that variations within *śim* or *shith* are immaterial, but there is no need here to go into them.) When you *samakh* your hands on somebody, you pour your personality—or a quality of yours which is relevant at this moment—into him. When you *śim* or *shith* your hands on somebody, you render concrete a wish you have for him. The difference is considerable and many consequences flow from it. For instance, whereas a feeble old man may still "place his hands" on a youth, invoking vigour and long life on him, a fool cannot "lean his hands" on a student so as to make him into a sage. In both the appointment of the seven servers and that of Paul and Barnabas, the ceremony is *samakh*,[87] which enjoyed a striking revival in the archaic Christian community.

What I failed to explain in my earlier discussion is that there are areas in which the two rites, "leaning" and "placing," overlap. This is indeed one of the factors accounting for their being thrown together in Greek and, accordingly, in English. (Another is the, to a non-Jewish public, outlandish nature of "a leaning of the hands," to this day an obstacle in the way of a proper understanding of the references to it.) The foremost example is healing. A healer may *śim* or *shith* his hand on the sick person, as in the case of any other blessing. Or alternatively, he may *samakh*, thereby conveying his own health to the sufferer. I do not think *samakh* underlies any of the New Testament passages about healing. However, it does occur in the Genesis Apocryphon. As the King of Egypt, having appropriated Sarah, is stricken with disease, Abraham is asked to pray for him and "lean his hands upon him"; and he does so successfully after his wife is restored.[88] I know of no Rabbinic parallel to this use of *samakh*. It may be an accident of transmission; there are, after all, not many places where one might expect such a parallel. But it is also possible that the ceremony was more prominent at Qumran,[89] as it was in the primitive Church.

[85] Acts 6:6.

[86] Daube, *The New Testament and Rabbinic Judaism*, 224 ff. [599 ff.], to which should be added J. Jeremias, "ΠΡΕΣΒΥΤΕΡΙΟΝ außerchristlich bezeugt," *ZNW*, 48 (1957), 127 ff.

[87] Acts 6:6; 13:3.

[88] 1 Qap Gen 20:22, 29. While the principal source of the Apocryphon is Gen 12:11 ff., several items are borrowed from 20:2 ff. One of these is Abraham's praying for the abducter of his wife, from Gen 20:7, 17.

[89] No support for this may be derived from a "leaning" in the *Dires de Moiae* 4:9 (D. Barthélemy and J. T. Milik, *Discoveries in the Judaean Desert*, 3 vols. [Oxford, 1955], I, 95). This merely takes up the traditional *samakh* in connection with sacrifice. The particular text behind it is most probably Lev 16:21.

On Acts 23: Sadducees and Angels

In Acts 23 Paul faces a hostile council and a multitude bent on mischief. The council is presided over by the high priest Ananias, a rabid ill-wisher of his, a "savage Sadducee" according to Josephus (*Ant.* 20.9.1.199). In fear of his life[1] he decides to make use of the animosity between Sadducees and Pharisees: he exclaims that the real grudge against him is his preaching the resurrection of the dead—that is, in general, even apart from the particular claim in regard to Jesus. His ruse works; a tumultuous dissension breaks out. "For the Sadducees say that there is no resurrection nor angel nor spirit, but the Pharisees profess both" (23:8).

"Both"—so the controversy must concern two phenomena. It is universally assumed that these are (1) resurrection, and (2), the existence of angels. But although Sadducean denial of resurrection is amply documented, nowhere else is there a trace of a denial of angels. Commentators divide into conservatives and liberals. The former go ahead without outside support. In this case, however, it just will not do. The Sadducees, though conceding no sanctity to rabbinic elaborations of scripture—the dogma of resurrection among them, in their view—are no less respectful than the Pharisees of the written text. Angels populate it from Genesis to 2 Chronicles: how could they discard them? Furthermore, supposing they did, is it conceivable that so flagrant an excision of a major element of biblical theology would never be criticized in the sources? The liberals hold that Luke (or whoever wrote Acts) is committing an error, but this is no more plausible. If it were a matter of rabbinic minutiae, it might pass. But angels are a popular subject; belief or disbelief in them among an important group is common knowledge; Luke cannot be less instructed about it than his cook. There is yet a quite different point speaking equally against conservatives and liberals, namely, that angelology as such has nothing to do with the contention stirred up by Paul, with the focus on resurrection.

The two phenomena are (1) as the prevalent opinion has it, resurrection, the final rising central in the message of Paul, who finds it anticipated by Jesus (so, of course, does Peter in a previous chapter of Acts, where he upsets the Sadducees by "proclaiming the resurrection of the dead, realized in Jesus" [Acts 4:2]); (2)—here I deviate—the span between death and resurrection, which, in widespread belief, a good person spends in the realm or mode of angel or spirit.

From early on, the two stages are coupled in accounts of the sectarian conflict. Josephus reports that, whereas for the Sadducees the soul perishes with the body, for

[1] A factor not, in general, adequately considered. But as it is not relevant to my specific thesis, I shall not enlarge.

the Pharisees it survives. It receives reward or punishment according to conduct on earth: interim. And the souls of the virtuous will in the end pass into a new body and new habitation: resurrection (*Bell.* 2.8.14.162–65; 3.8.5.374–75; *Ant.* 18.1.3–4.16; *Contra Apionem* 2.218.30). Angel and spirit are associated with the interim in Enoch. The author is shown "dwellings of the righteous with His [the Lord of the spirits'] angels." He denounces the Sadducees who "deny the dwelling of the holy ones and the Lord of the spirits; into heaven they shall not ascend," interim; "and on the earth they shall not come," resurrection (1 Enoch 39:5; 54:1–2). It should be noted that the seer goes on remarking on the utter dissimilarity of the final heavens and earth from the present ones—reminiscent of Jesus's refutation of a Sadducee's sarcasm about resurrection. What reinforces the impression of a common background is Jesus's comparison on that occasion of the resurrected to angels, a comparison, moreover, which Luke pushes toward identification. In Matthew and Mark, "they are like angels [*hōs aggeloi*] in heaven"; in Luke, "quasi angels [*isaggeloi*, an exceedingly rare term] they are" (1 Enoch 45:4-5; Matt 22:30; Mark 12:25; Luke 20:36). In Luke, indeed, angels play a role in the provisional completion of the deserving on death: Lazarus is carried by them into Abraham's bosom (16:22). The rabbis would speak of them as "Angels of the Service" (*Num. Rab.* 6:26, "and give thee peace").

As a rule, where the two stages are mentioned together, it is in the "natural" order, (1) interim (2) resurrection; in Acts 23:8 it is (1) resurrection (2) interim. The reason: this is not an academic exposition but a scene from the battlefield, a brilliant stroke in desperate straits. Resurrection is the apple of discord; by throwing it among the crowd, the apostle deflects their bellicosity from himself toward one another. It takes precedence.

It might perhaps be objected that a dead person is never explicitly introduced as an angel in extant early Jewish documents. However, for one thing, some passages do come close.[2] For another, they may be more numerous than meets the eye: where worthy dead ones are held to live on "as angels," Hebrew or Aramaic *kĕ* and Greek *hōs*, just like English "as," may denote anything from "resembling" or "equal to" to the actual "having the nature of."[3] No doubt many a text conveyed diverse nuances to diverse recipients: this is a field where we must not expect rigorous consistency. Above all, thirdly, we do hear of dead persons as spirits, both *en masse*—"hollow places that the spirits of the dead should assemble therein"—and with reference to an individual—"the spirit that went forth from Abel... makes suit" (1 Enoch 22:3, 7).[4] In Acts, angel and spirit are evidently on the same level.

To coin a modern parallel to the formulation before us. Suppose a Stalinist communiqué had declared that opponents despatched to concentration camps were all eventually released in great condition and were looked after by eminent psychiatrists

[2] 1 Enoch 104:4–6 and 2 Apoc. Bar. 51:1, 5, 10, 12 are quoted by J. H. Charlesworth, "The Portrayal of the Righteous as an Angel," in *Ideal Figures in Ancient Judaism: Profiles and Paradigms* ed. G. W. E. Nickelsburg and J. J. Collins; (1980) 136.

[3] An OT specimen of the latter usage in Neh 7:2: "I gave my brother charge... for he was of the nature of a man of truth."

[4] Among further relevant instances are 1 Enoch 49:3 and 103:3–4.

and caring nurses; and suppose Alexander Solzhenitsyn countered that there was no such release, nor eminent psychiatrists, nor caring nurses. Nobody would conclude that he was denying the existence of eminent psychiatrists and caring nurses throughout the universe and for all time. The restriction to the situation after arrest is obvious—but no more so than the restriction to afterlife in Acts. The idea of a wholesale rejection of celestial beings is utterly alien to this story.

There are 613 ways of characterizing the interval between death and resurrection. What accounts for the choice here of "angel or Spirit"? Partly, no doubt, the influence of Enoch and allied works; but, primarily, Paul's address on the previous day from the steps of the Antonia. This emerges from the verse immediately following, Acts 23:9, which, indeed, only now acquires its due force: "And… some of the scribes of the Pharisees' party arose and strove, saying, We find no evil in this man—but what if a spirit spoke to him or an angel." They are talking of the preacher's experiences on the road to Damascus and in the temple (Acts 22:6–10, 17–21). They cannot fall in with his interpretation of them—the risen Savior. But they do admit the possibility of a visit sponsored by God in order to transmit advice. To be sure, their motives are mixed, the wish to cross the Sadducees being the foremost: but for it, they might give Paul short shrift. Still, in the present connection, what counts is their envisaging the very same two phases following death as 23:8, the temporary "spirit or angel" and the total end-time change. The care with which the verse is crafted is indeed remarkable, betokening a high degree of historicity. This half acceptance of Paul's testimony—he was counseled not by Jesus resurrected but by Jesus on leave as, or represented by, an angel or spirit—is pretty subtle, not the kind of construction an ordinary member of the public would think up or even fully comprehend. It originates, we are told, from "scribes." Moreover, though it will anger the Sadducees, the bulk of Pharisees can hardly feel comfortable with such a concession to the Christian spokesman. Hence the qualification that it is embraced only by "some" scribes.[5]

Two more Lucan incidents corroborate the thesis here advanced. Toward the end of his Gospel (24:36–43), as Jesus appears to his disciple, they take him for "a spirit"—synonymous, surely, with "an angel." They look on him, that is, as being in the interim condition, on leave or a mission to meet with them, whereupon he proves to them that he is truly resurrected. The design finding expression in this episode is in striking harmony with that of Acts 22 and 23. The other evangelists and Paul, while they may well share it, do not formulate it in just this way (Matt 28:8–10; Mark 16:6–7, 14; John 20:19–20, 24–29; 1 Cor 15:5–11). The equation widely accepted of "spirit" (*pneuma*) here with "spectre" (*phantasma*), as used in the pericope about Jesus walking on the water (Matt 14:26; Mark 6:49; John 6:15–26),[6] though of great antiquity,[7] is misleading.

The relevance of a scene in Acts involving Peter is pointed out to me by my friend James Gordley. The apostle, after a miraculous nocturnal delivery from prison, calls out

[5] In medieval transmission, often one or the other or even both of the two refinements may be omitted.

[6] There is no parallel in Luke, and no "spectre" in the passage from John.

[7] *Phantasma* replaces *pneuma* in Codex Bezae and Marcion. Once the original sense was lost, this would be a plausible substitute; Marcion may also have reasons of his own.

at a house where Christians are gathered in prayer. A maid leaves the room to find out, recognizes his voice, and, instead of immediately opening, joyfully runs back to tell the assembly. They, however, conclude that it must be "his angel" (Acts 12:15). The current view I used to go by is that they have in mind a special type of guardian angel who is the exact image of his protégé.[8] According to Gordley, they assume that Peter was killed by Herod and is joining them in his angelic state. This seems to me to go well with the Greek, *ho aggelos estin autou,* translatable "it is the angel of him." What most recommends his suggestion is that the rabbinic evidence for that particular kind of guardian angel is thin—even apart from the fact that it has regard exclusively to alikeness in looks, not in voice. Of course, once Peter is admitted by his friends, he turns out to differ from an angel, not in being resurrected but in still continuing his earthly life—subject, I daresay, to a significant qualification. Henceforth this life, entirely due to a supernatural intervention of the Lord—as dreamlike while taking place as mighty in its effects—will be a foretaste, a token, of the ultimate glory.

Legends of deceased saints returning on special missions are common in rabbinic literature. Elijah is a regular consultant, comforter, critic, of Jose ben Halaphta and Joshua ben Levi.[9] Of greater interest, because more "archaic," is the treatment of Samuel's appearance at Endor (1 Sam 28:7–19). The plural in the witch's statement "gods I see ascending from the earth" is taken to indicate that he brings Moses with him: when aroused from sleep, he thought it was for the final judgment, so he called on Moses to accompany him and witness that he had been heedful of the commandments (*b. Hag.* 4b). His prediction to Saul, "thou and thy sons shall be with me tomorrow,"[10] is a message of forgiveness: "with me" means "in my [Samuel's and other deceased pious people's] compartment." It is, indeed, among the heavenly host: "the compartment of the pious will be amidst the Angels of the Service" (*Deut. Rab.* 1:10–11). Directly relevant is an episode where a Sadducee ridicules faith in the interim life of the dead in much the same fashion as his confreres ridicule resurrection in the Gospels (*b. Shab.* 152b). He asks how, if the virtuous dead are—as the Pharisees contend—"treasured," guarded as valuables, beneath the Throne of Glory, the necromancer could have interfered. The concept "treasure," verb or noun, is common in this area; the highest heaven is depicted as the place of "right, justice and compassion, the treasures of life, peace and blessing, the souls of the righteous, the spirits and the souls of those to be born, and the dew by which the Holy One will ultimately revive the dead. . . . There, too, are the Ophanim, Seraphim, Holy Living Creatures and Angels of the Service" (*b. Hag.* 12b). The answer, far from giving way, underlines the concreteness of afterlife: Samuel could be brought back because he had not been dead long, and for the first twelve months a soul will now ascend and now descend again. No need to expatiate.

[8] See Strack-Billerbeck, Vol. 2, 707.

[9] In *Collaboration with Tyranny in Rabbinic Law* (1965) 5–17 [*Talmudic Law*, 67–82], I discuss the prophet's contribution to the dilemma of a community ordered by the heathen government to extradite a political criminal or be otherwise annihilated.

[10] I cannot bring myself to modernize this into "you and your sons," feeling inseparably bound to Händel's oratorio.

Manifestly, here too the Sadducean attack is not indiscriminate, not directed against the Throne and its wonderful surroundings, justice, life, Ophanim, Angels of the Service, but specifically against assigning mortals a waiting room in that world, just as the Sadducees of the Gospels make fun of their ultimate restoration. From the description just quoted they would eliminate the portion starting "the souls of the righteous" and ending "will ultimately revive the dead." I need hardly add that I am not pronouncing on how much or how little of the rest they approve of—not, fortunately, essential to my argument.

Whether I am right or wrong, it seems astonishing that my simple explanation has not been proposed before. One cause may be that, say, from 1850 to 1925 NT research was dominated by a rationalist trend, shared or even exceeded by the Jewish scholars contributing. Old-fashioned orthodox Jews were not in general interested in the field. The progressives who were and set out to make the storehouse of Midrash and Talmud accessible to the uninitiated so its input could be grasped felt apologetic (and fearful too) about antiquated notions and *mores* among their forebears—hence tended to play them down both for their own satisfaction and for their public's.[11] Thus, calls from the next world are not made much of. For instance, the Gemara tells us of a bleeder (around A.D. 300) not learned in sacred lore but extremely conscientious and ethical, who received a greeting every Friday from the College of departed Sages (*b. Taan.* 216). This is routinely dubbed a legend. Yet the likelihood is that a good many people once thought of an actual delegation, and my relatives in Bene-Berak still do so. This is not to assert that every such anecdote wants to be understood literally. But it is always advisable to ask from what motivation, collective or individual, exegesis—including our own—may lean one way or the other. In the past fifty years or so, an increasing number of NT students do seriously explore long-neglected material, an opening-up helped on by Qumran. Also, the pendulum has definitely swung toward greater tolerance for the supernatural, and this irrespective of whether an expositor acknowledges it as a constituent of the datum being discussed.[12]

[11] See, e.g., my *Ancient Jewish Law* (1981) 16 [476].

[12] The volume cited in n. 2, *Ideal Figures in Ancient Judaism,* is representative of this welcome development. My thanks to Professors W. D. Davies and J. J. Collins for criticisms of an earlier draft.

"For they know not what they do": Luke 23:34

The following pages are intended to enquire whether this prayer was in the original Luke; on whose behalf it is offered; what kind of ignorance is envisaged by it; and whether a basis can be discovered in contemporary Jewish thought.

According to Luke 23:34 Jesus on the cross prayed: "Father, forgive them, for they know not what they do." The first problem is whether Luke wrote this. As it occurs in no other gospel, and as it is omitted even in Luke by the "weighty combination"[1] of B (Vaticanus, 4th century), D (Bezae, 6th), Syr. Sin. (4/5th) and the earliest representatives of the Itala, a and b (4/5th), the prevalent doctrine rejects it. Harnack defended it. He maintained that Luke intended it as a prayer for the Roman soldiers; later, it was misinterpreted as a prayer for the Jews; as such it offended sections of the Church—hence many scribes suppressed it. Nowadays, however, insertion is generally considered far more likely than elimination.

The case against Lukan origin is undoubtedly strong, and perhaps one could add a further argument. A virtually identical prayer is ascribed to James by Hegesippus, who is quoted by Eusebius.[2] It might be thought that a prayer already recognized as uttered by Jesus would not be given to James. On this basis, the prayer circulated in the name of James before it was transferred to Jesus; and possibly the transfer was not yet known to Hegesippus. This solution is in some ways the most satisfactory. It would not be the only case of the last words of a lesser figure coming to be attached to a greater one; and the textual position would become fully intelligible.

Nevertheless a doubt remains. For one thing, the first half—though not the second—is paralleled—though not literally repeated[3]—by the prayer of Stephanus as he is stoned: "Lord, lay not this sin to their charge."[4] But the second half fits no less well in Luke, who appears to be particularly interested in the relation of sin and ignorance, or we can put it more precisely, in their relation where the unsatisfactory response of men to God's manifestations is concerned. The theme occurs not only five times in Acts,[5] but also in a pericope peculiar to Luke,[6] where the servant who knew his mas-

[1] Creed, *The Gospel according to St. Luke* (New York, 1930), 286.

[2] *Eccl. Hist.* 2.23.16.

[3] The relation between the two passages is, therefore, quite different from that between Jesus's prayer and James's.

[4] Acts 7:60. In the Revelation of Stephen (James, *The Apocryphal New Testament*, corrected edition [Oxford, 1955], 565 f.) he offers this prayer when he is being beaten, and another when he is being killed: "Forgive them that stone us, for by their means we trust to enter into thy kingdom."

[5] Acts 3:17, 13:27, 14:16, 17:30, 26:9.

[6] Luke 12:47 f.

ter's will and disregarded it is said to deserve many stripes, but he who did not know, only few. It is also noteworthy that the prayer is to be found in Tatian, Irenaeus, Hippolytus, Origen, Clemens Romanus and the Didascalia.[7]

Whichever side one takes, the next question to be raised is on whose behalf intercession is made. Here again opinion is divided. Some contend that it is on behalf of the Roman soldiers who nailed Jesus to the cross and appropriated his raiment; it is these two actions which surround the prayer in verses 34 f. Others believe that Jesus is praying for the Jews and their rulers who had clamoured for his death; they find support in verses 28 ff., where he points to fearful consequences which even those among the crowd who weep cannot foresee, and where the verb "to do" is used of the conduct of his adversaries: "for if they do these things in a green tree."[8]

Both interpretations are old, the former adopted by Hippolytus,[9] the latter in the Didascalia;[10] those favouring the latter, however, might invoke, too, the fact that James's prayer in Hegesippus-Eusebius is definitely for the Jews. Either sense would be consonant with the spirit of Luke. That he attaches special importance to the idea of the gentiles being worthier than the Jews is suggested by his references to the widow of Sidon (visited by Elijah) and the Syrian Naaman (healed by Elisha),[11] references not to be met in the other gospels; and Luke has this pericope, not in the place of, but in addition to that about the queen of Sheba willing to listen to Solomon and the men of Nineveh to Jonah,[12] which is also in Matthew.[13] On the other hand, the ignorance of the Jewish people and their rulers in bringing about the death of Jesus is stressed as a mitigating circumstance in Acts.[14]

According as one refers the prayer to Romans or Jews, the second half, "for they know not what they do," assumes a very different meaning. If Jesus is praying for the Romans, it means "they have not been told, the gospel has not reached them, they lack information"; if for the Jews, it means "they do not grasp what they have been told, they do not see the truth of the gospel, they lack understanding." In the former case, a man is reprieved because he is not in possession of the relevant facts or doctrine. He "does not know" in the normal, commonplace sense: you can find out by straightforward enquiry that he does not know, that the soldiers have not been instructed. In the latter case, a man is reprieved because, though fully instructed, he fails to appreciate the implications of the facts or to rise to the doctrine offered. He "does not know" in a deeper sense: this is not so easy to verify, you deduce it from his make-up and the nature of his deed (which is quite deliberate), the Jews, it is thought, could not have compassed Jesus's death but for want of discernment.

[7] Zahn, *Das Evangelium des Lucas* (Leipzig, 1913), 699.

[8] Plummer, *The Gospel according to St. Luke* (London, 1896), 532.

[9] *Contra Judaeos* 3.

[10] *Didascalia* 2.16.1.

[11] Luke 4:25 ff.

[12] Luke 11:29 ff.

[13] Matt 12:40 ff.

[14] Acts 3:17 and 13:27.

Excuse on the ground of lack of information (if the Romans are meant)—excuse on the ground of lack of understanding (if the Jews are meant): though, as we shall see, the two may on occasion more or less coincide, they have not the same history by any means. To form a valid opinion about the prayer in Luke 23:34, it is necessary to pay attention to their respective antecedents.

It is obvious that the plea of lack of information antedates by far that of lack of understanding. In fact, certain instances of the former are met at an early stage in all legal or ethical systems. To quote a few examples—Abimelech, threatened with death by God for taking Sarah, escapes after pointing out that he was unaware of her status as Abraham's wife,[15] a defence recognized in the Assyrian laws.[16] The Draconian inscription[17] exempts from punishment him who in war mistakes a fellow-citizen for an enemy and kills him. Oedipus, to be sure, has to suffer for slaying his father and marrying his mother though he did not know them for what they were, but it is precisely his "innocence" which rouses terror and pity long before Sophocles follows up the Tyrannus with the Coloneus, with its striking formulations: "But all unwitting whither I went I went," "Murder and incest, deeds of horror, all I have borne, no willing sinner," "How canst thou with justice blame the all-unconscious hand?"[18] Antigone would presumably have lived had she been able to give a negative answer to Creon's preliminary question whether she was acquainted with the interdict denying burial to her brother.[19] In the New Testament itself, the affair of Paul's cursing of Ananias is closed as soon as it is found that he did not realize that the man before him was the High Priest.[20]

By contrast, the idea that the deliberate offender may deserve indulgence because of lack of understanding is relatively late and far from common among moralists—not to mention jurists. (We leave out of account the treatment of children, the insane and the like, confining ourselves to acts by in principle responsible persons.) Its most familiar and most radical version is the Socratic: no man ever does wrong but from ignorance of himself, his place in the world, the ultimate good. (That even with this tenet as starting-point one may arrive at a justification of punishment or repression is another matter.[21]) We need only transpose the examples just given to this category to realize how impossible they would become in their ancient settings. Suppose Abimelech had known Sarah to be Abraham's wife, would he have been let off because he might not have appreciated the wickedness of adultery? Is it conceivable that Draco should have done away with the punishment of murder—even of premeditated murder of a fellow-citi-

[15] Genesis 20; Daube, "Concerning Methods of Bible-Criticism: Late Law in Early Narratives," *Archiv Orientální,* 17 (1949), 91 ff.; "Error and Accident in the Bible," *RIDA,* 2 (1949), 139, 199; "Rechtsgedanken in den Erzählungen des Pentateuchs," *Von Ugarit nach Qumran: Festschrift für Eißfeldt* (Berlin, 1958), 38 ff.

[16] MAL Par. 14.

[17] Demosthenes, *In Aristidem* 53 ff. (637).

[18] *Oedipus at Colonus* 273, 962 ff., 976.

[19] *Antigone* 447 ff.

[20] Acts 23:5; Daube, "Error and Accident," 212 f. In contemporary Roman law also, apparently to assault the Emperor unaware of his position was not *maiestas*: Dio Cassius 61.9; Mommsen, *Römisches Strafrecht* (Leipzig, 1899), 582.

[21] We shall briefly return to it at the end of this paper.

zen—from such a consideration? Would an Oedipus who slew his father and married his mother in full knowledge have been an object of sympathy as one deficient in judgment? How Antigone ended we know. Would Paul have gone unpunished, on account of lack of understanding, if he had been aware that he was cursing the High Priest?

How different the two excuses are may be seen from the fact that even in the New Testament lack of understanding, blindness, is still apt to be thought of, not only as not exonerating, but as a reproach—in the Synoptics, for example, "that seeing they may see and not perceive, lest their sins should be forgiven them,"[22] or in Paul, "the god of this world hath blinded the minds of them which believe not, lest the light should shine unto them."[23] Renegation, relapse into darkness after once having entered into the truth, is indeed terrible.[24] It is not surprising, therefore, that with the exception of a remark by Philo, the Old Testament and Rabbinic parallels commonly cited in connection with our prayer or allied passages are concerned—at best—with the plea of lack of information (which would apply to the Roman soldiers), not with lack of understanding (which would apply to the Jews). For instance, we are referred to the distinction between a murderer and an unwitting homicide, who may escape into a city of refuge. But the point is that no refuge is granted to the murderer as one who lacks understanding—lack of understanding is no excuse in this context.

Let us survey the material of Strack-Billerbeck and Creed. Strack-Billerbeck ad Luke 23:34[25] adduce 1. Num 15:29 f., contrasting atonement in the case of sinning through ignorance and extirpation in that of sinning with a high hand. (In Deut 17:12, the unpardonable crime is called sinning from presumption.) Whatever the exact scope of sinning through ignorance, it does not in its original meaning refer to a conscious wrongdoer's lack of wisdom. 2. *y. Shebu.* 33a, *b. Yom.* 36b, interpreting the three classes of sins in Lev 16:21 as sins from presumption, rebellion and ignorance. Again, ignorance does not denote lack of understanding. 3. *b. B. B.* 60b, with the maxim "It is better the Israelites should transgress in ignorance than willfully." Certain precepts, that is, which the mass could not fulfil had better not be promulgated: ignorance plainly equals lack of information.[26] 4. *m. Makk.* 2:5, *b. Makk.* 10b, elaborating the distinction of Num 35:6 ff. between the murderer, who forfeits his life, and the unintentional homicide, who may live in a city of refuge. A man does not fall into the latter category because he lacks wisdom—if he did, the former category would be practically abolished.

To go on to Luke 12:47 f. (the servant who does not know his master's will is less blameworthy). Strack-Billerbeck[27] quote three further texts: 5. *m. Shab.* 7:1, about problems such as a person who, forgetful of the principle of the Sabbath, performs several acts of work: is he liable to one sin-offering or several? Not a case of deliberate

[22] Mark 4:12; Daube, *The New Testament and Rabbinic Judaism* (London, 1956), 149. [See 313].

[23] 2 Cor 4:4.

[24] 2 Pet 2:21; Heb 10:26.

[25] *Kommentar zum Neuen Testament aus Talmud und Midrasch*, 2 (München, 1924), 264.

[26] For the history of the principle see Daube, "Concessions to Sinfulness in Jewish Law," *JJS*, 10 (1959), 1 ff. [See *Talmudic Law*, 1 ff.].

[27] *Op. cit.*, 192.

wrongdoing excused on the ground of lack of understanding. 6. *m. Makk.* 3:7 f., about problems like a person who, in breach of Deut 22:11, wears a garment of diverse kinds for a day: ordinarily this counts as one transgression, but if he is formally warned, puts it off and then puts it on again, that is a second transgression. Again, no plea of lack of understanding. 7. *Deut. Rab.* on 28:1, a sinner who is not a student of the Torah is less culpable than one who is: lack of information.

Finally, ad John 9:41, exculpating those who have not had sufficient testimony of Jesus but declaring fully accountable the Pharisees who have seen him, 8. *b. B. M.* 33b, whereas a student's unwitting sin counts as intentional, an ignoramus's intentional sin counts as unwitting: the latter is not informed.

For the remaining statements in the New Testament which suggest forbearance where the offence is committed in ignorance, Strack-Billerbeck offer no parallels. As for Creed, he, in his comment on Luke 23:34[28] mentions Philo, *In Flaccum* 2.7, "I praise Flaccus to show up his villainy. For to one who sins through ignorance of the better, pardon may be extended, but one who does wrong in full knowledge has no defence, being already convicted in the court of his conscience." This does imply consideration for the criminal whose moral perception is defective, who is not sensible and sensitive enough to make the proper use of what he has learnt: though it does not go as far as Socrates's view, that the very commission of a crime proves defective perception.

At first sight one might be inclined to sum up that the prayer in Luke 23:34 is more likely to be for the soldiers, or that if it is for the Jews, its background must be Hellenistic. The former conclusion, however, would still leave us with ignorance as an exculpation of the Jews in Acts 3:17 and 13:27 and in James's prayer in Hegesippus-Eusebius to account for; and the latter conclusion (which would not necessarily involve the spuriousness of the prayer) is premature.

For one thing, as already indicated, the dividing line between excuse on the ground of lack of information and excuse on the ground of lack of understanding is not a very sharp one. On the one hand, such a notion as that the unlearned deserves less blame, though primarily concerned with lack of information, reaches into the field of lack of understanding; and this notion is firmly anchored in Rabbinism. Many references could be added to those given above—e.g. *Tanhuma* on Lev 4:2, distinguishing between an offence against the king committed by a provincial (the body) and one committed by a courtier (the soul).[29] Here we may also draw attention to the feeling, strong both in the New Testament and Rabbinism, that insofar as the gentiles have been vouchsafed no revelation, they are not responsible for their crimes.[30] While the main problem is lack of information, it does shade off into that of understanding: those without the Law are deficient in general wisdom as well as acquaintance with the proper rules of conduct.

[28] *Loc. cit.*

[29] Cp. the indulgence shewn by Roman law to *rusticitas*. In the New Testament, Jas 4:17 may be in point.

[30] E.g. Rom 1:18 ff.; Wisdom 13; Syr. Apoc. Baruch 72:4, 6, the nations not in contact with Israel will be spared, *Lev. Rab.* on 1:2, about the prophets and proselytes from whom the gentiles could learn, *Num. Rab.* on 7:89, about Balaam sent to the gentiles. The various ways in which it is argued that the gentiles have in fact received information would repay closer study.

On the other hand the ignorance of the Jews to whom facts and doctrine have been explained, though primarily a failing in insight, is not a failing of the general, natural kind which Socrates or, say, Philo in the passage cited above has in mind. It is a very particular and difficult phenomenon, the nature of Jesus, they are unable to appreciate. So there is, after all, some affinity with a gap in instruction, lack of a specific item of knowledge.

This overlapping of lack of information and lack of understanding would alone make one hesitate to postulate Hellenistic inspiration for the prayer under discussion. There are, besides, some significant data too much neglected.

Already in the Old Testament the sinning people are sometimes compared to erring sheep, and this does, of course, include those who sin in full possession of facts and doctrine: they none the less deserve mercy as, in a deeper sense, helpless and blind. "All we like sheep have gone astray," we read in the prophecy of the Suffering Servant.[31] As is well known, this very line is echoed in the New Testament.[32]

Two further developments, however, are of particular interest, having both of them to do with the liturgy of the Day of Atonement. One culminates in a remarkable exploitation of a verse from Numbers, i.e. 15:26, "And it shall be forgiven all the congregation of the children of Israel and the stranger that sojourneth among them, seeing that all the people were in ignorance." In its original context the verse contemplates an unwitting offence by the community at large—say, the mistaken dating of a festival. (A presumptuous offence by the whole community is not considered in this section, but the following one[33] opposes the unwitting and presumptuous offence of an individual, with full punishability of presumption; and as an example of the latter, the story of the man gathering sticks on a Sabbath is appended.[34]) On the eve of the Day of Atonement, it is boldly lifted from that context and placed towards the opening of the twenty-four hours' service. It thus becomes a request for and promise of forgiveness for all sin, unwitting or presumptuous, as flowing from ignorance—ignorance in a deeper sense, lack of understanding.

Hermann Cohen, in his *Die Religion der Vernunft aus den Quellen des Judentums* ["The Religion of Reason as it appears in Jewish Sources"],[35] notices an affinity with Socrates. But, not writing as a historian,[36] he was unconcerned about several points which we cannot discount. First, in order to harmonize the liturgical use of the verse with other pronouncements, Jewish and Greek, he held that really overweening sins, sins defying the divine and the human, were not covered; of such a reservation there is, however, no sign, the verse as employed in the liturgy is all-embracing. Secondly, he carried the modern, "Socratic" meaning of the verse back into the Pentateuch; a glance at the context, however, will show that that is untenable, in the Pentateuch the verse is confined to ignorance in the sense of lack of information. Thirdly, the verse, he

[31] Isa 53:6.

[32] 1 Pet 2:25.

[33] Num 15:27–31.

[34] Num 15:32 ff.

[35] (Leipzig, 1919), 255 ff., 234.

[36] Stressed by himself, 254.

assumed, expressed a central idea of the Day of Atonement from early times; but there is no evidence that it got into that liturgy prior to the Middle Ages.

This point needs following up: if the verse acquired its present role in the Middle Ages only, has it any bearing on the New Testament problem here raised? It has; for when we ask why it was given this role in the Middle Ages (if indeed the argument from silence proves that it had not obtained it before), we are taken right back into the first century A.D., when R. Eliezer the Great found an indication in this section that even a presumptuous sin would be treated by God as, in a deeper sense, unwitting.

The section from which the verse comes starts in 15:24: "If aught be committed by ignorance of the congregation." 15:25 contains the words "and it shall be forgiven them, for it is ignorance," and this is extended to the stranger in 15:26. The Rabbis fasten on the clause in 15:25, "for it is ignorance."[37] This is strictly superfluous, so in their usual manner they derive some additional teaching from it. According to an anonymous view it is intended to emphasize that the atonement in question can be for an unwitting sin only; that is to say, *ki* should be translated "if"—"if it is ignorance." Such a comment, supplying artificial support for the natural meaning of the text, is usually directed against a divergent interpretation, and in this case that is preserved, with the name of its author, Eliezer ben Hyrcanus. In his opinion, the clause indicates that even a presumptuous sin falls under this atonement. That is to say, he would translate *ki sheghagha* as one word, *kisheghagha*[38]—"it is like ignorance," "any sin, even a presumptuous one, receives the treatment of an unwitting one."

That this line of thought was not isolated is shewn by a Baraitha[39] which concludes from Exod 34:7, where God is represented as "forgiving iniquity [for the Rabbis: presumptuous sins] and transgression [rebellious sins] and sin [unwitting sins]," that when the Israelites had turned from true worship to worship of the golden calf, Moses besought god to accord their presumptuous sins the treatment of unwitting ones. It is noteworthy that the topic of this Baraitha is the High Priest's confession of sins on behalf of Israel on the Day of Atonement.

Curiously, Heb 5:2 deserves a place among the evidence, the Jewish High Priest—to whom Jesus is likened—being depicted as having "compassion on the ignorant and on them that are out of the way." There is surely no restriction intended to unconscious offenders. The whole tenor of the argument, which is about Jesus's sacrifice, shews that the writer is concerned about human guilt in its most serious aspects, that it is chiefly, if not exclusively, deliberate sinners for whom the High Priest is thought of as feeling and making atonement. Deliberate sinners—to be pitied as, in a deeper sense, ignorant, lost in the woods.

The medieval liturgists, then, in elevating Num 15:26 to its present station, were only continuing along a path opened up in the Tannaitic era. That they chose verse 26 rather than 25 is not surprising: 26 is not only wider—it includes the stranger—but also capable, as 25 is not, of figuring as an independent unit. It might perhaps be argued that

[37] *Siphre* on Num *ad loc.*

[38] The *plene* spelling of *ki* would be no obstacle to such an exegesis.

[39] *b. Yom.* 36b.

the Tannaitic idea that God forgives a presumptuous sin by treating it as an unwitting one is not quite the same as the Lukan and medieval Jewish idea that he forgives a presumptuous sin because it is, *au fond*, an unwitting one. But the difference between the two versions is slight: once the former has taken root, it is bound to imply something at least of the latter. Considering a doctrine like that of Eliezer the Great, and an intercession like that of Moses for his backsliding people (as the Rabbis understand it), it would be unreasonable to deny the possibility of Luke 23:34 being a prayer for the Jews and having a thoroughly Jewish background.

The other development to be mentioned here is attached to the Book of Jonah. While we know little about the selection of prophetic lessons for the various festivals in New Testament times, from a Baraitha[40] it is virtually certain that Jonah was, if not the prescribed, at least the usual reading for the afternoon of the Day of Atonement. (Which renders the wonderment of some modern scholars at its inclusion in the Jewish canon all the more unintelligible; there is indeed not the faintest trace of a controversy respecting this Book in our sources.) It tells of the power of repentance: Nineveh was saved through it, despite the prophecy of doom. But it ends on an even deeper note: "And should I not spare Nineveh that great city wherein are more than sixscore thousand persons that do not know between their right hand and their left hand, and also much cattle?"

Here forgiveness springs from what might be called divine humour in which this book abounds. Ultimately the sinners are poor, unknowing creatures, whom it would not do to destroy. No doubt as conceived by the author, there is in the ignorance of the Ninevites an element of lack of information: they are gentiles who had not heard God's word before he sent them Jonah. But we observed above that the gentiles' lack of information always shades off into lack of understanding. In the passage before us the latter element is predominant: that is clear from the phrase "they do not know between their right hand and their left hand," calling up a picture of children, and from the comparison with cattle (essential to the story[41]). Above all, however, from the moment this Book was read on the Day of Atonement, thus becoming expressive of the way in which God would deal with Jews, with his people calling on him, the assurance with which it closes referred exclusively to lack of understanding. Even he who is fully instructed may hope for mercy for his sins, because even he does not know himself, his place in the world, the right road to take.

The prayer in Luke 23:34, the exculpation of the people and their rulers in Acts 3:17 and 13:27 and James's prayer in Hegesippus-Eusebius are perfectly possible in a Jewish environment. A number of questions remain. For instance, from what moment and to what extent does recognition of lack of understanding play a part not only in theology, ethics, philosophy, but also in everyday law—say, when a thief comes before the court? What is the relation of this defence to that that the crime was committed from honest conviction, say a political murder? Here, in liberal systems, the penalty is

[40] *b. Meg.* 31a.

[41] Cp. Jonah 3:7 f.

reduced not because the criminal is regarded as blind, helpless, but because his unorthodox principles are respected.[42] There is an adumbration in Paul, when he says of Israel,[43] "For I bear them record that they have a zeal of God."

More fundamentally, we may ask in what kind of situation the excuse on the ground of lack of understanding is likely to come to the fore. The Book of Jonah, with its problem of sinning gentiles, may provide a clue. The most favourable situation seems to be where discrepant cultures, theologies, sets of values are in close contact and the representatives of one are not willing to abandon as irretrievably lost those of the other. So long as there is no contact it is possible to excuse the other side on the ground of lack of information; but once there is, with opportunities for everyone to find out, then, if an excuse is sought at all, it must be on the ground of lack of understanding.

As for reasons for seeking an excuse, the Book of Jonah may well go back to a milieu not unimpressed by the qualities of a civilised host-nation. The relative prominence of the idea in atonement theory of the early Tannaites is perhaps explicable by the serious divisions then existing: not only were there the well-known parties and sects, but we must remember that the bulk even of the Pharisaic following was slow in fully conforming to the code imposed by the Rabbinic leadership. That later Judaism did not allow the idea to operate much beyond its original range may be due to an awareness of its dangers: it might easily produce libertinism, denial of any responsibility of a man for his acts, and the like.

In the New Testament, the idea has plainly an important function in the clash between believers and unbelievers. The latter would more often than not be near and dear to the former—parents, for example. More than that, a believer might himself at one time have been a militant unbeliever. Excuse on the ground of lack of understanding would render bearable not only the terrible error of one's relations and friends—living or dead—but also one's own misguided past; it would moreover enable the community to welcome former enemies without too much reserve;[44] it would indeed facilitate conversion.

Some passages are suggestive. In Acts 3:17 Peter, exhorting a Jewish audience to believe, reassures them by saying, "And now, brethren, I wot that through ignorance ye did it, as did also your rulers." It looks a stock argument of this kind of address, since in Acts 13:26 f. Paul says, "Men and brethren, They that dwell at Jerusalem and their rulers, because they knew him not, nor yet the voices of the prophets which are read every sabbath day, they have fulfilled them in condemning him." A gentile audience is addressed by Paul in Acts 17:23 ff.: "Whom ye ignorantly worship, him I declare unto you. And the times of this ignorance God winked at, but now commandeth all men every where to repent." Finally, the convert himself speaks in 1 Tim 1:13 ff., describing himself as "before a blasphemer, but I obtained mercy because I did it ignorantly in unbelief; Christ Jesus came into the world to save sinners, of whom I am chief."

[42] In Germany the *Überzeugungsverbrechen* ["crime from conviction"] enjoyed certain privileges, abolished by the Hitler government as early as April 1933.

[43] Rom 10:2.

[44] Daube, "Error and Accident," 201.

Bearing in mind the setting of the idea, we can also say a little as to when lack of understanding is looked on as mitigating, and when as a reproach. Many factors are at work. But to mention one, maybe the tolerant judgment tends to prevail where there is a chance that encouragement will bear fruit. It is interesting that in nearly all cases, from Jonah onwards, where the excuse is accepted, the sinner either has come over or is about to come over. Conversely, in the absence of such a chance, lack of understanding is apt to be accounted a particularly damnable quality.

We have several times spoken of the Socratic ascription of evil to ignorance. Between it and its Biblical-Talmudic analogy there are enormous differences in approach, overtones, implications. Nevertheless it is not perhaps unthinkable that even in Greece the idea is not purely the result of detached, academic analysis, but was helped on by a conflict between differing basic attitudes the protagonists of which would not quite turn their backs on one another; the Socratic side at least would try to win over the others; and their outrages were explained as errors. (In the Apology the prosecution is invited to do the same for Socrates.[45]) It is at any rate noteworthy that in the Socratic system, too (at least as expounded by his disciples), if there is no chance of persuasion proving successful, blindness ceases to be an excuse and—no matter by virtue of what more or less ingenious justification—becomes liable to punishment and repression.[46]

[45] *Apology* 26A.13.

[46] On some aspects of the topic discussed, see now Daube, *Sin, Ignorance and Forgiveness in the Bible* (Claude Montefiore Lecture, 1960).

Neglected Nuances of Exposition in Luke-Acts

I. Encomium Prudentiae

1. It has long been seen that there are definite ties between the three Lucan parables of the Helper at Midnight, the Unjust Steward and the Unjust Judge.[1] Elsewhere I have drawn attention to a feature of theirs they share with other sections of this gospel: before reaching the evangelist, they were reworked by wisdom circles and, in the process, acquired a pronounced shame-cultural flavour.[2] Here I propose to concentrate on a further wisdom contribution, the introjection of the debate between realism and purism.

This struggle—not, of course, confined to Judaism and Christianity—bore on many issues. One that plays a part in all three pericopes is the motivation of correct behaviour, more precisely, the assessment of behaviour externally meritorious, yet flowing from a contaminated source. The Helper obliges, but not from friendship. The Steward aids debtors, but not from charity. The Judge does his job, but not from a sense of responsibility. Some types of discrepancy were unanimously condemned by the ethicists of the past—say, an action laudable in itself but, in the circumstances, deliberately injurious: punctilious return of a small deposit in order to be entrusted with and embezzle a large one,[3] a sop to a poor man which will just bring him up to a total excluding him from such privileges as gleaning in your field,[4] a Judas kiss.[5] An instance recurring again and again in the New Testament is piety for show; hypocrisy, always rebuked,[6] in accordance with long-standing tradition.[7] There are, however, varieties as to which opinion differed greatly. Cicero has nothing but praise for politicians being supportive to high and low with a view to gaining popularity:[8] realism. For Simeon ben

[1] Luke 11:5 ff.; 16:1 ff.; 18:1 ff. See J. M. Creed, *The Gospel according to St. Luke* (New York, 1930), 155 ff., 201 ff., 222 ff.; K. H. Rengstorf, *Das Evangelium nach Lukas*, 9th ed. (Göttingen, 1962), 146 f., 187 ff., 205 f.; J. Jeremias, *Die Gleichnisse Jesu*, 6th ed. (Göttingen, 1962), 42 ff., 85 f., 153 ff., 157 ff., 180 f.

[2] See ["Shame Culture in Luke"] *Paul and Paulinism: Essays in Honour of C .K. Barrett*, ed. M. D. Hooker and S. G. Wilson (London, 1982), 355 ff. [see 817 ff.] Several colleagues from England have written to me that my findings about the shame bias in Deuteronomy have been promulgated without acknowledgement by a scholar who attended one of my lectures on the subject in that country. As he is a product of the Western hemisphere, I shall leave him to his guilt—worse than exposure.

[3] Philo, *De Cherubim* 5.14, *Quod Deus Immutabilis Sit* 22.101, *De Plantatione* 23.101.

[4] *b. Sot.* 21b.

[5] Matt 26:49; Mark 14:45; Luke 22:48; Judg 14:15 ff., 16:5 ff.; Prov 27:6; Simeon ben Johai in *Siphre* on Num 9:10; Simeon ben Eleazar in *Gen. Rab.* on 33:4; Aeschylus, *Agamemnon* 783 ff.

[6] Starting Matt 6:1.

[7] E.g. Hillel in *m. Ab.* 1:13; Philo, *Quod Deus Immutabilis Sit* 22:102 f.

[8] Cicero, *De Officiis* 2.20.69 f.

Johai, if I have a loan from you—by way of grace, needless to say, as Scripture requires it[9]—and treat you with special politeness, I am guilty of illicit payment of interest:[10] purism. Even within the generally despised categories, exceptions were not unthinkable. Take hypocrisy. If a communal leader looked up to as representing superior values cannot resist the lures of a prostitute, a realist might prefer him to sin in secret so as to avoid bringing disrepute on his cause.[11]

Historical theologians have shown relatively little interest in the controversy, partly no doubt because the Christians among them like dwelling on the weight the gospels attach to the spirit informing a deed, while the Jews defensively collect parallel statements from the Talmud. (This mechanism dictates much inter-faith exploration. W. D. Davies, writing about the role of the land in the two religions,[12] reminds us that "the discussion of the interaction between Judaism and the Gospel has been governed almost entirely by those concerns that Christians themselves have deemed important.") Quite apart, however, from the adoption by both of a simplistic construction of spirit and deed, with hardly any awareness of modern psychological findings, and quite apart from the strained interpretation of texts and data engendered by competition—especially when it comes to ethereal conundrums like hoping or not hoping to be rewarded by God for doing his will—this narrow focus excludes a wealth of material throwing light on communal trends and individual authorities. A few sketchy illustrations must suffice.

Philo detects in the Biblical phrase "blessing I will bless" an application of the insight that, though even bad people can do the right thing, the wise man will do it from the right disposition: his benediction, then, will spring from a benedictory state.[13] Deuteronomy contains an episode when the Israelites embarked on a battle in the name of God though not supposed to do so: "They went up with violence." The result was defeat. This, Philo explains, read as an allegory, indicates that if you act dutifully not from genuine impulse but by doing violence to your undutiful nature, you will find no peace. The hypocrite figures among his examples, as does he who restores a deposit though he would love to withhold it; in fact, he labels these as little better than the scoundrel mentioned above who discharges a minor obligation on purpose to defraud on a big scale. (Whom, I wonder, had he in mind when he equally downrated uninspired scholars and artists who have to "do violence to themselves" to produce?[14]) Precisely what value—if any—he accords to approved conduct as such I shall not here attempt to unravel.

We have already come across a specimen of Simeon ben Johai's exacting stand. How this could affect, and be affected by, political convictions comes out in one of his numerous disagreements with Judah ben Ilai. While the latter, a moderate, pays tribute to the civilisation and order which the Romans are bringing the provinces, the former,

[9] Exod 22:24; Lev 25:25 ff.; Deut 23:20 f.

[10] *b. B. M.* 75b.

[11] *b. M. Kat.* 17a; *b. Kidd* 40a; see my *Ancient Jewish Law* (Leiden, 1981), 70.

[12] W. D. Davies, *The Gospel and the Land: Early Christianity and Jewish Territorial Doctrine* (Berkeley, 1974), 3.

[13] Philo, *Leg. All.* 3.74.210, on Gen 22:17.

[14] Philo, *Quod Deus Immutabilis Sit* 22:99 ff., on Deut 1:43.

implacable enemy of the foreign master, is contemptuous of these achievements induced, as they are, by self-interest and other objectionable aspirations.[15]

In the early third century, Rabh up to a point manages to bridge the gulf: right performance is commendable even if not due to high-mindedness since the habit of it will itself lead you to inner virtue.[16] "Through doing without thought of heaven, you will come to do with heaven in mind" has become proverbial in Jewish moral instruction. In its practical effects, the solution obviously leans towards realism. A hundred years after him, Raba compliments the rich ladies of his congregation on abstaining from work on Friday afternoon though they do so not in view of the approaching Sabbath but from indolence. He also discovers a Scriptural basis for a flexible approach. One psalm says "Your mercy is great above the heavens," another "Your mercy is great unto the heavens."[17] No contradiction: the former comforts those who take the proper course for the sake of God, the latter those who take it for a lesser end. Even these receive some recognition.

The preponderance of pragmatism or perfectionism in any given Rabbinic utterance is far from accidental. The former tends to be associated with the kind of wisdom dominant in the ancient Orient, including the Bible, i.e. mindful of God yet geared towards prosperity in this life, the latter with prophetic and mystical strivings, of a more other-worldly colour. Judah ben Ilai attributes to himself the "wisdom that makes a face to shine."[18] He contends that while the study of the Torah ranks highest, that of *derekh eretz*, guidelines concerning everyday affairs, is needful too: if you devote yourself fully to the Torah, you will be scorched, if to *derekh eretz*, you will be frost-bitten.[19] Bacher calls this simile odd;[20] but it is not if we pay heed to its author's general philosophy, his determined preference for the mean. It is significant that he professes himself quite human. He remarks that, unlike Noah who, when the earth had dried, still waited in the ark till God told him to leave it, he would have gotten out at once.[21] By contrast, Simeon ben Johai believes that, ideally, you should not even till the soil but spend all your time on Torah.[22] He and his son, he asserts, belong to the small number of true saints.[23]

Again, mostly, realism comes to the fore in settled conditions or where settled conditions are a major aim, and it is favoured by those comfortably situated, whereas purism flourishes in crises and among those hostile to the establishment. Judah ben Ilai, son of a prominent father, made it his task to reconstruct Palestinian Jewry when the Hadrianic persecution abated, admitting important—if limited—concessions to the Romans who actually conferred some honour on him. He preferred patient amelioration

15 *b. Shab.* 33b. See my *Collaboration with Tyranny in Rabbinic Law* Oxford, 1965), 39. [*Talmudic Law*, 90.]

16 *b. Pes.* 50b.

17 Pss 108:5; 57:11.

18 *y. Pes.* 31c; Eccl 8:1.

19 *Ab. de R. N.* 28i f.

20 See W. Bacher, *Die Agada der Tannaiten*, vol. 2. (Strasbourg, 1890), 196.

21 *Tanhuma Noah*, on Gen 8:15 f.

22 *Mek.* on Exod 16:5; *Siphre* on Deut 11:14.

23 *y. Ber.* 13d; *b. Sukk.* 45b.

to daring: he criticized Solomon's judgment which, had the true mother not come through, might have led to the baby's death.[24] Simeon ben Johai would have carried on resistance much longer, spending many years as an outlaw. He trusted in miraculous salvation: "If only Israel observed two Sabbaths meticulously, they would be redeemed at once."[25] Rabh and Raba lived in Babylonia in what was on the whole a very fortunate period. Both were scions of noble, wealthy families.

2. The primary message of the simile of the Helper at Midnight is that, since even our human neighbour will undergo considerable inconvenience for our sakes if we press him in an emergency, surely God is always ready to hear the needy. In my paper adverted to above, among the shame-cultural traits superimposed—though prior to the evangelist—I cite the explanation that the person aroused from sleep yields to the caller "because of his shamelessness." Now I would add that the same hand introduces the theme of dissonance between deed and spirit: he yields to his caller "not because he is his friend but because of his shamelessness."

The unexpanded parable enshrines a very old idea: though certain benefits habitually come to us from this or that fellow mortal, there is only one truly reliable and perfect saviour. Perhaps the most basic paradigm is parental care. That it is universal, extending to the unenlightened and, indeed, the beasts is a commonplace in the ancient world, traceable in Scripture,[26] made much of by Plutarch.[27] Even so, Isaiah preaches,[28] its divine mode surpasses its earthly one: "Can a woman forget the son of her womb? Yea, they may forget, yet will I not forget you." The service of the Helper at Midnight is less fundamental than a parent's—and, precisely for this reason, more appropriate for a parable. It would be too simple, too uninteresting, to put the case "Which of you shall have a father that is not nice to him?"

The "most basic paradigm" occurs in Q (to use a convenient symbol, without commitment):[29] "If you know how to give good gifts to your children, how much more your Father in heaven." Its presentation as a technical conclusion *a minori ad maius* should not surprise us: this argument enjoyed wide currency at the time.[30] The full text, however, contains a phrase which adumbrates the insertion "not because he is his friend"; it reads "If you, being evil, know" etc. The relatively naive contrast man—deity has become man intrinsically depraved—deity. On this level, where it is a question of flawed human nature in general and not of the flawed intent behind a specific action,

[24] *Eccl. Rab.* on 10:16 referring to 1 Kgs 3:25. The text slightly distorts the Rabbi's name, but there is no doubt as to his authorship; see W. Bacher, *op. cit.*, 216.

[25] *b. Shab.* 118b. See my *Collaboration*, 28 ff. [*Talmudic Law*, 83 ff.]

[26] Num 11:12; Deut 32:11; 2 Esdr 1:30; Matt 23:37; Luke 19:23.

[27] *De Amore Prolis* 2.494C ff., 4.496 ff.

[28] Isa 49:15.

[29] Matt 7:11; Luke 11:13.

[30] See my article "Rabbinic Methods of Interpretation and Hellenistic Rhetoric," *HUCA*, 22 (1949), 251 ff [*Talmudic Law*, 344–48]. Incidentally, it may not be without significance that the earliest *a fortiori* preserved in world literature, Gen 44:8, is propounded in a quasi-forensic setting, the defence of Joseph's brothers when accused of theft of his cup: "The money we found in our sacks we brought back, how then should we steal out of your lord's house silver or gold?"

the Rabbinic and early Christian attitude is uniformly accepting: despite our faultiness, that is, we can act decently.[31]

It is when we come to so sophisticated an analysis as "not because he is his friend but because of his shamelessness" that we are in the midst of the realist-purist battle. The interpolator is a realist. He does not give us to understand that the Helper's action is worthless. Certainly, it is below the saintly model, far below God's unalloyed mercy. But it is still a kind of foretaste of the latter. A purist verdict on behaviour not quite identical but not so different either is preserved in an anonymous Rabbinic warning: "If you give somebody all good gifts in the world but with a bad grace, you are accounted to have given him nothing."[32] A medieval treatise tones it down: "A small sum given joyfully is far more valuable than a large one given grudgingly."[33] The plain instruction to give at once is already set down in the Old Testament.[34] "God loves a cheerful giver" says Paul,[35] *Bis dat qui dat celerite* [He who gives quickly gives twice] Publilius Syrus.[36]

Quite possibly, whoever appended to the parable the Q portion with the verse about good gifts to children did so in awareness of the approximation here to the problem of the Helper's less than ideal state of mind. A slight deviation from the Matthean wording is perhaps worth noting. Matthew runs "If you, being (*ontes*) evil, know" etc., Luke "If you, from the outset (*hyparchontes*) evil, know" etc. Admittedly, *hyparcho*, "to be from the outset," often means no more than *eimi*, "to be"; in fact, this usage seems to be represented in the Third Gospel. Nevertheless, it is arguable that, in the passage under discussion, the verb is designed to add emphasis to the philosophical aspect.

3. The parable of the Unjust Steward counts as "an unedifying story,"[37] "one of the most difficult chapters of the gospels."[38] The stumbling-block, however, the glorification of a fraud, is due to a misunderstanding. As recently as when I penned the essay adverted to at the beginning of the present one,[39] I was still myself somewhat under its spell.[40] I must put it right before going into my dominant interest, pragmatism versus perfectionism in the rating of a fine deed from a dubious impulse. It is impossible, on the basis of the prevalent erroneous construction of the episode, to comprehend the intrusion and development of that dispute.

To leave aside anything but the nucleus—a tycoon's procurator, denounced as squandering the property in his charge, faces dismissal; so as his last move in office he forgives all debtors a portion of what they owe. His procedure is eulogized, which gravely troubles commentators who, misled by accretions—even these, on closer examina-

[31] Cp. Matt 19:16 ff.; Mark 10:17 ff.; Luke 18:18 ff.

[32] *Ab. de R. N.* 13i.f.

[33] *Sepher Hayashar* 841.

[34] Prov 3:28; cp. 22:9 in the LXX.

[35] 2 Cor 9:7.

[36] Publilius Syrus, *Sententiae* 274 (235).

[37] See J. M. Creed, *op. cit.*, 203.

[38] See K. H. Rengstorf, *op. cit.*, 188: "*gehört zu den schwierigsten Abschnitten der Evangelien.*"

[39] See above, n. 2.

[40] This is noticeable in the last paragraph but two, 367 [829], in the portion starting "A far stronger one is that, here and there, the evangelist tones down. . . ." Luckily, my chief result is not vitiated.

tion, not bearing them out—see him as "flagrantly dishonest,"[41] "a criminal"[42] or the like. Their embarrassment is unwarranted. In the situation as then conceived, he is committing no wrong whatever. It has been said that "the various attempts to whitewash him have all been unsuccessful."[43] Well, I dare damnation.

To begin with, he is plainly the kind of manager with *plein pouvoir* [full power]. That is indeed why he can be accused of running down the estate by his ineptness: he has discretionary power of disposal. Moreover, if it were otherwise, his very rebate to the debtors would be invalid or at least wide open to attack. Unless we have before us a simile extraordinarily clumsy and brittle, here is an agent who can freely negotiate and adjust his contracts. He might from the outset have charged his clients less; and he may at any time grant them a longer term for settlement, a lower interest rate or simply—as in the recital—a reduction in overall load. Certainly, if he blunders or, worse, embezzles, his employer will take whatever reprisals are appropriate. But, within these boundaries, he has plenty of room for manoeuvre. A second-century papyrus represents a fairly common practice:[44] "I have empowered you by this document to administer my estate in Arsinoe, and to collect the rents and, if need be, to arrange new leases or to cultivate some land yourself, and to give receipts in my name, and to transact any business connected with stewardship, just as I can transact it when I am present, and to distribute the plots in Karamis, restoring to me what remains over, as to which matter I rely on your good faith, and I confirm whatever you decide about them." The parable of the Talents or Pounds, it may be noticed, equally presupposes administrators of a high degree of independence.[45]

Next: he is a good servant. The verb *diaballo* used for "to denounce," no less than its noun *diabole*, as a rule—in the Greek Old Testament always—denotes a "diabolical" scheme: "to slander," "to calumniate." No reason to postulate an exception here.

So why is he called "a steward of unrighteousness," "an impious steward"? Precisely because, up to now, he has willingly executed a wealthy oppressor's bidding. It is for this role, and not for the new route he is entering on, that he deserves the damning predicate. Just so, in the first comment introduced by "And I say unto you"—"Make to yourselves friends with the mammon of unrighteousness"—the quality of unrighteousness palpably adheres to the principal's affluence. No less relevant is the fact that the Unjust Judge is called thus in the eulogy after he at long last resolves to do his duty: "Hear what the unjust judge says." Obviously, the pejorative characterizes his habitual unscrupulousness and not his overdue, proper act.

We must not forget that the tycoon, embodiment of mammon, is the villain of the plot. True, no offenses of his are detailed: he stands for the rich type (or "character," in the sense of Theophrastus's or Webster's "Characters") whose evildoing is taken for

[41] See J. M. Creed, *op. cit.*, 201.

[42] See J. Jeremias, *op. cit.*, 127.

[43] See J. Jeremias, *loc. cit.* The most recent one known to me is by J. D. M. Derrett: *Law in the New Testament* (London, 1970), 48 ff. Though containing valuable ideas, it, too, offers no convincing breakthrough.

[44] BGU I 300 of A.D. 148; see L. Wenger, *Die Stellvertretung im Rechte der Papyri* (Leipzig, 1906), 221 ff.

[45] Matt 25:14 ff.; Luke 19:12 ff.

granted. It is the same in the parable immediately following, of the Rich Man and Lazarus,[46] which, though it does depict the callous lifestyle of the former, singles out no particular wrongs. Once again, we are to take him as the familiar mould, hence that he is guilty of enough outrages to send him to hell goes without saying. Very similar considerations apply to the debtors. They, too, are stereotypes, on the other side from the creditor: we know, without being informed in so many words, that they are victims, sufferers, brutally exploited.

A close analogy is supplied by the tale of the Unjust Judge. Nothing whatever is said about the widow's case being sound. Since she represents a type, "the widow" as commonly situated or thought of, her adversary must be in the wrong, taking advantage of her helpless state.

Let us update the incident. "A landowner in Southern California used hundreds of illegal Mexican immigrants as slave labour. One of them only, whom he entrusted with laying down and enforcing the camp regulations, he paid and housed decently. After a while he decided that the fellow was not up to his job and told him that he would shortly be replaced. Whereupon this henchman of unrighteousness, this cruel overseer, changed his tune and proclaimed that a little shed should be built for the gravely ill." No reader, I suppose, will find here "a flagrant dishonesty" to the employer or connect the designation "of unrighteousness" or "cruel" to the final, humane step. But, then, neither are these conclusions appropriate to the parable of the Unjust Steward. It would indeed be worthwhile to examine why our instinctive reaction to the rebate is so different from that to the shed. But I shall be content with pointing out one major cause—that while the ruthlessly abandoned sick still represent an overriding demand in public imagination, debtors in distress have long lost this place which they occupied, say, when Solon came to their aid at Athens or Nehemiah at Jerusalem.[47] The New Testament, needless to say, is imbued with the traditional symbolism: "as we forgive our debtors" and so on.

Here is a sort of test. The prevalent doctrine has the steward perpetrate a swindle, praiseworthy as his only protection against ruin. I claim that he escapes ruin by bethinking himself of what religion requires—relief of the downtrodden. In the early 1950s, Alexander Kresling, of whose Russian choir at Freiburg University I was an early member in pre-Hitler days, told me of his war work as interpreter for the German General Staff. Towards the end, at Berlin, some Russian prisoners who, having shown themselves good collaborationists, were employed as valets let on to him a plan of murdering a German officer: that would help them with the soon-to-invade conquerors. He dissuaded them. But suppose he had not, could they be substituted for the steward? Surely not. A crime in desperation may be pardonable but, unlike a last-moment repair of harm, it is not fit to be held out for imitation. Had they proceeded to rescue a less lucky comrade from an extermination centre, the case would indeed be comparable.

At last I can embark on my topic. The parable in its *Ur*-form inculcates the urgency, in the endtime crisis that has arrived, of mending your wicked ways. My pre-

[46] Luke 16:19 ff.

[47] Aristotle, *Athenian Constitution* 6.1; Neh 5:6 ff.

vious study suggests that, just as in the parable of the Helper at Midnight, a shame consideration is inserted: a person of the procurator's standing thinks of himself as above begging or digging. To which I now add that, just as in the other parable, the same hand points out a selfish element in his kindly action: the hope that the grateful beneficiaries will look after him when he has lost his post. Once again, the implication is pragmatist. As they are placed, the verses express full understanding for his calculation.

The wisdom contact is manifest. That you should prepare while the going is good for hard times to come is among the hoariest lessons around the globe. The ant collects food in summer for the winter,[48] Joseph stored up corn in the seven plentiful years for the seven lean ones,[49] "Remember the time of famine in the time of fullness" we are cautioned by Sirach.[50] Wisdom input is noticeable also in the appendix to the parable which, in fact, starts with an explicit reference: Jesus is pleased with the steward for "having done wisely." The Greek is *phronimos*, "shrewdly," "prudently." It often ranks below *sophos*, "sage," "wise," being more down to earth, with an eye on the practicable. (A bit like German *klug*, used by Schiller's Gertrud Stauffacher when counselling timely prevention of disaster: "*Der kluge Mann baut vor* [A smart man is prepared]."[51] The line has become a proverb. It may be worth noting that what she feels entitles her to give advice is education in wisdom circles: for years in her father's home she listened to experienced, respected men exchanging views on matters of state.) But it is definitely a positive attribute.[52]

Jesus's praise is provided with an argument: "for the children of this age are wiser—*scil.* when acting thus—than the children of the light for their generation." This passage—which no expositor has attempted seriously to make sense of—leads on to another bone of contention between realism and purism. In judging a person, the former will and the latter will not take account of his environment and epoch. The pronouncement under discussion is realist. Conduct barely so-so at Boston or under Carter may be splendid at San Francisco or under Nixon.

Recently, I had occasion to write on a bold realist simile of Johanan ben Zaccai—first century A.D.—regarding milieu.[53] God, at Moses's instance, pardoned the children of Israel their worship of the calf, as a king, having divorced his adulterous wife, might be persuaded by friends that, considering her lowly origins, she deserved some leniency and might re-marry her. The sentence before us is concerned with the time in which you live. Quite likely, the phrase "for their generation," *eis ten genean heauton*, is a conscious allusion to Noah in Genesis, "just and perfect in his generation," *dikaios teleios en te genea autou*.[54] (I disregard the change of *en* into *eis*.) No need to go into the orig-

[48] Prov 6:6 ff.; Babrius, Fable 140.

[49] Genesis 41.

[50] Sir 18:25.

[51] Schiller, *Wilhelm Tell*, Act 1, Scene 2.

[52] Cp. Luke 12:42. It is positive even in Gen 3:1: see my *Civil Disobedience in Antiquity* (Edinburgh, 1972), 61. Philo, in *Leg. All.* 3.74.210, quoted above, footnote 13, employs *sophos*.

[53] See ["Biblical Landmarks in the Struggle for Women's Rights"] *JR*, 90 (n.s. 23) (1978), 195 f. [245 f.].

[54] Gen 6:9.

inal meaning. What matters here is that, for Philo,[55] "in his generation" signifies "by comparison with his generation"—not quite as good as absolute virtue but still a fine second prize. Similarly, Judah ben Ilai, whom we have already found to belong to the moderate camp, and who, as on other occasions, is no doubt drawing on earlier exegetes,[56] infers that Noah was exceptional only among his contemporaries. Had he lived in a less ungodly era, he would not have stood out. But as it was, his relative superiority sufficed to entitle him to be the founder of a new world. As may be expected, the austere Nehemiah, habitually in conflict with Judah, rejects this interpretation: purism requires Noah to have been absolutely dedicated. The line-up, in passing, conforms to my suggestion above—that realism is usually cultivated by the establishment, purism by those distrustful of it: whereas Judah ben Ilai, we saw, had a famous father, Nehemiah's is never mentioned.[57]

Their dispute involves other details of the narrative. For instance, Scripture records that Noah "walked with God," while Abraham was exhorted by God: "Walk before me."[58] Judah compares Noah to a toddler, Abraham to an adult son. The former's strength was no good, *ra'*, he had to walk "with" God, the latter's was beautiful, *yaphe*, he could walk "before" God. Once more, Nehemiah supplies a purist solution.[59] Again, Biblical chronology makes Enosh still live when Noah is born and Noah still live when the builders of the tower of Babel are scattered. For Judah, the Psalter's opening verse, "Blessed is the man" etc., is designed to tell us that Noah proved excellent in three generations, that of Enosh, that of the flood and that of the tower. Nehemiah denies that he could have been excellent in the generation of Enosh when he was still little. In Judah's system, even a child may reach the top—if allowance is made for his years; in Nehemiah's, there is only one unbending evaluation.[60]

A paraphrase, then, would run: There is a reason the Lord treats as a notable display of wisdom something so basic as the steward's (or campwarden's) seizure of his last, short opportunity for doing good. Considering their terrible background, the captives of this aeon—of whom the wealthy master's executive is obviously one—do indeed show more wisdom in such penitence than the aspirants to the kingdom for whom the waiving of debts (or provision for the sick) is a matter of course. Like Noah, they rise above their surroundings. This result is not affected if, as is conceivable, the pronouncement does not quote straight from Genesis or even if—highly improbable—the Genesis wording plays no role whatever. It is only by assuming something like Judah ben Ilai's approach that we can do justice to the text.

[55] Philo, *Abr.* 7.36 ff.

[56] *Gen. Rab.* on 6:9. On his acquaintance with ancient lore, see W. Bacher, *op. cit.*, 193 ff. In my article "Jewish Law in the Hellenistic World," in B.S. Jackson (ed.), *Jewish Law in Legal History and the Modern World*, *JLA*, Suppl. 2 (Leiden, 1980), 48ff. [*Talmudic Law*, 213–29], I record my impression that an interpretation common to Philo and the Rabbis is more often than not taken over by the former from the latter.

[57] See W. Bacher, *op. cit.*, 225.

[58] Gen 6:9; 17.1.

[59] *Gen. Rab.* on 6:9.

[60] *Gen. Rab.* on 5:32. W. Bacher, *op. cit.*, 269, fails to see the point.

The counsel "Make to yourselves friends" etc. generalizes for the benefit of the believers: the only proper use of mammon is in the service of God, hoping for higher reward. Maybe there is here a hint at yet a further realist point: even ill-gotten lucre can be turned to good purpose. An idealist might recommend walking away from it. I shall not, however, expand on this question which has a long, complicated history. In the Hebrew area, we should have to start with provisions such as that gain from prostitution may not be offered at the sanctuary.[61]

There follow three epigrams about faithfulness. The first—from the Q parable of the Talents or Pounds[62]—declares this virtue in small things to be a condition for promotion to great ones. The second extends the insight: if you are not faithful with, i.e. do not put to proper use, a specious thing like mammon, no one will entrust you with the genuine. The third repeats this in slightly different terms: if you are not faithful with, i.e. do not put to proper use, what is foreign from you, contrary to your concerns (*allotrion*), no one will give you what is your own—or, according to a variant, heaven's. The language of the second and third admonitions is pretty philosophical. Very likely, lack of sensibility to it from fairly early on fostered the formidable misconception here combated, first among the unlettered, then generally. The third saying was taken to speak of one not faithful with what belongs to another man, and there was seen in this a censure of the steward for making over to the debtors his principal's money. Once the idea took root, it was bound ultimately to affect, infect, all parts of the pericope. I cannot enlarge on the development but would point out that Theophilus of Antioch, adduced by Jerome, is still absolutely untouched. (Jerome is not.) The employer is God; I shall say nothing about how this interpretation came about. The steward is Paul, "of unrighteousness" prior to his vision on the road to Damascus, then, in fear of dismissal, preaching mercy without the Law to gentiles—borrowers of oil—as well as to Jews—borrowers of wheat.[63]

A rather purist Q affirmation[64] of total incompatibility of care for God and care for mammon forms the ending—chosen, I suspect, by Luke himself. Its position here corroborates my introductory comments: right to the close, the villain is the wealthy creditor. In fact, this continues in the ensuing appendix devoted to the reaction of the Pharisees. They hear of the parable, we are told, and, "loving money," deride Jesus. They side with the protagonist of evil, that is, instead of with his associate who, in the nick of time, separates from him.

4. In its pristine shape, the remaining parable introduces a judge who, with scant considerateness for the lowly, does listen to a widow who will not give up imploring him; and its moral is that all the more God can be relied on to vindicate the forlorn who persist in their trust. A shame-oriented elaboration has the judge relent lest the widow slap him in the face. This is the archetypal insult for Hebrews, Greeks and Romans; indeed,

[61] Deut 23:19.

[62] Matt 25:21, 23; Luke 19:17.

[63] Jerome, *Epistulae* 121 (151), *Ad Algasium*, in: Migne, *Patrologia Latina*, vol. 22 (Paris, 1877), 1120 f.

[64] Cp. Matt 6:24.

it figures as such in their laws,[65] so to represent it as uppermost in a lawyer's mind is particularly subtle. (A president of the Sanhedrin ordered it to be inflicted on Paul.[66]) Once more, the shame import is combined with the problem of blemished motivation. The Helper at Midnight, it will be remembered, rises not from friendship but from worry about shamelessness. The judge's deliberation exhibits an exactly corresponding antithesis: "though I fear not God nor regard man, I will avenge her lest she slap me."

Already the first sentence of the parable describes him as he here describes himself; and, probably, even in that sentence we have to do with wisdom expansion. From remote antiquity, it is a widely recognized mark of the rational, worthy citizen to balance the demands of heaven and those of society while the irrational, worthless one bothers about neither. Biblical wisdom's hero "will find favour in the eyes of God and man":[67] this scoundrel is its anti-hero. The formulation may owe something to Greek writings. In Dionysius of Halicarnassus, a gang of Roman conspirators are stigmatized as "neither fearing the wrath of the gods nor regarding the indignation of men."[68] At any rate, the repetition of the dreadful attributes in the judge's own reasoning is certainly due to the school whose contribution I am trying to elucidate.

So is the—distinctly realist—exhortation "Hear (plural, *akousate*) what the unjust judge says." However much his doing what his office requires may be prompted by fear of disgrace, it is still a good thing, actually, in certain situations, worthy of emulation. No doubt "hear" is the sage's appeal for earnest attention, common from early times.[69]

5. A realist need not be devoid of purist vision; none adhering to Judaeo-Christian tradition could be. The parables of the Helper at Midnight and the Unjust judge, as originally enunciated, teach that, as strenuous entreaty moves even a lazy neighbour or hardened judge, it is certain to move God, ever-caring. I have tried to demonstrate that the references to the Helper's and Judge's defective spirit are secondary, added by a realist, i.e. one who appreciates the action notwithstanding the defect. However, this approval does not imply that things might not be better. God, we are to understand, acts from absolute generosity. The parable of the Unjust Steward in its earliest form does not contrast him with anyone else at all: he makes amends in the nick of time—the best example for a depraved society. Again, a selfish aim is inserted; again, it does not ren-

[65] *m. B. K.* 6:8: "He who cuffs his fellow pays 400 zuz; if he slaps him in the face, 200 zuz." Aristotle, *Rhet.* 1.13.10: "If a man strikes, he is not always guilty of *hybris*, but only if he does so with intent to dishonour the other or to gratify himself." (The latter affirmative, "to gratify himself," would be worth closer inquiry.) The Roman pattern formula for this tort is quoted in *Collatio Legum Romanarum et Mosaicarum* 2.6.4: "Whereas plaintiff has had his face struck with the fist." See my *New Testament and Rabbinic Judaism* (London, 1956; repr. New York, 1973), 259 ff., discussing Matt 5:38 f. [181 ff.]

[66] Acts 23:2. See my *Ancient Jewish Law* (1981), 61.

[67] Prov 3:4; 1 Sam 2:26; Luke 2:40, 52.

[68] Dionysius of Halicarnassus, *Roman Antiquities* 10.10.7.

[69] Gen 49:2; Isa 28:23; often, of course, in the singular; Prov 4:10, for example. By the way, I do not know whether it has been seen that elements of the parable occur in an incident featuring Philip (Plutarch, Sayings of Kings and Commanders, *Moralia* 179C f.), Demetrius (Plutarch, *Parallel Lives*, Demetrius 42.3 f.), Antipater (Stobaeus, *Florilegium* 13.28) or Hadrian (Cassius Dio, *Roman History* 59.6.3), also in a similar one with Trajan, immortalized in Dante, *Divina Comedia*, Purgatorio 10.73 ff.

der his action worthless; and again, this does not mean blindness to a higher possibility. Actually, it is explained at length why, despite his calculating stance, he receives extraordinary commendation. The higher alternative is represented, not as in the other two parables by God, but by the children of light: their expectations are not of this world but of the next.[70]

Luke's personal view regarding the problem of motivation is hard to determine. To go by his treatment of other matters as to which extremists and moderates might clash, he steered a subtle course.

Take worldly attachments. On the one hand, he was quite radical. The extensive discussion of the Unjust Steward concludes, we saw, with "You cannot serve God and mammon." He alone of the Synoptics transmits Jesus's refusal to aid in the division of an inheritance[71] and the parable of the Rich Fool.[72] His Q insists more strongly than Matthew's on the renunciation of family ties.[73] Admittedly, Creed is right in labelling Jesus's dictum that his followers must "hate father, mother" and so on as hyperbole. But hyperboles are resorted to for a purpose: we are to pay heed, take the message seriously.[74] On the other hand, the account of the boy Jesus's debate with the Rabbis in the Temple and his parent's search for him[75] must originally have ended with his authoritative retort to the latter: "Did you not know that I had to concern myself with God's business?" Going back to the period when it was urgent to lend encouragement to the younger members of a family who, defying their elders, followed the new Messianic creed. In Luke, there is an addendum to the effect that Jesus returned with his parents and subjected himself to them. By now, full Christian families were in existence and, in general, obedience to hierarchical superiors took precedence of individual religious initiative. It is the same change of conditions that caused the toning down in Luke of Jesus's disavowal of his mother and brothers as they visit him compared with Matthew and Mark.[76]

These varying accounts of Jesus's response to his relatives, by the way, reinforce what emerged at the beginning of this section: a simple dichotomy realism—purism is quite inadequate. Certainly, in a sense, it is realist for the sake of order and harmony to set limits to heavenward soaring. Yet, insofar as the former do more for the ultimate success of the Church, they may become overriding purist goals. The tension is a major theme of 1 Corinthians; it is treated in masterly fashion; and priority is firmly assigned

[70] In passing—it would be unthinkable in that period to compare God with the steward, even on purpose to bring out a difference in conduct. God may be a friend, a judge, a principal creditor gracious or harsh (Matt 6:12, 18:23 ff.; Luke 11:4), but not an underling. Not a few depictions of Jesus—e.g. Matt 20:28; Luke 22:27; John 13:4 ff.—would be untransferable to God.

[71] Luke 12:13 ff.; see my note ("Inheritance in Two Lukan Perikopes") in *ZSS*, 72 (1955), Rom. Abt., 326 ff. [See 807 ff.]

[72] Luke 12:16 ff.

[73] Luke 9:59 ff. versus Matt 8:19 ff.; Luke 14:26 versus Matt 10:37.

[74] See J. M. Creed, *op. cit.*, 194. In substance correct K. H. Rengstorf, *op. cit.*, 180 f.

[75] Luke 2:42 ff. See my *Civil Disobedience*, 47 ff., and my article "Three Footnotes on *Civil Disobedience in Antiquity*," in *Humanities in Society*, vol. 2 (1979), 73 f.

[76] Matt 12:46 ff.; Mark 3:31 ff.; Luke 8:19 ff.

to "the upbuilding" (*oikodomeo*).[77] For example, if a heathen father and daughter embrace Christianity, since they are new creations, they can in principle marry one another. But—as already the Rabbis had decreed for their converts—such a union would damage the community's reputation in the outside world, hence is impermissible. You must serve the universality rather than bask in, boast of, your private miraculous freedom. It is in this spirit that Paul, as apostle, will fall in, up to a point, with the lower standards of those he hopes to win over: "though free of all, yet have I made myself servant unto all."[78] Luke, in Acts, shows him putting his preaching into practice: as it will further his mission among Jews, he waives his opposition to proselyte circumcision in the case of Timothy.[79] Realist? Purist? It depends on how we look at it. There are countless further nuances of this complexity. The huge field on institutionalized concessions to weakness belongs here:[80] kingship in deference to the people's inability to live under more direct divine guidance,[81] divorce because of the hardness of your heart,[82] marriage in order to forestall burning,[83] and so forth. I shall not go on with it.

One more point, however, about the evangelist. It looks as if he had confined his fiercer demands to insiders while showing a measure of indulgence to outsiders and even—or especially—sympathizers. In all three Synoptics, the Rich Young Man who craves Jesus's approval boggles at the requirement to give away all he has to the poor. But whereas according to Matthew and Mark he leaves and Jesus then addresses his entourage "It is easier for a camel" and so on,[84] according to Luke he keeps staying around and Jesus advances this reflection in his presence. No need to sever relations.[85] Naturally, if so much more was expected of those who pledged themselves, alerting would-be joiners to the risk must acquire particular importance. Thus Luke offers similes on the Cost of Discipleship not met in the other gospels.[86] The report about Ananias and Sapphira in Acts, too, is concerned with the peril of high commitment.[87] It does not, to be sure, contrast the ease outside the community with the rigour inside, but it does the ease of an ordinary member with the rigour if you profess to belong to a select band. Peter is careful to point out that they could without reproach have held on to their field or the sum they sold it for: it was by their pretence to be donating all of it—like Barnabas and many others—while in fact retaining a part that they incurred mortal

[77] See my paper ["Pauline Contributions to a Pluralistic Culture: Re-Creation and Beyond"] in *Jesus and Man's Hope*, ed. D. G. Miller and D. Y. Hadidian (Pittsburgh, 1971), vol. 2, 223 ff. [537 ff.], and my *Ancient Jewish Law*, 14 ff. [see 474 ff.]

[78] 1 Cor 9:20 ff.; cp. Rom 12:15. See my *The New Testament and Rabbinic Judaism*, 336 ff. [561 ff.]

[79] Acts 16:1 ff. See my *Ancient Jewish Law*, 26. [see 676.]

[80] See my lecture ("Concessions to Sinfulness in Jewish Law") in *JJS*, 10 (1959), 1 ff. [*Talmudic Law*, 1 ff.]

[81] 1 Sam 8:7.

[82] Matt 19:8; Mark 10:5.

[83] 1 Cor 7:9.

[84] Which saying has inspired a beautiful poem by Christian Morgenstern.

[85] Matt 19:16 ff.; Mark 10:17 ff.; Luke 18:18 ff.

[86] Luke 14:28 ff.

[87] Acts 5:1 ff.

guilt. It is well known that the episode is influenced by earlier texts. "When you vow a vow to the Lord," we read in Deuteronomy,[88] "you shall not slack to pay it; but if you forbear to vow it shall be no sin in you." "When you vow a vow to God, defer not to pay it; better that you should not vow than that you should vow and not pay," says Ecclesiastes,[89] echoed by Sirach.[90] But these passages do not envisage the peculiarly heinous aspects of the couple's design: the posing as having fulfilled the "vow," and a "vow," moreover, that qualifies them for a saintly elite.

6. New Testament ethics is enormously searching and variegated. Even of the single dilemma of right conduct from an egoistic consideration I have only scratched the surface. To comprehend it better, one would have to branch out in several directions. One would, for instance, have to look at the reverse: wrong conduct, or conduct in strictness wrong, from a noble impulse. One large group of cases I have already mentioned: the lowering of standards in the interest of (short-hand) "the upbuilding." But there are many others. The Jews, Paul says, go astray but with "a zeal of God."[91] An early text is Jesus's assault on the traders in the Temple-yard in defence of the sanctity of the place.[92] It is not accidental that the notion "zeal" recurs in this connection.[93] "Zeal" plays a tremendous role in the Jewish political thinking of the time as justifying procedures otherwise offensive.[94] In a way, the religiously zealous deed of that age corresponds to the amorous *crime passionnel* of the nineteenth century. Again, the then prevailing gradation of values and virtues ought to be taken account of far more meticulously than in this study. Present-day annotators of the three pericopes worry no end about the Steward and Judge, not at all about the Helper. To be sure, the two former, except for their final step, have been "given to unjustness"—which could not be said of the latter. Nevertheless, when we remember the sacred nature of friendship in Oriental philosophy, the latter's coming through merely in order to extricate himself from unpleasantness is almost as dubious as the Steward's in order to secure his comfort or the Judge's in order to avert a scandal.

An illustration not directly relevant to my main subject is the treatment of the children in the parable of the Helper at Midnight. After being used as a shield, they are totally disregarded when he feels it is time to satisfy the caller. This is so all right, the author does not comment on it, probably is not even conscious of it. Nowadays one hears a good deal of criticism of a man generous in the outside world at the expense of his dependents. A theological acquaintance whose attention I drew to it argued that the father was intending to teach his children how to serve. But there is not the faintest allusion to such an intent—no more than to an intent, at the opening of the scene, to teach

[88] Deut 23:22 f.

[89] Eccl 5:3 f.

[90] Sir 18:23.

[91] Rom 10:2; see my *Sin, Ignorance and Forgiveness in the Bible* (London, 1960), 29.

[92] Matt 21:12 ff.; Mark 11:15 ff.; Luke 19:45 f.; John 2:14 ff. See my *Civil Disobedience*, 101 ff.

[93] John 2:17, quoting Ps 69:10.

[94] See e.g. the articles "Zealot" by K. Kohler, in *The Jewish Encyclopaedia*, (New York–London, 1906), vol. 12, 639 ff., and by W. R. Farmer, in *The Interpreter's Dictionary of the Bible* (New York, 1962), vol. 4, 936 ff.

them how, if possible, to evade serving. It is futile to deny changes in sensibilities. In regard to friendship, as just remarked, on the whole the ancients may have been more serious than we are. When it comes to respecting children as persons, here and there we seem to be ahead. Of course, none of this occurs in a vacuum: natural environment, technical resources, social conditions, politics, economics are weighty contributory factors. In a functioning welfare state, friendship is less important for basic needs than in the world of the Book of Ruth. The recent increase in children's autonomy—slight enough—has much to do with affluence, loosening of communal ties, belief in experimentation, certain insecurities. Moreover, welcome though it is—given our circumstances—it is not achieved without a price.

To come back to wisdom, while it can be perfectionist, its preponderant thrust in Scripture, I noticed above,[95] is pragmatic. Its focus on daily successful living is apt to divert some attention from the stars. This in no way implies that it is Epicurean. In its motto "to find favour in the eyes of God and man," "of God" is to be taken seriously.[96] The closing words of Ecclesiastes are "Fear God and keep his commandments." Even if, as is widely supposed, they should be spurious, intended to make the work palatable to less speculative minds, they were presumably added by an initiate in wisdom: who else would bother.[97] Still, the distinctive note of wisdom comes out in "and man." Prophecy divulges the demands from on high. Wisdom, though fully acknowledging them, maps out a way to make it with our fellow-humans on earth. In connection with the Helper at Midnight, I adduced a rule from Proverbs to assist your neighbour without delay. There is, however, a little reservation: "if you have it available."[98] Stylistic peculiarities of this literature, such as the frequency of comparative expressions, reflect the balanced or balancing approach: "Better a dry morsel and quietness with it than a house full of quarrelsome sacrificial feasts,"[99] "A reproof enters more into a wise person than a hundred stripes into a fool,"[100] "Better a name than good oil"[101] (hardly, I fear, our government's devise). The form is employed in Paul's "It is better to marry than to burn" by which, we saw, a concession to frailty is supported.[102] For the genuine follower of this path, the task of weighing up and correctly adjusting a number of divergent aims, self-interest among them, may be as exacting as the single-minded pursuit of supreme virtue.

Similarly, while wisdom leaves plenty of room for guilt, its affinity with shame represents an essential part of its nature. With its eye on worldly success, it realizes how much depends on applause or disapproval. Conscience is inner; and though nowadays, wised up by Freud, we know that, in the long run, a good one may further your outer

[95] See 859 f., 864 f.

[96] Prov 3:4, cited above, 867, along with 1 Sam 2:26; Luke 2:40, 52. See H. Ringgren, in H. Ringgren and W. Zimmerli, *Sprüche/Prediger* (Göttingen, 1962), 20.

[97] Eccl 12:13. A stimulating treatment of the passage is provided by W. Zimmerli, *op. cit.*, 250 f.

[98] Prov 3:28; similarly 3:27.

[99] Prov 17:1.

[100] Prov 17:10.

[101] Eccl 7:1.

[102] 1 Cor 7:9; see above, 869.

career and a bad one mess it up (actually, the ancients, in their way, knew it too—think of Cain or Orestes), it remains the case that the good or bad impression your conduct creates brings you concrete benefit or hurt at once and with certainty. To put it from a slightly different angle—by and large, guilt culture presupposes a towering father or father-substitute directing you in reality or, internalized, in imagination, shame culture sets up a more diffuse and life-size authority: what will your neighbours, your peers, the respectable citizens think of you? Your fortune does greatly depend on these panels; it is towards their positive reaction that wisdom sets out to steer you. So strong is the preoccupation with appearances that even the summons just adverted to, "to find favour in the eyes of God and man," despite its emphatic inclusion of the religious tie, has this typical shame-cultural ring: what counts is how you strike the beholder. No wonder Sirach makes appropriate and misplaced shame into a major classification of sacred, ethical and practical precepts: you ought to be ashamed of whoredom etc., but not of observing the Law etc.[103] The roots of all this are deep indeed. Shame doubtless originates right in the domain of reproduction, at the centre, that is, of the shaping of mankind's dominant traits. Already among the primitives, an enormous genetic premium would reward couples that can escape detection and attack while copulating (in which situation they at once stir up most envy and are least ready for defence) and ensure good-will and respect while parenting. This is not the place, however, to probe further.

I am far from suggesting that relaxations of prophetic rigour entered Christianity only via wisdom. After "the first, fine careless rapture," institutionalization and expansion inevitably brought about a degree of adjustment to the pedestrian pull of an ongoing movement and to a membership—and candidates for membership—increasingly less uniform in provenance.[104] The Third Gospel would be especially affected, dating as it does from a relatively advanced state. Still, the particular cases here isolated, with a conscious giving credit for a helpful action though it is prompted by expediency, do bear the imprint of wisdom. After all, Luke more than the other Synoptics was in touch with the educated and well-to-do, the normal devotees of wisdom and tolerance. While he himself inclined to a stricter line, their voices are detectable in his material.

Perhaps the time has come for an upgrading of realism. It is one thing to yearn for purity, another to deny or condemn intrinsic components of our nature—of necessity being left with hatred of oneself and others. Not surprisingly, any system of ethics neglecting wisdom is driven to resort to contortions. Let us once more take up the debate between the pragmatic Judah ben Ilai and the perfectionist Nehemiah. King David, the Bible informs us, reigned "with justice and charity."[105] (Whatever the original import of the words, my rendering gives that from which these Rabbis proceeded.) According to Judah, David would sentence a man who had enriched himself at another's expense—justice—but if it was a poor fellow, he would then himself pay up in his

[103] Sir 4:20 ff., 41:16 ff.

[104] See e.g. W. D. Davies, *The Setting of the Sermon on the Mount* (Cambridge, 1964), 387 ff.

[105] 2 Sam 8:15.

stead—charity. Nehemiah objects that this might induce people to fake poverty, so the proper interpretation is that David compelled the debtor to make amends: in this way, he did justly by the recipient and charitably by the restorer—who was rid of his ill-gotten gains.[106] There is a very valid point in Nehemiah's stand. But it is easy to see how, with some more pressure and theorizing and self-deception, one could get from there to a doctrine such as that the execution of a felon springs from love of him.[107] I am aware that even Judah's David, who supports the destitute scoundrel, will be found on modern analysis to be far less high-minded than he was once held to be. At least, however, he does not make quite the claims of a radical idealist.[108]

[106] *Deut. Rab.* on 16:18; *b. Sanh.* 6b. As for the authorship of the two opinions, see W. Bacher, *op.cit.*, 241.

[107] See my article (cit. above, n. 75) in *Humanities in Society*, 2 (1979), 74.

[108] I am most grateful to, and a little angry with, Calum Carmichael whose criticism of my first draft of this section made me re-write it.

Τρία μυστήρια κραυγῆς: Ignatius, *Ephesians*, 19:1*

This phrase is generally interpreted as meaning "three mysteries to be proclaimed" or "proclaiming themselves", as if κραυγή were synonyomous with κήρυγμα.[1] (True, Kirsopp Lake in the Loeb Classical Library translates "three mysteries of a cry."[2]) If we look up dictionaries or the like for evidence for κραυγή in this sense, the only passage cited is that under notice.[3] I wonder whether Ignatius had not something more specific in mind, or at least at the back of his mind.

He is referring to (1) Mary's virginity, (2) her giving birth, (3) Jesus's death. (1) As for the *virginity*, in the Lucan infancy narrative, Mary, directly after the annunciation, visits Elisabeth and the latter ἀνεφώνησεν κραυγῇ μεγάλῃ, "spake out with a loud cry" (Luke 1:42), blessing the former and praising herself happy for receiving her; or, according to other readings, relevant because of what we shall find under (2) and (3), ἀνεφώνησεν φωνῇ μεγάλῃ or ἀνεβόησεν φωνῇ μεγάλῃ. Needless to say, Ignatius did not know Luke; but the story was doubtless forming much earlier than its appearance in the gospel. (2) As for the birth, in the infancy narrative of the Protevangelium of James, a great light appears so that the eyes cannot bear it (compare the light of Ignatius's star in *Ephesians* 19:2), and after it is gone the child becomes visible and the Hebrew midwife ἀνεβόησεν, "cried out" (19:2), praising herself happy. This work dates from the second century, but again the tradition may be quite old. (3) As for the death, Jesus's cry or cries on the cross—ἀνεβόησεν φωνῇ μεγάλῃ (Matt 27:46), κράξας φωνῇ μεγάλῃ (27:50), ἀφεὶς φωνὴν μεγάλην (Mark 15:37)—were discussed soon enough, by Gnostics and others, and even their omission from Luke and John is a sign of interest rather than the opposite. From Origen it is clear that the term "mystery" was here applied (e.g. *In Matthaeum Commentariorum Series*, 135).[4]

It may be added that there are not many "cries" in the accounts of the life of Jesus besides the three that would qualify: the importance attached to them is therefore understandable. Further, I have a feeling that the idea of these three "mysteries of a cry" being wrought in God's calm is more consistent with other texts where Ignatius contrasts speech and silence (such as *Magnesians* 8:2) than would be the idea of "mysteries of proclamation" being wrought in God's calm; but this is a minor point.

* Communication read in Professor H. Chadwick's Seminar at Oxford, June 1964.

[1] E.g. J. B. Lightfoot, *The Apostolic Fathers*, 2nd ed., II (1889), 79 f.; J. B. Lightfoot, ed. J. R. Harmer, *The Apostolic Fathers* (1926), 142; W. Bauer, *Die Briefe des Ignatius von Antiochia* (1920), 216.

[2] *The Apostolic Fathers*, I (1945), 193.

[3] E.g. W. Bauer, *Griechisch-Deutsches Wörterbuch zu den Schriften des Neuen Testaments*, 5th ed. (1958), col. 889.

[4] Migne, *P.G.*, *XIII* (1785).

ACKNOWLEDGEMENTS

The Robbins Collection and the editor wish to thank the various publishers for granting permission to reprint the essays contained in this volume. In particular, the following publishers are acknowledged: Verlag Hermann Böhlaus Nachfolger (copyright 1951, 1982), W.B. Eerdmans Publishing Co. (copyright 1987), E.J. Brill (copyright 1980), California Law Review Inc. (copyright 1971), Giuffrè (copyright 1954), Friends of the Midrashia (*Niv Hamidrashia* journal) (copyright 1971, 1972), Oxford University Press (copyright 1960), Hebrew Union College Annual (copyright 1949), Cambridge University Press (copyright 1982), Harvard University Divinity School (copyright 1968, 1975 by the President and Fellows of Harvard College).

Index of References

Biblical Sources

Deuteronomy

Joshua

Judges

Ruth

Psalms

Proverbs

Ecclesiastes

Song of Solomon (Canticles)

Isaiah

Mark

Luke

John

2 Corinthians

Galatians

Ephesians

Philippians

Colossians

1 Thessalonians

TARGUMS
(Onkelos and Jerusalemite)

APOCRYPHA AND PSEUDEPIGRAPHA

Dead Sea Scrolls

Josephus

PHILO

TALMUDIC SOURCES

MIDRASHIM AND OTHER JEWISH SOURCES

EARLY CHRISTIAN SOURCES

ANCIENT LEGAL SOURCES

CLASSICAL AUTHORS

Subject Index